THE
WRITER'S
HANDBOOK
2008

Barry Turner has worked on both sides of publishing, as a journalist and author, editor and marketing director. He started his career as a teacher before joining *The Observer* and then moving on to radio and television. His first book, a study of British politics in the early twentieth century, was published in 1970. He has written over twenty books including *A Place in the Country*, which inspired a television series, and a best-selling biography of the actor, Richard Burton. For many years he wrote on travel for *The Times* and now reviews and serialises books for the paper. Among his recent books are *Countdown to Victory* on the last months of World War II and *Suez 1956: The First Oil War*. As founding editor of *The Writer's Handbook* he has taken this annual reference title through to its twenty-first edition. For ten years, Barry has edited the annual *Statesman's Yearbook*. He is a founder and current chairman of the National Academy of Writing at the University of Central England.

THE
WRITER'S
HANDBOOK
2008

EDITOR
BARRY TURNER

MACMILLAN

First published 2007 by Macmillan
an imprint of Pan Macmillan Ltd
Pan Macmillan, 20 New Wharf Road,
London N1 9RR
Basingstoke and Oxford
Associated companies throughout the world
www.panmacmillan.com

ISBN: 978-0-2300-1637-8

9 8 7 6 5 4 3 2 1

Inclusion in *The Writer's Handbook* is entirely at the editor's discretion. Macmillan Publishers
Ltd makes no recommendation whatsoever by inclusion or omission of any agency, publisher
or organisation.
  While every effort has been made to ensure all of the information contained in this
publication is correct and accurate, the publisher cannot accept any responsibility for any
omission or errors that may occur or for any consequences arising therefrom.

A CIP catalogue record for this book is available from the British Library

Credits
Editor *Barry Turner*
Assistant Editor *Jill Fenner*
Editorial Assistant *Kenneth Hadley*
Poetry Editor *Chris Hamilton-Emery*
Contributors *Will Atkins*
           David Hooper
           Simon Tait
Tax and Finance Adviser *Ian Spring*

Typeset by HWA Text and Data Management, Tunbridge Wells
Printed and bound in Great Britain by Mackays of Chatham

Visit **panmacmillan.com** to read more about all our books and to buy them. You will also
find features, author interviews and news of author events, and you can sign up for e-news-
letters so that you are always first to hear about our new releases.

Contents

So You Want to be a Writer?

Barry Turner offers a helping hand

I have heard this story repeated on the festival circuit but I think I was first to use it and it really did happen. A lawyer friend, having prospered by his profession, confessed to me that he had lost the thrill of the court joust. 'Another couple of years will see me out of this,' he told me. 'And then I'm going to do what you do, make my living by writing.' I would like to say that the obvious riposte came immediately to mind. I should have said, 'Yeah, OK, and I'll be a rich QC.' Instead, a long stare of wonderment, which I guess he took as approval, lasted until the conversation moved on to less sensitive matters.

But it started me thinking. That anyone can write is as popular a myth as everyone having a book in them. If you set your standards by Jeffrey Archer maybe there is an inkling of truth in both propositions. Just don't count on it paying the bills.

What of talent? Well, what of it? There's a lot around, you say and I agree. But bringing it to fulfilment can be a problem. Many of those with writing talent remain unconscious of their gift until it is too late, or, wanting to write, are too easily discouraged by bad teaching or by bad advice. One option for testing talent is a creative writing course. They range from the justly renowned postgraduate degree at the University of East Anglia to weekend retreats pitched at would-be contributors to *Cat Lovers' Weekly*. The best courses focus on the craft of writing as opposed to promoting a particular style. Those to avoid put the stress on literary analysis or on hazy self-realisation; the writing course as a substitute for the psychiatrist's couch.

The truth is that talent, once discovered, needs to be nurtured. Ask any musician or architect or plumber. Don't, however, ask a successful writer. If you do, the chances are you will be peddled another literary myth, that genius blooms whatever its seed patch. In my time this dubious thesis was promoted, among others, by Kingsley Amis who, convinced of his own untutored brilliance, took the line that if you've got talent, flaunt it, otherwise shut up. Curiously, he did not extend the argument to brain surgery.

Now how about this? Writers write because they must. Don't you believe it. It is true that Robert Graves equated writing with a 'compulsion neurosis' and Hugh Leonard has said of his profession that it is 'an incurable illness'. But most writers have more mundane reasons for taking to print. As the critic D.J. Taylor has observed, money is the strongest motive. 'It tends to be forgotten ... that Johnson wrote *Rasselas* to defray the expenses of his mother's funeral or that Dumas's terse, interrogative dialogue was the result of being paid so many centimes a line.' He adds, 'If there is a single factor linking Joyce, Woolf and Conrad it is that they all at one time or another in their literary career submitted work to *Titbits*.' What a refreshing antidote to those pious reflections from authors who take themselves too seriously.

Writing can be hard graft, no doubt about it. You come up with the best story ever and no publisher or agent is in the least interested. Not at the start, anyway. Maybe somewhere there is a successful author who has not had to bear the pain of rejection. But this rare exception proves the rule. To take a few of my favourite examples – favourite because the authors concerned are by common consent among the best: J. P. Donleavy suffered thirty-six rejections before publishing *The Ginger Man* in 1955, George Orwell's *Animal Farm* (ten million copies sold) was turned down by three publishers who had an aversion to fables, while D.H. Lawrence took four years to find an imprint for *Women in Love*.

But if a few rejections are good for the memoirs there has to be hope of a breakthrough to keep going. This is where knowledge of how the book trade operates comes in useful. Too many aspiring authors think that it is just a matter of winging off a manuscript to the first big-name publishing house that comes to mind. But there is more, much more to it than that.

Start with the idea. What are you trying to say in this book of yours and, more to the point, are you confident enough that buyers will want to pay £15 or £20 to read what you have to say? In other words, does your book have marketing strength? That is the key word – marketing. Books have to be sold and sold hard. Long gone are the days, if they ever really existed, when publishers put literary excellence above all other factors. Now, the first line a publisher looks at is the bottom line. There is nothing inherently wrong in this, incidentally. Publishing is not and never has been a charitable enterprise although a few years ago there were still innocent souls who thought so. You can find them now, propping up a bar somewhere, wondering what went wrong.

Back to the writer. What must a writer do to get noticed by a publisher? I have said that everything depends on the strength of an idea. But how to get to the idea in the first place? First, study the market. Read what has made other authors successful. What have they got that you may be missing? I have come across writers who flatly refuse to read other books because they don't want to be influenced by a particular style and end up as imitators. This is just too precious. Nobody ever suffered by studying the opposition.

Next, don't get stuck on the quirky, one-off idea. True, the bestsellers that get most publicity are those that come out of the blue – Stephen Hawking's *A Brief History of Time* or Lyn Truss's *Eats, Shoots and Leaves*. But there is a huge amount of luck in all this. It makes more practical sense to ignore the oddballs and to focus on the books that fit some sort of pattern.

Take the airport novel. The outlets in the airport shopping malls are among the most profitable in the country. A sample of Borders, W.H. Smith and Waterstone's suggests that close on half of the airport sales are in the category of blockbuster fiction with authors such as Robert Ludlum, John Grisham, Jilly Cooper, Stephen King, Patricia Cornwell, Wilbur Smith and Danielle Steel leading the race to the cash register. Hardly surprising when the customers in most need of diversion are mostly long-haul travellers or tourists heading for the beach. The novels with the strongest appeal offer a rattling good story populated by larger-than-life characters in exotic locations where they engage in plenty of action laced with sex, intrigue, corruption, treachery, betrayal and more sex. An eye-catching cover and a memorable title are essential features.

This may not be the sort of book you want to write. Indeed you may feel that many front-of-shop titles are intended for customers with the intelligence of chewing gum. But at least you know what you are up against. Moreover, there are lessons to be learned from the perpetrators of pulp fiction, notably the appeal of a good story. If your idea for a book is to have sales potential, fiction or non-fiction, it must tell a story that holds the reader's attention over a hundred thousand words or more. Do you have a strong central character? A plot that gallops along? One that is not over-complex and keeps up the tension?

Beware giving out messages. You may think you have something vital to tell the world but the chances are, unless you happen to be a renowned expert with a reputation for polemics, the world will not want to know. This is not to deny that the literary imagination is a fertile source of original thinking but those in the genre of up-market fiction are a small sector of the company of novelists. In any case, even the brightest of intellectual writers must, above all, seek to entertain. Those inclined to lecture rarely find an audience.

Spot the trends. Peter Mayle scored a palpable hit with *A Year in Provence* and its sequels because he published during a recession when his middle-class readers dreamed of escaping to an affordable Shangri-la. Mayle was repeating the success of a now forgotten author, Winifred Fortescue, who brought some cheer to the dismal 1930s with *Perfume from Provence* and other similarly wistful titles. Come the next dip in the economy, someone else will make a fortune writing about a far-off place where the sun shines and the good life is to be had on a modest income. New Zealand, perhaps?

Some types of book have a long-running appeal. Novels of domestic upheaval in the shires, epitomised by the Jilly Cooper and Joanna Trollope titles, have been popular for twenty years or more and show no signs of losing their staying power.

Crime fiction is big. Some of the finest writers – Ian Rankin, Ruth Rendell, P.D. James, Peter Robinson, Henning Mankell – to pick names at random, find their inspiration in the lower depths.

Children's books are riding high on the Harry Potter broomstick but who can say how long the fantasy craze will last? For sure, publishers are wary of Harry Potter imitations. If young readers are quick to switch on to fashion they are just as liable to switch off if they begin to feel overloaded. The search is already on for the next big idea.

In adult non-fiction the current enthusiasms are for misery memoirs and celeb biographies. But here again, the vogue may be short lived. With many disappointed expectations in both categories, publishers will need a lot of convincing before they pay out for more of the same.

Enough of the speculation; what of the practicalities?

First, check out the publishers who focus on the books you want to write. Aspiring authors waste time and money submitting proposals that are at odds with a publisher's list. Romantic novels do not sit well with computer manuals.

Be businesslike. When corresponding with a publisher you are dealing with someone who has not much time to spare. She has neither the energy nor the optimism to wade through a weighty manuscript which just may turn out to be the blockbuster of the century but more probably will not.

All that is needed at the approach stage is a synopsis, a sample chapter, and a letter of introduction saying who you are and what there is in your life that makes you peculiarly qualified to write this particular book. Previous publications should be mentioned but not, please not, compliments on your literary skills from friends (however influential) and family. Equally irritating to the recipient are those anticipations of sharp practice such as the bold © at the end of a submission specifying 'First British rights only'.

The synopsis should begin with a line or two of what marketing people call the 'unique selling point'. Who is likely to buy this book and why? It is not enough to claim that the author will reach out to the general reader. We all like to think that a mass audience is waiting for us but the reality is that each book has a core appeal on which the sales potential will be judged.

Having settled on a snappy justification, the synopsis can be used to describe the book in some detail. It is impossible to specify length – where a single page may suffice for a beginner's guide to beekeeping, a closely argued case for energy conservation might require several thousand words. An idea for a novel has sparked interest on the strength of one paragraph. What is essential is for the synopsis to be a clear and logical description of the book.

It should end with a few pertinent details. What is the intended size of the book? This has an important bearing on production costs and thus on the sales forecast. The best estimate of size is the number of words, with the average book falling within the 80,000 – 100,000 bracket.

Will there be illustrations? If so, what sort? Library pictures can be expensive. Commissioned drawings raise the question of the role and standing of the illustrator in the origination of the book.

What about an index? All too often the non-fiction writer brushes aside such petty-fogging questions. Anyone can throw together an index. Wrong. Indexing is a highly skilled task and the quality of an index can make a significant impact on the quality of a book.

When will the manuscript be delivered? Publishers are rightly suspicious of authors who are vague on deadlines. The trouble is that after a few years, a book in the making can move out of range of any feasible sales forecast. Fashion changes, often with bewildering speed. A hot seller next year (linking in to an anniversary, for example, or a current political interest) could easily become a candidate for the remainder shelves if publication is delayed even by a few months. When specifying a delivery date keep in mind the time it takes to print and promote a book – a minimum of six months.

Submissions should be typewritten (with double spacing for the manuscript) and free of messy corrections. Publishers, being human, are liable to be put off by a grubby file of typescript patched together with Sellotape. How many others have seen and rejected this sad little offering?

Once a book proposal has been sent off, allow at least a month even for an acknowledgement and up to three months for a considered reply.

Don't be impatient. Writers are often sinned against but they can be unreasonable in their assumption of a quick decision on what, after all, is a risky investment. If, after a decent interval, nothing is heard, a telephone call is justified. But a polite enquiry is more likely to get results than a demand to know 'what the hell is going on'. It helps to have sent material to a named editor. That way you avoid the risk of being sucked into the whirlpool of internal company communications.

There is no harm in canvassing several publishers at the same time. And there is no need to make a secret of so doing. A little friendly competition may help to stimulate interest.

And so to the next leap forward. Assume that a book proposal has sparked a response from a publisher – say, a middle-range publisher with a respectable list of satisfied authors and a good name in the trade. A small celebration may be called for but this is no time to relax.

Every writer likes to think that somewhere out there is a sympathetic counsellor and friend. In theory, the publisher is ideally suited to the role – he knows the problems, understands the pressures and, after all, he is the one who has to make the book work. But publishing is like any other business. The purpose is to make money. There are some well-publicised practitioners of the art who claim that their minds are on higher things, but those who shout loudest about the glories of literature and the evils of materialism invariably end up with the biggest houses and the smartest cars. This is not to say they are dishonest. It is simply that in abiding by the first rule of elementary capitalism, they are out to maximise their profits.

Proceed, then, with caution.

For all but well-established authors the best that can be hoped for at this stage is an agreement in principle. The publisher may call for amendments to the proposal – more or fewer words or illustrations, a change of emphasis to help sharpen an argument or clarify an aspect of a plot. The timetable is bound to come up for discussion. Is it realistic? Can the author really turn out 100,000 words in two years? What other work does he have in hand?

If the outcome of the first meeting is encouraging, the next discussion should turn to money. Widely publicised stories of six-figure advances for unknown authors are misleading. So too are the figures attached to established names. It can happen that a first novel excites such interest as to start an offer war between publishers. But for most of us the sums involved are modest, bordering on derisory. There are non-fiction writers who settle for a few hundred pounds while a tenderfoot novelist is lucky to get more than £1,000. The standard formula is for the advance to equate with the 60 per cent of the estimated royalties payable on the first edition. Unsurprisingly, publishers favour pessimistic calculations.

The size of the advance should not be the sole criterion for choosing a publisher. The leading houses with their multi-million pound turnovers clearly have more to invest but you may feel happier with one of the smaller publishers that give more attention to individual writers but operate on tighter budgets. Whatever its size, the advance is important as a notification by the publisher of serious intent. The advance should be non-returnable, except when the author fails to deliver a manuscript. Usually, it is split three ways: part on signature of contract, part on delivery of the manuscript and part on publication.

Occasionally, there are good reasons for surrendering the advance in return for other benefits. Macmillan New Writing, a low-cost imprint aimed at attracting first-time authors, is a case in point (see p. 105). The thirty or so authors so far published under this banner are happy. Though no advances are paid, they get a 20 per cent royalty on sales, twice the standard rate.

It is often assumed that the cheques are more impressive when a literary agent represents the author. This may be so for best-selling authors who put their work up for auction but down the scale there may not be too much room for manoeuvre. Where an agent really proves his worth is in knowing which publishers are most likely to respond to a particular idea.

Moreover, the good agent understands the small print and, to greater advantage, spots the omissions – such as the failure to allow for higher royalties beyond a certain minimum sale. The agented author has a bigger say on bookclub deals, promotion budgets, cover design, the timing of publication, print number and on subsidiary rights – the latter capable of attracting earnings long after the book is out of print. The sheer range of potential subsidiary rights is mind-boggling – overseas publication (the publisher will try for world rights but when an agent is acting, US and translation rights may be reserved to the ultimate benefit of the author), film and television adaptations, talking books, digital retrieval – to mention only the most obvious. Above all, the good agent keeps a watching brief long after the contract has been signed, always ready to challenge the publisher to do better on behalf of his author.

But where is the efficient and sympathetic agent to be found? There is no sure way of matching a writer and agent merely by glancing through the list of names and addresses. The most powerful agencies are not necessarily suitable for a beginner, who may feel the need for the close personal contact offered by a smaller agency. On the other hand, the smaller agency may already have taken on its full quota of newcomers, by definition low earners who must, for a time, be subsidised by the more profitable sector of a client list. The agent who gets the balance wrong is heading for insolvency.

Advice frequently given by the agented to the agentless is to seek out the opinion of authors who have been through the mill and learn from their experiences. Writers' circles and seminars organised by the Society of Authors and the Writers' Guild are fruitful sources of gossip.

It is useful to know from the start what agents charge for their services. Ten per cent is customary but an increasing number go for 15 per cent and a few pitch as high as 17½ or 20 per cent – plus (for registered agencies) VAT. A vatable author can reclaim the tax. Others must add 17½ per cent to the commission to calculate the agent's deductions from earnings.

Reading fees are condemned by writers' associations and spurned by leading agents. It has been argued, by writers as well as agents, that a reading fee is a guarantee of serious intent; that if an agent is paid to assess the value of a manuscript, he is bound to give it professional attention. Sadly, this is not necessarily the case. While there are respectable agents who deserve a reading fee, the regular charging of fees can too easily end up as a means of exploiting the naïve. But some agents invoice certain administrative costs such as photocopying.

Do not be disappointed if one or even several agents give the thumbs down. They may be overloaded with clients. But even if this is not so, remember that all writing is in the realm of value judgement. Where one agent fails to see talent, another may be more perceptive.

When a writer does strike lucky, the first priority is to arrive at a clear understanding as to the scope of mutual commitment. Will the agent handle all freelance work – including, for example, journalism, personal appearances on radio and television, lecturing – or just books? Will the agent take a percentage of all earnings including those he does not negotiate? This is a touchy subject. Some writers think of their agency as an employment exchange. Any work they find themselves should not be subject to commission. But this is to assume a clear dividing line between what the agent does and what the writer achieves on his own account. In reality the distinction is not always apparent.

Understanding the market: what's needed, by whom, in what form, and in which media, is all part of an agent's job. Once he knows what his client can do, he is able to promote his talents to the people most likely to want to buy. Eventually, offers come out of the blue – an invitation to write for a newspaper, say, an editing job or a chance to present a television programme. It is at this point that the writer is tempted to by-pass his agent. 'Why should I pay him, he didn't get me the work?' But the chances are that he did, by making the author a saleable property in the first place.

There are authors who, preferring to remain unagented, show a creditable talent for wheeler-dealing. Others – the misguided or the hopelessly optimistic – enter complex publishing agreements without so much as a glance at the small print.

How can an author be sure that a contract is fair and above board? The writer who handles his own affairs is not entirely alone. A guide to good practice is available to members of the Society of Authors and the Writers' Guild (see *Professional Associations and Societies*). When it comes to signing, you may feel you have had to give way on a few points, but if the general principles set out by the writers' unions are followed, the chances of securing a reasonable deal are much enhanced.

Then there is the question of royalties. The conventional hardback royalty is 10 per cent on the first 2500 copies, 12½ per cent on the next 2500 copies and 15 per cent thereafter. On home (mass-market) paperback sales, the minimum royalty should be 7½ per cent, rising to 10 per cent after 30,000 copies.

Greater flexibility in the paying of royalties has followed the heavy discounting common to all the book chains. If an author's work is heavily discounted in the shop, is he entitled to a royalty on the original recommended price or on the marked-down price determined by the retailer? There is no set answer. Much depends on the author's negotiating muscle.

Similarly, generalisations on overseas royalties can be misleading – there are so many different ways in which publishers handle export sales. But as a rule of thumb, if the royalty is calculated on net receipts (when the publisher has sold in bulk at a special price), the percentages should not be less than the home royalty percentage. If the royalty is calculated on the published price, it should be no less than half the home royalty.

As a spot check, confirm four essential points before signing a contract.

First, there should be an unconditional commitment to publish the book within a specified time – say, twelve months from delivery of the typescript or, if the typescript is already with the publisher, from signature of the agreement.

The obligation to publish should not be subject to approval or acceptance of the manuscript. Otherwise what looks like a firm contract may be little more than an unenforceable declaration of intent to publish. Watch that advance payments are not dependent on 'approval' or 'acceptance'. The commitment to publish takes on added significance with editors changing jobs with increasing frequency. An author who has started a book with enthusiastic support from his editor may, when he delivers it, find he is in the hands of someone with quite different tastes and ideas. Provided the book, when delivered, follows the length and outline agreed, the publisher should hold to his contractual obligation.

Secondly, there should be a termination clause to come into play if the publisher breaks the contract or if the book goes out of print or falls below an agreed level of sales. Some publishers try it on but there is no way that a termination clause should be made dependent on the author refunding any unearned advance.

Thirdly, watch out for an option clause, giving the publisher first refusal on future work. Submitting to what may read like a flattering request could tie you to a deal you may come to regret. If an option clause is unavoidable it should be limited to one book on terms to be mutually agreed (not 'on the same terms') and enforceable only within a specified time limit – say, six weeks after delivery of a novel, or of a non-fiction synopsis.

Finally, the author should not be expected to contribute towards the cost of publication. Every writers' organisation warns against subsidised or vanity publishing. It is expensive, the quality of production is often inferior to that offered by conventional publishers, and the promises of vigorous marketing and impressive sales are rarely borne out by experience. Self-publishing is another matter. But the author who takes this route will not only have costs to bear but must also be prepared to take on the marketing and promotional roles of the publisher. Many have tried; few have prospered.

And the Web? Putting words on screen may be a good way to find out what people think of your talent. But, so far, the ability to make money by publishing on line has remained elusive. Maybe this will change as the public turns away from hard print to automatic readers. Until then, the best advice is to hold open any agreement on the shareout of income from downloading. What we do know is that whatever form reading takes someone will have to do the writing. Even if the means of delivering the words changes out of all recognition, the show will go on.

UK Publishers

AA Publishing
The Automobile Association, Fanum House, Basingstoke RG21 4EA
☎01256 491524 Fax 01256 491974
✉ AAPublish@TheAA.com
www.theAA.com
General Manager *Simon Davies*
Publisher *David Watchus*

Publishes maps, atlases and guidebooks, motoring, travel and leisure; also children's books. About 100 titles a year.

Abacus
See **Little, Brown Book Group UK**

ABC-CLIO
PO Box 1437, Oxford OX4 9AZ
☎01865 481403 Fax 01865 481482
✉ salesuk@abc-clio.com
www.abc-clio.com

Formerly Clio Press Ltd. Publishes academic and general reference works, social sciences and humanities. Markets, outside North America, the Web and reference books of the American parent company.

ROYALTIES twice-yearly.

Absolute Press
Scarborough House, 29 James Street West, Bath BA1 2BT
☎01225 316013 Fax 01225 445836
✉ info@absolutepress.co.uk
www.absolutepress.co.uk
Managing Director *Jon Croft*

Founded 1979. Publishes food and wine-related subjects. About 15 titles a year. No unsolicited mss. Synopses and ideas for books welcome.

ROYALTIES twice-yearly.

Abson Books London
5 Sidney Square, London E1 2EY
☎020 7790 4737 Fax 020 7790 7346
✉ absonbooks@aol.com
www.absonbooks.co.uk
Publisher *M.J. Ellison*
Manager *Sharon Wright*

Founded 1971 in Bristol. Publishes language

and dialect glossaries and curiosities. 2 titles in 2006. No unsolicited mss; synopses and ideas for books welcome.

ROYALTIES twice-yearly.

Academic Press
See **Elsevier Ltd**

Acair Ltd
7 James Street, Stornoway, Isle of Lewis HS1 2QN
☎01851 703020 Fax 01851 703294
✉ info@acairbooks.com
www.acairbooks.com

Specialising in matters pertaining to the Gaidhealtachd, Acair publishes books in Gaelic and English on Scottish history, culture and the Gaelic language. 75% of their children's books are targeted at primary school usage and are published exclusively in Gaelic.

ROYALTIES twice-yearly.

Acumen Publishing Limited
15A Lewins Yard, East Street, Chesham HP5 1HQ
☎01494 794398 Fax 01494 784850
✉ steven.gerrard@acumenpublishing.co.uk
www.acumenpublishing.co.uk
Managing Director *Steven Gerrard*

Founded in 1998 as an independent publisher for the higher education market. Publishes academic books on philosophy, classics and history of ideas. 15 titles in 2006. No unsolicited mss. Synopses and ideas for books welcome; send written proposal as per Acumen guidelines.

ROYALTIES annually.

Addison Wesley
See **Pearson Education**

Adlard Coles Nautical
See **A.&C. Black Publishers Ltd**

African Books Collective
Unit 13, Kings Meadow, Ferry Hinksey Road, Oxford OX2 0DP
www.africanbookscollective.com

Founded 1990. Collectively owned by its

17 founder publishers. Exclusive distribution in North America through Michigan State University Press, UK, Europe and Commonwealth countries outside Africa for 114 African participating publishers. Concentration is on scholarly/academic, literature and children's books. Mainly concerned with the promotion and dissemination of African-published material outside Africa. Supplies African-published books to African libraries and organisations, and publishes resource books on the African publishing industry. TITLES *The African Writers' Handbook*; *African Publishers Networking Directory*; *The Electronic African Bookworm: A Web Navigator*; *Courage and Consequence: Women Publishing in Africa*; *African Scholarly Publishing*.

Age Concern Books

1268 London Road, London SW16 4ER
☎020 8765 7200 Fax 020 8765 7211
✉ books@ace.org.uk
www.ageconcern.org.uk/bookshop
Approx. Annual Turnover £400,000+

Publishing arm of Age Concern England. Publishes non-fiction only (no fiction or biographies), including the *Your Rights* series, computing titles for the over 50s, financial handbooks and a series of *Carers Handbooks*; also a wide range of books and training packs for professionals. About 10 titles a year. Synopses and ideas welcome.

Airlife Publishing

See **The Crowood Press Ltd**

Akros Publications

33 Lady Nairn Avenue, Kirkcaldy KY1 2AW
☎01592 651522
www.akrospublications.co.uk

Publisher *Duncan Glen*

Founded 1965. Publishes poetry collections, pamphlets and anthologies; literary essays and studies; local histories. Also *Z2O* poetry magazine. No fiction. About 10 titles a year. No unsolicited mss.
ROYALTIES twice-yearly.

Alcemi

See **Y Lolfa Cyf**

Ian Allan Publishing Ltd

Riverdene Business Park, Molesey Road, Hersham KT12 4RG
☎01932 266600 Fax 01932 266601
✉ info@ianallanpublishing.co.uk
www.ianallanpublishing.com

Chairman *David Allan*
Managing Director *Tristan Hilderley*

Specialist transport publisher – atlases, maps, railway, aviation, road transport, military, maritime, reference. Manages distribution and sales for third party publishers. IMPRINTS **Midland Publishing** (see entry); **OPC** Railway titles; **Lewis Masonic**. About 120 titles a year. Send sample chapter and synopsis with s.a.e

J.A. Allen & Co.

An imprint of Robert Hale Ltd, Clerkenwell House, 45–47 Clerkenwell Green, London EC1R 0HT
☎020 7251 2661 Fax 020 7490 4958
✉ allen@halebooks.com

Publisher *Cassandra Campbell*
Approx. Annual Turnover £1 million

Founded 1926 as part of J.A. Allen & Co. (The Horseman's Bookshop) Ltd. Bought by **Robert Hale Ltd** in 1999. Publishes equine and equestrian non-fiction. About 20 titles a year. Mostly commissioned but willing to consider unsolicited mss of technical/instructional material related to all aspects of horses and horsemanship.
ROYALTIES twice-yearly.

Allen Lane

See **Penguin Group (UK)**

Allison & Busby

13 Charlotte Mews, London W1T 4EJ
☎020 7580 1080 Fax 020 7580 1180
✉ susie@allisonandbusby.com
www.allisonandbusby.com

Publishing Director *Susie Dunlop*
Approx. Annual Turnover £1 million

Founded 1967. Publishes literary fiction, fiction, crime fiction, true crime, pop culture and biography. TITLES *The Rabbit Factory* Marshall Karp; *Best British Mysteries* ed. Maxim Jakubowski; *Girls of Tender Age* Mary-Ann Tirone Smith; *Guns & Gangs* Graeme McLagan. About 90 titles a year. No unsolicited mss.

Authors' Rating 'A testament to the ability of smaller publishers to survive in the retail jungle' (*Publishing News*), A&B is putting its effort into promoting lead titles with crime at the top of the list.

Allyn & Bacon

See **Pearson Education**

Alma Books Ltd
London House, 243–253 Lower Mortlake Road, Richmond TW9 2LL
☎020 8948 9550 Fax 020 8948 5599
✉ info@almabooks.com
www.almabooks.com

Chairman *Elisabetta Minervini*
Managing Director *Alessandro Gallenzi*
Approx. Annual Turnover £350,000

Established in 2005 by founders of **Hesperus Press**. Publishes general fiction, biography, history. 20 titles in 2006. No unsolicited material. Approach through agents only.
Royalties annually.

Authors' Rating Alma is Spanish for 'soul', an apt name say the company founders for a publisher that 'regards a book as an aesthetic artefact rather than a mass produced commodity'.

Alpha Press
See **Sussex Academic Press**

Alphabet & Image Ltd
77 High Street, Totnes TQ9 5PB
☎01803 866946
✉ miranda@alphabetandimage.com
www.alphabetandimage.com

Publisher/Managing Director *Miranda Spicer*

Founded 1989. Publishes horticulture, beekeeping, architecture, ceramics and crafts. Imprints include **Marston House**. Unsolicited mss accepted with s.a.e.
Royalties/flat fee.

Alton Douglas Books
See **Brewin Books Ltd**

Amber Lane Press Ltd
Cheorl House, Church Street, Charlbury OX7 3PR
☎01608 810024 Fax 01608 810024
✉ info@amberlanepress.co.uk
www.amberlanepress.co.uk

Chairman *Brian Clark*
Managing Director/Editorial Head *Judith Scott*

Founded 1979 to publish modern play texts. Publishes plays and books on the theatre. Titles *Whose Life is it Anyway?* Brian Clark; *The Dresser* Ronald Harwood; *Once a Catholic* Mary O'Malley (play texts); *Strindberg and Love* Eivor Martinus. About 4 titles a year. 'Expressly *not* interested in poetry.' No unsolicited mss.
Royalties twice-yearly.

Amsco
See **Omnibus Press**

Andersen Press Ltd
20 Vauxhall Bridge Road, London SW1V 2SA
☎020 7840 8703/8701 Fax 020 7233 6263
✉ andersenpress@randomhouse.co.uk
www.andersenpress.co.uk

Managing Director/Publisher *Klaus Flugge*
Editorial Director *Rona Selby*
Editor, Fiction *Elizabeth Maude*

Founded 1976 by Klaus Flugge and named after Hans Christian Andersen. Publishes children's high-quality picture books and fiction sold in association with Random House Children's Books. Seventy per cent of the books are sold as co-productions abroad. Titles *Elmer* David McKee; *I Want My Potty* Tony Ross; *little.com* Ralph Steadman; *Cat in the Manger* Michael Foreman; *Preston Pig Books* Colin McNaughton; *Junk* Melvin Burgess; *You* Sandra Glover; *I Love You, Blue Kangaroo* Emma Chichester Clark. Unsolicited mss welcome for picture books; synopsis in the first instance for books for young readers up to age 12. No poetry or short stories.
Royalties twice-yearly.

Authors' Rating The secret of Andersen's success is publishing children's books that are loved by adults. That and a wicked sense of fun that has been known to upset the education establishment – and hooray for that.

Chris Andrews Publications
15 Curtis Yard, North Hinksey Lane, Oxford OX2 0LX
☎01865 723404 Fax 01865 725294
✉ chris.andrews1@btclick.com
www.cap-ox.co.uk

Partner *Chris Andrews*

Founded 1982. Publishes coffee-table, scenic travel guides. Also calendars, diaries, cards and posters. Titles *Romance of Oxford*; *Romance of the Cotswolds*; *Romance of the Thames & Chilterns*. Also owns the **Oxford Picture Library** (see entry under *Picture Libraries*). Unsolicited synopses and ideas for travel/guide books in the areas listed above will be considered; phone in the first instance.

Andromeda Children's Books
See **Pinwheel Limited**

The Angels' Share
See **Neil Wilson Publishing Ltd**

Anness Publishing Ltd
Hermes House, 88–89 Blackfriars Road,
London SE1 8HA
☎020 7401 2077 Fax 020 7633 9499
✉ info@anness.com
www.aquamarinebooks.com
www.lorenzbooks.com
www.southwaterbooks.com

Chairman/Managing Director *Paul Anness*
Publisher/Partner *Joanna Lorenz*
Approx. Annual Turnover £15.7 million

Founded 1989. Publishes highly illustrated co-edition titles: general non-fiction – cookery, crafts, interior design, gardening, photography, decorating, lifestyle, health, reference, military, transport and children's. IMPRINTS **Lorenz Books**; **Aquamarine**; **Hermes House**; **Southwater**. About 200 titles a year.

Anova Books
10 Southcombe Street, London W14 0RA
☎020 7610 5291
✉ info@anovabooks.com *or*
firstinitialsurname@anovabooks.com
www.anovabooks.com

CEO *Robin Wood*
Publishing Director *Polly Powell*
Approx. Annual Turnover £14 million

Anova Books, formerly Chrysalis Books Group, specialises in illustrated non-fiction, publishing under the IMPRINTS **B.T. Batsford**; **Collins & Brown**; **Conway**; **National Trust Books**; **Paper Tiger**; **Pavilion**; **Portico**; **Robson Books**; **Salamander**.

IMPRINTS **B.T. Batsford** Associate Publisher *Tina Persaud* Founded in 1843 as a bookseller, and began publishing in 1874. A world leader in books on chess, arts and craft. Publishes non-fiction, architecture, heritage, bridge and chess, film and entertainment, fashion, crafts and hobbies. About 100 titles a year.

Collins & Brown Associate Publisher *Katie Cowan* Publishes a range of lifestyle categories especially in the areas of practical art, photography and needlecrafts.

Conway Associate Publisher *John Lee* Publishes naval history, maritime culture, ship modelling and military history.

National Trust Books Associate Publisher *Tina Persaud* Imprint of Anova Books since 2005. Publishes heritage, gardening, architecture, gift and cookery-based titles. Unsolicited mss not welcome.

Paper Tiger Associate Publisher *Katie Cowan* (Part of Collins & Brown) Publishes science fiction and fantasy art.

Pavilion Associate Publisher *Polly Powell* Publishes illustrated books in biography, cookery, gardening, humour, art, interiors, music, sport and travel. Ideas and synopses for non-fiction titles considered.

Pavilion Children's Books Associate Publisher *Polly Powell* Publishes innovative, informative and fun books for children of all ages.

Portico Associate Publisher *Tom Bromley* Publishes cutting edge non-fiction which is fresh, funny and forthright.

Robson Books Associate Publisher *Barbara Phelan* Founded 1973. Publishes general non-fiction including biography, cookery, gardening, sport and travel. About 60 titles a year. Unsolicited synopses and ideas for books welcome (s.a.e. essential for reply).

Salamander Publisher *Polly Powell* Founded 1973. Publishes colour illustrated books on collecting, cookery, interiors, gardening, music, crafts, military, aviation, sport and transport. Also a wide range of books on American interest subjects. No unsolicited mss but synopses and ideas for the above subjects welcome.

Authors' Rating A cutback in new titles still leaves a varied collection of imprints each with a distinctive image. It can all be a bit confusing for authors who need to be clear on who precisely they are trying to target with ideas.

Anthem Press
See **Wimbledon Publishing Company**

Antique Collectors' Club
Sandy Lane, Old Martlesham, Woodbridge IP12 4SD
☎01394 389950 Fax 01394 389999
✉ sales@antique-acc.com
www.antiquecollectorsclub.com

Managing Director *Diana Steel*
Sales & Marketing Director *Mark Eastment*

Founded 1966. Publishes specialist books on antiques and collecting, decorative arts, architecture, gardening and fashion. The Price Guide series was introduced in 1968 with the first edition of *Price Guide to Antique Furniture*. Subject areas include furniture, silver and gold, metalwork, jewellery, glass, textiles, art reference, ceramics, horology. TITLES *Paul Nash – John Nash Design* Brian Webb and Peyton Skipwith; *Jean Muir – Beyond Fashion* Sinty Stemp; *Biba. The Biba Experience* Alwyn Turner; *Understanding Jewellery*

David Bennett and Daniela Mascetti. Also publishes subscription-only magazine, *Antique Collecting*, published 10 times a year. Unsolicited synopses and ideas for books welcome; no mss.

ROYALTIES twice-yearly as a rule, but can vary.

Anvil Press Poetry Ltd
Neptune House, 70 Royal Hill, London SE10 8RF
☎020 8469 3033 Fax 020 8469 3363
✉ anvil@anvilpresspoetry.com
www.anvilpresspoetry.com

Managing Director *Peter Jay*

Founded 1968. England's oldest independent publishing house dedicated to poetry. Publishes new poets and translated classics. Contemporary list includes Ros Barber, Martina Evans, Michael Hamburger, Dennis O'Driscoll, A.B. Jackson, Stanley Moss and Greta Stoddart. The backlist includes translations of Apollinaire, Baudelaire, Celan, Dante, Hikmet, Neruda, Tagore and Verlaine. Preliminary enquiry required for translations. Unsolicited book-length collections of poems are welcome from writers whose work has appeared in poetry magazines or literary journals. Please enclose adequate return postage.

Authors' Rating With a little help from the Arts Council, Anvil has become one of the foremost publishers of living poets.

Apollos
See **Inter-Varsity Press**

Apple
See **Quarto Publishing** under *UK Packagers*

Appletree Press Ltd
The Old Potato Station, 14 Howard Street South, Belfast BT7 1AP
☎028 9024 3074 Fax 028 9024 6756
✉ reception@appletree.ie
www.appletree.ie

Managing Director *John Murphy*

Founded 1974. Publishes gift books, plus general non-fiction of Irish and Scottish interest. TITLES *In St Patrick's Footsteps*; *Ireland's Ancient Stones*; *Scottish Lighthouses*; *Northern Ireland – International Football Facts*. No unsolicited mss; send initial letter or synopsis.

ROYALTIES twice-yearly in the first year, annually thereafter.

Aquamarine
See **Anness Publishing Ltd**

Arc Publications Ltd
Nanholme Mill, Shaw Wood Road, Todmorden OL14 6DA
☎01706 812338 Fax 01706 818948
✉ arc.publications@btconnect.com
www.arcpublications.co.uk

Editorial Director *Tony Ward*
Associate Editors *John Kinsella* (international), *Jo Shapcott* (UK), *Jean Boase-Beier* (translations), *Angela Jarman* (music)

Founded in 1969 to specialise in the publication of contemporary poetry from new and established writers both in the UK and abroad. AUTHORS John Kinsella, Anthony Lawrence and Katherine Gallagher (Australia), Juris Kronbergs (Latvia), Larissa Miller (Russia), Tony Curtis (Ireland), Mutsuo Takahashi (Japan), Remco Campert (Netherlands), David Baker and Terry Hummer (USA), Patrick Lane (Canada), Tomas Salamun (Slovenia), Joanna Boulter, Lorna Thorpe and Tariq Latif (UK). IMPRINT **Arc Music** specialises in profiles of contemporary composers (particularly where none have existed hitherto) and symposia which take a 'new approach' to well-visited territory. Commissioned work only. About 25 titles a year. Unable to accept unsolicited material for the foreseeable future. 'However, if authors feel impelled to submit material they should ensure that it is fully compatible with the current list, include a history of published works and enclose an s.a.e. if they wish mss to be returned.' Electronic submissions are not accepted.

ROYALTIES as per contracts.

Arcadia Books
15–16 Nassau Street, London W1W 7AB
☎020 7436 9898 Fax 020 7436 9898
✉ info@arcadiabooks.co.uk
www.arcadiabooks.co.uk

Managing Director *Gary Pulsifer*
Publishing Director *Daniela de Groote*
Commissioning Editor *Angeline Rothermundt*
Approx. Annual Turnover £500,000

Independent publishing house established in 1996. Specialises in quality translated fiction from around the world. IMPRINTS **Arcadia**; **BlackAmber**; **Bliss**; **EuroCrime**. TITLES *L'Oréal Took My Home: The Secrets of a Theft* Monica Waitzfelder; *Justice Under Siege* Eva Joly; *My Name is Anne, She Said, Anne Frank* Jacqueline van Maarsen; *Mistress* Anita Nair. Does not welcome unsolicited material.

ROYALTIES twice-yearly.

Authors' Rating A quality publisher that has great success with translated fiction.

Arcane
See **Omnibus Press**

Architectural Press
See **Elsevier Ltd**

Ardis
See **Gerald Duckworth & Co. Ltd**

Argentum
See **Aurum Press Ltd**

Aris & Phillips
See **Oxbow Books**

Armchair Traveller
See **Haus Publishing**

Arnefold Publishing
PO Box 22, Maidstone ME14 1AH
☎01622 759591 Fax 01622 209193
Chairman/Managing Director *I.G. Mann*

Publishes original non-fiction and selected fiction, and non-fiction reprints. No new fiction. IMPRINTS **Arnefold**; **George Mann Books**; **Recollections**. 'Will consider non-fiction titles (which authors find hard to place) on a joint venture/shared profit basis if they are worthy of publication or can be made so. Unsolicited material is welcomed provided it is understood that if not accompanied by return postage it will neither be read nor returned; that no new fiction is wanted and that joint-venture publications may be suggested. We are not vanity publishers.'
ROYALTIES annually.

Arris Publishing Ltd
12 Main Street, Adlestrop, Moreton in Marsh GL56 0YN
☎01608 658758 Fax 01608 659345
✉ gcs@arrisbooks.com
www.arrisbooks.com
Joint Managing Directors *Geoffrey Smith, Michel Moushabeck*
Publishing Director *Victoria Huxley*

Founded in 2001. Publishes politics, history, biography, travel, art and culture. IMPRINTS **Arris Books** *Geoffrey Smith* TITLES *9/11: The New Pearl Harbour; Hitler's British Slaves*; **Chastleton Travel** TITLES *Traveller's Wildlife Guides; A Traveller's History of Cyprus; 100 Best Paintings in London*. About 20 titles a year. No unsolicited mss; synopses and ideas for books welcome.

Send introductory letter, synopsis and specimen chapter by post; no e-mail submissions or CDs. No poetry or fiction.
ROYALTIES annually.

Arrow
See **The Random House Group Ltd**

Artech House
46 Gillingham Street, London SW1V 1AH
☎020 7596 8750 Fax 020 7630 0166
✉ ewillner@artechhouse.co.uk
www.artechhouse.com

CEO (USA) *William M. Bazzy*
Commissioning Editor *Tiina Ruonamaa*

Founded 1969. European office of Artech House Inc., Boston. Publishes books for practising professionals in biomedical engineering, bioinformatics, MEMS, nanotechnology, microwaves, radar, antennas and propagation, electromagnetic analysis, wireless communications, telecommunications, space applications, remote sensing, solid state technology and devices, technology management. 60–70 titles a year. Unsolicited mss and synopses in the specialised areas listed are considered.
ROYALTIES twice-yearly

Ashgate Publishing Ltd
Gower House, Croft Road, Aldershot GU11 3HR
☎01252 331551 Fax 01252 344405 (Ashgate and Gower)/020 7440 7530 (Lund Humphries)
✉ info@ashgatepublishing.com
www.ashgate.com
www.gowerpub.com
www.lundhumphries.com

Chairman *Nigel Farrow*

Founded 1967. Publishes business and professional titles under the Gower imprint, humanities, social sciences, law and legal studies under the Ashgate imprint, and art and art history under the Lund Humphries imprint. Acquired Lund Humphries, publisher of art books and exhibition catalogues in 1999. DIVISIONS **Ashgate** *Dymphna Evans* Social sciences; *John Smedley* History/Variorum collected studies; *Heidi May* Music; *Erika Gaffney* Literary studies; *Tom Gray* History; *Sarah Lloyd* Theology and religious studies; *Guy Loft* Aviation studies. **Gower** *Jonathan Norman* Business, management and training; *Alison Kirk* Law and legal studies. **Lund Humphries** *Lucy Myers*. Access the websites for information on submission of material.

Ashgrove Publishing

27 John Street, London WC1N 2BX
☎020 7831 5013 Fax 020 7831 5011
✉ gmo73@dial.pipex.com
www.ashgrovepublishing.com

Chairman/Managing Director *Brad Thompson*

Acquired by Hollydata Publishers in 1999, Ashgrove has been publishing for over 20 years. Publishes mind, body, spirit, health, cookery, sports. 3 titles in 2006. No unsolicited mss; approach with letter and outline in the first instance.

ROYALTIES twice-yearly.

Ashmolean Museum Publications

Ashmolean Museum, Beaumont Street, Oxford OX1 2PH
☎01865 278010 Fax 01865 278106
✉ publications@ashmus.ox.ac.uk
www.ashmolean.org

Contact *Declan McCarthy*

The Ashmolean Museum, which is wholly owned by Oxford University, was founded in 1683. The first publication appeared in 1890 but publishing did not really start in earnest until the 1960s. Publishes European and Oriental fine and applied arts, European archaeology and ancient history, Egyptology and numismatics, for both adult and children's markets. No fiction, American/African art, ethnography or post-medieval history. Most publications are based on and illustrated from the Museum's collections. About 8 titles a year. No unsolicited mss.

ROYALTIES annually.

Atlantic Books

26–27 Boswell Street, London WC1N 3JZ
☎020 7269 1610 Fax 020 7430 0916
✉ enquiries@groveatlantic.co.uk
www.groveatlantic.co.uk

Chairman *Morgan Entrekin*
Managing Director/Publisher *Toby Mundy*

Founded 2000. A subsidiary of **Grove/Atlantic Inc.** (see entry under *US Publishers*), New York. Publishes literary fiction, history, current affairs, autobiography, biography, memoir, politics and reference books. IMPRINT **Guardian/Observer Books** Editorial Director *Louisa Joyner* TITLE *The Guardian Year* (annual). 80 titles a year. Strictly no unsolicited material accepted.

ROYALTIES twice-yearly.

Authors' Rating The offshoot of US Grove/Atlantic has a reputation for punching above its weight. Clever marketing has a lot to do with it

but it is marketing based on an instinct for what sells - still not the most common attribute in trade publishing.

Atlantic Europe Publishing Co. Ltd

Greys Court Farm, Greys Court, Nr Henley on Thames RG9 4PG
☎01491 628188 Fax 01491 628189
✉ writers@atlanticeurope.com
www.AtlanticEurope.com
www.curriculumVisions.com

Director *Dr B.J. Knapp*

Publishes full-colour, highly illustrated primary school level text books. Not interested in any other material. Main focus is on National Curriculum titles, especially in the fields of religion, science, technology, social history and geography. About 50 titles a year. Unsolicited synopses and ideas for non-fiction curriculum-based books welcome by e-mail only – does not accept material sent by post.

FEES paid.

Atom

See **Little, Brown Book Group UK**

Aurora Metro

2 Oriel Court, The Green, Twickenham TW2 5AG
☎020 8898 4488 Fax 020 8898 0735
✉ info@aurorametro.com
www.aurorametro.com

Managing Director *Cheryl Robson*

Founded by writers in 1989 to publish new writing. Over 100 authors published including Germaine Greer, Meera Syal, Benjamin Zephaniah, Carole Hayman. International work in translation – fiction, children's, drama, biography, cookery, non-fiction. No unsolicited mss; send synopses and ideas by e-mail.

ROYALTIES annually.

Aurum Press Ltd

7 Greenland Street, London NW1 0ND
☎020 7284 7160 Fax 020 7485 4902
✉ editorial@aurumpress.co.uk
www.aurumpress.co.uk
www.jacquismallpub.com

Managing Director *Bill McCreadie*
Editorial Director *Graham Coster*
Approx. Annual Turnover £4.5 million

Founded 1976. Acquired by the Quarto Group in August 2004. High-quality, illustrated/non-illustrated adult non-fiction in the areas of biography, sport, current affairs, military history, travel, music and film. IMPRINTS **Argentum** Practical photography books; **Jacqui Small** High-quality lifestyle books. About 70 titles a year. No unsolicited mss or e-mailed submissions.

ROYALTIES twice-yearly.

Authors' Rating With an ever strengthening list, Aurum has thrived on the ambitions of parent company Quarto to expand from packaging into trade publishing.

Austin & Macauley Publishers

25 Canada Square, Canary Wharf, London E14 5LB
☎020 7038 8212 Fax 020 7038 8312
✉ editors@austinmacauley.com
www.austinmacauley.com

General Manager *Alan Forster*
Managing Editors *Annette Longman, Brenda Barclay*

Founded 2005. Publishes fiction and non-fiction, autobiography, biography, memoirs, post-1945 fiction, true life experiences, crime, romance, women's issues. Expanding educational list including reference books, IT, business studies, mathematics, English, world religions, sociology, mythology, politics, human interest, war, current affairs, music, sport, cinema and TV. About 25 titles a year. Unsolicited synopsis and ideas considered. Postal submissions must include return postage. No short stories or poetry.

ROYALTIES twice-yearly.

Authentic Media

9 Holdom Avenue, Bletchley, Milton Keynes MK1 1QR
☎01908 364200 Fax 01908 277169
✉ info@authenticmedia.co.uk
www.authenticmedia.co.uk

Publishing Director *Mark Finnie*
Editorial Coordinator *Charlotte Hubback*
Approx. Annual Turnover £2 million

A division of STL Ltd. Publishes Christian books on evangelism, discipleship and mission for Evangelical Alliance, Keswick Ministries, Icthus, Youth Work. IMPRINT **Paternoster** Founded 1935. Editorial Director *Robin Parry* Publishes academic, religion and learned/church/life-related books and journals. TITLES *Relational Leadership*; *After Christendom*. Over 50 titles a year. Unsolicited mss, synopses and ideas for books welcome. No poetry or fiction.

ROYALTIES twice-yearly.

AuthorHouse UK

500 Avebury Boulevard, Milton Keynes MK9 2BE
☎0800 197 4150 Fax 0800 197 4151
✉ info@authorhouse.co.uk
www.authorhouse.co.uk

President & CEO *Bryan S. Smith*
Vice President *W. Herbert Senft III*
UK Managing Director *Tim Davies*

Founded 1997. Acquired by Betram Capital in January 2007. Publishes fiction, biography and memoirs, current affairs, history, politics, humour, travel, health, spirituality, sport and academic. Provides a comprehensive range of publishing and promotional services including editorial, design, production, distribution and marketing paid for by the author who retains editorial and creative control.

Authors OnLine

19 The Cinques, Gamlingay, Sandy SG19 3NU
☎01767 652005 Fax 01767 652005
✉ theeditor@authorsonline.co.uk
www.authorsonline.co.uk

Submissions: Freephone 0800 107 2423

Managing Director *Richard Ovenden*
Editor *Richard Fitt*
Submissions Editor *Mrs Gaynor Johnson*
Approx. Annual Turnover £250,000

Founded 1998. A service for authors wishing to self-publish. Publishes new and reverted rights work in both electronic format via their website and traditional hard-copy mainly using digital Print-On-Demand technology. 70 titles in 2006. All genres welcome. Submit mss by e-mail or post (disk or CD-ROM) to the Submissions Editor.

PAYMENT 60% net, paid quarterly.

Autumn Publishing

Appledram Barns, Birdham Road, Chichester PO20 7EQ
☎01243 531660 Fax 01243 538160
✉ autumn@autumnpublishing.co.uk
www.autumnpublishing.co.uk

Managing Director *Michael Herridge*
Editorial Director *Lyn Coutts*

Founded 1976 Part of the Bonnier Group. Publishes baby and toddler books, children's activity, sticker and early learning books. About 200 titles a year. No responsibility accepted for the return of unsolicited mss.

Avon

See **HarperCollins Publishers Ltd**

Award Publications Limited

The Old Riding School, The Welbeck Estate, Worksop S80 3LR
☎01909 478170 Fax 01909 484632
✉ info@awardpublications.co.uk
www.awardpublications.co.uk
Founded 1958. Publishes children's books, both fiction and reference. IMPRINT **Horus Editions**. No unsolicited mss, synopses or ideas.

Azure

See **Society for Promoting Christian Knowledge**

Badger Publishing Ltd

15 Wedgwood Gate, Pin Green Industrial Estate, Stevenage SG1 4SU
☎01438 356907 Fax 01438 747015
✉ orders@badger-publishing.co.uk
www.badger-publishing.co.uk
Founded 1989. Educational publisher. 55 titles in 2006. No unsolicited mss; synopses and ideas for books considered. Approach by e-mail.
ROYALTIES twice-yearly.

Baillière Tindall

See **Elsevier Ltd**

Duncan Baird Publishers

Castle House, 75–76 Wells Street, London W1T 3QH
☎020 7323 2229 Fax 020 7580 5692
✉ info@dbairdpub.co.uk
Managing Director *Duncan Baird*
Editorial Director *Bob Saxton*
Approx. Annual Turnover £7.5 million
Founded in 1992 to publish and package co-editions overseas and went on to launch its own publishing operation in 1998. Publishes illustrated cultural reference, world religions, health, mind, body and spirit, lifestyle, graphic design. 80 titles in 2007. No unsolicited mss. Synopses and ideas welcome; approach in writing in the first instance with s.a.e. No fiction or UK-only subjects.
ROYALTIES twice-yearly.

Bantam/Bantam Press

See **Transworld Publishers**

Barefoot Books Ltd

124 Walcot Street, Bath BA1 5BG
☎01225 322400 Fax 01225 322499
✉ info@barefootbooks.co.uk
www.barefootbooks.com
Publisher *Tessa Strickland*

Founded 1993. Publishes high-quality children's picture books, particularly new and traditional stories from a wide range of cultures.
No unsolicited mss. See website for submission guidelines.
ROYALTIES twice-yearly.
Authors' Rating Writers of children's books would do well to keep track of Barefoot which, from small beginnings, is building a quality list that must be the envy of bigger publishers.

Barrington Stoke

18 Walker Street, Edinburgh EH3 7LP
☎0131 225 4113 Fax 0131 225 4140
✉ barrington@barringtonstoke.co.uk
www.barringtonstoke.co.uk
Chairman *David Croom*
Managing Director *Sonia Raphael*
Editorial Head *Kate Paice*
Approx. Annual Turnover £750,000
Founded in 1998 to publish books for 'dyslexic, struggling and disengaged' young readers. DIVISIONS **Fiction** for 8–12-year olds, reading at age 8+; **Teenage Fiction** for age 12+, reading at age 8+; **4u2read.OK** for children aged 8–13, with a reading age below 8; **gr8reads** for age 13+, with a reading age below 8; **fyi** for ages 10–14, fiction with stacks of facts; **Reality Checks** age 10–14, true-life stories. Also books for teachers and resources to accompany fiction books. Commissioned via literary agents only. *No* unsolicited material.
ROYALTIES twice-yearly.

B.T. Batsford

See **Anova Books**

BBC Active

See **Pearson Education**

BBC Books

See **The Random House Group Ltd**

BBC Children's Books

See **Penguin Group (UK)**

Beautiful Books Ltd

117 Sugden Road, London SW11 5ED
☎020 7738 2428 Fax 020 3070 0764
✉ office@beautiful-books.co.uk
www.beautiful-books.co.uk
Managing Director *Simon Petherick*
Approx. Annual Turnover £500,000
Founded 2004. Publishes adult and children's fiction and non-fiction. DIVISION **The Young Travellers Club** TITLE *Bonjour France!* IMPRINTS

Bloody Books Horror fiction; **Burning House** Contemporary fiction. Unsolicited mss, synopses and ideas welcome. Approach by letter in the first instance with outline and synopsis plus biographical information. Include s.a.e.

Belair
See **Folens Limited**

Berg Publishers
1st Floor, Angel Court, 81 St Clements Street, Oxford OX4 1AW
☎01865 245104 Fax 01865 791165
✉ enquiry@bergpublishers.com
www.bergpublishers.com
Managing Director *Kathryn Earle*
Editorial Director *Tristan Palmer*
Publishes scholarly books in the fields of fashion, cultural studies, social sciences, history and humanities. TITLES *Shoes* eds. Giorgio Riello and Peter McNeil; *Fashion* Roland Barthes; *The Hollywood Interviews* Cahiers du Cinema; *Sobibor: A History of a Nazi Death Camp* Jules Schelvis; *The World of the Anthropologist* Marc Auge. IMPRINT **Oswald Wolff Books**. About 65 titles a year plus six journals: *Fashion Theory, Home Cultures, Textile: The Journal of Cloth and Culture, Cultural Politics, The Senses and Society* and *Material Religion*. No unsolicited mss. Synopses and ideas for books welcome.
ROYALTIES annually.

Berghahn Books
3 Newtec Place, Magdalen Road, Oxford OX4 1RE
☎01865 250011 Fax 01865 250056
✉ publisher@berghahnbooks.com
www.berghahnbooks.com
Chairman/Managing Director *Marion Berghahn*
Approx. Annual Turnover £700,000
Founded 1994. Academic publisher of books and journals. TITLES *Imperial Germany, 1871–1918; Children of Palestine; Critical Interventions; A Different Kind of War.* OVERSEAS ASSOCIATE Berghahn Books Inc., New York. About 90 titles a year. No unsolicited mss; will consider synopses and ideas for books. Approach by e-mail in the first instance. No fiction or trade books.
ROYALTIES annually.

Berlitz Publishing
58 Borough High Stret, London SE1 1XF
☎020 7403 0284 Fax 020 7403 0290
✉ berlitz@apaguide.co.uk
www.berlitzpublishing.com
Managing Director *Jeremy Westwood*

Founded 1970. Acquired by the Langenscheidt Publishing Group in February 2002. Publishes travel and language-learning products only: visual travel guides, phrasebooks and language courses. SERIES *Pocket Guides; Berlitz Complete Guide to Cruising and Cruise Ships; Phrase Books; Pocket Dictionaries; Business Phrase Books; Self-teach: Rush Hour Commuter Cassettes; Think & Talk; Berlitz Kids*. No unsolicited mss.

BeWrite Books
See entry under *Electronic Publishing and Other Services*

BFI Publishing
British Film Institute, 21 Stephen Street, London W1T 1LN
☎020 7255 1444 Fax 020 7636 2516
www.bfi.org.uk
Founded 1980. Part of the **British Film Institute**. Publishes academic, schools and general film/television-related books and resources. TITLE *The Cinema Book*, revised edition, eds. Pam Cook and Mieke Bernink. SERIES *Film Classics; BFI Screen Guides; Modern Classics; World Directors*. About 30 titles a year. E-mail submissions preferred.
ROYALTIES annually.

BFP Books
Focus House, 497 Green Lanes, London N13 4BP
☎020 8882 3315 Fax 020 8886 3933
✉ mail@thebfp.com
Chief Executive *John Tracy*
Commissioning Editor *Stewart Gibson*
Founded 1982. The publishing arm of the Bureau of Freelance Photographers. Publishes illustrated books on photography, mainly aspects of freelancing and marketing pictures. No unsolicited mss but ideas welcome.

Clive Bingley Books
See **Facet Publishing**

Birlinn Ltd
West Newington House, 10 Newington Road, Edinburgh EH9 1QS
☎0131 668 4371 Fax 0131 668 4466
✉ info@birlinn.co.uk
www.birlinn.co.uk
Managing Director *Hugh Andrew*
Founded 1992. Publishes local and military history, adventure, Gaelic, humour, Scottish history, Scottish reference, guidebooks and folklore. IMPRINT **John Donald Publishers** (see

entry). Acquired **Polygon** in 2002 (see entry) and Tuckwell Press in 2005. 170 titles in 2005 across all imprints. No unsolicited mss; synopses and ideas welcome.

ROYALTIES paid.

Authors' Rating One of the fastest growing regional publishers.

Bitter Lemon Press
37 Arundel Gardens, London W11 2LW
☎020 7727 7927 Fax 020 7460 2164
✉ lcolchester@bitterlemonpress.com
www.bitterlemonpress.com

Directors *Laurence Colchester, François von Hurter*

Founded 2003. Specialises in thrillers, *romans noir* and other contemporary fiction from abroad. 7 titles in 2007. No unsolicited material; submissions from agents only.

ROYALTIES annually.

Black & White Publishing Ltd
99 Giles Street, Edinburgh EH6 6BZ
☎0131 625 4500 Fax 0131 625 4501
✉ mail@blackandwhitepublishing.com
www.blackandwhitepublishing.com

Director *Campbell Brown*

Founded 1990. Publishes general fiction and non-fiction, including memoirs, sport, cookery, humour and guidebooks. IMPRINTS **Itchy Coo** Scots language resources for use in schools; **Chroma** Literary fiction. Text only submissions via website, or synopsis and sample chapter by post with s.a.e. or return postage.

ROYALTIES twice-yearly.

A.&C. Black Publishers Ltd
38 Soho Square, London W1D 3HB
☎020 7758 0200 Fax 020 7758 0222
✉ enquiries@acblack.com
www.acblack.com

Chairman *Nigel Newton*
Managing Director *Jill Coleman*
Deputy Managing Director *Jonathan Glasspool*

Publishes children's and educational books, including music, for 0–16 year-olds, practical arts, visual arts, ceramics and glass, natural history, ornithology, nautical, reference, business books, dictionaries, fitness, sport, performing arts and writing books. Acquisitions brought the Herbert Press' art, design and general books, Adlard Coles' and Thomas Reed's sailing lists, plus *Reeds Nautical Almanac*, Christopher Helm, Pica Press and T&AD Poyser's natural history and ornithology lists, children's educational publisher Andrew Brodie and Whitakers Almanack into

A.&C. Black's stable. Bought by **Bloomsbury Publishing** in May 2000. Acquired **Methuen**'s drama list in 2006. IMPRINTS **Adlard Coles Nautical; Thomas Reed; Christopher Helm**; **T&AD Poyser; The Herbert Press; Andrew Brodie; Methuen Drama**. TITLES *Who's Who*; *Writers' & Artists' Yearbook*; *Children's Yearbook*; *Poetry Writers' Yearbook*; *Actors' Yearbook*; *Business: The Ultimate Resource*; *Steps to Success*; *Whitaker's World of Facts*; *Know the Game* sports series; *White Wolves* fiction series. 337 titles in 2006. Initial enquiry appreciated before submission of mss.

ROYALTIES vary according to contract.

Black Ace Books
PO Box 7547, Perth PH2 1AU
☎01821 642822 Fax 01821 642101
www.blackacebooks.com

Managing Director *Hunter Steele*

Founded 1991. Publishes new fiction, Scottish and general; some non-fiction including biography, history, philosophy and psychology. IMPRINTS **Black Ace Books**; **Black Ace Paperbacks** TITLES *Succeeding at Sex and Scotland, Or the Case of Louis Morel* Hunter Steele; *La Tendresse* Ken Strauss MD; *Count Dracula (The Authorized Version)* Hagen Slawkberg; *Caryddwen's Cauldron* Paul Hilton; *The Sinister Cabaret* John Herdman. No children's, poetry, cookery, DIY, religion. 36 titles in print. 'No submissions at all, please, without first checking our website for details of current requirements and submission guidelines.'

ROYALTIES twice-yearly.

Black Lace
See **Virgin Books Ltd**

Black Spring Press Ltd
Curtain House, 134–146 Curtain Road,
London EC2A 3AR
☎020 7613 3066 Fax 020 7613 0028
✉ general@blackspringpress.co.uk

Director *Robert Hastings*

Founded 1986. Publishes fiction and non-fiction, literary criticism, biography. TITLES *The Lost Weekend* Charles Jackson; *The Big Brass Ring* Orson Welles; *The Tenant* Roland Topor; *Julian Maclaren-Ross Collected Memoirs*. About 5 titles a year. No unsolicited mss.

ROYALTIES annually.

Black Swan
See **Transworld Publishers**

BlackAmber
See **Arcadia Books**

Blackstaff Press Ltd
4C Heron Wharf, Sydenham Business Park,
Belfast BT3 9LE
☎028 9045 5006 Fax 028 9046 6237
✉ info@blackstaffpress.com
www.blackstaffpress.com
Managing Editor *Patsy Horton*
Founded 1971. Publishes mainly, but not exclusively, Irish interest books, fiction, poetry, history, sport, cookery, politics, illustrated editions, natural history and humour. About 20 titles a year. Unsolicited mss considered, but preliminary submission of synopsis plus short sample of writing preferred. Return postage *must* be enclosed.
ROYALTIES twice-yearly.

Authors' Rating Regional and proud of it, this Belfast publisher is noted for bringing on young talent and for 'wonderfully well-presented catalogues and promotional material'.

Blackwell Publishing
See **Wiley-Blackwell**

John Blake Publishing Ltd
3 Bramber Court, 2 Bramber Road, London
W14 9PB
☎020 7381 0666 Fax 020 7381 6868
✉ words@blake.co.uk
Managing Director *John Blake*
Deputy Managing Director *Rosie Ries*
Founded 1991 and expanding rapidly. Bought the assets of Smith Gryphon Ltd in 1997 and acquired Metro Publishing in 2001. Publishes mass-market non-fiction. No fiction, children's, specialist or non-commercial. About 100 titles a year. No unsolicited mss; synopses and ideas welcome. Please enclose s.a.e.
ROYALTIES twice-yearly.

Authors' Rating One of the few publishers able to crack the market for celebrity memoirs, John Blake brings the tabloid touch to books.

Blandford Press
See **Octopus Publishing Group**

Bliss
See **Arcadia Books**

Bloodaxe Books Ltd
Highgreen, Tarset NE48 1RP
☎01434 240500 Fax 01434 240505
✉ editor@bloodaxebooks.com
www.bloodaxebooks.com
Managing/Editorial Director *Neil Astley*
Publishes poetry, literature and criticism, and related titles by British, Irish, European, Commonwealth and American writers. Ninety-five per cent of the list is poetry. TITLES include six major anthologies, *Staying Alive; real poems for unreal times* and *Being Alive*, both edited by Neil Astley; *The Bloodaxe Book of 20th Century Poetry* ed. Edna Longley; *The New Poetry* eds. Hulse, Kennedy and Morley; *Modern Women Poets* ed. Deryn Rees-Jones; collected editions of Fleur Adcock, David Constantine, Helen Dunmore, Roy Fisher, Brendan Kennelly, J.H. Prynne, Peter Reading, Carol Rumens, Ken Smith, Anne Stevenson and C.K. Williams. About 30–40 titles a year. Unsolicited poetry mss welcome; send a sample of no more than 10 poems with s.a.e., 'but if you don't read contemporary poetry, don't bother'. No e-mail submissions of any kind.
ROYALTIES annually.

Authors' Rating Assisted by regional Arts Council funding, Bloodaxe is one of the liveliest and most innovative of poetry publishers with a list that takes in some of the best of the younger poets.

Bloody Books
See **Beautiful Books Ltd**

Bloomsbury Publishing Plc
36 Soho Square, London W1D 3QY
☎020 7494 2111 Fax 020 7434 0151
www.bloomsbury.com
Chairman/Chief Executive *Nigel Newton*
Publishing Directors *Alexandra Pringle, Liz Calder, Kathy Rooney, Sarah Odedina, Arzu Tahsin, Michael Fishwick*
Approx. Annual Turnover £109 million
Founded in 1986 by Nigel Newton, David Reynolds, Alan Wherry and Liz Calder. Many of its authors have gone on to win prestigious literary prizes, most recently J.K. Rowling's *Harry Potter and the Philosopher's Stone, Harry Potter and the Chamber of Secrets* and *Harry Potter and the Prisoner of Azkaban* won the **Nestlé Smarties Book Prize** in 1997, 1998 and 1999 respectively. Margaret Atwood's *The Blind Assassin* won the **Booker Prize** in 2000. Started Bloomsbury USA in 1998. Acquired **A.&C. Black Publishers Ltd** in May 2000 (see entry), Peter Collin Publishing Ltd in September 2002, Berlin Verlag in 2003 and Walker Publishing Inc in New York in 2004. Publishes literary fiction

and non-fiction, including general reference; also audiobooks. AUTHORS include Margaret Atwood, T.C. Boyle, Sophie Dahl, Jeffrey Eugenides, Neil Gaiman, Daniel Goleman, David Guterson, Sheila Hancock, Ethan Hawke, John Irving, Jay McInerney, Tim Pears, Celia Rees, J.K. Rowling, Ben Schott, Will Self, Donna Tartt, Rupert Thomson, Barbara Trapido, Joanna Trollope, Benjamin Zephaniah. Unsolicited mss and synopses for adult titles only; no poetry.

ROYALTIES twice-yearly.

Authors' Rating With the seventh and final Harry Potter in the offing, Bloomsbury is in search of a new generation of mega sellers. A reported £12 million spree on celebrity memoirs and TV tie-ins, with an overall spend of £31 million on new authors, has so far failed to deliver the goods. But while City investors, mesmerised by Potter profits, are bound to be disappointed by the latest ventures, in publishing terms Bloomsbury is still a great success story with a stable of contented authors and a refreshing readiness to try new ideas.

BMM
See **SportsBooks Limited**

Boatswain Press
See **Kenneth Mason Publications Ltd**

Bobcat
See **Omnibus Press**

Bodleian Library
Communications & Publishing Office, Bodleian Library, Broad Street, Oxford OX1 3BG
☎01865 277627 Fax 01865 277187
✉ publishing@bodley.ox.ac.uk
www.bodleianbookshop.co.uk

Chairman *Dr Samuel Fanous*

Founded 1605. Publishes trade and academic works relating to the Bodleian Library collections of books and manuscripts. TITLES *A Month at the Front: The Diary of an Unknown Soldier; Queen Elizabeth's Book of Oxford; Laurel for Libby.* 10 titles in 2006. No unsolicited mss. Synopses and ideas for book related to the collections will be considered; approach should be made by post, addressed to the Commissioning Editor.

The Bodley Head/Bodley Head Children's Books
See **The Random House Group Ltd**

Boltneck Publications Limited
Head Office: Westpoint, 78 Queens Road, Clifton, Bristol BS8 1QX
☎0117 985 8709
✉ cfwb@radmorebirch.wanadoo.co.uk
www.boltneck.co.uk

Submissions: King's Cote, Valley Road, Finmere MK18 4AL

Managing Director *David Thomas*
Publishing Director *Clive Birch*

Founded 2004. Linked to Medavia Media Agency. Publishes fiction and popular non-fiction on topical subjects or people of interest. DIVISION **Medavia Publishing** *Clive Birch* TITLES *No Big Deal; A Decent Man.* IMPRINT **Boltneck Business Publications** *David Thomas.* 4 titles in 2006. No unsolicited mss. Initial letter, synopsis, sample chapter, c.v. and s.a.e.

ROYALTIES paid annually.

Bonnier Books (UK)
Appledram Barns, Birdham Road, Chichester PO20 7EQ
☎01243 531660 Fax 01243 774433

CEO *Des Higgins*

Founded in February 2007. Part of the Swedish media group, Bonnier AB. Publishes illustrated lifestyle and cookery titles. TITLES *Bride and Groom Cookbook; Healthy Heart Cookbook.* 45 titles in 2007.

Book Blocks
See **CRW Publishing Ltd**

The Book Guild Ltd
Pavilion View, 19 New Road, Brighton BN1 1UF
☎01273 720900 Fax 01273 723122
✉ info@bookguild.co.uk
www.bookguild.co.uk

Chairman *George M. Nissen, CBE*
Managing Director *Carol Biss*

Founded 1982. Publishes fiction, human interest, media, children's fiction, academic, naval and military, biography, art. Expanding mainstream list plus developing human interest and biography. DIVISIONS **Current Affairs** TITLE *The Truth About Cats and Dogs* Emma Milne. **Human Interest** TITLE *Debt Rescue* Gary Webster. **Biography** TITLES *More Dangerous Ground* Roger Cook; *In Sickness and in Health* Sir Richard Bayliss. **General Non-Fiction** TITLE *A Compost Kind of Girl* Bryony Hill. **Fiction** TITLES *A Doctor's Note* Julian Fane; *The Terrorist* Nigel Harris. **Children's** TITLE *Jemima's*

Mice David Moodie. About 90 titles a year. Unsolicited mss, ideas and synopses welcome. ROYALTIES twice-yearly.

Authors' Rating There are two sides to The Book Guild, not always coexisting in happy harmony. The favoured image is of a conventional publisher with a strong list of general titles. But also on offer is a service where authors cover the costs of publication. Unlike many vanity publishers, The Book Guild clearly sets out its terms of agreement. Still, the outlay can be high relative to sales and first-time authors should not be misled into believing that they have found an easy route to fame and fortune.

Border Lines Biographies
See **Seren**

Boulevard Books
& The Babel Guides
71 Lytton Road, Oxford OX4 3NY
☎01865 712931
✉ ray.keenoy@gmail.com
www.babelguides.com

Managing Director *Ray Keenoy*

Specialises in contemporary world fiction by young writers in English translation. Existing or forthcoming series of fiction from Brazil, Italy, Latin America, Low Countries, Greece, and elsewhere. The Babel Guides series of popular guides to fiction in translation started in 1995. DIVISONS **Latin American** *Ray Keenoy* TITLE *Hotel Atlantico* J.G. Noll. **Italian** *Fiorenza Conte* TITLE *The Toy Catalogue* Sandra Petrignani. **Brazil** *Dr David Treece* TITLE *The Jaguar*. **Babel Guides to Fiction in Translation** Series Editor *Ray Keenoy* TITLES *Babel Guide to Italian Fiction in Translation; Babel Guide to the Fiction of Portugal, Brazil & Africa in Translation; Babel Guide to French Fiction in English Translation; Babel Guide to Jewish Fiction; Babel Guide to Brazilian Fiction.* Suggestions and proposals for translations of contemporary fiction welcome. Also seeking contributors to forthcoming Babel Guides (all literatures).
ROYALTIES annually.

Bound Biographies Limited
Heyford Park House, Heyford Park, Bicester OX25 5HD
☎01869 232911 Fax 01869 232698
✉ office@boundbiographies.com
www.boundbiographies.com

Managing Director *Michael Oke*
Editorial Head *Dr A.J. Gray*

Approx. Annual Turnover £250,000

Founded in 1992 to assist in the writing and production of low numbers of private life stories. Print-on-demand facilities to provide short runs of paper or hardback books to complement the Bound Biographies leather-bound range. Publishes autobiographies predominantly although novels, poetry and special interest books are considered. TITLES *Red Tails in the Sunset* Bryn Williams; *The Long Straw* Mike Nicholson. 40 titles in 2006. Unsolicited material welcome; approach by post, telephone or e-mail.
ROYALTIES annually.

Bounty
See **Octopus Publishing Group**

Bowker (UK) Ltd
3rd Floor, Farringdon House, Wood Street, East Grinstead RH19 1UZ
☎01342 310450 Fax 01342 310486
✉ sales@bowker.co.uk
www.bowker.co.uk

Managing Director *Doug McMillan*

Part of the Cambridge Information Group (CIG). Publishes bibliographic references used by publishers, libraries and retailers throughout the world to source new book information. TITLES *Books In Print; Global Books in Print; Ulrich's Periodicals Directory.* Unsolicited material will not be read.

Boxtree
See **Macmillan Publishers Ltd**

Marion Boyars Publishers Ltd
24 Lacy Road, London SW15 1NL
☎020 8788 9522 Fax 020 8789 8122
✉ rebecca@marionboyars.com
www.marionboyars.co.uk

Editor *Rebecca Gillieron*
Editor, Non-fiction *Amy Christian*

Founded 1975, formerly Calder and Boyars. Publishes biography and autobiography, fiction, literature and criticism, music, philosophy, psychology, sociology and anthropology, theatre and drama, film and cinema, women's studies. AUTHORS include Georges Bataille, Ingmar Bergman, Heinrich Böll, Hortense Calisher, Jean Cocteau, Carlo Gébler, Julian Green, Ivan Illich, Pauline Kael, Ken Kesey, Toby Litt, Kenzaburo Oe, Hubert Selby, Igor Stravinsky, Frederic Tuten, Eudora Welty, Judith Williamson, Tom Wiseman, Hong Ying. About 30 titles a year. Unsolicited mss not welcome for fiction or poetry; submissions from agents only. Unsolicited synopses and ideas welcome for non-fiction. OVERSEAS ASSOCIATES Marion Boyars Publishers Inc. ROYALTIES annually.

Bradt Travel Guides

23 High Street, Chalfont St Peter SL9 9QE
☎01753 893444 Fax 01753 892333
✉ info@bradtguides.com
www.bradtguides.com

Managing Director *Donald Greig*
Editorial Director *Adrian Phillips*
Approx. Annual Turnover £1 million

Founded in 1974 by Hilary Bradt. Specialises in travel guides to off-beat places and quirky travel and wildlife-related titles. SERIES Country guides and island guides (Azores, Syria, Namibia); wildlife guides (Madagascar, Galapagos, Arctic, Antarctica, Southern Africa); mini guides to cities (Budapest, Dubrovnik, Bratislava, Tallinn) and the 'Eccentric' series (Britain, London, France, America, Oxford, Cambridge, Edinburgh). Worldwide distribution. 50 titles in 2007. No unsolicited mss; synopses and relevant ideas (not travelogues) welcome.
ROYALTIES twice-yearly.

Authors' Rating Bradt may well have hit on the antidote to online travel guides. A list of unlikely tourist destinations (Lapland and Kosovo are among forthcoming titles) has achieved such success to inspire plans for a doubling of the number of titles by 2010.

Nicholas Brealey Publishing

3–5 Spafield Street, London EC1R 4QB
☎020 7239 0360 Fax 020 7239 0370
✉ rights@nicholasbrealey.com
www.nicholasbrealey.com

Managing Director *Nicholas Brealey*

Founded 1992. Independent publishing group focusing on innovative trade/professional books covering business and economics, intelligent self-help, popular psychology and the increasingly active fields of travel writing and words and writing. The group has offices in Boston and includes Intercultural Press Inc. TITLES *It's All Greek to Me!*; *Almost French*; *Much Ado About English*; *Authentic Happiness*; *50 Psychology Classics*; *The Cult of the Luxury Brand*; *Tough Choices*. No fiction, poetry or leisure titles. 30 titles a year. No unsolicited mss; synopses and ideas welcome.

Authors' Rating Looks to be succeeding in breaking away from the usual computer-speak business manuals to publish information and literate texts. Lead titles have a distinct trans-Atlantic feel.

The Breedon Books Publishing Co. Ltd

3 The Parker Centre, Mansfield Rd, Derby DE21 4SZ
☎01332 384235 Fax 01332 292755
✉ steve.caron@breedonpublishing.co.uk
www.breedonbooks.co.uk

Owner/Managing Director *Steve Caron*
Approx. Annual Turnover £1 million

Founded 1983. Publishes football and sport, local history, old photographs, heritage. About 45 titles a year. Unsolicited mss, synopses and ideas welcome if accompanied by s.a.e. No poetry or fiction.

Martin Breese International

19 Hanover Crescent, Brighton BN2 9SB
☎01273 687555
✉ MBreese999@aol.com
www.abracadabra.co.uk

Chairman/Managing Director *Martin Ranicar-Breese*

Founded in 1975 to produce specialist conjuring books. No unsolicited submissions.

Brewin Books Ltd

Doric House, 56 Alcester Road, Studley B80 7LG
☎01527 854228 Fax 01527 852746
✉ admin@brewinbooks.com
www.brewinbooks.com

Chairman/Managing Director *Alan Brewin*
Company Secretary *Julie Brewin*
Art Editor *Alistair Brewin*

Founded 1976. Publishes books on all aspects of Midland life and history including social, hospital, police, military, transport and family histories as well as biographies and contemporary fiction. TITLES *Sounds Unlikely – Music in Birmingham* Margaret Handford; *The Haunted Midlands* Anne Bradford; *Black Country Memories* Carl Chinn. IMPRINTS **Alton Douglas Books**; **History Into Print**; **Brewin Books**. About 25 titles a year. Not interested in children's, poetry, short stories or novels. Approach by letter, but do not send full mss. Unsolicited synopses and ideas welcome with s.a.e.
ROYALTIES twice-yearly.

Bright 'I's

See **Infinite Ideas**

Bristol Classical Press
See **Gerald Duckworth & Co. Ltd**

Bristol Phoenix Press
See **University of Exeter Press**

British Academic Press
See **I.B. Tauris & Co. Ltd**

The British Academy
10 Carlton House Terrace, London
SW1Y 5AH
☎020 7969 5200 Fax 020 7969 5300
✉ secretary@britac.ac.uk
www.britac.ac.uk

Publications Officer *James Rivington*
Assistant Publications Officer *Janet English*
Publications Assistant *Amrit Bangard*

Founded 1902. The primary body for promoting scholarship in the humanities and social sciences, the Academy publishes many series stemming from its own long-standing research projects, or series of lectures and conference proceedings. Main subjects include history, philosophy and archaeology. SERIES *Auctores Britannici Medii Aevi; Early English Church Music; Fontes Historiae Africanae; Records of Social and Economic History*. About 20 titles a year. Proposals for these series are welcome and are forwarded to the relevant project committees. The British Academy is a registered charity and does not publish for profit.
ROYALTIES only when titles have covered their costs.

The British Computer Society
First Floor, Block D, North Star House, North Star Avenue, Swindon SN2 1FA
☎0845 300 4417 Fax 01793 480270
✉ publishing@hq.bcs.org.uk
www.bcs.org/books

Chief Executive *David Clarke*
Head of Publishing & Information Products
  Elaine Boyes
Commissioning Editor *Matthew Flynn*
Approx. Annual Turnover £20 million (Society)

Founded 1957. BCS is the leading professional and learned society in the field of computers and information systems. Publishes books which support the professional, academic and practical needs of the IT community. 6 titles in 2006. Unsolicited material welcome; submissions form and guide on website page: www.bcs. org/books/writer
ROYALTIES annually.

The British Library
96 Euston Road, London NW1 2DB
☎020 7412 7469 Fax 020 7412 7768
✉ blpublications@bl.uk
www.bl.uk

Head of Publishing *David Way*

Founded 1979 as the publishing arm of The British Library to publish works based on the historic collections and related subjects. Publishes bibliographical reference, manuscript studies, illustrated books based on the Library's collections, and book arts. TITLES *1000 Years of English Literature; The Books of Henry VIII and His Wives; Futurist Typography*. About 50 titles a year. Unsolicited mss, synopses and ideas welcome if related to the history of the book, book arts or bibliography. No fiction or general non-fiction.
ROYALTIES annually.

The British Museum Press
33 Russell Square, London WC1B 3QQ
☎020 7323 1234 Fax 020 7436 7315
www.britishmuseum.co.uk

Managing Director *Andrew Thatcher*
Director of Publishing *Rosemary Bradley*

The book publishing division of The British Museum Company Ltd. Founded 1973 as British Museum Publications Ltd; relaunched 1991 as British Museum Press. Publishes ancient history, archaeology, ethnography, art history, exhibition catalogues, guides, children's books and all official publications of the British Museum. TITLES *Michelangelo Drawings: Closer to the Master; The British Museum Concise Introduction to Ancient Egypt; Japanese Art in Detail; The Persian Empire: A History*. About 50 titles a year. Synopses and ideas for books welcome.
ROYALTIES twice-yearly.

Brockhampton Press Ltd
See **Caxton Publishing Group**

Andrew Brodie
See **A. &C. Black Publishers Ltd**

Brown Skin Books
PO Box 46504, London N1 3YA
☎020 8986 1115
✉ info@brownskinbooks.co.uk
www.brownskinbooks.co.uk

Chairman *Dr John Lake*
Managing Director *Vastiana Belfon*

Founded 2002. Publishes 'quality, intelligent erotic fiction by black women around the world' and a new series of erotic crime thrillers. TITLES

Body and Soul Jade Williams; *Personal Business* Isabel Baptiste; *Scandalous* and *A Darker Shade of Blue* Angela Campion; *Playthings* Faith Graham; *Online Wildfire* Crystal Humphries; *Strip Poker* Lisa Lawrence; *The Singer* Aisha DuQuesne; *Sorcerer* Tamzin Hall. 4 titles in 2006. No unsolicited mss; synopses and sample chapters welcome. Send by e-mail or post. No poetry.
ROYALTIES annually.

Brown, Son & Ferguson, Ltd
4–10 Darnley Street, Glasgow G41 2SD
☎0141 429 1234 Fax 0141 420 1694
✉ info@skipper.co.uk
www.skipper.co.uk
Chairman/Joint Managing Director *T. Nigel Brown*

Founded 1850. Specialises in nautical textbooks, both technical and non-technical. Also Scottish one-act/three-act plays. Unsolicited mss, synopses and ideas for books welcome.
ROYALTIES annually.

Bryntirion Press
Bryntirion, Bridgend CF31 4DX
☎01656 655886 Fax 01656 665919
✉ office@emw.org.uk
www.emw.org.uk
Publications Manager *Huw Kinsey*

Owned by the Evangelical Movement of Wales. Publishes Christian books in English and Welsh. No unsolicited mss; synopses and ideas welcome.
ROYALTIES annually.

Burning House
See **Beautiful Books Ltd**

Burns & Oates
See **The Continuum International Publishing Group Limited**

Business Education Publishers Ltd
The Teleport Doxford International, Sunderland SR3 3XD
☎0191 525 2410
✉ info@bepl.com
www.bepl.com
Managing Director *Mrs A. Murphy*
Approx. Annual Turnover £400,000

Founded 1981. Publishes business education, economics and law for BTEC and GNVQ reading. Currently expanding into further and higher education, computing, IT, business, travel and tourism, occasional papers for institutions and local government administration. Unsolicited mss and synopses welcome.
ROYALTIES annually.

Buster Books
See **Michael O'Mara Books Ltd**

Butterworth Heinemann
See **Elsevier Ltd**

Cadogan Guides
See **New Holland Publishers (UK) Ltd**

Calder Publications Ltd
51 The Cut, London SE1 8LF
☎020 7633 0599 Fax 020 7928 5930
✉ info@calderpublications.com
www.calderpublications.com
Chairman/Managing Director/Editorial Head *John Calder*

Acquired in April 2007 by independent publishers Alma Books/Oneworld Classics. A publishing company which has grown around the tastes and contacts of John Calder, the iconoclast of the literary establishment. The list has a reputation for controversial and opinion-forming publications; Samuel Beckett is perhaps the most prestigious name. The list includes all of Beckett's prose and poetry. Publishes autobiography, biography, drama, literary fiction, literary criticism, music, opera, poetry, politics, sociology, ENO opera guides. AUTHORS Antonin Artaud, Marguerite Duras, Martin Esslin, Erich Fried, P.J. Kavanagh, Robert Menasse, Robert Pinget, Luigi Pirandello, Alain Robbe-Grillet, Nathalie Sarraute, L.F. Celine, Eva Figes, Claude Simon, Howard Barker (plays). No new material accepted.
ROYALTIES annually.

Authors' Rating There was plenty of interest when this idiosyncratic publisher decided to put himself and his valuable backlist up for sale. In the event, the new owners are of the same breed of independent thinkers. Calder will continue to commission new work.

California University Press
See **University Presses of California, Columbia & Princeton Ltd**

Cambridge University Press
The Edinburgh Building, Shaftesbury Road, Cambridge CB2 2RU
☎01223 312393 Fax 01223 315052
www.cambridge.org
Chief Executive *Stephen R.R. Bourne*

Managing Director, Publishing, Academic
(books and journals in H&SS and STM)
A.M.C. Brown
Managing Director, Publishing, Cambridge
Learning (ELT and Education) *J.M. Pieterse*

The oldest printer and publisher in the world, now a global company with a regional structure operating in the UK, Europe, Middle East & Africa, in the Americas and in Asia-Pacific. Has warehousing centres in Cambridge, New York, Melbourne, Madrid, Cape Town, São Paulo, Singapore and New Delhi, with offices and agents in many other countries. Publishing includes major ELT courses; tertiary textbooks, monographs and journals; scientific and medical reference; professional lists in law, management and engineering; educational coursebooks for the National Curriculum; and e-learning materials for schools. Publishes academic/educational, ELT and reference books for markets worldwide, at all levels from primary school to postgraduate and professional. Also Bibles, prayer books and over 200 academic journals. Around 25,000 authors in 116 countries and between 1500 and 2000 new titles a year.

Synopses and ideas for books are welcome (and preferable to the submission of unsolicited mss). No fiction or poetry.
ROYALTIES twice-yearly.

Authors' Rating The reorganisation of publishing divisions at CUP indicates that the future is with primary and secondary education with the main growth areas in Middle East and Asian markets. Authors of academic monographs may soon have to look elsewhere for their natural outlet.

Camden Press Ltd
43 Camden Passage, London N1 8EA
☎020 7226 4673
Chairman *Bob Borzello*

Founded 1985. Publishes social issues; all books are launched in connection with major national conferences. DIVISION **Publishing for Change** *Bob Borzello* TITLE *Living with the Legacy of Abuse*. IMPRINT **Mindfield** TITLES *Hate Thy Neighbour: The Race Issue; Therapy on the Couch*. No unsolicited material. Approach by telephone in the first instance.
ROYALTIES annually.

Campbell Books
See **Macmillan Publishers Ltd**

Candle
See **Lion Hudson plc**

Canongate Books Ltd
14 High Street, Edinburgh EH1 1TE
☎0131 557 5111 Fax 0131 557 5211
✉ info@canongate.co.uk
www.canongate.net

Also at: Lower Basement, 151 Chesterton Road, London W10 6ET

Publisher/Managing Director *Jamie Byng*
Editorial Director *Anya Serota*
Publishing Director *Nick Davies*
Approx. Annual Turnover £5.81 million

Founded 1973. In 2002, won both 'Publisher of the Year' at the British Book Awards and The Booker Prize with *Life of Pi* by Yann Martel. Publishes a wide range of literary fiction and non-fiction. Historically, there is a strong Scottish slant to the list but its output is increasingly international, especially now with its joint venture with Grove Atlantic in the US and co-publishing agreement with Text Publishing in Australia. Canongate also has a growing reputation for originating unusual projects (typified by *The Pocket Canons* and more recently by *The Myths* series, launched in 2005). Key AUTHORS include Michel Faber, Yann Martel, Alasdair Gray, John Fante, James Meek and Louise Welsh.
ROYALTIES twice-yearly.

Authors' Rating It can't be long before Canongate emerges from the 'small publisher' category to compete on equal terms with the top names in the industry. More non-fiction titles are expected with a continuing emphasis on quality writing with marketing appeal.

Canterbury Press
See **SCM – Canterbury Press Ltd**

Capall Bann Publishing
Auton Farm, Milverton TA4 1NE
☎01823 401528 Fax 01823 401529
✉ enquiries@capallbann.co.uk
www.capallbann.co.uk

Chairman *Julia Day*
Editorial Head *Jon Day*

Founded in 1993, Capall Bann now has well over 300 titles in print. Family-owned and run company, 'operated by people with real experience in the topics we publish' which include British traditions, folklore, animals, alternative healing, environmental, Celtic lore, mind, body and spirit. TITLES *Tarot Therapy; How to Talk with Fairies; Mary Magdalene, Lost Goddess, Lost Gospels; Crystals Folklore & Healing; Understanding Star Children*. About 40 titles a year. Unsolicited proposals for books welcome. No fiction or poetry.

ROYALTIES twice-yearly.

Jonathan Cape/Jonathan Cape Children's Books

See **The Random House Group Ltd**

Capstone Publishing

(A Wiley Company)
John Wiley & Sons Ltd, The Atrium, Southern Gate, Chichester PO19 8SQ
☎01243 779777 Fax 01243 770638
✉ info@wiley-capstone.co.uk
www.wiley.com

Founded 1997. Part of **John Wiley & Sons Inc**. Publishes business, personal development, lifestyle and humour books.

Carcanet Press Ltd

4th Floor, Alliance House, 30 Cross Street, Manchester M2 7AQ
☎0161 834 8730 Fax 0161 832 0084
✉ info@carcanet.co.uk
www.carcanet.co.uk

Owner *Folio Holdings*
Chairman *Kate Gavron*
Managing Director/Editorial Director *Michael Schmidt, FRSL, OBE*

Having started the company as an undergraduate hobby, Robert Gavron bought the company in 1983 and established strong European, Commonwealth and American links. Winner of the **Sunday Times Small Publisher of the Year** award in 2000, it took over the Oxford Poets list from **Oxford University Press** in 1999, which it now publishes as a distinct imprint. Primarily a poetry publisher but also publishes academic, literary biography, fiction in translation and translations. AUTHORS John Ashbery, Eavan Boland, Donald Davie, Natalia Ginzburg, Robert Graves, Elizabeth Jennings, Hugh MacDiarmid, Edwin Morgan, Sinead Morrissey, Les Murray, Frank O'Hara, Richard Price, Frederic Raphael, C.H. Sisson, Charles Tomlinson, Jane Yeh. About 40 titles a year, including *PN Review* (six issues yearly). Poetry submissions (hard copy only): 6–10 poems with covering letter and return postage. Prospective writers should familiarise themselves with the Carcanet list before submitting work.

ROYALTIES annually.

Authors' Rating Now one of the UK's leading literary publishers with a diverse list of modern and classic poetry, Carcanet stays close to

the source of literary creativity with its own postgraduate Writing School at Manchester Metropolitan University (see entry under *Writers' Courses*).

Cardiff Academic Press

St Fagans Road, Fairwater, Cardiff CF5 3AE
☎029 2056 0333 Fax 029 2055 4909
✉ drakegroup@btinternet.co.uk
www.drakegroup.co.uk

Managing Director *R. G. Drake*

Academic publishers and Drake Audio Visual.

Carlton Publishing Group

20 Mortimer Street, London W1T 3JW
☎020 7612 0400 Fax 020 7612 0401
✉ enquiries@carltonbooks.co.uk
www.carltonbooks.co.uk

Managing Director *Jonathan Goodman*
Editorial Director *Piers Murray Hill*

Founded 1992. Carlton Publishing Group is an independent publishing house. It has three main divisions: **Carlton Books** Illustrated leisure and entertainment books aimed at the mass market. Subjects include history, sport, puzzles, health, popular science, children's non-fiction, popular culture, music, fashion and design. **André Deutsch** Autobiography, biography, history, current affairs, narrative non-fiction and the arts. **Prion Books** Humour, nostalgia, drink and classic literature. No unsolicited mss; synopses and ideas welcome. No novels, science fiction, poetry or children's fiction.

Carroll & Brown Publishers Limited

20 Lonsdale Road, London NW6 6RD
☎020 7372 0900 Fax 020 7372 0460
✉ mail@carrollandbrown.co.uk
www.carrollandbrown.co.uk

Editorial Director *Louise Dixon*
Approx. Annual Turnover £4 million

Publishes practical parenting, health, fitness, recreations, mind, body and spirit. TITLES *Your Pregnancy Bible*; *Practical Wabi Sabi*; *Beading for Beginners*. Synopses and ideas for illustrated books welcome; approach in writing in the first instance. No fiction

PAYMENT Fees or royalties paid.

Cassell Illustrated
See **Octopus Publishing Group**

Cassell Reference
See **The Orion Publishing Group Limited**

Kyle Cathie Ltd

122 Arlington Road, London NW1 7HP
☎020 7692 7215 Fax 020 7692 7260
✉ general.enquiries@kyle-cathie.com
www.kylecathie.co.uk

Founded 1990 to publish and promote 'books we have personal enthusiasm for'. Publishes non-fiction: cookery, food and drink, health and beauty, mind, body and spirit, gardening, homes and interiors, reference and occasional books of classic poetry. TITLES *The GI Diet* Antony Worrall Thompson; *Easy Entertaining* Darina Allen; *The Handbag Beauty Bible* Sarah Stacey and Josephine Fairley; *Free Yourself From Smoking* Christina Irvings; *The Gourmet Gardener* Bob Flowerdew. About 25 titles a year. No unsolicited mss. 'Synopses and ideas are considered in the fields in which we publish.'

ROYALTIES twice-yearly.

Catholic Truth Society (CTS)

40–46 Harleyford Road, London SE11 5AY
☎020 7640 0042 Fax 020 7640 0046
✉ f.martin@cts-online.org.uk
www.cts-online.org.uk

Chairman *Most Rev. Peter Smith*
General Secretary *Fergal Martin*

Founded originally in 1868 and re-founded in 1884. Publishes religious books – Roman Catholic; a variety of doctrinal, moral, biographical, devotional and liturgical publications, including a large body of Vatican documents and sources. Unsolicited mss, synopses and ideas welcome if appropriate to their list.

ROYALTIES annually.

Catnip Publishing Ltd

Islington Business Centre, 3–5 Islington High Street, London N1 9LQ
☎020 7745 2370 Fax 020 7745 2372
✉ martin@catnippublishing.co.uk
www.catnippublishing.co.uk

Managing Director *Robert Snuggs*
Approx. Annual Turnover £300,000

Children's books publisher formed from a merger of Southwood Books and Happy Cat Books in 2005. Concentrating on developing fiction, particularly the Happy Cat First Readers series and fiction for the 8–10 age group. IMPRINTS **Catnip** *Martin West* TITLES *The Riddle of the Poisoned Monk* Sarah Matthias; *Granny Was a Buffer Girl* Berlie Doherty; **Happy Cat** TITLE *Scaredy Squirrel* Melanie Watt; SERIES **Happy Cat First Readers** (5–7 years); **Talking it Through**. 45 titles in 2006. Unsolicited submis-sions welcome; send outline synopsis, including proposed age range and length, by letter or e-mail. No non-fiction and, currently, only limited interest in picture books as concentrating on fiction. 'We are actively looking for exciting new writers in our core areas.'

ROYALTIES twice-yearly.

Authors' Rating Shortlisted for Independent Children's Publisher of the Year for 2007, Catnip has all the makings of a star attraction for young readers.

Causeway Press

See **Pearson Education**

Caxton Publishing Group

20 Bloomsbury Street, London WC1B 3JH
☎020 7636 7171 Fax 020 7636 1922
✉ office@caxtonpublishing.com
www.caxtonpublishing.com

Managing Director *John Maxwell*
Approx. Annual Turnover £4 million

Founded 1999. Specialises in reprinting out-of-print works for the 'value' market worldwide and commissioning new general non-fiction publications in reference, cookery, gardening and children's. DIVISIONS/IMPRINTS **Brockhampton Press Ltd** Children's fiction and non-fiction. **Caxton Editions Ltd** General non-fiction, reference and military. **Knight Paperbacks Ltd** Fiction. **Chaucer Press** Art, architecture and literature. **Mercury Books** Illustrated non-fiction. **Mercury Junior** Children's books, illustrated, educational, novelty. 200 titles a year. No unsolicited mss; synopses and ideas welcome; send letter in the first instance.

ROYALTIES twice-yearly.

CBA Publishing

St Mary's House, 66 Bootham, York YO30 7BZ
☎01904 671417 Fax 01904 671384
www.britarch.ac.uk

Publications Officer *Catrina Appleby*
British Archaeology Editor *Mike Pitts*
Young Archaeologists' Club Communications
    Office *Nicky Milsted*
Approx. Annual Turnover £130,000

Publishing arm of the **Council for British Archaeology**. Publishes academic archaeology reports, practical handbooks, *Internet Archaeology*; *British Archaeology* (bi-monthly magazine), *Young Archaeologist* (Young Archaeologists' Club magazine), monographs, archaeology and education. TITLES *Historic Landscape Analysis: A Handbook*; *Archaeology in Northumberland*; *War Art*. Please contact by telephone before submitting mss and proposals.

CBD Research Ltd

Chancery House, 15 Wickham Road, Beckenham BR3 5JS
☎020 8650 7745 Fax 020 8650 0768
✉ cbd@cbdresearch.com
www.cbdresearch.com

Managing Director *S.P.A. Henderson*
Approx. Annual Turnover £500,000

Founded 1961. Publishes directories and other reference guides to sources of information. No fiction. IMPRINT **Chancery House Press** Non-fiction of an esoteric/specialist nature for 'serious researchers and the dedicated hobbyist'. About 6 titles a year.
ROYALTIES quarterly.

CCV

See **The Random House Group Ltd**

Centaur Press

See **Open Gate Press**

Century

See **The Random House Group Ltd**

CF4K

See **Christian Focus Publications**

CHA

See **The Random House Group Ltd**

Chambers Harrap Publishers Ltd

7 Hopetoun Crescent, Edinburgh EH7 4AY
☎0131 556 5929 Fax 0131 556 5313
✉ admin@chambersharrap.co.uk
www.chambersharrap.co.uk

Managing Director *Patrick White*
Office Manager *Esther Fulton*

Part of Hachette-Livre (UK). Publishes dictionaries and reference. The Chambers imprint was founded in the early 1800s to publish self-education books but soon diversified into dictionaries and other reference works. The current list covers a broad range of subject areas and includes crossword titles. The Harrap imprint dates from 1901 and is used for bilingual dictionaries and study aids. About 75 titles a year. Send synopsis with accompanying letter rather than completed mss.

Chancery House Press

See **CBD Research Ltd**

Channel 4 Books

See **Transworld Publishers**

Paul Chapman Publishing Ltd

See **Sage Publications**

Chapman Publishing

4 Broughton Place, Edinburgh EH1 3RX
☎0131 557 2207
✉ chapman-pub@blueyonder.co.uk
www.chapman-pub.co.uk

Managing Editor *Dr Joy Hendry*
Assistant Editor *Edmund O'Connor*

A venture devoted to publishing works by 'the best of Scottish writers, both up-and-coming and established, published in *Chapman*, Scotland's leading literary magazine'. Now publishing a wider range of works though the broad policy stands. Publishes poetry, drama, short stories, books of contemporary importance in 20th-century Scotland. TITLES *Winter Barley* George Gunn; *Lure* Dilys Rose; *Wild Women Series – Wild Women of a Certain Age* Magi Gibson; *Ye Cannae Win* Janet Paisley. About 4 titles a year. No unsolicited mss.
ROYALTIES annually.

Charnwood

See **F.A. Thorpe Publishing**

Chartered Institute of Personnel and Development (CIPD)

151 The Broadway, London SW19 1JQ
☎020 8612 6200 Fax 020 8612 6201
✉ publish@cipd.co.uk
www.cipd.co.uk/bookstore

Publishing Manager *Sarah Brown*
Approx. Annual Turnover £ 2.3 million

Part of CIPD Enterprises Limited. Publishes on personnel, training and management. A list of around 160 titles including looseleaf and online subscription products, student textbooks and professional information resources. New product proposals welcome.
ROYALTIES annually or flat fees paid.

Chastleton Travel

See **Arris Publishing Ltd**

Chatto & Windus

See **The Random House Group Ltd**

Chaucer Press

See **Caxton Publishing Group**

Cheek

See **Virgin Books Ltd**

Cherrytree Books
See **Evans Brothers Ltd**

Chicken House Publishing
2 Palmer Street, Frome BA11 1DS
☎01373 454488 Fax 01373 454499
✉ chickenhouse@doublecluck.com

Chairman/Managing Director *Barry Cunningham*

Children's publishing house founded in 2000. Acquired by Scholastic Inc. in May 2005. Publishes books 'that are aimed at real children' – fiction, original picture books, gift books. Aiming to publish about 25 titles a year. 'We are always on the lookout for new talent.' Unsolicited fiction and picture book material welcome; send letter with synopsis, three sample chapters and s.a.e.

ROYALTIES twice-yearly.

Authors' Rating Set up as a 'small, creative company', Chicken House is now part of Scholastic. But editorial freedom is preserved 'with no rules about what to publish as long as it's good'.

Child's Play (International) Ltd
Ashworth Road, Bridgemead, Swindon SN5 7YD
☎01793 616286 Fax 01793 512795
✉ office@childs-play.com
www.childs-play.com

Chief Executive *Neil Burden*

Founded in 1972, Child's Play is an independent publisher specialising in learning through play, whole child development, life-skills and values. Publishes books, games and A-V materials. TITLES *Big Hungry Bear; There Was an Old Lady; Our Cat Cuddles; Royston Knapper; Children of the Sun; Ten Beads Tall; Pocket Pals; Sliders; Roly Poly Books; Animal Lullabies; Monkey's Clever Tale; What's the Time, Mr Wolf?; Sign and Sing-Along; Arithmetic Lotto.* Unsolicited mss welcome. Send s.a.e. for return or response. Expect to wait two months for a reply.

ROYALTIES Outright or royalty payments are subject to negotiation.

Chimera
See **Pegasus Elliot Mackenzie Publishers Ltd**

Christian Focus Publications
Geanies House, Fearn, Tain IV20 1TW
☎01862 871011 Fax 01862 871699
✉ info@christianfocus.com
www.christianfocus.com

Owner *Balintore Holdings plc*
Chairman *R.W.M. Mackenzie*
Managing Director *William Mackenzie*
Editorial Manager *Willie Mackenzie*
Children's Editor *Catherine Mackenzie*
Approx. Annual Turnover £1.5 million

Founded 1979 to produce children's books for the co-edition market. Now a major producer of Christian books. Publishes adult and children's books, including some fiction for children but not adults. No poetry. Publishes for all English-speaking markets, as well as the UK. IMPRINTS **CF4K** Children's books; **Christian Focus** General books; **Mentor** Study books; **Christian Heritage** Classic reprints. About 90 titles a year. Unsolicited mss, synopses and ideas welcome from Christian writers. See website for submission criteria.

ROYALTIES annually.

Christian Heritage
See **Christian Focus Publications**

Chroma
See **Black & White Publishing Ltd**

Chrome Dreams
See entry under *Audio Books*

Chrysalis Books Group
See **Anova Books**

Churchill Livingstone
See **Elsevier Ltd**

Churchwarden Publications Ltd
PO Box 420, Warminster BA12 9XB
☎01985 840189 Fax 01985 840243
✉ churchwardens@btinternet.com
www.churchwardenbooks.co.uk

Managing Director *John Stidolph*

Founded 1974. Publishes books and stationery for churchwardens and church administrators including *The Churchwarden's Yearbook.*

Cicerone Press
2 Police Square, Milnthorpe LA7 7PY
☎01539 562069 Fax 01539 563417
✉ info@cicerone.co.uk
www.cicerone.co.uk

Managing/Editorial Director *Jonathan Williams*

Founded 1969. Guidebook publisher for outdoor enthusiasts. No fiction or poetry. TITLES *Hillwalker's Guide to Mountaineering; Tour of Mont Blanc; Coast to Coast Trail.* SERIES include *Alpine*

Walking; International Walking; British Long-Distance Trails, Cycling and *Winter Activities*. About 30 titles a year. No unsolicited mss; synopses and ideas considered.
ROYALTIES twice-yearly.

Cico Books
20–21 Jockey Fields, London WC1R 4BW
☎020 7025 2280 Fax 020 7025 2281
✉ mail@cicobooks.co.uk
Publisher *Cindy Richards*
Founded in 1999 and acquired by **Ryland, Peters & Small Limited** in 2006. Publishes highly illustrated lifestyle books covering interiors, crafts, mind, body and spirit and gift. About 30 titles a year. No unsolicited mss but synopses and ideas welcome.
ROYALTIES twice-yearly.

Cisco Press
See **Pearson Education**

Clairview Books Ltd
Hillside House, The Square, Forest Row RH18 5ES
☎0870 486 3526
✉ office@clairviewbooks.com
www.clairviewbooks.com
Managing Director *Mr S. Gulbekian*
Approx. Annual Turnover £100,000
Founded 2000. Publishes non-fiction. General books challenging conventional thinking: mind, body and spirit, current affairs, the arts, health and therapy. TITLES *Imperial America* Gore Vidal; *The Biodynamic Food and Cookbook* Wendy Cook; *My Descent Into Death* Howard Storm. 5 titles in 2006. No unsolicited material; send initial letter of enquiry. No poetry or fiction.
ROYALTIES annually.

Clarion
See **Elliot Right Way Books**

T&T Clark Intl
See **The Continuum International Publishing Group Ltd**

James Clarke & Co.
PO Box 60, Cambridge CB1 2NT
☎01223 350865 Fax 01223 366951
✉ publishing@jamesclarke.co.uk
www.jamesclarke.co.uk
Managing Director *Adrian Brink*
Parent company of **The Lutterworth Press** (see entry). Publishes scholarly titles, primarily theological, historical and reference. TITLES *Libraries*

Directory (book and CD-ROM); *Theology of William Tyndale; Henry VIII's Bishops; Armies of Pestilence*. Approach via written proposals.

Collector's Library
See **CRW Publishing Ltd**

Peter Collin Publishing Ltd
See **Bloomsbury Publishing Plc**

Collins
See **HarperCollins Publishers Ltd**

Collins & Brown
See **Anova Books**

Colourpoint Books
Colourpoint House, Jubilee Business Park, 21 Jubilee Road, Newtownards BT23 4YH
☎028 9182 0505 Fax 028 9182 1900
✉ info@colourpoint.co.uk
www.colourpoint.co.uk
Partners *Wesley Johnston, Malcolm Johnston, Norman Johnston* (transport editor), *Sheila M. Johnston* (commissioning editor)
Founded 1993. Publishes school textbooks and transport (covering the whole of the British Isles), plus books of Irish and general interest. No fiction. About 25 titles a year. Unsolicited material accepted but approach in writing in the first instance; include return postage, please.
ROYALTIES twice-yearly.

Columbia University Press
See **University Presses of California, Columbia & Princeton Ltd**

Communication Ethics
See **Troubador Publishing Ltd**

Compendium Publishing Ltd
43 Frith Street, London W1D 4SA
☎020 7287 4570 Fax 020 7494 0583
✉ alan.greene@compendiumpublishing.com
Managing Director *Alan Greene*
Editorial Director *Simon Forty*
Founded 2000. Publishes and packages for international publishing companies, general illustrated non-fiction: history, reference, hobbies, children's and educational transport and militaria. No unsolicited mss; synopses and ideas preferred.
ROYALTIES twice-yearly or fees per project.

Condor
See **Souvenir Press Ltd**

Conran Octopus
See **Octopus Publishing Group**

Constable & Robinson Ltd
3 The Lanchesters, 162 Fulham Palace Road,
London W6 9ER
☎020 8741 3663 Fax 020 8748 7562
✉ enquiries@constablerobinson.com
www.constablerobinson.com

Chairman *Nick Robinson*
Joint Managing Directors *Jan Chamier, Nova
    Jayne Heath*
Editorial Director, Crime list *Krystyna Green*
Editorial Director, Mammoth series *Pete
    Duncan*
Manager, Overcoming series *Fritha Saunders*

Archibald Constable, Walter Scott's publisher and
the originator of the '3 decker novel', published
his first titles in Edinburgh in 1795. Constable
& Robinson Ltd are now in the third century
of publishing under the Constable imprint,
still independent, with shareholders who work
or have worked in the business running the
company. IMPRINTS **Constable** Commissioning
Editors *Becky Hardie, Leo Hollis* Current
affairs, biography, general and military history,
psychology, travel, photography and crime fiction
mainly in hardback. **Robinson** Crime fiction in
paperback, the Mammoth Book Of series, the
Overcoming psychology series, popular health
and self-help, military history and true crime.
Unsolicited sample chapters, synopses and ideas
for books welcome. No mss; no e-mail submissions. Enclose return postage.

The Continuum International Publishing Group Limited
The Tower Building, 11 York Road, London
SE1 7NX
☎020 7922 0880 Fax 020 7922 0881
www.continuumbooks.com

CEO *Patrick Austen*
Approx. Annual Turnover £13.5 million

Founded in 1999 by a buy-out of the academic
and religious publishing of Cassell and the
acquisition of Continuum New York. Publishes
academic, religious and general books.
   DIVISIONS **Academic Humanities**
Publishing Director *Alexandra Webster* Education,
social sciences, literature, film and music, philosophy (including the **Thoemmes** imprint),
linguistics, biblical studies and theology printed
under the **T&T Clark** imprint. TITLES *Getting
the Buggers to Behave*; *Teaching in Further Education*;
What Philosophy Is; *The Guerrilla Film Makers*

Handbook. **General Trade & Continuum
Religion** Publishing Director *Robin Baird-Smith*
Publishes under **Continuum Burns & Oates**
(RC books) TITLES *Seven Basic Plots*; *Seven Last
Words*. IMPRINTS **Continuum**; **T&T Clark Intl**;
Thoemmes; **Burns & Oates**; **Hambledon
Continuum**. 550 titles in 2006. Unsolicited
synopses and ideas within the subject areas
listed above are welcome; approach in writing
in the first instance. OVERSEAS SUBSIDIARIES The
Continuum International Publishing Group
Inc., New York and Harrisburg.
   ROYALTIES twice-yearly.

Authors' Rating Noted for readable, often
controversial, religious and academic titles
which often qualify as trade books.

Conway
See **Anova Books**

Thomas Cook Publishing
Thomas Cook Business Park, Coningsby Road,
North Bretton, Peterborough PE3 8SB
☎01733 416477 Fax 01733 416688

Head of Travel Books *John Sadler*

Part of the Thomas Cook Group Ltd, publishing
commenced in 1873 with the first issue of *Cook's
Continental Timetable*. Publishes guidebooks,
maps and timetables. About 50 titles a year. No
unsolicited mss; synopses and ideas welcome as
long as they are travel-related.
   ROYALTIES annually.

Leo Cooper
See **Pen & Sword Books Ltd**

Corgi
See **Transworld Publishers**

Corgi Children's Books
See **The Random House Group Ltd**

Country Publications Ltd
The Water Mill, Broughton Hall, Skipton
BD23 3AG
☎01756 701381 Fax 01756 701326
✉ editorial@dalesman.co.uk
www.dalesman.co.uk

Book Editor *Mark Whitley*

Publishers of *Countryman, Dalesman, Cumbria*
and *Down Your Way* magazines, and regional
books covering the North of England. Subjects
include walking, guidebooks, history, humour
and folklore. About 10 titles a year. Will consider

mss on subjects listed above, relating to the North.

ROYALTIES annually.

Countryside Books

2 Highfield Avenue, Newbury RG14 5DS
☎01635 43816 Fax 01635 551004
✉ info@countrysidebooks.co.uk
www.countrysidebooks.co.uk

Publisher *Nicholas Battle*

Founded 1976. Publishes local interest paperbacks on regional subjects, generally by English county. Local history, dialects, genealogy, walking, photographic, aviation and military, some transport. Over 400 titles available. About 50 titles a year. Unsolicited mss and synopses welcome but no fiction, poetry, natural history or personal memories. Check the website for suitability before any submission.

ROYALTIES twice-yearly.

Crème de la Crime Ltd

PO Box 523, Chesterfield S40 9AT
☎01246 520835 Fax 01246 520835
✉ info@cremedelacrime.com
www.cremedelacrime.com

Managing Director *Lynne Patrick*
Approx. Annual Turnover £60,000

Founded in 2003 to discover and publish crime fiction by new authors. 6 titles scheduled for 2007, including new historical strand. Welcomes enquiries and unsolicited submissions, 'especially from talented but unpublished authors who are urged to read the detailed guidelines on the website; or send £2.50 with A4 s.a.e. and two first-class stamps for hard copy'.

ROYALTIES annually.

Crescent Books

See **Mercat Press Ltd**

Cressrelles Publishing Co. Ltd

10 Station Road Industrial Estate, Colwall, Malvern WR13 6RN
☎01684 540154 Fax 01684 540154
✉ simonsmith@cressrelles4drama.
fsbusiness.co.uk

Managing Director *Leslie Smith*

Publishes a range of local interest books and drama titles. IMPRINTS **J. Garnet Miller** Plays and theatre texts; **Kenyon-Deane** Plays and drama textbooks. About 6–12 new play titles a year. Submissions welcome.

Crombie Jardine Publishing Limited

Office 2, 3 Edgar Buildings, George Street, Bath BA1 2FJ
☎01225 464445
✉ catriona@crombiejardine.com
www.crombiejardine.com

Sales & Publishing Director *David Crombie*
Publishing Director *Catriona Jardine*

Founded in 2004. Specialises in fun, quirky and topical humour books only. TITLES *The Little Book of Chavs*; *The World's Funniest Proverbs*; *Shag Yourself Slim*; *The Sudoku & Kakuro Challenge*; *Britain's Rudest Place Names*. 40 titles in 2006. No postal submissions. Send synopsis by e-mail in the first instance.

PAYMENT Fees paid; no royalties.

Authors' Rating Having cut their teeth with Michael O'Mara Books, the co-founders of Crombie Jardine are out to grab a share of the young adult humour market.

Crossway

See **Inter-Varsity Press**

Crown House Publishing

Crown Buildings, Bancyfelin, Carmarthen SA33 5ND
☎01267 211345 Fax 01267 211882
✉ books@crownhouse.co.uk
www.crownhouse.co.uk

Managing Director *David Bowman*

Founded 1998. Publishes academic and trade titles in the areas of psychotherapy, education, business training and development, mind, body and spirit. No fiction. 'The aim of the list is to both demystify the latest psychological advances, particularly in the fields of Accelerated Learning, Neuro-Linguistic Programming (NLP) and hypnosis.' 30 titles in 2006. Unsolicited submissions, via the website, are welcome.

ROYALTIES twice-yearly.

The Crowood Press Ltd

The Stable Block, Crowood Lane, Ramsbury, Marlborough SN8 2HR
☎01672 520320 Fax 01672 520280
✉ enquiries@crowood.com
www.crowood.com

Chairman *John Dennis*
Managing Director *Ken Hathaway*

Publishes sport and leisure titles, including animal and land husbandry, climbing and walking, maritime, country sports, equestrian, fishing and shooting; also crafts, dogs, gardening, DIY, theatre, natural history, aviation, military history and motoring. IMPRINT **Airlife Publishing** Specialist aviation titles for pilots, historians and enthusiasts. About 70 titles a year. Preliminary letter preferred in all cases.

ROYALTIES annually.

CRW Publishing Ltd
69 Gloucester Crescent, London NW1 7EG
☎020 7485 5764 Fax 0870 751 7254
✉ marcus.clapham@crw-publishing.co.uk
www.collectors-library.com

Also at: 6 Turville Barns, Eastleach, Cirencester GL7 3QB

Chairman *Ken Webb*
Editorial Director *Marcus Clapham*
Approx. Annual Turnover £2 million

Founded 2003. Publishes literary classics, gift, children's, philosophy, boxed sets. IMPRINTS **Collector's Library**; **Book Blocks**; **Essential Thinkers**; **Poetry Library**; **Reference Library**. 24 titles in 2006. No unsolicited mss.

ROYALTIES annually.

Benjamin Cummings
See **Pearson Education**

James Currey Publishers
73 Botley Road, Oxford OX2 0BS
☎01865 244111 Fax 01865 246454
✉ editorial@jamescurrey.co.uk
www.jamescurrey.co.uk

Chairman *James Currey*
Managing Director/Editorial Director *Douglas H. Johnson*

Founded 1985. A specialist publisher of academic paperback books on Africa and the Third World: history, anthropology, economics, sociology, politics and literary criticism. Approach in writing by post with synopsis if material is 'relevant to our needs'.

ROYALTIES annually.

Custom Publishing
See **The Orion Publishing Group Limited**

D&B Publishing
PO Box 18, Hassocks BN6 9AA
☎01273 711443
✉ info@dandbpublishing.com
www.dandbpublishing.com

Joint Managing Directors *Dan Addelman, Byron Jacobs*

Founded 2002. Publishes games books, special-

ising in gambling, primarily. 8 titles in 2006. Unsolicited mss, synopses and ideas welcome; approach by e-mail in the first instance.

ROYALTIES annually.

Terence Dalton Ltd
Water Street, Lavenham, Sudbury CO10 9RN
☎01787 249291 Fax 01787 248267
www.terencedalton.com

Director/Editorial Head *Elisabeth Whitehair*

Founded 1967. Part of the Lavenham Group Plc, a family company. Non-fiction only. No unsolicited mss. Ideas welcome; telephone in the first instance.

ROYALTIES annually.

Darton, Longman & Todd Ltd
1 Spencer Court, 140–142 Wandsworth High Street, London SW18 4JJ
☎020 8875 0155 Fax 020 8875 0133
✉ tradesales@darton-longman-todd.co.uk
www.dltbooks.com

Editorial Director *Brendan Walsh*
Editor/Rights Officer *Claudine Nightingale*
Approx. Annual Turnover £1 million

A leading independent publisher of books on spirituality and religion. Unique among UK religious publishers in being jointly owned and managed by all its staff members. While predominantly Christian, DLT publishes books from different backgrounds and traditions. TITLES *Jerusalem Bible*; *New Jerusalem Bible*; *NRSV Bible*: *Catholic Edition*; *Return of the Prodigal Son*; *God of Surprises*; *The Enduring Melody*; *Hostage in Iraq*. About 45 titles a year. Information on submissions available on the website.

ROYALTIES twice-yearly.

David & Charles Publishers
Brunel House, Forde Close, Newton Abbot TQ12 4PU
☎01626 323200 Fax 01626 323317
✉ postmaster@davidandcharles.co.uk
www.davidandcharles.co.uk

Managing Director & Publisher *Sara Domville*
Head of Publishing *Alison Myer*

Founded 1960, owned by F+W Publications. Publishes illustrated non-fiction for international markets, specialising in needlecraft, crafts, art techniques, practical photography, military history and equestrian. No fiction, poetry or memoirs. TITLES *Kings & Queens*; *Tickets Please!*; *Not Tonight Darling I'm Knitting*; *Earthcam*; *Animal Portraits*; *Horse Bits n Pieces*. About 200 titles a year. Unsolicited mss will be considered if return postage is included; synopses and ideas welcome for the subjects listed above.

ROYALTIES twice-yearly or flat fees.

Christopher Davies Publishers Ltd
PO Box 403, Swansea SA1 4YF
☎01792 648825 Fax 01792 648825
✉ chris@cdaviesbookswales.com
Managing Director/Editorial Head *Christopher T. Davies*
Approx. Annual Turnover £20,000
Founded 1949 to promote and expand Welsh-language publications. Publishes biography, cookery, history, sport and literature of Welsh interest. TITLES *An A–Z of Wales and the Welsh; Welsh Birthplaces; Carwyn: A Personal Memoir; Who's Who in Welsh History.* About 2 titles a year. No unsolicited mss. Synopses and ideas for books welcome.

ROYALTIES twice-yearly.

Authors' Rating A favourite for Celtic readers and writers.

Giles de la Mare Publishers Ltd
PO Box 25351, London NW5 1ZT
☎020 7485 2533 Fax 020 7485 2534
✉ gilesdelamare@dial.pipex.com
www.gilesdelamare.co.uk
Chairman/Managing Director *Giles de la Mare*
Approx. Annual Turnover £30,000
Founded 1995 and commenced publishing in April 1996. Publishes mainly non-fiction, especially art and architecture, biography, history, music. TITLES *Short Stories, Vols I, II & III* Walter de la Mare; *Handsworth Revolution* David Winkley; *The Life of Henry Moore* Roger Berthoud; *Becoming an Orchestral Musician* Richard Davis; *Romanesque Churches of France: A Traveller's Guide* Peter Strafford; *Blindness and the Visionary* John Coles; *Tricks Journalists Play* Dennis Barker; *Venice: The Anthology Guide* Milton Grundy. Unsolicited mss, synopses and ideas welcome after initial telephone call.

ROYALTIES twice-yearly.

Debrett's Ltd
18–20 Hill Rise, Richmond TW10 6UA
☎020 8939 2250 Fax 020 8939 2251
✉ people@debretts.co.uk
www.debretts.co.uk
Head of Publishing *Liz Wyse*
Chairman *Conrad Free*
Biographical reference plus etiquette, correct form and other social guides; also diaries. Book TITLES include triennial *Debrett's Peerage &*

Baronetage and annual *People of Today* (as book, CD-ROM and online), *Etiquette for Girls; Correct Form; Debrett's Wedding Guide.* Book and article proposals welcome.

Dedalus Ltd
Langford Lodge, St Judith's Lane, Sawtry PE28 5XE
☎01487 832382
✉ info@dedalusbooks.com
www.dedalusbooks.com
Chairman *Juri Gabriel*
Managing Director *Eric Lane*
Approx. Annual Turnover £200,000
Founded 1983. Publishes contemporary European fiction and classics and original literary fiction. TITLES *The Dedalus Book of the Occult; The Arabian Nightmare* Robert Irwin; *Memoirs of a Gnostic Dwarf* David Madsen; *The Double Life of Daniel Glick* Maurice Caldera; *Music in a Foreign Language* Andrew Crumey (winner of the Saltire Best First Book Award in 1994).

DIVISIONS/IMPRINTS **Original Fiction in Paperback; Contemporary European Fiction 1992–2004; Dedalus Europe 1992–2012; Literary Concept Books**. Welcomes submissions for original fiction and books suitable for its list but 'most people sending work in have no idea what kind of books Dedalus publishes and merely waste their efforts'. Author guidelines on website. Particularly interested in intellectually clever and unusual fiction. A letter about the author should always accompany any submission. No replies without s.a.e.

ROYALTIES annually.

Authors' Rating A small, quality publisher which has taken a lead in promoting foreign language writers as well as home-grown authors with original ideas.

JM Dent
See **The Orion Publishing Group Ltd**

André Deutsch Ltd
See **Carlton Publishing Group**

Diggory Press Ltd
Three Rivers, Minions, Liskeard PL14 5LE
✉ publish@diggorypress.com
www.diggorypress.com
US Office: Diggory Press, Inc., 1646 N Litchfield Rd, Suite 200, Goodyear, AZ 85338
Managing Director *R. Franklin*
Founded 2005. Originally started as an imprint of Meadow Books, it has overtaken its parent

company in terms of productivity and profit. A Christian-run publisher of mainly nursing, military and Christian titles and Cornish/Cornwall books. Over 75 titles to date. 'Currently, Diggory Press is not taking on unsolicited mss on a traditional publishing basis.' IMPRINT **Exposure Publishing** Christian-run self publishing service for printed books and e-books. Publishes all subjects in any language: fiction, non-fiction, poetry, biography, autobiography, religious/spiritual (of all faiths), drama, humour, self-help, arts, literature, science and technology, business, military, law, pets, health, folklore, children's picture books, etc. Over 400 titles in 2006. Initial enquiries and submissions by e-mail; strictly no telephone calls from authors.

Digital Press
See **Elsevier Ltd**

Dinas
See **Y Lolfa Cyf**

Discovered Authors
50 Albemarle Street, London W1S 4BD
☎020 7529 3749 Fax 020 7493 9847
✉ authors@discoveredauthors.co.uk *and* authors@fouroclockpress.co.uk
www.discoveredauthors.co.uk

Managing Director *Graham Miller*

Founded 2006. Part of the Albemarle Group. Independent publisher offering various routes to publication, including self-publishing. Publishes fiction (adult and children's), non-fiction, academic and business. IMPRINTS **Discovered Authors Diamond** *Natalie Matthews* Traditional, mainstream publishing TITLES *Laughing Star*; *Haven't We Been Here Before?*; **Discovered Authors Revival** *Jennie Paterson* 'Enables out-of-print authors to get their work back into print and available for sale' TITLE *Harold the King*; **Four O Clock Press** *Jennie Paterson* Self-publishing imprint TITLE *Dwelling Place for Dragons*; **Horizon Press** *Jennie Paterson* Launched in March 2007. 60 titles in 2006. Unsolicited material welcome; approach by e-mail. New literary talent also sought via the Undiscovered Authors Literary Competition; details on the website.

ROYALTIES twice-yearly.

Authors' Rating It is yet to be seen if Discovered Authors can fulfil its objective of overlapping conventional and self publishing. As ever in these circumstances, first-time authors need to be entirely clear as to who pays for what.

John Donald Publishers Ltd
West Newington House, 10 Newington Road, Edinburgh EH9 1QS
☎0131 668 4371 Fax 0131 668 4466
✉ info@birlinn.co.uk
www.birlinn.co.uk

Managing Director *Hugh Andrew*
Commissioning Editor *John Tuckwell*

Bought by **Birlinn Ltd** in 1999. Publishes academic and scholarly, archaeology, architecture, textbooks, guidebooks, local, and social history. New books are published as an imprint of Birlinn Ltd. About 30 titles a year.

Donhead Publishing Ltd
Lower Coombe, Donhead St Mary, Shaftesbury SP7 9LY
☎01747 828422 Fax 01747 828522
✉ jillpearce@donhead.com
www.donhead.com

Contact *Jill Pearce*

Founded 1990 to specialise in publishing how-to books for building practitioners; particularly interested in architectural conservation material. Publishes building, architecture and heritage only. TITLES *Preserving Post-War Heritage*; *Stone Cleaning*; *Architecture 1900*; *Encyclopaedia of Architectural Terms*; *Cleaning Historic Buildings*; *Brickwork*; *Practical Stone Masonry*; *Conservation of Timber Buildings*; *Surveying Historic Buildings*; *English Heritage Directory of Building Limes*; *Heritage, Sands and Aggregates*; *Journal of Architectural Conservation* (3 issues yearly). 6 titles a year. Unsolicited mss, synopses and ideas welcome.

Dorling Kindersley Ltd
Part of the Penguin Group, 80 Strand, London WC2R 0RL
☎020 7010 3000 Fax 020 7010 6060
www.dk.com

CEO *Gary June*

Founded 1974. Packager and publisher of illustrated non-fiction: cookery, crafts, gardening, health, travel guides, atlases, natural history and children's information and fiction. Launched a US imprint in 1991 and an Australian imprint in 1997. Acquired Henderson Publishing in 1995 and was purchased by Pearson plc for £311 million in 2000.

DIVISIONS Adult: **Travel/Reference** Publisher *Douglas Amrine*; **General/Lifestyle** Publisher *John Roberts*. Children's: **Reference** Publisher *Miriam Farby*; **PreSchool/Primary** Publisher *Sophie Mitchell*. IMPRINTS **Ladybird**;

Ladybird Audio; Funfax; Eyewitness Guides; Eyewitness Travel Guides. TITLES *BMA Complete Family Health Encyclopedia; RHS A–Z Encyclopedia of Garden Plants; Children's Illustrated Encyclopedia; The Way Things Work*. Unsolicited synopses/ideas for books welcome.

Authors' Rating A much slimmed version of the old DK is heavily dependent on 'soft learning' products for education markets. The aim is to make Dorling Kindersley products distinctive against low priced rivals and retailers' own brand product, not to mention the Internet. Most titles are team efforts with writers and illustrators working closely with an in-house editor. A new stand-alone travel website will integrate DK content with consumer reviews and online bookings.

Doubleday
See **Transworld Publishers**

Doubleday Children's Books
See **The Random House Group Ltd**

Drake Educational Associates
St Fagans Road, Fairwater, Cardiff CF5 3AE
☎029 2056 0333 Fax 029 2956 0313
✉ info@drakeed.com
www.drakeed.com

Managing Director *R. G. Drake*

Literacy, phonics and language development games and activities. Ideas and scripts in these fields welcome. Also resources for subject areas in the primary school and modern languages at KS2.

Dref Wen
28 Church Road, Whitchurch, Cardiff
CF14 2EA
☎029 2061 7860 Fax 029 2061 0507
✉ gwilym@drefwen.com

Chairman *R. Boore*
Managing Director *G. Boore*

Founded 1970. Publishes Welsh language and bilingual children's books, Welsh and English educational books for Welsh learners.
ROYALTIES annually.

Gerald Duckworth & Co. Ltd
First Floor, 90–93 Cowcross Street, London
EC1M 6BF
☎020 7490 7300 Fax 020 7490 0080
✉ info@duckworth-publishers.co.uk
www.ducknet.co.uk

Managing Director *Peter Mayer*

Editorial Director (General) *Nick Webb*
Editorial Director (Academic) *Deborah Blake*
Approx. Annual Turnover £2 million

Founded 1898 by Gerald Duckworth. Original publishers of Virginia Woolf. Other early authors include Hilaire Belloc, John Galsworthy, D.H. Lawrence and George Orwell. Duckworth is a general trade publisher whose authors include John Bayley, Mary Warnock, Joan Bakewell and J.J. Connolly. In addition to its trade list, Duckworth has a strong academic division. Acquired by Peter Mayer in 2003.

IMPRINTS/DIVISIONS **Bristol Classical Press** Classical texts and modern languages; **Ardis** Russian literature; **Duckworth Academic**; **Duckworth General**. No unsolicited mss; synopses and sample chapters only. Enclose s.a.e. or return postage for response/return.

ROYALTIES twice-yearly at first, annually thereafter.

Dunedin Academic Press Ltd
Hudson House, 8 Albany Street, Edinburgh
EH1 3QB
☎0131 473 2397 Fax 01250 870920
✉ mail@dunedinacademicpress.co.uk
www.dunedinacademicpress.co.uk

Director *Anthony Kinahan*

Founded 2001. Publishes academic and serious general non-fiction. Considerable experience in academic and professional publishing. 18 titles in 2006. Not interested in science (other than earth sciences), poetry, fiction or children's. Check website for active subject areas. No unsolicited mss. Synopses and ideas welcome. Approach first in writing outlining proposal and identifying market.
ROYALTIES annually.

Ebury Publishing/Ebury Press
See **The Random House Group Ltd**

Economist Books
See **Profile Books**

Eden
See **Transworld Publishers**

Edinburgh University Press
22 George Square, Edinburgh EH8 9LF
☎0131 650 4218 Fax 0131 662 0053
www.eup.ed.ac.uk

Chairman *Timothy Rix*
Chief Executive *Timothy Wright*
Deputy Chief Executive/Head of Book
   Publishing *Jackie Jones*

Senior Commissioning Editors *Nicola Carr, Sarah Edwards*
Commissioning Editors *Carol Macdonald, Esmé Watson*

Publishes academic and scholarly books (and journals): African studies, ancient history and classics, film and media studies, Islamic studies, linguistics, literary criticism, philosophy, politics, Scottish studies and religious studies. About 100 titles a year. E-mail submissions accepted; consult website for guidelines.

Egmont UK Limited

239 Kensington High Street, London W8 6SA
☎020 7761 3500 Fax 020 7761 3510
www.egmont.co.uk

Vice President/UK General Manager *Robert McMenemy*
Director of Egmont Press *Cally Poplak*
Director of Egmont Publishing *David Riley*
Approx. Annual Turnover £40 million

Part of the Egmont Group (Copenhagen), Egmont Press publishes children's fiction and picture books, while Egmont Publishing publishes classic and contemporary characters, colouring and activity books. TITLES *Thomas the Tank Engine; Winnie the Pooh; Lemony Snicket; The Wind on Fire* trilogy; Enid Blyton. About 500 titles a year. See the website for current policy on ms submissions.

Authors' Rating The fourth largest children's book publishing group in the UK, Egmont is moving into animated books.

Eland Publishing Ltd

Third Floor, 61 Exmouth Market, London EC1R 4QL
☎020 7833 0762 Fax 020 7833 4434
✉ info@travelbooks.co.uk
www.travelbooks.co.uk

Directors *Rose Baring, John Hatt, Barnaby Rogerson*
Approx. Annual Turnover £250,000

Eland reprints classics of travel literature with a backlist of 60 titles, including *Naples '44* Norman Lewis; *Travels with Myself and Another* Martha Gelhorn; *Portrait of a Turkish Family* Irfan Orga; *Jigsaw* Sybille Bedford. No unsolicited mss. Postcards and e-mails welcome.

ROYALTIES annually.

Element
See **HarperCollins Publishers Ltd**

11:9
See **Neil Wilson Publishing Ltd**

Edward Elgar Publishing Ltd

Glensanda House, Montpellier Parade, Cheltenham GL50 1UA
☎01242 226934 Fax 01242 262111
✉ info@e-elgar.co.uk
www.e-elgar.com

Managing Director *Edward Elgar*

Founded 1986. International publisher in economics, the environment, public policy, business and management and law. TITLES *Who's Who in Economics* (3rd ed.); *Handbook of Environmental and Resource Economics; Who's Who in the Management Sciences.* 300 titles in 2006. No unsolicited mss; synopses and ideas in the subject areas listed above welcome. Approach by letter or e-mail; no telephone inquiries.

Elliot Right Way Books

Kingswood Buildings, Lower Kingswood, Tadworth KT20 6TD
☎01737 832202 Fax 01737 830311
✉ info@right-way.co.uk
www.right-way.co.uk

Managing Directors *A. Clive Elliot, Malcolm G. Elliot*

Founded 1946 by Andrew G. Elliot. Publishes paperback how-to and educative titles on an unlimited variety of home reference, indoor and outdoor leisure hobbies and pursuits, careers and business. Subjects include cookery, wine, family financial and legal matters, public speaking, weddings, jokes, parenting, etiquette, English skills, driving, fishing, horse riding, drawing, music, puzzles, crosswords and quizzes, job seeking, running your own company.

IMPRINTS **Right Way** Instructional paperbacks in B format for the most popular subjects; **Right Way Plus** Larger C format for more specialised subjects; **Clarion** B format for promotional/ultra low-price range. Unsolicited mss, synopses and ideas for books welcome.

ROYALTIES annually.

Elliott & Thompson

27 John Street, London WC1N 2BX
☎020 7831 5013 Fax 020 7831 5011
www.elliottthompson.com

Publishers *David Elliott, Brad Thompson*
Approx. Annual Turnover £100,000

Founded 2001. Publishes literary fiction, biography, belles lettres, reprints of classic male writers. 11 titles in 2006. New proposals welcome (send synopsis and sample pages initially) but s.a.e. essential.

Elm Publications/Training
(wholly owned subsidiary of **Elm Consulting Ltd**)
Seaton House, Kings Ripton, Huntingdon
PE28 2NJ
☎01487 773254
✉ elm@elm-training.co.uk
www.elm-training.co.uk

Managing Director *Sheila Ritchie*

Founded 1977. Publishes textbooks, teaching aids, educational resources and educational software in the fields of business and management for adult learners. Books and teaching/training resources are generally commissioned to meet specific business, management and other syllabuses. About 40 titles a year. Ideas are welcome; initial approach by e-mail with outline, or by a brief telephone call.

ROYALTIES annually.

Elsevier Ltd
The Boulevard, Langford Lane, Kidlington, Oxford OX5 1GB
☎01865 843000 Fax 01865 843010
www.elsevier.com

Managing Director *Anna Moon* (Oxford)
CEO, Science & Technology (books & journals) *Herman van Campenhout*

Parent company Reed Elsevier, Amsterdam. Now incorporates Pergamon Press and Harcourt Publishers International. Publishes academic and professional reference books, scientific, technical and medical books, journals, CD-ROMs and magazines. IMPRINTS **Academic Press; Architectural Press; Butterworth Heinemann; Digital Press; Elsevier; Elsevier Advanced Technology; Focal Press; Gulf Professional Press; JAI; Made Simple Books; Morgan Kauffman; Newnes; North-Holland.**

DIVISION **Elsevier (Health Sciences)** 32 Jamestown Road, London NW1 7BY ☎ 020 7424 4200 Fax 020 7483 2293 www.elsevier-health.com CEO Health Sciences (books & journals) *Brian Nairn*, Managing Director (UK & Netherlands) *Mary Ging* Publishes scientific, technical, medical books and journals. IMPRINTS **Baillière Tindall; Churchill Livingstone; Mosby; Pergamon; Saunders.** No unsolicited mss, but synopses and project proposals welcome.

ROYALTIES annually.

Emissary Publishing
PO Box 33, Bicester OX26 4ZZ
☎01869 323447 Fax 01869 322552

Editorial Director *Val Miller*

Founded 1992. Publishes mainly humorous paperback books including the complete set of Peter Pook novels; no poetry or children's. No unsolicited mss or synopses.

ROYALTIES paid according to contract.

Emma Treehouse Ltd
2nd Floor, The Old Brewhouse, Lower Charlton Trading Estate, Shepton Mallet BA4 5QE
☎01749 330529 Fax 01749 330544
✉ richard.powell4@virgin.net
and sales@emmatreehouse.com
www.emmatreehouse.com

Co-Directors *Richard Powell, David Bailey*
Approx. Annual Turnover £1 million

Founded 1992. Publishes children's pre-school novelty books. No mss. Illustrations, synopses and ideas for books welcome; write in the first instance.

FEES paid; no royalties.

Empiricus Books
See **Janus Publishing Company Ltd**

English Heritage (Publishing)
Kemble Drive, Swindon SN2 2GZ
☎01793 414497 Fax 01793 414769
www.english-heritage.org.uk

Head of Publishing *Rob Richardson*
Commercial Publishing Manager *Adèle Campbell*
Publishing Manager *Robin Taylor*

English Heritage's publishing programme is divided into two streams: commercial (titles commissioned to generate revenue) and not-for-profit, reflecting the organisation's academic and specialist publishing. 30 titles a year. 'All titles relate directly to the work of the organisation, so we do not accept unsolicited material.'

Enitharmon Press
26B Caversham Road, London NW5 2DU
☎020 7482 5967 Fax 020 7284 1787
✉ books@enitharmon.co.uk
www.enitharmon.co.uk

Director *Stephen Stuart-Smith*

Founded 1967. An independent company with an enterprising editorial policy, Enitharmon has established itself as one of Britain's leading literary presses. Patron of 'the new and the neglected', Enitharmon also prides itself on the success of its collaborations between writers and artists, now published by its associate company, **Enitharmon Editions**. Publishes poetry, literary criticism, fiction, art and photography. TITLES *Collected Poems* Alan Brownjohn; *The Apple That Astonished Paris* Billy Collins; *The Cut of the Light* Jeremy Hooker; *A Cypress Walk* Alun Lewis; *Thirteen Ways of Looking at Rillie* Edwin Morgan. No unsolicited mss.

ROYALTIES according to contract.

Epworth

c/o Methodist Publishing House, 4 John Wesley Road, Werrington, Peterborough PE4 6ZP
☎01733 325002 Fax 01733 384180
✉ natalie.watsor@mph.org.uk
www.mph.org.uk
www.scm-canterburypress.co.uk
Chair *The Revd Michael Townsend*
Head of Publishing *Dr Natalie K. Watson*

Publishes Christian books only: philosophy, theology, biblical studies, pastoralia, social concern and Methodist studies. No fiction, poetry or children's. About 12 titles a year. Unsolicited mss, synopses and ideas welcome; send sample chapter and contents with covering letter and s.a.e.

ROYALTIES annually.

The Erotic Print Society

17 Harwood Road, London SW6 4QP
☎020 7736 5800 Fax 020 7736 6330
✉ eros@eroticprints.org
www.eroticprints.org
Managing Director *Mr J. Maclean*

Publishes books of erotic art and photography and erotic literature. Unsolicited material accepted but approach in writing in the first instance with a summary or first chapter.

Essential Thinkers

See **CRW Publishing Ltd**

EuroCrime

See **Arcadia Books**

Euromonitor International

60–61 Britton Street, London EC1M 5UX
☎020 7251 8024 Fax 020 7608 3149
✉ info@euromonitor.com
www.euromonitor.com
Chairman *R.N. Senior*
Managing Director *T.J. Fenwick*
Approx. Annual Turnover £20 million
Founded 1972. International business informa-

tion publisher specialising in library and professional reference books, market reports, electronic databases. Publishes business reference, market analysis and information directories only.

DIVISIONS **Market Analysis** *A. Irwin*; **Reference Books & Directories** *S. Solomon*. About 2000 titles a year.

PAYMENT is generally by flat fee.

Evans Brothers Ltd

2A Portman Mansions, Chiltern Street, London W1U 6NR
☎020 7487 0920 Fax 020 7487 0921
✉ sales@evansbrothers.co.uk
www.evansbooks.co.uk
Managing Director *Stephen Pawley*
International Publishing Director *Brian Jones*
UK Publisher *Su Swallow*
Approx. Annual Turnover £4.5 million

Founded 1908 by Robert and Edward Evans. Publishes UK children's and educational books, and educational books for Africa, the Caribbean and Latin America. IMPRINTS **Cherrytree Books**; **Zero to Ten**. OVERSEAS ASSOCIATES in Kenya, Cameroon, Sierra Leone; Evans Bros (Nigeria Publishers) Ltd. About 175 titles a year.

ROYALTIES annually.

Everyman

See **The Orion Publishing Group Ltd**

Everyman Chess

See **Gloucester Publishers Plc**

Everyman's Library

Northburgh House, 10 Northburgh Street, London EC1V 0AT
☎020 7566 6350 Fax 020 7490 3708
✉ books@everyman.uk.com
Publisher *David Campbell*
Approx. Annual Turnover £3.5 million

Founded 1906. Publishes hardback classics of world literature, pocket poetry anthologies, children's books and travel guides. Publishes no new titles apart from poetry anthologies; only classics (no new authors). AUTHORS include Bulgakov, Bellow, Borges, Heller, Marquez, Nabokov, Naipaul, Orwell, Rushdie, Updike, Waugh and Wodehouse. No unsolicited mss.

ROYALTIES annually.

University of Exeter Press

Reed Hall, Streatham Drive, Exeter EX4 4QR
☎01392 263066 Fax 01392 263064
✉ uep@exeterpress.co.uk
www.exeterpress.co.uk

Publisher *Simon Baker*
Founded 1956. Publishes academic books: archaeology, classical studies and ancient history, history, maritime studies, English literature (especially medieval), European studies, modern languages and literature, film history, performance studies, Arabic studies and books on Exeter and the South West. IMPRINT **Bristol Phoenix Press** Commissioning Editor *John Betts* Classics and ancient history. About 30 titles a year. Proposals welcomed in the above subject areas.
ROYALTIES annually.

Exley Publications Ltd
16 Chalk Hill, Watford WD19 4BG
☎01923 248328 Fax 01923 800440
✉ editorial@exleypublications.co.uk
www.helenexleygiftbooks.com
Editorial Director *Helen Exley*
Founded 1976. Independent family company. Publishes giftbooks, quotation anthologies and humour. No submissions, please.

Expert Books
See **Transworld Publishers**

Exposure Publishing
See **Diggory Press Ltd**

Eyewitness Guides/ Eyewitness Travel Guides
See **Dorling Kindersley Ltd**

Faber & Faber Ltd
3 Queen Square, London WC1N 3AU
☎020 7465 0045 Fax 020 7465 0034
www.faber.co.uk
Chief Executive *Stephen Page*
Approx. Annual Turnover £14.5 million
Geoffrey Faber founded the company in the 1920s, with T.S. Eliot as an early recruit to the board. The original list was based on contemporary poetry and plays (the distinguished backlist includes Eliot, Auden and MacNeice). Publishes poetry and drama, children's, fiction, film, music, politics, biography. DIVISIONS **Fiction** *Lee Brackstone, Hannah Griffiths, Angus Cargill* AUTHORS P.D. James, Peter Carey, Rachel Cusk, Giles Foden, Michael Frayn, Tobias Hill, Kazuo Ishiguro, Barbara Kingsolver, Milan Kundera, Hanif Kureishi, John Lanchester, John McGahern, Rohinton Mistry, Lorrie Moore, Andrew O'Hagan, DBC Pierre, Jane Smiley; **Children's** *Julia Wells* AUTHORS Philip Ardagh, Terry Deary, Ricky Gervais, Russell Stannard, G.P. Taylor; **Film** *Walter Donohue* and

Plays *Dinah Wood* AUTHORS Samuel Beckett, Alan Bennett, David Hare, Brian Friel, Patrick Marber, Harold Pinter, Tom Stoppard, Woody Allen, John Boorman, Joel and Ethan Coen, John Hodge, Martin Scorsese; **Music** *Belinda Matthews* AUTHORS John Bridcut, Humphrey Burton, Rupert Christiansen, Nicholas Kenyon, Richard Morrison, Susan Tomes, John Tyrrell, Elizabeth Wilson; **Poetry** *Paul Keegan, Matthew Hollis* AUTHORS Simon Armitage, Douglas Dunn, Seamus Heaney, Ted Hughes, Paul Muldoon, Daljit Nagra, Tom Paulin; **Non-fiction** *Neil Belton, Julian Loose* AUTHORS John Carey, Simon Garfield, John Gray, Jan Morris, Francis Spufford, Frances Stonor Saunders, Jenny Uglow.
ROYALTIES twice-yearly.

Authors' Rating Named trade publisher of the year by the Independent Publishers Guild, Faber has experienced something of a rebirth with authors benefiting from more energetic and imaginative marketing. Plans are well ahead for an entry into the e-book market.

Facet Publishing
7 Ridgmount Street, London WC1E 7AE
☎020 7255 0590/0505 (text phone)
Fax 020 7255 0591
✉ info@facetpublishing.co.uk
www.facetpublishing.co.uk
Managing Director *John Woolley*
Publishing arm of **CILIP: The Chartered Institute of Library and Information Professionals** (formerly the Library Association). Publishes library and information science, monographs, reference, IT training materials and bibliography aimed at library and information professionals. IMPRINTS **Library Association Publishing**; **Clive Bingley Books**; **Facet Publishing**. Over 200 titles in print, including *The New Walford* and *AACR2*. 25–30 titles a year. Unsolicited mss, synopses and ideas welcome provided material falls firmly within the company's specialist subject areas.
ROYALTIES annually.

Fernhurst Books
John Wiley and Sons Ltd., The Atrium, Southern Gate, Arundel BN19 8SQ
☎01243 770439 Fax 01243 775878
✉ dpalmer@wiley.co.uk
www.fernhurstbooks.co.uk
Commissioning Editor *David Palmer*
Founded 1979. Books for people who love watersports. Publishes practical, highly-illustrated handbooks on sailing and watersports.

TITLES *The 32nd America's Cup; Laser Book; Rules in Practice; Wind Strategy; Weather at Sea; Simple Boat Maintenance; Electrics Afloat.* Synopses and ideas welcome.

David Fickling Books
See **The Random House Group Ltd**

Fig Tree
See **Penguin Group (UK)**

Findhorn Press Ltd
305A The Park, Findhorn IV36 3TE
☎01309 690582 Fax 01309 690036
✉ info@findhornpress.com
www.findhornpress.com

Director *Thierry Bogliolo*

Founded 1971. Publishes mind, body and spirit, New Age and healing. 24 titles in 2006. Unsolicited synopses and ideas via e-mail only if they come within Findhorn's subject areas. No children's books, fiction or poetry.
ROYALTIES twice-yearly.

Firefly Publishing
See **Helter Skelter Publishing**

First & Best in Education Ltd
Hamilton House, Earlstrees Court, Earlstrees Road, Corby NN17 4HH
☎01536 399005 Fax 01536 399012
✉ editorial@firstandbest.co.uk
www.firstandbest.co.uk
www.shop.firstandbest.co.uk

Publisher *Tony Attwood*
Editor *Anne Cockburn*

Publishers of over 1000 educational books of all types for all ages of children and for parents and teachers. Also small series of books on marketing. All books are published as being suitable for photocopying and/or as electronic books. 'Looking for new authors of educational books all the time. No fiction, please.' TITLES *Raising Grades Through Study Skills; Business Sponsorship of Secondary Schools; Policy Documents for Day Nurseries and Nursery Units.* IMPRINT **School Improvement Reports**. Check the website for submission guidelines.
ROYALTIES twice-yearly.

Fitzgerald Publishing
89 Ermine Road, Ladywell, London SE13 7JJ
☎020 8690 0597
✉ fitzgeraldbooks@yahoo.co.uk

Managing Editors *Tim Fitzgerald, Michael Fitzgerald*

General Editor *Andrew Smith*

Founded 1974. Specialises in scientific studies of insects and spiders. TITLES *The Tarantula; Keeping Spiders and Insects in Captivity; Tarantulas of the USA; Scorpions of Medical Importance* (books) and *Earth Tigers – Tarantulas of Borneo; Desert Tarantulas* (TV/video documentaries). 1–2 titles a year. Unsolicited mss, synopses and ideas for books welcome. Also considers video scripts for video documentaries.

Fitzjames Press
See **Motor Racing Publications**

Five Star
See **Serpent's Tail**

Floris Books
15 Harrison Gardens, Edinburgh EH11 1SH
☎0131 337 2372 Fax 0131 347 9919
✉ floris@florisbooks.co.uk
www.florisbooks.co.uk

Managing Director *Christian Maclean*
Editors *Christopher Moore, Gale Winskill*
Approx. Annual Turnover £350,000

Founded 1977. Publishes books related to the Steiner movement, including The Christian Community, as well as arts & crafts, children's (including fiction with a Scottish theme), history, religious, science, social questions and Celtic studies. No unsolicited mss except for the Kelpies children's books (not picture books). Synopses and ideas are welcome for all books except children's.
ROYALTIES annually.

Focal Press
See **Elsevier Ltd**

Folens Limited
Apex Business Centre, Boscombe Road, Dunstable LU5 4RL
☎0870 609 1235 Fax 0870 609 1236
✉ folens@folens.com
www.folens.com

Chairman *Dirk Folens*
Managing Director *Adrian Cockell*

Founded 1987. A leading educational publisher. IMPRINTS **Folens; Belair**. About 150 titles a year. Unsolicited mss, synopses and ideas for educational books welcome.
ROYALTIES annually.

Fort Publishing Ltd
Old Belmont House, 12 Robsland Avenue, Ayr KA7 2RW

☎01292 880693 Fax 01292 270134
✉ fortpublishing@aol.com
www.fortpublishing.co.uk
Chairman *Agnes Jane McCarroll*
Managing Director *James McCarroll*
Approx. Annual Turnover £95,000
Founded 1999. Publishes general non-fiction, history, sport, crime and local interest. TITLES *Glasgow Then and Now; Great Hull Stories; Evil Scotland; Ten Days That Shook Rangers.* 9 titles in 2005. No unsolicited mss; send synopses and ideas for books by post or e-mail.
ROYALTIES twice-yearly.

Foulsham Publishers

The Publishing House, Bennetts Close, Slough SL1 5AP
☎01753 526769 Fax 01753 535003
✉ reception@foulsham.com
www.foulsham.com
Chairman/Managing Director *B.A.R. Belasco*
Approx. Annual Turnover £2.5 million
Founded 1800 and now one of the few remaining independent family companies to survive takeover. Publishes non-fiction on most subjects including lifestyle, travel guides, family reference, cookery, diet, health, DIY, business, self improvement, self development, astrology, dreams, MBS. No fiction. IMPRINT **Quantum** Mind, body and spirit titles. TITLES *Classic 1000 Cocktails; A Brit's Guide to Orlando and Walt Disney World 2006; Old Moore's Almanack; Raphael's Astrological Ephemeris.* Around 60 titles a year. Unsolicited mss, synopses and ideas welcome – in hard copy.
ROYALTIES twice-yearly.

Fountain Press

Newpro UK Ltd., Old Sawmills Road, Faringdon SN7 7DS
☎01367 242411 Fax 01367 241124
✉ sales@newprouk.co.uk
www.newprouk.co.uk
Publisher *C.J. Coleman*
Approx. Annual Turnover £800,000
Founded 1923 when it was part of the Rowntree Trust Social Service. Owned by the British Electric Traction Group until 1982 when it was bought out by H.M. Ricketts. Acquired by Newpro UK Ltd in July 2000. Publishes mainly photography and natural history. TITLES *Photography and Digital 'Workshop'; Antique and Collectable Cameras; Camera Manual* (series). About 2 titles a year. Unsolicited mss and synopses welcome.

ROYALTIES twice-yearly.
Authors' Rating Highly regarded for production values, Fountain has the reputation for involving authors in every stage of the publishing process.

Four O Clock Press
See **Discovered Authors**

Fourth Estate
See **HarperCollins Publishers Ltd**

Free Association Books Ltd

PO Box 37664, London NW7 2XU
☎020 8906 0396 Fax 020 8906 0006
✉ info@fabooks.com
www.fabooks.com
Managing Director/Publisher *T.E. Brown*
Publishes psychoanalysis and psychotherapy, psychology, cultural studies, sexuality and gender, women's studies, applied social sciences. TITLES *Drug Use and Cultural Context* eds. Ross Coomber and Nigel South; *Skin Disease* Ann Maguire; *Caring for the Dying at Home* Gill Pharoah; *A History of Group Study and Psychodynamic Organizations* Amy L. Fraher. Always send a letter in the first instance accompanied by a book outline. OVERSEAS ASSOCIATES ISBS, USA; Astam, Australia.
ROYALTIES twice-yearly.

The Free Press
See **Simon & Schuster UK Ltd**

W.H. Freeman

Palgrave, Houndmills, Basingstoke RG21 6XS
☎01256 329242 Fax 01256 330688
www.palgrave.com
President *Elizabeth Widdicombe* (New York)
Editorial Director *Margaret Hewinson*
Following integration into the BFW (Bedford, Freeman, Worth) College Group, USA, W.H. Freeman now publishes academic educational and textbooks in biochemistry, biology and zoology, chemistry, economics, mathematics and statistics, natural history, neuroscience, palaeontology, physics. W.H. Freeman's editorial office is in New York (Basingstoke is a sales and marketing office only) but unsolicited mss can go through Basingstoke. Those which are obviously unsuitable will be sifted out; the rest will be forwarded to New York.
ROYALTIES annually.

Samuel French Ltd

52 Fitzroy Street, London W1T 5JR
☎020 7387 9373 Fax 020 7387 2161

✉ theatre@samuelfrench-london.co.uk
www.samuelfrench-london.co.uk

Chairman *Leon Embry*
Managing Director *Vivien Goodwin*

Founded 1830 with the object of acquiring acting rights and publishing plays. Publishes plays only. About 50 titles a year. Unsolicited mss considered only after introductory letter addressed to the Performing Rights Department.

ROYALTIES twice-yearly for books; performing royalties monthly, subject to a minimum amount.

Authors' Rating Thrives on the amateur dramatic societies who are forever in need of play texts. Editorial advisers give serious attention to new material but a high proportion of the list is staged before it goes into print. New writers are advised to try one-act plays, much in demand by the amateur dramatic societies but rarely turned out by established playwrights.

The Friday Project Ltd
83 Victoria Street, London SW1H 0HW
☎020 3008 8472 Fax 020 7078 6030
✉ authors@thefridayproject.co.uk
www.thefridayproject.co.uk

Chairman *Anthony Cheetham*
Managing/Publishing Director *Clare Christian*
Commercial Director *Scott Pack*
Approx. Annual Turnover £2.4 million

Founded in 2005, The Friday Project specialises in 'turning the best of the Web into the finest of books'. Publishes fiction and non-fiction. 44 titles in 2007. Unsolicited mss, synopses and ideas for books welcome; approach by e-mail. No academic books.

ROYALTIES twice-yearly.

David Fulton Publishers Ltd
2 Park Square, Milton, Abingdon OX14 4RN
☎020 7017 6000 Fax 020 8996 3622
✉ info@routledge.co.uk
www.routledge.co.uk

Owner *Taylor Francis Group*
Senior Publisher *Philip Mudd*
Approx. Annual Turnover £2.4 million

Founded 1987. Part of Routledge Education. Publishes books for trainee and working teachers at all levels of the curriculum (foundation stage to post compulsory), with particular emphasis on special educational needs (SEN) and inclusion. Special educational needs books also published in collaboration with the National Association for Special Educational Needs (NASEN); some overlap into other areas of health and social care, therapy, educational psychology, and speech and language therapy. A growing list of early years books for pre-school and nursery staff. About 100 titles a year. No unsolicited mss; synopses and ideas for books welcome.

ROYALTIES annually.

Funfax
See **Dorling Kindersley Ltd**

Fusion Press
See **Vision**

Gaia Books
See **Octopus Publishing Group**

J. Garnet Miller
See **Cressrelles Publishing Co. Ltd**

Garnet Publishing Ltd
8 Southern Court, South Street, Reading RG1 4QS
☎0118 959 7847 Fax 0118 959 7356
✉ dan@garnetpublishing.co.uk
www.garnetpublishing.co.uk

Editorial Manager *Dan Nunn*

Founded 1992 and purchased Ithaca Press in the same year. Publishes art, architecture, photography, archive photography, cookery, travel classics, comparative religion, Islamic culture and history, foreign fiction in translation. Core subjects are Middle Eastern but list is rapidly expanding to be more general.

IMPRINTS **Garnet Publishing** TITLES *Simply Lebanese; The Art and Architecture of Islamic Cairo.* **Ithaca Press** Specialises in post-graduate academic works on the Middle East, political science and international relations TITLES *The Making of the Modern Gulf States; The Palestinian Exodus; French Imperialism in Syria; Philby of Arabia.* About 20 titles a year. Unsolicited mss not welcome; write with outline and ideas first plus current c.v.

ROYALTIES twice-yearly.

Geddes & Grosset
David Dale House, New Lanark ML11 9DJ
☎01555 665000 Fax 01555 665694

Publishers *Ron Grosset, R. Michael Miller*
Approx. Annual Turnover £2.5 million

Founded 1989. Publisher of children's and reference books. Unsolicited mss, synopses and ideas welcome. No adult fiction.

GEE
See **Sweet & Maxwell Group**

The Geological Society Publishing House

Unit 7, Brassmill Enterprise Centre, Brassmill Lane, Bath BA1 3JN
☎01225 445046 Fax 01225 442836
✉ sales@geolsoc.org.uk *or* enquiries@geolsoc.org.uk
www.geolsoc.org.uk

Commissioning Editor *Angharad Hills*

Publishing arm of the Geological Society which was founded in 1807. Publishes postgraduate texts in the earth sciences. 30 titles a year. Unsolicited synopses and ideas welcome.

Stanley Gibbons Publications

7 Parkside, Christchurch Road, Ringwood BH24 3SH
☎01425 472363 Fax 01425 470247
✉ info@stanleygibbons.com
www.stanleygibbons.com

Chairman *P. Fraser*
Editorial Head *H. Jefferies*

Long-established force in the philatelic world with 150 years in the business. Publishes philatelic reference catalogues and handbooks. Reference works relating to other areas of collecting may be considered. TITLES *Stanley Gibbons British Commonwealth Stamp Catalogue; Stamps of the World.* Foreign catalogues include Japan and Korea, Portugal and Spain, Germany, Middle East, Balkans, China. Monthly publication: *Gibbons Stamp Monthly* (see entry under *Magazines*). www.collectorcafe.com – Internet site covering full range of collectables – editorial input always considered. About 20 titles a year. Unsolicited mss, synopses and ideas welcome.
ROYALTIES by negotiation.

Robert Gibson and Sons (Glasgow)

See **Hodder Gibson**

Gibson Square

47 Lonsdale Square, London N1 1EW
☎020 7096 1100 Fax 020 7993 2214
✉ info@gibsonsquare.com
www.gibsonsquare.com

Chairman *Martin Rynja*

Founded 2001. Publishes exclusively nonfiction: biography, current affairs, politics, cultural criticism, psychology, history, travel, art history, philosophy. Books must have high publicity profile. IMPRINTS **Gibson Square** TITLES *Londonistan* Melanie Phillips; *House of Bush House of Saud* Craig Unger; *Blowing up Russia* Alexander Litvinenko; *Two Lipsticks & a*

Lover Helena Frith Powell. Welcomes unsolicited mss, synopses and ideas. Send self-addressed, franked, return envelope. E-mailed submissions will be read but reply sent only if interested. No fiction.
ROYALTIES twice-yearly.

Ginn

See **Harcourt**

Gloucester Publishers Plc

10 Northburgh Street, London EC1V 0AT
☎020 7253 7887 Fax 020 7490 3708
✉ markbicknell@everyman.uk.com
www.everymanchess.com

Managing Director *Mark Bicknell*
Approx. Annual Turnover £1 million

Publishes exclusively academic and leisure books relating to chess. IMPRINT **Everyman Chess** TITLES *Garry Kasparov: My Great Predecessors, Vols 1–4; Play Winning Chess* Yasser Seirawan; *Art of Attack in Chess* Vladimir Vukovich. 30 titles in 2006/7. No unsolicited material.
ROYALTIES annually.

GMC Publications Ltd

166 High Street, Lewes BN7 1XU
☎01273 477374 Fax 01273 402866
✉ pubs@thegmcgroup.com
www.thegmcgroup.com

Joint Managing Directors *J.A.J. Phillips, J.A.B. Phillips*
Managing Editor *Gerrie Purcell*

Founded 1974. Publisher and distributor of craft and leisure books and magazines, covering topics such as woodworking, DIY, architecture, photography, gardening, cookery, art, puzzles and games, reference, humour, TV and film. About 50 illustrated books and 11 magazines a year. Unsolicited mss, synopses and ideas for books welcome. No fiction.
ROYALTIES twice-yearly.

Godsfield Press

See **Octopus Publishing Group**

Gollancz

See **The Orion Publishing Group Limited**

Gomer Press/Gwasg Gomer

Llandysul Enterprise Park, Llandysul SA44 4JL
☎01559 363090 Fax 01559 363758
✉ gwasg@gomer.co.uk
www.gomer.co.uk

Chairman/Managing Director *J.E. Lewis*
Publishing Director *Mairwen Prys Jones*

Editors (adult books – Welsh) *Bethan Mair, Bryan James*
Editor (adult books – English) *Ceri Wyn Jones*
Editors (children's books – Welsh) *Sioned Lleinau, Helen Evans, Rhiannon Davies*
Pont Books (children's books – English) Editor *Viv Sayer*

Founded 1892. Publishes adult fiction and non-fiction, children's fiction and educational material in English and in Welsh. IMPRINTS **Gomer**; **Pont Books**. 145 titles a year. Unsolicited mss welcome. Prior enquiry recommended.
ROYALTIES twice-yearly.

Gower
See **Ashgate Publishing Ltd**

Graham-Cameron Publishing & Illustration
The Studio, 23 Holt Road, Sheringham NR26 8NB
☎01263 821333 Fax 01263 821334
✉ enquiry@graham-cameron-illustration.com
www.graham-cameron-illustration.com

Also at: 59 Hertford Road, Brighton BN1 7GG
☎ 01273 385890

Editorial Director *Mike Graham-Cameron*
Art Director *Helen Graham-Cameron*

Founded 1984 as a packaging operation. Publishes illustrated books for children and adults for institutions and business. TITLES *Up From the Country*; *In All Directions*; *The Holywell Story*; *Flashbacks*; *Let's Look at Dairying*. Has 37 contracted book illustrators concentrating on educational and children's books. *Absolutely no unsolicited mss.*
ROYALTIES annually.

Granta Books
2–3 Hanover Yard, Noel Road, London N1 8BE
☎020 7704 9776 Fax 020 7354 3469
www.granta.com

Editorial Director *To be appointed*

Founded 1979. Acquired by Sigrid Rausing in 2006. Publishes general non-fiction and some literary fiction. About 35 titles a year. No unsolicited mss; synopses and sample chapters welcome.
ROYALTIES twice-yearly.

W. Green (Scotland)
See **Sweet & Maxwell Group**

Green Books
Foxhole, Dartington, Totnes TQ9 6EB
☎01803 863260 Fax 01803 863843
✉ edit@greenbooks.co.uk
www.greenbooks.co.uk

Chairman *Satish Kumar*
Publisher *John Elford*
Approx. Annual Turnover £500,000

Founded in 1987 with the support of a number of Green organisations. Closely associated with *Resurgence* magazine. Publishes high-quality books on a wide range of Green issues, including economics, politics and the practical application of Green thinking. No fiction or books for children. TITLES *The Organic Directory* ed. Clive Litchfield; *Timeless Simplicity* John Lane; *Allotment Gardening* Susan Berger. No unsolicited mss. Synopses and ideas welcome but check guidelines on the website in the first instance.
ROYALTIES twice-yearly.

Green Print
See **The Merlin Press Ltd**

Greenhill Books/ Lionel Leventhal Ltd
Park House, 1 Russell Gardens, London NW11 9NN
☎020 8458 6314 Fax 020 8905 5245
✉ michael.leventhal@greenhillbooks.com
www.greenhillbooks.com

Director *Michael Leventhal*

Founded 1984 by Lionel Leventhal (ex-Arms & Armour Press). Publishes aviation, military and naval books. Synopses and ideas for books welcome.
ROYALTIES twice-yearly.

Gresham Books Ltd
46 Victoria Road, Summertown, Oxford OX2 7QD
☎01865 513582 Fax 01865 512718
✉ info@gresham-books.co.uk
www.gresham-books.co.uk

Managing Director *Paul Lewis*
Approx. Annual Turnover £350,000

A small specialist publishing house. Publishes hymn and service books for schools and churches, school histories, also craft-bound choir and orchestral folders and Records of Achievement. No unsolicited material but ideas welcome.

Grisewood & Dempsey
See **Kingfisher Publications Plc**

Grub Street

4 Rainham Close, London SW11 6SS
☎020 7924 3966/7738 1008
Fax 020 7738 1009
✉ post@grubstreet.co.uk
www.grubstreet.co.uk

Managing Director *John Davies*

Founded 1982. Publishes cookery, food and wine, military and aviation history books. About 30 titles a year. Unsolicited mss and synopses welcome in the above categories but please enclose return postage.

ROYALTIES twice-yearly.

Guardian/Observer Books

See **Atlantic Books**

Guinness World Records Ltd

338 Euston Road, London NW1 3BD
☎020 7891 4567 Fax 020 7891 4501
✉ sales@guinnessworldrecords.com
www.guinnessworldrecords.com

Managing Director *Alistair Richards*

First published in 1955, the annual Guinness World Records book is published in more than 100 countries and 28 languages and is the highest-selling copyright book of all time, with more than 3 million copies sold annually across the globe. In addition to *Guinness World Records* the company publishes the annual industry-standard volume *British Hit Singles & Albums*. Guinness World Records is part of HIT Entertainment Ltd. Contact from prospective researchers, editors and designers welcome.

Gulf Professional Press

See **Elsevier Ltd**

Gullane Children's Books

See **Pinwheel Limited**

Gwasg Carreg Gwalch

12 Iard yr Orsaf, Llanrwst LL26 0EH
☎01492 642031 Fax 01492 641502
✉ books@carreg-gwalch.co.uk
www.carreg-gwalch.co.uk

Managing Editor *Myrddin ap Dafydd*

Founded in 1980. Publishes Welsh language; English books of Welsh interest – history, folklore, guides and walks. About 90 titles a year. Unsolicited mss, synopses and ideas welcome if of Welsh interest.

ROYALTIES paid.

Hachette Children's Books

338 Euston Road, London NW1 3BH
☎020 7873 6000
www.hachettechildrens.co.uk
www.franklinwatts.co.uk
www.orchardbooks.co.uk
www.hodderchildrens.co.uk
www.waylandbooks.co.uk

Owner *Hachette Book Group Inc.*
Managing Director *Marlene Johnson*
Approx. Annual Turnover £32 million

Formed by the combining of Watts Publishing Group with Hodder Children's Books in April 2005. Publishes children's non-fiction, reference, information, gift, fiction, picture and novelty books and audio books. IMPRINTS **Hodder Children's Books** *Anne McNeil* Fiction, picture books, novelty, general non-fiction and audio. **Orchard Press** Fiction & Picture *To be appointed*; Orchard Picture Books & Novelties *Kate Burns*; Orchard Fiction *Penny Morris*; **Franklin Watts** *Rachel Cooke* Non-fiction and information books. **Wayland** *Joyce Bentley* Non-fiction and information books. About 1100 titles a year. Unsolicited material is not considered.

ROYALTIES twice-yearly.

Hachette Livre

French publishing conglomerate which embraces **Chambers Harrap Publishers**, **Hachette Livre UK**, **Orion Publishing Group**, **Octopus Publishing Group**, **Little, Brown Book Group**. For further information, see imprint entries and entry under *European Publishers*.

Authors' Rating Now the largest UK trade publishing group with 16.4% of the total consumer market.

Hachette Livre UK

338 Euston Road, London NW1 3BH
☎020 7873 6000 Fax 020 7873 6024
www.hodderheadline.co.uk

Group Chief Executive *Tim Hely Hutchinson*
Approx. Annual Turnover £170 million

Hodder Headline was formed in June 1993 through the merger of Headline Book Publishing and Hodder & Stoughton and was renamed Hachette Livre UK in August 2007. The company was acquired by WHSmith plc in 1999 and subsequently by Hachette Livre S.A. in October 2004. Purchased John Murray (Publishers) Ltd in 2002. About 2000 titles a year.

DIVISIONS

Headline Book Publishing Managing Director *Martin Neild*, Deputy Managing

Director *Kerr MacRae*, Director of Non-fiction *Val Hudson*, Director of Fiction *Jane Morpeth* Publishes commercial and literary fiction (hardback and paperback) and popular non-fiction including autobiography, biography, food and wine, history, humour, popular science, sport and TV tie-ins. IMPRINTS **Headline**; **Headline Review**; **Little Black Dress**. AUTHORS Kate Adie, Catherine Alliott, Lyn Andrews, Emily Barr, Louise Bagshaw, Colin Bateman, Martina Cole, Janet Evanovich, Sophie Grigson, Wendy Holden, Matthew Jukes, Faye and Jonathan Kellerman, Jill Mansell, Maggie O'Farrell, Sheila O'Flanagan, James Patterson, Pamela Stephenson, Penny Vincenzi.

Hodder & Stoughton General Managing Director *Jamie Hodder-Williams*, Deputy Managing Director *Lisa Highton*; **Non-fiction** *Rowena Webb*; **Sceptre** *Carole Welch*; **Fiction** *Carolyn Mays*; **Audio** (see entry under *Audio Books*). Publishes commercial and literary fiction; biography, autobiography, history, self-help, humour, travel and other general interest non-fiction; audio. IMPRINTS **Hodder & Stoughton**; **Hodder Paperbacks**; **Sceptre**; **Mobius**. AUTHORS Melvyn Bragg, Jeffrey Deaver, Charles Frazier, Elizabeth George, Thomas Keneally, Stephen King, John le Carré, Andrew Miller, David Mitchell, Jodi Picoult, Rosamunde Pilcher, Mary Stewart, Fiona Walker. No unsolicited mss.

Hodder Children's Books (See **Hachette Children's Books**)

Hodder & Stoughton Religious Publishing Director *Judith Longman*, **Bibles & Hodder Christian Book**s *David Moloney*. Publishes TNIV, NIV and NIrV Bibles, Christian books, autobiography, biography, TV-tie-ins, gift/humour books, self-help. IMPRINTS **Hodder & Stoughton**; **Hodder Paperbacks**; **TNIV**; **NIV**; **NIrV**.

Hodder Education Group Managing Director *Philip Walters* Publishes in the following areas: **Schools** *Lis Tribe*; **Consumer Education** *Katie Roden*; **Further Education/Higher Education** Textbooks; **Health Sciences** *Philip Walters* (acting). Imprints **Hodder Murray**; **Teach Yourself**; **Hodder Arnold**; **Hodder Gibson** (see entry).

John Murray (Publishers) Ltd (see entry).

Authors' Rating Into its twentieth year, Hachette Livre UK, formerly known as Hodder Headline, is holding its reputation for publishing 'a broad range of stylish bestsellers'. The change of name does not imply a change of policy. While each imprint maintains its editorial independence, the joint strength of marketing muscle, at a time when bookselling is increasingly dominated by the high street chains and Amazon, will benefit brand name authors at the expense of those stuck in the midlist.

Halban Publishers

22 Golden Square, London W1F 9JW
☎020 7437 9300 Fax 020 7437 9512
✉ books@halbanpublishers.com
www.halbanpublishers.com

Directors *Peter Halban, Martine Halban*

Founded 1986. Independent publisher. Publishes biography, autobiography and memoirs, history, literature and Judaica. 8–10 titles a year. No unsolicited material. Approach by letter in first instance.

ROYALTIES twice-yearly for first two years, thereafter annually in December.

Robert Hale Ltd

Clerkenwell House, 45–47 Clerkenwell Green, London EC1R 0HT
☎020 7251 2661 Fax 020 7490 4958
✉ enquire@halebooks.com

Chairman/Managing Director *John Hale*

Founded 1936. Family-owned company. Publishes adult fiction (but not interested in category romance or science fiction) and non-fiction. No specialist material (education, law, medical or scientific). Acquired NAG Press Ltd in 1993 with its list of horological, gemmological, jewellery and metalwork titles, and **J.A. Allen & Co.** in 1999 with its extensive list of horse and dog books (see entry). TITLES Non-fiction: *Doctor's Latin* Keith Souter; *Watchmakers and Clockmakers of the World* Brian Loomes; *Rowing & Sculling* Bill Sayer; *Sussex* Peter Brandon; *Pets in Prospect* Malcolm D. Welshman. Fiction: *Laughter Class* Wendy Perriam; *Death's Dominion* Simon Clark. Over 250 titles a year. Unsolicited mss, synopses and ideas for books welcome.

ROYALTIES twice-yearly.

Authors' Rating Smiled upon in a Society of Authors survey on author relations, Robert Hale has carved out a profitable niche for popular non-fiction.

Halsgrove

Halsgrove House, Ryelands Farm Estate, Bagley Green, Wellington TA21 9PZ
☎01823 653777 Fax 01823 665294
✉ sales@halsgrove.com
www.halsgrove.com

Publisher *Simon Butler*

Founded in 1990 and now a leading publisher and distributor of regional books. Publishes books of regional interest throughout the UK: local history (including the *Community History* series), biography, photography and art, mainly in hardback. No fiction or poetry. 150 titles in 2006. Unsolicited mss, synopses and ideas for books of regional interest welcome.

ROYALTIES annually.

Hambledon Continuum
See **The Continuum International Publishing Grooup Limited**

Hamish Hamilton
See **Penguin Group (UK)**

Hamlyn Octopus
See **Octopus Publishing Group**

Hammersmith Press Ltd

496 Fulham Palace Road, London SW6 6JD
☎020 7736 9132 Fax 020 7348 7521
✉ gmb@hammersmithpress.co.uk
www.hammersmithpress.co.uk

Managing Director *Georgina Bentliff*

Founded 2004. Publishes health, nutrition, diet, academic medicine, and 'literary medicine', i.e. literary works that relate to the practice of medicine. TITLES *Your Thyroid and How to Keep it Healthy* Dr Barry Durrant Peatfield; *Playing God – poems about medicine* Dr Glenn Colquhoun. 3 titles in 2006. No unsolicited mss; synopses and ideas for books welcome; approach by e-mail. No fiction or children's material.

ROYALTIES twice-yearly.

Happy Cat
See **Catnip Publishing Ltd**

Harcourt

Halley Court, Jordan Hill, Oxford OX2 8EJ
☎01865 888000 (customer services)/311366
Fax 01865 314641
✉ enquiries@harcourt.co.uk (customer services)
www.harcourt.co.uk

Rights Director *Melissa Tombling*

Harcourt is a leading provider of educational resources for teachers and learners at primary, secondary and vocational level and the largest publisher of books and e-learning materials for schools and colleges in the UK. From May 2007, ownership of Harcourt switched from Reed Elsevier to Pearson. Under the **Heinemann, Rigby, Ginn, Payne-Gallway** and **Raintree** IMPRINTS, Harcourt provides a range of published resources, teachers' support, and pupil and student material in all core subjects for all ages. For submissions, write to 'Market Planning' at the address above.

ROYALTIES twice-yearly/annually, according to contract.

Harlequin Mills & Boon Limited

Eton House, 18–24 Paradise Road, Richmond TW9 1SR
☎020 8288 2800 Fax 020 8288 2898
www.eharlequin.com
www.millsandboon.co.uk

Managing Director *Guy Hallowes*
Editorial Director *Karin Stoecker*
Approx. Annual Turnover £18.97 million

Founded 1908. Owned by the Canadian-based Torstar Group. Publishes a wide range of women's fiction including romantic novels.

IMPRINTS **Mills & Boon Modern Romance** *Tessa Shapcott* (50–55,000 words) Alpha males and attractive women swept up in intense emotions set against a backdrop of international locations, luxury and wealth; passion is guaranteed. **Mills & Boon Modern Extra** *Bryony Green* (60,000 words) Delivers a feel-good experience, focusing on the kind of relationship that women aged 18 to 35 aspire to. Young characters in urban settings meet, flirt, share experiences, have great sex and fall in love, finally making a commitment that will bind them forever. Based around emotional issues, other concerns – e.g. jobs and friendships – are also touched upon and resolved in upbeat way. **Mills & Boon Romance** *Kimberley Young* (50–55,000 words) Contemporary upbeat and heroine-focused romance, driven by strongly emotional conflicts which are believable and relevant to today's women. Capturing the depth of emotion and sheer excitement of falling in love in a variety of international settings. **Mills & Boon Medical Romance** *Sheila Hodgson* (50–55,000 words) Modern medical practice provides a unique background to highly emotional contemporary romances. **Mills & Boon Historical Romance** *Linda Fildew* (80–95,000 words) Richly textured, emotionally intense historical novels covering a wide range of settings and periods from ancient civilisations up to and including the Second World War. Over 600 titles a year. Other submissions: also accepting submissions in all general women's fiction genres (contemporary and historical) for longer series and single title imprints. Tip sheets and guidelines are available from the Mills & Boon or eHarlequin websites (see above) or Harlequin Mills & Boon Editorial Dept. (telephone or write sending s.a.e.). Agented and unagented submissions accepted. Send query letter, synopsis and first three chapters in the first instance.

Authors' Rating M&B's dabbling in raw sex proved to have less appeal than the staple romance. This provides a good income for writers who can adapt to the clearly defined M&B formula. Just think, M&B has a network of 12,000 authors worldwide and every title scores six-figure sales. But be warned. M&B gets 2000 unsolicited manuscripts a year. The audio list has come to a premature end but the Christmas annual is to continue.

Harley Books

Martins, Great Horkesley, Colchester
CO6 4AH
☎01206 271216 Fax 01206 271182
✉ harley@harleybooks.co.uk
www.harleybooks.com

Managing Director *Basil Harley*
Owners *B.H. & A. Harley*

Founded 1983. Natural history publishers specialising in entomological and botanical books. Mostly definitive, high-quality illustrated reference works. TITLES *Liverwort Mosses and Ferns of Europe*; *Dragonflies of Europe*; *The Aurelian Legacy: British Butterflies and their Collectors*; *The Liverwort Flora of the British Isles*; *Maggots, Murder and Men: Memories and Reflections of a Forensic Entomologist*; *Freshwater Fishes in Britain*. 58 titles. No unsolicited material (no longer publishing new titles).

HarperCollins Publishers Ltd

77–85 Fulham Palace Road, London W6 8JB
☎020 8741 7070 Fax 020 8307 4440
www.harpercollins.co.uk

Also at: Westerhill Road, Bishopbriggs, Glasgow G64 2QT
☎ 0141 772 3200 Fax 0141 306 3119

Owner *News Corporation*
CEO/Publisher *Victoria Barnsley*
Approx. Annual Turnover £173.4 million (UK)

HarperCollins is one of the leading book publishers in the UK, with a wider range of books than any other publisher; from cutting-edge contemporary fiction to block-busting thrillers, from fantasy literature and children's stories to enduring classics. The wholly-owned division of News Corporation also publishes a wide selection of non-fiction including history, celebrity memoirs, biography, popular science, mind, body and spirit, dictionaries, maps and reference books. HarperCollins is also one of the largest education publishers in the UK. Authors include many award-winning and international bestsellers such as Isabel Allende, Paulo Coelho, Josephine Cox, Michael Crichton, Cathy Kelly, Judith Kerr, Doris Lessing, Frank McCourt, Tony Parsons, Nigel Slater and Diana Wynne Jones. Bestselling licensed properties include Dr Seuss and Noddy. About 1500 titles a year.

GENERAL BOOKS DIVISION
Managing Director *Amanda Ridout*
Harper Fiction Publisher *Lynne Drew* IMPRINTS **HarperCollins** Publishing Directors *Susan Watt, Julia Wisdom*; **Voyager** Fantasy/science fiction Publishing Director *Jane Johnson* General, historical fiction, crime and thrillers and women's fiction.

Harper Non-Fiction Managing Director/Publisher *Belinda Budge*, Publisher *Carole Tomkinson*, Editorial Directors *Viv Bowler* (cookery & lifestyle), *Natalie Jerome* (popular culture). **Avon** Managing Director *Caroline Ridding*, Editorial Director *Maxine Hitchcock* Popular fiction. IMPRINTS **HarperCollins** Publishing Director *David Brawn* (Agatha Christie, J.R.R. Tolkien, C.S. Lewis) Media-related books from film companions to celebrity autobiographies and TV tie-ins; **HarperSport** Publishing Director *Jonathan Taylor* Sporting biographies, guides and histories; **HarperCollins Audio** (see entry under *Audio Books*).

HarperThorsons/Element Publisher *Carole Tomkinson* (mind, body & spirit), *Sally Potter* (media tie-ins).

HarperCollins Children's Books Managing Director *Mario Santos*, Publisher *Ann-Janine Murtagh* Quality picture books for under-7s; fiction for age 6 up to young adult; TV and film tie-ins and properties Publishing Directors *Gillie Russell* (fiction), *Sue Buswell* (picture books)

PRESS BOOKS DIVISION
Managing Director *John Bond*
IMPRINTS **Fourth Estate** Publishing Director/Publisher *Nick Pearson* Fiction, literary fiction, current affairs, popular science, biography,

humour, travel; **HarperPress** General trade non-fiction and fiction Publishing Directors *Arabella Pike* (non-fiction), *Clare Smith* (fiction); **HarperPerennial** Paperback imprint. Publishing Director *Paul Baggaley*

COLLINS DIVISION
Managing Director *Thomas Webster*
Collins Reference Managing Director *Sarah Bailey* Guides and handbooks, Times World Atlases, Collins World Atlases, phrase books and manuals on popular reference, art instruction, illustrated, cookery and wine, crafts, DIY, gardening, military, natural history, pet care, pastimes Publishing Directors *Denise Bates* (illustrated reference), *Sheena Barclay* (world atlases), Associate Publisher *Myles Archibald* (natural history) IMPRINTS **Collins**; **Collins Gem**; **Times Books**; **Jane's**.
    Collins Dictionaries/COBUILD (division & imprint) **Collins Language** Managing Director *Robert Scriven* Bilingual and English dictionaries, English dictionaries for foreign learners. Publishing Directors *Helen Newstead* (digital development), *Elaine Higgleton* (editorial).
    Collins Education Managing Director *Jim Green* Books, CD-ROMs and online material for UK primary and secondary schools and colleges.
    Collins Maps and Road Atlases (division & imprint) Publishing Director *Helen Gordon* Maps, atlases, street plans and leisure guides.

Authors' Rating Rarely out of the bestseller lists, HarperCollins has enjoyed across the board growth with Fourth Estate's homegrown fiction, Thorson Element's non-fiction and the children's lists doing particularly well. HarperPress has launched a new fiction list.

Harrap
See **Chambers Harrap Publishers Ltd**

Harriman House Ltd
3A Penns Road, Petersfield GU32 2EW
☎01730 233870 Fax 01730 233880
✉ contact@harriman-house.com
www.harriman-house.com
Managing Director *Myles Hunt*
Founded 1994; commenced publishing in 2001. Independent publisher of finance, trading, business, economic and political books, covering a wide range of subjects from personal finance, small business and lifestyle through to stock market investing, trading and professional guides. 20 titles a year. Unsolicited mss, synopses

and ideas for book welcome. Initial approach by e-mail.
ROYALTIES twice-yearly.

Harvard University Press
Fitzroy House, 11 Chenies Street, London WC1E 7EY
☎020 7306 0603 Fax 020 7306 0604
✉ info@HUP-MITpress.co.uk
www.hup.harvard.edu
Director *William Sisler*
General Manager *Ann Sexsmith*
European office of **Harvard University Press**, USA. Publishes academic and scholarly works in history, politics, philosophy, economics, literary criticism, psychology, sociology, anthropology, women's studies, biological sciences, classics, history of science, art, music, film, reference. All mss go to the American office: 79 Garden Street, Cambridge, MA 02138 (see entry under *US Publishers*).

Harvill Secker
See **The Random House Group Ltd**

Haus Publishing
26 Cadogan Court, Draycott Avenue, London SW3 3BX
☎020 7584 6738 Fax 020 7584 9501
✉ haus@hauspublishing.com
www.hauspublishing.co.uk
Managing Director *Barbara Schwepcke*
DIVISIONS/IMPRINTS **Life&Times** Non-academic biographies of well-known and lesser-known personalities TITLES *Tito; Simone de Beauvoir; Prime Ministers of the 20th Century*. **ArmchairTraveller** Literary travel series TITLES *Mumbai to Mecca; Venice for Lovers*. **HausBooks** Hardback biographies TITLES *Ellen Terry; Rommel*. 26 titles in 2006. Unsolicited mss, synopses and ideas within the subject areas above are welcome; approach by e-mail or post only. No children's, fiction or poetry.
ROYALTIES twice-yearly.

Haynes Publishing
Sparkford, Near Yeovil BA22 7JJ
☎01963 440635 Fax 01963 440825
✉ info@haynes.co.uk
www.haynes.co.uk
Chairman *John H. Haynes, OBE*
Approx. Annual Turnover £30 million
Founded in 1960 by John H. Haynes. Listed public company with majority family ownership. The mainstay of its programme has been

the *Owners' Workshop Manual*, first published in the mid 1960s and still running off the presses today. Publishes DIY service and repair manuals for cars, motorbikes and leisure plus other related topics under the Haynes imprint.

AUTOMOTIVE DIVISION IMPRINT **Haynes** Editorial Director *Matthew Minter* Service and repair manuals; Editorial Director *Mark Hughes* Motoring, motor sport, cars, motorcycles, home, DIY and leisure titles. Unsolicited submissions welcome if they come within the subject areas covered. OVERSEAS SUBSIDIARIES Haynes Manuals Inc., California, USA; Haynes Publishing Nordiska AB, Sweden.

ROYALTIES twice-yearly.

Authors' Rating Having sold Sutton Publishing, Haynes is back to its core programme of publishing 'practical and hands-on' books.

Headline
See **Hachette Livre UK**

Heinemann
See **Harcourt**

William Heinemann
See **The Random House Group Ltd**

Helicon Publishing
RM plc, New Mill House, 183 Milton Park, Abingdon OX14 4SE
☎01235 823816
✉ helicon@rm.com
www.helicon.co.uk

Business Manager *Caroline Dodds*

A division of RM plc. Helicon is a general reference database publisher for the UK, US and Australian markets. Licenses quality reference content for online, print, and CD-ROM publications. TITLES include the flagship single-volume *Hutchinson 2005 Encyclopedia* published under licence from **Hodder Headline**. CD-ROM TITLES include *The Hutchinson Encyclopedia; The Hutchinson Science Reference Suite; The Hutchinson History Reference Suite; The Hutchinson Music Reference Suite*.

Christopher Helm
See **A.&C. Black Publishers Ltd**

Helm Information Ltd
Crowham Manor, Main Road, Westfield, Hastings TN35 4SR
☎01424 882422 Fax 01424 882817
✉ amandahelm@helm-information.co.uk
www.helm-information.co.uk

Director *Amanda Helm*

Founded 1990. Publishes academic books for students and university libraries. SERIES *The Critical Assessments of Writers in English* (collected criticism); *Literary Sources & Documents* (primary source material on themes/events/cultural/aesthetic movements ranging from the American Civil War to the Gothic Revival); *The Dickens Companions*; and *Icons*, a series which exposes the processes by which a figure, historical or fictional, achieves iconic status, e.g. Faust, Robin Hood. Will consider ideas and proposals provided they are relevant to the series listed above.

ROYALTIES annually.

Helter Skelter Publishing
South Bank House, Black Prince Road, London SE1 7SJ
☎020 7463 2204 Fax 020 7463 2295
✉ info@helterskelterpublishing.com
www.helterskelterpublishing.com

Editorial *Sean Body*
Art Director *Graeme Milton*

Founded 1995. Publishes music and film books only. IMPRINTS **Helter Skelter Publishing**; **Firefly Publishing**. 15 titles a year. Unsolicited mss, synopses and ideas welcome.

Ian Henry Publications Ltd
20 Park Drive, Romford RM1 4LH
☎01708 749119 Fax 01708 736213
✉ info@ian-henry.com
www.ian-henry.com

Managing Director *Ian Wilkes*

Founded 1976. Publishes local history, humour, transport history and Sherlockian pastiches. TITLES *People Who Mattered in Southend and Beyond*; *Deafness*. 1–2 titles a year. No unsolicited mss. Synopses and ideas for books welcome.

ROYALTIES twice-yearly.

The Herbert Press
See **A.&C. Black Publishers Ltd**

Hermes House
See **Anness Publishing Ltd**

Nick Hern Books
The Glasshouse, 49a Goldhawk Road, London W12 8QP
☎020 8749 4953 Fax 020 8735 0250
✉ info@nickhernbooks.demon.co.uk
www.nickhernbooks.co.uk

Chairman/Managing Director *Nick Hern*

Founded 1988. Fully independent since 1992. Publishes books on theatre and film: from how-to and biography to plays and screenplays.

About 40 titles a year. No unsolicited playscripts. Synopses, ideas and proposals for other theatre material welcome. Not interested in material unrelated to the theatre or cinema.

University of Hertfordshire Press

Learning and Information Services, Learning Resources Centre, College Lane, Hatfield
AL10 9AB
☎01707 284681 Fax 01707 284666
✉ UHPress@herts.ac.uk
www.herts.ac.uk/UHPress

Contact *Jane Housham*

Founded 1992. Publishes academic books on Gypsies, literature, regional and local history, parapsychology. IMPRINTS **University of Hertfordshire Press**; **Interface Collection**; **Hertfordshire Publications**. TITLES *Here to Stay: The Gypsies and Travellers of Britain* Colin Clark and Margaret Greenfields; *Selling Shakespeare to Hollywood: The marketing of filmed Shakespeare adaptations from 1989 into the new millennium* Emma French; *An Historical Atlas of Hertfordshire* ed. David Short. 15 titles a year

Hesperus Press Limited

4 Rickett Street, London SW6 1RU
☎020 7610 3331 Fax 020 7610 3217
www.hesperuspress.com

Managing Editor *Katherine Venn*

Founded 2001. Publishes lesser-known works in both original English and English translation by classic authors. TITLES *Hyde Park Gate News* Virginia Woolf; *Sarrasine* Honoré de Balzac; *No Man's Land* Graham Greene; *Hadji Murat* Lev Tolstoy; *Aller Retour New York* Henry Miller; *The Watsons* Jane Austen. *Modern Classics* series launched in 2005; contemporary European fiction in translation since 2005. 46 titles in 2007. Does not accept unsolicited mss.

ROYALTIES annually.

Authors' Rating Much praised for matching book design with quality content.

High Stakes

See **Oldcastle Books Ltd**

History Into Print

See **Brewin Books Ltd**

HMSO

See **TSO**

Hobsons Plc

Challenger House, 42 Adler Street, London E1 1EE
☎020 7958 5000 Fax 020 7958 5001

www.hobsons.uk.com

Chairman *Martin Morgan*
Group Managing Director *Christopher Letcher*

Founded 1974. Part of the Daily Mail & General Trust. Publishes course and career guides, under exclusive licence and royalty agreements for CRAC (Careers Research and Advisory Centre), directories and specialist titles for students and young professionals. TITLES *GET 2008*; *The Hobsons Study UK Guide 2008*; *The Hobsons Global MBA Guide 2008*.

Hodder & Stoughton

See **Hachette Livre UK**

Hodder Children's Books

See **Hachette Children's Books**

Hodder Gibson

2a Christie Street, Paisley PA1 1NB
☎0141 848 1609 Fax 0141 889 6315
✉ hoddergibson@hodder.co.uk
www.hoddereducation.co.uk

Managing Director *John Mitchell*

Part of the **Hodder Headline Group**. Publishes educational books specifically for Scotland. Combines the former Robert Gibson and Sons (Glasgow) with the Scottish branch of Hodder Murray (a merger of **John Murray** and **Hodder Stoughton Educational**). About 50 titles a year. Synopses/ideas preferred to unsolicited mss.

ROYALTIES annually.

Hodder Headline Ltd

See **Hachette Livre UK**

Honeyglen Publishing Ltd

56 Durrels House, Warwick Gardens, London W14 8QB
☎020 7602 2876 Fax 020 7602 2876

Directors *N.S. Poderegin, J. Poderegin*

Founded 1983. A small publishing house whose output is 'extremely limited'. Publishes history, philosophy of history, biography and selective fiction. No children's or science fiction. TITLES *The Soul of China*; *The Soul of India*; *Woman and Power in History*; *Lost World – Tibet*; *A Child of the Century* all by Amaury de Riencourt; *With Duncan Grant in South Turkey* Paul Roche; *Vladimir, The Russian Viking* Vladimir Volkoff; *The Dawning* Milka Bajic-Poderegin; *Quicksand* Louise Hide. Unsolicited mss welcome.

Honno Welsh Women's Press

c/o Canolfan Merched y Wawr, Vulcan Street, Aberystwyth SY23 1JH

☎01970 623150 Fax 01970 623150
✉ post@honno.co.uk
www.honno.co.uk

Editor *Caroline Oakley*

Founded in 1986 by a group of women who wanted to create more opportunities for women in publishing. A co-operative operation which publishes mainly fiction and autobiography. 'Contact us for current calls for short story submissions.' 7 titles a year. Welcomes mss and ideas for books from women who are Welsh or have a significant Welsh connection only Send as hard copy, not by e-mail.
ROYALTIES annually.

Horizon Press
See **Discovered Authors**

Horus Editions
See **Award Publications Limited**

How To Books Ltd
Spring Hill House, Spring Hill Road, Begbroke, Oxford OX5 1RX
☎01865 375794 Fax 01865 379162
✉ info@howtobooks.co.uk
www.howtobooks.co.uk

Managing Director *Giles Lewis*
Editorial Director *Nikki Read*

An independent publishing house, founded in 1991. Publishes non-fiction, self-help reference books. How To titles are practical, accessible books that enable their readers to achieve their goals in life and work. How To authors must have first-hand experience of the subject about which they are writing. Subjects covered include management, leisure learning, career choices and career development, living and working abroad, small business and self employment, study skills & student guides, creative writing and property. IMPRINTS **Transita** (see entry); **Springhill**. 250 titles a year. Submit outline followed by sample chapter.

Human Horizons
See **Souvenir Press Ltd**

John Hunt Publishing Ltd
See **O Books**

Hurst Publishers, Ltd
41 Great Russell Street, London WC1B 3PL
☎020 7255 2201
✉ hurst@atlas.co.uk
www.hurstpub.co.uk

Chairman/Managing Director/Editorial Head

Michael Dwyer

Founded 1967. An independent company publishing contemporary history, politics, religion (not theology) and anthropology.
About 25 titles a year. No unsolicited mss. Synopses and ideas welcome.
ROYALTIES annually.

Hutchinson/Hutchinson Children's Books
See **The Random House Group Ltd**

Hymns Ancient & Modern Ltd
St Mary's Works, St Mary's Plain, Norwich NR3 3BH
☎01603 612914 Fax 01603 624483
✉ admin@scm-canterburypress.co.uk
www.scm-canterburypress.co.uk

Chief Executive *Andrew Moore*
Publishing Director, SCM Press and
   Canterbury Press *Christine Smith*
Publisher, RMEP *Mary Mears*
Approx. Annual Turnover £4.4 million

Publishing subsidiary **SCM–Canterbury Press Ltd** (see entry) controls **SCM Press**, **Canterbury Press** and **RMEP** IMPRINTS which cover hymn books, liturgical material, academic and general religious books, and multi-faith religious and social education resources for pupils and teachers. Media subsidiary **G.J. Palmer & Sons Ltd** includes *Church Times* (see entry under *Magazines*); monthly magazine inserts *The Sign* and *Home Words* and *Crucible*, a quarterly magazine. About 100 titles a year. Ideas for new titles welcome but no unsolicited mss.
ROYALTIES annually.

Icon Books Ltd
The Old Dairy, Brook Road, Thriplow, Cambridge SG8 7RG
☎01763 208008 Fax 01763 208080
✉ info@iconbooks.co.uk
www.iconbooks.co.uk

Managing Director *Peter Pugh*
Publishing Director *Simon Flynn*
Editorial Director *Duncan Heath*

Founded 1992. SERIES *Introducing* Graphic introductions to key figures and ideas in the history of science, philosophy, psychology, religion and the arts. TITLE *Introducing Quantum Theory*. Publishes 'provocative and intelligent' non-fiction in science, politics and philosophy. TITLE *Why do People Hate America?* IMPRINT **Wizard Books** Children's non-fiction and game books including SERIES *Fighting Fantasy* (adventure gamebooks). Submit synopsis only. OVERSEAS ASSOCIATE Totem Books, USA, distributed by National Book Network.

ROYALTIES twice yearly.

Imprint Academic

PO Box 200, Exeter EX5 5YX
☎01392 851550 Fax 01392 851187
✉ keith@imprint.co.uk
www.imprint-academic.com

Publisher *Keith Sutherland*

Founded 1980. Publishes books and journals in politics, philosophy and psychology for both academic and general readers. Book series include *St. Andrews Studies in Philosophy and Public Affairs* and *Societas: Essays in political and cultural criticism*. Unsolicited mss, synopses and ideas welcome with return postage only.

The In Pinn

See **Neil Wilson Publishing Ltd**

Incomes Data Services

See **Sweet & Maxwell Group**

Independent Music Press

PO Box 69, Church Stretton SY6 6WZ
☎01694 720049 Fax 01694 720049
✉ info@impbooks.com
www.impbooks.com

Managing Director *Martin Roach*

Founded 1992. Publishes music biography and youth culture. No jazz or classical. TITLES include biographies of My Chemical Romance, Green Day, Muse, The Killers, The Cure, Dave Grohl, The Streets, Oasis, Prodigy as well as subculture classics such as *Scooter Boys* and Ian Hunter's *Diary of a Rock 'n' Roll Star*. 8 titles a year. Approach by e-mail, enclosing biography and synopsis only.

ROYALTIES twice-yearly.

Independent Voices

See **Souvenir Press Ltd**

Infinite Ideas

36 St Giles, Oxford OX1 3LD
☎01865 514888 Fax 01865 514777
✉ info@infideas.com
www.infideas.com

Joint Managing Directors *David Grant, Richard Burton*

Approx. Annual Turnover £1 million

Founded 2004. Publishes inspirational self-help. SERIES **52 Brilliant Ideas** Subject areas cover health and relationships; careers, finance and personal development; sports, hobbies and games; leisure and lifestyle; art, literature and music. No fiction, illustrated or children's books. IMPRINT **Bright 'I's** Business books, launched in 2006. 40 titles a year. No unsolicited mss. Synopses and ideas welcome; initial contact by e-mail or letter.

Flat FEES paid.

Informa Law

Informa House, 30–32 Mortimer Street, London W1W 7RE
☎020 7017 4600

Managing Director *Fotini Liontou*
Publishing Director *Wendy Gill*

Part of LLP Professional Publishing, a trading division of Informa Publishing Group Ltd. Publishes a range of maritime law, commercial law, insurance law, banking law, intellectual property law publications including newsletters, law reports, books, journals and magazines aimed at senior management and professional practices.

Inspire

c/o mph, 4 John Wesley Road, Werrington, Peterborough PE4 6ZP
☎01733 384188 Fax 01733 384180
✉ natalie.watson@mph.org.uk
www.mph.org.uk

Head of Publishing *Dr Natalie K. Watson*

Publishes accessible Christian books for the wider ecumenical market. Spirituality, social concern, worship resources, mission and evangelism, discipleship, prayer. No fiction or children's. 12 titles a year. Unsolicited mss, synopses and ideas welcome; send two sample chapters and proposal with covering letter and s.a.e. for return of mss.

ROYALTIES annually.

Inter-Varsity Press

IVP Book Centre, Norton Street, Nottingham NG7 3HR
☎0115 978 1054 Fax 0115 942 2694
✉ ivp@ivpbooks.com
www.ivpbooks.com

Chairman *Ralph Evershed*
Chief Executive *Brian Wilson*

Founded mid-1930s as the publishing arm of Universities and Colleges Christian Fellowship, it has expanded to wider Christian markets worldwide. Publishes Christian belief and lifestyle, reference and bible commentaries. No secular material or anything which fails to empathise with orthodox Protestant Christianity.

IMPRINTS **IVP**; **Apollos**; **Crossway** TITLES *The Bible Speaks Today*; *IVP Introduction to the Bible* Philip Johnston (ed.), *The Busy Christian's Guide to Busyness* Tim Chester. About 50 titles a year. Synopses and ideas welcome.

ROYALTIES twice-yearly.

Interface Collection
See **University of Hertfordshire Press**

Isis Publishing
7 Centremead, Osney Mead, Oxford OX2 0ES
☎01865 250333 Fax 01865 790358
✉ sales@isis-publishing.co.uk
www.isis-publishing.co.uk

Part of the Ulverscroft Group Ltd. Publishes large-print books – fiction and non-fiction – and unabridged audio books. Together with **Soundings** (see entry under *Audio Books*) produces around 4000 titles on audio tape and CD. AUTHORS Lee Child, Martina Cole, Terry Pratchett, Susan Sallis. No unsolicited mss as Isis undertakes no original publishing.

ROYALTIES twice-yearly.

Itchy Coo
See **Black & White Publishing Ltd**

Ithaca Press
See **Garnet Publishing Ltd**

IVP
See **Inter-Varsity Press**

Jacqui Small
See **Aurum Press Ltd**

JAI
See **Elsevier Ltd**

Jane's Information Group
Sentinel House, 163 Brighton Road, Coulsdon CR5 2YH
☎020 8700 3700 Fax 020 8763 1006
✉ info.uk@janes.com
www.janes.com

Owner *The Woodbridge Company Ltd*
Managing Director *Alfred Rolington*

Founded 1898 by Fred T. Jane with the publication of *All The World's Fighting Ships*. Now part of the Woodbridge Company Limited. In recent years management has been focusing on growth opportunities in its core business and in enhancing the performance of initiatives like Jane's information available online and on in-depth intelligence centres. Publishes Web journals, magazines and yearbooks on defence, aerospace, security and transport topics, with details of equipment and systems; plus directories. Full consulting arm offers bespoke offerings to clients. Also *Jane's Defence Weekly* (see entry under *Magazines*).

DIVISIONS **Magazines** Sean Howe TITLES *Jane's Defence Weekly*; *Jane's International Defence Review*; *Jane's Airport Review*; *Jane's Navy International*; *Jane's Islamic Affairs Analyst*; *Jane's Missiles and Rockets*. **Publishing for Defence, Aerospace, Transport** Ian Kay TITLES *Defence, Aerospace Yearbooks*. **Transport** TITLE *Transportation Yearbooks*. **Security** Sean Howe TITLES *Jane's Intelligence Review*; *Foreign Report*; *Jane's Sentinel* (regional security assessment); *Jane's Police Review*. CD-ROM and electronic development and publication. Over 100 titles a year. Unsolicited mss, synopses and ideas for reference/yearbooks welcome. OVERSEAS ASSOCIATES Jane's Information Group Inc., USA.

ROYALTIES twice-yearly.

Janus Publishing Company Ltd
105–107 Gloucester Place, London W1U 6BY
☎020 7486 6633 Fax 020 7486 6090
✉ publisher@januspublishing.co.uk
www.januspublishing.co.uk

Managing Director *Jeannie Leung*

Publishes fiction, human interest, memoirs, philosophy, mind, body and spirit, religion and theology, social questions, popular science, history, spiritualism and the paranormal, poetry and young adults. IMPRINTS **Janus Books** Subsidy publishing; **Empiricus Books** Non-subsidy publishing. TITLES *The Anarchists in the Spanish Civil War*; *Nature of the Self*; *Politics and Human Nature*; *Napoleon 1813*; *King David*; *Chameleon Candidate*; *Love Emporium*; *Digby*; *The Naked Emperor*. 'Two of our authors won the European Literary Award in 2002.' About 400 titles in print. Unsolicited mss welcome. Agents in the USA, Europe and Asia.

ROYALTIES twice-yearly.

Authors' Rating Authors may be asked to cover their own productions costs but Janus has moved into conventional publishing with its Empiricus imprint.

Jarrold Publishing
Whitefriars, Norwich NR3 1JR
☎01603 763300 Fax 01603 662748
✉ info@jarrold-publishing.co.uk
www.jarrold-publishing.co.uk

CEO (NPI Media Ltd) *Alan Sutton*

Founded in 1770, the book publishing division

was acquired by specialist heritage publisher NPI Media Group Ltd in January 2007. Publishes UK tourism, travel, leisure, history. Material tends to be of a high pictorial content. IMPRINTS **Pitkin**; **Unichrome**. About 30 titles a year. Unsolicited mss, synopses and ideas welcome but before submitting anything, approach in writing to the editorial department.

Michael Joseph
See **Penguin Group (UK)**

JR Books Ltd
10 Greenland Street, London NW1 0ND
☎020 7284 7163 Fax 020 7485 4902
✉ jeremyr@jrbooks.com
www.jrbooks.com

Chairman *Laurence Orbach*
Managing Director *Jeremy Robson*

Founded October 2006. Part of Quarto Publishing Group, JR Books publishes a wide range of non-fiction subjects, including biography, politics, music, humour, history, sport and self-help. First titles due to be launched in the autumn of 2007, featuring a number of high profile authors. Unsolicited synopses and ideas (with s.a.e.) welcome. Approach by mail. No fiction, children's or academic books.

ROYALTIES twice-yearly.

Kahn & Averill
9 Harrington Road, London SW7 3ES
☎020 8743 3278 Fax 020 8743 3278
✉ kahn@averill23.freeserve.co.uk

Managing Director *Mr M. Kahn*

Founded 1967 to publish children's titles but now specialises in music titles. A small independent publishing house. No unsolicited mss; synopses and ideas for books considered.

ROYALTIES twice-yearly.

Kamera Books
See **Oldcastle Books Ltd**

Kenilworth Press Ltd (An imprint of Quiller Publishing Ltd)
Wykey House, Wykey, Shrewsbury SY4 1JA
☎01939 261616 Fax 01939 260991
✉ info@quillerbooks.com
www.countrybooksdirect.com

Managing Director *Andrew Johnston*

Founded in 1989 and acquired by **Quiller Publishing Ltd** in 2005. Publishes equestrian books only. 10 titles in 2006. No unsolicited mss; synopses and ideas for books welcome. Send by post or e-mail.

ROYALTIES twice-yearly.

Kenyon-Deane
See **Cressrelles Publishing Co. Ltd**

Laurence King Publishing Ltd
4th Floor, 361-373 City Road, London EC1V 1LR
☎020 7841 6900 Fax 020 7841 6910
✉ enquiries@laurenceking.co.uk
www.laurenceking.co.uk

Chairman *Nick Perren*
Managing Director *Laurence King*
Commissioning Editor, Architecture *Philip Cooper*
Commissioning Editor, Design *Jo Lightfoot*
Approx. Annual Turnover £6 million

Launched in 1991, Laurence King publishes illustrated books on graphic design, contemporary architecture, fashion, interiors, product design, art history and the humanities. TITLES *A World History of Art*; *The Design Encyclopedia*; *A History of Western Architecture*; *How to Be a Graphic Designer Without Losing Your Soul*; *1000 New Designs and Where to Find Them* and the *Portfolio* series for students of art and design. About 50 titles a year. Unsolicited material welcome; send synopsis by post or e-mail.

Kingfisher Publications Plc
New Penderel House, 283–288 High Holborn, London WC1V 7HZ
☎020 7903 9999 Fax 020 7242 4979
✉ sales@kingfisherpub.com

Managing Director *John Richards*

Formerly Larousse plc until 1997 when the company name changed to Kingfisher Publications Plc. Founded 1994 when owners, Groupe de la Cité (also publishers of the Larousse dictionaries in France), merged their UK operations of Grisewood & Dempsey and **Chambers Harrap Publishers Ltd** (see entry). In 2002, Kingfisher officially became an imprint of **Houghton Mifflin Company** (see entry under *US Publishers*).

DIVISION **Kingfisher** Non-fiction Publishing Director *Melissa Fairley*, Fiction Publishing Director *Anne Marie Ryan*. Founded in 1973 by Grisewood & Dempsey Ltd. Publishes children's fiction and non-fiction in hardback and paperback: story books, rhymes and picture books, fiction and poetry anthologies, young non-fiction, activity books, general series and reference. No unsolicited mss accepted.

ROYALTIES twice-yearly where applicable.

Jessica Kingsley Publishers Ltd

116 Pentonville Road, London N1 9JB
☎020 7833 2307 Fax 020 7837 2917
✉ post@jkp.com
www.jkp.com

Also at: 400 Market Street, Suite 400,
Philadelphia, PA 19106, USA

Managing Director and Publisher *Jessica
Kingsley*
Senior Acquisitions Editor *Stephen Jones*

Founded 1987. Independent, international
publisher of books for professionals, academics
and the general reader on autism, disability,
special education, arts therapies, child psychology,
mental health, practical theology and social work.
150 titles a year. 'We are actively publishing and
commissioning in all these areas. We welcome
suggestions for books and proposals from
prospective authors. Proposals should consist of
an outline of the book, a contents list, assessment
of the market and author's c.v., and should be
addressed to *Jessica Kingsley*. Complete manuscript should not be sent.' OVERSEAS SUBSIDIARY
in Philadelphia, USA.

ROYALTIES twice-yearly.

Authors' Rating A twentieth anniversary year
was celebrated with two awards from the
Independent Publishers Guild - academic
publisher of the year and overall top publisher
of the year.

Kluwer Law International

Prospero House, Lower Ground Floor, 241
Borough High Street, London SE1 1GA
☎020 7357 0923
✉ simon.bellamy@kluwerlaw.com
www.kluwerlaw.com

Publisher *Simon Bellamy*

Founded 1995. Parent company: Wolters Kluwer
Group. Publishes international law. About 200
titles a year, including online, CD-ROM, looseleaf journals and monographs. Unsolicited
synopses and ideas for books on law at an international level welcome.

ROYALTIES annually.

Knight Paperbacks Ltd
See **Caxton Publishing Group**

Kogan Page Ltd

120 Pentonville Road, London N1 9JN
☎020 7278 0433 Fax 020 7837 3768/6348
✉ kpinfo@kogan-page.co.uk

www.kogan-page.co.uk
Chairman *Philip Kogan*
Managing Director *Helen Kogan*
Publishers *Jon Finch, Ian Hawsworth*
Approx. Annual Turnover £5.2 million

Founded 1967 by Philip Kogan to publish *The
Industrial Training Yearbook*. Publishes business and
management reference books and monographs,
careers, marketing, personal finance, personnel,
small business, training and industrial relations,
transport. Further expansion is planned, particularly in the finance and online development
areas, yearbooks and directories. Has initiated
a number of electronic publishing projects and
provision of EP content. About 150 titles a year.

ROYALTIES twice-yearly.

Authors' Rating Celebrating its fortieth anniversary, Kogan Page is one of the few, an independent publisher dedicated to books about and
for business. Founder and chairman Philip Kogan
has now handed over day-to-day management
to his daughter, Helen, who brings her own
individual style to the company. After two years
of losses, the company is back in profit.

Ladybird
See **Dorling Kindersley Ltd**

Landmark Publishing Ltd

Ashbourne Hall, Cokayne Avenue, Ashbourne
DE6 1EJ
☎01335 347349 Fax 01335 347303
✉ landmark@clara.net
www.landmarkpublishing.co.uk

Chairman *Mr R. Cork*
Managing Director *Mr C.L.M. Porter*
Approx. Annual Turnover £450,000

Founded in 1996. Publishes itinerary-based
travel guides, regional, industrial countryside
and local history. About 120 titles in 2006. No
unsolicited mss; telephone in the first instance.

ROYALTIES annually.

Lawrence & Wishart Ltd

99A Wallis Road, London E9 5LN
☎020 8533 2506 Fax 020 8533 7369
✉ lw@lwbooks.co.uk
www.lwbooks.co.uk

Managing Director/Editor *Sally Davison*

Founded 1936. An independent publisher with
a substantial backlist. Publishes current affairs,
cultural politics, economics, history, politics
and education. TITLES *After Blair; Labour Legends
Russian Gold; After Iraq; Making Sense of New
Labour*. 10 titles a year.

ROYALTIES annually, unless by arrangement.

The Learning Institute
Overbrook Business Centre, Blackford,
Wedmore BS28 4PA
☎01934 713563 Fax 01934 713492
✉ courses@inst.org
www.inst.org

Managing Director *Kit Sadgrove*

Founded 1994 to publish home-study courses
in vocational subjects such as garden design,
writing and computing. Publishes subjects that
show the reader how to work from home, gain a
new skill or enter a new career. Interests include
home working and self employment, especially
in 21st century jobs. TITLES *Diploma in Interior
Design*; *Become a Garden Designer*. Author's
guidelines sent on receipt of s.a.e. No unsolicited mss; send synopses and ideas only.
ROYALTIES quarterly.

Lionel Leventhal Ltd
See **Greenhill Books**

Dewi Lewis Publishing
8 Broomfield Road, Heaton Moor, Stockport
SK4 4ND
☎0161 442 9450 Fax 0161 442 9450
✉ mail@dewilewispublishing.com
www.dewilewispublishing.com

Contacts *Dewi Lewis, Caroline Warhurst*
Approx. Annual Turnover £250,000

Founded 1994. Publishes fiction, photography
and visual arts. TITLES *Industry of Souls* Martin
Booth (Booker Prize shortlist, 1998); *Wolfy and
the Strudelbakers* Zvi Jagendorf (Booker Prize
longlist, 2001; Sagittarius Prize, 2002); *Common
Sense* Martin Parr; *New York 1954–5* William
Klein. IMPRINT **Dewi Lewis Media** Publishes
non-fiction, biography, sports and celebrity
books. TITLES *David Beckham: Made in Manchester*
Eamonn and James Clarke; *500 Flowers* Roger
Camp. 16 titles in 2006. Not currently accepting
new fiction submissions. For any other submissions 'it is essential to check the website first'.
ROYALTIES annually.

Lewis Masonic
See **Ian Allan Publishing Ltd**

John Libbey Publishing
PO Box 276, Eastleigh SO50 5YS
☎01342 315440 Fax 023 8065 0259
✉ johnlibbey@aol.com
www.johnlibbey.com

Publisher *John Libbey*

Founded 1979. Publishes books and journals
on cinema, animation and media. Now the
publisher of the media series from University
of Luton Press. Synopses and ideas welcome.
OVERSEAS SUBSIDIARY John Libbey Eurotext Ltd,
France (medical publishers).

Library Association Publishing
See **Facet Publishing**

Library of Wales
See **Parthian**

Life&Times
See **Haus Publishing**

Frances Lincoln Ltd
4 Torriano Mews, Torriano Avenue, London
NW5 2RZ
☎020 7284 4009 Fax 020 7485 0490
✉ firstname and initial of surname
@frances-lincoln.com
www.franceslincoln.com

Managing Director *John Nicoll*
Approx. Annual Turnover £5 million

Founded 1977. Publishes highly illustrated non-
fiction: gardening, art and interiors, architec-
ture, parenting, walking and climbing, children's
picture and information books; and stationery.
DIVISIONS **Adult Non-fiction** *Jo Christian*
TITLES *Chatsworth* Duchess of Devonshire; *Grow
Your Own Vegetables* Joy Larkcom; *Pictorial Guides
to the Lakeland Fells* A. Wainwright; **Children's
General Fiction and Non-fiction** *Janetta
Otter-Barry* TITLE *The Wanderings of Odysseus*
Rosemary Sutcliffe, illus. Alan Lee; **Stationery**
Anna Sanderson TITLES *RHS Diary and Address
Book*; *British Library Diary*. About 100 titles a
year. Synopses and ideas for books considered.
ROYALTIES twice-yearly.

Linden Press
See **Open Gate Press**

Linford Romance/Linford Mystery/Linford Western
See **F.A. Thorpe Publishing**

Lion Hudson plc
Mayfield House, 256 Banbury Road, Oxford
OX2 7DH
☎01865 302750 Fax 01865 302757
✉ enquiries@lionhudson.com
www.lionhudson.com

Managing Director *Paul Clifford*
Approx. Annual Turnover £8.5 million

Founded 1971. A Christian book publisher, strong on illustrated books for a popular international readership, with rights sold in over 150 languages worldwide. Publishes a diverse list with Christian viewpoint the common denominator. All ages, from board books for children to multi-contributor adult reference, educational, paperbacks and colour co-editions and gift books. IMPRINTS **Lion** and **Lion Children's** *Kate Leech*; **Candle** and **Monarch** *Caroline Nicholls* (see **Monarch Books**). About 175 titles a year. Unsolicited mss accepted provided they have a positive Christian viewpoint intended for a Christian or wide general and international readership.

ROYALTIES twice-yearly.

Authors' Rating Market trends have not been kind but Lion Hudson remains strong in co-editions and international rights.

Literary Lions Publishing Company

Suite 35, 61 Praed Street, London W2 1NS
✉ info@literary-lions.com
corneliusvangraaf@googlemail.com
janecarlyle@googlemail.com
www.literary-lions.com

Publishing Manager *Cornelius van Graaf*
Editorial Manager *Jane Carlyle*

Founded 2006. Publishes fiction and non-fiction by Victorian and Edwardian writers but will consider new work. 'In selected cases we may seek a contribution to publishing costs. This depends entirely on the nature of the work and status of the author. No reading fee.' Essential that first contact is by e-mail with brief details and synopsis *only*. No CD, floppy disk or hard copy submissions. See website for those genres considered.

ROYALTIES annually.

Authors' Rating May ask authors to contribute towards publishing costs.

Little Black Dress

See **Hachette Livre UK**

Little Books Ltd

73 Campden Hill Towers, 112 Notting Hill Gate, London W11 3QW
☎ 020 7792 7929
www.littlebooks.net

Managing Director *Max Hamilton-Little*

Founded 2001. Publishes general trade books, history, biography, health, natural history. IMPRINT **Max** TITLES *Freud: A Life in Our Time*

Peter Gay; *Watching* Desmond Morris; *Lawrence of Arabia Letters* ed. Malcolm Brown. About 20–25 books a year. No unsolicited material.

ROYALTIES annually.

Little, Brown Book Group UK

Brettenham House, Lancaster Place, London WC2E 7EN
☎ 020 7911 8000 Fax 020 7911 8100
✉ uk@littlebrown.co.uk
www.littlebrown.co.uk

CEO/Publisher *Ursula Mackenzie*
Approx. Annual Turnover £50 million

Founded 1988 as Little, Brown & Co. (UK) and became Time Warner Book Group UK in 2002. Purchased by Hachette in March 2006 and renamed Little, Brown Book Group UK. Began by importing its US parent company's titles and in 1990 launched its own illustrated non-fiction list. Two years later the company took over former Macdonald & Co. Publishes hardback and paperback fiction, literary fiction, crime, science fiction and fantasy; and general non-fiction including true crime, biography and autobiography, cinema, history, humour, popular science, travel, reference, sport. IMPRINTS **Little, Brown** *Ursula Mackenzie, Richard Beswick, Stephen Guise, David Shelley, Hilary Hale* Hardback fiction and general non-fiction; **Abacus** *Richard Beswick, Stephen Guise* Literary fiction and non-fiction paperbacks; **Atom** *Tim Holman, Darren Nash* Young adult/teen paperbacks; **Hachette Audio** *Sarah Shrubb* (see entry under **Audio Books**); **Orbit** *Tim Holman, Darren Nash* Science fiction and fantasy; **Sphere** *Antonia Hodgson, Joanne Dickinson, Hilary Hale, David Shelley, Louise Davies, Adam Strange* Mass-market fiction and non-fiction hardbacks and paperbacks; **Virago Press** *Lennie Goodings* (see entry). Approach in writing in the first instance. 350 titles in 2006. No unsolicited mss.

ROYALTIES twice-yearly.

Authors' Rating After a highly successful 2006 there was an almost inevitable dip as Little, Brown accommodated itself to the merger with the Hachette group. But the core list remains one of the strongest in the market.

Little Tiger Press

An imprint of Magi Publications, 1 The Coda Centre, 189 Munster Road, London SW6 6AW
☎ 020 7385 6333 Fax 020 7385 7333
✉ info@littletiger.co.uk
www.littletigerpress.com

Publisher *Monty Bhatia*

Associate Publisher *Jude Evans*
Commissioning Editor *Stephanie Stansbie*
Junior Editor *Melinda Tallier*
Approx. Annual Turnover £5 million

Little Tiger Press imprint publishes children's picture and novelty books for ages 0–7. No texts over 750 words. About 30 titles a year. Unsolicited mss, synopses and new ideas welcome. See website for submission guidelines.

ROYALTIES annually.

Authors' Rating A thriving small publisher with imaginative output.

Liverpool University Press
4 Cambridge Street, Liverpool L69 7ZU
☎0151 794 2233 Fax 0151 794 2235
✉ robblo@liv.ac.uk
www.liverpool-unipress.co.uk

Managing Director/Editorial Head *Robin Bloxsidge*

LUP's primary activity is the publication of academic and scholarly books and journals but it also has a limited number of trade titles. Its principal focus is on the arts and social sciences, in which it is active in a variety of disciplines. TITLES *The Leaguers: The Making of Professional Football in England 1900–1939*; *Martin Mere: Lancashire's Lost Lake*; *Henry James: A Bibliographical Catalogue of a Collection of Editions to 1921*; *Transformations: The History of the Science Fiction Magazine from 1950 to 1970*; *Georges Brassens and Jacques Brel: Personal and Social Narratives in Post-War Chanson*; *Travellers' Visions: French Literary Encounters with Japan 1897–2004*; *Summer of Love: Psychedelic Art, Social Crisis and Counterculture in the 1960s*; *Faith, Fraternity and Fighting: The Orange Order and Irish Migrants in Northern England c. 1850–1920*. 30–40 titles a year.

ROYALTIES annually.

Livewire Books for Teenagers
See **The Women's Press**

Lonely Planet Publications Ltd
72–82 Rosebery Avenue, London EC1R 4RW
☎020 7841 9000 Fax 020 7841 9001
✉ go@lonelyplanet.co.uk
www.lonelyplanet.com

Owner *Lonely Planet (Australia)*
Editorial Head *Imogen Hall*
Approx. Annual Turnover £40 million

'For over 30 years, Lonely Planet's on-the-ground research and no-holds-barred opinion by our team of expert travel writers has inspired and guided independent travellers to explore the world around them.' With over 500 titles in print, publications include travel guidebooks, downloadable digital guides, phrasebooks, travel literature, pictorial books and How To guides. No unsolicited mss; synopses and ideas welcome. Author guidelines available at www.lonelyplanet.com/help/guide

Lorenz Books
See **Anness Publishing Ltd**

Lucky Duck Publishing
See **Sage Publications**

Lulu.com
www.lulu.com
A self publishing, print-on-demand service for individuals and companies. Produces a variety of digital content including books, music, video, software, calendars, photos and artwork with no set-up fee and no requirement to buy copies. Authors supply a digital file of their book and a print-ready version of the file is created by the company. Lulu handles sales and pays the royalty specified by the client with a small mark-up as commission. Offers two retail distribution services for a fee. Full details available on the website. Runs the **The Lulu Blooker Prize** (see entry under *Prizes*).

Authors' Rating Authors who find it hard to get into print now have recourse to an option that is not vanity publishing, at least not in the strict sense of the word. Launched in the US in 2002, Lulu is a website designed to carry anything that writers can throw at it, and for free. If browsers show an interest in a particular title, the book can be produced to order and shipped direct. To stay in business and, by all accounts, thrive Lulu takes a twenty per cent share of any royalties to which an author is entitled. Publishing services such as editing, proofing and marketing must be contracted separately. Anyone joining the game should not expect too much – as in all publishing luck plays a big part - but as an economic proposition Lulu has the edge on conventional vanity and self publishing operations. The company's list now extends to 90,000 titles. About half of the sales on Lulu are electronic.

Lund Humphries
See **Ashgate Publishing Ltd**

The Lutterworth Press
PO Box 60, Cambridge CB1 2NT
☎01223 350865 Fax 01223 366951
✉ publishing@jamesclarke.co.uk

www.lutterworth.com

Managing Director *Adrian Brink*

The Lutterworth Press dates back to the 18th century when it was founded as the Religious Tract Society. In the 19th century it was best known for its children's books and magazines, both religious and secular, including *The Boys' Own Paper*. Since 1984 it has been an imprint of **James Clarke & Co** (see entry). Publishes religious books for adults and children, adult non-fiction, children's fiction and non-fiction. TITLES *Artist of Wonderland* Frankie Morris; *A Spiritual Guide* Miguel de Molinos; *The Lost People of Malplaquet* Andrew Dalton; *From the Dairyman's Daughter to Worrals of the WAAF* ed. Dennis Butts. Approach in writing with ideas in the first instance.

ROYALTIES annually.

Macdonald & Co.

See **Little, Brown Book Group UK**

McGraw-Hill Education

McGraw-Hill House, Shoppenhangers Road, Maidenhead SL6 2QL
☎01628 502500 Fax 01628 770224
www.mcgraw-hill.co.uk

General Manager *Shona Mullen*

Owned by US parent company, founded in 1888. Began publishing in Maidenhead in 1965, having had an office in the UK since 1899. Publishes business, economics, finance, accounting, computing science, social sciences and engineering for the academic, student and professional markets. Acquired **Open University Press** in 2002 (see entry). Around 200 titles a year. See website for author guidelines. Unsolicited proposals via website only.

ROYALTIES twice-yearly.

Macmillan Publishers Ltd

The Macmillan Building, 4 Crinan Street, London N1 9XW
☎020 7833 4000 Fax 020 7843 4640
www.macmillan.com

Owner *Verlagsgruppe Georg von Holtzbrinck*
Chief Executive *Richard Charkin*
Approx. Annual Turnover £400 million (Book Publishing Group)

Founded 1843. Macmillan is one of the largest publishing houses in Britain, publishing approximately 1400 titles a year. In 1995, Verlagsgruppe Georg von Holtzbrinck, a major German publisher, acquired a majority stake in the Macmillan Group and in 1999 purchased the remaining shares. In 1996, Macmillan bought Boxtree, the successful media tie-in publisher and, in 1997, it purchased the Heinemann English language teaching list from Reed Elsevier. The educational publishing division was strengthened by the acquisitions of the Mexican list, Ediciones Castillo and the Argentine company Puerto de Palos. No unsolicited material, except for the **Macmillan New Writing** list.

DIVISIONS

Palgrave Macmillan Brunel Road, Houndmills, Basingstoke, Hampshire RG21 6XS ☎ 01256 329242 Fax 01256 328339 Managing Director *Dominic Knight*; **College** *Margaret Hewison*; **Scholarly & Reference** *Sam Burridge*; **Journals** *David Bull*. Publishes textbooks, monographs and journals in academic and professional subjects. Publications in both hard copy and electronic format.

Macmillan Education Macmillan Oxford, 4 Between Towns Road, Oxford OX4 3PP ☎ 01865 405700 Fax 01865 405701 ✉ info@macmillan.com www.macmillaneducation.com Executive Director *Christopher Paterson*, Managing Director *Chris Harrison*, Publishing Directors *Sue Bale* (ELT), *Alison Hubert* (education) Publishes a wide range of ELT titles and educational materials for the international education market from Oxford and through 30 subsidiaries worldwide.

Pan Macmillan 20 New Wharf Road, London N1 9RR ☎ 020 7014 6000 Fax 020 7014 6001 www.panmacmillan.com Managing Director *David North* Publishes under **Macmillan**, **Pan**, **Picador**, **Macmillan New Writing**, **Sidgwick & Jackson**, **Boxtree**, **Macmillan Children's Books**, **Macmillan Digital Audio**, **Campbell Books**, **Young Picador**, **Rodale**. No unsolicited mss. Visit the writers' area on www.panmacmillan.com for useful articles and information on books that may be helpful in getting your book published, or visit the Macmillan New Writing website (see below) for details of the MNW programme, which does accept unsolicited mss of first novels.

IMPRINTS

Macmillan (founded 1843) Fiction: Publisher *Andrew Kidd*, Publishing Director *Maria Rejt*, Editorial Director *Imogen Taylor* Publishes hardback commercial fiction including genre fiction, romantic, crime and thrillers. IMPRINT **Tor** (founded 2003) Publishes science fiction, fantasy and thrillers. Non-Fiction: Publisher *Richard Milner*, Editorial Director *Georgina Morley*

Publishes serious and general non-fiction: autobiography, biography, economics, history, philosophy, politics and world affairs, psychology, popular science, trade reference titles.

Pan (founded 1947) Paperback imprint for Pan Macmillan.

Picador (founded 1972) Publisher *Andrew Kidd*, Publishing Director *Maria Rejt*, Deputy Publisher *Ursula Doyle* Publishes literary international fiction, non-fiction and poetry.

Sidgwick & Jackson (founded 1908) Editorial Director *Ingrid Connell* Publishes popular non-fiction in hardback and trade paperback with strong personality or marketable identity, from celebrity and show business to music and sport. Also military history list.

Boxtree (founded 1986) Publisher *Richard Milner* Publishes brand and media tie-in titles, including TV, film, music and Internet, plus entertainment licences, pop culture, humour and event-related books. TITLES *Dilbert; James Bond; Purple Ronnie; Wallace & Gromit; The Onion.*

Macmillan Children's Books (New Wharf Road address) Managing Director *Emma Hopkin*, Publishing Director *To be appointed*; Fiction: Editorial Director *Sarah Dudman*; Non-Fiction and Poetry: Editorial Director *Gaby Morgan*; Picture Books & Gift Books: Editorial Director *Suzanne Carnell*. **Campbell Books** Editorial Director *Sarah Fabiny*; **Young Picador** Editorial Director *Sarah Dudman* Publishes fiction, non-fiction and poetry in paperback and hardback.

Macmillan New Writing (New Wharf Road address) Publishing Director *Maria Rejt*, Commissioning Editor *Will Atkins* Founded in 2006 as a way of finding talented new writers who might otherwise go undiscovered. MNW publishes full-length novels from authors who have not previously published a novel. All genres considered and all submissions assessed, but mss must be complete. No advance, but the author pays nothing and receives a royalty of 20% on net sales. Submissions must be sent by e-mail only via the MNW website (www.macmillannewwriting.com).

ROYALTIES annually or twice-yearly depending on contract.

Authors' Rating Macmillan New Writing has succeeded in its objective of attracting new talent. (See p. 105) The deal for first-time authors is a fixed contract with no advance but with a twenty per cent royalty. A new title appears each month. Pan Macmillan has entered the manga market, striking a deal with Tokyo-based Tokyopop. Crime and children's lists are thriving. On the academic side, Palgrave prospers on technological innovation ranging from hard print links to websites to print-on-demand. Macmillan CEO Richard Charkin sees an expansion of print-on-demand, a service that will offer speedier delivery at lower cost. Macmillan Science titles are now available as e-books to browse and buy (www.macmillansciencebookstore.com).

Made Simple Books
See **Elsevier Ltd**

Mainstream Publishing Co. (Edinburgh) Ltd
7 Albany Street, Edinburgh EH1 3UG
☎0131 557 2959 Fax 0131 556 8720
✉ bill.campbell@mainstreampublishing.com
www.mainstreampublishing.com

Directors *Bill Campbell, Peter MacKenzie*
Approx. Annual Turnover £3 million

Publishes art, autobiography/biography, current affairs, health, sport, history, illustrated and fine editions, photography, politics and world affairs, popular paperbacks. TITLES *Soldier Five* Mike Coburn; *The Real Nureyev* Carolyn Soutar; *Woodward's England* Mick Collins. Over 80 titles a year. Ideas for books considered, but they should be preceded by a letter, synopsis and s.a.e. or return postage.

ROYALTIES twice-yearly.

Authors' Rating Financial backing from Random House has strengthened marketing and editorial reach.

Management Books 2000 Ltd
Forge House, Limes Road, Kemble, Cirencester GL7 6AD
☎01285 771441 Fax 01285 771055
✉ info@mb2000.com
www.mb2000.com

Publisher *Nicholas Dale-Harris*
Approx. Annual Turnover £500,000

Founded 1993 to develop a range of books for executives and managers working in the modern world of business. 'Essentially, the books are working books for working managers, practical and effective.' Publishes business, management, self-development and allied topics as well as sponsored titles. Launched the *In Ninety Minutes* series of compact guide books for managers in 2004, offering advice, ideas and practical help across a range of highly relevant business topics in an hour and a half of study. New ideas for this series are welcome. About 24 titles a year.

Unsolicited mss, synopses and ideas for books welcome.

Manchester University Press

Oxford Road, Manchester M13 9NR
☎0161 275 2310 Fax 0161 274 3346
✉ mup@manchester.ac.uk
www.manchesteruniversitypress.co.uk

Publisher/Chief Executive *David Rodgers*
Head of Editorial *Matthew Frost*
Approx. Annual Turnover £2 million

Founded 1904. MUP is Britain's third largest university press, with a list marketed and sold worldwide. Remit consists of occasional trade publications but mainly A-level and under-graduate textbooks and research monographs. Publishes in the areas of: literature, TV, film, theatre and media, history and history of art, design, politics, economics and international law. DIVISIONS **Humanities** *Matthew Frost*; **History/Art History** *Alison Welsby*; **Politics and Law** *Tony Mason*. About 140 titles a year. Unsolicited mss welcome.
ROYALTIES annually.

George Mann Books

See **Arnefold Publishing**

Manson Publishing Ltd

73 Corringham Road, London NW11 7DL
☎020 8905 5150 Fax 020 8201 9233
✉ manson@mansonpublishing.com
www.mansonpublishing.com

Chairman/Managing Director *Michael Manson*

Founded 1992. Publishes highly illustrated book for study and reference. Subject areas covered include medicine, veterinary medicine, earth science, plant science, agriculture and microbi-ology. About 10 titles a year. No unsolicited mss; synopses and ideas will be considered.
ROYALTIES twice-yearly.

Marshall Cavendish Ltd

119 Wardour Street, London W1F 0UW
☎020 7565 6000
✉ mcelt@marshallcavendish.co.uk
www.marshallcavendish.co.uk
www.mcelt.com

Managing Director *Craig Tranter*

Founded 1956. Owned by Times Publishing, Singapore, Marshall Cavendish is a major publisher of books, directories, magazines and partworks. Publishes non-fiction, educational, children's and illustrated books. DIVISIONS **Trade** *Chris Jenner* TITLE *Football Handbook*; **Education**

Simon Ross TITLE *Real English Grammar*; **Marshall Cavendish Children** *Anne Nicholson*; **Marshall Cavendish Reference**; **Marshall Cavendish Benchmark**; **Times Editions**. About 100 titles a year. Unsolicited mss, synopses and ideas for books welcome; initial approach by e-mail.
ROYALTIES annually.

Marston House

See **Alphabet & Image Ltd**

Martin Books

See **Simon & Schuster UK Ltd**

Kenneth Mason Publications Ltd

The Book Barn, Westbourne, Emsworth PO10 8RS
☎01243 377977 Fax 01243 379136
✉ info@whitechimney.com
www.researchdisclosure.com

Chairman *Kenneth Mason*
Managing Director *Piers Mason*

Founded 1958. Publishes diet, health, fitness, nutrition and nautical. No fiction. IMPRINTS **Boatswain Press**; **Research Disclosure**. Initial approach by letter with synopsis only.
ROYALTIES twice-yearly in first year, annu-ally thereafter.

Matador

See **Troubador Publishing Ltd**

Max

See **Little Books Ltd**

Kevin Mayhew Publishers

Buxhall, Stowmarket IP14 3BW
☎01449 737978 Fax 01449 737834
✉ info@kevinmayhewltd.com
www.kevinmayhewltd.com

Chairman/Commissioning Editor *Kevin Mayhew*

Founded in 1976. One of the leading sacred music and Christian book publishers in the UK. Publishes religious titles – liturgy, sacramental, devotional, also children's books and school resources. IMPRINT **Palm Tree Press** Worldwide worship. Unsolicited synopses and mss welcome; telephone prior to sending material, please.
ROYALTIES annually.

Meadowside Children's Books

185 Fleet Street, London EC4A 2HS
☎020 7400 1092 Fax 020 7400 1037
✉ info@meadowsidebooks.com
www.meadowsidebooks.com

Owner *D. C. Thomson*
Publisher *Simon Rosenheim*
Editor *Lucy Cuthew*

Founded in September 2003. Publishes innovative books that range from picture books to novelty and junior fiction. Over 100 titles a year. Unsolicited mss, synopses and ideas accepted. Send to the editorial department by post or e-mail. Only successful submissions will be answered.

Medavia Publishing
See **Boltneck Publications Limited**

Melrose Books
St Thomas Place, Ely CB7 4GG
☎01353 646608 Fax 01353 646602
✉ info@melrosebooks.co.uk
www.melrosebooks.com

Chairman *Richard A. Kay*
Managing Director *Nicholas S. Law*
Approx. Annual Turnover £100,000

Independent subsidy publisher established by **Melrose Press** in 2004. To-date has published general and children's fiction, literature, fantasy, biography, travel, religion and science reference. Welcomes submissions by e-mail or post
ROYALTIES 65%.

Melrose Press Ltd
St Thomas Place, Ely CB7 4GG
☎01353 646600 Fax 01353 646601
✉ tradesales@melrosepress.co.uk
www.melrosepress.co.uk

Chairman *Richard A. Kay*
Managing Director *Nicholas S. Law*
Approx. Annual Turnover £2 million

Founded 1960. Took on its present name in 1969. Publishes biographical who's who reference only (not including *Who's Who*, which is published by **A. &C. Black**). About 10 titles a year.

Mentor
See **Christian Focus Publications**

Mercat Press Ltd
10 Coates Crescent, Edinburgh EH3 7AL
☎0131 225 5324 Fax 0131 226 6632
✉ enquiries@mercatpress.com
www.mercatpress.com

Directors *Seán Costello, Tom Johnstone*

Founded 1971. Publishes fiction and non-fiction, mainly of Scottish interest. The Press was established as a stand-alone company in 2002 in a management buy-out following the collapse of parent firm James Thin Booksellers. It began by publishing reprints of classic Scottish literature but now produces a wide range of new titles. Subject areas include biography, photography and walking guides. IMPRINT **Crescent Books** Adult fiction. TITLES *Edinburgh: A New Perspective* Jason Baxter; *The Worms of Euston Square* William Sutton; *Bruar's Rest* Jess Smith; *Mackerel at Midnight* Ethel G. Hofman; *West Highland Way, Official Guide* Bob Aitken and Roger Smith; *25 Walks* SERIES; *River of Memory* Joe Pieri; *Scottish Cookery* Catherine Brown. 20 titles in 2006. Unsolicited synopses, preferably with sample chapters, are welcome. No new poetry.
ROYALTIES annually.

Mercury Books/Mercury Junior
See **Caxton Publishing Group**

The Merlin Press Ltd
Suite 4, 96 Monnow Street, Monmouth NP25 3EQ
☎01600 775663 Fax 01600 775663
✉ info@merlinpress.co.uk
www.merlinpress.co.uk

Managing Director *Anthony W. Zurbrugg*
Director *Adrian Howe*

Founded 1956. Publishes in the area of history, philosophy and politics. No fiction. IMPRINTS **Merlin Press**; **Green Print**. TITLES *Socialist Register* (annual); the Chartist Studies SERIES; *Positive Education*. About 10 titles a year.
ROYALTIES annually.

Merrell Publishers Ltd
Head office: 81 Southwark Street, London SE1 0HX
☎020 7928 8880 Fax 020 7928 1199
✉ mail@merrellpublishers.com
www.merrellpublishers.com

US office: 49 West 24th Street, 8th Floor, New York, NY 10010
☎ 001 212 929 8344 Fax 001 212 929 8346
✉ info@merrellpublishersusa.com

Managing Director *Hugh Merrell*
Editorial Director *Julian Honer*
US Director *Joan Brookbank*
Approx. Annual Turnover £2.6 million

Founded 1993. Publishes art, architecture, design and photography. TITLE *Women Who Write* Stefan Bollman. 37 titles in 2006. Unsolicited synopses and ideas for books welcome. Send c.v. and synopsis giving details of the book's target markets and funding of illustrations.

Royalties annually.

Methodist Publishing House
See **mph**

Methuen Drama
See **A.&C. Black Publishers Ltd**

Methuen Publishing Ltd
11–12 Buckingham Gate, London SW1E 6LB
☎020 7798 1600 Fax 020 7828 2098
✉ sales@methuen.co.uk
www.methuen.co.uk

Managing Director *Peter Tummons*
Publishing Consultant *Max Eilenberg*

Founded 1889. Methuen was owned by Reed International until it was bought by Random House in 1997. Purchased by a management buy-out team in 1998. Acquired **Politico's Publishing** in 2003 (see entry). Publishes fiction and non-fiction; travel, sport, humour. No unsolicited mss; synopses and ideas welcome. Prefers to be approached via agents or a letter of inquiry. No first novels, cookery books, personal memoirs.
Royalties twice-yearly.

Metro Publishing
See **John Blake Publishing Ltd**

Michelin Maps & Guides
Hannay House, 39 Clarendon Road, Watford WD17 1JA
☎01923 205240/205254 (sales) Fax 01923 205241
www.Viamichelin.co.uk

Sales Manager *Ian Murray*

Founded 1900 as a travel publisher. Publishes travel guides, maps and atlases.

Midland Publishing
An imprint of Ian Allan Publishing Ltd, 4 Watling Drive, Hinckley LE10 3EY
☎01455 25549 Fax 01455 255495
✉ midlandbooks@compuserve.com

Publisher *Peter Waller*

Imprint of **Ian Allan Publishing Ltd**. Publishes aviation books. No wartime memoirs. No unsolicited mss; synopses and ideas welcome.
Royalties twice-yearly.

Milet Publishing Limited
See entry under *US Publishers*

Miller's
See **Octopus Publishing Group**

Millivres Prowler Limited
Unit M, Spectrum House, 32–34 Gordon House Road, London NW5 1LP
☎020 7424 7400 Fax 020 7424 7401
www.millivres.co.uk

Publishes various magazines including *Gay Times*, *Diva Magazine* and *The Pink Paper*, the national free gay newspaper.

Authors' Rating No longer interested in books; the focus is entirely on journals.

Mills & Boon
See **Harlequin Mills & Boon Ltd**

Milo Books Limited
The Old Weighbridge, Station Road, Wrea Green, Preston PR4 2PH
☎01772 672900 Fax 01772 687727
✉ info@milobooks.com
www.milobooks.com

Managing Director *Peter Walsh*

Founded 1997. Publishes non-fiction: true crime and sport. 12 titles in 2006. Unsolicited mss, synopses and ideas for books. 'Authors should note our specialist areas. We cannot promise to return all material submitted.' Approach in writing in the first instance. 'If we are interested in pursuing an idea, we will call to talk it through in more depth.' No fiction or poetry.
Royalties twice-yearly.

Mindfield
See **Camden Press Ltd**

Mitchell Beazley
See **Octopus Publishing Group**

Mobius
See **Hachette Livre UK**

Monarch Books
Lion Hudson plc, Mayfield House, 256 Banbury Road, Oxford OX2 7DH
☎01865 302750 Fax 01865 302757
✉ monarch@lionhudson.com

Editorial Director *Tony Collins*

An imprint of **Lion Hudson plc**. Publishes an independent list of Christian books across a wide range of concerns. Imprint **Monarch** Upmarket paperback list with Christian basis and strong social concern agenda including psychology, future studies, politics, mission, theology, leadership and spirituality. About 35 titles a year. Unsolicited mss, synopses and ideas welcome.

Morgan Kauffman
See **Elsevier Ltd**

Mosby
See **Elsevier Ltd**

Motor Racing Publications
PO Box 1318, Croydon CR9 5YP
☎020 8654 2711 Fax 020 8407 0339
✉ john@mrpbooks.co.uk
www.mrpbooks.co.uk
Chairman/Editorial Head *John Blunsden*
Founded soon after the end of World War II
to concentrate on motor-racing titles. Fairly
dormant in the mid 1960s but was reacti-
vated in 1968 by a new shareholding structure. John Blunsden later acquired a majority
share and major expansion followed in the
1970s. Publishes motor-sport history, classic and
performance car collection and restoration, race
track and off-road driving and related subjects.
IMPRINTS **Fitzjames Press**; **Motor Racing
Publications**. About 2–4 titles a year. No unsolicited mss. Send synopses and ideas in specified
subject areas in the first instance.
ROYALTIES twice-yearly.

mph
4 John Wesley Road, Werrington, Peterborough
PE4 6ZP
☎01733 325002 Fax 01733 384180
✉ chief.exec@mph.org.uk
www.mph.org.uk
Chair *Eric Jarvis*
Chief Executive *Martin Stone*
Head of Publishing *Dr Natalie K. Watson*
Approx. Annual Turnover £2 million
Founded 1800. Owned by the Methodist
Church. Publishes a wide range of books,
magazines and resources which are sold in the
UK and overseas. Also *Epworth Review* quar-
terly magazine. IMPRINTS **Epworth** (see entry);
Inspire (see entry); **Methodist Publishing
House**. Approx 30 titles a year. Unsolicited
mss, synopses and ideas welcome; send sample
chapter and contents with covering letter and
s.a.e. for return of mss.
ROYALTIES annually.

Murdoch Books UK Ltd
Erico House, 6th Floor North, 93–99 Upper
Richmond Road, London SW15 2TG
☎020 8785 5995 Fax 020 8785 5985
✉ info@murdochbooks.co.uk
www.murdochbooks.co.uk

Publisher *Kay Scarlett* (Australia)
Owned by Australian publisher Murdoch Books
Pty Ltd. Publishes full-colour non-fiction:
homes and interiors, gardening, cookery, craft,
DIY and narrative non-fiction. About 80 titles a
year. Contact: inquiry@murdochbooks.com.au
in the first instance.

John Murray (Publishers) Ltd
338 Euston Road, London NW1 3BH
☎020 7873 6000 Fax 020 7873 6446
✉ firstname.lastname@johnmurrays.co.uk
www.madaboutbooks.com
CEO *Martin Neild*
Managing Director *Roland Philipps*
Founded 1768. Part of **Hachette Livre UK**.
Publishes general trade books. **Non-fiction**
Eleanor Birne; **Fiction** *Heather Barrett, Kate
Parkin*. No unsolicited material; send prelimi-
nary letter.
ROYALTIES twice-yearly.
Authors' Rating Shifting towards mainstream
books since its acquisition by Hodder Headline,
Murray has more than doubled its sales in four
years.

Myriad Editions
59 Lansdowne Place, Brighton BN3 1FL
☎01273 720000
✉ info@myriadeditions.com
www.myriadeditions.com
Chairman *Robert J. Bennewick*
Managing Director *Candida Lacey*
Founded 1993. Independent publisher of literary
fiction and non-fiction, graphic novels and political atlases. TITLES *365 Ways to Change the World*
Michael Norton; *The Atlas of Climate Change*
(winner of the 2006 Planeta Environment Book
of the Year). 6 titles in 2006. No unsolicited mss.
Synopses and ideas for books in the specified
subject areas only. Approach by e-mail in the
first instance.
ROYALTIES annually.

Myrmidon Books
Rotterdam House, 116 Quayside, Newcastle
upon Tyne NE1 3DY
☎0191 206 4005 Fax 0191 206 4001
✉ submissions@myrmidonbooks.com
www.myrmidonbooks.com
Chairman/Managing Director *Ed Handyside*
Literary Editor *Anne Westgarth*
Approx. Annual Turnover £200,000
Founded 2006. Publishes adult trade fiction. 2
titles in 2006. Full mss from literary agents only;

first three chapters from unrepresented writers. No short stories, novellas or works under 65,000 words, children's books, graphic novels, non-fiction. Submit hard copy only after checking requirements on the website.

ROYALTIES quarterly.

NAG Press Ltd
See **Robert Hale Ltd**

The National Archives
Kew TW9 4DU
☎020 8392 5289 Fax 020 8487 1974
✉ catherine.bradley@nationalarchives.gov.uk
www.nationalarchives.gov.uk

Publisher *Catherine Bradley*

Publishes non-fiction books, guides relating to the thousand years of historical records held in The National Archives. Specialist areas: general history, family history, military history and intelligence history. TITLES *Germany 1944. A British Soldier's Pocketbook; All for Love. Seven centuries of illicit liaison* Val Horlser; *Cakes and Ale. The golden age of British feasting* Judy Spours; *Henry VIII. Church, court and conflict* David Loades; *Workhouse. The people, the places, the life behind bars* Simon Fowler. Also publishes *Ancestors*, a full-colour family history magazine. 20 titles in 2006.

National Trust Books
See **Anova Books**

Nautical Data Ltd
The Book Barn, Westbourne, Emsworth
PO10 8RS
☎01243 389352 Fax 01243 379136
✉ info@nauticaldata.com
www.nauticaldata.com

Managing Director *Piers Mason*

Founded 1999. Publishes pilots and nautical reference. No unsolicited mss; synopses and ideas welcome. No fiction or non-nautical themes.

ROYALTIES twice-yearly.

NCVO Publications
Regent's Wharf, 8 All Saints Street, London
N1 9RL
☎020 7713 6161/HelpDesk: 0800 2798 798
Fax 020 7713 6300
✉ ncvo@ncvo-vol.org.uk
www.ncvo-vol.org.uk/publications

Publications and Promotions Coordinator
Daniel Fluskey

Approx. Annual Turnover £140,000

Founded 1928. Publishing imprint of the National Council for Voluntary Organisations, embracing former Bedford Square Press titles and NCVO's many other publications. The list reflects NCVO's role as the representative body for the voluntary sector. Publishes directories, good practice information on management and trustee development, finance and employment titles and information of primary interest to the voluntary sector. TITLES *The Voluntary Agencies Directory; The Good Trustee Guide; The Good Campaigns Guide; The Good Financial Management Guide; The Good Employment Guide; The Good Management Guide; The Good Membership Guide; The UK Voluntary Sector Almanac.* No unsolicited mss as all projects are commissioned in-house.

Thomas Nelson & Sons Ltd
See **Nelson Thornes Limited**

Nelson Thornes Limited
Delta Place, 27 Bath Road, Cheltenham
GL53 7TH
☎01242 267100 Fax 01242 221914
✉ info@nelsonthornes.com
www.nelsonthornes.com

Owner *Wolters Kluwer*
Managing Director *Linden Harris*

Based in Cheltenham and a division of Wolters Kluwer, the Amsterdam based global publishing and services business, Nelson Thornes was formed by the merger of Thomas Nelson and Stanley Thornes publishing companies in 2000. Educational publisher of printed and electronic product, from pre-school to Higher Education. Unsolicited mss, synopses and ideas for books welcome if appropriate to specialised lists.

ROYALTIES annually.

New Beacon Books Ltd
76 Stroud Green Road, London N4 3EN
☎020 7272 4889 Fax 020 7281 4662
✉ newbeaconbooks@btconnect.com

Managing Director *Sarah White*
Approx. Annual Turnover £120,000

Founded 1966. Publishes fiction, history, politics, poetry and language, all concerning black people. No unsolicited material.

ROYALTIES annually.

New Holland Publishers (UK) Ltd
Garfield House, 86–88 Edgware Road, London
W2 2EA
☎020 7724 7773 Fax 020 7258 1293 (editorial)
✉ postmaster@nhpub.co.uk
www.newhollandpublishers.com

Managing Director *John Beaufoy*
Publishing Director *Rosemary Wilkinson*

Approx. Annual Turnover £8.5 million

With its headquarters in London, New Holland Publishers (UK) Ltd is the International Publishing Division of Johnnic Communications, one of Africa's leading publishing groups, with offices in Australia and New Zealand. Acquired Cadogan Guides in April 2007. Publishes non-fiction, practical and inspirational books across a range of categories, including food and drink, DIY, practical art, crafts, interiors, health and fitness, gardening, pets, humour and gift, reference, history, sports and outdoor pursuits, natural history, general travel books and Globetrotter travel guides. TITLES *Men and Sheds; The Allotment Handbook; The Big Book of Handmade Cards; The BTO Garden Bird Book; The Specialist Series; Dugouts; Diving with Giants; Party Knits; How to Decorate with Wallpaper, Meena Pathak Celebrates Indian Cooking; Abbeys and Priories of England*. No unsolicited mss; synopses and ideas welcome.

Authors' Rating Having taken over the highly regarded Cadogan Guides, New Holland is clearly confident of holding off the free travel websites. But for writers this is a highly competitive market.

Newnes
See **Elsevier Ltd**

Nexus
See **Virgin Books Ltd**

nferNELSON
The Chiswick Centre, 414 Chiswick High Road, London W4 5TF
☎020 8996 3333 Fax 020 8742 8390
www.nfer-nelson.co.uk

Founded 1981. A division of Granada Learning Ltd. Publishes educational and psychological tests and training materials. Main interest is in educational, clinical and occupational assessment and training material.

Nia
See **The X Press**

Nielsen BookData
3rd Floor, Midas House, 62 Goldsworth Road, Woking GU21 6LQ
☎0870 777 8710 Fax 0870 777 8711
✉ info@nielsenbookdata.co.uk
www.nielsenbookdata.co.uk

Commercial Director *Ann Betts*
Senior Manager, Publishing Services *Peter Mathews*

BookData creates and maintains a unique data-base of timely, accurate and content rich records for English-language books and other published media, collected from publishers in over 70 countries. The enriched data includes: price, availability, table of contents (where applicable), subject classifications, market rights, publisher and distributor details, cover/jacket images and book descriptions. The data is disseminated worldwide in a variety of formats: data feed, dynamic XML, CD-ROMs and online services.

Nightingale Books
See **Pegasus Elliot Mackenzie Publishers Ltd**

NMS Enterprises Limited – Publishing
National Museums Scotland, Chambers Street, Edinburgh EH1 1JF
☎0131 247 4026 Fax 0131 247 4012
✉ publishing@nms.ac.uk
www.nms.ac.uk

Director *Lesley A. Taylor*
Approx. Annual Turnover £123,000

Publishes non-fiction related to the National Museums of Scotland collections: academic and general; children's; archaeology, history, decorative arts worldwide, history of science, technology, natural history and geology, poetry. TITLES *Fonn's Duthchas: Land and Legacy; Beyond the Palace Walls: Islamic Art from the State Hermitage Museum; Nicholas and Alexandra: The Last Tsar and Tsarina; Minerals of Scotland; Audubon in Edinburgh; The Thin Red Line: War, Empire and Visions of Scotland; Weights and Measures in Scotland: a European Perspective* (2005 Saltire Society/National Library of Scotland Research Book of the Year). 8 titles in 2006. No unsolicited mss; only interested in synopses and ideas for books which are genuinely related to NMS collections and to Scotland in general.
ROYALTIES twice-yearly.

No Exit Press
See **Oldcastle Books Ltd**

North-Holland
See **Elsevier Ltd**

Northcote House Publishers Ltd
Horndon House, Horndon, Tavistock PL19 9NQ
☎01822 810066 Fax 01822 810034
✉ northcote.house@virgin.net
www.northcotehouse.co.uk

Managing Director *Brian Hulme*

Founded 1985. Publishes a series of literary critical studies, in association with the British Council, *Writers and their Work*; education management, literary criticism, educational dance and drama. 30 titles in 2006. 'Well-thought-out proposals, including contents and sample chapter(s), with strong marketing arguments welcome.'

ROYALTIES annually.

W. W. Norton & Company Ltd

Castle House, 75–76 Wells Street, London
W1T 3QT
☎020 7323 1579 Fax 020 7436 4553
✉ office@wwnorton.co.uk
www.wwnorton.co.uk

Managing Director *Alan Cameron*

Subsidiary of the US parent company founded in 1923 (see entry under *US Publishers*). Publishes non-fiction and academic books.

Nottingham University Press

Manor Farm, Church Lane, Thrumpton
NG11 0AX
☎0115 983 1011 Fax 0115 983 1003
✉ orders@nup.com
www.nup.com

Initially concentrated on agricultural and food sciences titles but has now branched into new areas including engineering, lifesciences, medicine and law. TITLES *Bovine Meat Inspection; Food, Farming and Countryside; Nutrition and Feeding of Poultry; Rumen Microbiology; The History of Meat Trading; Yields of Farm Species; Livestock and Wealth Creation.*

ROYALTIES twice-yearly.

NWP

See **Neil Wilson Publishing Ltd**

O Books/John Hunt Publishing Ltd

The Bothy, Deershot Lodge, Park Lane, Ropley
SO24 0BE
☎01962 773768 Fax 01962 773769
✉ office1@o-books.net
www.o-books.net
Approx. Annual Turnover £1.5 million

Publishes children's and world religions as well as mind, body and spirit titles. IMPRINTS **John Hunt Publishing**; **O Books**. About 50 titles a year. Unsolicited material welcome.

Oak

See **Omnibus Press**

Oberon Books

521 Caledonian Road, London N7 9RH
☎020 7607 3637 Fax 020 7607 3629
✉ info@oberonbooks.com
www.oberonbooks.com

Publishing Director *James Hogan*
Managing Director *Charles D. Glanville*
Editor *Dan Steward*

A leading theatre publisher, Oberon publishes play texts (usually in conjunction with a production), and books on theatre and dance. Specialises in contemporary plays and translations of European classics. IMPRINTS **Oberon Modern Plays**; **Oberon Classics**. Publishes for the National Theatre, Royal Opera House, Royal Court, English Touring Theatre, LAMDA, Gate Theatre, Bush Theatre, West Yorkshire Playhouse, Chichester Festival Theatre and many other London and regional theatre companies. Publishes over 300 writers and translators including Rodney Ackland, Tariq Ali, Howard Barker, John Barton, Ranjit Bolt, Pam Gems, Tanika Gupta, Sir Peter Hall, Bernard Kops, Adrian Mitchell, Sir John Mortimer, Adriano Shaplin, Laura Wade. An extensive classics list includes performance (edited) versions of Shakespeare including *King Lear; A Midsummer Night's Dream; Romeo and Juliet* and *Twelfth Night*, as well as new translations of plays by Chekhov, Molière, Strindberg and others. About 80 titles a year. Send manuscripts, with information about forthcoming productions to Will Hammond (will@oberonbooks.com). 'We do not provide readers' reports or feedback about work submitted.'

Octagon Press Ltd

78 York Road, London W1H 1DP
☎020 7193 6456 Fax 020 7117 3955
✉ info@octagonpress.com
www.octagonpress.com

Director *Saira Shah*
Approx. Annual Turnover £50,000

Founded 1960. Publishes travel, biography, literature, folklore, psychology, philosophy with the focus on East-West studies. 4–5 titles a year.

ROYALTIES annually.

Octopus Publishing Group

2–4 Heron Quays, London E14 4JP
☎020 7531 8400 Fax 020 7531 8650
www.octopus-publishing.co.uk

Chief Executive *Alison Goff*
Approx. Annual Turnover £45 million (Group)

Formed following a management buyout of

Reed Consumer Books from Reed Elsevier plc in 1998. Bought by French publishers Hachette-Livre in 2001 and acquired Cassell Illustrated and the lists of Ward Lock and Blandford Press; also, Gaia Books acquired in 2004.

Conran Octopus Fax 020 7531 8627 ✉ info-co@conran-octopus.co.uk www. conran-octopus.co.uk Publishing Director *Lorraine Dickey* Quality illustrated lifestyle books, particularly interiors, design, cookery, gardening and crafts TITLES *The Essential House Book* Terence Conran; *Fork to Fork* Monty Don; *Passion for Seafood* Gordon Ramsay; *New Retail* Rasshied Din.

Hamlyn Octopus Fax 020 7531 8562 ✉ info-ho@hamlyn.co.uk www.hamlyn.co.uk Publisher *Jane Birch* Popular non-fiction, particularly cookery, gardening, craft, sport, health, film and music TITLES *Larousse Gastronomique*; *Hamlyn All Colour Cookbook*; *Hamlyn Book of Gardening*; *Hamlyn Book of DIY & Decorating*.

Mitchell Beazley/Miller's Fax 020 7537 0773 ✉ info-mb@mitchell-beazley.co.uk www.mitchell-beazley.co.uk Publisher *David Lamb* Quality illustrated reference books, particularly food and wine, gardening, interior design and architecture, antiques, general reference TITLES *Hugh Johnson's Pocket Wine Book*; *The New Joy of Sex*; *Miller's Antiques and Collectibles Price Guides*.

Philip's Fax 020 7531 8460 ✉ george. philip@philips-maps.co.uk www.philips-maps. co.uk Managing Director *John Gaisford* World atlases, globes, astronomy, road atlases, encyclo-paedias, thematic reference TITLES *Philip's Atlas of the World*; *Philip's Modern School Atlas*; *Philip's Guide to the Stars and Planets*; *Ordnance Survey Street Atlas*; *Philip's Millennium Encyclopaedia*; *Philip's Atlas of World History*.

Bounty Fax 020 7531 8607 ✉ bountybooksinfo-bp@bountybooks.co.uk Publishing and International Sales Director *Polly Manguel* Bargain and promotional books. New, repackaged and reissued titles.

Cassell Illustrated Fax 020 731 8624 Publishing Director *Iain MacGregor* Serious non-fiction covering a wide range of topics from history and cookery to fitness and art.

Godsfield Press Fax 020 7531 8562 ✉ enquiries@godsfieldpress.com Publisher *Jane Birch* Mind, body and spirit encompassing original psychology, health and gift books.

Gaia Books Publisher *Jane Birch* Mind, body and spirit and natural/eco titles.

ROYALTIES twice-yearly/annually, according to contract in all divisions.

Authors' Rating There has been a move away from small run specialist titles to mainstream trade books at the popular end of the market.

Old Street Publishing Ltd

14 Bowling Green Lane, London EC1R 0BD
☎020 7253 3360 Fax 020 7251 6222
✉ info@oldstreetpublishing.co.uk
www.oldstreetpublishing.co.uk

Chairman *David Reynolds*
Managing Director *Ben Yarde-Buller*
Approx. Annual Turnover £5 million

Founded in 2006 by Ben Yarde-Buller and David Reynolds, co-founder of Bloomsbury Publishing. Publishes eclectic fiction including literary fiction, crime/thriller and translation. General non-fiction and humour 'of the better sort'. No poetry, technical or children's books. 20 titles in 2006. No unsolicited mss. Synopses and ideas welcome; approach by e-mail.

ROYALTIES twice-yearly.

Oldcastle Books Ltd

PO Box 394, Harpenden AL5 1XJ
☎01582 761264 Fax 01582 761264
www.noexit.co.uk
www.pocketessentials.com
ww.highstakespublishing.com
www.kamerabooks.com

Managing Director *Ion Mills*

Founded 1985. Publishes crime/noir fiction, gambling non-fiction, 160pp mini-reference titles on film, ideas, history, music. IMPRINTS **No Exit Press**; **High Stakes**; **Pocketessentials**; **Kamera Books**.

Olympia Publishers

78 Cannon Street, London EC4N 6NQ
☎020 7618 6424 Fax 020 7618 8001
✉ info@olympiapublishers.com
www.olympiapublishers.com

Managing Editor *G. Bartlett*
Assistant Editors *D. Absalom, B. Robinson*

Founded 2004. Publishes a wide range of non-fiction and some fiction. Educational books include textbooks on English language, TEFL, dyslexia and topics for university courses. General interest titles cover autobiography, children's, crime, history, humour, mind, body and soul, self help, science fiction. Specialises in books for international markets by Far Eastern authors and Europeans with relevant background experience. TITLES *The A-Z of Practical Wisdom*; *Essay Writing for TEFL*; *Slouching Towards America*; *The Amulet of Vichalace*. 40–50 titles a year. See website for submission guidelines. Unsolicited synopses, poetry and short stories also considered. Postal submissions must be accompanied by s.a.e.

ROYALTIES twice-yearly.

Michael O'Mara Books Ltd

16 Lion Yard, Tremadoc Road, London SW4 7NQ
☎020 7720 8643 Fax 020 7627 8953
✉ firstname.lastname@mombooks.com
www.mombooks.com
www.mombooks.com/busterbooks

Chairman *Michael O'Mara*
Managing Director *Lesley O'Mara*
Editorial Director *Toby Buchan*
Approx. Annual Turnover £6.5 million

Founded 1985. Independent publisher. Publishes general non-fiction, humour, anthologies, miscellanies, royalty and celebrity biographies. TITLES *The Timewaster Letters* Robin Cooper; *The Little Book of Sudoku; The Book of Senior Moments* Shelley Klein. IMPRINT **Buster Books** Children's TITLES *The Boys' Book; Do You Doodle?;* board books, picture books, novelty books, humour and quirky non-fiction. Unsolicited mss, synopses and ideas for books welcome.

ROYALTIES twice-yearly.

Authors' Rating Most of the creative work for bestselling humour titles is done in-house but strong ideas for the gift market may well attract interest. Children's publishing via the Buster Books imprint now accounts for close on half of turnover.

Omnibus Press

Music Sales Ltd, 14/15 Berners Street, London W1T 3LJ
☎020 7612 7400 Fax 020 7612 7545
✉ chris.charlesworth@musicsales.co.uk
www.omnibuspress.com

Owner *Robert Wise*
Editorial Head *Chris Charlesworth*

Founded 1971. Independent publisher of music books, rock and pop biographies, song sheets, educational tutors, cassettes, videos and software. A Division of the Music Sales Group of Companies. IMPRINTS **Amsco; Arcane; Bobcat; Oak; Omnibus; Vision On; Wise Publications**. About 25 titles a year. Unsolicited mss, synopses and ideas for music-related titles welcome.

Oneworld Publications

185 Banbury Road, Oxford OX2 7AR

☎01865 310597 Fax 01865 310598
✉ info@oneworld-publications.com
www.oneworld-publications.com

Editorial Director *Juliet Mabey*

Founded 1986. Publishes adult non-fiction across a range of subjects from world religions to psychology and philosophy, history, politics, and popular science. SERIES include short histories of countries and one on world religions (with authors such as Geoffrey Parrinder, Keith Ward, Klaus Klostermaier and John Hick); also concise encyclopedias on world religions. **Oneworld Philosophers** series was launched in 2001 and **Oneworld Beginners' Guides** in 2002. **Coping With** is a new series aimed at the self-help and counselling market; **Makers of the Muslim World** introduces key people from Muslim history, politics and religion to a broad audience, while a new popular science list explores scientific discoveries and ideas for the specialist and lay reader. TITLES *Pascal's Fire; Bioterror & Biowarfare: A Beginner's Guide; The New Imperialists; 25 Big Ideas: The Science that Changed our World.* About 45 titles a year. No unsolicited mss; synopses and ideas welcome, but should be accompanied by s.a.e. for return of material and/or notification of receipt. No autobiographies, fiction, poetry or children's.

ROYALTIES annually.

Onlywomen Press Ltd

40 St Lawrence Terrace, London W10 5ST
☎020 8354 0796
✉ onlywomenpress@btconnect.com
www.onlywomenpress.com

Editorial Director *Lilian Mohin*

Founded 1974. Publishes feminist lesbian literature: fiction, poetry, literary criticism and political theory. Unsolicited mss and proposals welcome. Submissions details on the website.

OPC

See **Ian Allan Publishing Ltd**

Open Gate Press incorporating Centaur Press

51 Achilles Road, London NW6 1DZ
☎020 7431 4391 Fax 020 7431 5129
✉ books@opengatepress.co.uk
www.opengatepress.co.uk

Managing Directors *Jeannie Cohen, Elisabeth Petersdorff*

Founded in 1989 to provide a forum for psychoanalytic social and cultural studies. Publishes psychoanalysis, philosophy, social sciences, politics, literature, religion, environment. SERIES *Psychoanalysis and Society.* IMPRINTS **Open Gate Press**; **Centaur Press**; **Linden Press**. No unsolicited mss.

ROYALTIES annually.

Open University Press

McGraw-Hill House, Shoppenhangers Road, Maidenhead SL6 2QL
☎01628 502500 Fax 01628 770224
✉ enquiries@openup.co.uk
www.openup.co.uk

Managing Director *Paul Maraviglia*

Founded 1977 as an imprint independent of the Open University's course materials. Acquired by **McGraw-Hill Education** in 2002. Publishes academic and professional books in the fields of education, sociology, health, psychology, psychotherapy and counselling, higher education and study skills materials. No economics or anthropology. Not interested in anything outside the social sciences. About 100 titles a year. No unsolicited mss; enquiries/proposals only.

ROYALTIES annually.

Orbit

See **Little, Brown Book Group UK**

Orchard Press

See **Hachette Children's Books**

The Orion Publishing Group Limited

Orion House, 5 Upper St Martin's Lane, London WC2H 9EA
☎020 7240 3444 Fax 020 7240 4822
www.orionbooks.co.uk/pub/index.htm

Chairman *Arnaud Nourry*
Chief Executive *Peter Roche*
Deputy Chief Executive *Malcolm Edwards*
Approx. Annual Turnover £70 million

Founded 1992. Incorporates Weidenfeld & Nicolson, JM Dent, Gollancz and Cassell.

DIVISIONS **Orion** Managing Director *Lisa Milton* IMPRINTS **Orion Fiction** Publishing Director *Jon Wood* Hardcover fiction; **Orion Media** Publishing Director *Ian Marshall* Hardcover non-fiction; **Orion Children's** Publisher *Fiona Kennedy* Children's fiction/non-fiction; **Gollancz** Editorial Directors *Simon Spanton, Jo Fletcher* Science fiction and fantasy.

Weidenfeld & Nicolson Managing Director *Malcolm Edwards*, Publisher *Alan Samson* IMPRINTS **Weidenfeld Illustrated** Editor-in-Chief *Michael Dover* Illustrated non-fiction; **Weidenfeld General** Publishing Director *Ian* *Drury* General non-fiction, history and military; **Weidenfeld Fiction** Editorial Director *Helen Garnons Williams* History; **Cassell Reference** General reference; **Custom Publishing** Director *Elizabeth Leath.*

Paperback Division Managing Director *Susan Lamb* IMPRINTS **Orion; Phoenix; Everyman**.

Osprey Publishing Ltd

Midland House, West Way, Botley, Oxford OX2 0PH
☎01865 727022 Fax 01865 727017/727019
✉ info@ospreypublishing.com
www.ospreypublishing.com

Also at: 443 Park Avenue, Suite 806, New York, NY 10016, USA

Chairman *Philip Sturrock*
Managing Director *Rebecca Smart*
Editorial Director *Anita Baker*

Publishes illustrated history of war and warfare and military aviation, also general military history. Founded 1969, Osprey became independent from **Reed Elsevier** in February 1998 and launched Osprey Publishing Inc. as a wholly owned subsidiary in North America in 2004. SERIES include *Men-at-Arms*; *Fortress*; *Campaign*; *Essential Histories*; *Warrior*; *Elite*; *New Vanguard*; *Osprey Modelling*; *Duel*; *Aircraft of the Aces*; *Aviation Elite Units*; *Combat Aircraft*. About 100 titles a year including 20 non-series titles a year. No unsolicited mss; ideas and synopses welcome.

ROYALTIES twice-yearly.

Peter Owen Publishers

73 Kenway Road, London SW5 0RE
☎020 7373 5628/7370 6093
Fax 020 7373 6760
✉ aowen@peterowen.com
www.peterowen.com

Chairman *Peter Owen*
Editorial Director *Antonia Owen*

Founded 1951. Publishes biography, general non-fiction, English-language literary fiction and translations, history, literary criticism, the arts and entertainment. 'No genre or children's fiction; the company is taking on no first novels or short stories at present.' AUTHORS Jane Bowles, Paul Bowles, Yuri Druzhnikov, Shusaku Endo, Philip Freund, Anna Kavan, Jean Giono, Anaïs Nin, Jeremy Reed, Peter Vansittart. About 25 titles a year. Unsolicited synopses welcome for non-fiction material. Please call in advance to submit fiction. Mss should be preceded by a descriptive letter and synopsis with s.a.e. OVERSEAS ASSOCIATES worldwide.

ROYALTIES twice-yearly.

Authors' Rating Peter Owen has been described as 'a publisher of the old and idiosyncratic school'. He has seven Nobel prizewinners on his list to prove it.

Oxbow Books
Park End Place, Oxford OX1 1HN
☎01865 241249 Fax 01865 794449
✉ oxbow@oxbowbooks.com
www.oxbowbooks.com

Editorial *Clare Litt*

Founded 1983. Publishes academic archaeology, Egyptology, ancient and medieval history. IMPRINT **Aris & Phillips** Greek, Latin and Hispanic texts and translations. About 60 titles a year.

Oxford University Press
Great Clarendon Street, Oxford OX2 6DP
☎01865 556767 Fax 01865 556646
✉ enquiry@oup.com
www.oup.com

Chief Executive *Henry Reece*
Approx. Annual Turnover £448 million

A department of Oxford University, OUP started as the university's printing business and developed into a major publishing operation in the 19th century. Publishes academic works in all formats (print and online): dictionaries, lexical and non-lexical reference, scholarly journals, student texts, schoolbooks, ELT materials, music, bibles, paperbacks, and children's books. Around 6000 titles a year.

DIVISIONS **Academic** *T.M. Barton* Academic and higher education titles in major disciplines, dictionaries, non-lexical reference and trade books. OUP welcomes first-class academic material in the form of proposals or accepted theses. **Journals** *M. Richardson* Academic and research journals. **Education** *K. Harris* National Curriculum courses and support materials as well as children's literature. **ELT** *P.R.C. Marshall* ELT courses and dictionaries for all levels.

OVERSEAS BRANCHES/SUBSIDIARIES Sister company in USA with branches or subsidiaries in Argentina, Australia, Brazil, Canada, China, East Africa, India, Japan, Malaysia, Mexico, Pakistan, Southern Africa, Spain and Turkey. Offices in France, Greece, Italy, Poland, Taiwan, Thailand.

ROYALTIES twice-yearly.

Authors' Rating The biggest publisher to benefit from charitable status, OUP is nervously looking to the Treasury as new rules are framed that could revoke its tax exempt status. English and bilingual dictionaries are the core activity with OUP capturing over half the English and a third of the bilingual market.

Palgrave Macmillan
See **Macmillan Publishers Ltd**

Palm Tree Press
See **Kevin Mayhew Publishers**

G.J. Palmer & Sons Ltd
See **Hymns Ancient & Modern Ltd**

Pan
See **Macmillan Publishers Ltd**

Paper Tiger
See **Anova Books**

Parthian
The Old Surgery, Napier Street, Aberteifi (Cardigan) SA43 1ED
☎01239 612059
✉ parthianbooks@yahoo.co.uk
www.parthianbooks.co.uk

Also: **Library of Wales**
Trinity College, Carmarthen SA31 3EP
Fax 01239 612059
www.libraryofwales.org

Publisher *Richard Davies*
Fiction/Poetry Editor *Jasmine Donahaye*
Editor, Library of Wales *Professor Dai Smith*

Founded 1993. Publishes contemporary Welsh writing in English including novels, poetry and drama, also translations from Welsh. A keen interest in short stories. Its list includes many young writers. TITLES *Fresh Apples* Rachel Trezise (winner of the EDS Dylan Thomas Award); *Luggage From Elsewhere* A.G. Thomas; *Martha, Jac and Shanco* Caryl Lewis. New non-fiction list planned for 2007. Increasing interest in translation with new titles planned from Catalan and Basque. Also publishes **Library of Wales** classic series including Raymond Williams' *Border Country*, ed. Prof. Dai Smith. 12–15 titles a year. Synopsis with first three sample chapters welcome. 'An idea of what we do is always an advantage.'

Paternoster
See **Authentic Media**

Pavilion/Pavilion Children's Books
See **Anova Books**

Payne–Gallway
See **Harcourt**

Pearson Education
Edinburgh Gate, Harlow CM20 2JE
☎01279 623623
www.pearsoned.com
The world's largest educational publisher was created by the merger of Addison Wesley Longman, Financial Times Management and **Simon & Schuster**'s educational list. Acquired **Harcourt Education** in May 2007. Publishes across a wide range of curriculum subjects from primary students to professional practitioners. IMPRINTS **Addison Wesley**; **Allyn & Bacon**; **BBC Active**; **Benjamin Cummings**; **Causeway Press**; **Cisco Press**; **Penguin Longman**; **Prentice Hall**; **Prentice Hall Business**; **QUE Publishing**; **SAM Publishing**; **Wharton**; **York Notes**. OVERSEAS ASSOCIATES worldwide. Unsolicited mss should be addressed to the appropriate department: **ELT** *Lyn Kitteridge*; **Schools** *Carol Hayward*; **University & Professional Level** *Anna Campling*.
ROYALTIES twice-yearly.

Pegasus Elliot Mackenzie Publishers Ltd
Sheraton House, Castle Park, Cambridge CB3 0AX
☎01223 370012 Fax 01223 370040
✉ editors@pegasuspublishers.com
www.pegasuspublishers.com
Senior Editor *D. W. Stern*
Editor *R. Sabir*
Publishes fiction and non-fiction, general interest, biography, autobiography, children's, history, humour, fantasy, self-help, educational, science fiction, poetry, travel, war, memoirs, crime and eroticism, also Internet and e-books. IMPRINTS **Vanguard Press**; **Nightingale Books**; **Chimera** TITLES *Count the Petals of the Moon Daisy* Martin Kirby; *Flowers of the Forest* Jan Carew; *Modern Day Hero* Nick Pettitt, GM, QGM; *Missing In Medway* Alex Mabon. Unsolicited mss, synopses and ideas considered if accompanied by return postage.
ROYALTIES twice-yearly.

Authors' Rating Liable to ask authors to contribute to production costs.

Pen & Sword Books Ltd
47 Church Street, Barnsley S70 2AS
☎01226 734222 Fax 01226 734438
✉ editorial@pen-and-sword.co.uk
www.pen-and-sword.co.uk
Commissioning Editor, Aviation *Peter Coles*
Commissioning Editor, Military & Maritime *Henry Wilson*
Commissioning Editor, History, Local History & Family History *Rupert Harding*
One of the leading military history publishers in the UK. Publishes non-fiction only, specialising in naval and aviation history, WW1, WW2, Napoleonic, autobiography and biography. Also publishes *Battleground* series for battlefield tourists. IMPRINTS **Leo Cooper**; **Pen & Sword Aviation**; **Pen & Sword Family History**; **Pen & Sword Maritime**; **Pen & Sword Military**; **Remember When** (see entry); **Wharncliffe Books** (see entry). About 200 titles a year. Unsolicited synopses and ideas welcome; no unsolicited mss.
ROYALTIES twice-yearly.

Penguin Group (UK)
A Pearson Company, 80 Strand, London WC2R 0RL
☎020 7010 3000 Fax 020 7010 6060
www.penguin.co.uk
Group Chairman & Chief Executive *John Makinson*
CEO Penguin UK *Peter Field*
Managing Director: Penguin *Helen Fraser*
Approx. Annual Turnover £121 million
Owned by Pearson plc. The world's best known book brand and for more than 70 years a leading publisher whose adult and children's lists include fiction, non-fiction, poetry, drama, classics, reference and special interest areas. Reprints and new work.

DIVISIONS
Penguin General Books Managing Director *Tom Weldon* Adult fiction and non-fiction is published in hardback under **Michael Joseph**, **Viking**, **Fig Tree** and **Hamish Hamilton** imprints. Paperbacks come under the **Penguin** imprint. IMPRINTS **Viking/Penguin** Publisher *Venetia Butterfield* Publishing Director *Tony Lacey*; **Hamish Hamilton** Publishing Director *Simon Prosser*; **Michael Joseph/Penguin** Managing Director *Louise Moore* Does not accept unsolicited mss.
    Penguin Press Managing Director *Stefan McGrath* Publishing Directors *Stuart Proffitt*, *Simon Winder* Academic adult non-fiction, reference, specialist and classics. IMPRINTS **Allen Lane**; **Penguin Reference** Publishing Director *Georgina Laycock* No unsolicited mss.
    Dorling Kindersley Ltd (see entry).

Frederick Warne Managing Director *Sally Floyer* Classic children's publishing and merchandising including *Beatrix Potter™*; *Flower Fairies*; *Orlando*. **Ventura** Publisher *Sally Floyer* Producer and packager of *Spot* titles by Eric Hill.

Ladybird (see **Dorling Kindersley Ltd**).

BBC Children's Books *Sally Floyer* Children's imprint launched in 2004.

Puffin Managing Director *Francesca Dow* (poetry and picture books) Publisher *Rebecca McNally* (fiction), Senior Editor *Fran Hammond* (media and popular non-fiction) Leading children's paperback list, publishing in virtually all fields including fiction, non-fiction, poetry, picture books, media-related titles. No unsolicited mss; synopses and ideas welcome.

Penguin Audiobooks (see entry under *Audio Books*).

ePenguin Penguin Digital Publisher *Jeremy Ettinghausen* E-books list launched in 2001. OVERSEAS ASSOCIATES worldwide.

ROYALTIES twice-yearly.

Authors' Rating One of the few publishers to boast a strong brand image, Penguin is in third place behind Random House and Hachette in terms of UK market share. Penguin holds the number one position for non-fiction. An ambitious digitisation programme is under way, 'testing the bounds of what's possible', according to CEO John Makinson. Puffin is roaring ahead in children's books while hardback fiction and non-fiction have benefited greatly from Amazon sales.

Penguin Longman
See **Pearson Education**

Pergamon
See **Elsevier Ltd**

Persephone Books
59 Lamb's Conduit Street, London WC1N 3NB
☎020 7242 9292 Fax 020 7242 9272
✉ sales@persephonebooks.co.uk
www.persephonebooks.co.uk

Managing Director *Nicola Beauman*

Founded 1999. Publishes reprint fiction and non-fiction, mostly 'by women, for women and about women'. TITLES *Miss Pettigrew Lives for a Day* Winifred Watson; *Kitchen Essays* Agnes Jekyll; *The Far Cry* Emma Smith; *The Priory* Dorothy Whipple. 4 titles a year. No unsolicited material.

ROYALTIES twice-yearly.

Phaidon Press Limited
Regent's Wharf, All Saints Street, London N1 9PA
☎020 7843 1000 Fax 020 7843 1010
✉ name@phaidon.com
www.phaidon.com

Group Chairman & Publisher *Richard Schlagman*
Chairman *Andrew Price*
Editorial Director *Amanda Renshaw*
Approx. Annual Turnover £24.5 million

Publishes quality books on the visual arts, including fine art, art history, architecture, design, photography, decorative arts, music and performing arts, cookery and children's books. Also produces videos. DIVISIONS/SERIES (with Editorial Heads) **Architecture and Design** *Emilia Terragni*; **Contemporary Art** Craig Garrett; **Photography** *Denise Wolff*; **Art & Academic** *David Anfam*; **Cooking/Food** *Emilia Terragni;* **Children's** *Amanda Renshaw.* About 100 titles a year. Unsolicited mss welcome but 'only a small amount of unsolicited material gets published'.

ROYALTIES twice-yearly.

Authors' Rating Claiming, with some justification, to have the best art and design list of any publisher, Phaidon is planning to have its own high street stores, a reaction to the book chains that have 'lost their way and their personality'. With French and German subsidiaries, Phaidon's European scope gives it added appeal here and in the US for titles that might not otherwise enter the English language market. Commended for tight management and strong marketing.

Philip's
See **Octopus Publishing Group**

Phillimore & Co. Ltd
Shopwyke Manor Barn, Chichester PO20 2BG
☎01243 787636 Fax 01243 787639
✉ bookshop@phillimore.co.uk
www.phillimore.co.uk

Managing Director *Noel Osborne*
Approx. Annual Turnover £1.45 million

Founded in 1897 by W.P.W. Phillimore, Victorian campaigner for local archive conservation in Chancery Lane, London. Became the country's leading publisher of historical source material and local histories. Somewhat dormant in the 1960s, it was revived by Philip Harris in 1968. Publishes British local and family history, including histories of institutions, buildings, villages, towns and counties, plus guides to research and writing in these fields. Acquired by NPI Media Group Ltd in November 2006. IMPRINT **Phillimore** *Noel Osborne* TITLES *Domesday Book; A History of Essex; Newcastle upon Tyne: A Modern History; The Haberdashers' Company; The North Downs; A History of Manchester; Warwickshire Country Houses.* About 50 titles a year. No unsolicited mss; synopses/ideas welcome for local or family histories.

ROYALTIES annually.

Phoenix
See **The Orion Publishing Group Limited**

Piatkus Books
5 Windmill Street, London W1T 2JA
☎020 7631 0710 Fax 020 7436 7137
✉ info@piatkus.co.uk
www.piatkus.co.uk
Managing Director *Judy Piatkus*
Deputy Managing Director *Philip Cotterell*
Approx. Annual Turnover £9.5 million

Founded in 1979 by Judy Piatkus, the company continues to be one of the UK's leading independent publishing houses. The Piatkus imprint specialises in lifestyle, health, self-help, mind, body and spirit, popular psychology and business titles. Piatkus fiction includes new novels from many of the world's bestselling international authors. Portrait imprint publishes biography, autobiography, history, popular culture, humour and serious non-fiction in both hardback and paperback. DIVISIONS **Non-fiction** Publisher *Judy Piatkus*, Editorial Director *Gill Bailey* IMPRINTS **Portrait** TITLES *Sour Gripes* Simon Carr; *Julie Andrews* Richard Stirling; *The Book of Origins* Trevor Homer; *The New School Rules* Francis Gilbert. **Piatkus** TITLES *The Holford Low GL Diet Made Easy* Patrick Holford; *Women Who Think Too Much* Susan Nolan-Hoeksema. **Fiction** Publisher *Judy Piatkus*, Fiction Director *Gillian Green* TITLES *High Noon* Nora Roberts; *It's in His Kiss* Julia Quinn; *Sex Wars* Marge Piercy. About 175 titles a year (70 of which are fiction). Piatkus is expanding its range of books and welcomes synopses together with first three chapters.

ROYALTIES twice-yearly.

Authors' Rating A thriving independent publisher, turnover has increased by 38% over two years, Piatkus is on the lookout for bright ideas. 'Company policy is to work closely with authors and to give every title time and attention and its own marketing budget. We feel if we are not going to do this for each book then there is

no point in our publishing it,' says Judy Piatkus. Unusually in the current climate, there is strong emphasis on pushing backlist sales.

Pica Press
See **A.&C. Black Publishers Ltd**

Picador/Young Picador
See **Macmillan Publishers Ltd**

Piccadilly Press
5 Castle Road, London NW1 8PR
☎020 7267 4492 Fax 020 7267 4493
✉ books@piccadillypress.co.uk
www.piccadillypress.co.uk
Publisher/Managing Director *Brenda Gardner*
Approx. Annual Turnover £1.4 million

Founded 1983. Independent publisher of children's and parental books. 30 titles in 2006. Welcomes approaches from authors 'but we would like them to know the sort of books we do. It is frustrating to get inappropriate material. They should check in their local libraries, bookshops or look at our website. We will send a catalogue (please enclose s.a.e.).' No adult or cartoon-type material.

ROYALTIES twice-yearly.

Pictorial Presentations
See **Souvenir Press Ltd**

Pimlico
See **The Random House Group Ltd**

Pinwheel Limited
Winchester House, 259–269 Old Marylebone Road, London NW1 5XJ
☎020 7616 7200 Fax 020 7616 7201
Managing Director *Andrew Flatt*

Acquired by Alligator Books in May 2007. Children's non-fiction, picture books and novelty titles. IMPRINTS **Andromeda Children's Books** Publishing/Creative Director *Linda Cole* Illustrated non-fiction for children from 3–12 years; **Gullane Children's Books** Creative Director *Paula Burgess* Picture books for children from 0–8 years; **Pinwheel Children's Books** Publishing/Creative Director *Linda Cole* Cloth and novelty books for children from 0–5 years. Unsolicited mss will not be returned.

Pitkin
See **Jarrold Publishing**

Pluto Press Ltd
345 Archway Road, London N6 5AA
☎020 8348 2724 Fax 020 8348 9133

pluto@plutobooks.com
www.plutobooks.com
Chair *Roger Van Zwanenberg*
Managing Director/Publisher *Anne Beech*
Founded 1970. Has developed a reputation for innovatory publishing in the field of non-fiction. Publishes academic and scholarly books across a range of subjects including cultural studies, politics and world affairs and more general titles on key aspects of currrent affairs. About 70 titles a year. Prospective authors are encouraged to consult the website for guidelines on submitting proposals.

Pocket Books
See **Simon & Schuster UK Limited**

Pocket Mountains Ltd
6 Church Wynd, Bo'ness EH51 0AN Fax 01506 500405
info@pocketmountains.com
www.pocketmountains.com
Managing Directors *Robbie Porteous, April Simmons*
Approx. Annual Turnover £100,000
Founded in 2003 to publish a series of guidebooks to the Scottish hills and now publishing other guides covering Europe: mountaineering, walking, cycling and wildlife books. 3 titles in 2006. Unsolicited mss, synopses and ideas welcome; approach by e-mail or letter. No fiction, children's or cookery.
ROYALTIES quarterly.

Pocketessentials
See **Oldcastle Books Ltd**

Poetry Library
See **CRW Publishing Ltd**

Poisoned Pen Press UK Ltd
6 Rodney Place, Clifton, Bristol BS8 4HY
0117 907 5949
info@poisonedpenpressuk.com
www.poisonedpenpressuk.com
Managing Director *Jennifer Muller*
Editorial Head *Barbara Peters*
UK subsidiary of Poisoned Pen Press US, founded in 1996. Publishes adult crime fiction and mystery books. Unsolicited mss welcome; electronic submissions only to: editor@poisonedpenpress.com
ROYALTIES annually.

The Policy Press
Fourth Floor, Beacon House, Queen's Road, Bristol BS8 1QU
0117 331 4054 Fax 0117 331 4093
tpp-info@bristol.ac.uk
www.policypress.org.uk
Managing Director *Alison Shaw*
Publishes social welfare and policy work for students, academics, practitioners, professionals and policy-makers.

Politico's Publishing
11–12 Buckingham Gate, London SW1E 6LB
020 7798 1600 Fax 020 7828 2098
sales@methuen.co.uk
www.politicospublishing.co.uk
Chairman/Managing Director *Peter Tummons*
Publishing Consultant *Alan Gordon Walker*
Founded 1998. Acquired by **Methuen Publishing Ltd** in April 2003. Publishes political books. 30 titles in 2006. Unsolicited mss, synopses and ideas welcome; telephone in the first instance.
ROYALTIES twice-yearly.

Polity Press
65 Bridge Street, Cambridge CB2 1UR
01223 324315 Fax 01223 461385
www.polity.co.uk
Founded 1984. Publishes archaeology and anthropology, criminology, economics, feminism, general interest, history, human geography, literature, media and cultural studies, medicine and society, philosophy, politics, psychology, religion and theology, social and political theory, sociology. Unsolicited synopses and ideas for books welcome. 'Please do not send mss.'
ROYALTIES annually.

Polygon
West Newington House, 10 Newington Road, Edinburgh EH9 1QS
0131 668 4371 Fax 0131 668 4466
info@birlinn.co.uk
www.birlinn.co.uk
Publishing Director *Neville Moir*
Managing Editor *Alison Rae*
Bought by **Birlinn Ltd** in 2002. Publishes literary fiction, crime fiction and poetry. About 40 titles a year.
ROYALTIES twice-yearly.

Pont Books
See **Gomer Press**

Pop Universal
See **Souvenir Press Ltd**

Portico
See **Anova Books**

Portland Press Ltd
3rd Floor, Eagle House, 16 Procter Street,
London WC1V 6NX
☎020 7280 4110 Fax 020 7280 4169
✉ editorial@portlandpress.com
www.portlandpress.com
Chairman *Professor A.J. Turner*
Managing Director *Rhonda Oliver*
Managing Editor *Pauline Starley*
Approx. Annual Turnover £2.5 million
Founded 1990 to expand the publishing activities of the Biochemical Society (1911). Publishes biochemisty and medicine for graduate, postgraduate and research students. Expanding the list to include schools and general readership. TITLES *The Biochemical Basis of the Health Effects of Exercise; The Cell Biology of Inositol Lipids and Phosphates; Fundamentals of Enzyme Kinetics.* 3 titles in 2006. Unsolicited mss, synopses and ideas welcome. No fiction.
ROYALTIES twice-yearly.

Portobello Books
Eardley House, 4 Uxbridge Street, Notting Hill Gate, London W8 7SY
☎020 7908 9892 Fax 020 7908 9899
✉ mail@portobellobooks.com
www.portobellobooks.com
Owners *Sigrid Rausing, Eric Abraham, Philip Gwyn Jones*
Managing Director *David Graham*
Administrative Assistant *Sophie Garland*
Founded in 2005 by Philip Gwyn Jones, formerly publishing director of HarperCollins' literary imprint Flamingo. Owners acquired **Granta** in 2005. Publishes international literature and activist non-fiction. About 25 titles a year. No unsolicited mss; synopses and ideas for books welcome. Approach by post in the first instance. No science fiction, romance or genre fiction of any kind, no gardening, cookery, mind, body and spirit or reference.

Portrait
See **Piatkus Books**

T&AD Poyser
See **A.&C. Black Publishers Ltd**

Prentice Hall/Prentice Hall Business
See **Pearson Education**

Prestel Publishing Limited
4 Bloomsbury Place, London WC1A 2QA
☎020 7323 5004 Fax 020 7636 8004
✉ sales@prestel-uk.co.uk
www.prestel.com
UK Editor *Philippa Hurd*
Editor-in-Chief (Germany) *Curt Holtz*
Founded 1924. Publishes art, architecture, photography, design, fashion, children's and general illustrated books. No fiction. Unsolicited mss, synopses and ideas welcome. Approach by post or e-mail.

Princeton University Press
See **University Presses of California, Columbia & Princeton Ltd**

Prion Books
See **Carlton Publishing Group**

Profile Books
3a Exmouth House, Pine Street, Exmouth Market, London EC1R 0JH
☎020 7841 6300 Fax 020 7833 3969
✉ info@profilebooks.com
www.profilebooks.com
Publisher & Managing Director *Andrew Franklin*
Editorial Director *Stephen Brough*
Approx. Annual Turnover £8.32 million
Founded 1996. Publishes general non-fiction: history, biography, current affairs, popular science, politics, business management. Also publishers of *The Economist* books. IMPRINTS **Serpent's Tail** (see entry). No unsolicited mss; phone or send preliminary letter.

Authors' Rating Reports that Profile was about to start a fiction list were overtaken by the revelation of the takeover of Serpent's Tail in a deal which 'brings together two of the most distinctive and fiercely independent small publishers in London'.

ProQuest CSA
The Quorum, Barnwell Road, Cambridge CB5 8SW
☎01223 215512 Fax 01223 215513
www.proquest.co.uk
Vice President, Technology/General Manager *John Taylor*
Part of Cambridge Information Group. Provides

access to and navigation of more than 125 billion digital pages of the world's scholarship, from arts and literature to science, technology and medicine. ProQuest CSA's content is available to researchers through libraries of all types, and includes the world's largest digital newspaper archive, periodical databases comprising the output of more than 9000 titles and covering more than 500 years.

Psychology Press (An imprint of Taylor & Francis Group, an Informa plc business)
27 Church Road, Hove BN3 2FA
☎020 7017 6000 Fax 020 7017 6336
www.psypress.co.uk
Managing Director *Mike Forster*
Deputy Managing Director *Rohays Perry*

Publishes psychology textbooks, monographs, professional books, tests and numerous journals which are available in both printed and online formats. Send detailed proposal plus c.v. and sample chapters. Proposal requirements and submission procedures available on the website. No poetry, fiction, travel or astrology.

ROYALTIES according to contract.

Publishing House
Trinity Place, Barnstaple EX32 9HG
☎01271 328892 Fax 01271 328768
✉ info@vernoncoleman.com
www.vernoncoleman.com
Managing Director *Vernon Coleman*
Publishing Director *Sue Ward*
Approx. Annual Turnover £750,000

Founded 1989. Self-publisher of fiction, health, humour, animals, politics. Over 90 books published. TITLES *Mrs Caldicot's Cabbage War; England our England; Bodypower; Bilbury Chronicles; Second Innings; It's Never Too Late; How to Publish Your Own Book; Alice's Diary; Rogue Nation; Food for Thought,* all by Vernon Coleman. No submissions.

Puffin
See **Penguin Group (UK)**

Pushkin Press Ltd
12 Chester Terrace, London NW1 4ND
☎020 7730 0750 Fax 020 7730 1341
✉ books@pushkinpress.com
www.pushkinpress.com
Chairman *Melissa Ulfane*
Editorial Head *Christopher Scott Vann*
Approx. Annual Turnover £250,000

Publishes novels and essays in translation drawn from the best of classic and contemporary European literature.

QED Publishing
226 City Road, London EC1V 2TT
☎020 7812 8600 Fax 020 7253 4370
✉ stevee@quarto.com
www.qed-publishing.co.uk
www.qeb-publishing.com
Owner *Quarto Publishing plc*
Chairman, Quarto Group *Laurence Orbach*
Director of Co-edition Publishing, Quarto Group *Piers Spence*
Publisher *Steve Evans*
Editorial Head *Hannah Ray*
Approx. Annual Turnover £2.4 million

Founded in 2003 by the Quarto Group. Publishes children's: education, reference, literacy, numeracy, fiction, geography, history, picture books, non-fiction. TITLES *QED Start Series; QED Learn Computing; QED Learn Art; QED You and Your Pet; QED Maths Club; QED Machines at Work; QED Down on the Farm.* 63 titles in 2007. No unsolicited material; initial approach by e-mail. No adult books. OVERSEAS SUBSIDIARY QEB Publishing Inc., USA.

FEES paid.

Quadrille Publishing Ltd
Alhambra House, 27–31 Charing Cross Road, London WC2H 0LS
☎020 7839 7117 Fax 020 7839 7118
✉ info@quadrille.co.uk
www.quadrille.co.uk
Chairman *Sir David Cooksey*
Managing Director *Alison Cathie*
Editorial Director *Jane O'Shea*
Approx. Annual Turnover £6 million

Founded in 1994 with a view to producing a small list of top-quality illustrated books. Publishes non-fiction, including cookery, gardening, interior design and decoration, craft, health. TITLES *Gordon Ramsay Fast; The Genius of Photography* Gerry Badger; *The Angel Way of Love and Light* Angela McGerr; *The Collectables* Erika Knight. 58 titles in 2006. Synopses and ideas for books welcome. No fiction or children's books.

ROYALTIES twice-yearly.

Authors' Rating The top publisher for cookbooks, Quadrille has achieved an enviable reputation for high production values.

Quantum
See **Foulsham Publishers**

Quartet Books

27 Goodge Street, London W1T 2LD
☎020 7636 3992 Fax 020 7637 1866
✉ quartetbooks@easynet.co.uk

Chairman *Naim Attallah*
Managing Director *Jeremy Beale*
Publishing Director *Stella Kane*

Founded 1972. Independent publisher. Publishes contemporary literary fiction including translations, popular culture, biography, music, history, politics and some photographic books. Unsolicited sample chapters with return postage welcome; no poetry, romance or science fiction. Submissions by disk or e-mail are not accepted.

ROYALTIES twice-yearly.

Quarto Publishing Plc

See entry under *UK Packagers*

QUE Publishing

See **Pearson Education**

Quercus Publishing

21 Bloomsbury Square, London WC1A 2NS
☎020 7291 7200 Fax 020 7291 7201
✉ mail@quercusbooks.co.uk

Chairman *Anthony Cheetham*
Managing Director *Mark Smith*
Approx. Annual Turnover £5 million

Founded in 2005 as a commercial publisher of quality fiction and non-fiction. DIVISIONS **Trade Publishing** Editorial Head *Nicolas Cheetham* TITLE *The Broken Shore*; **Children's Publishing** Editorial Head *Suzy Jenvey* TITLE *Hazel's Nightmares*; **Contract Publishing** Editorial Head *Wayne Davies* TITLE *Speeches That Changed the World*; **Quercus Audiobooks** *Laura Palmer* TITLE *The Tenderness of Wolves*. 50 titles in 2006. No unsolicited material.

ROYALTIES annually.

Authors' Rating Originally a contract publisher, forging deals directly with booksellers, Quercus is now into women's fiction and crime and has recently launched a range of audiobooks. Company policy is to focus on new and under-developed writers - 'refugees from big groups who weren't high enough up the pecking order to get into the sunshine of the big market spends'. The crime list has proved the greatest success with several previously middle-ranking authors benefiting from strong marketing to emerge as bestsellers.

Quiller Press (An imprint of Quiller Publishing Ltd)

Wykey House, Wykey, Shrewsbury SY4 1JA
☎01939 261616 Fax 01939 261606
✉ info@quillerbooks.com
www.countrybooksdirect.com

Managing Director *Andrew Johnston*

Specialises in sponsored books and publications sold through non-book trade channels as well as bookshops. Publishes architecture, biography, business and industry, collecting, cookery, DIY, gardening, guidebooks, humour, reference, sports, travel, wine and spirits. IMPRINTS **Kenilworth Press** (see entry); **The Sportsman's Press** (see entry); **Swan Hill Press** (see entry). About 10 titles a year. Unsolicited mss only if the author sees some potential for sponsorship or guaranteed sales.

ROYALTIES twice-yearly.

Quince Books Limited

209 Hackney Road, London E2 8JL
☎020 7033 4265
✉ info@quincebooks.com
www.quincebooks.com

Editor *Sara Hibbard*

Founded 2005. Publishes commercial ficton. About 15 books a year. Welcomes submissions; send synopsis and three chapters by e-mail.

ROYALTIES annually.

Radcliffe Press

See **I.B. Tauris & Co. Ltd**

Radcliffe Publishing Ltd

18 Marcham Road, Abingdon OX14 1AA
☎01235 528820 Fax 01235 528830
✉ contact.us@radcliffemed.com
www.radcliffe-oxford.com

Managing Director *Andrew Bax*
Editorial Director *Gillian Nineham*
Approx. Annual Turnover £2 million

Founded 1987. Medical publishing house which began by specialising in books for general practice and health service management. Publishes clinical, management, health policy books, training materials, journals and CD-ROMs. 110 titles in 2006. Unsolicited mss, synopses and ideas welcome. No non-medical books.

ROYALTIES twice-yearly.

Raintree

See **Harcourt**

The Random House Group Ltd

Random House, 20 Vauxhall Bridge Road, London SW1V 2SA

☎ 020 7840 8400 Fax 020 7233 6058

✉ enquiries@randomhouse.co.uk

www.randomhouse.co.uk

Chief Executive/Chairman *Gail Rebuck*
Deputy CEO *Ian Hudson*
Group Managing Director *Peter Bowron*

The Random House Group is the UK's leading trade publisher comprising 35 diverse imprints in five separate, substantially autonomous companies: **CCV**, **CHA**, **Ebury Publishing**, **Transworld** (see entry) and **Random House Children's Books**.

CCV

Managing Director *Richard Cable*, Publisher *Dan Franklin*

IMPRINTS **Jonathan Cape** ☎ 020 7840 8576 Fax 020 7233 6117 Publisher *Dan Franklin* Biography and memoirs, current affairs, fiction, history, photography, poetry, politics and travel. **Yellow Jersey Press** ☎ 020 7840 8637 Fax 020 7223 6117 Editorial Director *Tristan Jones* Narrative sports books. **Harvill Secker** ☎ 020 7840 8649 Fax 020 7233 6117 Publishing Director *Geoff Mulligan* Principally literary fiction with some non-fiction. Literature in translation, English literature, quality thrillers. **Chatto & Windus** ☎ 020 7840 8522 Fax 020 7233 6117 Publishing Director *Alison Samuel* Memoirs, current affairs, essays, literary fiction, history, poetry, politics, philosophy and translations. **Pimlico** ☎ 020 7840 8784 Fax 020 7233 6117 Publishing Director *Rachel Cugnoni* Quality non-fiction paperbacks, specialising in history. **Vintage** ☎ 020 7840 8784 Fax 020 7233 6117 Publishing Director *Rachel Cugnoni* Quality paperback fiction and non-fiction. Vintage (founded in 1990) has been described as one of the 'greatest literary success stories in recent British publishing'. **The Bodley Head** ☎ 020 7840 8553 Fax 020 7233 6117 Publishing Director *Will Sulkin* History, science, current affairs, politics, biography, popular culture.

CHA

Managing Director *Susan Sandon*

IMPRINTS **Century** ☎ 020 7840 8554 Fax 020 7233 6127 Publishing Director *Mark Booth* General fiction and non-fiction including commercial fiction, autobiography, biography, history and self-help. **William Heinemann** ☎ 020 7840 8400 Fax 020 7233 6127 Publishing Director *Jason Arthur* General non-fiction and fiction, especially history, literary fiction,

crime, science, thrillers and women's fiction. **Hutchinson** ☎ 020 7840 8564 Fax 020 7233 7870 Publishing Director *Caroline Gascoigne* General fiction and non-fiction including notably belles-lettres, current affairs, politics, travel and history. **Random House Books** (incorporating **Random House Business Books**) ☎ 020 7840 8666 Fax 020 7233 6127 Publisher *Nigel Wilcockson*. **Arrow** ☎ 020 7840 8557 Fax 020 7840 6127 Publishing Director *Kate Elton* Mass-market paperback fiction and non-fiction. **Random House Audio Books** (see entry under *Audio Books*)

EBURY PUBLISHING

(☎ 020 7840 8400 Fax 020 7840 8718)

Managing Director *Fiona MacIntyre*, Publisher *Jake Lingwood*

IMPRINTS **Ebury Press** Publishing Director (non-illustrated) *Hannah MacDonald*, Publishing Director (illustrated) *Carey Smith* Popular non-fiction, including memoir and popular history, humour, cookery, travel-writing, sport, music, TV tie-ins and reference. **Vermilion** Editorial Director *Clare Hulton* Personal development, health, diet, relationships and parenting. **Rider** Editorial Director *Judith Kendra* Psychology, philosophy, spirituality and personal development, travel, history, inspirational memoir, paranormal, divination. **Time Out Guides** Brand Manager *Luthfa Begum* Travel guides published in a unique partnership with *Time Out* magazine. **BBC Books** Publishing Director *Shirley Patton*, Editorial Director, TV & Media (entertainment, drama and comedy) *Mathew Clayton*, Editorial Director (history, art, science, religion, news/current affairs) *Martin Redfern*, Editorial Director (cookery, gardening, homes and interiors) *To be appointed*.

RANDOM HOUSE CHILDREN'S BOOKS

(at Transworld Publishers, 61–63 Uxbridge Road, London W5 5SA ☎ 020 8579 2652 Fax 020 8231 6737) Managing Director *Philippa Dickinson*, Publisher (fiction) *Annie Eaton*, Editorial Director (fiction) *Charlie Sheppard*, Senior Commissioning Editor (picture books) *Natascha Biebow*, Senior Commissioning Editor *Helen Mackenzie-Smith*, Publisher (Colour and Custom Publishing) *Fiona Macmillan*. Picture books, fiction, poetry, non-fiction and audio cassettes under IMPRINTS **Bodley Head Children's Books**; **Corgi Children's Books**; **Doubleday Children's Books**; **Hutchinson Children's Books**; **Jonathan Cape Children's Books**; **Red Fox Children's Books**; and **David Fickling Books** (31 Beaumont Street,

Oxford OX1 2NP ☎ 01865 339000 Fax 01865 339009 ✉ dfickling@randomhouse.co.uk www.davidficklingbooks.co.uk) Publisher *David Fickling*, Senior Editor *Bella Pearson* Children's fiction and picture books. Unsolicited mss, synopses and ideas for books welcome.

ROYALTIES twice-yearly for the most part.

Authors' Rating Responding to tougher market conditions for conventional bookselling, Random is putting a lot of effort into exploiting alternative ways of reaching out to customers. These include a £5 million plan for digitisation and a doubling of its print-on-demand programme. Expansion of a different sort started with the purchase of a 75% stake in BBC Books and a 90% share of Virgin Books, carrying with it the worldwide use of the Virgin brand for books, audio and digital publishing. Meanwhile, Ebury is branching into fiction with an erotica list produced in cooperation with the Ann Summers stores while Harvill, strong in translations, continues, to quote a critic, to 'enlarge the narrow cultural boundaries of the English'. No mean feat. According to Nielsen BookScan, the Virgin acquisition takes Random's UK market share to 15.7%, just behind the number one, Hachette Livre at 16.4%.

Ransom Publishing Ltd
Rose Cottage, Howe Hill, Watlington OX49 5HB
☎01491 613711 Fax 01491 613733
✉ jenny@ransom.co.uk
www.ransom.co.uk
Managing Director *Jenny Ertle*

Ransom's book programme is designed to develop reading skills (and an enthusiasm for reading) in everyone from young children through to adults. Many of Ransom's books are 'high interest age, low reading age'; both fact and fiction. Ransom is the only publisher to produce books for adults with a very low reading level. The first series of books in this area, Dark Man, won the Educational Resources Book Award in 2006. Interested in hearing from authors writing for reluctant and struggling readers. Initial enquiries by e-mail with details of the submission and three sample chapters. 'A response cannot be guaranteed but we try to respond to all submissions within a month.' Materials returned if supplied with s.a.e.

Reader's Digest Association Ltd
11 Westferry Circus, Canary Wharf, London E14 4HE

☎020 7715 8000 Fax 020 7715 8181
✉ gbeditorial@readersdigest.co.uk
www.readersdigest.co.uk

Managing Director *Andrew Lynam-Smith*
Editorial Director, Books *Julian Browne*

Editorial office in the USA (see entry under *US Publishers*). Publishes health, gardening, natural history, cookery, history, DIY, computer, travel and word books. About 30 titles a year through trade and direct marketing channels.

Reaktion Books
33 Great Sutton Street, London EC1V 0DX
☎020 7253 1071 Fax 020 7253 1208
✉ info@reaktionbooks.co.uk
www.reaktionbooks.co.uk
Managing Director *Michael R. Leaman*

Founded 1985. Publishes art history, architecture, animal studies, Asian studies, cultural studies, design, film, geography, history, natural history, photography and travel literature (*not* travel guides or journals). TITLE *Mad, Bad and Dangerous: The Scientist and the Cinema* Christopher Frayling; SERIES **Critical Lives** TITLES *Franz Kafka* Sander L. Gilman; *Marcel Duchamp* Caroline Cros; **Animal** TITLE *Bee* Claire Preston; **Edible** TITLES *Pancake* Ken Albala; *Hamburger* Andrew F. Smith. About 44 titles a year.

ROYALTIES twice-yearly.

Reardon Publishing
PO Box 919, Cheltenham GL50 9AN
☎01242 231800
✉ reardon@bigfoot.com
www.reardon.co.uk
www.cotswoldbookshop.com
www.antarcticbookshop.com
Managing Editor *Nicholas Reardon*

Founded in the mid-1970s. Family-run publishing house specialising in local interest and tourism in the Cotswold area and books on Antarctica. Member of the **Outdoor Writers & Photographers Guild**. Publishes walking and driving guides. TITLES *The Cotswold Way*; *The Cotswold Way Map*; *Cotswold Walkabout*; *Cotswold Driveabout*; *The Donnington Way*; *The Haunted Cotswolds*. Also distributes for other publishers such as Ordnance Survey. 10 titles a year. Unsolicited mss, synopses and ideas welcome with return postage only.

ROYALTIES twice-yearly.

Recollections
See **Arnefold Publishing**

Red Fox Children's Books
See **The Random House Group Ltd**

Thomas Reed
See **A.&C. Black Publishers Ltd**

William Reed Directories
Broadfield Park, Crawley RH11 9RT
☎01293 613400 Fax 01293 610322
✉ directories@william-reed.co.uk
www.grocerdirectories.co.uk

Head of Content *Daniel Verrells*

William Reed Directories, a division of William Reed Publishing, was established in 1990. Its portfolio includes 13 titles covering the food, drink, non-food, catering, retail and export industries, including European versions. The titles are produced as directories, market research reports, exhibition catalogues and electronic publishing.

Reed Elsevier Group plc
1–3 Strand, London WC2N 5JR
☎020 7930 7077
www.reedelsevier.com

Also at: 125 Park Avenue, 23rd Floor, New York, NY 10017, USA
☎ 001 212 309 5498 Fax 001 212 309 5480

And: Raderweg 29, 1043 NX Amsterdam, The Netherlands
☎ 00 31 20 485 2434 Fax 00 31 20 618 0325

Chief Executive Officer UK *Sir Crispin Davis*
Approx. Annual Turnover £5.4 million

Reed Elsevier Group plc is a world-leading publisher and information provider operating in the scientific, legal, educational and business-to-business sectors. It is owned equally by its two parent companies, Reed Elsevier Plc and Reed Elsevier NV.

No unsolicited material.

Authors' Rating After announcing the proposed sale of the education division, a deal was struck with Pearson in early May 2007. The transfer includes Harcourt Education International and Harcourt Assessment but Harcourt's US schools and publishing businesses remain with Reed Elsevier.

Reference Library
See **CRW Publishing Ltd**

Regency House Publishing Limited
Niall House, 24–26 Boulton Road, Stevenage SG1 4QX
☎01438 314488 Fax 01438 311303
✉ regency-house@btconnect.com
www.regencyhousepublishing.com

Chairman *Brian Trodd*
Managing Director *Nicolette Trodd*

Founded 1991. Publisher and packager of mass-market non-fiction. No fiction. No unsolicited material.

Remember When
47 Church Street, Barnsley S70 2AS
☎01226 734222 Fax 01226 734438
✉ enquiries@pen-and-sword.co.uk
www.rememberwhen.uk.com

Commissioning Editor *Fiona Shoop*

An imprint of **Pen & Sword Books Ltd**, Remember When covers the nostalgia and antiques collecting range of titles. No unsolicited mss; synopses and idea welcome.

ROYALTIES twice-yearly.

Research Disclosure
See **Kenneth Mason Publications Ltd**

Richmond House Publishing Company Ltd
70–76 Bell Street, Marylebone, London NW1 6SP
☎020 7224 9666 Fax 020 7224 9688
✉ sales@rhpco.co.uk
www.rhpco.co.uk

Managing Directors *Gloria Gordon, Spencer Block*

Publishes directories for the theatre and entertainment industries. TITLES *British Theatre Directory*; *Artistes and Agents*; *London Seating Plan Guide*. Synopses and ideas welcome.

Rider
See **The Random House Group Ltd**

Rigby
See **Harcourt**

Right Way/Right Way Plus
See **Elliot Right Way Books**

Rising Stars UK Ltd
22 Grafton Street, London W1S 4EX
☎020 7495 6793 Fax 020 7495 6796
✉ info@risingstars-uk.com
www.risingstars-uk.com

Chairman *David Fulton*
Managing Director *Andrea Carr*
Publishing Director *Ben Barton*
    (benbarton@risingstars-uk.com)
Approx. Annual Turnover £2.35 million

Founded 2006. Educational publishers for children aged 3–18. 85 titles in 2006. Unsolicited mss, synopses and ideas welcome; approach by e-mail.

ROYALTIES annually.

RMEP
See **Hymns Ancient & Modern Ltd**

Robinson
See **Constable & Robinson Ltd**

Robson Books
See **Anova Books**

Rodale
See **Macmillan Publishers Ltd**

RotoVision
Sheridan House, 114 Western Road, Hove
BN3 1DD
☎01273 727268 Fax 01273 727269
✉ sales@rotovision.com
www.rotovision.com
www.myspace.com/rotovision

Managing Director *Piers Spence*
Publisher *April Sankey*

Founded 1971. International publishers of graphic design, photography, digital design, advertising, film, product design and packaging design books. TITLES include *World's Top Photographers: Nudes*; *What Is Graphic Design For?*; *Designs of the Times*; *First Steps in Digital Design*; *500 Digital Photography Hints, Tips and Techniques*; *Print and Production Techniques for Brochures and Catalogues*. 35 titles a year. No unsolicited mss; written synopses and ideas welcome. No phone calls, please. No academic or fiction.

Flat FEE paid.

Roundhouse Group
Millstone, Limers Lane, Northam EX39 2RG
☎01237 474474 Fax 01237 474774
✉ roundhouse.group@tiscali.co.uk

Editorial Head *Alan Goodworth*

Founded 1991. Publishes cinema and media-related titles. TITLES *The Bent Lens: A World Guide to Gay & Lesbian Films*; *Cinema of Oliver Stone*; *Cinema of Martin Scorsese*. Represents and distributes (via Orca Books Services) a broad range of non-fiction publishing houses throughout the UK and Europe. No unsolicited mss.

ROYALTIES twice-yearly.

Routledge (An imprint of **Taylor & Francis Group**, an Informa plc business)
2 Park Square, Milton Park, Abingdon
OX14 4RN
☎020 7017 6000 Fax 020 7017 6699
www.routledge.com

CEO *Roger Horton*
Managing Director *Jeremy North*
Publishing Directors *Claire L'Enfant, Alan Jarvis*

Routledge is an international academic imprint publishing books primarily for university students, researchers, academics and professionals. Most Routledge authors are academics with specialist knowledge of their subject. Publishes everything from core text books to research monographs and journals in the following subject areas: humanities, including anthropology, archaeology, classical studies, communications and media studies, cultural studies, history, language and literature, music, philosophy, religious studies, theatre studies and sports studies; social sciences, including geography, politics, military and strategic studies, sociology and urban studies; business, management, law and economics; education; Asian and Middle Eastern studies. Over 1800 titles a year. Send a detailed proposal plus c.v. and sample chapters. Proposal requirements and submission procedures can be found on the website. No poetry, fiction, travel or astrology.

ROYALTIES annually or twice-yearly, according to contract.

RYA (Royal Yachting Association)
RYA House, Ensign Way, Hamble,
Southampton SO31 4YA
☎023 8060 4100 Fax 023 8060 4299
✉ phil.williamsellis@rya.org.uk
www.rya.org.uk

Chief Executive *Rod Carr*
Publishing Editor/Publications Manager *Phil Williams-Ellis*
Approx. Annual Turnover £12million+

The Royal Yachting Association, the UK governing body representing sailing, windsurfing, motorboating, powerboat racing both at sea and on inland waters, was founded in 1875. Publishes sports instruction books relating to specific training courses, technical, legal and boating advice, all written by experts in their field. TITLES *RYA Weather Handbook*; *RYA Navigation Exercises*; *RYA Powerboat Handbook*; *RYA Go Sailing!*. 10 titles a year. No unsolic-

ited mss; synopses and ideas for books welcome. Approach by e-mail or post in the first instance.
ROYALTIES twice-yearly.

Ryland Peters & Small Limited
20–21 Jockey's Fields, London WC1R 5BW
☎020 7025 2200 Fax 020 7025 2201
✉ info@rps.co.uk
www.rylandpeters.com
Managing Director *David Peters*
Publishing Director *Alison Starling*
Founded 1996. Publishes highly illustrated lifestyle books aimed at an international market, covering home and garden, food and drink, body and soul and gift. No fiction. Acquired **Cico Books** in 2006. No unsolicited mss; synopses and ideas welcome.
ROYALTIES twice-yearly.

Sage Publications
1 Oliver's Yard, 55 City Road, London EC1Y 1SP
☎020 7324 8500 Fax 020 7324 8600
✉ info@sagepub.co.uk
www.sagepub.co.uk
Managing Director *Stephen Barr*
Editorial Director *Ziyad Marar*
Founded 1971. Publishes academic books and journals in humanities and the social sciences, education and science, technology and medicine. Bought academic and professional books publisher Paul Chapman Publishing Ltd in 1998 and Lucky Duck Publishing in 2004.
ROYALTIES twice-yearly.

St Pauls Publishing
187 Battersea Bridge Road, London SW11 3AS
☎020 7978 4300 Fax 020 7978 4370
✉ editions@stpauls.org.uk
www.stpauls.ie
Publisher *Andrew Pudussery*
Publishing division of the Society of St Paul. Began publishing in 1914 but activities were fairly limited until around 1948. Publishes religious material mainly: theology, scripture, catechetics, prayer books and biography. About 20 titles a year. Unsolicited mss, synopses and ideas welcome with s.a.e.

Salamander
See **Anova Books**

SAM Publishing
See **Pearson Education**

Sangam Books Ltd
57 London Fruit Exchange, Brushfield Street, London E1 6EP
☎020 7377 6399 Fax 020 7375 1230
✉ sangambks@aol.com
Executive Director *Anthony de Souza*
Traditionally an educational publisher of school and college level textbooks. Also publishes art, India, medicine, science, technology, social sciences, religion, plus some fiction in paperback.

Saqi Books
26 Westbourne Grove, London W2 5RH
☎020 7221 9347 Fax 020 7229 7492
✉ enquiries@saqibooks.com
www.saqibooks.com
Chairman/Managing Director *André Gaspard*
Commissioning Editor *Lara Frankena*
Founded 1981, initially as a specialist publisher of books on the Middle East and Arab world but now includes Central Asia, South Asia and European fiction. Publishes non-fiction – academic and illustrated. About 30 titles a year. Welcomes unsolicited material; approach by post or e-mail.
ROYALTIES annually.

Authors' Rating A blunt warning from the managing editor that unsolicited manuscripts are not returned. Saqi is not alone in this. Authors should retain copies of everything they send out.

Saunders
See **Elsevier Ltd**

Savitri Books Ltd
See entry under *UK Packagers*

SB Publications
14 Bishopstone Road, Seaford BN25 2UB
☎01323 893498 Fax 01323 893860
✉ sbpublications@tiscali.co.uk
www.sbpublications.co.uk
Owner *Mrs Lindsay Woods*
Founded 1987. Specialises in local history, including themes illustrated by old picture postcards and photographs; also travel, guides (town, walking) and railways. TITLES *Sussex As She Was Spoke*; *The Neat and Nippy Guide to Brighton*; *Pre-Raphaelite Trail in Sussex*. Also provides marketing and distribution services for local authors. 12 titles a year.
ROYALTIES annually.

Sceptre
See **Hachette Livre UK**

Scholastic Ltd
Villiers House, Clarendon Avenue, Leamington Spa CV32 5PR
☎01926 887799 Fax 01926 883331
www.scholastic.co.uk
Chairman *M.R. Robinson*
Managing Director *Kate Wilson*
Approx. Annual Turnover £42 million

Founded 1964. Owned by US parent company, Scholastic Inc. who acquired **Chicken House Publishing** in May 2005. Publishes children's fiction and non-fiction and education for primary schools.

DIVISIONS
Scholastic Children's Books Managing Director *Elaine McQuade* Euston House, 24 Eversholt Street, London NW1 1DB ☎ 020 7756 7756 Fax 020 7756 7795 IMPRINT **Scholastic** TITLES *Horrible Histories* Terry Deary, illus. Martin Brown; *His Dark Materials Trilogy* Philip Pullman; *Mortal Engines* Philip Reeve.

Educational Publishing (Villiers House address) Managing Director *Denise Cripps* Professional books and classroom materials for primary teachers, plus magazines such as *Child Education, Junior Education, Junior Focus, Infant Projects, Nursery Education, Literacy Time.*

Scholastic Book Clubs, Getting Children Reading, Giving Books to Schools Managing Director *Miles Stevens-Hoare* Windrush Park, Witney, Oxford OX29 0YT ☎ 01993 893456 Fax 01993 776813 SBC is the UK's number one Schools Book Club. Offering five age specific clubs, it provides 'the best books at great prices and supports teachers in the process'.

School Book Fairs, Getting Children Reading, Giving Books to Schools Managing Director *Miles Stevens-Hoare* The Book Fair Division sells directly to children, parents and teachers in schools through 25,000 week-long book events held in schools throughout the UK.
ROYALTIES twice-yearly.

SCM – Canterbury Press Ltd
9–17 St Albans Place, London N1 0NX
☎020 7359 8033 Fax 020 7359 0049
✉ admin@scm-canterburypress.co.uk
www.scm-canterburypress.co.uk
Publishing Director *Christine Smith*
Commissioning Editor *Barbara Laing*
Approx. Annual Turnover £2.6 million

Part of **Hymns Ancient & Modern Ltd** (see entry). Has two publishing imprints: **SCM Press** Text and reference books for the study of theology, philosophy of religion, ethics and religious studies; **Canterbury Press** Religious titles for the general market, liturgy, spirituality and church resources. AUTHORS include Rowan Williams, Ronald Blythe, Helen Prejean. 100 titles a year. Refer to website for guidelines on submitting proposals.
ROYALTIES annually.

Authors' Rating Leading publisher of religious ideas with well-deserved reputation for fresh thinking. At SCM, 'questioning theology is the norm'.

Scottish Cultural Press/ Scottish Children's Press
Unit 6, Newbattle Abbey Business Park, Newbattle Road, Dalkeith EH22 3LJ
☎0131 660 6366 Fax 0870 285 4846
✉ info@scottishbooks.com
www.scottishbooks.com
Directors *Avril Gray, Brian Pugh*

Founded 1992. Publishes Scottish interest titles, including cultural literature, poetry, archaeology, local history. DIVISION **S.C.P. Children's Ltd** (trading as **Scottish Children's Press**) Children's fiction and non-fiction. Unsolicited mss, synopses and ideas accepted provided return postage is included, but *always* telephone before sending material, please. 'Mss sent without advance telephone call and return postage will be destroyed.'
ROYALTIES paid.

Scribner
See **Simon & Schuster UK Limited**

Seafarer Books Ltd
102 Redwald Road, Rendlesham, Woodbridge IP12 2TE
☎01394 420789 Fax 01394 461314
✉ info@seafarerbooks.com
www.seafarerbooks.com
Managing Director *Patricia M. Eve*

Founded 1968. Publishes sailing titles, with an emphasis on the traditional. AUTHORS Erskine Childers, Cecily Gould, Bjorn Larsson, John Leather, Jack London, Frank Mulville, Bob Roberts, Adrian Seligman. About 6 titles a year. No unsolicited mss; preliminary letter essential before making any type of submission.
ROYALTIES twice-yearly.

SeaNeverDry Publishing
13 Napoleon Road, St Margarets TW1 3EW
☎020 8892 2855
✉ orders@seaneverdrypub.com
www.seaneverdrypub.com

Chairman *B. de Vaatt*
Managing Director *D.R. Abbott*
Approx. Annual Turnover £300,000

Founded 2003. Publishes general fiction, erotica and humour. DIVISIONS **General Fiction** *S. Hytte* TITLES *Dropping in on Idi; The Book; Empire;* **Humour** *D.R. Abbott* TITLES *Fake Honesty; His/Her Words of Love.* Unsolicited mss, synopses and ideas for books welcome; approach by e-mail. No academic texts or science fiction.
ROYALTIES quarterly.

Authors' Rating Not to be confused with vanity publishing, SeaNeverDry Publishing offers advanced technology to produce a low cost, low volume print run to test the market. If the book takes off, well, good luck; the author gets a higher than average royalty of 15%. But there may be a long stretch between hope and realisation.

Search Press Ltd
Wellwood, North Farm Road, Tunbridge Wells TN2 3DR
☎01892 510850 Fax 01892 515903
✉ searchpress@searchpress.com
www.searchpress.com

Managing Director *Martin de la Bédoyère*
Commissioning Editor *Rosalind Dace*

Founded 1970. Publishes full-colour art, craft, needlecrafts – papermaking and papercrafts, painting on silk, art techniques and embroidery. No unsolicited mss; synopsis with sample chapter welcome.
ROYALTIES annually.

Seren
57 Nolton Street, Bridgend CF31 3AE
☎01656 663018 Fax 01656 649226
✉ general@seren-books.com
www.seren-books.com

Chairman *Cary Archard*
Publisher *Mick Felton*
Approx. Annual Turnover £150,000

Founded 1981 as a specialist poetry publisher but has now moved into general literary publishing with an emphasis on Wales. Publishes poetry, fiction, literary criticism, drama, biography, art, history and translations of fiction.

DIVISIONS **Poetry** *Amy Wack* AUTHORS Owen Sheers, Pascale Petit, Sheenagh Pugh, Kathryn Gray, Deryn Rees-Jones. **Drama** *Amy Wack* AUTHORS Edward Thomas, Charles Way, Lucinda Coxon. **Fiction** *Penny Thomas* AUTHORS Leonora Brito, Richard Collins, Lloyd Jones, Emyr Humphreys. **Art, Literary Criticism, History, Translations** *Mick Felton* IMPRINT **Border Lines Biographies** TITLES *Bruce Chatwin; Dennis Potter; Mary Webb; Wilfred Owen; Raymond Williams.* About 25 titles a year. Unsolicited mss, synopses and ideas for books welcome.
ROYALTIES twice-yearly or annually.

Serpent's Tail
3a Exmouth House, Pine Street, London EC1R 0JH
☎020 7841 6300 Fax 020 7833 3969
✉ info@serpentstail.com
www.serpentstail.com

Director *Pete Ayrton*

Founded 1986. An imprint of **Profile Books**. Publishes fiction and non-fiction in paperback; literary and mainstream work, and work in translation. IMPRINT **Five Star**. No unsolicited mss.

Authors' Rating Celebrating its twenty-first anniversary, Serpent's Tail has thrown in its lot with Profile to bring together two rising stars in publishing.

Severn House Publishers
9–15 High Street, Sutton SM1 1DF
☎020 8770 3930 Fax 020 8770 3850
✉ info@severnhouse.com
www.severnhouse.com

Chairman *Edwin Buckhalter*
Editorial *Amanda Stewart*

Founded 1974. A leader in library fiction publishing. Publishes hardback fiction: romance, science fiction, horror, fantasy, crime. Also large print and trade paperback editions of their fiction titles. About 140 titles a year. No unsolicited material. Synopses/proposals preferred through *bona fide* literary agents only. OVERSEAS ASSOCIATE Severn House Publishers Inc., New York.
ROYALTIES twice-yearly.

Authors' Rating Having established a strong hardback list, Severn House has now entered the paperback market with its crime and romance titles.

Sheldon Press
See **Society for Promoting Christian Knowledge**

Sheldrake Press

188 Cavendish Road, London SW12 0DA
☎020 8675 1767 Fax 020 8675 7736
✉ enquiries@sheldrakepress.co.uk
www.sheldrakepress.co.uk

Publisher *Simon Rigge*

Founded in 1979 as a book packager and commenced publishing under its own imprint in 1991. Publishes illustrated non-fiction: history, travel, style, cookery and stationery. TITLES *The Victorian House Book; The Shorter Mrs Beeton; The Power of Steam; The Railway Heritage of Britain; Wild Britain; Wild France; Wild Spain; Wild Italy; Wild Ireland; Amsterdam: Portrait of a City* and Kate Greenaway stationery books. 1 title in 2006. Synopses and ideas for books welcome, but not interested in fiction.

Shepheard-Walwyn (Publishers) Ltd

15 Alder Road, London SW14 8ER
☎020 7721 7666
✉ books@shepheard-walwyn.co.uk
www.shepheard-walwyn.co.uk

Managing Director *Anthony Werner*
Approx. Annual Turnover £120,000

Founded 1972. 'We regard books as food for the mind and want to offer a wholesome diet of original ideas and fresh approaches to old subjects.' Publishes general non-fiction in four main areas: gift books in calligraphy and/or illustrated; biography, ethical economics, perennial philosophy. About 6–7 titles a year. Synopses and ideas for books welcome.
ROYALTIES twice-yearly.

The Shetland Times Ltd

Gremista, Lerwick ZE1 0PX
☎01595 693622 Fax 01595 694637
✉ publishing@shetland-times.co.uk
www.shetland-books.co.uk

Managing Director *Brian Johnston*
Publications Manager *Charlotte Black*

Founded 1872 as publishers of the local newspaper. Book publishing followed thereafter plus publication of monthly magazine, *Shetland Life*. Publishes anything with Shetland connections – local and natural history, music, crafts, maritime. Prefers material with a Shetland theme/connection. 8 titles in 2006.
ROYALTIES annually.

Shire Publications Ltd

Cromwell House, Church Street, Princes Risborough HP27 9AA
☎01844 344301 Fax 01844 347080
✉ shire@shirebooks.co.uk
www.shirebooks.co.uk

General Manager *Sue Ross*

Founded 1962. Publishes original non-fiction paperbacks. About 25 titles a year. No unsolicited material; send introductory letter with detailed outline of idea.
ROYALTIES annually.

Authors' Rating You don't have to live in the country to write books for Shire but it helps. With titles like *Church Fonts, Haunted Inns* and *Discovering Preserved Railways* there is a distinct rural feel to the list. Another way of putting it, to quote owner John Rotheroe, Shire specialises in 'small books on all manner of obscure subjects'.

Short Books

3A Exmouth House, Pine Street, Exmouth Market, London EC1R 0JH
☎020 7833 9429 Fax 020 7833 9500
✉ emily@shortbooks.biz
www.shortbooks.co.uk

Editorial Directors *Rebecca Nicolson, Aurea Carpenter*

Founded 2001. Publishes general adult and children's non-fiction and fiction; biography, history and politics, humour and children's narrative history. No unsolicited mss.

Sidgwick & Jackson
See **Macmillan Publishers Ltd**

Sigma Press

5 Alton Road, Wilmslow SK9 5DY
☎01625 531035 Fax 01625 531035
✉ info@sigmapress.co.uk
www.sigmapress.co.uk

Owners *Diana Beech, Graham Beech*
Chairman/Managing Director *Graham Beech*

Founded in 1980 as a publisher of technical books, Sigma Press now publishes mainly in the leisure area. Publishes outdoor, local heritage, adventure and biography. DIVISION **Sigma Leisure** TITLES *Holiday Walks in the Loire Valley; The Bluebird Years: Donald Campbell and the pursuit of speed* (biography); *Walks in Ancient Wales; All-Terrain Pushchair Walks; Discovering Manchester.* About 10 titles a year. No unsolicited mss; synopses and ideas welcome. No poetry or novels required.
ROYALTIES twice-yearly.

Simon & Schuster UK Limited

Africa House, 64–78 Kingsway, London
WC2B 6AH
☎020 7316 1900 Fax 020 7316 0331
www.simonsays.co.uk

CEO/Managing Director *Ian S. Chapman*
Publishing Director *Suzanne Baboneau*
Publishers, Non-fiction *Andrew Gordon* (also
  The Free Press), *Angela Herlihy*
Publishers, Fiction *Suzanne Baboneau, Kate
  Lyall-Grant*
Approx. Annual Turnover £31.2 million

Founded 1986. Sister company of the leading
American company. Publishes hardback (**Simon
& Schuster**) and paperback (**Pocket Books**)
commercial and literary fiction and non-fiction,
including autobiography, biography, sport,
mind, body and spirit, humour, travel and other
general interest non-fiction. **The Free Press**
publishes serious non-fiction, including popular
science, politics, history and current business.
Literary international fiction and non-fiction is
published under the **Scribner** imprint.

DIVISIONS **Martin Books** Director *Janet
Copleston* Specialises in bespoke publishing and
branded editions, and the Simon & Schuster UK
cookery list. **Simon & Schuster Children's
Books** Publishing Director *Ingrid Selberg*, Editor
(fiction) *Venetia Gosling*, Editor (picture books)
Emma Blackburn Media tie-ins, picture books
and fiction titles. No unsolicited mss.
ROYALTIES twice-yearly.

Authors' Rating Back on track after reorganisation and a repositioning in the market, Simon
& Schuster is a medium-sized publisher with a
talent for spotting quality titles. A new fiction
list for young people has turned in a strong
performance. A US-led 'digital warehouse' will
increase market exposure.

Smith Gryphon Ltd
See **John Blake Publishing Ltd**

Colin Smythe Ltd

38 Mill Lane, Gerrards Cross SL9 8BA
☎01753 886000 Fax 01753 886469
✉ cs@colinsmythe.co.uk
www.colinsmythe.co.uk

Managing Director *Colin Smythe*
Approx. Annual Turnover £3.45 million

Founded 1966. Publishes Anglo-Irish literature,
drama; criticism and Irish history. Also acts as
agent for Terry Pratchett. About 5 titles a year.
No unsolicited mss.
ROYALTIES annually/twice-yearly.

Snowbooks Ltd

120 Pentonville Road, London N1 9JN
☎020 7837 6482 Fax 020 7837 6348
✉ submissions@snowbooks.com
www.snowbooks.com

Managing Director *Emma Barnes*
Approx. Annual Turnover £400,000

Founded 2003. Independent publisher of
mainly fiction and some non-fiction. 'Keen on
promoting open, friendly, productive relationships with authors and retailers.' TITLES *Adept*
Robert Finn; *Paradise Jazz* Kat Pomfret; *The Idle
Thoughts of an Idle Fellow* J.K. Jerome; *The London
Scene* Virginia Woolf; *Boxing Fitness* Ian Oliver;
The Romanian Bruce Benderson; *Plotting for
Beginners* Sue Hepworth and Jane Linfoot; *The
Other Eden* and *Sand Daughter* Sarah Bryant. 15–
30 titles a year. Unsolicited mss 'very welcome',
by e-mail only. Read the submission guidelines
in the authors' section of the website first: www.
snowbooks.com/authors.html

ROYALTIES vary according to contract 'but
tend to be higher than the industry average'.

Authors' Rating A welcome indication that
ideals and good business sense can go together.
There are only two conditions for taking on a
book: an editor must like it and believe it will
sell. Snowbooks has already chalked up a 'Nibbie'
award as Small Publisher of the Year.

Society for Promoting Christian Knowledge (SPCK)

36 Causton Street, London SW1P 4ST
☎020 7592 3900 Fax 020 7592 3939
www.spck.org.uk
www.sheldonpress.co.uk

Senior Executive Officer *Simon Kingston*

Founded 1698, SPCK is the third oldest
publisher in the country. IMPRINTS **SPCK**
Acting Publishing Director *Joanna Moriarty*
Theology, academic, liturgy, prayer, spirituality,
biblical studies, educational resources, mission,
pastoral care, gospel and culture, worldwide.
Sheldon Press Editor *Fiona Marshall* Popular
medicine, health, self-help, psychology. **Azure**
Senior Editor *Alison Barr* General spirituality.
ROYALTIES annually.

Authors' Rating Religion with a strong social
edge.

Sophia Books
See **Rudolf Steiner Press**

Southwater
See **Anness Publishing Ltd**

Souvenir Press Ltd

43 Great Russell Street, London WC1B 3PD
☎020 7580 9307 & 7637 5711
Fax 020 7580 5064
✉ souvenirpress@ukonline.co.uk

Chairman/Managing Director *Ernest Hecht*

Independent publishing house. Founded 1951. Publishes academic and scholarly, animal care and breeding, antiques and collecting, archaeology, autobiography and biography, business and industry, children's, cookery, crafts and hobbies, crime, educational, fiction, gardening, health and beauty, history and antiquarian, humour, illustrated and fine editions, magic and the occult, medical, military, music, natural history, philosophy, poetry, psychology, religious, sociology, sports, theatre and women's studies. Souvenir's Human Horizons series for the disabled and their carers is one of the most pre-eminent in its field and recently celebrated 33 years of publishing for the disabled.

IMPRINTS/SERIES **Condor**; **Human Horizons**; **Independent Voices**; **Pictorial Presentations**; **Pop Universal**; **The Story-Tellers**. TITLES *Farewell, Babylon* Naim Kattan; *How the Mind Forgets and Remembers* Daniel L. Schacter; *The Equation that Couldn't be Solved* Mario Livio; *Golf's Best Short Stories* ed. Paul D. Staudohar; *The Upside of Down* Thomas Homer-Dixon; *Rebuilt* Michael Chorost. About 55 titles a year. Unsolicited mss considered but initial letter of enquiry and outline always required in the first instance.

ROYALTIES twice-yearly.

Authors' Rating One of the last of the great independents, Souvenir covers every subject which happens to appeal to Ernest Hecht. But authors should not expect sentimentality. Commercial potential is the first priority.

SPCK

See **Society for Promoting Christian Knowledge**

Special Interest Model Books Ltd

Stanley House, 3 Fleets Lane, Poole BH15 3AJ
☎01202 649930 Fax 01202 649950
✉ chrlloyd@globalnet.co.uk
www.specialinterestmodelbooks.co.uk

Contact *Chris Lloyd*
Commissioning Editor *Bill Burkinshaw*

Publishes aviation, engineering, leisure and hobbies, modelling, electronics, wine and beer making. Send synopses rather than completed mss.

ROYALTIES twice-yearly.

Speechmark Publishing Ltd

8 Oxford Court, St James Road, Brackley NN13 7XY
☎01280 845570 Fax 01280 845584
✉ info@speechmark.net
www.speechmark.net

Managing Director *Sarah Miles*
Publishing Manager *Miranda Robson*
Approx. Annual Turnover £1.58 million

Speechmark publishes practical books, games and *ColorCards®* for health, education and special needs practitioners and students. 28 titles in 2006. Unsolicited mss, synopses and ideas welcome. Approach by letter or e-mail.

ROYALTIES twice-yearly.

Spellmount Ltd

The Mill, Brimscombe Port, Stroud GL5 2QG
☎01453 883300 Fax 01453 883233
✉ info@tempus-publishing.com
www.tempus-publishing.com

Managing Director *Jamie Wilson*
Approx. Annual Turnover £500,000

Founded 1983. Publishes history and military history. About 40 titles a year. Synopses/ideas for books in these specialist fields welcome but no personal memoirs. Enclose return postage.

ROYALTIES biannually for two years, then annually.

Sphere

See **Little, Brown Book Group UK**

SportsBooks Limited

PO Box 422, Cheltenham GL50 2YN
☎01242 256755 Fax 01242 254694
✉ randall@sportsbooks.ltd.uk
www.sportsbooks.ltd.uk

Chairman & Managing Director *Randall Northam*
Approx. Annual Turnover £150,000

Founded 1995. Publishes sports books including biographies, statistical and practical. TITLES *Wembley, the complete record 1923–2000*; *Growing up with Subbuteo*; *Fitba Gallimaufry*. IMPRINT **BMM** Editorial Head *Mark Jones*. 12 titles in 2007. No unsolicited mss. Synopses and ideas welcome. Approach by letter or e-mail.

The Sportsman's Press (An imprint of Quiller Publishing Ltd)

Wykey House, Wykey, Shrewsbury SY4 1JA
☎01939 261616 Fax 01939 261606

✉ info@quillerbooks.com
www.countrybooksdirect.com

Managing Director *Andrew Johnston*

Specialises in books on all country subjects and general sports including fishing, fencing, shooting, equestrian, cookery, gunmaking and wildlife art. About 10 titles a year.

ROYALTIES twice-yearly.

Springer-Verlag London Ltd

Ashbourne House, The Guildway, Old Portsmouth Road, Guildford GU3 1LP
☎01483 734666 Fax 01483 734411
www.springer.com

General Manager *Beverley Ford*
Approx. Annual Turnover £5 million

The UK subsidiary of Springer Science & Business Media. Publishes science, technical and medical books and journals. Specialises in computing, engineering, medicine, mathematics, chemistry, biosciences. All UK published books are sold through Springer's German and US companies as well as in the UK. Globally: 4000 books and 1250 journals; UK: 150 titles plus 27 journals. Not interested in social sciences, fiction or school books but academic and professional science mss or synopses welcome.

ROYALTIES annually.

Springhill

See **How To Books Ltd**

Stainer & Bell Ltd

PO Box 110, 23 Gruneisen Road, London
N3 1DZ
☎020 8343 3303 Fax 020 8343 3024
✉ post@stainer.co.uk
www.stainer.co.uk

Managing Directors *Carol Y. Wakefield, Keith M. Wakefield*
Publishing Director *Nicholas Williams*
Approx. Annual Turnover £816,000

Founded 1907 to publish sheet music. Publishes music and religious subjects related to hymnody. Unsolicited synopses/ideas for books welcome. Send letter enclosing brief précis.

ROYALTIES annually.

The Stationery Office

See **TSO**

Rudolf Steiner Press

Hillside House, The Square, Forest Row
RH18 5ES
☎01342 824433 Fax 01342 826437
✉ office@rudolfsteinerpress.com
www.rudolfsteinerpress.com

Chairman *Mr P. Martyn*
Manager *Mr S. Gulbekian*
Approx. Annual Turnover £170,000

Founded in 1925 to publish the work of Rudolf Steiner and related materials. Publishes non-fiction: spirituality and philosophy. IMPRINT **Sophia Books** *S. Gulbekian* TITLES *From Stress to Serenity*; *Homemaking as a Social Art*. 15 titles in 2006. No unsolicited material.

ROYALTIES annually.

The Story-Tellers

See **Souvenir Press Ltd**

Straightline Publishing Ltd

29 Main Street, Bothwell G71 8RD
☎01698 853000 Fax 01698 854208

Director *Patrick Bellew*
Editor *Colin Calder*

Founded 1989. Publishes magazines and directories – trade and technical – books of local interest. TITLES *Wired In*; *enterprisingglasgow*; *enterprisinglanarkshire*. No unsolicited material.

ROYALTIES annually.

Studymates Limited

PO Box 225, Abergele, Conwy LL18 9AY
☎01745 832863 Fax 01745 826606
✉ info@studymates.co.uk
www.studymates.co.uk

Managing Editor *Graham Lawler, MA*

Authors need to be practising or recently-retired teachers/lecturers, or published authors for the writers' guides. Ideas in writing first; unsolicited mss will not be considered. New list of business books planned under the IMPRINT **Studymates Professional** but again Studymates will not accept unsolicted mss. 'Please approach in writing in the first instance and outline how your idea will complement the current list.'

Summersdale Publishers Ltd

46 West Street, Chichester PO19 1RP
☎01243 771107 Fax 01243 786300
✉ submissions@summersdale.com
www.summersdale.com

Owners/Directors *Stewart Ferris, Alastair Williams*
Commissioning Editor *Jennifer Barclay*
Managing Editor *Carol Baker*
Approx. Annual Turnover £1.4 million

Founded 1990. Publishes travel literature, martial arts, self-help, cookery, humour and gift books. TITLES *Urban Legends Uncovered*; *How to Get*

Published; Sadistic Killers; Discover the New You; Real Crime Scene Investigations; Essential Questions To Ask When Buying a House in France. 75 titles a year. No unsolicited mss; synopses and ideas welcome by e-mail.

ROYALTIES paid.

Sussex Academic Press
PO Box 139, Eastbourne BN24 9BP
☎01323 479220 Fax 01323 478185
✉ edit@sussex-academic.co.uk
www.sussex-academic.co.uk

Managing Director *Anthony Grahame*
Approx. Annual Turnover £250,000

Founded 1994. Academic publisher. DIVISION/ IMPRINT **Sussex Academic** TITLES *Nazis in Pre-War London, 1930–1939; Cunning Folk and Familiar Spirits: Shamanistic Visionary Traditions in Early Modern British Witchcraft and Magic.* **Alpha Press** TITLE *The Financial Universe: Planning Your Investments Using Astrological Forecasting.* 45 titles in 2006. No unsolicited material; send letter of inquiry in the first instance.

ROYALTIES annually.

Sutton Publishing Ltd
Phoenix Mill, Thrupp, Stroud GL5 2BU
☎01453 731114 Fax 01453 731117
✉ publishing@sutton-publishing.co.uk

Managing Director *Alan Sutton*
Senior Commissioning Editors *Jaqueline Mitchell* (biography), *Jim Crawley* (general history), *Jonathan Falconer* (military), *Simon Fletcher* (local history)

Founded 1978. Acquired by NPI Media Group Ltd in January 2007. Publishes academic, archaeology, biography, countryside, history, military, aviation, regional interest, local history. About 200 titles a year. Send synopses rather than complete mss.

ROYALTIES twice-yearly.

Authors' Rating With Alan Sutton back in command of the company he founded plus four other companies in the heritage and regional publishing area (Jarrold, Phillimore, Oakland and US publisher History Press), his aim is to produce 2000 new titles from the combined operations. And he is likely to succeed. This is a niche that will attract many new non-fiction writers.

Swan Hill Press (An imprint of Quiller Publishing Ltd)
Wykey House, Wykey, Shrewsbury SY4 1JA
☎01939 261616 Fax 01939 261606

✉ info@quillerbooks.com
www.countrybooksdirect.com

Managing Director *Andrew Johnston*

Specialises in practical books on all country and field sports activities. Publishes books on fishing, shooting, gundog training, falconry, equestrian, deer, cookery, wildlife. About 20 titles a year. Unsolicited mss must include s.a.e.

ROYALTIES twice-yearly.

Sweet & Maxwell Group
100 Avenue Road, London NW3 3PF
☎020 7393 7000 Fax 020 7393 7010
✉ sweetandmaxwellcustomerservices@ thomson.com
www.sweetandmaxwell.thomson.com

Managing Director *Peter Lake*

Founded 1799. Part of the Thomson Corporation. Publishes materials in all media; looseleaf works, journals, law reports, CD-ROMs and online. The legal and professional list is varied and contains academic titles as well as treatises and reference works in the legal and related professional fields.

IMPRINTS **Sweet & Maxwell; GEE; W. Green (Scotland); Incomes Data Services; Thomson Round Hall (Ireland).** Over 1100 products, including 180 looseleafs, 80 periodicals, more than 40 digital products and online information services and 200 new titles each year. Ideas welcome. Writers with legal/professional projects in mind are advised to contact the Legal Business Unit at the earliest possible stage in order to lay the groundwork for best design, production and marketing of a project.

ROYALTIES and fees according to contract.

Tango Books Ltd
PO Box 32595, London W4 5YD
☎020 8996 9970 Fax 020 8996 9977
✉ sales@tangobooks.co.uk
www.tangobooks.co.uk

Directors *David Fielder, Sheri Safran*
Approx. Annual Turnover £1.1 million

Founded 1981. Children's books publisher with international co-edition potential: pop-ups, three-dimensional, novelty, picture and board books; 1000 words maximum. About 30 titles a year. Approach with preliminary letter, sample material and s.a.e. in the first instance.

Primarily, FEES paid.

Taschen UK
Fifth Floor, 1 Heathcock Court, 415 Strand, London WC2R 0NS

☎020 7845 8585 Fax 020 7836 3696
www.taschen.com
UK office of the German photographic, art and architecture publisher. Editorial office in Cologne (see entry under **European Publishers**).

I.B. Tauris & Co. Ltd
6 Salem Road, London W2 4BU
☎020 7243 1225 Fax 020 7243 1226
✉ mail@ibtauris.com
www.ibtauris.com
Chairman/Publisher *Iradj Bagherzade*
Managing Director *Jonathan McDonnell*
Founded 1984. Independent publisher. Publishes general non-fiction and academic in the fields of international relations, religion, current affairs, history, politics, cultural, media and film studies, Middle East studies. Distributes **Philip Wilson Publishers**, The Federal Trust and the Khalili Collections worldwide. IMPRINTS **Tauris Parke Books** Illustrated books on architecture, travel, design and culture. **Tauris Parke Paperbacks** Trade titles, including art, travel and biography. **British Academic Press** and **Tauris Academic Studies** Academic monographs. **Radcliffe Press** Colonial history and biography. Unsolicited synopses and book proposals welcome.
ROYALTIES twice-yearly.

Authors' Rating Imprint Radcliffe Press may require authors to contribute towards costs of publication.

Taylor & Francis (An imprint of Taylor & Francis Group, an Informa plc business)
2 Park Square, Milton Park, Abingdon OX14 4RN
☎020 7017 6000 Fax 020 7017 6699
www.tandf.co.uk
Managing Director (UK) *Jeremy North*
Managing Director (US) *Emmett Dages*
Publishing Director (US) *John Lavender*
Specialises in scientific and technical books for university students and academics in the following subjects: built environment, architecture, planning and civil engineering; biology, including genetics, plant architecture, molecular biology and biotechnology. About 2600 titles a year. Send detailed proposal plus c.v. and sample chapters. Proposal requirements and submission procedures can be found on the website. No poetry, fiction, travel or astrology.
ROYALTIES annually.

Authors' Rating One of those companies that barely registers with authors until they look at some of the famous imprints that are gathered under the corporate umbrella. Very much into higher education and reference. Further expansion is predicted, particularly in the US market.

Teach Yourself
See **Hachette Livre UK**

Telegram Books
26 Westbourne Grove, London W2 5RH
☎020 7229 2911 Fax 020 7229 7492
✉ info@telegrambooks.com
www.telegrambooks.com
Chairman/Managing Director *André Gaspard*
Commissioning Editor *Rebecca O'Connor*
New independent publisher of literary fiction from around the world. 15 titles a year. Welcomes unsolicited material; approach by post or e-mail.
ROYALTIES annually.

Telegraph Books
111 Buckingham Palace Road, London SW1W 0DT
☎020 7931 2887 Fax 020 7931 2929
www.books.telegraph.co.uk
Owner *Telegraph Media Group Ltd*
Publisher *Morven Knowles*
Approx. Annual Turnover £3 million
Concentrates on Telegraph branded books in association/collaboration with other publishers. Also runs Telegraph Books, a direct mail, phone-line bookselling service and off-the-page sales for other publishers' books. Publishes general non-fiction: reference, personal finance, health, gardening, cookery, heritage, guides, humour, puzzles and games. Mainly interested in books if a Telegraph link exists. About 55 titles a year. No unsolicited material.
ROYALTIES twice-yearly.

Temple Lodge Publishing Ltd
Hillside House, The Square, Forest Row RH18 5ES
☎01342 824000
✉ office@templelodge.com
www.templelodge.com
Chairman *Mr R. Pauli*
Chief Editor *Mr S. Gulbekian*
Approx. Annual Turnover £65,000
Founded in 1990 to develop the work of Rudolf Steiner (see also **Rudolf Steiner Press**). Publishes non-fiction: mind, body and spirit,

current affairs, health and therapy. 12 titles in 2006. No unsolicited material; send initial letter of enquiry. No poetry or fiction.

ROYALTIES annually.

Texere
See **Thomson Learning**

Thames and Hudson Ltd
181A High Holborn, London WC1V 7QX
☎020 7845 5000 Fax 020 7845 5050
✉ mail@thameshudson.co.uk
www.thamesandhudson.com

Chairman *Thomas Neurath*
Managing Director *Jamie Camplin*
Approx. Annual Turnover £30 million

Publishes art, archaeology, architecture and design, biography, fashion, garden and landscape design, graphics, history, illustrated and fine editions, mythology, photography, popular culture, style, travel and topography. SERIES *World of Art; Hip Hotels; StyleCity; New Horizons; Most Beautiful Villages; Earth From the Air; The Way We Live; Photofile.* TITLES *Art Since 1900; The Artist's Yearbook; Art Photography Now; The Great LIFE Photographers; Hockney's Pictures; Sensation; The Shock of the New; Germaine Greer's The Boy; Graffiti Woman; Balenciaga; Fashion Illustration Next; Factory Records; The Eco-Design Handbook; The Seventy Great Journeys in History; Roman Britain; Freemasonry; Reuters - The State of the World.* 200 titles a year. Send preliminary letter and outline before mss.

ROYALTIES twice-yearly.

Authors' Rating

Third Millennium Publishing
Third Millennium Information Ltd, 2–5 Benjamin Street, London EC1M 5QL
☎020 7336 0144 Fax 020 7608 1188
✉ info@tmiltd.com
www.tmiltd.com

Managing Director *Justin Tunstall*
Approx. Annual Turnover £750,000

Founded 1999 as a highly illustrated book publisher in the international museum, heritage and art gallery markets. Also some 'coffee-table' titles in association with various universities, Oxbridge colleges, independent schools and military organisations. 10–15 titles annually. Unsolicited material welcome; approach in writing with c.v., book synopsis, target market and any supporting information. No fiction.

ROYALTIES annually.

Thoemmes
See **The Continuum International Publishing Group Limited**

Thomson Learning
High Holborn House, 50–51 Bedford Row, London WC1R 4LR
☎020 7067 2500 Fax 020 7067 2600
www.thomson.com

CEO (Worldwide) *Ron Schlosser*
CEO/Managing Director (Thomson Learning EMEA) *Tom Davy*
Publishing Director (Thomson Learning EMEA) *John Yates*

Founded 1993. Formerly International Thomson Publishing, part of the Thomson Corporation and as such has offices worldwide with the UK office being reported to by Copenhagen (for Europe), Turkey (Middle East) and South Africa. Acquired Texere in 2003. Publishes education. TITLES *Management and Cost Accounting* Drury; *Strategy – Process, Content, Contact* DeWit and Meyer. Unsolicited material aimed at students is welcome but telephone in the first instance to check out the idea.

ROYALTIES vary according to contract.

Thomson Round Hall (Ireland)
See **Sweet & Maxwell Group**

Stanley Thornes (Publishers) Ltd
See **Nelson Thornes Ltd**

F.A. Thorpe Publishing
The Green, Bradgate Road, Anstey LE7 7FU
☎0116 236 4325 Fax 0116 234 0205

Group Chief Executive *Robert Thirlby*
Approx. Annual Turnover £6 million

Founded in 1964 to supply large print books to libraries. Part of the Ulverscroft Group Ltd. Publishes fiction and non-fiction large print books. No educational, gardening or books that would not be suitable for large print. IMPRINTS **Charnwood; Ulverscroft; Linford Romance; Linford Mystery; Linford Western.** No unsolicited material.

Thorsons
See **HarperCollins Publishers Ltd**

Time Out Guides
See **The Random House Group Ltd**

Times Books
See **HarperCollins Publishers Ltd**

Times Editions
See **Marshall Cavendish Ltd**

Timewell Press
10 Porchester Terrace, London W2 3TL
☎0870 760 5250 Fax 0870 760 5250
✉ info@timewellpress.com
www.timewellpress.com

Chairman *Gerard Noel*
Managing Director *Andreas Campomar*

Founded 1997. Publishes literary international fiction and non-fiction. AUTHORS include Anthony Blond, Francis Fulford, Leslie Grantham, Michael Winner, Ralph Lownie, C.S. Nicholls, M-J. Lancaster, Jonathan Gathorne-Hardy (J.R. Ackerley Prize, 2005), Charles Campion (Gourmand World Cookbook Awards, 2004), Anthony Powell, George Orwell, D.J. Taylor. 6 titles in 2006. No unsolicited mss; send synopses and ideas with letter and s.a.e.
ROYALTIES twice-yearly.

Titan Books
144 Southwark Street, London SE1 0UP
☎020 7620 0200 Fax 020 7803 1990
✉ editorial@titanemail.com
www.titanbooks.com

Managing Director *Nick Landau*
Editorial Director *Katy Wild*

Founded 1981. Now a leader in the publication of graphic novels and film and television tie-ins. Publishes comic books/graphic novels, film and television titles. IMPRINT **Titan Books** TITLES *Batman*; *Battlestar Galactica: The Official Companion: Season 3*; *The Simpsons*; *Stardust: The Film Companion*; *Star Wars*; *Superman*; *The Winston Effect: The Art and History of Stan Winston Studio*; *Transformers*; *24*; *The Official Companion Seasons 3&4*; *Wallace & Gromit*. About 200 titles a year. No unsolicited fiction or children's books. Ideas for film and TV titles considered; send synopsis/outline with sample chapter. No e-mail submissions. Author guidelines available.
ROYALTIES twice-yearly.

Tor
See **Macmillan Publishers Ltd**

Transita Ltd
Spring Hill House, Spring Hill Road,
Begbroke, Oxford OX5 1RX
☎01865 375794 Fax 01865 379162
✉ info@transita.co.uk
www.transita.co.uk

Managing Director *Giles Lewis*

Editorial Director *Nikki Read*

Imprint of **How To Books Ltd**. Specialises in contemporary fiction for women over 45. Synopsis and three chapters required.

Transworld Publishers, A division of the Random House Group Ltd
61–63 Uxbridge Road, London W5 5SA
☎020 8579 2652 Fax 020 8579 5479
✉ info@transworld-publishers.co.uk
www.booksattransworld.co.uk

Managing Director *Larry Finlay*
Publisher *Bill Scott-Kerr*
Senior Publishing Director *Francesca Liversidge*
Approx. Annual Turnover £85 million

Founded 1950. A subsidiary of **Random House, Inc.**, New York, which in turn is a wholly-owned subsidiary of **Bertelsmann AG**, Germany. Publishes general fiction and non-fiction, gardening, sports and leisure. IMPRINTS **Bantam** *Francesca Liversidge*; **Bantam Press** *Sally Gaminara*; **Corgi** & **Black Swan** *Linda Evans*; **Doubleday** *Marianne Velmans*; **Channel 4 Books** *Doug Young*; **Eden** *Susanna Wadeson*; **Expert Books** *Gareth Pottle*. AUTHORS Monica Ali, Kate Atkinson, Charlotte Bingham, Dan Brown, Bill Bryson, Lee Child, Jilly Cooper, Richard Dawkins, Ben Elton, Frederick Forsyth, David Gemmell, Tess Gerritsen, Robert Goddard, Joanne Harris, Stephen Hawking, D.G. Hessayon, John Irving, Sophie Kinsella, Anne McCaffrey, Paul McKenna, Andy McNab, John O'Farrell, Terry Pratchett, Patricia Scanlan, Gerald Seymour, Danielle Steel, Joanna Trollope, Robert Winston. No unsolicited mss. OVERSEAS ASSOCIATES Random House Australia Pty Ltd; Random House New Zealand; Random House (Pty) Ltd (South Africa).
ROYALTIES twice-yearly.

Authors' Rating In one of those delightful ironies, the fall away of sales of Dan Brown's *The Da Vinci Code* has been more than compensated by Richard Dawkins' bestseller, *The God Delusion*. Could they possibly be related?

Travel Publishing Ltd
7A Apollo House, Calleva Park, Aldermaston RG7 8TN
☎0118 981 7777 Fax 0118 940 8428
✉ info@travelpublishing.co.uk
www.travelpublishing.co.uk

Directors *Peter Robinson, Chris Day*

Founded in 1997 by two former directors of Reed Elsevier plc. Publishes travel guides covering places of interest, accommodation, food, drink and specialist shops in Britain and Ireland. SERIES *Hidden Places*; *Hidden Inns*; *Country Pubs*; *Country Living Rural Guides* (in conjunction with *Country Living* magazine); *Off the Motorway*. Over 40 titles in print. Welcomes unsolicited material; send letter in the first instance.

ROYALTIES twice-yearly.

Trentham Books Ltd

Westview House, 734 London Road, Stoke-on-Trent ST4 5NP
☎01782 745567/844699 Fax 01782 745553
www.trentham-books.co.uk

Directors *Dr Gillian Klein, Barbara Wiggins*
Approx. Annual Turnover £1 million

Publishes education (nursery, school to higher), social sciences, intercultural studies, gender studies and law for professional readers *not* for children and parents. Also academic and professional journals. No fiction, biography or poetry. Over 30 titles a year. Unsolicited mss, synopses and ideas welcome if relevant to their interests. Material only returned if adequate s.a.e. sent.

ROYALTIES annually.

Trident Press Ltd

Empire House, 175 Piccadilly, London W1J 9TB
☎020 7491 8770 Fax 020 7491 8664
✉ admin@tridentpress.com
www.tridentpress.com

Managing Director *Peter Vine*
Approx. Annual Turnover £550,000

Founded 1997. Publishes TV tie-ins, natural history, travel, geography, underwater/marine life, history, archaeology and culture. DIVISIONS **Fiction/General Publishing** *Paula Vine*; **Natural History** *Peter Vine*. TITLES *Red Sea Sharks*; *The Elysium Testament*; *BBC Wildlife Specials*; *UAE in Focus*. No unsolicited mss; synopses and ideas welcome, particularly TV tie-ins. Approach in writing or *brief* communications by e-mail, fax or telephone.

ROYALTIES annually.

Trotman & Co. Ltd

2 The Green, Richmond TW9 1PL
☎020 8486 1150 Fax 020 8486 1161
www.trotman.co.uk

Publishing Director *Mina Patria*
Approx. Annual Turnover £3 million

Publishes general careers books, higher education guides, teaching support material, employment and training resources. TITLES *Degree Course Offers*; *The Student Book*; *Trotman Green*

Guides; *Students' Money Matters*; *CRAC Degree Course Guides*; *Real Life Guides*; *Real Life Issues*; *Newscheck* (journal for careers professionals); *Careers 2006*. About 60 titles a year. Unsolicited material welcome.

ROYALTIES twice-yearly.

Troubador Publishing Ltd

9 De Montfort Mews, Leicester LE1 7FW
☎0116 255 9311 Fax 0116 244 9323
✉ books@troubador.co.uk
www.troubador.co.uk

Chairman *Jane Rowland*
Managing Director *Jeremy Thompson*
Approx. Annual Turnover £500,000

Founded 1998. Publishes fiction, children's, academic, non-fiction, translation and poetry. Offers self-publishing agreement for fiction or non-fiction under its Matador imprint. DIVISIONS **Academic** *Jane Rowland*; **Fiction/Non-Fiction** *Jeremy Thompson*. IMPRINTS **Matador**; **Troubador Italian Studies**; **Communication Ethics** TITLES *Energy Beyond Oil*; *Grazia Deledda: A Biography*; *The Ethics of Teaching Practice*. 90 titles in 2006. Unsolicited mss welcome, by e-mail only. No synopses or ideas for books.

ROYALTIES quarterly.

TSO (The Stationery Office)

St Crispins, Duke Street, Norwich NR3 1PD
☎01603 622211 Fax 01603 696501 (Editorial)
www.tso.co.uk

Chairman *Tim Hailstone*
Approx. Annual Turnover £250 million

Formerly HMSO, which was founded in 1786. Became part of the private sector in October 1996. Publisher of material sponsored by Parliament, government departments and other official bodies. Also commercial publishing in the following broad categories: business and professional, environment, transport, education and law. 11,000 new titles each year with 50,000 titles in print.

Tuckwell Press

See **Birlinn Ltd**

Twenty First Century Publishers Ltd

Braunton Barn, Kiln Lane, Isfield TN22 5UE
☎01892 522802
✉ TFCP@btinternet.com
www.twentyfirstcenturypublishers.com

Chairman *Fred Piechoczek*

Founded 2002. Publishes general fiction, financial thrillers and crime. Welcomes submissions by e-mail: manuscripts@connectfree.co.uk (contact *Fred Piechoczek*). Send brief synopsis in the body of the e-mail with extracts from the book in a file attachment (two to three chapters from anywhere in the book). No non-fiction or children's.

ROYALTIES twice-yearly.

20/20
See **The X Press**

Ulverscroft
See **F.A.Thorpe Publishing**

Unichrome
See **Jarrold Publishing**

University Presses of California, Columbia & Princeton Ltd
1 Oldlands Way, Bognor Regis PO22 9SA
☎01243 842165 Fax 01243 842167
✉ lois@upccp.demon.co.uk

Publishes academic titles only. US-based editorial offices. Enquiries only. Over 200 titles a year.

Usborne Publishing Ltd
83–85 Saffron Hill, London EC1N 8RT
☎020 7430 2800 Fax 020 7430 1562
✉ mail@usborne.co.uk
www.usborne.com

Managing Director *Peter Usborne*
Publishing Director *Jenny Tyler*
Approx. Annual Turnover £28 million

Founded 1973. Publishes non-fiction, fiction, art and activity books, puzzle books and music for children, young adults and pre-school. Some titles for parents. Up to 250 titles a year. Non-fiction books are written in-house to a specific format and therefore unsolicited mss are not normally welcome. Ideas which may be developed in-house are sometimes considered. Fiction for children will be considered. Keen to hear from new illustrators and designers.

ROYALTIES twice-yearly.

Authors' Rating The company has moved from specialising in children's reference books to being an 'all rounder'.

Vanguard Press
See **Pegasus Elliot Mackenzie Publishers Ltd**

Ventura
See **Penguin Group (UK)**

Vermilion
See **The Random House Group Ltd**

Verso
6 Meard Street, London W1F 0EG
☎020 7437 3546 Fax 020 7734 0059
✉ info@verso.co.uk
www.versobooks.com

Managing Director *Giles O'Bryen*
Approx. Annual Turnover £2 million

Formerly New Left Books which grew out of the *New Left Review*. Publishes politics, history, sociology, economics, philosophy, cultural studies, feminism. TITLES *The Occupation* Patrick Cockburn; *Planet of Slums* Mike Davis; *Polemics* Alain Badiou; *The Soviet Century* Moshe Lewin; *NHS plc: The Privatisation of our Health Care* Allyson M. Pollock; *Street-Fighting Years* Tariq Ali; *Planet of Slums* Mike Davis. No unsolicited mss; synopses and ideas for books welcome. OVERSEAS OFFICE in New York.

ROYALTIES annually.

Authors' Rating Dubbed by the *Bookseller* as 'one of the most successful small independent publishers'. The publishing programme is set to expand with the backlist supported by print-on-demand.

Viking
See **Penguin Group (UK)**

Vintage
See **The Random House Group Ltd**

Virago Press
Little, Brown Book Group UK, Brettenham House, Lancaster Place, London WC2E 7EN
☎020 7911 8000 Fax 020 7911 8100
✉ virago.press@littlebrown.co.uk
www.virago.co.uk

Publisher *Lennie Goodings*
Editor, Virago Modern Classics *Donna Coonan*

An imprint of **Little, Brown Book Group UK**. Founded in 1973 by Carmen Callil, Virago publishes women's literature, both fiction and non-fiction. IMPRINT **Virago Modern Classics** 19th and 20th-century fiction reprints by writers such as Daphne du Maurier, Angela Carter and Edith Wharton. Virago AUTHORS include Margaret Atwood, Maya Angelou, Jennifer Belle, Waris Dirie, Sarah Dunant, Germaine Greer, Michèle Roberts, Gillian Slovo, Talitha

Stevenson, Natasha Walter, Sarah Waters. 50 titles a year. 'We do not currently accept unsolicited fiction.'

ROYALTIES twice-yearly.

Authors' Rating The first name in women's publishing has gained marketing strength from its association with Time Warner. A team of young editors favours writers with something new to say.

Virgin Books Ltd

Thames Wharf Studios, Rainville Road, London W6 9HT
☎020 7386 3300 Fax 020 7386 3360
✉ info@virgin-books.co.uk
www.virgin.com/books

Managing Director *KT Forster*
Approx. Annual Turnover £10 million

The Virgin Group's book publishing company. Acquired by Random House Group in March 2007. Publishes non-fiction, reference books on lifestyle, health, music, sport, biography, crime, film, TV and current affairs. No poetry, short stories, individual novels, children's books.

DIVISIONS   **Non-fiction**   IMPRINT
Virgin Editorial Director *Carolyn Thorne*; Commissioning Editors *Ed Faulkner, Claire Kingston*. **Fiction** IMPRINTS **Virgin**; **Black Lace**; **Nexus**; **Cheek** Editor *Adam Nevill* Erotic fiction 'written by women for women'.

ROYALTIES twice-yearly.

Authors' Rating Prospects for this loss-making publisher have been transformed by its sale to Random House. With increased investment, the company is set to double its output.

Vision

101 Southwark Street, London SE1 0JF
☎020 7928 5599 Fax 020 7928 8822
✉ info@visionpaperbacks.co.uk
www.visionpaperbacks.co.uk

Managing Director *Sheena Dewan*

Founded 1996. Non-fiction publisher. IMPRINTS **Vision**; **Vision Paperbacks**; **Fusion Press**. 18 titles in 2006. Unsolicited mss, synopses and ideas for books welcome. Initial approach by e-mail, without attachments. No fiction or poetry.

ROYALTIES twice-yearly.

Vision On

See **Omnibus Press**

The Vital Spark

See **Neil Wilson Publishing Ltd**

Voyager

See **HarperCollins Publishers Ltd**

University of Wales Press

10 Columbus Walk, Brigantine Place, Cardiff CF10 4UP
☎029 2049 6899 Fax 029 2049 6108
✉ post@press.wales.ac.uk
www.uwp.co.uk

Director *Ashley Drake*
Commissioning Editor *Sarah Lewis*
Assistant Commissioning Editor *Ennis Akpinar*
Approx. Annual Turnover £500,000

Founded 1922. Publishes academic and scholarly books in English and Welsh in six main subject areas: History, Political Philosophy and Religious Studies, Welsh and Celtic Studies, Literary Studies, European Studies and Medieval Studies. SERIES include *Political Philosophy Now; Religion and Culture in the Middle Ages; Iberian and Latin American Studies; Gender Studies in Wales; Gothic Literary Studies; Kantian Studies; Television and Genre*. 55 titles a year. Unsolicited mss considered but see website for further guidance.

ROYALTIES annually.

Walker Books Ltd

87 Vauxhall Walk, London SE11 5HJ
☎020 7793 0909 Fax 020 7587 1123
✉ editorial@walker.co.uk
www.walkerbooks.co.uk

Managing Director *Helen McAleer*
Publisher *Jane Winterbotham*
Editors *Gill Evans* (fiction), *Deirdre McDermott* (picture books), *Caroline Royds* (early learning, non-fiction & gift books), *Denise Johnstone-Burt* (picture books, board & novelty), *Loraine Taylor* (new media, backlist and books plus)
Approx. Annual Turnover £47.7 million (Group)

Founded 1979. Publishes illustrated children's books, children's fiction and non-fiction. TITLES *Maisy* Lucy Cousins; *Where's Wally?* Martin Handford; *We're Going on a Bear Hunt* Michael Rosen and Helen Oxenbury; *Can't You Sleep, Little Bear?* Martin Waddell and Barbara Firth; *Guess How Much I Love You* Sam McBratney and Anita Jeram; *Alex Rider* series Anthony Horowitz. About 300 titles a year.

ROYALTIES twice-yearly.

Authors' Rating Dedicated to 'groundbreaking books' and much loved by its authors, Walker Books is enlivening its backlist with animated films of classic titles.

Wallflower Press
6 Market Place, London W1W 8AF
☎020 7436 9494
✉ info@wallflowerpress.co.uk
www.wallflowerpress.co.uk
Editorial Director *Yoram Allon*
Chief Editor *Del Cullen*
Approx. Annual Turnover £200,000

Founded 1999. Publishes trade and academic books devoted to cinema and the moving image. SERIES *Short Cuts* Introductory undergraduate books; *Director's Cuts* Studies on significant international film-makers; *24 Frames* Anthologies focusing on national and regional cinemas. Over 25 titles a year. Unsolicited mss, synopses and proposals welcome. No fiction or academic material not related to the moving image.
ROYALTIES annually.

Ward Lock
See **Octopus Publishing Group**

Ward Lock Educational Co. Ltd
BIC Ling Kee House, 1 Christopher Road, East Grinstead RH19 3BT
☎01342 318980 Fax 01342 410980
✉ wle@lingkee.com
www.wardlockeducational.com
Owner *Ling Kee (UK) Ltd*

Founded 1952. Publishes educational books (primary, middle, secondary, teaching manuals) for all subjects, specialising in maths, science, geography, reading and English and currently focusing on Key Stages 1 and 2.

Frederick Warne
See **Penguin Group (UK)**

Franklin Watts
See **Hachette Children's Books**

Wayland
See **Hachette Children's Books**

Weidenfeld & Nicolson
See **The Orion Publishing Group Ltd**

Wharncliffe Books
47 Church Street, Barnsley S70 2AS
☎01226 734222 Fax 01226 734438
✉ enquiries@wharncliffebooks.co.uk
www.wharncliffebooks.co.uk
Commissioning Editor *Rupert Harding*

An imprint of **Pen & Sword Books Ltd**. Wharncliffe is the book and magazine publishing arm of an old-established, independently owned newspaper publishing and printing house. Publishes local history throughout the UK, focusing on nostalgia and old photographs. SERIES *Foul Deeds*; *Local History Companions*; *Pals*; *Aspects*. No unsolicited mss; synopses and ideas welcome.
ROYALTIES twice-yearly.

Wharton
See **Pearson Education**

Which? Books
2 Marylebone Road, London NW1 4DF
☎020 7770 7000 Fax 020 7770 7660
✉ martin.chapman@which.co.uk
www.which.net
Editorial Director *Helen Parker*

Founded 1957. Publishing arm of Which? Publishes non-fiction: information and reference on personal finance, property, divorce, consumer law. All titles offer direct value to the consumer. IMPRINT **Which? Books** TITLES *The Good Food Guide*; *Wills and Probate*; *Be Your Own Financial Adviser*. 10–12 titles a year. No unsolicited mss; send synopses and ideas only.
ROYALTIES, if applicable, twice-yearly.

White Ladder Press
Great Ambrook, Near Ipplepen TQ12 5UL
☎01803 813343 Fax 01803 813928
✉ enquiries@whiteladderpress.com
www.whiteladderpress.com
Publisher *Roni Jay*

Founded 2002. Publishes non-fiction books which present a new angle on everyday living. Welcomes synopses and ideas by mail or e-mail. No fiction, poetry or children's titles.
ROYALTIES quarterly.

Whittet Books Ltd
Hill Farm, Stonham Road, Cotton, Stowmarket IP14 4RQ
☎01449 781877 Fax 01449 781898
✉ annabel@whittet.dircon.co.uk
www.whittetbooks.com
Owner *A. Whittet & Co.*
Managing Director *Annabel Whittet*

Publishes reference books on natural history, pets, poultry, horses, domestic livestock, horticulture, rural interest. 4 titles in 2006. Synopses and ideas for books on the subjects listed are welcome. Enclose s.a.e.
ROYALTIES twice-yearly.

Whydown Books Limited

Sedlescombe TN33 0RN
☎01424 870875 Fax 01424 870083
✉ readerspost@whydownbooks.com
www.whydownbooks.com

Chairman *Dick Nesbitt-Dufort*
Managing & Finance Director *Chris Martin*
Editorial Head *Pamela Richards*

Founded 2002. Publishes biography, fiction, general interest with a slant towards writers with first-hand experience of distant places and profound events. TITLES *Spies and Lovers* Adrian Hill; *Black Lysander* John Nesbitt-Dufort; *The Apothecary's Gift* Bradley Bernarde; *Chinnery's Hotel* Jaysinh Birje; *A Sussex Highlander Memoirs 1790–1815* Sergeant William Kenward. No children's or poetry at present. Developing their non-fiction list and film/television projects from fiction list. 2–3 books a year No unsolicited mss. Synopses and ideas welcome; even better a few chapters. Approach by letter or e-mail with idea and writing history.

ROYALTIES twice-yearly.

Wild Goose Publications

Iona Community, 4th Floor, The Savoy Centre, 140 Sauchiehall Street, Glasgow G2 3DH
☎0141 332 6292 Fax 0141 332 1090
✉ admin@ionabooks.com
www.ionabooks.com

Editorial Head *Sandra Kramer*

The publishing house of the Iona Community, established in the Celtic Christian tradition of St Columba, publishes books and CDs on holistic spirituality, social justice, political and peace issues, healing, innovative approaches to worship, song and material for meditation and reflection.

Wiley Europe Ltd

The Atrium, Southern Gate, Chichester PO19 8SQ
☎01243 779777 Fax 01243 775878
✉ europe@wiley.co.uk
www.wiley.com

Senior Vice President Europe & International Development *Stephen Smith*
Publishing Directors *Mike Davis, Stephen Smith*
Approx. Annual Turnover £103 million

Founded 1807. US parent company. Publishes professional, reference trade and text books, scientific, technical and biomedical.

Wiley-Blackwell

9600 Garsington Road, Oxford OX4 2DQ
☎01865 776868 Fax 01865 714591
www.blackwellpublishing.com

Senior Vice President, Wiley-Blackwell *Eric Swanson*
Chief Operating Officer *René Olivieri*

Wiley-Blackwell was formed from the acquisition of Blackwell Publishing (Holdings) Ltd by John Wiley & Sons, Inc. Blackwell's publishing programme has merged with Wiley's global scientific, technical and medical business. The merged operation is now the largest of the three of John Wiley & Sons, Inc.; its other businesses are Professional/Trade and Higher Education.

Authors' Rating Wiley's acquisition of Blackwell Publishing has prompted concern among librarians that it will reduce choice. But given that Blackwell was bound to be sold (and why not?) what better home could it find than one of the top educational and professional publishers. Academic authors are attracted by the American connection. Online publishing is set to increase.

Neil Wilson Publishing Ltd

Suite Ex 8 The Pentagon Centre, 44 Washington Street, Glasgow G3 8AZ
☎0141 221 1117 Fax 0141 221 5363
✉ info@nwp.co.uk
www.nwp.co.uk

Managing Director/Editorial Director *Neil Wilson*
Approx. Annual Turnover £110,000

Founded 1992. Publishes Scottish interest and history, biography, humour and hillwalking, whisky; also Scottish cookery and travel. IMPRINTS **The In Pinn** Outdoor pursuits; **The Angels' Share** Whisky, drink and food-related subjects; **The Vital Spark** Humour; **NWP** History, biography, reference, true crime; **11:9** Scottish fiction. About 6 titles a year. Unsolicited mss, synopses and ideas welcome. No politics, academic or technical.

ROYALTIES twice-yearly.

Philip Wilson Publishers Ltd

109 Drysdale Street, The Timber Yard, London N1 6ND
☎020 7033 9900 Fax 020 7033 9922
✉ pwilson@philip-wilson.co.uk
www.philip-wilson.co.uk

Chairman *Philip Wilson*

Founded 1976. Publishes art, art history, antiques and collectibles. About 14 titles a year.

Wimbledon Publishing Company

75–76 Blackfriars Road, London SE1 8HA
☎020 7401 4200 Fax 020 7401 4201

✉ info@wpcpress.com
www.wpcpress.com

Managing Director *Kamaljit Sood*
General Manager *Renu Sood*

Founded in 1992 as a publisher of school texts, going on to launch Anthem Press, an academic and trade imprint focusing on world history, politics, economics, international affairs, literature and culture. IMPRINTS **Anthem Press** *Tej Sood*; **WPC Education** *K. Sood*. Welcomes mss, synopses and ideas for books.

ROYALTIES annually.

Windhorse Publications

11 Park Road, Moseley B13 8AB
☎0121 449 9191 Fax 0121 449 9191
✉ jnanasiddhi@windhorsepublications.com
www.windhorsepublications.com

Chairman/Editorial Head *Jnanasiddhi*
Approx. Annual Turnover £250,000

Founded 1977. Publishes meditation and Buddhism. Associated with the FWBO, a worldwide Buddhist movement. Publishes across the Buddhist traditions. Unsolicited mss, synopses and ideas welcome; approach by letter or e-mail in the first instance.

ROYALTIES quarterly.

Wingedchariot Press

7 Court Royal, Eridge Road, Tunbridge Wells TN4 8HT
☎0779 127 3374
✉ info@wingedchariot.com
www.wingedchariot.com

Editor *Ann Arscott*

Founded in 2005 'to bring the best of children's books in translation to the UK for the first time'. 4 titles in 2006. Will consider books in their original language with illustrations. E-mail synopsis and scan of drawings. No English language books.

Wise Publications

See **Omnibus Press**

WIT Press

Ashurst Lodge, Ashurst, Southampton SO40 7AA
☎023 8029 3223 Fax 023 8029 2853
✉ marketing@witpress.com
www.witpress.com

Owner *Computational Mechanics International Ltd, Southampton*
Chairman/Managing Director/Editorial Head *Professor C.A. Brebbia*

Founded in 1980 as Computational Mechanics Publications to publish engineering analysis titles. Changed to WIT Press to reflect the increased range of publications. Publishes scientific and technical, mainly at postgraduate level and above, including architecture, environmental engineering, bioengineering. 50 titles in 2006. Unsolicited mss, synopses and ideas welcome; approach by post or e-mail. No non-scientific or technical material or lower level (school and college-level texts). OVERSEAS SUBSIDIARY Computational Mechanics, Inc., Billerica, USA.

ROYALTIES annually.

Wizard Books

See **Icon Books Ltd**

Oswald Wolff Books

See **Berg Publishers**

The Women's Press

27 Goodge Street, London W1T 2LD
☎020 7636 3992 Fax 020 7637 1866
www.the-womens-press.com

Managing Director *Stella Kane*
Approx. Annual Turnover £1 million

Part of the Namara Group. First title published in 1978. Publishes women only: quality fiction and non-fiction. Fiction usually has a female protagonist and a woman-centred theme. International writers and subject matter encouraged. Non-fiction: books for and about women generally; gender politics, race politics, disability, feminist theory, health and psychology, literary criticism. IMPRINTS **Women's Press Classics**; **Livewire Books for Teenagers** Fiction and non-fiction series for young adults. No mss without previous letter, synopsis and sample material.

ROYALTIES twice-yearly.

Woodhead Publishing Ltd

Abington Hall, Abington, Cambridge CB21 6AH
☎01223 891358 Fax 01223 893694
✉ wp@woodhead-publishing.com
www.woodheadpublishing.com

Chairman *Alan Jessup*
Managing Director *Martin Woodhead*
Approx. Annual Turnover £1.8 million

Founded 1989. Publishes engineering, materials technology, textile technology, finance and investment, food technology, environmental science. DIVISION **Woodhead Publishing** *Martin Woodhead*. About 60 titles a year. Unsolicited material welcome.

ROYALTIES annually.

Wordsworth Editions Ltd

8B East Street, Ware SG12 9HJ
☎01920 465167 Fax 01920 462267
✉ enquiries@wordsworth-editions.com
or dennis.hart@wordsworth-editions.com
(editorial)
www.wordsworth-editions.co.uk

Directors *E. G. Trayler, D.R. Hart*
Approx. Annual Turnover £4 million

Founded 1987. Publishes classics of English and world literature, reference books, poetry, children's classics, mystery and the supernatural and special editions. About 75 titles a year. No unsolicited mss.

WPC Education

See **Wimbledon Publishing Company**

The X Press

PO Box 25694, London N17 6FP
☎020 8801 2100 Fax 020 8885 1322
✉ vibes@xpress.co.uk
www.xpress.co.uk

Editorial Director *Dotun Adebayo*
Publisher *Steve Pope*

Launched in 1992 with the cult bestseller *Yardie*, The X Press is the leading publisher of Black-interest fiction in the UK. Also publishes general fiction and children's fiction. IMPRINTS **The X Press**; **Nia**; **20/20**. About 26 titles a year. Send mss rather than synopses or ideas (enclose s.a.e.). No poetry.

Authors' Rating A small company that has done an inestimable service by introducing Black writers to the publishing mainstream. Popular fiction is the mainstay but the list also covers reprints of classic Black fiction.

Y Lolfa Cyf

Talybont, Ceredigion SY24 5AP
☎01970 832304 Fax 01970 832782
✉ ylolfa@ylolfa.com
www.ylolfa.com/

Managing Director *Garmon Gruffudd*
General Editor *Lefi Gruffudd*
English Editor *Gwen Davies*
Approx. Annual Turnover £800,000

Founded 1967. Small company which publishes mainly in Welsh; has its own four-colour printing and binding facilities. Publishes Welsh language publications; Celtic language tutors; English language books for the Welsh and Celtic tourist trade. Expanding slowly. TITLES *My Kingdom of Books* Richard Booth; *The Welsh Learner's Dictionary* Heini Gruffudd; *The Fight for*

Welsh Freedom Gwynfor Evans; *Celtic Vision* John Merion Morris. IMPRINTS **Dinas** Part-author-subsidised imprint for non-mainstream books of Welsh interest in English and Welsh. **Alcemi** English language fiction. About 50 titles a year. Write first with synopses or ideas.
ROYALTIES twice-yearly.

Yale University Press (London)

47 Bedford Square, London WC1B 3DP
☎020 7079 4900 Fax 020 7079 4901
✉ sales@yaleup.co.uk
www.yalebooks.co.uk

Founded 1961. Owned by US parent company. Publishes art history, decorative arts, history, religion, music, politics, current affairs, biography and history of science. About 300 titles (worldwide) a year. Unsolicited mss and synopses welcome if within specialised subject areas.
ROYALTIES annually.

Authors' Rating A publisher with a marvellous talent for turning out serious books which appeal to the general reader.

Yellow Jersey Press

See **The Random House Group Ltd**

York Notes

See **Pearson Education**

The Young Travellers Club

See **Beautiful Books Ltd**

Zambezi Publishing Ltd

PO Box 221, Plymouth PL2 2YJ
☎01752 367300 Fax 01752 350453
✉ info@zampub.com
www.zampub.com

Chair *Sasha Fenton*
Managing Director *Jan Budkowski*

Founded 1999. Publishes non-fiction: mind, body and spirit, self-help, finance and business, including the 'Simply' series. About 12 titles a year. Send biography, synopsis and sample chapter by mail. Brief e-mail communication acceptable but *no* attachments, please.
ROYALTIES twice-yearly.

Zed Books Ltd

7 Cynthia Street, London N1 9JF
☎020 7837 4014 Fax 020 7833 3960
✉ sales@zedbooks.net
www.zedbooks.co.uk
Approx. Annual Turnover £1.4 million

Founded 1976. Publishes international and Third World affairs, development studies, women's studies, environmental studies, human rights and specific area studies. No fiction, children's or poetry. DIVISIONS **Development & Environment** *Susannah Trefgarne, Ellen McKinlay;* **Women's Studies.** TITLES *Rogue State: A Guide to the World's Only Superpower* William Blum; *Staying Alive* Vandana Shiva; *The Autobiography of Nawal* Nawal El Saadawi. About 60 titles a year. No unsolicited mss; synopses and ideas welcome.

ROYALTIES annually.

Zero to Ten
See **Evans Brothers Ltd**

Still Airborne

Will Atkins looks back on a year of Macmillan New Writing

The launch of Macmillan New Writing in 2006 provoked some unusually shrill denunciations from the British broadsheet press: apparently Macmillan was not only abdicating cultural responsibility but taking advantage of 'impressionable young authors'. A year later MNW has become established as part of Macmillan's mainstream publishing operation and increasingly is regarded as a prestigious forum for new novelists.

Like many publishers, Macmillan made the decision to stop accepting unsolicited manuscripts some years ago. Literary agents therefore effectively became the only source of new material. The paying of advances – advance payments to authors against the royalties they earn as their books are sold – is not a new practice, but the figures have been negotiated upwards by agents, whereas the sales of new novels have not grown. The consequence is often that the publisher is left with an 'unearned advance': the author's book fails to sell enough copies for the royalties earned to cover the value of the advance, the advance is not repaid, and the publisher must write off the amount unearned. The danger is that the route to market for those authors who may not be so obviously marketable and whose reputation takes time to build may be barred.

Macmillan New Writing was an attempt to address this situation. We decided to return to the practice of reading manuscripts received direct from authors and to set up a streamlined system for processing these. We also decided that we would not pay advances. Perhaps it should not have come as a surprise that this rather modest scheme wasn't exactly embraced by some literary agents.

But the fact is, the model of publishing we are practising is rather old-fashioned: we read manuscripts sent to us by authors and, if we like the novel and think we can sell enough copies to make it worthwhile for everyone, we publish it as a very handsome hardback. Our terms are standard and straightforward: we pay a royalty of 20% on net sales; we retain world rights and share any rights revenue 50/50, and we reserve the option to publish the author's second novel under the same terms as the first.

(To put the royalty figure in context, assuming the average discount at which a book sells is 50%: if 200 copies are sold the author gets about £260; if 1000 copies are sold the author gets about £1300; and if 10,000 are sold the author gets about £13,000.)

Having recently had his book published by a mainstream publisher, the journalist Nicholas Clee reported that he had been spending some time with his royalty statement and a calculator:

I have worked out that royalties from sales of my book are lower than they would have been under the terms of the Macmillan New Writing list. Given that

MNW has been described as 'the Ryanair of publishing', and that my contract benefited from the expert negotiations of my agent and conformed roughly to industry standards, this is a surprising discovery.[1]

★ ★ ★

It's true that we welcome unsolicited submissions – but there are a few important exceptions: we publish only full-length adult fiction (novels of over 50,000 words) by authors who have not previously had a novel published by a conventional publisher (so e-books, self-published books, or so-called 'vanity-published' books are OK). Which is to say, please send us your debut novel, but please don't send us your poetry, your children's book, your memoirs, history, self-help book, travelogue, etc. Full submission details can be found on our website (www.macmillannewwriting.com).

So what happens to your novel once you've emailed it to us? Assuming it meets the criteria above, it will be logged and read by one of our editors. If the editor likes the novel, it will be read by the rest of the team, and if there is general enthusiasm for it, you'll receive an e-mail with the good news. Unfortunately the sheer number of submissions makes it impossible for us to respond to those which we decide not to publish (and remember we only have space for twelve novels a year). At the time of writing, some 7,000 full-length novels have come in – on average we get about eighty submissions per week. What we can guarantee is that every novel that is sent to us will be given serious consideration.

If we decide to publish your novel, you will be assigned an editor and the novel will be copyedited, designed, typeset and proofread like any other Pan Macmillan novel. It will be sold by our very enthusiastic sales team, distributed by our formidable distribution network, and publicised by our tireless publicist. It may sell thousands of copies. It may not.

★ ★ ★

As I write, MNW is approaching its first anniversary. In the twelve months since April 2006, several of our titles have reprinted repeatedly and sold thousands of copies; a number of foreign rights deals have been struck, including a major two-book deal with a German publisher; rights have also been sold in Canada, Turkey and Russia. Jonathan Drapes's *Never Admit to Beige* was selected as BBC Five Live's Book of the Month and became one of our bestsellers as a result.

2007 looks set to be an exciting year for Macmillan New Writing, not least because we start publishing follow-up novels from authors who made their debut with MNW. One of our main aims in creating MNW was to find brilliant new writers who, in due course, would find a long-term home with Pan Macmillan's mainstream imprints, and that is already beginning to happen: Pan has recently announced a three-book deal with Brian McGilloway, an author who made his debut with MNW.

Submissions continue to pour in from all around the world, and our list remains very eclectic: 2007 alone boasts a terrorist thriller, a comic murder mystery, a literary saga, an American family drama, a police procedural and a historical novel set in Victorian Preston.

As for preying on 'impressionable young authors' – ask Brian Martin.The author of the critically acclaimed literary thriller *North* (published by MNW in 2006) describes himself as 'rivaling Mary Wesley' – in that he published his first novel at the age of sixty-eight.

Will Atkins is Commissioning Editor of Macmillan New Writing.

[1] *Nicholas Clee, 'Dividing the Spoils', The Bookseller, 14 July 2006.*

Further reading: Transparent Imprint *by Michael Barnard, Macmillan, 2006 (ISBN: 978-1405092425)*

The Making of an Author

Published for the first time under the Macmillan New Writing imprint, Ted Townsend tells Simon Tait how he made the grade

It was 19 May 2005 when Ted Townsend's wife called to him to listen to BBC Radio 4's *Open Book* on which Mariella Frostrup was talking to Mike Barnard, deviser of the Macmillan New Writing scheme.

Forty minutes later he had read the scheme's website, created the requisite pack and sent off the manuscript of his historical novel *In the Shadow of Lady Jane*.

And with the attention to detail that is the hallmark of his previous career, he tells what happened next: 'My manuscript was accepted on June 2nd that year, and published on May 5th the following year; and at sixty-four I was officially an author,' thereby putting the lie to the myth that publishers are not interested in older new authors. 'I think it depends on what you write, and I made a point of my age when I submitted the manuscript,' he says. 'It made no difference to Mike, and I think there's another twenty years of writing in me.'

His second novel, *Daughters of the Doge*, was published by Macmillan New Writing (MNW) in May 2007, he has completed his third, *Raphael's Secret*, and when we spoke it was being edited and he was half-way through his fourth. He writes under the name of Edward Charles.

Ted is now a full-time author, having finally retired from his career in December 2006, a career that could hardly have been more different from his new one. He was a finance director.

'I'd always wanted to be creative – I paint a bit, though not as well as I write – but after my first degree at Aberystwyth I was advised to get my PhD in finance and make my career, which I did,' he says.

He taught business studies, became a finance director in media businesses, a group development director in moneybroking, a chief executive, and a management consultant who project-managed dealing rooms around the world, including in New York's World Trade Center.

He had written all his life – academic finance books and magazine articles on economic subjects as well as numerous reports – and considered himself a man of the written word if not yet a man of letters. 'I've always believed I have a responsibility to the reader to be as accurate as I can, and not misleading,' he says.

Ten years ago he had attempted a book with a storyline from his professional life, a thriller about money-laundering, but it was 'lousy', and it was not until he had semi-retired and moved with his wife to Devon that he stumbled on the genre that was to bring him success.

Working part-time as a manager for a medical practice, he used some spare time to look at some old houses in the area. One, Shute House in east Devon (now a National Trust property called Shute Barton), with a mysterious gap in its history, was allegedly a home of the family of Lady Jane Grey, 'The Nine Days Queen' who was executed in 1554 by Mary I. There is an unchronicled interlude in 1551 when Lady Jane might have visited there.

'It was fascinating, that here was a gap in the knowledge of Jane's life, and I thought there might be a story to write.'

It was June 2000 when he took on Lady Jane as a 'what if' project and in November 2002 had decided there was a novel in it. Armed with a growing pile of reference books which included four complete biographies of Lady Jane and two of Edward VI, within eighteen months the experiment had become a book.

The secret, according to Ted, is that he sticks as closely as he can to historical fact, making a 'warp and weft' with real places and actual people and a precise timeline, to 'create a scaffold, as Will Atkins says'.

But his first draft wasn't good enough, and after consultation with his closest advisers – his wife and two daughters – he rewrote it in another four months, changing it from a third-person to a first-person narrative.

Then his book went on the familiar tour of agents. Over the next few months it went to half a dozen, with sometimes encouraging remarks but no acceptances. Then along came Macmillan New Writing, and the hardback had a reprint after its initial run of 500 and has now sold more than 2000. The paperback version was published in August 2007.

The second book, *Daughters of the Doge*, shifts the scene from England to Venice and employs the same formula of as much historical fact as possible interwoven with a credible fictional storyline, with only a brief visit to the city to help but meticulously researched though maps, guides, biographies, and often using Google. 'The Internet is a godsend for someone like me, but I'm also very good at reading maps,' he adds.

He will never make the kind of living he did in his previous career, but once the sparkle of becoming a published novelist for the first time has worn off, is the deal a fair one? There are fewer better qualified than Dr Townsend to judge.

'I've been very impressed with the way Mike worked it out – a new business model, I would say. He has kept expense to a minimum without making it cheap, and he's been very cost-effective.'

The scheme offers a generous royalty, but claims a half share of any rights revenue that may come. Is that fair?

'Absolutely. If I was to take part in *Dragons' Den* [the reality television show in which a panel of successful entrepreneurs are invited to invest in new ventures], I couldn't be interested in anyone who wanted less than 45 per cent of equity, and this shows that Macmillan are committed.'

He says he wanted three things from the arrangement: for the first book to go into paperback, for there to be a second one accepted, and to become part of the Macmillan family with the support of the experience and expertise 'where I could do my part in the exercise', and all of them have happened.

'I wrote the first book for my children, so I could talk to them through the books, and the test of whether it was worthwhile was to get it published.

'I always wanted to be creative, and I had to go off and do other things to make a living. But what MNW has done is to give me back my youth, because I can now do what I wanted to do when I was twenty, and be the real me.'

Irish Publishers

International Reply Coupons (IRCs) For return postage, IRCs are required (*not* UK postage stamps). These are available from post offices: letters, 60 pence; mss according to weight. For current postal rates from the Republic of Ireland to the UK go to www.letterpost.ie and click on 'Letterpost Services'.

An Gúm
27 Sr. Fhreidric Thuaidh, Baile Átha Cliath 1
☎00 353 1 889 2800 Fax 00 353 1 873 1140
✉ angum@forasnagaeilge.ie
www.gaeilge.ie
Senior Editor *Seosamh Ó Murchú*
Editors *Máire Nic Mheanman*
Founded 1926. Formerly the Irish language publications branch of the Department of Education and Science. Has now become part of the North/South Language Body, Foras na Gaeilge. Publishes educational, children's, young adult, music, lexicography and general. Little adult fiction or poetry. About 50 titles a year. Unsolicited mss, synopses and ideas for books welcome. Also welcomes reading copies of first and second level school textbooks with a view to translating them into the Irish language.
ROYALTIES annually.

Anvil Books
45 Palmerston Road, Dublin 6
☎00 353 1 497 3628
Managing Director *Rena Dardis*
Founded 1964 with emphasis on Irish history and biography. IMPRINT **The Children's Press**. Publishes Irish history, biography (particularly 1916–22), folklore and children's fiction. No adult fiction, poetry, fantasy, short stories or full-colour books for children. About 4 titles a year. 'Because of promotional requirements, only books by Irish-based authors considered and only books of Irish interest.' Send synopsis only with IRCs (no UK stamps); unsolicited mss not returned.
ROYALTIES annually.

Ashfield Press
30 Linden Grove, Blackrock, Co. Dublin
☎00 353 1 288 9808
✉ susanwaine@ashfieldpress.com
Directors *Susan Waine, John Davey, Gerry O'Connor*
Publishes Irish-interest non-fiction books. TITLES *Lady Icarus; The Weather is a Good Storyteller; Secret Sights II.*
Unsolicited mss and synopses welcome. ASSOCIATE COMPANY Ashfield Press Publishing Services.
ROYALTIES twice-yearly.

Atrium
See **Cork University Press**

Attic Press
See **Cork University Press**

Blackhall Publishing Ltd
33 Carysfort Avenue, Blackrock, Co. Dublin
☎00 353 1 278 5090 Fax 00 353 1 278 4446
✉ info@blackhallpublishing.com
www.blackhallpublishing.com
Managing Director *Gerard O'Connor*
Commissioning Editor *Elizabeth Brennan*
Publishes business, management, law and life issues. Main subject areas include accounting, finance, management, HRM and law books aimed at both students and professionals in the industry. Also provides legal publishing sevices including Statute Law Revision, Law Reporting, Legislative Drafting and Subscription Services. 15 titles a year. Unsolicited mss and synopses welcome.
ROYALTIES annually.

Bradshaw Books
Tigh Filí, Cork Arts Theatre, Carroll's Quay, Cork
☎00 353 21 450 9274
✉ info@tighfili.com
www.tighfili.com
Managing Director *Maire Bradshaw*
Project Manager *Leslie Ryan*
Founded 1985. Publishes poetry, women's issues, children's books. Organisers of the annual Cork Literary Review poetry manuscript competition. SERIES *Cork Literary Review*.
ROYALTIES not generally paid.

Brandon/
Mount Eagle Publications
Dingle, Co. Kerry
☎00 353 66 915 1463 Fax 00 353 66 915 1234
www.brandonbooks.com

Publisher *Steve MacDonogh*
Approx. Annual Turnover €500,000

Founded in 1997. Publishes Irish fiction, biography, memoirs and other non-fiction. About 15 titles a year. Not seeking unsolicited mss.

Brookside
See **New Island**

Edmund Burke Publisher
Cloonagashel, 27 Priory Drive, Blackrock, Co. Dublin
☎00 353 1 288 2159 Fax 00 353 1 283 4080
✉ deburca@indigo.ie
www.deburcararebooks.com

Managing Director *Eamonn De Búrca*
Publications Manager *Regina De Búrca-McAuley*
Approx. Annual Turnover €320,000

Small family-run business publishing historical and topographical and fine limited-edition books relating to Ireland. TITLES *The Great Book of Irish Genealogies*, 5 vols.; *The Annals of the Four Masters*, 7 vols; *Flowers of Mayo* (illus. Wendy Walsh); *O'Curry's Manners and Customs of the Ancient Irish*; *Joyce's Irish Names of Places*. Unsolicited mss welcome. No synopses or ideas.
ROYALTIES annually.

The Children's Press
See **Anvil Books**

Church of Ireland Publishing
Church of Ireland House, Church Avenue, Rathmines, Dublin 6
☎00 353 1 492 3979 Fax 00 353 1 492 4770
✉ susan.hood@rcbdub.org
www.cip.ireland.anglican.org

Owner *Representative Church Body of the Church of Ireland*
Chairman *Dr Kenneth Milne*
Publications Officer *Dr Susan Hood*

Founded 2004. Publishes official publications of the Church of Ireland: theological, doctrinal, historical and administrative, and facilitates publication for other church-related bodies. 3 titles in 2006. No unsolicited material.

Cló Iar-Chonnachta
Indreabhán, Connemara, Galway
☎00 353 91 593307 Fax 00 353 91 593362

✉ cic@iol.ie
www.cic.ie

Chairman/Director *Micheál Ó Conghaile*
Approx. Annual Turnover €400,000

Founded 1985. Publishes fiction, poetry, plays, teenage fiction and children's, mostly in Irish, including translations. Also publishes cassettes of writers reading from their own works. TITLES *Ag Greadadh Bas sa Reilig/Clapping in the Cemetery* Louis de Paorp; *Keening and Other Old Irish Musics* Breandán Ó Madagáin; *Máire Mhic Ghiolla Íosa: Beathaisnéis* Ray Mac Mánais; *Fardoras* Michael Daviett. 20 titles in 2006.
ROYALTIES annually.

The Collins Press
West Link Park, Doughcloyne, Wilton, Cork
☎00 353 21 434 7717
✉ enquiries@collinspress.ie
www.collinspress.ie

Managing Director *Con Collins*
Approx. Annual Turnover €750,000

Founded 1989. Publishes general non-fiction, Irish interest and children's books. 26 TITLES in 2006. No unsolicited mss; synopses and ideas welcome; approach by e-mail. See website for submission guidelines. No academic, technical, professional, fiction, poetry, literary criticism or short stories.

The Columba Press
55A Spruce Avenue, Stillorgan Industrial Park, Blackrock, Co. Dublin
☎00 353 1 294 2556 Fax 00 353 1 294 2564
✉ sean@columba.ie (editorial) *or*
info@columba.ie (general)
www.columba.ie

Chairman *Neil Kluepfel*
Managing Director *Seán O'Boyle*
Approx. Annual Turnover €1.02 million

Founded 1985. Small company committed to growth. Publishes religious and counselling titles. TITLES *Prism of Love* Donal O'Leary; *That Could Never Be* Kevin Dalton. IMPRINT **Currach Press** (see entry). 41 titles in 2006. Backlist of 250 titles. Unsolicited ideas and synopses rather than full mss preferred.
ROYALTIES twice-yearly.

Cork University Press
Youngline Industrial Estate, Pouladuff Road, Togher, Cork
☎00 353 21 490 2980 Fax 00 353 21 431 5329
✉ corkuniversitypress@ucc.ie
www.corkuniversitypress.com

Owner *University College Cork*
Publications Director *Mike Collins*
Editor *Sophie Watson*

Founded 1925. Relaunched in 1992, the Press publishes academic and some trade titles. TITLES *Staging the Easter Rising: 1916 as Theatre*; *Foreign Affections: Ireland and the Global Question*; *The Irish Red Setter*; *The Barrytown Trilogy*. Also a biannual journal, *The Irish Review*, an interdisciplinary cultural review. No fiction. IMPRINTS **Attic Press**; **Atrium**. 15 titles in 2007. Unsolicited synopses and ideas welcome for textbooks, academic monographs, belles lettres, illustrated histories and journals.
    ROYALTIES annually.

Currach Press
55A Spruce Avenue, Stillorgan Industrial Park, Blackrock, Co. Dublin
☎00 353 1 294 2556 Fax 00 353 1 294 2564
✉ jo@currach.ie
www.currach.ie

Publisher *Jo O'Donoghue*

Founded 2002. An imprint of **The Columba Press**. Publishes non-fiction titles of Irish interest, including politics, history, biography, sport, music and criticism. TITLES *A Memoir* Terry de Valera; *The Harcourt Street Line* Brian Mac Aongusa; *Short Hands, Long Pockets* Eddie Hobbs. Unsolicited ideas welcome; synopses rather than full mss preferred.

A. & A. Farmar Ltd
78 Ranelagh Village, Dublin 6
☎00 353 1 496 3625 Fax 00 353 1 497 0107
✉ afarmar@iol.ie
www.aafarmar.ie

Managing Director *Anna Farmar*
Production Director *Tony Farmar*

Founded 1992. Publishes Irish social history, business, food and wine. About 10 titles a year. No unsolicited mss. Synopses and ideas welcome; approach by letter or e-mail in the first instance.

Flyleaf Press
4 Spencer Villas, Glenageary, Co. Dublin
☎00 353 1 284 5906
✉ books@flyleaf.ie
www.flyleaf.ie

Managing Director *Dr James Ryan*
Sales & Administration *Brian Smith*

Founded 1981. Concentrates on family history/genealogy. No fiction. TITLES *Irish Records*; *Longford and its People*; *Tracing Your Kerry Ancestors*;

Tracing Your Limerick Ancestors. Unsolicited mss, synopses and ideas for books welcome.
    ROYALTIES twice-yearly.

Four Courts Press Ltd
7 Malpas Street, Dublin 8
☎00 353 1 453 4668 Fax 00 353 1 453 4672
✉ info@four-courts-press.ie
www.four-courts-press.ie

Chairman/Managing Director *Michael Adams*
Director *Martin Healy*

Founded 1972. Publishes mainly scholarly books in the humanities. About 65 titles a year. Synopses and ideas for books welcome.
    ROYALTIES annually.

The Gallery Press
Loughcrew, Oldcastle, Co. Meath
☎00 353 49 854 1779 Fax 00 353 49 854 1779
✉ gallery@indigo.ie
www.gallerypress.com

Managing Director *Peter Fallon*

Founded 1970. Publishes Irish poetry and drama. 9 titles in 2006. Currently, only interested in work from Irish poets and dramatists (plays must have had professional production). Unsolicited mss welcome but prefers to send submission notes to potential writers in the first instance.
    ROYALTIES paid.

Gill & Macmillan
10 Hume Avenue, Park West, Dublin 12
☎00 353 1 500 9500 Fax 00 353 1 500 9599
www.gillmacmillan.ie

Chairman *M.H. Gill*
Managing Director *Dermot O'Dwyer*
Approx. Annual Turnover €12 million

Founded 1968 when M.H. Gill & Son Ltd and Macmillan Ltd formed a jointly owned publishing company. Publishes biography/autobiography, history, current affairs, literary criticism (all mainly of Irish interest), guidebooks and cookery. Also educational textbooks for secondary and tertiary levels. Contacts: *Hubert Mahony* (educational), *Marion O'Brien* (college), *Fergal Tobin* (general). About 80 titles a year. Unsolicited synopses and ideas welcome.
    ROYALTIES subject to contract.

Hachette Livre Ireland
8 Castlecourt Centre, Castleknock, Dublin 15
☎00 353 1 824 6288 Fax 00 353 1 824 6289
✉ info@hhireland.ie
www.hhireland.ie

Managing Director *Breda Purdue*

Publisher *Ciara Considine*
Senior Commissioning Editor *Claire Rourke*
Editorial Manager *Ciara Doorley*
Founded 2002. Irish division of **Hachette Livre UK**. Publishes general fiction and non-fiction: memoirs, biography, sport, politics, current affairs, humour, food and drink. 25 titles in 2006. Consult the website for submission guidelines.
ROYALTIES twice-yearly.

Institute of Public Administration
57–61 Lansdowne Road, Dublin 4
☎00 353 1 240 3600 Fax 00 353 1 269 8644
✉ sales@ipa.ie
www.ipa.ie
Director-General *John Cullen*
Publisher *Eileen Kelly*
Approx. Annual Turnover €1.3 million

Founded in 1957 by a group of public servants, the Institute of Public Administration is the Irish public sector management development agency. The publishing arm of the organisation is one of its major activities. Publishes academic and professional books and periodicals: history, law, politics, economics and Irish public administration for students and practitioners. TITLES *Local Government in Ireland; E-Government and the Decentralisation of Service Delivery; Governance and Policy in Ireland; Crime, Punishment and the Search for Order in Ireland; Accountability in Irish Politics; Housing Contemporary Ireland: Policy, Society and Shelter*. About 10 titles a year. No unsolicited mss; synopses and ideas welcome. No fiction or children's publishing.
ROYALTIES annually.

Irish Academic Press Ltd
44 Northumberland Road, Ballsbridge, Dublin 4
☎00 353 1 668 8244 Fax 00 353 1 660 1610
✉ info@iap.ie
www.iap.ie
Chairman *Frank Cass* (London)
Dublin Office *Rachel Milotte*

Founded 1974. Publishes academic monographs and humanities. Unsolicited mss, synopses and ideas welcome.
ROYALTIES annually.

The Liffey Press Ltd
Ashbrook House, 10 Main Street, Raheny, Dublin 5
☎00 353 1 851 1458 Fax 00 353 1 851 1459
✉ info@theliffeypress.com
www.theliffeypress.com

Managing Director/Publisher *David Givens*
Founded 2001. Publishes general interest, Irish-focused non-fiction. 18 titles in 2006. Synopses, ideas and proposals with sample chapters welcome; approach by letter or e-mail in the first instance. No fiction, children's or books not of interest to Irish readers.
ROYALTIES twice-yearly.

The Lilliput Press
62–63 Sitric Road, Arbour Hill, Dublin 7
☎00 353 1 671 1647 Fax 00 353 1 671 1233
✉ info@lilliputpress.ie
www.lilliputpress.ie
Chair *Kathy Gilfillan*
Managing Director *Antony Farrell*
Approx. Annual Turnover €300,000+

Founded 1984. Publishes non-fiction: literature, history, autobiography and biography, ecology, essays; criticism; fiction and poetry. TITLES *Lark's Eggs; Wordgloss; The Bible War in Ireland; The Songman; Belios; Watching the Door* Kevin Myers; *The Dublin Edition of Ulysses* James Joyce. About 18 titles a year. Unsolicited mss, synopses and ideas welcome. No children's or sport titles.
ROYALTIES annually.

Marino Books
See **Mercier Press Ltd**

Maverick House Publishers
Main Street, Dunshaughlin, Co. Meath
☎00 353 1 824 0077 Fax 00 353 1 824 1638
✉ info@maverickhouse.com
www.maverickhouse.com
Managing Director *Jean Harrington*

Founded 2001. Publishes biography and auto-biography, current affairs, non-fiction (mainly of Irish interest), politics, sport. TITLES *Welcome to Hell: One Man's Fight for Life Inside the Bangkok Hilton* Colin Martin; *The General and I: The Untold Story of Martin Cahill's Hotdog Wars* Wolfgang Eulitz; *The Cup: How the 2006 Ryder Cup was Won* Philip Reid. Unsolicited material welcome; send by post. No fiction, children's books or poetry.
ROYALTIES twice-yearly.

Mercier Press Ltd
Douglas Village, Cork
☎00 353 21 489 9858 Fax 00 353 21 489 9887
✉ info@mercierpress.ie
www.mercierpress.ie
Chairman *John Spillaner*
Managing Director *Clodagh Feehan*

Founded 1944. One of Ireland's largest publishers with a list of approx 250 Irish interest titles. IMPRINTS **Mercier Press**; **Marino Books** Editorial Director *Mary Feehan* Children's, politics, history, folklore, biography, mind, body and spirit, current affairs, women's interest. TITLES *The Course of Irish History*; all of John B. Keane's works; *Beyond Prozac*; *It's a Long Way from Penny Apples*; *Ireland's Master Storyteller*. Unsolicited synopses and ideas welcome.
ROYALTIES annually.

Merlin Publishing
Newmarket Hall, Cork Street, Dublin 8
☎00 353 1 453 5866 Fax 00 353 1 453 5930
www.merlinwolfhound.com
Managing Director *Chenile Keogh*
Managing Editor *Aoife Barrett*
Founded 2000. Member of **Clé**. Publishes true crime, film, music, art, biography, general non-fiction, history and gift books. IMPRINT **Wolfhound Press** Founded 1974. Non-fiction. TITLES *Famine*; *Eyewitness Bloody Sunday*; *Father Browne's Titanic Album*. About 15 titles a year. Sample chapters of unsolicited mss (with synopses and s.a.e.) welcome by e-mail (aoife@merlin.ie). See Merlin website for submission guidelines and proposal form.

Mount Eagle
See **Brandon/Mount Eagle Publicaions**

National Library of Ireland
Kildare Street, Dublin 2
☎00 353 1 603 0200 Fax 00 353 1 676 6690
✉ info@nli.ie
www.nli.ie
Founded 1877. Publishes books and booklets based on the library's collections; folders of historical documents; academic and specialist books; reproduction folders and CD-ROMs. TITLES *Ulysses Unbound: A Reader's Companion to James Joyce's Ulysses* Terence Killeen; *Cooper's Ireland: Drawings and Notes from an Eighteenth Century Gentleman* Peter Harbison; *Into the Light: An Illustrated Guide to the Photographic Collections in the National Library of Ireland* Sarah Rouse; *Treasures from the National Library of Ireland* ed. Dr Noel Kissane. 1 title in 2006.

New Island
2 Brookside, Dundrum Road, Dundrum, Dublin 14
☎00 353 1 298 9937/298 3411
Fax 00 353 1 298 7912
✉ inka.hagen@newisland.ie
www.newisland.ie
Managing Director/Editorial Head *Edwin Higel*
Editorial Manager *Deirdre Nolan*
Founded 1990. Publishes fiction, Irish non-fiction, poetry and drama. Branching out into popular fiction and memoirs. IMPRINT **Brookside**. About 25 titles a year. Unsolicited mss, synopses and ideas welcome. Send three chapters and synopsis by post.
ROYALTIES twice-yearly

The O'Brien Press Ltd
12 Terenure Road East, Rathgar, Dublin 6
☎00 353 1 492 3333 Fax 00 353 1 492 2777
✉ books@obrien.ie
www.obrien.ie
Managing Director *Ivan O'Brien*
Publisher *Michael O'Brien*
Founded 1974. Publishes business, true crime, biography, music, travel, sport, Celtic subjects, food and drink, history, humour, politics, reference. Children's publishing – mainly fiction for every age from tiny tots to teenage. Illustrated fiction SERIES *Solos* (3 years+); *Pandas* (5 years+); *Flyers* (6 years+); *Red Flag* (8 years+). Novels (10 years+): contemporary, historical, fantasy. Some non-fiction: mainly historical, and art and craft, resource books for teachers. No poetry, adult fiction or academic. Unsolicited mss (sample chapters only), synopses and ideas for books welcome. No e-mail submissions. Submissions will not be returned.
ROYALTIES annually.

Oak Tree Press
19 Rutland Street, Cork
☎00 353 21 431 3855 Fax 00 353 21 431 3496
✉ info@oaktreepress.com
www.oaktreepress.com
Owners *Brian O'Kane, Rita O'Kane*
Managing Director *Brian O'Kane*
Founded 1991. Specialist publisher of business and professional books with a focus on small business start-up and development. 5 titles in 2006. Unsolicited mss and synopses welcome; send to the managing director, at the address above.
ROYALTIES annually.

On Stream Publications Ltd
Currabaha, Cloghroe, Co. Cork
☎00 353 21 438 5798
✉ info@onstream.ie
www.onstream.ie
Chairman/Managing Director *Roz Crowley*

Founded 1992. Formerly Forum Publications. Publishes academic, cookery, wine, general health and fitness, local history, railways, photography and practical guides. TITLES *The Health Squad Guide to Health and Fitness*; *A Kingdom of Wine: A Celebration of Ireland's Winegeese*; *At Home in Renvyle*. About 3 titles a year. Synopses and ideas welcome. No children's books.

ROYALTIES annually.

Penguin Ireland

25 St Stephen's Green, Dublin 2
☎00 353 1 661 7695 Fax 00 353 1 661 7696
✉ info@penguin.ie
www.penguin.ie

Managing Director *Michael McLoughlin*

Founded 2002. Part of the **Penguin Group UK**. DIVISIONS **Commercial fiction/non-fiction** Senior Editor *Patricia Deevy* TITLES *From Here to Maternity* Sinéad Moriaty; *Should Have Got Off at Sydney Parade* Ross O'Carroll Kelly; *This Man and Me* Alison Jameson; *HellFire* Mia Gallagher. **Literary fiction/non-fiction** Brendan Barrington TITLES *Connemara: Listening to the Wind* Tim Robinson; *In the Dark Room* Brian Dillon; *Notes from a Turkish Whorehouse* Philip Ó Ceallaigh. 24 titles in 2006. Unsolicited mss, synopses and ideas for books welcome; send by post.

ROYALTIES twice-yearly.

Poolbeg Press Ltd

123 Grange Hill, Baldoyle, Dublin 13
☎00 353 1 832 1477 Fax 00 353 1 832 1430
✉ poolbeg@poolbeg.com
www.poolbeg.com

Managing Director *Kieran Devlin*
Publisher *Paula Campbell*

Founded 1976 to publish the Irish short story and has since diversified to include all areas of fiction (literary and popular), children's fiction and non-fiction, and adult non-fiction: history, biography and topics of public interest. AUTHORS discovered and first published by Poolbeg include Maeve Binchy, Marian Keyes, Sheila O'Flanagan, Cathy Kelly and Patricia Scanlan. 'Our slogan is Poolbeg.com – The *Irish* for Bestsellers!' IMPRINTS **Poolbeg** (paperback and hardback); **Poolbeg For Children**. About 40 titles a year. Unsolicited mss, synopses and ideas welcome (mss preferred). No drama.

ROYALTIES twice-yearly.

Royal Dublin Society

Science Section, Ballsbridge, Dublin 4
☎00 353 1 240 7217 Fax 00 353 1 660 4014
✉ science@rds.ie
www.rds.ie/science

Development Executive, Science & Technology *Dr Claire Mulhall*

Founded 1731 for the promotion of agriculture, science and the arts, and throughout its history has published books and journals towards this end. Publishes conference proceedings, biology and the history of Irish science. TITLES *Agricultural Development for the 21st Century*; *The Right Trees in the Right Places*; *Agriculture & the Environment*; *Water of Life*; *Science, Technology & Realism*; *Science Centres for Ireland*; *Blueprint for a National Irish Science Centre*; *Science Education in Crisis*; *Science in the Service of the Fishing Industry*; occasional papers in *Irish Science & Technology* series.

ROYALTIES not generally paid.

Royal Irish Academy

19 Dawson Street, Dublin 2
☎00 353 1 676 2570 Fax 00 353 1 676 2346
✉ publications@ria.ie
www.ria.ie/publications

Executive Secretary *Patrick Buckley*
Managing Editor *Ruth Hegarty*

Founded in 1785, the Academy has been publishing since 1787. Core publications are journals but more books published in last 15 years. Publishes academic, Irish interest and Irish language. About 7 titles a year. Welcomes mss, synopses and ideas of an academic standard, but currently encourages publications which will popularise some aspect of the sciences and humanities. Address correspondence to the managing editor of publications.

Swordpoint Intercontinental Limited

'Solas Tobann', Ballyhillion, Malin Head, Co. Donegal
☎00 353 74 937 0278 Fax 00 353 1 6849930
✉ jgreenleaf@swordpoint.com
www.swordpoint.com

Chairman/Managing Director *Joseph A. Greenleaf*

Swordpoint was established in 1995 as a media company and branched out into books in 2003. Publishes fiction, children's, non-fiction, historical, travel, technical, Irish, poetry, plays, business, management, law, biography, fantasy, teenage fiction. Publication on cassettes and CDs as well as e-books. 17 titles in 2007. Unsolicited mss, synopses and ideas welcome by post with return postage. Enclosure of Microsoft Word CD in addition to mss is encouraged, but not required. E-mail submissions encouraged.

ROYALTIES twice-yearly.

Tír Eolas

Newtownlynch, Doorus, Kinvara, Co. Galway
☎00 353 91 637452 Fax 00 353 91 637452
✉ info@tireolas.com
www.tireolas.com

Publisher/Managing Director *Anne Korff*

Founded 1987. Publishes books and guides on ecology, archaeology, folklore and culture. TITLES *The Book of the Burren; The Shores of Connemara; Not a Word of a Lie; The Book of Aran; Kinvara, A Seaport Town on Galway Bay; A Burren Journal; Alive, Alive-O, The Shellfish and Shellfisheries of Ireland.* Unsolicited mss, synopses and ideas for books welcome. No specialist scientific and technical, fiction, plays, school textbooks or philosophy.

ROYALTIES annually.

Town House Dublin

Mountpleasant Business Centre, Mountpleasant Avenue, Ranelagh, Dublin 6
☎00 353 1 497 2399 Fax 00 353 1 497 0927
✉ books@townhouse.ie
www.townhouse.ie

Managing Director *Treasa Coady*

Irish interest trade non-fiction including, art, archaeology, biography, spirituality, sport, environment, human interest, anthologies etc. About 5 titles a year. Unsolicited mss, synopses and ideas welcome. No children's books.

ROYALTIES twice-yearly.

University College Dublin Press

Newman House, 86 St Stephen's Green,
Dublin 2
☎00 353 1 716 7397 Fax 00 353 1 716 7211
✉ ucdpress@ucd.ie
www.ucdpress.ie

Executive Editor *Barbara Mennell*

Founded 1995. Academic publisher. 15 titles in 2006. Unsolicited mss, synopses and ideas welcome by post. Approach in writing. No non-academic, journals, poetry, novels or books based on academic conferences.

ROYALTIES annually.

Veritas Publications

7–8 Lower Abbey Street, Dublin 1
☎00 353 1 878 8177 Fax 00 353 1 878 6507
✉ publications@veritas.ie
www.veritas.ie

Director *Maura Hyland*
Managing Editor *Ruth Garvey*

Founded 1969 to supply religious textbooks to schools and later introduced a wide-ranging general list. Part of the Catholic Communications Institute. Publishes books on religious, ethical, moral, societal and social issues. 30 titles a year. Unsolicited mss, synopses and ideas for books welcome.

ROYALTIES annually.

Wolfhound Press

See **Merlin Publishing**

Irish Literary Agents

The Book Bureau Literary Agency

7 Duncairn Avenue, Bray, Co. Wicklow
☎00 353 1 276 4996 Fax 00 353 1 276 4834
✉ thebookbureau@oceanfree.net

Contact *Ger Nichol*

Handles general and literary fiction. Special interest in women's fiction, crime and thrillers and some non-fiction. COMMISSION Home 10%; Overseas 20%. Works with foreign associates. Will suggest revision. Send preliminary letter, synopsis and first three chapters; return postage essential (IRCs only from UK and abroad). No reading fee.

Font International Literary Agency

Hollyville House, Hollybrook Road, Clontarf, Dublin 3
☎00 353 1 853 2356
✉ info@fontlitagency.com

Contacts *Aine McCarthy, Ita O'Driscoll*

Founded 2003. Handles book-length adult fiction and non-fiction from previously published writers (no children's, drama, sci-fi, erotic, technical or poetry). COMMISSION 15–20%; Translation 20–25%. ASSOCIATE The Marsh Agency, London for translation rights. No unsolicited mss. 'As an initial contact, please query our interest in your property either by e-mail or post.' Include details of writing and other media experience. S.a.e. required. 'We regret that we cannot discuss queries over the phone.' No reading fee.

Marianne Gunn O'Connor Literary Agency

Morrison Chambers, Suite 17, 32 Nassau Street, Dublin 2
✉ mgoclitagency@eircom.net

Contact *Marianne Gunn O'Connor*

Founded 1996. Handles commercial and literary fiction, non-fiction: biography, health and children's fiction. CLIENTS include Patrick McCabe, Morag Prunty, Claire Kilroy, Julie Dam, Cecelia Ahern, Paddy McMahon, Chris Binchy, Anita Notaro, Mike McCormack, Noelle Harrison, Claudia Carroll, John Lynch. COMMISSION UK 15%; Overseas 20%; Film & TV 20%. Translation rights handled by Vicki Satlow Literary Agency, Milan. No unsolicited mss; send preliminary enquiry letter plus half-page synopsis per e-mail.

The Lisa Richards Agency

108 Upper Leeson Street, Dublin 4
☎00 353 1 637 5000 Fax 00 353 1 667 1256
✉ faith@lisarichards.ie
www.lisarichards.ie

Contact *Faith O'Grady*

Founded 1998. Handles fiction and general non-fiction. CLIENTS include Charlie Bird, June Considine, Denise Deegan, Gary Duggan, Christine Dwyer Hickey, Neil Fetherstonhaugh, Karen Gillece, Tara Heavey, Paul Howard (Ross O'Carroll-Kelly), Arlene Hunt, Roisin Ingle, Alison Jameson, George Lee, Declan Lynch, Roisin Meaney, Pauline McLynn, Anna McPartlin, Sarah O'Brien (Helena Close and Trisha Rainsford), Marie O'Connor, Damien Owens, Kevin Rafter, Ray Scannell, Eirin Thompson. COMMISSION Home 10%; UK 15%; US & Translation 20%; Film & TV 15%. OVERSEAS ASSOCIATE The Marsh Agency for translation rights. Approach with proposal and sample chapter for non-fiction, and 3–4 chapters and synopsis for fiction (s.a.e. essential). No reading fee.

Jonathan Williams Literary Agency

Rosney Mews, Upper Glenageary Road, Glenageary, Co. Dublin
☎00 353 1 280 3482 Fax 00 353 1 280 3482

Contact *Jonathan Williams*

Founded 1980. Handles general trade books: fiction, auto/biography, travel, politics, history, music, literature and criticism, gardening, cookery, sport and leisure, humour, reference, social questions, photography. Some poetry. No plays, science fiction, children's books, mind, body and spirit, computer books, theology, multimedia, motoring, aviation. COMMISSION Home 10%; US & Translation 20%. OVERSEAS ASSOCIATES Piergiorgio Nicolazzini Literary Agency, Italy; Lora Fountain & Associates Agency, France; Linda Kohn, International Literature Bureau, Holland and Germany; Antonia Kerrigan Literary Agency, Spain; Tuttle-Mori Agency Inc., Japan. No reading fee 'unless the author wants a very fast opinion'. Initial approach by phone or letter.

Audio Books

AudioBooksForFree.Com Limited

25 Green Lane, Amersham HP6 6AS
☎01494 431119
✉ToUs@AudioBooksForFree.Com
www.AudioBooksForFree.Com
www.DVDAudioBooks.com
www.MobileAudioBooks.com

Managing Director *Ruslan G. Fedorovsky*
CTO *Peter Morris*

Founded 2000. Publishes and sells MP3 and DVD audiobooks on and offline. Genres: fiction, adventure, thrillers, crime, science fiction, children's, non-fiction, etc. AUTHORS include Michael Hartland, James Herlihy, Jon Schiller, Patrick Walsh, Jules Verne, Dumas. 120 titles in 2006.

Pays 100% royalties to 'contributors' (audiobook publishers, famous narrators or famous authors) for individual audiobook downloads.

BBC Audiobooks Ltd

St James House, The Square, Lower Bristol Road, Bath BA2 3BH
☎01225 335336 Fax 01225 310771
✉ bbcaudiobooks@bbc.co.uk
www.bbcworldwide.com

Managing Director *Paul Dempsey*
Publishing Director *Jan Paterson*

BBC Audiobooks Ltd was established in 2003 with the integration of BBC Radio Collection, Cover to Cover and Chivers Audio Books. Since then it has become a leading trade and library publisher in the UK, publishing a wide range of entertainment on a variety of formats including CD, cassette, MP3-CD and downloads, podcasts, etc.

DIVISIONS

Trade Titles range from original books and full-cast radio dramas through to abridged readings and full, unabridged recordings. TITLES *War and Peace; The Odyssey; Captain Corelli's Mandolin;* the complete Sherlock Holmes canon. IMPRINTS **BBC Audio – Children's** From pre-school nursery rhymes to modern classics. TITLES *The Chronicles of Narnia; His Dark Materials* trilogy. **BBC Audio – Radio Collection** Comedy classics from TV and radio. TITLES *The Goons; Hancock's Half Hour; Fawlty Towers; The News Quiz; Just a Minute.* **BBC Audio** Contemporary comedy. TITLES *Little Britain; Have I Got News For You; The League of Gentlemen.* **BBC Audio – Lifestyle** A range of titles to help the listener improve or learn. TITLES include the *Glenn Harrold's Ultimate Guide to ...* series. **BBC Audio – Radio 4** TITLES *This Sceptred Isle; Letter from America; A Suitable Boy.* **Science Fiction & Fantasy** TITLES *The Hitchhiker's Guide to the Galaxy; Doctor Who; Journey into Space; The Lord of the Rings.* **Library** IMPRINTS **Chivers Audio Books; Chivers Children's Audio Books** Founded 1980. Publishes over 500 titles annually. Complete and unabridged books for adults and children are sold to libraries and to the public by direct mail through **The Audiobook Collection**. CDs and cassettes covering best-selling fiction and popular non-fiction.

Bloomsbury Publishing

See entry under *UK Publishers*

Chivers Audio Books/ Chivers Children's Audio Books

See **BBC Audiobooks Ltd**

Chrome Dreams

12 Seaforth Avenue, New Malden KT3 6JP
☎020 8715 9781 Fax 020 8241 1426
✉ mail@chromedreams.co.uk
www.chromedreams.co.uk

Managing Director *Rob Johnstone*

A small record company and publisher founded 1998 to produce audio-biographies of current rock and pop artists and legendary performers on CD and, more recently, books on the same subjects. Ideas for biographies welcome.

Corgi Audio

Transworld Publishers, A division of the Random House Group Ltd, 61–63 Uxbridge Road, London W5 5SA
☎020 8579 2652
www.booksattransworldpublishers.co.uk

Managing Director *Larry Finlay*
Publisher *Bill Scott-Kerr*

Publishes fiction, autobiography and humour.

TITLES *Discworld Series* Terry Pratchett; *Down Under* Bill Bryson and other travel writing; *High Society*, *Past Mortem* and *Chart Throb* Ben Elton.

CSA Word

6a Archway Mews, 241a Putney Bridge Road, London SW15 2PE
☎020 8871 0220 Fax 020 8877 0712
✉ info@csaword.co.uk
www.csaword.co.uk

Managing Director *Clive Stanhope*
Audio Director *Victoria Williams*

Founded 1989. Publishes fiction, children's, short stories, poetry, travel, biographies, classics. Over 100 titles to-date on cassette and CD. Tends to favour quality/classic/nostalgic/timeless literature. TITLES *Carry on Jeeves* P.G. Wodehouse; *Alfie* Bill Naughton; *Decline and Fall* and *Brideshead Revisited* Evelyn Waugh; *Just William – Home for the Holidays* Richmal Crompton; *Lady Chatterley's Lover* D.H. Lawrence; *The Statement* Brian Moore; *Billy Bunter's Banknote* Frank Richards; *The Ragged Trousered Philanthropists* Robert Tressell; *Cautionary Verses* Hilaire Belloc.

CYP

The Fairway, Bush Fair, Harlow CM18 6LY
☎01279 444707 Fax 01279 445570
✉ enquiries@cyp.co.uk
www.kidsmusic.co.uk

Operations Director *Mike Kitson*

Founded 1978. Publishes music DVDs and audiobooks for young children; educational, entertainment, licensed characters (*Mr Men*; *Little Miss*; *Wheels On the Bus*). TV music and soundtrack production.

57 Productions

See entry under **Organisations of Interest to Poets**

Hachette Audio

Brettenham House, Lancaster Place, London WC2E 7EN
☎020 7911 8044 Fax 020 7911 8100
✉ sarah.shrubb@littlebrown.co.uk
www.littlebrown.co.uk

Publisher *Ursula Mackenzie*
Commissioning Editor *Sarah Shrubb*

Launched in 2003 with titles from bestselling authors Alexander McCall Smith, Mitch Albom and David Sedaris. Publishes fiction, humour, poetry and non-fiction. TITLES include new fiction from authors such as Patricia Cornwell and Mark Billingham, non-fiction such as

Sharon Osbourne's bestselling autobiography *Extreme*, and classics such as Maya Angelou's *I Know Why The Caged Bird Sings* and Michael Frayn's *Spies*. 92 titles in 2006.

HarperCollins AudioBooks

77–85 Fulham Palace Road, London W6 8JB
☎020 8741 7070 Fax 020 8307 4818
www.harpercollins.co.uk

Group Digital Publisher *Clive Malcher*
Senior Editor *Nicola Townsend*

The HarperCollins audio list was launched in 1990. Publishes a wide range including popular and classic fiction, non-fiction, children's, Shakespeare, poetry and self help (Thorsons' imprint) on cassette, CD and digital download. AUTHORS Agatha Christie, Ian McEwan, C.S. Lewis, Roald Dahl, Dr Seuss, Lemony Snicket, J.R.R. Tolkien, Bernard Cornwell, Enid Blyton, Nick Butterworth, Judith Kerr.

Hodder & Stoughton Audiobooks

338 Euston Road, London NW1 3BH
☎020 7873 6000 Fax 020 7873 6194
✉ rupert.lancaster@hodder.co.uk
www.madaboutbooks.co.uk

Publisher *Rupert Lancaster*

Launched in 1994 with the aim of publishing outstanding authors from within the Hodder group and commissioning independent audio titles. Publishes fiction and non-fiction. AUTHORS include Stephen King, John LeCarré, Alan Titchmarsh, Elizabeth George, Joanne Harris, Haruki Murakami, Jodi Picoult, Pam Ayres, David Mitchell, Linda Smith, John Humphries, Al Murray, Dickie Bird, Peter Robinson and Charles Frazier.

Ladybird Audio

See **Dorling Kindersley Ltd** under **UK Publishers**

Laughing Stock Productions

81 Charlotte Street, London W1T 4PP
☎020 7637 7943 Fax 020 7436 1666

Managing Director *Michael O'Brien*

Founded 1991. Issues a wide range of comedy cassettes/CDs from family humour to alternative comedy. TITLES *Red Dwarf*; *Shirley Valentine* (read by Willy Russell); *Rory Bremner*; *Peter Cook Anthology*; *Sean Hughes*; *John Bird and John Fortune*; *Eddie Izzard*. 12–16 titles a year.

Macmillan Digital Audio

20 New Wharf Road, London N1 9RR
☎020 7014 6040 Fax 020 7014 6141

✉ a.muirden@macmillan.co.uk
www.panmacmillan.co.uk
Owner *Macmillan Publishers Ltd*
Audio Publisher *Alison Muirden*
Founded 1995. Publishes adult fiction, non-fiction and autobiography, focusing mainly on lead book titles and releasing audio simultaneously with hard or paperback publication. Also publishes children's audio titles. Won Audio Publisher of the Year at the 2003 Spoken Word Awards and has won many other Spoken Word Awards for individual audio titles in previous years About 40–60 titles a year. Submissions not accepted.

Naxos AudioBooks
40a High Street, Welwyn AL6 9EQ
☎01438 717808 Fax 01438 717809
✉ naxos_audiobooks@compuserve.com
www.naxosaudiobooks.com
Owner *HNH International, Hong Kong / Nicolas Soames*
Managing Director *Nicolas Soames*
Founded 1994. Part of Naxos, the classical budget CD company. Publisher of the Year in the 2001 Spoken Word Awards. Publishes classic and modern fiction, non-fiction, children's and junior classics, drama and poetry. TITLES *Ulysses* Joyce; *King Lear* Shakespeare; *History of the Musical* Fawkes; *Just So Stories* Kipling.

Oakhill Publishing Ltd
PO Box 3855, Bath BA1 3WW
☎01225 317209 Fax 01225 317209
✉ info@oakhillpublishing.com
Managing Director *Julian Batson*
Founded in 2005 by Julian Batson, formerly with Chivers Press (now part of BBC Audiobooks) to offer a wider selection of titles for the library market. Produces complete and unabridged audiobooks of popular fiction and non-fiction for adults and children. TITLES *The Question* Jane Asher; *Rapids* Tim Parks; *Daughters of Britannia* Katie Hickman; *The Dragon Detective Agency* Gareth Jones; *Century* Sarah Singleton. 99 titles in 2006. Ideas for cassettes/CDs from literary agents only.

Orion Audio Books (Division of the Orion Publishing Group Ltd)
Orion House, 5 Upper St Martin's Lane, London WC2H 9EA
☎020 7520 4425 Fax 020 7379 6518
✉ pandora.white@orionbooks.co.uk
www.orionbooks.co.uk

Publisher *Pandora White*
Orion Audio has released over 500 titles since it was founded in 1998. Publishes fiction, non-fiction, humour, autobiographies, children's, poetry, science, crime and thrillers. AUTHORS Maeve Binchy, Ian Rankin, Robert Crais, Michael Connelly, Francesca Simon (*Horrid Henry* series), Harlan Coben, Dan Brown, Sally Gardner, Michelle Paver and Erica James. In 2006 all Orion audio titles became available for digital download on www.audible.co.uk

Penguin Audiobooks
80 Strand, London WC2R 0RL
☎020 7010 3000 Fax 020 7010 6695
✉ audio@penguin.co.uk
www.penguin.co.uk
Head of Audio Publishing *Jeremy Ettinghausen*
Launched in November 1993 and has rapidly expanded since then to reflect the diversity of Penguin Books' list. Publishes mostly fiction, both classical and contemporary, non-fiction, autobiography and an increasing range of digital audiobooks as well as children's titles under the **Puffin Audiobooks** imprint. Contemporary AUTHORS include: Zadie Smith, Anne Fine, Eoin Colfer, John Mortimer, Roald Dahl, Sue Townsend, Nicci French, Gervase Phinn, Charlie Higson, Marina Lewycka, Jonathan Coe, Niall Fergusson, Claire Tomalin. About 30 titles a year.

Puffin Audiobooks
See **Penguin Audiobooks**

Quercus Audiobooks
See **Quercus Publishing** under *UK Publishers*

Random House Audio Books
20 Vauxhall Bridge Road, London SW1V 2SA
☎020 7840 8519 Fax 020 7931 7672
Owner *The Random House Group Ltd*.
Commissioning Editor *Zoe Howes*
The audiobooks division of Random House started early in 1991. Acquired the Reed Audio list in 1997. Publishes fiction and non-fiction. AUTHORS include Monica Ali, Sebastian Faulks, John Grisham, Mark Haddon, Robert Harris, Thomas Harris, Tony Hawks, Andy McNab, Alison Pearson, Ruth Rendell, Kathy Reichs, Chris Ryan.

Rickshaw Productions
Suite 125, 99 Warwick Street, Leamington Spa
CV32 4RB

☎0780 3553214 Fax 01926 402490
✉ rickprod@aol.com
www.thelisteningzone.com
www.rickshawaudiobooks.co.uk

Commissioning Editor *L.J. Fairgrieve*

Founded in 1998, Rickshaw Productions have, for the time being, put on hold any further publication. Now concentrating solely on uploading their own and other audiobook/music publishers' titles on to www.thelisteningzone.com. This new website also features published and unpublished writers and musicians. Audiobook TITLES *Chinese Classic Stories; Chinese Women's Stories; The Carved Pipe/The Tall Woman and Her Short Husband; The Halfway-House Hotel; Wednesdays and Other Stories; The Tailor of Salisbury; Poems and Music Vol I; The First Line of Defence – The Kent Castles; The Churchills and their Palace.* Paperback TITLES: *Mary, a Nonagenarian's Story; The Tailor of Salisbury.* Enquiries by e-mail or telephone. Submissions by snail-mail *only*; salacious material will not be accepted. Two sample chapters, one-page synopsis and s.a.e. to cover return by Recorded Delivery.

Simon & Schuster Audio

Africa House, 64–78 Kingsway, London WC2B 6AH
☎020 7316 1900 Fax 020 7316 0332
✉ info@simonandschuster.co.uk
www.simonsays.co.uk

Audio Manager *Rumana Haider*

Simon & Schuster Audio began by distributing their American parent company's audio products. Moved on to repackaging products specifically for the UK market and in 1994 became more firmly established in this market with a huge rise in turnover. Publishes adult fiction, self help and business titles. TITLES *Above Suspicion* Lynda la Plante; *Rosie* Alan Titchmarsh; *The 7 Habits of Highly Effective People* Stephen R. Covey; *Chronicles* Bob Dylan; *Angels and Demons* and *Deception Point* Dan Brown; *Kate Remembered* A. Scott Berg.

SmartPass Ltd

15 Park Road, Rottingdean, Brighton BN2 7HL
☎01273 300742
✉ info@smartpass.co.uk
www.smartpass.co.uk
www.shakespeareappreciated.com
www.spaudiobooks.com

Managing Director *Phil Viner*
Creative Director *Jools Viner*

Founded 1999. SmartPass produces audio education study guides, full-cast drama with commentary analysis and study strategies for English Literature set texts – novels, plays and poetry. Available in student and teacher formats, including audio linked study materials. TITLES include *A Kestrel for a Knave; Animal Farm; Pride and Prejudice; Great Expectations; Shakespeare: the works; War Poetry.* IMPRINTS **SPAudiobooks** Full-cast unabridged dramas of classic and cult texts TITLES *The Antipope* Robert Rankin; *Othello.* **Shakespeare Appreciated** Full-cast unabridged dramas with commentary explaining who's who and what's going on plus historical insights and background information TITLES *Macbeth; Twelfth Night.* Welcomes ideas from authors who are teachers and from agents who represent the authors of studied texts.

Soundings Audio Books

Isis House, Kings Drive, Whitley Bay NE26 2JT
☎0191 253 4155 Fax 0191 251 0662
www.isis-publishing.co.uk

Founded in 1982. Part of the Ulverscroft Group Ltd. Together with Isis Publishing publishes fiction and non-fiction; crime, romance. AUTHORS include Lyn Andrews, Rita Bradshaw, Lee Child, Catherine Cookson, Alexander Fullerton, Joanne Harris, Anna Jacobs, Robert Ludlum, Patrick O'Brian, Pamela Oldfield, Susan Sallis, Judith Saxton, Mary Jane Staples, Sally Worboyes. About 190 titles a year. Many also available on CD.

SPAudiobooks
See **SmartPass Ltd**

The Globalisation of Poetry

Chris Hamilton-Emery

The publishing context

The publishing industry is in turmoil as it contends with heavy discounting, the growth of the wholesalers, centrally coordinated book-buying within the chains, pressure on high street bookstores from supermarkets and online retailers, the contraction of independent booksellers, the consolidation of the chains, computerised stock control, pressure on genres as stock turn is measured, shrinkage in broadsheet reviews coverage, book clubs, literary festivals, prizes and reading groups.

As publishers navigate these challenges they also face the massive, unpredictable expansion of the Web, with literary blogs, online stores, aggregators, specialist retailers, author portals, eBooks, free content, samples, community networks, polling, sharing, pirating, and, at some corner of this online cosmos, publishers selling straight to consumers. Add to this mix the extraordinary growth in the number of publishers utilising print-on-demand, audio books, podcasts, video, eBooks. Taken together we have a dynamic, dizzying and demanding new landscape for writers.

Looking down the supply chain, we see our customers faced with prizes, author publicity, TV tie-ins, choices and selections, three for twos, half-price offers, recommendations and price dumping. There is more publishing investment than ever before in publicity and support for reading groups, all trying to leverage the return on investment, constraining and focusing our choices, drowning out as many voices as possible in order to profit. Navigating this explosion of books and offers we all need advice, guidance and the constraint of choices. Managing the creation of choices has become big business, vital for turning debuts into blockbusters and increasing the profits for as few businesses, and as few writers, as possible. Competition is fierce. The consumer may feel that no writer is a writer without an award, that no book is a book without being a bargain, no cover price a real price unless it is half price.

In this context, poetry with its language of resistance and metaphor can seem a tiny, limited genre with no possibility of mass appeal; poetry keeps us apart, protecting us from the treacheries of language. Poetry's advocates and practitioners, its investors and consumers face a rapidly changing world, a world which is increasingly migrating to, or making use of, the World Wide Web; globalising, shifting from high street to hypertext, from introspection to Internet. We see poets as global citizens in ways never before envisaged.

Growth in poetry publishers

As the cost of entry for new poetry publishers has gone down over the past twenty years, so the number of new presses has increased. Software for desktop publishing has become cheap and ubiquitous, and new technologies in printing and distribution services have decreased the cost of supplying consumers. Community projects, writers groups and a wide range of writers' organisations as well as booksellers have all stepped into the world of publishing and this producer-dominated infrastructure has expanded with some judicious public sector support and investment. Poetry presses have appeared (and sometimes disappeared) with dizzying speed amid the turbulent industrial climate and changing patterns of consumption. There have never been more poetry presses. See *Poetry Presses* (p. 132).

In many cases poets have become their own publishers, supported by author services businesses; it has never been easier to get into print, and to place your talent before an audience, to market yourself and to print and sell your own books, to gain expertise in publicity and performance, sales and marketing on a micro level and to transform these skills into publishing success, working alone or in conjunction with friends and colleagues, arts organisations and literature development teams in every county.

Growth in poetry publications

With this growth in production capacity there has been an extraordinary growth in new writers and new writing, greater diversity and visibility for an extended poetic universe, and the boundaries of our national literatures have extended into a global poetry market. There are now thousands, tens of thousands, of new poetry publications produced in the English-speaking world and from a bedroom in Basingstoke a budding poet can sell books in Billericay or Barbados. This mass participation in poetry has created a bewildering new landscape of competing poetries and poets, whole new worlds of writing which have previously coexisted in ignorance or denial, and with wildly differing trajectories and ambitions. They have been brought together and our critical and commercial apparatuses are only now beginning to adjust. Few can keep up with the deluge of new books and pamphlets. Despite this massive growth in production and availability it is still a challenging world for the new writer. The dramatic expansion of production and of publications has not outstripped the even more dramatic growth in new writers and competition remains fierce and is increasing. Publishers may receive hundreds of postal submissions a month from all over the world, and hundreds more by e-mail.

No longer do production and distribution provide differentiation in the market; in this expanded world other factors have come into play in order to compete, to constrain and to profit. Publicity, sales and marketing, combined with hard-won publishing experience are separating out competing publishers. There are no longer any satisfactory or desirable mechanisms for measuring quality, and our poetic landscape is increasingly surveyed for its celebrity. For the market to continue to expand publishers need to build their skills and acquire a financially stable technical, sales and marketing infrastructure in order to keep and find new customers, and to find them anywhere in the world.

Changes in distribution, sales, marketing and publicity

As money has been invested in new presses, some has been invested in new alliances and new organisations to manage them. The introduction of some form of consolidation within the poetry market is a sensible step to maximise and focus any public sector investment, and we've never seen better sales and marketing as a result. Deals have been struck with sales representatives, distributors and publicists in order to market lists and events. Organisations such as the Independent Publishers Guild (see p. 498), Independent Northern Publishers, Inpress Books and Publishing North West (see *Useful Websites* p. 179), provide a wide range of developmental services, industry representation and support for publishers.

The Web and globalisation

It's impossible to understate or to summarise the impact of the Web on poetry, a simple Google search will yield a staggering array of portals, webzines, forums, workshops, discussion groups, listservs. The enemy of poetry is insularity and our national literature has now been transposed onto a world stage where the range of practices, voices and experimentation has helped to legitimise a vast range of different traditions and legacies. In the wake of this new visibility of poets and practices no one can discuss poetry without this new context of a global readership. For writers this provides a unique opportunity to engage with writers from every culture, to read, write and collaborate as never before. Directories like Contemporary Writers, the Electronic Poetry Center, the Poetry Archive, the Poetry Kit, UBUWEB, and more, provide a huge picture of this world of writers and writing, offering writers a new map of world writing, of literary heritage, and new contexts for their own work and the extension of the skills and indeed, themselves. The Web itself is giving rise to a digital poetics, where writing locates itself in the media of the Web and its users, participative, explorative, open-ended and non-deterministic. Writers are leading the way.

Diversity

As the world of poetry has expanded we have begun to see greater diversity in poetry and its reception, addressing political art, experimentation, tackling issues surrounding gender and sexuality, race and religion. Where economics and forms of bureaucracies had hidden the breadth of the art, now we see an explosion in new voices and new methodologies for writer and reader to come together, to participate, engage and occasionally enrage in a heady mix of social comment and mobilisation. As the Web extends its offer of interaction, access and resources, we can only expect to see literature transgress its own boundaries and discover new audiences and indeed, consumers. An art which is often confused with conservation and the preservation of moments can also be an art of change, collision and transformation. New publishers and new forms of publishing will inevitably occupy these spaces as innovative models for the delivery of literature emerge, from eBooks to interactive sites, multi-contributor online projects, mass collaborations, user-driven literature. The possibilities seem endless.

Competition

With such economically progressive and transformative changes, it is inevitable that the world of poetry will face increased competition. Competing ideologies, competing visions of investigation, recovery, extension and conservation pulling writers into communities all seeking a share of the consumer, but most of all challenging and channelling the available resources to serve their aims. This could be celebrated, invigorated, or controlled, yet poetry is an art of resistance and transubstantiation, of magic and alchemy, an ungovernable power which reaches past its adherents and advocates into and out of the silence of generations. No one can control the art, and here lies its strength and its sublimity.

The writer's context

Growth in courses, workshops and residential training programmes

The developing writer has never been in a better position for support and training. Creative writing courses, poetry workshops, distance learning, residencies and retreats, and mentoring opportunities abound. Writers should make use of these affordable and often life-changing services. It has never been easier to gain access to published poets with considerable teaching skills. Universities such as St Andrews, Aberystwyth, Bangor, Bath Spa, Birkbeck, Edge Hill, Exeter, Falmouth, Glasgow, Goldsmith's, Lancaster, MMU, the Open University, Plymouth, Roehampton, Sheffield, UEA and Warwick, to name only a handful, offer creative writing degrees and MAs, providing writers with the room to develop a wide range of technical skills and to nurture and hone their talents. See *UK and Irish Writers' Courses* (p. 543).

Training organisations such as the Poetry School and Writers Inc. offer short courses and workshops to build your skills in handling all aspects of technique and form, voice and performance. The Arvon Foundation, now a national institution and perhaps a treasure, offers residential courses to writers at all levels to find place, time and incentive to devote to extending your writing experience and your writing life.

Growth in promotional agencies

Organisations such as 57 Productions, Apples & Snakes, Commonword, Literature Northeast, the New Writing Partnership, the Poetry Society, Spread the Word and Survivors' Poetry, as well as many more, offer a wide range of services to writers, providing training, promotion, publicity, access to agents and publishers, as well as residencies, retreats, festivals, workshops, readings and tours, and even orchestrate national events. These organisations work extensively with writers to find new audiences, often in unexpected places. The Poetry Society's Poetry Landmarks website (www.poetrysociety.org.uk/content/landmarks/) provides a terrific geographic overview of poetry resources of all kinds.

New cooperatives such as Thrive will draw together some key London-based arts organisations including the Poetry Society, the Poetry Books Society and the Poetry School to improve the strategic delivery of books, to improve access, visibility, diversity and the support of poets. The National Association for Literature Development and the National Association for Writers in Education provide further support and guidance for freelance writers and educators.

Communities and writers' circles

Writers' collectives such as Oxford's Backroom Poets, the Joy of Six, Letchworth's Poetry ID, Wild Women or Writers Forum abound in the UK, drawing together groups of like-minded writers to test out new writing, workshop a poem, test out a performance and to promote, support and sustain local talent. Such groups can often extend in to reading groups, and performance groups, touring together and developing networks of writers and venues around the UK. Joining a writers' circle or workshop can provide you with the long-term support and friendship you need as you develop your writing and move towards performance, publication or both. See *Useful Websites* (p. 179)and *Writers' Circles and Workshops* (p. 559).

Performance

The reading circuit in the UK is extremely well developed and gigs at venues and festivals are highly sought after. The experience for poets can be a mixed bag, taking in back rooms in pubs and basements with fewer people than poets, to extravaganzas such as the Aldeburgh Poetry Festival or London's Poetry International. There can seem to be parallel universes in the performance scene. There is a growing network of new venues like The Spitz in London, or Manchester's Green Room, where blends of music, drama and monologue provide a heady mix for a large and committed audience as part of a revitalised oral tradition, comprising comedy, social issues, and crowd-pleasing, tub-thumping social commentary. The scope for literature in performance tends to oscillate around the sustained use of venues and the long-term support for writers and audiences. Festivals often bring with them a coherent audience, though ticket sales can still present a problem. Audiences create the literature they want, and extending and challenging those tastes can be difficult. Know which venues suit your writing, but recognise that a key part of writing life is to get out and read to folk. Nothing succeeds better in breaking down the barriers to poetry consumption than performance.

The import of slam and open mic sessions to bookshops and clubs has extended the possibility of new literature, and the opportunities for budding writers to step up and greet the audience and test out new pieces. Tackling hecklers and handling audible rejection is not for the faint-hearted. The boundaries between performance and more traditional page-based literatures are blurring. Some websites have emerged to promote live poetry, Poets on Fire is a good example (poetsonfire. blogspot.com/).

Financial support

There is a wide range of public and private sector financial awards made to writers. These can range from the Eric Gregory Awards for new poets under thirty to The Royal Literary Fund's assistance for writers in distress. Disbursements are rarely huge, but can provide support for research, travel, training or buying time to finalise manuscripts. The Arts Council's Grants for Writers provide successful applicants with the support they need to complete works, or start new ventures, to extend their skills and protect their writing life. Competition can be fierce for some awards and a proven track record of publishing experience in magazines and journals, as well as performances, can help in drawing together a successful application. See **Bursaries, Fellowships and Grants** (p. 567).

Competitions and prizes

One way to become a 'name' as a writer is to win a competition. One way to stay in the limelight is to win another. Prize culture is the principal language of reception in the UK, as well as the US and Australia. The range of competitions for best poem, best pamphlet, best first collection, best collection, lifetime achievement and so on is extensive to say the least. Some say literary prizes create a culture of 'losers'. For audiences, prizes have become a vital tool for navigating new literature; writers and publishers cannot fail to ignore them. They can be divisive, distracting, at times damaging; they serve to remind everyone in the poetry business that it is not a meritocracy, and the cultural field of writing outputs is worth a deeper and more engaged analysis. But prizes do matter, publishers pay attention as much as audiences, and the celebration of literature through prizes can certainly stimulate book sales. A Poetry Book Society Choice can guarantee a large book club audience as well as doubling trade sales, too. See **Prizes** (p. 573).

The audience

The high street bookshop, independents and chains

For published works, the local high street bookshop still provides access to the general public. Despite the contraction in the market, reduced range and high levels of returns, bookshops are important places for the poetry audience to browse, read at leisure and discover new voices and works. Consolidation in the book chains has led to the growing dominance of Waterstone's in the UK, superstores like Borders and academic specialists like Blackwell's all of which continue to support poetry, even though the shelves in some shops may offer less than 5 per cent of the poetry titles published that year. Competition for shelf space is fierce. Even if one succeeds in placing books within bookshops it is no guarantee of making sales, and it is incumbent on the publisher and the poet to do everything possible to drive potential customers in to bookshops in order to sell books and avoid returns.

Despite the dominance of the chains, independents are finding ways to compete: specialisation, events management, focus and expertise can build a dedicated customer base and businesses ranging from Foyle's of London to Salts Mill in Bradford have good poetry selections and sales to match.

Book fairs, festivals and readings

The small press scene regularly convenes book fairs especially in London and Oxford, dedicated book buyers looking for fugitive, non-mainstream publications, as well as highly crafted products congregate for weekend programmes of events, readings, displays, happenings and more. The audiences can be eccentric, eclectic and demanding often all at once. Such events can become staging posts for building author profile and making some handy sales. Festivals and regular reading venues can offer access to captive audiences who have already committed time and money to attend, and are ready to engage with a writer and to extend that connection by purchasing new books. Sessions can be exhausting and invigorating, but they provide rare opportunities to hear new talent and see what is happening in literature, on the scene, here and now.

Book clubs and subscription sales

For poetry, there is only one show in town when considering a book club. The Poetry Book Society has a membership of several thousand and provides a subscription-based offer of four choices a year and a wider range of recommendations. Members can buy any other title available in the UK at a substantial discount. The membership is loyal and conservative. In addition to their postal subscription services, the PBS has provided an online shop and a children's poetry bookshelf. The organisation is undergoing some rapid and exciting changes. Some publishers offer subscription sales, and customers can pre-buy a limited range of books guaranteeing publication. Such ventures work well with a defined audience and clear objectives within the publishing programme.

Magazines

Audiences are most likely to come across new talent in poetry magazines and journals. Paper based models and subscription sales are rapidly being replaced by blogzines and webzines which are capable of reaching tens of thousands of visitors a year, and in some cases tens of thousands a month. The poetry magazine scene is a constantly changing culture with a few notable exceptions, stalwarts like *Agenda, Ambit, Chapman, PN Review, Poetry London, Poetry Review, Poetry Saltzburg, The Rialto, Shearsman, Smiths Knoll, Stand* and *Stride*, offer a wide-ranging and shifting perspective of contemporary poets and poetry. This is by no means a fair representation of the poetry magazine scene. See **Poetry Magazines** (p. 142).

A superb directory for potential subscribers, as well as potential submitters, is run by the Poetry Library (www.poetrymagazines.org.uk/). This invaluable resource offers poets and readers an opportunity to come together and see not only contemporary magazines but a rich publishing history across the varied trajectories of the fragmented, bustling and occasionally combative world of poetry.

It is important to note that webzines like John Tranter's *Jacket*, Todd Swift's work at *Nthposition* and *Eye Wear*, Mark Thwaite's *ReadySteadyBook*, Tony Frazer's *Shearsman*, and Tim Allen's reviews webzine *Terrible Work* have helped to broaden poetry's reception in the UK. A characteristic of these changes in webzines is the broadening focus on international writers and a more extensive and expansive view of poetic possibilities. Nowhere is the globalisation of poetry more apparent than in online publications and forums. The audience, like the content, is increasingly international. Quite how these cultural collisions translate remains to be seen, but those who enjoy poetry are now worldwide, and addressing these markets is an important challenge for writers and publishers.

Online sales and the Web

As poetry publishing develops its offer around the world, finding new audiences through the Web, selling in an ever-widening range of countries and cultures we will see literary 'consumption' shifting its perceptions of the domestic and exotic, and the language of ideas, of conflict and compassion, of difference, diversity, coexistence and security will continue to permeate our literatures. Our identities and allegiances through vast migrations have already swelled beyond our national boundaries and our interdependence for energy, conservation and preservation are drawing peoples together. Poetry is international *and* local.

Audiences have migrated to the Web, to surf for pleasure, channel-hopping with stumbleupon.com, or making their purchases online from publishers and retailers. It seems an inescapable fact that the Web is the single most defining issue for new poetry in the twenty-first century. From the explosion in poetry Web cultures, portals, workshops, bulletin boards, author websites, blogs, sophisticated implementations of digital poetry artefacts, and innovative and highly sophisticated archives of performances, no writer or publisher can afford to avoid the power of search engines, eCommerce, networking sites like MySpace, Second Life or public archives of video clips at YouTube. By the time this book is in your hands, models and delivery systems will be available for readers and participants to work with, consume and collaborate in new writing ventures.

Chris Emery's poetry has appeared in The Age, Jacket, Magma, Poetry London, Poetry Review, Poetry Wales, PN Review, Quid *and* The Rialto. *He was anthologised in* New Writing 8 *in 1999. A first full-length poetry collection,* Dr Mephisto, *was published by Arc in 2002 and a new collection of poetry,* Radio Nostalgia, *was published by Arc in 2006. Chris Emery is publishing director of Salt Publishing, an independent literary press based in Cambridge. He was awarded an American Book Award in 2006.*

Poetry Presses

Abraxas Press
13 Copthall Gardens, London NW7 2NG
No unsolicited work considered.

Agenda Editions
The Wheelwrights, Fletching Street, Mayfield
TN20 6TL
✉ editor@agendapoetry.co.uk
Contact *Patricia McCarthy*
Separate collections of poetry. See also **Agenda** magazine.

Akros Publications
33 Lady Nairn Avenue, Kirkcaldy KY1 2AW
☎01592 651522
www.akrospublications.co.uk
Contact *Duncan Glen*
Publisher of Scottish poetry and literary criticism. See also **ZED20** magazine and entry under **UK Publishers**.

Anvil Press Poetry Ltd
Neptune House, 70 Royal Hill, London
SE10 8RF
☎020 8469 3033 Fax 020 8469 3363
✉ anvil@anvilpresspoetry.com
www.anvilpresspoetry.com
Contact *Peter Jay*
Contemporary British poetry and poetry in translation. See entry under **UK Publishers**.

Arc Publications Ltd.
Nanholme Mill, Shaw Wood Road, Todmorden
OL14 6DA
☎01706 812338 Fax 01706 818948
✉ arc.publications@btconnect.com
www.arcpublications.co.uk
Managing Director *Tony Ward*
Contemporary poetry from new and established writers using English as their first language from the UK and abroad. Also bi-lingual texts of poetry from around the world with a special interest in Eastern Europe and the minority languages See entry under **UK Publishers**.

Arrowhead Press
70 Clifton Road, Darlington DL1 5DX
✉ editor@arrowheadpress.co.uk
www.arrowheadpress.co.uk
Contact *Roger Collett*
Quality books and pamphlets of contemporary poetry.

Atlantean Publishing
38 Pierrot Steps, 71 Kursal Way, Southend on Sea SS1 2UY
✉ atlanteanpublishing@hotmail.com
www.geocities.com/dj_tyrer/
    atlantean-pub.html
Contact *David John Tyrer*
Single author broadsheets and poetry/prose booklets. See also **Awen, Monomyth, Bard, Garbaj** and **The Supplement** magazines.

Barque Press
70A Cranwich Road, London N16 5JD
☎020 7502 0906
✉ info@barquepress.com
www.barquepress.com
Contact *Andrea Brady*
Poetry.

BB Books
Spring Bank, Longsight Road, Copster Green, Blackburn BB1 9EU
☎01254 249128
Contact *Dave Cunliffe*
Post-Beat poetics and counterculture theoretic. Iconoclastic rants and anarchic psycho-cultural tracts. See also **Global Tapestry Journal**.

Beyond the Cloister Publications
74 Marina Street, St Leonards on Sea TN38 0BJ
☎01424 444072
✉ beyondcloister@hotmail.co.uk
www.beyondthecloister.com
Contact *Hugh Hellicar*
Anthologies of poetry and slim volumes to launch poets.

Big Little Poem Books
3 Park Avenue, Melton Mowbray LE13 0JB

Contact *Robert Richardson*

Effective contemporary approaches to the lyric and epigram. See also **Door-to-Everywhere** press.

Blinking Eye Publishing

PO Box 549, North Shields NE30 2WT
☎0191 257 3778
✉ jeanne@millview77.freeserve.co.uk
www.blinking-eye.co.uk

Contact *Jeanne Macdonald*
Co-editor *Judy Walker*

Promotes the work of writers over 50 – through annual poetry and short story competitions.

Bloodaxe Books Ltd

Highgreen, Tarset NE48 1RP
☎01434 240500 Fax 01434 240505
✉ editor@bloodaxebooks.com
www.bloodaxebooks.com

Contact *Neil Astley*

Britain's leading publisher of new poetry. No submissions by e-mail attachments. See entry under *UK Publishers*.

Blue Butterfly Publishers

13 Irvine Way, Invermurie AB51 4ZR
☎01467 625986 Fax 01467 625986
✉ blue7butterfly@which.net
homepages.which.net/~david.madill

Contact *Betty Madill*

Christian poetry.

Bluechrome

PO Box 109, Portishead, Bristol BS20 7ZJ
☎020 8123 1126
✉ anthony@bluechrome.co.uk
www.bluechrome.co.uk

Contact *Anthony Delgrado*

Founded 2002. Poetry, literary and experimental fiction. 30 titles a year. Submission details available on the website.

The Boho Press

Bluechrome, PO Box 109, Portishead, Bristol BS20 7ZJ
☎020 8123 1126 Fax 020 9227 3357
✉ info@bohopress.co.uk
www.bohopress.co.uk

Contact *Anthony Delgrado*

Publishes mainly poetry but the odd fiction title has made it onto the list, which includes work from Sam Smith, Poul Webb, Roger Elkin and Les Merton.

Bradshaw Books

Tigh Fili, Thompson House, Maccurtain Street, Cork, Republic of Ireland
☎00 353 21 450 9274 Fax 00 353 21 455 1617
✉ admin@cwpc.ie
www.tighfili.com

Contact *M. Bradshaw*

See entry under *Irish Publishers*.

Bridge Pamphlets

PO Box 309, Aylsham, Norwich NR11 6LN
✉ mail@therialto.co.uk
www.therialto.co.uk

Contact *Michael Mackmin*

An imprint of **Rialto Publications**.

The Brodie Press

www.brodiepress.co.uk
See entry under *Small Presses*.

Paula Brown Publishing

26 Orkney Road, Corsham, Portsmouth PO6 3UE
☎01202 672173
✉ paulabrownpublishing@btinternet.com
www.thepeoplespoet.com

Contact *Paula Brown*

Online poetry and arts community which publishes anthologies and single author collections.

Bullseye Publications

5 Camptoun, North Berwick EH39 5BA
☎01620 880311
✉ alancharlesgay@aol.com

Contact *Alan Gay*

Calder Wood Press

1 Beachmont Court, Dunbar EH42 1YF
☎01368 864953
✉ colin.will@zen.co.uk
www.calderwoodpress.co.uk

Contact *Colin Will*

Founded 1997. Publishes pamphlets and short-run publications. No unsolicited mss.

Carcanet Press Ltd

4th Floor, Alliance House, 30 Cross Street, Manchester M2 7AQ
☎0161 834 8730 Fax 0161 832 0084
✉ info@carcanet.co.uk
www.carcanet.co.uk

Contact *Michael Schmidt*

Major poetry publisher. See entry under **UK Publishers**; also publishes *PN Review* magazine.

Chapman Publishing
4 Broughton Place, Edinburgh EH1 3RX
☎0131 557 2207 Fax 0131 556 9565
✉ chapman-pub@blueyonder.co.uk
www.chapman-pub.co.uk

Contact *Joy Hendry*

Scottish writing, mainly from contributors to **Chapman** magazine. See entry under **UK Publishers**.

Cinnamon Press
Ty Meirion, Glan yr afon, Tanygrisiau, Blaenau Ffestiniog LL41 3SU
☎01766 832112
✉ jan@cinnamonpress.com
www.cinnamonpress.com

Editor *Dr Jan Fortune-Wood*

Poetry, fiction, some non-fiction. Growing list from Wales, UK & international. See also **Envoi** magazine.

The Collective Press
c/o Penlanlas Farm, Llantilio Pertholey, Y-fenni NP7 7HN
☎01873 856350 Fax 01873 859559
✉ jj@jojowales.co.uk
www.welshwriters.com

Contact *John Jones & Frank Olding*

Non-profit promoter and publishers of contemporary poetry.

Day Dream Press
39 Exmouth Street, Swindon SN1 3PU
☎01793 523927

Contact *Kevin Bailey*

Small poetry collections. Now associated with **Bluechrome Press**. See also *HQ Poetry Magazine (Haiku Quarterly)*.

The Dedalus Press
13 Moyclare Road, Baldoyle, Dublin 13, Republic of Ireland
☎00353 1 8392034 Fax 0870 127 2089
✉ office@dedaluspress.com
www.dedaluspress.com

Contact *Pat Boran*

Contemporary Irish poetry and poetry from around the world in English translation.

Diehard Publishers
91–93 Main Street, Callander FK17 8BQ
☎0131 229 7252

Contact *Ian W. King*

Poetry and drama, mainly Scottish. See also **Poetry Scotland** magazine.

Dionysia Press
127 Milton Road West, 7 Duddingston House Courtyard, Edinburgh EH15 1JG

Contact *Denise Smith*

Collections of poetry, short stories and translations. See also **Understanding** magazine.

DogHouse
PO Box 312, Tralee, Co. Kerry, Republic of Ireland
☎00 353 667 137547
✉ doghouse312@eircom.net
www.doghousebooks.ie

Contact *Noel King*

Poetry and short story collections by individuals (Irish born only).

Door-to-Everywhere
3 Park Avenue, Melton Mowbray LE13 0JB

Contact *Robert Richardson*

Poem card series – imagination first! See also **Big Little Poem Books** press.

Dreadful Night Press
82 Kelvin Court, Glasgow G12 0AQ
☎0141 339 9150 Fax 0141 339 9150
✉ dreadfulnight1@aol.com

Dream Catcher
Jasmine Cottage, 4 Church Street, Market Rasen LN8 3ET
☎01673 844325
✉ paulsuther@hotmail.com
www.inpressbooks.co.uk

Contact *Paul Sutherland*

Short fiction, poetry, reviews, artwork, biographies. See also *Dream Catcher* magazine.

Driftwood Publications
5 Timms Lane, Formby L37 7DW
☎01704 833911 Fax 0151 524 0216
✉ janet.speedy@tesco.net

Contact *Brian Wake*

New work by new and established poets more suited to the page than the stage.

Egg Box Publishing
25 Brian Avenue, Norwich NR1 2PH
☎01603 470191
✉ info@eggboxpublishing.com
www.eggboxpublishing.com

Contact *Nathan Hamilton & Gordon Smith*

New poetry and fiction; translations also considered. Mss by post only.

Enitharmon Press

26B Caversham Road, London NW5 2DU
☎020 7482 5967 Fax 020 7284 1787
✉ books@enitharmon.co.uk
www.enitharmon.co.uk

Contact *Stephen Stuart-Smith*

Poetry and criticism. See entry under **UK Publishers**.

Erran Publishing

43 Willow Road, Carlton, Nottingham
NG4 3BH
✉ erranpublishing@hotmail.com
www.poetichours.homestead.com

Contact *Nick Clark*

Non-profit supporter of Third World charities. See also **Poetic Hours** magazine.

Essence Press

8 Craiglea Drive, Edinburgh EH10 5PA
✉ jaj@essencepress.co.uk
www.essencepress.co.uk

Contact *Julie Johnstone*

Handbound editions of poetry, poetry postcards. Interested in concrete poetry and nature. See also **Island** magazine.

Etruscan Books

28 Fowler's Court, Fore Street, Buckfastleigh
TQ11 0AA
☎01364 643128 Fax 01364 643054
✉ etruscan@macunlimited.net
www.e-truscan.co.uk

Contact *Nicholas Johnson*

Modernist, sound, visual poetry, Gaelic, lyric poetry, US/UK poets.

Fal Publications

PO Box 74, Truro TR1 1XS
☎01208 851205
✉ info@falpublications.co.uk
www.falpublications.co.uk

Contact *Victoria Field*

Poetry and literature from Cornwall.

Feather Books

PO Box 438, Shrewsbury SY3 0WN
☎01743 872177 Fax 01743 872177
✉ john@waddysweb.freeuk.com
www.waddysweb.freeuk.com

Contact *Rev. J. Waddington-Feather*

Christian poetry, drama, hymns, novels. See entry under **Small Presses**; also **The Poetry Church** magazine.

Five Leaves Publications

PO Box 8786, Nottingham NG5 4ER
☎0115 969 3597
✉ info@fiveleaves.co.uk
www.fiveleaves.co.uk

Contact *Ross Bradshaw*

Fiction, poetry, Jewish interest, social history. See entry under **Small Presses**.

Flambard

Stable Cottage, East Fourstones, Hexham
NE47 5DX
☎01434 674360 Fax 01434 674178
www.flambardpress.co.uk

Contact *Peter Elfed Lewis & Will Mackie*

Concentrates on poetry and literary fiction.

Flarestack Publishing

8 Abbot's Way, Pilton BA4 4BN
☎01749 890019
✉ cannula.dementia@virgin.net
www.flarestack.co.uk

Contact *Charles Johnson*

Poetry. See also **Obsessed With Pipework** magazine.

Forward Press

Remus House, Coltsfoot Drive, Woodston,
Peterborough PE2 9JX
☎01733 898105 Fax 01733 313524
✉ info@forwardpress.co.uk
www.forwardpress.co.uk

Contact *Kerrie Pateman*

General poetry and short fiction anthologies.

Fras Publications

The Atholl Browse Bookshop, Blair Atholl
PH18 5SG

Contact *John Herdman & Walter Perrie*

The Frogmore Press

42 Morehall Avenue, Folkestone CT19 4EF
☎07751 251689
www.frogmorepress.co.uk

Contact *Jeremy Page*

A forum for contemporary poetry, prose and artwork. See also **The Frogmore Papers** magazine.

The Gallery Press
Loughcrew, Oldcastle, Co. Meath, Republic of Ireland
☎00 353 49 854 1779 Fax 00 353 49 854 1779
✉ gallery@indigo.ie
www.gallerypress.com
Contact *Peter Fallon*

Poems, plays and prose by contemporary Irish writers.

The Goldsmith Press
Newbridge, Co. Kildare, Republic of Ireland
☎00 353 45 433613 Fax 00 353 45 434648
✉ viv1@iol.ie
Contact *Vivienne Abbott*

Gomer Press/Gwasg Gomer
Llandysul Enterprise Park, Llandysul SA44 4JL
☎01559 363090 Fax 01559 363758
www.gomer.co.uk
Welsh interest. See entry under **UK Publishers**.

Green Arrow Publishing
2 Chambers Cottages, Underlyn Lane, Marden, Tonbridge TN12 9BD
☎01622 832485
✉ mail@johndench.demon.co.uk
Contact *John Dench*

Collaborative publishing scheme and other services for writers. See also **Scriptor** magazine.

Happenstance Press
21 Hatton Green, Glenrothes KY7 4SD
✉ nell@happenstancepress.com
www.happenstancepress.com
Contact *Helena Nelson*

Poetry publishing; mainly chapbooks and usually first collections. See also **Sphinx** magazine.

Harpercroft
24 Castle Street, Crail KY10 3SH
☎01333 451744
✉ jarvie522@btinternet.com
Contact *Gordon Jarvie*

Poetry, local interest.

Headland Publications
Ty Coch, Galltegfa, Ruthin LL15 2AR
☎0151 625 9128 Fax 0151 625 9128
✉ headlandpublications@hotmail.co.uk
www.headlandpublications.co.uk
Contact *Gladys Mary Coles*

Fine editions of poetry; anthologies.

Hearing Eye
Box 1, 99 Torriano Avenue, London NW5 2RX
www.torriano.org/hearing_eye
Contact *John Rety*

Poetry/literature publishers based in Kentish Town.

Heaventree Press
PO Box 3342, Coventry CV1 5YB
☎07833 150277
✉ info@heaventreepress.co.uk
www.heaventreepress.co.uk
Contact *Jon Morley*

'A new poetry press which already shows immense promise.' See also **Avocado** magazine.

Hilltop Press
4 Nowell Place, Almondbury, Huddersfield HD5 8PD
booksmusicfilmstv.com/HilltopPress.htm
Contact *Steve Sneyd*

Specialist publisher of science fiction and dark fantasy poetry, and background material.

Hippopotamus Press
22 Whitewell Road, Frome BA11 4EL
☎01373 466653 Fax 01373 466653
✉ rjhippopress@aol.com
Contact *Roland John*

First collections of verse from those with a track record in the magazines. See also **Outposts** magazine.

Honno Welsh Women's Press
Canolfan Merched Y Wawr, Vulcan Street, Aberystwyth SY23 1JH
☎01970 623150 Fax 01970 623150
✉ post@honno.co.uk
www.honno.co.uk
Contact *Lindsay Ashford*

The Welsh women's press – novels, short stories, poetry and autobiographical anthologies. Must have a Welsh connection. See entry under **UK Publishers**.

I★D Books
Connah's Quay Library, Wepre Drive, Connah's Quay, Deeside
☎01244 830485

Poetry, short fiction, local history – mainly self-publishing by associated writers' group.

Iron Press
5 Marden Terrace, Cullercoats, North Shields
NE30 4PD
☎0191 253 1901 Fax 0191 253 1901
✉ ironpress@blueyonder.co.uk
www.ironpress.co.uk
Contact *Peter Mortimer*
Poetry and fiction.

Katabasis
10 St Martin's Close, London NW1 0HR
☎020 7485 3830
✉ katabasis@katabasis.co.uk
www.katabasis.co.uk
Contact *Dinah Livingstone*
Down-to-earth and Utopian poetry and prose
from home an abroad – English and Latin
American. No unsolicited mss.

Kates Hill Press
126 Watsons Green Road, Kates Hill, Dudley
DY2 7LG
www.kateshillpress.co.uk
Fiction and social history from the West Midlands
or with a West Midlands theme. Some poetry.

Kettillonia
24 South Street, Newtyle PH12 8UQ
☎01828 650615
✉ james@kettillonia.co.uk
www.kettillonia.co.uk
Contact *James Robertson*

The King's England Press
Cambertown House, Commercial Road,
Goldthorpe, Rotherham S63 9BL
☎01484 663790 Fax 01484 663790
✉ steve@kingsengland.com
www.kingsengland.com
www.pottypoets.com
Contact *Steve Rudd*
History, folklore, children's poetry.

KT Publications
16 Fane Close, Stamford PE9 1HG
☎01780 754193
Contact *Kevin Troop*
Always looking for new material of the highest
standard. See also **The Third Half** magazine.

Leaf Books
Gti Suite, Valleys Innovation, Navigation Park,
Abercynon CF45 4SN
☎01443 665704
✉ contact@leafbooks.co.uk
www.leafbooks.co.uk
Bite-sized reads.

Leafe Press
4 Cohen Close, Chilwell, Nottingham
NG9 6RW
✉ leafepress@hotmail.com
www.leafepress.com
Contact *Alan Baker*
Pamphlets of contemporary poetry with occasional full-length collections.

Luath Press Ltd
543/2 Castlehill, The Royal Mile, Edinburgh
EH1 2ND
☎0131 225 4326 Fax 0131 225 4324
✉ gavin.macdougall@luath.co.uk
www.luath.co.uk
Contact *Gavin MacDougall*
Committed to publishing well-written books
worth reading. Over 150 titles in print including
poetry and fiction. See entry under **Small
Presses**.

Malfunction Press (1969)
Rose Cottage, 3 Tram Lane, Buckley CH7 3JB
✉ rosecot@presford.freeserve.co.uk
Contact *Peter E. Presford*
Mainly dedicated to science fiction, fantasy, light
horror.

Mare's Nest
41 Addison Gardens, London W14 0DP
☎020 7603 3969
✉ maresnest@tesco.net
www.maresnest.co.uk
Contact *Pamela Cluines-Ross*
Icelandic.

Mariscat Press
10 Bell Place, Edinburgh EH3 5HT
☎0131 343 1070
✉ hamish.whyte@virgin.net
Contact *Hamish Whyte & Diana Hendry*
Currently publishing poetry pamphlets only.

Masque Publishing
PO Box 3257, 84 Dinsdale Gardens,
Littlehampton BN16 9AF
✉ masque_pub@tiscali.co.uk
myweb.tiscali.co.uk/masquepublishing
Contact *Lisa Stewart*
For self-publishers. See also **Decanto** magazine.

Mews Press
English Department, Sheffield Hallam University, Collegiate Crescent, Sheffield S10 2BP
☎0114 225 2241
✉ s.l.earnshaw@shu.ac.uk
extra.shu.ac.uk/mews-press
Contact *Dr Steven Earnshaw*
Work by poets associated with Sheffield Hallam University's MA in Writing.

The Moving Finger Press
PO Box 4867, Birmingham B3 3HD
Contact *Dave Reeves*
See also **Raw Edge Magazine**.

Mudfog Press
Arts Development, The Stables, Stewart Park, The Grove, Marton, Middlesborough TS7 8AR
www.mudfog.co.uk
Community press publishing poetry and short fiction only from writers in the Tees Valley.

New Fountainhead Press
10 Frenchlands Hatch, Ockham Road South, East Horsley KT24 6SJ
☎01483 285396
✉ stanleyt5@aol.com
Stanley Trevor writ large.

New Hope International
20 Werneth Avenue, Gee Cross, Hyde SK14 5NL
www.geraldengland.co.uk
Contact *Gerald England*
Poetry booklet publisher. No longer considering unsolicited mss.

New Island
2 Brookside, Dundrum Road, Dublin 14, Republic of Ireland
☎00 353 1 298 9937 Fax 00 353 1 298 7912
www.newisland.ie
Contact *Edwin Higel*
See entry under **Irish Publishers**.

nthposition
38 Allcroft Road, London NW5 4NE
☎020 7485 5002
✉ val@nthposition.com
www.nthposition.com
Editor *Val Stevenson*
Poetry Editor *Todd Swift* (toddswift@clara.co.uk)

Eclectic and award-winning mix of politics and opinion, travel writing, fiction and poetry, reviews and interviews and some high weirdness.

Object Permanence
First Floor, 16 Ruskin Terrace, Glasgow G12 8DY
✉ robinpurves@yahoo.co.uk
www.objectpermanence.co.uk
Contact *Robin Purves*

The Old Stile Press
Catchmays Court, Llandogo, Nr Monmouth NP25 4TN
☎01291 689226
✉ oldstile@dircon.co.uk
www.oldstilepress.com
Contact *Frances & Nicolas McDowall*
Fine, hand-printed books with text and images. No unsolicited mss.

The Once Orange Badge Poetry Press
PO Box 184, South Ockenden RM15 5WT
☎01708 852827
✉ orangebadge@poetry.fsworld.co.uk
Contact *D.M. Heath*
A4 and A5 pamphlets – ideal for first collections. E-mail submissions preferred. See also **The Once Orange Badge Poetry Supplement** magazine.

The One Time Press
Model Farm, Linstead Magna, Halesworth IP19 0DT
☎01986 785422
www.onetimepress.com
Contact *Peter Wells*
Poetry of the forties and occasionally some contemporary work in limited editions. Illustrated.

Original Plus
Flat 3, 18 Oxford Grove, Ilfracombe EX34 9HQ
☎01271 862708
✉ smithsssj@aol.com
members.aol.com/smithsssj/index.html
Contact *Sam Smith*
Requires something extra – another language or markedly original. See also **The Journal** magazine.

Palores Publishing
11a Penryn Street, Redruth TR15 2SP
☎01209 218209
✉ les.merton@tesco.net
Editor *Les Merton*
Non-profit-making publisher helping writers and poets to self publish.

Parthian
The Old Surgery, Napier Street, Cardigan
SA43 1ED
☎01239 612059 Fax 01239 612059
✉ parthianbooks@yahoo.co.uk
www.parthianbooks.co.uk
Contact *Jasmine Donahaye*
New Welsh writing. See entry under **UK Publishers**.

Partners
289 Elmwood Avenue, Feltham TW13 7QB
✉ partners_writing_group@hotmail.com
Contact *Ian Deal*
Competitions and poetry pamphlets. See also **A Bard Hair Day**, **Imagenation** and **Poet Tree** magazines.

Peepal Tree Press Ltd
17 King's Avenue, Leeds LS6 1QS
☎0113 245 1703 Fax 0113 246 8368
✉ contact@peepaltreepress.com
www.peepaltreepress.com
Contact *Jeremy Poynting*
Best in Caribbean, Black British and south Asian writing from around the world.

Peterloo Poets
The Old Chapel, Sand Lane, Calstock
PL18 9QX
☎01822 833473 Fax 01822 833473
✉ info@peterloopoets.com
www.peterloopoets.com
Publishing Director *Harry Chambers*

Pigasus Press
13 Hazely Combe, Arreton, Isle of Wight
PO30 3AJ
✉ mail@pigasuspress.co.uk
www.pigasuspress.co.uk
Contact *Tony Lee*
Publisher of science fiction magazine and genre poetry.

Pikestaff Press
Ellon House, Harpford, Sidmouth EX10 0NH
☎01395 568941
Contact *Robert Roberts*
Contemporary poetry belonging to the English tradition, mainly 24-page pamphlets.

Pipers' Ash Ltd
Pipers Ash, Church Road, Christian Malford, Chippenham SN15 4BW
☎01249 720563 Fax 0870 056 8916
✉ pipersash@supamasu.com
www.supamasu.com
Contact *Mr A. Tyson*
Collections of 60 poems arranged in their best order, grouped on common themes, with an appropriate title. See entry under **Small Presses**.

Poems in the Waiting Room
PO Box 488, Richmond TW9 4SW
✉ pitwr@blueyonder.co.uk
Contact *Michael Lee*
Pamphlets for medical waiting rooms.

Poetry Now
Remus House, Coltsfoot Drive, Woodston, Peterborough PE2 8JX
☎01733 8998101 Fax 01733 313524
✉ poetrynow@forwardpress.co.uk
www.forwardpress.co.uk
Contact *Steve Twelvetree*
Lively, personal and contemporary; also deals with womenswords. See also **Forward Press**.

Poetry Powerhouse Press
See **Performance Poetry Society** under *Organisations of Interest to Poets*

Poetry Press Ltd
26 Park Grove, Edgware HA8 7SJ
☎020 8958 6499
✉ poetrypress@yahoo.co.uk
www.poetrypress.co.uk
Contact *Judy Karbritz*
Anthologies – rhyming poetry welcome.

Poetry Salzburg
Dept. of English, University of Salzburg, Akademiestr. 24, A–5020 Salzburg, Austria
☎00 43 662 8044 4424
Fax 00 43 662 8044 167
✉ editor@poetrysalzburg.com
www.poetrysalzburg.com
Contact *Wolfgang Görtschacher*

See also **Poetry Salzburg Review** magazine.

Poetry Wednesbury
25 Griffiths Road, West Bromwich B71 2EH
☎07950 591455
✉ ppatch66@hotmail.com
www.poetrywednesbury.co.uk
Contact *Geoff Stevens*

Occasional CDs, DVDs, leaflets and booklets. See also **The Firing Squad** and **Purple Patch** magazines. Public meetings for readings, workshops, etc. monthly at Wednesbury Library.

Poets Anonymous
70 Aveling Close, Purley CR8 4DW
✉ poets@poetsanon.org.uk
www.poetsanon.org.uk
Contact *Peter L. Evans*

Anthologies and collections of predominantly south London poets. See also **Poetic Licence** magazine.

Precious Pearl Press
41 Grantham Road, Manor Park, London E12 5LZ
Contact *P.G.P.Thompson*

Romantic, lyrical, spiritual, inspirational and mystical poetry; a traditionalist poetry press. See also **Rubies in the Darkness** magazine.

PS Avalon
Box 1865, Glastonbury BA6 8YR
✉ info@psavalon.com
www.psavalon.com
Contact *Will Parfitt*

Quality books of contemplative, inspirational and ecstatic poetry.

Puppet State Press
1 West Colinton House, 40 Woodhall Road, Edinburgh EH13 0DU
☎0131 441 9693
✉ richard@puppetstate.com
www.puppetstate.com
Contact *Richard Medrington*

QQ Press
York House, 15 Argyle Terrace, Rothesay, Isle of Bute PA20 0BD
Contact *Alan Carter*

Collections of poetry plus poetry anthologies. Submissions should be marked 'Collections' and sent with an s.a.e. or two IRCs if from abroad. See also **Quantum Leap** magazine.

Rack Press
The Rack, Kinnerton, Presteigne LD8 2PF
☎01547 560411
✉ rackpress@britishlibrary.net
pages.britishlibrary.net/nicholas.murray/ RackPress.htm
Contact *Nicholas Murray*

Welsh poetry pamphlet imprint with an international vision.

Ragged Raven Press
1 Lodge Farm, Snitterfield, Stratford upon Avon CV37 0LR
☎01789 730320
✉ raggedravenpress@aol.com
www.raggedraven.co.uk
Contact *Bob Mee & Janet Murch*

Poetry. See also **Iota** magazine.

Raunchland Publications
26 Alder Grove, Dunfermline KY11 8RP
✉ raunchland@hotmail.com
www.raunchland.co.uk
Contact *John Mingay*

Limited edition poetry/graphics booklets and online publications.

Reality Street Editions
63 All Saints Street, Hastings TN34 3BN
✉ info@realitystreet.co.uk
www.realitystreet.co.uk
Contact *Ken Edwards*

New writing from Britain, Europe and America. No unsolicited mss.

Red Candle Press
50 Manbey Grove, London E15 1EX
✉ rcp@poetry7.fsnet.co.uk
www.members.tripod.com/redcandlepress
Contact *M.L. McCarthy*

Traditionalist poetry press. See also **Candelabrum Poetry** magazine.

Rialto Publications
PO Box 309, Aylsham, Norwich NR11 6LN
✉ mail@therialto.co.uk
www.therialto.co.uk
Contact *Michael Mackmin*

'We want to publish first collections by poets of promise.' See also **The Rialto** magazine and **Bridge Pamphlets** press.

Rive Gauche Publishing
69 Lower Redland Road, Bristol BS6 6SP

☎0117 974 5106
✉ twinset1969@hotmail.com
Contact *PVT West*

Poetry by women writing and/or performing in Bristol.

Route Publishing
PO Box 167, Pontefract WF8 4WW
☎01977 797695
✉ info@route-online.com
www.route-online.com
Contact *Ian Daley & Isabel Galan*

Contemporary fiction and performance poetry. Online magazine publishes downloadable books.

Salt Publishing
PO Box 937, Great Wilbraham, Cambridge CB1 5JX
☎01223 882220 Fax 01223 882260
✉ sales@saltpublishing.com
www.saltpublishing.com
Contact *Chris Hamilton-Emery*

International poetry and poetics.

Scriberazone
PO Box 3849, Sheffield S2 9AG
✉ peterjohnson@scriberazone.co.uk
www.scriberazone.co.uk
Contact *Peter Johnson & Sarah Annetts*

Poetry and other vibes.

Second Light Publications
9 Greendale Close, London SE22 8TG
☎020 8299 0088
✉ dilyswood@tiscali.co.uk
Contact *Dilys Wood*

Seren
57 Nolton Street, Bridgend CF31 3AE
☎01656 663018 Fax 01656 649226
✉ seren@seren-books.com
www.seren-books.com
Contact *Mick Felton*

Poetry, fiction, lit crit, biography, essays. See entry under **UK Publishers**; also **Poetry Wales** magazine.

Shearsman Books
58 Velwell Road, Exeter EX4 4LD
☎01392 434511 Fax 01392 434511
✉ editor@shearsman.com
www.shearsman.com
Contact *Tony Frazer*

Publishes poetry almost exclusively. Contact editor before submitting. See also **Shearsman** magazine.

Shoestring Press
19 Devonshire Avenue, Beeston, Nottingham NG9 1BS
☎0115 925 1827
✉ lucasbeeston@aol.com
www.shoestring-press.com
Contact *John Lucas*

Poetry.

Sixties Press
89 Connaught Road, Sutton SM1 3PJ
☎020 8286 0419
Contact *Barry Tebb*

Small press concentrating on poetry and novellas. See also **Leeds Poetry Weekly** and **Literature and Psychoanalysis** magazines.

Smokestack Books
PO Box 408, Middlesbrough TS5 6WA
☎01642 813997
✉ info@smokestack-books.co.uk
Contact *Andy Croft*

Champions poets who are unconventional, unfashionable, radical or left-field.

Spectacular Diseases
83b London Road, Peterborough PE2 9BS
Contact *Paul Green*

Innovative poetry and some prose. Translations of both.

Stinging Fly Press
PO Box 6016, Dublin 8, Republic of Ireland
✉ stingingfly@gmail.com
www.stingingfly.org

New Irish and international writing. See also **The Stinging Fly** magazine.

Stride
4b Tremayne Close, Devoran, Truro TR3 6QE
✉ editor@stridebooks.co.uk
www.stridebooks.co.uk
Contact *Rupert Loydell*

Innovative poetry, criticism and music, essays and interviews. See entry under **Small Presses**.

Talking Pen
12 Derby Crescent, Moorside, Consett DH8 8DZ
☎01207 505724
Contact *Steve Urwin*

See also **Moodswing** magazine.

Templar Poetry
PO Box 7082, Bakewell DE45 9AF
☎01629 582500
✉ info@templarpoetry.co.uk
www.templarpoetry.co.uk

Contact *Alexander McMillen*

Publishes new poets and poetry via an annual open pamphlet and collection competition. Poets are also occasionally commissioned to submit work for publication. 'Templar Poetry is committed to the professional publication and development of excellent contemporary poetry.'

Troubador Publishing Ltd
9 De Montfort Mews, Leicester LE1 7FW
☎0116 255 9311
www.troubador.co.uk

See entry under *UK Publishers*.

Tuba Press
Tunley Cottage, Tunley, Near Cirencester GL7 6LW
☎01285 760424

Contact *Charles Graham*

Vane Women Press
31 Garthorne Avenue, Darlington DL3 9XL
☎01325 468464
✉ marg.rule@ntl.com
www.vanewomen.co.uk

Contact *Margaret Rule*

Work by women of the North East.

Waterloo Press
126 Furze Croft, Hove BN3 1PF
☎01273 202876
www.waterloopress.com

Contact *Simon Jenner*

Poetry and periodical publisher; please phone for submissions. See also **Eratica** magazine.

Waywiser Press
9 Woodstock Road, London N4 3ET
☎020 8374 5526 Fax 020 8374 5736
✉ waywiserpress@aol.com
www.waywiser-press.com

Managing Editor *Philip Hoy*

Independent literary press. See entry under *Small Presses*.

Wendy Webb Books
9 Walnut Close, Taverham, Norwich NR8 6YN
✉ tipsforwriters@yahoo.co.uk

Contact *Wendy Webb*

Poetry books with rules of new and traditional forms; Arthur legend, Norfolk, Pantoums. See also **Norfolk Poets and Writers – Tips Newsletter** magazine.

West House Books
40 Crescent Road, Nether Edge, Sheffield S7 1HN
☎0114 258 6035
✉ alan@nethedge.demon.co.uk
www.westhousebooks.co.uk

Contact *Alan Halsey*

Contemporary poetry, poets' prose and related work.

Wild Women Press
Flat 10, The Common, Windermere LA23 1JH
www.wildwomenpress.com

Not-for-profit small press run by founders Victoria Bennett and Adam Clarke. 'We publish from within our collective and do not accept any unsolicited material. Please do not send, we will not reply.'

Woodburn Press
Kendalmere, Caledonian Road, Peebles EH45 9DL
☎01721 720031

Worple Press
See entry under *Small Presses*.

Poetry Magazines

Acumen
6 The Mount, Higher Furzeham, Brixham
TQ5 8QY
☎01803 851098 Fax 01803 851098
✉ patricia@acumen-poetry.co.uk
www.acumen-poetry.co.uk
Contact *Patricia Oxley*
Good poetry, intelligent articles and wide-ranging reviews.

Aesthetica
PO Box 371, York YO23 1WL
☎01904 674500
✉ info@aestheticamagazine.com
www.aestheticamagazine.com
Managing Editor *Cherie Federico*
Poetry Editor *Kate North*
Fiction Editor *David Martin*
Contemporary glossy: literature, art, music, film, sci-art, news, reviews, interviews and features.

Agenda
The Wheelwrights, Fletching Street, Mayfield
TN20 6TL
✉ editor@agendapoetry.co.uk
Contact *Patricia McCarthy*
Poems, essays, reviews. See **Agenda Editions** press.

Aireings
Dean Head Farm, Scotland Lane, Horsforth, Leeds LS18 5HU
Contact *Lesley Quayle & Linda Marshall*
Biannual poetry mag: poetry, prose, reviews, b&w artwork.

The Amsterdam Review
Columbusplein 19-111, 1057 TT Amsterdam, The Netherlands
www.amsterdamreview.nl
Contact *Duncan Bush & P.C. Evans*
Magazine for European literature.

Anon
67 Learmouth Grove, Edinburgh EH4 1BL
✉ mike@volta1.fsworld.co.uk
www.blanko.org.uk/anon

Contact *Mike Stocks*
Poems selected anonymously; for submission guidelines see website or send s.a.e.

Aquarius
Flat 4, Room B, 116 Sutherland Avenue, London W9 2QP
☎020 7289 4338
www.geocities.com/eddielinden
Contact *Eddie S. Linden*
Literary magazine; prose and poetry.

Areopagus
48 Cornwood Road, Plympton, Plymouth
PL7 1AL Fax 0870 134 6384
✉ editor@areopagus.org.uk
www.areopagus.org.uk
Contact *Julian Barritt*
A Christian-based arena for creative writers. Subscription: £12 p.a.

Avocado
The Heaventree Press, PO Box 3342, Coventry
CV1 5YB
✉ info@heaventreepress.co.uk
www.heaventreepress.co.uk
Contact *Jonathan Morley*
'No first person whining, please.' See also **Heaventree Press**.

Awen
38 Pierrot Steps, 71 Kursaal Way, Southend on Sea SS1 2UY
✉ atlanteanpublishing@hotmail.com
www.geocities.com/dj_tyrer/awen.html
Contact *David John Tyrer*
Poetry and vignette-length fiction of any style/genre. See also **Bard**, **Monomyth**, **Garbaj** and **The Supplement** magazines and **Atlantean Publishing** press.

Banipal
PO Box 22300, London W13 8ZQ
☎020 8568 9747 Fax 020 8568 8509
✉ info@banipal.co.uk
www.banipal.co.uk
Contact *Margaret Obank*

Assistant Editor *Samuel Shimon* (samuel@ banipal.co.uk)

Contemporary Arab authors in English translation: poetry, fiction, interviews, reviews.

Bard

38 Pierrot Steps, 71 Kursal Way, Southend on Sea SS1 2UY

✉ atlanteanpublishing@hotmail.com

www.geocities.com/dj_tyrer/bard.html

Contact *David John Tyrer*

Short poetry. See also **Awen**, **Garbaj**, **Monomyth** and **The Supplement** magazines and **Atlantean Publishing** press.

A Bard Hair Day

289 Elmwood Avenue, Feltham TW13 7QB

Contact *Ian Deal*

Contemporary poetry magazine. See also **Partners** press, **Imagenation** and **Poet Tree** magazines.

Blithe Spirit

12 Eliot Vale, Blackheath, London SE3 0UW

☎020 8318 4677

www.britishhaikusociety.org

Contact *Graham High*

Journal of the British Haiku Society. Haiku and related forms.

Borderlines

Nant Y Brithyll, Llangynyw, Welshpool SY21 0JS

☎019388 810263

Contact *Angie Quinn & Kevin Bamford*

Open poetry mag with no axe to grind published by the Anglo-Welsh Poetry Society.

Braquemard

229 Hull Road, Hull HU6 8QZ

✉ braquemard@hotmail.com

www.braquemard.fsnet.co.uk

Contact *David Allenby*

A5, 52 pages, poetry and artwork. No doggerel.

Brittle Star

PO Box 56108, London E17 0AY

☎020 8802 1507

✉ magazine@brittlestar.org.uk

www.brittlestar.org.uk

Contact *Louise Hooper*

Poetry, short stories and articles on contemporary poetry.

Candelabrum Poetry Magazine

50 Manbey Grove, London E15 1EX

✉ rcp@poetry7.fsnet.co.uk

www.members.tripod.com/redcandlepress

Contact *M.L. McCarthy*

Formalist poetry magazine for people who like poetry rhythmic and shapely. See also **Red Candle Press**.

Cannon's Mouth

22 Margaret Grove, Harborne, Birmingham B17 9JH

☎0121 426 6413

✉ canmouth@yahoo.co.uk

www.cannonpoets.co.uk

Contact *Greg Cox*

New poetry, criticism, articles, information.

Carillon

19 Godric Drive, Bainsworth, Rotherham S60 5NA

✉ editor@carillonmag.org.uk

www.carillonmag.org.uk

Contact *Graham Rippon*

Eclectic poetry and prose.

Cauldron

10 Glyn Road, Wirral CH44 1AB

☎07900 966061 Fax 0151 200 9402

✉ terence.grogan50@ntlworld.com

www.thenewcauldron.co.uk

Contact *Terence Grogan*

Prose and poetry of all genres and styles, plus articles and regular features.

CFUK

105b Fidlas Road, Llanishen, Cardiff CF14 0LY

☎07786 988836

✉ cfuk@hotmail.co.uk

www.cfukmagazine.net

Contact *Dylan Moore*

Cardiff's brightest litzine: fiction, poetry, essays, interviews and reviews from Wales and the world.

Chanticleer Magazine

6/1 Jamaica Mews, Edinburgh EH3 6HN

✉ richard@livermore8304.freeserve.co.uk

Contact *Richad Livermore*

Poetry and ideas; not afraid to be different.

Chapman

4 Broughton Place, Edinburgh EH1 3RX

☎0131 557 2207

✉ chapman-pub@blueyonder.co.uk
www.chapman-pub.co.uk

Contact *Joy Hendry*

The best in Scottish and international writing, well-established writers and the up-and-coming. See entry under **Magazines**.

Connections
4 Shipwrights Lee, Island Wall, Whitstable CT5 1EW
☎01227 277773
✉ jane@hardy91.fsnet.co.uk

Contact *Jane Hardy*

Poetry and prose by new and established writers.

Current Accounts
16–18 Mill Lane, Horwich, Bolton BL6 6AT
✉ bswscribe@aol.com
hometown.ao.co.uk/bswscribe/myhomepage/writing.html

Contact *Rod Riesco*

Poetry, short fiction, articles. Magazine of the Bank Street Writers' Group.

Dandelion Arts Magazine
24 Frosty Hollow, East Hunsbury NN4 0SY
☎01604 701730 Fax 01604 701730

Editor/Publisher *Jacqueline Gonzalez-Marina*

Biannual, international publication. No religious or political material. Essential to become a subscriber when seeking publication: UK, £16 p.a.; Europe, £30; RoW, US$70. See also **The Student Magazine**.

Decanto
PO Box 3257, 84 Dinsdale Gardens, Littlehampton BN16 9AF
✉ masque_pub@tiscali.co.uk
myweb.tiscali.co.uk/masquepublishing

Contact *Lisa Stewart*

Non-conformist poetry magazine; any style considered, not just contemporary. See also **Masque Publishing** press.

Dream Catcher
Jasmine Cottage, 4 Church Street, Market Rasen LN8 3ET
☎01673 844325
✉ paulsuther@hotmail.com

Editor *Paul Sutherland*

Short fiction and poetry. More information at www.poetrymagazines.org.uk (select *Dream Catcher*). See also **Dream Catcher** press.

Dreams That Money Can Buy
24 Dunkirk Rise , College Bank, Rochdale OL12 6UH
☎01706 648040 Fax 01706 648040
✉ editorial@dreamsthatmoneycanbuy.co.uk
www.dreamsthatmoneycanbuy.co.uk

Contact *Benjamin Ware & Sarah Lomax*

Quarterly journal of avant-garde poetry, prose-fiction, manifestoes and art.

Earth Love
PO Box 11219, Paisley PA1 2WH
homepage.ntlworld.com/earth.love/earthlove.htm

Contact *Tracy Patrick*

Poetry magazine for the environment; proceeds to conservation charities.

Eastern Rainbow
17 Farrow Road, Whaplode Drove, Spalding PE12 0TS
✉ p_rance@yahoo.co.uk
uk.geocities.com/p_rance/pandf.htm

Contact *Paul Rance*

Focuses on 20th century culture via poetry, prose and art. See also **Peace and Freedom** magazine.

Echoes of Gilgamesh
18 Craighead Way, Barrhead, Glasgow G78 2RS
✉ paul.mcdonagh@virgin.net
www.gilgamesh.fsworld.co.uk

Contact *Paul McDonagh*

Long poem magazine, short stories, community groups, Barrhead and Neilston sports and arts festival.

The Engine
3 Ardgreenan Drive, Belfast BT4 3FQ
☎028 9065 9866 Fax 028 9032 2767
✉ clitophon@yahoo.com
www.theengine.net

Contact *Paul Murphy*

Journal of art, poetry, reviews and short stories.

Envoi
Ty Meirion, Glan yr afon, Tanygrisiau, Blaenau Ffestiniog LL41 3SU
☎01766 832112

Contact *Jan Fortune-Wood*

Poetry, sequences, features, reviews, letters pages, competitions. Celebrating 50th anniversary and 150th issue in 2008. See also **Cinnamon Press**.

Equinox

134b Joy Lane, Whitstable CT5 4ES
☎01227 282718
✉ dordi@talktalk.net
www.poetrymagazines.org.uk/equinox
Contact *Barbara Dordi*

Contemporary poetry invited. No email
submissions.

Eratica

126 Furze Croft, Hove BN3 1PF
☎01273 202876
✉ drjenner@ntlworld.com
Contact *Simon Jenner*

Biannual journal with colour plates – focus
on poetry, strong on music and art. See also
Waterloo Press.

Federation Magazine

Burslem School of Art, Queen Street, Stoke-
on-Trent ST6 3EJ
☎01792 822327
✉ fedmag@tiscali.co.uk
www.thefwwcp.org.uk

Articles, reviews, news for people working in
community publishing. 12-page broadsheet.

Fire

Field Cottage, Old Whitehill, Tackley,
Kidlington OX5 3AB
☎01869 331300
www.poetical.org
Contact *Jeremy Hilton*

Poetry: alternative, unfashionable, experimental,
spiritual, demotic; occasional experimental
prose.

The Firing Squad

36 Rooth Street, Wednesbury WS10 9QP
☎077364 11089
www.purplepatchpoetry.co.uk/firingsquad
Contact *Alex Barzdo*

Protest poetry website. See also **Purple Patch**
magazine and **Poetry Wednesbury** press.

First Offense

Syringa, The Street, Stodmarsh, Canterbury
CT3 4BA
☎01227 721249
✉ tim@firstoffense.co.uk
www.firstoffense.co.uk
Contact *Tim Fletcher*

Magazine for contemporary poetry; not traditional but is received by most ground-breaking
poets.

Flaming Arrows

Sligo–Leitrim Arts, V E C, Riverside, Sligo,
Republic of Ireland
☎00 353 71 914 7304 Fax 00 353 71 914 3093
✉ leojregan@yahoo.ie
Contact *Leo Regan*

Poetry of the spirit: mystical, contemplative,
metaphysical, grounded in the senses. Worldwide.
Written submissions by post only with e-mail
address for reply.

The Frogmore Papers

18 Nevill Road, Lewes BN7 1PF
www.frogmorepress.co.uk
Contact *Jeremy Page*

Founded 1983. Biannual. Poetry, prose and
artwork. See also **The Frogmore Press**.

Gabriel

27 Headingley Court, North Grange Road,
Leeds LS6 2QU
Contact *Thelma Laycock*

Annual Christian poetry magazine.

Garbaj

38 Pierrot Steps, 71 Kursaal Way, Southend on
Sea SS1 2UY
✉ atlanteanpublishing@hotmail.com
www.geocities.com/dj_tyrer/garbaj.html
Contact *D.J. Tyrer*

Humourous/non-pc poetry, vignette-length
fiction, fake news, etc. See also **Awen**, **Bard**,
Monomyth and **The Supplement** magazines
and **Atlantean Publishing** press.

Global Tapestry Journal

Spring Bank, Longsight Road, Copster Green,
Blackburn BB1 9EU
☎01254 249128
Contact *Dave Cunliffe*

Global Bohemia, post-Beat and counterculture
orientation. See also **BB Books** press.

Green Queen

BM Box 5700, London WC1N 3XX
✉ eandk@lineone.net
Contact *Elsa Wallace*

Occasional magazine, Green issues, lesbian and
gay fiction, articles, poetry.

Haiku Scotland
2 Elizabeth Gardens, Stoneyburn EH47 8PB
✉ haiku.scotland@btinternet.com
Contact *Frazer Henderson*

Haiku, senryu, aphorism, epigram, reviews and articles.

Handshake
5 Cross Farm, Station Road North, Fearnhead, Warrington WA2 0QG
Contact *John Francis Haines*

Newsletter of **The Eight Hand Gang**, an association of UK sci-fi poets.

Harlequin
PO Box 23392, Edinburgh EH8 7YZ
✉ harlequinmagazine@yahoo.com
www.harlequinmagazine.com
Contact *Jim Sinclair*

High quality poetry and artwork of intense beauty, mysticism and wisdom.

HQ Poetry Magazine (Haiku Quarterly)
39 Exmouth Street, Swindon SN1 3PU
☎ 01793 523927
Contact *Kevin Bailey*

General poetry mag with slight bias towards imagistic/haikuesque work

Imagenation
289 Elmwood Avenue, Feltham TW13 7QB
Contact *Ian Deal*

Poetry and artwork magazine. See also **Partners** press, **A Bard Hair Day** and **Poet Tree** magazines.

Inclement
White Rose House, 8 Newmarket Road, Fordham, Ely CB7 5LL
✉ inclement_poetry_magazine@hotmail.com
Contact *Michelle Foster*

All forms and styles of poetry. Responses within a month.

Interlude
Limehouse Town Hall, 646 Commercial Road, London E14 7HA
☎ 020 8673 2256
✉ submissions@interludemagazine.co.uk
www.interludemagazine.co.uk
Contact *Francesca Ricci, Helen Nodding, Becky Philp*

Poetry, writings and visual work; multidiscipli-

nary projects and work in progress. See entry under *Magazines*.

The Interpreter's House
19 The Paddox, Oxford OX2 7PN
www.interpretershouse.org.uk
Contact *Merryn Williams*

Poems and stories up to 2500 words; new and established writers. Check website for subscription details.

Iota
1 Lodge Farm, Snitterfield, Stratford upon Avon CV37 0LR
☎ 01789 730320
✉ iotapoetry@aol.com
www.iotapoetry.co.uk
Contact *Bob Mee & Janet Murch*

Poetry, reviews; long and short poems welcome. No epics. See also **Ragged Raven Press**.

Irish Pages
The Linen Hall Library, 17 Donegall Square North, Belfast BT1 5GB
☎ 028 9043 4800
✉ irishpages@yahoo.co.uk
www.irishpages.org
Contact *Chris Agee*

'Ireland's premier literary journal.' Outstanding writing from Ireland and overseas: poetry, short fiction, essays, literary journalism, nature-writing, etc. See entry under *Magazines*.

Island
8 Craiglea Drive, Edinburgh EH10 5PA
✉ jaj@essencepress.co.uk
www.essencepress.co.uk
Contact *Julie Johnstone*

A distinctive space for writing inspired by nature and exploring our place within the natural world. See also **Essence Press**.

The David Jones Journal
The David Jones Society, 22 Gower Road, Sketty, Swansea SA2 9BY
☎ 01792 206144 Fax 01792 470385
✉ anne.price-owen@sihe.ac.uk
www.sihe.ac.uk/davidjones
Contact *Anne Price-Owen*

Articles, poetry, information, reviews and inspired works.

The Journal
17 High Street, Maryport CA15 6BQ
☎ 01900 812194

✉ smithsssj@aol.com
members.aol.com/smithsssj/index.html

Contact *Sam Smith*

Poems in translation alongside poetry written in English. See also **Original Plus** press.

Knight-Vision
103 Westminster Crescent, Lodge Moor, Sheffield S10 4EU

Contact *Richard Middlebrook*

Sheffield's poetry and art.

Krax
63 Dixon Lane, Wortley, Leeds LS12 4RR

Contact *Andy Robson*

Light-hearted, contemporary poetry, short fiction and graphics.

Leeds Poetry Weekly
89 Connaught Road, Sutton SM1 3PJ
☎020 8286 0419

Contact *Barry Tebb*

New poems, reviews, articles on literary and psychoanalytic matters. See also **Sixties Press** and **Literature and Psychoanalysis** magazine.

Linear B Publishing
PO Box 23614, 5/17 Saunders Street, Edinburgh EH3 6TT
☎0131 314 4527 Fax 0131 334 5353
✉ linearb26@hotmail.com

Contact *Jamie Kelly*

Poetry, literary fiction, short stories.

Linkway
The Shieling, The Links, Burry Port SA16 0HU
☎01554 834486 Fax 01554 834486

Contact *Fay C. Davies*

A publication for writers and friends; a general interest magazine for the whole family. No crude language.

Literature and Psychoanalysis
89 Connaught Road, Sutton SM1 3PJ
☎020 8286 0419

Contact *Barry Tebb*

New poems, reviews, articles on literary and psychoanalytical matters. See also **Sixties Press** and **Leeds Poetry Weekly** magazine.

The London Magazine
32 Addison Grove, London W4 1ER

☎020 8400 5882 Fax 020 8994 1713
✉ admin@londonmagazine.net
www.londonmagazine.net

Contacts *Christopher Arkell/Sebastian Barker*

A review of literature and the arts. See entry under **Magazines**.

Magma
43 Keslake Road, London NW6 6DH
✉ magmapoetry@ntlworld.com
www.magmapoetry.com

Contact *David Boll*

New poetry plus poetry reviews and interviews.

Modern Poetry in Translation
The Queen's College, Oxford OX1 4AW
☎01865 244701
✉ administrator@mptmagazine.com
www.mptmagazine.com

Contact *David & Helen Constantine*

Publishes and promotes poetry in English translation.

Monkey Kettle
✉ monkeykettle@hotmail.com
www.monkeykettle.co.uk

Editor *Matthew Taylor*

Biannual poetry, prose, photos, articles in Milton Keynes and further afield.

Monomyth
38 Pierrot Steps, 71 Kursaal Way, Southend on Sea SS1 2UY
✉ atlanteanpublishing@hotmail.com
www.geocities.com/dj_tyrer/monomyth.html

Contact *David John Tyrer*

Poetry, prose and articles; all genres, styles and lengths considered. New writers welcome. See also **Awen**, **Bard**, **Garbaj** and **The Supplement** magazines and **Atlantean Publishing** press.

Moodswing
12 Derby Crescent, Moorside, Consett DH8 8DZ
☎01207 505724

Contact *Steve Urwin*

Short poems, short prose, light/dark psychologically charged. See also **Talking Pen** press.

Mslexia
PO Box 656, Newcastle upon Tyne NE99 1PZ
☎0191 261 6656
✉ postbag@mslexia.demon.co.uk

www.mslexia.co.uk

National quarterly magazine for women who write. Advice, inspiration, news, reviews, interviews, etc. See entry under *Magazines*.

Neon Highway
37 Grinshill Close, Liverpool L8 8LD
✉ poetshideout@yahoo.com
www.neonhighway.co.uk

Contact *Alice Lenkiewicz*

Innovative and experimental poetry/arts magazine.

Never Bury Poetry
Bracken Clock, Troutbeck Close, Hawkshaw, Bury BL8 4LJ
☎01204 884080
✉ n.b.poetry@zen.co.uk
www.nbpoetry.care4free.net

Contact *Jean Tarry*

Founded 1989. Quarterly. International reputation. Each issue has a different theme.

New Welsh Review
PO Box 170, Aberystwyth SY23 1WZ
☎01970 628410
✉ admin@newwelshreview.com
www.newwelshreview.com

Contact *Francesca Rhydderch*

Vibrant literary quarterly magazine which showcases the best new writing from Wales. Also includes features and reviews. See entry under *Magazines*.

Norfolk Poets and Writers – Tips Newsletter
9 Walnut Close, Taverham, Norwich NR8 6YN
✉ tipsforwriters@yahoo.co.uk

Editor *Wendy Webb*

Tips for Writers, 4 mags, 6 newssheets, theme challenges and comps, annual Davidian – rules of poetry forms. See also **Wendy Webb Books** press.

The North
The Poetry Business, The Studio, Byram Arcade, Westgate, Huddersfield HD1 1ND
☎01484 434840 Fax 01484 426566
✉ edit@poetrybusiness.co.uk
www.poetrybusiness.co.uk

Contact *Peter Sansom & Janet Fisher*

Contemporary poetry and articles, extensive reviews.

Obsessed With Pipework
8 Abbot's Way, Pilton BA4 4BN
☎01749 890019
✉ cannula.dementia@virgin.net
www.flarestack.co.uk

Contact *Charles Johnson*

Quarterly magazine of new poetry 'to surprise and delight'. See also **Flarestack Publishing** press.

The Once Orange Badge Poetry Supplement
PO Box 184, South Ockendon RM15 5WT
☎01708 852827
✉ onceorangebadge@poetry.fsworld.co.uk

Contact *D. Martyn Heath*

A4 poetry supplement for everyone whose life has been touched by disability in some way. See also **The Once Orange Badge Poetry Press**.

Open Wide
The Flat, Yew Tree Farm, Sealand Road, Chester CH1 6BS
☎07790 962317
✉ contact@openwidemagazine.co.uk
www.openwidemagazine.co.uk

Contact *James Quinton*

80 pages of punchy short fiction, poetry, reviews and interviews.

Other Poetry
29 Western Hill, Durham DH1 4RL
☎0191 386 4058
www.otherpoetry.com

Managing Editor *Michael Standen*

Thrice-yearly 60–70 poems per issue. Process of selection involves all four editors. Token payment. Submit up to four poems (with name on each sheet) plus s.a.e.

Outposts
22 Whitewell Road, Frome BA11 4EL
☎01373 466653 Fax 01373 466653
✉ rjhippopress@aol.com

Contact *Roland John*

Longest-surviving independent poetry magazine in the UK. See also **Hippopotamus Press**.

Parameter
PO Box 220, Wythenshawe, Manchester M23 0WE
✉ editor@parametermagazine.org
www.parametermagazine.org

Partners Annual Poetry Competition

289 Elmwood Avenue, Feltham TW13 7QB

✉ partners_writing_group@hotmail.com

Contact *Ian Deal*

Showcases poems entered into the Partners annual open poetry competitions.

Peace and Freedom

17 Farrow Road, Whaplode Drove, Spalding PE12 0TS

☎01406 330242

✉ p_rance@yahoo.co.uk

uk.geocities.com/p_rance/pandf.htm

Contact *Paul Rance*

Poetry, prose, art mag; humanitarian, environmental, animal welfare. See also **Eastern Rainbow** magazine.

Peer Poetry International

26 (wh) Arlington House, Bath Street BA1 1QN

☎01225 445298

✉ peerpoetry@msn.com

www.publish-your-poetry.com

Contact *Paul Amphlett*

Biannual; 60 poets per issue.

The Penniless Press

100 Waterloo Road, Ashton, Preston PR2 1EP

☎01772 736421

www.pennilesspress.co.uk

Contact *Alan Dent*

Quarterly for the poor pocket and the rich mind. Poetry, fiction, essays, reviews.

Pennine Ink Magazine

The Gallery, Mid-Pennine Arts, Yorke Street, Burnley BB11 1HD

☎01282 703657

✉ sheridansdandl@yahoo.co.uk

Contact *Laura Sheridan*

Quality poetry reflecting traditional and modern trends.

Pennine Platform

Frizingley Hall, Frizinghall Road, Bradford BD9 4LD

☎01274 541015

✉ nicholas.bielby@virgin.co.uk

www.pennineplatform.co.uk

Contact *Nicholas Bielby*

Biannual poetry magazine; eclectic and serious-minded. Considers hard copy submissions only.

Planet

PO Box 44, Aberystwyth SY23 3ZZ

☎01970 611255 Fax 01970 611197

✉ planet.enquiries@planetmagazine.org.uk

www.planetmagazine.org.uk

Contact *John Barnie*

The Welsh Internationalist: current affairs, arts, environment.

Poet Tree

289 Elmwood Avenue, Feltham TW13 7QB

Contact *Ian Deal*

Contemporary poetry magazine. See also **Partners** press, **A Bard Hair Day** and **Imagenation** magazines.

Poetic Hours

43 Willow Road, Carlton, Nottingham NG4 3BH

✉ erranpublishing@hotmail.com

www.poetichours.homestead.com

Contact *Nick Clark*

Non-profit supporter of Third World charities. See also **Erran Publishing**.

Poetic Licence

70 Aveling Close, Purley CR8 4DW

✉ poets@poetsanon.org.uk

www.poetsanon.org.uk

Contact *Peter L. Evans*

Original unpublished poems and drawings. See also **Poets Anonymous** press.

The Poetry Church

Feather Books, PO Box 438, Shrewsbury SY3 0WN

☎01743 872177 Fax 01743 872177

✉ john@waddysweb.freeuk.com

www.waddysweb.freeuk.com

Contact *Rev. J. Waddington-Feather*

Quarterly magazine of Christian poetry and prayers. See **Feather Books** under *Small Presses*.

Poetry Combination Module

PEF Productions, 196 High Road, London N22 8HH

✉ page84direct@yahoo.co.uk

www.geocities.com/andyfloydplease

Contact *Mr PEF*

Poetry, anti-poetry, aphorism and artwork magazine by PEF and guest artists. Submissions welcome.

Poetry Cornwall/ Bardhonyeth Kernow

11a Penryn Street, Redruth TR15 2SP
☎01209 218209
✉ poetrycornwall@yahoo.com
www.poetrycornwall.freeservers.com

Editor *Les Merton*

Publishes poets from around the world, including 'Meet the Editors', poetry in its original language with English translation and poetry in Kernewek and Cornish dialect. Three issues a year. Submission guidelines on the website.

Poetry Express

Studio 11, Bickerton House, 25–27 Bickerton Road, London N19 5JT
☎020 7281 4654
✉ alan@survivorspoetry.org.uk
www.survivorspoetry.com

Contact *Alan Morrison & Others*

Quarterly newsletter from **Survivors' Poetry** (see entry under *Organisations of Interest to Poets*).

Poetry Ireland News

2 Proud's Lane, Dublin 2, Republic of Ireland
☎00 353 1 478 9974 Fax 00 353 1 478 0205
✉ publications@poetryireland.ie
www.poetryireland.ie

Contact *Paul Lenehan*

Bi-monthly newsletter. See also **Poetry Ireland Review** magazine.

Poetry Ireland Review/ Eigse Eireann

2 Proud's Lane, Dublin 2, Republic of Ireland
☎00 353 1 478 9974 Fax 00 353 1 478 0205
✉ poetry@iol.ie
www.poetryireland.ie

Contact *Peter Sirr*

Quarterly journal of poetry and reviews. See also **Poetry Ireland News** magazine.

Poetry London

1a Jewel Road, London E17 4QU
☎020 8521 0776 Fax 020 8521 0776
✉ editors@poetrylondon.co.uk
www.poetrylondon.co.uk

Poetry Editor *Maurice Riordan*

Poetry, listings, reviews, features and information.

Poetry Nottingham

11 Orkney Close, Stenson Fields, Derby DE24 3LW
✉ adrian.buckner@btopenworld.com

Contact *Adrian Buckner*

Poetry, articles, reviews, published quarterly.

Poetry Review

Poetry Society, 22 Betterton Street, London WC2H 9BU
☎020 7420 9883 Fax 020 7240 4818
✉ poetryreview@poetrysociety.org.uk
www.poetrysoc.org.uk

Contact *Fiona Sampson*

The senior review of contemporary poetry. Quarterly.

Poetry Salzburg Review

Dept. of English, University of Salzburg, Akademiestr. 24, A–5020 Salzburg, Austria
☎00 43 662 8044 4424
Fax 00 43 662 8044 167
✉ editor@poetrysalzburg.com
www.poetrysalzburg.com

Contact *Wolfgang Görtschacher*

Editorial board: *David Miller* (99 Mitre Road, London SE1 8PT); *Robert Dassanowsky* (Dept. of Languages & Cultures, University of Colorado, 1420 Austin Bluffs, Colorado CO 80933, USA)

Poetry magazine, formerly *The Poet's Voice*. Published at the University of Salzburg. Publishes new poetry, translations, interviews, review–essays and artwork.

Poetry Scotland

91–93 Main Street, Callander FK17 8BQ
www.poetryscotland.co.uk

Contact *Sally Evans*

All-poetry broadsheet with Scottish emphasis. See also **Diehard Publishers** press.

Poetry Wales

57 Nolton Street, Bridgend CF31 3BN
☎01656 663018 Fax 01656 649226
✉ poetrywales@seren-books.com
www.poetrywales.co.uk

Contact *Robert Minhinnick*

An international magazine with a reputation for fine writing and criticism. See also **Seren Books** under *UK Publishers*.

Premonitions

13 Hazely Combe, Arreton, Isle of Wight PO30 3AJ

☎01983 865668
✉ mail@pigasus.press.co.uk
www.pigasuspress.co.uk

Contact *Tony Lee*

Magazine of science fiction and horror stories, with genre poetry and artwork. See also **Pigasus Press**.

Presence

12 Grovehall Avenue, Leeds LS11 7EX
✉ martin.lucas2@btinternet.com
freespace.virgin.net/haiku.presence

Contact *Martin Lucas*

Haiku, senryu, tanka, renku and related poetry in English.

Pulsar Poetry Magazine

34 Lineacre Close, Grange Park, Swindon SN5 6DA
☎01793 875941
✉ pulsar.ed@btopenworld.com
www.pulsarpoetry.com

Contact *David Pike*

Hard-hitting/inspirational poetry with a message and meaning. Biannual.

Purple Patch

25 Griffiths Road, West Bromwich B71 2EH
☎07950 591455
✉ ppatch66@hotmail.com
www.purplepatchpoetry.co.uk

Contact *Geoff Stevens*

Poetry mag founded 1976. Includes reviews and gossip column. See also **The Firing Squad** magazine and **Poetry Wednesbury** press.

Quantum Leap

York House, 15 Argyle Terrace, Rothesay, Isle of Bute PA20 0BD

Contact *Alan Carter*

User-friendly magazine – encourages new writers; all types of poetry – pays. Mark envelope 'Guidelines' and enclose s.a.e. or two IRCs if from abroad. See also **QQ Press**.

Quattrocento

Bodnant, 11 Llwynon Gardens, Llandudno LL30 2HP
☎07986 824336

Contact *Malcolm Bradley*

An independent journal of the arts made in Wales.

The Quiet Feather

St Mary's Cottage, Church Street, Dalton in Furness LA15 8BA
☎01229 468967
✉ editors@thequietfeather.co.uk
www.thequietfeather.co.uk

Contact *Dominic Hall & Taissa Csaky*

Lively and eclectic quarterly: short stories, poetry, travel, essays, cartoons, photographs, line drawings; all welcome.

The Radiator

Flat 10, 21 Greenheys Road, Liverpool L8 0SX

Contact *Scott Thurston*

Publishes commissioned essays on poetry by contemporary poets.

Rainbow Poetry News

14 Lewes Crescent, Brighton BN2 1FH
☎01273 687053
✉ beyondcloister@hotmail.co.uk

Contact *Hugh C. Hellicar*

Quarterly with poems, articles and news of poetry recitals in London and the South East.

Raw Edge Magazine

PO Box 4867, Birmingham B3 3HD

Contact *Dave Reeves*

New writing, free from outlets in ACE, West Midlands area. Writers with a regional connection only. See also **The Moving Finger Press**.

Read the Music

20 Wharfedale Street, Wednesbury WS10 9AG
☎07970 441110
✉ mooncrow@tiscali.co.uk
www.poetrywednesbury.co.uk

Contact *Brendan Hawthorne*

Original poetry based on music and its influences.

The Reater

Wrecking Ball Press, 24 Cavendish Square, Hull HU3 1SS
☎01482 210226
✉ editor@wreckingballpress.com
www.wreckingballpress.com

Contact *Shane Rhodes*

No flowers, just blunt, chiselled poetry.

Red Poets – Y Beirdd Coch

26 Andrew's Close, Heolgerrig, Merthyr Tydfil CF48 1SS
☎01685 376726

✉ marc.jones@phonecoop.com

Contact *Mike Jenkins & Marc Jones*

A magazine of left-wing poetry from Wales and beyond: socialist, republican and anarchist.

Reflections

PO Box 178, Sunderland SR1 1DU

✉ reflections1@fastmail.fm

Poetry by and for men and women of goodwill.

The Rialto

PO Box 309, Aylsham, Norwich NR11 6LN

✉ mail@therialto.co.uk

www.therialto.co.uk

Contact *Michael Mackmin*

Excellent poetry in a clear environment. Buy online at www.impressbooks.co.uk See also **Rialto Publications** press.

Roundyhouse

3 Crown Street, Port Talbot SA13 1BG

✉ srjones@alunbooks.co.uk

Contact *Sally R. Jones*

Poems and articles on poetry. Reviews. Eclectic approach.

Rubies In the Darkness

41 Grantham Road, Manor Park, London E12 5LZ

Contact *P.G.P.Thompson*

Romantic, lyrical, spiritual, inspirational, traditional and mystical poetry. See also **Precious Pearl Press**.

Sable

PO Box 33504, London E9 7YE

✉ info@sablelitmag.org

Contact *Kadija Sesay*

Literary magazine for writers of African, Caribbean and Asian descent. Poetry, prose, memoirs, travel, etc.

Saw

4 Masefield Avenue, Pilton, Barnstaple EX31 1QJ

☎01271 342999

✉ sawpoems@btinternet.com

Contact *Colin Shaddick*

Poems that are radical, multicultural and international in outlook.

Scar Tissue

Pigasus Press, 13 Hazley Combe, Arreton, Isle of Wight PO30 3AJ

Contact *Tony Lee*

SF genre poetry, short fiction, cartoons and artwork.

Scribbler!

Remus House, Coltsfoot Drive, Woodston, Peterborough PE2 9JX

☎01733 890066 Fax 01733 313524

✉ youngwriters@forwardpress.co.uk

www.youngwriters.co.uk

Contact *Lynsey Hawkins*

Quarterly magazine by 7–11-year-olds: poetry, stories, guest authors, workshops, features.

Scriptor

2 Chambers Cottages, Underlyn Lane, Marden, Tonbridge TN12 9BD

☎01622 832485

✉ mail@johndench.demon.co.uk

Contact *John Dench*

Poetry, short stories, essays from the UK; publishes biennially. See also **Green Arrow Publishing** press.

The Seventh Quarry

Dan-Y-Bryn, 74 Cwm Level Road, Brynhyfryd, Swansea SA5 9DY

Fax 01792 774070

Contact *Peter Thabit Jones*

Poetry from Swansea and beyond.

Shearsman

58 Velwell Road, Exeter EX4 4LD

☎01392 434511 Fax 01392 434511

✉ editor@shearsman.com

www.shearsman.com

Contact *Tony Frazer*

Mainly poetry, some prose, some reviews. Poetry in the modernist tradition. No fiction. See also **Shearsman Books** press.

The ShOp: A Magazine Of Poetry

Skeagh, Schull, Co. Cork, Republic of Ireland

✉ Theshop@theshop-poetry-magazine.ie

(Not for submissions)

www.theshop-poetry-magazine.ie

Contact *John Wakeman & Hilary Wakeman*

International but with emphasis on Irish poetry.

Skald

6 Hill Street, Menai Bridge LL59 5AG

☎01248 712880

✉ editors@skald.co.uk

www.skald.co.uk

Contact *Zoe Skoulding*

Poetry, prose and artwork. Open to experimental/innovative writing.

Smiths Knoll

Goldings, Goldings Lane, Leiston IP16 4EB

Contact *Joanna Cutts & Michael Laskey*

Poems worth re-reading; two-week turnaround for submissions.

Smoke

The Windows Project, 96 Bold Street, Liverpool L1 4HY

☎0151 709 3688

www.windowsproject.demon.co.uk

Contact *Dave Ward*

Poetry, graphics, short prose. Biannual; 24pp.

South

PO Box 5369, Poole BH14 0XN

Contact *Richard Hicks*

Poetry magazine from the southern counties of England that welcomes poets from across the world. Poems judged anonymously.

Southword

84 Douglas Street, Cork, Republic of Ireland

www.munsterlit.ie

Contact *Frank O'Connor House*

Biannual, 120 pages of poetry, fiction, visual art and book reviews.

Sphinx

21 Hatton Green, Glenrothes KY7 4SD

✉ nell@happenstancepress.com

www.happenstancepress.com

Contact *Helena Nelson*

A feature & review-based magazine focusing on poetry publishing: who, how and why. No unsolicited submissions. See also **Happenstance Press**.

SPL Newsletter

Scottish Poetry Library, 5 Crichton's Close, Canongate, Edinburgh EH8 8DT

☎0131 557 2876 Fax 0131 557 8393

✉ inquiries@spl.org.uk

www.spl.org.uk

Contact *Robyn Marsack*

Newsletter of the Scottish Poetry Library.

Springboard

Corrimbla, Ballina, Co. Mayo, Republic of Ireland

✉ bobgroom@eircom.net

Contact *Robert Groom*

Short fiction, poetry and articles.

The Stinging Fly

PO Box 6016, Dublin 8, Republic of Ireland

✉ stingingfly@gmail.com

www.stingingfly.org

Contact *Declan Meade*

New Irish and international writing. Poetry, short fiction, author interviews, essays and book reviews. See also **Stinging Fly Press**.

The Student Magazine

24 Frosty Hollow, East Hunsbury NN4 0SY

☎01604 701730 Fax 01604 701730

Contact *Jacqueline Gonzalez-Marina*

Poetry, articles, interviews, art and illustration. Biannual magazine. No religious or political material. 'Essential to become a subscriber when seeking publication': UK, £16 p.a.; Europe, £30; RoW, US$70. See also **Dandelion Arts Magazine**.

The Supplement

38 Pierrot Steps, 71 Kursaal Way, Southend on Sea SS1 2UY

✉ atlanteanpublishing@hotmail.com

www.geocities.com/dj_tyrer/mms.html

Contact *D.J. Tyrer*

Non-fiction: articles, news, reviews, letters, etc. See also **Awen**, **Bard**, **Garbaj** and **Monomyth** magazines and **Atlantean Publishing** press.

Taliesin

Academi, Mount Stuart House, Mount Stuart Square, Cardiff CV10 5FQ

☎029 2047 2266 Fax 029 2049 2930

✉ taliesin@academi.org

www.academi.org

Contact *Manon Rhys & Christine James*

Wales' leading Welsh language literary journal, published three times a year.

Tears in the Fence

38 Hod View, Stourpaine, Nr Blandford Forum DT11 8TN

☎01258 456803 Fax 01258 454026

✉ david@davidcaddy.wanadoo.co.uk

www.tearsinthefence.co.uk

Contact *David Caddy*

A magazine looking for the unusual, perceptive, risk-taking, lived and visionary literature.

Temenos Academy Review
PO Box 203, Ashford TN25 5ZT
✉ stephenovery@onetel.com
www.temenosacademy.org

10th Muse
33 Hartington Road, Southampton
SO14 0EW
✉ andyj@noplace.screaming.net

Contact *Andrew Jordan*

Publishes poetry and reviews as well as short prose (usually no more than 2000 words) and graphics.

The Third Half
16 Fane Close, Stamford PE9 1HG
☎01780 754193

Contact *Kevin Troop*

Searches for good poetry and fiction. See also **KT Publications** press.

Time Haiku
Basho-an, 105 King's Head Hill, London
E4 7JG
☎020 8529 6478
✉ facey@aol.com

Contact *Erica Facey*
Editor *Doreen King*

Founded 1994. Promotes haiku and haiku-related forms. Aims to increase accessibility through education by encouraging school and college activities as well as providing a biannual journal and newsletter.

Understanding
127 Milton Road West, 7 Duddingston House Courtyard, Edinburgh EH15 1JG

Contact *Denise Smith*

Original poetry, short stories, parts of plays, reviews and articles. See also **Dionysia Press**.

The Unruly Sun
Rising Sun Arts Centre, 30 Silver Street, Reading RG1 2ST
✉ submissions@hotmail.com
www.unrulysun.co.uk

Contact *Jennifer Hoskins & Others*

Contemporary poetry from the margins. 'If we love it, we print it.'

Urthona
Old Abbey House, Abbey Road, Cambridge CB5 8HQ
☎01223 306513
✉ urthonamag@onetel.com
www.urthona.com

Contact *Ratnagarbha*

The only Buddhist arts magazine: artists, poetry, essays, world culture from a Buddhist perspective.

Wasafiri
The Open University in London, 1–11 Hawley Crescent, Camden Town, London NW1 8NP
☎020 7556 6110 Fax 020 7556 6187
✉ wasafiri@open.ac.uk
www.wasafiri.org

Literary journal of international and diasporic writing with special focus on Asia, Africa and the Caribbean.

Wordsmith
Remus House, Coltsfoot Drive, Woodston, Peterborough PE2 9JX
☎01733 890066 Fax 01733 313524
✉ youngwriters@forwardpress.co.uk
www.youngwriters.co.uk

Contact *Allison Dowse*

Poetry, stories, guest authors, features in a quarterly magazine for 11–18-year-olds. See also **Scribbler!** magazine.

Zed20
33 Lady Nairn Avenue, Kirkcaldy KY1 2AW
☎01592 651522

Contact *Duncan Glen*

See also **Akros Publications** press.

Organisations of Interest to Poets

A survey of some of the societies, groups and other bodies which may be of interest to practising poets. Organisations not listed should send details to the Editor for inclusion in future editions.

Academi – The Welsh National Literature Promotion Agency and Society for Writers

3rd Floor, Mount Stuart House, Mount Stuart Square, Cardiff Bay CF10 5FQ
☎029 2047 2266 Fax 029 2049 2930
✉ post@academi.org
www.academi.org

North Wales Office: Ty Newydd, Llanystumdwy, Cricieth, Gwynedd LL52 0LW
West Wales Office: Dylan Thomas Centre, Somerset Place, Swansea SA1 1RR
Glyn Jones Centre: Wales Millennium Centre, Cardiff

Chief Executive *Peter Finch*

The writers' organisation of Wales with special responsibility for literary activity, writers' residencies, writers on tour, festivals, writers' groups, readings, tours, exchanges and other development work. Academi awards financial bursaries annually, runs a criticism service and organises the **Welsh Book of the Year Awards**. **Yr Academi Gymreig/The Welsh Academy** operates the Arts Council of Wales franchise for Wales-wide literature development. It has offices in Cardiff and fieldworkers elsewhere in Wales. Publisher of the lottery-funded *Encyclopedia of Wales*, the Welsh-medium literary magazine *Taliesin*, the *Academi English-Welsh Dictionary*, co-publisher of *The New Welsh Review* along with a number of other projects. The Academi sponsors a range of annual contests including the John Tripp Award For Spoken Poetry and the prestigious **Academi Cardiff International Poetry Competition**. Publishes *A470*, a bi-monthly literary information magazine.

Apples & Snakes

Battersea Arts Centre, Lavender Hill, London SW11 5TN
☎020 7924 3410 Fax 020 7924 3763
✉ info@applesandsnakes.org
www.applesandsnakes.org

Director *Geraldine Collinge*

Set up in 1982 as a platform for poetry which would be popular, relevant, cross-cultural and accessible to the widest possible range of people, A&S aims to stretch the boundaries of Poetry in Education and performance. Currently undergoing an extensive programme of expansion, bringing performance poetry to new places and new audiences across England.

The Arvon Foundation

See entry under *UK Writers' Courses*

Back Room Poets

✉ matt@brpoets.org
www.myspace.com/backroompoets

Oxford-based poetry group. Membership gives access to workshops, open mic evenings, guest readings and opportunities to take part in literary festivals. E-mail for more information.

The British Haiku Society

38 Wayside Avenue, Hornchurch RM12 4LL
☎01772 251827
www.britishhaikusociety.org

General Secretary *Doreen King*

Formed in 1990. Promotes the appreciation and writing of haiku, senryu, tanka, haibun and renku, and welcomes overseas members. It provides tutorials, workshops, readings, critical comment and information. The Society runs a haiku library and administers a haiku contest. The journal, *Blithe Spirit*, is produced quarterly. The Society has active local groups and issues a regular newsletter. Current membership details can be obtained from the website.

Contemporary Poetics Research Centre

School of English and Humanities, Birkbeck College, Malet Street, London WC1E 7HX
✉ w.rowe@bbk.ac.uk *or* c.watts@bbk.ac.uk
www.bbk.ac.uk/eh/research/
   contemppoeticscentre

Contacts *Will Rowe & Carol Watts*

Dedicated to fostering research, performance and practice in all modes and formats of contemporary poetry. It runs a Creative Reading

Workshop, holds readings, performances, talks and debates and organises conferences, the latest of which was E Poetry London 2005. It collaborates closely with Royal Holloway University of London and the Centre for Cultural Poetics at the University of Southampton, e.g. on the British Electronic Poetry Centre at www.soton.ac.uk/~bepc Poets associated with the Centre include Ulli Freer, Caroline Bergvall and Bill Griffiths. The Centre publishes the web journal www.pores.bbk.ac.uk

The Eight Hand Gang

5 Cross Farm, Station Road North, Fearnhead, Warrington WA2 0QG

Secretary *John F. Haines*

An association of SF poets. Publishes *Handshake*, a single-sheet newsletter of SF poetry and information available free in exchange for an s.a.e.

57 Productions

57 Effingham Road, Lee Green, London SE12 8NT

☎020 8463 0866 Fax 020 8463 0866
✉ info@57productions.com
www.57productions.com

Contact *Paul Beasley*

Specialises in the promotion of poetry and its production through an agency service, a programme of events and a series of audio publications. Services are available to event promoters, festivals, education institutions and the media. Poets represented include Jean 'Binta' Breeze, Adrian Mitchell, John Cooper Clarke and Liz Lochhead. 57 Productions' series of audio cassettes, CDs and Poetry in Performance compilations offer access to some of the most exciting poets working in Britain today – check their Poetry Jukebox on their excellent website.

The Football Poets

4 The Retreat, Butterow, Stroud GL5 2LS

☎01453 757376
✉ editors@footballpoets.org *and*
ctm@crispinthomas.orangehome.co.uk
www.footballpoets.org

Editor & Performance *Crispin Thomas*
Co-Editors *Simon Williams, Peter Goulding*

The Football Poets exist to promote and encourage the writing, reading and performing of football poetry. Formed in 1995, they perform extensively and also provide comprehensive football poetry workshops in schools, football clubs, prisons and communities. Their website is a fast, free and entertaining mix of literature and

soccer poetry from around the world. Anyone may contribute. The site has recently been archived by the British Library.

Performance Poetry Society

PO Box 11178, Birmingham B11 4WP
✉ performancepoetry@yahoo.com
Branch contact and rehearsal room: The Old Meeting House, behind 20/22 Wolverhampton Street, Dudley
Contact *Sandra Dennis*
Dudley Branch contact: *Jim MacCool*
    (☎ 01384 258191)

PPS was founded in 1999 by members of the Birmingham Midland Institute to serve the interests of performance poets and poetry in performance throughout the UK and Ireland. Initiated October as National Poetry Month in 2000. Organises an extensive national tour each autumn, visiting small halls, colleges, schools and prisons. The Society has an in-house publishing company, Poetry Powerhouse Press.

The Poetry Archive

PO Box 286, Stroud GL6 1AL
☎01453 832090 Fax 01453 836450
✉ info@poetryarchive.org
www.poetryarchive.org

Directors *Richard Carrington, Andrew Motion*

A permanent online archive of audio recordings of work by poets who write in English. New 60-minute recordings are made for the Archive by a wide-ranging list of poets; extracts from those recordings are available on their website launched in 2005. The site also contains a wealth of educational and intepretative information and the full-length recordings are available on CD for purchase by mail order. A registered charity, the Archive intends to ensure that all significant poets are recorded for posterity and that their recordings are fully valued and enjoyed.

The Poetry Book Society

Fourth Floor, 2 Tavistock Place, London WC1H 9RA
☎020 7833 9247 Fax 020 7833 5990
✉ info@poetrybooks.co.uk
www.poetrybooks.co.uk
www.poetrybookshoponline.com
www.childrenspoetrybookshelf.co.uk

Director *Chris Holifield*
Editorial/Marketing Officer *Sian Lambert*
Sales/Membership Officer *James Knapton*

For readers, writers, students and teachers of poetry. Founded in 1953 by T.S. Eliot and funded by the Arts Council, the PBS is a unique membership organisation and book club providing up-to-date and comprehensive information about poetry from publishers in the UK and Ireland. Members receive the quarterly *Poet Selectors' Choice* and the quarterly *PBS Bulletin* packed with articles by poets, poems, news, listings and access to discounts of at least 25% off featured titles. Subscriptions start at £10. The relaunched PBS website (www.poetrybooks.co.uk) has a recruitment area and a closed section for members. PBS also offers a range of over 30,000 poetry titles at www.poetrybookshoponline.com. During 2005 the PBS relaunched the children's Poetry Bookshelf (www.childrenspoetrybookshelf.co.uk) range of books and new membership schemes for parents, grandparents and libraries. Also runs the annual **T.S. Eliot Prize** for the best collection of new poetry. In 2004 it ran the Next Generation Poets promotion.

The Poetry Business

The Studio, Byram Arcade, Westgate, Huddersfield HD1 1ND
☎01484 434840 Fax 01484 426566
✉ edit@poetrybusiness.co.uk
www.poetrybusiness.co.uk
Directors *Peter Sansom, Janet Fisher*

Founded in 1986, the Business publishes *The North* magazine and books and pamphlets under the Smith/Doorstop imprint. It runs an annual competition and organises writing days and a Writing School. Send an s.a.e. for full details.

Poetry Can

Unit 11, 20–22 Hepburn Road, Bristol BS2 8UD
☎0117 942 6976 Fax 0117 944 1478
✉ admin@poetrycan.co.uk
www.poetrycan.co.uk
Director *Colin Brown*
Administrator *Peter Hunter*

Founded in 1995, Poetry Can is a poetry development agency working across Bristol and the South West Region areas. It organises an education programme and events such as the annual Bristol Poetry Festival, lifelong learning projects and provides information and advice concerning all aspects of poetry to individuals, agencies and organisations. It also hosts the Literature South West website.

Poetry Ireland/Eigse Eireann

2 Proud's Lane, Dublin 2, Republic of Ireland
☎00 353 1 478 9974 Fax 00 353 1 478 0205

✉ poetry@iol.ie
www.poetryireland.ie

Education ☎ 00 353 671 4216
Writers in Schools scheme
☎ 00 353 1 475 8601
Acting Director *Jane O'Hanlon*

Poetry Ireland is the national organisation for poetry in Ireland, with its four core activities being readings, publications, education and an information and resource service. Organises readings by Irish and international poets countrywide. Through its website, telephone, post and public enquiries, Poetry Ireland operates as a clearing house for everything pertaining to poetry in Ireland. Operates the Writers in Schools scheme. Publishes *Poetry Ireland News*, a bi-monthly newsletter containing information on events, competitions and opportunities. *Poetry Ireland Review* appears quarterly and is the journal of record for poetry in Ireland; current editor: *Peter Sirr*.

The Poetry Library

Royal Festival Hall, Level 5, London SE1 8XX
☎020 7921 0943/0664 Fax 020 7921 0939
✉ info@poetrylibrary.org.uk
www.poetrylibrary.org.uk
www.poetrymagazines.org.uk
Librarian *Simon Smith*

Founded by the Arts Council in 1953. A collection of 90,000 titles of modern poetry since 1912, from Georgian to Rap, representing all English-speaking countries and including translations into English by contemporary poets. Two copies of each title are held, one for loan and one for reference. A wide range of poetry magazines and ephemera from all over the world are kept along with cassettes, records and videos for consultation, with many available for loan. There is a children's poetry section with teacher's resource collection. An information service compiles lists of poetry magazines, competitions, publishers, groups and workshops which are available from the Library on receipt of a large s.a.e., or direct from the website. The main website also has a noticeboard for lost quotations through which it tries to identify lines or fragments of poetry which have been sent in by other readers.

Poetry London

1a Jewel Road, London E17 4QU
✉ editors@poetrylondon.co.uk
www.poetrylondon.co.uk

Contacts *Gyonghi Vegh* (listings), *Maurice Riordan* (poetry editor), *Scott Verner* (reviews)

Published three times a year, *Poetry London* includes poetry by new and established writers, reviews of recent collections and anthologies, articles on issues relating to poetry, and an encyclopædic listings section of virtually everything to do with poetry in the capital and elsewhere in the UK.

The Poetry School

1a Jewel Road, London E17 4QU
☎0845 223 5274 Fax 020 8223 0439
✉ jacqueline@poetryschool.com
www.poetryschool.com

Administrator *Julia Bird*
Marketing Manager *Jacqueline Gabbitas*

Funded by Arts Council England, London, The Poetry School offers a wide range of courses and workshops on writing and reading poetry and is open to anyone regardless of experience or formal qualifications. Tutors include Mimi Khalvati, Stephen Knight, Linda Chase, Graham Fawcett, Pascale Petit, Myra Schneider and Penelope Shuttle. The School provides a forum for practitioners to share experiences, develop skills and extend appreciation of the traditional and innovative aspects of their art. There are Special Events with visiting poets such as Marilyn Hacker, Jorie Graham, Molly Peacock, Galway Kinnell, Paul Muldoon, Alfred Corn and Sharon Olds. The Poetry School is a Registered Charity No. 1069314.

The Poetry Society

22 Betterton Street, London WC2H 9BX
☎020 7240 9881 Fax 020 7240 4818
✉ info@poetrysociety.org.uk
www.poetrysociety.org.uk

Director *Jules Mann*

Founded in 1909 which ought to make it venerable, the Society exists to help poets and poetry thrive in Britain. In the past decade it has undergone a renaissance, reaching out from its Covent Garden base to promote the national health of poetry in a range of imaginative ways. Membership costs £35 for individuals. *Poetry News* membership is £15. Current activities include:

★ Quarterly magazine of new verse, views and criticism, *Poetry Review*.

★ Quarterly newsletter, *Poetry News*, with lively relevant articles for members.

★ Promotions, events and cooperation with Britain's many literature festivals, poetry venues and poetry publishers.

★ Competitions and awards, including the annual **National Poetry Competition** with a £5000 first prize.

★ A manuscript diagnosis service, *The Poetry Prescription*, which gives detailed reports on submissions. Reduced rates for members.

★ Provides information and advice, publishes books, posters and resources for schools and libraries. Education membership costs £50 (secondary) or £30 (primary) which includes free poetry anthologies, lesson plans and a subscription to Poems on the Underground. Publications include *The Poetry Book For Primary Schools* and *Jumpstart Poetry for the Secondary School*, colourful poetry posters for Keystages 1, 2, 3 and 4. Many of Britain's most popular poets – including Michael Rosen, Roger McGough and Jackie Kay – contribute, offering advice and inspiration.

★ The Society's online poetry classroom is at www.poetryclass.net

★ The Poetry Café serving snacks and drinks to members, friends and guests, part of The Poetry Place, a venue for many poetry activities – readings, workshops and poetry launches. This space is available for bookings (☎ 020 7420 9887).

★ *Poetry Landmarks of Britain*, a free resource on the Society's website, packed with regional poetry places, publishers, venues and regular events.

The Poetry Trust

The Cut, 9 New Cut, Halesworth IP9 8BY
☎01986 835950
✉ info@thepoetrytrust.org
www.thepoetrytrust.org

Director *Naomi Jaffa*

The flagship literature organisation for the East of England, funded by Arts Council England. The Trust promotes high quality contemporary poetry and works to increase people's enjoyment of reading, writing and teaching poetry. It organises the renowned international **Aldeburgh Poetry Festival**, held annually over the first weekend in November; the **Jerwood Aldeburgh First Collection Prize**; and a range of poetry events, workshops and residential writing courses. Its creative education programme, funded by the Paul Hamlyn Foundation, includes writing workshops for teachers and students and poetry tours to schools. The Poetry Trust, Registered Charity No. 1102893.

Point

Ithaca, Apdo. 125, E–03590 Altea, Spain

☎00 34 96 584 2350 Fax 00 34 96 688 2767
✉ elpoeta@point-editions.com
www.point-editions.com

Also at: Schapenstraat 157, B–1750 Lennik, Belgium

Director *Germain Droogenbroodt*

Founded as POetry INTernational in 1984, Point is based in Spain and Belgium. A multilingual publisher of contemporary verse from *established* poets, the organisation has brought out more than 80 titles in at least eight languages, including English. Point Editions runs the original work alongside a verse translation into Dutch made in cooperation with the poet. The organisation's website features the world's best known and unknown poets in English, Spanish and Dutch. Point also co-organises an annual international poetry festival.

The Railway Prism

myweb.tiscali.co.uk/railwayprism

The Ralway Prism website is a focal point for lovers of railway poetry. Preferably unpublished submissions welcome about railways old and new, reflecting industrial history, childhood nostalgia and modern rail travel both above and below ground level. 'We're after atmosphere rather than dry facts.'

Regional Arts Councils

See **Arts Councils and Regional Offices**, pages 541–542.

Scottish Pamphlet Poetry

No 4 Cottage, High Swinton, Masham HG4 4JH
✉ hazel@scottish-pamphlet-poetry.biz
www.scottish-pamphlet-poetry.com

Administrator *Hazel Cameron*

A publisher collective of more than 50 mainly Scottish-based presses promoting poetry published as pamphlets. A pamphlet is defined as not less than six pages but no more than 30 and with a first edition of less than 300 copies. The organisation has an excellent website, publishes a video, runs book fairs and events, and administers the annual Callum Macdonald Memorial Award created to recognise publishing skill and effort in the pamphlet form.

Scottish Poetry Library

5 Crichton's Close, Canongate, Edinburgh EH8 8DT
☎0131 557 2876 Fax 0131 557 8393
✉ inquiries@spl.org.uk

www.spl.org.uk

Director *Robyn Marsack*
Librarian *Julie Johnstone*

A comprehensive reference and lending collection of work by Scottish poets in Gaelic, Scots and English, plus the work of British, European and international poets. Stock includes books, audio, videos, news cuttings and magazines. Borrowing is free to all. Services include a postal lending scheme, for which there is a small fee; enquiries; schools workshops throughout Scotland on application; exhibitions; bibliographies; publications; general information in the field of poetry. Also available is an online catalogue and index to Scottish poetry periodicals. There is a Friends' scheme costing £20 annually. Friends receive a newsletter and other benefits and support the library.

Second Light

9 Greendale Close, London SE22 8TG
✉ dilyswood@tiscali.co.uk

Director *Dilys Wood*

A network of over 350 women poets, major names and less well-known. With its publishing arm, Second Light Publications, the network aims to develop and promote women's poetry. Issues a twice-yearly newsletter with poetry, articles and reviews; runs an annual poetry competition; holds residential workshops, readings; has published three anthologies of women's poetry.

Spiel Unlimited

20 Coxwell Street, Cirencester GL7 2BH
☎01285 640470/07814 830031
✉ spiel@arbury.freeserve.co.uk *or* info@spiel.wanadoo.co.uk
www.thepeoplespoet.com/spiel

Directors *Marcus Moore, Sara-Jane Arbury*

'Spoken word, written word, anywhere, everywhere' with two writers who put a positive charge in live literature by organising quirky and original events such as Slam!Fests, Spontaneity Days and Living Room Poetry performances, hosting UK poetry slams and running *word*shops for schools and adults. Also produce *SPIEL*, a monthly e-mail newsletter. Specialists in breathing new life into literature.

Survivors' Poetry

Studio 11, Bickerton House, 25–27 Bickerton Road, London N19 5JT
☎020 7281 4654
✉ info@survivorspoetry.org.uk
www.survivorspoetry.com

National Outreach:
royb@survivorspoetry.org.uk
National Mentoring Scheme & Poetry Express:
alan@survivorspoetry.org.uk

A unique national literature organisation promoting poetry by survivors of mental distress through workshops, readings and performances to audiences all over the UK. It was founded in 1991 by four poets with first-hand experience of the mental health system. Survivors' community outreach work provides training and performance workshops and publishing projects. For the organisation's quarterly magazine, see *Poetry Express*. Survivors work with those who have survived mental distress and those who empathise with their experience.

Ty Newydd Writers' Centre

Llanystumdwy, Cricieth LL52 0LW
☎01766 522811 Fax 01766 523095
✉ post@tynewydd.org
www.tynewydd.org
Executive Director *Sally Baker*

Run by the Taliesin Trust, an independent, Arvon-style residential writers centre established in the one-time home of Lloyd George in North Wales. The programme (in both Welsh and English) has a regular poetry content. (See also *UK Writers' Courses*.) Fees start at £205 for weekends and £410 for week-long courses. Bursaries available. Among the many tutors to-date have been: Gillian Clarke, Owen Sheers, Robert Minhinnick, Liz Lochhead, Michael Longley, Ian Macmillan and Jo Shapcott. Send for the centre's descriptive leaflets and programme of courses.

The Western Writers' Centre / Ionad Scriobhneoirí Chaitlin Maud

34 Nuns Island, Galway, Republic of Ireland
☎00 353 91 533595
✉ westernwriters@eircom.net
www.twwc.ie
Director *Fred Johnston*

Founded 2001. The only writers' centre in the West Shannon region, named after the late Caitlin Maud, prominent Irish-language activist, poet and singer. Courses, organised readings and workshops are held in the Galway City and County area. Small library of literary periodicals. News and reviews of books in the 'Kiosque!' section of the website. Publishes new short stories and poems in Gaelic and English. Accepts original work for online publication in Gaelic, English and French. No payment for publication.

Small Presses

Aard Press
c/o Aardverx, 31 Mountearl Gardens, London
SW16 2NL
Managing Editors *Dawn Redwood, D. Jarvis*
Founded 1971. Publishes artists' bookworks,
experimental/visual poetry and art theory, topo-
graphics, ephemera and ibnternational mail-art
documentation. Very small editions. No unsolicited material or proposals.
ROYALTIES not paid. No sale-or-return deals.

Accent Press
The Old School, Upper High Street, Bedlinog
CF46 6SA
☎01443 710930 Fax 0870 130 6934
✉ info@accentpress.co.uk
www.accentpress.co.uk
Managing Editor *Hazel Cushion*
Founded 2002. Publishes general fiction, erotic
fiction, health, humour and biography. 24 titles a
year. Visit the website for submission guidelines.
ROYALTIES twice-yearly.

Allardyce, Barnett, Publishers
14 Mount Street, Lewes BN7 1HL
☎01273 479393
www.abar.net
Publisher *Fiona Allardyce*
Managing Editor *Anthony Barnett*
Founded 1981. Publishes art, literature and
music. IMPRINT **Allardyce Book**. About 3 titles
a year. Unsolicited mss and synopses cannot be
considered.

Anglo-Saxon Books
25 Brocks Road, Swaffham PE37 7XG
☎0845 530 4200/0845 430 4200
www.asbooks.co.uk
Managing Editor *Tony Linsell*
Founded 1990 to promote a greater awareness
of and interest in early English history, language
and culture. Publishes Anglo-Saxon history,
culture, language. About 5 titles a year. Please
phone before sending mss.
ROYALTIES at standard rate.

Apex Publishing Ltd
PO Box 7086, Clacton on Sea CO15 5WN
☎01255 428500 Fax 0870 046 6536
✉ enquiry@apexpublishing.co.uk
www.apexpublishing.co.uk
Managing Editor *Susan Kidby*
Production Manager *Chris Cowlin*
Founded 2002. Subsidy publishing company
for unknown and established authors. Publishes
poetry, self-help, non-fiction, fiction, crime, sci-
fi, history, humour, sport, education and textbooks, economics, children's books, biography,
autobiography, academic, women's interests,
medical, philosophy, law, pets, quizzes, religion
and travel. 75 titles in print. Welcomes unsolicited
mss, synopses and ideas for books. Approach in
writing to the address above with a copy of the
full ms.
ROYALTIES twice-yearly.

M. & M. Baldwin
24 High Street, Cleobury Mortimer,
Kidderminster DY14 8BY
☎01299 270110
✉ mb@mbaldwin.free-online.co.uk
Managing Editor *Dr Mark Baldwin*
Founded 1978. Publishes local interest/history,
WW2 codebreaking and inland waterways
books. Up to 5 titles a year. Unsolicited mss,
synopses and ideas for books welcome (not
general fiction).
ROYALTIES paid.

Barny Books
Hough on the Hill, near Grantham NG32 2BB
☎01400 250246/01522 790009 Fax 01400
251737
www.barnybooks.biz
Managing Director/Editorial Head *Molly
Burkett*
Business Manager *Jayne Thompson*
Founded with the aim of encouraging new
writers and illustrators. Publishes a wide variety
of books including adult fiction and non-
fiction. Offers schools' projects where students
help to produce books. Too small a concern to
have the staff/resources to deal with unsolicited

mss. Writers with strong ideas should approach Molly Burkett by letter in the first instance. Also runs a readership and advisory service for new writers (£20 fee for short stories or illustrations; £50 for full-length stories).

Division of profits 50/50.

BB Books

See entry under *Poetry Presses*

The Better Book Company Ltd

Forum House, Stirling Road, Chichester PO19 7DN
☎01243 530113
✉ editors@thebetterbookcompany.com
www.thebetterbookcompany.com
Managing Editor *Jill Field*
Business Director *John Littlefield*

Founded 1996. Editorial, proof reading, book design and printing services together with a marketing advisory service to authors wishing to self-publish their work in all genre. Produces fiction, histories, memoirs, poetry, religious, scientific, company histories. A free guide, *A Complete Guide to Self-Publishing*, is available on request. 25 titles in 2006.

Between the Lines

9 Woodstock Road, London N4 3ET
☎020 8374 5526 Fax 020 8374 5736
✉ btluk@aol.com
www.interviews-with-poets.com
Editorial Board *Peter Dale, Philip Hoy,
    J.D. McClatchy*
Editorial Assistant *Ryan Roberts*

Founded 1998. Publishes in book form extended interviews with leading contemporary poets. Thirteen volumes currently in print, featuring Peter Dale, John Ashbery, Charles Simic, Ian Hamilton, Donald Justice, Seamus Heaney, Richard Wilbur, Thom Gunn, Donald Hall, Anthony Hecht, Anthony Thwaite, Michael Hamburger and W.D. Snodgrass. Each volume includes a career sketch, a comprehensive bibliography and a representative selection of quotations from the poets' critics and reviewers. More recent volumes include photographs as well as previously uncollected poems. A second series, featuring slightly younger poets, was launched in autumn 2006. The first volumes in that series feature Dick Davis, Rachel Hadas and Timothy Steele.

ROYALTIES not paid.

Bluemoose Books Limited

25 Sackville Street, Hebden Bridge HX7 7DJ
☎01422 842731
✉ dufk@aol.com
www.bluemoosebooks.com
Managing Editor *Hetha Duffy*

Founded 2006. Publishes fiction, non-fiction and children's books. 2 titles in 2006. No unsolicited mss; send first three chapters and synopsis either by post (include s.a.e.) or via e-mail.

ROYALTIES annually.

The Book Castle

12 Church Street, Dunstable LU5 4RU
☎01582 605670 Fax 01582 662431
✉ bc@book-castle.co.uk
www.book-castle.co.uk
Managing Editor *Paul Bowes*
Assistant Editor *Sally Siddons*

Founded 1986. Publishes non-fiction of local interest (Bedfordshire, Hertfordshire, Buckinghamshire, Oxfordshire, the Chilterns). Over 120 titles in print. 12 titles a year. Unsolicited mss, synopses and ideas for books welcome.

ROYALTIES paid.

Brilliant Publications

1 Church View, Sparrow Hall Farm, Edlesborough, Dunstable LU6 2ES
☎01525 222292 Fax 01525 222720
✉ info@brilliantpublications.co.uk
www.brilliantpublications.co.uk
Publisher *Priscilla Hannaford*

Founded 1993. Publishes practical resource books for teachers, parents and others working with 0–13-year-olds. About 10–15 titles a year. Submit synopsis and sample pages in the first instance. Most of the books have black and white insides and many have pupil sheets that may be photocopied. Potential authors are strongly advised to look at the format of existing books before submitting synopses. 'We do not publish children's picture books.'

ROYALTIES twice-yearly.

The Brodie Press

✉ thebrodiepress@hotmail.com
www.brodiepress.co.uk
Managing Editors *Hannah Sheppard, Tom
    Sperlinger*

Founded 2002. Publishes poetry and anthologies. SERIES *The Brodie Poets*, launched in 2003, including Julie-ann Rowell, Poetry Book Society Pamphlet Choice, Winter 2003. Send synopses and proposals by e-mail in the first instance.

Charlewood Press
7 Weavers Place, Chandlers Ford SO53 1TU
☎023 8026 1192
✉ gponting@clara.net
www.home.clara.net/gponting/
    index-page11.html
Managing Editors *Gerald Ponting, Anthony Light*
Founded 1987. Publishes local history books and walks booklets on Hampshire and adjacent counties, especially around the Fordingbridge area. Mss in field of Hampshire local history (only) considered.

Chrysalis Press
7 Lower Ladyes Hills, Kenilworth CV8 2GN
☎01926 855223
✉ editor@margaretbuckley.com
www.margaretbuckley.com
Managing Editor *Brian Boyd*
Founded 1994. Publishes fiction, literary criticism and biography. No unsolicited mss.
    ROYALTIES paid.

CNP Publications
See **Lyfrow Trelyspen**

Contact Publishing Ltd
Unit 346, 176 Finchley Road, London
NW3 6BT
☎020 7871 6990
✉ info@contact-publishing.co.uk
www.contact-publishing.co.uk
Managing Director *Anne Kontoyannis*
Founded 2003. Publishes general fiction, non-fiction, self help and New Age. No children's, political, sports or westerns.'Interested in seeing mss by new authors with original angles and new ideas.' See website for author guidelines. Send synopsis, three sample chapters and outline in the first instance.
    ROYALTIES twice-yearly.

Corvo Books
64 Duncan Terrace, London N1 8AG
☎020 7288 0651
✉ editor@corvobooks.com
www.corvobooks.com
Managing Director *Scott McDonald*
Editorial Head *Julia Rochester*
Founded 2002. Small independent publisher of serious non-fiction: biography, memoir, history, philosophy. 2 titles in 2006. No unsolicited mss. Synopses and ideas welcome; send by mail or e-mail. No fiction.
    ROYALTIES twice-yearly.

The Cosmic Elk
68 Elsham Crescent, Lincoln LN6 3YS
☎01522 820922
✉ post@cosmicelk.co.uk
www.cosmicelk.co.uk
Contact *Heather Hobden*
Founded 1988. Publishes easily updated books on science, history and the history of science. Websites designed and maintained, with or without associated printed books. 'Please check our website first where you will find the information you need and contact us by e-mail.'

Crescent Moon Publishing and Joe's Press
PO Box 393, Maidstone ME14 5XU
☎01622 729593
✉ cresmopub@yahoo.co.uk
www.crescentmoon.org.uk
Managing Editor *Jeremy Robinson*
Founded 1988 to publish critical studies of figures such as D.H. Lawrence, Thomas Hardy, André Gide, Walt Disney, Rilke, Leonardo da Vinci, Mark Rothko, C.P. Cavafy and Hélène Cixous. Publishes literature, criticism, media, art, feminism, painting, poetry, travel, guidebooks, cinema and some fiction. Literary magazine, *Passion*, launched February 1994 (quarterly). *Pagan America*, twice-yearly anthology of American poetry. About 15–20 titles per year. Unsolicited synopses and ideas welcome but approach in writing first and send an s.a.e. Do not send whole mss.
    ROYALTIES negotiable.

Crossbridge Books
Tree Shadow, Berrow Green, Martley
WR6 6PL
☎01886 821128
✉ crossbridgebooks@btinternet.com
www.crossbridgebooks.com
Managing Director *Eileen Mohr*
Founded 1995. Publishes Christian books for adults and children. IMPRINT **Mohr Books**. No new submissions for the foreseeable future.

Day Books
Orchard Piece, Crawborough, Charlbury
OX7 3TX
☎01608 811196 Fax 01608 811196
✉ diaries@day-books.com
www.day-books.com
Managing Editor *James Sanderson*
Founded in 1997 to publish a series of great

diaries from around the world. Unsolicited mss, synopses and ideas welcome. Include postage if return of material is required.

The Dragonby Press
4-A Enterprise Way, Roxby Road, Winterton
DN15 9SU
☎01724 733011
✉ rich@rah2williams.freeserve.co.uk
Managing Editor *Richard Williams*

Founded 1987 to publish affordable bibliography for reader, collector and dealer. About 3 titles a year. Unsolicited mss, synopses and ideas welcome for bibliographical projects only.
ROYALTIES paid.

Dramatic Lines
PO Box 201, Twickenham TW2 5RQ
☎020 8296 9502 Fax 020 8296 9503
✉ mail@dramaticlinespublishers.co.uk
www.dramaticlines.co.uk
Managing Editor *John Nicholas*

Founded to promote drama for all. Publications with a wide variety of theatrical applications including classroom use and school assemblies, drama examinations, auditions, festivals, theatre group performance, musicals and handbooks. Unsolicited drama-related mss, proposals and synopses welcome; enclose s.a.e.
ROYALTIES paid.

Edgewell Publishing
5A Front Street, Prudhoe NE42 5HJ
☎01661 835330 Fax 01661 835330
✉ keithminton@btconnect.com
www.tynedale-languages.co.uk
Editor *Keith Minton*

Quarterly short story and poetry magazine (*Lively Tales*) to encourage writing from new and established writers, also children. Writers from the North East especially welcome.

Educational Heretics Press
113 Arundel Drive, Bramcote Hills,
Nottingham NG9 3FQ
☎0115 925 7261 Fax 0115 925 7261
www.edheretics.gn.apc.org
Directors *Janet & Roland Meighan*

Non-profit venture which aims to question the dogmas of schooling in particular and education in general, and establish the logistics of the next personalised learning system. No unsolicited material. Enquiries only.
ROYALTIES not paid but under review.

Eilish Press
4 Collegiate Crescent, Broomhall Park,
Sheffield S10 2BA
☎07973 353964
✉ eilishpress@hotmail.co.uk
eilishpress.tripod.com
Head of Marketing *Suzi Kapadia*

Specialises in academic work and popular non-fiction in the areas of women's studies, human rights and anti-racism. Also produces children's literature with humanitarian themes. No adult fiction. Unsolicited mss cannot be accepted at this time. However, ideas for children's books may be sent by e-mail.
ROYALTIES annually.

Enable Enterprises
PO Box 1974, Coventry CV3 1YF
☎0800 358 8484 Fax 0800 358 8484
✉ writers@enableenterprises.com
www.enableenterprises.com
Chief Executive *Simon Stevens*

Enable Enterprises provides a wide range of accessibilty and disability services including publications on relevant issues. Welcomes unsolicited material related to accessibility and disability issues.

Fand Music Press
Glenelg, 10 Avon Close, Petersfield GU31 4LG
☎01730 267341 Fax 01730 267341
✉ Paul@fandmusic.com
www.fandmusic.com
Managing Editor *Peter Thompson*

Founded in 1989 as a sheet music publisher, Fand Music Press has expanded its range to include CD recordings and books on music. Also publishes poetry and short stories. 10 titles a year. No unsolicited mss. Write with ideas in the first instance.

Feather Books
PO Box 438, Shrewsbury SY3 0WN
☎01743 872177 Fax 01743 872177
✉ john@waddysweb.freeuk.com
www.waddysweb.freeuk.com
Managing Director *Rev. John Waddington-Feather*
Music Director *David Grundy*
Drama Director/Recordings Manager *Tony Reavil*

Founded 1980 to publish writers' group work. All material has a strong Christian ethos. Publishes poetry (mainly, but not exclusively, religious); Christian mystery novels (the Revd. D.I. Blake Hartley series); Christian children's

Quill Hedgehog novels; seasonal poetry collections and *The Poetry Church* quarterly magazine. Produces poetry, drama and hymn CD/cassettes; also the anthology 'Pilgrimages' ed. Professor Walter Nash ('a milestone in Christian poetry publishing'). About 20 titles a year. All correspondence to include s.a.e., please.

Fidra Books
60 Craigcrook Road, Edinburgh EH4 3PJ
☎0131 343 3118
✉ vanessa@fidrabooks.com
www.fidrabooks.com
Managing Editor *Vanessa Robertson*

Founded 2005. Publishes children's fiction, specialising in reprints of sought-after 20th century children's fiction. No unsolicited material; initial approach by letter or e-mail.
ROYALTIES quarterly.

Five Leaves Publications
PO Box 8786, Nottingham NG1 9AW
☎0115 969 3597
✉ info@fiveleaves.co.uk
www.fiveleaves.co.uk
Contact *Ross Bradshaw*

Founded 1995 (taking over the publishing programme of Mushroom Bookshop). Publishes fiction, poetry, social history, politics and Jewish interest. Also publishes for the Anglo-Catalan Society. Titles normally commissioned. About 10 titles a year.
ROYALTIES paid.

Frontier Publishing
Windetts, Kirstead NR15 1EG
☎01508 558174
✉ frontier.pub@macunlimited.net
www.frontierpublishing.co.uk
Managing Editor *John Black*

Founded 1983. Publishes travel, photography, sculptural history and literature. 2–3 titles a year. No unsolicited mss; synopses and ideas welcome.
ROYALTIES paid.

Galactic Central Publications
Imladris, 25A Copgrove Road, Leeds LS8 2SP
✉ gcp@philsp.com
www.philsp.com
Managing Editor *Phil Stephensen-Payne*

Founded 1982 in the US. Publishes science fiction bibliographies. All new publications originate in the UK. About 4 titles a year.

Unsolicited mss, synopses and ideas (for bibliographies) welcome.

Galore Park Publishing Ltd
19/21 Sayer's Lane, Tenterden TN30 6BW
☎0870 234 2304 Fax 0870 234 2305
✉ info@galorepark.co.uk
www.galorepark.co.uk
Managing Director *Nicholas Oulton*

Founded 1999. Publishes school textbooks and children's books. 17 titles in 2006. No unsolicited mss. Synopses and ideas welcome; send by e-mail.
ROYALTIES twice-yearly.

Glosa Education Organisation
PO Box 18, Richmond TW9 2GE
www.glosa.org
Managing Editor *Wendy Ashby*

Founded 1981. Publishes textbooks, dictionaries and translations for the teaching, speaking and promotion of Glosa (an international, auxiliary language); also a newsletter, *Plu Glosa Nota* and journal, *PGN*. Unsolicited mss and ideas for Glosa books welcome.

Godstow Press
60 Godstow Road, Wolvercote, Oxford OX2 8NY
☎01865 556215
✉ info@godstowpress.co.uk
www.godstowpress.co.uk
Managing Editors *Linda Smith, David Smith*

Founded in 2003 for the publication of creative work with a philosophical/spiritual content. 2–3 titles a year. Considers works self-published by the author for inclusion in the catalogue. The press works on direct sales rather than through usual trade outlets. Synopses and ideas welcome but no unsolicited mss.

Graffeg
2 Radnor Court, 256 Cowbridge Road East, Cardiff CF5 1GZ
☎029 2037 7312 Fax 029 2039 8101
✉ info@graffeg.com
www.graffeg.com
Managing Editor *Peter Gill*

Founded 2002. Publishes travel, food and drink, Wales, landscapes, photography. 2 titles in 2006. Unsolicited material welcome by post.
ROYALTIES twice-yearly.

Grant Books

The Coach House, New Road, Cutnall Green, Droitwich WR9 0PQ

☎01299 851588 Fax 01299 851446

✉ golf@grantbooks.co.uk

www.grantbooks.co.uk

Managing Editor *H.R.J. Grant*

Founded 1978. Publishes golf-related titles only: course architecture, history, biography, etc., but not instructional, humour or fiction material. New titles and old, plus limited editions. About 6 titles a year. Mss, synopses and ideas welcome.

ROYALTIES paid.

Great Northern Publishing

PO Box 202, Scarborough YO11 3GE

☎01723 581329 Fax 01723 581329

✉ books@greatnorthernpublishing.co.uk

www.greatnorthernpublishing.co.uk

Production Manager *Mark Marsay*
Senior Editor *Diane Crowther*

Small, independent, award-winning, family-owned company founded in 1999. Publishers of books, magazines and journals. Also provides full book, magazine and print production services to individuals, businesses, charities, museums and other small publishers. Publishes non-fiction (mainly military), adult erotic material and, occasionally, fiction. No romance, religious, political, feminist, New Age, medical or children's books. Publishers of the bi-monthly magazines, *The Great War*, *The Second World War* and *Jade* (see entries under **Magazines**). Mail order and Internet-based bookshop stocking selected titles alongside its own. Website provides submission guidelines and current publishing requirements. No unsolicited phone calls or mss; send letter or text-only e-mail in the first instance.

ROYALTIES twice-yearly.

Griffin Publishing Associates

61 Grove Avenue, London N10 2AL

☎020 8444 0815/0778 842 5262

✉ griffin.publishing.associates@
   googlemail.com

Managing Editor *Ali Ismail*

Founded 2007. Publishes all kinds of fiction (plays, poetry and prose) with an emphasis on science fiction, fantasy and horror. Unsolicited mss, synopses and ideas for books welcome. Approach by post (return postage must be included) or telephone.

ROYALTIES annually.

GSSE

11 Malford Grove, Gilwern, Abergavenny NP7 0RN

☎01873 830872

✉ GSSE@zoo.co.uk

www.gsse.org.uk

Owner/Manager *David P. Bosworth*

Publishes books and booklets describing classroom practice (at all levels of education and training). Ideas welcome – particularly from practising teachers, lecturers and trainers describing how they use technology in their teaching.

ROYALTIES by arrangement.

Haunted Library

Flat 1, 36 Hamilton Street, Hoole, Chester CH2 3JQ

☎01244 313685

✉ pardos@globalnet.co.uk

www.users.globalnet.co.uk/~pardos/GS.html

Managing Editor *Rosemary Pardoe*

Founded 1979. Publishes the *Ghosts and Scholars M.R. James Newsletter* two or three times a year, featuring articles, news and reviews (no fiction).

ROYALTIES not paid.

Headpress

Suite 306, The Colourworks, 2a Abbot Street, London E8 3DP

☎0845 330 1844 Fax 020 7249 6395

✉ info@headpress.com

www.headpress.com

Managing Editor *David Kerekes*

Founded 1991. Publishes *Headpress* journal and books devoted to film, music, popular culture, the strange and esoteric. No fiction or poetry. Unsolicited material welcome; send letter and outline in the first instance.

ROYALTIES/flat fees vary.

Heart of Albion Press

2 Cross Hill Close, Wymeswold, Loughborough LE12 6UJ

☎01509 880725 Fax 01509 881715

✉ albion@indigogroup.co.uk

www.hoap.co.uk

Managing Editor *R.N. Trubshaw*

Founded 1990 to publish local history. Publishes folklore, local history and mythology. 12–14 titles a year. Synopses relating to these subjects welcome.

ROYALTIES negotiable.

Immanion Press

8 Rowley Grove, Stafford ST17 9BJ
☎01785 613299
✉ editorial@immanion-press.com
www.immanion-press.com

Managing Editor *Storm Constantine*

Founded 2003. Publishes genre fiction (science fiction, fantasy, horror), slipstream fiction; esoteric non-fiction. IMPRINT **Megalithica Books** Commissioning Editor *Taylor Ellwood* (info@immanion-press.com) Non-fiction, specifically cutting edge esoteric work. Submissions by e-mail or post (enclose s.a.e.). Website gives full submission details.

ROYALTIES paid.

Infinity Junction

PO Box 64, Neston DO CH64 0WB
✉ infin-info@infinityjunction.com
www.infinityjunction.com

Managing Editor *Neil Gee*

Established originally as a self-publishing, self-help organisation in 1991, Infinity Junction became a publisher in 2001. Currently offers a variety of services to authors, including advice, free web display space and full commercial publication. Authors are strongly advised to read the detailed information on the website before making contact. E-mail communication preferred. 'We cannot undertake to read unsolicited whole mss.'

Inner Sanctum Publications

75 Greenleaf Gardens, Polegate BN26 6PQ
☎01323 484058
www.innersanctumpublications.com

Managing Editor *Mary Hession*

Founded in 1999 to publish spiritual books. Unsolicited mss, synopses and ideas welcome; initial approach via e-mail (address available on the website) or by post, including s.a.e.

Iolo

38 Chaucer Road, Bedford MK40 2AJ
☎01234 301718/07909 934866
Fax 01234 301718
✉ dedwydd1@ntlworld.com
www.dedwyddjones.co.uk

Managing Director *Dedwydd Jones*

Publishes Welsh theatre-related material and campaigns for a Welsh National Theatre. Ideas on Welsh themes welcome; approach in writing.

Ivy Publications

72 Hyperion House, Somers Road, London SW2 1HZ
☎020 8671 6872

Proprietor *Ian Bruton-Simmonds*

Founded 1989. Publishes educational, science, fiction, philosophy, children's, travel, literary criticism, history, film scripts. No unsolicited mss; send two pages, one from the beginning and one from the body of the book, together with synopsis (one paragraph) and s.a.e. No cookery, gardening or science fiction.

ROYALTIES annually.

The Jupiter Press

The Coach House, Gatacre, Claverley, Nr Wolverhampton WV5 7AW
☎01746 710694 Fax 01746 710158
✉ gordonthomasdrury@btinternet.com

Managing Editor *Gordon Thomas Drury*

Founded 1995. Looking for niche market and information publications, also quiz and game subjects. Interested in holistic, clairvoyance and esoteric subjects. Synopses and ideas for books welcome. Send idea and sample chapter (include contact telephone number). Unsolicited mss welcome 'but may request a reader's fee'. Currently seeking books for SERIES entitled *How To Make Money At* ....

ROYALTIES paid.

Kittiwake

3 Glantwymyn Village Workshops, Glantwymyn, Nr Machynlleth SY20 8LY
☎01650 511314 Fax 01650 511314
✉ perrographics@btconnect.com
www.kittiwake-books.com

Managing Editor *David Perrott*

Founded 1986. Publishes guidebooks only, with an emphasis on careful design/production. Specialist research, writing, cartographic and electronic publishing services available. Unsolicited mss, synopses and ideas for guidebooks welcome.

ROYALTIES paid.

Legend Press Limited

13a Northwold Road, London N16 7HL
☎020 7249 6901
✉ info@legendpress.co.uk
www.legendpress.co.uk

Managing Director *Tom Chalmers*
Publishing Executive *Emma Howard*

'New and innovative publisher, publishing cutting-edge contemporary fiction for the mainstream market.' Also offers writing competitions, talks, articles, online shop, free monthly e-bulletin and a text-setting and layout service. 5 titles in 2007; doubling list year-on-year. Send three chapters and synopsis with s.a.e. for return.

ROYALTIES twice-yearly.

The Lindsey Press

Unitarian Headquarters, 1–6 Essex Street, Strand, London WC2R 3HY
☎020 7240 2384 Fax 020 7240 3089
✉ ga@unitarian.org.uk
Convenor *Kate Taylor*

Established at the end of the 18th century as a vehicle for disseminating liberal religion. Adopted the name of The Lindsey Press at the beginning of the 20th century (after Theophilus Lindsey, the great Unitarian Theologian). Publishes books reflecting liberal religious thought or Unitarian denominational history. Also worship material – hymn books, collections of prayers, etc. 2 titles in 2006. No unsolicited mss; synopses and ideas welcome.

ROYALTIES not paid.

The Linen Press

75c (13) South Oswald Road, Edinburgh EH9 2HH
✉ lynn@linenpressbooks.co.uk
www.linenpressbooks.co.uk
Managing Editor *Lynn Michell*

Founded 2006. Publishes fiction and memoirs. Unsolicited submissions of synopsis and first three chapters, sent by post, are welcome as long as the website has been consulted in the first instance.

ROYALTIES paid.

Logaston Press

Logaston, Woonton, Almeley HR3 6QH
☎01544 327344
www.logastonpress.co.uk
Managing Editors *Andy Johnson, Ron Shoesmith*

Founded 1985. Publishes guides, archaeology, social history, rural issues and local history for Wales, the Welsh Border and West Midlands. 10–15 titles a year. Unsolicited mss, synopses and ideas welcome. Return postage appreciated.

ROYALTIES paid.

Luath Press Ltd

543/2 Castlehill, The Royal Mile, Edinburgh EH1 2ND
☎0131 225 4326 Fax 0131 225 4324
✉ gavin.macdougall@luath.co.uk
www.luath.co.uk
Managing Editor *G.H. MacDougall*

Founded 1981. Publishes mainly books with a Scottish connection. Current list includes fiction, poetry, guidebooks, walking and outdoor, history, folklore, politics and global issues, cartoons, biography, food and drink, environment, music and dance, sport and *On the Trail Of* and *The Quest For* SERIES. About 20–30 titles a year. Unsolicited mss, synopses and ideas welcome; 'committed to publishing well-written books worth reading'.

ROYALTIES paid.

Lyfrow Trelyspen

The Roseland Institute, Gorran, St Austell PL26 6NT
☎01726 843501 Fax 01726 843501
✉ trelispen@care4free.net
Managing Editor *Dr James Whetter*

Founded 1975. Publishes works on Cornish history, biography, essays, etc. Also **CNP Publications** which publishes the quarterly journal *The Cornish Banner/An Baner Kernewek*. 1–2 titles a year. Unsolicited mss, synopses and ideas welcome.

ROYALTIES not paid.

The Maia Press

82 Forest Road, London E8 3BH
☎020 7683 8141 Fax 020 7683 8141
✉ maggie@maiapress.com
www.maiapress.com
Contacts *Maggie Hamand, Jane Havell*

Founded 2002. Publishes fiction by known and new writers. 6 titles a year. No unsolicited mss, write with c.v. and synopsis only. S.a.e. essential.

ROYALTIES twice-yearly.

Meadow Books

35 Stonefield Way, Burgess Hill RH15 8DW
✉ publish@diggorypress.com
www.diggorypress.com

Founded 1990. Publisher of nursing history books and nursing picture archive. IMPRINT **Diggory Press** (see entry under *UK Publishers*). 'No longer taking on new titles; referring all contacts to Diggory Press instead. No telephone calls from author.'

Megalithica Books

See **Immanion Press**

Mercia Cinema Society

29 Blackbrook Court, Durham Road,
Loughborough LE11 5UA
☎01509 218393
✉ Mervyn.Gould@virgin.net
www.merciacinema.org.uk
Managing Editor *Kate Taylor*
Series Editor *Mervyn Gould*

Founded 1980 to foster research into the history of picture houses. Publishes books and booklets on the subject, including cinema circuits and chains. Books are often tied in with specific geographical areas. Quarterly journal: *Mercia Bioscope*, editor *Paul Smith* (Paul@Smith2004.fs.net.co.uk). 60 titles to date. Unsolicited mss (preferably on disk); synopses and ideas.

ROYALTIES not paid. Six free copies to the author.

Meridian Books

40 Hadzor Road, Oldbury B68 9LA
☎0121 429 4397
✉ meridian.books@btopenworld.com
Managing Editor *Peter Groves*

Founded 1985 as a small home-based enterprise following the acquisition of titles from Tetradon Publications Ltd. Publishes walking and regional guides. 4–5 titles a year. Unsolicited mss, synopses and ideas welcome if relevant. Send s.a.e. if mss to be returned.

ROYALTIES paid.

Neil Miller Publications

c/o Ormonde House, 49 Ormonde Road,
Hythe CT21 6DW
www.neilmillerbooks.co.uk

Also at: 4 Rue D'Equiire Bergueneuse, Pas de Calais, France 62134
Managing Editor *Neil Miller*

Founded 1994. Publishes novels and collections of short stories on any subject, fact or fiction: memoirs, autobiography, mystery, horror, war, comedy, science fiction. Interested in working with new and published writers. Evaluation and critique service available. 'Send your novel or selection of short stories for consideration plus our reader's fee of £22. For this you receive a critique plus two of our latest authors' books and have the opportunity of being published by us.' Enclose s.a.e. for return of work. No unrequested tales.

Millers Dale Publications

7 Weavers Place, Chandlers Ford, Eastleigh
SO53 1TU

☎023 8026 1192
✉ gponting@clara.net
www.home.clara.net/gponting/
    index-page10.html
Managing Editor *Gerald Ponting*

Founded 1990. Publishes books on local history related to central Hampshire. Also books related to slide presentations by Gerald Ponting. Ideas for local history books on Hampshire (only this topic) considered.

Mirage Publishing

PO Box 161, Gateshead NE8 1WY
☎0870 720 9498
✉ sales@miragepublishing.com
www.miragepublishing.com
Managing Director *Sharon Anderson*

Founded 1998. Publishes mind, body and spirit, autobiography, biography. 3 titles in 2006. No unsolicited mss; send synopses and ideas by mail or e-mail.

ROYALTIES twice-yearly.

Mohr Books

See **Crossbridge Books**

Natzler Enterprises (Entertainments)

1 Wakeford Cottages, Selden Lane, Worthing
BN11 2LQ
☎01903 211785 Fax 01903 211519
✉ info@natzler.com
www.natzler.com
www.paulgordon.net
Managing Editor *Paul Gordon*

Founded 1993. Publishes magic (entertainment) books only. No unsolicited mss; send synopses and ideas by post.

Need2Know

Remus House, Coltsfoot Drive, Woodston
PE2 9JX
☎01733 898105 Fax 01733 313524
✉ info@forwardpress.co.uk
www.n2kbooks.com

Founded 1995 'to fill a gap in the market for self-help books'. Need2Know is an imprint of **Forward Press** (see entry under **Poetry Presses**). Publishes contemporary health and lifestyle issues. No unsolicited mss. Call in the first instance.

ROYALTIES Advance plus 15% royalties.

Jane Nissen Books

Swan House, Chiswick Mall, London W4 2PS

☎020 8994 8203 Fax 020 8742 8198
✉ jane@nissen.demon.co.uk
www.janenissenbooks.co.uk

Managing Editor *Jane Nissen*

Founded 2000. Publishes reprints of children's fiction only. 3 titles in 2006. Does not consider submitted material as all titles published are reprints of classics or fogotten children's books.

Norvik Press Ltd

School of Language, Linguistic & Translation Studies, University of East Anglia, Norwich NR4 7TJ
☎01603 593356 Fax 01603 250599
✉ norvik.press@uea.ac.uk
www.uea.ac.uk/llt/norvik_press

Managing Editors *Janet Garton, Michael Robinson*

Small academic press. Publishes the journals *Scandinavica* and *Swedish Book Review* and both translations of and books related to Scandinavian literature. About 6 titles a year. Interested in synopses and ideas for books within its *Literary History and Criticism* SERIES. No unsolicited mss.
ROYALTIES paid.

The Nostalgia Collection

Silver Link Publishing Ltd, The Trundle, Ringstead Road, Great Addington, Kettering NN14 4BW
☎01536 330588 Fax 01536 330588
✉ sales@nostalgiacollection.com
www.nostalgiacollection.com

Managing Editor *Will Adams*

Founded 1985. Small independent company specialising in illustrated post-war nostalgia titles including railways, trams, ships and other transport subjects, towns and cities, villages and rural life, rivers and inland waterways, and industrial heritage under the **Silver Link** and **Past and Present** imprints.
FEES/ROYALTIES paid.

Nyala Publishing

4 Christian Fields, London SW16 3JZ
☎020 8764 6292/0115 981 9418
Fax 020 8764 6292/0115 981 9418
✉ nyala.publishing@geo-group.co.uk
www.geo-group.co.uk

Editorial Director *J.F.J. Douglas*

Founded 1996. Publishing arm of Geo Group. Publishes biography, travel and general nonfiction. Also offers a wide range of printing and publishing services. 'Quality low-cost printing a speciality.' No unsolicited mss; synopses and ideas considered.
ROYALTIES annually.

Orpheus Publishing House

4 Dunsborough Park, Ripley Green, Ripley, Guildford GU23 6AL
☎01483 225777 Fax 01483 225776
✉ orpheuspubl.ho@btinternet.com

Managing Editor *J.S. Gordon*

Founded 1996. Publishes 'well-researched and properly argued' books in the fields of occult science, esotericism and comparative philosophy/religion. 'Keen to encourage good (but sensible) new authors.' In the first instance, send maximum three-page synopsis with s.a.e.
ROYALTIES by agreement.

Packard Publishing Limited

Forum House, Stirling Road, Chichester PO19 7DN
☎01243 537977 Fax 01243 537977
✉ info@packardpublishing.co.uk
www.packardpublishing.com

Chairman/Managing Director *Michael Packard*

Founded in 1977 to distribute overseas publishers' lists in biology, biochemistry and ecology. Publishes academic & professional: school/university interface, postgraduate – mainly in land management and applied ecology; agriculture, forestry, nature conservation, rural studies, landscape architecture and garden design; some languages (French, Arabic). SERIES Instructional books on garden and landscape design, and monographs or critical biographies in garden and landscape design and history. 30 titles to date. No unsolicited mss. Synopses and ideas in relevant areas welcome. Telephone first.
ROYALTIES twice-yearly in first year, then annually.

Panacea Press Limited

86 North Gate, Prince Albert Road, London NW8 7EJ
☎020 7722 8464 Fax 020 7586 8187
✉ ebrecher@panaceapress.net
www.panaceapress.net

Managing Editor *Erwin Brecher, PhD*

Founded as a self-publisher but now open for non-fiction from other authors. Material of academic value considered provided it commands a wide general market. No unsolicited mss; synopses and ideas welcome. Approach by fax or letter. No telephone calls.
ROYALTIES annually.

PaperBooks Ltd
Neville House, Station Approach, Wendens Ambo CB11 4LB
☎01799 544657 Fax 01799 541747
✉ submissions@paperbooks.co.uk or info@paperbooks.co.uk
www.paperbooks.co.uk
Managing Director *Keirsten Clark*
Founded 2004. Publishes fiction – literary and commercial biography and other non fiction. Unsolicited material welcome.
ROYALTIES twice-yearly.

Parapress Ltd
The Basement, 9 Frant Road, Tunbridge Wells TN2 5SD
☎01892 512118 Fax 01892 512118
✉ office@parapress.eclipse.co.uk
www.parapress.co.uk
Managing Editor *Elizabeth Imlay*
Founded 1993. Publishes animals, autobiography, biography, history, literary criticism, military and naval, music, self-help. Some self-publishing. About 3 titles a year.

Past and Present
See **The Nostalgia Collection**

Paupers' Press
37 Quayside Close, Turney's Quay, Trent Bridge, Nottingham NG2 3BP
☎0115 986 3334 Fax 0115 986 3334
✉ books@pauperspress.com
www.pauperspress.com
Managing Editor *Colin Stanley*
Founded 1983. Publishes extended essays in booklet form (about 15,000 words) on literary criticism and philosophy. 'Sometimes we stray from these criteria and produce full-length books, but only to accommodate an exceptional ms.' Limited hardback editions of bestselling titles. About 6 titles a year. No unsolicited mss but synopses and ideas for books welcome.
ROYALTIES paid.

Peepal Tree Press Ltd
See entry under *Poetry Presses*

Pen Press Publishers Ltd
25 Eastern Place, Brighton BN2 1GJ
☎0845 108 0530 Fax 01273 261434
✉ info@penpress.co.uk
www.penpress.co.uk
Managing Director *Lynn Ashman*
Founded 1996. Publishing across a wide range of categories, Pen Press helps new authors to self-publish. Distribution, promotion and marketing included in self-publishing deal. Publisher, not author, pays for reprints and shares in sales revenue. 400 titles to date. Write, phone or e-mail for submission form and full details. Return form with full ms (digital or hard copy).
ROYALTIES 45%, payable twice-yearly.

Perfect Publishers Ltd
23 Maitland Avenue, Cambridge CB4 1TA
☎01223 424422 Fax 01223 424414
✉ editor@perfectpublishers.co.uk
www.perfectpublishers.co.uk
Managing Editor *Shahida Rahman*
Founded 2005. Publishes books of all genres. 8 titles in 2006. No unsolicited mss; send synopses and ideas for books by e-mail.
ROYALTIES: 'We pay 100% royalties twice-yearly.'

Pipers' Ash Ltd
'Pipers' Ash', Church Road, Christian Malford, Chippenham SN15 4BW
☎01249 720563 Fax 0870 0568916
✉ pipersash@supamasu.com
www.supamasu.com
Managing Editor *Mr A. Tyson*
Founded 1976. The company's publishing activities include individual collections of contemporary short stories, science fiction short stories, poetry, plays, short novels, local histories, children's fiction, philosophy, biographies, translations and general non-fiction. 12 titles a year. Synopses and ideas welcome; 'new authors with potential will be actively encouraged'. Offices in New Zealand and Australia.
ROYALTIES annually.

Playwrights Publishing Co.
70 Nottingham Road, Burton Joyce NG14 5AL
☎0115 931 3356
✉ playwrightspublishingco@yahoo.com
geocities.com/playwrightspublishingco
Managing Editors *Liz Breeze, Tony Breeze*
Founded 1990. Publishes one-act and full-length plays. Unsolicited scripts welcome. No synopses or ideas. Reading fees: £15 one act; £30 full length (waived if evidence of professional performance or if writer is unwaged).
ROYALTIES paid.

Pomegranate Press

Dolphin House, 51 St Nicholas Lane, Lewes BN7 2JZ
☎01273 470100 Fax 01273 470100
✉ pomegranatepress@aol.com
www.pomegranate-press.co.uk

Managing Editor *David Arscott*

Founded in 1992 by writer/broadcaster David Arscott, who also administers the **Sussex Book Club**. Specialises in books about Sussex and self publishing. IMPRINT **Pomegranate Practicals** How-to books.

ROYALTIES twice-yearly.

David Porteous Editions

PO Box 5, Chudleigh, Newton Abbot TQ13 0YZ
☎01626 853310 Fax 01626 853663
✉ editorial@davidporteous.com
www.davidporteous.com

Publisher *David Porteous*

Founded 1992 to produce colour illustrated books on hobbies and leisure for the UK and international markets. Publishes crafts, hobbies, art techniques and needlecrafts. No poetry or fiction. 3–4 titles a year. Unsolicited mss, synopses and ideas welcome if return postage included.

ROYALTIES twice-yearly.

Praxis Books

Crossways Cottage, Walterstone HR2 0DX
☎01873 890695
✉ author@rebeccatope.fsnet.co.uk
www.rebeccatope.com

Proprietor *Rebecca Smith*

Founded 1992. Publishes reissues of the works of Sabine Baring-Gould, memoirs, diaries and local interest. 21 titles to date. Unsolicited mss accepted with s.a.e. No fiction. Editing and advisory service available. Funding negotiable. 'I am most likely to accept work with a clearly identifiable market.'

QueenSpark Books

49 Grand Parade, Brighton BN2 9QA
☎01273 571710
✉ info@queensparkbooks.org.uk
www.queensparkbooks.org.uk

A community writing and publishing group. Since the early 1970s QueenSpark Books has published 87 titles, mainly featuring the lives of local people. Writing workshops and groups held on a regular basis. No unsolicited mss, please.

Radikal Phase Publishing House Ltd

Willow Court, Cordy Lane, Underwood NG16 5FD
☎01773 764288 Fax 01773 764282
✉ sales@radikalbooks.com
www.radikalbooks.com

Joint Managing Directors *Philip Gardiner, Kevin Marks*

Founded 2001. Publishes radical revelation and technical electrical books. IMPRINTS **William Ernest** *Kevin Marks*; **Radikal Phase** *Philip Gardiner*. Welcomes unsolicited material; approach in writing in the first instance.

ROYALTIES twice-yearly.

Ravenhall Books

PO Box 357, Welwyn Garden City AL6 6WJ
Fax 01707 325230
✉ info@ravenhallbooks.com
www.ravenhallbooks.com

Managing Editor *Evgenia North*

Founded 2004. Publishes history books. 5 titles in 2006. No unsolicited mss; send synopsis with sample chapter by post.

ROYALTIES twice-yearly.

Robinswood Press

30 South Avenue, Stourbridge DY8 3XY
☎01384 397475 Fax 01384 440443
✉ info@robinswoodpress.com
www.robinswoodpress.com

Managing Editor *Christopher J. Marshall*

Founded 1985. Publishes children's, educational, teaching resources, SEN. Also collaborative publishing, e.g., with Camphill Foundation. About 30–50 titles a year. Unsolicited mss, synopses and ideas welcome. See website.

ROYALTIES paid.

St James Publishing

Earsby Street, London W14 8SH
☎020 7348 1799 Fax 020 7348 1795
✉ stjamespublishing@stjamesschools.co.uk

Managing Editors *Linda Smith, David Smith*

Founded in 1995 to provide teaching materials with spiritual substance for St James Independent Schools: 'Good Books for Fine Minds'. Also many workbooks and textbooks for the study of English and mathematics. No unsolicited mss, synopses or ideas.

Serif

47 Strahan Road, London E3 5DA
☎020 8981 3990 Fax 020 8981 3990

✉ stephen@serif.demon.co.uk

Managing Editor *Stephen Hayward*

Founded 1993. Publishes cookery, Irish and African studies, travel writing and modern history; no fiction. Ideas and synopses welcome; no unsolicited mss.

ROYALTIES paid.

Silver Link
See **The Nostalgia Collection**

Spacelink Books
115 Hollybush Lane, Hampton TW12 2QY
☎020 8979 3148
www.spacelink.fsworld.co.uk

Managing Director *Lionel Beer*

Founded 1967. Named after a UFO magazine published in the 1960/70s. Publishes non-fiction titles connected with UFOs, Fortean phenomena and paranormal events. Publishers of *TEMS News* for the Travel and Earth Mysteries Society and *MWB Railway Society News Brief* newsletters. Distributors of a wide range of related titles and magazines. No unsolicited mss; send synopses and ideas.

ROYALTIES/FEES according to contract.

Stenlake Publishing Limited
54–58 Mill Square, Catrine KA5 6RD
☎01290 552233
✉ enquiries@stenlake.co.uk
www.stenlake.co.uk

Publishes illustrated local history, railways, shipping, aviation and industrial. 20 titles in 2006. Unsolicited mss, synopses and ideas welcome if accompanied by s.a.e. or sent by e-mail. Freelance writers with experience in above fields also sought for specific commissions.

ROYALTIES or fixed fee paid.

Stone Flower Limited
PO Box 1513, Ilford IG1 3QU
✉ stoneflower10622@aol.com

Managing Editor *L. G. Norman*

Founded 1989. Publishes humour and general fiction. Will consider mss, synopses and ideas only if sent with s.a.e. or IRC ('this also means NO electronic submissions.') Approach in writing in the first instance. 'No anthropomorphism, illiteracy or anyone incapable of accepting any comment or criticism, please.'

Stride
4b Tremayne Close, Devoran, Truro TR3 3QE
✉ editor@stridebooks.co.uk
www.stridebooks.co.uk

Managing Editor *Rupert Loydell*

Founded in 1982 as a magazine and booklet series. Since the mid-1980s, the press has published paperback editions of imaginative new writing. Publishes poetry, prose-poems, criticism, reviews, interviews, arts (particularly experimental music and literary criticism). No unsolicited submissions required at this time.

ROYALTIES sometimes paid; free copies usually.

Superscript
404 Robin Square, Newtown SY16 1HP
☎01588 650452
✉ drjbford@yahoo.co.uk
www.dubsolution.org

Editor *Julie Ford*
Chair *Bernard Burgoyne*
Secretary *Ray Pahl*

Founded 2002. Publishes literary, philosophical and political fiction, humanities and social sciences. 11 titles in 2006. Initial enquiries by letter, telephone or e-mail to the editor.

ROYALTIES vary with each contract.

Tamarind Ltd
PO Box 52, Northwood HA6 1UN
☎020 8866 8808 Fax 020 8866 5627
✉ info@tamarindbooks.co.uk
www.tamarindbooks.co.uk

Managing Editor *Verna Wilkins*

Founded 1987 to publish picture books which give a high, positive profile to black children. They feature regularly on the SATs List for National Curriculum, on BBC Words and Pictures, CBBC and 'Balamory'. Regularly chosen among the Best Books of the Year. All titles sold into both trade and educational markets. Age range: 0–12.

Tan House Publishing Limited
Tan House, 15 South End, Bassingbourn, Royston SG8 5NJ
www.tanhouse.net

Managing Editor *Nigel Spence*

Founded 2005. Publishes fiction and special interest. 1 title in 2006. Unsolicited mss, synopses and ideas for books welcome. Approach by post.

Tarquin Publications
99 Hatfield Road, St Albans AL1 4JL

☎0870 143 2568 Fax 0845 456 6385
✉ sales@tarquinbooks.com
www.tarquinbooks.com

Managing Editor *Andrew Griffin*

Founded 1970 as a hobby which gradually grew and now publishes mathematical, cut-out models, teaching and pop-up books. Other topics covered if they involve some kind of paper cutting or pop-up scenes. About 5 titles a year. No unsolicited mss; letter with 1–2 page synopses welcome.

ROYALTIES paid.

Tartarus Press

Coverley House, Carlton-in-Coverdale, Leyburn DL8 4AY
☎01969 640399 Fax 01969 640399
✉ tartarus@pavilion.co.uk
www.tartaruspress.com

Proprietor *Raymond Russell*
Editor *Rosalie Parker*

Founded 1987. Publishes fiction, short stories, reprinted classic supernatural fiction and reference books. About 10 titles a year. 'Please do not send submissions. We cater to a small, collectable market and commission the fiction we publish.'

Tindal Street Press Ltd

217 The Custard Factory, Gibb Street, Birmingham B9 4AA
☎0121 773 8157 Fax 0121 693 5525
✉ emma@tindalstreet.co.uk
www.tindalstreet.co.uk

Managing Editor *Emma Hargrave*

Founded in 1998 to publish contemporary original fiction from the English regions. Publishes original fiction only – novels and short story anthologies. No local history, memoirs or poetry. Published *Astonishing Splashes of Colour* by Clare Morrall, shortlisted for the 2003 **Man Booker Prize for Fiction**. 6 titles in 2006. Approach with a letter, synopsis and three chapters and include s.a.e. for return of ms.

ROYALTIES paid.

Tlön Books Publishing Ltd

64 Arthurdon Road, London SE4 1JU
☎020 8690 0642 Fax 020 8690 0642
✉ mark.reid@tlon.co.uk
www.tlon.co.uk

Managing Editor *Jason Shelley*

Founded 2002. Publishes fiction, art, photography, poetry and children's books. 8 titles

in 2006. Unsolicited mss, synopses and ideas welcome; approach by e-mail.

ROYALTIES twice-yearly.

Wakefield Historical Publications

19 Pinder's Grove, Wakefield WF1 4AH
☎01924 372748
✉ kate@airtime.co.uk

Managing Editor *Kate Taylor*

Founded 1977 by the Wakefield Historical Society to publish well-researched, scholarly works of regional (namely West Riding) historical significance. 1–2 titles a year. Unsolicited mss, synopses and ideas for books welcome.

ROYALTIES not paid.

Watling Street Publishing Ltd

33 Hatherop, Nr Cirencester GL7 3NA
☎01285 750212
✉ chris.mclaren@saltwaypublishing.co.uk

Managing Director *Chris McLaren*
Editorial Head *Christine Kidney*

Founded 2001. Publishes non-fiction titles on London and its history; children's and adult. No unsolicited mss. Ideas and synopses welcome. Approach in writing or by e-mail with a one-page proposal. 'Not interested in anything not related to London.'

Waywiser Press

9 Woodstock Road, London N4 3ET
☎020 8374 5526 Fax 020 8374 5736
✉ waywiserpress@aol.com
www.waywiser-press.com

Managing Editor *Philip Hoy*
Editorial Advisers *Joseph Harrison, Clive Watkins, Greg Williamson*

Founded 2002. An independent literary press, publishing poetry, fiction and other kinds of literary work by new as well as established writers. The press also runs a literary award, the **Anthony Hecht Poetry Prize** (see entry under *Prizes*). Submission details available on the website.

ROYALTIES paid.

Whitchurch Books Ltd

67 Merthyr Road, Whitchurch, Cardiff CF14 1DD
☎029 2052 1956
✉ whitchurchbooks@btconnect.com

Managing Director *Gale Canvin*

Founded 1994. Publishes local interest, particularly local history. Welcomes unsolicited mss,

synopses and ideas on relevant subjects. Initial approach by phone or in writing.
ROYALTIES twice-yearly.

Whittles Publishing
Dunbeath Mains Cottages, Dunbeath
KW6 6EY
☎01593 731333 Fax 01593 731400
✉ info@whittlespublishing.com
www.whittlespublishing.com

Publisher *Dr Keith Whittles*

Publisher in geomatics, civil and structural engineering and applied science. Also publishes non-technical books within the following areas: maritime, military history, landscape and nature writing. Unsolicited mss, synopses and ideas welcome on appropriate themes.
ROYALTIES annually.

William Ernest
See **Radikal Phase Publishing House Ltd**

Willow Bank Publishers Ltd
16A Bunters Road, Wickhambrook,
Newmarket CB8 8XY
☎0800 731 5258
✉ editorial@willowbankpublishers.co.uk
www.willowbankpublishers.co.uk

Managing Editor *Christopher Sims*

Founded 2005. Publishes all genres, fiction and non-fiction. Unsolicited mss, synopses and ideas for books welcome; send via post in the first instance.
ROYALTIES annually.

Witan Books
Cherry Tree House, 8 Nelson Crescent, Cotes Heath, via Stafford ST21 6ST
☎01782 791673
✉ witan@mail.com

Managing Editor *Jeff Kent*

Founded in 1980 for self-publishing and commenced publishing other writers in 1991. Publishes general books, including biography, education, environment, geography, history, politics, popular music and sport. 1 or 2 titles a year. Unsolicited mss, synopses and ideas welcome (include s.a.e.).
ROYALTIES paid.

Worple Press
PO Box 328, Tonbridge TN9 1WR
☎01732 368958
✉ theworpleco@aol.com
www.theworplepress.co.uk

Managing Editors *Peter Carpenter, Amanda Knight*

Founded 1997. Independent publisher specialising in poetry, art and alternative titles. Write or phone for catalogue and flyers. 4 titles a year. No unsolicited mss.
ROYALTIES paid.

Zymurgy Publishing
Hoults Estate, Walker Road, Newcastle upon Tyne NE6 2HL
☎0191 276 2425 Fax 0191 276 2425
✉ martin.ellis@ablibris.com
zymurgypublishing.com

Chairman *Martin Ellis*

Founded 2000. Publishes adult non-fiction, ranging from full colour illustrated hardbacks to mass market paperbacks. 4 titles in 2006. Synopses and ideas for books welcome but no unsolicited mss. Contact by telephone or e-mail.
ROYALTIES twice-yearly.

Electronic Publishing and Other Services

www.ABCtales.com

Unit 3N, Leroy House, 436 Essex Road, London N1 3QP
☎020 7682 1865 Fax 020 7682 1867
✉ tcook@abctales.com
www.abctales.com

Owner *Burgeon Creative Ideas Ltd*
Editor *Tony Cook*

Founded by A. John Bird, MBE, co-founder of the *Big Issue* magazine, Tony Cook and Gordon Roddick. ABCtales is a free website dedicated to publishing and developing new writing. Content is predominantly short stories, autobiography and poetry. Anyone can upload creative writing to the website.

Arbour E-Books

2 Clonmel Road, Stirchley, Birmingham B30 2BU
☎0121 459 5659
✉ mike@arbour-ebooks.com
www.arbour-ebooks.com

Owner/Editor *Mike Hill*

Electronic publisher. 'A small fee is charged for electronic submission checking by a specialist. If accepted, the e-book is produced, published and sold for a negotiated percentage of sales.' Short stories, serials or poems of social comedy/ drama preferred. A negotiable fee is applicable to commercial artists and companies for catalogues and marketing e-books published. Some website work may be undertaken for all clients. Submissions must be Microsoft Word compatible, English and to a high standard of spelling and casual grammar. Paper submissions not accepted.

Authors OnLine

See entry under *UK Publishers*

BeWrite Books

32 Bryn Road South, Wigan WN4 8QR
✉ contact@bewrite.net
www.bewrite.net

Managing Director *Cait Myers*
Editorial Director *Neil Marr*

A multi-genre publishing house founded in 1999 and especially geared toward the encouragement and publication of first-time authors. About 20 titles a year. Unsolicited mss and synopses welcome (using the online form on the website). 'All offers promptly acknowledged and draft manuscript-to-publication time shorter than most other publishing houses.'
ROYALTIES quarterly (no advance).

Books 4 Publishing

Drovers House, The Auction Yard, Craven Arms SY7 9BZ
☎0870 777 3339 Fax 01588 673623
✉ editor@books4publishing.com
www.books4publishing.com

Owner *Corvedale Media Ltd*
Managing Director *Mark Oliver*

Founded 2000. Specialises in showcasing unpublished books and helping new authors gain recognition for their work by displaying synopses and up to 5000 words on the Books 4 Publishing website and promoting titles to publishers and literary agents. Mss, synopses and ideas welcome; initial enquiries by e-mail, post or submission form on website.

Claritybooks.com

Colt Farm, Bromley Green Road, Ashford TN26 2EQ
✉ ed@claritybooks.com
www.claritybooks.com

Internet e-book publisher and distributor. Has proprietary e-book technology which simplifies the process of downloading and reading of purchased works for the reader while still providing authors with copyright protection/ encryption. Mss or synopses welcomed from new or published authors. No charges to authors. Will consider all works of a good standard. E-mail communication preferred. If paper submission, please include s.a.e.

e-book-downloads-uploads.com

63 Lulworth Avenue, Preston PR2 2BE
☎07722 209009
✉ editor@e-book-downloads-uploads.com *or*
    info@e-book-downloads-uploads.com
www.e-book-downloads-uploads.com

Contact *H. Pritchard*

A new e-book publisher, established in 2006, 'willing to give opportunities to writers who by no fault of their own cannot get their work to market'. Will consider all submissions and all categories apart from poetry. Approach by e-mail with short synopsis attached.

ROYALTIES twice-yearly.

Fern HousE-Publishing
19 High Street, Haddenham, Ely CB6 3XA
☎01353 740222
✉ epub@fernhouse.com
www.fernhouse.com

Managing Editor *Rodney Dale*

Founded 1995. Has published mainly non-fiction (13 titles in print) but now entering the field of e-publishing. Open to submissions – 'but only of the highest quality'.

50 Connect – www.50connect.co.uk
5 Church Street, Windsor SL4 1PE
☎01753 847340 Fax 01753 857174
✉ admin@50connect.com
www.50connect.co.uk

Editor *Rachael Hannan* (rhannan@50connect.com)

Launched in 2000, www.50connect.co.uk is a leading content-driven website for the over 45's. Covers everything from finance to health, travel, overseas retirement, food, theatre, music, gardening and much more. Also strong community element including forums and a chat room. Please contact via e-mail in the first instance.

Fledgling Press Limited
7 Lennox Street, Edinburgh EH4 1QB
☎0131 332 6867
✉ info@fledglingpress.co.uk
www.fledglingpress.co.uk

Director *Zander Wedderburn*

Founded 2000. Internet publisher, aiming to be a launching pad for new authors. Special interest in authentic writing about the human condition, including autobiography, diaries, poetry and fictionalised variations on these. Monthly online competition (www.canyouwrite.com) with small prizes for short pieces. Also free books and reports in the areas of shiftwork and working time. Send mss and other details by e-mail from the website or by post. Links into short-run book production. 20 titles to date.

Justis Publishing Ltd
Grand Union House, 20 Kentish Town Road, London NW1 9NR
☎020 7267 8989 Fax 020 7267 1133
✉ enquiries@justis.com
www.justis.com

Founded 1986. Electronic publisher of UK and European legal and offical information on CD-ROM, online and the Internet.

Lulu
See entry under *UK Publishers*

The Male Alliance UK
✉ admin@themalealliance.info
www.themalealliance.info

Established in 2001. Non-profit Internet-based campaign group devoted to serious gay male issues: politics, law, support, information, protest and male rights. Articles should promote positive images of gay men, challenge ignorance and stereotypical concepts of homosexual males. Unsolicited material from gay men will be considered for publication on the website as a free contribution.

New Authors Showcase
See **Barrie James Literary Agency** under *UK Literary Agents*

Online Originals
Priory Cottage, Wordsworth Place, London NW5 4HG
☎020 7267 4244
✉ editor@onlineoriginals.com
www.onlineoriginals.com

Managing Director *David Gettman*
Technical Director *Neill Sanders*

Publishes book-length works on the Internet and as print-on-demand or short run library editions. Acquires global electronic rights in literary fiction, intellectual non-fiction, drama, and youth fiction (ages 8–16). No poetry, fantasy, how-to, self-help, picture books, cookery, hobbies, crafts or local interest. TITLES *Being and Becoming* Christopher Macann (4 vols.); *The Dreamer and the Beast* Keith Stevens; *Lard and Speck* Andrew Cogan; *Quintet* Frederick Forsyth; *The Angels of Russia* Patricia Leroy. 6 titles in 2006. Unsolicited mss, synopses and proposals for books welcome. *All* authors must have Internet access. Unique peer-review, automated submissions system, accessed via the website address above. No submissions on paper or disk.

ROYALTIES paid annually (50% royalties on e-book price of £6).

Research Bureau
Digital Publishing

81 Hillhead Crescent, Belfast BT11 9FW

☎028 9087 4769/07849 020205

✉ info@researchbureau.co.uk

www.researchbureau.co.uk

Offers a range of book publishing services, including self-publishing, book promotion, print-on-demand from other publishers and e-book publishing. Primarily interested in non-fiction books, manuals and reports but also fiction considered. See website for further details. Text should be sent in electronic format (e-mail, pdf file) but will consider finished book or ms by post (include s.a.e).

WritersServices

See entry under *Useful Websites*

Useful Websites

Many of these and other useful websites for writers can be found in *The Internet for Writers* by Nick Daws (ISBN 1-84025-308-8), one of a series of books published by Internet Handbooks; *The Incredibly Indispensable Web Directory* by Clive and Bettina Zietman, published by Kogan Page (ISBN 0-7494-3617-4); *thegoodwebguide for writers* by Paul Chronnell, published by The Good Web Guide Limited (ISBN 1-903282-38-1).

A2A Access to Archives
www.a2a.org.uk

Database of UK archive catalogues dating from the eighth century to the present day. Now contains '10 million records relating to 9.2 million items held in 410 record offices and other repositories'.

AbeBooks
www.abebooks.co.uk

Includes new and second-hand books search engine and 'The Rare Book Room' for antiquarian, rare and collectible titles online. Also features a search engine for textbooks and reference publications, both new and second-hand.

Academi (Welsh Academy/ Yr Academi Gymreig)
www.academi.org

News of events, publications and funding for Welsh-based literary events. (See entry under *Professional Associations and Societies*.)

Alibris
www.alibris.com

Over 60 million used, new and hard-to-find books online. Bargain books, text and reference listings and rare books. ISBN search engine. Also movies and music.

Alliance of Literary Societies
www.sndc.demon.co.uk/als.htm

Details of societies and events. (See entry under *Professional Associations and Societies*.)

Amazon
www.amazon.co.uk

The online shop for books, music, videos and DVDs, electronics, software, photographic, toys and games, home and garden.

Ancestry
www.ancestry.co.uk

Family history information – databases, articles and other sources of genealogical data.

Arts Council England
www.artscouncil.org.uk

Includes information on funding applications, publications and the National Lottery. (See entry under *Arts Councils and Regional Offices*.)

Arts Council of Northern Ireland
www.artscouncil-ni.org

Information on funding and awards, events and free E-Newsletter service. (See entry under *Arts Councils and Regional Offices*.)

Arts Council of Wales/ Cyngor Celfyddydau Cymru
www.acw-ccc.org.uk

Information on publications, grants, council meetings, the arts in Wales. (See entry under *Arts Councils and Regional Offices*.)

Arvon Foundation
www.arvonfoundation.org

See entry under *UK and Irish Writers' Courses*.

Association for Scottish Literary Studies
www.asls.org.uk

The educational charity promoting the languages and literature of Scotland. (See entry under *Professional Associations and Societies*.)

Association of Authors' Agents (AAA)
www.agentsassoc.co.uk

UK agents' organisation including list of current members. (See entry under *Professional Associations and Societies*.)

Association of Authors' Representatives (AAR)
www.aar-online.org

US agents' organisation including search engine for current members. (See entry under *Professional Associations and Societies*.)

Author-Network
www.author-network.com

Writers' resource site run by Karen Scott.

Author.co.uk
www.author.co.uk

Links to advice and information for writers.

Authorbank
www.authorbank.com

Registration for a fee enables authors to present book ideas to publishers online and access to a free advice service.

Authors' Licensing and Collecting Society Limited (ALCS)
www.alcs.co.uk

Details of membership, news and publications. (See entry under *Professional Associations and Societies*.)

Bartleby.com
www.bartleby.com

An ever-expanding list of books published online for reference, free of charge.

BBC
www.bbc.co.uk

Access to all BBC departments and services.

bibliofind
www.bibliofind.com

Millions of second-hand and rare books, periodicals and ephemera for sale online via Amazon.com.

Bibliomania
www.bibliomania.com

Over 2000 classic texts, study guides and reference resources available online for free. Also selected books for sale in the Bibliomania shop.

book2book/booktrade.info
www.book2book.co.uk

Established by a group of publishers, booksellers, website developers and trade journalists to provide up-to-date news, features and useful information for the book trade.

Booktrust
www.booktrust.org.uk

Book information service, guide to prizes and awards, factsheets on getting published. (See entry under *Professional Associations and Societies*.)

British Association of Picture Libraries and Agencies (BAPLA)
www.bapla.org.uk

Website includes the BAPLA Online Database search facility by category or name. (See entry under *Professional Associations and Societies*.)

British Centre for Literary Translation
www.literarytranslation.com

A joint website with the British Council with workshops by leading translators, contacts and networks, and search engine for translation conferences, seminars and events. (See entry under *Professional Associations and Societies*.)

The British Council
www.britishcouncil.org

Information on the Council's English Language services, education programmes, society and science links. (See entry under *Professional Associations and Societies*.)

British Film Institute (bfi)
www.bfi.org.uk

Information on the services offered by the Institute. (See entry under *Professional Associations and Societies*.)

British Library
www.bl.uk

Reader service enquiries, access to main catalogues, information on collections, links to the various reading rooms and exhibitions. (See related entries under *Library Services*.)

Chapter One Promotions
www.chapteronepromotions.com

Provides services to writers at various stages of their writing career: news, story and poetry critique services, proof reading, 'Kids Korner'.

Chartered Institute of Linguists (IoL)
www.iol.org.uk

Discussion forum, news on regional societies, job opportunities, 'Find a Linguist' service and *The Linguist* magazine. (See entry under *Professional Associations and Societies*.)

CILIP
www.cilip.org.uk

The professional body for librarians and information professionals. (See entry under *Professional Associations and Societies*.)

Commonword
www.commonword.org.uk

Resource site for writers (website currently under development).

Complete Works of William Shakespeare
www-tech.mit.edu/Shakespeare/works.html

Access to the text of the complete works.

Copyright Licensing Agency Ltd (CLA)
www.cla.co.uk

Copyright information, customer support and information on CLA services. (See entry under *Professional Associations and Societies*.)

Crime Writers' Association (CWA)
www.thecwa.co.uk

Website of the professional crime writers' association. (See entry under *Professional Associations and Societies*.)

Daily Express
www.express.co.uk

Daily Express online.

Daily Mail/The Mail on Sunday
www.mail.co.uk

Daily Mail and *The Mail on Sunday* online.

Daily Mirror
www.mirror.co.uk

Daily Mirror online.

Daily Telegraph
www.telegraph.co.uk

Daily Telegraph online.

Dictionary of Slang
dictionaryofslang.co.uk

A guide to slang 'from a British perspective'. Research information and search facility.

The Eclectic Writer
www.eclectics.com/writing/writing.html

US website offering a selection of articles giving advice for writers and an online discussion board.

Encyclopædia Britannica
www.britannica.com

Subscription access to the entire *Encyclopædia Britannica*.

The English Association
www.le.ac.uk/engassoc

News, publications, conference and membership information. (See entry under *Professional Associations and Societies*.)

Federation of Worker Writers and Community Publishers (FWWCP)
myweb.tiscali.co.uk/thefwwcp/Info.htm

Links to members of the FWWCP, the Federation magazine, information on membership. (See entry under *Professional Associations and Societies*.)

Film Angel
www.filmangel.co.uk

Established in conjunction with Hammerwood Films to create a shop window for writers and would-be film angels alike. Submitted synopses are displayed for a pre-determined period, for a fee, while would-be angels are invited to finance a production of their choice.

Filmmaker Store
www.filmmakerstore.com

US site giving scriptwriting resources, listings and advice.

Financial Times
www.ft.com

Financial Times online.

Frankfurt Book Fair
www.frankfurt-book-fair.com/en/portal.html

Provides latest news and market analysis of the book business plus information on the annual Book Fair.

The Froebel Archive for Childhood Studies
www.roehampton.ac.uk/froebel/froebelarchive/index.html

Collection of children's literature. Supports courses at Roehampton University and is available to *bona fide* researchers. Catalogue available online.

The Good Web Guide Ltd
www.thegoodwebguide.co.uk

Guide to the best websites. Provides thousands

of detailed and independent reviews of a wide range of websites.

The Guardian/Observer
www.guardian.co.uk

Website of the *Guardian* and *Observer* newspapers online.

Guide to Grammar and Style
www.andromeda.rutgers.edu/~jlynch/Writing

A guide to grammar and style, organised alphabetically, plus articles and links to other grammatical reference sites.

Hansard
www.parliament.the-stationery-office.co.uk/pa/cm/cmhansrd.htm

The official record of debates and written answers in the House of Commons. The transcript of each day's business appears at noon on the following weekday.

The Herald
www.theherald.co.uk

Scottish daily broadsheet.

House of Commons Research Library
www.parliament.uk/parliamentary_publications_and_archives/research_papers.cfm

Gives access to the text of research reports prepared for MPs on a wide range of current issues.

The HTML Writers Guild
www.hwg.org

US organisation offering resources, support and training for Web authors. (See entry under *Professional Associations and Societies*.)

The Independent
www.independent.co.uk

The *Independent* newspaper online.

Independent Northern Publishers
www.northernpublishers.co.uk

Promotes the work of new writers across the region.

IngentaConnect
www.ingentaconnect.com

A comprehensive online UK academic research service. The site offers access to more than 21 million articles, chapters and reports online.

Inpress Books
www.inpressbooks.co.uk

Provides sales, marketing and distribution for small independent publishers.

Institute of Translation and Interpreting (ITI)
www.iti.org.uk/indexMain.html

Website of the professional association of translators and interpreters, with the ITI directory of members, publications, training and membership information. (See entry under *Professional Associations and Societies*.)

Internet Classics Archive
classics.mit.edu

Includes works of classical literature; mostly Greek and Roman with some Chinese and Persian. All are in English translation

Internet Movie Database (IMDb)
www.imdb.com

Essential resource for film buffs and researchers with search engine for cast lists, screenwriters, directors and producers; film and television news, awards, film preview information, video releases.

The Irish Arts Council/ An Chomhairle Ealaíon
www.artscouncil.ie

Monthly e-mail newsletter available giving latest information on grants and awards, news and events, etc. (See entry under *Arts Councils and Regional Offices*.)

Journalism UK
www.journalismuk.co.uk

A website for UK-based print journalists who write for text-based publications. Includes links to newspapers, magazines, e-zines, news sources plus information on training and organisations.

The Library Association see CILIP

Literature North East
www.literaturenortheast.co.uk

Monthly e-newsletter; listings of events and readings in the region; writing courses and local training opportunities.

Literature North West
www.publishingnorthwest.co.uk

Promotional agency for the region's independent presses and literature organisations

literaturetraining
www.literaturetraining.com

Online directory of training and professional development opportunities for UK writers and literature professionals. Includes information on courses, workshops, jobs, residencies, submissions, competitions, organisations and funding for professional development. Also, information sheets and specially commissioned features.

Location Register of 20th-Century English Literary Manuscripts and Letters
www.library.rdg.ac.uk/colls/projects/ locreg.html

Reference source for the study of English literature. Information about the manuscript holdings of repositories of all sizes, from the British Library to small-town museums, of literary authors – from major poets to minor science fiction writers.

Mr William Shakespeare and the Internet
shakespeare.palomar.edu

Guide to scholarly Shakespeare resources on the Internet.

National Union of Journalists (NUJ)
www.nuj.org.uk

Represents those journalists who work in all sectors of publishing, print and broadcasting. (See entry under *Professional Associations and Societies*.)

New Writers Consultancy
www.new-writers-consultancy.com

Advice for writers and critiques, offered by Karen Scott and Diana Hayden.

New Writing North
www.newwritingnorth.com

Essentially for writers based in the north of England but also a useful source of advice and guidelines. (See entry under *Professional Associations and Societies*.)

New Writing Partnership
www.newwritingpartnership.org.uk

Promotes and supports creative writing in Eastern England.

Newnovelist
www.newnovelist.com

Novel-writing software. Aids research, characterisation, structure and plot, and breaks down the process of writing a novel into manageable chunks.

PEN
www.englishpen.org

Website of the English Centre of International PEN. News of events, information on prizes, membership details. (See entry under *Professional Associations and Societies*.)

PlaysOnTheNet
www.playsonthenet.com

Information and help for new playwrights.

Poets and Writers, Inc
www.pw.org

A US site containing information and advice for writers.

Producers Alliance for Cinema and Television (PACT)
www.pact.co.uk

Publications, training, production companies, membership details. (See entry under *Professional Associations and Societies*.)

The Publishers Association
www.publishers.org.uk

Information about the Association and careers in publishing; also 'Getting Published' pages. (See entry under *Professional Associations and Societies*.)

Publishing North West
See **Literature North West**.

RefDesk.com
refdesk.com

Free facts and statistics on every country in the world plus charts and maps, illustrations and related sources.

Royal Society of Literature
www.rslit.org

Information on lectures, discussions and readings; membership details and prizes. (See entry under *Professional Associations and Societies*.)

The Scotsman
www.scotsman.com

The Scotsman newspaper online.

Scottish Arts Council
www.sac.org.uk

Information on funding and events. (See entry under *Arts Councils and Regional Offices*.)

Scottish Book Trust
www.scottishbooktrust.com

Information on the Trust's activities. (See entry under *Professional Associations and Societies*.)

Scottish Library Association (SLAINTE: Information & Libraries Scotland)
www.slainte.org.uk

Links to various services and information on librarianship and information management in Scotland. (See entry under *Professional Associations and Societies*.)

Scottish Publishers Association
www.scottishbooks.org

Links to websites of members of the Association, information on activities and publications. (See entry under *Professional Associations and Societies*.)

Screenwriters Online
screenwriter.com/insider/news.html

US website, described as the '*only* professional screenwriter's site run by major screenwriters who get their scripts and screenplays made into movies'. Contains screenplay analysis, expert articles and *The Insider Report*.

The SF Hub
www.sfhub.ac.uk/

Science fiction research website created by the University of Liverpool. Includes links to the Science Fiction Foundation collection and the John Wyndham archives.

Shots Magazine
www.shotsmag.co.uk

Electronic magazine of crime and mystery fiction.

Society for Editors and Proofreaders (SfEP)
www.sfep.org.uk

Information about the Society including online directory of members. (See entry under *Professional Associations and Societies*.)

The Society of Authors
www.societyofauthors.org

Includes FAQs for new writers, diary of events,

membership details, prizes and awards. (See entry under *Professional Associations and Societies*.)

Society of Indexers
www.indexers.org.uk/

Indexing information for publishers and authors, 'Find an Indexer' pages. Membership information. (See entry under *Professional Associations and Societies*.)

South Bank Centre, London
www.sbc.org.uk

Links to the Royal Festival Hall, Purcell Room, Queen Elizabeth Hall, the Hayward Gallery and Poetry Library; news of literature events.

Story Wizard
www.storywizard.co.uk

Software to enable children to write creative stories.

The Sun
www.thesun.co.uk

The Sun online.

The Times
www.thetimes.co.uk

The Times online.

trAce Online Writing Centre
tracearchive.ntu.ac.uk

Online archive of work published by the trAce Online Writing Centre between 1995 -- 2005. Also holds articles and transcripts of discussions.

UK Children's Books Directory
www.ukchildrensbooks.co.uk

Website created by Steve and Diana Kimpton to 'increase the profile of UK children's books on the Internet'.

The UK Public Libraries Page
dspace.dial.pipex.com/town/square/ac940/ weblibs.html

Website links to public libraries throughout the UK, compiled by Sheila and Robert Harden.

Webster Dictionary/Thesaurus
www.m-w.com/home.htm

Merriam-Webster Online. Includes a search facility for words in the Webster Dictionary or Webster Thesaurus; word games and daily podcast.

Welsh Academy see **Academi**

**Welsh Books Council
(Cyngor Llyfrau Cymru)**
www.cllc.org.uk

Information about books from Wales, editorial and design services, publishing grants. (See entry under *Professional Associations and Societies*.)

The Word Pool
www.wordpool.co.uk

Children's book site with information on writing for children and a thriving discussion group for children's writers. Also Word Pool Design (www.wordpooldesign.co.uk): Web design for writers, illustrators and publishers.

WordCounter
www.wordcounter.com

Highlights the most frequently used words in a given text. Use as a guide to see what words are overused. Also Political Vocabulary Analysis which measures indications of political leanings in given text.

Write4kids.com
www.write4kids.com

US website for children's writers, whether published or beginners. Includes special reports, articles, advice, news on the latest bestsellers and links to related sites.

Writernet
www.writernet.org.uk

Information, advice and guidance for writers on all aspects of live and recorded performance. (See entry under *Professional Associations and Societies*.)

The Writers' Guild of Great Britain
www.writersguild.org.uk

Information on contracts, copyright, news, writers' resources and industry regulations. (See entry under *Professional Associations and Societies*.)

Writers Nexus International
www.writersnexus.com

Enables writers to place their work online and for publishers, agents and readers to access it quickly and effectively.

Writers' Circles
www.writers-circles.com

Directory of writers' circles, courses and workshops. Free listings.

Writers, Artists and their Copyright Holders (W.A.T.C.H.)
tyler.hrc.utexas.edu

Database of copyright holders in the UK and North America. (See entry under *Professional Associations and Societies*.)

WritersNet
www.writers.net

A directory of writers, editors, publishers and literary agents.

WritersServices
www.WritersServices.com

Established in March 2000 by Chris Holifield, former deputy managing director and publisher at Cassell. Offers factsheets, book reviews, advice, links and other resources for writers including editorial services, contract vetting and self-publishing.

The Writing Centre
www.thewritingcentre.com

A new resource for writers in Cornwall and the South West. Covers all genres from poetry to business writing, from novels to radio comedy. Helps find mentors, run workshops, seminars and short courses. Details of training and a Work Opportunities board; listings of magazines and publishers in the region.

Writing-World.com
writing-world.com

'A world of writing tips ... for writers around the world.'

UK Packagers

Aladdin Books Ltd
2/3 Fitroy Mews, London W1T 6DF
☎020 7383 2084 Fax 020 7388 6391
✉ sales@aladdinbooks.co.uk
www.aladdinbooks.co.uk

Managing Director *Charles Nicholas*

Founded in 1979 as a packaging company but with joint publishing ventures in the UK and USA. Commissions children's fully illustrated, non-fiction reference books. IMPRINTS **Aladdin Books** *Bibby Whittaker* Children's reference; **Nicholas Enterprises** *Charles Nicholas* Adult non-fiction; **The Learning Factory** *Charles Nicholas* Early learning concepts 0–4 years. TITLES *World Issues*; *Science Readers*; *The Atlas of Animals*. About 40 titles a year. Will consider synopses and ideas for children's non-fiction with international sales potential only. No fiction.

FEES usually paid instead of royalties.

The Albion Press Ltd
Spring Hill, Idbury OX7 6RU
☎01993 831094 Fax 01993 831982

Chairman/Managing Director *Emma Bradford*

Founded 1984. Commissions illustrated trade titles, particularly children's. TITLES *The Great Circle: A History of the First Nations* Neil Philip; *Fairy Tales of Hans Christian Andersen* Isabelle Brent. About 2 titles a year. Unsolicited synopses and ideas for books not welcome.

ROYALTIES paid; fees paid for introductions and partial contributions.

Amber Books Ltd
Bradleys Close, 74–77 White Lion Street, London N1 9PF
☎020 7520 7600 Fax 020 7520 7606/7
✉ enquiries@amberbooks.co.uk
www.amberbooks.co.uk

Managing Director *Stasz Gnych*
Rights Director *Sara Ballard*
Publishing Manager *Charles Catton*

Founded 1989. Commissions history, encyclopedias, military, aviation, transport, sport, combat, survival and fitness, cookery, lifestyle, naval history, crime, childrens and general reference. No fiction, poetry or biography. 100 titles in 2006. No unsolicited material outside subject areas listed above.

FEES paid.

BCS Publishing Ltd
2nd Floor, Temple Court, 109 Oxford Road, Cowley OX4 2ER
☎01865 770099 Fax 01865 770050
✉ bcs-publishing@dsl.pipex.com

Managing Director *Steve McCurdy*
Approx. Annual Turnover £150,000

Commissions general interest non-fiction for the international co-edition market.

Bender Richardson White
PO Box 266, Uxbridge UB9 5BD
☎01895 832444 Fax 01895 835213
✉ brw@brw.co.uk

Partners *Lionel Bender, Kim Richardson, Ben White*

Founded 1990 to produce illustrated non-fiction for children, adults and family reference for publishers in the UK and abroad. 80 titles in 2004. Unsolicited material not welcome.

FEES paid.

Book House
See **Salariya Book Company Ltd**

Breslich & Foss Ltd
Unit 2A, Union Court, 20–22 Union Road, Clapham, London SW4 6JP
☎020 7819 3990 Fax 020 7819 3998
✉ sales@breslichfoss.com

Directors *Paula Breslich, K.B. Dunning*
Approx. Annual Turnover £650,000

Packagers of adult non-fiction titles, including interior design, crafts, gardening, health and children's non-fiction and picturebooks. Unsolicited mss welcome but synopses preferred. Include s.a.e. with all submissions.

ROYALTIES paid twice-yearly.

Brown Wells and Jacobs Ltd
Forresters Hall, 25–27 Westow Street, London SE19 3RY
☎020 8771 5115 Fax 020 8771 9994

✉ graham@bwj-ltd.com
www.bwj.org

Managing Director *Graham Brown*

Founded 1979. Commissions non-fiction, novelty, pre-school and first readers, natural history and science. About 40 titles a year. Unsolicited synopses and ideas for books welcome.

FEES paid.

Cameron & Hollis

PO Box 1, Moffat DG10 9SU

☎01683 220808 Fax 01683 220012

✉ info@cameronbooks.co.uk
www.cameronbooks.co.uk

Directors *Ian A. Cameron, Jill Hollis*

Approx. Annual Turnover £400,000

Commissions contemporary art, design, collectors' reference, decorative arts, architecture, children's non-fiction and film (serious critical works only). About 6 titles a year.

PAYMENT varies with each contract.

Compendium Publishing Ltd

See entry under *UK Publishers*

Diagram Visual Information Ltd

195 Kentish Town Road, London NW5 2JU

☎020 7482 3633 Fax 020 7482 4932

✉ brucerobertson@diagramgroup.com

Managing Director *Bruce Robertson*

Founded 1967. Producer of library, school, academic and trade reference books. About 10 titles a year.

FEES paid; no payment for sample material/ submissions for consideration.

Eddison Sadd Editions

St Chad's House, 148 King's Cross Road, London WC1X 9DH

☎020 7837 1968 Fax 020 7837 2025

✉ info@eddisonsadd.com
www.eddisonsadd.com

Managing Director *Nick Eddison*
Editorial Director *Ian Jackson*

Approx. Annual Turnover £2.5 million

Founded 1982. Produces a wide range of popular illustrated non-fiction – mind, body, spirit and complementary therapies are particular strengths – with books and interactive kits published in 30 countries. Many titles suit gift markets. Ideas and synopses, rather than mss, are welcome but titles must have international appeal.

ROYALTIES paid twice-yearly; fees paid when appropriate.

Erskine Press

The White House, Sandfield Lane, Eccles, Norwich NR16 2PB

☎01953 887277 Fax 01953 888361

✉ erskpres@aol.com
www.erskine-press.com

Chief Executive *Crispin de Boos*

Approx. Annual Turnover £65,000

Specialist publisher of books on Antarctic exploration – facsimiles, diaries, previously unpublished works and first English translations of expeditions of the late 19th and early 20th centuries. Publisher of general interest biographies with special reference to Norfolk. Recent publications include a number of Second World War related subjects. Also produces scholarly reprints and limited edition publications for academic/business organisations ranging from period print reproductions to facsimiles of rare and important books no longer available. 7 titles in 2006. No unsolicited mss. Ideas welcome.

ROYALTIES paid twice-yearly.

Expert Publications Ltd

Sloe House, Halstead CO9 1PA

☎01787 474744 Fax 01787 474700

✉ expert@lineone.net

Chairman *Dr. D. G. Hessayon*

Founded 1993. Produces the *Expert* series of books by Dr. D.G. Hessayon. Currently 24 titles in the series, including *The Flower Expert*; *The Evergreen Expert*; *The Vegetable & Herb Expert*; *The Flowering Shrub Expert*; *The Container Expert*. No unsolicited material.

Haldane Mason Ltd

PO Box 34196, London NW10 3YB

☎020 8459 2131 Fax 020 8728 1216

✉ info@haldanemason.com

Editorial Director *Samuel Francis*
Art Director *Ron Samuel*

Founded 1994. Commissions mainly children's illustrated non-fiction. Children's books are published under the **Red Kite Books** imprint. Adult list consists mainly of mind, body and spirit plus alternative health books under the Neal's Yard Remedies banner; children's age range 0–15. Unsolicited synopses and ideas welcome but approach by phone or e-mail first. No adult fiction.

FEES paid.

The Ilex Press Limited

The Old Candlemakers, West Street, Lewes BN7 2NX

☎01273 487440 Fax 01273 487441
✉ surname@ilex-press.com
www.ilex-press.com

Managing Director *Stephen Paul*
Associate Publisher *Robin Pearson*

Founded 1999. Sister company of **The Ivy Press Limited**. Commissions titles on digital art, design and photography as well as on all aspects of website design and graphics software. No fiction. Unsolicited synopses and ideas welcome; send a *brief* idea outline (3 or 4 pages) and a letter.

FEES paid.

The Ivy Press Limited

The Old Candlemakers, West Street, Lewes BN7 2NZ
☎01273 487440 Fax 01273 487441
✉ surname@ivy-group.co.uk
www.ivy-press.com

Managing Director *Stephen Paul*
Publisher *Jason Hook*

Founded 1996. Sister company of **The Ilex Press Limited**. Commissions illustrated non-fiction books covering subjects such as art, lifestyle, popular culture, health, self-help and humour. No fiction. Unsolicited synopses and ideas welcome; send a *brief* idea outline (3 or 4 pages) and a letter.

FEES paid.

The Learning Factory

See **Aladdin Books Ltd**

Lennard Associates Ltd

Windmill Cottage, Mackerye End, Harpenden AL5 5DR
☎01582 715866 Fax 01582 715866
✉ stephenson@lennardqap.co.uk

Chairman/Managing Director *Adrian Stephenson*

Founded 1979. Sponsored and commissioned projects only. IMPRINTS **Lennard Publishing**; **Queen Anne Press**. Acquired the latter and most of its assets in 1992. Now operating as a packager/production company only with no trade distribution. 2 titles in 2006. No unsolicited mss.

PAYMENT Both fees and royalties by arrangement.

Lexus Ltd

60 Brook Street, Glasgow G40 2AB
☎0141 556 0440 Fax 0141 556 2202
✉ peterterrell@lexusforlanguages.co.uk

www.lexusforlanguages.co.uk

Managing/Editorial Director *P.M. Terrell*

Founded 1980. Compiles bilingual reference, language and phrase books. TITLES Rough Guide phrasebooks; Langenscheidt dictionaries; *HarperCollins English-Chinese*; *Oxford Italian Pocket Dictionary*. Own series of *Travelmates* published in 2004 including a new beginner's course for learning Chinese, *The Chinese Classroom*. About 5 titles a year. Unsolicited material considered although books are mostly commissioned. Freelance contributors employed for a wide range of languages.

PAYMENT Generally flat fee.

Lionheart Books

10 Chelmsford Square, London NW10 3AR
☎020 8459 0453 Fax 020 8451 3681
✉ Lionheart.Brw@btinternet.com

Senior Partner *Lionel Bender*
Partner *Madeleine Samuel*

A design/editorial packaging team. Titles are primarily commissioned from publishers. Highly illustrated non-fiction for children aged 8–14, mostly natural history, history and general science. See also **Bender Richardson White**. About 20 titles a year.

PAYMENT Generally flat fee.

M&M Publishing Services

33 Warner Road, Ware SG12 9JL
☎01920 466003
✉ mikemoran@moran01.wanadoo,co.uk
www.photography-london.co.uk

Proprietors *Mike Moran, Maggie Copeland*

Project managers, production and editorial, packagers and publishers. TITLES *MM Publisher Database*; *MM Printer Database* (available in UK, European and international editions).

Market House Books Ltd

Suite B, Elsinore House, 43 Buckingham Street, Aylesbury HP20 2NQ
☎01296 484911 Fax 01296 437073
✉ books@mhbref.com
www.markethousebooks.com

Directors *John Daintith, Peter Sapsed*

Founded 1970. Formerly Laurence Urdang Associates. Compiles dictionaries, encyclopedias and reference. TITLES *Collins English Dictionary*; Facts on File dictionaries; *Grolier Bibliographical Encyclopedia of Scientists* (10 vols); *Larousse Thematica* (6 vols); *The Macmillan Encyclopedia*; Macmillan Dictionaries; Oxford Dictionaries of: *Business, Science, Medicine*, etc.; *Penguin Dictionary*

of *Electronics*; *Penguin Rhyming Dictionary*, etc. About 15 titles a year. Unsolicited material not welcome as most books are compiled in-house.
FEES paid.

Monkey Puzzle Media Ltd
Gissing's Farm, Fressingfield IP21 5SH
☎01379 588044 Fax 01379 588055
✉ info@monkeypuzzlemedia.com
Chairman/Managing Director *Roger Goddard-Coote*
Commissioning and List Development *Paul Mason*
Founded 1998. Packager of adult and children's non-fiction for trade, school, library and mass markets. No fiction or textbooks. About 80 titles a year. Synopses and ideas welcome. Include s.a.e. for return.
FEES paid; no royalties.

Nicholas Enterprises
See **Aladdin Books Ltd**

Orpheus Books Limited
6 Church Green, Witney OX28 4AW
☎01993 774949 Fax 01993 700330
✉ info@orpheusbooks.com
www.orpheusbooks.com
Directors *Nicholas Harris, Sarah Hartley*
Founded 1993. Commissions children's non-fiction. 25 titles in 2006. No unsolicited material.
FEES paid.

Playne Books Limited
Park Court Barn, Trefin, Haverfordwest SA62 5AU
☎01348 837073 Fax 01348 837063
✉ playne.books@virgin.net
Editorial Director *Gill Davies*
Design & Production *David Playne*
Founded 1987. Commissions early learning titles for young children – fun ideas with an educational slant and novelty books. Also highly illustrated and practical books on any subject. Synopses and ideas by prior arrangement only. Vanity publications welcomed.
ROYALTIES paid on payment from publishers. Fees sometimes paid instead of royalties.

Mathew Price Ltd
The Old Glove Factory, Bristol Road, Sherborne DT9 4HP
☎01935 816010 Fax 01935 816310
✉ mathewp@mathewprice.com
www.mathewprice.com

Chairman/Managing Director *Mathew Price*
Approx. Annual Turnover £500,000
Commissions full-colour novelty and picture books and fiction for young children plus children's non-fiction for all ages. TITLES *Magnificent Mazes*; *Creepies*; *Tractor Factory*; *Join-In Stories for the Very Young*; *Treasure Hunt*. Mss should be double-spaced, typed on one side of paper. Enclose s.a.e. with submission and keep a copy of everything that is sent.
FEES sometimes paid instead of royalties.

Quarto Publishing plc
The Old Brewery, 6 Blundell Street, London N7 9BH
☎020 7700 6700 Fax 020 7700 4191
www.quarto.com
Chairman & CEO *Laurence Orbach*
Director of Co-edition Publishing *Piers Spence*
Founded 1976. Britain's largest book packager. Acquired Marshall Editions in 2002. Commissions illustrated non-fiction, including painting, graphic design, how-to, lifestyle, visual arts, history, cookery, gardening, crafts. Publishes under the Apple imprint. Unsolicited synopses/ ideas for books welcome.
PAYMENT Flat fees paid.

Queen Anne Press
See **Lennard Associates Ltd**

Red Kite Books
See **Haldane Mason Ltd**

Regency House Publishing Limited
See entry under *UK Publishers*

Salariya Book Company Ltd
25 Marlborough Place, Brighton BN1 1UB
☎01273 603306 Fax 01273 693857
✉ salariya@salariya.com
www.salariya.com
www.book-house.co.uk
www.scribblersbook.com
Managing Director *David Salariya*
Editor *Steven Hayes*
Art Director *Carolyn Franklin*
Founded 1989. Books for children: history, art, music, science, architecture, education, nature, environment, fantasy, folktales, multicultural, fiction, young readers and picture books. IMPRINTS **Book House**; **Scribblers** Highly illustrated books in all subjects for babies and children, from pre-school board books to teenage graphic novels. For fiction, submit complete c.v., ms for picture books; outline/synopsis and one

sample story or chapter for collections, novels or graphic novels. Response in four months if s.a.e. included. Illustrations: no original artwork. Send c.v., promotion sheet to be kept on file. Samples returned if s.a.e. included.

PAYMENT by arrangement.

Savitri Books Ltd
25 Lisle Lane, Ely CB7 4AS
☎01353 654327 Fax 01353 654327
✉ munni@savitribooks.demon.co.uk
Managing Director *Mrinalini S. Srivastava*
Approx. Annual Turnover £200,000

Founded 1983 and since 1998, Savitri Books has also become a publisher in its own right (textile crafts). Keen to work 'very closely with authors/illustrators and try to establish long-term relationships with them, doing more books with the same team of people'. Commissions illustrated non-fiction: biography, history, travel. About 7 titles a year. Unsolicited synopses and ideas for books 'very welcome'.

Scribblers
See **Salariya Book Company Ltd**

Stonecastle Graphics Ltd
Highlands Lodge, Chartway Street, Sutton Valence ME17 3HZ
☎01622 844414
✉ paul@stonecastle-graphics.co.uk *or*
sue@stonecastle-graphics.co.uk
www.stonecastle-graphics.co.uk
Partner *Paul Turner*
Editorial Head *Sue Pressley*
Approx. Annual Turnover £300,000

Founded 1976. Formed additional design/packaging partnership, **Touchstone**, in 1983 (see entry). Commissions illustrated non-fiction general books: motoring, health, sport, leisure, lifestyle and children's non-fiction. TITLES *Polar Regions*; *Penguins*; *Spirit of the Ocean*; *Africa*; *Classic Cars*; *Classic Motorbikes*; *Celebrating the Horse*. 20 titles in 2006. Unsolicited synopses and ideas for books welcome

FEES paid.

Templar Publishing
Pippbrook Mill, London Road, Dorking RH4 1JE
☎01306 876361 Fax 01306 889097
✉ editorial@templarco.co.uk
www.templarco.co.uk
Managing Director/Editorial Head *Amanda Wood*
Approx. Annual Turnover £14 million

Founded 1981. A division of The Templar Company plc. Commissions quality novelty and gift books, picture books and children's illustrated non-fiction. 100 titles a year. Synopses and ideas for books welcome. 'We are particularly interested in picture book mss and ideas for new novelty concepts.'

ROYALTIES by arrangement.

Toucan Books Ltd
Third Floor, 89 Charterhouse Street, London EC1M 6HR
☎020 7250 3388 Fax 020 7250 3123
Managing Director *Ellen Dupont*

Founded 1985. Specialises in international co-editions and fee-based editorial, design and production services. Commissions illustrated non-fiction for children and adults. No fiction or non-illustrated titles. About 5–10 titles a year.

ROYALTIES paid twice-yearly; fees paid in addition to or instead of royalties.

Touchstone Books Ltd
Highlands Lodge, Chartway Street, Sutton Valence ME17 3HZ
☎01622 844414 Fax 01622 844414
✉ paul@touchstone-books.com *or*
sue@touchstone-books.com
www.touchstone-books.com
Directors *Paul Turner, Sue Pressley, Nick Wigley, Trevor Legate*

Founded in 2006, Touchstone Books Ltd is an independent publisher of lavishly-illustrated books on motoring, art and general-interest subjects. TITLES *Cobra – The First 40 Years*; *100 Years of Grand Prix*; *The Very Best of Volkswagen*; *In the Company of Dali*. 6 titles in 2006. Unsolicited synopses and ideas for books welcome.

FEES paid.

David West Children's Books
7 Princeton Court, 55 Felsham Road, London SW15 1AZ
☎020 8780 3836 Fax 020 8780 9313
✉ dww@btinternet.com
www.davidwestchildrensbooks.com

Founded 1992. Commissions children's illustrated reference books. No fiction or adult books. 140 titles in 2006. Unsolicited ideas and synopses welcome; approach in writing in the first instance

FEES/ROYALTIES paid annually.

Working Partners Ltd
1 Albion Place, London W6 0QT

☎020 8748 7477 Fax 020 8748 7450
✉ enquiries@workingpartnersltd.co.uk
www.workingpartnersltd.co.uk

Chairman *Ben Baglio*
Managing Director *Chris Snowdon*
Contact *James Noble*

Specialises in quality mass-market fiction for leading children's publishers including Bloomsbury, HarperCollins, Hodder, Macmillan, Orchard, OUP, Random House and Scholastic. First chapter books to young adult. No picture books. **Working Partners Two** handles adult fiction across all popular genres on a similar basis. Welcomes approaches from interested writers.

PAYMENT Both fees and royalties by arrangement.

Zoë Books

15 Worthy Lane, Winchester SO23 7AB
✉ enquiries@zoebooks.co.uk
www.zoebooks.co.uk

Managing Director *Imogen Dawson*

Founded 1990. Specialises in full-colour information and reference books for schools and libraries worldwide. Does *not* publish picture books or fiction. No freelance work available. Unsolicited material not considered.

FEES paid.

Book Clubs

David Arscott's Sussex Book Club
Dolphin House, 51 St Nicholas Lane, Lewes
BN7 2JZ
☎01273 470100 Fax 01273 470100
✉ sussexbooks@aol.com
Founded January 1998. Specialises in books about the county of Sussex. Represents all the major publishers of Sussex books and offers a wide range of titles. Free membership without obligation to buy.

Artists' Choice
PO Box 3, Huntingdon PE28 0QX
☎01832 710201 Fax 01832 710488
www.artists-choice.co.uk
Specialises in books for the amateur artist at all levels of ability.

Baker Books
Manfield Park, Cranleigh GU6 8NU
☎01483 267888 Fax 01483 267409
✉ bakerbooks@dial.pipex.com
www.bakerbooks.co.uk
Book clubs for schools: Funfare for ages 3–8 and Bookzone, ages 8–13. Four issues per year operated in the UK and overseas.

BCA (Book Club Associates)
Greater London House, Hampstead Road,
London NW1 7TZ
☎020 7760 6500 Fax 020 7760 6505
www.bca.co.uk
BCA, a wholly-owned subsidiary of Bertelsmann AG, is Britain's largest book club organisation. Clubs include: The Arts Guild, Books For Children (BFC), Escape Fiction Club, Fantasy & SF, History Guild, Mango, Military & Aviation Book Society, World of Mystery & Thriller, Quality Paperbacks Direct (QPD), Railway Book Club, The Softback Preview (TSP), WorldBooks.

Bibliophile Books
5 Thomas Road, London E14 7BN
☎020 7515 9222 Fax 020 7538 4115
✉ orders@bibliophilebooks.com
www.bibliophilebooks.com
New books covering a wide range of subjects at discount prices. Write, phone, fax or e-mail for free catalogue of 3000 titles issued 10 times a year.

Book Club Associates
See **BCA**.

Cygnus Books
PO Box 15, Llandeilo SA19 6YX
☎01550 777701 Fax 01550 777569
✉ enquiries@cygnus-books.co.uk
www.cygnus-books.co.uk
'Bookseller offering books for your next step in spirituality and complementary health care.' Over 1000 hand-picked titles. Publishes *The Cygnus Review* magazine which features 30–40 reviews on new mind, body and spirit titles each month.

The Folio Society
44 Eagle Street, London WC1R 4FS
☎020 7400 4222 Fax 020 7400 4242
✉ enquiries@foliosoc.co.uk
www.foliosociety.com
Fine editions of classic fiction, history and memoirs; also some children's classics.

Letterbox Library
71–73 Allen Road, London N16 8RY
☎020 7503 4801 Fax 020 7503 4800
✉ info@letterboxlibrary.com
www.letterboxlibrary.com
Children's book cooperative. Hard and softcover specialist in inclusive books for children from one to teenage.

Poetry Book Society
See entry under *Organisations of Interest to Poets*

Readers' Union Ltd
Brunel House, Forde Close, Newton Abbot
TQ12 4PU
☎01626 323200 Fax 01626 323318
www.readersunion.co.uk
Book clubs with specific interests: Anglers' Book Club, The Craft Club, Craftsman's Book Club, Country Sports Book Club, Equestrian Society, The Gardeners Society, Needlecrafts with Cross Stitch, Painting for Pleasure, Photographers' Book Club, Puzzles Plus.

Scholastic Book Clubs
See **Scholastic Ltd** under *UK Publishers*

The New Gatekeepers

Simon Tait asks the literary agents where book publishing goes from here

British publishing is producing more books than ever to more readers, having experienced an earth-shift which has seen literary agents emerge as the vital element. Yet it is in crisis on several fronts. The most recent figures show a satisfyingly steady increase in business, particularly in the vast fiction market, but there are different interpretations of it. To listen to some in British publishing the prospects could hardly be rosier, yet to others they are distinctly gloomy.

Richard Charkin, chairman of Macmillan and former president of the Publishers' Association, encapsulates the cross-currents neatly in the PA's most recent Statistics Yearbook, for 2005. 'Book sales must be increasing hugely because of reading groups,' he reckons. But then, he adds, 'book sales must be decreasing because of the Internet; students get all their information electronically'. Then again, 'Harry Potter has created a whole new generation of readers.' And what about the influence of supermarkets, of the government's backing for schoolbook buying, of the decline in public libraries as book-lending outlets? What about the Richard and Judy quotient?

The statistical truth is that in 2005 unit sales were up 4 per cent on the previous year to the enormous figure of nearly 800 million books, of which 459 million were sold in this country. This comes down to a staggering average of eight books per year per person, or nineteen per household. 'But take a longer view,' says Mr Charkin, 'and you find that over four years the total growth has been only 5 per cent, significantly lower than inflation and thus representing an absolute decline. Although we sold a total of 215 million novels in 2005, that represented only a 1.5 per cent increase, and without the thriving foreign market for our fiction there would hardly have been any increase at all.'

Agents don't necessarily see it that way. 'We're having the most fantastic time,' says Carole Blake, speaking from forty years' experience as an agent and, she adds, strictly from the point of view of her own company, Blake Friedmann. Her own 1999 book, *From Pitch to Publication*, was a primer for those wanting to know how to get a novel published. 'Publishing has become bigger business,' she says, adding cautiously, 'but authors need more help now than they used to.'

Publishing in the United Kingdom has become a far more complex business in recent years, too, and in the middle of the mix now, rather than on the peripheries as they used to be, are the agents. 'Publishers used to call the shots,' one says. 'Now the agents do.' Well, up to a point as we shall see, but the roles have changed significantly in the last two decades. 'The old traditional cosy relationship between a publisher and an author has largely gone now. Publishers don't make discoveries any more, they regard agents as the filter,' says Mark Le Fanu, general secretary of the Society of Authors. 'Literary agents are the gatekeepers now.'

Literary agents have a long pedigree, the longest established being A.P.Watt which is still prospering more than 130 years after it was founded, and representing now children's authors, novelists and particularly non-fiction writers such as Michael Holroyd, Jan Morris and Susie Orbach. But literary agents have been a peculiarly anglophone element in the publishing chain, and until very recently all publishers in other languages tended to deal with their authors direct. Now, agents in the British market deal with publishers in Italy, France and Germany and in other languages, working through intermediaries who, as well as keeping their British links, are beginning to represent authors themselves.

It is hard to say precisely how many agents there are working in British publishing now because no qualification is required. At the end of the 1930s there were known to be around fifty, and the number rose slowly over the next thirty years, until there was a rapid expansion in the 1990s so that there are now about 170. They claim an average of 15 per cent of an author's fees. About half of the 170 are registered members of the Association of Authors' Agents, which acts as an information forum for its members for whom it organises talks and social events, giving them a pool of knowledge on what is happening in the industry – who is doing well and who is not, for instance – and potential trends. It is also a good starting point for writers looking for representation. Not all respected agents are AAA members, though, with one agent with four decades' experience of British publishing saying, 'they don't actually do anything – when things get tough they back off', a perception which may be a misconception of the Association's role as it sees itself.

Agencies come in three sizes. There are sole traders, often agents just starting out, but not always. Deborah Owen, an esteemed agent since 1971, claims a lower percentage than many, but represents only two authors, Delia Smith and Amos Oz, expressly discouraging new ones. Other sole trading agents specialise in niche areas, such as children's writers and illustrators, sports subjects or scripts for film, television and theatre, and they often cultivate a more personal relationship with their clients.

By far the largest category, not surprisingly, is the middle-scale agency which includes A.P. Hall and Blake Friedmann, each working with a small number of primary agents mostly on books and mostly on fiction, but each drawing in categories such as children's literature, biography, history, other non-fiction and leisure subjects.

At the other end of the scale are the groups, middle-scale agencies who have often merged to create larger ones. A.D. Peters began business off The Strand in 1924 and quickly established a reputation which was to last. It later absorbed the Fraser & Dunlop agency, and then the June Hall Agency, so that for a while the new conglomerate was known as Peters, Fraser, Dunlop & Hall. It is now Peters Fraser & Dunlop, trading even more pragmatically as PFD, and represents not only authors but screenplay writers, playwrights, and even actors and TV presenters.

The large groups include Curtis Brown, more than a century old but now employing upwards of a dozen agents one of whom, Giles Gordon, was a doyen among agents. Before his untimely death in 2003 he wrote of the modern heartbreak of having to turn down good new writers because they did not fit market demands: 'Much as I have admired their talent I haven't believed I would be able to find or persuade a publisher to take their work. Ultimately, failing to find a good publisher for an author means that the agent has failed the writer.'

The literary agent has become so much more key to the process because of the development of the large global publishing conglomerates that have developed, such as Random House and HarperCollins, swallowing smaller publishers so that there are far fewer houses with which to negotiate on behalf of authors, with more cognisance of market forces and less enthusiasm for risk among publishers. A number of successful agents are former publishers, and some are also published authors. Many of the tasks that once were performed by publishers now fall to agents, not only the negotiation of fees and rights on behalf of authors but also the safeguarding of authors' wishes.

The old-fashioned publisher would also have had a 'mid-list', a category often encapsulating new authors taken on as a hunch or as an investment in the future who were nurtured, sometimes over years, to eventual success but without great expectations for early big sales. In the twenty-first century, conglomerates tend to be hunch-averse. 'No one likes to think they've got a mid-list because they're seen as the books that didn't make it,' Carole Blake says. 'These days authors are expected to explode on to the market fully formed as bestsellers, but how do they learn if they're not working up their craft through something like the mid-list?'

On the face of it, the job of the literary agent is simple enough: to represent the interests of a writer to the publisher, and help steer him or her through the increasingly complicated forest of contracts and royalties towards a successful career. Within that, however, is an essential expertise that requires not only experience but also a finely tuned ear for changes in the publishing ethos, and an eye for talent.

Modern agents need to know the exact state of the market on any day – which can change overnight – and the dynamics that are at work. They need to be able to judge a range of appropriate publishers for a particular work, and to negotiate separately on foreign markets for their authors in other languages as well as in English – world rights are largely a thing of the past, or so agents would hope as they try to create parallel income streams for their writers that are not interdependent. They have to be financially numerate, able to spot the nuances in a proposal and negotiate through them for the best possible deal.

Agents need to be sales people who can convey a completely credible belief in their product, which means that, like the authors they represent, their lives are committed to the business. They must be vigilant, watching for any subtle change in publishers' 'boilerplates', the standard contracts publishers have; often each publisher has several to meet different cases. These tend to be weighted in favour of the publisher, and agents see them as a starting point for negotiation rather than the result.

They have to be prepared to be tough with their own clients, too, because struggling authors can sometimes feel inclined to accept a deal for a quicker cash return, a deal the agent might feel is disadvantageous in the long term. Agents have taken on the role of talent spotter, and the 'slush piles' of manuscripts publishers used to have from promising authors who should be published when the opportunity arises now tend to be vetted by agents. Publicising a book remains the responsibility of publishers, but agents are often a part of that process, too, with such ploys as encouraging novelists to write short stories which can be released for publication in magazines to coincide with the publication of, or as a taster for, a major novel.

The publicising phenomenon that neither publisher nor agent can have any influence on, though, is *Richard & Judy*. In 2001 Cactus TV, the producers of the popular daytime chat show, negotiated a deal which moved it from ITV to Channel 4 with a new format devised by producer Amanda Ross. This was 'Richard & Judy's Choice' in which the presenters, Richard Madeley and Judy Finnegan, picked new books to be discussed with guests, and which incorporated a short film about the author.

Those in the trade were sceptical to say the least – how likely was an audience of bored housewives to be influenced into buying books? Yet the impact cannot be over-estimated, and some agents have even tried to get written in to contracts that a publisher will try to get the book on the programme. They can't, they can only submit, and Ms Ross gets about 650 submissions a year.

The effect can be explosive. In 2005 Joseph O'Connor's book *The Star of the Sea* was doing all right in the lists, but not spectacularly well – it is a fine book but one that requires close reading to absorb essential detail. It went out on the programme at 5 p.m. one day and by the end of the evening was top of the Amazon lists, selling 750,000 copies that year.

'It was met with almost universal cynicism at the start,' says Luigi Bonomi, of Luigi Bonomi Associates, who adds that it was telling that it was not an initiative that had come from publishers: it would have shown their faith in their authors. 'But it's been a godsend to the industry, and although book programmes haven't really worked in the past, Richard and Judy have shown how it can be done and I think we shall see more in the future from other broadcasters,' he says.

J.K. Rowling's Harry Potter has been a phenomenon which has not only added a new readership to the market, but a new string to the bows of the likes of the comedian Ricky Gervaise and the actor Nichola McAuliffe, who have penned moderately successful children's fiction.

There are issues which agents see as seriously threatening to writers. One of the biggest is the arrival of the supermarkets as a new dynamic in the mix, ordering bulk numbers of a publication but demanding substantial discounts, the effects of which will be passed on to the hapless author.

'They are too powerful,' says Toby Eady of Toby Eady Associates, 'and the serious problem is discounting.' A typical scenario would have an author pressured by a publisher into accepting 10 per cent of the price received on a book with the recommended retail price of £7.99, with the prospect of huge supermarket sales. But the supermarket then sells the book for £3.50 paying the publisher £1.30, and the author then has to accept 10 per cent of that – 13p. And supermarket selling can have a flip side. The popular historian William Dalrymple's first book was taken by supermarkets and scored a great success, but for no apparent reason the second was not taken, a disaster for the publisher. 'How can they make a profit when they are discounting at 50% from day one?' Mr Eady asks.

Discounts, which operate not only in the supermarkets, used to be controlled by the Net Book Agreement, which was a price fixing deal between publishers and booksellers. It was finally abolished in 1997 after a long wrangle. 'Ending the NBA was a terrible mistake for both authors and publishers,' says Mr Eady, 'and I can't see any immediate solution to discounting.'

'It has become a much more ruthless, big money business,' says Luigi Bonomi, 'with publishers willing to offer huge advances for the right name.' Alongside traditional writers he represents such celebrity authors as Alan Titchmarsh, John Humphrys and Richard Madeley himself, authors who are known for success in other domains where their names are universally familiar.

'Publishers are only reflecting the demand from the marketplace. You have to be a brand now to succeed, and so there are bigger and bigger advances for fewer and fewer books, and inevitably that means that there's less room for other authors in the market,' he says. 'But that doesn't mean that celebrity books always work, some of them have bombed terribly, but the right celebrity book can make a publisher's financial year – they are that important. An agent's ultimate goal is to transform traditional authors into brand names in their own right.' He doesn't deal in ghosted books, such as those with the names of sports celebrities on the cover, and believes their days are numbered. 'They're costing too much, and although there are often serial rights that go with the deal, they're a lot of hassle.' Toby Eady thinks the whole payment system needs to change, with an end to royalties and advances and instead authors being paid a simple fee for every copy sold. 'But to change publishing in this country would be like turning a fleet of tankers around,' he says.

A major peril seen by Carole Blake lies in new technology and Internet rights, of which publishers and agents are struggling for control. 'The premise of all of our contracts is that any right not specifically and explicitly granted to a publisher in a contract will remain the author's', she says – specifically with audio downloads. 'It's the knottiest problem of all, every agent I know expects it to become an enormous part of the market.' More and more 'readers' are taking spoken readings of books off the Web, and the problem remains unresolved with most big publishers prepared to offer 15 per cent to the authors while agents think at least 50% would be fairer, especially as, in contrast to printed books, there are no overheads for storage and packaging. At best, agents are prepared to give publishers a licence for a year, to be renegotiated.

'This is such an immature market it's foolish to set down in stone figures you will not be able to change in the future,' says Ms Blake. 'I'm even worried about a one-year licence, because in my experience no renegotiation ever gets better for an author.' What is sure is that, despite the complexity of modern publishing and the increasingly convoluted fee and rights negotiations agents have to do, enthusiasm for publishing among literary agents seems to be undiminished.

'I've been in the business since 1968, and there's nothing I'd rather be doing,' Toby Eady says. 'It's the most fascinating living, it's a gift.'

UK Literary Agents

★ = Members of the Association of Authors' Agents

Sheila Ableman Literary Agency★
48–56 Bayham Place, London NW1 0EU
☎020 7388 7222
✉ sheila@sheilaableman.co.uk
Contact *Sheila Ableman*
Founded 1999. Handles non-fiction including history, science, biography and autobiography. Specialises in celebrity ghostwriting and TV tie-ins. No poetry, children's, gardening or sport. COMMISSION Home 15%; US & Translation 20%. Unsolicited mss welcome. Approach in writing with publishing history, c.v., synopsis, three chapters and s.a.e. for return. No reading fee.

The Agency (London) Ltd★
24 Pottery Lane, London W11 4LZ
☎020 7727 1346 Fax 020 7727 9037
✉ info@theagency.co.uk
Contacts *Stephen Durbridge, Leah Schmidt, Norman North, Julia Kreitman, Bethan Evans, Hilary Delamere, Katie Haines, Faye Webber, Nick Quinn, Fay Davies, Ian Benson*
Founded 1995. Deals with writers and rights for TV, film, theatre, radio scripts and children's fiction. Also handles directors. Only existing clients for adult fiction or non-fiction. COMMISSION Home 10%; US by arrangement. Send letter with s.a.e. No unsolicited mss. No reading fee.

Aitken Alexander Associates Ltd★
18–21 Cavaye Place, London SW10 9PT
☎020 7373 8672 Fax 020 7373 6002
✉ recep@gillonaitken.co.uk
www.gillonaitkenassociates.co.uk
Contacts *Gillon Aitken, Clare Alexander, Lesley Thorne* (also film/TV)
Associated Agents *Anthony Sheil, Mary Pachnos*
Founded 1977. Handles fiction and non-fiction. No plays, scripts or children's fiction unless by existing clients. CLIENTS include Caroline Alexander, Pat Barker, Nicholas Blincoe, Gordon Burn, Jung Chang, John Cornwell, Josephine Cox, Sarah Dunant, Susan Elderkin, Sebastian Faulks, Helen Fielding, Russell Grant, Jane Goldman, Germaine Greer, Mark Haddon, Susan Howatch, Liz Jensen, John Keegan, V.S. Naipaul, Jonathan Raban, Piers Paul Read, Michèle Roberts, Nicholas Shakespeare, Gillian Slovo, Matt Thorne, Colin Thubron, Salley Vickers, A.N. Wilson, Robert Wilson. COMMISSION Home 10%; US & Translation 20%; Film/TV 10%. Send preliminary letter, with half-page synopsis and first 30pp of sample material, and adequate return postage, in the first instance. No reading fee.

The Ampersand Agency Ltd★
Ryman's Cottages, Little Tew OX7 4JJ
☎01608 683677 Fax 01608 683449
✉ peter@theampersandagency.co.uk
www.theampersandagency.co.uk
Contacts *Peter Buckman, Anne-Marie Doulton*
Consultants *Peter Janson-Smith, Patrick Neale*
Founded 2003. Handles literary and commercial fiction and non-fiction; contemporary and historical novels, crime, thrillers, biography, women's fiction, history, memoirs. No scripts unless by existing clients. No poetry, science fiction, fantasy or illustrated children's books. CLIENTS Sharon Bolton, Georgette Heyer estate, Druin Burch, Will Davis, Cora Harrison, Michael Hutchinson, Beryl Kingston, Philip Purser, Ivo Stourton, Vikas Swarup, Nick van Bloss, Michael Walters. COMMISSION Home 10–15%; US 15–20%; Translation 20%. Translation rights handled by The Buckman Agency. Unsolicited mss, synopses and ideas welcome, as are e-mail enquiries, but send sample chapters and synopsis by post (s.a.e. required if material is to be returned). No reading fee.

Darley Anderson Literary, TV & Film Agency★
Estelle House, 11 Eustace Road, London SW6 1JB
☎020 7385 6652 Fax 020 7386 5571
✉ enquiries@darleyanderson.com
www.darleyanderson.com
www.darleyandersonchildrens.com
Contacts *Darley Anderson* (crime, mystery, thrillers, women's fiction), *Zoe King* (non-fiction), *Julia Churchill* (children's books), *Emma White* (rights), *Rosi Bridge* (finance),

Ella Andrews (agency assistant)

Founded 1988. Run by an ex-publisher with a knack for spotting talent and making great deals – many for six and seven figure advances. Handles commercial fiction and non-fiction, children's fiction and non-fiction; also selected scripts for film and TV. No academic books or poetry. Special fiction interests: all types of thrillers and crime (American/hard boiled/cosy/historical); women's fiction (sagas, chick-lit, contemporary, love stories, 'tear jerkers', women in jeopardy) and all types of American and Irish novels. Non-fiction interests: celebrity autobiographies, biographies, sports books, 'true life' women in jeopardy, revelatory history and science, popular psychology, self improvement, diet, beauty, health, finance, fashion, animals, humour/cartoon, gardening, cookery, inspirational and religious. CLIENTS include Anne Baker, Alex Barclay, Constance Briscoe, Paul Carson, Cathy Cassidy, Lee Child, Martina Cole, John Connolly, Margaret Dickinson, Clare Dowling, Tana French, Joan Jonker, Danny King, Adrienne Kress, Patrick Lennon, Freda Lightfoot, Carole Matthews, Lesley Pearse, Lynda Page, Adrian Plass, Sheila Quigley, Carmen Reid, Rebecca Shaw, Elizabeth Waite, Ahmet Zappa. COMMISSION Home 15%; US & Translation 20%; Film/TV/Radio 20%. OVERSEAS ASSOCIATES APA Talent and Literary Agency (LA/Hollywood); Liza Dawson Literary Agency (New York); and leading foreign agents throughout the world. Send letter, synopsis and first three chapters; plus s.a.e. for return. No reading fee.

Anubis Literary Agency
7 Birdhaven Close, Lighthorne, Warwick CV35 0BE
☎01926 642588 Fax 01926 642588

Contact *Steve Calcutt*

Founded 1994. Handles genre fiction in the following categories: science fiction, fantasy and horror. No other material considered. COMMISSION Home 15%; US & Translation 20%. Works with the Marsh Agency on translation rights. In the first instance send 50 pages with a one-page synopsis (s.a.e. essential). No telephone calls. No reading fee.

Artellus Limited
30 Dorset House, Gloucester Place, London NW1 5AD
☎020 7935 6972 Fax 020 7487 5957
www.artellusltd.co.uk

Chairman *Gabriele Pantucci*
Director *Leslie Gardner*
Associates *Darryl Samaraweera, Elizabeth Mallett*

Founded 1986. Full-length and short mss. Handles crime, science fiction, historical, contemporary and literary fiction; non-fiction: art history, current affairs, biography, general history, science. Works directly in the USA and with agencies internationally. COMMISSION Home 10%; Overseas 20%. Sample chapters in the first instance. Selective reader's service available for a fee. Return postage essential.

Author Literary Agents
53 Talbot Road, London N6 4QX
☎020 8341 0442/0776 7022659 (mobile)
Fax 020 8341 0442
✉ agile@authors.co.uk

Contact *John Havergal*

Founded 1997. 'We put to leading publishers and producers strong new novels, thrillers and graphic media ideas.' COMMISSION (VAT extra) Book, Screen & Internet production rights – Home 12½%; Overseas & Translation 22½%. Send s.a.e. with first chapter, scene or section writing sample, plus half-to-one page outline. Please include graphics samples, if applicable. No reading fee.

The Bell Lomax Moreton Agency
James House, 1 Babmaes Street, London SW1Y 6HF
☎020 7930 4447 Fax 020 7925 0118
✉ agency@bell-lomax.co.uk

Executives *Eddie Bell, Pat Lomax, Paul Moreton, June Bell*

Established 2002. Handles quality fiction and non-fiction, biography, children's, business and sport. No unsolicited mss without preliminary letter. No scripts. No reading fee.

Lorella Belli Literary Agency (LBLA)★
54 Hartford House, 35 Tavistock Crescent, Notting Hill, London W11 1AY
☎020 7727 8547 Fax 0870 787 4194
✉ info@lorellabelliagency.com
www.lorellabelliagency.com

Contact *Lorella Belli*

Founded 2002. Handles full-length fiction (from literary to genre) and general non-fiction. Particularly interested in first novelists, journalists, multi-cultural and international writing, books on or about Italy. No children's, fantasy, science fiction, poetry, plays, scripts or academic books. CLIENTS include Michael Bess, Sean Bidder, Zöe Brân, Annalisa Coppolaro-Nowell, Dario Fo, Emily Giffin, Paul Martin, Nisha Minhas, Alanna Mitchell, Rick Mofina, Angela Murrills, Jennifer Ouellette, Robet Ray, Grace Saunders, Dave Singleton, Rupert Steiner, Diana Winston. COMMISSION Home 15%; US, Translation & Dramatic Rights 20%. Works in conjunction with leading associate agencies in most countries and a film/TV agency in London. Also represents in the USA: Paula Balzer Literary Agency, The Imprint Agency, Sarah Lazin Books, Marmur Associates Ltd, Norris Literary Agency, LLC; Canada: The Harding Agency; Kathryn Mulders Literary Agency; Australia: Calidris Literary Agency; Italy: Boroli Editore Group; Nabu Literary Agency. Welcomes approaches from new authors. Send full proposal plus two chapters for non-fiction, and short synopsis plus first three chapters for fiction. S.a.e. essential. No reading fee. Revision suggested where appropriate.

Blake Friedmann Literary Agency Ltd★

122 Arlington Road, London NW1 7HP
☎020 7284 0408 Fax 020 7284 0442
✉ firstname@blakefriedmann.co.uk
www.blakefriedmann.co.uk

Contacts *Carole Blake* (books), *Julian Friedmann* (film/TV), *Conrad Williams* (original scripts/radio), *Isobel Dixon* (books), *Oli Munson* (books)

Founded 1977. Handles all kinds of fiction from genre to literary; a varied range of specialist and general non-fiction, plus scripts for TV, radio and film. No poetry, science fiction or short stories (unless from existing clients). Special interests: commercial women's fiction, intelligent thrillers, literary fiction, upmarket non-fiction. CLIENTS include Gilbert Adair, Jane Asher, Edward Carey, Elizabeth Chadwick, Anne de Courcy, Anna Davis, Barbara Erskine, Ann Granger, Ken Hom, Billy Hopkins, Peter James, Glenn Meade, Deon Meyer, Lawrence Norfolk, Gregory Norminton, Joseph O'Connor, Sheila O'Flanagan, Siân Rees, Michael Ridpath, Craig Russell, Tess Stimson, Michael White. COMMISION Home 15%; US & Translation 20%. Radio/TV/Film: 15%. OVERSEAS ASSOCIATES 24 worldwide. Unsolicited mss welcome but initial letter with synopsis and first two chapters preferred. Letters should contain as much information as possible on previous writing experience, aims for the future, etc. No reading fee.

Luigi Bonomi Associates Limited (LBA)★

91 Great Russell Street, London WC1B 3PS
☎020 7637 1234 Fax 020 7637 2111
✉ info@bonomiassociates.co.uk

Contacts *Luigi Bonomi, Amanda Preston, Molly Stirling*

Handles commercial and literary fiction, thrillers, crime and women's fiction; non-fiction: history, science, parenting, lifestyle, diet, health; teen and young adult fiction. CLIENTS include James Barrington, Chris Beardshaw, Terry Brighton, Gennaro Contaldo, Nick Foulkes, David Gibbins, Richard Hammond, Jane Hill, John Humphrys, Graham Joyce, Simon Kernick, James May, Niki Monaghan, Mike Morley, Dr Gillian McKeith, Richard Madeley & Judy Finnigan, Sue Palmer, William Petre, Melanie Phillips, Jem Poster, John Rickards, Prof. Bryan Sykes, Mitch Symons, Alan Titchmarsh, Sally Worboyes, Sir Terry Wogan. COMMISSION Home 15%; US & Translation 20–25%. 'We are very keen to find new authors and help them develop their careers.' No scripts, poetry, science fiction/fantasy, children's storybooks. Send synopsis and first chapter only. 'We do *not* reply by e-mail so return postage/s.a.e. essential for reply.' No reading fee.

BookBlast Ltd

PO Box 20184, London W10 5AU
☎020 8968 3089
www.bookblast.com

Contact *Address material to the Company*

Handles fiction and non-fiction. Memoir, travel, popular culture, multicultural writing only. Reading very selectively. No new authors taken on except by recommendation. Editorial advice given to own authors. Initiates in-house projects. Also offers translation consultancy. Film, TV and radio rights mainly sold in works by existing clients. COMMISSION Home 12%; US & Translation 20%; Film, TV & Radio 20%. No reading fee.

Bookseeker Agency

PO Box 7535, Perth PH2 1AF
☎01738 620688
✉ bookseeker@blueyonder.co.uk

Contact *Paul Thompson*

Founded 2005. Handles poetry and any creative writing except non-fiction; also some illustration and visual art. COMMISSION negotiable 'but not exceeding 10%'. Approach in writing, giving a personal introduction, a summary of work so far and any current projects. No mss or sample chapters; synopsis or half-a-dozen poems acceptable. No reading fee.

Alan Brodie Representation Ltd

6th Floor, Fairgate House, 78 New Oxford Street, London WC1A 1HB
☎020 7079 7990 Fax 020 7079 7999
✉ info@alanbrodie.com
www.alanbrodie.com

Contacts *Alan Brodie, Sarah McNair, Lisa Foster*

Founded 1989. Handles theatre, film and TV scripts. No books. COMMISSION Home 10%; Overseas 15%. Preliminary letter plus professional recommendation and c.v. essential. No reading fee but s.a.e. required.

Jenny Brown Associates★

33 Argyle Place, Edinburgh EH9 1JT
☎0131 229 5334 Fax 0131 229 6695
✉ info@jennybrownassociates.com
www.jennybrownassociates.com

Contacts *Jenny Brown, Mark Stanton*
Children's *Lucky Juckes*
Crime *Allan Guthrie*

Founded 2002. Handles literary fiction, crime writing, writing for children; non-fiction: biography, history, sport, music, popular culture. No poetry, science fiction, fantasy or academic. CLIENTS include Lin Anderson, Jeff Connor, Mary Contini, Jennie Erdal, Alex Gray, Laura Hird, Roger Hutchinson, Laura Marney, Janet Morgan, Jonathan Rendall, Suhayl Saadi, Paul Torday. COMMISSION Home 12½%; US & Translation 20%. No unsolicited mss. Approach in writing with letter, synopsis and first two chapters. Include c.v. and s.a.e.

Felicity Bryan★

2A North Parade, Banbury Road, Oxford OX2 6LX
☎01865 513816 Fax 01865 310055
✉ agency@felicitybryan.com
www.felicitybryan.com

Agents *Felicity Bryan, Catherine Clarke, Sally Holloway, Caroline Wood*

Founded 1988. Handles fiction of various types and non-fiction with emphasis on history, biography, science and current affairs. No scripts for TV, radio or theatre. No crafts, picture books, how-to, science fiction or light romance. CLIENTS include Karen Armstrong, Simon Blackburn, Michael Buerk, Artemis Cooper, Isla Dewar, John Dickie, A.C. Grayling, Tim Harford, Julie Hearn, Colin Jones, Liz Kessler, Diarmaid MacCulloch, John Man, Martin Meredith, James Naughtie,

John Julius Norwich, Gemma O'Connor, Iain Pears, Robin Pilcher, Rosamunde Pilcher, Matt Ridley, Meg Rosoff, Miriam Stoppard, Roy Strong, Adrian Tinniswood, Colin Tudge, Eleanor Updale and the estates of Robertson Davies and Humphrey Carpenter. COMMISSION Home 15%; US & Translation 20%. OVERSEAS ASSOCIATES Andrew Nurnberg, Europe; several agencies in US. Please approach by letter. See website for submission guidelines. No e-mail submissions. No reading fee.

The Buckman Agency

Ryman's Cottages, Little Tew OX7 4JJ
☎01608 683677 Fax 01608 683449
✉ r.buckman@talk21.com *or*
  j.buckman@talk21.com

Partners *Rosie Buckman, Jessica Buckman*

Founded in the early 1970s, the agency specialises in foreign rights and represents leading authors and agents from the UK and US. COMMISSON 20% (including sub-agent's commission). No unsolicited mss.

Brie Burkeman★

14 Neville Court, Abbey Road, London NW8 9DD
☎0870 199 5002 Fax 0870 199 1029
✉ brie.burkeman@mail.com

Contact *Brie Burkeman, Isabel White*

Founded 2000. Handles commercial and literary full-length fiction and non-fiction. Film and theatre scripts. No academic, text, poetry, short stories, musicals or short films. Also associated with Serafina Clarke Ltd and independent film/TV consultant to literary agents. CLIENTS include Richard Askwith, Alexandra Carew, Alastair Chisholm, Kitty Ferguson, Joanne Harris, Shaun Hutson, Robin Norwood, David Savage, Steven Sivell, Gerald Wilson. COMMISSION Home 15%; Overseas 20%. Unsolicited e-mail attachments will be deleted without opening. No reading fee but return postage essential.

Juliet Burton Literary Agency

2 Clifton Avenue, London W12 9DR
☎020 8762 0148 Fax 020 8743 8765
✉ juliet.burton@btinternet.com

Contact *Juliet Burton*

Founded 1999. Handles fiction and non-fiction. Special interests crime and women's fiction. No plays, film scripts, articles, poetry or academic material. COMMISSION Home 15%; US & Translation 20%. Approach in writing in the first instance; send synopsis and two sample chapters with s.a.e. No e-mail submissions. No unsolicited mss. No reading fee.

Campbell Thomson & McLaughlin Ltd★

11/12 Dover Street, London W1S 4LJ
☎020 7399 2808 Fax 020 7399 2801
✉ submissions@ctmcl.co.uk
Contact *Charlotte Bruton*

Founded 1931. Handles fiction and general non-fiction, excluding children's. No plays, film/TV scripts, articles, short stories or poetry. Translation rights handled by The Marsh Agency. No unsolicited mss or synopses. Preliminary enquiry essential, by letter or e-mail. No reading fee.

Capel & Land Ltd★

29 Wardour Street, London W1D 6PS
☎020 7734 2414 Fax 020 7734 8101
✉ robert@capelland.co.uk
www.capelland.com
Contact *Georgina Capel*

Handles fiction and non-fiction. Also film and TV. CLIENTS Kunal Basu, John Gimlette, Andrew Greig, Dr Tristram Hunt, Liz Jones, Andrew Roberts, Simon Sebag Montefiore, Stella Rimington, Diana Souhami, Louis Theroux, Fay Weldon. COMMISSION Home, US & Translation 15%. Send sample chapters and synopsis with covering letter and s.a.e. (if return required) in the first instance. No reading fee.

Casarotto Ramsay and Associates Ltd

Waverley House, 7–12 Noel Street, London W1F 8GQ
☎020 7287 4450 Fax 020 7287 9128
✉ agents@casarotto.co.uk
www.casarotto.uk.com

Film/TV/Radio *Jenne Casarotto, Charlotte Kelly, Jodi Shields, Elinor Burns, Miriam James, Holly Nicholson, Rachel Holroyd*
Stage *Tom Erhardt, Mel Kenyon*

Handles scripts for TV, theatre, film and radio. CLIENTS include: **Theatre** Alan Ayckbourn, Caryl Churchill, Christopher Hampton, David Hare, Sarah Kane estate, Mark Ravenhill. **Film** Laura Jones, Neil Jordan, Nick Hornby, Shane Meadows, Purvis & Wade, Lynne Ramsay. **TV** Howard Brenton, Amy Jenkins, Susan Nickson, Jessica Stevenson. COMMISSION Home 10%. OVERSEAS ASSOCIATES worldwide. No unsolicited material without preliminary letter.

Celia Catchpole

56 Gilpin Avenue, London SW14 8QY
☎020 8255 4835
www.celiacatchpole.co.uk
Contact *Celia Catchpole*

Founded 1996. Handles children's books – artists and writers. No TV, film, radio or theatre scripts. No poetry. COMMISSION Home 10% (writers) 15% (artists); US & Translation 20%. Works with associate agents abroad. Will consider complete picture books and the first two chapters of longer scripts. S.a.e. essential.

Chapman & Vincent★

7 Dilke Street, London SW3 4JE
☎020 7352 5582 Fax 01763 243033
✉ chapmanvincent@hotmail.co.uk
Directors *Jennifer Chapman, Gilly Vincent*

A small agency handling almost entirely non-fiction work – often highly illustrated – and whose clients come mainly from personal recommendation. The agency is not actively seeking clients but is happy to consider really original work. CLIENTS include George Carter, Leslie Geddes-Brown, Rowley Leigh and Eve Pollard. COMMISSION Home 15%; US & Europe 20%. Works with The Elaine Markson Agency. Please do not submit by fax. Send submissions, two sample chapters and s.a.e. to The Mount, Sun Hill, Royston SG8 9AT. Will consider e-mail submissions without attachments. No reading fee.

Mic Cheetham Literary Agency

11–12 Dover Street, London W1S 4LJ
☎020 7495 2002 Fax 020 7399 2801
✉ info@miccheetham.com
www.miccheetham.com
Contacts *Mic Cheetham, Simon Kavanagh*

Established 1994. Handles general and literary fiction, crime and science fiction, and some specific non-fiction. No film/TV scripts apart from existing clients. No children's, illustrated books or poetry. CLIENTS include Iain Banks, Simon Beckett, Carol Birch, Anita Burgh, Laurie Graham, M. John Harrison, Toby Litt, Ken MacLeod, China Miéville, Antony Sher, Janette Turner Hospital. COMMISSION Home 15%; US & Translation 20%. Works with The Marsh Agency for all translation rights. No unsolicited mss. Approach in writing with publishing history, first two chapters and return postage. No reading fee.

Judith Chilcote Agency★
8 Wentworth Mansions, Keats Grove, London
NW3 2RL
☎020 7794 3717
✉ judybks@aol.com
Contact *Judith Chilcote*
Founded 1990. Handles commercial fiction, TV tie-ins, health and nutrition, popular psychology, biography and celebrity autobiography and current affairs. COMMISSION Home 15%; Overseas 20–25%. *No* academic, science fiction, children's, short stories, film scripts or poetry. *No approaches by e-mail.* Send letter with c.v., synopsis, three chapters and s.a.e. for return. No reading fee.

Teresa Chris Literary Agency Ltd★
43 Musard Road, London W6 8NR
☎020 7386 0633
Contacts *Teresa Chris, Charles Brudenell-Bruce*
Founded 1989. Handles crime, general, women's, commercial and literary fiction, and non-fiction: history, biography, health, cookery, lifestyle, sport and fitness, gardening, etc. Specialises in crime fiction and commercial women's fiction. No scripts. Film and TV rights handled by co-agent. No poetry, short stories, fantasy, science fiction or horror. CLIENTS include Stephen Booth, Martin Davies, Tamara McKinley, Marguerite Patten, Eileen Ramsay, Debby Holt. COMMISSION Home 10%; US & Translation 20%. OVERSEAS ASSOCIATES Patty Moosbrugger Literary Agency, USA; representatives in all other countries. Unsolicited mss welcome. Send query letter with first two chapters plus two-page synopsis (s.a.e. *essential*) in first instance. No reading fee.

Mary Clemmey Literary Agency★
6 Dunollie Road, London NW5 2XP
☎020 7267 1290 Fax 020 7482 7360
Contact *Mary Clemmey*
Founded 1992. Handles fiction and non-fiction – high-quality work with an international market. No science fiction, fantasy or children's books. TV, film, radio and theatre scripts from existing clients only. US clients: Frederick Hill Bonnie Nadell Inc., Lynn C. Franklin Associates Ltd, The Miller Agency, Roslyn Targ, Weingel-Fidel Agency Inc, Betsy Amster Literary. COMMISSION Home 15%; US & Translation 20%. OVERSEAS ASSOCIATE Elaine Markson Literary Agency, New York. No unsolicited mss. Approach by letter only in the first instance giving a description of the work (include s.a.e.). No reading fee.

Jonathan Clowes Ltd★
10 Iron Bridge House, Bridge Approach,
London NW1 8BD
☎020 7722 7674 Fax 020 7722 7677
Contacts *Ann Evans, Lisa Whadcock*
Founded 1960. Pronounced 'clewes'. Now one of the biggest fish in the pond and not really for the untried unless they are true high-flyers. Fiction and non-fiction, plus scripts. No textbooks or children's. Special interests: situation comedy, film and television rights. CLIENTS include David Bellamy, Len Deighton, Elizabeth Jane Howard, Doris Lessing, David Nobbs, Gillian White and the estate of Kingsley Amis. COMMISSION Home & US 15%; Translation 19%. OVERSEAS ASSOCIATES Andrew Nurnberg Associates; Sane Töregard Agency. No unsolicited mss; authors come by recommendation or by successful follow-ups to preliminary letters.

Elspeth Cochrane Personal Management
16 Old Town, Clapham, London SW4 0JY
☎020 7819 6256 Fax 020 7819 4297
✉ info@elspethcochrane.co.uk
Contact *Elspeth Cochrane*
Founded 1960. Handles fiction, non-fiction, biographies, screenplays and plays. No children's fiction. CLIENTS include Alex Jones, Dominic Leyton, Royce Ryton, F.E. Smith, Robert Tanitch. COMMISSION 12½%. No unsolicited mss. Phone before submitting work.

Rosica Colin Ltd
1 Clareville Grove Mews, London SW7 5AH
☎020 7370 1080 Fax 020 7244 6441
Contact *Joanna Marston*
Founded 1949. Handles all full-length mss, plus theatre, film, television and sound broadcasting but few new writers being accepted. COMMISSION Home 10%; US & Translation 20%. Preliminary letter with return postage essential; writers should outline their writing credits and whether their mss have previously been submitted elsewhere. May take 3–4 months to consider full mss; synopsis preferred in the first instance. No reading fee.

Conville & Walsh Limited★
2 Ganton Street, London W1F 7QL
☎020 7287 3030 Fax 020 7287 4545
✉ firstname@convilleandwalsh.com
Directors *Clare Conville, Patrick Walsh, Peter Tallack* (book rights), *Alan Oliver* (finance)

Book Development *Jake Smith-Bosanquet, Susan Armstrong*

Established in 2000 by Clare Conville (ex-A.P. Watt) and Patrick Walsh (ex-Christopher Little Literary Agency). Handle all genres of fiction and non-fiction worldwide but no poetry, screenplays or short stories. Film/television rights handled by Sam North (Booker long-listed author with *The Unnumbered*). 'Agency taste is generally upmarket to mass-market: literary and commercial fiction.' Fiction CLIENTS range from the Booker winner DBC Pierre to recent short-list nominees such as Sarah Hall and Hisham Matar, and the Orwell Prize winner Delia Jarrett-Macauley. Commercial novelists include Isabel Wolff, Matt Dunn and Michael Cordy. Non-fiction CLIENTS Tom Holland, Helen Castor, Simon Singh, Richard Wiseman, Ian Stewart, Tahir Shah, Ruth Padel, Misha Glenny, Michael Bywater. Also handles the estate of artist, Francis Bacon. Prestigious children's and young adult list ranges from John Burningham to Steve Voake and the estate of Astrid Lindgren. COMMISSION Home 15%; US & Translation 20%. Send first three chapters, one-page synopsis, covering letter and s.a.e. No reading fee.

Jane Conway-Gordon Ltd★
1 Old Compton Street, London W1D 5JA
☎020 7494 0148 Fax 020 7287 9264

Contact *Jane Conway-Gordon*

Founded 1982. Works in association with Andrew Mann Ltd. Handles fiction and general non-fiction. No poetry, science fiction, children's or short stories. COMMISSION Home 15%; US & Translation 20%. OVERSEAS ASSOCIATES McIntosh & Otis, Inc., New York; plus agencies throughout Europe and Japan. Unsolicited mss welcome; preliminary letter and return postage essential. No reading fee.

Rupert Crew Ltd★
1A King's Mews, London WC1N 2JA
☎020 7242 8586 Fax 020 7831 7914
✉ info@rupertcrew.co.uk (correspondence only)
www.rupertcrew.co.uk

Contacts *Doreen Montgomery, Caroline Montgomery*

Founded 1927. International representation, handling volume and subsidiary rights in fiction and non-fiction properties. No screenplays, plays or poetry, journalism or short stories, science fiction or fantasy. COMMISSION Home 15%;

Elsewhere 20%. Preliminary letter and return postage essential. No reading fee.

Curtis Brown Group Ltd★
Haymarket House, 28/29 Haymarket, London SW1Y 4SP
☎020 7393 4400 Fax 020 7393 4401
✉ cb@curtisbrown.co.uk
www.curtisbrown.co.uk

CEO *Jonathan Lloyd*
Director of Operations *Ben Hall*
Directors *Jacquie Drewe, Jonny Geller, Nick Marston*
Books *Jonny Geller* (MD, Book Division), *Camilla Hornby, Jonathan Lloyd, Jonathan Pegg, Vivienne Schuster, Elizabeth Sheinkman, Janice Swanson, Gordon Wise*
Foreign Rights (books) *Kate Cooper, Carol Jackson, Betsy Robbins*
Film/TV/Theatre *Nick Marston* (MD, Media Division), *Tally Garner, Ben Hall, Joe Phillips, Sally Whitehill*
Actors *Grace Clissold, Maxine Hoffman, Sarah MacCormick, Sarah Spear, Kate Staddon, Claire Stannard*
Presenters *Jacquie Drewe*

Founded 1899. Agents for the negotiation in all markets of novels, general non-fiction, children's books and associated rights (including multimedia) as well as play, film, theatre, TV and radio scripts. OVERSEAS ASSOCIATES in Australia and the US. Send outline for non-fiction and short synopsis for fiction with two/three sample chapters and autobiographical note. No reading fee. Return postage essential. No submissions by e-mail. See further submission guidelines on website. Also represents playwrights, film and TV writers and directors, theatre directors and designers, TV and radio presenters and actors.

Judy Daish Associates Ltd
2 St Charles Place, London W10 6EG
☎020 8964 8811 Fax 020 8964 8966

Contacts *Judy Daish, Tracey Elliston, Howard Gooding*

Founded 1978. Theatrical literary agent. Handles scripts for film, TV, theatre and radio. No books. Preliminary letter essential. No unsolicited mss.

Caroline Davidson Literary Agency★
5 Queen Anne's Gardens, London W4 1TU
☎020 8995 5768 Fax 020 8994 2770
www.cdla.co.uk

Contact *Caroline Davidson*

Founded 1988. Handles fiction and non-fiction, including archaeology, architecture, art, astronomy, biography, design, gardening, health, history, medicine, natural history, reference, science. CLIENTS Peter Barham, Nigel Barlow, Catherine Beale, Andrew Beatty, Andrew Dalby, Emma Donoghue, Chris Greenhalgh, Ed Husain, Tom Jaine, Huon Mallalieu, David Saffery, Simon Unwin, Caroline Williams. COMMISSION Home & Commonwealth, US, Translation 12½%; 20% if sub-agents are involved in foreign sales. Finished, polished first novels positively welcomed. No thrillers, crime, occult, short stories, children's, plays or poetry. Writers should send an initial letter giving details of their project and/or book proposal, including the first 50 pages of their novel if a fiction writer, together with c.v. and s.a.e. No response to submissions without return postage or to those sent by fax or e-mail.

Merric Davidson Literary Agency
See **MBA Literary Agents Ltd**

Felix de Wolfe
Kingsway House, 103 Kingsway, London WC2B 6QX
☎020 7242 5066 Fax 020 7242 8119
✉ info@felixdewolfe.com

Contact *Felix de Wolfe*

Founded 1938. Handles quality fiction only, and scripts. No non-fiction or children's. CLIENTS include Jan Butlin, Jeff Dowson, Brian Glover, Sheila Goff, Aileen Gonsalves, John Kershaw, Ray Kilby, Bill MacIlwraith, Angus Mackay, Gerard McLarnon, Malcolm Taylor, David Thompson, Paul Todd, Dolores Walshe. COMMISSION Home 12½%; US 20%. No unsolicited mss. No reading fee.

The Dench Arnold Agency
10 Newburgh Street, London W1F 7RN
☎020 7437 4551 Fax 020 7439 1355
✉ contact@den07charnold.co.uk
www.den07charnold.co.uk

Contacts *Elizabeth Dench, Michelle Arnold*

Founded 1972. Handles scripts for TV and film. CLIENTS include Peter Chelsom. COMMISSION Home 10–15%. OVERSEAS ASSOCIATES include William Morris/Sanford Gross and C.A.A., Los Angeles. Unsolicited mss will be read, but a letter with sample of work and c.v. (plus s.a.e.) is required.

Dorian Literary Agency (DLA)★
Upper Thornehill, 27 Church Road, St Marychurch, Torquay TQ1 4QY
☎01803 312095

Contact *Dorothy Lumley*

Founded 1986. Handles popular genre fiction: romance, historicals, sagas; crime and thrillers; science fiction, fantasy, horror; some general fiction. No short stories, poetry, autobiography, film/TV scripts or plays. CLIENTS include Gillian Bradshaw, Gary Gibson, Kate Hardy, Stephen Jones, Brian Lumley, Amy Myers, Rosemary Rowe, Lyndon Stacey. COMMISSION Home 12½% for new clients; US 15%; Translation 20–25%. Works with agents in most countries for translation. Introductory letter with outline and 1–3 chapters (with return postage/s.a.e.) only, please. No enquiries or submissions by telephone, fax or e-mail. No reading fee.

Toby Eady Associates Ltd
9 Orme Court, London W2 4RL
☎020 7792 0092 Fax 020 7792 0879
✉ toby@tobyeady.demon.co.uk
www.tobyeadyassociates.co.uk

Contact *Toby Eady*

Handles fiction, and non-fiction. Special interests: China, Middle East, Africa, India. CLIENTS include Nada Awar Jarrar, Mark Burnell, Chris Cleave, Bernard Cornwell, John Carey, Yasmin Crowther, Rana Dasgupta, Fadia Faqir, Kuki Gallmann, Sophie Gee, Samson Kambalu, Richard Lloyd Parry, Julia Lovell, Francesca Marciano, Linda Polman, Fiammetta Rocco, Deborah Scroggins, Rachel Seiffert, Samia Serageldin, John Stubbs, Diane Wei Liang, Robert Winder, Fan Wu Xinran Xue. COMMISSION Home 15%; Elsewhere 20%. OVERSEAS ASSOCIATES USA: ICM; France: La Nouvelle Agence; Holland: Jan Michael; Italy, Spain, Germany, Portugal, Scandinavia: Deal Direct; China, Taiwan: The Bardon Chinese Media Agency; Japan: The English Agency; Korea: The Eric Yang Agency; Eastern Europe/Russia: Prava I Prevodi; Turkey: Akcali Copyright; Czech Republic: Kristin Olson; Hungary: Katai & Bolza; Greece: JLM. Approach by personal recommendation. No film/TV scripts or poetry.

Eddison Pearson Ltd
West Hill House, 6 Swains Lane, London N6 6QS
☎020 7700 7763 Fax 020 7700 7866
✉ info@eddisonpearson.com

Contact *Clare Pearson*

Founded 1996. Small, personally-run agency. Handles children's books, fiction and non-fiction, poetry. CLIENTS include Sue Heap, Robert Muchamore, Valerie Bloom. COMMISSION Home 10%; US & Translation 15–20%. Submissions by e-mail only. Please e-mail for up-to-date submission guidelines by return. No reading fee.

Edwards Fuglewicz★
49 Great Ormond Street, London WC1N 3HZ
☎020 7405 6725 Fax 020 7405 6726

Contacts *Ros Edwards, Helenka Fuglewicz, Julia Forrest*

Founded 1996. Handles literary and commercial fiction (not children's, science fiction, horror or fantasy); non-fiction: biography, history, popular culture. COMMISSION Home 15%; US & Translation 20%. No unsolicited mss or e-mail submissions.

Faith Evans Associates★
27 Park Avenue North, London N8 7RU
☎020 8340 9920 Fax 020 8340 9410
✉ faithevanslituk@hotmail.com

Founded 1987. Small agency. CLIENTS include Melissa Benn, Shyam Bhatia, Cherie Booth, Eleanor Bron, Caroline Conran, Alicia Foster, Midge Gillies, Ed Glinert, Vesna Goldsworthy, Cate Haste, Jim Kelly, Helena Kennedy, Seumas Milne, Tom Paulin, Sheila Rowbotham, the estate of Lorna Sage, Rebecca Stott, Harriet Walter, Francesca Weisman, Elizabeth Wilson. COMMISSION Home 15%; US & Translation 20%. OVERSEAS ASSOCIATES worldwide. List full; no submissions, please.

Lisa Eveleigh Literary Agency★
c/o Pollinger Ltd, 9 Staple Inn, London WC1V 7QH
☎020 7404 0342 Fax 020 7242 5737
✉ lisaeveleigh@dial.pipex.com

Contact *Lisa Eveleigh*

Founded 1996. Handles literary and commercial fiction and non-fiction. No children's picture books, plays, scripts, poetry or horror. CLIENTS include Christina Balit, Robin Brooks, Samit Basu, Philip Casey, Kimberley Jane Chambers, Matthew Collins, Jonathan Gornall, Jonathan Meres, Lynn Peters, Relate, Grace Wynne-Jones. COMMISSION Home 15%; US & Translation 20%. Send synopsis with covering letter and c.v. rather than full mss. No reading fee but return postage essential. Please restrict e-mail contact to preliminary letter only.

Laurence Fitch Ltd
Mezzanine, Quadrant House, 80–82 Regent Street, London W1B 5AU
☎020 7734 9911
✉ information@laurencefitch.com
www.laurencefitch.com

Contact *Brendan Davis*

Founded 1952, incorporating the London Play Company (1922) and in association with Film Rights Ltd (1932). Handles children's and horror books, scripts for theatre, film, TV and radio only. CLIENTS include Carlo Ardito, Hindi Brooks, John Chapman & Ray Cooney, Jeremy Lloyd, Dave Freeman, John Graham, Robin Hawdon, Glyn Robbins, Lawrence Roman, Gene Stone, the estate of Dodie Smith, Edward Taylor. COMMISSION UK 10%; Overseas 15%. OVERSEAS ASSOCIATES worldwide. No unsolicited mss. Send synopsis with sample scene(s)/first chapters in the first instance. No reading fee.

Jill Foster Ltd
9 Barb Mews, Brook Green, London W6 7PA
☎020 7602 1263 Fax 020 7602 9336
✉ agents@jflagency.com

Contacts *Jill Foster, Alison Finch, Simon Williamson, Dominic Lord, Gary Wild*

Founded 1976. Handles scripts for TV, drama and comedy. No fiction, short stories or poetry. CLIENTS include Ian Brown, Jan Etherington and Gavin Petrie, Phil Ford, Nev Fountain and Tom Jamieson, Rob Gittins, Jenny Lecoat, Jim Pullin and Fraser Steele, Pete Sinclair, Peter Tilbury, Susan Wilkins. COMMISSION Home 12½%; Books, US & Translation 15%. No unsolicited mss; approach by letter in the first instance. No approaches by e-mail. No reading fee.

Fox & Howard Literary Agency
4 Bramerton Street, London SW3 5JX
☎020 7352 8691 Fax 020 7352 8691

Contacts *Chelsey Fox, Charlotte Howard*

Founded 1992. A small agency, specialising in non-fiction, that prides itself on 'working closely with its authors'. Handles biography, history and popular culture, reference, business, mind, body and spirit, health and fitness. COMMISSION Home 15%; US & Translation 20%. No unsolicited mss; send letter and synopsis with s.a.e. for response. No reading fee.

FRA★
17 Deanhill Road, London SW14 7DQ
☎020 8255 7755 Fax 020 8286 4860
✉ guy@futermanrose.co.uk

www.futermanrose.co.uk

Biography/Non-Fiction/Screenplays *Guy Rose* (guy@futermanrose.co.uk)

Adult Fiction *Betty Schwartz* (betty@futermanrose.co.uk)

TV & Screenplay *Barnaby Fisher-Taylor* (barney@@futermanrose.co.uk)

Teen Fiction *Alexandra Groom* (alexandra@futermanrose.co.uk)

Founded 1984. Handles fiction, scripts for film and TV, biography, show business, current affairs and teenage fiction. No science fiction, fantasy or young children's. CLIENTS include Larry Barker, Christian Piers Betley, Shirley Clarkson, Iain Duncan Smith, Royston Ellis, Sir Martin Ewans, Yvette Fielding, Susan George, Stephen Griffin, Anita Harris, Brian Harvey, Paul Hendy, Russell Warren Howe, Keith R. Lindsay, Stephen Lowe, Eric MacInnes, Paul Marx, Max Morgan-Witts, Ciarán O'Keeffe, Erin Pizzey, John Repsch, Liz Rettig, Peter Sallis, Pat Silver-Lasky, Paul Stinchcombe, Gordon Thomas, Bill Tidy, Mark White, Toyah Willcox, Simon Woodham, Tappy Wright, Allen Zeleski. No unsolicited mss. Send preliminary letter with brief resumé, detailed synopsis, first 20 pages (approx.) and s.a.e.

Fraser Ross Associates

6 Wellington Place, Edinburgh EH6 7EQ
☎0131 657 4412/0131 553 2759
✉ kjross@tiscali.co.uk *and*
lindsey.fraser@tiscali.co.uk
www.fraserross.co.uk

Contacts *Lindsey Fraser, Kathryn Ross*

Founded 2002. Handles children's books, adult literary and mainstream fiction. No poetry, short stories, adult fantasy and science fiction, academic, scripts. CLIENTS Thomas Bloor, Sally J. Collins, Chris Fisher, Vivian French, Janey Louise Jones, Tanya Landman, Iain MacIntosh, Jack McLean, Michaela Morgan, Dugald Steer, Linda Strachan. Send preliminary letter, synopsis, first three chapters or equivalent, c.v. and s.a.e. No reading fee.

Futerman, Rose & Associates

See FRA

Jüri Gabriel

35 Camberwell Grove, London SE5 8JA
☎020 7703 6186

Contact *Jüri Gabriel*

Handles quality fiction and non-fiction and (almost exclusively for existing clients) film, TV and radio rights. Jüri Gabriel worked in televi-
sion, wrote books for 20 years and is chairman of Dedalus publishers. No short stories, articles, verse or books for children. CLIENTS include Maurice Caldera, Diana Constance, Gerry and Joanne Dryansky, Miriam Dunne, Matt Fox, Paul Genney, Pat Gray, Mikka Haugaard, Robert Irwin, John Lucas, David Madsen, Richard Mankiewicz, Karina Mellinger, David Miller, Andy Oakes, John Outram, Philip Roberts, Dr Stefan Szymanski, Frances Treanor, Dr Terence White, Chris Wilkins, Dr Robert Youngson. COMMISSION Home 10%; US & Translation 20%. Unsolicited mss ('two-page synopsis and three sample chapters in first instance, please') welcome if accompanied by return postage and letter giving sufficient information about author's writing experience, aims, etc.

Eric Glass Ltd

25 Ladbroke Crescent, London W11 1PS
☎020 7229 9500 Fax 020 7229 6220
✉ eglassltd@aol.com

Contacts *Janet Glass, Sissi Lichtenstein*

Founded 1934. Handles fiction, non-fiction and scripts for publication or production in all media. No poetry, short stories or children's works. CLIENTS include Herbert Appleman, Pierre Chesnot, Charles Dyer, Henry Fleet, Tudor Gates, Philip Goulding, Pauline Macaulay, Brendan Murray and the estates of Rodney Ackland, Marc Camoletti, Jean Cocteau, Warwick Deeping, William Douglas Home, Philip King, Robin Maugham, Alan Melville, Beverley Nichols, Jack Popplewell, Jean-Paul Sartre. COMMISSION Home 15%; US & Translation 20%. OVERSEAS ASSOCIATES in the US, Australia, Czech Republic, France, Germany, Greece, Holland, Italy, Japan, Poland, Scandinavia, Slovakia, South Africa, Spain. No unsolicited mss. Return postage required. No reading fee.

David Godwin Associates

55 Monmouth Street, London WC2H 9DG
☎020 7240 9992 Fax 020 7395 6110
✉ assistant@davidgodwinassociates.co.uk
www.davidgodwinassociates.co.uk

Contact *David Godwin*

Founded 1996. Handles literary and general fiction, non-fiction, biography. No scripts, science fiction or children's. No reading fee. COMMISSION Home 15%; Overseas 15%. 'Please contact the office before making a submission.'

Annette Green Authors' Agency★

1 East Cliff Road, Tunbridge Wells TN4 9AD
☎01892 514275 Fax 01892 518124

annettekgreen@aol.com
www.annettegreenagency.co.uk

Contact *Address material to the Agency*

Founded 1998. Handles literary and general fiction and non-fiction, popular culture and current affairs, science, music, film, history, biography, older children's and teenage fiction. No dramatic scripts or poetry. CLIENTS include Andrew Baker, Duncan Bannatyne, Bill Broady, Meg Cabot, Simon Conway, Fiona Gibson, Justin Hill, Mary Hogan, Anvar Khan, Maria McCann, Adam Macqueen, Ian Marchant, Professor Charles Pasternak, Kirsty Scott, Bernadette Strachan, Elizabeth Woodcraft. COMMISSION Home 15%; US & Translation 20%. Letter, synopsis, sample chapters and s.a.e. essential. No reading fee.

Christine Green Authors' Agent★

6 Whitehorse Mews, Westminster Bridge Road, London SE1 7QD
☎020 7401 8844 Fax 020 7401 8860
info@christinegreen.co.uk
www.christinegreen.co.uk

Contact *Christine Green*

Founded 1984. Handles fiction (general and literary) and general non-fiction. No scripts, poetry or children's. COMMISSION Home 10%; US & Translation 20%. Initial letter, synopsis and first three chapters preferred. No reading fee but return postage essential.

Louise Greenberg Books Ltd★

The End House, Church Crescent, London N3 1BG
☎020 8349 1179 Fax 020 8343 4559
louisegreenberg@msn.com

Contact *Louise Greenberg*

Founded 1997. Handles full-length literary fiction and serious non-fiction only. COMMISSION Home 15%; US & Translation 20%. DRAMATIC ASSOCIATE Micheline Steinberg Associates; CHILDREN'S ASSOCIATE Sarah Manson Literary Agent. *No telephone approaches.* No reading fee. S.a.e. essential.

Greene & Heaton Ltd★

37 Goldhawk Road, London W12 8QQ
☎020 8749 0315 Fax 020 8749 0318
www.greeneheaton.co.uk

Contacts *Carol Heaton, Judith Murray, Antony Topping, Linda Davis* (children's), *Will Francis*

A medium-sized agency with a broad range of clients. Handles all types of fiction and non-fiction. No original scripts for theatre, film or TV.

CLIENTS include Mark Barrowcliffe, Bill Bryson, Jan Dalley, Marcus du Sautoy, Hugh Fearnley-Whittingstall, Michael Frayn, P.D. James, William Leith, Mary Morrissy, C.J. Sansom, William Shawcross, Sarah Waters. COMMISSION Home 15%; US & Translation 20%. OVERSEAS ASSOCIATES worldwide. No reply to unsolicited submissions without s.a.e. and/or return postage.

Gregory & Company Authors' Agents★
(formerly **Gregory & Radice**)

3 Barb Mews, London W6 7PA
☎020 7610 4676 Fax 020 7610 4686
info@gregoryandcompany.co.uk
(general enquiries)
www.gregoryandcompany.co.uk

Contact *Jane Gregory*
Editorial Manager *Emma Dunford*
Rights Manager *Claire Morris*
Administration *Jemma McDonagh*

Founded 1987. Handles all kinds of fiction and general non-fiction. Special interest fiction – literary, commercial, women's fiction, crime, suspense and thrillers. 'We are particularly interested in books which will also sell to publishers abroad.' No original plays, film or TV scripts (only published books are sold to film and TV). No science fiction, fantasy, poetry, academic or children's books. No reading fee. Editorial advice given to own authors. COMMISSION Home 15%; US, Translation, Radio/TV/Film 20%. Is well represented throughout Europe, Asia and US. No unsolicited mss; send a preliminary letter with c.v., synopsis, first three chapters and future writing plans (plus return postage). Short submissions by fax or e-mail (maryjones@ gregoryandcompany.co.uk) in the first instance; maximum five pages.

David Grossman Literary Agency Ltd

118b Holland Park Avenue, London W11 4UA
☎020 7221 2770 Fax 020 7221 1445

Contact *Submissions Dept.*

Founded 1976. Handles full-length fiction and general non-fiction – good writing of all kinds and anything healthily controversial. No verse or technical books for students. No original screenplays or teleplays (only works existing in volume form are sold for performance rights). Generally works with published writers of fiction only but 'truly original, well-written novels from beginners' will be considered. COMMISSION Rates vary for different markets.

OVERSEAS ASSOCIATES throughout Europe, Asia, Brazil and the US. Best approach by preliminary letter giving full description of the work and, in the case of fiction, with the first 50 pages. 'Please ensure material is printed in at least 1½ spacing on one side of paper only; that all pages are numbered consecutively throughout and in minimum 11pt typeface.' All material must be accompanied by return postage. No approaches or submissions by fax or e-mail. No unsolicited mss. No reading fee.

Gunn Media Associates
8 Lower James Street, London W1F 9EL
☎0207 534 5757
✉ ali@gunnmedia.co.uk

Contacts *Ali Gunn, Alice Goodwin-Hudson*
Head of Foreign Rights *Diana McKay*

Founded 2005. Handles commercial fiction and non-fiction. No scripts. CLIENTS include Jenny Colgan, Brian Freeman, Mil Millington, Martina Reilly, Sarah Webb, Alison Penton Harper. COMMISSION Home 15%; US & Translation 20%. ASSOCIATES Gelfman Schneider, LJK Literary, Fletcher Parry. Unsolicited mss, sample chapters and synopses welcome; approach in writing. No reading fee.

The Rod Hall Agency Limited
6th Floor, Fairgate House, 78 New Oxford Street, London W1A 1HB
☎020 7079 7987 Fax 0845 638 4094
✉ office@rodhallagency.com
www.rodhallagency.com

Contact *Charlotte Knight*

Founded 1997. Handles drama for film, TV and theatre and writers-directors. Does not represent writers of episodes for TV series where the format is provided but represents originators of series. CLIENTS include Simon Beaufoy (*The Full Monty*), Jeremy Brock (*Mrs Brown*), Liz Lochhead (*Perfect Days*), Martin McDonagh (*The Pillowman*), Simon Nye (*Men Behaving Badly*). COMMISSION Home 10%; US & Translation 15%. No reading fee.

Margaret Hanbury Literary Agency★
27 Walcot Square, London SE11 4UB
☎020 7735 7680 Fax 020 7793 0316
✉ maggie@hanburyagency.demon.co.uk

Contacts *Margaret Hanbury, Genevieve Carden*

Personally run agency representing quality fiction and non-fiction. No plays, scripts, poetry, children's books, fantasy, horror. CLIENTS include

George Alagiah, J.G. Ballard, Simon Callow, Jane Glover, Bernard Hare, Judith Lennox, Katie Price. COMMISSION Home 15%; Overseas 20%. No unsolicited approaches via e-mail.

Roger Hancock Ltd
4 Water Lane, London NW1 8NZ
☎020 7267 4418 Fax 020 7267 0705
✉ info@rogerhancock.com

Contact *Material should be addressed to the Submissions Department*

Founded 1960. Special interests: comedy drama and light entertainment. COMMISSION Home 10%; Overseas 15%. Unsolicited mss not welcome. Initial phone call required.

Antony Harwood Limited
103 Walton Street, Oxford OX2 6EB
☎01865 559615 Fax 01865 310660
✉ mail@antonyharwood.com
www.antonyharwood.com

Contacts *Antony Harwood, James Macdonald Lockhart*

Founded 2000. Handles fiction and non-fiction. CLIENTS Amanda Craig, Peter F. Hamilton, Alan Hollinghurst, A.L. Kennedy, Douglas Kennedy, Chris Manby, George Monbiot, Tim Parks. COMMISSION Home 15%; US & Translation 20%. Send letter and synopsis with return postage in the first instance. No reading fee.

A.M. Heath & Co. Ltd★
6 Warwick Court, London WC1R 5DJ
☎020 7242 2811 Fax 020 7242 2711
www.amheath.com

Contacts *Bill Hamilton, Sara Fisher, Sarah Molloy, Victoria Hobbs, Euan Thorneycroft*

Founded 1919. Handles fiction, general non-fiction and children's. No dramatic scripts, poetry or short stories. CLIENTS include Christopher Andrew, Bella Bathurst, Anita Brookner, Geoff Dyer, Katie Fforde, Lesley Glaister, Graham Hancock, Conn Iggulden, Hilary Mantel, Hilary Norman, Susan Price, John Sutherland, Adam Thorpe, Barbara Trapido. COMMISSION Home 15%; US & Translation 20%; Film & TV 15%. OVERSEAS ASSOCIATES in the US, Europe, South America, Japan and the Far East. Preliminary letter and synopsis essential. No reading fee.

Rupert Heath Literary Agency
177a Old Winton Road, Andover SP10 2DR
☎020 7788 7807 Fax 020 7691 9331
✉ emailagency@rupertheath.com

Contact *Rupert Heath*

Founded 2000. Handles literary and general fiction and non-fiction, including history, biography and autobiography, current affairs, popular science, the arts and popular culture. No scripts or poetry. COMMISSION Home 15%; US & Translation 20%. OVERSEAS ASSOCIATES worldwide. Approach with e-mail ('initially telling us about yourself and the book you wish to submit'), or letter (first 50 pages and s.a.e.). E-mail enquiries preferred. No reading fee.

hhb agency ltd★
6 Warwick Court, London WC1R 5DJ
☎020 7405 5525
✉ heather@hhbagency.com
www.hhbagency.com
Contact *Heather Holden-Brown*

Founded in 2005 by Heather Holden-Brown, a publishing editor for 20 years with Waterstone's, Harrap, BBC Books and Headline. Handles non-fiction: history and politics, contemporary autobiography/biography, popular culture, entertainment and TV, business, family memoir, food and cookery. No scripts. COMMISSION Home 15%. No unsolicited mss; please contact by e-mail or telephone before sending any material. No reading fee.

David Higham Associates Ltd★
5−8 Lower John Street, Golden Square, London W1F 9HA
☎020 7434 5900 Fax 020 7437 1072
✉ dha@davidhigham.co.uk
www.davidhigham.co.uk
Books *Anthony Goff, Bruce Hunter, Veronique Baxter, Lizzy Kremer, Caroline Walsh* (children's), *Georgia Glover, Alice Wilson*
Scripts *Nicky Lund, Georgina Ruffhead, Gemma Hirst, Jessica Cooper*

Founded 1935. Handles fiction, general non-fiction (biography, history, current affairs, etc.) and children's books. Also scripts. CLIENTS include John le Carré, J.M. Coetzee, Stephen Fry, Jane Green, James Herbert, Alexander McCall Smith, Lynne Truss, Jacqueline Wilson. COMMISSION Home 15%; US & Translation 20%; Scripts 10%. Preliminary letter with synopsis essential in first instance. No e-mail submissions. No reading fee. See website for further information.

Vanessa Holt Ltd★
59 Crescent Road, Leigh-on-Sea SS9 2PF
☎01702 473787 Fax 01702 473787
Contact *Vanessa Holt*
Founded 1989. Handles general fiction, non-

fiction and non-illustrated children's books. No scripts, poetry, academic or technical. Specialises in crime fiction, commercial and literary fiction, and particularly interested in books with potential for sales abroad and/or to TV. COMMISSION Home 15%; US & Translation 20%; Radio/TV/Film 15%. Represented in all foreign markets. Approach by letter only and no unsolicited mss.

Kate Hordern Literary Agency
18 Mortimer Road, Clifton, Bristol BS8 4EY
☎0117 923 9368
✉ katehordern@blueyonder.co.uk
Contact *Kate Hordern*
Founded 1999. Handles quality fiction and general non-fiction. CLIENTS Richard Bassett, Jeff Dawson, Leigh Eduardo, Kylie Fitzpatrick, Duncan Hewitt, J.T. Lees, Will Randall. COMMISSION Home 15%; US & Translation 20%. OVERSEAS ASSOCIATES VVV Agency, France; Carmen Balcells Agency, Spain; Synopsis Agency, Russia and various agencies in Asia. Approach in writing (or by e-mail) in the first instance with details of project. New clients taken on very selectively. Synopsis required for fiction; proposal/chapter breakdown for non-fiction. Sample chapters on request only. S.a.e. essential. No reading fee.

Valerie Hoskins Associates Limited
20 Charlotte Street, London W1T 2NA
☎020 7637 4490 Fax 020 7637 4493
✉ vha@vhassociates.co.uk
Contacts *Valerie Hoskins, Rebecca Watson*
Founded 1983. Handles scripts for film, TV and radio. Special interests feature films, animation and TV. COMMISSION Home 12½%; US 20% (maximum). No unsolicited scripts; preliminary letter of introduction essential. No reading fee.

ICM★
Oxford House, 76 Oxford Street, London W1D 1BS
☎020 7636 6565 Fax 020 7323 0101
Contacts *Sue Rodgers, Jessica Sykes, Cathy King, Greg Hunt, Hugo Young, Michael McCoy, Duncan Heath, Paul Lyon-Maris*
Founded 1973. Specialises in scripts for film, theatre, TV and radio. No reading fee.

ICM Books★
International Creative Management Ltd, 4−6 Soho Square, London W1D 3PZ
☎020 7432 0800 Fax 020 7432 0808
www.icmtalent.com

Contacts *Kate Jones, Margaret Halton*

Handles fiction and non-fiction; no plays or scripts. OVERSEAS ASSOCIATE International Creative Management Inc., Worldwide Plaza, 825 Eighth Ave., New York, NY 10019, USA. Submissions must include sample chapters and letter. No reading fee.

Indepublishing CIA – Consultancy for Independent Authors

77 Acre Road, Kingston upon Thames KT2 6ES
☎07768 864364
✉ joanna@indepublishing.com
www.indepublishing.com

Contact *Joanna Anthony*

Founded 2005. Handles women's fiction, crime fiction, contemporary fiction, travelogues and biographies. No TV, film, radio or theatre scripts. COMMISSION Home 10%. Send e-mail with synopsis and publishing plans in the first instance. £75 reading fee 'only upon invitation'.

The Inspira Group

5 Bradley Road, Enfield EN3 6ES
☎020 8292 5163 Fax 0870 139 3057
✉ darin@theinspiragroup.com
www.theinspiragroup.com

Managing Director *Darin Jewell*

Founded 1996. Handles children's books, crime fiction, lifestyle/relationships, science fiction/fantasy. No scripts. CLIENTS Dominic Wyse, C.W. Reed, Mike Haskins, Steve Arnott. COMMISSION Home & US 15%. Unsolicited mss and synopses welcome; approach by e-mail or telephone. No reading fee.

Intercontinental Literary Agency★

Centric House, 391 Strand, London WC2R 0LT
☎020 7379 6611 Fax 020 7240 4724
✉ ila@ila-agency.co.uk
www.ila-agency.co.uk

Contacts *Nicki Kennedy, Sam Edenborough*

Founded 1965. Handles translation rights only for, among others, the authors of PFD, London; PFD, New York; LAW Ltd, London; Harold Matson Co. Inc., New York.

International Scripts

1A Kidbrooke Park Road, London SE3 0LR
☎020 8319 8666 Fax 020 8319 0801
✉ internationalscripts@btinternet.com

Contacts *Bob Tanner, Pat Hornsey, Jill Lawson*

Founded 1979 by Bob Tanner. Handles most

types of books (non-fiction and fiction) and scripts for most media. No poetry, articles or short stories. CLIENTS include Jane Adams, Zita Adamson, Ashleigh Bingham, Simon Clark, Ann Cliff, Dr James Fleming, June Gadsby, Julie Harris, Robert A. Heinlein, Anna Jacobs, Anne Jones, Richard Laymon, Trevor Lummis, Margaret Muir, Nick Oldham, Chris Pascoe, Christine Poulson, John and Anne Spencer, Janet Woods. COMMISSION Home 15%; US & Translation 20%. OVERSEAS ASSOCIATES include Ralph Vicinanza, USA; Thomas Schlück, Germany. Preliminary letter, one-page synopsis, wordage, plus s.a.e. required. No unsolicited manuscripts by post or e-mail accepted.

Barrie James Literary Agency (including **New Authors Showcase**)

Rivendell, Kingsgate Close, Torquay TQ2 8QA
☎01803 326617
✉ mail@newauthors.org.uk
www.newauthors.org.uk

Contact *Barrie James*

Founded 1997. No unsolicited mss. First approach should be made by sending s.a.e. or e-mail. No reading fee but small charge is made for display on the Internet.

Janklow & Nesbit (UK) Ltd★

33 Drayson Mews, London W8 4LY
☎020 7376 2733 Fax 020 7376 2915
✉ queries@janklow.co.uk

Agents *Tif Loehnis, Claire Paterson, Jenny McVeigh*
Head of Rights *Rebecca Folland*

Founded 2000. Handles fiction and non-fiction; commercial and literary. (See also Janklow & Nesbit Associates, New York, under *US Literary Agents*.) Send full outline (non-fiction), synopsis and three sample chapters (fiction) plus informative covering letter and return postage. No e-mail submissions.

Johnson & Alcock★

Clerkenwell House, 45–47 Clerkenwell Green, London EC1R 0HT
☎020 7251 0125 Fax 020 7251 2172
✉ info@johnsonandalcock.co.uk
www.johnsonandalcock.co.uk

Contacts *Andrew Hewson, Michael Alcock, Anna Power*

Founded 1956. Handles literary and commercial fiction, children's 9+ fiction; general non-fiction including current affairs, biography, memoirs, history, culture, design, lifestyle and health. No poetry, screenplays, technical or academic material. COMMISSION Home 15%; US & Translation 20%. No unsolicited mss. For fiction and non-fiction approach by letter in the first instance giving details of writing and other media experience, plus synopsis. S.a.e. essential for response. No reading fee.

Jane Judd Literary Agency*
18 Belitha Villas, London N1 1PD
☎020 7607 0273 Fax 020 7607 0623

Contact *Jane Judd*

Founded 1986. Handles general fiction and non-fiction: women's fiction, crime, thrillers, literary fiction, humour, biography, investigative journalism, health, women's interests and travel. 'Looking for good contemporary women's fiction but not Mills & Boon-type; also historical fiction and non-fiction.' No scripts, academic, gardening, short stories or DIY. CLIENTS include Andy Dougan, Cliff Goodwin, Jill Mansell, Jonathon Porritt, Rosie Rushton, Manda Scott, David Winner. COMMISSION Home 10%; US & Translation 20%. Approach with letter, including synopsis, first chapter and s.a.e. Initial telephone call helpful in the case of non-fiction.

Michelle Kass Associates*
85 Charing Cross Road, London WC2H 0AA
☎020 7439 1624 Fax 020 7734 3394
✉ office@michellekass.co.uk

Contacts *Michelle Kass*

Founded 1991. Handles literary fiction, film and television primarily. COMMISSION Home 10%; US & Translation 15–20%. No mss accepted without preliminary phone call. No reading fee.

Frances Kelly*
111 Clifton Road, Kingston upon Thames KT2 6PL
☎020 8549 7830 Fax 020 8547 0051

Contact *Frances Kelly*

Founded 1978. Handles non-fiction, including illustrated: biography, history, art, self-help, food & wine, complementary medicine and therapies, finance and business books; and academic non-fiction in all disciplines. No scripts except for existing clients. COMMISSION Home 10%; US & Translation 20%. No unsolicited mss. Approach by letter with brief description of work or synopsis, together with c.v. and return postage.

Knight Features
20 Crescent Grove, London SW4 7AH
☎020 7622 1467 Fax 020 7622 1522

✉ peter@knightfeatures.co.uk

Contacts *Peter Knight, Samantha Ferris, Gaby Martin, Andrew Knight*

Founded 1985. Handles motor sports, cartoon books, puzzles, business, history, factual and biographical material. No poetry, science fiction or cookery. CLIENTS include Frank Dickens, Gray Jolliffe, Angus McGill, Chris Maslanka, Barbara Minto. COMMISSION dependent upon authors and territories. OVERSEAS ASSOCIATES United Media, US; Auspac Media, Australia; Puzzle Co., New Zealand. No unsolicited mss and no e-mail submissions. Send letter accompanied by c.v. and s.a.e. with synopsis of proposed work.

LAW*
14 Vernon Street, London W14 0RJ
☎020 7471 7900 Fax 020 7471 7910

Contacts *Mark Lucas, Julian Alexander, Araminta Whitley, Alice Saunders, Lucinda Bettridge, Peta Nightingale, Lizzie Jones, Philippa Milnes-Smith* (children's), *Aisha Mobin* (children's)

Founded 1996. Handles full-length commercial and literary fiction, non-fiction and children's books. No fantasy (except children's), plays, poetry or textbooks. Film and TV scripts handled for established clients only. COMMISSION Home 15%; US & Translation 20%. OVERSEAS ASSOCIATES worldwide. Unsolicited mss considered; send brief covering letter, short synopsis and two sample chapters. S.a.e. essential. No e-mailed or disk submissions.

LBA
See **Luigi Bonomi Associates Limited**

Barbara Levy Literary Agency*
64 Greenhill, Hampstead High Street, London NW3 5TZ
☎020 7435 9046 Fax 020 7431 2063

Contacts *Barbara Levy, John Selby*

Founded 1986. Handles general fiction, non-fiction, and film and TV rights. COMMISSION Home 15%; US 20%; Translation by arrangement, in conjunction with The Buckman Agency. US ASSOCIATE Writers House, New York. No unsolicited mss. No reading fee.

Limelight Management*
33 Newman Street, London W1T 1PY
☎020 7637 2529 Fax 020 7637 2538
✉ limelight.management@virgin.net
www.limelightmanagement.com

Contacts *Fiona Lindsay, Linda Shanks*

Founded 1991. Handles general non-fiction:

cookery, gardening, antiques, interior design, wine, art and crafts and health. No fiction, TV, film, radio or theatre. Specialises in illustrated books. COMMISSION Home 15%; US & Translation 20%. Unsolicited mss welcome; send preliminary letter (s.a.e. essential). No reading fee.

The Christopher Little Literary Agency★

Eel Brook Studios, 125 Moore Park Road, London SW6 4PS

☎020 7736 4455 Fax 020 7736 4490

✉ info@christopherlittle.net *or* firstname@christopherlittle.net

www.christopherlittle.net

Contacts *Christopher Little, Patrick Janson-Smith*

Founded 1979. Handles commercial and literary full-length fiction and non-fiction. No poetry, plays, science fiction, fantasy, textbooks, illustrated children's or short stories. Film scripts for established clients only. AUTHORS include Steve Barlow and Steve Skidmore, Paul Bajoria, Andrew Butcher, Janet Gleeson, Carol Hughes, Alastair MacNeill, Robert Mawson, Haydn Middleton, Andrew Quinnell, Christopher Matthew, Robert Radcliffe, J.K. Rowling, Darren Shan, Wladyslaw Szpilman, John Watson, Pip Vaughan-Hughes, Gorillaz, Christopher Hale, Peter Howells, Gen. Sir Mike Jackson, Lauren Liebenberg, Shiromi Pinto, Dr Nicholas Reeves, Shayne Ward, Angela Woolfe, Anne Zouroudi. COMMISSION Home 15%; US, Canada, Translation, Audio & Motion Picture 20%. Send detailed preliminary letter in the first instance with synopsis, first 2–3 chapters and s.a.e. No reading fee.

London Independent Books

26 Chalcot Crescent, London NW1 8YD

☎020 7706 0486 Fax 020 7724 3122

Proprietor *Carolyn Whitaker*

Founded 1971. A self-styled 'small and idiosyncratic' agency. Handles fiction and non-fiction reflecting the tastes of the proprietor. All subjects considered (except computer books and young children's), providing the treatment is strong and saleable. Scripts handled only if by existing clients. Special interests: boats, travelogues, commercial fiction, science fiction and fantasy, teenage fiction. COMMISSION Home 15%; US & Translation 20%. No unsolicited mss; letter, synopsis and first two chapters with return postage the best approach. No reading fee.

The Andrew Lownie Literary Agency★

36 Great Smith Street, London SW1P 3BU

☎020 7222 7574 Fax 020 7222 7576

✉ lownie@globalnet.co.uk

www.andrewlownie.co.uk

Contact *Andrew Lownie*

Founded 1988. Specialises in non-fiction, especially history, biography, current affairs, military history, UFOs, reference and packaging celebrities and journalists for the book market. No poetry, short stories or science fiction. Formerly a journalist, publisher and himself the author of 12 non-fiction books, Andrew Lownie's CLIENTS include Richard Aldrich, Juliet Barker, the Joyce Cary estate, Tom Devine, Jonathan Fryer, Laurence Gardner, Timothy Good, David Hasselhoff, Robert Holden, Lawrence James, Robert Jobson, Julian Maclaren-Ross estate, Patrick MacNee, Norma Major, Sir John Mills, Tom Pocock, Nick Pope, John Rae, Desmond Seward, David Stafford. COMMISSION Worldwide 15%. Preferred approach by e-mail in format suggested on website.

Lucas Alexander Whitley

See **LAW**

Lucy Luck Associates

20 Cowper Road, London W3 6PZ

☎020 8992 6142

✉ lucy@lucyluck.com

www.lucyluck.com

Contact *Lucy Luck*

Founded 2006. Handles quality fiction and non-fiction. No TV, film, radio or theatre scripts; no illustrated or children's books. CLIENTS include Ewan Morrison, Jon Hotten, Doug Johnstone, Philip Ó Ceallaigh, Catherine O'Flynn, Lorelei Mathias. COMMISSION Home 10%; US & Translation 20% Send sample chapters by post. No reading fee.

Lutyens and Rubinstein★

231 Westbourne Park Road, London W11 1EB

☎020 7792 4855 Fax 020 7792 4833

Partners *Sarah Lutyens, Felicity Rubinstein*

Submissions *Susannah Godman*

Founded 1993. Handles adult fiction and non-fiction books. No TV, film, radio or theatre scripts. COMMISSION Home 15%; US & Translation 20%. Unsolicited mss accepted; send introductory letter, c.v., two chapters and return postage for all material submitted. No reading fee.

Duncan McAra

28 Beresford Gardens, Edinburgh EH5 3ES
☎0131 552 1558 Fax 0131 552 1558
✉ duncanmcara@hotmail.com

Contact *Duncan McAra*

Founded 1988. Handles fiction (literary fiction) and non-fiction, including art, architecture, archaeology, biography, military, travel and books of Scottish interest. COMMISSION Home 10%; Overseas 20%. Preliminary letter, synopsis and sample chapter (including return postage) essential. No reading fee.

McKernan Agency

5 Gayfield Square, Edinburgh EH1 3NW
☎0131 557 1771
✉ maggie@mckernanagency.co.uk
www.mckernanagency.co.uk

Contact *Maggie McKernan*

Founded 2005. Works in conjunction with Capel & Land Ltd. Handles fiction, both literary and commercial; also TV, film, radio and theatre scripts. COMMISSION Home 15%; US & Translation 15%. Send s.a.e. for return of ms. No reading fee.

Bill McLean Personal Management

23B Deodar Road, London SW15 2NP
☎020 8789 8191

Contact *Bill McLean*

Founded 1972. Handles scripts for all media. No books. CLIENTS include Dwynwen Berry, Graham Carlisle, Pat Cumper, Jane Galletly, Patrick Jones, Tony Jordan, Bill Lyons, John Maynard, Michael McStay, Les Miller, Ian Rowlands, Jeffrey Segal, Richard Shannon, Ronnie Smith, Barry Thomas, Garry Tyler, Frank Vickery, Laura Watson, Mark Wheatley. COMMISSION Home 10%. No unsolicited mss. Phone call or introductory letter essential. No reading fee.

Eunice McMullen Ltd

Low Ibbotsholme Cottage, Off Bridge Lane, Troutbeck Bridge, Windermere LA23 1HU
☎01539 448551
✉ eunicemcmullen@totalise.co.uk
www.eunicemcmullen.co.uk

Contact *Eunice McMullen*

Founded 1992. Handles all types of children's fiction. Especially interested in 9plus and has 'an excellent' list of picture book authors and illustrators. CLIENTS include Wayne Anderson, Jon Berkeley, Sam Childs, Caroline Jayne Church, Jason Cockcroft, Ross Collins, Charles Fuge,

Angela McAllister, David Melling, Angie Sage, Gillian Shields, David Wood. COMMISSION Home 10%; US 15%; Translation 20%. *No unsolicited scripts.* Telephone enquiries only.

Andrew Mann Ltd★

1 Old Compton Street, London W1D 5JA
☎020 7734 4751 Fax 020 7287 9264
✉ info@manscript.co.uk

Contacts *Anne Dewe, Tina Betts, Louise Burns*

Founded 1975. Handles fiction, general non-fiction, children's and film, TV, theatre, radio scripts. COMMISSION Home 15%; US & Translation 20%. OVERSEAS ASSOCIATES various. Unsolicited mss accepted only with preliminary letter, synopsis, first three chapters; s.a.e. essential. E-mail submissions for synopses only, but 'we do not open attachments'. No reading fee.

Sarah Manson Literary Agent

6 Totnes Walk, London N2 0AD
☎020 8442 0396
✉ info@sarahmanson.com
www.sarahmanson.com

Contact *Sarah Manson*

Founded 2002. Handles quality fiction for children and young adults. COMMISSION Home 10%; Overseas & Translation 20%. Please consult website for submission guidelines. No reading fee.

Marjacq Scripts Ltd

34 Devonshire Place, London W1G 6JW
☎020 7935 9499 Fax 020 7935 9115
✉ subs@marjacq.com
www.marjacq.com

Contact *Philip Patterson* (books), *Luke Speed* (film/TV)

Handles fiction and non-fiction, literary and commercial as well as film, TV, radio scripts. No poetry. COMMISSION Home 10%; Overseas 20%. New work welcome; send brief letter, synopsis and approx. first 50 pages plus s.a.e. No reading fee.

The Marsh Agency Ltd★

11/12 Dover Street, London W1S 4LJ
☎020 7399 2800 Fax 020 7399 2801
✉ submissions@marsh-agency.co.uk
www.marsh-agency.co.uk

Managing Director *Paul Marsh*
Contacts *Geraldine Cooke, Jessica Woollard, Leyla Moghadam, Caroline Hardman*
Foreign Rights *Camilla Ferrier*

Founded in 1994 as international rights

specialist for British, American and Canadian agencies. Expanded to act as agents handling fiction and non-fiction. Specialises in authors with international potential. See website for further information on individual agents' areas of interest. COMMISSION Home 15%; Elsewhere 20%; Film & TV 15%. See also Paterson Marsh Ltd. No plays, scripts or poetry. Unsolicited mss considered. Brief e-mail enquiry preferred, with outline (non-fiction) synopsis and two chapters (fiction).

MBA Literary Agents Ltd★
62 Grafton Way, London W1T 5DW
☎020 7387 2076 Fax 020 7387 2042
✉ firstname@mbalit.co.uk
www.mbalit.co.uk
Contacts *Diana Tyler, John Richard Parker, Meg Davis, Laura Longrigg, David Riding, Sophie Gorell Barnes, Susan Smith, Jean Kitson*
Founded 1971. Handles fiction and non-fiction, TV, film, radio and theatre scripts. Works in conjunction with agents in most countries. Also UK representative for Donald Maass Agency, Frances Collin Literary Agency, Martha Millard Literary Agency and the JABberwocky Agency. In November 2006, the Merric Davidson Literary Agency became part of MBA. COMMISSION Home 15%; Overseas 20%; Theatre/TV/Radio 10%; Film 10–20%. See website for submission details.

Christy Moore Ltd
See **Sheil Land Associates Ltd**

William Morris Agency (UK) Ltd★
CentrePoint Tower, 103 Oxford Street, London WC1A 1DD
☎020 7534 6800 Fax 020 7534 6900
www.wma.com
Managing Director *Caroline Michel*
London office founded in 1965. Worldwide talent and literary agency with offices in New York, Beverly Hills, Nashville, Miami and Shanghai. Handles fiction, general non-fiction, TV and film scripts. COMMISSION TV 10%; UK Books 15%; US Books & Translation 20%. Mss for books including covering letter to Book Department; single page synopsis, s.a.e. Limit submission to one title; sample to 50 pages or less. Telephone in the first instance for screenplay and TV submissions. No reading fee.

Michael Motley Ltd
The Old Vicarage, Tredington, Tewkesbury GL20 7BP

☎01684 276390 Fax 01684 297355
Contact *Michael Motley*
Founded 1973. Handles only full-length mss (adult: 60,000+; children's – all ages – and humour: length variable). No short stories or journalism. No science fiction, horror, poetry or original dramatic material. COMMISSION Home 10%; US 15%; Translation 20%. New clients by referral only: no unsolicited material considered. No reading fee.

Judith Murdoch Literary Agency★
19 Chalcot Square, London NW1 8YA
☎020 7722 4197
Contact *Judith Murdoch*
Founded 1993. Handles full-length fiction only, especially accessible literary and popular women's fiction. No science fiction/fantasy, children's, poetry or short stories. CLIENTS include Anne Bennett, Alison Bond, Meg Hutchinson, Lisa Jewell, Pamela Jooste, Eve Makis. Translation rights handled by The Marsh Agency. COMMISSION Home 15%; US & Translation 20%. No unsolicited mss; approach in writing only enclosing first two chapters and brief synopsis. Submissions by e-mail cannot be considered. Return postage/s.a.e. essential. Editorial advice given. No reading fee.

The Narrow Road Company
182 Brighton Road, Coulsdon CR5 2NF
☎020 8763 9895 Fax 020 8763 2558
✉ richardireson@narrowroad.co.uk
Contact *Richard Ireson*
Founded 1986. Part of the Narrow Road Group. Theatrical literary agency. Handles scripts for TV, theatre, film and radio. No novels or poetry. CLIENTS include Ron Aldridge, Geoff Aymer, Steve Gooch, Joe Graham, Renny Krupinski, Simon McAllum, Tim Sanders. No unsolicited mss or e-mail attachments; approach by letter with c.v. only. Interested in writers with some experience in theatre and radio

The Maggie Noach Literary Agency★
Unit 4, 246 Acklam Road, London W10 5YG
☎020 8748 2926
✉ info@mnla.co.uk
www.mnla.co.uk
Contact *Address material to the Company.*
Founded 1982. Pronounced 'no-ack'. Will consider high quality full-length fiction and general non-fiction (especially biography, travel, history) only. No short stories, poetry, plays,

screenplays, cookery, gardening, mind, body and spirit, scientific/academic or specialist non-fiction. Absolutely no illustrated books. COMMISSION Home 15%; US & Translation 20%. No submissions from authors resident outside the UK. Initial approach should consist of a brief description plus two/three sample chapters. Return postage essential. 'We do not open e-mail attachments or consider faxed submissions.' No reading fee.

Andrew Nurnberg Associates Ltd★
Clerkenwell House, 45–47 Clerkenwell Green, London EC1R 0QX
☎020 7417 8800 Fax 020 7417 8812
✉ all@nurnberg.co.uk

Directors *Andrew Nurnberg, Sarah Nundy, D. Roger Seaton, Vicky Mark*

Founded in the mid-1970s. Specialises in foreign rights, representing leading authors and agents. Branches in Moscow, Budapest, Prague, Sofia, Warsaw, Riga, Beijing and Taipei. COMMISSION Home 15%; US & Translation 20%.

Alexandra Nye
'Craigower', 6 Kinnoull Avenue, Dunblane FK15 9JG
☎01786 825114

Contact *Alexandra Nye*

Founded 1991. Handles fiction and topical non-fiction. Special interests: literary fiction and history. CLIENTS include Dr Tom Gallagher, Harry Mehta, Robin Jenkins. COMMISSION Home 10%; US 20%; Translation 15%. Unsolicited mss welcome (s.a.e. essential for return). No phone calls. Preliminary approach by letter, with synopsis, preferred. Reading fee for supply of detailed report.

David O'Leary Literary Agents
10 Lansdowne Court, Lansdowne Rise, London W11 2NR
☎020 7229 1623 Fax 020 7229 1623
✉ d.oleary@dsl.pipex.com

Contact *David O'Leary*

Founded 1988. Handles fiction, both popular and literary, and non-fiction. Areas of interest include thrillers, history, popular science, Russia and Ireland (history and fiction). No poetry or science fiction. CLIENTS include David Crackanthorpe, James Kennedy, Nick Kochan, Jim Lusby, Derek Malcolm, Ken Russell. COMMISSION Home & US 10%. OVERSEAS ASSOCIATES Lennart Sane, Scandinavia/Spain/South America; Tuttle Mori, Japan. No unsolicited mss

but happy to discuss a proposal. Ring or write in the first instance. No reading fee.

Deborah Owen Ltd★
78 Narrow Street, Limehouse, London E14 8BP
☎020 7987 5119/5441 Fax 020 7538 4004

Contact *Deborah Owen*

Founded 1971. Small agency specialising in only representing two authors direct around the world. *No new authors.* CLIENTS Amos Oz and Delia Smith. COMMISSION Home 10%; US & Translation 15%.

Paterson Marsh Ltd★
11/12 Dover Street, London W1S 4LJ
☎020 7399 2800 Fax 020 7399 2801
✉ submissions@patersonmarsh.co.uk
www.patersonmarsh.co.uk

Contact *Stephanie Ebdon*

Originally founded in 1961 as Mark Paterson & Associates. World rights representatives of authors and publishers with specialisation in psychoanalysis, psychotherapy and related fields. CLIENTS include the estates of Sigmund and Anna Freud, Donald Winnicott, Michael Balint and Wilfred Bion. Also interested in narrative non-fiction, health and neuroscience. Visit website for further information. COMMISSION 20% (including sub-agent's commission). See also The Marsh Agency Ltd. No fiction, scripts, poetry, children's, articles or short stories. Unsolicited mss considered. Send outline and sample chapter.

John Pawsey
60 High Street, Tarring, Worthing BN14 7NR
☎01903 205167 Fax 01903 205167

Contact *John Pawsey*

Founded 1981. Handles non-fiction only: biography, current affairs, popular culture, sport. Special interests: sport and biography. No fiction, children's, drama scripts, poetry, short stories, journalism, academic or submissions from outside the UK. CLIENTS include David Rayvern Allen, Elwyn Hartley Edwards, William Fotheringham, Don Hale, Patricia Hall, Gary Imlach, Anne Mustoe, Matt Rendell. COMMISSION Home 12½%; US & Translation 19–25%. OVERSEAS ASSOCIATES in the US, Japan, South America and throughout Europe. Preliminary letter with s.a.e. essential (no e-mail submissions). No reading fee.

Maggie Pearlstine Associates★
31 Ashley Gardens, Ambrosden Avenue,
London SW1P 1QE
☎020 7828 4212 Fax 020 7834 5546
✉ maggie@pearlstine.co.uk
Contact *Maggie Pearlstine*
Founded 1989. Small agency representing a
select few authors. CLIENTS include Matthew
Baylis, Roy Hattersley, Claire Macdonald, Prof.
Raj Persaud, Prof. Lesley Regan, Henrietta
Spencer-Churchill, Prof. Robert Winston. No
new authors. Translation rights handled by
Aitken Alexander Associates Ltd.

Peters Fraser & Dunlop Group Ltd
See **PFD**

PFD★
Drury House, 34–43 Russell Street, London
WC2B 5HA
☎020 7344 1000
Fax 020 7836 9539/7836 9541
✉ postmaster@pfd.co.uk
www.pfd.co.uk
Joint Chairmen *St John Donald, Maureen Vincent*
Books *Caroline Dawnay, Michael Sissons, Pat
Kavanagh, Charles Walker, Rosemary Canter,
Robert Kirby, Simon Trewin, James Gill, Anna
Webber*
Serial *Pat Kavanagh, Carol MacArthur*
Film/TV *Anthony Jones, Tim Corrie, Charles
Walker, St John Donald, Natasha Galloway,
Jago Irwin, Louisa Thompson, Lynda Mamy,
Andrew Naylor, Alice Dunne*
Actors *Maureen Vincent, Dallas Smith, Lindy
King, Ruth Young, Duncan Hayes, Hannah
Begbie, Duncan Millership*
Theatre *Kenneth Ewing, St John Donald, Nicki
Stoddart, Rose Cobbe*
Children's *Rosemary Canter*
PFD represents authors of fiction and non-
fiction, children's writers, screenwriters, play-
wrights, documentary makers, technicians,
presenters and actors throughout the world.
Consult the website for submission guidelines.

Pollinger Limited★
9 Staple Inn, London WC1V 7QH
☎020 7404 0342 Fax 020 7242 5737
✉ info@pollingerltd.com
www.pollingerltd.com
Managing Director *Lesley Pollinger*
Agents *Lesley Pollinger, Joanna Devereux, Tim
Bates, Ruth Needham*

Permissions *Electronic form available on website*
Rights Manager *rightsmanager@pollingerltd.com*
Consultants *Leigh Pollinger, Joan Deitch*
CLIENTS include Michael Coleman, Catherine
Fisher, Philip Gross, Kelly McKain, Sue
Mongredien, Jeremy Poolman, Nicholas Rhea
and Michal Snunit. Also the estates of H.E.
Bates, Erskine Caldwell, Rachel Carson, D.H.
Lawrence, John Masters, Carson McCullers,
Alan Moorehead, W. Heath Robinson, Eric
Frank Russell, Clifford D. Simak and other nota-
bles. COMMISSION Home 15%; Translation 20%.
Overseas, theatrical and media associates. No
unsolicited material.

Shelley Power Literary Agency Ltd★
13 rue du Pré Saint Gervais, 75019 Paris,
France
☎00 33 1 42 38 36 49 Fax 00 33 1 40 40 70 08
✉ shelley.power@wanadoo.fr
Contact *Shelley Power*
Founded 1976. Shelley Power works between
London and Paris. This is an English agency
with London-based administration/accounts
office and the editorial office in Paris. Handles
general commercial fiction, quality fiction, business books, self-help, true crime, investigative
exposés, film and entertainment. No scripts,
short stories, children's or poetry. COMMISSION
Home 10%; US & Translation 19%. Preliminary
letter with brief outline of project (plus return
postage as from UK or France) essential. 'We do
not consider submissions by e-mail.' No reading
fee.

Puttick Agency★
46 Brookfield, Highgate West Hill, London
N6 6AT
☎020 8340 6383 Fax 0870 751 8098
✉ enquiries@puttick.com
www.puttick.com
Contact *Liz Puttick*
Founded 1995. Handles general non-fiction
with special interest in self-help, health and
popular culture. Also interested in current affairs,
biography, history, philosophy, science. No
fiction, poetry, scripts, drama or children's books.
COMMISSION Home 15%; US & Translation 20%.
Works with associates in the US for translation
rights. Preliminary enquiries and c.v. by e-mail.
No reading fee, but s.a.e. essential.

PVA Management Limited
Hallow Park, Worcester WR2 6PG

☎01905 640663 Fax 01905 641842
✉ pvamanltd@aol.com
www.pva.co.uk

Managing Director *Paul Vaughan*

Founded 1978. Handles non-fiction only. COMMISSION 15%. Send synopsis and sample chapters together with return postage.

Real Creatives Worldwide

14 Dean Street, London W1D 3RS
☎020 7437 4188
✉ malcolm.rasala@realcreatives.com
www.TVmyworld.com

Contacts *Mark Maco, Malcolm Rasala*

Founded 1984. Specialises in drama, science, technology, factual and entertainment. Represents Hollywood TV and film writers and directors. Has a production arm making motion pictures, television, commercials, etc. Send first 30 pages only initially.

Redhammer Management Ltd★

186 Bickenhall Mansions, Bickenhall Street, London W1U 6BX
☎020 7486 3465 Fax 020 7000 1249
✉ info@redhammer.info
www.redhammer.info

Vice President *Peter Cox*

'Provides in-depth management for a small number of highly talented authors.' Willing to take on unpublished authors who are professional in their approach and who have major international potential, ideally for, book, film and/or tv. CLIENTS Martin Bell OBE, John Brindley, Brian Clegg, Joe Donnelly, Audrey Eyton, Maria Harris, Senator Orrin Hatch, Amanda Lees, David McIntee, Hon. Nicholas Monson, Michelle Paver, Carolyn Soutar, Carole Stone, Donald Trelford, Justin Wintle, David Yelland. Submissions considered only if the guidelines given on the website have been followed. Do not send unsolicited mss by post. No radio or theatre scripts. No reading fee.

Rogers, Coleridge & White Ltd★

20 Powis Mews, London W11 1JN
☎020 7221 3717 Fax 020 7229 9084

Chairman *Deborah Rogers*
Managing Director *Peter Straus*
Directors *Gill Coleridge, Pat White, David Miller, Zoe Waldie, Laurence Laluyaux, Stephen Edwards*

Founded 1967. Handles full-length mss fiction, non-fiction and children's books. COMMISSION

Home 15%; US & Translation 20%. No submissions by fax or e-mail.

Uli Rushby-Smith Literary Agency

72 Plimsoll Road, London N4 2EE
☎020 7354 2718 Fax 020 7354 2718

Contact *Uli Rushby-Smith*

Founded 1993. Handles fiction and non-fiction, commercial and literary, both adult and children's. Film and TV rights handled in conjunction with a sub-agent. No plays or poetry. COMMISSION Home 15%; US & Translation 20%. Represents UK rights for 2.13.61 USA and Columbia University Press. Approach with an outline, two or three sample chapters and explanatory letter in the first instance (s.a.e. essential). No disks. No reading fee.

Rosemary Sandberg Ltd

6 Bayley Street, London WC1B 3HB
☎020 7304 4110
✉ rosemary@sandberg.demon.co.uk

Contact *Rosemary Sandberg*

Founded 1991. In association with Ed Victor Ltd. Specialises in children's writers and illustrators. COMMISSION 10%. No unsolicited mss as client list is currently full.

The Sayle Literary Agency★

1 Petersfield, Cambridge CB1 1BB
☎01223 303035 Fax 01223 301638
www.sayleliteraryagency.com

Contact *Rachel Calder*

Handles literary, crime and general fiction, current affairs, social issues, travel, biography, history, general non-fiction. No plays, poetry, children's, textbooks, technical, legal or medical books. COMMISSION Home 15%; US & Translation 20%. OVERSEAS ASSOCIATES Dunow & Carlson & Lerner Literary Agency; Darhansoff, Verrill Feldman; Anne Edelstein Literary Agency; New England Publishing Associates, USA; translation rights handled by The Marsh Agency; film rights by Sayle Screen Ltd. No unsolicited mss. Preliminary letter essential, including a brief biographical note and a synopsis plus two or three sample chapters. Return postage essential. No reading fee.

Sayle Screen Ltd

11 Jubilee Place, London SW3 3TD
☎020 7823 3883 Fax 020 7823 3363
✉ info@saylescreen.com
www.saylescreen.com

Agents *Jane Villiers, Matthew Bates, Toby Moorcroft*

Specialises in writers and directors for film and television. Also deals with theatre and radio. Works in association with The Sayle Literary Agency and Greene & Heaton Ltd representing film and TV rights in novels and non-fiction. CLIENTS include Shelagh Delaney, Marc Evans, Margaret Forster, John Forte, Rob Green, Mark Haddon, Christopher Monger, Paul Morrison, Gitta Sereny, Sue Townsend. No unsolicited material without preliminary letter. No e-mail submissions.

The Sharland Organisation Ltd
The Manor House, Manor Street, Raunds
NN9 6JW
☎01933 626600 Fax 01933 624860
✉ tsoshar@aol.com
www.sharlandorganisation.co.uk
Contacts *Mike Sharland, Alice Sharland*

Founded 1988. Specialises in national and international film and TV negotiations. Also negotiates multimedia, interactive TV deals and computer game contracts. Handles scripts for film, TV, radio and theatre; also non-fiction. Markets books for film and handles stage, radio, film and TV rights for authors. No scientific, technical or poetry. COMMISSION Home 15%; US & Translation 20%. OVERSEAS ASSOCIATES various. No unsolicited mss. Preliminary enquiry by letter or phone essential.

Sheil Land Associates Ltd★
(incorporating **Richard Scott Simon Ltd 1971** and **Christy Moore Ltd 1912**)
52 Doughty Street, London WC1N 2LS
☎020 7405 9351 Fax 020 7831 2127
✉ info@sheilland.co.uk
Agents, UK & US *Sonia Land, Vivien Green, Ben Mason*
Film/Theatrical/TV *Emily Hayward, Sophie Janson*
Foreign *Gaia Banks, Sophie LeGrande*

Founded 1962. Handles full-length general, commercial and literary fiction and non-fiction, including: social politics, business, history, science, military history, gardening, thrillers, crime, romance, drama, biography, travel, cookery and humour, UK and foreign estates. Also theatre, film, radio and TV scripts. CLIENTS include Peter Ackroyd, Hugh Bicheno, Melvyn Bragg, David Cohen, Catherine Cookson estate, Anna del Conte, Seamus Deane, Greg Dyke, Bonnie Greer, Susan Hill, Richard Holmes, HRH The Prince of Wales, Mark Irving, Richard Mabey,

Patrick O'Brian estate, Jean Rhys estate, Graham Rice, Martin Riley, Catherine Sampson, Diane Setterfield, Tom Sharpe, Martin Stephen, Brian Sykes, Jeffrey Tayler, Andrew Taylor, Rose Tremain, Barry Unsworth, John Wilsher, Toby Young. COMMISSION Home 15%; US & Translation 20%. OVERSEAS ASSOCIATES Georges Borchardt, Inc. (Richard Scott Simon). US film and TV representation: CAA, APA, and others. Welcomes approaches from new clients either to start or to develop their careers. Preliminary letter with s.a.e. essential. No reading fee.

Caroline Sheldon Literary Agency Ltd★
70–75 Cowcross Street, London EC1M 6EJ
☎01983 760205/020 7336 6550
✉ carolinesheldon@carolinesheldon.co.uk *and*
pennyholroyde@carolinesheldon.co.uk
www.carolinesheldon.co.uk

Also at: Thorley Manor Farm, Thorley, Yarmouth PO41 0SJ
Contacts *Caroline Sheldon, Penny Holroyde*

Founded 1985. Handles fiction and children's books. Special interests: all fiction for women, sagas, suspense, contemporary, chick-lit, historical fiction, fantasy and comic novels. Non-fiction: true life stories, memoirs, humour, quirky, animal interest. Children's books: fiction for all age groups, contemporary, comic, fantasy and all major genres including fiction series. Picture book stories. Non-fiction. Children's illustration: all quality illustrations. COMMISSION Home 15%; US & Translation 20%; Film & TV 15%. Send submissions by post or e-mail to Thorley address above. 'Include introductory information about yourself and ambitions and the first three chapters of your book.' If sending by e-mail, type 'Submission' in subject line. Send large s.a.e. for postal submissions. No reading fee. 'We do not represent TV or film scripts except for current clients. Editorial advice given on work of exceptional promise.'

Dorie Simmonds Agency★
Riverbank House, 1 Putney Bridge Approach, London SW6 3JD
☎020 7736 0002 Fax 020 7569 8696
✉ dhsimmonds@aol.com
Contact *Dorie Simmonds*

Handles a wide range of subjects including commercial fiction and non-fiction, children's books and associated rights. Specialities include contemporary personalities and historical biographies, commercial women's fiction and children's books. COMMISSION Home & US 15%; Translation 20%. Outline required for non-fiction; a short synopsis for fiction with 2–3 sample chapters, and a c.v. with writing experience/publishing history. No reading fee. Return postage essential.

Jeffrey Simmons
15 Penn House, Mallory Street, London NW8 8SX
☎020 7224 8917
✉ jasimmons@btconnect.com
Contact *Jeffrey Simmons*
Founded 1978. Handles biography and autobiography, cinema and theatre, fiction (both quality and commercial), history, law and crime, politics and world affairs, parapsychology and sport (but not exclusively). No science fiction/fantasy, children's books, cookery, crafts, hobbies or gardening. Film scripts handled only if by book-writing clients. Special interest in personality books of all sorts and fiction from young writers (i.e. under 40) with a future. COMMISSION Home 10–15%; US & Foreign 15%. Writers become clients by personal introduction or by letter, enclosing a synopsis if possible, a brief biography, a note of any previously published books, plus a list of any publishers and agents who have already seen the mss.

Richard Scott Simon Ltd
See **Sheil Land Associates Ltd**

Sinclair-Stevenson
3 South Terrace, London SW7 2TB
☎020 7581 2550 Fax 020 7581 2550
Contact *Christopher Sinclair-Stevenson*
Founded 1995. Handles biography, current affairs, travel, history, fiction, the arts. No scripts, children's, academic, science fiction/fantasy. CLIENTS include Jennifer Johnston, J.D.F. Jones, Ross King, Christopher Lee, Andrew Sinclair and the estates of Alec Guinness, John Cowper Powys and John Galsworthy. COMMISSION Home 10%; US 15%; Translation 20%. OVERSEAS ASSOCIATE T.C. Wallace Ltd, New York. Translation rights handled by David Higham Associates. Send synopsis with s.a.e. in the first instance. No reading fee.

Robert Smith
Literary Agency Ltd★
12 Bridge Wharf, 156 Caledonian Road, London N1 9UU
☎020 7278 2444 Fax 020 7833 5680
✉ robertsmith.literaryagency@virgin.net

Contact *Robert Smith*
Founded 1997. Handles non-fiction; biography, memoirs, current affairs, entertainment, true crime, cookery and lifestyle. No scripts, fiction, poetry, academic or children's books. CLIENTS Kate Adie (serialisations), Martin Allen, Amanda Barrie (serialisations), Kevin Booth, Judy Cook, Stewart Evans, Neil and Christine Hamilton, James Haspiel, Nikola T. James, Muriel Jakubait, Lois Jenkins, Roberta Kray, Jean MacColl, Ann Ming, Theo Paphitis, Mike Reid, Frances Reilly, Professor Bill Rubinstein, Keith Skinner. COMMISSION Home 15%; US & Translation 20%. No unsolicited mss. Send a letter and synopsis in the first instance. No reading fee.

The Standen Literary Agency
41b Endymion Road, London N4 1EQ
☎020 8292 0541 Fax 020 8292 0541
✉ info@standenliteraryagency.com
www.standenliteraryagency.com
Contact *Mrs Yasmin Standen*
Founded 2004. Handles fiction, both adult and children's. 'We are interested in first time writers.' No TV/radio scripts. CLIENTS include Jonathan Yeatman Biggs, Zara Kane, Zoe Marriott, Andrew Murray. COMMISSION Home 15%; Overseas 20%. Follow the submissions procedure on the website. 'With regard to non-fiction, please contact us in the first instance.' No reading fee.

Elaine Steel
110 Gloucester Avenue, London NW1 8HX
☎020 8348 0918 Fax 020 8341 9807
✉ ecmsteel@aol.com
Contact *Elaine Steel*
Founded 1986. Handles scripts, screenplays and books. No technical or academic. CLIENTS include Les Blair, Anna Campion, Michael Eaton, Pearse Elliott, Gwyneth Hughes, Brian Keenan, Troy Kennedy Martin, James Lovelock, Rob Ritchie, Albie Sachs, Ben Steiner. COMMISSION Home 10%; US & Translation 20%. Initial phone call preferred.

Abner Stein★
10 Roland Gardens, London SW7 3PH
☎020 7373 0456 Fax 020 7370 6316
Contact *Arabella Stein*
Founded 1971. Mainly represents US agents and authors but handles some full-length fiction and general non-fiction. No scientific, technical, etc. No scripts. COMMISSION Home 10%; US & Translation 20%.

Micheline Steinberg Associates

104 Great Portland Street, London W1W 6PE
☎020 7631 1310
✉ info@steinplays.com
www.steinplays.com

Contacts *Micheline Steinberg, Matt Connell, Helen MacAuley*

Founded 1988. Specialises in plays for stage, TV, film, animation and radio. Represents writers for film and TV rights in fiction and non-fiction on behalf of book agents. COMMISSION Home 10%; Overseas 15–20%. Works in association with agents in the USA and overseas. Return postage essential.

Shirley Stewart Literary Agency★

3rd Floor, 4A Nelson Road, London SE10 9JB
☎020 8293 3000 Fax 05601 161121

Director *Shirley Stewart*

Founded 1993. Handles fiction and non-fiction. No scripts, children's, science fiction, fantasy or poetry. COMMISSION Home 10–15%; US & Translation 20%. OVERSEAS ASSOCIATE Curtis Brown Ltd, New York; Carolyn Swayze Agency, Canada. Will consider unsolicited material; send letter with two or three sample chapters in the first instance. S.a.e. essential. Submissions by fax or on disk not accepted. No reading fee.

Sarah Such Literary Agency

81 Arabella Drive, London SW15 5LL
☎020 8876 4228 Fax 020 8878 8705
✉ sarah@sarahsuch.com

Director *Sarah Such*

Founded 2006. Former publisher with 17 years' experience. Handles high-quality literary and commercial non-fiction and fiction. 'Always looking for original work and new talented writers.' OVERSEAS ASSOCIATES worldwide. COMMISSION Home 15%; US & Translation 20%. Works by recommendation but welcomes unsolicited synopsis and sample chapter submissions. TV/film scripts for established clients only. No radio or theatre scripts, poetry, fantasy, self-help or short stories. Contact by e-mail with brief synopsis, author biog and first two chapters (as Word attachment). S.a.e. essential if postal submission. No unsolicited mss and no telephone submissions. No reading fee.

Sunflower Literary Agency

BP 14, Lauzerte 82110 France
✉ submission@sunflowerliteraryagency.com
www.sunflowerliteraryagency.com

Senior Editor *Paul Muller*

Correspondence Secretary *David Sherriff*

Founded 2003. Handles full-length fiction, especially thrillers (techno a plus); literary fiction, especially political and/or social satire (controversy a plus); erotica, in any of the above genres. No poetry, screenplays, non-fiction, short fiction, 'who-dunnits' or autobiography. COMMISSION Home 15% (first book), 10% (later books); USA & Translation: additional 5% to base rate. 'We *only* consider work from *unpublished* authors (or major changes of genre).' Electronic submissions preferred: first contact via the website then e-mail only. Please do not write to the above in the first instance. All requirements listed on the Web page must be fulfilled before e-mail contact is made. No fees charged.

The Susijn Agency Ltd

3rd Floor, 64 Great Titchfield Street, London W1W 7QH
☎020 7580 6341 Fax 020 7580 8626
✉ info@thesusijnagency.com
www.thesusijnagency.com

Contacts *Laura Susijn, Nicola Barr*

Founded April 1998. Specialises in selling rights worldwide in literary fiction and non-fiction. Also represents non-English language authors and publishers for UK, US and translation rights worldwide. COMMISSION Home 15%; US & Translation 15–20%. Send preliminary letter, synopsis and first two chapters by post. No reading fee.

The Tennyson Agency

10 Cleveland Avenue, Wimbledon Chase, London SW20 9EW
☎020 8543 5939
✉ submissions@tenagy.co.uk
www.tenagy.co.uk

Contacts *Christopher Oxford, Adam Sheldon*

Founded 2001. Specialises in theatre, radio, television and film scripts. Related material considered on an ad hoc basis. No short stories, children's, poetry, travel, military/historical, academic, fantasy, science fiction or sport. CLIENTS Vivienne Allen, Tony Bagley, Kristina Bedford, Alastair Cording, Caroline Coxon, Iain Grant, Jonathan Holloway, Julian Howell, Philip Hurd-Wood, Joanna Leigh, Antony Mann, Ken Ross, John Ryan, Walter Saunders, Diane Speakman, Diana Ward. COMMISSION Home 12½–15%; Overseas 17½–20%. No unsolicited material; send introductory letter with author's résumé and proposal/outline of work. No reading fee.

Lavinia Trevor Literary Agency★
29 Addison Place, London W11 4RJ
☎020 7603 5254 Fax 0870 129 0838
www.laviniatrevor.co.uk

Contact *Lavinia Trevor*

Founded 1993. Handles general fiction (literary and commercial) and non-fiction, including popular science. No fantasy, science-fiction, poetry, academic, technical or children's books. No TV, film, radio, theatre scripts. COMMISSION rate by agreement with author. 'Sorry - no unsolicited submissions.'

Jane Turnbull★
Mailing address: Barn Cottage, Veryan, Truro TR2 5QA
☎01872 501317
✉ jane.turnbull@btinternet.com

London office: 58 Elgin Crescent, London W11 2JJ
☎ 020 7727 9409

Contact *Jane Turnbull*

Founded 1986. Handles fiction and non-fiction but specialises in biography, history, current affairs, self-help and humour. Translation rights handled by Aitken Alexander Associates Ltd. COMMISSION Home 10%; US & Foreign 20%. No unsolicited mss. Approach with letter in the first instance. No reading fee.

Ed Victor Ltd★
6 Bayley Street, Bedford Square, London WC1B 3HE
☎020 7304 4100 Fax 020 7304 4111
✉ mary@edvictor.com

Contacts *Ed Victor, Maggie Phillips, Sophie Hicks, Grainne Fox, Charlie Campbell*
Foreign Rights Manager *Morag O'Brien*

Founded 1976. Handles a broad range of material but leans towards the more commercial ends of the fiction and non-fiction spectrums. Excellent children's book list. No poetry, scripts or academic. Takes on very few new writers and does not accept unsolicited submissions. After trying his hand at book publishing and literary magazines, Ed Victor, an ebullient American, found his true vocation. Strong opinions, very pushy and works hard for those whose intelligence he respects. Loves nothing more than a good title auction. CLIENTS include John Banville, Herbie Brennan, Eoin Colfer, Frederick Forsyth, A.A. Gill, Josephine Hart, Jack Higgins, Nigella Lawson, Kathy Lette, Allan Mallinson, Andrew Marr, Janet Street-Porter and the

estates of Douglas Adams, Raymond Chandler, Dame Iris Murdoch, Sir Stephen Spender and Irving Wallace. COMMISSION Home & US 15%; Translation 20%. No unsolicited mss.

Wade & Doherty Literary Agency Ltd
33 Cormorant Lodge, Thomas More Street, London E1W 1AU
☎020 7488 4171 Fax 020 7488 4172
✉ rw@rwla.com *or* bd@rwla.com
www.rwla.com

Contacts *Robin Wade, Broo Doherty*

Founded 2001. Handles general fiction and non-fiction including children's books. Specialises in military history and crime books. No scripts, poetry, plays or short stories. CLIENTS include Louise Cooper, Adam Guillain, Georgina Harding, Caroline Kington, Helen Oyeyemi, Lance Price, Ewen Southby-Tailyour. COMMISSION Home 10%; Overseas & Translation 20%. 'Fees negotiable if a contract has already been offered.' Send detailed synopsis and first 10,000 words by e-mail with a brief biography. No reading fee.

Cecily Ware Literary Agents
19C John Spencer Square, London N1 2LZ
☎020 7359 3787 Fax 020 7226 9828
✉ info@cecilyware.com

Contacts *Cecily Ware, Gilly Schuster, Warren Sherman*

Founded 1972. Primarily a film and TV script agency representing work in all areas: drama, children's, series/serials, adaptations, comedies, etc. COMMISSION Home 10%; US 10–20% by arrangement. No unsolicited mss or phone calls. Approach in writing only. No reading fee.

Watson, Little Ltd★
48–56 Bayham Place, London NW1 0EU
☎020 7388 7529 Fax 020 7388 8501
✉ office@watsonlittle.com
www.watsonlittle.com

Contacts *Mandy Little, James Wills, Isabel Atherton*

Handles fiction, commercial women's fiction, crime and literary fiction. Non-fiction special interests include history, science, popular psychology, self-help and general leisure books. Also children's fiction and non-fiction. No short stories, poetry, TV, play or film scripts. Not interested in purely academic writers. COMMISSION Home 15%; US & Translation 20%. OVERSEAS ASSOCIATE The Marsh Agency; FILM & TV ASSOCIATES The Sharland Organisation Ltd; MBA

Literary Agents Ltd; USA Howard Morhaim Literary Agency (adult); The Chudney Agency (children). Informative preliminary letter and synopsis with return postage essential.

A.P. Watt Ltd★

20 John Street, London WC1N 2DR
☎020 7405 6774 Fax 020 7831 2154
✉ apw@apwatt.co.uk
www.apwatt.co.uk

Directors *Caradoc King, Linda Shaughnessy, Derek Johns, Georgia Garrett, Natasha Fairweather, Sheila Crowley*

Founded 1875. The oldest-established literary agency in the world. Handles full-length type-scripts, including children's books, screenplays for film and TV. No poetry, academic or specialist works. CLIENTS include Trezza Azzopardi, David Baddiel, Sebastian Barry, Quentin Blake, Marika Cobbold, Michael Cox, Helen Dunmore, Nicholas Evans, Giles Foden, Esther Freud, Janice Galloway, Martin Gilbert, Nadine Gordimer, Linda Grant, Reginald Hill, Michael Holroyd, Michael Ignatieff, Mick Jackson, Philip Kerr, Dick King-Smith, India Knight, John Lanchester, Alison Lurie, Jan Morris, Andrew O'Hagan, Susie Orbach, Tony Parsons, Caryl Phillips, Philip Pullman, James Robertson, Jancis Robinson, Jon Ronson, Elaine Showalter, Zadie Smith, Graham Swift, Fiona Walker and the estates of Graves and Maugham. COMMISSION Home 15%; US & Translation 20%. No unsolicited mss accepted.

Josef Weinberger Plays

12–14 Mortimer Street, London W1T 3JJ
☎020 7580 2827 Fax 020 7436 9616
✉ general.info@jwmail.co.uk
www.josef-weinberger.com

Contact *Michael Callahan*

Josef Weinberger is both agent and publisher of scripts for the theatre. CLIENTS include Ray Cooney, John Godber, Peter Gordon, Debbie Isitt, Arthur Miller, Sam Shepard, John Steinbeck. OVERSEAS REPRESENTATIVES in the USA, Canada, Australia, New Zealand, India, South Africa and Zimbabwe. No unsolicited mss; introductory letter essential. No reading fee.

John Welch, Literary Consultant & Agent

Mill Cottage, Calf Lane, Chipping Camden GL55 6JQ
☎01386 840237 Fax 01386 840568
✉ johnwelch@cyphus.co.uk

Contact *John Welch*

Founded 1992. Handles military aviation and naval history, and history in general. No fiction, poetry, children's books or scripts for radio, TV, film or theatre. Already has a full hand of authors so no new authors being considered. CLIENTS include Alexander Baron, Michael Calvert, Patrick Delaforce, Timothy Jenkins, Sybil Marshall, Ewart Oakeshott, Peter Reid, Norman Scarfe, Anthony Trew, Peter Trew, David Wragg. COMMISSION Home 10%.

Eve White Literary Agent

1a High Street, Kintbury RG17 9TJ
☎01488 657656
✉ evewhite@btinternet.com
www.evewhite.co.uk

Contact *Eve White*

Founded 2003. Handles full-length adult and children's fiction and non-fiction. No poetry, short stories or textbooks. CLIENTS Teresa Cooper, Susannah Corbett, Jimmy Docherty, Rae Earl, Steve Emmerson, Shanta Everington, David E. Flavell, Marguerite Hann Syme, Peter J. Murray, Vijay Medtia, Alex Parsons, Gillian Rogerson, Andy Stanton. COMMISSION Home 15%; US & Translation 20%. Please see website for up-to-date submission requirements. No initial approach by e-mail or telephone. No reading fee.

Dinah Wiener Ltd★

12 Cornwall Grove, Chiswick, London W4 2LB
☎020 8994 6011 Fax 020 8994 6044

Contact *Dinah Wiener*

Founded 1985. Handles fiction and general non-fiction: auto/biography, popular science, cookery. No scripts, children's or poetry. CLIENTS include Valerie-Anne Baglietto, Malcolm Billings, Guy Burt, David Deutsch, Wendy K. Harris, Jenny Hobbs, Mark Jeffery, Michael Lockwood, Daniel Snowman, Mitchell Tonks, Rachel Trethewey, Marcia Willett. COMMISSION Home 15%; US & Translation 20%. Approach with preliminary letter in first instance, giving full but brief c.v. of past work and future plans. Mss submitted must include s.a.e. and be typed in double-spacing.

Rebecca Winfield Literary Agency

84 Cowper Road, London W7 1EJ
☎020 8567 6738 Fax 020 8567 6738
✉ rebecca.winfield@btopenworld.com

Contact *Rebecca Winfield*

Founded 2003; part of Luxton Harris Ltd

since January 2007. Specialises in non-fiction; biography, popular culture, history and narrative non-fiction. No children's books, science fiction, fantasy, horror or poetry. COMMISSION Home 15%; US & Translation 20%. Send letter, synopsis and no more than three sample chapters in the first instance together with s.a.e. for return of material. Submissions on disk or by e-mail not accepted. No reading fee.

The Wylie Agency (UK) Ltd

17 Bedford Square, London WC1B 3JA
☎020 7908 5900 Fax 020 7908 5901
✉ mail@wylieagency.co.uk

Handles fiction and non-fiction. No scripts or children's books. COMMISSION Home 10%; US 15%; Translation 20%. The Wylie Agency does not accept unsolicited submissions. Enquire by letter or e-mail before submitting. Any submission must be accompanied by return postage/s.a.e.

AGENCY CONSULTANTS

Agent Research & Evaluation, Inc. (AR&E)

425 North 20th Street, Philadelphia, PA 19130, USA
☎001 215 563 1867 Fax 001 215 563 6797
✉ info@agentresearch.com
www.agentresearch.uk.net

Contact *Bill Martin*

US consultancy founded in 1996. Provides authors, editors and other professionals with data on clients and sales made by literary agents in the USA, UK and Canada, i.e. who sells what to whom for how much. Information is culled from the trade and general press, and collection has been continuous since 1980. Individual reports on specific agents and various forms of manuscript-agent match-up services are available. See website for pricing or send s.a.e. Publishes *Talking Agents*, the AR&E newsletter (10 p.a.). The website offers a free service of agent verification: information on whether or not the database reflects that a given agent has created a public record of sales.

UK Literary Scouts

Literary scouts gather information from UK agents, publishers and editors on behalf of foreign clients. They are not literary agents and work only with material that is already commissioned or being handled by an agent. They do **not** accept unsolicited material and do **not** deal directly with writers.

Louise Allen-Jones Literary Scouts

5c Old Town, London SW4 0JT
☎020 7720 2453 Fax 020 7627 3510

Contacts *Louise Allen-Jones*
(louise@louiseallenjones.com), *Mira Popken* (mira@louiseallenjones.com), *Lucy Abrahams* (lucy@louiseallenjones.com)

Scouts for Ullstein Buchverlage (Ullstein hc/ ppbk, List, Claassen, Marion von Schroeder, Econ, Propyläen), Germany; AW Bruna (Bruna, VIP, Signature) and J.M. Meulenhoff Boekerij (Boekerij, Forum, Mynx, Arena, Meulenhoff), The Netherlands; Distribuidora Record, Brazil; Sperling & Kupfer, Italy; Keter Books, Israel; Oceanida, Greece; Bazar, Scandinavia (all four territories); The English Agency, Japan; BBC TV Drama, UK.

Badcock & Rozycki Literary Scouts

1 Old Compton Street, London W1D 5JA
☎020 7734 7997 Fax 020 7734 6886

Contacts *June Badcock*
(june@badcock-rozycki.co.uk), *Barbara Rozycki* (barbara@badcock-rozycki.co.uk), *Claire Holt* (claire@badcock-rozycki.co.uk)

Scouts for Wilhelm Heyne Verlag and Diana Verlag, Germany; Unieboek BV, The Netherlands; RCS Libri Group, Italy; Editions Jean-Claude Lattès, France; Ediciones Salamandra, Spain; Ellinika Grammata, Greece; Werner Söderström Osakeyhtiö, Finland; Forum, Sweden; NW Damm & Son A/S, Norway; Aschehoug Dansk Forlag, Denmark; Edda Media, Iceland.

Natasha Farrant

77 Starfield Road, London W12 9SN
☎020 8746 1857
✉ natasha.farrant@btinternet.com

Contact *Natasha Farrant*

Scouts for children's fiction on behalf of Hachette Jeunesse, France; Edizione Piemme, Italy; Lerner Publishing Group, USA; Carlsen Verlag, Germany; Jane Southern Literary Scout.

Anne Louise Fisher

29 D'Arblay Street, London W1F 8EP
☎020 7494 4609 Fax 020 7494 4611
✉ annelouise@alfisher.co.uk

Contacts *Anne Louise Fisher, Catherine Eccles*

Scouts for Doubleday/Broadway Books/Nan Talese/Spiegel & Grau, US; Doubleday/Bond Street Books, Canada; Librairie Plon, Univers Poche/Pocket Jeunesse, France; Karl Blessing Verlag, C. Bertelsmann, Knaus, Blanvalet, DVA/ Siedler/Pantheon, C. Bertelsmann Jugenbuch, Germany; Arnoldo Mondadori Editore, Oscar and Mondadori Ragazzi, Italy; Albert Bonniers Forlag, Sweden; Otava, Finland; Gyldendal Norsk Forlag, Norway; Gyldendal, Denmark; Mouria, Holland; Random House Mondadori and Montena, Spain; Patakis Publications, Greece, Heyday Films, UK.

Folly Marland, Literary Scout

6 Elmcroft Street, London E5 0SQ
☎020 8986 0111 Fax 020 8986 0111
✉ fmarland@pobox.com

Contact *Folly Marland*

Scouts for Scherz Verlag, Krüger Verlag, Germany; Livani, Greece; FMG: Truth & Dare, Pimento, The Netherlands.

Rosalind Ramsay Limited

First Floor, 2 Ingate Place, London SW8 3NS
☎020 7622 3336
✉ ros@rosalindramsay.com
www.rosalindramsay.com

Contacts *Rosalind Ramsay, Naomi Colvin*
Assistant *Ben Fowler*
Office Manager *Lindsey Clarke*

Scouts for Ambo Anthos and Uitgeverij Artemis, The Netherlands; Kadokawa Shoten, Japan; Kiepenheuer and Witsch, Germany; Droemer Knaur, Germany; Kinneret Zmora Bitan Dvir, Israel; Norstedts Forlagsgrupp, Sweden; Il Saggiatore, Italy; Santillana Ediciones General, Spain; Editora Objetiva, Brazil; Channel 4 and FilmFour, UK.

Heather Schiller

✉ heather.schiller@virgin.net

Contact *Heather Schiller*

Scouts for Prometheus, The Netherlands; Cappelen, Norway; Piper, Germany; Lindhardt & Ringhof, Denmark.

Petra Sluka

3 Dry Bank Road, Tonbridge TN10 3BS
☎01732 353694
✉ petrasluka@petrasluka.plus.com

Contact *Petra Sluka*

Scouts for Verlagsgruppe Lübbe, Gemany; De Fontein/De Kern, Holland; J'ailu, France; Bra Böcker, Sweden; Japan Uni Agency, Inc., Japan; Harlenic Hallas, Greece.

Jane Southern

11 Russell Avenue, Bedford MK40 3TE
☎01234 400147

✉ jane.southern@ntlworld.com

Contact *Jane Southern*

UK Scout for Der Club, Germany; The House of Books, The Netherlands; Belfond, Presses de la Cité and France Loisirs, France; Newton Compton, Italy; Damm Forlag, Sweden; Planeta Group, Spain; Dom Quixote, Portugal; Minoas, Greece; Owls Agency, Japan.

Sylvie Zannier-Betts

114 Springfield Road, Brighton BN1 6DE
☎01273 557370 Fax 01273 557370
✉ szannier@lineone.net

Contact *Sylvie Zannier-Betts*

Scouts for Uitgeverij De Geus, The Netherlands; S. Fischer Verlag, Germany; Gummerus Publishers, Finland; Alfabeta Bokfoerlag, Sweden; Borgen Forlag, Denmark. Exclusive agent in the UK for S. Fischer Verlag, Germany.

PR Consultants

Claire Bowles Publicity
Ashley Court, Ashley, Market Harborough
LE16 8HF
☎01858 565800 Fax 01858 565811
www.clairebowlespr.co.uk
Contact *Claire Bowles*
Represents non-fiction: The Good Pub Guide;
Oz Clarke. CLIENTS include Workman (US);
Artisan; BBC Books; Ebury Press; Time Out;
David & Charles; Little, Brown; Weidenfeld &
Nicolson; Virgin Books.

Maria Boyle Communications
36 Shalstone Road, Mortlake SW14 7HR
☎020 8876 8444
✉ maria@mbcomms.co.uk
www.mbcomms.co.uk
Director *Maria Boyle*
Handles PR projects for some of the UK's leading
publishers. Named as one of the top seven PRs
in the UK by the Institute of Public Relations.
Works for a range of consumer and corporate
clients. 'One area of specialism includes developing and delivering media campaigns that
jump off the books pages and feature in the
main body of newspapers and magazines, on
national high profile TV and radio programmes
and online.' CLIENTS include Penguin Classics;
Pearson Booktime.

Cameron Publicity and Marketing
35 Edward Road, Farnham GU9 8NP
☎07903 951957
✉ ben@cameronpm.co.uk
www.cameronpm.co.uk
Contact *Ben Cameron*
Represents publishers and authors. CLIENTS
include Anova Books; Anthem Press; Hachette
Children's Books (Hodder and Orchard);
Pinwheel.

Colbert Macalister PR
7 Killieser Avenue, London SW2 5NU
☎020 8671 6615
✉ ailsa@colmacpr.co.uk
www.colbertmacalister.co.uk
Contacts *Ailsa Macalister, Diana Colbert*

Represents publishers' lists and authors. CLIENTS
include John Blake Publishing; Random House;
Faber & Faber; Hay House; Bonnie; Robert
Hale; Absolute Press.

Colman Getty
28 Windmill Street, London W1T 2JJ
☎020 7631 2666 Fax 020 7631 2699
✉ info@colmangetty.co.uk
www.colmangetty.co.uk
Handles prizes, book campaigns, authors,
publishers' lists, professional associations. CLIENTS
include The Man Booker Prize for Fiction;
World Book Day; National Poetry Day; Icon
Books; Frankfurt Book Fair.

Day Five Ltd
1 Archibald Road, London N7 0AN
☎020 7619 0098
✉ eobr@blueyonder.co.uk
Contact *Emma O'Bryen*
Represents publishers' lists and individual book
projects. CLIENTS include Frances Lincoln
Publishers; Macmillan; Natural History
Museum.

FMcM Associates
3rd Floor, Colonial Buildings, 59–61 Hatton
Garden, London EC1N 8LS
☎020 7405 7422 Fax 020 7405 7424
✉ publicity@fmcm.co.uk
www.fmcm.co.uk
Managing Director *Fiona McMorrough*
Founded 1998. Represents authors, publishers'
lists, literary festivals, industry associations.
Winner of two Publishers Publicity Circle
Awards, and the inaugural Hospital Award for
Creative Contribution to Book Publishing.
Specialises in publishing, literature, the arts
and events. CLIENTS include Margaret Atwood;
Marian Keyes; Maggie O'Farrell; Tracy Chevalier;
Althorp Literary Festival; Cadogan Guides;
Frommer's Guides; Canongate; Cape; Penguin;
Little, Brown; Headline; HarperCollins; Fourth
Estate; Short Books; Independent Alliance.

Cathy Frazer PR

Old Hayle Barn, Hayle Farm, Marle Place Road, Horsmonden TN12 8DZ
☎01892 724156 Fax 01892 724155
✉ cathyfrazer@hotmail.com

Contact *Cathy Frazer*

Handles illustrated non-reference, consumer education, children's books; subjects include wine, food, antiques, sport, languages, health, parenting. Individual authors also represented. Over 20 years of publishing experience. CLIENTS include Hodder Education; Hodder Children's Books; Virgin; Mitchell Beazley; Millers; DBP; Kingfisher; Carol Vorderman; Uri Geller; Viscount Linley; Sir Patrick Moore; Carol Smillie; Lorraine Kelly; Peter Allis; Jonty Hearnden; Eric Knowles; Judith Miller; Marguerite Patten; Sarah Kennedy.

Gotch Solutions

Flat 1, 10 Holmdene Avenue, London SE24 9LF
☎020 7733 0882
✉ gotchsolutions@btinternet.com

Contact *Corinne Gotch*

Represents authors, publishers' lists, including children's; awards. CLIENTS include Romantic Novelists' Association; Wingedchariot Press; Hodder Arnold.

Idea Generation

11 Chance Street, London E2 7JB
☎020 7428 4949 Fax 020 7428 4948
✉ hector@ideageneration.co.uk
www.ideageneration.co.uk

Managing Director *Hector Proud*

Arts and entertainment PR consultancy, working across the arts, photography, publishing, museums, film, TV, media and lifestyle sectors. Specialises in PR for illustrated, arts and photographic books. CLIENTS include Gloria Books; Genesis Publications; Vision On Publishing; Dazed Publishing; Waddell Publishing.

Andrea Marks Public Relations

146 Edgwarebury Lane, Edgware HA8 8NE
☎020 8958 4398 Fax 020 8905 3727
✉ info@andreamarks.co.uk
www.andreamarks.co.uk

Contacts *Andrea Marks, Melanie Abbey*

Corporate PR for publishers, booksellers, publishers' lists (not individual titles), prizes and awards, events, projects and initiatives, professional associations. CLIENTS include Borders UK; Egmont UK; Romantic Novel of the Year.

MGA

190 Shaftesbury Avenue, London WC2H 8JL
☎020 7836 4774 Fax 020 7836 4775
✉ mag@mga-pr.com
www.mga-pr.com

Managing Director *Beth Macdougall*
Director *Bethan Jones*

Formerly Macdougall Gabriel Associates. Handles publishers' lists and authors. CLIENTS include (publishers' lists) English Heritage; National Archives; Chaucer Press; Mercury Books; Mercury Junior; Ravenhall Books; Asia Ink. Selected books for Penguin; Constable & Robinson; Spellmount; Tempus. Authors include Brian Aldiss; Bowvayne; Dinah Lampitt/Deryn Lake.

Louise Page PR

☎020 8741 5663 Fax 020 8741 5663
✉ louise@lpagepr.co.uk

Contact *Louise Page*

PR for fiction and non-fiction authors. CLIENTS include Maeve Binchy; Martina Cole; Wendy Holden.

Platypus PR

2 Tidy Street, Brighton BN1 4EL
☎01273 692215
✉ info@platypuspr.com

Contact *Jeff Scott*

Represents publishers, authors, including self-published authors. CLIENTS include Cambridge University Press; Simon & Schuster; Dorling Kindersley; Pearson Education; various independent publishers. Books handled have won the Sunday Times Political Book of the Year 2005 and Economist Best Book 2006: Politics & Current Affairs.

Nicky Potter

181 Alexandra Park Road, London N22 7UL
☎020 8889 9735
✉ nicpot@dircon.co.uk

Contact *Nicky Potter*

Represents publishers' lists, prizes and professional organisations. CLIENTS include Booktrust (for the Children's Laureate); School Library Association (SLA School Librarian of the Year Award); Marsh Award for Children's Literature in Translation; Frances Lincoln; Barrington Stoke.

Publishing Services

9 Curwen Road, London W12 9AF
☎020 8222 6800 Fax 020 8222 6799

✉ susanne@publishing-services.co.uk
www.publishing-services.co.uk
Handles publishers and authors. Third-party associates include book distributor Central Books; sales agency Signature Book Services; and Edgar Book Services. Publishers: mainly niche publishers such as Green Books and educational/reference publisher Lucas Publications. Authors: the emphasis is on media-friendly authors capable of selling a minimum of 5000 copies. Areas of interest include country/green; politics/current affairs; English language/reference; history, biography, autobiography; quirky idiosyncratic books. No children's books, poetry, plays or screenplays.

Sonia Pugh PR
☎01375 891063
✉ sonia.pugh@ntlworld.com
Contact *Sonia Pugh*
Independent PR consultancy which handles illustrated non-fiction books in all areas including launches, etc.

Sally Randall PR
Forty Acre Oast, Woodchurch, Ashford
TN26 3PW
☎01233 860670
✉ sallyrandall@reynoldsm.f2s.com
Contact *Sally Randall*
Handles general fiction and non-fiction, independent publishers' lists, individual authors/titles, arts. CLIENTS include Meet the Author; Galore Park; Simon & Schuster; Michael O'Mara.

Claire Sawford PR
Studio One, 7 Chalcot Road, London
NW1 8LH
☎020 7722 4114
✉ cs@cspr.uk.net
www.cspr.uk.net
Contact *Claire Sawford*
Handles authors, publishers, prizes and professional associations. Specialises in non-fiction: art, architecture, fashion, design, biography. CLIENTS include V&A Publications; RIBA Bookshops; Royal Academy of Arts; National Portrait Gallery; Gill Hicks.

National Newspapers

Departmental e-mail addresses are too numerous to include in this listing. They can be obtained from the newspaper's main switchboard or the department in question

Daily Express
The Northern & Shell Building, No. 10 Lower Thames Street, London EC3R 6EN
☎0871 434 1010
www.express.co.uk
Owner *Northern & Shell Media/Richard Desmond*
Editor *Peter Hill*
Circulation 760,086

Under owner Richard Desmond, publisher of *OK!* magazine, the paper features a large amount of celebrity coverage. The general rule of thumb is to approach in writing with an idea; all departments are prepared to look at an outline without commitment. Ideas welcome but already receives many which are 'too numerous to count'.

News Editor *Greg Swift*
Diary (Hickey Column) *Kathryn Spencer*
Features Editor *Heather Preen*
City Editor *Stephen Kahn*
Political Editor *Macer Hall*
Sports Editor *Bill Bradshaw*
Planning Editor (News Desk) should be circulated with copies of official reports, press releases, etc., to ensure news desk cover at all times.
Saturday magazine. Editor *Graham Bailey*
PAYMENT negotiable.

Daily Mail
Northcliffe House, 2 Derry Street, London W8 5TT
☎020 7938 6000
Owner *Associated Newspapers/Lord Rothermere*
Editor *Paul Dacre*
Circulation 2.3 million

In-house feature writers and regular columnists provide much of the material. Photo-stories and crusading features often appear; it's essential to hit the right note to be a successful Mail writer. Close scrutiny of the paper is strongly advised. Not a good bet for the unseasoned. Accepts news on savings, building societies, insurance, unit trusts, legal rights and tax.

News Editor *Keith Poole*
City Editor *Alex Brummer*
'Money Mail' Editor *Tony Hazell*

Political Editor *Benedict Brogan*
Education Correspondent *Sarah Harris*
Diary Editor *Richard Kay*
Features Editor *Leaf Kalfayan*
Literary Editor *Jane Mays*
Head of Sport *Tim Jotischky*
Femail Editor *Lisa Collins*
Weekend Saturday supplement. Editor *Charlotte Kemp*

Daily Mirror
1 Canada Square, Canary Wharf, London E14 5AP
☎020 7293 3000 Fax 020 7293 3409
www.mirror.co.uk
Owner *Trinity Mirror plc*
Editor *Richard Wallace*
Circulation 1.54 million

No freelance opportunities for the inexperienced, but strong writers who understand what the tabloid market demands are always needed.

Deputy Editor *Conor Hanna*
News Editor *Anthony Harwood*
Features Editor *Carole Watson*
Political Editor *Oonagh Blackman*
Business Editor *Clinton Manning*
Showbusiness Diary Editor *Eva Simpson*
Sports Editor *Dean Morse*

Daily Record
One Central Quay, Glasgow G3 8DA
☎0141 309 3000 Fax 0141 309 3340
✉ reporters@dailyrecord.co.uk
www.record-mail.co.uk
Owner *Trinity Mirror plc*
Editor *Bruce Waddell*
Circulation 404,187

Mass-market Scottish tabloid. Freelance material is generally welcome.

News Editor *Tom Hamilton*
Features Editor *Melanie Harvey*
Political Editor *Magnus Gardham*
Assistant Editor (Sport) *James Traynor*
Magazine Editor *Jayne Savva*

Scotland Means Business Quarterly business magazine, launched 2002. Editor *Magnus Gardham*

Daily Sport

19 Great Ancoats Street, Manchester M60 4BT
☎0161 236 4466 Fax 0161 236 4535
www.dailysport.co.uk
Owner *Sport Newspapers Ltd*
Editor *David Beevers*
Circulation 200,000

Tabloid catering for young male readership. Unsolicited material welcome; send to News Editor, *Jane Field-Harris*
Sports Editor *Marc Smith*

Lads Mag Monthly glossy magazine. Editor *Mark Harris.*

Daily Star

The Northern & Shell Building, No. 10 Lower Thames Street, London EC3R 6EN
☎0871 434 1010
Owner *Northern & Shell Media/Richard Desmond*
Editor *Dawn Neesom*
Circulation 770,313

In competition with *The Sun* for off-the-wall news and features. Freelance opportunities available.
Deputy Editor *Ben Knowles*
Assistant Editor, Features *Lizzie Hosking*
Sports Editor *Howard Wheatcroft*

Daily Star Sunday

The Northern & Shell Building, No. 10 Lower Thames Street, London EC3R 6EN
☎0871 434 1010 Fax 0871 434 2941
✉ michael.booker@dailystar.co.uk
www.dailystar.co.uk
Owner *Northern & Shell Media/Richard Desmond*
Editor *Gareth Morgan*
Circulation 383,231

Launched in September 2002 in direct competition with *News of the World* and *The People.*

Supplement: *Take5* Lifestyle/showbiz magazine.

The Daily Telegraph

111 Buckingham Palace Road, London SW1W 0DT
☎020 7931 2000
www.telegraph.co.uk
Owner *Telegraph Media Group*
Editor *William Lewis*
Circulation 898,817

Unsolicited mss not generally welcome – 'all are carefully read and considered, but very few published'. Contenders should approach the paper in writing, making clear their authority for writing on that subject. No fiction.
Arts Editor *Sarah Crompton*
City Editor *Damien Reece*
Political Editor *George Jones*
Diary Editor *Celia Walden* Always interested in diary pieces.
Education *John Clare*
Environment *Charles Clover*
Features Editor *Liz Hunt* Most material supplied by commission from established contributors. New writers are tried out by arrangement with the features editor. Approach in writing. Maximum 1500 words.
Literary Editor *Sam Leith*
Sports Editor *Keith Perry* Occasional opportunities for specialised items.
Style Editor *Georgina Cover*
PAYMENT by arrangement.

Daily Telegraph Weekend Saturday supplement. Editor *Jon Stock*
Telegraph Magazine. Editor *Michele Lavery*

Financial Times

1 Southwark Bridge, London SE1 9HL
☎020 7873 3000 Fax 020 7873 3076
✉ firstname.lastname@ft.com
www.ft.com
Owner *Pearson*
Editor *Lionel Barber*
Circulation 452,930

Founded 1888. UK and international coverage of business, finance, politics, technology, management, marketing and the arts. All feature ideas must be discussed with the department's editor in advance. Not snowed under with unsolicited contributions – they get less than any other national newspaper. Approach by e-mail with ideas in the first instance.
News Editor *Robert Shrimsley*
Features Editor *Brian Groom*
Arts Editor *Jan Dalley*
Financial Editor *Andrew Hill*
Book and Art Editor, *FT Magazine Rosie Blau*
Literary Editor *Jan Dalley*
Education *Jon Boone*
Environment *Fiona Harvey*
Political Editor *James Blitz*
Leisure Industries *Roger Blitz*

Weekend FT Editor *Michael Skapinker*
How to Spend It Monthly magazine. Editor *Gillian de Bono*

The Guardian

119 Farringdon Road, London EC1R 3ER
☎020 7278 2332 Fax 020 7837 2114
✉ firstname.secondname@guardian.co.uk
www.guardian.co.uk

Owner *The Scott Trust*
Editor *Alan Rusbridger*
Circulation 366,556

Of all the nationals *The Guardian* probably offers the greatest opportunities for freelance writers, if only because it has the greatest number of specialised pages which use freelance work. Read specific sections before submitting mss.

Deputy Editor *Paul Johnson* No opportunities except in those regions where there is presently no local contact for news stories.

Literary Editor *Claire Armitstead*
City Editor *Julia Finch*
G2 Editor *Katharine Viner*
Technology Editor *Charles Arthur* Thursday supplement.
Diary Editor *Jon Henley*
Education Editor *Rebecca Smithers*
Environment *John Vidal*
Features Editor *Katharine Viner*
Guardian Society Patrick Butler Focuses on all public service activity.
Media Editor *Matt Wells*
Political Editor *Patrick Wintour*
Sports Editor *Ben Clissitt*
Women's Page *Kira Cochrane* Runs three days a week.

The Guardian Weekend Glossy Saturday issue.
Editor *Merope Mills*
The Guide Editor *Malik Meer*

The Herald (Glasgow)

200 Renfield Street, Glasgow G2 3PR
☎0141 302 7000 Fax 0141 302 7007
www.theherald.co.uk

Owner *Gannett UK Ltd*
Editor *Charles McGhee*
Circulation 73,834

One of the oldest national newspapers in the English-speaking world, *The Herald*, which dropped its 'Glasgow' prefix in February 1992, was bought by Scottish Television in 1996 and by Newsquest in 2003. Lively, quality, national Scottish daily broadsheet. Approach with ideas in writing or by phone in first instance.

News Editor *Magnus Llewellin*
Arts Editor *Keith Bruce*
Business Editor *Ian McConnell*
Diary *Ken Smith*
Education *Andrew Denholm*

Sports Editor *Donald Cowey*
Herald Magazine Editor *Kathleen Morgan*

The Independent

Independent House, 191 Marsh Wall, London E14 9RS
☎020 7005 2000 Fax 020 7005 2999
www.independent.co.uk

Owner *Independent Newspapers*
Editor *Simon Kelner*
Circulation 249,536

Founded 1986. Particularly strong on its arts/media coverage, with a high proportion of feature material. Theoretically, opportunities for freelancers are good. However, unsolicited mss are not welcome; most pieces originate in-house or from known and trusted outsiders. Ideas should be submitted in writing.

Executive News Editor *Dan Gledhill*
Features *Adam Leigh*
Arts Editor *David Lister*
Business Editor *Jeremy Warner*
Education *Richard Garner*
Environment *Michael McCarthy*
The Independent Extra Editor *Ruth Metzstein*
Literary Editor *Boyd Tonkin*
Political Editor *Andrew Grice*
Sports Editor *Matt Tench*
Travel Editor *Simon Calder*

The Independent Magazine Saturday supplement.
Editor *Laurence Earle*
The Independent Traveller 32-page Saturday magazine
The Information Editor *Jo Ellison*

Independent on Sunday

Independent House, 191 Marsh Wall, London E14 9RS
☎020 7005 2000 Fax 020 7005 2999
www.independent.co.uk

Owner *Independent Newspapers*
Editor *Tristan Davies*
Circulation 244,809

Founded 1986. Regular columnists contribute most material but feature opportunites exist. Approach with ideas in first instance.

Executive Editor (News) *Andy Malone*
News Editor *Peter Victor*
Focus Editor *Cole Moreton*
Arts Editor *Ian Irvine*
Comment Editor *James Hanning*
Business Editor *Andrew Murram-Watson*
Literary Editor *Suzi Feay*
Environment *Geoffrey Lean*
Political Editor *Marie Woolf*

Sports Editor *Neil Morton*
Travel Editor *Kate Simon*
The New Review supplement. Editor *Bill Tuckey*

International Herald Tribune

6 bis, rue des Graviers, 92521 Neuilly, Paris
☎0033 1 4143 9322
Fax 0033 1 4143 9338 (editorial)
✉ iht@iht.com
www.iht.com

Executive Editor *Michael Oreskes*
Managing Editor *Alison Smale*
Features Editor *Katherine Knorr*
Circulation 241,000
Published in France, Monday to Saturday, and circulated in Europe, the Middle East, North Africa, the Far East and the USA. General news, business and financial, arts and leisure. Uses regular freelance contributors. Contributor policy can be found on the website at: www.iht.com/contributor.htm

The Mail on Sunday

Northcliffe House, 2 Derry Street, London W8 5TS
☎020 7938 6000 Fax 020 7937 3829

Owner *Associated Newspapers/Lord Rothermere*
Editor *Peter Wright*
Circulation 2.33 million

Sunday paper with a high proportion of newsy features and articles. Experience and judgement required to break into its band of regular feature writers.

News Editor *David Dillon*
Financial Editor *Lisa Buckingham*
Diary Editor *Katie Nicholl*
Features Editor/Women's Page *Sian James*
Books *Marilyn Warnick*
Political Editor *Simon Walters*
Sports Editor *Malcolm Vallerius*
Live Night & Day Editor *Gerard Greaves*
Review Editor *George Thwaites*

You – The Mail on Sunday Magazine Colour supplement. Many feature articles, supplied entirely by freelance writers. Editor *Sue Peart*, Features Editor *Rosalind Lowe*

Morning Star

William Rust House, 52 Beachy Road, London E3 2NS
☎020 8510 0815 Fax 020 8986 5694
✉ morsta@geo2.poptel.org.uk

Owner *Peoples Press Printing Society*
Editor *John Haylett*
Circulation 9000

Not to be confused with the *Daily Star*, the *Morning Star* is the farthest left national daily. Those with a penchant for a Marxist reading of events and ideas can try their luck, though feature space is as competitive here as in the other nationals.

News Editor *Dan Coysh*
Features & Arts Editor/Political Editor *Richard Bagley*
Foreign Editor *Dave Williams*
Sports Editor *Karl Stewart*

News of the World

1 Virginia Street, London E98 1NW
☎020 7782 1000 Fax 020 7583 9504
www.newsoftheworld.co.uk

Owner *News International plc/Rupert Murdoch*
Editor *Colin Myler*
Circulation 3.28 million

Highest circulation Sunday paper. Freelance contributions welcome. News and features editors welcome tips and ideas.

Deputy Editor *Neil Wallis*
Assistant Editor (News) *Ian Edmondson*
Features Editor *Jules Stenson*
Political Editor *Ian Kirby*
Sports Editor *Mike Dunn*

Sunday Magazine Colour supplement. Editor *Louise Oswald* Showbiz interviews and strong human-interest features make up most of the content, but there are no strict rules about what is 'interesting'. Unsolicited mss and ideas welcome.

The Observer

3–7 Herbal Hill, London EC1R 5EJ
☎020 7278 2332 Fax 020 7837 7817
✉ firstname.surname@observer.co.uk
www.observer.co.uk

Owner *Guardian Newspapers Ltd*
Editor *Roger Alton*
Circulation 463,128

Founded 1791. Acquired by Guardian Newspapers from Lonrho in May 1993. Occupies the middle ground of Sunday newspaper politics.

Unsolicited material is not generally welcome, 'except from distinguished, established writers'. Receives far too many unsolicited offerings already. No news, fiction or special page opportunities. The newspaper runs annual competitions which change from year to year. Details are advertised in the newspaper.

Executive Editor, News *Kamal Ahmed*
Home News Editor *Lucy Rock*

Foreign News Editor *Tracy McVeigh*
Crime Correspondent *Mark Townsend*
Foreign Affairs Editor *Peter Beaumont*
Home Affairs Editor *Jamie Doward*
Investigations Editor *Antony Barnett*
Sports News and Social Affairs Correspondent *Denis Campbell*
Culture and Society Correspondent *Amelia Hill*
Political Editor *Gaby Hinsliff*
Chief Political Correspondent *Ned Temko*
Arts Editor *Sarah Donaldson*
Review Editor *Jane Ferguson*
Comment Editor *Ruaridh Nicoll*
Deputy Business Editor/City Editor *Richard Wachman*
Business Editor *Ruth Sunderland*
Personal Finance Editor *Jill Insley*
Science Editor *Robin McKie*
Education Correspondent *Anushka Asthana*
Environment and Transport Editor *Juliette Jowit*
Literary Editor *Robert McCrum*
Travel Editor *Joanne O'Connor*
Sports Editor *Brian Oliver*

The Observer Magazine Glossy arts and lifestyle supplement. Editor *Allan Jenkins*
The Observer Sport Monthly Magazine supplement launched in 2000. Editor *Brian Oliver*
The Observer Food Monthly Launched in 2001. Editor *Nicola Jeal*
The Observer Music Monthly Launched in 2003. Editor *Caspar Llewellyn Smith*
Observer Woman Launched in 2006. Editor *Nicola Jeal*

The People
1 Canada Square, Canary Wharf, London E14 5AP
☎020 7293 3437 Fax 020 7293 3517
www.people.co.uk
Owner *Trinity Mirror plc*
Editor *Mark Thomas*
Circulation 721,667

Slightly up-market version of *The News of the World*. Keen on exposés and big-name gossip. Interested in ideas for investigative articles. Phone in first instance.
News Editor *Lee Harpin*
Features Editor *Chris Bucktin*
Political Editor *Nigel Nelson*
Sports Editor *Lee Horton*

Take It Easy Magazine supplement. Editor *Maria Coole* Approach by phone with ideas in first instance.

Scotland on Sunday
Barclay House, 108 Holyrood Road, Edinburgh EH8 8AS
☎0131 620 8620 Fax 0131 620 8491
www.scotlandonsunday.com
Owner *Scotsman Publications Ltd*
Editor *Les Snowdon*
Circulation 75,240

Scotland's top-selling quality broadsheet. Welcomes ideas rather than finished articles.
Assistant Editor *Kenny Farquharson*
News Editor *Peter Laing*
Arts Editor *Fiona Leith*

Spectrum Colour supplement. Features on personalities, etc. Editor *Clare Trodden*

The Scotsman
Barclay House, 108 Holyrood Road, Edinburgh EH8 8AS
☎0131 620 8620 Fax 0131 620 8616 (editorial)
✉ enquiries@scotsman.com
www.scotsman.com
Owner *Johnston Press*
Editor *Mike Gilson*
Circulation 58,128

Scotland's national newspaper. Many unsolicited mss come in, and stand a good chance of being read, although a small army of regulars supply much of the feature material not written in-house. See website for contact details.
News Editor *James Hall*
Business Editor *Nick Bevens*
Education *Kevin Schofield*
Features Editor *Jackie Hunter*
Arts Editor *Andy Eaton*
Book Reviews *David Robinson*
Sports Editor *Donald Walker*

The Sun
1 Virginia Street, London E98 1SN
☎020 7782 4000 Fax 020 7782 4108
✉ firstname.lastname@the-sun.co.uk
www.the-sun.co.uk
Owner *News International Ltd/Rupert Murdoch*
Editor *Rebekah Wade*
Circulation 3.05 million

Highest circulation daily. Populist outlook; very keen on gossip, pop stars, TV soap, scandals and exposés of all kinds. No room for non-professional feature writers; 'investigative journalism' of a certain hue is always in demand, however.
Head of News *Chris Pharo*
Head of Features *Dominic Mohan*
Head of Sport *Steve Waring*
Woman's Editor *Sharon Hendry*

Health Editor *Jane Symons*
Fashion Editor *Erica Davies*

Sunday Express

The Northern & Shell Building, Number 10 Lower Thames Street, London EC3R 6EN
☎0871 434 1010 Fax 0871 434 7300
Owner *Northern & Shell Media/Richard Desmond*
Editor *Martin Townsend*
Circulation 739,298

The general rule of thumb is to approach in writing with an idea; all departments are prepared to look at an outline without commitment.

News Editor *Stephen Rigley*
Features Editor *Giulia Rhodes*
Business Editor *Lawrie Holmes*
Political Editor *Julia Hartley-Brewer*
Sports Editor *Scott Wilson*

S Fashion and lifestyle magazine for women. Editor *Louise Robinson* No unsolicited mss. All contributions are commissioned. Ideas in writing only.

PAYMENT negotiable.

Sunday Herald

200 Renfield Street, Glasgow G2 3QB
☎0141 302 7800 Fax 0141 302 7815
✉ editor@sundayherald.com
www.sundayherald.com

Owner *Newsquest*
Editor *Richard Walker*
Circulation 56,611

Also at: 9/10 St Andrew Square, Edinburgh EH2 2AF
☎ 0131 718 6040 Fax 0131 718 6105

Launched February 1999. Scottish seven-section compact.

Deputy Editor *David Milne*
News Editor *Charlene Sweeney*
Political Editor *Paul Hutcheon*
Sports Editor *Stephen Penman*
Entertainment Editor *Graeme Virtue*
Magazine Editor *Jane Wright*

Sunday Mail

One Central Quay, Glasgow G3 8DA
☎0141 309 3000 Fax 0141 309 3587
www.sundaymail.co.uk

Owner *Trinity Mirror plc*
Editor *Allan Rennie*
Circulation 507,279

Popular Scottish Sunday tabloid.

News Editor *Brendan McGinty*
Sports Editor *George Cheyne*

7Days Weekly supplement. Editor *Liz Cowan*

Sunday Mirror

1 Canada Square, Canary Wharf, London E14 5AP
☎020 7293 3000 Fax 020 7293 3939 (news desk)
www.sundaymirror.co.uk

Owner *Trinity Mirror*
Editor *Tina Weaver*
Circulation 1.4 million

In general terms contributions are welcome, though the paper patiently points out it has more time for those who have taken the trouble to study the market. Initial contact in writing preferred, except for live news situations. No fiction.

News Editor *James Saville* The news desk is very much in the market for tip-offs and inside information. Contributors would be expected to work with staff writers on news stories. Approach by telephone or fax in the first instance.

Finance *Melanie Wright*
Features Editor *Nicky Dawson* 'Anyone who has obviously studied the market will be dealt with constructively and courteously.' Cherishes its record as a breeding ground for new talent.

Sports Editor *David Walker*

Celebs on Sunday Colour supplement. Editor *Mel Brodie*

Sunday Post

2 Albert Square, Dundee DD1 9QJ
☎01382 575791 Fax 01382 201064
✉ tmckay@sundaypost.com
www.sundaypost.com

Owner *D.C. Thomson & Co. Ltd*
Editor *David Pollington*
Circulation 468,414

Contributions should be addressed to the editor.

post plus Monthly colour supplement. Editor *Jan Gooderham*

Sunday Sport

19 Great Ancoats Street, Manchester M60 4BT
☎0161 236 4466 Fax 0161 236 4535
www.sundaysport.com

Owner *David Sullivan*
Editor *Paul Carter*
Circulation 98,682

Founded 1986. Sunday tabloid catering for a particular sector of the male 15–35 readership. As concerned with 'glamour' (for which, read:

'page 3') as with human interest, news, features and sport. Unsolicited mss are welcome; receives about 90 a week. Approach should be made by phone in the case of news and sports items, by letter for features. All material should be addressed to the news editor.

News Editor *Nick Appleyard* Off-beat news, human interest, preferably with photographs.

Showbiz Editor *Tanya Jones* Regular items: showbiz, television, films, pop music and gossip.

Sports Editor *Marc Smith* Hard-hitting sports stories on major soccer clubs and their personalities, plus leading clubs/people in other sports. Strong quotations to back up the news angle essential.

PAYMENT negotiable and on publication.

The Sunday Telegraph
111 Buckingham Palace Road, London SW1W 0DT
☎020 7931 2000 Fax 020 7531 2936
www.telegraph.co.uk
Owner *Press Holdings Limited*
Editor *Patience Wheatcroft*
Circulation 666,905

Right-of-centre quality Sunday paper which, although traditionally formal, has pepped up its image to attract a younger readership. Unsolicited material from untried writers is rarely ever used. Contact with idea and details of track record.

News Editor *Tim Woodward*
Seven Editor *Ross Jones*
City Editor *Dan Roberts*
Political Editor *Patrick Hennessy*
Education Editor *Julie Henry*
Arts Editor *To be appointed*
Environment Editor *David Harrison*
Literary Editor *Michael Prodger*
Diary Editor *Tim Walker*
Sports Editor *Jon Ryan*

Stella Magazine Colour supplement. Editor *Anna Murphy*

The Sunday Times
1 Pennington Street, London E98 1ST
☎020 7782 5000 Fax 020 7782 5658
www.sunday-times.co.uk
Owner *News International plc/Rupert Murdoch*
Editor *John Witherow*
Circulation 1.23 million

Founded 1820. Tendency to be anti-establishment, with a strong crusading investigative tradition. Approach the relevant editor with an idea in writing. Close scrutiny of the style of each section of the paper is strongly advised before sending mss. No fiction. All fees by negotiation.

News Editor *Charles Hymas* Opportunities are very rare.

News Review Editor *Eleanor Mills* Submissions are always welcome, but the paper commissions its own, uses staff writers or works with literary agents, by and large. The features sections where most opportunities exist are *Style* and *The Culture*.

Culture Editor *Helen Hawkins*
Business Editor *John Waples*
City Editor *Grant Ringshaw*
Education Correspondent *Geraldine Hackett*
Science and Environment Editor *Jonathan Leake*
Literary Editor *Susannah Herbert*
Sports Editor *Alex Butler*
Style Editor *Tiffanie Darke*

Sunday Times Magazine Colour supplement. Editor *Robin Morgan* No unsolicited material. Write with ideas in first instance.

The Times
1 Pennington Street, London E98 1TT
☎020 7782 5000 Fax 020 7488 3242
www.thetimes.co.uk
Owner *News International plc/Rupert Murdoch*
Editor *Robert Thomson*
Circulation 629,157

Generally right (though features can range in tone from diehard to libertarian). *The Times* receives a great many unsolicited offerings. Writers with feature ideas should approach by letter in the first instance. No fiction.

Deputy Editor *Ben Preston*
News Editor *John Wellman*
Features Editor *Michael Harvey*
City/Financial Editor *James Hardwig*
Diary Editor *Hugo Rifkind*
Arts Editor *Alex O'Connell*
Literary Editor *Erica Wagner*
Political Editor *Phil Webster*
Sports Editor *Tim Hallissey*

The Times Magazine Saturday supplement. Editor *Gill Morgan*
Times 2 Editor *Sandra Parsons*

Regional Newspapers

ENGLAND

Berkshire

Reading Evening Post
8 Tessa Road, Reading RG1 8NS
☎0118 918 3000 Fax 0118 959 9363
✉ editorial@reading-epost.co.uk
Owner *Guardian Media Group*
Editor *Andy Murrill*
Circulation 15,720

Unsolicited mss welcome; one or two received every day. Fiction rarely used. Interested in local news features, human interest, well-researched investigations. Special sections include holidays & travel; children's page (Tues); style page (Wed); business (Mon–Fri); motorcycling; food page; gardening; reviews; rock music (Thurs); motoring (Fri). Also magazines, *Food Monthly* and *Business Monthly*.

Cambridgeshire

Cambridge Evening News
Winship Road, Milton, Cambridge CB4 6PP
☎01223 434434 Fax 01223 434415
Owner *Cambridge Newspapers Ltd*
Editor *Murray Morse*
Circulation 28,371
  Deputy Editor *James Foster*
  News Editor *John Deex*
  Business Editor *Jenny Chapman*
  Sports Editor *Chris Gill*

Cheshire

Trinity Mirror Cheshire
Chronicle House, Commonhall Street, Chester CH1 2AA
☎01244 340151 Fax 01244 606498
✉ eric.langton@cheshirenews.co.uk
www.iccheshireonline.co.uk
Owner *Trinity Mirror Plc*
Editor-in-Chief *Eric Langton*

All unsolicited feature material will be considered.

Cleveland

Hartlepool Mail
New Clarence House, Wesley Square, Hartlepool TS24 8BX
☎01429 239333 Fax 01429 869024
✉ mail.news@northeast-press.co.uk
www.hartlepooltoday.co.uk
www.peterleetoday.co.uk
Owner *Johnston Press Plc*
Editor *Joy Yates*
Circulation 18,992
  Deputy Editor *Brian Nuttney*
  News Editor *Pete McCusker*
  Sports Editor *Roy Kelly*

Cumbria

News & Star
Newspaper House, Dalston Road, Carlisle CA2 5UA
☎01228 612600 Fax 01228 612601
Owner *Cumbrian Newspaper Group Ltd*
Editor *Neil Hodgkinson*
Circulation 24,053
  Deputy Editor *Richard Eccles*
  Sports Editor *Vic Gibson*
  Women's Page *Jane Loughran*

North West Evening Mail
Abbey Road, Barrow in Furness LA14 5QS
☎01229 821835 Fax 01229 840164
✉ news@nwemail.co.uk
www.nwemail.co.uk
Owner *Robin Burgess*
Editor *Stephen Brauner*
Circulation 19,280

All editorial material should be addressed to the editor.
  Sports Editor *Frank Cassidy*

Derbyshire

Derby Evening Telegraph
Northcliffe House, Meadow Road, Derby DE1 2DW
☎01332 291111
✉ newsdesk@derbytelegraph.co.ukA

Owner *Northcliffe Media Group Ltd*
Editor *Steve Hall*
Circulation 45,522
  Acting News Editor *Emma Slee*
  (newsdesk@derbytelegraph.co.uk)
  Sports Editor *Peter Green*
  (sports@derbytelegraph.co.uk)
  Motoring Editor *Bob Maddox*

Devon

Express & Echo
Heron Road, Sowton, Exeter EX2 7NF
☎01392 442211 Fax 01392 442294 (editorial)
✉ echonews@expressandecho.co.uk
www.thisisexeter.co.uk
Owner *Westcountry Publications Limited*
Editor *Marc Astley*
Circulation 22,179
Weekly supplements: *Business Week*; *Property Echo*; *Wheels*; *Weekend Echo*.
  Head of Content *Sue Kemp*
  Features Editor *Lynne Turner*
  Sports Editor *Richard Davies* (Fax 01392 442416)

Herald Express
Harmsworth House, Barton Hill Road, Torquay TQ2 8JN
☎01803 676000 Fax 01803 676228 (editorial)
✉ newsdesk@heraldexpress.co.uk
www.thisissouthdevon.co.uk
Owner *Northcliffe Media Group Ltd*
Editor *Andy Phelan*
Circulation 25,261
Drive scene, property guide, *On The Town* (leisure and entertainment guide), Monday sports, special pages, rail trail, Saturday surgery, nature and conservation column, dance scene, shop scene, The Business. Supplements: *Gardening* (weekly); *Visitors Guide* and *Antiques & Collectables* (fortnightly). Unsolicited mss generally not welcome. All editorial material should be addressed to the editor in writing.

The Herald
17 Brest Road, Derriford Business Park, Derriford, Plymouth PL6 5AA
☎01752 765500 Fax 01752 765527
✉ news@eveningherald.co.uk
www.thisisplymouth.co.uk
Owner *Northcliffe Media Group Ltd*
Editor *Bill Martin*
Circulation 40,736

All editorial material to be addressed to the editor or the News Editor, *James Garnett*.

Western Morning News
17 Brest Road, Derriford Business Park, Derriford, Plymouth PL6 5AA
☎01752 765500 Fax 01752 765535
✉ wmnnewsdesk@westernmorningnews.co.uk
www.thisisdevon.co.uk
www.thisiscornwall.co.uk
Owner *Northcliffe Media Group Ltd*
Editor *Alan Qualtrough*
Circulation 43,036
Unsolicited mss welcome, but must be of topical and local interest and addressed to the Deputy Editor, *Philip Bowern*.
  News Editor *Steve Grant*
  Features Editor *Su Carroll*
  Sports Editor *Mark Stephens*

Dorset

Daily Echo
Richmond Hill, Bournemouth BH2 6HH
☎01202 554601 Fax 01202 299543
Owner *Newsquest Media Group Ltd (a Gannett company)*
Editor *Neal Butterworth*
Circulation 33,347
Founded 1900. Has a strong news and features content and invites specialist articles, particularly on unusual subjects, either contemporary or historical, but only with a local angle or flavour. Special review sections each day, including sport, property, entertainment and culture, heritage, motoring, gardening, the environment and the coastline. Also *Saturday Magazine* and monthly *Society* glossy magazine. All editorial material should be addressed to the Editor, *Neal Butterworth*. PAYMENT on publication.

Dorset Echo
Fleet House, Hampshire Road, Granby Industrial Estate, Weymouth DT4 9XD
☎01305 830930 Fax 01305 830956
www.dorsetecho.co.uk
Owner *Newsquest Media Group Ltd (a Gannett company)*
Editor *David Murdock*
Circulation 19,112
By-gone days, films, arts, showbiz, brides, motoring, property, weekend leisure and entertainment including computers and gardening and weekend magazine.

News Editor *Paul Thomas*
Sports Editor *Nigel Dean*

Durham

The Northern Echo
Priestgate, Darlington DL1 1NF
☎01325 381313 Fax 01325 380539
✉ echo@nne.co.uk
www.thenorthernecho.co.uk
Owner *Newsquest (North East) Ltd (a Gannett company)*
Editor *Peter Barron*
Circulation 50,675

Founded 1870. Freelance pieces welcome but telephone first to discuss submission.

Assistant Editor (News) *Nigel Burton* Interested in reports involving the North East or North Yorkshire. Preferably phoned in.

Features Editor *Lindsay Jennings* Background pieces to topical news stories relevant to the area. Must be arranged with the features editor before submission of any material.

Business Editor *Julia Breen*
Sports Editor *Nick Loughlin*
PAYMENT and length by arrangement.

Essex

Echo Newspapers
Newspaper House, Chester Hall Lane, Basildon SS14 3BL
☎0844 477 4512 Fax 0844 477 4286
Owner *Newsquest Media Group (a Gannett company)*
Editor *Martin McNeill*
Circulation 36,531

Relies almost entirely on staff and regular outside contributors, but will very occasionally consider material sent on spec. Approach the editor in writing with ideas. Although the paper is Basildon-based, its largest circulation is in the Southend area.

Evening Gazette (Colchester)
Oriel House, 43–44 North Hill, Colchester CO1 1TZ
☎01206 506000 Fax 01206 508274
✉ gazette_newsdesk@nqe.com
www.evening-gazette.co.uk
Owner *Newsquest (Essex) Ltd*
Editor *Irene Kettle*
Circulation 23,142

Monday to Friday daily newspaper servicing north and mid-Essex including Colchester,

Harwich, Clacton, Braintree, Witham, Maldon and Chelmsford. Unsolicited mss not generally used. Relies heavily on regular contributors.

Features Editor *Iris Clapp*

Gloucestershire

The Citizen
6–8 The Oxebode, Gloucester GL1 1RZ
☎01452 424442 Fax 01452 420664 (editorial)
✉ citizen.news@glosmedia.co.uk
www.thisisgloucestershire.co.uk
Owner *Northcliffe Newspapers Group Ltd*
Editor *Ian Mean*
Circulation 26,907

News or features material should be addressed to News Editor, *Jenny Eastwood* or Features Editor, *Tanya Gledhill*.

Gloucestershire Echo
1 Clarence Parade, Cheltenham GL50 3NY
☎01242 271900 Fax 01242 271848
www.thisisgloucestershire.co.uk
Owner *Northcliffe Media Group Ltd*
Editor *Anita Syvret*
Circulation 22,033

All material, other than news, should be addressed to the editor.

News Editor *Sam Shepherd*

Hampshire

The News
The News Centre, Hilsea, Portsmouth PO2 9SX
☎023 9266 4488 Fax 023 9267 3363
✉ newsdesk@thenews.co.uk
www.portsmouth.co.uk
Owner *Portsmouth Printing & Publishing Ltd*
Acting Editor *Mark Acheson*
Circulation 60,663

Unsolicited mss not generally accepted. Approach by letter.

Assistant Editor *Colin McNeill*

Features Editor *Graeme Patfield* General subjects of S.E. Hants interest. Maximum 600 words. No fiction.

Sports Editor *John Carter* Sports background features. Maximum 600 words.

The Southern Daily Echo
Newspaper House, Test Lane, Redbridge, Southampton SO16 9JX
☎023 8042 4777 Fax 023 8042 4545
www.thisishampshire.net

Owner *Newsquest Plc*
Editor *Ian Murray*
Circulation 40,461

Unsolicited mss 'tolerated'. Approach the editor in writing with strong ideas; staff supply almost all the material.

Kent

Kent Messenger
6 & 7 Middle Row, Maidstone ME14 1TG
☎01622 695666 Fax 01622 664988
✉ messengernews@thekmgroup.co.uk
www.kentonline.co.uk

Owner *Kent Messenger Group*
Editor *Bob Bounds*
Circulation 53,987

Very little freelance work is commissioned.

Medway Messenger
Medway House, Ginsbury Close, Sir Thomas Longley Road, Medway City Estate, Strood, Rochester ME2 4DU
☎01634 227800 Fax 01634 715256
✉ medwaymessenger@thekmgroup.co.uk
www.kentonline.co.uk

Owner *Kent Messenger Group*
Editor *Bob Bounds*
Circulation 12,485 (Mon)/20,000 (Fri)

Published Mondays and Fridays with the free *Medway Extra* on Wednesday.

 Business Editor *Trevor Sturgess*
 Community Editor *David Jones*
 Sports Editor *Mike Rees*

Lancashire

The Bolton News
Newspaper House, Churchgate, Bolton BL1 1DE
☎01204 522345 Fax 01204 365068
✉ newsdesk@boltonnews.co.uk
www.theboltonnews.co.uk

Owner *Newsquest Media Group Ltd (a Gannett company)*
Editor *Steve Hughes*
Circulation 30,799

Business, children's page, travel, local services, motoring, fashion and cookery.
 News Editor *James Higgins*
 Features Editor/Women's Page *Andrew Mosley*

The Gazette (Blackpool)
Avroe House, Avroe Crescent, Blackpool FY4 2DP
☎01253 400888 Fax 01253 361870
✉ jon.rhodes@blackpoolgazette.co.uk
www.blackpoolgazette.co.uk

Owner *Johnston Press plc*
Managing Director *Darren Russell*
Editor *David Helliwell*
Circulation 31,114

Unsolicited mss welcome in theory. Approach in writing with an idea. Supplements: *Eve* (women, Tues); *All Stars* (football, youth sport, Wed); *Homes* (Thurs); *The Weekend* (entertainment, Fri); *Wheels* (motoring, Fri); *Life!* magazine (entertainment & leisure, Sat); *Jobs Plus* (jobs and careers, Sat).

Lancashire Evening Post
Olivers Place, Eastway, Fulwood, Preston PR2 9ZA
☎01772 254841 Fax 01772 880173
www.lep.co.uk

Owner *Johnston Press plc*
Editor *Simon Reynolds*
Circulation 32,783

Unsolicited mss are not generally welcome; many are received and not used. All ideas in writing to the editor.

Lancashire Telegraph
Newspaper House, High Street, Blackburn BB1 1HT
☎01254 678678 Fax 01254 680429
✉ let_editorial@lancashire.newsquest.co.uk
www.lancashiretelegraph.co.uk

Owner *Newsquest Media Group Ltd (a Gannett company)*
Editor *Kevin Young*
Circulation 32,716

News stories and feature material with an East Lancashire flavour (a local angle, or written by local people) welcome. Approach in writing with an idea in the first instance. No fiction.
 News Editor *Andrew Turner*
 Features Editor *John Anson*
 Sports Editor *Paul Plunkett*
 Pictures Editor *Neil Johnson*

Oldham Evening Chronicle
PO Box 47, Union Street, Oldham OL1 1EQ
☎0161 633 2121 Fax 0161 652 2111
✉ editorial@oldham-chronicle.co.uk

Owner *Hirst Kidd & Rennie Ltd*
Editor *Jim Williams*

Circulation 22,584

Motoring, food and wine, lifestyle supplement, business page.

News Editor *Mike Attenborough*

Leicestershire

Leicester Mercury
St George Street, Leicester LE1 9FQ
☎0116 251 2512 Fax 0116 253 0645
www.thisisleicestershire.co.uk
Owner *Northcliffe Media Group Ltd*
Editor *Nick Carter*
Circulation 73,634
   News Editor *Mark Charlton*
   Features Editor *Alex Dawson*

Lincolnshire

Grimsby Telegraph
80 Cleethorpe Road, Grimsby DN31 3EH
☎01472 360360 Fax 01472 372257
✉ newsdesk@gsmg.co.uk
Owner *Northcliffe Media Group Ltd*
Editor *Michelle Lalor*
Circulation 37,247

Sister paper of the *Scunthorpe Telegraph*. Unsolicited mss generally welcome. Approach in writing. No fiction. Weekly supplements: *Business Telegraph*; *Property Telegraph*; *Motoring*; *Sports Telegraph* (Sat). All material to be addressed to the News Editor, *Lucy Wood*. Particularly welcomes hard news stories; approach in haste by telephone.
   Production Editor *B. Farnsworth*

Lincolnshire Echo
Brayford Wharf East, Lincoln LN5 7AT
☎01522 820000 Fax 01522 804493
✉ news@lincolnshireecho.co.uk
Owner *Northcliffe Media Group Ltd*
Editor *Jon Grubb*
Circulation 23,420

Best buys, holidays, motoring, dial-a-service, restaurants, sport, leisure, home improvement, record reviews, gardening corner, stars.

Scunthorpe Telegraph
4–5 Park Square, Scunthorpe DN15 6JH
☎01724 273273 Fax 01724 273101
Owner *Northcliffe Media Group Ltd*
Editor *Jane Manning*
Circulation 21,278

All correspondence should go to the Deputy Editor, *Dave Atkin*.

London

Evening Standard
Northcliffe House, 2 Derry Street, London
W8 5EE
☎020 7938 6000 Fax 020 7937 2648
www.standard.co.uk/e-editions
Owner *Associated Newspapers/Lord Rothermere*
Editor *Veronica Wadley*

Long-established evening paper, serving Londoners with both news and feature material. Genuine opportunities for London-based features. Produces a weekly colour supplement, *ES Magazine* (Fri) and *Homes & Property* (Wed).
   Deputy Editor *Andrew Bordiss*,
   Executive Editor *Anne McElvoy*
   Managing Editor *Doug Wills*
   Features Editor *Simon Davies*
   News Editor *Hugh Dougherty*
   Arts Editor *Fiona Hughes*
   Sports Editor *Martin Chilton*
   ES Editor *Catherine Ostler*
   Homes & Property Editor *Janice Morley*

Manchester

Manchester Evening News
Number 1 Scott Place, Manchester M3 3RN
☎0161 832 7200 Fax 0161 211 2030
www.manchesteronline.co.uk
Owner *Manchester Evening News Ltd*
Editor *Paul Horrocks*
Circulation 94,018

One of the country's major regional dailies. Initial approach in writing preferred. No fiction. *Personal Finance* (Mon); *Health*; *Holidays* (Tues); *Homes & Property* (Wed); *Small Business* (Thurs); *Lifestyle* (Fri/Sat).
   News Editor *Sarah Leste*
   Features Editor *Deanna Delamotta* Regional news features, personality pieces and showbiz profiles considered. Maximum 1200 words.
   Sports Editor *Peter Spencer*
   Women's Page *Helen Tither*
   PAYMENT based on house agreement rates.

Merseyside

Liverpool Daily Post
PO Box 48, Old Hall Street, Liverpool
L69 3EB
☎0151 227 2000 Fax 0151 472 2506
www.icliverpool.co.uk
Owner *Trinity Mirror Plc*
Editor *Jane Wolstenholme*

Circulation 17,103

Unsolicited mss welcome. Receives about six a day. Approach in writing with an idea. No fiction. Local, national/international news, current affairs, profiles (with pictures). Maximum 800–1000 words.

Features Editor *Emma Johnson*
News Editor *Andy Kelly*
Business Editor *Bill Gleeson*
Sports Editor *Richard Williamson*

Liverpool Echo

PO Box 48, Old Hall Street, Liverpool L69 3EB
☎0151 227 2000 Fax 0151 236 4682
✉ letters@liverpoolecho.co.uk

Owner *Trinity Mirror Merseyside*
Editor *Alastair Machray*
Circulation 110,804

One of the country's major regional dailies. Unsolicited mss welcome; initial approach with ideas in writing preferred.

News Editor *Alison Gow*
Features Editor *Jane Haase*
Sports Editor *John Thompson*
Women's Editor *Susan Lee*

Norfolk

Eastern Daily Press

Prospect House, Rouen Road, Norwich NR1 1RE
☎01603 628311 Fax 01603 623872
✉ EDP@archant.co.uk
www.EDP24.co.uk

Owner *Archant Regional*
Editor *Peter Franzen, OBE*
Circulation 67,004

Most pieces by commission only. Supplements: *Centro* (daily); rental, motoring, business, property pages, agriculture, employment (all weekly); *Event* full-colour magazine (Fri); *Saturday* full colour magazine; *Sunday* 24-page supplement.

Deputy Editor *Peter Waters*
Assistant Editor (News) *Paul Durrant*
Head of Feature Content *Sarah Hardy*
Head of Sport *Richard Willner*
Assistant Editor (*Saturday*) *Steve Snelling*

Evening News

Prospect House, Rouen Road, Norwich NR1 1RE
☎01603 628311 Fax 01603 219060
✉ tim.williams@archant.co.uk
www.eveningnews24.co.uk

Owner *Archant Ltd*
Circulation 26,014
Acting Editor *Tim Williams*

Includes special pages on local property, motoring, pop, fashion, arts, entertainments and TV, gardening, local music scene, home and family.

Assistant Editor *Zoe Catchpole*
(zoe.catchpole@archant.co.uk)
Features Editor *Derek James*
(derek.james@archant.co.uk)

Northamptonshire

Chronicle and Echo

Upper Mounts, Northampton NN1 3HR
☎01604 467000 Fax 01604 467190

Owner *Northamptonshire Newspapers*
Editor *Mark Edwards*
Circulation 21,114

Unsolicited mss are 'not necessarily unwelcome but opportunities to use them are rare'. Approach in writing with an idea. No fiction. Supplements: *Sport* (Mon); *Business Week* (Tues); *Property Today* (Wed); *Jobs Today* (Thurs); *Motors Today* and *The Guide* (Friday); *Weekend Life* (Sat).

News Editor *Richard Edmondson*
Features Editor/Women's Page *Lily Canter*
Sports Editor *Steve Pitts*

Evening Telegraph

Newspaper House, Ise Park, Rothwell Road, Kettering NN16 8GA
☎01536 506100 Fax 01536 506195 (editorial)
✉ et.newsdesk@northantsnews.co.uk
www.northantset.co.uk

Owner *Johnston Press Plc*
Editor *Jeremy Clifford*
Circulation 24,018

Northamptonshire Business Guide (weekly); *Entertainment Guide* and *Jobs* supplements (Thurs); films and eating out (Fri); and *Home & Garden* – monthly lifestyle supplement including gardening, etc.

Assistant Editor *Nick Tite*
News Editor *Kristy Ward*
Sports Editor *Jim Lyon*

Nottinghamshire

Evening Post Nottingham

Castle Wharf House, Nottingham NG1 7EU
☎0115 948 2000 Fax 0115 964 4032

Owner *Northcliffe Media Group Ltd*
Editor *Malcolm Pheby*

Circulation 62,077

Unsolicited mss occasionally used. Good local interest only. Maximum 800 words. No fiction. Send ideas in writing.

News Editor *Steven Fletcher*
Deputy Editor *Martin Done*
Sports Editor *Dave Parkinson*

Oxfordshire

Oxford Mail

Osney Mead, Oxford OX2 0EJ
☎01865 425262 Fax 01865 425554
✉ nqonews@nqo.com
www.thisisoxfordshire.co.uk

Owner *Newsquest (Oxfordshire) Ltd*
Editor *Simon O'Neill*
Circulation 25,838

Unsolicited mss are considered but a great many unsuitable offerings are received. Approach in writing with an idea, rather than by phone. No fiction.

PAYMENT All fees negotiable.

Shropshire

Shropshire Star

Ketley, Telford TF1 5HU
☎01952 242424 Fax 01952 254605

Owner *Shropshire Newspapers Ltd*
Editor *Sarah-Jane Smith*
Circulation 74,083

No unsolicited mss; approach the editor with ideas in writing in the first instance. No news or fiction.

Head of Features *Carl Jones* Limited opportunities; uses mostly in-house or syndicated material. Maximum 1200 words.

Sports Editor *Dave Ballinger*

Somerset

The Bath Chronicle

Windsor House, Windsor Bridge Road, Bath BA2 3AU
☎01225 322322 Fax 01225 322291
www.thisisbath.com

Owner *Northcliffe Media Group Ltd*
Editor *Sam Holliday*
(s.holliday@bathchron.co.uk)
Circulation 12,363

Local news and features especially welcomed (news@bathchron.co.uk).

Deputy Editor *John McCready*
News Editor *Paul Wiltshire*

Features Editor *Georgette McCready*
Sports Editor *Julie Riegal*

Evening Post

Temple Way, Bristol BS99 7HD
☎0117 934 3000 Fax 0117 934 3575
✉ epnews@bepp.co.uk
www.thisisbristol.co.uk

Owner *Bristol News & Media Ltd (part of Northcliffe Media Group Ltd)*
Editor *Mike Norton*
Circulation 54,699

News Editor *Robin Perkins*
Newsdesk *Jane Westhead*
Features Editor *David Webb*
Sports Editor *Chris Spittles*

Western Daily Press

Temple Way, Bristol BS99 7HD
☎0117 934 3000 Fax 0117 934 3574
✉ WDEditor *or* WDNews *or* WDFeats@bepp.co.uk
www.westerndailypress.co.uk

Owner *Bristol Evening Post & Press Ltd*
Editor *Andy Wright*
Circulation 43,512

Sports Editor *Steve Mellen*
Women's Page *Susie Weldon* (Features Production)

Staffordshire

Burton Mail

65–68 High Street, Burton upon Trent DE14 1LE
☎01283 512345 Fax 01283 515351
✉ editorial@burtonmail.co.uk

Owner *Staffordshire Newspapers Ltd*
Editor *Paul Hazeldine*
Circulation 15,483

Fashion, health, wildlife, environment, nostalgia, financial/money; consumer; women's world, rock; property; motoring, farming; what's on, leisure *Weekend Supplement* (Sat).

News Editor *Steve Doohan*
Features *Louise Elliott*
Sports Editor *Rex Page*

The Sentinel/Sentinel Sunday

Sentinel House, Etruria, Stoke on Trent ST1 5SS
☎01782 602525 Fax 01782 280781 (Sentinel)/201167 (Sentinel Sunday)
www.thisisthesentinel.co.uk

Owner *Staffordshire Sentinel Newspapers Ltd*

Editor-in-Chief *Mike Sassi*
Circulation 65,294 (Sentinel)/13,126 (Sentinel Sunday)

Weekly sports final supplement. All material should be sent to the Assistant Editor, *Martin Tideswell*.

Suffolk

East Anglian Daily Times

Press House, 30 Lower Brook Street, Ipswich IP4 1AN
☎01473 230023 Fax 01473 324776
✉ news@eadt.co.uk
www.eadt.co.uk

Owner *Archant Ltd*
Editor *Terry Hunt*
Circulation 35,806

Founded 1874. Unsolicited mss generally not welcome; three or four received a week and almost none are used. Approach in writing in the first instance. No fiction. Supplements: sport (Mon); business (Tues); jobs (Wed); property (Thurs); motoring (Fri); magazine (Sat).

News Editor *Brad Jones* Hard news stories involving East Anglia (Suffolk, Essex particularly) or individuals resident in the area are always of interest.

Features *Julian Ford* Mostly in-house, but will occasionally buy in when the subject is of strong Suffolk/East Anglian interest. Photo features preferred (extra payment). Special advertisement features are regularly run. Some opportunities here. Maximum 1000 words.

Sports Editor *Nick Garnham*
Women's Page *Victoria Hawkins*

Evening Star

30 Lower Brook Street, Ipswich IP4 1AN
☎01473 230023 Fax 01473 324850

Owner *Archant Ltd*
Editor *Nigel Pickover*
Circulation 21,352
News Editor *Jess Nicholls*

Sussex

The Argus

Argus House, Crowhurst Road, Hollingbury, Brighton BN1 8AR
☎01273 544544 Fax 01273 505703
✉ editor@theargus.co.uk
www.theargus.co.uk

Owner *Newsquest (Sussex) Ltd*
Editor *Michael Beard*
Circulation 33,860

News Editor *Frankie Taggart*
Sports Editor *Chris Giles*

Teesside

Evening Gazette

Borough Road, Middlesbrough TS1 3AZ
☎01642 234242 Fax 01642 232014
www.gazettelive.co.uk

Owner *Trinity Mirror plc*
Editor *Darren Thwaites*
Circulation 53,739

Special pages: health, education, family, business, property, entertainment, leisure, motoring, recruitment.

News Editor *Jim Horsley*
Business Features/Commercial Features *Helen Logan*
Sports Editor *Phil Tallentire*
Councils *Sandy McKenzie*
Health *Audrey Forbes*
Crime *Simon Haworth*

Tyne & Wear

Evening Chronicle

Groat Market, Newcastle upon Tyne NE1 1ED
☎0191 232 7500 Fax 0191 232 2256
✉ ec.news@ncjmedia.co.uk
www.icnewcastle.co.uk

Owner *Trinity Mirror Plc*
Editor *Paul Robertson*
Circulation 77,056

Receives a lot of unsolicited material, much of which is not used. Family issues, gardening, pop, fashion, cooking, consumer, films and entertainment guide, home improvements, motoring, property, angling, sport and holidays. Approach in writing with ideas. Limited opportunities for features due to full-time feature staff.

News Editor *James Marley*
Sports Editor *Paul New*
Women's Interests *Jennifer Bradbury*

Gazette

Chapter Row, South Shields NE33 1BL
☎0191 427 4800 Fax 0191 456 8270
www.southtynesidetoday.co.uk

Owner *Northeast Press Ltd*
Editor *John Szymanski*
Circulation 19,899
News & Features Editor *Helen Charlton*

The Journal

Groat Market, Newcastle upon Tyne NE1 1ED
☎0191 232 7500/201 6344 (Newsdesk)

Fax 0191 232 2256/201 6044
✉ jnl.newsdesk@ncjmedia.co.uk
www.journallive.co.uk

Owner *Trinity Mirror Plc*
Editor *Brian Aitken*
Circulation 37,822

Daily platforms include farming and business.
Deputy Editor *Graham Pratt*
Sports Editor *Kevin Dinsdale*
Arts & Entertainment Editor
David Whetstone
Environment Editor *Tony Henderson*
Business Editor *Iain Laing*

Sunday Sun

ncjMedia, Groat Market, Newcastle upon Tyne
NE1 1ED
☎0191 201 6299 Fax 0191 201 6180
✉ colin.patterson@ncjmedia.co.uk

Owner *Trinity Mirror Plc*
Editor *Colin Patterson*
Circulation 70,904

All material should be addressed to the appropriate editor (phone to check), or to the editor.
Sports Editor *Neil Farrington*

Sunderland Echo

Echo House, Pennywell, Sunderland SR4 9ER
☎0191 501 5800 Fax 0191 534 5975
✉ rob.lawson@northeast-press.co.uk

Owner *Johnston Press Plc*
Editor *Rob Lawson*
Circulation 43,496

All editorial material to be addressed to the
News Editor, *Gavin Foster*(echo.news@northeast-press.co.uk).

Warwickshire

Coventry Telegraph

Corporation Street, Coventry CV1 1FP
☎024 7663 3633 Fax 024 7655 0869
✉ news@coventry-telegraph.co.uk
www.IcCoventry.co.uk

Owner *Trinity Mirror Plc*
Editor *Alan Kirby*
Circulation 49,571

Unsolicited mss are read, but few are published.
Approach in writing with an idea. No fiction.
All unsolicited material should be addressed to
the editor. Maximum 600 words for features.
News Managers *Steve Chilton, Steve Williams*
Features Manager/Women's Page *Tara Cain*
Sports Editor *Rob Madill*
PAYMENT negotiable.

Leamington Spa Courier

32 Hamilton Terrace, Leamington Spa
CV32 4LY
☎01926 457755 Fax 01926 339960
✉ editorial@leamingtoncourier.co.uk
www.leamingtontoday.co.uk

Owner *Heart of England Newspapers (Johnston
Press)*
Editor *Martin Lawson*
Circulation 14,247

One of the Leamington Spa Courier series
which also includes the *Warwick Courier* and
Kenilworth Weekly News. Unsolicited feature articles considered, particularly matter with a local
angle. Telephone with idea first.
News Editor *Peter Ormerod*

West Midlands

Birmingham Mail

PO Box 78, Weaman Street, Birmingham
B4 6AT
☎0121 234 5688 Fax 0121 233 0271 (editorial)
✉ Steve_dyson@mrn.co.uk
www.birminghammail.net

Owner *Trinity Mirror Plc*
Editor *Steve Dyson*
Circulation 72,218

Freelance contributions are welcome, particularly topics of interest to the West Midlands
and feature pieces offering original and lively
comment on family issues, health or education. Also news tips and community picture
contributions.
Deputy Editor *Carole Cole*
Assistant Editor (Content) *Alf Bennett*
Features *Paul Fulford*
News *Andy Richards*
Sport *Ken Montgomery*
Pictures *Steve Murphy*
Business *Jon Griffin*

Birmingham Post

Weaman Street, Birmingham B4 6AY
☎0121 234 5301 Fax 0121 234 5625

Owner *Trinity Mirror Plc*
Editor *Marc Reeves*
Circulation 13,251

One of the country's leading regional newspapers. Freelance contributions are welcome.
Topics of interest to the West Midlands and
pieces offering lively, original comment are
particularly welcome.
News Editor *Mo Ilyas*
Features Editor *Sarah Probert*

Express & Star
Queen Street, Wolverhampton WV1 1ES
☎01902 313131 Fax 01902 319721
Owner *Midlands News Association*
Editor *Adrian Faber*
Circulation 142,433
    Deputy Editor *Keith Harrison*
    Assistant Editor *Roy Williams*
    Head of News *Mark Drew*
    Features Editor *Emma Farmer*
    Business Editor *Jim Walsh*
    Sports Editor *Tim Walters*
    Women's Editor *Maria Cusine*

Sunday Mercury (Birmingham)
Weaman Street, Birmingham B4 6AY
☎0121 234 5567 Fax 0121 234 5877
✉ sundaymercury@mrn.co.uk
www.icbirmingham.co.uk
Owner *Trinity Mirror Plc*
Editor *David Brookes*
Circulation 62,009
    Deputy Editor (Features) *Paul Cole*
    Head of Content (News) *Tony Larner*
    Assistant Editor (Sport) *Lee Gibson*
    Lifestyle Editor *Zoe Chamberlain*

Wiltshire

Swindon Advertiser
100 Victoria Road, Swindon SN1 3BE
☎01793 528144 Fax 01793 501888
✉ editor@newswilts.co.uk
www.swindonadvertiser.co.uk
Owner *Newsquest (Wiltshire) Ltd*
Editor *Mark Waldron*
Circulation 21,856
Copy and ideas invited. 'All material must be strongly related or relevant to the town of Swindon or the county of Wiltshire.' Little scope for freelance work. Fees vary depending on material.
    Deputy Editor *Pauline Leighton*
    News Editor *Tom Morton*
    Sports Editor *Steve Butt*

Worcestershire

Worcester News
Berrow's House, Hylton Road, Worcester
WR2 5JX
☎01905 748200 Fax 01905 742277
Owner *Newsquest (Midlands South) Ltd*
Editor *Stewart Gilbert*
Circulation 18,425

Community (Tues); jobs (Wed); property (Thurs); entertainment and motoring (Fri).
    News Editor *Stephanie Summers*
    Features Editor *Stewart Gilbert*
    Sports Editor *Paul Ricketts*

Yorkshire

The Doncaster Star
Sunny Bar, Doncaster DN1 1NB
☎01302 348500 Fax 01302 348528
✉ doncaster@sheffieldnewspapers.co.uk
Owner *Sheffield Newspapers Ltd*
Editor *Alan Powell*
Circulation 4,567
All editorial material to be addressed to the editor.
    News *David Kessen*
    Sports Writer *Steve Hossack*

Huddersfield Daily Examiner
Queen Street South, Huddersfield HD1 2TD
☎01484 430000 Fax 01484 437789
Owner *Trinity Mirror Plc*
Editor *Roy Wright*
Circulation 27,046
Home improvement, home heating, weddings, dining out, motoring, fashion, services to trade and industry.
    Deputy Editor *Michael O'Connell*
    News Editor *Neil Atkinson*
    Features Editor *Andrew Flynn*
    Sports Editor *Mel Booth*
    Women's Page *Hilarie Stelfox*

Hull Daily Mail
Blundell's Corner, Beverley Road, Hull
HU3 1XS
☎01482 327111 Fax 01482 315353
✉ news@mailnewsmedia.co.uk
www.thisishullandeastriding.co.uk
Owner *Northcliffe Media Group Ltd*
Editor *John Meehan*
Circulation 59,859
    News Editor *Paul Baxter*
    Features Editor *Paul Johnson*

The Press
PO Box 29, 76–86 Walmgate, York YO1 9YN
☎01904 653051 Fax 01904 612853
✉ newsdesk@ycp.co.uk
www.yorkpress.co.uk
Owner *Newsquest Media Group (a Gannett company)*
Editor *Kevin Booth*

Circulation 34,070

Unsolicited mss not generally welcome, unless submitted by journalists of proven ability. *Business Press Pages* (daily); *Property Press* (Thurs); *Twenty4Seven* – entertainment (Fri).

Assistant Editor *Fran Clee*
Head of Content *Scott Armstrong*
Picture Editor *Martin Oates*
Sports Editor *Martin Jarred*
PAYMENT negotiable.

Scarborough Evening News

17–23 Aberdeen Walk, Scarborough YO11 1BB
☎01723 363636 Fax 01723 379033
✉ editorial@scarborougheveningnews.co.uk
www.scarboroughtoday.co.uk

Owner *Yorkshire Regional Newspapers Ltd*
Editor *Ed Asquith*
Circulation 14,431

Special pages include property (Mon); jobs (Thurs); motors (Fri).

Deputy Editor *Sue Wilkinson*
News Editor *Steven Hartley*
Sports Editor *Charles Place*
All other material should be addressed to the editor.

The Star

York Street, Sheffield S1 1PU
☎0114 276 7676 Fax 0114 272 5978

Owner *Sheffield Newspapers Ltd*
Editor *Alan Powell*
Circulation 55,307

Unsolicited mss not welcome, unless topical and local.

News Editor *Charles Smith* Contributions only accepted from freelance news reporters if they relate to the area.

Features Editor *Martin Smith* Very rarely requires outside features, unless on specialised local subjects.

Sports Editor *Bob Westerdale*
Women's Page *Jo Davison*
PAYMENT negotiable.

Telegraph & Argus (Bradford)

Hall Ings, Bradford BD1 1JR
☎01274 729511 Fax 01274 723634
www.thetelegraphandargus.co.uk

Owner *Newsquest Media Group Ltd (a Gannett company)*
Editor *Perry Austin-Clarke*
Circulation 38,716

No unsolicited mss – approach in writing with samples of work. No fiction.

Head of News *Martin Heminway*
Features Editor *David Barnett*
Local features and general interest. Showbiz pieces. 600–1000 words (maximum 1500).

Yorkshire Evening Post

Wellington Street, Leeds LS1 1RF
☎0113 243 2701 Fax 0113 238 8536
✉ eped@ypn.co.uk

Owner *Johnston Press*
Editor *Paul Napier*
Circulation 58,114

Evening sister of the Yorkshire Post.

News Editor *Gillian Haworth*
Features Editor *Jayne Dawson*
Sports Editor *Phil Rostron*
Women's Editor *Jayne Dawson*

Yorkshire Post

Wellington Street, Leeds LS1 1RF
☎0113 243 2701 Fax 0113 238 8537
✉ yp.editor@ypn.co.uk
www.yorkshireposttoday.co.uk

Owner *Johnston Press*
Editor *Peter Charlton*
Circulation 51,777

A serious-minded, quality regional daily with a generally conservative outlook. Three or four unsolicited mss arrive each day; all will be considered but initial approach in writing preferred. All submissions should be addressed to the editor. No fiction, poetry or family histories.

Deputy Editor *Duncan Hamilton*
Features Editor *Sarah Freeman* Open to suggestions in all fields (though ordinarily commissioned from specialist writers).
Sports Editor *Matt Reeder*

NORTHERN IRELAND

Belfast News Letter

Johnson Press, Northern Ireland Division, 2 Esky Drive, Portadown BT63 5YY
☎028 3839 3939 Fax 028 3839 3940

Owner *Johnson Press*
Editor *Darwin Templeton*

Weekly supplements: *Farming Life; Business News Letter, Female Times; Spectrum; Sports Ulster.*

News Editors *Ric Clark, Steven Moore, Karen Quinn*
Features Editor *Geoff Hill*
Sports Editor *Brian Millar*
Business Editor *Adrienne McGill*

Agricultural Editor *David McCoy*
Political Editor *Stephen Dempster*

Belfast Telegraph

Royal Avenue, Belfast BT1 1EB
☎028 9026 4000 Fax 028 9055 4506/4540
✉ newseditor@belfasttelegraph.co.uk
www.belfasttelegraph.co.uk

Owner *Independent News & Media (UK)*
Editor *Martin Lindsay*
Circulation 87,782

Weekly business, property and recruitment supplements.

Deputy Editor *Paul Connolly*
News Editor *Ronan Henry*
Features Editor *Gail Walker*
Sports Editor *Steven Beacom*
Business Editor *Nigel Tilson*

The Irish News

113/117 Donegall Street, Belfast BT1 2GE
☎028 9032 2226 Fax 028 9033 7505
✉ newsdesk@irishnews.com

Owner *Irish News Ltd*
Editor *Noel Doran*
Circulation 48,518

All material to appropriate editor (phone to check), or to the news desk.

Assistant Editor *Fiona McGarry*
Sports Editor *Thomas Hawkins*
Arts Editor/Women's Page *Joanna Braniff*

Sunday Life

124–144 Royal Avenue, Belfast BT1 1EB
☎028 9026 4300 Fax 028 9055 4507
✉ m.hill@belfasttelegraph.co.uk
www.sundaylife.co.uk

Owner *Independent News & Media (UK)*
Editor *Jim Flanagan*
Circulation 77,506

Deputy Editor *Martin Hill*
Sports Editor *Jim Gracey*
Features Editor *Audrey Watson*

SCOTLAND

The Courier and Advertiser

80 Kingsway East, Dundee DD4 8SL
☎01382 223131 Fax 01382 454590
✉ courier@dcthomson.co.uk
www.thecourier.co.uk

Owner *D.C. Thomson & Co. Ltd*
Editor *Bill Hutcheon*
Circulation 75,435

Circulates in East Central Scotland. Features occasionally accepted on a wide range of subjects, particularly local/Scottish interest, including finance, insurance, agriculture, motoring, modern homes, lifestyle and fitness. Maximum length, 500 words.

News Editor *Arliss Rhind*
Features Editor/Women's Page *Catriona McInnes*
Sports Editor *Graeme Dey*

Daily Record (Glasgow)

See *National Newspapers*

Evening Express (Aberdeen)

PO Box 43, Lang Stracht, Mastrick, Aberdeen AB15 6DF
☎01224 690222 Fax 01224 699575
✉ ee.news@ajl.co.uk

Owner *D.C. Thomson & Co. Ltd*
Editor *Damian Bates*
Circulation 55,938

Circulates in Aberdeen and the Grampian region. Local, national and international news and pictures, sport. Family platforms include *What's On, Counter* (consumer news), *Eating Out Guide, Family Days Out*. Unsolicited mss welcome 'if on a controlled basis'.

Deputy Editor *Richard Prest* Freelance news contributors welcome.

PAYMENT negotiable.

Evening News

Barclay House, 108 Holyrood Road, Edinburgh EH8 8AS
☎0131 620 8620 Fax 0131 620 8696
www.edinburghnews.com

Owner *Scotsman Publications Ltd*
Editor *John McLellan*
Circulation 55,503

Founded 1873. Circulates in Edinburgh, Fife, Central and Lothian. Coverage includes: entertainment, gardening, motoring, shopping, fashion, health and lifestyle, showbusiness. Occasional platform pieces, features of topical and/or local interest. Unsolicited feature material welcome. Approach the appropriate editor in writing.

News Editor *Euan McGrory*
Sports Editor *Graham Lindsay*
PAYMENT NUJ/house rates.

Evening Telegraph

80 Kingsway East, Dundee DD4 8SL
☎01382 223131 Fax 01382 454590
✉ general@eveningtelegraph.co.uk

www.eveningtelegraph.co.uk
Owner *D.C.Thomson & Co. Ltd*
Editor *Gordon Wishart*
Circulation 24,716

Circulates in Tayside, Dundee and Fife. All material should be addressed to the editor.

Evening Times
200 Renfield Street, Glasgow G2 3QB
☎0141 302 7000 Fax 0141 302 6677
✉ times@eveningtimes.co.uk
Owner *Newsquest*
Editor *Donald Martin*
Circulation 85,637

Circulates in Glasgow and the west of Scotland.
Supplements: *Job Search*; *City Living*; *Drive times*; *Extra times*; *Times Out*; *etc* magazine.

News Editor *Yvonne Flynn*
Features Editor *Garry Scott*
Sports Editor *David Stirling*

Greenock Telegraph
2 Crawfurd Street, Greenock PA15 1LH
☎01475 726511 Fax 01475 783734
Owner *Clyde & Forth Press Ltd*
Editor *Tom McConigley*
Circulation 17,962

Circulates in Greenock, Port Glasgow, Gourock, Kilmacolm, Langbank, Bridge of Weir, Inverkip, Wemyss Bay, Skelmorlie, Largs. Unsolicited mss considered 'if they relate to the newspaper's general interests'. No fiction. All material to be addressed to the editor.

The Herald/Sunday Herald (Glasgow)
See *National Newspapers*

Paisley Daily Express
14 New Street, Paisley PA1 1YA
☎0141 887 7911 Fax 0141 887 6254
✉ pde@s-un.co.uk
Owner *Scottish & Universal Newspapers Ltd*
Editor *Jonathan Russell*
Circulation 10,158

Circulates in Paisley, Linwood, Renfrew, Johnstone, Elderslie, Neilston and Barrhead. Unsolicited mss welcome only if of genuine local (Renfrewshire) interest. The paper does not commission work and will consider submitted material. Maximum 1000–1500 words. All submissions to the news editor.

News Editor *Anne Dalrymple*
Sports Reporter *Paul Behan*

The Press and Journal
PO Box 43, Lang Stracht, Mastrick, Aberdeen
AB15 6DF
☎01224 690222 Fax 01224 663575
Owner *D.C.Thomson & Co. Ltd*
Editor *Derek Tucker*
Circulation 82,496

A well-established daily that circulates in Aberdeen, Grampians, Highlands, Tayside, Orkney, Shetland and the Western Isles. Most material is commissioned but will consider ideas.

News Editor *Andrew Hebden* Wide variety of hard or off-beat news and features relating especially, but not exclusively, to the north of Scotland.

Sports Editor *Alex Martin*
Women's Page *Victoria Banks*
Your Life *Sonja Cox* Saturday lifestyle tabloid pullout. Features food, fashion, travel, books, arts and lifestyle.

PAYMENT by arrangement.

Scotland on Sunday (Edinburgh)
See *National Newspapers*

The Scotsman (Edinburgh)
See *National Newspapers*

Sunday Mail (Glasgow)
See *National Newspapers*

Sunday Post (Dundee)
See *National Newspapers*

WALES

Daily Post
PO Box 202, Vale Road, Llandudno Junction, Conwy LL31 9ZD
☎01492 574455 Fax 01492 574433
✉ welshnews@dailypost.co.uk
Owner *Trinity Mirror Plc*
Editor *Rob Irvine*
Circulation 38,332

Features Editor *Mark Brittain*
News Editor *Maria Breslin*
Sports Editor *Andy Gilpin*

Evening Leader
Mold Business Park, Wrexham Road, Mold
CH7 1XY
☎01352 707707 Fax 01352 752180
✉ news@eveningleader.co.uk

Owner *North Wales Newspapers*
Editor-in-Chief *Barrie Jones*
Circulation 21,838
Circulates in Wrexham, Flintshire, Deeside and Chester. Special pages/features: motoring, travel, arts, women's, children's, local housing, information and news for the disabled, music and entertainment.

Deputy Editor *Martin Wright*
Assistant Editor *Jonathon Barnett*
Sports Editor *Nick Harrison*

South Wales Argus

Cardiff Road, Maesglas, Newport NP20 3QN
☎01633 810000 Fax 01633 777202
www.southwalesargus.co.uk
Owner *Newsquest*
Editor *Gerry Keighley*
Circulation 28,818
Circulates in Newport, Gwent and surrounding areas.

News Editor *Maria Williams*
Sports Editor *Phil Webb*

South Wales Echo

Thomson House, Havelock Street, Cardiff CF10 1XR
☎029 2058 3622 Fax 029 2058 3624
✉ echo.newsdesk@wme.co.uk
www.icwales.co.uk
Owner *Trinity Mirror Plc*
Editor *Richard Williams*
Circulation 52,740
Circulates in South and Mid Glamorgan and Gwent.

Head of News *Cathy Owen*
Head of Features *Jonah Webb, Alison Stokes*
Head of Sport *Delme Parfitt*

South Wales Evening Post

Adelaide Street, Swansea SA1 1QT
☎01792 510000 Fax 01792 514697
✉ postbox@swwmedia.co.uk
www.thisissouthwales.co.uk
Owner *Northcliffe Media Group Ltd*
Editor *Spencer Feeney*
Circulation 54,745
Circulates throughout south west Wales.

News Editor *Peter Slee*
Features Editor *Catherine Ings*
Sports Editor *David Evans*

Wales on Sunday

Thomson House, Havelock Street, Cardiff CF10 1XR

☎029 2058 3733 Fax 029 2058 3725
Owner *Trinity Mirror plc*
Editor *Tim Gordon*
Circulation 43,129
Launched 1989. Tabloid with sports supplement. Does not welcome unsolicited mss.

Head of Content *Laura Kemp*
Show Biz/Features Editor *Rachel Mainwaring*
Sports Editor *Nick Rippington*

Western Mail

Thomson House, Havelock Street, Cardiff CF10 1XR
☎029 2058 3583 Fax 029 2058 3652
www.icwales.co.uk
Owner *Trinity Mirror Plc*
Editor *Alan Edmunds*
Circulation 39,776
Circulates in Cardiff, Merthyr Tydfil, Newport, Swansea and towns and villages throughout Wales. Mss welcome if of a topical nature, of Welsh interest. No short stories or travel. Approach in writing to the features editor. 'Usual subjects already well covered, e.g. motoring, travel, books, gardening. We look for the unusual.' Maximum 1000 words. Opportunities also on women's page. Supplements: *Saturday Magazine*; *Education*; *WM*; *Box Office*; *Welsh Homes*; *Business*; *Sport*; *Motoring*; *Country & Farming*.

Deputy Editor *Ceri Gould*
News Editor *Pal Carey*
Sports Editor *Philip Blanche*
Features Editor *Peter Morrell*

CHANNEL ISLANDS

Guernsey Press & Star

Braye Road, Vale, Guernsey GY1 3BW
☎01481 240240 Fax 01481 240235
✉ newsroom@guernsey-press.com
www.guernsey-press.com
Owner *Guiton Group*
Editor *Richard Digard*
Circulation 16,249
Special pages include children's and women's interest, gardening and fashion.

News Editor *Paul Baker*
Sports Editor *Rob Batiste*
Features Editor *Diane Digard*

Jersey Evening Post

PO Box 582, Jersey JE4 8XQ
☎01534 611611 Fax 01534 611622
✉ editorial@jerseyeveningpost.com
www.thisisjersey.com

Owner *Claverley Company*
Editor *Chris Bright*

Circulation 21,237
Special pages: gardening, motoring, property, boating, technology, young person's (16–25), food and drink, personal finance, rock reviews, health, business.

News Editor *Sue Le Ruez*
Features Editor *Carl Walker*
Sports Editor *Ron Felton*

Magazines

Abraxas Unbound
57 Eastbourne Road, St Austell PL25 4SU
☎01726 64975 Fax 01726 64975
✉ lordcrashingbore@btinternet.com
www.stormloader.com/users/abrax7
Owner *Paul Newman*
Editors *Paul Newman, Pamela Smith-Rawnsley*
Founded 1991. Large Crown Quarto, biannual paperback of over 250 pages, available both from address above and Lulu Publishing (www.lulu.com/lord-crashingbore). Combines leading articles by Colin Wilson and other scholars and critics with short stories, poems, reviews, translations and features on philosophy, existentialism and ideas. Favours challenging essays on the new and radical slants on the old (e.g. Colin Wilson on Edmund Husserl). Contributors include D.M. Thomas, Beryl Bainbridge, John Shand, Matthew Coniam, Gary Allen, Roger Morris and A.R. Lamb.

FICTION Flexible but prefers short stories of 1000–2000 words. 'Think of a writer like Wolfgang Borchert who wrote briefly, vividly and fiercely.'

POETRY Open to all styles, rhymed and irregular but prefers a creative, original use of language rather than prosy verse.

PAYMENT 'Flattery' and complimentary copy.

Acclaim
See **The New Writer**

Accountancy
145 London Road, Kingston Upon Thames KT2 6SR
☎020 8247 1389 Fax 020 8247 1424
✉ accountancynews@cch.co.uk
www.accountancymagazine.com
Owner *Wolters Kluwer UK*
Editor *Chris Quick*
Circulation 149,586
Founded 1889. MONTHLY. Written ideas welcome.

FEATURES *Lesley Bolton* Accounting, tax, business-related articles of high technical content aimed at professional/managerial readers. Maximum 2000 words. PAYMENT by arrangement.

Accountancy Age
32–34 Broadwick Street, London W1A 2HG
☎020 7316 9000 Fax 020 7316 9250
✉ accountancy_age@vnu.co.uk
www.accountancyage.com
Owner *Incisive Media*
Editor-in-Chief *Damian Wild*
Editor *Gavin Hinks* (☎ 020 7316 9608)
Circulation 60,368
Founded 1969. WEEKLY. Unsolicited mss welcome. Ideas may be suggested in writing provided they are clearly thought out.

FEATURES *Rachel Fielding, Michelle Perry* Topics right across the accountancy, business and financial world. Max. 2000 words. PAYMENT negotiable.

ACE Tennis Magazine
Advantage Publishing, Barry House, 20–22 Worple Road, London SW19 4DH
☎020 8947 0100
✉ paul.morgan@acemag.co.uk
Owner *Tennis GB*
Editor *Paul Morgan*
Circulation 46,036
Founded 1996. MONTHLY specialist tennis magazine. News (250 words max.) and features (2000 words max.). No unsolicited mss; send feature synopses by e-mail in the first instance. No tournament reports. PAYMENT £200 per 1000 words.

Acoustic
Oyster House Media Ltd, Oyster House, Hunter's Lodge, Kentisbeare EX15 2DY
☎01884 266100 Fax 01884 266101
✉ editor@acousticmagazine.com
www.acousticmagazine.com
Owner *Oyster House Media Ltd*
Editor *Steve Harvey*
Circulation 15,000
Launched 2004. BI-MONTHLY. Reviews, news, features and interviews related to acoustic guitars, acoustic instruments and acoustic instru-

ment manufacturing. Unsolicited contributions welcome; particularly interested in hard-to-secure interviews with well known acoustic guitarists. Approach by e-mail.

Acumen

See under *Poetry Magazines*

Aeroplane

IPC Media Ltd., The Blue Fin Building, 110 Southwark Street, London SE1 0SU
☎020 3148 4100
✉ aeroplane_monthly@ipcmedia.com
www.aeroplanemonthly.com

Owner *IPC Country & Leisure Media Ltd*
Editor *Michael Oakey*
Circulation 36,656

Founded 1973. MONTHLY. Historic aviation and aircraft preservation from its beginnings to the 1960s. No poetry. Will consider news items and features written with authoritative knowledge of the subject, illustrated with good quality photographs.

NEWS *Tony Harsmworth* Max. 500 words.
FEATURES *Michael Oakey* Max. 3000 words.
Approach by letter or e-mail in the first instance.

PAYMENT £60 per 1000 words; £10–40 per picture used.

Air International

PO Box 100, Stamford PE9 1XQ
☎01780 755131 Fax 01780 757261
✉ malcolm.english@keypublishing.com
www.airinternational.com

Owner *Key Publishing Ltd*
Editor *Malcolm English*
Circulation 12,636

Founded 1971. MONTHLY. Civil and military aircraft magazine. Unsolicited mss welcome but initial approach by phone or in writing preferred.

AirForces Monthly

PO Box 100, Stamford PE9 1XQ
☎01780 755131 Fax 01780 757261
✉ edafm@keypublishing.com

Owner *Key Publishing Ltd*
Editor *Alan Warnes*
Circulation 20,015

Founded 1988. MONTHLY. Modern military aviation magazine. Unsolicited contributions welcome but initial approach by phone or in writing preferred.

All About Soap

Hachette Filipacchi (UK) Ltd, 64 North Row, London W1K 7LL
☎020 7150 7000 Fax 020 7150 7681
✉ allaboutsoap@hf-uk.com
www.allaboutsoap.co.uk

Editor *Johnathon Hughes*
Circulation 74,856

Founded 1999. FORTNIGHTLY. Soap opera story-lines, television gossip and celebrity features.

FEATURES *Kerry Barrett* Freelance cover for staff holidays; occasional commissions. No unsolicited contributions; make initial contact by phone or e-mail.

Amateur Gardening

Westover House, West Quay Road, Poole BH15 1JG
☎01202 440840 Fax 01202 440860

Owner *IPC Media (A Time Warner Company)*
Editor *Tim Rumball*
Circulation 45,146

Founded 1884. WEEKLY. New contributions are welcome especially if they are topical and informative. All articles/news items should be supported by colour pictures (which may or may not be supplied by the author).

FEATURES Topical and practical gardening articles; will only consider those accompanied by photos. Max. 1000 words.

NEWS Compiled and edited in-house generally but all stories welcomed.

PAYMENT negotiable.

Amateur Photographer

IPC Media Ltd., The Blue Fin Building, 110 Southwark Street, London SE1 0SU
☎020 3148 4138
✉ amateurphotographer@ipcmedia.com

Owner *IPC Media (A Time Warner Company)*
Editor *Damien Demolder*
Circulation 26,068

Founded 1884. WEEKLY. For the competent amateur with a technical interest. Freelancers are used but writers should be aware that there is ordinarily no use for words without pictures.

Amateur Stage

Hampden House, 2 Weymouth Street, London W1W 5BT
☎020 7636 4343 Fax 020 7636 2323
✉ cvtheatre@aol.com

Owner *Platform Publications Ltd*
Editor *Charles Vance*

Some opportunity here for outside contributions. Topics of interest include amateur premières, technical developments within the amateur forum and items relating to landmarks or anniversaries in the history of amateur societies. Approach in writing only (include s.a.e. for return of mss). No PAYMENT.

Ancestors
See **The National Archives** under
UK Publishers

Angler's Mail
IPC Media Ltd., The Blue Fin Building, 110 Southwark Street, London SE1 0SU
☎020 3148 4159
✉ anglersmail@ipcmedia.com
www.anglersmail.com
Owner *IPC Media (A Time Warner Company)*
Editor *Tim Knight*
Circulation 32,639
Founded 1965. WEEKLY. Angling news and matches. Interested in pictures, stories, tip-offs and features. Approach the news desk by telephone. PAYMENT £10–40 per 200 words; pictures, £20–40.

Animal Action
Wilberforce Way, Southwater, Horsham RH13 9RS
☎0870 754 0392 Fax 0870 753 0392
✉ publications@rspca.org.uk
www.rspca.org.uk
Owner *RSPCA*
Editor *Sarah Evans*
Circulation 50,000
BI-MONTHLY RSPCA youth membership magazine. Articles (pet care, etc.) are written in-house. Good-quality animal photographs welcome.

Animals and You
D.C. Thomson & Co. Ltd, 2 Albert Square, Dundee DD1 9QJ
☎01382 223131 Fax 01382 322214
✉ animalsandyou@dcthomson.co.uk
Owner *D.C. Thomson & Co. Ltd*
Editor *Margaret Monaghan*
Circulation 75,000
Founded 1998. MONTHLY magazine aimed at girls, aged 7–11 years who love animals. Contains cute 'n' cuddly pin-ups, pet tips and advice, animal charity information, photo stories, puzzles, readers' pictures and drawings. Most work done in-house but will consider short features, photographic or with good illustrations. Approach by e-mail.

Antiquesnews incorporating Antiques & Art Independent
PO Box 483, Winchester SO23 3BL
☎07000 268478
✉ antiquesnews@hotmail.com
www.antiquesnews.co.uk
Owners *A.J. & M.K. Keniston*
Publisher/Editor *Tony Keniston*
Founded 1997. WEEKLY. Up-to-date information online for the British antiques and art trade. News, photographs, gossip and controversial views on all aspects of the fine art and antiques world welcome. Articles on antiques and fine arts themselves are not featured. Approach in writing with ideas.

Apex Advertiser
PO Box 7086, Clacton-on-Sea CO15 5WN
☎01255 428500 Fax 0870 046 6536
✉ mail@apexadvertiser.co.uk
www.apexadvertiser.co.uk
Owner *Apex Publishing Ltd*
Editor *Chris Cowlin*
Circulation 12,000
Founded 2002. MONTHLY advertising magazine including guides and information, features, listings and reviews. Approach by post, only.

Apollo Magazine
22 Old Queen Street, London SW1H 9HP
☎020 7961 0107
✉ editorial@apollomag.com
www.apollo-magazine.com
Owner *The Spectator (1828) Ltd*
Chief Executive *Andrew Neil*
Editor *Michael Hall*
Founded 1925. MONTHLY. Specialist articles on art and antiques, exhibition and book reviews, information on dealers and auction houses. Unsolicited mss welcome but please make initial contact by e-mail. Interested in new research on fine and decorative arts of all eras, and architecture.

The Architects' Journal
151 Rosebery Avenue, London EC1R 4GB
☎020 7505 6700 Fax 020 7505 6701
www.ajplus.co.uk
Owner *Emap Construct*
Editor *Isabel Allen*
Circulation 11,680
WEEKLY trade magazine dealing with all aspects of the industry. No unsolicited mss. Approach in writing with ideas.

Architectural Design

John Wiley & Sons, 3rd Floor, International House, Ealing Broadway Centre, London W5 5DB
☎020 8326 3800 Fax 020 8326 3801

Owner *John Wiley & Sons Ltd*
Editor *Helen Castle*
Development Editor *Mariangela Palazzi-Williams*
Circulation 5000

Founded 1930. Bɪ-ᴍᴏɴᴛʜʟʏ. Sold as a book and journal as well as online, *AD* charts theoretical and topical developments in architecture. Format consists of 128pp, the first part dedicated to a theme compiled by a specially commissioned guest-editor; the back section (AD+) carries series and more current one-off articles. Unsolicited mss not welcome generally, though journalistic contributions will be considered for the back section.

The Architectural Review

151 Rosebery Avenue, London EC1R 4GB
☎020 7505 6725 Fax 020 7505 6701
www.arplus.com

Owner *Emap Construct*
Editor *Paul Finch*
Circulation 21,583

Mᴏɴᴛʜʟʏ international professional magazine dealing with architecture and all aspects of design. No unsolicited mss. Approach in writing with ideas.

Arena

Endeavour House, 189 Shaftesbury Avenue, London WC2H 8JG
☎020 7437 9011
✉ hollie.moat@emap.com

Owner *Emap East*
Editor *Giles Hattersley*
Circulation 34,556

Mᴏɴᴛʜʟʏ style and general interest magazine for men. Intelligent articles and profiles.

Fᴇᴀᴛᴜʀᴇs Fashion, lifestyle, film, television, politics, business, music, media, design, art and architecture. Ideas for articles will be considered; send by e-mail.

The Armourer Magazine

PO Box 161, Congleton CW12 3WJ
☎01260 278044 Fax 01260 278044
✉ editor@armourer.co.uk
www.armourer.co.uk

Owner *Beaumont Publishing Ltd*
Editor *Irene Moore*

Circulation 15,000

Founded 1994. Bɪ-ᴍᴏɴᴛʜʟʏ. Militaria, military antiques, military history, events and auctions, with an emphasis on the First and Second World Wars. Unsolicited military-related contributions are welcome but 'we do not have an editorial budget'. Approach by e-mail in the first instance.

Art Monthly

4th Floor, 28 Charing Cross Road, London WC2H 0DB
☎020 7240 0389 Fax 020 7497 0726
✉ info@artmonthly.co.uk
www.artmonthly.co.uk

Owner *Britannia Art Publications Ltd*
Editor *Patricia Bickers*
Circulation 6000

Founded 1976. Tᴇɴ ɪssᴜᴇs ʏᴇᴀʀʟʏ. News and features of relevance to those interested in modern and contemporary visual art. Unsolicited mss welcome. Contributions should be addressed to the deputy editor, accompanied by s.a.e.

Fᴇᴀᴛᴜʀᴇs Always commissioned. Interviews and articles of up to 2000 words on art theory, individual artists, contemporary art history and issues affecting the arts (e.g. funding and arts education). Exhibition and book reviews: 750–1000 words.

Nᴇᴡs Brief reports (250–300 words) on art issues.

Pᴀʏᴍᴇɴᴛ negotiable.

The Art Newspaper

70 South Lambeth Road, London SW8 1RL
☎020 7735 3331 Fax 020 7735 3332
✉ contact@theartnewspaper.com
www.theartnewspaper.com

Owner *Umberto Allemandi & Co. Publishing*
Editor *Cristina Ruiz*
Circulation 22,000

Founded 1990. Mᴏɴᴛʜʟʏ. Tabloid format with hard news on the international art market, news, museums, exhibitions, archaeology, conservation, books and current debate topics. Length 250–2000 words. No unsolicited mss. Approach with ideas in writing. Commissions only.

Art Review

1 Sekforde Street, London EC1R 0BE
☎020 7107 2760 Fax 020 7107 2761
✉ office@artreview.com
www.artreview.com

Owner *Dennis Hotz*

Editor *Mark Rappolt*
Deputy Editor *Skye Sherwin*
Circulation 35,000

Founded 1949. MONTHLY magazine of international contemporary art. Features, profiles, previews and reviews of artists and exhibitions worldwide. 'We have a very international focus so it's important that the artist is exhibiting internationally and has good gallery representation.'
FEATURES *Mark Rappolt* Max. 1500 words. E-mail pitch and c.v. at least three months in advance of related show/publication. PAYMENT £400–500.
NEWS All items written in-house.

The Artist

Caxton House, 63–65 High Street, Tenterden TN30 6BD
☎0158076 3673 Fax 0158076 5411
www.theartistmagazine.co.uk
Owner/Editor *Sally Bulgin*
Circulation 21,500

Founded 1931. MONTHLY. Art journalists, artists, art tutors and writers with a good knowledge of art materials are invited to write to the editor with ideas for practical and informative features about art, materials, techniques and artists.

Athletics Weekly

83 Park Road, Peterborough PE1 2TN
☎01733 898440 Fax 01733 898441
✉ results@athletics-weekly.co.uk
www.athleticsweekly.com
Owner *Descartes Publishing*
Editor *Jason Henderson*
Results Editor *Paul Halford*
Circulation 14,000

Founded 1945. WEEKLY. Covers track and field, road, fell, cross-country, race walking. Results, fixtures, interviews, technical coaching articles and news surrounding build up to 2012 Olympics.
NEWS *Jon Mulkeen* Max. 400 words.
FEATURES *Jason Henderson* Max. 2000 words. Approach in writing.
PAYMENT negotiable.

Attitude

Northern & Shell Tower, City Harbour, 4 Selsdon Way, London E14 9GL
☎020 7308 5090 Fax 020 7308 5377
✉ attitude@attitudemag.co.uk
www.myspace.com/attitude_mag
Owner *Giant Clipper*
Editor *Adam Mattera*

Deputy Editor *Jamie Hakim*
Circulation 60,000

Founded 1994. MONTHLY. Style magazine aimed primarily, but not exclusively, at gay men. Celebrity, fashion and cultural coverage. Brief summaries of proposed features, together with details of previously published work, should be sent by post or e-mail only. 'It sounds obvious, but anyone wanting to contribute to the magazine should read it first.'

The Author

84 Drayton Gardens, London SW10 9SB
☎020 7373 6642
✉ theauthor@societyofauthors.org
Owner *The Society of Authors*
Editor *Andrew Rosenheim*
Manager *Kate Pool*
Circulation 9000

Founded 1890. QUARTERLY journal of the **Society of Authors**. Most articles are commissioned.

Auto Express

30 Cleveland Street, London W1T 4JD
☎020 7907 6200 Fax 020 7907 6234
✉ editorial@autoexpress.co.uk
www.autoexpress.co.uk
Owner *Dennis Publishing*
Editor *David Johns*
Associate Editor *Tom Johnston*
Features Editor *Mat Watson*
Circulation 88,000

Founded 1988. WEEKLY consumer motoring title with news, drives, tests, investigations, etc.
NEWS News stories and tip-offs welcome. Fillers 100 words max.; leads 300 words.
FEATURES Ideas welcome. No fully-written articles – features will be commissioned if appropriate. Max. 2000 words.
PAYMENT £350 per 1000 words.

Autocar

Haymarket Publishing, Teddington Studios, Broom Road, Teddington TW11 9BE
☎020 8267 5630 Fax 020 8267 5759
✉ autocar@haymarket.com
www.autocar.co.uk
Owner *Haymarket Publishing Ltd*
Editor *Chas Hallett*
News Editor *Dan Stevens*
Circulation 62,577

Founded 1895. WEEKLY. All news stories, features, interviews, scoops, ideas, tip-offs and photographs welcome. PAYMENT negotiable.

Aviation News

HPC, Drury Lane, St Leonards on Sea
TN38 9BJ
☎01424 205536 Fax 01424 443693
✉ editor@aviation-news.co.uk
www.aviation-news.co.uk

Owner *Hastings Printing Company*
Editor *David Baker*
Circulation 21,000

Founded 1939. MONTHLY review of aviation for those interested in military, commercial and business aircraft and equipment – old and new. Will consider articles on military and civil aircraft, airports, air forces, current and historical subjects. No fiction.

FEATURES 'New writers always welcome and if the copy is not good enough it is returned with guidance attached.' Max. 5000 words.

NEWS Items are always considered from new sources. Max. 300 words.

PAYMENT negotiable.

Balance

Diabetes UK, 10 Parkway, London NW1 7AA
☎020 7424 1000 Fax 020 7424 1001
✉ balance@diabetes.org.uk

Owner *Diabetes UK*
Editor *Martin Cullen*
Circulation 250,000

Founded 1935. BI-MONTHLY. Unsolicited mss are not accepted. Writers may submit a brief proposal in writing. Only topics relevant to diabetes will be considered.

NEWS Short pieces about activities relating to diabetes and the lifestyle of people with diabetes. Max. 150 words.

FEATURES Medical, diet and lifestyle features written by people with diabetes or with an interest and expert knowledge in the field. General features are mostly based on experience or personal observation. Max. 1500 words.

PAYMENT NUJ rates.

The Banker

Tabernacle Court, 16–28 Tabernacle Street,
London EC2A 4DD
☎020 7382 8507 Fax 020 7382 8586
✉ stephen.timewell@ft.com
www.thebanker.com

Owner *FT Business*
Editor-in-Chief *Stephen Timewell*
Circulation 26,089

Founded 1926. MONTHLY. News and features on banking, finance and capital markets worldwide and technology.

BBC Gardeners'World Magazine

Woodlands, 80 Wood Lane, London W12 0TT
☎020 8433 3959 Fax 020 8433 3986
✉ adam.pasco@bbc.co.uk
www.gardenersworld.com

Owner *BBC Worldwide Publishing Ltd*
Editor *Adam Pasco*
Deputy Editor *Lucy Hall*
Commissioning Editor *Kevin Smith*
Circulation 236,207

Founded 1991. MONTHLY. Gardening advice, ideas and inspiration. No unsolicited mss. Approach by phone or in writing with ideas – interested in features about exceptional small gardens. Also interested in any exciting new gardens showing good design and planting ideas as well as new plants and the stories behind them. 'The magazine aims to be the first to bring news of new trends and developments, and always welcomes ideas from contributors.'

BBC Good Food

Woodlands, 80 Wood Lane, London W12 0TT
☎020 8433 2000 Fax 020 8433 3931
✉ goodfood.magazine@bbc.co.uk
www.bbcgoodfood.com

Owner *BBC Worldwide Publishing Ltd*
Editor *Gillian Carter*
Circulation 350,391

Founded 1989. MONTHLY recipe magazine featuring celebrity chefs. No unsolicited mss.

BBC History Magazine

Tower House, Fairfax Street, Bristol BS1 3BN
☎0117 927 9009
✉ historymagazine@bbcmagazinesbristol.com
www.bbcmagazinesbristol.com

Owner *Bristol Magazines Ltd*
Editor *Dave Musgrove*
Circulation 53,783

Founded 2000. MONTHLY. General news and features on British and international history, with books and CD reviews, listings of history events, TV and radio history programmes and regular features for those interested in history and current affairs. Winner, British Society of Magazine Editors 'Editor of the Year Award', 2002, for general interest and current affairs titles. Will consider submissions from academic or otherwise expert historians/archaeologists as well as, occasionally, from historically literate journalists who include expert analysis and historiography with a well-told narrative. Ideas for regular features are welcome. Also publishes cartoons, quizzes and crosswords. 'We cannot guarantee to acknowledge all unsolicited mss.'

FEATURES should be pegged to anniversaries or forthcoming books/TV programmes, current affairs topics, etc. 750–3000 words.

NEWS 400–500 words. Send short letter or e-mail with synopsis, giving appropriate sources, pegs for publication dates, etc.

PAYMENT negotiable.

BBC Homes & Antiques

14th Floor, Tower House, Fairfax Street, Bristol BS1 3BN

☎0117 927 9009

www.bbcmagazinesbristol.com

Owner *BBC Worldwide Publishing Ltd*
Editor *Angela Linforth*
Circulation 100,212

Founded 1993. MONTHLY traditional home interest magazine with a strong bias towards antiques and collectibles. Opportunities for free-lancers are limited; most features are commissioned from regular stable of contributors. No fiction, health and beauty, fashion or general showbusiness. Approach with ideas by phone or in writing.

FEATURES *Natasha Goodfellow* At-home features: inspirational houses – people-led items. Pieces commissioned on recce shots and cuttings. Guidelines available on request. Send cuttings of relevant work published. Max. 1500 words. PAYMENT negotiable.

BBC Music Magazine

9th Floor, Tower House, Fairfax Street, Bristol BS1 3BN

☎0117 927 9009 Fax 0117 934 9008

✉ music@bbcmagazinesbristol.com

www.bbcmusicmagazine.com

Owner *BBC Worldwide Publishing Ltd*
Editor *Oliver Condy*
Circulation 47,091

Founded 1992. MONTHLY. All areas of classical music. Not interested in unsolicited material. Approach with ideas by e-mail or fax.

BBC Top Gear Magazine

Room A1004, Woodlands, 80 Wood Lane, London W12 0TT

☎020 8433 3716 Fax 020 8433 3754

www.topgear.com

Owner *BBC Magazines*
Editor *Michael Harvey*
Circulation 190,032

Founded 1993. MONTHLY general interest

motoring magazine. No unsolicited material as most features are commissioned.

BBC Wildlife Magazine

14th Floor, Tower House, Fairfax Street, Bristol BS1 3BN

☎0117 927 9009 Fax 0117 927 9008

✉ wildlifemagazine@bbcmagazinesbristol.com

www.bbcwildlifemagazine.com

Owner *Bristol Magazines Ltd*
Editor *Sophie Stafford*
Features Editor *Fergus Collins*
News & Travel Editor *James Fair*
Circulation 47,007

Founded 1963. Formerly *Wildlife*; became *BBC Wildlife Magazine* in 1983. THIRTEEN ISSUES A YEAR. Welcomes idea pitches but not unsolicited mss. Read guidelines on website to improve chances of success.

FEATURES Most features commissioned from excellent writers with expert knowledge of wildlife or conservation subjects. Max. 2000 words.

NEWS Most news stories commissioned from known freelancers. Max. 400 words. PAYMENT Features, £200–450; news, £80–120.

Bee World

See **Journal of Apicultural Research**

Bella

H. Bauer Publishing, Academic House, 24–28 Oval Road, London NW1 7DT

☎020 7241 8000 Fax 020 7241 8056

Owner *H. Bauer Publishing*
Editor-in-Chief *Jayne Marsden*
Circulation 316,281

Founded 1987. WEEKLY. Women's magazine specialising in real-life, human interest stories.

FEATURES *Bridget Cowan* Contributions welcome for some sections of the magazine: readers' letters, 'Blush with Bella'.

Best

33 Broadwick Street, London W1F 0DQ

☎020 7339 4000 Fax 020 7339 4580

✉ best@acp-natmag.co.uk

Owner *National Magazine Company/ACP*
Editor *Michelle Hather*
Circulation 362,417

Founded 1987. WEEKLY women's magazine. Multiple features, news, short stories on all topics of interest to women. Important for would-be contributors to study the magazine's style which differs from many other women's weeklies. Approach in writing with s.a.e.

FEATURES *Helen Garston, Charlotte Seligman* Max. 1500 words. No unsolicited mss.

FICTION *Pat Richardson* Short story slot: 900–1200 words. Send s.a.e. for guidelines.

PAYMENT negotiable.

Best of British

Church Lane Publishing Ltd, Bank Chambers, 27a Market Place, Market Deeping PE6 8EA
☎01778 342814
✉ mail@british.fsbusiness.co.uk
www.bestofbritishmag.co.uk

Owner *Church Lane Publishing Ltd*
Editor-in-Chief *Ian Beacham*
Assistant Editor *Linne Matthews*

Founded 1994. MONTHLY magazine celebrating all things British, both past and present. Emphasis on nostalgia – memories from the 1940s, 1950s and 1960s. Study of the magazine is advised in the first instance. All preliminary approaches should be made in writing or by e-mail.

The Big Issue

1–5 Wandsworth Road, London SW8 2LN
☎020 7526 3200 Fax 020 7526 3201
www.bigissue.com

Editor-in-Chief *A. John Bird*
Editor *Charles Howgego*
Deputy Editor *Judy Kerr*
Circulation 68,853; 144,750 (Group)

Founded 1991. WEEKLY. An award-winning campaigning and street-wise general interest magazine sold in London, the Midlands, the North East and South of England. Separate regional editions sold in Manchester, Scotland, Wales and the South West.

NEWS *Judy Kerr* Hard-hitting exclusive stories with emphasis on social injustice aimed at national leaders.

ARTS *Charles Howgego* Interested in interviews and analysis ideas. Reviews written in-house. Send synopses to arts editor.

FEATURES Interviews, campaigns, comment, opinion and social issues reflecting a varied and informed audience. Balance includes social issues but mixed with arts and cultural features. Freelance writers used each week commissioned from a variety of contributors. Best approach in the first instance is to e-mail or post synopses to Editor *Charles Howgego* with examples of work. Max. 1500 words.

The Big Issue Cymru

55 Charles Street, Cardiff CF10 2GD
☎029 2025 5670 Fax 029 2025 5672
✉ editor@bigissuecymru.co.uk
www.bigissuecymru.co.uk
Editor *Rachell Howells*
Circulation 7,484

Founded 1993. WEEKLY. Hard-hitting social and news features plus arts and entertainment.

FEATURES/NEWS *Rachel Howells* Welcomes contributions but must be relevant to a Welsh readership. Approach by e-mail. Lead in of four to six weeks. Max. 1000 words (features); 350 (news). No poetry or fiction.

The Big Issue in Scotland

MirVillage, 71 Oxford Street, Glasgow G5 9EP
☎0141 418 7000 Fax 0141 418 7061
✉ editorial@bigissuescotland.com
www.bigissuescotland.com
Editor *Clare Harris*
Circulation 24,212

WEEKLY. Coverage of social issues, arts and culture, sport, interviews; news and hard-hitting journalism.

The Big Issue in the North

135–141 Oldham Street, Manchester M4 1LN
☎0161 834 6300 Fax 0161 832 3237
✉ editorial@bigissueinthenorth.com
www.thebiglifecompany.com

Owner *The Big Life Company*
Editor *Matt Baker*
Circulation 30,824

Launched 1992. WEEKLY. Entertainment, celebrity interviews, environmental issues and issues from the social sector as well as homelessness. Welcomes news stories not covered by the national press; approach by e-mail.

The Big Issue South West

5 Brunswick Court, Brunswick Square, Bristol BS2 8PT
☎0117 916 6593 Fax 0017 916 6599
✉ editorial@bigissuesouthwest.co.uk
Editor *Rachell Howells*
Circulation 13,377

Founded 1994. WEEKLY. Hard-hitting, socially aware news and features, local arts and entertainment. Welcomes news features with a regional relevance. No poetry or fiction.

FEATURES/NEWS *Rachell Howells* Items must be regionally specific, date pegged, new information and people-based. Approach by e-mail. Max. 1000 words (features); 350 (news).

Bike

Emap Automotive Ltd, Media House, Lynch Wood, Peterborough PE2 6EA
☎01733 468181 Fax 01733 468196
✉ bike@emap.com
www.bikemagazine.co.uk
Owner *Emap Plc*
Editor *John Westlake*
Circulation 90,013
Founded 1971. MONTHLY. Broad-based motor-cycle magazine. Approach by e-mail.

Bird Life Magazine

The RSPB, UK Headquarters, The Lodge, Sandy SG19 2DL
☎01767 680551 Fax 01767 683262
✉ derek.niemann@rspb.org.uk
Owner *Royal Society for the Protection of Birds*
Editor *Derek Niemann*
Circulation 90,000
Founded 1965. BI-MONTHLY. Bird, wildlife and nature conservation for 8–12-year-olds (RSPB Wildlife Explorers members). No unsolicited mss. No 'captive/animal welfare' articles.
FEATURES Unsolicited material rarely used.
NEWS News releases welcome. Approach in writing in the first instance.

Bird Watching

Emap Active, Bretton Court, Peterborough PE3 8DZ
☎0870 062 0200 Fax 01733 465376
✉ kevin.wilmot@emap.com
www.birdwatching.co.uk
Owner *Emap Active*
Editor *Kevin Wilmot*
Circulation 20,296
Founded 1986. MONTHLY magazine for bird-watchers at all levels of experience. Offers practical advice of where and when to see birds, how to identify them, product reviews (particularly binoculars, telescopes and digiscoping equipment), extensive bird sightings, 'Go Birding' walks (10 each issue), news and general articles.
FEATURES Interested in authoratative articles on bird behaviour and bird watching/sites in the UK. Please send synopsis, not the whole piece. Max. 1000 words.
NEWS UK news pre-eminent, preferably with pictures. Max. 350 words.
FEES negotiable.

Birds

The RSPB, UK Headquarters, The Lodge, Sandy SG19 2DL
☎01767 680551 Fax 01767 683262
✉ rob.hume@rspb.org.uk
www.rspb.org.uk
Owner *Royal Society for the Protection of Birds*
Editor *R.A. Hume*
Circulation 620,780
QUARTERLY magazine which covers not only wild birds but also other wildlife and related conservation topics. No interest in features on pet birds or 'rescued' sick/injured/orphaned ones. Content refers mostly to RSPB work so opportunities for freelance work on other subjects are limited but some freelance submissions are used in most issues. Phone or e-mail to discuss.

Birdwatch

B403A The Chocolate Factory, 5 Clarendon Road, London N22 6XJ
☎020 8881 0550 Fax 020 8881 0990
✉ editorial@birdwatch.co.uk
www.birdwatch.co.uk
Owner *Solo Publishing*
Editor *Dominic Mitchell*
Circulation 13,000
Founded 1992. MONTHLY magazine featuring illustrated articles on all aspects of birds and birdwatching, especially in Britain. No unsolicited mss. Approach in writing with synopsis of 100 words max. Annual **Birdwatch Bird Book of the Year** award (see entry under *Prizes*).
FEATURES *Dominic Mitchell* Unusual angles/personal accounts, if well-written. Articles of an educative or practical nature suited to the readership. Max. 2000 words.
FICTION *Dominic Mitchell* Very little opportunity although occasional short story published. Max. 1500 words.
NEWS *Simon Papps* Very rarely use external material.
PAYMENT £50 per 1000 words.

Bizarre

30 Cleveland Street, London W1T 4JD
☎020 7907 6000 Fax 020 7907 6516
✉ bizarre@dennis.co.uk
www.bizarremag.com
Owner *Dennis Publishing*
Editor *Alex Godfrey*
Circulation 60,667
Founded 1997. MONTHLY magazine featuring amazing stories and images from around the world. No fiction, poetry, illustrations, short snippets.

FEATURES *Kate Hodges* No unsolicited mss. Send synopsis by post or e-mail. PAYMENT negotiable.

Black Beauty & Hair

2nd Floor, Culvert House, Culvert Road, Battersea, London SW11 5HD
☎020 7720 2108 Fax 020 7498 3023
✉ info@blackbeautyandhair.com
www.blackbeautyandhair.com
Owner *Hawker Consumer Publications Ltd*
Publisher *Pat Petker* (☎ ext. 207)
Editor *Irene Shelley*
Circulation 19,697

BI-MONTHLY with one annual special: *The Hairstyle Book* in October; and a *Bridal Supplement* in the April/May issue. Black hair and beauty magazine with emphasis on authoritative articles relating to hair, beauty, fashion, health and lifestyle. Unsolicited contributions welcome.

FEATURES Beauty and fashion pieces welcome from writers with a sound knowledge of the Afro-Caribbean beauty scene plus bridal features. Minimum 1000 words.

PAYMENT £100 per 1000 words.

Black Static

5 Martins Lane, Witcham, Ely CB6 2LB
✉ andy@ttapress.demon.co.uk
www.ttapress.com
Owner *TTA Press*
Editor *Andy Cox*
Formerly *The Third Alternative*, founded 1993. BIMONTHLY colour horror magazine: short fiction, news and gossip, film and television, manga and anime books. Publishes talented newcomers alongside famous authors. Unsolicited mss welcome if accompanied by s.a.e. or e-mail address for overseas submissions (max. 8000 words). Fiction submissions as hard copy only; feature suggestions can be e-mailed. Potential contributors are advised to study the magazine. Contracts are exchanged and payment made upon acceptance. Winner of several British Fantasy Awards.

Bliss Magazine

Coach and Horses Passage, The Pantiles, Tunbridge Wells TN2 5UJ
☎01892 5001008 Fax 01892 545666
✉ bliss@panini.co.uk
www.mybliss.co.uk
Owner *Panini UK Ltd*
Editor *Leslie Sinoway*
Features Editor *Angeli Milburn* (amilburn@

panini.co.uk)
Circulation 151,729
Founded 1995. MONTHLY teenage lifestyle magazine for girls. No unsolicited mss; 'e-mail the Features Editor with an idea and then follow up with a call.'

NEWS Worldwide teenage news. Max. 200 words.

FEATURES Real life teenage stories with subjects willing to be photographed. Reports on teenage issues. Max. 1500 words.

Blueprint

6–14 Underwood Street, London N1 7JQ
☎020 7549 2542
✉ vrichardson@wilmington.co.uk
www.blueprintmagazine.co.uk
Owner *Wilmington Media*
Editor *Vicky Richardson*
Deputy Editor *Tim Abrahams*
Senior Staff Writer *Peter Kelly*
Circulation 10,000

Founded 1983. MONTHLY. 'Crossing the boundaries of design and architecture (from graphics and product design to interiors and urban development), Blueprint examines their impact on society in general.' Features, news and reviews. Welcomes ideas and pitches for articles on topics relevant to the magazine; no completed features. Approach by e-mail.

The Book Collector

PO Box 12426, London W11 3GW
☎020 7792 3492 Fax 020 7792 3492
✉ editor@thebookcollector.co.uk (editorial)
www.thebookcollector.co.uk
Owner *The Collector Ltd*
Editor *Nicolas J. Barker*
Founded 1950. QUARTERLY magazine on bibliography and the history of books, book-collecting, libraries and the book trade.

Book World Magazine

2 Caversham Street, London SW3 4AH
☎020 7351 4995 Fax 020 7351 4995
✉ leonard.holdsworth@btinternet.com
Owner *Christchurch Publishers Ltd*
Editor *James Hughes*
Circulation 5500
Founded 1980. MONTHLY news and reviews for serious book collectors, librarians, antiquarian and other booksellers. No unsolicited mss. Interested in material relevant to literature, art and book collecting. Send letter in the first instance.

The Bookseller

Endeavour House, 5th Floor, 189 Shaftesbury Avenue, London WC2H 8TJ
☎020 7420 6006 Fax 020 7420 6103
www.theBookseller.com
Owner *VNU Entertainment Media*
Editor-in-Chief *Neill Denny*

Trade journal of the book trade, publishing, retail and libraries – the essential guide to the book business since 1858. Trade news and features, including special features, company news, publishing trends, bestseller data, etc. Unsolicited mss rarely used as most writing is either done in-house or commissioned from experts within the trade. Approach in writing first.

Boxing Monthly

40 Morpeth Road, London E9 7LD
☎020 8986 4141 Fax 020 8986 4145
✉ mail@boxing-monthly.demon.co.uk
www.boxing-monthly.co.uk
Owner *Topwave Ltd*
Editor *Glyn Leach*
Circulation 25,000

Founded 1989. MONTHLY. International coverage of professional boxing; previews, reports and interviews. Unsolicited material welcome. Interested in small hall shows and grass-roots knowledge. No big fight reports. Approach in writing in the first instance.

Boyz

18 Brewer Street, London W1F 0SH
☎020 7025 6120 Fax 020 7025 6109
✉ hudson@boyz.co.uk
Editor *David Bridle*
Circulation 55,000

Founded 1991. WEEKLY entertainment and features magazine aimed at a gay readership covering clubs, fashion, TV, films, music, theatre, celebrities and the UK gay scene in general. Unsolicited mss are looked at but not often used.

Brides

Vogue House, Hanover Square, London W1S 1JU
☎020 7499 9080 Fax 020 7152 3369
www.bridesmagazine.co.uk
Owner *Condé Nast Publications Ltd*
Editor *Deborah Joseph*
Circulation 67,181

Founded 1955. BI-MONTHLY. Much of the magazine is produced in-house, but a good, relevant feature on cakes, jewellery, music, flowers, etc. is always welcome. Max. 1000 words. Prospective contributors should make initial contact by e-mail.

British Birds

4 Harlequin Gardens, St Leonards-on-Sea TN37 7PF
☎01424 755155 Fax 01424 755155
✉ editor@britishbirds.co.uk
Editor *Dr R. Riddington*
Circulation 6000

Founded 1907. MONTHLY ornithological journal. Features main papers on topics such as behaviour, distribution, ecology, identification and taxonomy; annual *Report on Rare Birds in Great Britain* and *Rare Breeding Birds in the UK*; sponsored competition for Bird Photograph of the Year. Unsolicited mss welcome from ornithologists.

FEATURES Well-researched, original material relating to Western Palearctic birds welcome.

NEWS *Adrian Pitches* (adrian.pitches@ blueyonder.co.uk) Items ranging from conservation to humour. Max. 200 words.

PAYMENT for photographs, drawings, paintings and main papers.

British Chess Magazine

The Chess Shop, 44 Baker Street, London W1U 7RT
☎020 7486 8222 Fax 020 7486 3355
✉ bcmchess@compuserve.com
www.bcmchess.co.uk
Director/Editor *John Saunders*

Founded 1881. MONTHLY. Emphasis on tournaments, the history of chess and chess-related literature. Approach in writing with ideas. Unsolicited mss not welcome unless from qualified chess experts and players.

British Journalism Review

Sage Publications Ltd, 1 Oliver's Yard, 55 City Road, London EC1Y 1Sp
☎020 7324 8500 Fax 020 7324 8600
✉ bill.hagerty@btinternet.com
www.bjr.org.uk
www.bjr.sagepub.com
Owner *BJR Publishing Ltd*
Editor *Bill Hagerty*

Founded 1988. QUARTERLY. Media magazine providing a forum for the news media. Freelance contributions welcome: non-academic articles on all aspects of the news media only. No academic papers. Approach by e-mail. Max. 2000 words.

British Medical Journal

BMA House, Tavistock Square, London
WC1H 9JR
☎020 7387 4499 Fax 020 7383 6418
✉ editor@bmj.com
www.bmj.com
Owner *British Medical Association*
Editor *Dr Fiona Goodlee*
Circulation 122,982

One of the world's leading general medical journals.

British Philatelic Bulletin

Royal Mail, 148 Old Street, London
EC1V 9HQ
☎020 7250 2038 Fax 020 7250 2389

Owner *Royal Mail*
Editor *John Holman*
Circulation 20,000

Founded 1963. MONTHLY bulletin giving details of forthcoming British stamps, features on older stamps and postal history, and book reviews. Welcomes photographs of interesting, unusual or historic letter boxes.

FEATURES Articles on all aspects of British philately. Max. 1500 words.

NEWS Reports on exhibitions and philatelic events. Max. 500 words. Approach in writing in the first instance.

PAYMENT £75 per 1000 words.

British Railway Modelling

The Maltings, West Street, Bourne PE10 9PH
☎01778 391027 Fax 01778 425437
✉ johne@warnersgroup.co.uk
www.brmodelling.co.uk
Owner *Warners Group Publications Plc*
Managing Editor *David Brown*
Editor *John Emerson* Assistant Editor *Tony Wright*
Circulation 25,000

Founded 1993. MONTHLY. A general magazine for the practising modeller. Ideas are welcome. Interested in features on quality models, from individual items to complete layouts. Approach in writing first.

FEATURES Articles on practical elements of the hobby, e.g. locomotive construction, kit conversions, etc. Layout features and articles on individual items which represent high standards of the railway modelling art. Max. length 6000 words (single feature).

NEWS News and reviews containing the model railway trade, new products, etc. Max. length 1000 words.

Broadcast

33–39 Bowling Green Lane, London
EC1R 0DA
☎020 7505 8014 Fax 020 7505 8050
Owner *Emap Communications*
Editor *Lisa Campbell*
Circulation 10,997

Founded 1960. WEEKLY. Opportunities for freelance contributions. Write to the relevant editor in the first instance.

FEATURES *Emily Booth* Any broadcasting issue. Max. 1500 words.

NEWS *Chris Curtis* Broadcasting news. Max. 350 words.

PAYMENT £250 per 1000 words.

Build It

1 Canada Square, Canary Wharf, London
E14 5AP
☎020 7772 8440 Fax 020 7772 8584
✉ buildit@oceanmedia.co.uk
www.buildit-online.co.uk
Owner *Ocean Media*
Editor *Catherine Monk*
Circulation 23,663

Founded 1990. MONTHLY magazine covering self-build, conversion and renovation. Unsolicited material welcome on self-build case studies as well as articles on technical construction, architecture and design and dealing with builders. Max. length 2500 words. Approach by post or e-mail.

Building Magazine

8th Floor, Ludgate House, 245 Blackfriars Road, London SE1 9UY
☎020 7560 4141 Fax 020 7560 4080
✉ dchevin@cmpi.biz
www.building.co.uk
Owner *CMP Information Ltd*
Editor *Denise Chevin*
Circulation 24,193

WEEKLY magazine for the whole construction industry, from architects and engineers to contractors and house builders. News and features. No unsolicited contributions as all material is commissioned, although legal items welcome.

The Burlington Magazine

14–16 Duke's Road, London WC1H 9SZ
☎020 7388 1228 Fax 020 7388 1230
✉ editorial@burlington.org.uk
www.burlington.org.uk
Owner *The Burlington Magazine Publications Ltd*

Managing Director *Kate Trevelyan*
Editor *Richard Shone*
Deputy Editor *Bart Cornelis*
Associate Editor *Jane Martineau*
Contributing Editor *John-Paul Stonard*
Founded 1903. MONTHLY. Unsolicited contributions welcome on the subject of art history provided they are previously unpublished. All preliminary approaches should be made in writing.

EXHIBITION REVIEWS Usually commissioned, but occasionally unsolicited reviews are published if appropriate. Max. 1000 words.

ARTICLES Max. 4500 words. PAYMENT Max. £150.

SHORTER NOTICES Max. 2000 words. PAYMENT Max. £80.

Business Brief

PO Box 582, Five Oaks, St Saviour JE4 8XQ
☎01534 611600 Fax 01534 611610
✉ mspeditorial@msppublishing.com
Owner *MSP Publishing*
Editor *Peter Body*
Circulation 6500 (Jersey & Guernsey)

Founded 1989. MONTHLY magazine covering business developments in the Channel Islands and how they affect the local market. Styles itself as the magazine for business people rather than just a magazine about business. Interested in business-orientated articles only – 800 words max. Approach the editor by e-mail in the first instance with telephone follow-up.

PAYMENT negotiable.

Business Traveller

2nd Floor, Cardinal House, Albemarle Street, London W1S 4TE
☎020 7647 6330 Fax 020 7647 6331
✉ editorial@businesstraveller.com
www.businesstraveller.com
Owner *Panacea Publications*
Editorial Director *Tom Otley*
Circulation 500,000 (worldwide)

MONTHLY. Consumer publication. Opportunities exist for freelance writers. Would-be contributors are strongly advised to study the magazine or the website first. Approach in writing with ideas.

PAYMENT varies.

The Business

Press Holdings Media Group, 22 Old Queen Street, London SW1H 9HP
☎020 7961 0000

www.thebusiness.co.uk
Editor-in-Chief *Andrew Neil*
Editor *Allister Heath*
Political Editor *Fraser Nelson*
City Editor *Rupert Steiner*
Investments Editor *Tom Burroughs*

Launched in 1998 as a Sunday national newspaper dedicated to business, finance and politics. Relaunched as a magazine in 2007, published on a Thursday. No unsolicited material. All ideas must be discussed with the department's editor in advance.

Campaign

174 Hammersmith Road, London W6 7JP
☎020 8267 4683 Fax 020 8267 4914
✉ campaign@haymarket.com
www.brandrepublic.com
Owner *Haymarket Publishing Ltd*
Editor *Claire Beale*
Circulation 10,309

Founded 1968. WEEKLY. Lively magazine serving the advertising and related industries. Freelance contributors are best advised to write in the first instance.

FEATURES Ideas welcome.

NEWS Relevant news stories of up to 320 words.

PAYMENT negotiable.

Camping and Caravanning

Greenfields House, Westwood Way, Coventry CV4 8JH
☎0845 130 7631 Fax 024 7647 5413
Owner *The Camping and Caravanning Club*
Editor *Nick Harding*
Circulation 201,827

Founded 1901. MONTHLY. Interested in journalists with camping and caravanning knowledge. Write with ideas for features in the first instance.

FEATURES Outdoor pieces in general, plus items on specific regions of Britain. Max. 1200 words. Illustrations to support text essential.

Canals and Rivers

PO Box 618, Norwich NR7 0QT
☎01603 708930
✉ chris@themag.fsnet.co.uk
www.canalsandrivers.com
Owner *A.E. Morgan Publications Ltd*
Editor *Chris Cattrall*
Circulation 14,000

Covers all aspects of waterways, narrow boats

and cruisers. Contributions welcome. Make initial approach by post or e-mail.

FEATURES Waterways, narrow boats and motor cruisers, cruising reports, practical advice, etc. Unusual ideas and personal comments are particularly welcome. Max. 2000 words. Articles should be supplied in PC Windows format disk or e-mailed with JPEG images.

NEWS Items of up to 200 words welcome on the Inland Waterways System, plus photographs if possible.

PAYMENT Features, around £60 per page; news, £20.

Candis

Newhall Lane, Hoylake CH47 4BQ
☎0870 745 3001 Fax 0870 745 3003
✉ jenny@candis.co.uk
Owner *Newhall Publications*
Editor *Debbie Atwell*
Circulation 301,309

MONTHLY. General features on health and family life – no fashion or beauty items or first-person accounts of illness. No unsolicited contributions as most features are individually commissioned but fiction will be considered (max. 2000 words). Send by e-mail to Fiction Editor *John Jenkins*.

Car Mechanics

Kelsey Publishing Group, Cudham Tithe Barn, Berry's Hill, Cudham TN16 3AG
☎01959 541444/01733 771292 (editor)
Fax 01959 541400
✉ cm.mag@kelsey.co.uk
Owner *Kelsey Publishing Group*
Editor *Peter Simpson*
Circulation 35,000

MONTHLY. Practical guide to maintenance and repair of post-1978 cars for DIY and the motor trade. Unsolicited mss, with good-quality colour prints or transparencies, sent 'at sender's risk'. Initial approach by letter or phone strongly recommended, 'but please study a recent copy for style first'. No non-technical material, 'travelogues', cartoons or fiction.

FEATURES Good, entertaining and well-researched technical material welcome, especially anything presenting complex matters clearly and simply. PAYMENT negotiable 'but generous for the right material'.

Caravan Magazine

IPC Media Ltd, Leon House, 233 High Street, Croydon CR9 1HZ
☎020 8726 8000 Fax 020 8726 8299
✉ caravan@ipcmedia.com

www.caravanmagazine.co.uk
Owner *IPC Media (A Time Warner Company)*
Editor *Steve Rowe*
Circulation 13,655

Founded 1933. MONTHLY. Unsolicited mss welcome. Approach in writing with ideas. All correspondence should go direct to the editor.

FEATURES Touring with strong caravan bias, technical/DIY features and how-to section. Max. 1500 words.

PAYMENT by arrangement.

Cat World

Ancient Lights, 19 River Road, Arundel BN18 9EY
☎01903 884988 Fax 01903 885514
✉ laura@catworld.co.uk
www.catworld.co.uk
Owner *Ashdown Publishing Ltd*
Editor *Laura Quiggen*

Founded 1981. MONTHLY. Unsolicited mss welcome but initial approach in writing preferred. No poems or fiction.

FEATURES Lively, first-hand experience features on every aspect of the cat. Breeding features and veterinary articles by acknowledged experts only. Preferred length 750 or 1700 words. Accompanying pictures should be good quality and sharp. Submissions by e-mail (MS Word attachment) if possible, or by disk with accompanying hard copy and s.a.e. for return.

The Catholic Herald

Lamb's Passage, Bunhill Row, London EC1Y 8TQ
☎020 7448 3603 Fax 020 7256 9728
✉ editorial@catholicherald.co.uk
www.catholicherald.co.uk
Editor *Luke Coppen*
Features Editor *Christina Farrell*
Literary Editor *Stav Sherez*
Circulation 22,000

WEEKLY. Interested mainly in straight Catholic issues but also in general humanitarian matters, social policies, the Third World, the arts and books. PAYMENT by arrangement.

Chapman

4 Broughton Place, Edinburgh EH1 3RX
☎0131 557 2207
✉ chapman-pub@blueyonder.co.uk
www.chapman-pub.co.uk
Owner/Editor *Dr Joy Hendry*
Assistant Editor *Edmund O'Connor*
Circulation 2000

Founded 1970. Scotland's quality literary magazine. Features poetry, short works of fiction, criticism, reviews and articles on theatre, politics, language and the arts. Gives priority to Scottish writers but also has work from UK and international authors. Unsolicited material welcome if accompanied by s.a.e. Approach in writing unless discussion is needed. Priority is given to full-time writers.

FEATURES Topics of literary interest, especially Scottish literature, theatre, culture or politics. Max. 5000 words.

FICTION Short stories, occasionally novel extracts if self-contained. Max. 6000 words.

SPECIAL PAGES Poetry, both UK and non-UK in translation (mainly, but not necessarily, European).

PAYMENT by negotiation.

Chat

IPC Connect Ltd., The Blue Fin Building, 110 Southwark Street, London SE1 0SU
☎020 3148 6145
www.ipcmedia.com/pubs/chat.htm
Owner *IPC Media*
Editor *Gilly Sinclair*
Circulation 537,464

Founded 1985. WEEKLY general interest women's magazine. Unsolicited mss considered; approach in writing with ideas. Not interested in contributors 'who have never bothered to read *Chat* and therefore don't know what type of magazine it is. *Chat* does not publish fiction.'

FEATURES *Ingrid Millar* Human interest and humour. Max. 1000 words.

PAYMENT up to £1500 maximum.

Chemist & Druggist

Riverbank House, Angel Lane, Tonbridge TN9 1SE
☎01732 377487 Fax 01732 367065
✉ chemdrug@cmpmedica.com
www.dotpharmacy.com
Owner *CMP Medica*
Editor *Gary Paragpuri*
Circulation 13,956

Founded 1859. WEEKLY news magazine for the UK community pharmacy.

FEATURES practice, politics, professional matters, clinical articles and business advice. Contact by phone or e-mail to discuss features ideas.

NEWS Contact News Editor with news articles relating to local pharmacy matters, local pharmaceutical industry events and pharmacists in the news. Max. 200 words.

PAYMENT standard rates.

Child Education

Scholastic Ltd, Villiers House, Clarendon Avenue, Leamington Spa CV32 5PR
☎01926 887799 Fax 01926 883331
www.scholastic.co.uk
Owner *Scholastic Ltd*
Editor *Mike Ward*
Deputy Editor *Charlotte Ronalds*
Circulation 21,121

Founded 1923. MONTHLY magazine aimed at teachers of children aged 4–7 years. Practical articles from teachers about education for this age group are welcome. Max. 900 words. Approach in writing with synopsis.

Choice

First Floor, 2 King Street, Peterborough PE1 1LT
☎01733 555123 Fax 01733 427500
✉ editorial@choicemag.co.uk
Owner *Choice Publishing Ltd*
Editor *Norman Wright*
Circulation 90,000

Monthly full-colour, lively and informative magazine for people aged 50 plus which helps them get the most out of their lives, time and money after full-time work.

FEATURES Real-life stories, hobbies, interesting (older) people, British heritage and countryside, involving activities for active bodies and minds, health, relationships, book/entertainment reviews. Unsolicited mss read (s.a.e. for return of material); write with ideas and copies of cuttings if new contributor. No phone calls, please.

RIGHTS/MONEY All items affecting the magazine's readership are written by experts. Areas of interest include pensions, state benefits, health, finance, property, legal.

PAYMENT by arrangement.

Church Music Quarterly

19 The Close, Salisbury SP1 2EB
☎01722 424848 Fax 01722 424849
✉ cmq@rscm.com
www.rscm.com
Owner *Royal School of Church Music*
Editor *Esther Jones*
Circulation 15,500

QUARTERLY. Contributions welcome. Phone in the first instance.

FEATURES Articles on church music or related

subjects considered. Max. 2100 words. PAYMENT £60 per page.

Church of England Newspaper

Central House, 142 Central Street, London
EC1V 8AR
☎020 7417 5800 Fax 020 7216 6410
✉ cen@churchnewspaper.com
www.churchnewspaper.com
Owner *Religious Intelligence*
Editor *Colin Blakely*
Circulation 9,500

Founded 1828. WEEKLY. Almost all material is commissioned but unsolicited mss are considered.
FEATURES Preliminary enquiry essential. Max. 1200 words.
NEWS Items must be sent promptly to the e-mail address above and should have a church/Christian relevance. Max. 200–400 words.
PAYMENT negotiable.

Church Times

33 Upper Street, London N1 0PN
☎020 7359 4570 Fax 020 7226 3073
✉ news@churchtimes.co.uk *or* features@churchtimes.co.uk
www.churchtimes.co.uk
Owner *Hymns Ancient & Modern*
Editor *Paul Handley*
Circulation 29,500

Founded 1863. WEEKLY. Unsolicited mss considered.
FEATURES *Christine Miles* Articles and pictures (any format) on religious topics. Max. 1500 words.
NEWS *Helen Saxbee* Occasional reports (commissions only) and up-to-date photographs.
PAYMENT Features, £120 per 1000 words; news, by arrangement.

Classic & Sports Car

Teddington Studios, Broom Road, Teddington
TW11 9BE
☎020 8267 5399 Fax 020 8267 5318
✉ letters.c&sc@haymarket.com
www.classicandsportscar.com
Owner *Haymarket Publishing Ltd*
Editor *James Elliott* -
Circulation 81,766

Founded 1982. MONTHLY. Best-selling classic car magazine covering all aspects of buying, selling, owning and maintaining historic vehicles. Will consider news stories and features involving classic cars but 'be patient because hundreds of unsolicited material received monthly'. Initial contact by e-mail (james.elliott@haymarket. com).

Classic Bike

EMAP Automotive, Media House, Lynchwood, Peterborough Business Park, Peterborough
PE2 6EA
☎01733 468465 Fax 01733 468466
✉ classic.bike@emap.com
www.classicbike.co.uk
Owner *Emap Automotive Ltd*
Editor *Hugo Wilson*
Features Editor *Jim Moore*
Circulation 39,463

Founded 1978. MONTHLY. Mainly pre-1980 classic motorcycles. Freelancers must contact the editor before making submissions. Approach in writing or by e-mail.
NEWS Genuine news with good illustrations, if possible, suitable for a global audience. Max. 400 words.
FEATURES British motorcycle industry inside stories, technical features 'that can be understood by all', German, Spanish and French machine features, people. Restoration features, riding features; 'good reads'. Max. 2000 words.
SPECIAL PAGES How-to features, oddball machines, stunning pictures, features with a fresh slant.
PAYMENT £150–200 per 1000 words, plus pictures.

Classic Boat

IPC Media Ltd, Leon House, 233 High Street, Croydon CR9 1HZ
☎020 8726 8000 Fax 020 8726 8195
✉ cb@ipcmedia.com
www.classicboat.co.uk
Owner *IPC Media (A Time Warner Company)*
Editor *Dan Houston*
Circulation 12,304

Founded 1987. MONTHLY. Traditional boats and classic yachts, old and new; maritime history. Unsolicited mss, particularly if supported by good photos, are welcome. Sail and power boat pieces considered. Approach in writing with ideas. Interested in well-researched stories on all nautical matters. News reports welcome. Contributor's notes available online.
FEATURES Boatbuilding, boat history and design, events, yachts and working boats. Material must be well-informed and supported where possible by good-quality or historic

photos. Max. 3000 words. Classic is defined by excellence of design and construction – the boat need not be old and wooden!

NEWS New boats, restorations, events, boat-builders, etc. Max. 500 words.

PAYMENT Features, £75–100 per published page; news, according to merit.

Classic Cars
Media House, Peterborough Business Park, Lynchwood, Peterborough PE2 6EA
☎01733 468219 Fax 01733 468888
✉ classic.cars@emap.com
www.classiccarsmagazine.co.uk

Owner *Emap Automotive Ltd*
Editor *Phil Bell*
Circulation 42,634

Founded 1973. TWELVE ISSUES YEARLY. International classic car magazine containing entertaining and informative articles about classic cars, events and associated personalities. Contributions welcome. PAYMENT negotiable.

Classic Land Rover World
See **Land Rover World**

Classic Stitches
D.C.Thomson & Co. Ltd, 80 Kingsway East, Dundee DD4 8SL
☎01382 223131 Fax 01382 452491
✉ editorial@classicstitches.com
www.classicstitches.com

Owner *D.C.Thomson & Co. Ltd*
Editor *Mrs Bea Neilson*
Circulation 10,000

Founded 1994. BI-MONTHLY magazine with exclusive designs to stitch, textile-based features, designer profiles, book reviews and 'what's new shopping' information. Will consider features covering textiles – historical and modern, designer profiles and original designs in context with the style of the magazine (no items on knit-ting or crochet). Approach by e-mail or letter with short synopsis to avoid clashes. For designs, send sketches, swatches and brief description of the idea.

FEATURES *Bea Neilson* Three features per issue with accompanying photography. Max. 2000 words.

NEWS *Liz O'Rourke* Max. 300 words.

SPECIAL PAGES *Susan Kydd* Details only.

Classic Guitar
1 & 2 Vance Court, Trans Britannia Enterprise Park, Blaydon on Tyne NE21 5NH
☎0191 414 9000 Fax 0191 414 9001
✉ classicalguitar@ashleymark.co.uk
www.classicalguitarmagazine.com

Owner *Ashley Mark Publishing Co.*
Editor *Maurice Summerfield*
Founded 1982. MONTHLY.

FEATURES *Oliver McGhie* Usually written by staff writers. Max. 1500 words.

News *Thérèse Wassily Saba* Small paragraphs and festival concert reports welcome.

Reviews *Tim Panting* Concert reviews of up to 250 words are usually written by staff reviewers.

PAYMENT features, by arrangement; no payment for news.

Classical Music
241 Shaftesbury Avenue, London WC2H 8TF
☎020 7333 1742 Fax 020 7333 1769
✉ classical.music@rhinegold.co.uk
www.rhinegold.co.uk

Owner *Rhinegold Publishing Ltd*
Editor *Keith Clarke*

Founded 1976. FORTNIGHTLY. A specialist maga-zine using precisely targeted news and feature articles aimed at the music business. Most mate-rial is commissioned but professionally written unsolicited mss are occasionally published. Freelance contributors may approach in writing with an idea but should familiarise themselves beforehand with the style and market of the magazine. PAYMENT negotiable.

Climber
Warners Group Publications plc, West Street, Bourne PE10 9PH
☎01778 392425
✉ climber@bernardnewman.demon.co.uk
www.climber.co.uk

Owner *Warners Group Publications plc*
Editor *Bernard Newman*

Founded 1962. MONTHLY. Features articles and news on climbing and mountaineering in the UK and abroad. No unsolicited mss.

Closer
Endeavour House, 189 Shaftesbury Avenue, London WC2H 8JG
☎020 7437 9011 Fax 020 7859 8600
✉ closer@emap.com

Owner *Emap élan Ltd*
Editor *Jane Johnson*
Circulation 614,141

Launched 2002. WEEKLY celebrity magazine with a 'tongue-in-cheek' approach. No unsolicited material; approach by e-mail with idea in the first instance.

Club International
2 Archer Street, London W1D 7AW
☎020 7292 8000 Fax 020 7734 5030
✉ mattb@paulraymond.com
Owner *Paul Raymond*
Editor *Matt Berry*
Circulation 80,000

Founded 1972. MONTHLY. Features and short humorous items aimed at young male readership aged 18–30.
FEATURES Max. 1000 words.
SHORTS 200–750 words.
PAYMENT negotiable.

Coach and Bus Week
Rouncy Media Ltd, 3 The Office Village, Forder Way, Cygnet Park, Hampton, Peterborough PE7 8GX
☎01733 293240 Fax 0845 280 2927
✉ jacqui.grobler@rouncymedia.co.uk
www.CBWonline.com
Owner *Rouncy Media*
Editorial Director *Andrew Sutcliffe*
Circulation 4575

WEEKLY magazine, aimed at coach and bus operators. Interested in coach and bus industry-related items only: business, financial and legal. Contact by letter, e-mail, telephone or via website.

Coin News
Token Publishing Ltd, Orchard House, Duchy Road, Heathpark, Honiton EX14 1YD
☎01404 46972 Fax 01404 44788
✉ info@tokenpublishing.com
www.tokenpublishing.com
Owners *J. W. Mussell, Carol Hartman*
Editor *J. W. Mussell*
Circulation 10,000

Founded 1964. MONTHLY. Contributions welcome. Approach by phone in the first instance.
FEATURES Opportunity exists for well-informed authors 'who know the subject and do their homework'. Max. 2000 words.
PAYMENT by arrangement.

Company
National Magazine House, 72 Broadwick Street, London W1F 9EP
☎020 7439 5000 Fax 020 7312 3797
✉ company.mail@natmags.co.uk
www.company.co.uk
Owner *National Magazine Co. Ltd*
Editor *Victoria White*
Circulation 264,095

MONTHLY. Glossy women's magazine appealing to the independent and intelligent young woman. A good market for freelancers: 'We look for great newsy features relevant to young British women'. Keen to encourage bright, new, young talent, but uncommissioned material is rarely accepted. Feature outlines are the only sensible approach in the first instance. Max. 1500–2000 words. Send to *Claire Askew*, Features Editor.
PAYMENT £250 per 1000 words.

Computer Arts
30 Monmouth Street, Bath BA1 2BW
☎01225 442244 Fax 01225 732295
✉ ca.mail@futurenet.co.uk
www.computerarts.co.uk
Owner *The Future Network*
Editor *Paul Newman*
Circulation 21,362

Founded 1995. MONTHLY. The world of computer arts – 3D, web design, photoshop, digital video. No unsolicited mss. Interested in tutorials, profiles, tips, software and hardware reviews. Approach by post or e-mail.

Computer Weekly
Quadrant House, The Quadrant, Sutton SM2 5AS
☎020 8652 3122 Fax 020 8652 8979
✉ computer.weekly@rbi.co.uk
www.computerweekly.com
Owner *Reed Business Information*
Editor *Hooman Bassirian*
Circulation 143,000

Founded 1966. Freelance contributions welcome.
FEATURES Always looking for good new writers with specialised industry knowledge. Max. 1800 words.
NEWS *Christian Annesley* Some openings for regional or foreign news items. Max. 300 words.
PAYMENT negotiable.

Computeractive
VNU Business Publications, VNU House, 32–34 Broadwick Street, London W1A 2HG
☎020 7316 9000 Fax 020 7316 9520
✉ news@computeractive.co.uk
www.computeractive.co.uk
Owner *VNU Business Publications Ltd*
Editor *Dylan Armbrust*
Circulation 216,031

Launched 1998. FORTNIGHTLY. Consumer and computer technology magazine. No unsolicited material.

Computing

VNU Business Publications, VNU House, 32–34 Broadwick Street, London W1A 2HG
☎020 7316 9000 Fax 020 7316 9160
✉ feedback@computing.co.uk
www.computing.co.uk

Owner *VNU Business Publications Ltd*
Editor-in-Chief *Toby Wolpe*
Editor, computing.co.uk *Bryan Glick*
Circulation 115,000

Founded 1973. WEEKLY newspaper for IT professionals. Unsolicited articles welcome. Please enclose s.a.e. for return.
NEWS *Emma Nash*
Payment up to £300 per 1000 words.

Condé Nast Traveller

Vogue House, Hanover Square, London W1S 1JU
☎020 7499 9080 Fax 020 7493 3758
✉ editorcntraveller@condenast.co.uk
www.cntraveller.com

Owner *Condé Nast Publications*
Editor *Sarah Miller*
Circulation 84,783

Founded 1997. MONTHLY travel magazine. Proposals rather than completed mss preferred. Approach in writing in the first instance. No unsolicited photographs. 'The magazine has a no freebie policy and no writing can be accepted on the basis of a press or paid-for trip.'

Construction News

Emap Construct, 151 Rosebery Avenue, London EC1R 4GB
☎020 7505 6868 Fax 020 7505 6867
✉ cneditorial@emap.com
www.cnplus.co.uk

Owner *Emap*
Editor *Aaron Morby*
Circulation 26,835

WEEKLY. Since 1871, *Construction News* has provided news to the industry. Readership ranges from construction site to the boardroom, from building and specialist construction through to civil engineering. Initial approach by e-mail.
Features Editor *Emma Crates*
News Editor *Grant Prior*

Contemporary Review

PO Box 1242, Oxford OX1 4FJ
✉ editorial@contemporaryreview.co.uk
www.contemporaryreview.co.uk

Owner *Contemporary Review Co. Ltd*
Editor *Dr Richard Mullen*

Founded 1866. QUARTERLY. Covers international affairs and politics, literature and the arts, history and religion. No fiction. Max. 3000 words.

Literary Editor *Dr James Munson* Quarterly book section with reviews which are always commissioned.

Coop Traveller

River Publishing, Victory House, 14 Leicester Place, London WC2H 7BZ
☎020 7413 9308 Fax 020 7306 0304
✉ cooptraveller@riverltd.co.uk
www.riverltd.co.uk

Owner *River Publishing*
Editor *Heather Farmborough*
Circulation 300,000

Founded 2001. BIANNUAL. Magazine for Co-op Travel customers. Travel articles and travel-related news for the independent traveller. No unsolicted material; approach by telephone, fax, letter or e-mail in the first instance.

FEATURES Ideas for exciting travel features, including destinations, accommodation, activities etc. Max. 1000 words.

NEWS Stories that reveal fascinating facts for holidaymakers, including interesting products, new destinations and developments in the travel market. Max. 300 words.

PAYMENT negotiable.

CosmoGIRL!

National Magazine House, 72 Broadwick Street, London W1F 9EP
☎020 7439 5000 Fax 020 7439 5400
✉ cosmogirl.mail@natmags.co.uk
www.cosmogirl.co.uk

Owner *National Magazine Co. Ltd*
Editor *Celia Duncan*
Circulation 131,956

Founded 2001. MONTHLY glossy magazine for teenagers, median age 15. Fashion, beauty advice and boys.

FEATURES *Natalie Glenford* Interested in ideas. Send synopsis by mail; no finished articles.

Cosmopolitan

National Magazine House, 72 Broadwick Street, London W1F 9EP
☎020 7439 5000 Fax 020 7439 5016

✉ cosmo.mail@natmags.co.uk
www.cosmopolitan.co.uk
Owner *National Magazine Co. Ltd*
Editor *Louise Court*
Deputy Editor *Helen Daly*
Circulation 455,649

MONTHLY. Designed to appeal to the mid-twenties, modern-minded female. Popular mix of articles, with emphasis on relationships and careers, and hard news. No fiction. Will rarely use unsolicited mss but always on the look-out for 'new writers with original and relevant ideas and a strong voice'. All would-be writers should be familiar with the magazine. E-mail for submission guidelines.

Counselling at Work

Association for Counselling at Work, BACP, BACP House, 15 St John's Business Park, Lutterworth LE17 4HB
☎0870 443 5252 Fax 0870 443 5161
✉ acw@bacp.co.uk
www.counsellingatwork.org.uk
Owner *British Association for Counselling and Psychotherapy*
Editor *Rick Hughes*
Circulation 1600

Founded 1993. QUARTERLY official journal of the Association for Counselling at Work, a Division of BACP. Looking for well-researched articles (500–2400 words) about *any* aspect of work-place counselling. Mss from those employed as counsellors or in welfare posts are particularly welcome. Photographs accepted. No fiction or poetry. Send A4 s.a.e. for writer's guidelines and sample copy of the journal. No PAYMENT.

Country Homes and Interiors

IPC Media Ltd., The Blue Fin Building, 110 Southwark Street, London SE1 0SU
☎020 3148 5000
✉ countryhomes@ipcmedia.com
Owner *IPC Media*
Editor *Rhoda Parry*
Circulation 80,709

Founded 1986. MONTHLY. The best approach for prospective contributors is with an idea in writing as unsolicited mss are not welcome.

FEATURES *Jean Carr* Monthly personality interviews of interest to an intelligent, affluent readership (women and men), aged 25–44. Max. 1200 words.

HOUSES *Vivienne Ayers* Country-style homes with excellent design ideas. Length 1000 words. PAYMENT negotiable.

Country Life

IPC Media Ltd., The Blue Fin Building, 110 Southwark Street, London SE1 0SU
☎020 3148 4444
www.countrylife.co.uk
Owner *IPC Media (A Time Warner Company)*
Editor-in-Chief *Mark Hedges*
Circulation 42,693

Established 1897. WEEKLY. *Country Life* features articles which relate to architecture, country-side, wildlife, rural events, sports, arts, exhibitions, current events, property and news articles of interest to town and country dwellers. Strong informed material rather than amateur enthusiasm. 'Uncommissioned material is rarely accepted. We regret we cannot be liable for the safe custody or return of any solicited or unsolicited materials.'

Country Living

National Magazine House, 72 Broadwick Street, London W1F 9EP
☎020 7439 5000 Fax 020 7439 5093/5077
www.countryliving.co.uk
Owner *National Magazine Co. Ltd*
Editor *Susy Smith*
Circulation 193,372

Magazine aimed at both country dwellers and town dwellers who love the countryside. Covers people, conservation, wildlife, houses (gardens and interiors) and rural businesses. No unsolicited mss

Country Smallholding

Archant Publishing, Fair Oak Close, Exeter Airport Business Park, Clysts Honiton, Nr Exeter EX5 2UL
☎01392 888475 Fax 01392 888550
✉ editorial.csh@archant.co.uk
www.countrysmallholding.com
Owner *Archant Publishing*
Editor *Diane Cowgill*
Circulation 20,896

Founded 1975. MONTHLY magazine for small farmers, smallholders, practical landowners and for anyone interested in self sufficiency at all levels both in town and in the country. Articles welcome on organic growing, keeping poultry, livestock and other animals, crafts, cookery, herbs, building and energy. Articles should be detailed and practical, based on first-hand knowledge and experience. Approach in writing or by e-mail.

Country Walking

Bretton Court, Bretton, Peterborough
PE3 8DZ
☎01733 282614
✉ country.walking@emap.com
www.countrywalking.co.uk
Owner *Emap Plc*
Editor *Jonathan Manning*
Circulation 47,822

Founded 1987. MONTHLY magazine focused on walking in the finest landscapes of the UK and Europe. News, gear tests and profiles of celebrity walkers also feature. Special monthly pull-out section of detailed walking routes. Original high quality photography and ideas for features considered, although very few unsolicited mss accepted. Approach by letter or e-mail.

SPECIAL PAGES Routes section of magazine, including outline Ordnance Survey map and step-by-step directions. Accurately and recently researched walk and fact file including photographs and points of interest en route. Please contact *Jane Ward* for guidelines (unsolicited submissions generally not accepted for this section).

PAYMENT not negotiable.

The Countryman

The Water Mill, Broughton Hall, Skipton
BD23 3AG
☎01756 701381 Fax 01756 701326
✉ editorial@thecountryman.co.uk
www.thecountryman.co.uk
Owner *Country Publications Ltd*
Editor *Paul Jackson*
Circulation 22,870

Founded 1927. Monthly. Feature ideas welcome by e-mail, phone or in writing. Articles supplied with top quality illustrations (colour transparencies, archive b&w prints and line drawings) are far more likely to be used. Max. article length 1200 words.

The Countryman's Weekly
(incorporating **Gamekeeper and Sporting Dog**)

Yelverton PL20 7PE
☎01822 855281 Fax 01822 855372
✉ editorial@countrymanswweekly.com
Owner *Diamond Publishing Ltd*
Editor *David Venner*

Founded 1895. WEEKLY. Unsolicited material welcome.

FEATURES on any country sports topic. Max. 1000 words.
PAYMENT rates available on request.

Countryside Alliance Update

The Old Town Hall 367 Kennington Road,
London SE1 4PT
☎020 7840 9200 Fax 020 7793 8484
www.countryside-alliance.org
Owner *Countryside Alliance*
Editor *Georgina Kester*
Circulation 70,000

Founded 1996. QUARTERLY membership magazine on country sports and conservation issues. No unsolicited mss.

The Creative Writer

28 Howard Mews, Denmark Road, Norwich
NR3 4JU
☎01603 484424 Fax 01603 484424
✉ CreativeWriter@btconnect.com
Editor *Inna Zabrodskaya*
Circulation 3500

QUARTERLY glossy magazine featuring the work of new creative writers from around the world. 'We particularly welcome articles from novice writers wishing to see their first piece of work published. Articles welcomed on any subject/genre but must be interesting, different, unique and, above all, creative!'

The Cricketer International
See **The Wisden Cricketer**

Crimewave

5 Martins Lane, Witcham, Ely CB6 2LB
✉ andy@ttapress.demon.co.uk
www.ttapress.com
Owner *TTA Press*
Editor *Andy Cox*

Founded 1998. QUARTERLY B5 colour magazine of crime fiction. 'The UK's only magazine specialising in crime short stories, publishing the very best from across the spectrum.' Every issue contains stories by authors who are household names in the crime fiction world but room is found for lesser known and unknown writers. Submissions welcome (not via e-mail) with appropriate return postage. Potential contributors are advised to study the magazine. Contracts exchanged upon acceptance. PAYMENT on publication.

Crucible
See **Hymns Ancient & Modern Ltd** under **UK Publishers**

Cumbria

The Water Mill, Broughton Hall, Skipton
BD23 3AG
☎01756 701381 Fax 01756 701326
✉ editorial@dalesman.co.uk
www.dalesman.co.uk

Owner *Country Publications Ltd*
Editor *Terry Fletcher*
Circulation 13,713

Founded 1951. MONTHLY. County magazine of strong regional and countryside interest, focusing on the Lake District. Unsolicited mss welcome. Max. 1500 words. Approach in writing, by phone or e-mail with feature ideas. PAYMENT negotiable.

Cycle Sport

IPC Media Ltd, Leon House, 233 High Street, Croydon CR9 1HZ
☎020 8726 8463 Fax 020 8726 8499
✉ cyclesport@ipcmedia.com *and*
cycling@ipcmedia.com
www.cyclesport.co.uk

Owner *IPC Media (A Time Warner Company)*
Managing Editor *Robert Garbutt*
Deputy Editor *Nigel Wynn*
Circulation 18,996

Founded 1993. MONTHLY magazine dedicated to professional cycle racing. Unsolicited ideas for features welcome.

Cycling Weekly

IPC Media Ltd, Leon House, 233 High Street, Croydon CR9 1HZ
☎020 8726 8463 Fax 020 8726 8499
✉ cycling@ipcmedia.com
www.cyclingweekly.co.uk

Owner *IPC Media (A Time Warner Company)*
Publishing Director *Keith Foster*
Editor *Robert Garbutt*
Circulation 28,137

Founded 1891. WEEKLY. All aspects of cycle sport covered. Unsolicited mss and ideas for features welcome. Approach in writing with ideas. Fiction rarely used. 'It is important that you are familiar with the format so read the magazine first.'

FEATURES Cycle racing, coaching, technical material and related areas. Max. 2000 words. Most work commissioned but interested in seeing new work.

NEWS Short news pieces, local news, etc. Max. 300 words.

PAYMENT Features, around £60–120 per

1000 words (quality permitting); news, £15 per story.

Dalesman

The Water Mill, Broughton Hall, Skipton
BD23 3AG
☎01756 701381 Fax 01756 701326
✉ editorial@dalesman.co.uk
www.dalesman.co.uk

Owner *Country Publications Ltd*
Editor *Terry Fletcher*
Circulation 43,935

Founded 1939. Now the biggest-selling regional publication of its kind in the country. MONTHLY magazine with articles of specific Yorkshire interest. Unsolicited mss welcome; receives approximately ten per day. Initial approach in writing, by phone or e-mail. Max. 1500 words. PAYMENT negotiable.

Dance Theatre Journal

Laban, Creekside, London SE8 3DZ
☎020 8691 8600 Fax 020 8691 8400
✉ dtj@laban.org
www.laban.org

Owner *Laban*
Editor *Martin Hargreaves*
Circulation 2000

Founded 1982. QUARTERLY. Interested in features on every aspect of the contemporary dance scene, particularly issues such as the funding policy for dance, critical assessments of choreographers' work and the latest developments in the various schools of contemporary dance. Unsolicited mss welcome. Length 1000–3000 words

Dance Today

Dancing Times Ltd, Clerkenwell House, 45–47 Clerkenwell Green, London EC1R 0EB
☎020 7250 3006 Fax 020 7253 6679
✉ dancetoday@dancing-times.co.uk
www.dancing-times.co.uk

Owner *Dancing Times Ltd*
Editor *Katie Gregory*
Editorial Assistants *Alison Kirkman, Jon Gray*
Circulation 3500

Founded in 1956 as the *Ballroom Dancing Times* and relaunched as *Dance Today* in 2001. MONTHLY magazine for anyone interested in social and competitive dance. Styles include ballroom and Latin American, salsa, tango, flamenco, tea dancing and sequence. Related topics covered include health and fitness and dance fashion.

Contributions welcome; send c.v. with sample work by post or e-mail to the editor.

The Dancing Times

The Dancing Times Ltd, 45–47 Clerkenwell Green, London EC1R 0EB
☎020 7250 3006 Fax 020 7253 6679
✉ editorial@dancing-times.co.uk
www.dancing-times.co.uk

Owner *The Dancing Times Ltd*
Editors *Mary Clarke, Jonathan Gray*

Founded 1910. MONTHLY. Freelance suggestions welcome from specialist dance writers and photographers only. Approach in writing.

The Dandy

D.C. Thomson & Co. Ltd, Albert Square, Dundee DD1 8QJ
☎01382 223131 Fax 01382 322214
www.dandy.com

Owner *D.C. Thomson & Co. Ltd*
Editor *Craig Graham*

Founded 1937. WEEKLY comic. Original, humorous comic strips for 7–12-year-olds, featuring established characters such as Desperate Dan as well as new ones like Jak. Generally, unsolicited contributions are welcome but 'please read the comic before sending any material. Try a one-off script for an established, current *Dandy* character. Send by e-mail or post but never send your only copy.' Include s.a.e. for reply. No non-script material such as puzzles, poetry, etc.

Darts World

81 Selwood Road, Croydon CR0 7JW
☎020 8650 6580 Fax 020 8654 4343
✉ dartsworld@blueyonder.co.uk
www.dartsworld.com

Owner *World Magazines Ltd*
Editor *A.J. Wood*
Circulation 12,263

FEATURES Single articles or series on technique and instruction. Max. 1200 words.

FICTION Short stories with darts theme. Max. 1000 words.

NEWS Tournament reports and general or personality news required. Max. 800 words.

PAYMENT negotiable.

Day by Day

Woolacombe House, 141 Woolacombe Road, London SE3 8QP
☎020 8856 6249

Owner *Loverseed Press*
Editor *Patrick Richards*

Circulation 25,000

Founded 1963. MONTHLY. News commentary and digest of national and international affairs, with reviews of the arts (books, plays, art exhibitions, films, opera, musicals) and county cricket and Test reports among regular slots. Unsolicited mss welcome (s.a.e. essential). Approach in writing with ideas. Contributors are advised to study the magazine in the first instance. (Specimen copy £1.25) UK subscription £14.85; Europe £18.85; RoW £22.85.

NEWS *Ronald Mallone* Interested in themes connected with non-violence and social justice only. Max. 600 words.

FEATURES No scope for freelance contributions here.

POEMS *Michael Gibson* Short poems in line with editorial principles considered. Max. 20 lines.

PAYMENT negotiable.

Dazed & Confused

112–116 Old Street, London EC1V 9BG
☎020 7549 6816 Fax 020 7336 0966
✉ rod@dazedgroup.com
www.dazeddigital.com

Owner *Waddell Ltd*
Editor *Rod Stanley*
Circulation 80,000

Founded 1992. MONTHLY. Cutting edge fashion, music, film, art, interviews and features. No unsolicited material. Approach in writing with ideas in the first instance.

Decanter

First Floor, Broadway House, 2–6 Fulham Broadway, London SW6 1AA
☎020 7610 3929 Fax 020 7381 5282
✉ decanter_editorial@decanter.com
www.decanter.com

Editor *Guy Woodward*
Circulation 35,000

FOUNDED 1975. Glossy wines magazine. Feature ideas welcome; send to editor by post, fax or e-mail. No fiction.

NEWS/FEATURES All items and articles should concern wines, food and related subjects.

PAYMENT £230 per 1000 words.

Delicious

Seven Publishing, 20 Upper Ground, London SE1 9PD
☎020 7775 7757 Fax 020 7775 7705
✉ info@deliciousmagazine.co.uk
www.deliciousmagazine.co.uk

Owner *Seven Publishing*
Editor *Matthew Drennan*
Circulation 100,631
Launched 2003. MONTHLY publication for people who love food and cooking. Recipes – from the simple to the sophisticated – plus features on food and where it comes from. Welcomes freelance contributions; approach by e-mail.

Derbyshire Life and Countryside
61 Friar Gate, Derby DE1 1DJ
☎01332 227850 Fax 01332 227860
Owner *Archant Life*
Editor *Joy Hales*
Circulation 13,297
Founded 1931. MONTHLY county magazine for Derbyshire. Unsolicited mss and photographs of Derbyshire welcome, but written approach with ideas preferred.

Descent
Wild Places Publishing, PO Box 100, Abergavenny NP7 9WY
☎01873 737707
✉ descent@wildplaces.co.uk
www.caving.uk.com
Owner *Wild Places Publishing*
Editor *Chris Howes*
Assistant Editor *Judith Calford*
Founded 1969. BI-MONTHLY magazine for cavers and mine enthusiasts. Submissions welcome from freelance contributors who can write accurately and knowledgeably and in the style of existing content on any aspect of caves, mines or underground structures.

FEATURES General interest articles of under 1000 words welcome, as well as short foreign news reports, especially if supported by photographs/illustrations. Suitable topics include exploration (particularly British, both historical and modern), expeditions, equipment, techniques and regional British news. Max. 2000 words.

PAYMENT on publication according to page area filled.

Desire
9 Harmsworth Street, London SE17 3TJ
☎020 7820 8844 Fax 020 7820 9944
✉ editorial@moondancemedia.co.uk
www.desire.co.uk
Owner *Moondance Media Ltd*
Editor *Ian Jackson*
Founded 1994. FIVE ISSUES YEARLY. Britain's only

erotic magazine for both women and men, celebrating sex and sensuality with a mix of features, reviews, interviews, photography and erotic fantasy. For a sample copy of the magazine plus contributors' guidelines and rates, please enclose four loose first class stamps.

Destination France
151 Station Street, Burton on Trent DE14 1BG
☎01283 742950 Fax 01283 742957
✉ alison.bell@wwonline.co.uk
Owner *Waterways World*
Editor *Alison Bell*
Circulation 12,000
Founded in 2005 as *Camping in France*. MONTHLY. Aimed at the Francophile – the British holidaymaker in France and for those who wish to move there. Features include sports, general tourism, property and regional information. Photographs to accompany articles. Approach in writing, preferably by e-mail, in the first instance.

PAYMENT negotiable.

Director
116 Pall Mall, London SW1Y 5ED
☎020 7766 8950 Fax 020 7766 8840
✉ director-ed@iod.com
Editor *Joanna Higgins*
Circulation 58,371
1991 Business Magazine of the Year. Published by Director Publications Ltd. for members of the Institute of Directors. Wide range of features from political and business profiles and management thinking to employment and financial issues. Also book reviews. Regular contributors used. Send letter with synopsis/published samples rather than unsolicited mss.

PAYMENT negotiable.

Disability Now
6 Market Road, London N7 9PW
☎020 7619 7323 Fax 020 7619 7331
✉ editor@disabilitynow.org.uk
www.disabilitynow.org.uk
Owner *SCOPE*
Acting Editor *John Pring*
Circulation 20,856
Founded 1984. Leading MONTHLY newspaper with fortnightly supplement for disabled people in the UK – people with all disabilities, as well as their families, carers and relevant professionals. Freelance contributions welcome. No fiction. Approach in writing or by e-mail.

FEATURES Covering new initiatives and services, personal experiences and general issues of interest to a wide national readership. Max. 900 words. Disabled contributors welcome.

NEWS Max. 300 words.

SPECIAL PAGES Possible openings for cartoonists.

PAYMENT by arrangement.

Diva, lesbian life and style

Spectrum House, 32–34 Gordon House Road, London NW5 1LP

☎020 7424 7400 Fax 020 7424 7401

✉ edit@divamag.co.uk

www.divamag.co.uk

Owner *Millivres-Prowler Group*
Editor *Jane Czyzselska*

Founded 1994. MONTHLY glossy magazine featuring lesbian news and culture including fashion, lifestyle and satire. Welcomes news, features and photographs. No poetry. Contact the news editor at the e-mail address above with news items and feature ideas and photo/fashion photographs.

Dog World

Somerfield House, Wotton Road, Ashford TN23 6LW

☎01233 621877 Fax 01233 645669

www.dogworld.co.uk

Owner *DW Media Holdings Ltd*
Editor *Stuart Baillie*
Circulation 18,706

Founded 1902. WEEKLY newspaper for people who are seriously interested in pedigree dogs. Unsolicited mss occasionally considered but initial approach in writing preferred.

FEATURES Well-researched historical items or items of unusual interest concerning dogs. Max. 1000 words. Photographs of unusual 'doggy' situations occasionally of interest.

NEWS Freelance reports welcome on court cases and local government issues involving dogs.

PAYMENT Features, up to £50; photos, £15.

Dogs Monthly

Ascot House, High Street, Ascot SL5 7HG

☎0870 730 8433 Fax 0870 730 8431

✉ dm@rtc-mail.org.uk

www.dogsmonthly.co.uk

Owner *Mr D. Cavill*
Editor *Meriel France*
Circulation 11,000

Founded 1983. MONTHLY magazine suitable for serious dog owners whose dog is more than just a pet.

FEATURES Articles on breeds and topical news. Approach the editor first by e-mail. Max. length for features, news, fiction or other articles, 2000 words.

PAYMENT negotiable.

Dorset Life – The Dorset Magazine

7 The Leanne, Sandford Lane, Wareham BH20 4DY

☎01929 551264 Fax 01929 552099

✉ editor@dorsetlife.co.uk

www.dorsetlife.co.uk

Owner/Editor *John Newth*
Circulation 10,000

Founded 1968. MONTHLY magazine about Dorset, both present and past. Unsolicited contributions welcome if specifically about Dorset.

Eastern Eye

Unit 2, 65 Whitechapel Road, London E1 1DU

☎020 7650 2000 Fax 020 7650 2001

www.ethnicmedia.co.uk

Owner *Ethnic Media Group*
Editor *Hamant Verma*
Circulation 20,844

Founded 1989. WEEKLY community paper for the Asian community in Britain. Interested in relevant general, local and international issues. Approach in writing with ideas for submission.

Easy Living

68 Old Bond Street, London W1S 4PH

☎020 7499 9080 Fax 020 7399 2625

✉ easylivingeditorial@condenast.co.uk

www.easylivingmagazine.com

Owner *Condé Nast*
Editor *Susie Forbes*
Circulation 200,116

Launched 2005. MONTHLY magazine aimed at women aged 30–50-plus. Focuses on aspects of fashion, home life, beauty and health, food, relationships; stylish and glossy with real-life, practical and useful items.

The Ecologist

Unit 102, Lana House Studios, 116–118 Commercial Street, London E1 6NF

☎020 7422 8100 Fax 020 7422 8101

✉ editorial@theecologist.org

www.theecologist.org

Owner *Ecosystems Ltd*
Managing Editor *Jeremy Smith*
Editor *Zac Goldsmith*

Circulation 25,000

Founded 1970. MONTHLY. Unsolicited mss welcome but best approach is a brief proposal to the editor by e-mail (address above), outlining experience and background and summarising suggested article.

FEATURES Radical approach to political, economic, social and environmental issues, with an emphasis on rethinking the basic assumptions that underpin modern society. Articles of between 500 and 3000 words.

PAYMENT negotiable.

The Economist

25 St James's Street, London SW1A 1HG
☎020 7830 7000 Fax 020 7839 2968
www.economist.com

Owner *Pearson/individual shareholders*
Editor *John Micklethwait*
Circulation 170,038 (UK edition)

Founded 1843. WEEKLY. Worldwide circulation. Approaches should be made in writing to the editor. No unsolicited mss.

The Edge

65 Guinness Buildings, Hammersmith, London W6 8BD
☎0845 456 9337
✉ davec@theedge.abelgratis.co.uk
www.theedge.abelgratis.co.uk

Editor *Dave Clark*

QUARTERLY. Reviews and features: film (indie, arts), books, popular culture. Fiction: modern crime, horror, SF, erotica, imaginative non-mainstream. Sample issue £5 post-free (cheques payable to 'The Edge'). Writers' guidelines available on website.

PAYMENT up to £75 per 1000 words.

Edinburgh Review

22A Buccleugh Place, Edinburgh EH8 9LN
☎0131 651 1415
✉ edinburgh.review@ed.ac.uk
www.edinburghreview.org.uk

Owner *Dept. of English Literature, University of Edinburgh*
Editor *Brian McCabe*

Founded 1802. THREE ISSUES YEARLY. Cultural and literary magazine. Articles on Scottish and international culture, history, art, literature and politics. Each issue is themed (e.g. Latina, Chicana and Scottish Women Writers; Voices of Africa). Unsolicited contributions welcome, particularly articles, fiction and poetry; send by post or e-mail. 'Writers offering unsolicited

essays should contact us by e-mail in the first instance.'

Electrical Times

Media House, Swanley BR8 8HU
☎01322 611276 Fax 01322 616376
✉ louise.frampton@purplems.com

Owner *Purple Media Solutions Ltd*
Editor *Louise Frampton*
Circulation 10,613

Founded 1891. MONTHLY. Aimed at electrical contractors, designers and installers. Unsolicited mss welcome but initial approach preferred.

Elle

64 North Row, London W1K 7LL
☎020 7150 7000 Fax 020 7150 7670

Owner *Hachette Filipacchi*
Editor *Lorraine Candy*
Features Director *Anna Pursglove*
Circulation 209,172

Founded 1985. MONTHLY fashion glossy. Prospective contributors should approach the relevant editor in writing in the first instance, including cuttings.

FEATURES Max. 2000 words.

HOT LIST Short articles on hot trends, events, fashion and beauty. Max. 500 words.

PAYMENT negotiable.

Embroidery

PO Box 42B, East Molesey KT8 9BB
☎01260 273891
✉ jo.editor@btinternet.com
www.embroiderersguild.com

Owner *Embroiderers' Guild*
Editor *Joanne Hall*
Circulation 12,000

Founded 1933. BI-MONTHLY. Features articles on historical and foreign embroidery, and contemporary artists' work with illustrations. Covers all forms of textile art, historical and contemporary. Also reviews. Unsolicited material welcome. Max. 1000 words.

PAYMENT negotiable.

Empire

4th Floor, Mappin House, 4 Winsley Street, London W1W 8HF
☎020 7182 8781 Fax 020 7182 8703
✉ empire@emap.com
www.empireonline.co.uk

Owner *Emap East*
Editor *Mark Dinning*
Circulation 175,854

Founded 1989. Launched at the Cannes Film Festival. MONTHLY guide to the movies which aims to cover the world of films in a 'comprehensive, adult, intelligent and witty package'. Although most of *Empire* is devoted to films and the people behind them, it also looks at the developments and technology behind television and DVDs plus music, multimedia and books. Wide selection of in-depth features and stories on all the main releases of the month, and reviews of over 100 films and videos. Contributions welcome but approach in writing first.

FEATURES Behind-the-scenes features on films, humorous and factual features.

PAYMENT by agreement.

The Engineer

50 Poland Street, London W1F 7AX
☎020 7970 4000 Fax 020 7970 4123
✉ andrew.lee@centaur.co.uk
www.theengineer.co.uk
Owner *Centaur Media*
Editor *Andrew Lee*
Circulation 31,367

FOUNDED 1856. FORTNIGHTLY news magazine for technology and innovation.

FEATURES Most outside contributions are commissioned but good ideas are always welcome. Max. 2000 words.

NEWS Scope for specialist regional freelancers, and for tip-offs. Max. 500 words.

TECHNOLOGY Technology news from specialists. Max. 500 words.

PAYMENT by arrangement.

The English Garden

Archant Specialist, Jubilee House, 2 Jubilee Place, London SW3 3TQ
☎020 7751 4800 Fax 020 7751 4848
✉ theenglishgarden@archant.co.uk
www.theenglishgarden.co.uk
Owner *Archant Specialist*
Editor *Janine Wookey*
Circulation 33,031

Founded 1996. MONTHLY. Features on beautiful gardens with practical ideas on design and planting. No unsolicited mss.

FEATURES *Jackie Bennett* Max. 800 words. Approach in writing in the first instance; send synopsis of 150 words with strong design and planting ideas, feature proposals, or sets of photographs of interesting gardens.

ES

See **Evening Standard** under *Regional Newspapers*

Esquire

National Magazine House, 72 Broadwick Street, London W1F 9EP
☎020 7439 5000 Fax 020 7439 5675
Owner *National Magazine Co. Ltd*
Editor *Jeremy Langmead*
Circulation 52,468

Founded 1991. MONTHLY. Quality men's general interest magazine. No unsolicited mss or short stories.

Essentials

IPC Media Ltd., The Blue Fin Building, 110 Southwark Street, London SE1 0SU
☎020 3148 7211
Owner *IPC Media (A Time Warner Company)*
Editor *Julie Barton-Breck*
Circulation 73,046

Founded 1988. MONTHLY women's interest magazine. Unsolicited mss (not originals) welcome if accompanied by s.a.e. Initial approach in writing preferred. Prospective contributors should study the magazine thoroughly before submitting anything. No fiction.

FEATURES Max. 2000 words (double-spaced on A4).

PAYMENT negotiable.

Essex Life

3 Tustin Court, Portway, Preston PR2 2YQ
☎01772 329362
www.essexlife.net
Owner *Archant*
Editor *Robyn Bechelet*
Circulation 17,000

Founded 1952. MONTHLY county magazine 'celebrating all that is best about Essex'. No unsolicited contributions. Send c.v. and covering letter in the first instance.

The Essex Magazine

See **The Journal Magazines**

Eve

Griffin House, 174 Hammersmith Road, London W6 7JP
☎020 8267 8223 Fax 020 8267 8222
✉ evrp@servicehelpline.co.uk
www.evemagazine.co.uk
Owner *Haymarket Publishing*
Editor *Sara Cremer*
Deputy Editor *Rachael Ashley*
Features Director *Emma Elms*
Features Editor *Linda Gray*
Circulation 172,419

Founded 2000. MONTHLY. Wide-ranging general interest – aimed at the intelligent 30+ woman. No unsolicited material. Send introductory letter, *recent* writings and outlines for ideas aimed at a specific section. It is essential that would-be contributors familiarise themselves with the magazine.

Eventing
See **Horse and Hound**

Evergreen
PO Box 52, Cheltenham GL50 1YQ
☎01242 537900 Fax 01242 537901
Editor *S. Garnett*
Circulation 75,000

Founded 1985. QUARTERLY magazine featuring articles and poems about Britain. Unsolicited contributions welcome.

FEATURES Britain's natural beauty, towns and villages, nostalgia, wildlife, traditions, odd customs, legends, folklore, crafts, etc. Length 250–2000 words.

PAYMENT £15 per 1000 words; poems £4.

Executive Woman
2 Chantry Place, Harrow HA3 6NY
☎020 8420 1210 Fax 020 8420 1691
✉ info@execwoman.com
www.execwoman.com
Owner *Saleworld*
Managing Editor *Angela Giveon*
Circulation 85,000

Founded 1987. BI-MONTHLY magazine for female executives in the corporate field and female entrepreneurs.

FEATURES New and interesting business issues and 'Women to Watch'. Health and conferencing, profiles, technology, beauty, fashion, training and arts items. 700 words per page.

LEGAL/FINANCIAL Opportunities for lawyers/accountants to write on issues in their field. Max. 600 words.

Eye: The international review of graphic design
174 Hammersmith Road, London W6 7JP
☎020 8267 8046 Fax 020 8264 4900
✉ john.walters@haynet.com
www.eyemagazine.com
Owner *Haymarket Brand Media*
Editor *John L. Walters*
Circulation 9,000

Founded 1990. QUARTERLY. 'The world's most beautiful and authoritative magazine about graphic design and visual culture.' Unsolicited contributions not generally welcomed.

FEATURES Specialist articles about graphic design and designers. Design history by experts. Max. 3000 words.

REVIEWS Max. 200–1000 words.

PAYMENT negotiable.

Fairgame Magazine
The Baltic Business Centre, Gateshead NE8 3DA
☎0191 442 4003 Fax 0191 442 4002
✉ info@fgmag.com
www.fgmag.com
Editor *Jennifer O'Neill*
Circulation 15,000

Founded 2003. BI-MONTHLY magazine for women football players. Contributions welcome.

FEATURES *Jennifer O'Neill* International reports, player and team profiles, interviews, diet, health and fitness, tactics, training advice, play improvement, fund-raising. Max. 1500 words.

NEWS *Wilf Frith* Match reports, team news, transfers, injuries, results and fixtures. Max. 600 words.

Family Tree Magazine
61 Great Whyte, Ramsey, Huntingdon PE26 1HJ
☎01487 814050 Fax 01487 711361
✉ sue.f@family-tree.co.uk
www.family-tree.co.uk
Owner *ABM Publishing Ltd*
Editor *Peter Watson*
Circulation 50,000

Founded 1984. MONTHLY. News and features on matters of genealogy. Not interested in own family histories. Approach in writing with ideas. All material should be addressed to *Peter Watson*.

FEATURES Any genealogically related subject. Max. 2000 words. No puzzles or fictional articles.

PAYMENT News and features, negotiable.

Fancy Fowl
The Publishing House, Station Road, Framlingham IP13 9EE
☎01728 622030 Fax 01728 622031
✉ fancyfowl@todaymagazines.co.uk
www.fancyfowl.com
Owner *TP Publications*
Editor *Liz Fairbrother*
Circulation 3000

Founded 1979. MONTHLY. Devoted entirely to

poultry, waterfowl, turkeys, geese, pea fowl, etc. – management, breeding, rearing and exhibition. Outside contributions of knowledgeable, technical poultry-related articles and news welcome. Max. 1000 words. Approach by letter. PAYMENT negotiable.

Farmers Weekly

Quadrant House, Sutton SM2 5AS
☎020 8652 4911 Fax 020 8652 4005
✉ farmers.weekly@rbi.co.uk
www.fwi.co.uk

Owner *Reed Business Information*
Editor *Jane King*
Circulation 71,349

WEEKLY. PPA Awards 2006. For practising farmers and those in the ancillary industries. Unsolicited mss considered.

FEATURES A wide range of material relating to farmers' problems and interests: specific sections on arable and livestock farming, farm life, practical and general interest, machinery and business.

NEWS General farming news.
PAYMENT negotiable.

Fast Car

Future Publishing Ltd, 30 Monmouth Streeet, Bath BA1 2BW
www.fastcar.co.uk

Owner *Future Publishing Ltd*
Editor *Steve Chalmers*
Circulation 95,893

Founded 1987. THIRTEEN ISSUES YEARLY. Lad's magazine about performance tuning and modifying cars. Covers all aspects of this youth culture including the latest street styles and music. Features cars and their owners, product tests and in-car entertainment. Also includes a free reader ads section.

NEWS Any item in line with the above.
FEATURES Innovative ideas in line with the above and in the *Fast Car* writing style. Generally two to four pages in length. No Kit-car features, race reports or road test reports of standard cars. Copy should be as concise as possible.
PAYMENT negotiable.

FHM

Mappin House, 4 Winsley Street, London W1W 8HF
☎020 7182 8028 Fax 020 7182 8021
✉ general@fhm.com
www.fhm.com

Owner *Emap Plc*

Editor-in-Chief *Anthony Noguera*
Circulation 371,263

Founded in 1986 as a free fashion magazine, FHM evolved to become more male oriented but without much public acclaim until Emap bought the title in 1994. Since then it has become the best-selling men's magazine in the world covering all areas of men's lifestyle. Published MONTHLY with 18 international editions worldwide. No unsolicited mss. Synopses and ideas welcome by e-mail. PAYMENT negotiable.

The Field

IPC Media Ltd., The Blue Fin Building, 110 Southwark Street, London SE1 0SU
☎020 3148 4772 Fax 020 3148 8179
✉ beatrice_gray@ipcmedia.com
www.thefield.co.uk

Owner *IPC Media (A Time Warner Company)*
Editor-in-Chief *Jonathan Young*
Circulation 31,855

Founded 1853. MONTHLY magazine for those who are serious about the British countryside and its pleasures. Unsolicited mss (and transparencies) welcome but initial approach should be made in writing or by phone.

FEATURES Exceptional work on any subject concerning the countryside. Most work tends to be commissioned.
PAYMENT varies.

50 Connect – www.50connect.co.uk

See entry under *Electronic Publishing and Other Services*

Film Review

Visual Imagination Ltd, 9 Blades Court, Deodar Road, London SW15 2NU
☎020 8875 1520 Fax 020 8875 1588
✉ filmreview@visimag.com
www.visimag.com

Owner *Visual Imagination Ltd*
Editor *Nikki Baughan*
Circulation 50,000

FOUR-WEEKLY. Reviews, profiles, interviews and special reports on films. Unsolicited material considered. PAYMENT negotiable.

Fishing News

4th Floor, Albert House 1–4 Singer Street, London EC2A 4BQ
☎020 7017 4531 (editor) Fax 020 7017 4536
✉ tim.oliver@informa.com
www.fishingnews.co.uk

Owner *Informa Group Plc*
Editor *Tim Oliver*
Circulation 8739

Founded 1913. WEEKLY. All aspects of the commercial fishing industry in the UK and Ireland. No unsolicited mss; telephone inquiry in the first instance. Max. 600 words for news and 1500 words for features. PAYMENT £100 per 1000 words.

The Fix

5 Martins Lane, Witcham, Ely CB6 2LB
✉ andy@ttapress.demon.co.uk
www.ttapress.com

Owner *TTA Press*

Founded 1994. BI-MONTHLY. Features detailed contributors' guidelines and reviews of international short story publications, plus varied articles, news, views and interviews.

FEATURES Unsolicited articles welcome on any aspect of short story publishing: market information, writing, editing, illustrating, interviews and reviews. All genres. Submissions should include adequate return postage. 'Please study the magazine: this will greatly enhance your chances of acceptance.' No fiction or poetry.

Flight International

Quadrant House, The Quadrant, Sutton SM2 5AS
☎ 020 8652 3842 Fax 020 8652 3840
✉ flight.international@flightglobal.com
www.flightglobal.com

Owner *Reed Business Information*
Editor *Murdo Morrison*
Circulation 52,222

Founded 1909. WEEKLY. International trade magazine for the aerospace industry, including civil, military and space. Unsolicited mss considered. Commissions preferred – phone with ideas and follow up with letter. E-mail submissions encouraged.

FEATURES *Murdo Morrison* Technically informed articles and pieces on specific geographical areas with international appeal. Analytical, in-depth coverage required, preferably supported by interviews. Max. 1800 words.

NEWS *Andrew Doyle* Opportunities exist for news pieces from particular geographical areas on specific technical developments. Max. 350 words.

PAYMENT NUJ rates.

Flora International

The Fishing Lodge Studio, 77 Bulbridge Road, Wilton, Salisbury SP2 0LE
☎ 01722 743207 Fax 01722 743207
✉ floramag@aol.com

Publisher/Editor *Maureen Foster*
Circulation 16,000

Founded 1974. BI-MONTHLY magazine for flower arrangers and florists. Unsolicited mss welcome. Approach in writing with ideas. Not interested in general gardening articles.

FEATURES Fully illustrated: colour photographs, transparencies or CD. Flower arranging, flower arrangers' gardens and flower crafts. Floristry items written with practical knowledge and well illustrated are particularly welcome. Average 1000 words.

PAYMENT £60 per 1000 words plus additional payment for suitable photographs, by arrangement.

FlyPast

PO Box 100, Stamford PE9 1XQ
☎ 01780 755131 Fax 01780 757261
✉ flypast@keypublishing.com
www.flypast.com

Owner *Key Publishing Ltd*
Editor *Ken Ellis*
Circulation 39,177

Founded 1981. MONTHLY. Historic aviation and aviation heritage, mainly military, Second World War period up to c.1970. Unsolicited mss welcome.

Focus

Bristol Magazines Ltd, Tower House, Fairfax Street, Bristol BS1 3BN
☎ 0117 927 9009 Fax 0117 934 9008
✉ focus@bbcmagazinesbristol.com
www.bbcfocusmagazine.com

Owner *Bristol Magazines Ltd, a subsidiary of BBC Worldwide*
Editor *Paul Parsons*
News & Features *Sally Palmer*
Reviews *Ian Taylor*
Circulation 59,318

Founded 1992. FOUR-WEEKLY. Popular science and discovery. Welcomes *relevant* summaries of original feature ideas by e-mail.

Fortean Times: The Journal of Strange Phenomena

PO Box 2409, London NW5 4NP
☎ 020 7907 6235 Fax 020 7907 6406
✉ david_sutton@dennis.co.uk

www.forteantimes.com
Editor *David Sutton*
Circulation 23,776
Founded 1973. THIRTEEN ISSUES YEARLY.
Accounts of strange phenomena and experiences, curiosities, mysteries, prodigies and portents. Unsolicited mss welcome. Approach in writing with ideas. No fiction, poetry, rehashes or politics.

FEATURES Well-researched and referenced material on current or historical mysteries, or first-hand accounts of oddities. Max. 3000 words, preferably with good relevant photos/illustrations.

NEWS Concise copy with full source references essential.

PAYMENT negotiable.

FQ Magazine
Seymour House, South Street, Bromley
BR1 1RH
☎020 8460 6060 Fax 020 8460 6050
✉ andy@touchline.com
www.fqmagazine.co.uk
Owner *3D Media Ltd*
Editor *Andy Tonge*
Launched 2003. BI-MONTHLY. Lifestyle magazine for young fathers. Interviews, reviews, finance, kids' toys, child issues, parenting tips and general fatherhood advice. Ideas welcome; contact the Editor by e-mail.

France Magazine
Archant House, Oriel Road, Cheltenham
GL50 1BB
☎01242 216050 Fax 01242 216094
✉ editorial@francemag.com
www.francemag.com
Owner *Archant (Life South) Ltd*
Editor *Carolyn Boyd*
Circulation 37,082 (Group); 19,351 (UK edition)
FOUNDED 1989. MONTHLY magazine containing all things of interest to Francophiles – in English. Approach by e-mail in the first instance.

Freelance Market News
Sevendale House, 7 Dale Street, Manchester
M1 1JB
☎0161 228 2362 Fax 0161 228 3533
✉ fmn@writersbureau.com
www.freelancemarketnews.com
Editor *Angela Cox*
MONTHLY. News and information on the freelance writers' market, both inland and overseas.

Includes market information, competitions, seminars, courses, overseas openings, etc. Short articles (700 words max.). Unsolicited contributions welcome.
PAYMENT by negotiation.

The Freelance
See **National Union of Journalists** under *Professional Associations and Societies*

Front Magazine
Flip Media, 4 Selsdon Way, Crossharbour, London E14 9GL
☎020 7308 5302
✉ front@frontmag.co.uk
Owner *Flip Media*
Acting Editor *Joe Barnes*
Circulation 85,000
Founded 1998. MONTHLY men's interest magazine. Includes features on sport (including extreme sport), crime, war, humour, sex, real life stories and irreverent celebrity interviews. Welcomes contributions but nothing on food, health and fitness, finance items or 'how to pull women' stories. Approach by e-mail.

Garden Answers
Bretton Court, Bretton, Peterborough
PE3 8DZ
☎01733 264666 Fax 01733 282695
Owner *Emap Active Publications Ltd*
Editor *Justine Thompson*
Circulation 38,707
Founded 1982. MONTHLY. 'It is unlikely that unsolicited manuscripts will be used, as articles are usually commissioned and must be in the magazine style.' Prospective contributors should approach the editor in writing. Interested in hearing from gardening writers on any subject, whether flowers, fruit, vegetables, houseplants or greenhouse gardening.

Garden News
Bretton Court, Bretton, Peterborough
PE3 8DZ
☎01733 264666 Fax 01733 282695
Owner *Emap Active Publications Ltd*
Editor *Neil Pope*
Circulation 49,629
Founded 1958. Britain's biggest-selling, full-colour gardening WEEKLY. News and advice on growing flowers, fruit and vegetables, plus colourful features on all aspects of gardening especially for the committed gardener. News and features welcome, especially if accompanied

by top-quality photos or illustrations. Contact the editor before submitting any material.

The Garden, Journal of the Royal Horticultural Society

RHS Publications, 4th Floor, Churchgate New Road, Peterborough PE1 1TT
☎01733 775775 Fax 01733 775819
✉ thegarden@rhs.org.uk
www.rhs.org.uk

Owner *The Royal Horticultural Society*
Editor *Ian Hodgson*
Circulation 353,547

Founded 1866. MONTHLY journal of the Royal Horticultural Society. Covers all aspects of the art, science and practice of horticulture and garden making. 'Articles must have depth and substance.' Approach by letter with a synopsis in the first instance. Max. 2500 words.

Gardens Illustrated

Bristol Magazines Ltd, Tower House, Fairfax Street, Bristol BS1 3BN
☎0117 314 8774 Fax 0117 933 8032
✉ gardens@bbcmagazinesbristol.com
www.gardensillustrated.com

Owner *Bristol Magazines Ltd*
Editor *Juliet Roberts*
Circulation 25,692

Founded 1993. MONTHLY. 'Britain's most distinguished garden magazine' with a world-wide readership. The focus is on garden design, with a strong international flavour. Unsolicited mss are rarely used and it is best that prospective contributors approach the editor with ideas in writing, supported by photographs.

Gardens Monthly

Berwick House, 8–10 Knoll Rise, Orpington BR6 0EL
☎01689 899297 Fax 01689 899266
✉ liz.dobbs@magicalia.com
www.gardening.co.uk

Owner *Magicalia Publishing Ltd*
Editor *Liz Dobbs*
Circulation 26,017

Launched 2002. MONTHLY consumer magazine for amateur gardeners with some experience. Practical advice on plants, gardens, garden design and equipment.

Gay Times

See **GT**

Gibbons Stamp Monthly

Stanley Gibbons, 7 Parkside, Christchurch Road, Ringwood BH24 3SH
☎01425 472363 Fax 01425 470247
✉ hjefferies@stanleygibbons.co.uk
www.gibbonsstampmonthly.com

Owner *Stanley Gibbons Ltd*
Editor *Hugh Jefferies*
Circulation 22,000

Founded 1890. MONTHLY. News and features. Unsolicited mss welcome. Make initial approach in writing by telephone or e-mail to avoid disappointment.

FEATURES *Hugh Jefferies* Unsolicited material of specialised nature and general stamp features welcome. Max. 3000 words but longer pieces can be serialised.

NEWS *John Moody* Any philatelic news item. Max. 500 words.

Payment Features, £40–50 per 1000 words; news, no payment.

Girl Talk / Girl Talk Extra

80 Wood Lane, London W12 0TT
☎020 8433 2758
✉ samantha.robinson@bbc.co.uk
www.bbcgirltalk.com

Owner *BBC Worldwide*
Editor *Sam Robinson*
Circulation 90,000

Founded 1995. FORTNIGHTLY/MONTHLY. Lifestyle magazine for girls aged 7–12. Friendship and belonging, celebrity. No unsolicited submissions; send c.v. by e-mail.

Glamour

6–8 Old Bond Street, London W1S 4PH
☎020 7499 9080 Fax 020 7491 2551
✉ letters@glamourmagazine.co.uk
www.condenast.co.uk

Owner *Condé Nast*
Editor *Jo Elvin*
Circulation 588,539

Founded 2001. Handbag-size glossy women's magazine – fashion, beauty and celebrities. No unsolicited mss; send ideas for features in synopsis form to the Features Editor, *Corrie Jackson*.

Golf Monthly

IPC Media Ltd., The Blue Fin Building, 110 Southwark Street, London SE1 0SU
☎020 4138 4530 Fax 020 4138 8130
✉ golfmonthly@ipcmedia.com
golf-monthly.co.uk

Owner *IPC Media (A Time Warner Company)*

Editor *Michael Harris*
Assistant Editor *John Thynne*
Instruction Editor *Neil Tappin*
Travel Editor *Alicia Harney*
News Editor *Luke Norman*
Circulation 73,775

Founded 1911. MONTHLY. Player profiles, golf instruction, general golf features and columns. Not interested in instruction material from outside contributors. Unsolicited mss welcome. Approach in writing with ideas.

FEATURES Max. 1500–2000 words.

PAYMENT by arrangement.

Golf World

Bushfield House, Orton Centre, Peterborough PE2 5UW
☎01733 237111 Fax 01733 288025
✉ paul.hamblin@emap.com
www.email.golfworldmagazine.co.uk

Owner *Emap Active Ltd*
Editor *Paul Hamblin*
Office Manager *Linda Manigan*
Circulation 42,696

Founded 1962. MONTHLY. No unsolicited mss. Approach in writing with ideas.

The Golf

IPC Media Ltd, Leon House, 233 High Street, Croydon CR9 1HZ
☎020 8726 8000 Fax 020 8726 8296
✉ thegolfmag@ipcmedia.com
www.thegolf.co.uk

Owner *IPC Media (A Time Warner Company)*
Editor *Fabian Cotter*
Circulation 25,000

Founded 1995. MONTHLY. Features Volkswagen Golfs and other VAG cars. Articles on tuning, styling, performance, technical and potential feature cars. 'Not interested in anything to do with the game of golf.' Submissions should be made directly to the editor. Articles must show excellent specialist knowledge of the subject matter. PAYMENT by negotiation.

Good Holiday Magazine

27A High Street, Esher KT10 9RL
☎01372 468140 Fax 01372 470765
✉ edit@goodholidayideas.com
www.goodskiguide.com

Editor *John Hill*
Circulation 100,000

Founded 1985. QUARTERLY aimed at better-off holiday-makers rather than travellers. Worldwide destinations including Europe and domestic. No

unsolicited material but approach in writing or by e-mail with ideas and/or synopsis.

PAYMENT negotiable.

Good Homes Magazine

Woodlands, 80 Wood Lane, London W12 0TT
☎020 8433 2391 Fax 020 8433 2691
✉ deargoodhomes@bbc.co.uk
www.bbcgoodhomes.com

Owner *BBC Worldwide Publishing Ltd*
Editor *Bernie Herlihy*
Circulation 127,024

Founded 1998. MONTHLY. Decorating, interiors, readers' homes, shopping, makeovers, property and consumer information. No fiction.

FEATURES *Emily Peck*

PROPERTY & READERS' HOMES *Rachel Watson* Property features from specialists. Approach by letter with cuttings.

Good Housekeeping

National Magazine House, 72 Broadwick Street, London W1F 9EP
☎020 7439 5000 Fax 020 7439 5616
✉ firstname.lastname@natmags.co.uk
www.goodhousekeeping.co.uk

Owner *National Magazine Co. Ltd*
Editor *Louise Chunn*
Circulation 463,645

Founded 1922. MONTHLY glossy. No unsolicited mss. Write with ideas in the first instance to the appropriate editor.

FEATURES *Lucy Moore* Most work is commissioned but original ideas are always welcome. No ideas are discussed on the telephone. Send short synopsis, plus relevant cuttings, showing previous examples of work published. No unsolicited mss.

HEALTH *Julie Powell*. Submission guidelines as for features; no unsolicited mss.

Good Motoring

Station Road, Forest Row RH18 5EN
☎01342 825676 Fax 01342 824847
✉ editor@motoringassist.com
www.roadsafety.org.uk

Owner *Gem Motoring Assist*
Editor *James Luckhurst*
Circulation 52,000

Founded 1932. QUARTERLY motoring, road safety, travel and general features magazine. 1500 words max. Prospective contributors should approach in writing only.

Good News

25 Ridley Road, Bournemouth BH9 1LD
☎01202 522177 Fax 01202 522177
✉ goodnews@pepr.co.uk
www.goodnews-paper.org.uk
Owner *Good News Fellowship*
Editor *Paul Eddy*
Circulation 50,000

Founded 2001. MONTHLY evangelistic newspaper which welcomes contributions. No
fiction. Send for sample copy of writers' guidelines in the first instance. No poetry or children's
stories.

NEWS Items of up to 500 words (preferably with pictures) 'showing God at work, and
human interest photo stories. "Churchy" items
not wanted. Testimonies of how people have
come to personal faith in Jesus Christ and the
difference it has made are always welcome. They
do not need to be dramatic!'

WOMEN'S PAGE Relevant items of interest
welcome.

PAYMENT negotiable.

The Good Ski Guide

27A High Street, Esher KT10 9RL
☎01372 468140 Fax 01372 470765
✉ info@goodholidayideas.com
www.goodskiguide.com
Owner *Good Holiday Group*
Editors *John Hill, Nick Dalton*
Circulation 250,000

Founded 1976. FOUR ISSUES YEARLY. Unsolicited
mss welcome from writers with a knowledge
of skiing and ski resorts. Prospective contributors are best advised to make initial contact
in writing as ideas and work need to be seen
before any discussion can take place. PAYMENT
negotiable.

GQ

Vogue House, Hanover Square, London
W1S 1JU
☎020 7499 9080 Fax 020 7495 1679
www.gqmagazine.co.uk
Owner *Condé Nast Publications Ltd*
Editor *Dylan Jones*
Circulation 127,505

Founded 1988. MONTHLY. Men's style magazine.
No unsolicited material. Write or fax with an
idea in the first instance.

Granta

2–3 Hanover Yard, Noel Road, London
N1 8BE
☎020 7704 9776 Fax 020 7704 0474
✉ editorial@granta.com
www.granta.com
Editor *Jason Cowley*
Deputy Editor *Matt Weiland*

QUARTERLY magazine of new writing, including
fiction, memoirs, reportage and photography
published in paperback book form. Highbrow,
diverse and contemporary, with a thematic
approach. Unsolicited mss (including fiction)
considered. A lot of material is commissioned.
Vital to read the magazine first to appreciate its
very particular fusion of cultural and political
interests. No reviews or news articles. No poetry.
Access the website for submission guidelines.

PAYMENT negotiable.

Grazia

Emap Consumer Media, Endeavour House,
189 Shaftesbury Avenue, London WC2H 8JG
☎020 7437 9011 Fax 020 7520 6589
✉ feedback@graziamagazine.co.uk
www.graziamagazine.co.uk
Owner *Emap Consumer Media*
Editor *Jane Bruton*
Circulation 210,200

Launched February 2005. Britain's first WEEKLY
glossy aimed at women aged 25 to 45. Features
articles on fashion, celebrity, news, beauty and
lifestyle. Approach by e-mail.

The Great Outdoors

See **TGO**

The Great War (1914–1918)

PO Box 202, Scarborough YO11 3GE
☎01723 581329 Fax 01723 581329
✉ books@greatnorthernpublising.co.uk
www.greatnorthernpublishing.co.uk
Owner *Great Northern Publishing*
Editor *Mark Marsay*

Founded 2001. BI-MONTHLY subscription only,
non-academic magazine published in A5 format.
'The little magazine dedicated to the Great War
(1914–19) and to those who perished and those
who returned.' Articles, personal stories and
accounts of those who served (men and women
of all nationalities) and their families: diaries,
anecdotes, letters, postcards, poetry, unit histories,
events and memorials, etc. Absolutely no fiction
or long academic works expounding historian's personal views. New material welcome but
contact editor prior to sending. See website for
submission guidelines and editorial content.
'Open door policy: all welcome regardless of

ability to write to high standard as all work is carefully edited. No subject or topic excluded.' Sample copy £5.

GrowYour Own
25 Phoenix Court, Hawkins Road, Colchester CO2 8JY
☎01206 505979 Fax 01206 505945
✉ georgina.wroe@aceville.co.uk
www.growfruitandveg.co.uk
Owner *Helen Tudor*
Editor *Craig Drever*
Launched 2005. MONTHLY magazine aimed at aspiring self-sufficients giving information on the best ways to grow (and cook) seasonal produce. Contributions are welcome on anything relevant to fruit, vegetables and herbs. Approach by e-mail.
FEATURES & NEWS *Craig Drever* (e-mail address above).

GT (Gay Times)
Unit M, Spectrum House, 32–34 Gordon House Road, London NW5 1LP
☎020 7424 7400 Fax 020 7424 7401
✉ edit@gaytimes.co.uk
www.gaytimes.co.uk
Owner *Millivres-Prowler Group*
Editor *Joseph Galliano*
Circulation 65,000
Covers all aspects of gay life, plus general interest likely to appeal to the gay community, art reviews, fashion, style and news. Regular freelance writers used. PAYMENT negotiable.

Guardian Weekend
See **The Guardian** under *National Newspapers*

Guiding magazine
17–19 Buckingham Palace Road, London SW1W 0PT
☎020 7834 6242 Fax 020 7828 5791
✉ guiding@girlguiding.org.uk
www.girlguiding.org.uk
Owner *Girlguiding UK*
Editor *Wendy Kewley*
Circulation 79,000
Founded 1914. MONTHLY. Unsolicited mss welcome provided topics relate to the Movement and/or women's role in society. Ideas in writing appreciated in first instance. No nostalgic,'when I was a Guide', pieces, please.
ACTIVITY IDEAS Interesting, contemporary ideas and instructions for activities for girls aged

5 to 18+ to do during unit meetings – crafts, games (indoor/outdoor), etc.
FEATURES Topics relevant to today's women. 500 words.
NEWS Items likely to be of interest to members. Max. 100–150 words.
PAYMENT negotiable.

H&E Naturist
Burlington Court, Carlisle Street, Goole DN14 5EG
☎01405 760298/766769 Fax 01405 763815
✉ editor@henaturist.co.uk
www.healthandefficiency.co.uk
Owner *New Freedom Publications Ltd*
Editor *Sara Backhouse*
Circulation 20,000
Founded 1898. MONTHLY naturist magazine.
FEATURES Will consider short features on social nudism, longer features on nudist holidays and nudist philosophy. 90% of every issue is by freelance contributors. 800–1500 words.
NEWS 'We are always on the lookout for national and international nudist news stories.' 250–500 words. No soft porn, 'sexy' stories or sleazy photographs. Approach by post, e-mail or telephone.

Hair
IPC Media Ltd.,The Blue Fin Building, 110 Southwark Street, London SE1 0SU
☎020 3148 7274
Owner *IPC Media (A Time Warner Company)*
Editor *LouiseWhite*
Circulation 83,962
Founded 1977. TEN ISSUES YEARLY hair and beauty magazine. No unsolicited mss, but always interested in good photographs. Approach with ideas in writing.
FEATURES Fashion pieces on hair trends and styling advice.
PAYMENT negotiable.

Hairflair & Beauty
Haversham Publications Ltd, Freebournes House, Freebournes Road,Witham CM8 3US
☎01376 534540 Fax 01376 534546
Owner *Haversham Publications Ltd*
Editor *Ruth Page*
Circulation 21,000
Founded 1982. BI-MONTHLY. Original and interesting hair and beauty-related features written in a young, lively style to appeal to a readership aged 16–35 years. Freelancers are not used.

Harper's Bazaar

National Magazine House, 72 Broadwick
Street, London W1F 9EP
☎020 7439 5000 Fax 020 7439 5506
harpersandqueen.co.uk

Owner *National Magazine Co. Ltd*
Editor *Lucy Yeomans*
Circulation 105,731

MONTHLY. Up-market glossy combining the
stylish and the streetwise. Approach in writing
(not by phone) with ideas.

FEATURES *Harriet Green* Ideas only in the first
instance.

NEWS Snippets welcome if very original.
PAYMENT negotiable.

Health & Fitness Magazine

2 Balcombe Street, London NW1 6NW
☎020 7042 4000
✉ mary.comber@futurenet.co.uk
www.healthandfitnessonline.co.uk

Owner *Future Publishing Ltd*
Editor *Mary Comber*
Circulation 65,000

Founded 1983. MONTHLY. Target reader: active,
health-conscious women aged 25–40.

FEATURES news and articles on nutrition,
exercise, healthy eating, holistic health and well-
being. Will consider ideas; approach in writing
in the first instance.

Healthy

River Publishing, 14 Leicester Place, London
WC2H 7BZ
☎020 7413 9359 Fax 020 7306 0314
✉ hberesford@riverltd.co.uk
www.healthy-magazine.co.uk

Owner *River Publishing*
Editor *Heather Beresford*
Circulation 229,769

TEN ISSUES YEARLY. Health magazine with
authoritative and accessible information and
advice. Will consider holistic health and lifestyle
features; approach by e-mail.

Heat

Endeavour House, 189 Shaftesbury Avenue,
London WC2H 8JG
☎020 7437 9011 Fax 020 7859 8670
✉ heat@emap.com

Owner *Emap Entertainment*
Editor *Mark Frith*
Circulation 598,623

Founded January 1999. WEEKLY entertainment
magazine dealing with TV, film and radio infor-

mation, fashion and features, with an emphasis
on celebrity interviews and news. Targets 18 to
40-year-old readership, male and female. Articles
written both in-house and by trusted freelancers.
No unsolicited mss.

Hello!

Wellington House, 69–71 Upper Ground,
London SE1 9PQ
☎020 7667 8700 Fax 020 7667 8716
www.hellomagazine.com

Owner *Hola! (Spain)*
Editor *Ronnie Whelan*
Commissioning Editor *Linda Newman*
Circulation 412,807

WEEKLY. Owned by a Madrid-based publishing
family, *Hello!* has grown faster than any other
British magazine since its launch here in 1988.
The magazine has editorial offices both in
Madrid and London. Major colour features plus
regular news pages. Although much of the material is provided by regulars, good proposals do
stand a chance. Approach the commissioning
editor with ideas in the first instance. No unsolicited mss.

FEATURES Interested in celebrity-based
features, with a newsy angle, and exclusive
interviews from generally unapproachable
personalities.

PAYMENT by arrangement.

Hi-Fi News

IPC Media Ltd, Leon House, 233 High Street,
Croydon CR9 1HZ
☎020 8726 8000 Fax 020 8726 8397
✉ hi-finews@ipcmedia.com

Owner *IPC Media (A Time Warner Company)*
Editor *Paul Miller*
Circulation 17,211

Founded 1956. MONTHLY. Write in the first
instance with suggestions based on knowledge
of the magazine's style and subject. All articles
must be written from an informed technical
or enthusiast viewpoint. PAYMENT negotiable,
according to technical content.

High Life

37–43 Sackville Street, London W1S 3EH
☎020 7534 2400 Fax 020 7534 2555
✉ high.life@cedarcom.co.uk
www.cedarcom.co.uk

Owner *Cedar Communications*
Editor *Kerry Smith*
Circulation 207,382

Founded 1973. MONTHLY glossy. British Airways

in-flight magazine. Almost all the content is commissioned. No unsolicited mss. Few opportunities for freelancers.

History Today

20 Old Compton Street, London W1D 4TW
☎020 7534 8000
✉ p.furtado@historytoday.com
www.historytoday.com
Owner *History Today Trust for the Advancement of Education*
Editor *Peter Furtado*
Circulation 26,191

Founded 1951. MONTHLY. General history and archaeology worldwide, history behind the headlines. Serious submissions only; no 'jokey' material. Approach by post only with s.a.e.

Home & Family

Mary Sumner House, 24 Tufton Street, London SW1P 3RB
☎020 7222 5533 Fax 020 7222 1591
Owner *MU Enterprises Ltd*
Editor *Jill Worth*
Circulation 50,600

Founded 1976. QUARTERLY. Unsolicited mss considered. No fiction or poetry. Features on family life, social issues, marriage, Christian faith, etc. Max. 1000 words. PAYMENT 'modest'.

Homes & Gardens

IPC Media Ltd., The Blue Fin Building, 110 Southwark Street, London SE1 0SU
☎020 3148 5000 Fax 020 3148 8165
www.homesand gardens.com
Owner *IPC Media (A Time Warner Company)*
Editor *Deborah Barker*
Circulation 138,323

Founded 1919. MONTHLY. Almost all published articles are specially commissioned. No fiction or poetry. Best to approach in writing with an idea, enclosing snapshots if appropriate.

Horse

IPC Media Ltd., The Blue Fin Building, 110 Southwark Street, London SE1 0SU
☎020 3148 4609
✉ joanna_pyatt@ipcmedia.com
www.ipcmedia.com
Owner *IPC Media (A Time Warner Company)*
Editor *Jo Pyatt*
Circulation 24,302

Founded 1997. MONTHLY magazine aimed at dedicated leisure riders and keen competitors who are committed to improving their riding

skills and horsecare knowledge. Also features veterinary developments and interviews with leading equestrian celebrities. Send feature ideas with a short synopsis to the editor.

Horse and Hound

IPC Media Ltd., 9th Floor, The Blue Fin Building, 110 Southwark Street, London SE1 0SU
☎020 3148 4562
✉ jenny_sims@ipcmedia.com
www.horseandhound.co.uk
Owner *IPC Media (A Time Warner Company)*
Editor *Lucy Higginson*
Circulation 71,128

Founded 1884. WEEKLY. The oldest equestrian magazine on the market. Contains regular veterinary advice and instructional articles, as well as authoritative news and comment on fox hunting, international and national show-jumping, horse trials, dressage, driving and endurance riding. Also weekly racing and point-to-points, breeding reports and articles. Regular books and art reviews, and humorous articles and cartoons are frequently published. Plenty of opportunities for freelancers. Unsolicited contributions welcome. Also publishes a sister monthly publication, *Eventing*, which covers the sport of horse trials comprehensively; Editor *Julie Harding*.

PAYMENT NUJ rates.

Horse and Rider

Headley House, Headley Road, Grayshott GU26 6TU
☎01428 601020 Fax 01428 601030
✉ djm@djmurphy.co.uk
www.horseandrideruk.co.uk
Owner *D.J. Murphy (Publishers) Ltd*
Editor *Alison Bridge*
Deputy Editor *Nicky Moffatt*
Circulation 46,000

Founded 1949. MONTHLY. Adult readership, largely horse-owning. News and instructional features, which make up the bulk of the magazine, are almost all written in-house or commissioned. New contributors and unsolicited articles are occasionally used. Approach the editor in writing with ideas.

Hotline

The River Group, Victory House, Leicester Square, London WC2H 7BZ
☎020 7306 0304
✉ arayner@riverltd.co.uk

Editor *Alex Rayner*
Circulation 178,163
Founded 1997. QUARTERLY on-board magazine for Virgin trains. UK celebrity and travel-based features. Ideas and outlines welcome by post or e-mail.

House & Garden

Vogue House, Hanover Square, London W1S 1JU
☎020 7499 9080 Fax 020 7629 2907
www.houseandgarden.co.uk
Owner *Condé Nast Publications Ltd*
Editor *Susan Crewe*
Circulation 141,074

Founded 1947. MONTHLY. Most feature material is produced in-house but occasional specialist features are commissioned from qualified freelancers, mainly for the interiors, wine and food sections and travel.

FEATURES *Hatta Byng* Suggestions for features, preferably in the form of brief outlines of proposed subjects, will be considered.

House Beautiful

National Magazine House, 72 Broadwick Street, London W1F 9EP
☎020 7439 5000 Fax 020 7439 5141
Owner *National Magazine Co. Ltd*
Editor *Julia Goodwin*
Circulation 188,160

Founded 1989 and relaunched in November 2003. MONTHLY. Lively magazine offering sound, practical information and plenty of inspiration for those who want to make the most of where they live. Over 100 pages of easy-reading editorial. Regular features about decoration, DIY, food, gardening and occasionally property, plus topical features with a newsy slant to fit the 'Hot Topics' slot. Approach in writing with synopses in the first instance including a brief outline of areas of specialism and examples of previously published articles in a similar vein.

i-D Magazine

124 Tabernacle Street, London EC2A 4SA
☎020 7490 9710 Fax 020 7490 9737
✉ editor@i-dmagazine.co.uk
www.i-dmagazine.com
Owner *Levelprint*
Editor *Ben Reardon*
Circulation 73,016

Founded 1980. MONTHLY lifestyle magazine for both sexes with a fashion bias. International. Very hip. Does not accept unsolicited contributions but welcomes new ideas from the fields of fashion, music, clubs, art, film, technology, books, sport, etc. No fiction or poetry. 'We are always looking for freelance non-fiction writers with new or unusual ideas.' A different theme each issue – past themes have included Green politics, taste, films, sex, love and loud dance music – means it is advisable to discuss feature ideas in the first instance.

Ideal Home

IPC Media Ltd., The Blue Fin Building, 110 Southwark Street, London SE1 0SU
☎020 3148 7357
Owner *IPC Media (A Time Warner Company)*
Editor *Susan Rose*
Circulation 231,643

Founded 1920. MONTHLY glossy. Unsolicited feature ideas are welcome only if appropriate to the magazine. Prospective contributors wishing to submit ideas should do so in writing to the editor. No fiction.

FEATURES Furnishing and decoration of houses, kitchens or bathrooms; interior design, soft furnishings, furniture and home improvements, lifestyle, consumer, gardening, property, food and readers' homes. Length to be discussed with editor.

PAYMENT negotiable.

Image Magazine

Upper Mounts, Northampton NN1 3HR
☎01604 467000 Fax 01604 467190
✉ image@northantsnews.co.uk
www.northantsnews.co.uk
Owner *Northamptonshire Newspapers Ltd*
Editor *Ruth Supple*
Circulation 12,000

Founded 1905. MONTHLY general interest regional magazine. No unsolicited mss.

FEATURES Local issues, personalities, businesses, etc., of Northamptonshire, Bedfordshire, Buckinghamshire interest. Max. 500 words.

NEWS No hard news as such, just monthly diary column.

OTHER Regulars on motoring, fashion, beauty, lifestyle, travel and horoscopes. Max. 500 words.

PAYMENT for features negotiable.

In Britain

Jubilee House, 2 Jubilee Place, London SW3 3TQ
☎020 7751 4800 Fax 020 7751 4848
✉ inbritain@archant.co.uk

Editor *Andrea Spain*
Circulation 40,000
Founded in the 1930s. BI-MONTHLY. Travel magazine of 'VisitBritain'. Not much opportunity for unsolicited work – approach (by e-mail) with ideas and samples. Words and picture packages preferred (good quality transparencies or digital images by CD only).

Independent Magazine
See **The Independent** under *National Newspapers*

Inspire
CPO, Garcia Estate, Canterbury Road, Worthing BN13 1BW
☎01903 264556 Fax 01903 821081
✉ russbravo@cpo.org.uk
www.inspiremagazine.org.uk

Owner *Christian Publishing & Outreach Ltd*
Editor *Russ Bravo*
Circulation 65,000

MONTHLY. Upbeat, good news Christian magazine featuring human interest stories, growing churches and community transformation. Limited freelance articles used. Contributor's guidelines available.

InStyle
IPC Media Ltd., The Blue Fin Building, 110 Southwark Street, London SE1 0SU
☎020 3148 7399 Fax 020 3148 8166
✉ firstname_lastname@instyleuk.com

Owner *IPC Media (A Time Warner Company)*
Senior Editor *Kate O'Donnell*
Editor *Trish Halpin*
Deputy Editor *Charlotte Moore*
Executive Fashion & Beauty Director
  Sophie Hedley
Features Editor *Kate Bussman*
Fashion Director *Fiona Rubie*
Circulation 181,909

Launched March 2001. MONTHLY. UK edition of US fashion, beauty, celebrity and lifestyle magazine. Unsolicited material welcome; send by e-mail to individual editors.

Interlude
Limehouse Town Hall, 646 Commercial Road, London E14 7HA
☎020 8673 2256
✉ info@interludemagazine.co.uk
www.interludemagazine.co.uk

Editors *Helen Nodding, Becky Philp, Francesca Ricci*

Launched 2005. Magazine for writing and visual work with a focus on multidisciplinary projects and 'work in progress'. Pages are formatted and illustrated by the author. Unsolicited contributions welcome by e-mail, particularly experimental writing (max. 2500 words); no extracts from published books. See website for submission guidelines.

Interzone: Science Fiction & Fantasy
TTA Press, 5 Martins Lane, Witcham, Ely CB6 2LB
✉ andy@ttapress.demon.co.uk
www.ttapress.com

Owner *TTA Press*
Editor *Andy Cox*
Circulation 10,000

Founded 1982. BI-MONTHLY magazine of science fiction and fantasy. Unsolicited mss are welcome 'from writers who have a knowledge of the magazine and its contents'. S.a.e. essential for return.

FICTION 2000–6000 words.

FEATURES Book/film reviews, interviews with writers and occasional short articles. Length by arrangement.

PAYMENT fiction, £30 per 1000 words; features, negotiable.

Investors Chronicle
Number One, Southwark Bridge, London SE1 9HL
☎020 7775 6582 Fax 020 7382 8105
www.investorschronicle.co.uk

Owner *Pearson*
Editor *Matthew Vincent*
Deputy Editor *Rosie Carr*
Circulation 34,919

Founded 1860. WEEKLY. Opportunities for freelance contributors in the survey section only. All approaches should be made in writing. Over forty surveys are published each year on a wide variety of subjects, generally with a financial, business or investment emphasis. Copies of survey list and synopses of individual surveys are obtainable from the surveys editor.

PAYMENT negotiable.

The Irish Book Review
Ashbrook House, 10 Main Street, Raheny, Dublin 5, Republic of Ireland
☎00 353 1 851 1459
✉ editor@irishbookreview.com
www.irishbookreview.com

Editor *Eugene O'Brien*
Publisher *David Givens*

Founded 2005. QUARTERLY. Reviews books of Irish interest and/or by Irish authors. Also publishes features,extracts,articles relating to Irish books, publishing and the book trade. 'Would like to hear from potential reviewers/writers.'

Irish Pages

The Linen Hall Library, 17 Donegall Square North, Belfast BT1 5GB
☎028 9043 4800
✉ irishpages@yahoo.co.uk
www.irishpages.org

Editor *Chris Agee*
Circulation 1400

Founded 2002. BIANNUAL non-partisan, non-sectarian journal publishing writing from Ireland and abroad.'The most important cultural journal in Ireland at the present moment' (Jonathan Allison, Director of the Yeats Summer School).

FEATURES Poetry, short fiction, essays, non-fiction, memoirs, nature-writing, translated work, literary journalism and other autobiographical, historical and scientific writing of literary distinction. Irish language and Ulster Scots writing are published in the original, with English translations. Equal editorial attention is given to established, emergent and new writers. Send submissions to the editor by post.

IRRV Valuer

IRRV, 41 Doughty Street, London WC1N 2LF
☎01843 290919 Fax 01843 290919
✉ jcroberts54@hotmail.com
www.irrv.org.uk

Owner *Institute of Revenues, Rating and Valuation*
Managing Editor *Kate Miller*
Circulation 2000

Founded 2001. FOUR issues yearly for property valuation professionals.Well-qualified commentary, analysis and news covering issues affecting valuers, including reforms, legislation and technology. Small amount of appropriate lifestyle coverage. No unsolicited material; approach by telephone, fax, letter or e-mail in the first instance.

FEATURES Ideas for stories must be well sourced and informed.

NEWS Stories relevant to property professionals. Max. 300 words.

PAYMENT negotiable.

It's Hot! Magazine

Rm A1136, BBC Worldwide,Woodlands, 80 Wood Lane, London W12 0TT
☎020 8433 3910 Fax 020 8433 2763
✉ rosalie.snaith@bbc.co.uk

Owner *BBC Worldwide Publishing Ltd*
Editor *Rosalie Snaith*
Deputy Editor *Shelley Moulden* (shelley. moulden@bbc.co.uk)
Circulation 57,013

Founded 2002. MONTHLY magazine aimed at 9–13 year old girls featuring music, film & TV gossip, plus fashion, beauty and lifestyle features. Interested in exclusive celebrity interviews relevant to their market, lifestyle features and quizzes. Rarely accept on-spec features/ideas as they have an in-house editorial team. To put yourself forward for freelance work approach the Deputy Editor by e-mail but 'please read the magazine first for style'. PAYMENT negotiable.

Jade

PO Box 202, Scarborough YO11 3GE
☎01723 581329 Fax 01723 581329
✉ books@greatnorthernpublishing.co.uk
www.greatnorthernpublishing.co.uk

Owner *Great Northern Publishing*
Editor *Mark Marsay*

Founded 2002. BI-MONTHLY uncensored, adult subscription-only magazine in A5 format. Official magazine of the Guild of Erotic Artists. Features new and established international photographers, artists, sculptors and writers in all erotic genres from around the world. No editorial articles, features or advice columns. Contributors (photographers, artists, sculptors and writers) should consult the website for submission guidelines and current requirements; contact the editor prior to sending material. Sample copy £5 (contains strong adult content).

Jane's Defence Weekly

Sentinel House, 163 Brighton Road, Coulsdon CR5 2YH
☎020 8700 3700 Fax 020 8763 1007
✉ jdw@janes.com
www.janes.com

Owner *Jane's Information Group*
Editor *Peter Felstead*
Circulation 25,500

Founded 1984. WEEKLY. No unsolicited mss. Approach in writing with ideas in the first instance.

FEATURES Current defence topics of worldwide interest. No history pieces. Most features are commissioned. Max. 4000 words.

Jazz Journal International
3 & 3A Forest Road, Loughton IG10 1DR
☎020 8532 0456/0678 Fax 020 8532 0440

Owner *Jazz Journal Ltd*
Editor *Janet Cook*
Circulation 8000+

Founded 1948. MONTHLY. A specialised jazz magazine, for record collectors, principally using expert contributors whose work is known to the editor. Unsolicited mss not welcome, with the exception of news material (for which no payment is made). It is not a gig guide, nor a free reference source for students.

Jersey Now
PO Box 582, Five Oaks, St Saviour JE4 8XQ
☎01534 611743 Fax 01534 611610
✉ eperchard@msppublishing.com

Owner *MSP Publishing*
Managing Editor *Peter Body*
Editor *Elisabeth Perchard*
Circulation 24,000

Founded 1987. QUARTERLY lifestyle magazine for Jersey covering homes, gardens, the arts, Jersey heritage, motoring, boating, fashion, beauty, food and drink, health, travel and technology. Upmarket glossy aimed at an informed and discerning readership. Interested in Jersey-orientated articles only; 1200 words max. Approach the editor initially. PAYMENT negotiable.

Jewish Chronicle
25 Furnival Street, London EC4A 1JT
☎020 7415 1500 Fax 020 7405 9040
✉ editorial@thejc.com
www.thejc.com

Owner *Kessler Foundation*
Editor *David Rowan*
Circulation 35,427

WEEKLY. Unsolicited mss welcome if 'the specific interests of our readership are borne in mind by writers'. Approach in writing, except for urgent current news items. No fiction. Max. 1500 words for all material.
    FEATURES *Alan Montague*
    NEWS EDITOR *Jenni Frazer*
    FOREIGN NEWS *Daniella Peled*
    SUPPLEMENTS *Angela Kiverstein*
    PAYMENT negotiable.

Jewish Quarterly
PO Box 37645, London NW7 1WB

☎020 8343 4675
✉ editor@jewquart.freeserve.co.uk
www.jewishquarterly.org

Publisher *Jewish Literary Trust*
Editor *Matthew Reisz*

Founded 1953. QUARTERLY illustrated magazine featuring Jewish literature and fiction, politics, art, music, film, poetry, history, dance, community, autobiography, Hebrew, Yiddish, Israel and the Middle East, Judaism, interviews, Zionism, philosophy and holocaust studies. Features a major books and arts section. Unsolicited mss welcome but letter or phone call preferred in first instance.

Jewish Telegraph Group of Newspapers
Telegraph House, 11 Park Hill, Bury Old Road, Prestwich, Manchester M25 0HH
☎0161 740 9321 Fax 0161 740 9325
✉ editor@jewishtelegraph.com
www.jewishtelegraph.com

Editor *Paul Harris* (☎ 0161 741 2633)
Circulation 16,000

Founded 1950. WEEKLY publication with local, national and international news and features. (Separate editions published for Manchester, Leeds, Liverpool and Glasgow.) Unsolicited features on Jewish humour and history welcome.

The Journal Magazines (Norfolk, Suffolk, Cambridgeshire)/The Essex Magazine
Cambridge Newspapers Ltd, Winship Road, Milton CB24 6PP
☎01223 434409 Fax 01223 434415

Owner *Cambridge Newspapers Ltd*
Editor *Debbie Tweedie*
Circulation 12,000 each

Founded 1990. MONTHLY magazines covering items of local interest – history, people, conservation, business, places, food and wine, fashion, homes and sport.
    FEATURES 750–1500 words max., plus pictures. Approach the editor with ideas in the first instance.

Journal of Apicultural Research
(including **Bee World**)
IBRA, 18 North Road, Cardiff CF10 3DT
☎029 2037 2409 Fax 029 2066 5522
✉ mail@ibra.org.uk
www.ibra.org.uk

Owner *International Bee Research Association*
Editor *Professor Keith Delaplane*
Circulation 1700

Bee World, founded 1919; Journal of Apicultural Research, 1962. QUARTERLY. High-quality factual journal, including peer-reviewed articles, with international readership. Features on apicultural science and technology. Unsolicited mss welcome but authors should write to the editor for guidelines before submitting material.

Kerrang!

Mappin House, 4 Winsley Street, London W1W 8HR
☎020 7182 8000 Fax 020 7182 8910
✉ kerrang@emap.com
www.kerrang.com

Owner *Emap Performance*
Editor *Paul Brannigan*
Circulation 85,377

Founded 1981. WEEKLY rock, punk and metal magazine.'Written by fans for fans.'Will consider ideas for features but not actively seeking new contributors unless expert in specialist fields such as black metal and hardcore, emo, etc.

The Lady

39–40 Bedford Street, London WC2E 9ER
☎020 7379 4717 Fax 020 7836 4620

Editor *Arline Usden*
Circulation 31,752

Founded 1885. WEEKLY. Unsolicited mss are accepted provided they are not on the subject of politics or religion, or on topics covered by staff writers or special correspondents, i.e. fashion and beauty, health, cookery, household, gardening, finance and shopping.

FEATURES Well-researched pieces on British and foreign travel, historical subjects or events; interviews and profiles and other general interest topics. Max. 1200 words for illustrated two-page articles; 900 words for one-page features; 420 words for first-person 'Viewpoint' pieces. All material should be addressed to the editor with s.a.e. enclosed. Photographs supporting features may be supplied as colour transparencies, b&w prints or on disk. Telephone enquiries about features are not encouraged.

Lake District Life

3 Tustin Court, Port Way, Preston PR2 2YQ
☎01772 722022 Fax 01772 736496
✉ roger.borrell@lakedistrict-life.co.uk
www.lakedistrict-life.co.uk

Owner *Archant Life*

Editor *Roger Borrell*
Circulation 23,000

Founded 1947. MONTHLY. A celebration of life in the Lake District, both past and present. Unsolicited contributions welcome; approach the editor by e-mail.

Lancashire Life

3 Tustin Court, Port Way, Preston PR2 2YQ
☎01772 722022 Fax 01772 736496
✉ roger.borrell@lancashirelife.co.uk
www.lancashirelife.co.uk

Owner *Archant Life*
Editor *Roger Borrell*
Circulation 23,000

Founded 1947. MONTHLY county magazine. Features and pictures about Lancashire. Unsolicited contributions welcome; approach the editor by e-mail.

Land Rover World

IPC Media Ltd, Leon House, 233 High Street, Croydon CR9 1HZ
☎020 8726 8371 Fax 020 8726 8398
✉ landroverworld@ipcmedia.co.uk
www.landroverworld.co.uk

Owner *IPC Media (A Time Warner Company)*
Editor *John Carroll*
Circulation 30,000

Founded 1994. MONTHLY. Incorporates *Practical Land Rover World* and *Classic Land Rover World*. Unsolicited material welcome, especially if supported by high-quality illustrations.

FEATURES All articles with a Land Rover theme of interest. Potential contributors are strongly advised to examine previous issues before starting work.

PAYMENT negotiable.

Lawyer 2B

50 Poland Street, London W1F 7AX
☎0207 970 4622
www.lawyer2b.com

Owner *Centaur Media plc*
Editor *Husnara Begum*
Circulation 30,000

Launched in 2001, *Lawyer 2B* is a sister publication of *The Lawyer*, circulated to law students and trainees. FIVE ISSUES PER ACADEMIC YEAR. Occasional opportunities for profiles/features relating to legal education and law students.

The Lawyer

50 Poland Street, London W1F 7AX
☎020 7970 4000

✉ editorial@thelawyer.com
www.thelawyer.com
Owner *Centaur Media plc*
Editor *Catrin Griffiths*
Circulation 31,475 (print); 126,413 (online)
Launched 1987. WEEKLY plus daily news e-mail alerts and commentaries. Leading news magazine for City and commercial lawyers. Strong international coverage and leading-edge research.
FEATURES *Gemma Westacott* Technical legal content, written in an accessible style. No unsolicited contributions; initial approach by e-mail with specific idea. 'Read the magazine first!'

Lincolnshire Life
County Life Ltd, PO Box 81, Lincoln LN1 1HD
☎01522 527127 Fax 01522 560035
✉ editorial@lincolnshirelife.co.uk
www.lincolnshirelife.co.uk
Publisher *C. Bingham*
Executive Editor *Judy Theobald*
Circulation 10,000
Founded 1961. MONTHLY county magazine featuring geographically relevant articles on local culture, history, personalities, etc. Max. 1500 words. Contributions supported by three or four good-quality photographs welcome. Approach in writing. PAYMENT varies.

The Lincolnshire Poacher
County Life Ltd, PO Box 81, Lincoln LN1 1HD
☎01522 527127 Fax 01522 560035
✉ editorial@lincolnshirelife.co.uk
www.lincolnshirelife.co.uk
Publisher *C. Bingham*
Executive Editor *Judy Theobald*
Circulation 5000
QUARTERLY county magazine featuring geographically relevant but nostalgic articles on history, culture and personalities of Lincolnshire. Max. 2000 words. Contributions supported by three or four good-quality photographs/illustrations appreciated. Approach in writing. PAYMENT varies.

The List
14 High Street, Edinburgh EH1 1TE
☎0131 550 3050 Fax 0131 550 3050
✉ editor@list.co.uk
www.list.co.uk
Owner *The List Ltd*
Publisher *Robin Hodge*
Editor *Claire Prentice*

Circulation 17,500
Founded 1985. FORTNIGHTLY. Events guide covering Glasgow and Edinburgh. Interviews and profiles of people working in film, theatre, music and the arts. Max. 1200 words. No unsolicited mss. News material tends to be handled in-house.

Literary Review
44 Lexington Street, London W1F 0LW
☎020 7437 9392 Fax 020 7734 1844
✉ editorial@literaryreview.co.uk
www.literaryreview.co.uk
Editor *Nancy Sladek*
Circulation 15,000
Founded 1979. MONTHLY. Publishes book reviews (commissioned), features and articles on literary subjects. Prospective contributors are best advised to contact the editor in writing. Unsolicited mss not welcome. Runs a monthly competition for 'poems which rhyme, scan and make sense'.
PAYMENT 'minuscule'.

Living France
Archant House, Oriel Road, Cheltenham GL50 1BB
☎01242 216086 Fax 01242 216094
✉ editorial@livingfrance.com
www.livingfrance.com
Owner *Archant Life*
Editor *Eleanor O'Kane*
Founded 1989. FOUR-WEEKLY. A magazine for people who are considering or actively purchasing a home in France. Editorial consists of travel features as well as practical, friendly information and advice on becoming an owner of French property. Will consider articles describing different regions of France, interviews with owners of property and aspects of living in France. Interested in hearing from professional writers who could do interviews. No unsolicited mss; approach in writing or by e-mail with an idea.

Loaded
IPC Media Ltd., The Blue Fin Building, 110 Southwark Street, London SE1 0SU
☎020 3148 5000 Fax 020 3148 8107
✉ andy_sherwood@ipcmedia.com
Owner *IPC Media (A Time Warner Company)*
Editor *Martin Daubney*
Features Editor *Andy Sherwood*
Circulation 162,554
Founded 1994. MONTHLY men's lifestyle maga-

zine featuring music, sport, sex, humour, travel, fashion, hard news and popular culture. Will consider material which comes into these categories; approach the features editor in writing or by e-mail in the first instance. No fiction or poetry.

Logos

5 Beechwood Drive, Marlow SL7 2DH
☎01628 483371 Fax 01628 477577
✉ logos-marlow@dial.pipex.com
www.logos-journal.org
Owner *LOGOS International Educational Publishing Foundation*
Editor (New York) *Charles M. Levine* (Charlev@Nyc.rr.com)
Editor Emeritus *Gordon Graham* (Marlow address)
Business Manager *Betty Graham* (Marlow address)

Founded 1990. QUARTERLY. Aims to 'deal in depth with issues which unite, divide, excite and concern the world of books', with an international perspective. Each issue contains six to eight articles of between 3500 and 7000 words. 'Logos is a non-profit making professional forum, not a scholarly journal.' Suggestions and ideas for contributions are welcome, and should be addressed to the editor. 'Guidelines for Contributors' available. Contributors write from their experience as authors, publishers, booksellers, librarians, etc.

PAYMENT Contributors receive off-prints, a copy of the issue in which their article appears and a 50% concession on the subscription rate.

The London Magazine

Editorial office: 70 Wargrave Road, London N15 6UB
☎020 8400 5882 (Admin. office)
Fax 020 8994 1713
✉ admin@thelondonmagazine.net
www.londonmagazine.net
Publisher *Christopher Arkell*
Editor *Sebastian Barker*
Circulation 1200

Founded originally in 1732 and relaunched in 2002. BI-MONTHLY review of literature and the arts. Publishes poems, short stories, features, memoirs, and book and performance reviews. Not interested in overtly political material. Do *not* send anything by e-mail or fax. No phonecalls. All submissions should be made by post with an s.a.e. to the editorial office.
FEATURES Max. 6000 words.

FICTION Max. 6000 words.
POEMS 'Any length within reason.'
PAYMENT negotiable with the editor. Standard fees for most items.

London Review of Books

28 Little Russell Street, London WC1A 2HN
☎020 7209 1101 Fax 020 7209 1102
✉ edit@lrb.co.uk
www.lrb.co.uk
Owner *LRB Ltd*
Editor *Mary-Kay Wilmers*
Circulation 43,469

Founded 1979. FORTNIGHTLY. Reviews, essays and articles on political, literary, cultural and scientific subjects. Also poetry. Unsolicited contributions welcome (approximately 50 received each week). No pieces under 2000 words. Contact the editor in writing. Please include s.a.e.
PAYMENT £200 per 1000 words; poems, £125.

Lothian Life

Ballencrieff Cottage, Ballencrieff Toll, Bathgate EH48 4LD
☎01506 632728
✉ editor@lothianlife.co.uk
www.lothianlife.co.uk
Owner *Pages Editorial & Publishing Services*
Editor *Susan Coon*

Online county magazine for people who live, work or have an interest in the Lothians. Features on successful people, businesses or initiatives. Regular articles by experts in the Lifestyle section including Homes & Gardens, Tastebuds, Out & About, The Arts and Health & Fitness. Phone first to discuss content and timing.
PAYMENT See the website.

Machine Knitting Monthly

PO Box 1479, Maidenhead SL6 8YX
☎01628 783080 Fax 01628 633250
✉ mail@machineknittingmonthly.net
www.machineknittingmonthly.net
Owner *RPA Publishing Ltd*
Editor *Anne Smith*

Founded 1986. MONTHLY. Unsolicited mss considered 'as long as they are applicable to this specialist publication. We have our own regular contributors each month but we're always willing to look at new ideas from other writers.' Approach in writing in the first instance.

MacUser
30 Cleveland Street, London W1T 4JD
☎020 7907 6000
✉ mailbox@macuser.co.uk
www.macuser.co.uk
Owner *Dennis Publishing*
Editor *Nik Rawlinson*
Circulation 18,906
Launched 1985. FORTNIGHTLY computer magazine.

Management Today
174 Hammersmith Road, London W6 7JP
☎020 8267 5000
✉ editorial@mtmagazine.co.uk
Owner *Haymarket Specialist*
Managing Director *Nick Simpson*
Editor *Matthew Gwyther*
Circulation 100,258

General business topics and features. Ideas welcome. Send brief synopsis to the features editor.

marie claire
IPC Media Ltd., The Blue Fin Building, 110 Southwark Street, London SE1 0SU
☎020 3148 7513 Fax 020 3148 8120
✉ marieclaire@ipcmedia.com
www.ipcmedia.com
Owner *European Magazines Ltd*
Editor *Marie O'Riordan*
Circulation 334,729

Founded 1988. MONTHLY. An intelligent glossy magazine for women, with strong international features and fashion. No unsolicited mss. Approach with ideas in writing or by e-mail (marieclaireideas@ipcmedia.com). No fiction.

FEATURES *Miranda McMinn* Detailed proposals for feature ideas should be accompanied by samples of previous work.

Marketing Week
St Giles House, 50 Poland Street, London W1F 7AX
☎020 7970 4000 Fax 020 7970 6721
✉ mw.editorial@centaur.co.uk
www.marketingweek.co.uk
Owner *Centaur Communications*
Editor *Stuart Smith*
Circulation 39,163

WEEKLY trade magazine of the marketing industry. Features on all aspects of the business, written in a newsy and up-to-the-minute style. Approach with ideas in the first instance.

FEATURES *Daney Parker*

PAYMENT negotiable.

Match
Bushfield House, Orton Centre, Peterborough PE2 5UW
☎01733 288138 Fax 01733 288150
✉ match.magazine@emap.com
www.matchmag.co.uk
Owner *Emap Active Ltd*
Editor *Ian Foster*
Circulation 117,844

Founded 1979. WEEKLY. The UK's biggest-selling football magazine aimed at 10–15-year-olds. All material is generated in-house by a strong news and features team. Work experience placements often given to trainee journalists and students; several staff have been recruited through this route. Approach in writing or by phone.

Maxim
30 Cleveland Street, London W1T 4JD
☎020 7907 6410 Fax 020 7907 6439
✉ editorial.maxim@dennis.co.uk
www.maximmag.co.uk
Owner *Dennis Publishing*
Editor *Derek Harbison*
Circulation 131,497

Established 1995. MONTHLY glossy men's lifestyle magazine featuring sex, grooming, girls, fun-stuff, cars and fashion. No fiction or poetry. Approach in writing in the first instance, sending outlines of ideas only together with examples of published work.

Mayfair
2 Archer Street, Piccadilly Circus, London W1D 7AW
☎020 7292 8000 Fax 020 7734 5030
✉ mayfair@paulraymond.com
www.sexclub.co.uk
Owner *Paul Raymond Publications*
Editor *David Spenser*
Circulation 331,760

Founded 1966. THIRTEEN ISSUES YEARLY. Unsolicited material accepted if pertinent to the magazine and if accompanied by suitable illustrative material. 'We will *only* publish work if we can illustrate it.' Interested in features and humour aimed at men aged 18 to 80; 800–1000 words. Punchy, bite-sized humour, top ten features, etc. 'Must make the editor laugh.' Also considers erotica.

Mayfair Times

1 Blandel Bridge House, 56 Sloane Square,
London SW1W 8AX
☎020 7259 1050 Fax 020 7901 9042
✉ erik.brown@pubbiz.com
www.pubbiz.com
Owner *Publishing Business Ltd*
Editor *Selma Day*
Circulation 17,000

Founded 1985. MONTHLY. Features on Mayfair of interest to residents, local workers, visitors and shoppers.

Medal News

Token Publishing, Orchard House, Duchy Road, Heathpark, Honiton EX14 1YD
☎01404 46972 Fax 01404 44788
✉ info@tokenpublishing.com
www.tokenpublishing.com
Owners *J. W. Mussell, Carol Hartman*
Editor *J. W. Mussell*
Circulation 5500

Founded 1989. TEN ISSUES YEARLY. Unsolicited material welcome but initial approach by phone or in writing preferred.

FEATURES 'Opportunities exist for well-informed authors who know the subject and do their homework. It would help if a digital copy of the contribution is provided in the form of an e-mail or CD. Relevant illustrations welcome.' Max. 2500 words.

PAYMENT £30 per 1000 words.

Media Week

Griffin House, 161 Hammersmith Road,
London W6 8BS
☎020 8267 5000 Fax 020 8267 8020
✉ firstname.surname@haymarket.com
www.mediaweek.co.uk
Owner *Haymarket Publishing Ltd*
Editor *Steve Barrett*
Circulation 13,297

Founded 1986. WEEKLY trade magazine. UK and international coverage on all aspects of commercial media. Approach in writing with ideas. See website for e-mail addresses.

Melody Maker

See **New Musical Express**

Men's Health

National Magazine House, 33 Broadwick Street, London W1F 0DQ
☎020 7339 4400 Fax 020 7339 4444
www.menshealth.co.uk

Owner *Natmag-Rodale Publishing*
Editor *Morgan Rees*
Circulation 238,568

Founded 1994. MONTHLY men's healthy lifestyle magazine covering health, fitness, nutrition, stress and sex issues. No unsolicited mss; will consider ideas and synopses tailored to men's health. No fiction or extreme sports. Approach in writing in the first instance.

MiniWorld Magazine

IPC Media Ltd, Leon House, 233 High Street, Croydon CR9 1HZ
☎020 8726 8000 Fax 020 8726 8399
✉ miniworld@ipcmedia.com
www.miniworld.co.uk
Owner *IPC Media (A Time Warner Company)*
Editor *Monty Watkins*
Circulation 37,000

Founded 1991. THIRTEEN ISSUES YEARLY. Car magazine devoted to the Mini. Unsolicited material welcome but prospective contributors are advised to contact the editor.

FEATURES Maintenance, tuning, restoration, technical advice, classified, sport, readers' cars and social history of this cult car.

PAYMENT negotiable.

Mizz

Panini UK, Panini House, Coach & Horses Passage, Tunbridge Wells TN2 5UJ
☎01892 500100 Fax 01892 545666
✉ mizz@panini.co.uk
www.mizz.com
Owner *Panini UK Ltd*
Editor *Karen Brown*
Circulation 59,934

Founded 1985. FORTNIGHTLY magazine for the 10–14–year-old girl.

FEATURES 'We have a full features team and thus do not accept freelance features.'

Mobilise

Mobilise Organisation, Ashwellthorpe, Norwich NR16 1EX
☎01508 489449 Fax 01508 488173
✉ enquiries@mobilise.info
www.mobilise.info
Owner *Mobilise Organisation*
Editor *Nicky Rogers*
Circulation 30,000

MONTHLY publication of the Mobilise Organisation, which aims to promote and protect the interests and welfare of disabled people and help and encourage them in gaining increased mobility.Various discounts available for members; membership costs £14 p.a. (single), £18 (joint).The magazine includes information for members plus members' letters. Approach in writing with ideas. Unsolicited mss welcome.

Model Collector
IPC Focus Network, Leon House, 233 High Street, Croydon CR9 1HZ
☎020 8726 8000 Fax 020 8726 8299
✉ modelcollector@ipcmedia.com
www.modelcollector.com
Owner *AOL Time Warner/IPC Media*
Editor *Lindsey Amrani*
Circulation 11,605

Founded 1987.THIRTEEN ISSUES YEARLY Britain's best selling die cast magazine. From the latest models to classic 1930's Dinkys. Interested in historical articles about particular models or ranges and reviews of the latest products. Photographs welcome. Not interested in radio controlled models or model railways.
FEATURES Freelancers should contact the editor. Unsolicited material may be considered.
NEWS Trade news welcome. Call *Lindsey Armrani* (☎ 020 8726 8238) to discuss details.

Mojo
Mappin House, 4 Winsley Street, London W1W 8HF
☎020 7182 8616 Fax 020 7182 8596
✉ mojo@emap.com
www.mojo4music.com
Owner *Emap Performance*
Editor-in-Chief *Phil Alexander*
Circulation 114,183

Founded 1993. MONTHLY magazine containing features, reviews and news stories about all types of music and its influences. Receives about five mss per day. No poetry, think-pieces on dead rock stars or similar fan worship.
FEATURES Amateur writers discouraged except as providers of source material, contacts, etc.
NEWS All verifiable, relevant stories considered.
REVIEWS Write to Reviews Editor, *Jenny Bulley* with relevant specimen material.
PAYMENT negotiable.

Moneywise
1st Floor, Standon House, Mansell Street, London E1 8AA
☎020 7680 3600 Fax 020 7702 0710
✉ hannah.ricci@moneywise.co.uk
www.moneywise.co.uk

Owner *Capital Accumulation Services Ltd*
Editor-in-Chief *Emma-Lou Montgomery*
Editor *Rachel Williams*
Circulation 30,151
Founded 1990. MONTHLY. No unsolicited mss; ideas welcome. Make initial approach in writing to Editorial Department (c.v. preferred).

More
Endeavour House, 189 Shaftesbury Avenue, London WC2H 8JG
☎020 7208 3165 Fax 020 7208 3595
www.moremagazine.co.uk
Owner *Emap élan Publications*
Editor *Lisa Smosarski*
Circulation 271,629
Founded 1988. FORTNIGHTLY women's magazine aimed at the working woman aged 18–26. Features on sex and relationships plus celebrity news, style and fashion. Most items are commissioned; approach features director with idea. Prospective contributors are strongly advised to study the magazine's style before submitting anything.

The Morley Review
Dept. of Humanities, Morley College, 61 Westminster Bridge Road, London SE1 7HT
☎020 7450 1846
✉ paul.laffan@morleycollege.ac.uk
Editor *Paul Laffan*
ANNUAL poetry and fiction magazine. One piece of fiction (a short story or first chapter of a novel) or four poems may be submitted per edition. Fiction: max. 2000 words; poems: max. 40 lines. All submissions should be accompanied by an s.a.e. Advisable to keep a copy of any work submitted. 'Copyright is retained by the author, but by submitting authors agree to their work being published and edited by *The Morley Review*.'
PAYMENT Complimentary copy of the magazine in which author's work appears.

Mother and Baby
Greater London House, Hampstead Road, London NW1 7EJ
☎020 7347 1869 Fax 020 7874 0201
✉ mother&baby@emap.com
Owner *Emap Esprit*
Editor *Elena Dalrymple*
Circulation 72,345
Founded 1956. MONTHLY. Welcomes suggestions for feature ideas about pregnancy, newborn basics, practical babycare, baby development and

childcare subjects. Approaches may be made by telephone, e-mail or in writing to the Features Editor, *Wendy Golledge.*

Motor Boat & Yachting

IPC Media Limited, The Blue Fin Building, 100 Southwark Street, London SE1 0SU
☎020 3148 4643
✉ mby@ipcmedia.com
www.mby.com

Owner *Time Warner*
Editor *Hugo Andreae*
Technical Editor *David Marsh*
Circulation 17,134

Founded 1904. MONTHLY for those interested in motor boats and motor cruising.

FEATURES *Hugo Andreae* Cruising features and practical features especially welcome. Illustrations/photographs (colour) are just as important as text. Max. 3000 words.

NEWS *Rob Peake* Factual pieces. Max. 200 words.

PAYMENT Features: from £100 per 1000 words or by arrangement; news: up to £50 per item.

Motor Boats Monthly

Room 2220, The Blue Fin Building, 110 Southwark Street, London SE1 0SU
☎020 3148 4664 Fax 020 3148 8128
✉ mbm@ipcmedia.com

Owner *IPC Media*
Editor *Simon Collis*
Circulation 16,000

Founded 1987. MONTHLY magazine devoted to motor boating in the UK. Unsolicited contributions welcome: cruising articles, DIY and human interest. No powerboat racing or any sailing-related material. Approach by e-mail.

Motor Caravan Magazine

IPC Media Ltd, Leon House, 233 High Street, Croydon CR9 1HZ
☎020 8726 8000
✉ helen_avery@ipcmedia.com
www.motorcaravanmagazine.co.uk

Owner *IPC Media (A Time Warner Company)*
Editor *Helen Avery*
Circulation 12,000

Founded 1986. MONTHLY magazine with ideas about where to go in your motor caravan, expert advice to keep trips fun and practical advice on vans and kit. Interested in features on touring, unusual motorhomes, and activities people

pursue while out and about in their van. E-mail the editor with ideas. PAYMENT £60 a page.

Motor Cycle News

Media House, Lynchwood, Peterborough Business Park, Peterborough PE2 6EA
☎01733 468000 Fax 01733 468028
✉ MCN@emap.com
www.motorcyclenews.com

Owner *Emap plc*
Editor *Marc Potter*
Circulation 135,017

Founded 1955. WEEKLY. Interested in short news stories and features on motorcyles and motor-cycle racing. Contact relevant desks direct.

Motorcaravan Motorhome Monthly (MMM)

PO Box 88, Tiverton EX16 7ZN
✉ mmmeditor@warnersgroup.co.uk
www.mmmonline.co.uk

Owner *Warners Group Publications Plc*
Editor *Mike Jago*
Circulation 34,803

Founded 1966. MONTHLY. 'There's no money in motorcaravan journalism but for those wishing to cut their first teeth ...' Unsolicited mss welcome if relevant, but ideas in writing preferred in first instance.

FEATURES Caravan site reports. Max. 500 words.

TRAVEL Motorcaravanning trips (home and overseas). Max. 2000 words.

NEWS Short news items for miscellaneous pages. Max. 200 words.

FICTION Must be motorcaravan-related and include artwork/photos if possible. Max. 2000 words.

SPECIAL PAGES DIY – modifications to motorcaravans. Max. 1500 words.

OWNER REPORTS Contributions welcome from motorcaravan owners. Contact the editor for requirements. Max. 2000 words.

PAYMENT varies.

Mountain Magic

27A High Street, Esher KT10 9RL
☎01372 468140 Fax 01372 470765
✉ info@goodholidayideas.com

Editor *John Hill*
Circulation 50,000

New QUARTERLY magazine covering mountain travel worldwide. No unsolicited material but approach in writing or by e-mail with ideas and/or synopsis. PAYMENT negotiable.

Mslexia (For Women Who Write)

PO Box 656, Newcastle upon Tyne NE99 1PZ
☎0191 261 6656
✉ postbag@mslexia.demon.co.uk
www.mslexia.co.uk

Owner *Mslexia Publications Limited*
Editor *Daneet Steffens*
Circulation 10,000

Founded 1997. QUARTERLY. Articles, advice, reviews, interviews, events for women writers plus new poetry and prose. Will consider fiction, poetry, features and letters but contributors *must* send for guidelines first or see website for details.

Music Week

Ludgate House, 245 Blackfriars Road, London SE1 9UR
☎020 7921 5000 Fax 020 7921 8327
✉ mwletters@musicweek.com
www.musicweek.com

Owner *CMP Information*
Publisher *Ajax Scott*
Managing Editor *Paul Williams*
Editor *Martin Talbot*
Circulation 8810

Britain's only WEEKLY music business magazine. Also produces a subscriber-only news and data website. Annual music industry contacts book – the *Music Week Directory*. Free Daily news e-mail. No unsolicited mss. Approach in writing with ideas.

FEATURES Analysis of specific music business events and trends.

NEWS Music industry news only.

Musical Opinion

2 Princes Road, St Leonards on Sea TN37 6EL
☎01424 715167 Fax 01424 712214
✉ musicalopinion2@aol.com
www.musicalopinion.com

Owner *Musical Opinion Ltd*
Editor *Denby Richards*
Circulation 8500

Founded 1877. Glossy, full-colour BI-MONTHLY magazine. Classical music content, with topical features on music, musicians, festivals, etc., and reviews (concerts, festivals, opera, ballet, jazz, CDs, DVDs, videos, books and printed music). International readership. No unsolicited mss; commissions only. Ideas always welcome though; approach by phone, fax or e-mail, giving telephone number. Visit the website for full information.

PAYMENT negotiable.

My Weekly

80 Kingsway East, Dundee DD4 8SL
☎01382 223131 Fax 01382 452491
✉ myweekly@dcthomson.co.uk
www.dcthomson.co.uk

Owner *D. C. Thomson & Co. Ltd*
Editor *Sally Hampton*
Deputy Editor *Fiona Brown*
  (fbrown@dcthomson.co.uk)
Fiction Editor *Liz Smith*
  (lsmith@dcthomson.co.uk)
Circulation 195,809

Weekly title aimed at women 50+. Mix of fiction, true-life stories, emotional features, fashion, food, craft, finance, gardening, travel. Ideas welcome. Approach in writing.

FEATURES Particularly interested in human interest pieces (1200 words approx.) which appeal to the 50-plus age-group.

FICTION Three stories a week, ranging in content from the emotional to the off-beat and unexpected. 1000–4000 words.

PAYMENT negotiable.

My Weekly Story Collection

D.C. Thomson & Co. Ltd, Albert Square, Dundee DD1 9QJ
☎01382 575810 Fax 01382 322214
✉ tsteele@dcthomson.co.uk

Owner *D. C. Thomson & Co. Ltd*
Editor *Tracey Steele*

MONTHLY. Publishes 25,000 – 30,000-word romantic stories aimed at the adult market. Send first three chapters and synopsis by mail.

The National Trust Magazine

Heelis, Kemble Drive, Swindon SN2 2NA
☎01793 817716 Fax 01793 817401
✉ magazine@nationaltrust.org.uk

Owner *The National Trust*
Editor *Sue Herdman*
Deputy Editor *Gemma Hall*
Circulation 1.71 million

Founded 1968. THREE ISSUES YEARLY. Conservation of historic houses, coast and countryside in England, Northern Ireland and Wales. No unsolicited mss. Approach in writing with ideas.

The Naturalist

c/o University of Bradford, Bradford BD7 1DP
☎01274 234212 Fax 01274 234231
✉ m.r.d.seaward@bradford.ac.uk

Owner *Yorkshire Naturalists' Union*
Editor *Prof. M.R.D. Seaward*

Circulation 5000

Founded 1875. QUARTERLY. Natural history, biological and environmental sciences for a professional and amateur readership. Unsolicited mss and b&w illustrations welcome. Particularly interested in material – scientific papers – relating to the north of England. No PAYMENT.

Nature

The Macmillan Building, 4–6 Crinan Street, London N1 9XW
☎020 7833 4000 Fax 020 7843 4596
✉ nature@nature.com
www.nature.com/nature

Owner *Nature Publishing Group*
Editor *Philip Campbell*
Circulation 65,000

Covers all fields of science, with articles and news on science and science policy only. Scope only for freelance writers with specialist knowledge in these areas.

NB

105 Judd Street, London WC1H 9NE
☎020 7388 1266
www.rnib.org.uk/nbmagazine

Owner *Royal National Institute of the Blind*
Editor *Ann Lee*
Circulation 5000

Founded 1917. MONTHLY. Published in print, braille and on audio, CD, disk and e-mail. Unsolicited mss accepted. Authoritative items by professionals or volunteers working in the field of sight loss welcome. Max. 1500 words.
PAYMENT negotiable.

New Humanist

1 Gower Street, London WC1E 6HD
☎020 7436 1151 Fax 020 7079 3588
✉ editor@newhumanist.org.uk
www.newhumanist.org.uk

Owner *Rationalist Association*
Editor *Caspar Melville*
Circulation 5000

Founded 1885. BI-MONTHY. Unsolicited mss welcome. No fiction.

FEATURES Articles with a humanist perspective welcome in the following fields: religion (critical), humanism, human rights, philosophy, current events, literature, history and science. 2000 words.

BOOK REVIEWS 750–1000 words, by arrangement with the editor.

PAYMENT for features is nominal, but negotiable.

New Internationalist

55 Rectory Road, Oxford OX4 1BW
☎01865 811400 Fax 01865 793152
✉ ni@newint.org
www.newint.org/

Owner *New Internationalist Trust*
Co-Editors *Vanessa Baird, David Ransom, Adam Ma'anit, Jess Worth*
Circulation 80,000

Radical and broadly leftist in approach, but unaligned. Concerned with world poverty and global issues of peace and politics, feminism and environmentalism, with emphasis on the Third World. Difficult to use unsolicited material as they work to a theme each month and features are commissioned by the editor on that basis. The way in is to send examples of published or unpublished work; writers of interest are taken up.

New Magazine

The Northern & Shell Building, 10 Lower Thames Street, London EC3R 6EN
☎0871 520 7016
✉ karmel.doughty@express.co.uk

Owner *Richard Desmond*
Editor *Kirsty Mouatt*
Circulation 458,751

Founded 2003. Celebrity WEEKLY with true life content plus fashion and beauty. Celebrity interviews and true life submissions welcome. Approach by e-mail.

New Musical Express

IPC Media Ltd.,The Blue Fin Building, 110 Southwark Street, London SE1 0SU
☎020 3148 5000 Fax 020 3148 8107
www.nme.com

Owner *IPC Media (A Time Warner Company)*
Editor *Conor McNicholas*
Circulation 73,008

Britain's best-selling musical WEEKLY. Now incorporates *Melody Maker*. Freelancers used, but always for reviews in the first instance. Specialisation in areas of music is a help.

REVIEWS: ALBUMS *Julian Marshall* Send in examples of work, either published or specially written samples.

New Nation

Unit 2, 65 Whitechapel Road, London E1 1DU
☎020 7650 2000 Fax 020 7650 2004
✉ theeditor@newnation.co.uk
www.newnation.co.uk

Owner *Ethnic Media Group*
Editor *Michael Eboda*
Circulation 73,000

Founded 1996. WEEKLY community paper for the black community in Britain. Interested in relevant general, local and international issues. Approach in writing with ideas for submission.

New Scientist

8th Floor, Lacon House, 84 Theobalds Road, London WC1X 8NS
☎020 8652 3500 Fax 020 7611 1250 (news)
www.newscientist.com

Owner *Reed Business Information Ltd*
Editor *Jeremy Webb*
Circulation 175,000 (Worldwide)

Founded 1956. WEEKLY. No unsolicited mss. Approach with ideas (one A4-page synopsis) by fax or e-mail.

FEATURES Commissions only, but good ideas welcome. Max. 3500 words.

NEWS *Matt Walker* Mostly commissions, but ideas for specialist news welcome. Max. 1000 words.

REVIEWS are commissioned.

OPINION Unsolicited material welcome if of general/humorous interest and related to science. Max. 1000 words.

PAYMENT negotiable.

The New Shetlander

Market House, 14 Market Street, Lerwick ZE1 0JP
☎01595 743902 Fax 01595 696787
✉ scss@shetland.org
www.shetlandcss.co.uk

Owner *Shetland Council of Social Service*
Editors *Brian Smith, Laureen Johnson*
Circulation 1400

Founded 1947. QUARTERLY literary magazine containing short stories, essays, poetry, historical articles, literary criticism, political comment, arts and books. The magazine has two editors and an editorial committee who all look at submitted material. Interested in considering short stories, poetry, historical articles with a northern Scottish or Scandinavian flavour, literary pieces and articles on Shetland. As a rough guide, items should be between 1000 and 2000 words although longer mss are considered. Initial approach in writing, please.

PAYMENT Complimentary copy.

New Statesman

3rd Floor, 52 Grosvenor Gardens, London SW1W 0AU
☎020 7730 3444 Fax 020 7259 0181
✉ info@newstatesman.co.uk
www.newstatesman.com

Publisher *Spencer Neal*
Editor *John Kampfner*
Deputy Editor *Sue Matthias*
Circulation 30,036

WEEKLY magazine, the result of a merger (1988) of *New Statesman* and *New Society*. Coverage of news, book reviews, arts, current affairs, politics and social reportage. Unsolicited contributions with s.a.e. will be considered. No short stories.

Arts Editor *Alice O'Keefe*
Books Editor *Rachel Aspden*

New Theatre Quarterly

Oldstairs, Kingsdown, Deal CT14 8ES
☎01304 373448
✉ simontrussler@btinternet.com
www.uk.cambridge.org

Publisher *Cambridge University Press*
Editors *Simon Trussler, Maria Shevtsova*

Founded 1985 (originally launched in 1971 as *Theatre Quarterly*). Articles, interviews, documentation and reference material covering all aspects of live theatre. Recommend preliminary e-mail enquiry before sending contributions. No theatre reviews or anecdotal material.

New Welsh Review

PO Box 170, Aberystwyth SY23 1WZ
☎01970 628410 Fax 01970 628410
✉ editor@newwelshreview.com
www.newwelshreview.com

Owner *New Welsh Review Ltd*
Editor *Francesca Rhydderch*
Circulation 3500

Founded 1988. QUARTERLY Welsh literary magazine in the English language. Welcomes material of literary and cultural relevance to Welsh readers and those with an interest in Wales. Approach in writing in the first instance.

FEATURES Max. 3000 words.
FICTION Max. 5000 words.
REVIEWS Max. 800 words.

PAYMENT average of £150 (features); £75 (fiction); £40 (reviews); £25 per poem.

New Woman

Endeavour House, 189 Shaftesbury Avenue, London WC2H 8JG
☎020 7437 9011 Fax 020 7208 3585

www.newwoman.co.uk

Owner *Emap élan Ltd*
Editor *Lauren Libbert*
Circulation 222,076

MONTHLY women's interest magazine. 'The only magazine to combine gorgeous fashion and beauty pages, glamorous celebrity features and real life experiences with a sense of humour. All our core subjects – fashion, beauty, relationships, money, work – are covered in a witty tone and style.'

The New Writer

PO Box 60, Cranbrook TN17 2ZR
☎01580 212626 Fax 01580 212041
✉ editor@thenewwriter.com
www.thenewwriter.com

Publisher *Merric Davidson*
Editor *Suzanne Ruthven*

Founded 1996. Published BI-MONTHLY following the merger between *Acclaim* and *Quartos* magazines. Available by subscription only, TNW continues to offer practical 'nuts and bolts' advice on creative writing but with the emphasis on *forward-looking* articles and features on all aspects of the written word that demonstrate the writer's grasp of contemporary writing and current editorial/publishing policies. Plenty of news, views, competitions, reviews; writers' guidelines available with s.a.e. Monthly e-mail News bulletin is included free of charge in the subscription package.

FEATURES Unsolicited mss welcome. Interested in lively, original articles on writing in its broadest sense. Approach with ideas in writing in the first instance. No material is returned unless accompanied by s.a.e.

FICTION Publishes short-listed entries from competitions and subscriber-only submissions.

POETRY Unsolicited poetry welcome. Both short and long unpublished poems, providing they are original and interesting.

PAYMENT Features, £20 per 1000 words; fiction, £10 per story; poetry, £3 per poem. Full guidelines and details of annual Prose & Poetry Prizes at the website.

New Writing Scotland

Association for Scottish Literary Studies, c/o Department of Scottish Literature, 7 University Gardens, University of Glasgow G12 8QH
☎0141 330 5309 Fax 0141 330 5309
✉ nws@asls.org.uk
www.asls.org.uk

Contact *Duncan Jones*

ANNUAL anthology of contemporary poetry and prose in English, Gaelic and Scots, produced by the **Association for Scottish Literary Studies** (see entry under *Professional Associations and Societies*). Will consider poetry, drama, short fiction or other creative prose but not full-length plays or novels, though self-contained extracts are acceptable. Contributors should be Scottish by birth or upbringing, or resident in Scotland. Max. length of 3500 words is suggested. Send no more than one short story and no more than four poems. Submissions should be accompanied by two s.a.e.s (one for receipt, the other for return of mss). Mss, which must be sent by 30 September, should be typed, double-spaced, on one side of the paper only with the sheets secured at top left-hand corner. Provide covering letter with full contact details but do not put name or address on individual work(s). Prose pieces should carry an approximate word count. PAYMENT £20 per printed page.

newbooks

4 Froxfield Close, Winchester SO22 6JW
✉ guy@newbooksmag.com
www.newbooksmag.com

Owner/Editor *Guy Pringle*
Circulation 80,000

Founded 2000. BI-MONTHLY magazine for readers and reading groups with extracts from the best new fiction and free copies to be claimed. No unsolicited contributions. Also publishes *tBkmag* for 8–12-year-olds.

The North

See under *Poetry Magazines*

Now

IPC Media Ltd., The Blue Fin Building, 110 Southwark Street, London SE1 0SU
☎020 3148 6373

Owner *IPC Media (A Time Warner Company)*
Editor *Helen Johnston*
Circulation 540,132

Founded 1996. WEEKLY magazine of celebrity gossip, news and topical features aimed at the working woman. Unlikely to use freelance contributions due to specialist content – e.g. exclusive showbiz interviews – but ideas will be considered. Approach in writing; no faxes.

Nursery Education

Scholastic Ltd, Villiers House, Clarendon Avenue, Leamington Spa CV32 5PR
☎01926 887799 Fax 01926 883331
✉ earlyyears@scholastic.co.uk

www.scholastic.co.uk
Owner *Scholastic Ltd*
Publishing Editor *Helen Freeman*
Circulation 20,000

Founded 1997. MONTHLY magazine for early years professionals.Welcomes contributions from freelance journalists specialising in education.
FEATURES Early years issues explored. Max. 1500 words.
NEWS Relevant and timely news for the early years sector. Max. 400 words.
PRACTICAL IDEAS Themed activities that support the Foundation Stage curriculum and Birth-to-Three activites. Max. 800 words. Approach by letter or e-mail.

Nursing Times

Greater London House, Hampstead Road, London NW1 7EJ
☎020 7874 0500 Fax 020 7874 0505
www.nursingtimes.net
Owner *Emap Healthcare*
Editor *Rachel Downey*
Circulation 72,166

Some of *Nursing Times'* feature content is from unsolicited contributions sent on spec. Articles on all aspects of nursing and health care, including clinical information, written in a contemporary style, are welcome.

Nuts

IPC Media Ltd.,The Blue Fin Building, 110 Southwark Street, London SE1 0SU
☎020 3148 5000
✉ nutsmagazine@ipcmedia.com
www.nuts.co.uk
Owner *IPC Media (A Time Warner Company)*
Editor *Dominic Smith*
Circulation 295,002

Launched 2004.WEEKLY magazine for men aged 16–45 'who like chat, women, gossip, cars and football'. Welcomes true life stories and items on gadgets. Approach by e-mail in the first instance.

OK! Magazine

The Northern & Shell Building, 10 Lower Thames Street, London EC3R 6EN
☎0871 434 1010 Fax 0871 434 7305
✉ firstname.lastname@express.co.uk
Owner *Northern & Shell Media/Richard Desmond*
Editor *Lisa Byrne*
Circulation 624,091

Founded 1996. WEEKLY celebrity-based maga-zine. Welcomes interviews and pictures on well known personalities, and ideas for general features.Approach the editor by phone or fax in the first instance.

Old Glory

Mortons Heritage Media, Mortons Way, Horncastle LN9 6JR
☎01507 529300 Fax 01507 529495
✉ editor@oldglory.co.uk
www.oldglory.co.uk
Owner *Mortons Media Ltd*
Editor *Colin Tyson*

Founded 1988. MONTHLY magazine covering all aspects of transport and industrial heritage both in the UK and overseas. Specialises in vintage vehicles and steam preservation.Unsolicited articles are welcome. Approach by letter addressed to the editor.
FEATURES Restoration projects from steam rollers to windmills. Max. 2000 words.
NEWS Steam and transport rally reports. News concerning industrial and heritage sites and buildings.

The Oldie

65 Newman Street, London W1T 3EG
☎020 7436 8801 Fax 020 7436 8804
✉ theoldie@theoldie.co.uk
www.theoldie.co.uk
Owner *Oldie Publications Ltd*
Editor *Richard Ingrams*
Circulation 24,769

Founded 1992. MONTHLY general interest maga-zine with a strong humorous slant for the older person. Submissions welcome; enclose s.a.e. No poetry.

Olive

BBC Worldwide, 80 Wood Lane, London W12 0TT
☎020 8433 1389
✉ firstname.surname@bbc.co.uk
www.olivemagazine.co.uk
Owner *BBC Worldwide Publishing Ltd*
Editorial Coordinator *Paula Stain*
Deputy Editor/Food Editor *Lulu Grimes*
Features Editor *Jessica Gunn*
(jess.gunn@bbc.co.uk)
Circulation 60,041

Launched 2003. MONTHLY food magazine. Recipes, restaurants and food lovers' travel. Unsolicited pitches are welcome 'but please note that we will reply *only* to those we plan to commission'.

Opera

36 Black Lion Lane, London W6 9BE
☎020 8563 8893 Fax 020 8563 8635
✉ editor@opera.co.uk
www.opera.co.uk

Owner *Opera Magazine Ltd*
Editor *John Allison*
Circulation 11,500

Founded 1950. MONTHLY review of the current opera scene. Almost all articles are commissioned and unsolicited mss are not welcome. All approaches should be made in writing.

Opera Now

241 Shaftesbury Avenue, London WC2H 8TF
☎020 7333 1740 Fax 020 7333 1769
✉ opera.now@rhinegold.co.uk
www.rhinegold.co.uk

Publisher *Rhinegold Publishing Ltd*
Editor-in-Chief *Ashutosh Khandekar*
Deputy Editor *Antonia Couling*

Founded 1989. BI-MONTHLY. News, features and reviews aimed at those involved as well as those interested in opera. No unsolicited mss. All work is commissioned. Approach with ideas in writing.

Organic Gardening

The Garden Flat, 22b Hayburn Crescent, Glasgow G11 5AY
✉ gaby@organicgardeningmagazine.co.uk

Editor *Gaby Bartai*
Circulation 20,000

Founded 1988. MONTHLY. Articles and features on all aspects of gardening based on organic methods. Unsolicited material welcome; 800–2000 words for features and 100–300 for news items. Poetry not published. Prefers 'hands-on' accounts of projects, problems, challenges and how they are dealt with. Approach in writing.
PAYMENT by arrangement.

OS (Office Secretary) Magazine

15 Grangers Place, Witney OX28 4BS
☎01993 775545 Fax 01993 778884
✉ paul.ormond@peeblesmedia.com
www.peeblesmedia.com

Owner *Peebles Media Group Ltd*
Editor *Paul Ormond*
Circulation 24,977

Founded 1986. BI-MONTHLY. Features articles of interest to secretaries and personal assistants aged 25–60. No unsolicited mss.
FEATURES Informative pieces on technology and practices, office and employment-related

topics. Length 1000 words. Approach with ideas by telephone or in writing.
PAYMENT by negotiation.

Park Home & Holiday Caravan

IPC Media Ltd, Leon House, 233 High Street, Croydon CR9 1HZ
☎020 8726 8000 Fax 020 8726 8299
✉ em_bartlett@ipcmedia.com
www.phhc.co.uk

Owner *IPC Inspire*
Editor *Emma Bartlett*
Circulation 15,000

Founded 1960. THIRTEEN ISSUES YEARLY. News of parks, models, legislation, accessories, lifestyle for those living in residential park homes or owning holiday caravans. Welcomes material specifically related to park home and holiday caravan sites; no general touring features. Approach by e-mail.

PC Format

Future Publishing, 30 Monmouth Street, Bath BA1 2BW
☎01225 442244 Fax 01225 732295
✉ pcfmail@futurenet.co.uk
www.pcformat.co.uk

Owner *Future Publishing*
Publisher *Stuart Anderton*
Editor *Adam Ifans*
Circulation 28,439

Founded 1991. FOUR-WEEKLY magazine covering everything for the consumer PC – games, software and hardware. Welcomes feature and interview ideas in the first instance; approach by telephone or e-mail.

Pensions World

2 Addiscombe Road, Croydon CR9 5AF
☎020 8212 1946 Fax 020 8212 1920

Owner *Reed Elsevier*
Editor *Stephanie Hawthorne*
Circulation 7372

Launched 1972. MONTHLY magazine for pensions professionals. Pensions, law, investment and retirement issues. Specialist contributors only. No consumer pension stories. Approach by e-mail.
FEATURES Max. 1500 words.
NEWS Max. 400 words.
PAYMENT negotiable.

People Management

Personnel Publications Ltd., 17–18 Britton Street, London EC1M 5TP

☎020 7324 2729 Fax 020 7296 4215
✉ editorial@peoplemanagement.co.uk
www.peoplemanagement.co.uk
Editor *Steve Crabb*
Deputy Editor *Rima Evans*
Circulation 124,964

FORTNIGHTLY magazine on human resources, industrial relations, employment issues, etc. Welcomes submissions but apply for 'Guidelines for Contributors' in the first instance.

FEATURES *Jane Pickard/ Claire Warren*
NEWS *Anna Scott*
LAW AT WORK *Jill Evans*

People's Friend Story Collection
D.C.Thomson & Co. Ltd, Albert Square, Dundee DD1 9QJ
☎01382 575938 Fax 01382 322214
✉ shheron@dcthomson.co.uk

Owner *D.C. Thomson & Co. Ltd*
Editor *Sheelagh Heron*

Founded 1938. TWICE-MONTHLY. Family and romantic stories of 50,000–55,000 words, aimed at the 30+ age group. Unsolicited contributions welcome. Phone, write or e-mail for guidelines; synopsis and first three chapters to be sent initially.

The People's Friend
80 Kingsway East, Dundee DD4 8SL
☎01382 223131 Fax 01382 452491
✉ peoplesfriend@dcthomson.co.uk

Owner *D.C. Thomson & Co. Ltd*
Editor *Margaret McCoy*
Circulation 346,962

The *Friend* is a fiction magazine, with two serials and several short stories each week. Founded in 1869, it has always prided itself on providing 'a good read for all the family'. Stories should be about ordinary, identifiable characters with the kind of problems the average reader can understand and sympathise with. 'We look for the romantic and emotional developments of characters, rather than an over-complicated or contrived plot. We regularly use period serials and, occasionally, mystery/adventure.' Guidelines on request with s.a.e.

SHORT STORIES Can vary in length from 1000 words or less to 4000.
SERIALS Serials of 8–12 instalments.
ARTICLES Short fillers welcome.
PAYMENT on acceptance.

Period Living
St Giles House, 50 Poland Street, London W1F 7AX
☎020 7970 4433 Fax 020 7970 4438
✉ period.living@centaur.co.uk

Owner *Centaur*
Editor-in-Chief *Michael Holmes*
Editor *Sara Whelan*
Circulation 48,792

Founded 1992. Formed from the merger of *Period Living* and *Traditional Homes*. Covers interior decoration in a period style, period house profiles, traditional crafts, renovation of period properties.

PAYMENT varies according to length/type of article.

The Philosopher
Centre for Lifelong Learning, Newcastle University, Newcastle upon Tyne NE3 7RU
✉ thephilosophicalsociety@yahoo.co.uk
www.the-philosopher.co.uk

Owner *The Philosophical Society*
Editor *Martin Cohen*

Founded 1913. BIANNUAL journal of the Philosophical Society of Great Britain with an international readership made up of members, libraries and specialist booksellers. Wide range of philosophical interests, but leaning towards articles that present philosophical investigation which is relevant to the individual and to society in our modern era. Accessible to the non-specialist. Will consider articles and book reviews. Notes for Contributors available; see website. As well as short philosophical papers, will accept:

NEWS about lectures, conventions, philosophy groups. Ethical issues in the news. Max. 1000 words.
REVIEWS of philosophy books (max. 600 words); discussion articles of individual philosophers and their published works (max. 2000 words).
MISCELLANEOUS items, including graphics, of philosophical interest and/or merit.
PAYMENT Free copies.

Piano
241 Shaftesbury Avenue, London WC2H 8TF
☎020 7333 1724 Fax 020 7333 1769
✉ piano@rhinegold.co.uk
www.rhinegold.co.uk

Owner *Rhinegold Publishing*
Editor *Jeremy Siepmann*
Deputy Editor *Sarah Smith*

Circulation 11,000

Founded 1993. Bi-monthly magazine containing features, profiles, technical information, news, reviews of interest to those with a serious amateur or professional concern with pianos or their playing. No unsolicited material. Approach with ideas in writing only.

Picture Postcard Monthly

15 Debdale Lane, Keyworth, Nottingham NG12 5HT
☎0115 937 4079 Fax 0115 937 6197
✉ reflections@postcardcollecting.co.uk
www.postcardcollecting.co.uk

Owners *Brian & Mary Lund*
Editor *Brian Lund*
Circulation 4000

Founded 1978. Monthly. News, views, clubs, diary of fairs, sales, auctions, and well-researched postcard-related articles. Might be interested in general articles supported by postcards. Unsolicited mss welcome. Approach by phone, e-mail or in writing with ideas.

Pilot

Archant Specialist, The Mill, Bearwalden Business Park, Wendens Ambo, Saffron Walden CB11 4GB
☎01799 544200 Fax 01799 544201
✉ nick.bloom@pilotweb.aero
www.pilotweb.co.uk

Publisher *Archant Specialist*
Editor *Nick Bloom*
Circulation 19,485

Founded 1966. Monthly magazine for private plane pilots. Much of the magazine is written by outside contributors – mostly regulars. Unsolicited mss welcome but ideas in writing preferred. Perusal of any issue of the magazine will reveal the type of material bought. 700 words of 'Advice to would-be contributors' sent on receipt of s.a.e. (mark envelope 'Advice'), or see the website for details.

News Contributions, preferably with photographs, need to be as short as possible. See *Pilot Notes* and *Old-Timers* in the magazine.

Features Many articles are unsolicited personal experiences/travel accounts from pilots of private planes; good photo coverage is very important. Max. 5000 words.

Pink Paper

Unit M, Spectrum House, 32–34 Gordon House Road, London NW5 1LP
☎020 7424 7400 Fax 020 7424 7401
✉ editorial@pinkpaper.com

Owner *Millivres Prowler Group*
Editor *Tris Reid-Smith*
Circulation 39,758

Founded 1987. Fortnightly. Only national newspaper for lesbians and gay men covering politics, social issues, health, the arts, celebrity interviews and all areas of concern to lesbian/gay people. Unsolicited mss welcome. Initial approach by post with an idea preferred. Interested in profiles, reviews, in-depth features and short news pieces.

Payment by arrangement.

Poetry Ireland Review
See under *Poetry Magazines*

Poetry Review
See under *Poetry Magazines*

Poetry Scotland
See under *Poetry Magazines*

Poetry Wales
See under *Poetry Magazines*

PONY

D.J. Murphy (Publishers) Ltd, Headley House, Headley Road, Grayshott GU26 6TU
☎01428 601020 Fax 01428 601030
✉ djm@djmurphy.co.uk (text only)
www.ponymag.com

Owner *D.J. Murphy (Publishers) Ltd*
Editor *Janet Rising*
Assistant Editor *Louise Bland*
Circulation 40,274

Founded 1948. Lively Monthly aimed at 10–16-year-olds. News, instruction on riding, stable management, veterinary care, interviews. Approach in writing with an idea.

Features welcome. Max. 900 words.

News Written in-house. Photographs and illustrations (serious/cartoon) welcome.

Payment £65 per 1000 words.

post plus
See **Sunday Post** under *National Newspapers*

PR Week

174 Hammersmith Road, London W6 7JP
☎020 8267 4429 Fax 020 8267 4509
✉ prweek@haynet.com
www.prweek.com

Owner *Haymarket Business Publications Ltd*
Editor *Daniel Rogers*
Circulation 16,326

Founded 1984. WEEKLY. Contributions accepted from experienced journalists. Approach in writing with an idea.
PAYMENT negotiable.

Practical Boat Owner

IPC Media Ltd, Westover House, West Quay Road, Poole BH15 1JG
☎01202 440820 Fax 01202 440860
✉ sarah_norbury@ipcmedia.com and pbo@ipcmedia.com
www.pbo.co.uk
Owner *IPC Media (A Time Warner Company)*
Editor *Sarah Norbury*
Circulation 48,637

Britain's biggest selling boating magazine. MONTHLY magazine of practical information for cruising boat owners. Receives about 1500 mss per year.

FEATURES Technical articles about maintenance, restoration, modifications to cruising boats, power and sail up to 45ft. European and British regional pilotage articles and cruising guides. Approach in writing with synopsis in the first instance.
PAYMENT negotiable.

Practical Caravan

Teddington Studios, Broom Road, Teddington TW11 9BE
☎020 8267 5629 Fax 020 8267 5725
✉ practical.caravan@haymarket.com
www.practicalcaravan.com
Owner *Haymarket Magazines Ltd*
Editor *David Motton*
Circulation 44,062

Founded 1967. MONTHLY. Contains caravan reviews, travel features, investigations, products, park reviews. Unsolicited mss welcome on travel relevant only to caravanning/touring vans. No motorcaravan or static van stories. Approach with ideas by phone, letter or e-mail.

FEATURES Must refer to caravanning. Written in friendly, chatty manner. Pictures essential. Max. length 2000 words.
PAYMENT negotiable.

Practical Fishkeeping

Bretton Court, Bretton, Peterborough PE3 8DZ
☎01733 264666 Fax 01733 465246
✉ karen.youngs@emap.com
www.practicalfishkeeping.co.uk
Owner *Emap Active Publications Ltd*
Editor *Karen Youngs*

Circulation 15,446

THIRTEEN ISSUES YEARLY. Practical articles on all aspects of fishkeeping. Unsolicited mss welcome; approach in writing with ideas. Quality photographs of fish always welcome. No fiction or verse.

Practical Land Rover World

See **Land Rover World**

Practical Parenting

IPC Media Ltd., The Blue Fin Building, 110 Southwark Street, London SE1 0SU
☎020 3148 7551
Owner *IPC Media (A Time Warner Company)*
Editor *Susie Boone*
Circulation 42,660

Founded 1987. MONTHLY. Practical advice on pregnancy, birth, babycare and childcare, 0–4 years. Submit ideas/synopses by e-mail. Interested in feature articles of up to 3000 words in length, and in readers' experiences/personal viewpoint pieces of between 750–1000 words. All material must be written for the magazine's specifically targeted audience and in-house style. Submissions to: *Amy Benson* (amy_benson@ ipcmedia.com).
PAYMENT negotiable.

Practical Photography

Bretton Court, Bretton, Peterborough PE3 8DZ
☎01733 264666 Fax 01733 465246
✉ practical.photography@emap.com
www.practicalphotography.co.uk
Owner *Emap Active Publications Ltd*
Editor *Andrew James*
Circulation 61,078

MONTHLY All types of photography, particularly technique-orientated pictures. No unsolicited mss. Preliminary approach may be made by e-mail. Always interested in new, especially unusual, ideas.

FEATURES Anything relevant to the world of photography, but not 'the sort of feature produced by staff writers. Features on technology, digital imaging techniques and humour are three areas worth exploring. Bear in mind that there is a three-month lead-in time.' Max. 2000 words.
PAYMENT varies.

Practical Wireless

Arrowsmith Court, Station Approach, Broadstone BH18 8PW
☎0870 224 7810 Fax 0870 224 7850

✉ rob@pwpublishing.ltd.uk
www.pwpublishing.ltd.uk
Owner *PW Publishing Ltd*
Editor *Rob Mannion (G3XFD/EI5IW)*
Circulation 20,000

Founded 1932. MONTHLY. News and features relating to amateur radio, radio construction and radio communications. Unsolicited mss welcome. Author's guidelines available and are essential reading (send s.a.e.). Approach by phone or e-mail with ideas in the first instance. Only interested in hearing from people with a thorough knowledge of amateur radio. Copy (typed only) should be supported where possible by artwork, either illustrations, diagrams or photographs.
PAYMENT £54–70 per page.

Practical Woodworking

Magicali Publishing Ltd, Berwick House, 8–10 Knoll Rise, Orpington BR6 0EL
☎01442 831128 Fax 01442 831128
✉ practicalwoodworking@magicalia.com
www.getwoodworking.com
Owner *Magicalia Publishing Ltd*
Editor *Mark Chisholm*
Circulation 7000

Founded 1965. THIRTEEN ISSUES YEARLY. Contains articles relating to woodworking: projects, techniques, new products, tips, letters, etc. Unsolicited mss welcome. No fiction. Approach with ideas in writing, by phone or e-mail.
FEATURES Projects, techniques, etc.
PAYMENT by arrangement.

The Practitioner

245 Blackfriars Road, London SE1 9UY
☎020 7921 8113
✉ cshort@cmpmedica.com
www.practitioner-i.co.uk
Owner *CMPi*
Editor *Corinne Short*
Circulation 43,000

Founded 1868. MONTHLY publication that keeps General Practitioners up to date on clinical issues. All articles are independently commissioned.

Prediction

IPC Focus Network, Leon House, 233 High Street, Croydon CR9 1HZ
☎020 8726 8000 Fax 020 8726 8296
✉ prediction@ipcmedia.com
www.predictionmagazine.co.uk
Owner *IPC Media (A Time Warner Company)*
Editor *Marion Williamson*

Circulation 14,903
Founded 1936. MONTHLY. Covering astrology and mind, body, spirit topics. Unsolicited material in these areas welcome (about 200–300 mss received every year). Writers' guidelines available on request.
ASTROLOGY Pieces should be practical and of general interest.
FEATURES Articles on divination, shamanism, alternative healing, psychics and other supernatural phenonema considered. Please read a recent copy of the magazine before sending unsolicited material.

Pregnancy & Birth

Greater London House, Hampstead Road, London NW1 7EJ
☎020 7347 1885
Owner *Emap Esprit*
Editor *Sarah Hart*
Features Editor *Tatty Good*
Circulation 48,600

MONTHLY magazine covering all aspects of pregnancy from health to fashion. Regularly commissions features from health journalists. Freelancers should approach by post in the first instance.
PAYMENT varies.

Pregnancy, Baby & You

2 Balcombe Street, London NW1 6NW
☎020 7042 4000
✉ claire.roberts@futurenet.co.uk
Owner *Future Publishing Ltd*
Editor *Claire Roberts*
Deputy Editor *Emma Hartfield*
Circulation 20,048

THIRTEEN ISSUES YEARLY focusing on issues affecting the family as a whole. No unsolicited mss; e-mail the editor with ideas only.

Press Gazette

6–14 Underwood Street, London N1 7JQ
☎020 7324 2385 Fax 020 7566 5769
✉ pged@pressgazette.co.uk
www.pressgazette.co.uk
Owner *Wilmington Media Limited*
Editor *Dominic Ponsford*
Circulation 5010

WEEKLY magazine for all journalists – in regional and national newspapers, magazines, broadcasting and online – containing news, features and analysis of all areas of journalism, print and broadcasting. Unsolicited mss welcome; interested in profiles of magazines, broadcasting companies and news agencies, personality profiles, technical and current affairs relating to the world of journalism. Also welcomes gossip for diary page. Approach with ideas by phone, e-mail, fax or post.

Pride
Pride House, 55 Battersea Bridge Road, London SW11 3AX
☎020 7228 3110 Fax 020 7228 3121
✉ info@pridemagazine.com
Owner *Carl Cushnie Junior*
Editor *Sherry Dixon*
Circulation 40,000

Founded 1991. MONTHLY lifestyle magazine for Black women with features, beauty, arts and fashion. Approach in writing or by e-mail with ideas.

FEATURES Issues pertaining to the Black community. 'Ideas and solicited mss are welcomed from new freelancers.' Max. 2000 words.

FICTION Publishes the occasional short story. Max. 3000 words.

HEALTH, BEAUTY, LIFESTYLE *Sherry Dixon* Freelancers used for short features. Max. 1000 words.

Prima
National Magazine House, 72 Broadwick Street, London W1F 9EP
☎020 7439 5000
✉ prima@natmags.co.uk
www.natmags.co.uk
Owner *National Magazine Company*
Editor *Maire Fahey*
Circulation 315,149

Founded 1986. MONTHLY women's magazine.

HEALTH & FEATURES Coordinator *Ruth Tierney* Mostly practical and real life, written by specialists or commissioned from known freelancers. Unsolicited mss not welcome.

Private Eye
6 Carlisle Street, London W1D 3BN
☎020 7437 4017 Fax 020 7437 0705
✉ strobes@private-eye.co.uk
www.private-eye.co.uk
Owner *Pressdram*
Editor *Ian Hislop*
Circulation 208,979

Founded 1961. FORTNIGHTLY satirical and investigative magazine. Prospective contributors are best advised to approach the editor in writing.

News stories and feature ideas are always welcome, as are cartoons.

Prospect
2 Bloomsbury Place, London WC1A 2QA
☎020 7255 1344 (editorial)/1281 (publishing)
Fax 020 7255 1279
✉ editorial@prospect-magazine.co.uk *or* publishing@prospect-magazine.co.uk
www.prospect-magazine.co.uk
Owner *Prospect Publishing Limited*
Editor *David Goodhart*
Circulation 22,269

Founded 1995. MONTHLY. Essays, reviews, short fiction and research on current/international affairs and cultural issues. No news features. Unsolicited contributions welcome, although more useful to approach in writing with ideas in the first instance.

Psychic News
The Coach House, Stansted Hall, Stansted CM24 8UD
☎01279 817050 Fax 01279 817051
✉ pnadverts@btconnect.com
www.psychicnewsbookshop.co.uk
Owner *Psychic Press 1995 Ltd*
Editor *Tony Ortzen*
Circulation 40,000

Founded 1932. *Psychic News* is the world's only WEEKLY spiritualist newspaper. It covers subjects such as psychic research, hauntings, ghosts, poltergeists, spiritual healing, survival after death and paranormal gifts. Unsolicited material considered.

Psychologies
64 North Row, London W1K 7LL
☎020 7150 7000
✉ psychologies@hf-uk.com
www.psychologies.co.uk
Owner *Hachette Filipacchi UK*
Editor *Maureen Rice*
Features Editor *Rebecca Alexander* (rebecca.alexander@hf-uk.com)
Assistant Editor *Sarah Maber* (sarah.maber@hf-uk.com)
Circulation 115,398

Founded 2005. MONTHLY. Women's lifestyle magazine covering relationships, family and parenting, health, beauty, social trends, travel, personality and behaviour, spirituality and sex. Consult the submissions guidelines on the website before submitting ideas for features.

Publishing News

7 John Street, London WC1N 2ES
☎0870 870 2345 Fax 0870 870 0385
✉ mailbox@publishingnews.co.uk
www.publishingnews.co.uk

Owner *Publishing News Ltd*
Editor *Liz Thomson*
Deputy Editor *Roger Tagholm*

WEEKLY newspaper of the book trade. Hardback
and paperback reviews and extensive listings of
new paperbacks and hardbacks. Interviews with
leading personalities in the trade, authors, agents,
and features on specialist book areas. 'Almost no
submissions accepted.'

Q

Mappin House, 4 Winsley Street, London
W1W 8HF
☎020 7182 8482 Fax 020 7182 8547
✉ firstname.surname@emap.com
www.q4music.com

Owner *Emap Consumer Media*
Editor *Paul Rees*
Circulation 140,282

Founded 1986. MONTHLY. Glossy aimed at
educated popular music enthusiasts of all
ages. Few opportunities for freelance writers.
Prospective contributors should approach in
writing only to the relevant section editor.

Q-News, The Muslim Magazine

PO Box 4295, London W1A 7YH
☎07985 143263
✉ info@q-news.com
www.q-news.com

Owner *Fuad Nahdi*
Editor *Fareena Alam*
Circulation 40,000

Founded 1992. MONTHLY British Muslim
community magazine concerned with shaping
the debate about Muslims in Britain. Covers
recruitment, news, opinion and reviews.

FEATURES *Abdul-Rehman Malik* 'Writers
wishing to focus on areas of interest to our readership will gain access and credibility among the
relevant people.' Max. 3000 words.

OTHER *Fareena Alam* Analysis on news and
current affairs – alternative rather than mainstream viewpoint preferred. Max. 2000 words.
PAYMENT None.

Quarterly Review

PO Box 36, Mablethorpe LN12 9AB
☎01507 339056 Fax 01507 339056
✉ editor@quarterly-review.org

www.quarterly-review.org

Owner *Quarterly Review*
Editor *Derek Turner*

Founded 2007. A revival of the classic journal
founded by Sir Walter Scott, Robert Southey
and George Canning in 1809. QUARTERLY
journal of politics, ideas and culture, with an
emphasis on regionalism, small-scale economics,
ecology and socio-biology. Approach in writing
in the first instance. Articles from 1000 – 8000
words. No PAYMENT.

Quartos Magazine

See **The New Writer**

QWF Magazine

234 Brook Street, Unit 2, Waukesha
WI 53188, USA
☎01788 334302
✉ info@allwriters.org *and*
qwfsubmissionsusa@yahoo.com *(submissions)*
www.allwriters.org (click on QWF)

Semi-annual literary magazine published in
January and July. Founded in 1994 in the UK,
QWF is now published through AllWriters'
Workplace & Workshop in the US. Evoking
emotion is the most important characteristic of a
QWF story. There is no room for a dry reporting
of the facts here. The stories should present the
expanse that is every woman's emotional lifetime
and experience. Only considers fiction written
by women that are previously unpublished
and of less than 5000 words. Submissions by e-
mail only. Submit only during reading periods:
September 1 and November 31 and March 1
and May 31. Submissions received outside of
the reading period will be returned unread. For
further information and detailed guidelines,
please access the website or contact the editor at
the e-mail address above.

RA Magazine (Royal Academy of Arts Magazine)

Royal Academy of Arts, Burlington House,
Piccadilly, London W1J 0BD
☎020 7300 5820 Fax 020 7300 5032
✉ ramagazine@royalacademy.org.uk
www.ramagazine.org.uk

Owner *Royal Academy of Arts*
Editor *Sarah Greenberg*
Circulation 100,000

Founded 1983. QUARTERLY visual arts, architecture and culture magazine distributed to Friends
of the RA, promoting exhibitions and publishing
articles on art shows, books and news worldwide.

'There are opportunities for freelancers who can write about art in an accessible way. Most articles need to be tied in to forthcoming exhibitions, books and projects.' No unsolicited contributions. Approach by telephone or e-mail.

Racecar Engineering
IPC Media Ltd, Leon House, 233 High Street, Croydon CR9 1HZ
☎020 8726 8364 Fax 0208 726 8398
✉ racecar@ipcmedia.com
www.racecar-engineering.co.uk
Owner *IPC Media (A Time Warner Company)*
Editor *Charles Armstrong-Wilson*
Circulation 15,000
Founded 1990. MONTHLY. In-depth features on motorsport technology plus news and products. Interested in receiving news and features from freelancers.
FEATURES Informed insight into current motorsport technology. 3000 words max.
NEWS New cars, products or business news relevant to motorsport. No items on road cars or racing drivers. 500 words max. Call or e-mail to discuss proposal.

Racing Post
1 Canada Square, Canary Wharf, London E14 5AP
☎020 7293 3000 Fax 020 7293 3758
✉ editor@racingpost.co.uk
www.racingpost.co.uk
Owner *Trinity Mirror Plc*
Editor *Chris Smith*
Circulation 64,728
Founded 1986. DAILY horse racing paper with some general sport. In 1998, following an agreement between the owners of *The Sporting Life* and the *Racing Post*, the two papers merged.

Radio Times
80 Wood Lane, London W12 0TT
☎020 8433 3400 Fax 020 8433 3160
✉ radio.times@bbc.co.uk
www.radiotimes.com
Owner *BBC Worldwide Limited*
Editor *Gill Hudson*
Circulation 1.08 million
WEEKLY. UK's leading broadcast listings magazine. The majority of material is provided by freelance and retained writers, but the topicality of the pieces means close consultation with editors is essential. Very unlikely to use unsolicited material. Detailed BBC, ITV, Channel 4, Channel 5 and satellite television and radio listings are accompanied by feature material relevant to the week's output.
PAYMENT by arrangement.

Radio User
Arrowsmith Court, Station Approach, Broadstone BH18 8PW
☎0870 224 7810 Fax 0870 224 7850
✉ elaine@pwpublishing.ltd.uk
www.pwpublishing.ltd.uk
Owner *PW Publishing Ltd*
Editor *Elaine Richards*
Circulation 19,000
Founded 1937. In 2006, *Shortwave Magazine* merged with *Radio Active* magazine to become *Radio User*. MONTHLY. Specialist electronics and radio enthusiasts' magazine covering all aspects of listening to radio signals. Features, news, regular columns and projects. Will consider contributions but recommends that contact be made prior to submission to check publishing plans.

Rail
Bretton Court, Bretton, Peterborough PE3 8DZ
☎01733 264666 Fax 01733 282720
✉ rail@emap.com
www.rail-magazine.co.uk
Owner *Emap Active Ltd*
Managing Editor *Nigel Harris*
Circulation 25,502
Founded 1981. FORTNIGHTLY magazine dedicated to modern railway. News and features, and topical newsworthy events. Unsolicited mss welcome. Approach by phone with ideas. Not interested in personal journey reminiscences. No fiction.
FEATURES By arrangement with the editor. All modern railway British subjects considered. Max. 2000 words.
NEWS Any news item welcome. Max. 500 words.
PAYMENT Features, varies/negotiable; news, up to £100 per 1000 words.

Railway Gazette International
Quadrant House, Sutton SM2 5AS
☎020 8652 8608 Fax 020 8652 3738
✉ railway.gazette@rbi.co.uk
www.railwaygazette.com
Owner *Reed Business Information*
Editor *Chris Jackson*
Industry Editor *Andrew Gratham*
Circulation 9752

Founded 1835. MONTHLY magazine for senior railway, metro and tramway managers, engineers and suppliers worldwide. 'No material for railway enthusiast publications.' Telephone to discuss ideas in the first instance.

The Railway Magazine

IPC Media Ltd., The Blue Fin Building, 110 Southwark Street, London SE1 0SU
☎020 3148 4638 Fax 020 3148 8122
✉ railway@ipcmedia.com
www.ipcmedia.com

Owner *IPC Media (A Time Warner Company)*
Editor *Nick Pigott*
Circulation 30,783

Founded 1897. MONTHLY. Articles, photos and short news stories of a topical nature, covering modern railways, steam preservation and railway history, welcome. Max. 2000 words, with sketch maps of routes, etc., where appropriate. Unsolicited mss welcome. No poetry.
    PAYMENT negotiable.

Random Acts of Writing

Lower Knock-na-Shalavaig, Struy, Beauly IV4 7JU
✉ randomactsofwriting@fsmail.net
www.randomactsofwriting.co.uk
Owners/Editors *Vikki Trelfer, Jennifer Thomson*
Circulation 200

Founded 2005. THREE ISSUES YEARLY. Promotes the short story. 'Unsolicited short fiction (max. 3000 words) welcomed from all, regardless of previous publication history. Will give advice and feedback.' Approach by e-mail. PAYMENT Complimentary copy of the magazine plus discounts on further copies.

Reader's Digest

11 Westferry Circus, Canary Wharf, London E14 4HE
☎020 7715 8000 Fax 020 7715 8716
www.readersdigest.co.uk

Owner *Reader's Digest Association Ltd*
Editor-in-Chief *Katherine Walker*
Circulation 717,285

Although in theory, a good market for general interest features of around 2500 words very few are ever accepted. However, 'a tiny proportion' comes from freelance writers, all of which are specially commissioned. Opportunities exist for short humorous contributions to regular features – 'Life's Like That', 'Laughter, the Best Medicine', 'All in a Day's Work'. Issues a helpful

booklet called 'Writing for Reader's Digest', available by post at £4.50.
    PAYMENT up to £100.

The Reader

Reader Office, 19 Abercromby Square, Liverpool L69 7ZG
☎0151 794 2830
✉ readers@liv.co.uk
www.thereader.co.uk

Editor *Jane Davis*
Circulation 1200

Founded 1997. QUARTERLY. Poetry, short fiction, literary articles and essays, thought, reviews, recommendations. Contributions from internationally lauded and new voices. Welcomes articles/essays about reading, max. 2000 words. Recommendations for good reading, max. 1000 words. Short stories, max. 2500 words. No theoretical style literary discourses. Approach in writing.
    PAYMENT negotiable.

Readers' Review Magazine
See **The Self Publishing Magazine**

Real

Essential Publishing, Phoenix Square, Colchester CO4 9HU
☎01206 851117
www.essentialpublishing.co.uk

Owner *Essential Publishing Ltd*
Editor *David Claridge*
Circulation 131,525

FORTNIGHTLY women's magazine. Real life stories

Record Collector

Room 101, 140 Wales Farm Road, Acton, London W3 6UG
☎0870 732 8080 Fax 0870 732 6060
✉ alan.lewis@metropolis.co.uk
www.recordcollectormag.com

Owner *Metropolis*
Editor *Alan Lewis*

Founded 1979. MONTHLY. Detailed, well-researched articles welcome on any aspect of record collecting or any collectable artist in the field of popular music (1950s to present day), with complete discographies where appropriate. Unsolicited mss welcome. Approach with ideas by phone or e-mail.
    PAYMENT negotiable.

Red

64 North Row, London W1K 7LL

☎020 7150 7000 Fax 020 7150 7684
✉ harriet.cooper@hf-uk.com
www.redmagazine.co.uk
Owner *Hachette Filipacchi UK Ltd*
Editor *Sam Baker*
Circulation 224,072
Founded 1998. MONTHLY magazine aimed at the 30-something woman. Will consider ideas sent in 'on spec' but tends to rely on regular contributors.

Report

ATL, 7 Northumberland Street, London WC2N 5RD
☎020 7930 6441 Fax 020 7782 1618
www.atl.org.uk
Owner *Association of Teachers and Lecturers*
Joint Editors *Guy Goodwin, Victoria Poskitt*
Circulation 160,000
Founded 1978. TEN ISSUES YEARLY during academic terms. Contributions welcome. All submissions should go directly to the editor. Articles should be no more than 800 words and must be of practical interest to the classroom teacher and F.E. lecturers.

Retail Week

33–39 Bowling Green Lane, London EC1R 0DA
☎020 7505 8000
✉ editorial@retail-week.com
www.retail-week.com
Owner *Emap*
Editor *Tim Danaher*
Circulation 12,000
Founded 1988. WEEKLY. Leading news publication for the multiple retail sector. No unsolicited contributions. Limited opportunities for both features and news. Approach by e-mail.
FEATURES *Liz Morrell* Max. 1600 words.
NEWS *Jessica Price-Brown*

Reveal

National Magazine Co., National Magazine House, 33 Broadwick Street, London W1F 0DQ
☎020 7339 4500 Fax 020 7339 4529
✉ michael@acp-natmag.co.uk
www.natmags.co.uk
Owner *ACP – Natmag*
Editor *Michael Butcher*
Circulation 345,508
Launched 2004. WEEKLY glossy lifestyle magazine with celebrities, real-life stories, cookery,

beauty and seven-day TV guide. No unsolicited contributions.

Rugby World

IPC Media Ltd., The Blue Fin Building, 110 Southwark Street, London SE1 0SU
☎020 3148 4708
✉ paul_morgan@ipcmedia.com
www.rugbyworld.com
Owner *IPC Media (A Time Warner Company)*
Editor *Paul Morgan*
Circulation 41,896
Founded 1960. MONTHLY. Features of special rugby interest only. Unsolicited contributions welcome but s.a.e. essential for return of material. Prior approach by phone or in writing preferred.

Runner's World

33 Broadwick Street, London W1F 0AD
☎020 7339 4400 Fax 020 7339 4220
✉ rwedit@natmag-rodale.co.uk
www.runnersworld.co.uk
Owner *Natmag – Rodale Press*
Editor *Andy Dixon*
Circulation 83,527
Founded 1979. MONTHLY magazine giving practical advice on all areas of distance running including products and training, travel features, news and cross-training advice. Personal running-related articles, famous people who run or off-beat travel articles are welcome. No elite athlete or training articles. Approach with ideas in writing in the first instance.

Running Fitness

1st Floor, South Wing, Broadway Court, Broadway, Peterborough PE1 1RP
☎01733 353363 Fax 01733 891342
✉ rf.ed@kelsey.pb.co.uk
www.runningfitnessmag.com
Owner *Kelsey Publishing*
Editor *David Castle*
Circulation 26,000
Founded 1985. MONTHLY. Instructional articles on running, fitness, and lifestyle, plus running-related activities and health.
FEATURES Specialist knowledge an advantage. Opportunities are wide, but approach with ideas in first instance.
NEWS Opportunities for people stories, especially if backed up by photographs.

Saga Magazine
Saga Publishing Ltd,The Saga Building, Enbrook Park, Sandgate, Folkstone CT20 3SE
☎01303 771523 Fax 01303 776699
✉ editor@saga.co.uk
www.saga.co.uk/magazine

Owner *Saga Publishing Ltd*
Editor *Emma Soames*
Circulation 610,771

Founded 1984. MONTHLY magazine that sets out to celebrate the role of older people in society, reflecting their achievements, promoting their skills, protecting their interests, and campaigning on their behalf. A warm personal approach, addressing the readership in an up-beat and positive manner. It has a hard core of celebrated commentators/writers (e.g. Keith Waterhouse, Alexander Chancellor, Sally Brampton) as regular contributors. Articles mostly commissioned or written in-house but exclusive celebrity interviews welcome if appropriate/relevant. Length 1000–1200 words (max. 1600). No short stories or poems, please.

Sailing Today
Swanwick Marina, Lower Swanwick, Southampton SO31 1ZL
☎01489 585225 Fax 01489 565054
✉ john.goode@sailingtoday.co.uk
www.sailingtoday.co.uk

Owner *Edisey Ltd*
Editor *John Goode*

Founded 1997. MONTHLY practical magazine for cruising sailors. *Sailing Today* covers owning and buying a boat, equipment and products for sailing and is about improving readers' skills, boat maintenance and product tests. Most articles are commissioned but will consider practical features and cruising stories with photos. Approach by telephone or in writing in the first instance.

Sainsbury's Magazine
20 Upper Ground, London SE1 9PD
☎020 7633 0266 Fax 020 7401 9423
✉ edit@sevenpublishing.co.uk

Owner *Seven Publishing Ltd*
Editor *Sue Robinson*
Consultant Director *Delia Smith*
Circulation 382,792

Founded 1993. MONTHLY featuring a main core of food and cookery with features, health, beauty, home and gardening. No unsolicited mss. Approach in writing with ideas only in the first instance.

The Salisbury Review
33 Canonbury Park South, London N1 2JW
☎020 7226 7791 Fax 020 7354 0383
✉ salisburyreview@tiscali.co.uk
www.salisburyreview.co.uk

Managing Editor *Merrie Cave*
Consulting Editors *Roger Scruton, Sir Richard Body, Myles Harris, Lord Charles Cecil*
Literary Editor *Ian Crowther*
Circulation 1700

Founded 1982. QUARTERLY magazine of conservative thought. Editorials and features from a right-wing viewpoint. Unsolicited material welcome. No fiction or poetry.
FEATURES Max. 2000 words.
REVIEWS Max. 1000 words. Small PAYMENT.

Scotland in Trust
91 East London Street, Edinburgh EH7 4BQ
☎0131 556 2220 Fax 0131 556 3300
✉ trust@cmyk-design.co.uk
www.scotlandintrust.co.uk

Owner *National Trust for Scotland*
Editor *Iain Gale*
Contact *Neil Braidwood*
Circulation 195,034

Founded 1983. THREE ISSUES YEARLY. Membership magazine of the National Trust for Scotland. Magazine containing heritage/conservation features relating to the Trust, their properties and work. No unsolicited mss.

Scotland on Sunday Magazine
See **Scotland on Sunday** under *National Newspapers*

The Scots Magazine
D.C.Thomson & Co., 2 Albert Square, Dundee DD1 9QJ
☎01382 223131 Fax 01382 322214
✉ mail@scotsmagazine.com
www.scotsmagazine.com

Owner *D.C.Thomson & Co. Ltd*
Editor *John Methven*
Circulation 41,698

Founded 1739. MONTHLY. Covers a wide field of Scottish interests ranging from personalities to wildlife, climbing, reminiscence, history and folklore. Outside contributions welcome; 'staff delighted to discuss in advance by letter or e-mail'.
EVENTS LISTING *Christina Dolan*
PHOTOGRAPHY/MUSIC *Ian Neilson*
Books *Alison Cook*

The Scottish Farmer

Newsquest Magazines, 200 Renfield Street, Glasgow G2 3QB
☎0141 302 7727 Fax 0141 302 7799
✉ ken.fletcher@thescottishfarmer.co.uk

Owner *Newsquest Magazines*
Editor *Alasdair Fletcher*
Circulation 20,279

Founded 1893. WEEKLY. Farmer's magazine covering most aspects of Scottish agriculture. Unsolicited mss welcome. Approach with ideas in writing, by fax or e-mail.

FEATURES *Ken Fletcher* Technical articles on agriculture or farming units. 1000–2000 words.

NEWS *Ken Fletcher* Factual news about farming developments, political, personal and technological. Max. 800 words.

WEEKEND FAMILY PAGES Rural and craft topics.

Scottish Field

Special Publications, Craigcrook Castle, Craigcrook Road, Edinburgh EH4 3PE
☎0131 312 4550 Fax 0131 312 4551
✉ editor@scottishfield.co.uk
www.scottishfield.co.uk

Owner *Wyvex Media Ltd*
Editor *Archie Mackenzie*
Circulation 13,469

Founded 1903. MONTHLY. Scotland's quality lifestyle magazine. Unsolicited mss welcome but writers should study the magazine first.

FEATURES Articles of general interest on Scotland and Scots abroad with good photographs or, preferably, e-mailed images at 300 DPI. Approx. 1000 words.

PAYMENT negotiable.

Scottish Home & Country

42 Heriot Row, Edinburgh EH3 6ES
☎0131 225 1724 Fax 0131 225 8129
✉ magazine@swri.demon.co.uk

Owner *Scottish Women's Rural Institutes*
Editor *Liz Ferguson*
Circulation 11,000

Founded 1924. MONTHLY. Scottish or rural-related issues, health, travel, women's issues and general interest. Unsolicited mss welcome. Commissions are rare and tend to go to established contributors only.

Scouting Magazine

Gilwell House, Gilwell Park, Chingford E4 7QW
☎020 8433 7100 Fax 020 8433 7103
✉ scouting.magazine@scout.org.uk
www.scouts.org.uk

Owner *The Scout Association*
Editors *Chris James, Hilary Galloway, Matthew Oakes*
Circulation 75,000

BI-MONTHLY magazine for adults connected to or interested in the Scout Movement. Interested in Scouting-related submissions only.

PAYMENT by negotiation.

Screen

Gilmorehill Centre for Theatre, Film and Television, University of Glasgow, Glasgow G12 8QQ
☎0141 330 5035 Fax 0141 330 3515
✉ screen@arts.gla.ac.uk
www.screen.arts.gla.ac.uk
screen.oxfordjournals.org

Publisher *Oxford University Press*
Editorial Office *Caroline Beven* Editors *Annette Kuhn, John Caughie, Simon Frith, Karen Lury, Jackie Stacey, Sarah Street*
Circulation 1200

QUARTERLY, refereed academic journal of film and television studies for a readership ranging from undergraduates to screen studies academics and media professionals. There are no specific qualifications for acceptance of articles. Straightforward film reviews are not normally published. Check the magazine's style and market in the first instance.

Screen International

33–39 Bowling Green Lane, London EC1R 0DA
☎020 7505 8000
✉ michael.gubbins@emap.com
www.screendaily.com

Owner *Emap Communications*
Editor *Michael Gubbins*
Circulation 7107

The voice of the international film industry. Expert freelance writers used in all areas. No unsolicited mss. Approach by e-mail.

NEWS *Wendy Mitchell*
FEATURES *Leon Forde*
INTERNATIONAL *Finn Halligan*
BOX OFFICE *Diana Lodderhose*
PAYMENT negotiable on NUJ basis.

Screentrade Magazine

Screentrade Media Ltd, PO Box 144, Orpington BR6 6LZ
☎01689 833117 Fax 01689 833117

✉ philip@screentrademagazine.co.uk
www.screentrademagazine.co.uk
Owner *Screentrade Media Ltd*
Editor *Philip Turner*
US Representative, Screentrade Media Ltd
  Pamala Stanton (pamscreentrade@aol.com)
Circulation 3000+

Founded 2002. QUARTERLY journal for British, European and American exhibitors and film distributors. Now also serving Russia and India.

FEATURES Items on cinema management, technical, cinema building history, nostalgia, showmanship, book reviews, concession supply, ticketing issues, trade articles including seating, screening, projection/career tips and other managerial matters. Also film and producer/director opinions. Some film reviews but no 'film star' interviews. Most contributions are from within the industry. Items on the state of cinema exhibition, film distribution, cinema architecture, interviews with key industry personnel frequently undertaken. 1500–3000 words.

NEWS Topical items (if substantiated) welcome. Events coverage (e.g. festivals, premières) from an exhibitor's viewpoint preferred.

ScriptWriter Magazine
2 Elliott Square, London NW3 3SU
☎020 7586 4853 Fax 020 7586 4853
✉ info@scriptwritermagazine.com
www.scriptwritermagazine.com
Owner *Scriptease Ltd*
Managing Editor *Jonquil Florentin*
Editor *Julian Friedmann*
Circulation 1500

Launched November 2001. SIX ISSUES PER YEAR. Magazine for professional scriptwriters covering all aspects of the business and craft of writing for the small and large screen. Interested in serious, in-depth analysis; max. 1500–3500 words. E-mail with synopsis sample material and c.v.

Sea Breezes
Mannin Media Group Ltd, Media House, Cronkbourne IM4 4SB
☎01624 696573 Fax 01624 661655
✉ seabreezes@manninmedia.co.im
www.seabreezes.co.im
Owner *Print Centres*
Editor *Captain A.C. Douglas*
Circulation 17,000

Founded 1919. MONTHLY. Covers virtually everything relating to ships and seamen. Unsolicited mss welcome; they should be thoroughly researched and accompanied by relevant photographs. No fiction, poetry, or anything which 'smacks of the romance of the sea'.

FEATURES Factual tales of ships, seamen and the sea, Royal or Merchant Navy, sail or power, nautical history, shipping company histories, epic voyages, etc. Length 1000–4000 words. 'The most readily acceptable work will be that which shows it is clearly the result of first-hand experience or the product of extensive and accurate research.' PAYMENT £14 per page (about 800 words).

The Second World War – WWII (1939–1945)
PO Box 202, Scarborough YO11 3GE
☎01723 581329 Fax 01723 581329
✉ books@greatnorthernpublishing.co.uk
www.greatnorthernpublishing.co.uk
Owner *Great Northern Publishing*
Editor *Mark Marsay*

Launched October 2005. BI-MONTHLY subscription only, non-academic magazine published in A5 format (sister magazine to *The Great War*). 'The magazine dedicated to the struggle for freedom – the voice and record of those who served between 1939 and 1945.' Articles, personal stories and accounts of those who served (men and women of all nationalities) on the war and home fronts and their families; diaries, anecdotes, letters, postcards, poetry, unit histories, events and memorials, etc. Absolutely no fiction or academic works expounding historian's personal views. New material welcome; contact the editor prior to sending. Submission guidelines and editorial content on the website. 'Open door policy: all welcome regardless of ability to write to a high standard as all work is carefully edited. No subject or topic excluded.' Sample copy £5.

The Self Publishing Magazine (incorporating Readers' Review Magazine)
9 De Montfort Mews, Leicester LE1 7FW
☎0116 255 9311 Fax 0116 255 9323
✉ readersreview@troubador.co.uk
www.troubador.co.uk/selfpublishing
Owner *Troubador Publishing Ltd*
Editor *Jane Rowland*
Circulation 2000

Launched 2006. THREE ISSUES YEARLY. Articles on self publishing. Submissions welcome on aspects of authors publishing their own books (design, production, editing, print, marketing). Approach by e-mail. Max. 2000 words.

BOOK REVIEWS Self-published books only. Max. 300 words.

She Magazine

National Magazine House, 72 Broadwick Street, London W1F 9EP
☎020 7439 5000 Fax 020 7312 3940
www.she.co.uk
Owner *National Magazine Company Ltd*
Editor *Sian Rees*
Circulation 151,713

Glossy MONTHLY for the 35-plus woman, addressing her needs as a modern individual, a parent and a homemaker. Talks to its readers in an intelligent, humorous and informative way.

FEATURES Approach with feature ideas in writing or e-mail to Deputy Editor, *Carmen Bruegmann* (carmen.bruegmann@natmags.co.uk). No unsolicited material.
PAYMENT negotiable.

Ships Monthly

IPC Inspire, 222 Branston Road, Burton-upon-Trent DE14 3BT
☎01283 542721 Fax 01283 546436
shipsmonthly@ipcmedia.com
www.shipsmonthly.com
Owner *IPC Inspire*
Editor *Iain Wakefield*
Deputy Editor *Nicholas Leach*
Circulation 22,000

Founded 1966. MONTHLY A4 format magazine for ship enthusiasts and maritime professionals. News, photographs and illustrated articles on all kinds of ships – mercantile and naval, past and present. No yachting. Welcomes contributions on port histories. Most articles are commissioned; prospective contributors should telephone or e-mail in the first instance.

Shoot Monthly Magazine

IPC Media Ltd., The Blue Fin Building, 110 Southwark Street, London SE1 0SU
☎020 3148 4727 Fax 020 3148 8130
shoot@ipcmedia.com
www.shoot.co.uk
Owner *IPC Media (A Time Warner Company)*
Editor *Colin Mitchell*
Circulation 29,947

Founded 1969. MONTHLY football magazine. No unsolicited mss. Present ideas for news, features or colour photo-features to the editor by letter or e-mail.

FEATURES Hard-hitting, topical and off-beat. Very limited opportunities for freelance work.

PAYMENT negotiable.

Shooting and Conservation

BASC, Marford Mill, Rossett, Wrexham LL12 0HL
☎01244 573000 Fax 01244 573001
jeffrey.olstead@basc.org.uk
Owner *The British Association for Shooting and Conservation (BASC)*
Editor *Jeffrey Olstead*
Circulation 120,000

SIX ISSUES PER YEAR. Good articles and stories on shooting, conservation and related areas may be considered although most material is produced in-house. Max. 1500 words.
PAYMENT negotiable.

The Shooting Gazette

PO Box 225, Stamford PE9 2HS
☎01780 485350 Fax 01780 485390
will_hetherington@ipcmedia.com
Owner *IPC Media (A Time Warner Company)*
Editor *Will Hetherington*
Circulation 17,022

Launched 1989. MONTHLY aimed at those who enjoy driven game shooting in the UK and around the world.

FEATURES *Will Hetherington* Welcomes articles directly related to interesting or unusual game shooting stories; max. 2000 words. Approach by e-mail.

NEWS *Darren Crush* Max. 2000 words.

Shooting Times & Country Magazine

IPC Media Ltd., The Blue Fin Building, 110 Southwark Street, London SE1 0SU
☎020 3148 4741
steditorial@ipcmedia.com
www.shootingtimes.co.uk
Owner *IPC Media (A Time Warner Company)*
Editor *Camilla Clark*
Circulation 28,178

Founded 1882. WEEKLY. Covers shooting, fishing and related countryside topics. Unsolicited contributions considered.
PAYMENT negotiable.

Shout Magazine

D.C. Thomson & Co., Albert Square, Dundee DD1 9QJ
☎01382 223131 Fax 01382 200880
shout@dcthomson.co.uk
www.shoutmag.com
Owner *D.C. Thomson Publishers*

Editor *Maria T. Welch*
Circulation 82,000
Founded 1993. FORTNIGHTLY. Pop music, quizzes, emotional, beauty, fashion, soap features.

Shout!

PO Box YR46, Leeds LS9 6XG
☎0113 248 5700 Fax 0113 295 6097
✉ shout.magazine@ntlworld.com
www.shoutweb.co.uk

Owner/Editor *Mark Michalowski*
Circulation 7000
Founded 1995. MONTHLY lesbian/gay and bisexual news, views, arts and scene for Yorkshire; lgb health and politics. Interested in reviews of Yorkshire lgb events, happenings, news, analysis – 300 to 1000 words max. No fiction, fashion or items with no reasonable relevance to Yorkshire and the north.
PAYMENT £40 per 1000 words.

Showing World

The Publishing House, Station Road, Framlingham IP13 9EE
☎01728 622030 Fax 01728 622031
✉ info@showingworldonline.co.uk
www.showingworldonline.co.uk

Owner *Robin Aldwood Publications Ltd*
Editor *Sandy Lee*
Circulation 8000
Founded 1991. Features every aspect of showing horses and ponies plus natives, miniatures and donkeys. Knowledgeable and how-to-do-it articles welcome. Photos essential.
PAYMENT negotiable.

Shropshire Magazine

Waterloo Road, Telford TS1 5HU
☎01952 288822 Fax 01952 288820

Owner *Shropshire Newspapers Ltd*
Editor *Henry Carpenter*
Founded 1950. MONTHLY. Unsolicited mss welcome but ideas in writing preferred.
FEATURES Personalities, topical items, historical (e.g. family) of Shropshire; also general interest: homes, weddings, antiques, etc. Max. 1000 words.
PAYMENT negotiable 'but modest'.

Sight & Sound

British Film Institute, 21 Stephen Street, London W1T 1LN
☎020 7255 1444 Fax 020 7436 2327
✉ s&s@bfi.org.uk
www.bfi.org.uk/sightandsound

Owner *British Film Institute*
Editor *Nick James*
Founded 1932. MONTHLY. Topical and critical articles on international cinema, with regular columns from the USA and Europe. Length 1000–5000 words. Relevant photographs appreciated. Also book, film, DVD and video release reviews. Approach in writing with ideas.
PAYMENT by arrangement.

The Skier and Snowboarder Magazine

Mountain Marketing Ltd., PO Box 386, Sevenoaks TN13 1AQ
☎0845 310 8303
✉ skierandsnowboarder@hotmail.com

Publisher *Mountain Marketing Ltd*
Editor *Frank Baldwin*
Circulation 30,000
SEASONAL (from July to May). FIVE ISSUES YEARLY. Outside contributions welcome.
FEATURES Various topics covered, including race and resort reports, fashion, equipment update, dry slope, club news, new products, health and safety. Crisp, tight, informative copy of 800 words or less preferred.
NEWS All aspects of skiing news covered.
PAYMENT negotiable.

Slightly Foxed: The Real Reader's Quarterly

67 Dickinson Court, 15 Brewhouse Yard, London EC1V 4JX
☎020 7549 2121/2111 Fax 0870 199 1245
✉ all@foxedquarterly.com
www.foxedquarterly.com

Owner *Slightly Foxed Ltd*
Editors *Gail Pirkis, Hazel Wood*
Circulation 4000
Founded 2004. 'Reviews of books (fiction and non-fiction) that have stood the test of time or books that have been published recently and are of real quality but which have been overlooked by reviewers and bookshops.' Unsolicited contributions of 'lively, personal, idiosyncratic writing of real quality' are welcome but it is recommended that would-be contributors read the magazine first to gauge its approach. Send e-mail with sample work in the first instance. Not interested in anything that is not actually a review of a book or author.

Smallholder

Hook House, Wimblington March PE15 0QL
☎01354 741538 Fax 01354 741182

✉ liz.wright1@btconnect.com
www.smallholder.co.uk
Owner *Newsquest Plc*
Editor *Liz Wright*
Circulation 20,000
Founded 1982. MONTHLY. Outside contributions welcome. Send for sample magazine and editorial schedule before submitting anything. Follow up with samples of work to the editor so that style can be assessed for suitability. No poetry or humorous, unfocused personal tales; no puzzles.

FEATURES New writers always welcome, but must have high level of technical expertise – 'not textbook stuff'. 'How to do it' articles with photos welcome. Illustrations and photos paid for. Length 750–1500 words.

NEWS All agricultural and rural news welcome. Length 200–500 words.

PAYMENT negotiable.

SmartLife International
21–23 Phoenix Court, Hawkins Road, Colchester CO2 8JY
☎01206 505924 Fax 01206 505929
✉ stuart@smartlifeint.com
www.smartlifeint.com
Owner *Aceville Publications Ltd*
Editor *Stuart Pritchard*
Circulation 19,411

Launched 2000. TEN ISSUES YEARLY. High-end lifestyle magazine: consumer technology, interior design, luxury cars, travel, fashion and grooming. Welcomes proposals by e-mail.

FEATURES *Hamish McNair-Wilson* 'No good feature ideas that fit the remit are ruled out.' Max. 2000 words.

NEWS *Jake Stow* Generally compiled in-house.

Snooker Scene
Hayley Green Court, 130 Hagley Road, Hayley Green, Halesowen, Birmingham B63 1DY
☎0121 585 9188 Fax 0121 585 7117
✉ clive.everton@talk21.com
www.snookersceneonline.com
Owner *Everton's News Agency*
Editor *Clive Everton*
Circulation 10,000

Founded 1971. MONTHLY. No unsolicited mss. Approach in writing with an idea.

Spanish Magazine
Merricks Media Ltd, Units 3–4 Riverside Court, Lower Bristol Road, Bath BA2 6RN

☎01225 786857 Fax 01225 786801
✉ spanish.edit@spanishmagazine.co.uk
www.spanishmagazine.co.uk
Owner *Merricks Media Ltd*
Editor *Adam Waring*
Circulation 15,000

Founded 2003. MONTHLY. Travel, property and lifestyle in Spain. Unsolicited contributions welcome. Travel and culture pieces must have high-resolution photography. E-mail for guidelines. Max. 1200–1600 words.

Spear's Wealth Management Survey
Spear Media, Enterprise House, 36a Notting Hill Gate, London W11 3HX
☎020 7985 0002 Fax 020 7792 9244
✉ info@spearmedia.co.uk
www.spearswms.com
Owner/Editor *William Cash*
Circulation 30,000

Launched 2005. QUARTERLY specialist guide for 'high and ultra-high net worth' individuals to all aspects of wealth management and the super-rich lifestyle. Subscription is by invitation, only. No unsolicited contributions.

Speciality Food
25 Phoenix Court, Hawkins Road, Colchester CO2 8JY
☎01206 505981 Fax 01206 505945
✉ nicola.mallett@aceville.co.uk
www.specialityfoodmagazine.co.uk
Owner *Aceville Publications Ltd*
Editor *Nicola Mallett*
Circulation 8733

Founded 2002. NINE ISSUES PER YEAR. Trade magazine focusing on premium food and drink relevant for the fine food retail sector. Unsolicited contributions not generally welcome.

FEATURES Subjects such as cheese, dairy and chocolate; also organic food. Approach by e-mail. Max. 1800 words. PAYMENT negotiable.

The Spectator
22 Old Queen Street, London SW1H 9HP
☎020 7961 0020 Fax 020 7961 0058
✉ editor@spectator.co.uk
www.spectator.co.uk
Owner *The Spectator (1828) Ltd*
Editor *Matthew d'Ancona*
Deputy Editor *Stuart Reid*
Books *Mark Amory*
Circulation 72,034

Founded 1828. WEEKLY political and literary magazine. Prospective contributors should write in the first instance to the relevant editor. Unsolicited mss welcome, but no 'follow up' phone calls, please.

PAYMENT nominal.

Staffordshire Life

The Publishing Centre, Derby Street, Stafford ST16 2DT

☎01785 257700 Fax 01785 253287

✉ editor@staffordshirelife.co.uk

www.staffordshirelife.co.uk

Owner *Staffordshire Newspapers Ltd*
Editor *Philip Thurlow-Craig*
Circulation 17,000

Founded 1982. MONTHLY. Full-colour county magazine devoted to Staffordshire, its surroundings and people. Contributions welcome. Approach in writing with ideas.

FEATURES Max. 1200 words.
PAYMENT NUJ rates.

Stage

Stage House, 47 Bermondsey Street, London SE1 3XT

☎020 7403 1818 Fax 020 7357 9287

✉ editor@thestage.co.uk

www.thestage.co.uk

Owner *The Stage Newspaper Ltd*
Editor *Brian Attwood*
Circulation 24,781

Founded 1880. WEEKLY. No unsolicited mss. Prospective contributors should write with ideas in the first instance.

FEATURES Preference for middle-market, tabloid-style articles. 'Puff pieces', PR plugs and extended production notes will not be considered. Max. 800 words. Profiles: 1200 words.

NEWS News stories from outside London are always welcome. Max. 300 words.

PAYMENT £100 per 1000 words.

Stamp Lover

National Philatelic Society, 107 Charterhouse Street, London EC1M 6PT

☎020 7490 9610

✉ nps@ukphilately.org.uk

www.ukphilately.org.uk/nps

Owner *National Philatelic Society*
Editor *David Alford*
Circulation 800

Founded 1908. SIX ISSUES YEARLY. Magazine of the National Philatelic Society. Welcomes articles about the hobby; stamps, old and new. Approach by e-mail or letter.

NEWS Information about worldwide philately. Max. 1000 words. No payment.

Stamp Magazine

IPC Media Ltd, Leon House, 233 High Street, Croydon CR9 1HZ

☎020 8726 8243 Fax 020 8726 8299

✉ guy_thomas@ipcmedia.com

Owner *IPC Media (A Time Warner Company)*
Editor *Guy Thomas*
Circulation 12,000

Founded 1934. MONTHLY news and features on the world of stamp collecting from the past to the present day. Interested in articles by experts on particular countries or themes such as subject matter illustrated on stamps – dogs, politics, etc. Approach in writing.

NEWS *Julia Lee* News of latest stamp issues or industry news. Max. 500 words.

FEATURES *Guy Thomas* Any features welcome on famous stamps, rarities, postmarks, postal history, postcards, personal collections. Must be illustrated with colour images ('we can arrange for photography of original stamps').

PAYMENT negotiable.

Steam Railway Magazine

Bretton Court, Bretton, Peterborough PE3 8DZ

☎01733 264666 Fax 01733 282720

✉ steam.railway@emap.com

Owner *Emap Active Limited*
Editor *Danny Hopkins*
Circulation 32,315

Founded 1979. FOUR-WEEKLY magazine targeted at all steam enthusiasts interested in the modern preservation movement. Unsolicited material welcome. News reports, photographs, steam-age reminiscences. Approach in writing or by e-mail.

The Strad

Orpheus Publications, Newsquest Specialist Media Ltd, 2nd Floor, 30 Cannon Street, London EC4M 6YJ

☎020 7618 3095 Fax 020 7618 3483

✉ thestrad@orpheuspublications.com

www.thestrad.com

Owner *Newsquest Specialist Media Group*
Editor *Ariane Todes*
Circulation 17,500

Founded 1890. MONTHLY for classical string musicians, makers and enthusiasts. Unsolicited mss accepted occasionally 'though acknowledgement/return not guaranteed'.

FEATURES Profiles of string players, teachers, luthiers and musical instruments, also relevant research. Max. 2000 words.
REVIEWS *Matthew Rye*
PAYMENT £150 per 1000 words.

Stuff

Teddington Studios, Broom Road, Teddington TW11 9BE
☎020 8267 5036
✉ stuff@haymarket.com
www.stuff.tv
Owner *Haymarket Publishing Ltd*
Editor *Fraser MacDonald*
Circulation 100,265

Launched 1998. MONTHLY guide to new technology with information on all the latest gadgets and gear. Includes a 'Buyers' Guide' with information about the top tried and tested items. No unsolicited contributions.

Suffolk and Norfolk Life

The Publishing House, Framlingham IP13 9EE
☎01728 622030 Fax 01728 622031
Owner *Today Magazines Ltd*
Editor *Kevin Davis*
Circulation 17,000

Founded 1989. MONTHLY. General interest, local stories, historical, personalities, wine, travel, food. Unsolicited mss welcome. Approach by phone or in writing with ideas. Not interested in anything which does not relate specifically to East Anglia.
FEATURES *Kevin Davis* Max. 1500 words, with photos.
NEWS *Kevin Davis* Max. 1000 words, with photos.
SPECIAL PAGES *William Locks* Study the magazine for guidelines. Max. 1500 words.
PAYMENT £40–60.

Sugar Magazine

64 North Row, London W1K 7LL
☎020 7150 7087 Fax 020 7150 7678
✉ sugarreaders@sugarmagazine.co.uk
www.sugarmagazine.co.uk
Owner *Hachette Filipacchi (UK)*
Editor *Annabel Brog*
Circulation 200,541

Founded 1994. MONTHLY. Everything that might interest the teenage girl. No unsolicited mss. Will consider ideas or contacts for real-life features. No fiction. Approach in writing in the first instance.

Sunday Times Magazine

See **The Sunday Times** under *National Newspapers*

SuperBike Magazine

IPC Media Ltd, Leon House, 233 High Street, Croydon CR9 1HZ
☎020 8726 8455 Fax 020 8726 8499
✉ kenny_pryde@ipcmedia.com
www.superbike.co.uk
Owner *IPC Media (A Time Warner Company)*
Publishing Director *Keith Foster*
Editor *Kenny Pryde*
Circulation 50,023

Founded 1977. MONTHLY. Dedicated to all that is best and most exciting in the world of motorcycling. Unsolicited mss, synopses and ideas by e-mail are welcome.

Sussex Life

Baskerville Place, 28 Teville Road, Worthing BN11 1UG
☎01903 218719 Fax 01903 820193
✉ jonathan.keeble@sussexlife.co.uk
www.sussexlife.com
Owner *Archant Life*
Editor *Jonathan Keeble*
Circulation 42,000

Founded 1965. MONTHLY. Sussex and general interest magazine. Regular supplements on education, fashion, homes and gardens. Interested in investigative, journalistic pieces relevant to the area and celebrity profiles. Unsolicited mss, synopses and ideas welcome but approach by telephone in the first instance.

Swimming Times Magazine

41 Granby Street, Loughborough LE11 3DU
☎01509 632230 Fax 01509 632233
Owner *Amateur Swimming Association*
Editor *P. Hassall*
Circulation 20,000

Founded 1923. MONTHLY about competitive swimming and associated subjects. Unsolicited mss welcome.
FEATURES Technical articles on swimming, water polo, diving or synchronised swimming. Length and payment negotiable.

The Tablet

1 King Street Cloisters, Clifton Walk, London W6 0QZ
☎020 8748 8484 Fax 020 8748 1550
✉ thetablet@tablet.co.uk
www.thetablet.co.uk

Owner *The Tablet Publishing Co Ltd*
Editor *Catherine Pepinster*
Circulation 23,628
Founded 1840. WEEKLY. Quality international Roman Catholic periodical featuring articles (political, social, cultural, theological or spiritual) of interest to concerned Christian laity and clergy.'We welcome ideas for articles; please send a brief outline in advance, setting out what you propose to write about and explaining your credentials.' Unsolicited material is not accepted.
PAYMENT negotiable.

Take a Break
Academic House, 24–28 Oval Road, London NW1 7DT
☎020 7241 8000
✉ tab.features@bauer.co.uk
Owner *H. Bauer Publishing Ltd*
Editor *John Dale*
Circulation 1.3 million
Founded 1990. WEEKLY. True-life feature magazine. Approach with ideas in writing.
NEWS/FEATURES Always on the look-out for good, true-life stories. Max. 1200 words.
FICTION Sharp, succinct stories which are well told and often with a twist at the end. All categories, provided it is relevant to the magazine's style and market. Max. 1000 words.
PAYMENT negotiable.

Tate Etc
Millbank, London SW1P 4RG
☎020 7887 8030 Fax 020 7887 3940
✉ tateetc@tate.org.uk
www.tate.org.uk
Owner *Tate*
Editorial Director *Bice Curiger*
Editor *Simon Grant*
Circulation 90,000
Relaunched May 2004. THREE ISSUES YEARLY. Visual arts magazine aimed at a broad readership with articles blending the historic and the contemporary. Please send material by post.

Tatler
Vogue House, Hanover Square, London W1S 1JU
☎020 7499 9080 Fax 020 7493 1641
www.tatler.co.uk
Owner *Condé Nast Publications Ltd*
Editor *Geordie Greig*
Features Director *Vassi Chamberlain*
Senior Features Editor *Camilla Long*

Features Editor *Kate Bernard*
Editor's Assistant *Fiona Kent*
Editorial Assistant *Richard Dennen*
Circulation 90,372
Up-market glossy from the Condé Nast stable. New writers should send in copies of either published work or unpublished material; writers of promise will be taken up. The magazine works largely on a commission basis: they are unlikely to publish unsolicited features, but will ask writers to work to specific projects.

The Teacher
Hamilton House, Mabledon Place, London WC1H 9BD
☎020 7380 4708 Fax 020 7383 7230
✉ teacher@nut.org.uk
www.teachers.org.uk
Owner *National Union of Teachers*
Editor *Elyssa Campbell-Barr*
Circulation 320,000
Journal of the National Union of Teachers, published EIGHT TIMES YEARLY. News, advice, information and special features on educational matters relating to classroom teaching. Will consider 'anything on spec'. Approach by letter or e-mail.

TGO (The Great Outdoors)
Newsquest (Herald & Times) Magazines Ltd., 200 Renfield Street, Glasgow G2 3QB
☎0141 302 7700 Fax 0141 302 7799
✉ cameron.mcneish@tgomagazine.co.uk
www.tgomagazine.co.uk
Owner *Newsquest*
Editor *Cameron McNeish*
Circulation 11,569
Founded 1978. MONTHLY. Deals with walking, backpacking and wild country topics. Unsolicited mss are welcome.
FEATURES Well-written and illustrated items on relevant topics. Max. 2500 words. Quality high resolution digital colour images only, please.
NEWS Short topical items (or photographs). Max. 300 words.
PAYMENT negotiable.

That's Life!
3rd Floor, Academic House, 24–28 Oval Road, London NW1 7DT
☎020 7241 8000 Fax 020 7241 8008
✉ firstname.lastname@bauer.co.uk
www.bauer.co.uk
Owner *H. Bauer Publishing Ltd*

Editor *Jo Checkley*
Circulation 464,762
Founded 1995.WEEKLY.True-life stories,puzzles, health, homes, parenting, cookery and fun.
FEATURES *Karen Bryans* Max. 1600 words.
FICTION *Emma Fabian* 1200 words.
PAYMENT Features, varies; fiction, £300.

The Third Alternative
See **Black Static**

This England
PO Box 52, Cheltenham GL50 1YQ
☎01242 537900 Fax 01242 537901
Owner *This England Ltd*
Editor *Roy Faiers*
Circulation 200,000
Founded 1968. QUARTERLY, with a strong overseas readership. Celebration of England and all things English: famous people, natural beauty, towns and villages, history, traditions, customs and legends, crafts, etc. Generally a rural basis, with the 'Forgetmenots' section publishing readers' recollections and nostalgia. Up to a hundred unsolicited pieces received each week. Unsolicited mss/ideas welcome. Length 250–2000 words.
PAYMENT £25 per 1000 words.

Time
The Blue Fin Building, 110 Southwark Street, London SE1 0SU
☎020 3148 3000
✉ edit_office@timemagazine.com
www.time.com
Owner *Time Warner*
International Editor *Michael Elliott*
Circulation 143,519 (UK)
Founded 1923.WEEKLY current affairs and news magazine.There are few opportunities for freelancers on *Time* as almost all the magazine's content is written by staff members from various bureaux around the world. No unsolicited mss.

Time Out
Universal House, 251 Tottenham Court Road, London W1T 7AB
☎020 7813 3000 Fax 020 7813 6001
www.timeout.com
Managing Director *David Pepper*
Editor *Gordon Thomson*
Circulation 92,233
Founded 1968.WEEKLY magazine of news, arts, entertainment and lifestyle in London plus listings.

FEATURES *Alan Rutter* 'Usually written by staff writers or commissioned, but it's always worth submitting an idea if particularly apt to the magazine.' Word length varies; up to 2000 max.
CONSUMER SECTION Food and drink, shopping, services, travel, design, property, health and fitness.
PAYMENT negotiable.

The Times Educational Supplement
Admiral House, 66–68 East Smithfield, London E1W 1BX
☎020 7782 3000 Fax 020 7782 3200
www.tes.co.uk
Owner *Exponent*
Editor *Judith Judd*
Circulation 70,533
Founded 1910. WEEKLY. New contributors are welcome and should fax or e-mail ideas on one sheet of A4 for news (newsdesk@tes.co.uk), features (features@tes.co.uk) or reviews. The main newspaper accepts contributions in the following sections:
COMMENT Weekly slot for a well-informed and cogently argued viewpoint. Max. 750 words. (comment@tes.co.uk).
LEADERSHIP Practical issues for school governors and managers. Max. 500 words.
FE FOCUS Weekly pull-out section covering post-16 education and training in colleges, work and the wider community. Aimed at everyone from teachers/lecturers to leaders and opinion formers in lifelong learning. News, features, comment and opinion on all aspects of college life welcome. Length from 350 words (news) to 1000 max. (features). Contact *Ian Nash* (ian. nash@tes.co.uk).
TES Magazine Weekly magazine for teachers focusing on looking at their lives, inside and outside the classroom, investigating the key issues of the day and highlighting good practice. Max. 800 words. (features@tes.co.uk).

The Times Educational Supplement Scotland
Scott House, 10 South St Andrew Street, Edinburgh EH2 2AZ
☎0131 557 1144 Fax 0131 558 1155
✉ scoted@tes.co.uk
www.tes.co.uk/scotland
Owner *TSL Education Ltd*
Editor *Neil Munro*
Circulation 6118

Founded 1965. WEEKLY. Unsolicited mss welcome.
FEATURES Articles on education in Scotland. Max. 1000 words.
NEWS Items on education in Scotland. Max. 600 words.

The Times Higher Education Supplement

Admiral House, 66–68 East Smithfield, London E1W 1BX
☎020 7782 3000 Fax 020 7782 3300
✉ editor@thes.co.uk
www.thes.co.uk
Owner *Exponent Private Equity*
Editor *Gerard Kelly*
Circulation 23,902

Founded 1971. WEEKLY. Unsolicited items are welcome but most articles and almost all book reviews are commissioned. 'In most cases it is better to write or e-mail, but in the case of news stories it is all right to phone.'
FEATURES *Mandy Garner* Most articles are commissioned from academics in higher education.
News *Alan Thomson* Freelance opportunities very occasionally.
SCIENCE *Steve Farrar*
SCIENCE BOOKS *Gerard Kelly*
FOREIGN *David Jobbins*
PAYMENT by negotiation.

The Times Literary Supplement

Times House, 1 Pennington Street, London E98 1BS
☎020 7782 5000 Fax 020 7782 4966
www.the-tls.co.uk
Owner *The Times Literary Supplement Ltd*
Editor *Peter Stothard*
Circulation 33,323

Founded 1902. WEEKLY review of literature, history, philosophy, science and the arts. Contributors should approach in writing and be familiar with the general level of writing in the *TLS*.
LITERARY DISCOVERIES *Alan Jenkins*
POEMS *Mick Imlah*
NEWS Reviews and general articles concerned with literature, publishing and new intellectual developments anywhere in the world. Length by arrangement.
PAYMENT by arrangement.

Titbits

2 Caversham Street, London SW3 4AH

☎020 7351 4995 Fax 020 7351 4995
Owner *Sport Newspapers Ltd*
Editor *James Hughes*
Circulation 150,000

Founded 1895. MONTHLY. Consumer magazine for men covering show business and general interests. Ideas in writing welcome. Max. 3000 words. News, features, particularly photofeatures (colour) and fiction. Always send letter or telephone first.
PAYMENT negotiable.

Today's Flyfisher

DHP Ltd, 2 Stephenson Close, Drayton Fields, Daventry NN11 8RF
☎01327 311999 Fax 01327 311190
✉ timsmith@dhpub.co.uk
www.dhponline.com
Owner *David Hall*
Editor *Tim Smith*
Circulation 17,000

Founded 2003. MONTHLY instructional fly fishing magazine. Welcomes contributions including fishery reports and fly tying articles. No foreign features or advanced skills. Approach by e-mail.
FEATURES Stillwater trout tactics, salmon tactics, river trout/grayling tactics, UK saltwater tactics. Max. 2500 words. PAYMENT (including pictures) £280.
NEWS Stories relevant to UK fly fishers.
FICTION Funny fishing stories. Max. 400 words. PAYMENT £60.

Today's Golfer

Bushfield House, Orton Centre, Peterborough PE2 5UW
☎01733 237111 Fax 01733 288014
✉ editorial@todaysgolfer.co.uk
www.todaysgolfer.co.uk
Owner *Emap Active Ltd*
Editor *Andy Calton*
Deputy Editor *Chris Jones*
Circulation 104,000

Founded 1988. MONTHLY. Golf instruction, features, player profiles and news. Most features written in-house but unsolicited mss will be considered. Approach in writing with ideas. Not interested in instruction material from outside contributors.
FEATURES/NEWS *Kevin Brown* Opinion, player profiles and general golf-related features.

Top of the Pops Magazine

Room A1136, Woodlands, 80 Wood Lane,
London W12 0TT
☎020 8433 3910

Owner *BBC Worldwide Publishing Ltd*
Editor *Peter Hart*
Circulation 105,025

Founded 1995. FOUR-WEEKLY teenage celebrity magazine with a lighthearted and humorous approach. No unsolicited material.

Total Coarse Fishing

DHP Ltd, 2 Stephenson Close, Drayton Fields,
Daventry NN11 8RF
☎01327 311999 Fax 01327 311190
✉ gareth@dhpub.co.uk
www.total-fishing.com

Owner *David Hall*
Editor *Gareth Purnell*
Circulation 35,000

Founded 2006. MONTHLY magazine for anglers who like to keep their fishing varied and target quality coarse fish from exceptional venues. No unsolicited contributions.
FEATURES Overseas freshwater angling features with 'exceptional' photographs. Max. 2200 words. PAYMENT £200. Approach by e-mail.

Total Film

2 Balcombe Street, London NW1 6LY
☎020 7042 4000 Fax 020 7042 4839
✉ totalfilm@futurenet.co.uk

Owner *Future Publishing*
Editor *Nev Pierce*
Reviews *Jonathan Dean* (jonathan.dean@ futurenet.co.uk) Features *Jamie Graham* (jamie.graham@futurenet.co.uk), *Andy Lowe* (andy.lowe@futurenet.co.uk), News *Jonathan Crocker* (jonathan.crocker@futurenet.co.uk)
Circulation 90,642

Founded 1997. MONTHLY reviews-based movie magazine. Interested in ideas for features, not necessarily tied in to specific releases, and humour items. No reviews or interviews with celebrities/directors. Approach by post or e-mail.

Total TV Guide

H. Bauer Publishing, Academic House, 24–28 Oval Road, London NW1 8DT
☎020 7241 8000 Fax 020 7241 8042
✉ barbara.miller@bauer.co.uk
www.bauer.co.uk

Owner *H. Bauer Publishing*
Editor *Jon Peake*
Circulation 92,004

Founded 2003. WEEKLY TV listings for those with access to multichannel television, covering everything from movies to sport, drama to children's programmes.
FEATURES *Ben Lawrence* Commissions features relating to current TV programmes; chiefly celebrity interviews and set visits. No unsolicited contributions.

Total Vauxhall

Future Publishing, 30 Monmouth Street, Bath
BA1 2BW
☎01225 442244 Fax 01225 446019
✉ info@totalvauxhall.co.uk
www.totalvauxhall.co.uk

Owner *Future Publishing*
Editor *Barton Brisland*
Circulation 20,000

Founded 2001. MONTHLY independent newsstand magazine aimed at the Vauxhall enthusiast. Covers new, modified, historical/classic, race and rally Vauxhalls of all kinds. Substantial amount of technical content. Also covers the more interesting parts of the GM family, particularly Opel and Holden. Uses a lot of freelance contributors; 'those who hit deadlines and fulfil the brief get regular work and lots of it.' Feature ideas, news items, historical pieces and potential feature cars welcome but must have a Vauxhall/GM tilt. Call the editor directly for an informal discussion on style, approach and angle.
PAYMENT 'surprisingly generous'.

Traditional Woodworking

151 Station Street, Burton on Trent DE14 1BG
☎01283 742950 Fax 01283 742966
✉ twproductions@twonline.co.uk

Owner *Waterways World*
Editor *Carmen Conopka*
Circulation 8,034

Founded 1988. MONTHLY. Features workshop projects, techniques, reviews of the latest woodworking tools and equipment, general articles on woodworking and furniture making. Supplement: *Power Tool Guide*.
FEATURES Technical features and furniture projects welcome. The latter must include drawings and cutting lists. A photograph of the piece is required before commissioning. Approach in writing in the first instance.
PAYMENT negotiable.

Trail

Bretton Court, Bretton, Peterborough
PE3 8DZ
☎01733 264666 Fax 01733 282653
✉ trail@emap.com
www.trailroutes.com
Owner *Emap Active Publishing Ltd*
Editor *Matthew Swain*
Circulation 40,552

Founded 1990. MONTHLY. Gear reports, where to walk and practical advice for the hillwalker and long distance walker. Inspirational reads on people and outdoor/walking issues. Health, fitness and injury prevention for high level walkers and outdoor lovers. Approach by phone or in writing in the first instance.

FEATURES *Simon Ingram* Very limited requirement for overseas articles, 'written to our style'. Ask for guidelines. Max. 2000 words. Limited requirement for guided walks articles. Specialist writers only. Ask for guidelines. 750–2000 words (depending on subject).

PAYMENT £100 per 1000 words.

Traveller

45–49 Brompton Road, London SW3 1DE
☎020 7589 0500 Fax 020 7581 8476
✉ traveller@wexas.com
www.traveller.org.uk
Owner *Wexas International Ltd*
Editor *Amy Sohanpaul*
Circulation 28,831

Founded 1970. QUARTERLY travel magazine.

FEATURES High quality, personal narratives of remarkable journeys. Articles should be off-beat, adventurous, authentic. For guidelines, see website. Articles may be accompanied by professional quality, original slides or high-res digital photographs. Freelance articles considered. Max. 1000 words. Initial contact by e-mail.

PAYMENT £200 per 1000 words.

Tribune

9 Arkwright Road, London NW3 6AN
☎020 7433 6410 Fax 020 7433 6410
✉ tribuneweb@btconnect.com
Owner *Tribune Publications*
Editor *Chris McLaughlin*

Founded 1937. WEEKLY. Independent Labour publication covering parliament, politics, trade unions, public policy and social issues, international affairs and the arts. Welcomes freelance contributions; approach by telephone or e-mail.

FEATURES *George Osgerby* Anything in line with the topics above. Max. 1000 words.

NEWS *Barckley Sumner* Breaking or forthcoming news events/stories. Max. 480 words.
OTHER Interviews, reviews, cartoons.

Trout Fisherman

EMAP Active Ltd, Bushfield House, Orton Centre, Peterborough PE2 5UW
☎01733 237111 Fax 01733 465820
✉ russell.hill@emap.com
www.troutfisherman.co.uk
Owner *Emap Active Ltd*
Editor *Russell Hill*
Circulation 27,734

Founded 1977. MONTHLY instructive magazine on trout fishing. Most of the articles are commissioned, but unsolicited mss and quality colour transparencies welcome.

FEATURES Max. 2500 words.
PAYMENT varies.

TVTimes

IPC Media Ltd., The Blue Fin Building, 110 Southwark Street, London SE1 0SU
☎020 3148 5615 Fax 020 3148 8115
Owner *IPC Media (A Time Warner Company)*
Editor *Ian Abbott*
Circulation 377,473

Founded 1955. WEEKLY magazine of listings and features serving the viewers of independent television, BBC, satellite and radio. Freelance contributions by commission only. No unsolicited contributions.

Ulster Business

5b Edgewater Business Park, Belfast Harbour Estate, Belfast BT3 9JQ
☎028 9078 3200 Fax 028 9078 3210
✉ davidcullen@greerpublications.com
www.ulsterbusiness.com
Owner *James Greer*
Editor *David Cullen*
Circulation 8,274

Founded 1987. MONTHLY. General business content with coverage of all sectors: ICT, retail, agriculture, commercial property, etc. 'Opportunities exist for well-written local orientated features, particularly those dealing with local firms or the issues they face; local business personality interviews also useful.' Contact the editor by e-mail. Max. 1000 words.

Ulster Tatler

39 Boucher Road, Belfast BT12 6UT
☎028 9066 3311 Fax 028 9038 1915
✉ edit@ulstertatler.com

www.ulstertatler.com
Owner/Editor *Richard Sherry*
Circulation 10,480

Founded 1965. MONTHLY. Articles of local interest and social functions appealing to Northern Ireland's ABC1 population. Welcomes unsolicited material; approach by phone or in writing in the first instance.
FEATURES *Noreen Dorman* Max. 1500 words.
FICTION *Richard Sherry* Max. 3000 words

Ultimate Advertiser

PO Box 7086, Clacton on Sea CO15 5WN
☎01255 428500 Fax 0870 046 6536
✉ sales@ultimateadvertiser.co.uk
www.ultimateadvertiser.co.uk
Owner *Apex Publishing Ltd*
Editor *Susan Kidby*
Circulation 5000

Founded 2005. MONTHLY advertising magazine including guides and information, features, listings and reviews. Approach by post, only.

Uncut

IPC Media Ltd., The Blue Fin Building, 110 Southwark Street, London SE1 0SU
☎020 3148 6985 Fax 020 3148 8105
✉ farah_ishaq@ipcmedia.com
www.uncut.co.uk
Owner *IPC Media (A Time Warner Company)*
Editor *Allan Jones*
Associate Editor *Michael Bonner*
Music Editor *John Mulvey*
Picture Editor *May Starey*
Production Editor *Mark Bentley*
Art Editor *Marc Jones*
Uncut.co.uk Editor *Ben Perreau*
Uncut.co.uk News Editor *Farah Ishaq*
Circulation 93,678

Launched 1997. MONTHLY music and film magazine with free CD each issue. Welcomes music and film reviews; approach by e-mail.

The Universe

Gabriel Communications Ltd., 4th Floor, Landmark House, Station Road, Cheadle Hulme SK8 7JH
☎0161 744 1700 Fax 0161 744 1701
✉ joseph.kelly@totalcatholic.com
www.totalcatholic.com
Owner *Gabriel Communications Ltd*
Editor *Joseph Kelly*
Circulation 60,000

Occasional use of new writers, but a substantial network of regular contributors already exists.

Interested in a very wide range of material: all subjects which might bear on Christian life. Fiction not normally accepted.
PAYMENT negotiable.

The Vegan

Donald Watson House, 7 Battle Road, St Leonards on Sea TN37 7AA
☎01424 427393 Fax 01424 717064
✉ editor@vegansociety.com
www.vegansociety.com
Owner *Vegan Society*
Editor *Rosamund Raha*
Circulation 7000

Founded 1944. QUARTERLY. Deals with the ecological, ethical and health aspects of veganism. Unsolicited mss welcome. Max. 2000 words.
PAYMENT negotiable.

Vogue

Vogue House, Hanover Square, London W1S 1JU
☎020 7499 9080 Fax 020 7408 0559
www.vogue.co.uk
Owner *Condé Nast Publications Ltd*
Editor *Alexandra Shulman*
Circulation 219,026

Launched 1916. Condé Nast Magazines tend to use known writers and commission what's needed, rather than using unsolicited mss. Contacts are useful.
FEATURES *Harriet Quick* Upmarket general interest rather than 'women's'. Good proportion of highbrow art and literary articles, as well as travel, gardens, food, home interest and reviews.

The Voice Newspaper

GV Media Group Ltd., Northern & Shell Tower, 6th Floor, 4 Selsdon Way, London London E14 9GL
☎020 7510 0340 Fax 020 7510 0341
✉ yourviews@gvmedia.co.uk
www.voice-online.co.uk
Acting Managing Director *George Ruddock*
News Editor *Andrew Clunis*
Circulation 40,000

Founded 1982. Leading WEEKLY newspaper for black Britons and other minority communities. Includes news, features, arts, sport and a comprehensive jobs section. Also includes a weekly glossy entertainment section. Illustrations: colour and b&w photos. Open to ideas for news and features on sport, business, community events and the arts.

W.I. Life

104 New Kings Road, London SW6 4LY
☎020 7731 5777 Fax 020 7736 4061
Owner *National Federation of Women's Institutes*
Editor *Joanna Grey*
Circulation 200,000

Women's Institute membership magazine. First issue February 2007. EIGHT ISSUES YEARLY. Contains articles on a wide range of subjects of interest to women. Strong environmental country slant with crafts and cookery plus gardening. Contributions, photos and illustrations from WI members welcome. PAYMENT by arrangement.

Walk Magazine

2nd Floor, Camelford House, 87–90 Albert Embankment, London SE1 7TW
☎020 7339 8500 Fax 020 7339 8501
✉ ramblers@ramblers.org.uk
www.ramblers.org.uk
Owner *Ramblers' Association*
Editor *Chris Ord*
Assistant Editor *Denise Noble*
Circulation 115,000

QUARTERLY. Official magazine of the Ramblers' Association, available to members only. Unsolicited mss welcome. S.a.e. required for return.

FEATURES Freelance features are invited on any aspect of walking in Britain. Length up to 1500 words, preferably with good photographs. No general travel articles.

The War Cry

101 Newington Causeway, London SE1 6BN
☎020 7367 4900 Fax 020 7367 4710
✉ warcry@salvationarmy.org.uk
www.salvationarmy.org.uk/warcry
Owner *The Salvation Army*
Editor *Major Nigel Bovey*
Circulation 58,000

Founded 1879. WEEKLY full-colour magazine containing Christian comment on current issues. Unsolicited mss welcome if appropriate to contents. No fiction or poetry. Approach by phone with ideas.

NEWS relating to Christian Church or social issues. Max. length 500 words.

FEATURES Human interest articles aimed at the 'person-in-the-street'. Max. 500 words.

PAYMENT negotiable.

Waterways World

151 Station Street, Burton on Trent DE14 1BG
☎01283 742950 Fax 01283 742957
✉ admin@wwonline.co.uk
www.waterwaysworld.com
Owner *Waterways World Ltd*
Editor *Richard Fairhurst*
Circulation 16,782

Founded 1972. MONTHLY magazine for inland waterway enthusiasts. Unsolicited mss welcome, provided the writer has a good knowledge of the subject. No fiction.

FEATURES *Richard Fairhurst* Articles (preferably illustrated) are published on all aspects of inland waterways in Britain and abroad but predominantly recreational boating on rivers and canals.

NEWS *Chris Daniels* Max. 500 words.

PAYMENT £70 per published page.

Web User

IPC Media Ltd., The Blue Fin Building, 110 Southwark Street, London SE1 0SU
☎020 3148 5000 Fax 020 3148 8122
✉ letters@webuser.co.uk
www.webuser.co.uk
Owner *IPC Media (A Time Warner Company)*
Editor *Claire Woffenden*
Circulation 34,376

Founded 2001. FORTNIGHTLY bestseller Internet magazine for all users of the Internet. No unsolicited material; send e-mail or letter of enquiry in the first instance.

Wedding

IPC Media Ltd., The Blue Fin Building, 110 Southwark Street, London SE1 0SU
☎020 3148 7800
✉ wedding@ipcmedia.com
Owner *IPC Media (A Time Warner Company)*
Editor *Catherine Westwood*
Circulation 50,000

Founded 1985. BI-MONTHLY offering ideas and inspiration for women planning their wedding. Most features are written in-house or commissioned from known freelancers. Unsolicited mss are not welcome, but approaches may be made in writing.

Weekly News

D.C. Thomson & Co. Ltd., Albert Square, Dundee DD1 9QJ
☎01382 223131 Fax 01382 201390
✉ weeklynews@dcthomson.co.uk
Owner *D.C. Thomson & Co. Ltd*
Editor *David Burness*
Circulation 78,417

Founded 1855. WEEKLY. Newsy, family-orientated magazine designed to appeal to the busy housewife. Regulars include true-life stories told in the first person, showbiz, royals and television. One or two general interest fiction stories each week. Usually commissions, but writers of promise will be taken up. PAYMENT negotiable.

Welsh Country Magazine

Aberbanc, Llandysul SA44 5NP

☎01559 372010 Fax 01559 371995

✉ editor@welshcountry.co.uk

www.welshcountry.co.uk

Owner *Equine Marketing Limited*

Editor *Kath Rhodes*

Circulation 19,195

Founded 2004. BI-MONTHLY. Outside contributions welcome. Contact the editor with samples of work before submitting full article. The magazine contains a couple of pages in Welsh but is predominantly written in English.

FEATURES Pesonal experiences or viewpoints, historical or modern, but there needs to be a strong Welsh connection in some form.

NEWS All Welsh news welcome; anything at all commercial is not paid for.

PAYMENT negotiable.

What Car?

Teddington Studios, Teddington Lock, Broom Road, Teddington TW11 9BE

☎020 8267 5688

✉ editorial@whatcar.com

www.whatcar.com

Owner *Haymarket Motoring Publications Ltd*

Editor *Steve Fowler*

Circulation 111,093

MONTHLY. The car buyer's bible, *What Car?* concentrates on road test comparisons of new cars, news and buying advice on used cars, as well as a strong consumer section. Some scope for freelancers. No unsolicited mss.

PAYMENT negotiable.

What Hi-Fi? Sound & Vision

Teddington Studios, Teddington Lock, Broom Road, Teddington TW11 9BE

☎020 8943 5000 Fax 020 8267 5019

www.whathifi.com

Owner *Haymarket Media Ltd*

Managing Director *Kevin Costello*

Editor *Clare Newsome*

Circulation 67,531

Founded 1976. THIRTEEN ISSUES YEARLY. Features on hi-fi and home cinema. No unsolic-

ited contributions. Prior consultation with the editor essential.

FEATURES General or more specific items on hi-fi and home cinema pertinent to the consumer electronics market.

REVIEWS Specific product reviews. All material is now generated by in-house staff. Freelance writing no longer accepted.

What Investment

Vitesse Media, Octavia House, 50 Banner Street, London EC1Y 8ST

☎020 7250 7026 Fax 020 7250 7011

✉ keiron.root@vitessemedia.co.uk

Owner *Vitesse Media plc*

Editor *Keiron Root*

Circulation 21,800

Founded 1982. MONTHLY. Features articles on a variety of savings and investment matters. E-mail ideas to the editor.

FEATURES Max. 2500 words.

PAYMENT £200 per 1000 words.

What Mortgage

Arnold House, 36–41 Holywell Lane, London EC2A 3SF

☎020 7827 5454 Fax 020 7827 0567

✉ ajarvis@ccplcemail.co.uk

www.whatmortgage.co.uk

Owner *Charterhouse Communications*

Editor *Amanda Jarvis*

Founded 1982. MONTHLY magazine on property purchase and finance. No unsolicited material; prospective contributors may make initial contact with ideas either by telephone or in writing.

FEATURES Particularly welcomes new angles, ideas or specialities relevant to mortgages.

PAYMENT varies.

What Satellite and Digital TV

2 Balcombe Street, London NW1 6NW

☎020 7042 4000

✉ wotsat@futurenet.co.uk

www.wotsat.com

Owner *Future Publishing Ltd*

Editor *Alex Lane*

Circulation 40,000

Founded 1986. MONTHLY including news, technical information, equipment tests, programme background, listings. Contributions welcome – phone first.

FEATURES Unusual installations and users. In-depth guides to popular/cult shows. Technical tutorials.

News Industry and programming. Max. 250 words.

What's New in Building

Ludgate House, 245 Blackfriars Road, London SE1 9UY
☎020 7921 4245 Fax 020 7921 4134
✉ mpennington@cmpi.biz

Owner *CMP Information*
Editor *Mark Pennington*
Circulation 29,000

Monthly. Specialist magazine covering new products for building. Unsolicited mss not generally welcome. The only freelance work available is rewriting press release material. This is offered on a monthly basis of 25–50 items of about 150 words each. Payment £5.25 per item.

Which Caravan

Warners Group Publications plc, The Maltings, West Street, Bourne PE10 9PH
☎01778 391165 Fax 01778 425437
✉ marks@warnersgroup.co.uk

Editor *Mark Sutcliffe*
Founded 1987. Buyers' guide for first-time and experienced caravanners and enthusiasts providing product information, advice and testing. Opportunities for caravanning, relevant touring and travel material, also monthly reviews of the best tow cars, all with good-quality colour photographs.

Wild Times

The RSPB, UK Headquarters, The Lodge, Sandy SG19 2DL
☎01767 680551 Fax 01767 683262
✉ derek.niemann@rspb.org.uk

Owner *Royal Society for the Protection of Birds*
Editor *Derek Niemann*
Founded 1965. Bi-monthly. Bird, wildlife and nature conservation for under-8-year-olds (RSPB Wildlife Explorers members). No unsolicited mss. No 'captive/animal welfare' articles.

Features Unsolicited material rarely used.

News News releases welcome. Approach in writing in the first instance.

Wine & Spirit

William Reed Publishing, Broadfield Park, Crawley RH11 9RT
☎01293 613400 Fax 01293 610317
✉ david.williams@williamreed.co.uk
www.wine-spirit.com

Owner *William Reed Publishing Ltd*
Editor *David Williams*

Circulation 35,000

Monthly. New owner, William Reed, has merged *Wine Magazine* with its sister title *Wine & Spirit International* to create *Wine & Spirit*. Still a consumer/specialist magazine, covering wine, spirit and beer, plus food and food/wine-related travel. No unsolicited mss. Prospective contributors should approach in writing or by e-mail.

Wingbeat

The RSPB, UK Headquarters, The Lodge, Sandy SG19 2DL
☎01767 680551 Fax 01767 683262
✉ derek.niemann@rspb.org.uk

Owner *Royal Society for the Protection of Birds*
Editor *Derek Niemann*
Founded 1965. Bi-monthly. Bird, wildlife and nature conservation for 14–18-year-olds (RSPB Wildlife Explorers members). No unsolicited mss. No 'captive/animal welfare' articles.

Features Unsolicited material rarely used.

News News releases welcome. Approach in writing in the first instance.

The Wisden Cricketer

1.4 Shepherds Building, Charecroft Way, London W14 0EE
☎020 7471 6900 Fax 020 7471 6901
✉ twc@wisdengroup.com
www.thewisdencricketer.com

Owner *BSkyB Publications*
Editor *John Stern*
Deputy Editor *Edward Craig*
Features Editor *Paul Coupar*
Staff Writer *Daniel Brigham*
Circulation 35,000

Founded 2003. Monthly. Result of a merger between *The Cricketer International* (1921) and *Wisden Cricket Monthly* (1979). Very few uncommissioned articles are used, but would-be contributors are not discouraged. Approach in writing. Payment varies.

Woman

IPC Media Ltd., The Blue Fin Building, 110 Southwark Street, London SE1 0SU
☎020 3148 6491
✉ woman@ipcmedia.com
www.ipcmedia.com

Owner *IPC Media (A Time Warner Company)*
Editor *Jackie Hatton*
Deputy Editor *Abigail Blackburn*
Circulation 388,998

Founded 1937. Weekly. Long-running, popular women's magazine which boasts a readership of over 2.5 million. No unsolicited mss. Most work commissioned. Approach with ideas in writing.

FEATURES *Jenny Vereker* Max. 1250 words.

BOOKS *Claire Snewin*

Woman and Home

IPC Media Ltd., The Blue Fin Building, 110 Southwark Street, London SE1 0SU

☎020 3148 7836

✉ w&hmail@ipcmedia.com

www.womanandhome.com

Owner *IPC Media (A Time Warner Company)*

Editor *Sue James*

Circulation 316,034

Founded 1926. MONTHLY. No unsolicited mss. Prospective contributors are advised to write with ideas, including photocopies of other published work or details of magazines to which they have contributed. S.a.e. essential for return of material. All freelance work is specially commissioned.

Woman's Own

IPC Media Ltd., The Blue Fin Building, 110 Southwark Street, London SE1 0SU

☎020 3148 5000 Fax 207 3148 8112

Owner *IPC Media (A Time Warner Company)*

Editor *Karen Livermore*

Acting Features Editor *Sally Windsor*

Circulation 356,811

Founded 1932. WEEKLY. Prospective contributors should contact the features editor *in writing* in the first instance before making a submission. No unsolicited fiction.

Woman's Weekly

IPC Media Ltd., The Blue Fin Building, 110 Southwark Street, London SE1 0SU

☎020 3148 6628

✉ womansweeklypostbag@ipcmedia.com

Owner *IPC Media (A Time Warner Company)*

Editor *Sheena Harvey*

Deputy Editor *Geoffrey Palmer*

Features Editor *Sue Pilkington*

Fiction Editor *Gaynor Davies*

Circulation 387,098

Founded 1911. Mass-market WEEKLY for the mature woman.

FEATURES General features covering anything and everything of interest to women of forty-plus. Can be newsy and/or emotional but should be informative. Could be campaigning, or nostalgic, first or third person. Words: ranging from 800 to 2000. Only experienced journalists.

Synopses and ideas should be submitted by e-mail to susan_archer@ipcmedia.com

FICTION Short stories, 1000–2500 words; serials, 12,000–30,000 words. Guidelines for serials: 'a strong emotional theme with a conflict not resolved until the end'; short stories should have warmth and originality. Short stories up to 5000 words considered for *Woman's Weekly Fiction Specials* (see entry). E-mails to maureen_street@ipcmedia.com

Woman's Weekly Fiction Special

IPC Media Ltd., The Blue Fin Building, 110 Southwark Street, London SE1 0SU

☎020 3148 6600

Owner *IPC Media (A Time Warner Company)*

Editor *Gaynor Davies*

Launched 1998. EIGHT ISSUES A YEAR. Welcomes short stories of between 1000 and 5000 words. Guidelines are available from the Fiction Department. See also *Woman's Weekly*.

Women & Golf

IPC Media Ltd., The Blue Fin Building, 110 Southwark Street, London SE1 0SU

☎020 3148 4530

✉ women&golf@ipcmedia.com

Owner *IPC Media (A Time Warner Company)*

Editor *Ben Evans*

Circulation 24,000

Founded 1991. NINE ISSUES YEARLY. Consumer magazine aimed at amateur lady golfers of all ability levels. Features and photography and news welcome; approach by e-mail or post.

The Woodworker

Magicalia Publishing Ltd., Berwick House, 8–10 Knoll Rise, Orpington BR6 0EL

☎01689 899256

✉ mark.ramuz@magicalia.com

www.getwoodworking.com

Owner *Magicalia Publishing Ltd.*

Editor *Mark Ramuz*

Circulation 45,000

Founded 1901. MONTHLY. Contributions welcome; approach with ideas in writing.

FEATURES Articles on woodworking with good photo support appreciated. Max. 2000 words.

Payment £150+ per 1000 words.

World Fishing

Mercator Media Ltd., The Old Mill, Lower Quay, Fareham PO6 0RA

☎01329 825335 Fax 01329 825330

✉ cwills@mercatormedia.com
Owner *Mercator Media Ltd*
Editor *Carly Wills*
Circulation 3401
Founded 1952. MONTHLY. Unsolicited mss welcome; approach by phone or in writing with an idea.

NEWS/FEATURES of a technical or commercial nature relating to the commercial fishing and fish processing industries worldwide (the magazine is read in over 100 different countries). Max. 1500 words.

PAYMENT by arrangement.

The World of Interiors

Vogue House, Hanover Square, London
W1S 1JU
☎020 7499 9080 Fax 020 7493 4013
✉ interiors@condenast.co.uk
www.worldofinteriors.co.uk

Owner *Condé Nast Publications Ltd*
Editor *Rupert Thomas*
Circulation 65,085

Founded 1981. MONTHLY. Best approach by fax or letter with an idea, preferably with reference snaps or guidebooks.

FEATURES *Rupert Thomas* Most feature material is commissioned. 'Subjects tend to be found by us, but we are delighted to receive suggestions of interiors, archives, little-known museums, collections, etc. unpublished elsewhere, and are keen to find new writers.'

World Soccer

IPC Media Ltd., The Blue Fin Building, 110 Southwark Street, London SE1 0SU
☎020 3148 4817 Fax 020 3148 8130
✉ world_soccer@ipcmedia.com
www.worldsoccer.com

Owner *IPC Media (A Time Warner Company)*
Editor *Gavin Hamilton*
Circulation 51,911

Founded 1960. MONTHLY. Unsolicited material welcome but initial approach by e-mail or in writing. News and features on world soccer.

Writers' Forum incorporating World Wide Writers

PO Box 3229, Bournemouth BH1 1ZS
☎01202 589828 Fax 01202 587757
✉ editorial@writers-forum-com
www.writers-forum.com

Owner *Writers International Ltd*
Editor *Carl Styants*
Assistant Editor *Laura Fennimore*

Founded 1993. MONTHLY. Magazine covers all aspects of the craft of writing. Well written articles welcome. Write to the editor in the first instance.

Writers Forum Short Story Competition Prizes: £300 (1st), £150 (2nd), £100 (3rd) with winning entries published in an anthology. Entrance fee: non-subscribers: £10; subscribers: £7. Winners published in every issue.

Writers' Forum Poetry Competition First prize £100; runners up receive a dictionary. Entrance fee: £5 for one poem or £7 for two. Winners published in every issue. Annual subscription: £33 UK; £46 Worldwide. Send s.a.e. with 66p in stamps for free back issue.

Writers' News/Writing Magazine

Warners Group Publications, Fifth Floor,
31–32 Park Row, Leeds LS1 5JD
☎0113 200 2929 Fax 0113 200 2928
www.writersnews.co.uk

Owner *Warners Group Publications plc*
Publisher *Janet Davison*
Editor, Writers' News *Jonathan Telfer*
Editor, Writing Magazine *Hilary Bowman*

Founded 1989. MONTHLY magazines containing news and advice for writers. *Writers' News* is available exclusively by subscription; *Writing Magazine*, a full-colour glossy publication, is available by subscription or on newsstands. No poetry or general items on 'how to become a writer'. Receive 1000 mss each year. Approach in writing or by e-mail.

NEWS Exclusive news stories of interest to writers. Max. 350 words.

FEATURES How-to articles of interest to professional writers. Max. 1000 words.

Yachting Monthly

IPC Media Ltd., The Blue Fin Building, 110 Southwark Street, London SE1 0SU
☎020 3148 4872 Fax 020 3148 8128
✉ paul_gelder@ipcmedia.com
www.yachtingmonthly.com

Owner *IPC Media (A Time Warner Company)*
Editor *Paul Gelder*
Circulation 35,012

Founded 1906. MONTHLY magazine for yachting and cruising enthusiasts – not racing. Unsolicited mss welcome, but many are received and not used. Prospective contributors should make initial contact in writing.

FEATURES A wide range of features concerned with maritime subjects and cruising under sail; well-researched and innovative material always welcome, especially if accompanied by high resolution digital images. Max. 1800 words. PAYMENT £80–110 per 1000 words.

Yachting World

IPC Media Ltd., The Blue Fin Building, 110 Southwark Street, London SE1 0SU
☎020 3148 4846 Fax 020 3148 8127
✉ yachting_world@ipcmedia.com
www.yachtingworld.com

Owner *IPC Media (A Time Warner Company)*
Editor *Andrew Bray*
Circulation 26,830

Founded 1894. MONTHLY with international coverage of yacht racing, cruising and yachting events. Will consider well researched and written sailing stories. Preliminary approaches should be by phone for news stories and in writing for features.
PAYMENT by arrangement.

Yorkshire Women's Life Magazine

PO Box 113, Leeds LS8 2WX
✉ ywlmagenquiries@btinternet.com
www.yorkshirewomenslife.co.uk

Editor/Owner *Dawn Maria France*
Fashion *Sky Taylor*
Magazine PA *Anna Jenkins*
Diary *Giles Smith*
Circulation 15,000

Founded 2001. THREE ISSUES YEARLY. Features of interest to women along with regional, national, international news and lifestyle articles. Past issues covered health, stress management, living with domestic abuse, pampering breaks for city women, coping with a difficult boss, Windrush awards. 'It is important to study the style of the magazine before submitting material. Send A4 s.a.e. with 46p stamp for copy of submission guidelines. Unsolicited mss and new writers actively encouraged; approach in writing in the first instance with s.a.e.' Magazine available on subscription at the website address.

You & Your Wedding

National Magazine Company, 72 Broadwick Street, London W1F 9EP
☎020 7439 5000 (editorial) Fax 020 7439 2985
www.youandyourwedding.co.uk

Owner *The National Magazine Company Ltd*
Editor *Colette Harris*
Circulation 58,059

Founded 1985. BI-MONTHLY. Anything relating to weddings, setting up home, and honeymoons.

No unsolicited mss. Submit ideas by e-mail only, especially travel features. No phone calls.

You – The Mail on Sunday Magazine

See **The Mail on Sunday** under *National Newspapers*

Young Voices

GV Media Group Ltd, Northern & Shell Tower, 6th Floor, 4 Selsdon Way, London E14 9GL
☎020 7510 0340 Fax 020 7510 0341
✉ yourviews@gvmedia.co.uk
www.young-voices.co.uk

News Editor *Andrew Clunis*

Founded 2003. MONTHLY glossy magazine aimed at 11–19-year-olds. 'Provides a new outlet for today's youth.' Latest news features, showbiz insight and reviews. Also covers current affairs topics that affect readers' lives.

Young Writer

Glebe House, Weobley, Hereford HR4 8SD
☎01544 318901 Fax 01544 318901
✉ editor@youngwriter.org
www.youngwriter.org

Editor *Kate Jones*

Describing itself as 'The Magazine for Children with Something to Say', *Young Writer* is issued three times a year, at the back-to-school times of September, January and April. A forum for young people's writing – fiction and non-fiction, prose and poetry – the magazine is an introduction to independent writing for young writers aged five to 18. PAYMENT from £20 to £100 for freelance commissioned articles (these can be from adult writers).

Your Cat Magazine

Roebuck House, 33 Broad Street, Stamford PE9 1RB
☎01780 766199 Fax 01780 766416
✉ yourcat@bournepublishinggroup.co.uk
www.yourcat.co.uk

Owner *BPG (Stamford) Ltd*
Editor *Sue Parslow*

Founded 1994. MONTHLY magazine giving practical information on the care of cats and kittens, pedigree and non-pedigree, plus a wide range of general interest items on cats. Will consider 'true life' cat stories (max. 900 words) and quality fiction by published novelists. Send synopsis in the first instance. 'No articles written as though by a cat and no poetry.'

Your Dog Magazine

Roebuck House, 33 Broad Street, Stamford
PE9 1RB
☎01780 766199 Fax 01780 766416
✉ s.wright@bournepublishinggroup.co.uk
www.yourdog.co.uk
Owner *BPG (Stamford) Ltd*
Editor *Sarah Wright*
Circulation 29,651

Founded 1995. MONTHLY. Practical advice for pet dog owners. Will consider practical features and some personal experiences (no highly emotive pieces or fiction). Telephone in the first instance.

NEWS Max. 300–400 words.
FEATURES Max. 2500 words; limited opportunities.
PAYMENT negotiable.

Your Horse

Bretton Court, Bretton, Peterborough
PE3 8DZ
☎01733 264666 Fax 01733 465200
www.yourhorse.co.uk
Owner *Emap Active Ltd*
Editor *Nicola Dela-Croix*
Circulation 45,729

'The magazine that aims to make owning and riding horses more rewarding.' Most writing produced in-house but well-targeted articles will always be considered.

Yours Magazine

Emap Esprit, Bretton Court, Bretton,
Peterborough PE3 8DZ
☎01733 264666 Fax 01733 465266
Owner *Emap Esprit*
Editor *Valery McConnell*
Circulation 383,577

Founded 1973. FORTNIGHTLY. Aimed at a readership aged 50 and over. Submission guidelines on request.

FEATURES Unsolicited mss welcome but must enclose s.a.e. Max. 1400 words.
FICTION One or two short stories used in each issue. Max. 1500 words.
PAYMENT negotiable.

Zest

National Magazine House, 72 Broadwick Street, London W1F 9EP
☎020 7439 5000 Fax 020 7312 3750
✉ zest.mail@natmags.co.uk
www.zest.co.uk
Owner *National Magazine Company*
Editor *Alison Pylkkanen*
Deputy Editors *Rebecca Frank, Charlotte Bradshaw*
Circulation 93,176

Founded 1994. MONTHLY. Health, beauty, fitness, nutrition and general well-being. No unsolicited mss. Prefers ideas in synopsis form; approach in writing.

Zoo

Emap Consumer Media, Mappin House, 4 Winsley Street, London W1W 8HF
☎020 7182 8355 Fax 020 7208 3586
www.zooweekly.co.uk
Owner *Emap Consumer Media*
Editor *Anthony Noguera*
Circulation 204,564

Launched 2004. WEEKLY men's lifestyle magazine featuring showbiz, sport, humour, sex, fashion and news. Will consider ideas; see 'Work for Us' page on the website for freelance quidelines.

News Agencies

Associated Press Limited
12 Norwich Street, London EC4A 1BP
☎020 7353 1515
Fax 020 7353 8118 (Newsdesk)

Material is either generated in-house or by regulars. Hires the occasional stringer. No unsolicited mss.

Dow Jones Newswires
10 Fleet Place, London EC4M 7QN
☎020 7842 9900 Fax 020 7842 9361

A real-time financial and business newswire operated by Dow Jones & Co., publishers in the USA of *The Wall Street Journal*. No unsolicited material.

National News Press and Photo Agency
4–5 Academy Buildings, Fanshaw Street, London N1 6LQ
☎020 7684 3000 Fax 020 7684 3030
✉ news@nationalnews.co.uk

All press releases are welcome. Most work is ordered or commissioned. Coverage includes courts, tribunals, conferences, general news, etc. – words and pictures – as well as PR.

The Press Association Ltd
292 Vauxhall Bridge Road, London SW1V 1AE
☎020 7963 7000
Fax 020 7963 7192 (news desk)
✉ copy@pa.press.net
www.pressassociation.co.uk

No unsolicited material. Most items are produced in-house though occasional outsiders may be used. A phone call to discuss specific material may lead somewhere 'but this is rare'.

Reuters
30 South Colonnade, Canary Wharf, London E14 5EP
☎020 7250 1122

No unsolicited material.

Solo Syndication Ltd
17–18 Hayward's Place, London EC1R 0EQ
☎020 7566 0360 Fax 020 7566 0388
✉ wgardiner@solosyndication.com
www.solosyndication.com

Founded 1978. Specialises in worldwide newspaper syndication of photos, features and cartoons. Professional contributors only.

South Yorkshire Sport
6 Sharman Walk, Apperknowle, Sheffield S18 4BJ
☎01246 414767/07970 284848 (mobile)
Fax 01246 414767
✉ Nicksport1@aol.com

Contact *Nick Johnson*

Provides written/broadcast coverage of sport in the South Yorkshire area.

Space Press News and Pictures
Bridge House, Blackden Lane, Goostrey CW4 8PZ
☎01477 533403
✉ Scoop2001@aol.com

Editor *John Williams*
Pictures *Emma Williams*

Founded 1972. Press and picture agency covering Cheshire and the North West, North Midlands, including Knutsford, Macclesfield, Congleton, Crewe and Nantwich, Wilmslow, Alderley Edge, serving national, regional and local press, TV, radio, and digital picture transmission. Copy and pictures produced for in-house publications and PR. Property, countryside and travel writing. A member of the National Association of Press Agencies (NAPA).

Television and Radio

For the latest information on broadcast rates for freelancers access the following websites: the National Union of Journalists' 'The Freelance Fees Guide' database link (www.gn.apc.org/media); the Producers Alliance for Cinema and Television (www.pact.co.uk); the Society of Authors (www.societyofauthors.org); and the Writers' Guild (www.writersguild.org.uk).

BBC Vision, BBC Audio & Music

www.bbc.co.uk

Director-General *Mark Thompson*
Deputy Director-General *Mark Byford*
Reorganisation of the BBC operational structure has resulted in the following groups: BBC Vision Group which runs three main areas: production, commissioning and services and includes the terrestrial and digital television channels; Drama, Entertainment and Children's; Factual and Learning. The Audio & Music Group - responsible for TV Music Entertainment; In-house Factual, Specialist Factual and Drama Audio production. The Journalism Group covers News; Sport; Global News, Nations and Regions.

BBC Television Centre, Wood Lane, London W12 7RJ
☎ 020 8743 8000
Broadcasting House, Portland Place, London W1A 1AA
☎ 020 7580 4468

TV & RADIO COMMISSIONING:
www.bbc.co.uk/commissioning
Director, BBC Vision *Jana Bennett*
Director of Audio & Music Group *Jenny Abramsky*
Controller, BBC One *Peter Fincham*
Controller, BBC Two *Roly Keating*
Controller, Daytime *Jay Hunt*
Controller, BBC Three *Danny Cohen*
Controller, BBC Four *Janice Hadlow*

Controller, Radio 1 *Andy Parfitt*
Radio 1 documentary submission enquiries:
Sam Steele, Executive Producer, Speech & Campaigns
(sam.steele@bbc.co.uk; 020 7765 3827)
Controller, Radio 2 & 6 Music *Lesley Douglas*
Radio 2 commissioning enquiries:
Robert Gallacher, Editor, Planning & Station Sound
(robert.gallacher@bbc.co.uk; 020 7765 4373)
Controller, Radio 3 *Roger Wright*
Radio 3 commissioning enquiries:

David Ireland, Commissions & Schedules Manager
(david.ireland@bbc.co.uk; 020 7765 4943)
Controller, Radio 4 & BBC 7 *Mark Damazer*
Radio 4 proposals must be submitted through an in-house department or a registered independent production company (lists of departments and companies are available at www.bbc.co.uk/commissioning/radio/network/radio4.shtml).
Controller, Radio Five Live & Asian Network *Bob Shennan*
Radio 5 Live commissioning enquiries:
Moz Dee, Commissioning Editor
(moz.dee@bbc.co.uk; 020 8624 8948)

BBC Drama, Comedy and Children's

BBC *writersroom* champions new writers across all BBC platforms for drama, comedy and children's programmes, running targeted schemes and workshops linked directly to production. It accepts and assesses unsolicited scripts for all departments: film, TV drama, radio drama, TV narrative comedy and radio narrative comedy.

The *writersroom* website (www.bbc.co.uk/writersroom) offers a diary of events, opportunities, competitions, interviews with established writers, submission guidelines and free formatting software. BBC *writersroom* also has a Manchester base which focuses on new writing in the north of England. Writers should address hard copies of original, completed scripts to: Development Manager, BBC *writersroom*, Grafton House, 379–381 Euston Road, London NW1 3AU. Before sending in scripts, please log on to the website, or send an A5 s.a.e. to *writersroom* at the Grafton House address above for the latest guidelines on submitting unsolicited work. See also www.bbc.co.uk/commissioning/structure/public.shtml

COMMISSIONERS
Controller, Fiction *Jane Tranter*
Head of Drama Commissioning and Drama

Wales *Julie Gardner*
Acting Controller, Comedy Commissioning *Cheryl Taylor*
Continuing Comedy Commissioning *Lucy Lumsden*

DRAMA
Controller, Drama *John Yorke*
Head of Series and Serials, BBC Drama Production *Kate Harwood*
Creative Director, BBC Drama Productions *Manda Levin*
Director, BBC Drama Productions *Nicolas Brown*
Executive Producer, EastEnders *Diederick Santer*
Head of Films and Single Drama *David Thompson*
Creative Director, New Writing *Kate Rowland*
Head of Radio Drama *Alison Hindell*
Executive Producer (Birmingham) & Editor, The Archers *Vanessa Whitburn*
Executive Producer (World Service Drama) *Marion Nancarrow*
Executive Producer (Manchester Radio Drama) *Sue Roberts*
Editor, Silver Street *James Peries*

COMEDY
Head of Comedy *Jon Plowman*
Head of Radio Entertainment *Paul Schlesinger*

CHILDREN'S
Controller, BBC Children's *Richard Deverell*
Creative Director, CBBC *Anne Gilchrist*
Creative Director, CBeebies *Michael Carrington*
Head of CBBC Drama *Jon East*
Head of CBBC Entertainment *Joe Godwin*
Head of News, Factual & Learning *Reem Nouss*
Head of CBeebies Production, Animation & Acquisitions *Kay Benbow*

BBC News

www.bbc.co.uk/news
news.bbc.co.uk

BBC News is the world's largest news-gathering organisation with over 2500 journalists, 45 bureaux worldwide and 15 networks and services across TV, radio and new media.

Director, News *Helen Boaden*
Deputy Director, News/Controller, News Production *Adrian Van Klaveren*
Head of Television Current Affairs *George Entwistle*
Head of Newsgathering *Francesca Unsworth*
Head of Radio News *Stephen Mitchell*
Deputy Head of Radio News *Mary Hockaday*
Head of Television News *Peter Horrocks*

Deputy Head of Television News *Rachel Attwell*
Controller, BBC News 24 *Kevin Bakhurst*

TELEVISION
Editor, Daytime *Amanda Farnsworth*
Editor, 10 o'clock News *Craig Oliver*
Editor, Newsnight *Peter Barron*
Editor, Breakfast *David Kermode*

RADIO
Editor, Today *Ceri Thomas*
Editor, The World at One/World This Weekend *Colin Hancock*
Editor, PM/Broadcasting House *Peter Rippon*
Head of News, Five Live *Matt Morris*
Editor, The World Tonight *Alistair Burnett*
Editor, World Service News Programmes & Current Affairs *Liliane Landor*

CEEFAX
Room 7540, BBC Television Centre, Wood Lane, London W12 7RJ
☎ 020 8576 1801
Editor, Ceefax *Paul Brannan*

SUBTITLING
Red Bee Media, Broadcast Centre, 201 Wood Lane, London W12 7TP
www.redbeemedia.com

Available via Ceefax page 888.

BBC Sport

www.bbc.co.uk/sport

Director, Sport *Roger Mosey*
Head of Programmes & Planning *Philip Bernie*
Head of Football *Niall Sloane*

Sports news and commentaries across television, online and Radios 1, 4 and 5 Live.

BBC Religion

New Broadcasting House, Oxford Road, Manchester M60 1SJ
☎0161 200 2020 Fax 0161 244 3183

Head of Religion and Ethics *Michael Wakelin*

Regular programmes for television include *Heaven & Earth*; *Songs of Praise*. Radio output includes *Good Morning Sunday*; *Sunday Half Hour*; *Thought for the Day*; *The Daily Service*.

BBC New Talent

www.bbc.co.uk/newtalent

The BBC's search for new talent covers a constantly changing range of outlets that has included radio producers, presenters, young storytellers, filmmakers and comedy writers. Access the website for latest information.

BBC World Service

PO Box 76, Bush House, Strand, London
WC2B 4PH
☎020 7240 3456 Fax 020 7557 1900
www.bbc.co.uk/worldservice

Director, World Service *Nigel Chapman*
Director, English Networks & News, BBCWS
  Phil Harding

The World Service broadcasts in English and 32 other languages. The English service is round-the-clock, with news and current affairs as the main component. With over 160 million listeners, excluding countries where research is not possible, it reaches a bigger audience than its five closest competitors combined. The World Service is increasingly available throughout the world on local FM stations, via satellite and online as well as through short-wave frequencies. Coverage includes world business, politics, people/events/opinions, development issues, the international scene, developments in science and technology, sport, religion, music, the arts. BBC World Service broadcasting is financed by a grant-in-aid voted by Parliament amounting to £246 million for 2007/2008.

BBC writersroom

See **BBC Drama, Comedy and Children's**

BBC Northern Ireland

Broadcasting House, Ormeau Avenue, Belfast
BT2 8HQ
☎028 9033 8000
www.bbc.co.uk/northernireland

Controller *Peter Johnston*
Head of Broadcasting *Ailsa Orr*
Head of Production Planning & Development
  Stephen Beckett
Head of News & Current Affairs *Andrew
  Colman*
Head of Interactive and Learning *Kieran
  Hegarty*
Head of Drama *Patrick Spence*
Head of Entertainment, Events & Sport *Mike
  Edgar*
Head of Radio *Susan Lovell*
Head of Factual TV *Paul McGuigan*
Commissioning Editor Broadcasting *Fergus
  Keeling*
Editor Learning *Jane Cassidy*
Editor New Media *David Sims*
Senior Producer Irish Language *Antaine
  O'Donnaile*
Editor, TV News *Angelina Fusco*
Editor, Radio News *Kathleen Carragher*

Editor, News Gathering *Michael Cairns*
Editor TV Current Affairs *Jeremy Adams*
Editor News Online *Eddie Fleming*
Editor - Foyle *Paul McCauley*

Regular television programmes include *BBC Newsline 6.30* and a wide range of documentary, popular factual and entertainment programmes. Radio stations: BBC Radio Foyle and BBC Radio Ulster (see entries). For further details on television and film scripts contact: *Susan Carson*, Development Co-ordinator Television, BBC Northern Ireland Drama, Room 3.07, Blackstaff House, Great Victoria Street, Belfast, BT2 7BB. (☎ 028 9033 8498; tvdrama.ni@bbc.co.uk) Radio scripts contact: *Anne Simpson*, Manager, Radio Drama at the same address.

BBC Scotland

Broadcasting House, 40 Pacific Quay, Glasgow
G51 1DA
☎0141 422 6000
www.bbc.co.uk/scotland

Controller *Ken MacQuarrie*
Chief Operating Officer *Bruce Malcolm*
Head of Programme and Services *Donalda
  MacKinnon, Maggie Cunningham*
Head of Drama, Television *Anne Mensah*
Head of Drama, Radio *Patrick Rayner*
Head of Factual Programmes *Andrea Miller*
Head of Gaelic *Margaret Mary Murray*
Head of Radio *Jeff Zycinski*
Head of News and Current Affairs *Atholl
  Duncan*
Head of Sport & Commissioning Editor,
  Television *Ewan Angus*
Head of Children's *Simon Parsons*
Head of New Media, Learning & Communities
  Julie Adair

Headquarters of BBC Scotland with centres in Aberdeen, Dundee, Edinburgh, Dumfries, Inverness, Orkney, Shetland and Stornaway. Regular and recent programmes include *Reporting Scotland, Sportscene* and *River City* on television and *Good Morning Scotland* and *Macaulay and Co.* on radio.

Aberdeen
Broadcasting House, Beechgrove Terrace,
Aberdeen AB9 2ZT
☎ 01224 625233

Dundee
Nethergate Centre, 66 Nethergate, Dundee
DD1 4ER
☎ 01382 202481

Edinburgh
The Tun, Holyrood Road, Edinburgh EH8 8JF

☎ 0131 557 5677
Dumfries
Elmbank, Lover's Walk, Dumfries DG1 1NZ
Inverness
7 Culduthel Road, Inverness 1V2 4ADT
☎ 01463 720720
Editor *Ishbel MacLennan*

Orkney
Castle Street, Kirkwall, Orkney KW15 1DF
Shetland
Pitt Lane, Lerwick, Shetland ZE1 0DW
Stornaway
Rosebank, Church Street, Stornoway, Isle of Lewis PA87 2LS
☎ 01851 705000
Radio Nan Gaidheal
Rosebank, Church Street, Stornoway, Isle of Lewis PA87 2LS
☎ 01851 705000

BBC Wales
Broadcasting House, Llandaff CF5 2YQ
☎029 2032 2000 Fax 029 2055 2973
www.bbc.co.uk/wales

Controller *Menna Richards*
Head of Programmes (Welsh Language) *Keith Jones*
Head of Programmes (English Language) *Clare Hudson*
Head of News & Current Affairs *Mark O'Callaghan*
Head of Drama *Julie Gardner*
Commissioning Editor, Independents and BBC2W *Martyn Ingram*
Producer, Pobol y Cwm *Bethan Jones*
Editor, New Media *Iain Tweedale*

Headquarters of BBC Wales, with regional centres in Bangor, Aberystwyth, Carmarthen, Wrexham and Swansea. BBC Wales television produces up to 12 hours of English language programmes a week, 12 hours in Welsh for transmission on **S4C** and an increasing number of hours on network services, including *Doctor Who*, *Tribe* and *Torchwood*. BBC2W, the digital channel, was launched in 2001. Regular programmes include *Wales Today*; *Newyddion* (Welsh-language daily news); *Week In Week Out*, *X-Ray* and *Pobol y Cwm* (Welsh-language soap) on television and *Good Morning Wales*; *Good Evening Wales*; *Post Cyntaf* and *Post Prynhawn* on Radio Wales and Radio Cymru. Ideas for programmes should be submitted either by post to *Martyn Ingram*, Commissioning Editor,

Room 3021 at the address above or by e-mail to commissioning@bbc.co.uk
Bangor
Broadcasting House, Meirion Road, Bangor LL57 2BY
☎ 01248 370880 Fax 01248 351443
Head of Centre *Marian Wyn Jones*

BBC Asian Network
The Mailbox, Birmingham B1 1RF
☎0121 567 6000/0116 201 6772 (newsdesk)
✉ asian.network@bbc.co.uk
www.bbc.co.uk/asiannetwork
Managing Editor *Vijay Sharma*
Commenced broadcasting in November 1996. Broadcasts nationwide. Programmes in English, Bengali, Gujerati, Hindi, Punjabi and Urdu.

BBC Birmingham
The Mailbox, Birmingham B1 1RF
☎0121 567 6767 Fax 0121 567 6875
✉ birmingham@bbc.co.uk
www.bbc.co.uk/birmingham
Head of Regional and Local Programmes *David Holdsworth*
Output Editor *Dave Hart*

BBC Birmingham's Documentaries & Contemporary Factual Department produces a broad range of programming for BBC ONE, BBC TWO and BBC THREE, including *Gardener's World*; *Coast*; *Pay off your mortgage in two years*; *Bunking Off*; *Conflicts*; *Pakistani Actually*; *Mind Your Own Business*; *Desi DNA*; *To Buy or Not to Buy*. Network radio includes: Radio 2: Janice Long, Paul Jones, Alex Lester, Mo Dutta. Radio 4: *The Archers*; *Farming Today*; *Ramblings*; *On the Ropes*. The Asian Network: Adil Ray. Regional & Local Programmes: TV: *Midlands Today*; *Inside Out*; *The Politics Show*; Radio: BBC WM (see entry). BBC Birmingham is the head-quarters for BBC English Regions. There is a television Drama Village at the University of Birmingham.

BBC Birmingham Drama
Archibald House, 1059 Bristol Road, Selly Oak, Birmingham B29 6LT
☎ 0121 567 7350
Programmes produced include *Dalziel and Pascoe*; *Doctors*; *The Afternoon Play* and *Brief Encounters* (which champions new writers).

BBC East Midlands (Nottingham)
East Midlands Broadcasting Centre, London Road, Nottingham NG2 4UU
☎ 0115 955 0500 Fax 0115 902 1983

www.bbc.co.uk/nottingham
Head of Regional Programming *Aziz Rashid*
Output Editor *Sally Bowman*

BBC East (Norwich)
The Forum, Millennium Plain, Norwich
NR2 1AW
☎ 01603 284700 Fax 01603 284399
www.bbc.co.uk/norfolk
Head of Regional Programming *Tim Bishop*
Output Editor *Dave Betts*

BBC Bristol
Broadcasting House, Whiteladies Road, Bristol
BS8 2LR
☎0117 973 2211
bbc.co.uk/bristol
Head of Regional and Local Programmes *Lucio Mesquita*
Managing Editor *Tim Pemberton*
Head of Programmes Leisure and Factual
Entertainment *Tom Archer*
Head of Natural History Unit *Neil Nightingale*
BBC Bristol is the home of the BBC's Natural History Unit, producing programmes such as *Blue Planet; Life of Mammals; British Isles, A Natural History; Abyss* and *Planet Earth* for BBC ONE and BBC TWO. It also produces natural history programmes for Radio 4 and Radio 5 Live. The Factual department produces a wide range of television programmes, including *DIY SOS; Antiques Roadshow; Soul Deep* and *Ray Mears* in addition to radio programmes specialising in history, travel, literature and human interest features for Radio 4.

BBC London
35 Marylebone High Street, London
W1U 4QA
☎020 7224 2424
www.bbc.co.uk/london
Executive Editor *Mike MacFarlane* (Responsible for BBC tri-media: BBC London News, BBC London 94.9FM and the BBC London website)
Planning Editor *Duncan Williamson*

BBC South East (Tunbridge Wells)
The Great Hall, Mount Pleasant Road,
Tunbridge Wells TN1 1QQ
☎01892 670000
www.bbc.co.uk/kent
Head of Regional and Local Programmes *Mike Hapgood* (Responsible for BBC South East [TV], BBC Radio Kent and BBC Southern Counties Radio)

Editor, South East Today *Quentin Smith*
Managing Editor, Southern Counties Radio
Nicci Holiday
Managing Editor, Radio Kent *Paul Leaper*
Editor, Newsgathering *Mark Hayman*
Producer, Inside Out *Linda Bell*

BBC West/BBC South/BBC South West
The three regional television stations, BBC West, BBC South and BBC South West produce the lunchtime and nightly news magazine programmes, as well as *Inside Out*, regular 30-minute local current affairs programmes and regional parliamentary programmes, *The Politics Show*. Each of the regions operates a comprehensive local radio service as well as a range of correspondents specialising in subjects such as health, education, business, home affairs and the environment.

BBC West (Bristol)
Broadcasting House, Whiteladies Road, Bristol
BS8 2LR
☎ 0117 973 2211
Head of Regional and Local Programmes *Lucio Mesquita* (Responsible for the BBC West region. TV: BBC Points West (regional news programme), Inside Out West (regional current affairs series) and The Politics Show West. Local Radio: BBC Radio Bristol, BBC Somerset Sound, BBC Radio Gloucestershire, BBC Radio Wiltshire, BBC Radio Swindon and the regional BBC Where I Live websites)
Daily TV Output Editor *Stephanie Marshall*
TV Features Editor *Roger Farrant*
Political Editor *Dave Harvey*

BBC South (Southampton)
Broadcasting House, Havelock Road,
Southampton SO14 7PU
☎ 023 8022 6201
Head of BBC South *Eve Turner* (Responsible for BBC South TV, BBC Radio Berkshire, BBC Radio Oxford, BBC Radio Solent and online content for the region)
Output Editor, BBC South Today *Lee Desty*
Series Producer, Inside Out *Andrew Head*

BBC South West (Plymouth)
Broadcasting House, Seymour Road,
Mannamead, Plymouth PL3 5BD
☎ 01752 229201
Head of BBC South West *John Lilley* (Responsible for the BBC South West region. TV: BBC Spotlight (regional news

programme), Spotlight Channel Islands (regional news programme), Inside Out (regional current affairs series) and The Politics Show South West. Local Radio: BBC Radio Devon, BBC Radio Cornwall, BBC Radio Guernsey, BBC Radio Jersey and the regional BBC Where I Live websites)

Output Editor *Simon Read*

Series Producer, Inside Out *Simon Willis*

Political Editor *Chris Rogers*

BBC Yorkshire/BBC North West/ BBC North East & Cumbria

The regional centres at Leeds, Manchester and Newcastle make their own programmes on a bi-media approach, each centre having its own head of regional and local programmes.

BBC Yorkshire

Broadcasting Centre, 2 St Peter's Square, Leeds LS9 8AH

☎ 0113 244 1188

Head of Regional and Local Programmes *Helen Thomas*

Editor, News *Tim Smith*

Assistant News Editors, Look North *Denise Wallace*/Acting Editor *Sean Stowell*

Political Editor, North of Westminster *Len Tingle*

Weeklies Editor, Close Up North *Ian Cundall*

Producers, Close Up North *Richard Taylor, Paul Greenan*

BBC North West (Manchester)

New Broadcasting House, Oxford Road, Manchester M60 1SJ

☎ 0161 200 2020

Head of Regional and Local Programmes *Tamsin O'Brien* Editor, Newsgathering *Jim Clarke*

Output Editor *Cerys Griffiths*

Producer, Northwest Tonight *Helen Griffiths*

Producer, Inside Out *Deborah van Bishop*

Producer, The Politics Show *Michelle Mayman*

BBC North East & Cumbria (Newcastle upon Tyne)

Broadcasting Centre, Barrack Road, Newcastle Upon Tyne NE99 2NE

☎ 0191 232 1313

Head of Regional and Local Programmes *Wendy Pilmer*

News Editor *Andy Cooper*

BBC Local Radio

bbc.co.uk/england

There are 40 local BBC radio stations across England transmitting on FM and medium wave. These present local news, information and entertainment to local audiences and reflect the life of the communities they serve. Each has its own newsroom which supplies local bulletins and national news service. Many have specialist producers. A comprehensive list of programmes for each is unavailable and would soon be out of date. For general information on programming visit the BBC website and select the local station you want or contact the relevant station direct.

BBC Radio Berkshire

PO Box 104.4, Reading RG4 8FH

☎0118 946 4200 (news) Fax 0118 946 4555

www.bbc.co.uk/berkshire

Editor *Marianne Bell*

BBC Radio Bristol

PO Box 194, Bristol BS99 7QT

☎0117 974 1111 Fax 0117 923 8323

✉ radio.bristol@bbc.co.uk

www.bbc.co.uk/bristol/local_radio

Managing Editor *Tim Pemberton*

Wide range of feature material used.

BBC Radio Cambridgeshire

104 Hills Road, Cambridge CB2 1LD

☎01223 259696 Fax 01223 460832

✉ cambs@bbc.co.uk

www.bbc.co.uk/radiocambridgeshire

Managing Editor *Jason Horton*

Commenced broadcasting in May 1982.

BBC Radio Cleveland

PO Box 95FM, Broadcasting House, Newport Road, Middlesbrough TS1 5DG

☎01642 225211 Fax 01642 211356

✉ cleveland.studios@bbc.co.uk (programmes) *and* cleveland.news@bbc.co.uk (news)

www.bbc.co.uk/tees/local_radio

Managing Editor *Matthew Barraclough*

Assistant Editor *Ben Thomas*

Material used is local to Teesside, Co. Durham and North Yorkshire. News, current affairs and features about life in the north east.

BBC Radio Cornwall

Phoenix Wharf, Truro TR1 1UA

☎01872 275421 Fax 01872 240679

✉ cornwall@bbc.co.uk

www.bbc.co.uk/radiocornwall

Editor *Pauline Causey*

On air from 1983 serving Cornwall and the Isles of Scilly. Broadcasts 117 hours of local programmes weekly including news, phone-ins and specialist music.

BBC Coventry and Warwickshire

Priory Place, Coventry CV1 5SQ

☎024 7655 1000

✉ coventry@bbc.co.uk *and* warwickshire@bbc.co.uk

www.bbc.co.uk/coventrywarwickshire

Editor *David Clargo*

Commenced broadcasting in January 1990 as CWR. News, current affairs, public service information and community involvement, relevant to its broadcast area.

BBC Radio Cumbria

Annetwell Street, Carlisle CA3 8BB

☎01228 592444 Fax 01228 511195

✉ radio.cumbria@bbc.co.uk

bbc.co.uk/cumbria

Editor *Nigel Dyson*

Occasional opportunities for plays and short stories are advertised on-air.

BBC Radio Cymru

Broadcasting House, Llandaff, Cardiff CF5 2YQ

☎029 20 322018 Fax 029 20 322473

✉ radio.cymru@bbc.co.uk

www.bbc.co.uk/radiocymru

Editor *Siân Gwynedd*

Welsh language station serving Welsh speaking communities. Rich mix of news, music, sport, features, current affairs, drama, comedy, religion and education. Writing opportunities: DRAMA During 2007–08, up to 30 adaptations of Welsh literary classics will be broadcast and over nine further hours of new radio drama each year. COMEDY Occasional series during the year (for details of independent commissions see www. bbc.co.uk/wales/commissioning/).

BBC Radio Derby

PO Box 104.5, Derby DE1 3HL

☎01332 361111 Fax 01332 290794

✉ radio.derby@bbc.co.uk

www.bbc.co.uk/derby

Editor *Simon Cornes*

News, sport, information and entertainment.

BBC Radio Devon

PO Box 1034, Plymouth

☎01752 260323

✉ radio.devon@bbc.co.uk

www.bbc.co.uk/devon

Also at: Walnut Gardens, St David's Hill, Exeter EX4 4DB

☎ 01392 215651 Fax 01392 425570

Managing Editor *Robert Wallace*

Head of News *Sarah Solftley*

On air since 1983.

BBC Essex

PO Box 765, Chelmsford CM2 9XB

☎01245 616000 Fax 01245 492983

✉ essex@bbc.co.uk

www.bbc.co.uk/essex

Managing Editor *Gerald Main*

Programmes are a mix of news, interviews, expert contributors, phone-ins, sport and special interest such as gardening.

BBC Radio Foyle

8 Northland Road, Londonderry BT48 7GD

☎028 7137 8600 Fax 028 7137 8666

www.bbc.co.uk/northernireland

Managing Editor *Paul McCauley*

News Producer *Paul McFadden*

Radio Foyle broadcasts about seven hours of original material a day, seven days a week to the north west of Northern Ireland. Other programmes are transmitted simultaneously with Radio Ulster. The output ranges from news, sport, and current affairs to live music recordings and arts reviews.

BBC Radio Gloucestershire

London Road, Gloucester GL1 1SW

☎01452 308585 Fax 01452 309491

✉ radio.gloucestershire@bbc.co.uk

www.bbc.co.uk/radiogloucestershire

Managing Editor *Mark Hurrell*

Assistant Editor *Mark Jones*

News and information covering the large variety of interests and concerns in Gloucestershire. Leisure, sport and music, plus African Caribbean and Asian interests. Regular book reviews and interviews with local authors in the *Steve Kitchen Show*.

BBC Guernsey

Broadcasting House, Bulwer Avenue, St Sampson's, Guernsey GY2 4LA

☎01481 200600 Fax 01481 200361

✉ radio.guernsey@bbc.co.uk
www.bbc.co.uk/guernsey

Managing Editor *David Martin*

Opened with its sister station, BBC Radio Jersey, in March 1982. Broadcasts 80 hours of local programming a week.

BBC Hereford & Worcester
Hylton Road, Worcester WR2 5WW
☎01905 748485 Fax 01905 748006
✉ bbchw@bbc.co.uk
www.bbc.co.uk/herefordworcester

Also at: 43 Broad Street, Hereford HR4 9HH
☎ 01432 355252 Fax 01432 356446

Managing Editor *James Coghill*

Has an interest in writers/writing with local connections

BBC Radio Humberside
Queen's Court, Queen's Gardens, Hull HU1 3RH
☎01482 323232 Fax 01482 621403
✉ radio.humberside@bbc.co.uk
www.bbc.co.uk/radiohumberside

Managing Editor *Derek McGill*

On air since 1971. BBC Radio Humberside has broadcast short pieces by local writers. Interested in ideas for longer form comedy from local writing talent. Two short story competitions were broadcast in 2007 as part of the BBC RaW 'Read and Write' project.

BBC Radio Jersey
18 & 21 Parade Road, St Helier, Jersey JE2 3PL
☎01534 837200 Fax 01534 732569
✉ radiojersey@bbc.co.uk
www.bbc.co.uk/jersey

Managing Editor *Denzil Dudley*
Assistant Editor *Matthew Price*

Local news, current affairs and community items.

BBC Radio Kent
The Great Hall, Mount Pleasant Road, Tunbridge Wells TN1 1QQ
☎01892 670000 Fax 01892 549118
✉ radio.kent@bbc.co.uk
www.bbc.co.uk/radiokent

Managing Editor *Paul Leaper*

Occasional commissions are made for local interest documentaries and other one-off programmes.

BBC Radio Lancashire
20–26 Darwen Street, Blackburn BB2 2EA
☎01254 262411
✉ lancashire@bbc.co.uk
www.bbc.co.uk/radiolancashire

Editor *John Clayton*

Journalism-based radio station, interested in interviews with local writers. Contact *Alison Brown*, Daily Programmes Producer, Monday to Friday (alison.brown.01@bbc.co.uk).

BBC Radio Leeds
2 St Peters Square, Leeds LS9 8AH
☎0113 244 2131 Fax 0113 224 7316
✉ radioleeds@bbc.co.uk
www.bbc.co.uk/radioleeds

Managing Editor *Phil Roberts*

BBC Radio Leeds is the station for West Yorkshire, serving 1.3 million potential listeners since 1968. Broadcasts a mix of news, sport, talk, music and entertainment, 24 hours a day.

BBC Radio Leicester
9 St Nicholas Place, Leicester LE1 5LB
☎0116 251 6688 Fax 0116 251 1463
✉ radio.leicesternews@bbc.co.uk
www.bbc.co.uk/leicester

Managing Editor *Kate Squire*

The first local station in Britain. Occasional interviews with local authors.

BBC Radio Lincolnshire
Newport, Lincoln LN1 3XY
☎01522 511411 Fax 01522 511058
✉ radio.lincolnshire@bbc.co.uk
www.bbc.co.uk/radiolincolnshire

Managing Editor *Charlie Partridge*

Unsolicited material considered only if locally relevant. Maximum 1000 words: straight narrative preferred, ideally with a topical content.

BBC London
PO Box 94.9, Marylebone High Street, London W1A 6FL
☎020 7743 8000 Fax 020 7208 9661 (news)
✉ ldn-planning@bbc.co.uk
www.bbc.co.uk/london

Managing Editor *David Robey*

Formerly Greater London Radio (GLR), launched in 1988, BBC London 94.9 broadcasts news, information, travel bulletins, sport and music to Greater London and the Home Counties.

BBC Radio Manchester

PO Box 951, Oxford Road, Manchester
M60 1SJ
☎0161 200 2000 Fax 0161 236 5804
✉ radiomanchester@bbc.co.uk
www.bbc.co.uk/radiomanchester

Managing Editor *John Ryan*
News Editor *Mark Elliot*

One of the largest of the BBC local radio stations, broadcasting news, current affairs, phone-ins, help, advice and sport.

BBC Radio Merseyside

PO Box 95.8, Liverpool L69 1ZJ
☎0151 708 5500 Fax 0151 794 0988
✉ radio.merseyside@bbc.co.uk
www.bbc.co.uk/radiomerseyside
www.bbc.co.uk/liverpool

Managing Editor *Mick Ord*

First Friday – a monthly poetry slot between 1.30 pm and 2.00 pm on the first Friday of every month in the Roger Phillips lunchtime programme. Merseyside writers can offer poetry by e-mailing roger.phillips@bbc.co.uk or send copies with name/address attached, to 'First Friday Poetry', c/o BBC Radio Merseyside at the address above. Only the poets used will be acknowledged and contacted.

BBC Radio Newcastle

Broadcasting Centre, Barrack Road, Newcastle upon Tyne NE99 1RN
☎0191 232 4141
✉ radionewcastle.news@bbc.co.uk
www.bbc.co.uk/tyne
www.bbc.co.uk/wear

Managing Editor *Andrew Robson*
Senior Producer (Programmes) *Sarah Miller*

Commenced broadcasting in January 1971. One of the BBC's big city radio stations in England, Radio Newcastle reaches an audience of 233,000.

BBC Radio Norfolk

The Forum, Millennium Plain, Norwich NR2 1BH
☎01603 617411 Fax 01603 284488
✉ radionorfolk@bbc.co.uk
www.bbc.co.uk/radionorfolk

Managing Editor *David Clayton*

Good local ideas and material welcome for features and documentaries *if* directly related to Norfolk.

BBC Radio Northampton

Broadcasting House, Abington Street, Northampton NN1 2BH
☎01604 239100 Fax 01604 230709
✉ northampton@bbc.co.uk
www.bbc.co.uk/northamptonshire

Managing Editor *Laura Moss*

Books of local interest are regularly featured. Authors and poets are interviewed on merit. Poems and short stories are reviewed occasionally, but not broadcast. Runs occasional competitions for local writers.

BBC Radio Nottingham

London Road, Nottingham NG2 4UU
☎0115 955 0500 Fax 0115 902 1983
✉ radio.nottingham@bbc.co.uk
www.bbc.co.uk/radionottingham

Editor *Sophie Stewart*

Rarely broadcasts scripted pieces of any kind but interviews with authors form a regular part of the station's output.

BBC Radio Orkney

Castle Street, Kirkwall KW15 1DF
☎01856 873939 Fax 01856 872908
✉ radio.orkney@bbc.co.uk

Senior Producer *John Fergusson*

Regular programmes include *Around Orkney* (news magazine programme), *Bruck* (swapshop and general features) and *Orky-Ology* (archaeology magazine). As a BBC Community station, all Radio Orkney's programme material is generated from within the Orkney Islands.

BBC Oxford

269 Banbury Road, Oxford OX2 7DW
☎08459 311444 Fax 08459 311555
✉ oxford@bbc.co.uk
www.bbc.co.uk/oxford/local_radio

Executive Editor *Steve Taschini*

Restored to its original name in 2000 having been merged with BBC Radio Berkshire in 1995 to create BBC Thames Valley. The station frequently carries interviews with local authors and offers books as prizes.

BBC Radio Scotland (Dumfries)

Elmbank, Lover's Walk, Dumfries DG1 1NZ
☎01387 268008 Fax 01387 252568
✉ dumfries@bbc.co.uk

Senior Producer *Willie Johnston*

Previously Radio Solway. The station mainly outputs news bulletins (four daily) although it has become more of a production centre with programmes being made for Radio Scotland as well as BBC Radio 2 and 5 Live. Freelancers of a high standard, familiar with Radio Scotland, should contact the producer.

BBC Radio Scotland (Selkirk)
Unit 1, Ettrick Riverside, Dunsdale Road, Selkirk TD7 5EB
☎01750 724 567 Fax 01750 724555
✉ selkird.news@bbc.co.uk
Senior Broadcaster *Cameron Buttle*
Formerly BBC Radio Tweed. Local news bulletins only.

BBC Radio Sheffield
54 Shoreham Street, Sheffield S1 4RS
☎0114 273 1177 Fax 0114 267 5454
✉ radio.sheffield@bbc.co.uk
www.bbc.co.uk/radiosheffield
Managing Editor *Gary Keown*
Programmes Editor *Mike Woodcock*
News Editor *Emma Gilliam*
Writer interviews, writing-related topics and readings on the Rony Robinson show at 11.00 am.

BBC Radio Shetland
Pitt Lane, Lerwick ZE1 0DW
☎01595 694747 Fax 01595 694307
✉ radio.shetland@bbc.co.uk
Senior Producer *Caroline Moyes*
Regular programmes include *Good Evening Shetland.* An occasional books programme highlights the activities of local writers and writers' groups.

BBC Radio Shropshire
2–4 Boscobel Drive, Shrewsbury SY1 3TT
☎01743 248484 Fax 01743 237018
✉ radio.shropshire@bbc.co.uk
bbc.co.uk/shropshire
Managing Editor *Tim Beech*
On air since 1985. Unsolicited literary material rarely used, and then only if locally relevant.

BBC Radio Solent
Broadcasting House, Havelock Road, Southampton SO14 7PW
☎023 8063 2811 Fax 023 8033 9648 (news)
✉ radio.solent.news@bbc.co.uk
www.bbc.co.uk/radiosolent
Managing Editor *Mia Costello*
Broadcasting since 1970.

BBC Somerset Sound
Broadcasting House, Park Street, Taunton TA1 4DA
☎01823 323956 Fax 01823 332539
✉ somerset.sound@bbc.co.uk
www.bbc.co.uk/somerset
Managing Editor *Simon Clifford*
Informal, speech-based programming with strong news and current affairs output and regular local interest features, including local writing. Poetry and short stories on the *Adam Thomas Programme.*

BBC Southern Counties Radio
Broadcasting House, 40–42 Queens Road, Brighton BN1 3XB
☎01483 306306
✉ southerncounties.radio@bbc.co.uk
www.bbc.co.uk/southerncounties
Also at: Broadcasting Centre, Guildford GU2 7AP
Managing Editor *Nicci Holliday*
Regular programmes include the breakfast shows: *Breakfast Live in Surrey with Fred Maden* and *Breakfast Live in Sussex with Neil Pringle.*

BBC Radio Stoke
Cheapside, Hanley, Stoke on Trent ST1 1JJ
☎01782 208080 Fax 01782 289115
✉ radio.stoke@bbc.co.uk
www.bbc.co.uk/radiostoke
Managing Editor *Sue Owen*
On air since 1968, one of the first eight 'experimental' BBC stations. Emphasis on news, current affairs and local topics. Music represents one fifth of total output. Unsolicited material of local interest is welcome – send to *Tim Wedgwood.*

BBC Radio Suffolk
Broadcasting House, St Matthew's Street, Ipswich IP1 3EP
☎01473 250000 Fax 01473 210887
✉ radiosuffolk@bbc.co.uk
www.bbc.co.uk/suffolk
Managing Editor *Peter Cook*
Strongly locally speech-based, dealing with news, current affairs, community issues, the arts, agriculture, commerce, travel, sport and leisure. Programmes sometimes carry interviews with writers.

BBC Radio Swindon
BBC Broadcasting House, Prospect Place, Swindon SN1 3RW

☎01793 513626 Fax 01793 513650
✉ radio.swindon@bbc.co.uk
www.bbc.co.uk/england/radiowiltshire
Managing Editor *Tony Worgan*

Local news and current affairs. Local authors are interviewed on Mark Seaman's *Afternoon Show.*

BBC Three Counties Radio
1 Hastings Street, Luton LU1 5XL
☎01582 637400 Fax 01582 401467
✉ threecounties@bbc.co.uk
www.bbc.co.uk/threecounties
Managing Editor *Angus Moorat*

Encourages freelance contributions from the community across a wide range of radio output, including interview and feature material. Interested in local history topics (five minutes maximum).

BBC Radio Ulster
Broadcasting House, Ormeau Avenue, Belfast BT2 8HQ
☎028 9033 8000
Head of Radio Ulster *Susan Lovell*

Programmes broadcast from 6.30 am to midnight weekdays and from 6.55 am to midnight at weekends. Programmes include: *Good Morning Ulster; The Stephen Nolan Show; Gerry Anderson*; *Talk Back*; *Evening Extra*; *On Your Behalf*; *Your Place and Mine*; *Sunday Sequence* and *Saturday Magazine*. Comedy, documentary and community programming are also included.

BBC Radio Wales
Broadcasting House, Llandaff, Cardiff CF5 2YQ
☎029 2032 2000 Fax 029 2032 2674
✉ radio.wales@bbc.co.uk
www.bbc.co.uk/radiowales
Editor *Sally Collins*
Editor, Radio Wales News *Geoff Williams*

Broadcasts news on the hour and half hour throughout weekday daytime programmes; hourly bulletins in the evenings and at weekends. Programmes include *Good Morning Wales*; *Roy Noble & Nicola Heywood-Thomas*. Access line number: 08700 100110.

BBC Radio Wiltshire
BBC Broadcasting House, Prospect Place, Swindon SN1 3RW
☎01793 513626 Fax 01793 513650
✉ radio.wiltshire@bbc.co.uk
www.bbc.co.uk/england/radiowiltshire

Editor *Tony Worgon*

Sister company of BBC Radio Swindon. Regular programmes include Mark Seaman's *Afternoon Show* (reviews and author interviews).

BBC WM
The Mailbox, Birmingham B1 1RF
☎08453 009956 Fax 0121 567 6025
✉ bbcwm@bbc.co.uk
www.bbc.co.uk/radiowm
Managing Editor *Keith Beech*

Commenced broadcasting in November 1970 as BBC Birmingham and has won four gold Sony awards in recent years. Speech-based station broadcasting to the West Midlands, South Staffordshire and North Worcestershire. Two regular programmes showcase writers, particularly writers from the West Midlands: *The Carl Chinn Show*, Sunday, 1.00 pm - 4.00 pm and *The Jimmy Franks Show*, Monday to Thursday, 10.00 pm - 1.00 am. The producers are, respectively, *Anna Winkles* (anna.winkles@bbc.co.uk) and *Fiona Dye* (fiona.dye@bbc.co.uk).

BBC Radio York
20 Bootham Row, York YO30 7BR
☎01904 641351 Fax 01904 610937
✉ northyorkshire.news@bbc.co.uk
www.bbc.co.uk/northyorkshire
Editor *Sarah Drummond*

Books of local interest are sometimes previewed.

Independent Television

Channel 4
124 Horseferry Road, London SW1P 2TX
☎020 7396 4444 Fax 020 7306 8356
www.channel4.com

Chief Executive *Andy Duncan*
Director of Television *Kevin Lygo*
Head of Channel 4 *Julian Bellamy*
Head of Features *Sue Murphy*
Head of Specialist Factual *Hamish Mykura*
Head of News & Current Affairs *Dorothy Byrne*
Head of Education and Managing Editor,
     Commissioning *Janey Walker*
Director of Acquisitions *Jeff Ford*
Head of More4 *Peter Dale*
Head of E4 *Angela Jain*

COMMISSIONING EDITORS
Head of Drama and Film Four *Tessa Ross*
Commissioning Editor, Comedy and Head of

Comedy Films *Caroline Leddy*
Head of Entertainment *Andrew Newman*
Head of Sport *Andrew Thompson*
Controller of Broadcasting *Rosemary Newell*
Head of Schedules and T4 *Julie Oldroyd*
Commissioning Editor, Daytime *Adam MacDonald*
Head of Documentaries *Angus Macqueen*

Channel 4 started broadcasting as a national channel in November 1982. It enjoys unique status as the world's only major public service broadcaster funded entirely by its own commercial activities. All programmes are commissioned from independent production companies and are broadcast across the whole of the UK except those parts of Wales covered by S4C. Its FilmFour channel, launched in 1998, is a premium pay-TV channel featuring modern independent cinema. A second digital entertainment channel, E4, was launched in January 2001, focusing on young audiences. More4, launched in October 2005, features news, current affairs, documentaries and drama targeted at older audiences.

Channel Television

Television Centre, La Pouquelaye, St Helier, Jersey JE1 3ZD
☎01534 816816 Fax 01534 816817
www.channelonline.tv

Also at: Television House, Bulwer Avenue, St Sampsons, Guernsey GY2 4LA
☎ 01481 241888 Fax 01481 241878

Managing Director *Michael Lucas*
Director of Programmes *Karen Rankine*
Director of Sales *Mike Elsey*
Director of Resources & Transmission *Kevin Banner*

Channel Television is the independent television broadcaster to the Channel Islands, serving 150,000 residents, most of whom live on the main islands, Jersey, Guernsey, Alderney and Sark. The station has a weekly reach of more than 83% with local programmes (in the region of five and a half hours each week) at the heart of the ITV service to the islands.

Five

22 Long Acre, London WC2E 9LY
☎020 7550 5555
www.five.tv
CEO *Jane Lighting*
Managing Director of Content *Lisa Opie*
Controller of Children's Programmes *Nick Wilson*
Senior Programme Controller (News &

Current Affairs) *Chris Shaw*
Commissioning Editor Drama *Abigail Webber*

Channel 5 Broadcasting Ltd won the franchise for Britain's third commercial terrestrial television station in 1995 and came on air at the end of March 1997. Regular programmes include *The Wright Stuff* (weekday morning chat show), *The Trisha Goddard Show* (talk show), *CSI: NY* (drama) and *House* (drama).

GMTV

The London Television Centre, Upper Ground, London SE1 9TT
☎020 7827 7000 Fax 020 7827 7001
✉ talk2us@gm.tv
www.gm.tv

Managing Director *Paul Corley*
Director of Programmes *Peter McHugh*
Managing Editor *John Scammell*
Editor *Martin Frizell*

Winner of the national breakfast television franchise. Jointly owned by ITV plc and Disney. GMTV took over from TV-am on 1 January 1993, with live programming from 6.00 am to 9.25 am. Regular news bulletins, current affairs, topical features, showbiz and lifestyle. Also competitions, travel and weather reports. The week's news and political issues are reviewed on Sundays, followed by children's programming. Launched its digital service, GMTV2, in January 1999, with daily broadcasts from 6.00 am to 9.25 am. Children's programming with some simulcast with GMTV1.

ITN (Independent Television News Ltd)

200 Gray's Inn Road, London WC1X 8XZ
☎020 7833 3000 Fax 020 7430 4868
✉ contact@itn.co.uk
www.itn.co.uk

Chief Executive *Mark Wood*
Editor-in-Chief, ITV News *David Mannion*
Editor, Channel 4 News *Jim Gray*

Provider of the main national and international news for ITV and Channel 4 and radio news for IRN. Programmes on ITV: *Lunchtime News; London Today; Evening News; London Tonight; News at 10.30,* plus regular news summaries and three programmes a day at weekends. Programmes on Channel 4 include the in-depth news analysis programmes *Channel 4 News at Noon* and *Channel 4 News.*

ITV plc

200 Gray's Inn Road, London WC1X 8HF

☎020 7843 8000
www.itvplc.com
www.itv.com

Executive Chairman *Michael Grade*
Chief Operating Officer *John Cresswell*

See listings below for ITV Anglia, ITV Border, ITV Central, ITV Granada, ITV London, ITV Meridian, ITV Tyne Tees, ITV Wales, ITV West, ITV Westcountry and ITV Yorkshire.

ITV Network

ITV1 comprises 15 regional channels with ITV plc holding the English and Welsh regional ITV licences (Anglia, Border, Central, Granada, London, Meridian, Thames Valley, Tyne Tees, Wales, West, Westcountry and Yorkshire) as well as the digital channels, ITV2, ITV3, ITV4, CiTV and ITV Play. The remaining ITV licences belong to: SMG plc (Grampian and Scottish), Ulster Television plc (UTV) and Channel Television. Granada is the production arm of ITV plc.

ITV Anglia Television

Anglia House, Norwich NR1 3JG
☎01603 615151
www.angliatv.com

Managing Director & Controller of New Programmes *Neil Thompson*

Broadcasting to the east of England, Anglia Television is a major producer of programmes for the ITV network. Its network factual department currently boasts the largest portfolio of North American documentary commissions for a UK-based production company.

ITV Border Television

Television Centre, Durranhill, Carlisle CA1 3NT
☎01228 525101 Fax 01228 541384
www.border-tv.com

Managing Director *Douglas Merrall*

Border's region covers three different cultures – English, Scottish and Manx. Programming concentrates on documentaries rather than drama. Most scripts are supplied in-house but occasionally there are commissions. Apart from notes, writers should not submit written work until their ideas have been fully discussed.

ITV Central

Gas Street, Birmingham B1 2JT
☎0121 643 9898/0808 100 7888 (newsdesk)

Managing Director *Ian Squires*

Formed in 2004 by the merger of Carlton and Granada, ITV Central is the largest of the UK

commercial television networks outside of London.

ITV Granada

Quay Street, Manchester M60 9EA
☎0161 832 7211 Fax 0161 827 2180
www.granadatv.com

Director of Production *Claire Poyser*
Controller of Regional Programmes *Duncan Rycroft*
Controller of Drama *Keiron Roberts*
Controller of Factual North *Jeff Anderson*
Controller of Documentaries, History and Science *Bill Jones*

The longest continuous ITC licence holder, broadcasting for over 50 years. Programmes include *Coronation Street* and *Disappearing World*. See also **ITV Productions** under *Film, TV and Radio Producers*.

ITV London

London Television Centre, Upper Ground, London SE1 9LT
☎020 7261 8163
✉ newsdesk@itvlondon.com

Managing Director *Christy Swords*

ITV London, formed in February 2004 by the merger of Carlton and LWT, broadcasts to the Greater London region, extending into the counties on its border.

ITV Meridian

Solent Business Park, Whiteley PO15 7PA
☎0844 881 2000
www.www.itvlocal.com/meridian

Managing Director *Mark Southgate*

Serves viewers across the South and South-East region. Long-running programmes include *Country Ways* and *Monkey Business*.

ITV Thames Valley

Solent Business Park, Whiteley PO15 7PA
☎0844 881 2000

Head of News *Robin Britton*

Formed in December 2004 from the two former ITV sub-regions, Central South and Meridian West, ITV Thames Valley is ITV's newest regional news service. It covers an area stretching from Banbury in the north to Winchester in the south, from Swindon in the west to Bracknell in the east.

ITV Tyne Tees

Television House, The Watermark, Gateshead NE11 9SZ

☎0191 404 8700 Fax 0191 404 8710
www.tynetees.tv
Managing Director/Controller of Programmes
   Graeme Thompson
Head of News & Sport Graham Marples
Executive Producer & Head of Development,
   Granada Factual North Mark Robinson
Regional Affairs Manager Brenda Mitchell
Programming covers politics, news and current
affairs, regional documentaries and sport.
Regular programmes include North East Tonight
with Jonathan Morrell and Philippa Tomson and
Around the House (politics).

ITV Wales

The Television Centre, Culverhouse Cross,
Cardiff CF5 6XJ
☎029 2059 0590 Fax 029 2059 7183
✉ info@itvwales.com
Managing Director Elis Owen
Fomerly HTV Wales. Programmes include the
consumer affairs magazine, The Ferret and current
affairs series, Wales this Week. The company also
makes Welsh language programming for S4C,
including the series voted the most popular with
viewers on the Welsh channel – Cefn Gwlad and
the current affairs series, Y Byd ar Bedwar.

ITV West

Television Centre, Bath Road, Bristol
BS4 3HG
☎0117 972 2722 Fax 0117 972 3122
✉ itvwestnews@itv.com (newsdesk)
Managing Director Mark Haskell
Director of Programmes Jane McCloskey
Formerly HTV. Broadcasts to over two million
viewers in the West of England.

ITV West Country

Langage Science Park, Western Wood Way,
Plymouth PL7 5BQ
☎01752 333333 Fax 01752 333444
Managing Director Mark Haskell
Director of Programmes Jane McCloskey
Broadcasts to Cornwall, Devon, Somerset and
west Dorset. Produces regional news, current
affairs and features programmes.

ITV Yorkshire

The Television Centre, Leeds LS3 1JS
☎0113 243 8283 Fax 0113 244 5107
www.itv.com/yorkshire
Managing Director David Croft
Controller of Drama, Leeds Keith Richardson
Controller of Comedy Drama and Drama

Features David Reynolds
Drama series, comedy drama, single drama, adaptations and long-running series like Emmerdale
and Heartbeat. Always looking for strong writing
in these areas, but prefers to find it through an
agent. Documentary/current affairs material
tends to be supplied by producers; opportunities in these areas are rare but adaptations of
published work as a documentary subject are
considered. In theory, opportunity exists within
series, episode material but the best approach is
through a good agent.

S4C

Parc Ty Glas, Llanishen CF14 5DU
☎029 2074 7444 Fax 029 2075 4444
✉ s4c@s4c.co.uk
www.s4c.co.uk
Chief Executive Iona Jones
Director of Commissioning Programmes Rhian
   Gibson
The Welsh 4th Channel, established by the
Broadcasting Act 1980, is responsible for a
schedule of Welsh and English programmes on
the Fourth Channel in Wales. Known as S4C,
the analogue service is made up of about 34
hours per week of Welsh language programmes
and more than 85 hours of English language
output from Channel 4. S4C digidol broadcasts in Welsh exclusively for 80 hours per week.
Ten hours a week of the Welsh programmes
are provided by the BBC; the remainder are
purchased from ITV1 Wales and independent
producers. Drama, comedy, sport, music and
documentary are all part of S4C's programming.
Commissioning guidelines can be viewed on
www.s4c.co.uk/production

stv

Pacific Quay, Glasgow G51 1PQ
☎0141 300 3000 Fax 0141 300 3030
www.stv.tv

Also at: Television Centre, Craigshaw Business
Park, West Tullos, Aberdeen AB12 3QH
☎ 01224 848848 Fax 01224 848800
Managing Director, Broadcasting, SMG
   Television Bobby Hain
Deputy Managing Director, Broadcasting,
   SMG Television Derrick Thomson
Head of News & Current Affairs (Glasgow)
   Gordon Macmillan
Head of News & Current Affairs (Aberdeen)
   Craig Wilson
Head of Sport Henry Eagles
stv is the ITV (Channel 3) licence holder for

the north and central regions of Scotland. The company produces a range of television programmes, covering current affairs, sport, entertainment, documentary and drama, as well as flagship news programmes *Scotland Today* and *North Tonight*.

Teletext Ltd

Building 10, Chiswick Park, 566 Chiswick High Road, London W4 5TS
☎0870 731 3000 Fax 0870 731 3001
www.teletext.co.uk
Managing Director *Dr Mike Stewart*
Editor-in-Chief *John Sage*

Broadcasts TV text services on analogue TV on ITV, Channel 4 and Five. Also broadcasts digital text services on Freeview and satellite on Channel 4 and, since 2005, on ITV. In addition, Teletext runs a holidays website and mobile services.

UTV

Ormeau Road, Belfast BT7 1EB
☎028 9032 8122 Fax 028 9024 6695
✉ info@u.tv
www.u.tv
Head of Television *Michael Wilson*
Head of News, Current Affairs and Sport *Rob Morrison*

Regular programmes on news and current affairs, sport and entertainment.

Cable and Satellite Television

British Sky Broadcasting Ltd (BSkyB)

6 Centaurs Business Park, Grant Way, Isleworth TW7 5QD
☎020 7705 3000 Fax 020 7705 3030
www.sky.com
Chief Executive *James Murdoch*
Managing Director, Sky Networks *Sophie Turner-Laing*
Chief Operating Officer *Mike Darcey*
Head of Sky News *John Ryley*
Managing Director, Sky Sports *Vic Wakeling*

Launched in 1989, British Sky Broadcasting gives over 21 million viewers (in more than 8.2 million households) access to movies, news, entertainment and sports channels, and interactive services on Sky digital. Launched in October 1998, Sky digital has more than 500 channels and offers a range of innovative interactive serv-

ices. 2006 saw the introduction of high definition television (HDTV). Sky Broadband was launched later that year.

WHOLLY-OWNED SKY CHANNELS
Sky Movies/Sky Cinema
Largest TV movie service outside the US with 10 Sky Movie channels and 2 Sky Movie HD channels. Sky Movies show over 90% of the top 100 grossing box-office films of the previous year including classic films, from Westerns to Film Noir, Chaplin to Chevy Chase, as well as a World Cinema strand that includes UK premières of new and old movies.

Sky News Award-winning 24-hours news service with hourly bulletins and expert comment.

Sky One/Sky Two/Sky Three
One of the most frequently watched non-terrestrial channel.

Sky Sports 1/Sky Sports 2/Sky Sports 3/ Sky Sports News/Sky Sports Extra/Sky Sports HD1 & HD2
Around 40,000 hours of sport are broadcast every year across the five Sky Sports channels. Sky Sports 1, 2 and 3 are devoted to live events, support programmes and in-depth sports coverage seven days a week. Sky Sports News provides sports news and the latest results and information 24 hours a day. Sky Sports Extra carries additional sports programming including the award-winning live interactive coverage.

Sky Travel/Sky Travel Extra Magazine shows, documentaries and teleshopping.

Sky Arts
Wholly-owned Sky channel showcasing the best of the world's arts programmes, 18 hours a day, seven days a week.

JOINT VENTURES
National Geographic; Nickelodeon; Nick Jr; The History Channel; Paramount Comedy Channel; MUTV; Adventure One; The Biography Channel; Attheraces; Chelsea Digital Media.

CNBC Europe

10 Fleet Place, London EC4M 7QS
☎020 7653 9300 Fax 020 7653 5956
www.cnbc.com
Managing Director *Mick Buckley*

A service of NBC Universal. 24-hour business and financial news service. Programmes include *Today's Business*; *Worldwide Exchange*; *Power Lunch Europe*; *European Closing Bell*; *Squawk Box Europe*.

CNN International

Turner House, 16 Great Marlborough Street,
London W1P 1DF
☎020 7693 1000 Fax 020 7693 0892
edition.cnn.com

Managing Editor, CNN International Europe,
Middle East & Africa *Nick Wrenn*

CNN, the leading global 24-hour news network, is available to one billion people worldwide via the 26 CNN branded TV, Internet, radio and mobile services produced by CNN News Group, a Time Warner company. CNN has major production centres in Atlanta, New York, Los Angeles, London, Hong Kong and Mexico City. The London bureau, the largest outside the USA, is CNN's European headquarters and produces over 50 hours of programming per week. Live business and news programmes, including *Business International; World News* and *World Business Today*.

MTV Networks International

180 Oxford Street, London W1D 1DS
☎020 7284 7777 Fax 020 7284 7788
www.mtv.co.uk

Vice Chairman *Bill Roedy*

Established 1987. Europe's 24-hour music and youth entertainment channel, available on cable, via satellite and digitally. Transmitted from London in English across Europe.

Travel Channel

64 Newman Street, London W1T 3EF
☎020 7636 5401 Fax 020 7636 6424
www.travelchannel.co.uk

Launched in February 1994. Broadcasts programmes and information on the world of travel. Destinations reports, lifestyle programmes plus food and drink, sport and leisure pursuits.

National Commercial Radio

Classic FM

30 Leicester Square, London WC2H 7LA
☎020 7343 9000 Fax 020 7766 6100
www.classicfm.com

Station Manager *Darren Henley*

Classic FM, Britain's largest national commercial radio station, started broadcasting in September 1992. Plays accessible classical music 24 hours a day and broadcasts news, weather, travel, business information, political/celebrity/general interest

talks, features and interviews. Winner of the 'Station of the Year' Sony Award in 2000.

Digital One

30 Leicester Square, London WC2H 7LA
☎020 7288 4600 Fax 020 7288 4601
✉ info@digitalone.co.uk
www.ukdigitalradio.com

The UK's only national commercial digital radio multiplex operator. Backed by GCap Media and Arqiva, Digital One began broadcasting on 15 November 1999. Digital One broadcast stations include **Classic FM**, **talkSPORT**, **Virgin Radio** and, digital-only stations, **Oneword**, Planet Rock, Core, theJazz and Capital Life as well as an electronic programme guide and the BT Movio television channels.

Oneword Radio

50 Lisson Street, London NW1 5DF
www.oneword.co.uk

Station Manager *Simon Blackmore*
Head of Programmes *Paul Kent*

The first commercial radio station dedicated solely to the transmission of books, comedy, drama and discussions. Jointly owned by UBC Media and Channel 4, the station broadcasts from 6.00 am to midnight on DAB digital radio and 24 hours a day on Sky, Freeview and ntl cable. Winner of the 'Station of the Year' Sony Radio Awards in 2001 and 2002, the NTL Commercial Radio Award in 2003 and the Clarion Broadcast Radio Award in 2005.

talkSPORT

PO Box 1089, London SE1 8WQ
☎020 7959 7800
✉ pressreleases@talksport.co.uk
www.talksport.net

Programme Director *Bill Ridley*

Commenced broadcasting in February 1995 as Talk Radio UK. Re-launched January 2000 as TalkSport, the UK's first sports radio station. Acquired by Ulster Television in 2005. Broadcasts 24 hours a day. News items can be e-mailed via the website.

Virgin Radio

1 Golden Square, London W1F 9DJ
☎020 7434 1215 Fax 020 7434 1197
www.virginradio.co.uk

Programme Director *Paul Jackson*

Music-based station launched in 1973, bought by Chris Evans' Ginger Media Group in December

1997 and acquired by the Scottish Media Group in March 2000.

Independent Local Radio

Capital Radio London

30 Leicester Square, London WC2H 7LA
☎020 7766 6000 Fax 020 7766 6012
www.capitalradio.com

Programme Director *Scott Muller*

Commenced broadcasting in October 1973 as the country's second commercial radio station (the first being LBC, launched a week earlier). Europe's largest commercial radio station.

Central FM Ltd

201–203 High Street, Falkirk FK1 1DU
☎01324 611164 Fax 01324 611168
✉ email@centralfm.co.uk
www.centralfm.co.uk

Programme Controller *Tom Bell*

Broadcasts music, sport and local news to central Scotland, 24 hours a day.

Clyde 1/Clyde 2

Clydebank Business Park, Clydebank
G81 2RX
☎0141 565 2200 Fax 0141 565 2265
www.clyde1.com
www.clyde2.com

Owner *Emap Radio*
Managing Director *Paul Cooney*

Programmes usually originate in-house or by commission. All documentary material is made in-house. Good local news items always considered. There are two book programmes presented by Alex Dickson each week on Clyde 2 at 10.00 pm – 10.30 pm: *Authors* (Monday) features author interviews and *Paperback Bookcase* (Wednesday) reviews latest titles.

Cool FM

See **Downtown Radio**

Downtown Radio/Cool FM

Newtownards, Co. Down BT23 4ES
☎028 9181 5555 Fax 028 9181 5252
✉ programmes@downtown.co.uk
www.downtown.co.uk

Managing Director *Gary Robinson*

Downtown Radio first ran a highly successful short story competition in 1988, attracting over 400 stories. The competition is now an annual event and writers living within the station's transmission area are asked to submit material during the winter and early spring. The competition is promoted in association with Eason Shops. For further information, write to *Anita Downey* at the station.

Forth One/Forth 2

Forth House, Forth Street, Edinburgh EH1 3LF
☎0131 556 9255 Fax 0131 558 3277
✉ moira.miller@radioforth.com
www.forth.com

Programme Director *Luke McCullough*
Programme Producer, Forth 2 *Moira Millar*
News Editor *Paul Robertson*
Book Reviewer *Lesley Fraser-Taylor*

News stories welcome from freelancers. Music-based programming.

Isle of Wight Radio

Dodnor Park, Newport PO30 5XE
☎01983 822557 Fax 01983 821690
www.iwradio.co.uk

Station Manager *Andy Shier*
Programme Controller *Tom Stroud*

Part of The Local Radio Company, Isle of Wight Radio is the island's only radio station broadcasting local news, music and general entertainment including phone-ins and interview based shows. Music, television, film, popular culture are the main areas of interest.

kmfm

Head Office: Express House, 34–36 North Street, Ashford TN24 8JR
☎01233 895825
www.kmfm.co.uk

Group Programme Controller *Steve Fountain*

A wide range of music programming plus news, views and local interest. Part of the Kent Messenger Group.

LBC Radio Ltd

The Chrysalis Building, Bramley Road, London W10 6SP
☎020 7314 7300
www.lbc.co.uk

Controller *Scott Solder*
Editorial Director *Jonathan Richards*

LBC 97.3 FM is a talk-based station broadcasting 24 hours a day, providing entertainment, interviews, celebrity guests, music, chat shows, local interest, news and sport. LBC News 1152 AM, the sister station of LBC 97.3 FM, provides 24-hour rolling news.

NorthSound Radio

Abbotswell Road, Aberdeen AB12 3AJ
☎01224 337000
www.northsound1.com
www.northsound2.com

Managing Director *Ken Massie*
Programme Controller *Chris Thomson*

Features and music programmes 24 hours a day including, mid-morning (9.00 am – midday), *Northsound 2* feature programme.

Premier Radio

22 Chapter Street, London SW1P 4NP
☎020 7316 1300 Fax 020 7233 6706
✉ premier@premier.org.uk
www.premier.org.uk

Managing Director *Peter Kerridge*

Broadcasts programmes that reflect the beliefs and values of the Christian faith, 24 hours a day on 1305, 1413, 1332 MW, Sky digital 0123, ntl 886, Freeview channel 725 and on the Web.

Radio XL 1296 AM

KMS House, Bradford Street, Birmingham B12 0JD
☎0121 753 5353 Fax 0121 753 3111

Managing Director *Arun Bajaj*

Asian broadcasting for the West Midlands, 24 hours a day. Broadcasts *Love Express* featuring love stories and poems. Writers should send material for the attention of *Sukhjinder Ghataore*.

Sabras Radio

Radio House, 63 Melton Road, Leicester LE4 6PN
☎0116 261 0666 Fax 0116 266 7776
www.sabrasradio.com

Programme Controller *Don Kotak*

Programmes for the Asian community, broadcasting 24 hours a day.

Spectrum Radio

4 Ingate Place, London SW8 3NS
☎020 7627 4433 Fax 020 7627 3409
✉ enquiries@spectrumradio.net
www.spectrumradio.net

Managing Director *Toby Aldrych*
General Manager *Paul Hogan*

Programmes for a broad spectrum of ethnic groups in London.

Spire FM

City Hall Studios, Malthouse Lane, Salisbury SP2 7QQ
☎01722 416644 Fax 01722 416688
www.spirefm.co.uk

Station Director *Karen Bosley*

Music, news current affairs, quizzes and sport. Broadcasts to south Wiltshire and west Hampshire.

Sunrise Radio (Yorkshire)

Sunrise House, 30 Chapel Street, Bradford BD1 5DN
☎01274 735043 Fax 01274 728534
www.sunriseradio.fm

Programme Controller, Chief Executive & Chairman *Usha Parmar*

Programmes for the Asian community in West Yorkshire.

Swansea Sound 1170 MW/ 96.4 FM The Wave

Victoria Road, Gowerton, Swansea SA4 3AB
☎01792 511170 (MW)/ 511964 (FM)
Fax 01792 511171 (MW)/511965 (FM)
www.swanseasound.co.uk

Station Director *Carrie Mosley*
Programme Controller *Steve Barnes*
News Editor *Emma Thomas*

Music-based programming on FM while Swansea Sound is interested in a wide variety of material, though news items must be of local relevance. An explanatory letter, in the first instance, is advisable.

Talk 107

9 South Gyle Crescent, Edinburgh Park, Edinburgh EH12 9EB
☎0131 316 3107
✉ studio@talk107.co.uk
www.talk107.co.uk

Station Director *Peter Gillespie*
News Editor *Gwen Lawrie*

Talk 107 is the first commercial speech radio station to be launched in the UK outside London. Commenced broadcasting in February 2006. Serves Edinburgh, Fife and the Lothians in Scotland. News, sport and debate.

Film, TV and Radio Producers

Aardman

Gas Ferry Road, Bristol BS1 6UN
☎0117 984 8485 Fax 0117 984 8486
www.aardman.com

Development Assistant (Features) *Andrea Redman*
Development Executive (Television) *Dick Hansom*

Founded 1976. Award-winning animation studio producing films, television series, videos, commercials and new media properties. OUTPUT includes: *Creature Comforts; Wallace and Gromit; Angry Kid; Chicken Run; Flushed Away; Shaun The Sheep; Chop Socky Chooks; Purple and Brown*. No unsolicited submissions.

Above The Title

Level 2, 10/11 St Georges Mews, London NW1 8XE
☎020 7916 1984 Fax 020 7722 5706
✉ mail@abovethetitle.com
www.abovethetitle.com

Contacts *Bruce Hyman, Helen Chattwell*

Producer of radio drama, comedy and factual programmes. OUTPUT includes *Clive Anderson's Chat Room* and *Till the End of the Day – The Kinks Story* (Radio 2); *Unreliable Evidence; The Glittering Prizes* and *The Hitchhiker's Guide to the Galaxy* (Radio 4); *The Joy of Sax* and *Features Like Mine* (Radio 3). Unsolicited mss and ideas welcome with s.a.e. See website for details of how to approach in the first instance by e-mail. 'We encourage and support new writing in every way we can.'

Abstract Images

117 Willoughby House, Barbican, London EC2Y 8BL
☎020 7638 5123
✉ productions@abstract-images.co.uk

Contact *Howard Ross*

Television documentary and drama programming. Also theatre productions. OUTPUT includes *Balm in Gilead; Road* and *Bent* (all dramas); *God: For & Against* (documentary); *This Is a Man* (drama/doc). New writers should send synopsis in the first instance.

Acacia Productions Ltd

80 Weston Park, London N8 9TB
☎020 8341 9392
✉ acacia@dial.pipex.com
www.acaciaproductions.co.uk

Contact *J. Edward Milner*

Producer of award-winning television and video documentaries; also news reports, corporates and programmes for educational charities. Undertakes basic video training and has a video manual in preparation. OUTPUT includes documentary series entitled *Last Plant Standing; A Farm in Uganda; Montserrat: Under the Volcano; Spirit of Trees* (8 progs.); *Vietnam: After the Fire; Macroeconomics – the Decision-makers; Greening of Thailand; A Future for Forests*. No unsolicited mss.

Actaeon Films Ltd

50 Gracefield Gardens, London SW16 2ST
☎020 8769 3339 Fax 0870 134 7980
✉ info@actaeonfilms.com
www.actaeonfilms.com

Producer *Daniel Cormack*
Head of Development *Becky Connell*

Founded 2004. Specialises in short and feature length theatrical motion pictures. OUTPUT includes *Amelia and Michael* (short drama starring Anthony Head). In development: *Golden Apples* (feature-length drama); *The Dead Letters* (feature-length psychological thriller); *My Brother's Keeper* (feature-length psychological thriller). Actaeon Films is a member of the **New Producers Alliance, The Script Factory** and the London Filming Partnership. 'We actively encourage new writers and new writing. However, we can only give feedback on scripts with strong potential for developments (all mss are read by a professional reader within four weeks of submission). Scripts returned only if accompanied by s.a.e.'

All Out Productions

50 Copperas Street, Manchester M4 1HS
☎0161 834 9955 Fax 0161 834 6978
✉ mail@allout.co.uk
www.allout.co.uk

Contact *David Cook*

Producer of documentaries, features and current affairs programmes for radio. OUTPUT includes *Five Live Report* (BBC Five Live – weekly news documentary); *Lamacq Live* (BBC Radio One – music and social affairs). Ideas welcome but not mss. Approach by e-mail.

Alomo Productions

See **FremantleMedia Ltd**

Anglo/Fortunato Films Ltd

170 Popes Lane, London W5 4NJ
☎020 8932 7676 Fax 020 8932 7491
✉ anglofortunato@aol.com

Contact *Luciano Celentino*

Film, television and video producer/director of action comedy and psych-thriller drama. No unsolicited mss.

Arlington Productions Limited

Cippenham Court, Cippenham Lane,
Cippenham, Nr Slough SL1 5AU
☎01753 516767 Fax 01753 691785

Television producer. Specialises in popular international drama, with *occasional* forays into other areas. 'We have an enviable reputation for encouraging new writers but only accept unsolicited submissions via agents.'

Art & Training Films Ltd

PO Box 3459, Stratford upon Avon CV37 6ZJ
☎01789 294910
✉ andrew.haynes@atf.org.uk
www.atf.org.uk

Contact *Andrew Haynes*

Producer of documentaries, drama, commecials and corporate films and video. Submissions via agents considered.

The Ashford Entertainment Corporation Ltd

20 The Chase, Coulsdon CR5 2EG
☎020 8660 9609 Fax 087 0116 4142
✉ info@ashford-entertainment.co.uk
www.ashford-entertainment.co.uk

Managing Director *Frazer Ashford*

Founded in 1996 by award-winning film and TV producer Frazer Ashford whose credits include *Great Little Trains* (Mainline Television for Westcountry/Ch4, starring the late Willie Rushton); *Street Life* and *Make Yourself at Home* (both for WTV). Produces theatrical films and television – drama, lifestyle and documentaries. Happy to receive ideas for documentaries

but submit a one-page synopsis only in the first instance, enclosing s.a.e. 'Be patient, allow up to four weeks for a reply. Be precise with the idea; specific details rather than vague thoughts. Attach a back-up sheet with credentials and supporting evidence, i.e., can you ensure that your idea is feasible?'

Beckmann International

Milntown Lodge, Lezayre Road, Ramsey
IM8 2TG
☎01624 816585 Fax 01624 816589
✉ sales@beckmanngroup.co.uk
www.beckmanngroup.co.uk

Contacts *Jo White, Stuart Semark*

Isle of Man-based company. Video and television documentary distributor. OUTPUT *Practical Guide to Europe* (travel series); *Maestro* (12-part series on classical composers); *Above and Beyond – The Story of British Aviation* (a celebration of aviation technology).

Big Heart Media

✉ info@bigheartmedia.com
www.bigheartmedia.com

Contacts *Colin Izod, Beth Newell*

Producer of drama and documetaries for television and video. Ideas/outlines welcome by e-mail, but not unsolicited mss. 'We will respond as soon as we can. We're very keen to enourage new writing.'

Blackwatch Productions Limited

2/1, 104 Marlboro Avenue, Glasgow G11 7LE
☎0141 339 9996
✉ info@blackwatchtv.com
www.blackwatchtv.com

Company Director *Nicola Black*
Production Manager *Anke Hilt*

Film, television, video producer of drama and documentary programmes. OUTPUT includes *The Paranormal Peter Sellers*; *Snorting Coke with the BBC*; *When Freddie Mercury Met Kenny Everett*; *Designer Vaginas*; *Bonebreakers*; *Luv Bytes*; and *Can We Carry On, Girls?* for Ch4. Also coordinates *Mesh*, animation scheme. Does not welcome unsolicited mss.

Bona Broadcasting Limited

Media Suitie 1, 43 Cavalry Park Drive,
Edinburgh EH15 3QG
☎0131 661 7550 Fax 0131 661 7558
✉ enquiries@bonabroadcasting.com
www.bonabroadcasting.com

Contact *Turan Ali*

Producer of award winning-drama and documentary programmes for BBC radio, TV and film projects. No unsolicted mss but send a one-paragraph summary by e-mail in the first instance. 'Writers new to BBC radio should expect to write a whole script on spec to win a commission.' Runs radio and TV drama training courses in the UK and internationally.

Buccaneer Films
5 Rainbow Court, Oxhey WD19 4RP
☎01923 254000

Contact *Michael Gosling*

Corporate video production and still photography specialists in education and sport. No unsolicited mss.

Calon Limited
3 Mount Stuart Square, Butetown, Cardiff CF10 5EE
☎029 2048 8400 Fax 029 2048 5962
✉ enquiries@calon.tv

Contact *Andrew Offiler*

Animated series, mainly for children. OUTPUT includes *Meeow*; *Hilltop Hospital*; *The Hurricanes*; *Tales of the Toothfairies*; *Billy the Cat*; *The Blobs*, as well as the feature films, *Under Milk Wood* and *The Princess and the Goblin*. Write with ideas and sample script in the first instance.

Carnival (Films & Theatre) Ltd
47 Marylebone Lane, London W1U 2NT
☎020 7317 1370 Fax 020 7317 1380
✉ info@carnival-films.co.uk
www.carnival-films.co.uk

Managing Director *Gareth Neame*
Head of Development *Clova McCallum*

Film, TV and theatre producer. OUTPUT FILM: *The Mill on the Floss* (BBC); *Firelight* (Hollywood Pictures/Wind Dancer Productions); *Up on the Roof* (Rank/Granada); *Shadowlands* (Savoy/Spelling); *The Infiltrator* (Home Box Office); *Under Suspicion* (Columbia/Rank/LWT). TELEVISION: *Rosemary & Thyme* (ITV/Granada); *The Grid* (BBC/TNT); *As If* (Ch4/Columbia); *Lucy Sullivan is Getting Married* (ITV); *The Tenth Kingdom* (Sky/NBC); *Agatha Christie's Poirot* (ITV/LWT/A&E); *Every Woman Knows a Secret* and *Oktober* (both for ITV Network Centre); *Hotel Babylon*; *Blott on the Landscape*; *Crime Traveller* and *Bugs 1–4* (all for BBC); *Anna Lee* and *All Or Nothing At All* (LWT); *Head Over Heels* (Carlton); *Jeeves & Wooster* I–IV (Granada); *The Fragile Heart*; *Traffik* and *Porterhouse Blue* (all for Ch4). THEATRE: *What a Performance*; *Juno &*

the Paycock; *Murder is Easy*; *Misery*; *Ghost Train*; *Map of the Heart*; *Shadowlands*; *Up on the Roof*. No unsolicited mss

Cartwn Cymru
32 Wordsworth Avenue, Roath, Cardiff CF24 3FR
☎029 2046 3556/07771 640400
✉ production@cartwn-cymru.com

Producer *Naomi Jones*

Animation production company. OUTPUT *Toucan 'Tecs* (YTV/S4C); *Funnybones* and *Turandot: Operavox* (both for S4C/BBC); *Testament: The Bible in Animation* (BBC2/S4C); *The Miracle Maker* (S4C/BBC/British Screen/Icon Entertainment International); *Faeries* (HIT Entertainment plc for CITV); *Otherworld* (animated feature film for S4C Films, British Screen, Arts Council of Wales).

Celador Films
39 Long Acre, London WC2E 9LG
☎020 7845 6988 Fax 020 7845 6977
✉ ljames@celador.co.uk
www.celador.co.uk

Story Editor *Diarmud McKeown*

Producer of feature films. OUTPUT includes *Dirty Pretty Things*, Julian Fellowes–helmed romantic drama, *Separate Lives* and Neil Marshall's second feature, *The Descent*. No unsolicited mss.

Celador Productions
39 Long Acre, London WC2E 9LG
☎020 7240 8101 Fax 020 7845 6979
✉ tvhits@celador.co.uk
www.celadorproductions.com

Director of Production *Heather Hampson*
Head of Factual *Murray Boland*
Head of Radio *Liz Anstee*

Producer of TV and radio comedies and light entertainment. OUTPUT *You Are What You Eat*; *Perfect Strangers*; *Popcorn*; *It's Been a Bad Week*; *Commercial Breakdown*; *How to Dump Your Mates* and *Three Off the Tee*. 'We are interested in radio scripts but do not accept unsolicited proposals for comedy or entertainment formats. As a relatively small company our script-reading resources are limited.'

Celtic Films Entertainment Ltd
Lodge House, 69 Beaufort Street, London SW3 5AH
☎020 7351 0908 Fax 020 7351 4139
✉ info@celticfilms.co.uk
www.celticfilms.co.uk

Contact *Steven Russell*

Film and television drama producer. OUTPUT includes 15 feature-length *Sharpe* TV films for Carlton and *A Life for a Life – The True Story of Stefan Kiszko* TV film for ITV. Devised *Hornblower* series for ITV. No unsolicited submissions.

Chameleon Television Ltd
Great Minster House, Lister Hill, Horsforth, Leeds LS18 5DL
☎0113 205 0040 Fax 0113 281 9454
✉ allen@chameleontv.com

Contacts *Allen Jewhurst, Julia Kirby-Smith*

Film and television drama and documentary producer. OUTPUT includes *Edge of the City*; 'Dispatches' – *Channel 4 News*; *The Family Who Vanished*; *Killing for Honour*; *College Girls*; *Ken Dodd in the Dock* (all for Ch4); *Diary of a Mother on the Edge*; *Divorces From Hell*; *Shipman*; *Love to Shop*; *The Marchioness* (all for ITV); *Ted & Sylvia – Love, Loss*; *Hamas Bombers* (BBC); *Liverpool Poets* (Ch5). Scripts not welcome unless via agents but new writing is encouraged.

Channel Television Ltd
Television Centre, St Helier, Jersey JE1 3ZD
☎01534 816873 Fax 01534 816889
✉ david@channeltv.co.uk
www.channeltvco.uk

Senior Producer *David Evans*

Producer of TV commercials and corporate material: information, promotional, sales, training and events coverage. CD and DVD production; promotional videos for all types of businesses throughout Europe. No unsolicited mss; new writing/scripts commissioned as required. Interested in hearing from local writers resident in the Channel Islands.

The Children's Film & Television Foundation Ltd
✉ annahome@cftf.org

Chief Executive *Anna Home*

Involved in the development and co-production of films for children and the family, both for the theatric market and for TV.

Cinema Verity Productions Ltd
11 Addison Avenue, London W11 4QS
☎020 7460 2777 Fax 020 7371 3329

Contact *Verity Lambert*

Leading television drama producer whose credits include *She's Out* by Lynda la Plante; *Class Act* by Michael Aitkens; *May to December* (BBC series); *Running Late* by Simon Gray (Screen 1);

The Cazalets adapt. of *The Cazalet Chronicle* by Elizabeth Jane Howard (BBC).

Cleveland Productions
5 Rainbow Court, Oxhey, Near Watford WD19 4RP
☎01923 254000

Contact *Michael Gosling*

Communications in sound and vision A/V production and still photography specialists in education and sport. No unsolicited mss.

COI
Hercules Road, London SE1 7DU
☎020 7928 2345

Government advertising and marketing communications, and public information films.

Collingwood O'Hare Entertainment Ltd
10–14 Crown Street, London W3 8SB
☎020 8993 3666 Fax 020 8993 9595
✉ info@crownstreet.co.uk
www.collingwoodohare.com

Producer *Christopher O'Hare*
Head of Development *Helen Stroud*

Film and TV; specialises in children's animation. OUTPUT *The Secret Show* (BBC/BBC Worldwide); *RARG* (award-winning animated film); *Yoko! Jakamoko! Toto!* (CITV); *Daisy-Head Mayzie* (Dr Seuss animated series for Turner Network and Hanna-Barbera); *Gordon the Garden Gnome* (CBBC); *Eddy and the Bear* and *The King's Beard* (both for CITV). Unsolicited mss not welcome 'as a general rule as we do not have the capacity to process the sheer weight of submissions this creates. We therefore tend to review material from individuals recommended to us through personal contact with agents or other industry professionals. We like to encourage new writing and have worked with new writers but our ability to do so is limited by our capacity for development. We can usually only consider taking on one project each year, as development/finance takes several years to put in place.'

The Comedy Unit
Glasgow TV & Film Studios, Glasgow Media Park, Craigmont Street, Glasgow G20 9BT
☎0141 305 6666 Fax 0141 305 6600
✉ scripts@comedyunit.co.uk
www.comedyunit.co.uk

Managing Directors *April Chamberlain, Colin Gilbert*

Producers of comedy entertainment for children's TV, radio, video and film. OUTPUT *Still Game; Karen Dunbar Show; Offside; Chewin' the Fat; Only An Excuse; Yo! Diary* and *Watson's Wind Up.* Unsolicited mss welcome by post or e-mail.

Cosgrove Hall Films
8 Albany Road, Chorlton–cum–Hardy
M21 0AW
☎0161 882 2500 Fax 0161 882 2555
✉ animation@cosgrovehall.com

Contact *Lee Marriott*

Children's animation producer; film video and television. OUTPUT includes *Noddy* and *Rotten Ralph* (both for BBC); *Lavender Castle* by Gerry Anderson; *The Fox Busters; Animal Shelf; Rocky & the Dodos;* Alison Uttley's *Little Grey Rabbit* (all for children's ITV); Terry Pratchett's *Discworld* (Ch4). Submissions accepted only via an agent.

The Creative Partnership
13 Bateman Street, London W1D 3AF
☎020 7439 7762
✉ sally.chapman@thecreativepartnership.co.uk
www.thecreativepartnership.co.uk

Contacts *Christopher Fowler, Sally Chapman*

'Europe's largest "one-stop shop" for advertising and marketing campaigns for the film and television industries.' Clients include most major and independent film companies. No scripts. 'We train new writers in-house, and find them from submitted c.v.s. All applicants must have previous commercial writing experience.'

Cricket Ltd
Medius House, 63–69 New Oxford Street,
London WC1A 1EA
☎020 7845 0300 Fax 020 7845 0303
✉ team@cricket-ltd.com
www.cricket-ltd.com

Head of Recruitment *Mary McDonnell*

Film and video, live events and conferences, print and design. 'Communications solutions for business clients wishing to influence targeted external and internal audiences.'

CSA Word
6A Archway Mews, 241A Putney Bridge Road,
London SW15 2PE
☎020 8871 0220 Fax 020 8877 0712
✉ victoria@csaword.co.uk
www.csaword.co.uk

Contacts *Victoria Williams, Clive Stanhope*

Producer of drama, documentaries and readings for radio. OUTPUT *Alfie Elkins & His Little Life*

(drama for BBC World Service); *The Hungry Years* (reading for BBC R4); *A Stable Relationship* (feature for BBC R4); *Bob Dylan's Chronicles 1* (reading for BBC R2); *It's a Girl; Chat Snaps & Videotape – Two* (documentaries for BBC World Service Learning); *The Glenn Miller Story, Berlin…Soundz Decadent* and *Original Soundtrack Recordings* (documentaries for BBC R2), Unsolicited drama ideas welcome by post or e-mail. 'We encourage new drama, and documentary/feature ideas.'

Cutting Edge Productions Ltd
27 Erpingham Road, London SW15 1BE
☎020 8780 1476 Fax 020 8780 0102
✉ juliannorridge@btconnect.com

Contact *Julian Norridge*

Corporate and documentary video and television. OUTPUT includes US series on evangelicalism, 'Dispatches' on US tobacco and government videos. No unsolicited mss; 'we commission all our writing to order, but are open to ideas.'

Diverse Production Limited
6 Gorleston Street, London W14 8XS
☎020 7603 4567 Fax 020 7603 2148
www.diverse.tv

Independent production company specialising in popular prime-time formats, strong documentaries, specialist factual, historical, cultural, religious, arts, music and factual entertainment. Recent OUTPUT includes *Ballet Changed My Life: Ballet Hoo!; Mission Africa; Codex; Bear Grylls' Man vs. Wild; Tribal Wife; Musicality; Operatunity; Who Wrote the Bible; Who You Callin' Nigger?; In Search of Tony Blair; Britain AD; Shock Treatment; Beyond Boundaries; Escape to the Legion.*

DMS Films Ltd
89 Sevington Road, London NW4 3RU
☎020 8203 5540 Fax 0870 762 5871
✉ danny@dmsfilms.co.uk
www.dmsfilms.co.uk

Producer *Daniel San*

Film producer. OUTPUT includes *Understanding Jane; Hard Edge; Popcorn.* Unsolicited screenplays not welcome: phone, fax or e-mail synopsis or outline in first instance.

Double Exposure
See **Flashback Television Limited**

DoubleBand Films
3 Crescent Gardens, Belfast BT7 1NS
☎028 9024 3331 Fax 028 9023 6980

✉ info@doublebandfilms.com
www.doublebandfilms.com

Contacts *Michael Hewitt, Dermot Lavery*

Specialises in documentaries and some drama. Recent productions include *Seven Days that Shook the World* and *War in Mind* (both for Ch4); *Christine's Children* (BBC Northern Ireland; nominated for both the RTS and Celtic Film Festival); *D-Day: Triumph and Tragedy* (BBC NI). No unsolicited scripts.

Drake A-V Video Ltd

89 St Fagans Road, Fairwater, Cardiff CF5 3AE
☎029 2056 0333 Fax 029 2055 4909
www.drakeav.com

Contact *Ian Lewis*

Corporate A-V film and video, mostly promotional, training or educational. Scripts in these fields welcome. Design and installation of AV systems.

Charles Dunstan Communications Ltd

42 Wolseley Gardens, London W4 3LS
☎020 8994 2328 Fax 020 8994 2328

Contact *Charles Dunstan*

Producer of film, video and TV for documentary and corporate material. OUTPUT *Renewable Energy* for broadcast worldwide in 'Inside Britain' series; *The Far Reaches* travel series; *The Electric Environment*. No unsolicited scripts.

Electric Airwaves Ltd (Ladbroke Radio)

Essel House, 29 Foley Street, London
W1W 7JW
☎020 7323 2770 Fax 020 7079 2080
✉ neil@electricairwaves.com
www.electricairwaves.com

Contacts *Neil Gardner, Richard Bannerman*

Producer of radio drama, documentary, corporate, music, music documentaries and readings. OUTPUT includes *The Woman in White*; *The Darling Buds of May*; *The True History of British Pop*; *The World on a String*; *The Colour of Music* (all for BBC Radio 2); *Don Carlos*; *In the Company of Men* (BBC Radio 3 drama); *Sitting in Limbo* (BBC World Service drama); *Your Vote Counts* (Electoral Commision audio CDs). Unsolicited mss and ideas welcome; send letter in the first instance. 'We are willing to help develop for possible submission to the BBC.'

Farnham Film Company Ltd

34 Burnt Hill Road, Lower Bourne, Farnham
GU10 3LZ
☎01252 710313 Fax 01252 725855
www.farnfilm.com

Contact *Ian Lewis*

Television and film: intelligent full-length film and children's drama. Unsolicited mss usually welcome but prefers a letter or e-mail to be sent in the first instance. Check website for current requirements.

Fast Films

Christmas House, 213 Chester Road, Castle Bromwich, Solihull B36 0ET
☎0121 749 7147/4144
✉ gavinprime@mac.com

Contact *Gavin Prime*

Film and television: comedy, entertainment and animation. No unsolicited mss.

Festival Film and Television Ltd

Festival House, Tranquil Passage, Blackheath, London SE3 0BJ
☎020 8297 9999 Fax 020 8297 1155
✉ info@festivalfilm.com
www.festivalfilm.com

Managing Director *Ray Marshall*
Producer *Matt Marshall*

Television drama and feature films. Best known for its Catherine Cookson Dramas, which became one of ITV's long-running brands. Now developing both TV drama and features. Generally accept material submitted through an agent. However, will consider unsolicited material but prefers a treatment or synopsis in the first instance.

Fiction Factory

14 Greenwich Church Street, London
SE10 9BJ
☎020 8853 5100 Fax 020 8293 3001
✉ radio@fictionfactory.co.uk
www.fictionfactory.co.uk

Creative Director *John Taylor*

Production company specialising in intelligent entertainments. Recent OUTPUT for BBC Radio includes Marcel Proust's *A La Recherche du Temps Perdu*; *Scam* John Arden; *The Coup* Annie Caulfield. Ideas considered if sent by e-mail. Mss only from agents or writers with a professional track record in the broadcast media.

Film and General Productions Ltd

4 Bradbrook House, Studio Place, London
SW1X 8EL
☎020 7235 4495 Fax 020 7245 9853
✉ cparsons@filmgen.co.uk

Contacts *Clive Parsons, Davina Belling*

Film and television drama. Feature films include *True Blue*; *Tea with Mussolini* and *I Am David*. Also *Seesaw* (ITV drama), *The Greatest Store in the World* (family drama, BBC) and *The Queen's Nose* (children's series, BBC). Interested in considering new writing but subject to prior telephone conversation.

Firehouse Productions

42 Glasshouse Street, London W1B 5DW
☎020 7439 2220
✉ postie@firehouse.biz
www.firehouse.biz

Contacts *Peter Granger, Mike McLeod*

Corporate films and websites, commercials, DRTV and live production events. OUTPUT includes work for De Beers; Prudential; government and various agencies.

The First Film Company Ltd

3 Bourlet Close, London W1W 7BQ
☎020 7436 9490 Fax 020 7637 1290
✉ info@firstfilmcompany.com

Producers *Roger Randall-Cutler, Robert Cheek*

Founded 1984. Cinema screenplays. All submissions should be made through an agent.

First Writes Theatre Company

Lime Kiln Cottage, High Starlings, Banham,
Norwich NR16 2BS
☎01953 888525 Fax 01953 888974
✉ ellen@firstwrites.fsnet.co.uk
www.first-writes.co.uk

Contact *Ellen Dryden*

Producer of numerous afternoon, Friday and Saturday plays, classic serials and comedy narrative series for BBC Radio 3, 4 and World Service. Welcomes unsolictied mss or ideas by post. 'As an independent company it is difficult to obtain commissions for new writers and in-house should be your first port of call. However, we are committed to producing new work by established writers.'

Flannel

21 Berwick Street, London W1F 0PZ
☎020 7287 9277 Fax 020 7287 7785
✉ mail@flannel.net

Contact *Kate Haldane*

Producer of drama, documentaries and comedy for television and radio. OUTPUT includes *Woman's Hour* (BBC R4); *The Hendersons' Christmas Party* (five-part Christmas drama, BBC R4). No unsolicited mss. 'Keen to encourage new writing, but must come via an agent. Particularly interested in 45–50 minute dramas for radio. Not in a position to produce plays for stage, but very happy to consider adaptations. Welcomes comedy with some track record.'

Flashback Television Limited

11 Bowling Green Lane, London EC1R 0BG
☎020 7490 8996 Fax 020 7490 5610
✉ mailbox@flashbacktv.co.uk
www.flashbacktelevision.com

Contact *Tim Ball*

Producer of documentaries and factual entertainment since 1982. Based in London and Bristol. Acquired education producer Double Exposure in 2004. Recent credits include *Married to the Prime Minister* and *The Hiroshima Pictures* (both for Ch4); *Discovery Superhomes* and *Top Tens* (both for Discovery).

Focus Films Ltd

The Rotunda Studios, Rear of 116–118
Finchley Road, London NW3 5HT
☎020 7435 9004 Fax 020 7431 3562
✉ focus@focusfilms.co.uk
www.focusfilms.co.uk

Managing Director *David Pupkewitz*
Head of Development *Malcolm Kohll*
Contact *Raimund Berens*

Film producer. OUTPUT *The Book of Eve* (Canadian drama); *The Bone Snatcher* (Horror, UK/Can/SA); *Julia's Ghost* (German co-production); *The 51st State* (feature film); *Secret Society* (comedy drama feature film); *Crimetime* (feature thriller); *Diary of a Sane Man*; *Othello*. Projects in development include *Heaven and Earth*; *Tainted Desert*; *The Complete History of the Breast*; *Triomf*. No unsolicited scripts.

Mark Forstater Productions Ltd

11 Keslake Road, London NW6 6DJ
☎020 8933 4375 Fax 020 8933 4375

Contact *Mark Forstater*

Active in the selection, development and production of material for film and TV. OUTPUT *Monty Python and the Holy Grail*; *The Odd Job*; *The Grass is Singing*; *Xtro*; *Forbidden*; *Separation*; *The Fantasist*; *Shalom Joan Collins*; *The Silent Touch*; *Grushko*; *The Wolves of Willoughby Chase*;

Between the Devil and the Deep Blue Sea; *Doing Rude Things*. No unsolicited scripts.

FremantleMedia Ltd

1 Stephen Street, London W1T 1AL
☎020 7691 6000 Fax 020 7691 6100
www.fremantlemedia.com

CEO *Tony Cohen*
CEO, talkbackTHAMES *Lorraine Heggessey*

FremantleMedia, formerly known as Pearson Television, is the production arm of the RTL Group, Europe's largest TV and radio company. Acquired Thames Television in 1993 (producer of *The Bill*) and Grundy Worldwide (*Neighbours*) in 1995. Further acquisitions were Witzend Productions (*Lovejoy*) and Alomo Productions in 1996 and TalkBack Productions in 2000. FremantleMedia produces more than 260 programmes in over 40 countries and territories a year. *No unsolicited submissions, please.*

Gaia Communications

Sanctuary House, 35 Harding Avenue,
Eastbourne BN22 8PL
☎01323 734809/727183 Fax 01323 734809
✉ production@gaiacommunications.co.uk
www.gaiacommunications.co.uk

Producer *Robert Armstrong*
Script Editor *Loni Webb*

Established 1987. Video and TV corporate and documentary. OUTPUT *Discovering* (south east regional tourist and local knowledge series); *Holistic* (therapies and general information); local interest audiobooks.

Noel Gay Television

Shepperton Studios, Studios Road, Shepperton TW17 0QD
☎01932 592569 Fax 01932 592172
✉ charles.armitage@virgin.net

CEO *Charles Armitage*

OUTPUT *The Fear* (BBC Choice); *Second Chance* and *I-Camcorder* (both for Ch4); *Hububb* Series 1–5 (BBC); *Frank Stubbs Promotes* and *10%ers* Series 2 (both for Carlton/ITV); *Call Up the Stars* (BBC1); *Smeg Outs* (BBC video); *Red Dwarf*; *Dave Allen* (ITV); *Windrush* (BBC2). Joint ventures and companies include a partnership with Odyssey, a leading Indian commercials, film and TV producer, and the Noel Gay Motion Picture Company, whose credits include *Virtual Sexuality*; *Trainspotting* (with Ch4 and Figment Films); *Killer Tongue*; *Dog Soldiers*; *Fast Sofa* and *Pasty Faces*. Associate NGTV companies are Grant Naylor Productions and Pepper

Productions. NGTV is willing to accept unsolicited material from writers but 1–2-page treatments only. No scripts, please.

Ginger Productions

See **SMG Productions & Ginger Productions**

Goldcrest Films International Ltd

65–66 Dean Street, London W1D 4PL
☎020 7437 8696 Fax 020 7437 4448
✉ info@goldcrestfilms.com
www.goldcrestfilms.com

Chairman *John Quested*
Contact *Wayne Godfrey*

Since it was established in 1977, Goldcrest Films has become a leading independent film production company winning many prizes at international festivals including 19 Academy Awards and 28 Baftas. Finances, produces and distributes films and television programmes. OUTPUT includes *Chariots of Fire*; *Gandhi*; *The Killing Fields*; *A Room With a View*; *Local Hero*; *The Mission*; *To End All Wars*. 'We are currently seeking film projects to invest equity in through our Finishing Fund in return for International Sales Rights.' Scripts via agents only.

The Good Film Company Ltd

The Studio, 5–6 Eton Garages, Lambolle Place, London NW3 4PE
☎020 7794 6222 Fax 020 7794 4651
✉ yanina@goodfilms.co.uk
www.goodfilms.co.uk

Contact *Yanina Barry*

Commercials and pop videos. Clients include Suzuki, Burberry, Totally London, Hugo Boss, Cadbury's. *No* unsolicited mss.

Granite Film & Television Productions Ltd

10 Margaret Street, London W1W 8RL
☎020 3008 8498 Fax 020 3008 6171

Contact *Simon Welfare*

Producer of television documentary programmes such as *Nicholas & Alexandra*; *Victoria & Albert* and *Arthur C. Clarke's Mysterious Universe*.

Grant Naylor Productions

See **Noel Gay Television**

Green Umbrella Ltd

59 Cotham Hill, Cotham, Bristol BS6 6JR
☎0117 906 4336 Fax 0117 923 7003
✉ postmaster@umbrella.co.uk
www.umbrella.co.uk

Film producers specialising in science and natural history documentaries. OUTPUT includes episodes for *The Natural World*, *Wildlife on One* and original series such as *Living Europe* and *Triumph of Life*. Unsolicited treatments relating to natural history and science subjects are welcome.

Greenwich Village Productions

14 Greenwich Church Street, London
SE10 9BJ
☎020 8853 5100 Fax 020 8293 3001
✉ tv@fictionfactory.co.uk
www.fictionfactory.co.uk

Contact *John Taylor*

Features, arts and educational projects, web-movies and new-media productions. Recent OUTPUT includes *The Rings of Saturn* and *Beastworlds*. Mss only via agents or from writers with a professional track record in the chosen medium.

H2 Business Communications

Shepperton Studios, Shepperton TW17 0QD
☎01932 593717 Fax 01932 593718
✉ mail@h2bc.co.uk
www.h2bc.co.uk

Contact *Julie Knight*

Conferences, videos, awards presentations and speaker training.

Hammerwood Film Productions

www.filmangel.co.uk

Film, video and TV drama. OUTPUT *Iceni* (film; co-production with Pan-European Film Productions and Boudicca Film Productions Ltd); *Boudicca – A Celtic Tragedy* (TV series). In pre-production: *The Black Egg* (witchcraft in 17th century England); *The Ghosthunter*; *Iceni* (documentary of the rebellion of AD61); *No Case to Answer* (legal series). 'Authors are recommended to access www.filmangel.co.uk' (see *Useful Websites*).

Hartswood Films Ltd

Twickenham Studios, The Barons, St Margarets
TW1 2AW
☎020 8607 8736 Fax 020 8607 8744
✉ films.tv@hartswoodfilms.co.uk

Contact *Elaine Cameron*

Film and TV production for drama, comedy and documentary. OUTPUT *Men Behaving Badly*; *Border Cafe*; *Coupling*; *Carrie & Barry*; *Jekyll*; *Fear, Stress and Anger* (all for BBC); *After Thomas* (ITV drama).

Hat Trick Productions Ltd

10 Livonia Street, London W1F 8AF
☎020 7434 2451 Fax 020 7287 9791
✉ info@hattrick.com
www.hattrick.com

Managing Director *Jimmy Mulville*

Television programmes.

Healthcare Productions Limited

The Great Barn, Godmersham, Canterbury
CT4 7DT
☎01227 738279 Fax 01227 732145
✉ penny@healthcareproductions.co.uk
www.healthcareproductions.co.uk

Contact *Penny Webb*

Television and video: documentary and drama. Produces training and educational material, in text, video, CD-ROM and DVD, mostly health-related, social care issues, law and marriage.

Heritage Theatre Ltd

Unit 1, 8 Clanricarde Gardens, London
W2 4NA
☎020 7243 2750 Fax 020 7792 8584
✉ rm@heritagetheatre.com
www.heritagetheatre.com

Contact *Robert Marshall*

Video recordings of successful stage plays for distribution on DVD and broadcast. 'We cannot deal with scripts of unproduced plays.'

David Hill

107 Wellington Road North, Stockport
SK4 2LP
☎0161 477 9090 Fax 0161 477 9191
✉ david.hill@acrobat-tv.co.uk
www.acrobat-tv.co.uk

Contact *David Hill*

All script genres for broadcast and coporate television, including training and promotional scripts, comedy and drama-based material. OUTPUT includes *Make a Stand* (Jack Dee, Gina Bellman and John Thompson for Video Arts); *The Customer View* (Roy Barraclough for Air Products); *Serious About Waves* series (Peter Hart for the Royal Yachting Association); *Fat Face Night* series (Extreme). No unsolicited mss.

Holmes Associates

The Studio, 37 Redington Road, London
NW3 7QY
☎020 7813 4333
✉ holmesassociates@blueyonder.co.uk

Contact *Andrew Holmes*

Prolific originator, producer and packager of documentary, drama and music television and films. OUTPUT has included *Ashes and Sand* (Film 4); *Chunky Monkey* (J&V Films); *Prometheus* (Ch4 'Film 4'); *The Shadow of Hiroshima* (Ch4 'Witness'); *The House of Bernarda Alba* (Ch4/WNET/Amaya); *Piece of Cake* (LWT); *The Cormorant* (BBC/Screen 2); *John Gielgud Looks Back*; *Rock Steady*; *Well Being*; *Signals*; *Ideal Home?* (all Ch4); *Timeline* (with MPT, TVE Spain & TRT Turkey); *Seven Canticles of St Francis* (BBC2). Submissions only accepted by e-mail in synopsis form.

Hourglass Productions
27 Prince's Road, London SW19 8RA
☎020 8540 8786
✉ productions@hourglass.co.uk
www.hourglass.co.uk

Partners *Martin Chilcott, Jacqueline Chilcott*

Film and video; documentary and drama. OUTPUT BAFTA nominated scientific television documentaries and educational programming. Also current affairs, health and social issues.

Icon Films
✉ info@iconfilms.co.uk
www.iconfilms.co.uk

Contact *Harry Marshall*

Film and TV documentaries. OUTPUT *Nick Baker's Weird Creatures* (five/Animal Planet/Granada International); *Tom Harrisson – The Barefoot Anthropologist* (BBC). Specialises in factual documentaries. Open-minded to new documentary proposals.

Imari Entertainment Ltd
PO Box 158, Beaconsfield HP9 1AY
☎01494 677147 Fax 01494 677147
✉ info@imarientertainment.com

Contact *Jonathan Fowke*

TV and video producer, covering all areas of drama, documentary and corporate productions.

Isis Productions
387b King Street, Hammersmith, London W6 9NJ
☎020 8748 7634 Fax 020 8748 3046
✉ isis@isis-productions.com
www.isisproductions.co.uk

Directors *Nick de Grunwald, Jamie Rugge-Price*

Formed in 1991, Isis Productions focuses on the production of music and documentary programmes. OUTPUT *Imagine – Yusuf Islam*

(BBC); *Pet Shop Boys – A Life in Pop*; *Rufus Wainwright*; *Brian Ferry – The Dylan Sessions*; *Ray Davies – The World from My Window*; *James Brown – Soul Survivor* (Ch4); *Bernie Taupin* (ITV 'South Bank Show'); *Iron Maiden, Judas Priest* (Five 'Rock Classics'); Films on *Deep Purple, Metallica, Def Leppard, Lou Reed, Elton John, Elvis Presley, Sex Pistols* (ITV 'Classic Albums 3'); *Simply Red, Nirvana, Cream, Pink Floyd, Motorhead* ('Classic Albums 4'); *England's Other Elizabeth – Elizabeth Taylor* (BBC 'Omnibus').

Isolde Films
28 Twyford Avenue, London W3 9QB
☎020 8896 2860
✉ isolde@btinternet.com
www.tonypalmer.org

Contact *Michela Antonello*

Film and TV documentaries. OUTPUT *Wagner; Margot; Menuhin; Maria Callas; Testimony; In From the Cold; Pushkin; England, My England* (by John Osborne). Unsolicited material is read, but please send a written outline first.

ITV Productions
The London Television Centre, Upper Ground, South Bank, London SE1 9LT
☎020 7620 1620 Fax 020 7261 3041
www.itv.com

Controller of ITV Productions (Drama),
   London *Michele Buck*
Director *John Whiston*

ITV Productions is the largest commercial TV production company in the UK. Produces original programmes, co-productions and TV movies for ITV channels and other broadcasters, both in the UK and abroad. OUTPUT includes *Hornblower; Poirot; Miss Marple; Touching Evil; Where the Heart Is; The Last Detective; Jericho*.

JAM Pictures and Jane Walmsley Productions
8 Hanover Street, London W1S 1YE
☎020 7290 2676 Fax 020 7256 6818
✉ producers@jampix.com

Contacts *Jane Walmsley, Michael Braham*

JAM Pictures was founded in 1996 to produce drama for film, TV and stage. Projects include: *Hillary's Choice* (TV film, A&E Network); *Son of Pocahontas* (TV film, ABC); *Rudy: the Rudy Giuliani Story* (TV film, USA Network); *One More Kiss* (feature, directed by Vadim Jean); *Bad Blood* (UK theatre tour). Jane Walmsley Productions, formed in 1985 by TV producer, writer and broadcaster, Jane Walmsley, has completed award-winning documentaries and features such as *Hot House People* (Ch4). No unsolicited mss. 'Letters can be sent to us, asking if we wish to see mss; we are very interested in quality material, from published or produced writers only, please'

Justice Entertainment Ltd
PO Box 4377, London W1A 7SX
☎020 7287 2355 Fax 020 7287 2354
✉ info@timwestwood.com
www.timwestwood.com
Producer of shows for Radio 1. No unsolicited material.

Keo Films.com Ltd
101 St John Street, London EC1M 4AS
☎020 7490 3580 Fax 020 7490 8419
✉ keo@keofilms.com
www.keofilms.com
Contact *Katherine Perry*
Television documentaries and factual entertainment. OUTPUT includes *Atlantic Britain* and *Surviving Extremes* (both for Ch4/NatGeo Europe); *Beyond River Cottage*; *Where's Your F***ing Manners?*; *Road Trip*; *Tales From River Cottage*; *How To Be a Man*; *Running for God*; *Heavy*; *My Body My Business*; *A Dangerous Obsession*; *Sperm Bandits* (all for Ch4); *10 Years Younger* (Discovery Health). No unsolicited mss.

Kingfisher Television Productions Ltd
Martindale House, The Green, Ruddington, Nottingham NG11 6HH
☎0115 945 6581 Fax 0115 921 7750
Contact *Tony Francis*
Broadcast television production.

Kudos Film and Televison Ltd
12–14 Amwell Street, London EC1R 1UQ
☎020 7812 3270 Fax 020 7812 3271
✉ info@kudosfilmandtv.com
www.kudosfilmandtv.com
Joint Managing Directors *Jane Featherstone, Stephen Garrett*
Commercial Director *Daniel Isaacs*
Director of Drama *Simon Crawford Collins*
Television dramas include *Life on Mars*; *Spooks*; *Hustle*; *Tsunami – The Aftermath*; *The Amazing Mrs Pritchard*; *Wide Sargasso Sea*; *Scars*; *MI High*; *Child of Mine*; *Comfortably Numb*; *Pleasureland*; *The Magician's House* and *Psychos*. Feature films such as *Among Giants* and *Pure*. No unsolicited mss.

Lagan Pictures Ltd
21 Tullaghbrow, Tullaghgarley, Ballymena BT42 2LY
☎028 2563 9479/077 9852 8797
Fax 028 2563 9479
✉ laganpictures@tullaghbrow.freeserve.co.uk
Producer/Director *Stephen Butcher*
Film, video and TV: drama, documentary and corporate. OUTPUT *A Force Under Fire* (Ulster TV). In development: *Into the Bright Light of Day* (drama-doc); *The £10 Float* (feature film); *The Centre* (drama series). 'We are always interested in hearing from writers originating from or based in Northern Ireland or anyone with, preferably unstereotypical, projects relevant to Northern Ireland. We do not have the resources to deal with unsolicited mss, so please write with a brief treatment/synopsis in the first instance.'

Landseer Productions Ltd
140 Royal College Street, London NW1 0TA
☎020 7485 7333
✉ ken@landseerproductions.com
www.landseerfilms.com
Directors *Derek Bailey, Ken Howard*
Film and video production: documentary, drama, music and arts. OUTPUT *Swinger* (BBC2/ Arts Council); *Auld Lang Syne* and *Retying the Knot – The Incredible String Band* (both for BBC Scotland); *Benjamin Zander* ('The Works', BBC2); *Zeffirelli, Johnnie Ray, Petula Clark, Bing Crosby, Maxim Vengerov* (all for 'South Bank Show', LWT); *Death of a Legend – Frank Sinatra* ('South Bank Show' special); *Routes of Rock* (Carlton); *See You in Court* (BBC); *Nureyev Unzipped, Gounod's Faust, The Judas Tree, Ballet Boyz, 4Dance* and *Bourne to Dance* (all for Ch4), *Proms in the Park* (Belfast).

Lilyville Screen Entertainment Ltd
7 Lilyville Road, London SW6 5DP
☎020 7471 8989
✉ tony.cash@btclick.com
Contact *Tony Cash*
Drama and documentaries for TV. OUTPUT *Poetry in Motion* (series for Ch4); 'South Bank Show': *Ben Elton* and *Vanessa Redgrave*; *Musique Enquête* (drama-based French language series, Ch4); *Sex and Religion* (ITV); *Landscape and Memory* (arts documentary series for the BBC); Jonathan Miller's production of the *St Matthew Passion* for the BBC; major documentary on the BeeGees for the 'South Bank Show'. Scripts with an obvious application to TV may be

considered. Interested in new writing for documentary programmes.

Loftus Productions Ltd

2a Aldine Street, London W12 8AN
☎020 8740 4666
✉ ask@loftusproductions.co.uk
www.loftusproductions.co.uk
Contact *Matt Thompson* (radio drama) ☎ 01620 893876

Producers of factual radio programmes, documentaries, readings (mostly non-fiction) and drama, as well as audio books and audio guides for museums and galleries. OUTPUT includes numerous titles for Radio 4's 'Book of the Week'. 'We are happy to look at brief emailed synopses of radio plays suitable for broadcast in the available drama slots on BBC Radio 3 or 4.'

London Scientific Films Ltd

Dassels House, Dassels, Braughing, Ware SG11 2RW
☎01763 289905
✉ lsf@londonscientificfilms.co.uk
Contact *Mike Cockburn*

Film and video documentary and corporate programming. No unsolicited mss.

Lucida Productions

5 Alleyn Crescent, London SE21 8BN
☎020 8761 4344
✉ pj.lucida@tiscali.co.uk
Contact *Paul Joyce*

Television and cinema: arts, adventure, current affairs, documentary, drama and music. OUTPUT has included *Motion and Emotion: The Films of Wim Wenders*; *Dirk Bogarde – By Myself*; *Sam Peckinpah – Man of Iron*; *Kris Kristofferson – Pilgrim*; *Wild One: Marlon Brando*; *Stanley Kubrick: 'The Invisible Man'*; *2001: the Making of a Myth* (Ch4); *Mantrap – Straw Dogs, the final cut* (with Dustin Hoffman). Restoration of the Director's Cut of *The Devils* plus the documentary *Hell on Earth* with Ken Russell and Vanessa Redgrave. Currently in development for documentary projects.

Malone Gill Productions Ltd

27 Campden Hill Road, London W8 7DX
☎020 7937 0557 Fax 020 7460 3750
✉ malonegill@aol.com
Contact *Georgina Denison*

Mainly documentary but also some drama. OUTPUT includes *The Face of Russia* (PBS); *Vermeer* ('South Bank Show'); *Highlanders* (ITV);

Storm Chasers; *Nature Perfected* and *The Feast of Christmas* (all for Ch4); *The Buried Mirror: Reflections on Spain and the New World* by Carlos Fuentes (BBC2/Discovery Channel). Approach by letter with proposal in the first instance.

Marchmont Films Ltd

24 Three Cups Yard, Sandland Street, London WC1R 4PZ
✉ office@marchmontfilms.com
www.marchmontfilms.com
Development Executives *Beverley Hills, Daniel Hayes, Andrew Cussens*

Producer of short films and feature projects. OUTPUT includes *Out In the Cold*; *The Green Wave*; *Punch*; *Shag & Go*. Welcomes new writers. See website for current submission criteria.

Jane Marshall Productions

The Coach-House, Westhill Road, Blackdown, Leamington Spa CV32 6RA
☎01926 831680
✉ jane@jmproductions.freeserve.co.uk
Contact *Jane Marshall*

Producer of readings of published work both fiction and non-fiction for BBC Radio. Published work only.

Maverick Television

Progress Works, Heath Mill Lane, Birmingham B9 4AL
☎0121 771 1812 Fax 0121 771 1550
✉ mail@mavericktv.co.uk
www.mavericktv.co.uk
Contact *Juliet Howell*

Established in 1994, Maverick has a strong reputation for popular factual programming as well as drama. It is now one of network television's most prolific independent suppliers. OUTPUT includes *10 Years Younger*; *Who'll Age Worst?*; *Bollywood Star*; *Fat Chance*; *Born Too Soon*; *Vee TV*; *Trade Secrets*; *Embarrassing Illnesses*; *10 Things You Didn't Know About ...*; *How To Live Longer*; *The Property Chain*; *Male, 33, Seeks Puberty*; *Extreme Engineering*; *Picture This: Accidental Hero*; *Up Your Street*; *The Property Chain*; *Motherless Daughters*; *Highland Bollywood: Black Bag*; *Health Alert: My Teenage Menopause*; *Long Haul*; *Learning to Love the Grey*.

Maya Vision International Ltd

6 Kinghorn Street, London EC1A 7HW
☎020 7796 4842 Fax 020 7796 4580
www.mayavisionint.com
Contact *Tamsin Ranger*

Film and TV: drama and documentary. OUTPUT *Saddam's Killing Fields* (for 'Viewpoint', Central TV); *3 Steps to Heaven* and *A Bit of Scarlet* (feature films for BFI/Ch4); *A Place in the Sun* and *North of Vortex* (dramas for Ch4/Arts Council); *The Real History Show* (Ch4); *In Search of Myths and Heroes*; *In Search of Shakespeare*; *In the Footsteps of Alexander the Great*; *Conquistadors* (BBC documentaries); *Hitler's Search for the Holy Grail*; *Once Upon a Time in Iran* (Ch4 documentaries). Absolutely no unsolicited material; commissions only.

MBP TV

Saucelands Barn, Coolham, Horsham
RH13 8QG
☎01403 741620 Fax 01403 741647
✉ info@mbptv.com
www.mbptv.com

Contact *Phil Jennings*

Maker of film and video specialising in programmes covering equestrianism and the countryside. No unsolicited scripts, but always looking for new writers who are fully acquainted with the subject.

Melendez Films

Julia House, 44 Newman Street, London
W1T 1QD
☎020 7323 5273 Fax 020 7323 5373

Contact *Steven Melendez*

Independent production company specialising in 2D animation. Also involved in production and film design for clients in England, Spain, Sweden, India and the US, plus website design and 3D animation on the Web. Clients include book publishers, TV companies and advertisers. Winner of international awards for films, particularly of classic books, stories and comic characters. 'We will look at unsolicited projects in outline or synopsis form only. Enclose s.a.e.'

Mendoza Film Productions

3–5 Barrett Street, London W1U 1AY
☎020 7935 4674 Fax 020 7935 4417
✉ office@mendozafilms.com
www.mendozafilms.com

Contacts *Wynn Wheldon, Debby Mendoza*

Commercials, title sequences (e.g. Alan Bleasdale's *G.B.H.*); party political broadcasts. Currently in pre-production on a feature-length comedy film. Involved with the **Screenwriters' Workshop**. Unsolicited mss welcome but 'comedies only, please'. Material will not be returned without s.a.e.

Merseyfilm

Tirley Garth, Utkinton, Near Tarporley
CW6 0LZ
☎01829 731860 Fax 01829 732265
www.merseyfilm.biz

Chairman *Prof. Phil Redmond, CBE*

Creators of television dramas *Brookside, Hollyoaks, The Courtroom* (Ch4) and *Grange Hill* (BBC).

Moonstone Films Ltd

☎020 7870 7180 Fax 0870 005 6839
✉ info@moonstonefilms.co.uk
www.moonstonefilms.co.uk

Contact *Tony Stark*

Television: current affairs, science and history documentaries. OUTPUT *Arafat's Authority* and *Arafat Investigated*, both for BBC 'Correspondent'. Plus various Ch4 News commissions. Unsolicited mss welcome.

Neon

Studio Two, 19 Marine Crescent, Glasgow
G51 1HD
☎0141 429 6366 Fax 0141 429 6377
✉ stephy@go2neon.com
www.go2neon.com

Contact *Stephanie Pordage*

Television and radio: drama and documentary producers. OUTPUT includes *Brand New Country*; *Asian Overground*; *Peeking Past the Gates of Skibo*. Supports and encourages new writing 'at every opportunity'. Welcomes unsolicited material but telephone in the first instance.

Number 9 Films

Linton House, 24 Wells Street, London
W1T 3PH
☎020 7323 4060 Fax 020 7323 0456
✉ info@number9films.co.uk

Contacts *Stephen Woolley, Elizabeth Karlsen*

Leading feature film producer. OUTPUT includes *Breakfast on Pluto*; *Stoned*; *Mrs Harris*. Forthcoming productions: *And When Did You Last See Your Father?*; *How to Lose Friends and Alienate People*; *Edith and the Lonely Doll*. No unsolicited material.

Odyssey Productions Ltd

72 Tay Street, Newport-on-Tay DD6 8AP
☎01382 542070 Fax 01382 542070
✉ billykay@sol.co.uk
www.sol.co.uk/b/billy

Contact *Billy Kay*

Producer of radio documentaries. OUTPUT

includes *Scotland's Black History*; *Gentle Shepherds* (oral history); *Street Kids* (Scottish missionaries working with street kids in Brazil). Ideas for radio documentaries welcome; send letter with one page outlining the idea and programme content.

Omnivision
Pinewood Studios, Iver Heath SL0 0NH
☎01753 656329 Fax 01753 631146
✉ info@omnivision.co.uk
www.omnivision.co.uk

Contacts *Christopher Morris, Nick Long*

TV and video producers of documentary, corporate, news and sport programming. Also equipment and facilities hire. Interested in ideas; approach by letter or e-mail.

Orlando TV Productions
Up-the-Steps, Little Tew, Chipping Norton OX7 4JB
☎01608 683218 Fax 01608 683364
✉ info@orlandomedia.co.uk
www.orlandomedia.co.uk

Contact *Mike Tomlinson*

Producer of TV documentaries and digital multimedia content, with science, health and information technology subjects as a specialisation. Approaches by established writers/journalists to discuss proposals for collaboration are welcome.

Orpheus Productions
6 Amyand Park Gardens, Twickenham TW1 3HS
☎020 8892 3172 Fax 020 8892 4821
✉ richard-taylor@blueyonder.co.uk

Contact *Richard Taylor*

Television documentaries and corporate work. OUTPUT has included programmes for the BBC, ITV and Ch4 as well as documentaries for the United Nations, the Shell Film Unit and Video Arts. Unsolicited scripts are welcomed with caution. 'Our preference is for the more classically structured documentary that, while being hard-hitting, explores the subtleties and the paradox of an issue – and is not presented by unqualified celebrities.'

Ovation
Upstairs at the Gatehouse, Highgate, London N6 4BD
☎020 8340 4256 Fax 020 8340 3466

Contact *John Plews*

Corporate video and conference scripts.

Unsolicited mss not welcome. 'We talk to new writers from time to time.' Ovation also runs the fringe theatre, 'Upstairs at the Gatehouse'.

Paper Moon Productions
Wychwood House, Burchetts Green Lane, Littlewick Green, Nr. Maidenhead SL6 3QW
☎01628 829819 Fax 01628 829819
✉ david@paper-moon.co.uk

Contact *David Haggas*

Broadcast documentaries and corporate communications. Recent OUTPUT includes *Bilbo & Beyond*, an affectionate glimpse into the life and work of the dedicated philologist and fantasy writer J.R.R. Tolkien.

Parallax Independent Ltd
St Runwald Street, Colchester CO1 1HF
☎01206 574909 Fax 01206 575311
www.parallaxindependent.co.uk

Contact *Sally Hibbin*

Feature films/television drama. OUTPUT *A Very British Coup*; *Riff-Raff*; *Bad Behaviour*; *Raining Stones*; *Ladybird, Ladybird*; *i.d.*; *Land and Freedom*; *The Englishman Who Went up a Hill But Came Down a Mountain*; *Bliss*; *Jump the Gun*; *Carla's Song*; *The Governess*; *My Name Is Joe*; *Stand and Deliver*; *Dockers*; *Hold Back the Night*; *Bread and Roses*; *Princesa*; *The Navigators*; *Sweet Sixteen*; *Innocence*; *The Intended*; *Blind Flight*; *Yasmin*; *Almost Adult*.

Passion Pictures
3rd Floor, 33–34 Rathbone Place, London W1T 1JN
☎020 7323 9933 Fax 020 7323 9030
✉ info@passion-pictures.com

Managing Director *Andrew Ruhemann*

Documentary and drama includes: *One Day in September* (Academy Award-winner for Best Feature Documentary, 2000); also commercials and music videos: Carphone Warehouse, Mini, Aero, Gorillaz, Coldplay and Robbie Williams. Unsolicited mss welcome.

Pathé Pictures
14–17 Kenthouse, Market Place, London W1W 8AR
☎020 7323 5151 Fax 020 7631 3568

Head of Creative Affairs *Celine Haddad*

Produces 4–6 theatrical feature films each year. 'We are pleased to consider all material that has representation from an agent or production company.'

Pearson Television
See **FremantleMedia Ltd**

Pelicula Films
59 Holland Street, Glasgow G2 4NJ
☎0141 287 9522

Contact *Mike Alexander*

Television producer. Maker of drama documentaries and music programmes for the BBC and Ch4. OUTPUT *As an Eilean (From the Island); The Trans-Atlantic Sessions 1 & 2; Nanci Griffith, Other Voices 2; Follow the Moonstone.*

Pennine Productions LLP
Kilmagadwood Cottage, Scotlandwell, Kinross KY13 9HY
☎05600 472247
✉ mike@pennine.biz
www.pennine.biz

Contact *Mike Hally*
Producers *Mark Whitaker, Janet Graves, Clare Jenkins*

Producer of radio documentaries, features and short story readings. OUTPUT includes *The Pennine Way, Manchester Crime Wave* and *Northern Creative Writing Groups* (all for Radio 4). No unsolicited material.

Pepper Productions
See **Noel Gay Television**

Photoplay Productions Ltd
21 Princess Road, London NW1 8JR
☎020 7722 2500 Fax 020 7722 6662
✉ info@photoplay.co.uk

Contact *Patrick Stanbury*

Documentaries for film, television and video plus restoration of silent films and their theatrical presentation. OUTPUT includes *The Cat and the Canary; Orphans of the Storm; Cecil B. DeMille: American Epic* and the 'Channel 4 Silents' series of silent film restoration, including *The Wedding March* and *The Iron Mask.* Recently completed *Garbo* and *I'm King Kong!* No unsolicited mss; 'we tend to create and write all our own programmes'.

Picardy Media & Communication
1 Park Circus, Glasgow G3 6AX
☎0141 333 5554 Fax 0141 332 6002
✉ jr@picardy.co.uk
www.picardy.co.uk

Head of Production *John Rocchiccioli*

Produces screen-based content for education, training, sales and marketing, HR and induc-

tion. Operates in a variety of areas including health, education, social policy, etc. 'Aims to inform through entertainment.' Unsolicited mss welcome; 'keen to encourage new writing.'

Picture Palace Films Ltd
13 Egbert Street, London NW1 8LJ
☎020 7586 8763 Fax 020 7586 9048
✉ info@picturepalace.com
www.picturepalace.com

Contacts *Malcolm Craddock, Katherine Hedderly*

Leading independent producer of film and TV drama. OUTPUT *Rebel Heart* (BBC1); *Sharpe's Challenge; Extremely Dangerous; A Life for A Life* and *Frances Tuesday* (all for ITV); *Sharpe's Rifles* (14 films for Carlton TV); *Little Napoleons* (comedy drama, Ch4); *The Orchid House* (drama serial, Ch4); *Tandoori Nights; 4 Minutes; When Love Dies* (all for Ch4); *Ping Pong* (feature film); *Acid House* (Picture Palace North). Material will only be considered if submitted through an agent.

Planet24 Pictures Ltd
39 Meadow Road, Trimdon Village TS29 6JN
☎0870 765 8780
✉ planet24picture@aol.com
www.planet24pictures.co.uk

Contact *Mercedes de Dunewíc*

Producer of television and video documentaries plus community/infomercials. OUTPUT includes *Jack the Ripper: The Conspiracies; Truth to Tell; Pitmen and Politics: The County Built on Coal.* Mss, plot outlines and screenplays considered but e-mail for information first. 'Welcome the input of new writers with radical points of view.'

Plantagenet Films Limited
Ard-Daraich Studio B, Ardgour, Nr Fort William PH33 7AB
☎01855 841384 Fax 01855 841384
✉ plantagenetfilms@aol.com

Contact *Norrie Maclaren*

Film and television: documentary and drama programming such as *Dig* (gardening series for Ch4); various 'Dispatches' for Ch4 and 'Omnibus' for BBC. Keen to encourage and promote new writing; unsolicited mss welcome.

Portobello Pictures
Eardley House, 4 Uxbridge Street, Notting Hill Gate, London W8 7SY
☎020 7908 9890 Fax 020 7908 9899
✉ mail@portobellopictures.com
www.portobellopictures.com

Producer *Eric Abraham*
Associate Producer *Kate McCullagh*

Oscar-winning film, television and theatre production company.

Pozzitive Television

Paramount House, 162–170 Wardour Street, London W1F 8AB
☎020 7734 3258 Fax 020 7437 3130
✉ david@pozzitive.co.uk

Contact *David Tyler*

Producer of comedy and entertainment for television and radio. OUTPUT *Dinner Ladies; Coogan's Run; The 99p Challenge; The Comic Side of 7 Days; Armando Iannucci's Charm Offensive.* Unsolicited mss of TV and radio comedy welcome. 'No screenplays or stage plays or novels, please. Send hard copy of full sample script. We read everything submitted this way. Sorry, we don't return scripts unless you send an s.a.e.'

Promenade Enterprises Limited

6 Russell Grove, London SW9 6HS
☎020 7582 9354
✉ info@promenadeproductions.com
www.promenadeproductions.com

Contact *Nicholas Newton*

Producer of drama for radio and theatre predominantly. Supports new writing but only accepts unsolicited mss via agents or producers.

Redweather

Easton Business Centre, Felix Road, Easton BS5 0HE
☎0117 941 5854 Fax 0117 941 5851
✉ production@redweather.co.uk
www.redweather.co.uk

Broadcast documentaries on arts and disability, corporate video and CD-ROM, Water Aid, British Oxygen, etc.

Renaissance Vision

256 Fakenham Road, Taverham, Norwich NR8 6QW
☎01603 260280 Fax 01603 260280
✉ bfg@renvision.co.uk

Contact *B. Gardner*

Video: full range of corporate work (training, sales, promotional, etc.). Producers of educational and special-interest video publications. Willing to consider good ideas and proposals.

Richmond Films & Television Ltd

PO Box 33154, London NW3 4AZ
☎020 7722 6464 Fax 020 7722 6232

✉ mail@richmondfilms.com

Contact *Development Executive*

Film and TV: drama and comedy. OUTPUT *Press Gang; The Lodge; The Office; Wavelength; Privates; in2minds. No* unsolicited scripts.

RS Productions

191 Trewhitt Road, Newcastle upon Tyne NE6 5DY
☎0191 224 4301/00 49 89 5111 5895/07710 064632 (Mobile)
✉ enquiries@rsproductions.co.uk
www.rsproductions.co.uk

Contact *Mark Lavender*

Feature films and television: drama series/serials and singles. TV documentaries and series. Working with established and new talent.

Sands Films

119 Rotherhithe Street, London SE16 4NF
☎020 7231 2209 Fax 020 7231 2119
✉ sands@sandsfilms.co.uk
www.sandsfilms.co.uk

Contacts *Christine Edzard, Olivier Stockman*

Film and TV drama. OUTPUT *Little Dorrit; The Fool; As You Like It; A Dangerous Man; The Long Day Closes; A Passage to India; Topsy Turvy; Nicholas Nickleby; The Gangs of New York; The Children's Midsummer Night's Dream. No* unsolicited scripts.

Scala Productions Ltd

2nd Floor, 37 Foley Street, London W1W 7TN
☎020 7637 5720 Fax 020 7637 5734
✉ scalaprods@aol.com

Contacts *Ian Prior, Nick Powell*

Production company set up by ex-Palace Productions Nik Powell and Stephen Woolley, who have an impressive list of credits including *Company of Wolves; Absolute Beginners; Mona Lisa; Scandal; The Crying Game; Backbeat; Neon Bible; 24:7; Little Voice; Divorcing Jack; The Last September; Wild About Harry; Last Orders; A Christmas Carol – The Movie; Black and White; Leo; The Night We Called It A Day; Ladies in Lavender; Stoned.* In development: *The Coat; Du Cane's Boys; Meek; Johnny Bollywood; The Rough; Black Cockatoo.*

Scope Productions Ltd

180 West Regent Street, Glasgow G2 4RW
☎0141 221 4312
✉ laurakingwell@scopeproductions.co.uk
www.scopeproductions.co.uk

Corporate *Laura Kingwell*

Corporate film and video and multimedia communications for clients across all sectors.

Screen First Ltd
The Studios, Funnells Farm, Down Street,
Nutley TN22 3LG
☎01825 712034
✉ paul.madden@virgin.net
Contacts *M. Thomas, P. Madden*
Television dramas, documentaries, arts and animation programmes. Developing major drama series, feature films, animated specials and series. No unsolicited scripts.

Screen Ventures Ltd
49 Goodge Street, London W1T 1TE
☎020 7580 7448 Fax 020 7631 1265
✉ info@screenventures.com
www.screenventures.com
Contacts *Christopher Mould, Michael Evans*
Film and TV sales and production: documentary, music videos and drama. OUTPUT *Life and Limb* (documentary, Discovery Health Channel); *Pavement Aristocrats* (SABC); *Woodstock Diary*; *Vanessa Redgrave* and *Genet* (both for LWT 'South Bank Show'); *Mojo Working*; *Burma: Dying for Democracy* (Ch4); *Dani Dares* (Ch4 series on strong women); *Pagad* (Ch4 news report).

Screenhouse Productions Ltd
Chapel Allerton House, 114 Harrogate Road, Leeds LS7 4NY
☎0113 266 8881 Fax 0113 266 8882
✉ paul.bader@screenhouse.co.uk
www.screenhouse.co.uk
Contacts *Paul Bader, Barbara Govan*
Specialises in science TV, documentary, stunts and events, including outside broadcasts. Science prop. and demo workshop supplying working models to, e.g., BBC History *What the Past Did For Us*; ITV, Discovery and museums. OUTPUT includes *Stardate* (BBC2 astronomy series); *Zapped* (Discovery/US/Canada); *The Man Who Invented the Aeroplane* (UKTV/BBC North); *Science Shack, Local Heroes*, BBC2, presented by Adam Hart-Davis. 'More likely to consider written up proposals.'

September Films Ltd
Glen House, 22 Glenthorne Road, London W6 0NG
☎020 8563 9393 Fax 020 8741 7214
✉ september@septemberfilms.com
www.septemberfilms.com
Director of Production *Elaine Day*

Factual entertainment and documentary specialists. Feature film OUTPUT includes *Breathtaking*; *House of America*; *Solomon & Gaenor*. No unsolicited submissions, please.

Shell Like
81 Whitfield Street, London W1T 4HG
☎020 7255 5204 Fax 020 7255 5255
✉ enquiries@shellike.com
www.shelllike.com
Contact *Anna Pollard*
Produces radio commercials. Unsolicited mss and ideas welcome; send by e-mail.

Sianco Cyf
36 Y Maes, Caernarfon LL55 2NN
☎01286 676100/07831 726111 (mobile)
Fax 01286 677616
✉ post@sianco.tv
Contact *Siân Teifi*
Children's, youth and education programmes, children's drama, people-based documentaries for adults. 'Please note, *we do not accept any unsolicited scripts*.'

Silent Sound Films Ltd
Cambridge Court, Cambridge Road, Frinton on Sea CO13 9HN
☎01255 676381 Fax 01255 676381
✉ thj@silentsoundfilms.co.uk
www.silentsoundfilms.co.uk
www.londonfoodfilmfiesta.co.uk
Contact *Timothy Foster*
Active in European film co-production with mainstream connections in the USA. Special interest in developing stage and film musicals, art house and documentaries on the arts. Synopses considered via e-mail or post.

Skyline Productions
10 Scotland Street, Edinburgh EH3 6PS
☎0131 557 4580 Fax 0131 556 4377
✉ leslie@skyline.uk.com
www.skyline.uk.com
Producer/Writer *Leslie Hills*
Produces film and television drama and documentary.

SMG Productions & Ginger Productions
SMG: Pacific Quay, Glasgow G3 7TG
☎0141 300 3000
www.smgproductions.tv

Also: Ginger Productions, 3 Waterhouse Square, 138–142 Holborn London EC1N 2NY
☎ 020 7882 1020 www.ginger.tv

Managing Director (SMG Productions & Ginger Productions) *Elizabeth Partyka*
Head of Drama *Eric Coulter*
Head of Business Development *Helen Alexander*

SMG Productions, which incorporates Ginger Productions, makes programmes for the national television networks, including ITV, Ch4 and Sky. Specialises in drama, factual entertainment and children's programming. OUTPUT includes *Taggart; Rebus; Our Daughter Holly; Club Reps.*

Somethin Else

Units 1–4, 1A Old Nichol Street, London E2 7HR
☎020 7613 3211 Fax 020 7739 9799
✉ info@somethin-else.com
www.somethin-else.com

Contact *Jez Nelson*

Producer of television, video and radio documentaries, DVD and interactive content. Ideas for TV shows welcome; send letter in the first instance.

Soundplay

17 Gleneagles Drive, Henbury, Bristol BS10 7PS
☎07818 271659
✉ enquiries@soundplay.co.uk
www.soundplay.co.uk

Contact *Tom Bennett*

Producer of radio drama and documentaries. OUTPUT includes *In Search of the Picturesque* (dramatised radio feature by Tom Bennett); *The Hearts and Lives of Men* (radio drama by Fay Weldon); *Remember the Day* (radio thriller by Tom Bennett).

Specific Films

25 Rathbone Street, London W1T 1NQ
☎020 7580 7476 Fax 020 7636 6866
✉ info@specificfilms.com

Contact *Michael Hamlyn*

Founded 1991. OUTPUT includes *Mr Reliable* (feature film co-produced by PolyGram and the AFFC); *The Adventures of Priscilla, Queen of the Desert*, co-produced with Latent Image (Australia) and financed by PolyGram and AFFC; *U2 Rattle and Hum*, full-length feature – part concert film/part cinema verité documentary; *Paws* (executive producer); *The Last Seduction 2* (Polygram); and numerous pop promos for major international artists.

Spice Factory (UK) Ltd

14 Regent Hill, Brighton BN1 3ED
☎01273 739182 Fax 01273 749122
✉ shirine@spicefactory.co.uk
www.spicefactory.co.uk

Contacts *Lucy Shuttleworth, Shirine Best*

Founded 1995. Film producers. OUTPUT *Plots With a View* (Christopher Walken, Brenda Blethyn, Alfred Molina, Lee Evans); *Bollywood Queen* (Preeya Kallidas, James McAvoy, Ian McShane); *The Bridge of San Luis Rey* (Robert De Niro, Kathy Bates, Harvey Keitel); *A Different Loyalty* (Sharon Stone, Rupert Everett); *Head in the Clouds* (Charlize Theron, Penelope Cruz); *The Merchant of Venice* (Al Pacino, Jeremy Irons, Joseph Fiennes, Lynn Collins). No unsolicited material accepted.

'Spoken' Image Ltd

8 Hewitt Street M15 4GB
☎0161 236 7522 Fax 0161 236 0020
✉ info@spoken-image.com
www.spoken-image.com

Contacts *Geoff Allman, Steve Foster*

Film, video and TV production for documentary and corporate material. Specialises in high-quality brochures and reports, CD-ROMs, exhibitions, conferences, film and video production for broadcast, industry and commerce.

Tony Staveacre Productions

Channel View, Blagdon BS40 7TP
☎01761 462161 Fax 01761 462161
✉ newstaving@btinternet.com

Contact *Tony Staveacre*

Producer of dramas and documentaries as well as music, arts and comedy progammes. Recent OUTPUT *The Wodehouse Notebooks; The Liberation of Daphne, Speaking from the Belly; Standing Up for Liverpool* (Radio 4); *The Very Thought of You* and *Jigsy* (theatre); *Tango Maestro* (BBC4); *The Old Boys Band* (BBC1); *Mendip Voices* (CD). No unsolicited mss.

Stirling Film & TV Productions Limited

137 University Street, Belfast BT7 1HP
☎028 9033 3848 Fax 028 9043 8644
✉ anne@stirlingtelevision.co.uk

Contact *Anne Stirling*

Producer of broadcast and corporate programming – documentary, sport, entertainment and lifestyle programmes.

Straight Forward Film & Television Productions Ltd

Building 2, Lesley Office Park, 393 Hollywood Road, Belfast BT4 2LS
☎028 9065 1010 Fax 028 9065 1012
✉ enquiries@straightforwardltd.co.uk

Contacts *John Nicholson, Ian Kennedy*

Northern Ireland-based production company specialising in documentary, feature and lifestyle series for both regional and network transmission. OUTPUT includes *We Shall Overcome* (winner of Best Documentary at 1999 Celtic Television Festival for BBC); *Conquering the Normans* (Ch4 Learning – history of Normans in Ireland); *Gift of the Gab* (Ch4 Learning – contemporary Irish writing); *Sportsweek* (BBC Radio Ulster); *On Eagle's Wing* (full stage musical/TV material; story of the Scots/Irish in America); *Fire School*; *Mission Employable*; *Sweet Child of Mine*; *School Challenge*, 3rd series; *World Indoor Bowls* (all for BBC NI); *Awash With Colour* (series, BBC Daytime).

Sunset + Vine Productions Ltd

30 Sackville Street, London W1S 3DY
☎020 7478 7300 Fax 020 7478 7403
www.sunsetvine.co.uk

Sports, children's and music programmes for television. No unsolicited mss. 'We hire freelancers only upon receipt of a commission.'

Table Top Productions

1 The Orchard, Chiswick, London W4 1JZ
☎020 8742 0507 Fax 020 8742 0507
✉ alvin@tabletopproductions.com

Contact *Alvin Rakoff*

TV and film. OUTPUT *Paradise Postponed*; *The Adventures of Don Quixote*; *A Voyage Round My Father*; *The First Olympics 1896*; *Dirty Tricks*; *A Dance to the Music of Time*; *Too Marvellous for Words*. Also Dancetime Ltd. No unsolicited mss.

talkbackTHAMES

20–21 Newman Street, London W1T 1PG
☎020 7861 8000 Fax 020 7861 8001
✉ reception@talkbackthames.tv
www.talkbackthames.tv

Chief Executive Officer *Lorraine Heggessey*
Chief Operating Officer *Sara Geater*

talkackTHAMES Productions is a **FremantleMedia** company. OUTPUT includes: comedy, comedy drama, drama, entertainment, documentary and lifestyle programmes. OUTPUT *The Apprentice*; *Green Wing*; *The Bill*; *The X Factor*; *Never Mind the Buzzcocks*; *Grand Designs*; *Unteachables*; *Property Ladder*.

Talkingheads Production Ltd

2–4 Noel Street, London W1F 8GB
☎020 7292 7575 Fax 020 7292 7576
✉ johnsachs@talkingheadsproductions.com
www.talkingheadsproductions.com

Contact *John Sachs*

Feature films. OUTPUT includes *The Merchant of Venice* starring Al Pacino. Will consider scripts; contact by e-mail. 'Somewhere out there is the new Tom Stoppard.'

Tandem TV & Film Ltd

Suite 206, Charleston House, Hemel Hempstead HP1 3AA
☎01442 261576 Fax 01442 219250
✉ info@tandemtv.com
www.tandemtv.com

Production Director *Barbara Page*
Creative Director *Terry Page*
Production Controller *Jevan Green*

Internal and external communications, documentaries, drama-documentaries, public relations, sales, marketing and training programmes for, amongst others, the construction, civil engineering, transport, local government and charitable sectors. Welcomes unsolicited mss.

Taylor Made Broadcasts Ltd

3B Cromwell Park, Chipping Norton OX7 5SR
☎01608 646444
✉ post@tmtv.co.uk

Contact *Trevor Taylor*

Producer of *Gardeners' Question Time* (BBC Radio 4). No unsolicited mss.

Telemagination Ltd

Royalty House, 72–74 Dean Street, London W1D 3SG
☎020 7434 1551 Fax 020 7434 3344
✉ mail@tmation.co.uk
www.telemagination.co.uk

Contact *Beth Parker*

Animation production company. CREDITS include *The Animals of Farthing Wood*; *Noah's Island*; *The Last Polar Bears*; *Little Ghosts*; *Pongwiffy*; *Heidi*; *The Cramp Twins ll*; *Pettson and Findus*; *Rudi and Trudi*. In production: *Littlest Pet Shop*.

Tern Television Productions Ltd

73 Crown Street, Aberdeen AB11 6EX

☎01224 211123 Fax 01224 211199
✉ aberdeen@terntv.com
www.terntv.com

Also at: 4th Floor, 114 Union Street, Glasgow
G1 3QQ
☎ 0141 204 1717
✉ glasgow@terntv.com

And: 1st Floor, Cotton Court, 38–42 Waring
Street, Belfast BT1 2ED
☎ 02890 241433
✉ belfast@terntv.com

Contacts *David Strachan, Gwyneth Hardy*
(Aberdeen), *Harry Bell* (Glasgow)

Broadcast, television and corporate video
productions. Specialises in factual entertainment. Currently developing drama.

Testimony Films
12 Great George Street, Bristol BS1 5RS
☎0117 925 8589 Fax 0117 925 7608
✉ steve.humphries@testimonyfilms.com

Contact *Steve Humphries*

TV documentary producer. Specialises in social
history exploring Britain's past using living
memory. OUTPUT includes *Hooked: History of
Addictions*; *Married Love* (both Ch4 series); *A
Secret World of Sex* (BBC series); *The 50s & 60s
in Living Colour*; *Some Liked It Hot* (both ITV
series). Welcomes ideas from those working on
life stories and oral history.

Tiger Aspect Productions
7 Soho Street, London W1D 3DQ
☎020 7434 6700 Fax 020 7434 1798
✉ general@tigeraspect.co.uk
www.tigeraspect.co.uk

Contact *Charles Brand*

Part of IMG Media. Television producer for
comedy, drama, documentary and entertainment. OUTPUT *Births, Marriages & Deaths*; *Kid
in the Corner*; *Country House*; *Gimme Gimme
Gimme*; *Harry Enfield & Chums*; *Howard Goodalls'
Big Bangs*; *Playing the Field I, II & III*; *Streetmate
I & II*; *Let Them Eat Cake*; *The Vicar of Dibley*.
Only considers material submitted via an agent
or from writers with a known track record.

Touch Productions Ltd
18 Queen Square, Bath BA1 2HN
☎01225 484666 Fax 01225 483620
✉ erica@touchproductions.co.uk

Contacts *Erica Wolfe-Murray, Malcolm Brinkworth*

Over the last 20 years, Touch has made a wide
range of programmes including award–winning

investigations, popular documentaries, medical
and science films, revelatory history productions
as well as observational, social, religious and arts
programmes. Current commissions include *The
Human Footprint*, a Ch4 documentary special
and various series and documentaries for the
BBC, National Geographic, TLC and Animal
Planet. Other projects include *Transplanting
Memories?*; *The Boy Who Couldn't Stop Running*;
Parish in the Sun; *Revival* and *Angela's Dying
Wish*.

Transatlantic Films Production and Distribution Company
Cabalva Studios, Whitney-on-Wye HR3 6EX
☎01497 831428 Fax 01497 831677
✉ revel@transatlanticfilms.com
www.transatlanticfilms.com

Executive Producer *Revel Guest*

Producer of TV documentaries. OUTPUT *Belzoni*
(Ch4 Schools); *Science of Sleep and Dreams*; *Science
of Love* and *Extreme Body Parts* (all for Discovery
Health); *Legends of the Living Dead* (Discovery
Travel/S4C International); *2025* (Discovery
Digital); *How Animals Tell the Time* (Discovery);
Trailblazers (Travel Channel). No unsolicited scripts. Interested in new writers to write
'the book of the series', e.g. for *Greek Fire* and
History's Turning Points, but not usually drama
script writers.

TV Choice Ltd
PO Box 597, Bromley BR2 OYB
☎020 8464 7402 Fax 020 8464 7845
✉ tvchoiceuk@aol.com
www.tvchoice.uk.com

Contact *Norman Thomas*

Produces a range of educational videos for
schools and colleges on subjects such as history,
geography, business studies and economics. No
unsolicited mss; send proposals only.

Twentieth Century Fox Film Co
Twentieth Century House, 31–32 Soho Square,
London W1D 3AP
☎020 7437 7766
www.fox.co.uk

London office of the American giant. Does not
accept unsolicited material.

Twofour Group Limited
Twofour Studios, Estover, Plymouth PL6 7RG
☎01752 727400 Fax 01752 727450
✉ enq@twofour.co.uk
www.twofour.co.uk

Chief Executive *Charles Wace*

Managing Director, Twofour Broadcast *Melanie Leach*

One of the largest broadcast television and corporate communications producers in the UK, comprising Twofour Broadcasting, Twofour Communications and Twofour Digital. The Group produces over 200 hours of factual entertainment broadcast programming and 100 hours of corporate communications each year. Content is distributed over a range of multimedia platforms including websites, intranets, CD-ROM, DVD, mobile devices and Internet video streaming.

Tyburn Film Productions Limited

Cippenham Court, Cippenham Lane, Cippenham, Nr Slough SL1 5AU

☎01753 516767 Fax 01753 691785

Feature films. Subsidiary of **Arlington Productions Limited**. No unsolicited submissions.

UK Film and TV Production Company Plc

3 Colville Place, London W1T 2BH

☎020 7255 1650

Contact *Henrietta Fudakowski*

Film producers. OUTPUT includes *Tsotsi*, winner of the 2005 Oscar for Foreign Film. Currently looking for feature films, with a preference for stories with humour. No TV, please. Return postage and list of credits essential. Please phone before submitting material.

Vera Productions

66–68 Margaret Street, London W1W 8SR

☎020 7436 6116 Fax 020 7436 6117

Contact *Phoebe Wallace*

Produces television comedy such as *Bremner, Bird and Fortune*.

Video Enterprises

12 Barbers Wood Road, High Wycombe HP12 4EP

☎01494 534144/07831 875216 (mobile)
Fax 01494 534145

✉ videoenterprises@ntlworld.com
www.videoenterprises.co.uk

Contact *Maurice R. Fleisher*

Video and TV, mainly corporate: business and industrial training, promotional material and conferences. No unsolicited material 'but always ready to try out good new writers'.

VIP Broadcasting

8 Bunbury Way, Epsom KT17 4JP

☎01372 721196 Fax 01372 726697

✉ mail@vipbroadcasting.co.uk

Contact *Chris Vezey*

Produces a wide range of radio programmes, particularly interviews, documentaries, music programmes and live concerts. Won award for 'Best Sound' at New York Festival 2000. Approach with idea by e-mail in the first instance; no unsolicited mss.

Wall to Wall

8–9 Spring Place, London NW5 3ER

☎020 7485 7424 Fax 020 7267 5292

www.walltowall.co.uk

Chief Executive *Alex Graham*

Factual and drama programming. OUTPUT includes *Who Do You Think You Are?*; *New Tricks*; *A Rather English Marriage*; *Glasgow Kiss*; *Sex, Chips & Rock 'n' Roll*; *The 1940s House*; *Body Story*; *Neanderthal*; *The Mafia*; *Not Forgotten*; *H. G. Wells*.

Jane Walmsley Productions

See **JAM Pictures**

Walsh Bros. Limited

4 The Heights, London SE7 8JH

☎020 8858 6870

✉ john@walshbros.co.uk
www.walshbros.co.uk

Producer/Director *John Walsh*

Producer/Head of Finance *David Walsh, ACA*

Producer/Head of Development *Maura Walsh*

BAFTA-nominated producers of television, film drama and documentaries. OUTPUT *Monarch* (feature film); *Don't Make Me Angry* (Ch 4); *Headhunting the Homeless* (BBC programme on the perception of homeless people in the work place); *Trex* (factual series on teenagers at work in China, Mexico, Vancouver and Alaska); *Trex2* (follow-up series covering Romania, India, Iceland and Louisiana); *Boyz & Girlz* (Derbyshire dairy farm documentary series); *Cowboyz & Cowgirlz* (US sequel to hit series of Brit teens working on a ranch in Montana). Also arts documentaries: *The Comedy Store* and *Ray Harryhausen* (the work of Hollywood special effects legend). Drama: *The Sleeper*; *The Sceptic and the Psychic*; *A State of Mind*.

Paul Weiland Film Company

14 Newburgh Street, London W1F 7RT

☎020 7287 6900 Fax 020 7434 0146

✉ info@weilands.co.uk
www.weilands.co.uk
Television commercials and pop promos.

Whistledown Productions Ltd
66 Southwark Bridge Road, London SE1 0AS
☎020 7922 1120
✉ davidprest@whistledown.net
www.whistledown.net

Managing Director *David Prest*

Producer of Sony Award-winning Landmark Series for BBC Radio 4. Features and documentaries on a wide range of social and historical subjects, contemporary issues and popular culture. OUTPUT includes *Questions Questions* and *The Reunion* (Radio 4); music-based documentaries for Radio 2. 'We welcome contributions and ideas, but phone or e-mail first.'

Wise Buddah Creative Ltd
74 Great Titchfield Street, London W1W 7QP
☎020 7307 1600 Fax 020 7307 1602
✉ info@wisebuddah.com
www.wisebuddah.com

Contacts *Chris North, Paul Plant*

Radio production company: documentaries and commercials. Also studio facilities, sound-to-picture/sound design, talent management. No unsolicited material.

Witzend Productions
See **FremantleMedia Ltd**

Working Title Films Ltd
Oxford House, 76 Oxford Street, London
W1D 1BS
☎020 7307 3000 Fax 020 7307 3001/2/3

Co-Chairmen (films) *Tim Bevan, Eric Fellner*
Head of Development (films) *Natascha Wharton*
Executive Producer (films) *Debra Hayward*
Development Executives (films) *Amelia Granger, Rachael Prior*
Television *Simon Wright*

Feature films OUTPUT *United 93*; *Smokin' Aces*; *Sixty Six*; *Catch a Fire*; *Gone*; *Nanny McPhee*; *Pride & Prejudice*; *The Interpreter*; *Wimbledon*; *Bridget Jones 2*; *Edge of Reason*; *Shaun of the Dead*; *Love Actually*; *Thunderbirds*; *Ned Kelly*; *Johnny English*; *Bridget Jones's Diary*; *Captain Corelli's Mandolin*; *Ali G Indahouse*; *Billy Elliot*; *Notting Hill*; *Elizabeth*; *Fargo*; *Dead Man Walking*; *French Kiss*; *Four Weddings and a Funeral*; *The Hudsucker Proxy*; *The Tall Guy*; *Wish You Were Here*; *My Beautiful Laundrette*.

Television (drama, family/children's entertainment, comedy) OUTPUT *The Robber Bride*; *Perfect Strangers*; *The Other Woman*; *Dr Jekyll & Mr Hyde*; *Ready When You Are Mr McGill*; *Come Together*; *Lucky Jim*; *Randall & Hopkirk (deceased) I & II*; *The Last of the Blonde Bombshells*; *Doomwatch*; *More Tales of the City*; *Tales of the City*; *Lano and Woodley I & II*; *The Baldy Man I & II*; *The Borrowers I & II*; *News Hounds*. No unsolicited mss at present.

Wortman Productions UK
48 Chiswick Staithe, London W4 3TP
☎020 8994 8886/07976 805976 (mobile)
✉ nevillewortman@beeb.net

Producer *Neville Wortman*

Co-producers with Polestar Pictures Ltd. Feature film and TV production for drama, documentary, entertainment and corporate. OUTPUT 'Lost Ships' series: *White Gold of the Dragon Sea* (Discovery Channel, US); *Neffertiti*; *Resurrected*; *Who Killed Julius Caesar* (Discovery Channel, US/Ch 5, UK); 'Days That Shook the World' series: *Conspiracy to Kill*; *Hitler Bomb Plot*; *Assassinate De Gaulle* (BBC); 'Surviving Disaster' series: *Munich Air Crash*; *Eruption at Mount St Helen*; *Murder in Paradise* (Lion TV/Ch4) *Pevkovsky* ('Nuclear Spies' BBC2 series). Open to new writing, preferably through agents; single page outline, some pages of dialogue; s.a.e. for reply.

Theatre Producers

For latest minimum rates for writers of plays for subsidised repertory theatres (not Scotland) access the following websites: Theatrical Management Association at www.tmauk.org; and the Writers' Guild at www.writersguild.org.uk

Almeida Theatre Company

The Almeida Theatre, Almeida Street, London N1 1TA
☎020 7288 4900 Fax 020 7288 4901
www.almeida.co.uk
Artistic Director *Michael Attenborough*

Founded 1980. The Almeida is a full-time producing theatre, presenting a year-round theatre programme in which new light is shed on an eclectic mix of new plays, classic revivals, adaptations and new versions of international work. Previous productions: *Festen*; *The Goat, or Who is Sylvia?*; *The Lady From the Sea*; *The Late Henry Moss*; *Enemies*. No unsolicited mss.

Alternative Theatre Company Ltd

Bush Theatre, Shepherds Bush Green, London W12 8QD
☎020 7602 3703 Fax 020 7602 7614
✉ info@bushtheatre.co.uk
www.bushtheatre.co.uk
Literary Manager *Abigail Gonda*

Founded 1972. Trading as The Bush Theatre. Produces nine new plays a year (principally British) including up to three visiting companies also producing new work: 'we are a writer's theatre'. Previous productions include: *Kiss of the Spiderwoman* Manuel Puig; *Raping the Gold* Lucy Gannon; *The Wexford Trilogy* Billy Roche; *Love and Understanding* Joe Penhall; *This Limetree Bower* Conor McPherson; *Discopigs* Enda Walsh; *The Pitchfork Disney* Philip Ridley; *Caravan* Helen Blakeman; *Beautiful Thing* Jonathan Harvey; *Killer Joe* Tracy Letts; *Shang-a-Lang* Catherine Johnson; *Howie the Rookie* Mark O'Rowe; *The Glee Club* Richard Cameron; *Adrenalin ... Heart* Georgia Fitch. Scripts are read by a team of associates, then discussed with the management, a process which takes about four months. The theatre offers a small number of commissions, recommissions to ensure further drafts on promising plays, and a guarantee against royalties so writers are not financially penalised even though the plays are produced in a small house. Writers should send scripts (full-length plays only) with small s.a.e. for acknowledgement and large s.a.e. for return of script.

ATC (Actors Touring Company)

15–16 Nassau Street, London W1W 7AB
☎020 7580 7723 Fax 020 7580 7724
✉ info@atc-online.com
www.atc-online.com
Artistic Director *Bijan Sheibani*

Collaborates with writers on adaptation and/or translation work and unsolicited mss will be considered in this category as well as new writing. 'We endeavour to read mss but do not have the resources to do so quickly.' As a small-scale company, all plays must have a cast of six or less.

Birmingham Repertory Theatre

Centenary Square, Broad Street, Birmingham B1 2EP
☎0121 245 2000 Fax 0121 245 2100
www.birmingham-rep.co.uk
Contact *Literary Assistant*

The Birmingham Repertory Theatre aims to provide a platform for the best work from new writers from both within and beyond the West Midlands region. The Rep is committed to the production of new work which reflects both the diversity of contemporary experience and of approaches to writing for the stage. The commissioning of new plays takes place across the full range of the theatre's activities: in the Main House, The Door (which is a dedicated new writing space) and on tour to community venues in the region. The theatre runs a programme of writers' attachments every year in addition to its commissioning policy and maintains close links with *Script* (the regional writers' training agency) and the MPhil in Playwriting Studies at the University of Birmingham. For more information contact the Literary Assistant.

Black Theatre Co-op

See **NITRO**

Bootleg Theatre Company

23 Burgess Green, Bishopdown, Salisbury
SP1 3El
☎01722 421476
✉ colin281@btinternet.com

Contact *Colin Burden*

Founded 1984. Tries to encompass as wide an audience as possible and has a tendency towards plays with socially relevant themes. A good bet for new writing since unsolicited mss are very welcome. 'Our policy is to produce new and/or rarely seen plays and anything received is given the most serious consideration.' Actively seeks to obtain grants to commission new writers for the company. Productions include: *Asking for It; 17th Valentine; King Squealer*.

Borderline Theatre Company

Darlington New Church, North Harbour
Street, Ayr KA8 8AA
☎01292 281010 Fax 01292 618685
✉ enquiries@borderlinetheatre.co.uk
www.borderlinetheatre.co.uk

Producer *Eddie Jackson*

Founded 1974. Borderline is one of Scotland's leading touring companies. Tours to main-house theatres and small venues throughout Scotland. Productions include the world premières of *The Angels' Share* by Chris Dolan; *The Prince and the Pilot* Anita Sullivan. Previous writers have included Dario Fo, Liz Lochhead and John Byrne. Borderline is also committed to commissioning and touring new plays for young people. Please contact the company before submitting synopsis or script.

Bristol Old Vic Theatre Company (Old Vic, Studio & Basement)

King Street, Bristol BS1 4ED
☎0117 949 3993 Fax 0117 949 3996
✉ admin@bristol-old-vic.co.uk
www.bristol-old-vic.co.uk

Bristol Old Vic actively seeks new writers for development and commission. 'We do not offer a formal reading service but are keen to build relationships with local writers in particular.' NB The theatre is closed until late 2008 for a £7 million refurbishment; no submissions during this period.

Bush Theatre

See **Alternative Theatre Company Ltd**

Carnival (Films & Theatre) Ltd

See entry under *Film, TV and Radio Producers*

Citizens Theatre

Gorbals, Glasgow G5 9DS
☎0141 429 5561 Fax 0141 429 7374
✉ info@citz.co.uk
www.citz.co.uk

Artistic Directors *Jeremy Raison, Guy Hollands*
General Manager *Anna Stapleton*

No formal new play policy. The theatre has a play reader but opportunities to do new work are limited.

Clwyd Theatr Cymru

Mold, Flintshire CH7 1YA
☎01352 756331 Fax 01352 701558
✉ drama@celtic.co.uk
www.clwyd-theatr-cymru.co.uk

Literary Manager *William James* (william.james@clwyd-theatr-cymru.co.uk)

Clwyd Theatr Cymru produces plays performed by a core ensemble in Mold and tours them throughout Wales (in English and Welsh). Productions are a mix of classics, revivals and contemporary drama. Recent new writing includes: *Memory* Jonathan Lichtenstein; *Stone City Blue* Ed Thomas; *The Rabbit* Meredydd Barker; *The Journey of Mary Kelly* Siân Evans; *And Now What?* Tim Baker and Sarah Argent; *The Way It Was, Flights of Fancy; Pocketful of Memories; The Ballad of Megan Morgan; Flora's War/Rhyfel Flora; Word for Word/Gair am Air* and *The Secret/Y Gyfrinach*: all Tim Baker. Plays by Welsh writers or on Welsh themes will be considered.

Michael Codron Plays Ltd

Aldwych Theatre Offices, Aldwych, London
WC2B 4DF
☎020 7240 8291 Fax 020 7240 8467

Michael Codron Plays Ltd manages the Aldwych Theatre in London's West End. The plays it produces don't necessarily go into the Aldwych but always tend to be big-time West End fare. Previous productions: *Bedroom Farce; Blue Orange; Copenhagen; The Invention of Love; Hapgood; Uncle Vanya; Rise and Fall of Little Voice; Arcadia; Dead Funny; My Brilliant Divorce; Dinner; Democracy; Glorious!*. No particular rule of thumb on subject matter or treatment. The acid test is whether 'something appeals to Michael'. Straight plays rather than musicals.

Colchester Mercury Theatre Limited

Balkerne Gate, Colchester CO1 1PT
☎01206 577006 Fax 01206 769607
✉ info@mercurytheatre.co.uk

www.mercurytheatre.co.uk

Chief Executive *Dee Evans*
Associate Director *Adrian Stokes*

Producing theatre with a wide-ranging audience. New writing encouraged. The theatre has a free playwright's group for adults with a serious commitment to writing plays.

The Coliseum, Oldham

Fairbottom Street, Oldham OL1 3SW
☎0161 624 1731 Fax 0161 624 5318

Chief Executive/Artistic Director *Kevin Shaw*

The artistic policy of the theatre is to present a high quality and diverse theatre programme with the ambition to commission a new play each year. Unsolicited scripts will be read; please enclose s.a.e.

Concordance

Finborough Theatre, 118 Finborough Road, London SW10 9ED
☎020 7244 7439 Fax 020 7835 1853
✉ admin@concordance.org.uk
www.concordance.org.uk

Artistic Director *Neil McPherson*

Founded in 1981, Concordance is the resident company based at the **Finborough Theatre** (see entry). Presents world premières of new writing and revivals of neglected work with a special commitment to music theatre as well as integrating music into its work and productions featuring the writing of non-theatrical artists – poets, artists, novelists, etc. – presenting their work in a theatrical setting. We accept unsolicited scripts through the Finborough Theatre's submission department. Further details at www.finboroughtheatre.co.uk

Contact Theatre Company

Oxford Road, Manchester M15 6JA
☎0161 274 3434 Fax 0161 274 0640
✉ info@contact-theatre.org.uk
www.contact-theatre.org

Artistic Director *John E. McGrath*

The RAW Theatre Department at Contact looks at new writing and new work. The title RAW: Rhythm and Words in Theatre emphasises the fact that the new writing department will concentrate on all forms of writing for theatre – including lyrical writing, and experiments with other artists as well as plays. Works primarily with the 13–30 age group and is particularly interested in materials that relate to the lives and culture of young people. 'We guarantee to read the first ten pages of whatever you

send at Pitch Party, which comprises a group of people from Contact and the BBC. From there your writing could be entered into Flip the Script (our monthly no-holds-barred playwriting "slam" night where professional actors and directors put 5–7 minutes of your script on stage), BBC Writers Room, or you can access our RAW writing workshop programme.'

Crucible Theatre

55 Norfolk Street, Sheffield S1 1DA
☎0114 249 5999 Fax 0114 249 6003

Associate Director *Ellie Jones*
Literary Associate *Matthew Byam Shaw*

'Although we are interested in all new writing, most of the new work we present will be the result of commissions or prolonged script development with writers in whom we have expressed an interest.'

Derby Playhouse

Eagle Centre, Derby DE1 2NF
☎01332 363271 Fax 01332 547200
www.derbyplayhouse.co.uk

Chief Executive *Karen Hebden*
Creative Producer *Stephen Edwards*

Derby Playhouse is interested in new work and has produced several world premières over the last year. 'We have a discrete commissioning budget but already have several projects under way. Due to the amount of scripts we receive, we now ask writers to send a letter accompanied by a synopsis of the play, a résumé of writing experience and any ten pages of the script they wish to submit. We will then determine whether we think it is suitable for the Playhouse, in which case we will ask for a full script.' Writers are welcome to send details of rehearsed readings and productions as an alternative means of introducing the theatre to their work.

Druid Theatre Company

Flood Street, Galway, Republic of Ireland
☎00 353 91 568660 Fax 00 353 91 563109
✉ info@druidtheatre.com
www.druidtheatre.com

New Writing Manager *Thomas Conway*

Founded 1975. Based in Galway and playing nationally and internationally, the company operates a major programme for the development of new writing. While focusing on Irish work, the company also accepts unsolicited material from outside Ireland.

The Dukes

Moor Lane, Lancaster LA1 1QE
☎01524 598505 Fax 01524 598519
✉ info@dukes-lancaster.org
www.dukes-lancaster.org

Chief Executive *Amanda Belcham*
Artistic Director *Ian Hastings*

Founded 1971. The only producing house in Lancashire. Wide target market for cinema and theatre. Plays in a 313-seater end-on auditorium and in a 198-seater in-the-round studio. Host for **Litfest** – Lancaster's annual festival of literature. In the summer months open-air promenade performances are held in Williamson Park. DT3 – The Education Centre is the Dukes' newly refurbished space dedicated to work by and for young people.

Dundee Repertory Theatre

Tay Square, Dundee DD1 1PB
☎01382 227684 Fax 01382 228609
✉ hwatson@dundeereptheatre.co.uk
www.dundeereptheatre.co.uk

Artistic Directors *Dominic Hill, James Brining*

Founded 1939. Plays to a varied audience. Translations and adaptations of classics, and new local plays. Most new work is commissioned. Interested in contemporary plays in translation and in new Scottish writing. No scripts except by prior arrangement.

Eastern Angles Theatre Company

Sir John Mills Theatre, Gatacre Road, Ipswich IP1 2LQ
☎01473 218202 Fax 01473 384999
✉ admin@easternangles.co.uk
www.easternangles.co.uk

Artistic Director *Ivan Cutting*
General Manager *Jill Streatfeild*

Founded 1982. Plays to a rural audience for the most part. New work only: some commissioned, some devised by the company, some researched documentaries. Unsolicited mss welcome but scripts or writers need to have some connection with East Anglia. 'We are always keen to develop and produce new writing, especially that which is germane to a rural area.'

Edinburgh Royal Lyceum Theatre

See **Royal Lyceum Theatre Company**

English Touring Theatre

25 Short Street, London SE1 8LJ
☎020 7450 1990 Fax 020 7450 1991
✉ admin@ett.org.uk

www.ett.org.uk

Director *Stephen Unwin*

Founded 1993. National touring company visiting middle-scale receiving houses and arts centres throughout the UK. Mostly mainstream. Largely classical programme, but with increasing interest to tour one modern English play per year. Strong commitment to education work. No unsolicited mss.

Finborough Theatre

118 Finborough Road, London SW10 9ED
☎020 7244 7439 Fax 020 7835 1853
✉ admin@finboroughtheatre.co.uk
www.finboroughtheatre.co.uk

Artistic Director *Neil McPherson*

Founded 1980. 'One of London's leading new writing venues' (*Time Out*). Presents revivals of neglected work from 1850 onwards, music theatre and UK premières of foreign work, particularly from Ireland, the United States and Canada. The theatre is available for hire and the fee is sometimes negotiable to encourage interesting work. Premièred work by Chris Lee, Anthony Neilson, Naomi Wallace, Tony Marchant, Diane Samuels and Mark Ravenhill. Three times winner of the Pearson Award. Unsolicited scripts are accepted, but please read carefully the details on submissions policy on the website before sending any scripts.

Gate Theatre Company Ltd

11 Pembridge Road, London W11 3HQ
☎020 7229 5387 Fax 020 7221 6055
✉ gate@gatetheatre.co.uk
www.gatetheatre.co.uk

Artistic Director *Thea Sharrock*

Founded 1979. Plays to a mixed, London-wide audience, depending on production. Aims to produce British premières of plays which originate from abroad and translations of neglected classics. Runs a biennial Translation Award. Recent productions include: *The Chairs* by Eugène Ionesco, transl. Martin Crimp; *The Emperor Jones* by Eugene O'Neill; *Tshepang* by Lara Foot Newton; *Woyzeck* by George Büchner, adapted by Daniel Kramer; *Tejas Verdes* by Fermín Cabal, transl. by Robert Shaw. Positively encourages writers from abroad to send in scripts or translations. Most unsolicited scripts are read but plays by writers from the UK will not be accepted. Please address submissions to the Literary Manager. Always enclose s.a.e. if play needs returning.

Graeae Theatre Company
LVS Resource Centre, 356 Holloway Road, London N7 6PA
☎020 7700 2455 Fax 020 7609 7324
✉ info@graeae.org
www.graeae.org
Minicom 020 7700 8184
CEO/Artistic Director *Jenny Sealey*
Europe's premier theatre company of disabled people, the company tours nationally and internationally with innovative theatre productions highlighting both historical and contemporary disabled experience. Graeae also runs educational programmes available to schools, youth clubs, students and disabled adults nationally and provides vocational training in theatre arts (including playwriting). Unsolicited scripts, from disabled writers, welcome. New work is commissioned.

Hampstead Theatre
Eton Avenue, Swiss Cottage, London NW3 3EU
☎020 7449 4200 Fax 020 7449 4201
✉ literary@hampsteadtheatre.com
www.hampsteadtheatre.com
Contact *Katy Silverton*
A brand new Hampstead Theatre opened in 2003. The building is an intimate space with a flexible stage and an auditorium capable of expanding to seat 325. The artistic policy continues to be the production of British and international new plays and the development of important young writers. 'We are looking for writers who recognise the power of theatre and who have a story to tell. All plays are read and discussed. We give feedback to all writers with potential.' Writers produced in the last five years at Hampstead include Gregory Burke, Dennis Kelly, Nell Leyshon, Sharman Macdonald, Tamsin Oglesby, Debbie Tucker Green and Roy Williams. In earlier years, breakthrough plays by Harold Pinter, David Hare, Mike Leigh, Pam Gems and Stephen Jeffreys were produced.

Harrogate Theatre
Oxford Street, Harrogate HG1 1QF
☎01423 502710 Fax 01423 563205
✉ firstname.surname@harrogatetheatre.co.uk
www.harrogatetheatre.co.uk
Artistic Director *To be appointed*
Produces four to five productions a year on the main stage, one of which may be a new play but is most likely to be commissioned. Annual mainstage Youth Theatre production may also be commissioned. (Policy on new writing unknown at the time of going to press as a new artistic director had not been appointed.)

Headlong Theatre
Chertsey Chambers, 12 Mercer Street, London WC2H 9QD
☎020 7438 9940 Fax 020 7438 9941
✉ info@headlongtheatre.co.uk
www.headlongtheatre.co.uk
Artistic Director *Rupert Goold*
Formerly Oxford Stage Company. A middle-scale touring company producing established and new plays. On average, one new play or new adaptation a year. Due to forthcoming projects the company is not considering unsolicited scripts at present.

Heritage Theatre Ltd
See entry under *Film, TV and Radio Producers*

Horsecross Arts Ltd
185 High Street, Perth PH1 5UW
☎01738 472700 Fax 01738 624576
✉ info@horsecross.co.uk
www.horsecross.co.uk
Creative Directors *Ian Grieve, Graham McLaren*
General Manager *Paul Hackett*
Founded 1935. Combination of one to four-weekly repertoire of plays and musicals, incoming tours and studio productions. Unsolicited mss are read when time permits, but the timetable for return of scripts is lengthy. New plays staged by the company are usually commissioned under the SAC scheme.

Hull Truck Theatre Company
Spring Street, Hull HU2 8RW
☎01482 224800 Fax 01482 581182
✉ admin@hulltruck.co.uk
www.hulltruck.co.uk
Executive Director *Joanne Gower*
General Manager *Nigel Penn*
Artistic Directors *John Godber, Gareth Tudor-Price*
Associate Director *Nick Lane*
Literary Development Manager *Steven J. Atkinson*
John Godber, of *Teechers, Bouncers* and *Up 'n' Under* fame (the artistic director of this high-profile Northern company since 1984), has very much dominated the scene in the past with his own successful plays. The emphasis is still on new writing but Godber's works continue to be toured extensively. Recent premieres include *Christmas Crackers; Crown Prince; My Favourite*

Summer, Ladies Down Under, Sully. Most new plays are commissioned. Recent Commissions: *A Kick in the Baubles* and *Kissing Married Women* Gordon Steel; *Ladies Day* Amanda Whittington; *Up on Roof* Richard Bean; *1984* adapted by Nick Lane and *I Want That Hair* Jane Thornton, plus various family shows by Nick Lane. 'New scripts should be addressed to the Literary Development Manager who will attempt as quick a response as possible. Bear in mind the artistic policy of Hull Truck, which is accessibility and popularity.' In general, not interested in musicals or in plays with casts of more than seven.

Stephen Joseph Theatre

Westborough, Scarborough YO11 1JW
☎01723 370540 Fax 01723 360506
www.sjt.uk.com

Artistic Director *Alan Ayckbourn*

A two-auditoria complex housing a 165-seat end stage theatre/cinema (the McCarthy) and a 400-seat theatre-in-the-round (the Round). Positive policy on new work. For obvious reasons, Alan Ayckbourn's work features quite strongly but a new writing programme ensures plays from other sources are actively encouraged. Also runs a lunchtime season of one-act plays each summer. Writers are advised however that the SJT is very unlikely to produce an unsolicited script – synopses are preferred. Recent commissions and past productions include: *Soap* Sarah Woods; *Fields of Gold* Alex Jones; *For Starters* Nick Warburton; *Bedtime Stories* Lesley Bruce; *Making Waves* Stephen Clark; *Larkin with Women* Ben Brown; *Amaretti Angels* Sarah Phelps; *Something Blue* Gill Adams; *Clockwatching* and *A Listening Heaven* Torben Betts; *The Star Throwers* Paul Lucas; *Safari Party* Tim Firth; *Drowning on Dry Land*; *Private Fears in Public Places* and *My Sister Sadie* Alan Ayckbourn. 'Writers are welcome to send details of rehearsed readings and productions as an alternative means of introducing the theatre to their work.' Submit to the Literary Department enclosing an s.a.e. for return of mss.

Bill Kenwright Ltd

BKL House, 106 Harrow Road, London W2 1RR
☎020 7446 6200 Fax 020 7446 6222

Contact *Bill Kenwright*

Presents both revivals and new shows for West End and touring theatres. Although new work tends to be by established playwrights, this does not preclude or prejudice new plays from new writers. The company has an in-house dramaturg. Scripts should be addressed to Bill Kenwright with a covering letter and s.a.e. 'We have enormous amounts of scripts sent to us although we very rarely produce unsolicited work. Scripts are read systematically. Please do not phone; the return of your script or contact with you will take place in time.'

Komedia

44–47 Gardner Street, North Laine, Brighton BN1 1UN
☎01273 647101 Fax 01273 647102
✉ admin@komedia.co.uk
www.komedia.co.uk

Contact *David Lavender*

Founded in 1994, Komedia promotes, produces and presents new work. Mss of new plays welcome.

Leicester Haymarket Theatre

Belgrave Gate, Leicester LE1 3YQ
☎0116 253 0021 Fax 0116 251 3310
✉ enquiries@lhtheatre.co.uk
www.lhtheatre.co.uk

Artistic Directors *Kully Thiarai, Paul Kerryson*

Leicester Haymarket Theatre aims for a balanced programme of original and established works. It is a multi-cultural integrated company with educational projects that support all productions and areas of work. Current programme includes work by Brecht and Stephen Sondheim. There is a thriving young peoples theatre company, *Young Blood*, plus a New Writing Theatre initiative. (The Haymarket Theatre closed in 2007 and the company is due to move to a new, state-of-the-art theatre in Rutland Street in spring 2008.)

Library Theatre Company

St Peter's Square, Manchester M2 5PD
☎0161 234 1913 Fax 0161 228 6481
✉ jwong@manchester.gov.uk
www.librarytheatre.com

Artistic Director *Chris Honer*

Produces new and contemporary work, as well as the classics. No unsolicited mss. Send outline of the nature of the script first. Encourages new writing through the commissioning of new plays and through a programme of rehearsed readings to help writers' development.

Live Theatre Company

7/8 Trinity Chare, Newcastle upon Tyne NE1 3DF
☎0191 261 2694 Fax 0191 232 2224

✉ info@live.org.uk
www.live.org.uk

Artistic Director *Max Roberts*
Executive Director *Jim Beirne*

Founded 1973. Produces shows at its refurbished 200-seat venue, and also tours regionally and nationally. Company policy is to produce work that is rooted in the culture of the region, particularly for those who do not normally get involved in the arts. The company is particularly interested in promoting new writing. As well as full-scale productions the company organises workshops, rehearsed readings and other new writing activities. The company also enjoys a close relationship with **New Writing North** and is funded to support new writing through the BBC's *Northern Exposure* project. Productions include *Falling Together* Tom Hadaway; *Cooking With Elvis* Lee Hall; *Bones* Peter Straughan; *ne1* and *Tales From the Backyard* Alan Plater; *Double Lives* Julia Darling and Sean O'Brien; *Smack Family Robinson* Richard Bean; *Keepers of the Flame* and *Laughter When We're Dead* Sean O'Brien.

London Bubble Theatre Company

5 Elephant Lane, London SE16 4JD
☎020 7237 4434 Fax 020 7231 2366
✉ admin@londonbubble.org.uk
www.londonbubble.org.uk

Artistic Director *Jonathan Petherbridge*

Produces workshops, plays and events for a mixed audience of theatregoers and non-theatregoers, wide-ranging in terms of age, culture and class. Previous productions: *Punchkin, Enchanter; You Can't Say You Can't Play*. Unsolicited mss are received but 'our reading service is extremely limited and there can be a considerable wait before we can give a response'. Commissions approximately one new project a year, often inspired by a promenade site, specific community of interest or workshop group.

Lyric Hammersmith

Lyric Square, King Street, London W6 0QL
☎08700 500 511 Fax 020 8741 5965
✉ enquiries@lyric.co.uk
www.lyric.co.uk

Artistic Director *David Farr*
Executive Director *Jessica Hepburn*

The main theatre stages an eclectic programme of new and revived classics. Interested in developing projects with writers, translators and adaptors. The Lyric does not accept unsolicited

scripts. Its 110-seat studio focuses on work for children, young people and families.

mac

Cannon Hill Park, Birmingham B12 9QH
☎0121 440 3838 Fax 0121 446 4372
✉ enquiries@macarts.co.uk
www.macarts.co.uk

Director *Dorothy Wilson*

Innovative creative arts activities, including theatre, music, comedy, plays for children, literature and poetry events, courses and workshops, family show at Christmas, films and free exhibitions.

Manchester Library Theatre

See **Library Theatre Company**

New Vic Theatre

Etruria Road, Newcastle under Lyme ST5 0JG
☎01782 717954 Fax 01782 712885
✉ admin@newvictheatre.org.uk
www.newvictheatre.org.uk

Artistic Director *Theresa Heskins*

The New Vic is a purpose-built theatre-in-the-round. Produces ten in-house plays each year and is active within the education sector and community. New plays produced are the result of specific commissions. Send synopses *not* unsolicited scripts. 'We cannot guarantee that unsolicited scripts will be read; they will be returned on receipt of an s.a.e.'

Newpalm Productions

26 Cavendish Avenue, London N3 3QN
☎020 8349 0802 Fax 020 8346 8257

Contact *Lionel Chilcott*

Very rarely produces new plays (*As Is* by William M. Hoffman, which came from Broadway to the Half Moon Theatre, was an exception to this). National tours and West End productions such as *Peter Pan (The Musical); Noises Off; Seven Brides for Seven Brothers* and *Rebecca*, at regional repertory theatres, are more typical examples of Newpalm's work. Both plays and musicals are, however, welcome; synopses are preferable to scripts.

Nimax Theatres

1 Lumley Court, off 402 Strand, London WC2R 0NB
☎0845 434 9290

CEO *Nica Burns*

West End theatre managers of the Apollo,

Duchess, Garrick, Lyric and Vaudeville theatres. Unsolicited scripts are not considered.

NITRO
6 Brewery Road, London N7 9NH
☎020 7609 1331 Fax 020 7609 1221
✉ info@nitro.co.uk
www.nitro.co.uk
Artistic Director *Felix Cross*

Founded 1978. Formerly Black Theatre Co-op. Plays to a mixed audience, approximately 65% female. Usually tours nationally twice a year. 'A music theatre company, we are committed in the first instance to new writing by Black British writers and work which relates to the Black culture and experience throughout the Diaspora.' Unsolicited mss welcome.

Northcott Theatre
Stocker Road, Exeter EX4 4QB
☎01392 223999 Fax 01392 223996
www.northcott-theatre.co.uk
Artistic Director *Ben Crocker*

Founded 1967. The Northcott is the South-west's principal subsidised producing theatre, situated on the University of Exeter campus. Describes its audience as 'geographically diverse, with a core audience of AB1s (40–60 age range)'. Continually looking to broaden the base of its audience profile, targeting younger and/or non-mainstream theatregoers. Aims to develop, promote and produce quality new writing which reflects the life of the region and addresses the audience it serves. Generally works on a commission basis but occasionally options existing new work. Unsolicited mss welcome. No mss can be returned unless a correct value s.a.e. is included with the original submission. The theatre is closed until October 2007 for refurbishment.

Norwich Puppet Theatre
St James, Whitefriars, Norwich NR3 1TN
☎01603 615564 Fax 01603 617578
✉ info@puppettheatre.co.uk
www.puppettheatre.co.uk
Artistic Director *Luis Boy*
General Manager *Ian Woods*

Plays to a young audience (aged 3–12) but developing shows for adult audiences interested in puppetry. All year round programme plus tours to schools and arts venues. Most productions are based on traditional stories but unsolicited mss welcome if relevant.

Nottingham Playhouse
Nottingham Playhouse Trust, Wellington Circus, Nottingham NG1 5AF
☎0115 947 4361 Fax 0115 947 5759
www.nottinghamplayhouse.co.uk
Artistic Director *Giles Croft*

Aims to make innovation popular, and present the best of world theatre, working closely with the communities of Nottingham and Nottinghamshire. Unsolicited mss will be read. It normally takes about six months, however, and 'we have never yet produced an unsolicited script. All our plays have to achieve a minimum of 60 per cent audiences in a 732-seat theatre. We have no studio.'

Nottingham Playhouse Roundabout Theatre in Education
Wellington Circus, Nottingham NG1 5AF
☎0115 947 4361
✉ andrewb@nottinghamplayhouse.co.uk
www.nottinghamplayhouse.co.uk
Contact *Andrew Breakwell*

Founded 1973. Theatre-in-Education company of the **Nottingham Playhouse**. Plays to a young audience aged 5–18 years of age. 'We are committed to the encouragement of new writing and commission at least two new plays for young people each year. With other major producers in the East Midlands we share the resources of the *Theatre Writing Partnership* which is based at the Playhouse. See website for philosophy and play details. Please make contact before submitting scripts.'

N.T.C. Touring Theatre Company
The Playhouse, Bondgate Without, Alnwick NE66 1PQ
☎01665 602586 Fax 01665 605837
✉ admin@ntc-touringtheatre.co.uk
www.ntc-touringtheatre.co.uk
Contact *Gillian Hambleton*
General Manager *Anna Flood*

Founded 1978. Northumberland Theatre Company. An Arts Council England revenue funded organisation. Predominantly rural, small-scale touring company, playing to village halls and community centres throughout the Northern region, the Scottish Borders and countrywide. Productions range from established classics to new work and popular comedies, but must be appropriate to their audience. Unsolicited scripts welcome but are unlikely to be produced. All scripts are read and returned with constructive criticism within six months. Writers whose style is of interest may then be commissioned. The company encourages new writing and commissions when possible. Financial constraints restrict casting to a *maximum* of six.

Nuffield Theatre

University Road, Southampton SO17 1TR
☎023 8031 5500 Fax 023 8031 5511
✉ alison.thurley@nuffieldtheatre.co.uk
www.nuffieldtheatre.co.uk

Artistic Director *Patrick Sandford*
Script Executive *John Burgess*

Well known as a good bet for new playwrights, the Nuffield gets an awful lot of scripts. Produces two new main stage plays every season. Previous productions: *Exchange* by Yuri Trifonov (transl. Michael Frayn) which transferred to the Vaudeville Theatre; *The Floating Light Bulb* Woody Allen (British première); *Nelson*, a new play by Pam Gems; *Dogspot* and *The Dramatic Attitudes of Miss Fanny Kemble* Claire Luckham; and *The Winter Wife* by Claire Tomalin. Open-minded about subject and style, producing musicals as well as straight plays. Also opportunities for some small-scale fringe work. Scripts preferred to synopses in the case of writers new to theatre. All will, eventually, be read 'but please be patient. We do not have a large team of paid readers. We read everything ourselves.'

Octagon Theatre Trust Ltd

Howell Croft South, Bolton BL1 1SB
☎01204 529407 Fax 01204 556502
✉ info@octagonbolton.co.uk
www.octagonbolton.co.uk

Executive Director *John Blackmore*

Founded in 1967 and celebrating its 40th anniversary from September 2007 to July 2008, the award-winning Octagon Theatre stages at least eight main auditorium home-produced shows a year, and hosts UK touring companies such as the National Theatre, John Godber's Hull Truck Theatre Company, Peshkar Productions and Alan Ayckbourn's Stephen Joseph Theatre. Also hosts the work of partner companies as part of its commitment to creative partnerships. The theatre boasts a thriving and constantly developing participatory department, activ8, which operates a highly successful Youth Theatre as well as initiating and facilitating exciting education and outreach programmes. The theatre is keen to encourage new writing but, due to the lack of a dedicated literary department, is unable to accept and process new and unsolicited scripts;

the theatre uses **North West Playwrights** as a reading service instead.

Orange Tree Theatre

1 Clarence Street, Richmond TW9 2SA
☎020 8940 0141 Fax 020 8332 0369
✉ admin@orange-tree.demon.co.uk
www.orangetreetheatre.co.uk

Artistic Director *Sam Walters*

The Orange Tree, a theatre-in-the-round venue, presents a broad cross section of work. Past productions have included plays by Rodney Ackland, John Galsworthy and a new translation of Lorca as well as new plays by Oliver Ford Davies, David Lewis, Ben Brown and Kenneth Jupp. The theatre no longer considers unsolicited mss; writers who may wish to approach the theatre are asked to write first.

Out of Joint

7 Thane Works, Thane Villas, London N7 7NU
☎020 7609 0207 Fax 020 7609 0203
✉ ojo@outofjoint.co.uk
www.outofjoint.co.uk

Director *Max Stafford-Clark*
Producer *Graham Cowley*
Literary Associate *Alex Roberts*

Founded 1993. Award-winning theatre company with new writing central to its policy. Produces new plays which reflect society and its concerns, placing an emphasis on education activity to attract young audiences. Welcomes unsolicited mss. Productions include: *Blue Heart* Caryl Churchill; *Our Lady of Sligo*, *The Steward of Christendom* and *Hinterland* Sebastian Barry; *Shopping and Fucking* and *Some Explicit Polaroids* Mark Ravenhill; *Rita, Sue and Bob Too* Andrea Dunbar; *A State Affair* and *Talking to Terrorists* Robin Soans; *Sliding with Suzanne* Judy Upton; *The Positive Hour* and *A Laughing Matter* April De Angelis; *Duck* and *O go my Man* Stella Feehily; *The Permanent Way* David Hare.

Oxford Stage Company

See **Headlong Theatre**

Paines Plough

4th Floor, 43 Aldwych, London WC2B 4DN
☎020 7240 4533 Fax 020 7240 4534
✉ office@painesplough.com
www.painesplough.com

Artistic Director *Roxana Silbert*
Literary Manager *Pippa Ellis*

Founded 1975. Award-winning company

commissioning and producing new plays by British and international playwrights. Tours 2–4 plays a year nationally and worldwide for small and middle-scale. Also runs a range of projects focused on identifying and launching emerging playwrights (see website for details). 'We welcome unsolicited scripts and will respond to all submissions. We are looking for original plays that engage with the contemporary world and are written in a distinctive voice.' Recent productions: *Product* Mark Ravenhill; *Long Time Dead* Rona Munro; *After the End* Dennis Kelly; *If Destroyed True* Douglas Maxwell; *Pyrenees* David Greig; *Mercury Fur* Philip Ridley; *The Small Things* Edna Walsh.

Perth Repertory Theatre
See **Horsecross Arts Ltd**

Plymouth Theatre Royal
See **Theatre Royal**

Polka Theatre for Children
240 The Broadway, Wimbledon SW19 1SB
☎020 8543 4888 (box office)
Fax 020 8545 8365
✉ info@polkatheatre.com
www.polkatheatre.com
Artistic Director *Jon Lloyd*
Executive Director *Stephen Midlane*
Associate Director, New Writing *Richard Shannon*

Founded in 1968 and moved into its Wimbledon base in 1979. Leading children's theatre committed to commissioning and producing new plays. Programmes are planned two years ahead and at least three new plays are commissioned each year. 'Many of our scripts are commissioned from established writers. We are, however, keen to develop work from writers new to children's and young people's theatre. We run a new writing programme which includes master classes and workshops. Potential new writers' work is read and discussed on a regular basis; thus we constantly add to our pool of interesting and interested writers. This department is headed by *Richard Shannon*, Associate Director for New Writing.'

Queen's Theatre, Hornchurch
Billet Lane, Hornchurch RM11 1QT
☎01708 462362 Fax 01708 462363
✉ info@queens-theatre.co.uk
www.queens-theatre.co.uk
Artistic Director *Bob Carlton*

The Queen's Theatre is a 503-seat theatre producing eight main house productions per year, including pantomime. Aims for distinctive and accessible performances in an identifiable house style focused upon actor/musician shows but, in addition, embraces straight plays, classics and comedies. 'New play/musical submissions are welcome but should be submitted in treatment and not script form.' Also runs a writers' social group which meets on the first Monday of each month, and writers' groups for adults (contact the Education Manager for information). These groups have close links with the Queen's Community Company (of amateur actors as well as the main house company) which workshops and showcases the groups' work. The theatre also runs a biannual New Writing Award scheme which culminates in a festival called Writenow!.

The Really Useful Group Ltd
22 Tower Street, London WC2H 9TW
☎020 7240 0880 Fax 020 7240 1204
www.reallyuseful.com

Commercial/West End, national and international theatre producer/co-producer/licensor whose output has included *Joseph and the Amazing Technicolor Dreamcoat*; *Jesus Christ Superstar*; *Cats*; *Evita*; *Song & Dance*; *Daisy Pulls It Off*; *Lend Me a Tenor*; *Starlight Express*; *The Phantom of the Opera*; *Aspects of Love*; *Sunset Boulevard*; *By Jeeves*; *Whistle Down the Wind*; *The Beautiful Game*; *Tell Me On a Sunday*; *Bombay Dreams*; *The Woman in White*; *The Sound of Music*.

Red Ladder Theatre Company
3 St Peter's Buildings, York Street, Leeds LS9 8AJ
☎0113 245 5311 Fax 0113 245 5351
✉ rod@redladder.co.uk
www.redladder.co.uk
Artistic Director/Literary Manager *Rod Dixon*
Administrator *Leyla Asadi*

Founded 1968. National company touring 1–2 shows a year with a strong commitment to new work and new writers. Aimed at an audience of young people aged between 13–25 years who have little or no access to theatre. Performances held in youth clubs and theatre venues. Recent productions: *Kaahini* Maya Chowdhry; *Worlds Apart* Mick Martin; *Free Falling* and *Silent Cry* Madani Younis. The company is particularly keen to enter into a dialogue with writers with regard to creating new work for young people. E-mail the artistic director for more information at the address above.

Red Shift Theatre Company

TRG2 Trowbray House, 108 Weston Street,
London SE1 3QB
☎020 7378 9787 Fax 020 7378 9789
✉ mail@redshifttheatreco.co.uk
www.redshifttheatreco.co.uk

Contact *Jonathan Holloway* (Artistic Director)
General Manager *Emma Rees*

Founded 1982. Small-scale touring company
which plays to a theatre-literate audience.
Welcomes contact with writers – 'we try to
see their work' – and receipt of c.v.s and treatments, new translations and adaptations. Recent
productions: *The Third Man*; *Get Carter* and
Vertigo.

Ridiculusmus

BAC, Lavender Hill, London SW11 5TN
✉ enquiries@ridiculusmus.com
www.ridiculusmus.com

Artistic Directors *Jon Haynes, David Woods*

Founded 1992. Touring company which plays
to a wide range of audiences. Productions have
included adaptations of *The Importance of Being
Earnest*; *Three Men In a Boat*; *The Third Policeman*;
At Swim Two Birds and original work: *The
Exhibitionists*; *Yes, Yes, Yes*; *Say Nothing* and *Ideas
Men*. Unsolicited scripts not welcome.

Royal Court Theatre

Sloane Square, London SW1W 8AS
☎020 7565 5050
Fax 020 7565 5002 (Literary office)
www.royalcourttheatre.com

Literary Manager *Graham Whybrow*

The Royal Court is a leading international
theatre producing up to 17 new plays each year
in its 400-seat proscenium theatre and 80-seat
studio. In 1956 its first director George Devine
set out to find 'hard-hitting, uncompromising
writers whose plays are stimulating, provocative
and exciting'. This artistic policy helped transform post-war British theatre, with new plays by
writers such as John Osborne, Arnold Wesker,
John Arden, Samuel Beckett, Edward Bond
and David Storey, through to Caryl Churchill,
Jim Cartwright, Kevin Elyot and Timberlake
Wertenbaker. Since 1994 it has produced a new
generation of playwrights such as Joe Penhall,
Rebecca Prichard, Sarah Kane, Jez Butterworth,
Martin McDonagh, Mark Ravenhill, Ayub
Khan-Din, Conor McPherson, Roy Williams
and many other first-time writers. The Royal
Court has programmes for young writers and
international writers, and it is always searching
for new plays and new playwrights.

Royal Exchange Theatre Company

St Ann's Square, Manchester M2 7DH
☎0161 615 6709 Fax 0161 832 0881
✉ jo.combes@royalexchange.co.uk
www.royalexchange.co.uk

Associate Artistic Director *Sarah Frankcom*
Associate Director (Literary) *Jo Combes*

Founded 1976. The Royal Exchange has developed a new writing policy which it finds is
attracting a younger audience to the theatre.
The company has recently produced new
plays by Nick Leather, Chloe Moss, Simon
Stephens, Shelagh Stephenson, Brad Fraser, Jim
Cartwright and Owen McCafferty. Currently
has Gurpreet Bhatti, Linda Marshall Griffiths,
Owen McCafferty, Abi Morgan, Sharif Samad,
Simon Stephens and Roy Williams on commission. 'We accept unsolicited work from writers
based in the UK, and as we will often include
a full script report, we limit our reading to one
script per writer per year. If you would like your
script returned at the end of the process, please
include the appropriate postage. Please note that
we do not accept musicals or electronic copies
of scripts and our current turnaround time is
four months. Send scripts to *Jo Combes*.'

Royal Lyceum Theatre Company

Grindlay Street, Edinburgh EH3 9AX
☎0131 248 4800 Fax 0131 228 3955
www.lyceum.org.uk

Artistic Director *Mark Thomson*
Administration Manager *Ruth Butterworth*

Founded 1965. Repertory theatre which plays
to a mixed urban Scottish audience. Produces
classic, contemporary and new plays. Would
like to stage more new plays, especially Scottish.
No full-time literary staff to provide reports on
submitted scripts.

Royal National Theatre

South Bank, London SE1 9PX
☎020 7452 3333 Fax 020 7452 3344
www.nationaltheatre.org.uk

Literary Manager *Jack Bradley*

The majority of the National's new plays come
about as a result of direct commission or from
existing contacts with playwrights. There is no
quota for new work, though many of the plays
presented have been the work of living playwrights especially in the Cottesloe Theatre.
Writers new to the theatre would need to be of

exceptional talent to be successful with a script here, however the Royal NationalTheatre Studio helps a limited number of playwrights, through readings, workshops and discussions. Scripts considered but not by e-mail (send s.a.e).

Royal Shakespeare Company

1 Earlham Street, London WC2H 9LL
☎020 7845 0515
✉ Daniel.Usztan@rsc.org.uk
www.rsc.org.uk
Literary Manager *Jeanie O'Hare*

The RSC is a classical theatre company based in Stratford upon Avon. As well as Shakespeare, the RSC produces English classics, foreign classics in translation, adaptations and new plays. The Literary Department is proactive rather than reactive and seeks out the plays and playwrights it wishes to commission. 'We can only read contemporary works where the writer is known. Sadly we are unable to read unsolicited work from less established writers but we do monitor the work of emerging playwrights in production nationally and internationally.'

7:84 Theatre Company Scotland

Film City Glasgow, 4 Summertown Road,
Glasgow G51 2LY
☎0141 445 7245
✉ admin@784theatre.com
www.784theatre.com
Artistic Director *Lorenzo Mele*

Founded 1973. One of Scotland's foremost touring theatre companies committed to producing work that addresses current social, cultural and political issues. Recent productions include commissions by Scottish playwrights such as Stephen Greenhorn, Rona Munro and Martin McArdie (*Reasons to be Cheerful*); Christopher Dean (*Boiling a Frog*); Peter Arnott (*A Little Rain*); Stephen Greenhorn (*Dissent*); David Greig (*Caledonia Dreaming*) and the Scottish premières of Tony Kushner's *Angels in America* and Athol Fugard's *Valley Song*. 'The company is committed to a new writing policy that encourages and develops writers at every level of experience, to get new voices and strong messages on to the stage.' New writing development has always been central to 7:84's core activity and has included Summer Schools and rehearsed readings. The company continues to be committed to this work and its development.

Shared Experience

The Soho Laundry, 9 Dufour's Place, London
W1F 7SJ
☎020 7434 9248 Fax 020 7287 8763
✉ admin@sharedexperience.org.uk
www.sharedexperience.org.uk
Joint Artistic Directors *Nancy Meckler, Polly Teale*

Founded 1975. Varied audience depending on venue, since this is a touring company. Recent productions have included: *Anna Karenina, Mill on the Floss*, and *War and Peace* (all adapt. by Helen Edmundson); *Jane Eyre* (adapt. Polly Teale); *The House of Bernarda Alba* (transl. Rona Munro); *Mother Courage* (transl. Lee Hall); *A Doll's House* (transl. Michael Meyer); *The Magic Toyshop* (adapt. Bryony Lavery); *The Clearing* and *Gone to Earth* Helen Edmundson; *A Passage to India* (adapt. Martin Sherman); *After Mrs Rochester and Brönte* Polly Teale. No unsolicited mss. Primarily not a new writing company. New plays always commissioned.

Sherman Theatre Company

Senghennydd Road, Cardiff CF24 4YE
☎029 2064 6901 Fax 029 2064 6902
www.shermantheatre.co.uk
Artistic Director *Phil Clark*

Founded 1973. Theatre for Young People, with main house and studio. Encourages new writing; has produced 86 new plays in the last ten years. Previous productions include a David Wood adaptation of Roald Dahl's *Danny the Champion of the World*, plays by Frank Vickery (*Pullin the Wool*); Helen Griffin (*Flesh and Blood*); Patrick Jones (*Everything Must Go*); Terry Deary (*Horrible Histories Crackers Christmas*); Mike Kenny (*Puff the Magic Dragon*); Brendan Murray (*Something Beginning With ...*); Roald Dahl (*The Enormous Crocodile*); Roger Williams (*Pop*); Arnold Wesker (*Break, My Heart*). Runs a new scheme called WriteHere for which scripts can be submitted. Interesting ideas go through to ScriptSlam during which an audience votes for their favourite excerpt to be developed further.

Show of Strength

74 Chessel Street, Bedminster, Bristol
BS3 3DN
☎0117 902 0235 Fax 0117 902 0196
✉ info@showofstrength.org.uk
www.showofstrength.org.uk
Creative Producer *Sheila Hannon*

Founded 1986. Plays to an informal, younger than average audience. Aims to stage at least one new play each season with a preference for work from Bristol and the SouthWest. Will read unsolicited scripts but a lack of funding means they are unable to provide written reports. Output:

The Wills Girls Amanda Whittington; *Lags* Ron Hutchinson; *So Long Life* and *Nicholodeon* Peter Nichols. Also, rehearsed readings of new work.

Soho Theatre Company
21 Dean Street, London W1D 3NE
☎020 7287 5060 Fax 020 7287 5061
✉ writers@sohotheatre.com
www.sohotheatre.com
Artistic Director *Lisa Goldman*

Dedicated to new writing, the company has an extensive research and development programme consisting of a free script-reading service, workshops and readings. Also runs many courses for new writers. Soho Young Writers hold free 'Taster Workshops' and longer courses for promising playwrights aged 15–25. The company produces around four plays a year. Recent productions include: *Other Hands* and *Colder than Here* Laura Wade (recipient of the Critics' Circle Most Promising New Playwright and Olivier Award nominated for Outstanding Achievement); *On Ego* Mick Gordon with Paul Broks; *On Religion* Mick Gordon and A.C. Grayling (co-production with On Productions); *Shoreditch Madonna* Rebecca Lenkiewicz. Runs the **Verity Bargate Award**, a biennial competition (see entry under *Prizes*).

Sphinx Theatre Company
25 Short Street, London SE1 8LJ
☎020 7401 9993 Fax 020 7401 9995
✉ info@sphinxtheatre.co.uk
www.sphinxtheatre.co.uk
Artistic Director *Sue Parrish*
General Manager *Susannah Kraft Levene*
Administrator *Bailey Lock*

'Sphinx is a feminist theatre company that places women at the centre of its artistic endeavour.' Since 1973 the company has toured groundbreaking productions to small and mid-scale venues. Synopses and ideas are welcome by e-mail or post with s.a.e.

Talawa Theatre Company Ltd
3rd Floor, 23–25 Great Sutton Street, London EC1V 0DN
☎020 7251 6644 Fax 020 7251 5969
✉ hq@talawa.com
www.talawa.com

Founded 1985. 'Aims to provide high quality productions that reflect the significant creative role that Black theatre plays within the national and international arena and also to enlarge theatre audiences from the Black community.' Previous productions include *High Heel Parrotfish*; *Blues for Mister Charlie*; *The Key Game*. Seeks to provide a platform for new work from up and coming Black British writers. Send a copy of the script by post or e-mail. Runs a Black script development project and Black writers' group. Talawa is funded by Arts Council England, London.

Theatre Absolute
57–61 Corporation Street, Coventry CV1 1GQ
☎024 7625 7380 Fax 024 7655 0680
✉ julia@theatreabsolute.co.uk
www.theatreabsolute.co.uk
Artistic Director/Writer *Chris O'Connell*
Producer *Julia Negus*

Founded 1992. An independent theatre company which commissions, produces and tours new plays based on a strong narrative text and aimed at audiences aged 15 and upwards. Productions include: *Car*; *Kid*; *Street Trilogy*; *Hang Lenny Pope*. The company also runs The Writing House, a script development scheme.

Theatre Royal Plymouth & Drum Theatre Plymouth
Royal Parade, Plymouth PL1 2TR
☎01752 230347 Fax 01752 230499
✉ d.prescott@theatreroyal.com
www.theatreroyal.com
Artistic Director *Simon Stokes*
Artistic Associate *David Prescott*

Stages small, middle and large-scale drama and music theatre. Commissions and produces new plays. The theatre no longer accepts unsolicited playscripts but will consider plays through known channels, i.e. theatre practitioners, regional and national scriptwriters' groups and agents.

Theatre Royal Stratford East
Gerry Raffles Square, London E15 1BN
☎020 8279 1104 Fax 020 8534 8381
✉ sramamurthy@stratfordeast.com
www.stratfordeast.com
New Writing Manager *Sita Ramamurthy*

Situated in the heart of the East End, the theatre caters for a very mixed audience, in terms of both culture and age range. Produces plays and musicals, youth theatre and local community plays/events, all of which is new work. Special interest in plays and musicals reflecting the culturally diverse communities of London and the UK. New initiatives in developing contemporary British musicals. No longer accepts unsolicited scripts but instead asks for a) synopsis of script, b) sample ten pages of writing, c) brief writer's biography. 'From this information we will decide whether or not to ask for full-length script.'

Theatre Royal Windsor

Windsor SL4 1PS
☎01753 863444 Fax 01753 831673
✉ info@theatreroyalwindsor.co.uk
www.theatreroyalwindsor.co.uk

Executive Producer *Bill Kenwright*
Executive Director *To be appointed*

Plays to a middle-class, West End-type audience. Produces thirteen plays a year and 'would be disappointed to do fewer than two new plays in a year; always hope to do half a dozen'. Modern classics, thrillers, comedy and farce. Only interested in scripts along these lines.

Theatre Workshop Edinburgh

34 Hamilton Place, Edinburgh EH3 5AX
☎0131 225 7942 Fax 0131 220 0112
www.theatre-workshop.com

Artistic Director *Robert Rae*

First ever professional producing theatre to fully include disabled actors in all its productions. Plays to a young, broad-based audience with many pieces targeted towards particular groups or communities. Output has included *D.A.R.E.*; *Threepenny Opera*; *Black Sun Over Genoa*. Particularly interested in issues-based work for young people and minority groups. Frequently engages writers for collaborative work and devised projects. Commissions a significant amount of new writing for a wide range of contexts, from large-scale community plays to small-scale professional productions. Favours writers based in Scotland, producing material relevant to a contemporary Scottish audience.

The Torch Theatre

St Peter's Road, Milford Haven SA73 2BU
☎01646 694192 Fax 01646 698919
✉ info@torchtheatre.co.uk
www.torchtheatre.co.uk

Artistic Director *Peter Doran*

Founded 1977. Stages a mixed programme of in-house and middle-scale touring work. Unsolicited scripts will be read and guidance offered but production unlikely due to restricted funding. Please include s.a.e. for return of script and notes; mark clearly, 'FAO Peter Doran'. Torch Theatre Company productions include: *Dancing*

at Lughnasa; *Neville's Island*; *The Woman in Black*; *Abigail's Party*; *Taking Steps*; *Blue Remembered Hills*; *A Prayer for Wings*; *Little Shop of Horrors*; *The Caretaker*; *One Flew Over the Cuckoo's Nest*; *One for the Road* plus annual Christmas musicals.

Traverse Theatre

Cambridge Street, Edinburgh EH1 2ED
☎0131 228 3223 Fax 0131 229 8443
✉ louise@traverse.co.uk
www.traverse.co.uk

Artistic Director *Philip Howard*
Literary Manager *Katherine Mendelsohn*
Literary Assistant *Louise Stephens*

The Traverse is Scotland's only new writing theatre, with a particular commitment to producing new Scottish plays. However, it also has a strong international programme of work in translation and visiting companies. Previous productions include *The People Next Door* Henry Adam; *Dark Earth* David Harrower; *15 Seconds* François Archambarlt, version by Isabel Wright; *Iron* Rona Munro; *Outlying Islands* David Greig; *Gagarin Way* Gregory Burke; *Perfect Days* Liz Lochhead. Please address hard copies of unsolicited scripts to *Louise Stephens*, Literary Assistant.

Trestle Theatre Company

Trestle Arts Base, Russet Drive, St Albans AL4 0JQ
☎01727 850950 Fax 01727 855558
✉ admin@trestle.org.uk
www.trestle.org.uk

Artistic Director *Emily Gray*

Founded 1981. Some devised work, but increasing collaboration with writers to create new writing for touring visual/physical performance work nationally and internationally and also local community projects. No unsolicited scripts.

Tricycle Theatre

269 Kilburn High Road, London NW6 7JR
☎020 7372 6611 Fax 020 7328 0795
www.tricycle.co.uk

Artistic Director *Nicolas Kent*

Founded 1980. Plays to a very mixed audience, in terms of both culture and class. Previous productions: *Stones in his Pockets* Marie Jones; *The Stephen Lawrence Enquiry – The Colour of Justice* adapt. from the enquiry transcripts by Richard Norton-Taylor; *Nuremberg* adapt. from transcripts of the trials by Richard Norton-Taylor; *Joe Turner's Come and Gone*, *The Piano Lesson* and *Two Trains Runnin'* all by August Wilson; *Kat and the Kings* David Kramer. New writing welcome from women and ethnic minorities (particularly Black, Asian and Irish). Looks for a strong narrative drive with popular appeal, not 'studio' plays. Fee: £14 per script. Supplies written reader's report. Can only return scripts if postage coupons or s.a.e. are enclosed with original submission.

Tron Theatre Company
63 Trongate, Glasgow G1 5HB
☎0141 552 3748 Fax 0141 552 6657
✉ gregory.thompson@tron.co.uk
www.tron.co.uk
Artistic Director *Gregory Thompson*

Founded 1981. Plays to a broad cross-section of Glasgow and beyond, including international tours. Recent productions: *Pyrenees* David Greig (co-production with Paines Plough); *Half Life* John Mighton (co-production with Necessary Angel Theatre Company, Canada and Perth Rep); *Ubu the King* adapted by David Greig (co-production with Dundee Rep, BITE05, Barbican and the Young Vic as part of 'Young Genius'); *The Patriot* Grae Cleugh (Tron Theatre production). Interested in ambitious plays by UK and international writers. No unsolicited scripts.

Unicorn Theatre for Children
147 Tooley Street, More London, London SE1 2HZ
☎020 7645 0500 Fax 020 7645 0550
✉ stagedoor@unicorntheatre.com
www.unicorntheatre.com
Artistic Director *Tony Graham*
Associate Director *Carl Miller*

Founded 1947, resident at the Arts Theatre from 1967 to 1999 and now based at the new Unicorn Children's Centre with two theatres. Produces full-length professionally performed plays for children and adults. Recent work includes *Tom's Midnight Garden* by Philippa Pearce, adapt. David Wood; *Yikes* by Bryony Lavery; *Oz* by Patrick Shanahan; *Journey to the River Sea* by Eva Ibbotson, adapt. Carl Miller. Does not produce unsolicited scripts but works with commissioned writers. Writers interested in working with the company should send an e-mail (artistic@unicorntheatre.com), requesting further information.

Upstairs at the Gatehouse
See **Ovation Productions** under *Film, TV and Radio Producers*

Charles Vance
Hampden House, 2 Weymouth Street, London W1W 5BT
☎020 7636 4343 Fax 020 7636 2323
✉ cvtheatre@aol.com
Contact *Charles Vance*

In the market for medium-scale touring productions and summer-season plays. Hardly any new work and no commissions but writing of promise stands a good chance of being passed on to someone who might be interested in it. Occasional try-outs for new work in the Sidmouth repertory theatre. Send s.a.e. for return of mss.

Warehouse Theatre
Dingwall Road (adjacent to East Croydon Station), Croydon CR0 2NF
☎020 8681 1257 Fax 020 8688 6699
✉ info@warehousetheatre.co.uk
www.warehousetheatre.co.uk
Artistic Director *Ted Craig*

South London's new writing theatre seats 90–100 and produces up to six new plays a year. Also co-produces with, and hosts, selected touring companies who share the theatre's commitment to new work. The theatre continues to build upon a tradition of discovering and nurturing new writers through the **International Playwriting Festival** (see entry under *Festivals*). Also runs a vigorous writers' workshop and hosts youth theatre workshops and Saturday morning children's theatre. Scripts will get a faster response if submitted through the International Playwriting Festival.

Watford Palace Theatre
Clarendon Road, Watford WD17 1JZ
☎01923 235455 Fax 01923 819664
✉ enquiries@watfordtheatre.co.uk
www.watfordtheatre.co.uk
Contact *Assistant Producer*

Reopened in Autumn 2004, following an £8.7 million refurbishment. An important part of artistic policy is developing new work suitable for this 600-seat proscenium arch theatre, which generally means the writer has some professional production experience. 'We run a writers' group for local playwrights, by invitation. We regret we are unable to offer a script reading and reporting service for unsolicited scripts and are unable to return unsolicited mss.'

West Yorkshire Playhouse
Playhouse Square, Leeds LS2 7UP

☎0113 213 7800 Fax 0113 213 7250
✉ alex.chisholm@wyp.org.uk
www.wyp.org.uk

Associate Director *Alex Chisholm*

Committed to working with new writing originating from or set in the Yorkshire and Humberside region. New writing from outside the region is programmed usually where writer or company is already known to the theatre. For more information contact ☎ 0113 213 7286 or e-mail to address above. Scripts should be submitted with s.a.e. for return. 'Not all submitted scripts will be read. You are strongly advised to check guidelines on the website *before* submitting.'

Whirligig Theatre

14 Belvedere Drive, Wimbledon, London SW19 7BY
☎020 8947 1732 Fax 020 8879 7648
✉ whirligig-theatre@virgin.net

Contact *David Wood*

Occasional productions and tours to major theatre venues, usually a musical for primary school audiences and weekend family groups. Interested in scripts which exploit the theatrical nature of children's tastes. Previous productions: *The See-Saw Tree; The Selfish Shellfish; The Gingerbread Man; The Old Man of Lochnagar; The Ideal Gnome Expedition; Save the Human; Dreams of Anne Frank; Babe, the Sheep-Pig*.

White Bear Theatre Club

138 Kennington Park Road, London SE11 4DJ
www.whitebeartheatre.co.uk

Administration: 3 Dante Road, Kennington, London SE11 4RB
☎ 020 7793 9193
Fax 020 7793 9193

Contact *Michael Kingsbury*
Administrator *Julia Parr*

Founded 1988. Output primarily new work for an audience aged 20–35. Unsolicited scripts welcome, particularly new work with a keen eye on contemporary issues, though not agitprop. *Absolution* by Robert Sherwood was nominated by the Writers' Guild for 'Best Fringe Play' and *Spin* by the same author was the *Time Out* Critics' Choice in 2000. The theatre received the *Time Out* award for Best Fringe Venue in 2001 and a Peter Brook award for best up-and-coming venue. In 2004 *Round the Horne ... Revisited* transferred to The Venue, Leicester Square.

Windsor Theatre Royal

See **Theatre Royal Windsor**

The Young Vic

66 The Cut, London SE1 8LZ
☎020 7922 2800 Fax 020 7922 2801
✉ info@youngvic.org
www.youngvic.org

Artistic Director *David Lan*
Executive Director *Kevin Fitzmaurice*
Dramaturg *Ruth Little*

Founded 1970. The Young Vic is a theatre for everyone but, above all, for younger artists and audiences. Produces revivals of classics – old and new – as well as new plays and annual events that embrace both young people and adults.

Festivals

Aberdeen Arts Carnival
Aberdeen Arts Centre, 33 King Street,
Aberdeen AB24 5AA
☎01224 635208
www.aberdeenartscentre.org.uk
Venue Manager *Paula Gibson*
Performances – mainly by local amateurs and
arts workshops in drama, music, art, dance and
creative writing – take place each summer
during the school holidays.

University of Aberdeen Writers Festival
See **Word**

The Aldeburgh Literary Festival
44 High Street, Aldebugh IP15 5AB
☎01728 452389 Fax 01728 452389
✉ johnandmary@aldeburghbookshop.co.uk
www.aldeburghbookshop.co.uk
Festival Organisers *John and Mary James*
Founded 2002. Held on the first weekend in
March. The programme includes literary work-
shops, a literary dinner, and talks. Previous
speakers have included Beryl Bainbridge, Alan
Bennett, Craig Brown, Richard Dawkins,
Lady Antonia Fraser, Michael Frayn, Anthony
Horowitz, P.D. James, Doris Lessing, David
Lodge, Ian McEwan, Harold Pinter, Matt Ridley,
Alexander McCall Smith, Claire Tomalin, Salley
Vickers, A.N. Wilson.

Aldeburgh Poetry Festival
The Poetry Trust, The Cut, 9 New Cut,
Halesworth IP19 8BY
☎01986 835950
✉ info@thepoetrytrust.org
www.thepoetrytrust.org
Director *Naomi Jaffa*
Founded 1989. One of the UK's biggest celebrations of international contemporary poetry,
held in the small coastal town of Aldeburgh on
the first weekend in November. Features poetry
readings, performances, talks, public master-
class, workshops, discussions, family events and
a writer-in-residence. Also includes a reading by
the winner of the annual **Jerwood Aldeburgh**

First Collection Prize (see entry under
Prizes).

Aspects Literature Festival
North Down Borough Council, Town Hall,
The Castle, Bangor BT20 4BT
☎028 9127 8032 Fax 028 9127 1370
✉ gail.prentice@northdown.gov.uk
Festival Coordinator/Arts Officer *Gail Prentice*
Founded 1992. 'Ireland's Premier Literary
Festival' is held at the end of September and
celebrates the richness and diversity of living
Irish writers with occasional special features on
past generations. It draws upon all disciplines –
fiction (of all types), poetry, theatre, non-fiction,
cinema, song-writing, etc. It also includes a day
of writing for young readers and sends writers to
visit local schools during the festival. Highlights
of recent festivals include appearances by Bernard
MacLaverty, Marion Keyes, Alice Taylor, Frank
Delaney, Seamus Heaney, Brian Keenan and
Fergal Keane.

Aye Write! Bank of Scotland Book Festival
The Mitchell Library, North Street, Glasgow
G3 7DN
☎0141 287 2999/2876 Fax 0141 287 2815
✉ lil@cls.glasgow.gov.uk
www.ayewrite.com
Festival Director *Karen Cunningham*
Festival Programmers *Andrew Kelly, Melanie
Kelly*
Launched 2005. Annual festival (15th–24th
February in 2008) which aims to increase the use
of libraries, encourage a love of books, reading
and writing and an awareness of Glasgow's
writing heritage. The 2007 Festival guests
included Iain Banks, John Banville, Steve Bell,
Alasdair Gray, Simon Hoggart, A.L. Kennedy,
Liz Lochhead, Andrea Levy, Andrew Motion,
William McIlvanney.

Bath Festival of Children's Literature
✉ info@bathfestivalofchildrensliterature.co.uk
www.bathfestivalofchildrensliterature.co.uk

Festival Director *John McLay*

Founded 1007. Annual event held in September (19th–28th in 2008). Events for readers aged up to 16. Guest authors have included Jacqueline Wilson, Eoin Colfer, Anthony Horowtiz, Darren Shan, Lauren Child, Louise Rennison, Tony Ross, Francesca Simon, Michelle Paver, Allan Ahlberg, Chris Riddell and Paul Stewart.

Bath Literature Festival

Bath Festivals, Abbey Chambers, Kingston Buildings, Bath BA1 1NT

☎01225 462231 Fax 01225 445551

✉ info@bathfestivals.org.uk

www.bathlitfest.org.uk

Box Office: Bath Festivals Box Office, 2 Church Street, Abbey Green, Bath BA1 1NL

☎ 01225 463362

✉ boxoffice@bathfestivals.org.uk

Artistic Director *Sarah LeFanu*

Founded 1995. This annual festival (held in March) programmes over 100 different literary events from debates and lectures to readers' groups and workshops in venues throughout the city. In addition there are a number of events for children and young people. Previous featured writers include Tony Benn, Kazuo Ishiguro, Andrea Levy, Peter Porter, Oliver Sacks and Sue Townsend.

BayLit Festival

Academi, Mount Stuart House, Mount Stuart Square, Cardiff CF10 5FQ

☎029 2047 2266 Fax 029 2049 2930

✉ post@academi.org

www.academi.org

Chief Executive *Peter Finch*

Annual literature festival held in Cardiff Bay, featuring writers from Wales and beyond. Lectures, readings, performances, workshops and book launches in English and Welsh. Dates and further details available on the Academi website. Writers who appeared in recent festivals include: Ian McMillan, Fay Weldon, Simon Singh, Howard Marks and Will Self.

Belfast Festival at Queen's

8 Fitzwilliam Street, Belfast BT9 6AW

☎028 9097 1034 Fax 028 9097 1336

✉ g.farrow@qub.ac.uk

www.belfastfestival.com

Director *Graeme Farrow*

Founded 1964. Annual three-week festival held in October/November (19th–3rd in 2007).

Organised by Queen's University, the festival covers a wide variety of events, including literature. Programme available in September.

Beverley Literature Festival

Wordquake, Libraries and Information, Council Offices, Skirlaugh HU11 5HN

☎01482 392745 Fax 01482 392710

✉ john@bevlit.org

www.beverley-literature-festival.org

Festival Director *John Clarke*

Founded 2002. Annual October festival which has acquired 'a national reputation for commissioning and hosting quality poetry events'. Also covers all other literary genres and mixes readings and performances with author-led readers' groups and creative writing workshops. Held in intimate and historic venues across Beverley.

Birmingham Book Festival

c/o Unit 116, The Custard Factory, Gibb Street, Birmingham B9 4AA

☎0121 246 2770 Fax 0121 246 2771

✉ jonathan@bookcommunications.co.uk

www.birminghambookfestival.org

Contact *Jonathan Davidson*

Founded 1999. Annual literature festival held during October at venues around Birmingham. Also promotes events throughout the year. Includes performances, lectures, discussion events and workshops.

Book Now –
Richmond Literature Festival

The Arts Team, Orleans House Gallery, Riverside, Twickenham TW1 3DJ

✉ artsinfo@richmond.gov.uk

www.richmond.gov.uk/literature

Founded 1992. Annual three-week literature festival held in November, delivered by the Arts Service of Richmond Borough. Previous guests include Gerald Scarfe, Hanif Kureishi, Ben Fogle, Claire Tomalin, Salley Vickers, Sir David Attenborough, Kate Adie, The Kumars.

Bournemouth Literary Festival

☎01202 417535

✉ info@bournemouthliteraryfestival.co.uk

www.bournemouthliteraryfestival.co.uk

Director & Founder *Lilly Avon*

Founded in 2004, the Festival fuses literature with performing arts. Events throughout the year, in venues all over Bournemouth, with a focus on September and October.

Bradford Book Festival

Central Library, Princes Way, Bradford
BD1 1NN
☎01274 433915
✉ paula.truman@bradford.gov.uk

Contact *Paula Truman*

Founded in 1999, the festival is organised by Bradford Libraries, runs for two weeks and is usually held during May or June.

Brighton Festival

Festival Office, 12a Pavilion Buildings, Castle Square, Brighton BN1 1EE
☎01273 700747 Fax 01273 707505
✉ info@brightonfestival.org
www.brightonfestival.org

Contact *General Manager*

Founded 1966. For 24 days every May, Brighton hosts England's largest mixed arts festival. Music, dance, theatre, film, opera, literature, comedy and exhibitions. Literary enquiries will be passed to the literature officer. Deadline October for following May.

Bristol Poetry Festival

See **Poetry Can** under *Organisations of Interest to Poets*

Broadstairs Dickens Festival

10 Lanthorne Road, Broadstairs CT10 3NH
☎01843 861827 Fax 01843 861827
www.broadstairs.gov.uk/DickensFestival.html

Organiser *Sylvia Hawkes*

Founded 1937 to commemorate the 100th anniversary of Charles Dickens' first visit to Broadstairs in 1837, which he continued to visit until 1859. The Festival lasts for nine days in June and events include an opening gala concert, a parade, a performance of a Dickens play (*Pickwick Papers* in 2007), duels, melodramas, Dickens readings, a Victorian cricket match, Victorian bathing parties, talks, music hall, three-day Victorian country fair. Costumed Dickensian ladies in crinolines with top-hatted escorts promenade during the week.

Buxton Festival

3 The Square, Buxton SK17 6AZ
☎01298 70395 Fax 01298 72289
✉ info@buxtonfestival.co.uk
www.buxtonfestival.co.uk

Chief Executive *Glyn Foley*

Founded 1979. Held annually in July, this 17-day opera, literature and music festival includes a varied literary programme, attracting those with a broad interest in well-crafted writing, whether in biography, fiction, politics or personal memoir.

Cambridge Wordfest

☎01223 264404
✉ cam.wordfest@btinternet.com
www.cambridgewordfest.co.uk

Festival Director *Cathy Moore*
Festival Patrons *Dame Gillian Beer, Rowan Pelling, Ali Smith*

An annual spring festival for writers as well as readers which takes place at various venues across Cambridge and the surrounding area. A weekend event packed with the best of contemporary writing, poetry, political debate, events for children and writing workshops.

Camelford Poetry Festival Workshops

The Indian King, Garmoe Cottage, 2 Trefrew Road, Camelford PL32 9TP
☎01840 212161

Director *Helen Wood*

Founded 1997 as the Jon Silkin Memorial Poetry Festival. Jon Silkin taught annual poetry workshops and readings to raise funds for the Centre, and the festival was held to honour his life and work. Held annually in Camelford, the central town in North Cornwall, the festival now consists of workshops, readings and performances for a small number of poetry writing participants. Previous guests have included Fred d'Aguiar, Sara Jane Arbury, John Branfield, Ann Gray, John Greening, Philip Gross, Derrek Hines, Christopher Logue, William Oxley, Ian Parks, Fiona Sampson, Myra Schneider, Penelope Shuttle and Dilys Wood. Book for one or more days.

Canterbury Festival

Christ Church Gate, The Precincts, Canterbury CT1 2EE
☎01227 452853 Fax 01227 781830
✉ info@canterburyfestival.co.uk

Festival Director *Rosie Turner*

Canterbury provides a unique location for the largest festival of arts and culture in the region, showcasing local, national and international talent in classical and contemporary music, world theatre, opera, comedy, dance, talks, walks and community events.

Centre for Creative & Performing Arts Spring Literary Festival at UEA

University of East Anglia, School of Literature and Creative Writing, Norwich NR4 7TJ
☎01603 592810
✉ v.striker@uea.ac.uk
www.uea.ac.uk/eas/events/intro.shtml

Contact *Val Striker*

Founded 1993. Annual event held in the spring and summer.

Charleston Festival

The Charleston Trust, Charleston, Nr Firle, Nr Lewes BN8 6LL
☎01323 811626
✉ info@charleston.org.uk
www.charleston.org.uk

Festival Programmer *Diana Reich*

Annual literary festival held in May over nine days. Novelists, biographers, travel writers, broadcasters, poets, food writers, actors and artists gather at Charleston, the country home of the Bloomsbury Group. Past speakers include Margaret Atwood, Alan Bennett, Jeanette Winterson, Louis de Bernières, Patti Smith, Paula Rego, Clive James, Ali Smith, Roger McGough, Germaine Greer and Harold Pinter.

Cheltenham Literature Festival

Town Hall, Imperial Square, Cheltenham GL50 1QA
☎01242 263494 Fax 01242 256457
✉ clair.greenaway@cheltenham.gov.uk
www.cheltenhamfestivals.com

Festival Manager *Clair Greenaway*

Founded 1949. Annual festival held in October. The first purely literary festival of its kind, this festival has over the past decade developed from an essentially local event into the largest and most popular in Europe. A wide range of events including talks and lectures, poetry readings, novelists in conversation, exhibitions, discussions and a large bookshop.

Chester Literature Festival

Viscount House, River Lane, Saltney, Chester CH4 8RH
☎01244 674020 Fax 01244 680037
✉ info@chesterlitfest.org.uk
www.chesterlitfest.org.uk

Chairman *Bill Hughes*

Founded 1989. Annual festival (30th September–27th October in 2006). Events include international and nationally known writers, as well as events by local literary groups. There is a Literary Lunch and a Festival Dinner, events for children, workshops and competitions. Free mailing list.

Children's Books Ireland – Annual Festival

See **Children's Books Ireland** under *Professional Associations*

Dartington Literary Festival

See **Ways With Words**

Derby's Festival of Words

Derby City Council, Roman House, Friar Gate, Derby DE1 1XB
☎01332 715434
✉ alex.davis@derby.gov.uk

Literature Development Officer *Alex Davis*

A biannual celebration of words in all their forms. Derby's Festival of Words takes in poetry, novels, storytelling, graphic novels, children's writing, reading and games. Runs for ten days in mid-October.

Derbyshire Literature Festival

c/o Arts Office, Derbyshire County Council, Cultural & Community Services Department, Alfreton Library, Severn Square, Alfreton DE55 7BQ
☎01773 832497 Fax 01773 831359
✉ ann.wright@derbyshire.gov.uk
www.derbyshire.gov.uk

Festival Organiser *Ann Wright*

Founded 2000. The festival takes place in June every two years and covers the whole county. The festival programming includes all types of live literature events; performance poetry, theatre, talks, readers' groups, workshops, dramatised readings, signings, storytelling and literary trails, as well as a number of cross-art form events. The festival takes place in libraries and many other community venues including heritage centres, industrial buildings, stately homes, parks and moors, churches and schools and is specifically designed to reach as many different communities and geographical areas in the county as possible.

Dorchester Festival

Dorchester Arts Centre, School Lane, The Grove, Dorchester DT1 1XR
☎01305 266926 Fax 01305 266143
✉ enquiries@dorchesterarts.org.uk
www.dorchesterarts.org.uk

Artistic Director *Sharon Hayden*

Founded 1996. A biennial five-day international festival held over early May Bank Holiday (next takes place in 2008) which includes performance, live music and visual arts with associated educational and community projects. Also three days of free events various venues around the town, including literature and poetry. The theme for the 2007 festival was Eastern and Central Europe including a tribute to the 200th Anniversary of the Abolition of the Slave Trade.

The Daphne du Maurier Festival of Arts & Literature

Restormel Borough Council, 39 Penwinnick Road, St Austell PL25 5DR
☎01726 223535 (24-hr answerphone)
Fax 01726 223301
✉ rbc@dumaurierfestival.co.uk
www.dumaurierfestival.co.uk
Founded 1997. Annual festival, held in Fowey over ten days in May. Guests at the 2007 Festival included John Mortimer, Wendy Cope, Brian Patten, Nina Auerbach, Justine Picardie, Claire Tomalin, Jan Morris, Michael Portillo.

Dumfries and Galloway Arts Festival

Gracefield Arts Centre, 28 Edinburgh Road, Dumfries DG1 1JQ
☎01387 260447 Fax 01387 260447
✉ info@dgartsfestival.org.uk
www.dgartsfestival.org.uk
Festival Organiser *Mrs Barbara Kelly*
Founded 1980. Annual week-long festival held at the end of May with a variety of events including classical and folk music, theatre, dance, literary events, exhibitions and children's events.

Durham Literature Festival

Durham City Arts, 2 The Cottages, Fowlers Yard, Back Silver Street, Durham DH1 3RA
☎0191 375 0763
✉ enquiries@durhamcityarts.org.uk
Festival Coordinator *John McGagh*
Founded 1989. Annual 2–3-week festival held in September/October at various locations in the city. Performances and readings plus workshops, cabaret, exhibitions and other events.

Edinburgh International Book Festival

5a Charlotte Square, Edinburgh EH2 4DR
☎0131 718 5666 Fax 0131 226 5335
✉ admin@edbookfest.co.uk
www.edbookfest.co.uk

Director *Catherine Lockerbie*
Founded 1983. 'The world's largest and most dynamic annual book event.' Takes place over 17 days in Edinburgh each August. An extensive programme showcases the work of the world's top authors and thinkers to an audience of over 200,000 adults and children. Featuring workshops, readings, lectures and a high profile debate and discussion series.

Falmouth Festival of Literature & Arts

56 Killigrew Street, Falmouth TR11 3PP
☎01326 211522
✉ admin@falmouthfestival.co.uk
www.falmouthfestival.co.uk
Festival Director *Kirsten Whiting*
Founded 2003. Held annually in October, the Festival brings together international and local authors for adults and children alike at various venues in the seaside town of Falmouth. Talks, readings, workshops, music, discussion, art and performance make up three full days and nights of literary and artistic celebration.

Folkestone Literary Festival

The Glassworks, Mill Bay, Folkestone CT20 1JG
☎01303 211300
✉ info@folkestonelitfest.com
www.folkestonelitfest.com
Festival Director *Nick Ewbank*
Annual festival. Tours, discussions, talks, live performances and readings. 2007 festival: 2nd–10th November.

Frome Festival

25 Market Place, Frome BA11 1AH
☎01373 453889
✉ office@fromefestival.co.uk
www.fromefestival.co.uk
Festival Director *Martin Bax, MBE*
An annual festival held from the first Friday in July for ten days celebrating all aspects of visual and performing arts and entertainment and with a strong literary element. Features music, film, dance, drama and visual arts plus readings, talks and workshops. Previous literary guests have included nationally renowned writers as well as local authors.

Graham Greene Festival

See **Graham Greene Birthplace Trust** under *Literary Societies*

The Guardian Hay Festival

25 Lion Street, Hay-on-Wye HR3 5AD
☎0870 787 2848 Fax 01497 821066
✉ admin@hayfestival.com
www.hayfestival.com

Festival Director *Peter Florence*

Founded 1988. Annual May festival sponsored by *The Guardian*. Also has a children's programme which began in 2003. The event coincides with half term and caters for young children through to teenage. Guests have included Paul McCartney, Bill Clinton, Salman Rushdie, Toni Morrison, Stephen Fry, Joseph Heller, Carlos Fuentes, Maya Angelou, Amos Oz, Arthur Miller.

Guildford Book Festival

c/o Tourist Information Centre, 14 Tunsgate, Guildford GU1 3QT
☎01483 444334
✉ deputy@guildfordbookfestival.co.uk
www.guildfordbookfestival.co.uk

Book Festival Director *Glenis Pycraft*

Founded 1990. Patrons: Elizabeth Buchan, Michael Buerk, Sandi Toksvig, Fay Weldon, Timothy West and Jacqueline Wilson. Held annually, during October in venues throughout the ancient town of Guildford. The festival includes events with established and new writers, workshops, poetry performances, children's events, adult short story competition and the **Jelf Group First Novel Award** (see entry under *Prizes*). This diverse festival aims to involve, instruct and entertain all who care about literature. Guest authors in 2006 included Brenda Blethyn, Sarah Dunant, Miles Kington, Fay Weldon, Maureen Lipman, Nigel Havers, Frances Fyfield, Ian Rankin, Simon Brett, Claire Tomalin, Richard Holmes, Kevin McCloud, Alison Weir, Conn Iggulden.

Harrogate Crime Writing Festival

See **Theakstons Old Peculier Harrogate Crime Writing Festival**

Harrogate International Festival

Raglan House, Raglan Street, Harrogate HG1 1LE
☎01423 562303 Fax 01423 521264
✉ info@harrogate-festival.org.uk
www.harrogate-festival.org.uk

Festival Director *William Culver-Dodds*
Festival Manager *Sharon Canavar*

Founded 1966. Annual two-week festival at the end of July and beginning of August. Events include international symphony orchestras, chamber concerts, ballet, celebrity recitals, contemporary dance, opera, drama, jazz and comedy.

Harwich Festival of the Arts

2A Kings Head Street, Harwich CO12 3EG
☎01255 503571
✉ anna@rendell-knights.freeserve.co.uk

Contact *Anna Rendell-Knights*

Founded 1980. Annual ten-day summer festival held in June/July. Events include concerts, drama, film, dance, art, exhibitions, historic town walks. The Festival in 2007 commemorated Christopher Newport and the founding of James Town, Virginia.

The Hay Festival

See **The Guardian Hay Festival**

Hebden Bridge Arts Festival

New Oxford House, Albert Street, Hebden Bridge HX7 8AH
☎01422 842684
✉ hbfestival@gmail.com *or* enid.stephenson@3-c.coop
www.hebdenbridge.co.uk/festival

Contact *Enid Stephenson*

Founded 1994. Annual arts festival with increasingly strong adult and children's literature events. Previous guest writers include Roger McGough, Benjamin Zephaniah, Anne Fine, Juliet Barker, Jacqueline Wilson, Quentin Blake, Ian McMillan, Adele Geras, George Alagiah.

Humber Mouth – Hull Literature Festival

City Arts Unit, Central Library, Albion Street, Kingston upon Hull HU1 3TF
☎01482 616961 Fax 01482 616827
✉ humbermouth@gmail.com
www.humbermouth.org.uk

Contact *Maggie Hannan*, City Arts Unit

Founded 1992. Hull's largest festival, held in the summer, and one of the region's liveliest events. Features readings, talks, performances and workshops by writers and artists from around the world and from the city.

Ilkley Literature Festival

The Manor House, 2 Castle Hill, Ilkley LS29 9DT
☎01943 601210 Fax 01943 817079
✉ admin@ilkelyliteraturefestival.org.uk
www.ilkleyliteraturefestival.org.uk

Director *Rachel Feldberg*
Founded 1973. Major literature festival in the north held over 17 days every October. Includes children's literature weekend and Festival fringe. Recent guests include Maya Angelou, Alan Bennett, Sarah Waters, Claire Tomalin, Benjamin Zephaniah, Richard Ford, P.D. James, Donna Tartt, Kate Adie, Liz Lochhead, Tony Harrison, Ian Rankin. Telephone or e-mail to join free mailing list.

Imagine: Writers and Writing for Children
See **Royal Festival Hall Literature & Talks**

The International Festival of Mountaineering Literature
15 Ednaston Court, Ednaston, Ashbourne DE6 3BA
☎01335 360581 Fax 01333 439148
✉ t.gifford@chi.ac.uk
www.festivalofmountaineeringliterature.co.uk
Director *Terry Gifford*
Founded 1987. Annual one-day festival held at the Kendal Mountaineering Book Festival, Kendal, Cumbria. Taking place in November, the Festival celebrates recent books, commissions new writing, gives overviews of national literatures, holds debates of issues, book signings. Announces the winner of the festival writing competition run in conjunction with *Climb* magazine. Write to join free mailing list.

International Playwriting Festival
Warehouse Theatre, Dingwall Road, Croydon CR0 2NF
☎020 8681 1257 Fax 020 8688 6699
✉ info@warehousetheatre.co.uk
www.warehousetheatre.co.uk/ipf.html
Festival Administrator *Rose Marie Vernon*
The Warehouse Theatre Company's International Playwriting Festival celebrated 22 successful years in 2007. It is held in two parts: the *first* is the competition with entries accepted between January and June from all over the world and judged by a panel of distinguished theatre practitioners. The *second* is the festival itself which showcases the selected plays from the competition. This takes place in November each year. The IPF also showcases plays in Europe in association with its partners Extra Candoni in Italy and Theatro Ena in Cyprus. Rules and entry form on webpage above. Previous winners produced at the theatre include: Guy Jenkin *Fighting for the Dunghill*; James Martin Charlton *Fat Souls*; Peter

Moffat *Iona Rain*; Dino Mahoney *YoYo*; Dominic McHale *The Resurrectionists*; Philip Edwards *51 Peg*; Roumen Shomov *The Dove*; Maggie Nevill *The Shagaround*; Andrew Shakeshaft *Just Sitting*; Des Dillon *Six Black Candles*.

Isle of Man Literature Festival
Isle of Man Arts Council, St Andrew's House, Finch Road, Douglas IM1 2PX
☎01624 694598 Fax 01624 686709
✉ dawn.maddrell@iomartscouncil.dtl.gov.im
Contact *Arts Development Manager*
Founded 1997. Regular programme of literature events throughout the year.

King's Lynn, The Fiction Festival
19 Tuesday Market Place, King's Lynn PE30 1JW
☎01553 691661 (office hours) or 761919
Fax 01553 691779
✉ tony.ellis@hawkins-solicitors.com
Contact *Anthony Ellis*
Founded 1989. Annual weekend festival held in March. Over the weekend there are readings and discussions, attended by guest writers of which there are usually twelve. Previous guests have included Beryl Bainbridge, Louis de Bernière, John Buchan, J.P. Donleavy and D.J. Taylor.

King's Lynn, The Poetry Festival
19 Tuesday Market Place, King's Lynn PE30 1JW
☎01553 691661 (office hours) or 761919
Fax 01553 691779
✉ tony.ellis@hawkins-solicitors.com
Contact *Anthony Ellis*
Founded 1985. Annual weekend festival held at the end of September, with guest poets (usually eight). Previous guests have included Clive James, Les Murray, Peter Porter, D.M. Thomas, C.K. Williams and Kit Wright.

Knutsford Literature Festival
☎01565 722738/07050 183417
✉ knutsfordlitfest@yahoo.co.uk
www.knutsfordlitfest.blogspot.com
Contact *Charlotte Peters Rock*
An annual two-week festival, held at the beginning of October to celebrate writing and performance by distinguished national, international and local authors. Events include readings and discussions, a literary lunch and theatrical performances.

Lambeth Readers & Writers Festival

London Borough of Lambeth, Brixton Library, Brixton Oval, London SW2 1JQ
☎020 7926 1105
✉ to'dell@lambeth.gov.uk
www.lambethgov.uk/Services/LeisureCulture/Libraries

Contact *Tim O'Dell*

Founded in 2001. Held annually in May, the festival brings together internationally recognised, new and local authors for a month of talks, poetry and writing courses focusing on the reading experience. Previous guests have included, Peter Ackroyd, Monica Ali, Armando Iannucci, Polly Toynbee, Linton Kwesi Johnson, John O'Farrell, Buchi Emecheta, Jo Brand and Lionel Shriver.

Lancaster LitFest

PO Box 751, Lancaster LA1 9AJ
☎01524 62166
✉ all@litfest.org
www.litfest.org

Founded 1978. Regional Literature Development Agency, organising workshops, readings, residencies, publications. Year-round programme of literature-based events and annual festival in November featuring a wide range of writers from the UK and overseas. Publishes new Lancashire and Cumbrian prose and poetry writers under the Flax Books imprint.

Ledbury Poetry Festival

Church Lane, Ledbury HR8 1DH
☎0845 458 1743
✉ info@poetry-festival.com
www.poetry-festival.com

Festival Director *Chloe Garner*

Founded 1997. Annual ten-day festival held in June/July. Includes readings, discussions, workshops, exhibitions, music and walks. There is also an extensive year-round community programme and a national poetry competition. Past guests have included James Fenton, Helen Dunmore, Bernard MacLaverty, Andrew Motion, Benjamin Zephaniah, Simon Armitage, Roger McGough, John Hegley. Full programme available in May.

Lewes Live Literature Festival

PO Box 2766, Lewes BN7 2WF
☎01273 483181 Fax 01273 483181
✉ info@leweslivelit.co.uk
www.leweslivelit.co.uk

Artistic Director *Mark Hewitt*

Founded 1995. Lewes Live Literature Festival is a three-day intensive event, held in late October/early November. Events include readings, performances, lectures, workshops, screenings of film and video, exhibitions. LLL also runs year-round creative writing workshops led by established professionals.

Lichfield Festival

7 The Close, Lichfield WS13 7LD
☎01543 306270 Fax 01543 306274
✉ lichfield.fest@lichfield-arts.org.uk
www.lichfieldfestival.org

Festival Director *Richard Hawley*

Founded 1982. Annual July festival with events taking place in the 13th century Cathedral, the new Lichfield Garrick Theatre, and various country churches and outdoor venues. Mainly music but a growing programme of literary events such as poetry, plays and talks.

City of London Festival

12–14 Mason's Avenue, London EC2V 5BB
☎020 7796 4949
✉ admin@colf.org
www.colf.org

Director *Ian Ritchie*

Founded 1962. Annual three-week festival held in June and July. Features over fifty classical and popular music events alongside poetry and prose readings, street theatre and open-air extravaganzas, in some of the most outstanding performance spaces in the world.

Lowdham Book Festival

The Bookcase, 50 Main Street, Lowdham NG14 7BE
☎0115 966 4143
✉ janestreeter@thebookcase.co.uk
www.lowdhambookfestival.co.uk

Contact *Jane Streeter*

Founded 1999. Annual nine-day festival held in June combining a village fête atmosphere with that of a major literature festival. Guests have included Carol Ann Duffy, Polly Toynbee, Ian McMillan, Alan Sillitoe, Jackie Kay, Gary Younge and Carole Blake. Talks on everything from St Kilda to the Jewish roots of rock 'n' roll.

Manchester Literature Festival

3rd Floor, 24 Lever Street, Manchester M1 1DZ
☎0161 236 5725
✉ admin@manchesterliteraturefestival.co.uk

www.manchesterliteraturefestival.co.uk

Contact *Administrator*

Held in October (4th–14th in 2007), Manchester Literature Festival offers 'unique and imaginative literature experiences to its audiences' with a programme that features readings by some of the world's finest authors, freshly commissioned work, and a series of cutting-edge events exploring the crossover between new technology and literature.

Mere Literary Festival

Lawrence's, Old Hollow, Mere BA12 6EG
☎01747 860475/861211 (Tourist Information)
www.merewilts.org.uk

Contact *Adrienne Howell*

Founded 1997. Annual festival held in the second week of October in aid of registered charity, The Mere & District Linkscheme. Events include readings, quiz, workshop, writer's lunch and talks. Finale is adjudication of the festival's writing competition (see entry under *Prizes*) and presentation of awards.

Metrowords

Arts Team, Room M25, Harrow Council, Civic Centre, Station Road, Harrow HA1 2UW
☎020 8424 1803

'Subject to funding', Metrowords is an annual programme of readings and workshops held at venues throughout Harrow during April and May. Check the website (select 'Metrowords' in What's On) for details.

Arthur Miller Centre Literary Festival at UEA

University of East Anglia, School of American Studies, Norwich NR4 8TJ
☎01603 592810
✉ v.striker@uea.ac.uk
www.uea.ac.uk/eas/events/intro.shtml

Contact *Val Striker*

Founded 1991. Annual festival, held in the autumn

National Association of Writers' Groups (NAWG) Open Festival of Writing

The Arts Centre, Washington NE38 2AB
☎01262 609228
✉ nawg@tesco.net
www.nawg.co.uk

Festival Administrator *Mike Wilson*

Founded 1995. Annual Festival held at St Aidan's

College, University of Durham, 31st August–2nd September 2007. Three days of creative writing tuition covering poetry, short and long fiction, playwriting, journalism, TV sitcom and many other subjects all led by professional writer-tutors. Workshops, one-to-one tutorials and fringe events. Saturday gala dinner and awards ceremony. Full or part-residential weekend, or single workshops only. Open to all, no qualifications or NAWG membership required.

National Eisteddfod of Wales

40 Parc Ty Glas, Llanishen, Cardiff CF14 5WU
☎029 2076 3777 Fax 029 2076 3737
✉ info@eisteddfod.org.uk
www.eisteddfod.org.uk

The National Eisteddfod, held in August, is the largest arts festival in Wales, attracting over 170,000 visitors during the week-long celebration of more than 800 years of tradition. Competitions, bardic ceremonies and concerts.

National Student Drama Festival

See **University of Hull** under *UK Writers' Courses*

Northern Children's Book Festival

Schools Library Service, Sandhill Centre, Grindon Lane, Sunderland SR3 4EN
☎0191 553 8866/7/8 Fax 0191 553 8869
✉ schools.library@sunderland.gov.uk
www.ncbf.org.uk

Secretary *Eleanor Dowley*

Founded 1984. Annual two-week festival during November. Events in schools and libraries for children in the North East region. One Saturday during the festival sees the staging of a large book event hosted by one of the local authorities involved.

Off the Page Literature Festival

County Library Support Services, Glaisdale Parkway, Nottingham NG8 4GP
☎0115 928 6029 Fax 0115 928 6400
✉ alison.hirst@nottscc.gov.uk

Contact *Alison Hirst*

Author visits aimed at making authors accessible to readers. Programme is available from late summer/early autumn.

Off the Shelf Literature Festival

Central Library, Surrey Street, Sheffield S1 1XZ
☎0114 273 4716/4400 Fax 0114 273 5009
✉ offtheshelf@sheffield.gov.uk
www.offtheshelf.org.uk

Festival Organisers *Maria de Souza, Susan*

Walker, Lesley Webster

Founded 1992. Annual two-week festival held during the last fortnight in October. Lively and diverse mix of readings, workshops, children's events, storytelling and competitions. Previous guests have included Stephen Fry, Madhur Jaffrey, Nicholas Parsons, Nick Hornby, Doris Lessing, Benjamin Zephaniah, Terry Pratchett, Michael Palin, Carol Ann Duffy and Louis de Bernières.

Oundle Festival of Literature
2 New Road, Oundle PE8 4LA
☎01832 273050
✉ enquiries@oundlelitfest.org.uk
www.oundlelitfest.org.uk

Festival Deputy Chair *Liz Dillarstone*

Founded 2002. Annual festival running in the first two weeks of March for adults and children. Features talks by high profile authors and poets, writing workshops, poetry and prose showcases for local writers, children's writing competitions, school events, drama productions and community readings for young and old.

Oxford Literary Festival
See **The** *Sunday Times* **Oxford Literary Festival**

Poetry Otherwise
Emerson College, Forest Row RH18 5JX
☎01342 822238 Fax 01342 826055
✉ mail@emerson.org.uk
www.emerson.org.uk
www.poetryotherwise.org

Director *Paul Matthews*

Held in August. A summer gathering of poets, writers and all lovers of language. Workshops, readings, talks, conversation, practice in the art of speaking poetry. Contributors have included Andrea Hollander Budy, John Freeman, Ashley Ramsden, Andie Lewenstein, Paul Matthews, Peter Abbs, Katherine Pierpoint, Fiona Owen, Lee Harwood, Jay Ramsay, Mimi Khalvati and Roselle Angwin. 'Wholesome food, wonderful Sussex countryside.'

Purple Patch Poetry Convention
25 Griffiths Road, West Bromwich B71 2EH
✉ ppatch66@hotmail.com
www.purplepatchpoetry.co.uk

Contact *Geoff Stevens*

Held at the Barlow Theatre near Birmingham this event celebrates the strength of small press poets. The Purple Patch Poetry Convention is a three-day event of poetry readings, talks, workshops and discussions. Admission charges are kept very low, payments to participants being low to non-existent. The Convention's aims are quality and an opportunity to participate. Poets at past festivals have included Ray Avery, R.G. Bishop, Tilla Brading, Gerald England, J.F. Haines, Brendan Hawthorne, Martin Holroyd, Mike Hoy, Eamer O'Keeffe, Carolyn King, Paul McDonald, Bob Mee, Les Merton, Michael Newman, Simon Pitt, Andy Robson, Sam Smith and Steve Sneyd. Monthly poetry readings are held at the Barlow Theatre with open mic, guest poet, music and residents Unleaded Petrels.

Redbridge Book and Media Festival
3rd Floor, Central Library & Museum, Clements Road, Ilford IG1 1EA
☎020 8708 2855 Fax 020 8708 2431
✉ mark.etherington@redbridge.org.uk
www.redbridge.gov.uk

Contact *Arts Development Officer*

Founded in 2003, the festival celebrates literature in all its forms, and takes place annually over two weeks in April/May. Features a programme of author readings, book signings, creative writing classes, school-based workshops, community events, performance poetry evenings, competitions, exhibitions and panel debates.

Royal Court Young Writers Programme
The Site, Royal Court Theatre, Sloane Square, London SW1W 8AS
☎020 7565 5050 Fax 020 7565 5001
✉ ywp@royalcourttheatre.com
www.royalcourttheatre.com

Associate Director *Ola Animashawun*

Open to young people up to the age of 25. The YWP focuses on the process of playwriting by running a series of writers' groups throughout the year at its base in Sloane Square. Additionally the YWP welcomes unsolicited scripts from all young writers from across the country. 'We are always looking for scripts for development and possible production (not film scripts).'

Royal Festival Hall Literature & Talks
Performing Arts Department, Royal Festival Hall, London SE1 8XX
☎020 7921 0906 Fax 020 7921 0700
✉ mpenney@rfh.org.uk
www.rfh.org.uk

Head of Literature & Talks *Ruth Borthwick*

The Royal Festival Hall presents a year-round literature programme covering all aspects of writing. Regular series range from A Life Indeed! to Fiction International and there are two biennial festivals: Poetry International and Imagine: Writers and Writing for Children. Literature events are now programmed in the Purcell Room and Queen Elizabeth Hall. To join the free mailing list, call 020 7921 0971 or e-mail: Literature&Talks@rfh.org.uk

Saffron Walden Literary Festival

Harts Bookshop, 5 King Street, Saffron Walden CB10 1HT

☎01799 508150 (box office)

✉ events@harts1836.co.uk

www.hartsbooks.co.uk

Festival Director *Jo Burch*

Founded 2006. Annual event run by family-owned Harts Bookshop, held over a long weekend (27th Sept–1st Oct in 2007) with events and workshops for adults and children. 2007 Festival speakers: John Hegley, Nick Hornby, Meg Rosoff, Kathryn Hughes, JoJo Moyes, James Mayhew, Tony Mitton and Clare Beaton.

The Scottish Book Town Festival

Festival Office, County Buildings, Wigtown DG8 9JH

☎01988 403222

✉ jenny@wigtownbookfestival.com

www.wigtownbookfestival.com

Festival Director *Michael McCreath*

Festival Admin *Jennifer Bradley*

Founded 1999. Annual Festival held over ten days (last week September/first week October). Author readings, poetry events, workshops, drama, music. Children's events and school outreach programme. Also Spring Festival (founded 2005) held over first May Bank Holiday weekend.

Southwold Festival

See **Ways with Words**

StAnza: Scotland's Poetry Festival

Registered Office: 57 Lade Braes, St Andrews KY16 9DA

☎05600 433847

✉ info@stanzapoetry.org

www.stanzapoetry.org

Festival Director *Brian Johnstone*

(admin@stanzapoetry.org)

Artistic Director *Eleanor Livingstone*

(arts@stanzapoetry.org)

Press Officer *Annie Kelly*

(press@stanzapoetry.org)

The only regular festival dedicated to poetry in Scotland, StAnza is international in outlook. Held annually in March in the ancient university town of St Andrews, the festival is an opportunity to hear world class poets reading in exciting and atmospheric venues. The 2007 festival themes were *Homelands & Exile* and *Poetry & the Moving Image* and featured, readings, discussions, conversations, performance poetry, poetry in exhibition, workshops and children's poetry. It had a strong showing of poets from across the UK and overseas as well as the festival's signature foreign language readings. Free programmes can be ordered from Fife Council Arts on 01592 414714 or by e-mail to arts.development@fife.gov.uk

Stratford-upon-Avon Poetry Festival

The Shakespeare Centre, Henley Street, Stratford-upon-Avon CV37 6QW

☎01789 204016/292176 (box office)

Fax 01789 296083

✉ director@shakespeare.org.uk

www.shakespeare.org.uk

Festival Director *Roger Pringle*

Sponsored by the Shakespeare Birthplace Trust, this Festival, now in its 54th year, features weekly recitals during July and August. These are given by established poets and by actors who present themed evenings of verse. The 2007 Festival included a programme of poems written by local children for National Poetry Day, a Local Poets evening and a Poetry Mass. Full details available from late May and can be accessed on the Trust's website.

Strokestown International Poetry Festival

See **Strokestown International Poetry Prize** under *Prizes*

The *Sunday Times* Oxford Literary Festival

301 Woodstock Road, Oxford OX2 7NY

☎01865 514149

✉ angela@sundaytimes-oxfordliteraryfestival.co.uk

www.sundaytimes-oxfordliteraryfestival.co.uk

Directors *Sally Dunsmore, Angela Prysor-Jones*

Founded 1997. Annual week-long festival held

in March/April. Authors speaking about their books, covering a wide variety of writing: fiction, poetry, biography, travel, food, gardening, children's art. Previous guests have included William Boyd, Andrew Motion, Beryl Bainbridge, Sophie Grigson, Philip Pullman, Doris Lessing, Seamus Heaney, Richard Dawkins, Zandra Rhodes, Kazuro Ishiguro.

Swindon Festival of Literature

Lower Shaw Farm, Shaw, Swindon SN5 5PJ
☎01793 771080 Fax 01793 771080
✉ swindonlitfest@lowershawfarm.co.uk
www.swindonfestivalofliterature.co.uk

Festival Director Matt Holland

Founded 1994. Annual festival held in May, starting with 'Dawn Chorus' at sunrise. Includes a wide range of authors, speakers, discussions, performances and workshops, plus the Swindon Performance Poetry Slam competition. Guests at the 2006 Festival included Kate Adie, Matthew Parris, Anne Widdecombe, Satish Kumar, Bettany Hughes, Melvin Burgess, Marina Lewyzka, Christian Wolmar and John Carey.

Tears in the Fence Festival

38 Hod View, Stourpaine, Blandford Forum DT11 8TN
☎01258 456803
✉ david@davidcaddy.wanadoo.co.uk
www.thewordtravels.com

Festival Director David Caddy

Founded 1995. Annual international poetry festival based in London with readings, talks, discussions and workshops continuing the work begun by the Wessex Poetry Festivals, 1995–2001. Previous guests have included Lee Harwood, Elizabeth Cook, Jeremy Reed, Alice Notley, Fred Voss, Joan Jobe Smith, Irina Ratushinskaya, Michele Roberts, Edwin Morgan and Kim Taplin.

Theakstons Old Peculier Harrogate Crime Writing Festival

Raglan House, Raglan Street, Harrogate HG1 1LE
☎01423 562303 Fax 01423 521264
✉ crime@harrogate-festival.org.uk
www.harrogate-festival.org.uk

Operations Director Sharon Canavar
Festival Manager Adina Watt

Launched 2003. Weekend of events at the end of July each year featuring the best of British and American crime writers. The winner of the **Theakstons Old Peculier Prize for the**

Crime Novel of the Year is announced at the Festival (see entry under **Prizes**). Events also include industry 'How to ...' sessions, social events and late night shows. Part of the **Harrogate International Festival**.

Dylan Thomas Festival

Dylan Thomas Centre, Somerset Place, Swansea SA1 1RR
☎01792 463980 Fax 01792 463993
✉ dylanthomas.lit@swansea.gov.uk
www.dylanthomas.com

Contacts *David Woolley, Jo Furber*

Two weeks of performances, talks, lectures, films, music, poetry, exhibitions and celebrity guests held in October/November (27th–9th in 2007). The Dylan Thomas Centre also runs a year-round programme of literary events; please e-mail for details.

Torbay Weekend Festival of Poetry

6 The Mount, Higher Furzeham, Brixham TQ5 8QY
☎01803 851098
✉ pwoxley@aol.com
www.acumen-poetry.co.uk/events

Festival Organiser Patricia Oxley

Founded 2001. Held annually at the end of October, Thursday evening until Monday afternoon with workshops, poetry readings, talks and debates. Programme for adults and children. Encourages active participation through workshops, open mike events, etc. Guest poets include internationally known writers as well as local authors.

Ty Newydd Festival

Ty Newydd, Llanystumdwy, Criccieth LL52 0LW
☎01766 522811 Fax 01766 523095
✉ post@tynewydd.org
www.tynewydd.org

Director Sally Baker

Biennial, bilingual literature festival held on alternate years. Held in June and run by the National Writers' Centre for Wales, it is located at Ty Newydd Writers' Centre and other venues near Criccieth. Features writers and poets from Wales (working in both English and Welsh) and worldwide. Ty Newydd also holds an annual weekend festival in November devoted solely to Cynghanedd – Welsh strict meter poetry.

Warwick Words

The Court House, Jury Street, Warwick
CV34 4EW
☎01926 427056
✉ info@warwickwords.co.uk
www.warwickwords.co.uk

Founded 2002. Annual festival featuring both living writers and those who have had connections with Warwick – Tolkien, Larkin and Landor in particular. Also workshops and an education programme. A weekend festival of literature and spoken word for all the family. Events at the Bridge House Theatre, St Mary's Church, the Lord Leycester Hospital and other historic buildings around Warwick over the first weekend in October. 2007 Festival: 4th–7th October.

Ways with Words

Droridge Farm, Dartington, Totnes TQ9 6JG
☎01803 867373 Fax 01803 863688
✉ admin@wayswithwords.co.uk
www.wayswithwords.co.uk

Festival Director *Kay Dunbar*

Ways With Words runs three major annual literature festivals. Dartington Hall in south Devon for ten days in July, features over 200 writers giving lectures, readings, interviews, discussions, performances, masterclasses and workshops. Words by the Water is a ten-day festival held in Keswick in March. Also a five-day festival at Southwold, Suffolk in November. Also organises writing, reading and painting courses in Italy.

Wellington Literary Festival

Civic Offices, Larkin Way, Tan Bank, Wellington, Telford TF1 1LX
☎01952 567697 Fax 01952 567690
✉ welltowncl@aol.com
www.wellington-shropshire.gov.uk

Contact *Derrick Drew*

Founded 1997. Annual festival held throughout October. Events include storytelling, writers' forum, 'Pints and Poetry', children's poetry competition, story competition, theatre review and guest speakers.

Wells Festival of Literature

25 Chamberlain Street, Wells BA5 2PQ
☎01749 670929
www.somersite.co.uk/wellsfest.htm

Founded 1992. Annual week-long festival held in the middle of October. Main venue is the historic, moated Bishop's Palace. A wide range of speakers caters for different tastes in reading.

Recent guests include: Sir Roy Strong, Kate Adie, Libby Purves, Melvyn Bragg, Margaret Drabble, William Dalrymple, Timothy West. Short story and poetry competitions and writing workshops are run in conjunction with the Festival.

Wessex Poetry Festivals

See **Tears in the Fence Festival**

Wigtown Book Festival

See **The Scottish Book Town Festival**

Winchester Writers' Conference, Bookfair & Workshops

See entry under *UK Writers' Courses*

Wonderful Words

c/o Penzance Library, Morrab Road, Penzance TR18 4EY
☎07968 892196
✉ agunderson@cornwall.gov.uk
www.cornwall.gov.uk/library

Festival Organiser *Alison Gunderson*

Founded 1994. Biennial literature festival hosted throughout Cornwall. Organised by the Cornwall Library Service, Wonderful Words has grown into a prestigious event for children and adults, offering author talks, writers' workshops, poetry performances, theatre and storytelling. Guest authors have included Doris Lessing, Ruth Rendell, Margaret Drabble, Simon Callow and Dick King-Smith.

Word – University of Aberdeen Writers Festival

Office of External Affairs, University of Aberdeen, King's College, Aberdeen AB24 3FX
☎01224 283726
www.abdn.ac.uk/word

Artistic Director *Alan Spence*
Festival Producer *Fiona Christie*

Held annually in May, the Festival takes place over six days at the historic King's College Campus and at venues throughout the city. Attracts over 70 authors and over 10,000 visitors to a weekend of readings, lectures, debates, music, art exhibitions and film screenings. Also includes an extended schools' and children's programme and a Festival of Gaelic.

Word Market

PO Box 150, Barrow-in-Furness LA14 3WF
☎07812 178193
✉ janice@word-market.co.uk
www.wordmarket.org.uk

Project Coordinator *Janice Benson*

Annual festival and programme of activities throughout the year, offering workshops, masterclasses, tasters and a host of events for all ages and abilities. Word Market supports writers, readers, storytellers, lyricists and performers through events, training and advice. Individuals and groups who wish to develop their work and potential are welcome to get in touch. Check the website for further details.

Words by the Water
See **Ways with Words**

WordStar
Leicester City Council, Libraries, A12 New Walk Centre, Leicester LE1 6ZG
☎0116 252 7347
✉ damien.walter@leicester.gov.uk
Literature Development Officer *Damien Walter*
Year-round programme of live literature including author events, poetry, storytelling, graphic novels and new media.

The Wordsworth Trust
Dove Cottage, Grasmere LA22 9SH
☎015394 35544 Fax 015394 35748
✉ enquiries@wordsworth.org.uk
www.wordsworth.org.uk
Contact *Literature Officer*
Ongoing contemporary poetry programme held over the summer and one-off events held around the country. Readers include Simon Armitage, Seamus Heaney, Paul Muldoon, Sharon Olds, Philip Pullman and Don Paterson as well as a 'support' reader at most events. The Trust also operates an artists-in-residence programme throughout the year, giving time and space for new writers to develop their work in this setting: a cottage and stipend are supplied and no demands are made upon the artist. Past artists-in-residence include Henry Shukman, Owen Sheers, Paul Farley, Helen Farish, Jack Mapanje, Rebecca O'Connor, Jacob Polley and Neil Rollinson.

Writenow!
See **Queen's Theatre, Hornchurch** under *Theatre Producers*

Writing on the Wall
60 Duke Street, Liverpool L1 5AA
☎0151 707 4313
✉ info@writingonthewall.org.uk
www.writingonthewall.org.uk
Festival Coordinator *Madeline Heneghan*
Annual festival held in Liverpool that works alongside schools, young people, local communities and broader audiences to celebrate writing, diversity, tolerance, story-telling and humour through controversy, inquiry and debate. Performances, readings, workshops, screenings, high profile debates and discussions. Guest speakers have included Noam Chomsky, Irvine Welsh, Howard Marks, Roddy Doyle.

Voices of Experience

Writers who write about writing fall into two categories – those who add to the mystery of creativity largely by proclaiming their own supposedly innate talent and those who get down to fundamentals. In the second group George Orwell gives the best value. Here he is on the English language with its two outstanding characteristics, a large vocabulary and simplicity of grammar. Moreover, 'the greatest quality of English is its enormous range not only of meaning but of *tone*. It is capable of endless subtleties and of everything from the most high-flown rhetoric to the most brutal coarseness. On the other hand, its lack of grammar makes it easily compressible. It is the language of lyric poetry, and also of headlines.'

But English has one great weakness.

> Just because it is so easy to use, it is easy to use *badly*. To write or even to speak English is not a science but an art. There are no reliable rules: there is only the general principle that concrete words are better than abstract ones, and that the shortest way of saying anything is always the best. Mere correctness is no guarantee whatever of good writing. A sentence such as 'an enjoyable time was had by all present' is perfectly correct English, and so is the unintelligible mess of words on an income-tax return. Whoever writes English is involved in a struggle that never lets us free even for a sentence. He is struggling against vagueness, against obscurity, against the lure of the decorative adjective, against the encroachment of Latin and Greek, and, above all, against the worn-out phrases and dead metaphors with which the language is cluttered up.

English, says Orwell, is peculiarly subject to jargons:

> Doctors, scientists, businessmen, officials, sportsmen, economists, and political theorists all have their characteristic perversion of the language … But probably the deadliest enemy of good English is what is called 'standard English'. This dreary dialect, the language of leading articles, White Papers, political speeches and B.B.C. news bulletins … Its characteristic is its reliance on ready-made phrases – *in due course, take the earliest opportunity, warm appreciation, deepest regret, explore every avenue, ring the changes, take up the cudgels, legitimate assumption, the answer is in the affirmative*, etc. etc. – which may once have been fresh and vivid, but have now become mere thought-saving devices, having the same relation to living English as a crutch has to a leg.

Orwell's observations on his craft appeared in *The English People* first published in 1947 and recently reprinted as part of an anthology, *Orwell's England* (Penguin Books, 2001).

Less on the 'don'ts' and more on the 'dos' of writing may be culled from John Braine's *Writing a Novel* which first appeared in 1974. To follow Braine is to avoid the usual mistakes committed by novices. His advice, neatly parcelled into memorable axioms, applies across the range of literary endeavour, from fiction to faction, from documentary to drama. For example:

> A good beginning means a good book. A good beginning is one which takes the reader straight into the action. It must also tell us who and what the novel will be about. It doesn't give away the story, but it doesn't leave us in any doubt. It shouldn't ever begin with a foreword, nor should it be leisurely and discursive. Summary – 'This is the story of what happened to an ordinary English family in the year of the Apollo Moonshot' – must never be used. It need not mention the main characters, but it's much preferable that they be brought in straight away.

Dialogue, says Braine, must always be speakable. If you can't speak it aloud, it's no good. Writers can spend too long on dialogue. The attention to detail needed to develop a story with a consistent theme can produce stilted dialogue which would never be spoken in real life. On the other hand:

> Those who can't write credible dialogue can't write good prose either. And there is an inextricable relationship between the fact that Scott Fitzgerald writes superb narrative and superb dialogue. It isn't that the dialogue is merely an extension of his narrative. It could never be so, for its function is to give us words that we can accept as having been spoken in real life. But the same standards of craftsmanship apply to both. I suspect that the reason that the ability to write good prose and good dialogue go hand-in-hand is simply that a good writer knows how to listen.

There is much more on the same lines: sound common sense on writing clear and understandable prose – from compiling synopses and creating characters (people who make a novel happen) to cutting down on the adjectives and rejecting clichés.

Write from experience, says Braine, but experience does not have to be wildly exotic to serve its purpose.

> It doesn't matter now limited your experience has been. (It is hardly possible for it to have been more limited than mine.) If you've lived in the same house all your life, if you've had the same dull routine job ever since leaving school, if nothing remarkable has ever happened to you, if you have never even had such basic experiences as making love or seeing someone close to you die, you still have the material for a thousand novels.

The evidence for believing that a little experience goes a long way can be found throughout literature. What is needed, argues Allan Massie, is a combination of experience and imagination. An example is Hemingway's First World War masterpiece *A Farewell to Arms*.

> Hemingway's experience of battle was brief and limited – he had served with an ambulance unit for a few weeks until he was wounded. Yet, drawing on this,

he imagined battle so well and thoroughly that he convinced his readers, and in time also perhaps himself, that he was a veritable veteran and war hero: an interesting example of the imagination coming first, and the presumed experience only after the creation of the work of art.

Massie goes on:

The essential part of a writer's life is lived in the imagination. Of course all his experience, of a variety of sorts – everything that he does, everything that happens to him, everything that he sees, hears, touches, feels and importantly – reads – may serve as food for the imagination to brood on and transform. ... a very little experience, the merest whiff of a situation or story, may be sufficient stimulus for a writer's imagination. Stendhal found the germ of *Scarlet and Black* in a newspaper report a couple of paragraphs long. Tolstoy also found his inspiration for *Anna Karenina* in a similarly brief report.

The only condition that John Braine puts on the exercise of imagination is that the writer does not go out of his way to be wildly experimental. In words that should be up in lights over every publishing house, Braine proclaims the simple truth:

There is nothing which you cannot say within the framework of the straightforward realistic novel. It is the people in your story who should astound us. The great failing of the novel in England is a self-imposed restriction of subject and its stereotyped attitudes towards every aspect of life, particularly class. To be shockingly original with your first novel you don't have to discover a new technique: simply write about people as they are and not as the predominantly liberal and humanist literary Establishment believes that they ought to be.

Of his own choice of books that seem to improve our understanding of the creative process, Braine puts Dorothea Brande's *Becoming a Writer* at the top of his list. First published in 1934, it was in print until the 1980s. You can see why. Her advice is specific; she avoids abstractions. And she faces up to problems every writer has encountered. Here she is on the Four Difficulties in getting going as a writer:

First there is the difficulty of writing *at all*. The full abundant flow that must be established if the writer is to be heard from simply will not begin. The stupid conclusion that if he cannot write easily he has mistaken his career is sheer nonsense. There are a dozen reasons for the difficulty which should be canvassed before the teacher is entitled to say that he can see no signs of hope for his pupil ...

Second, there is the writer who has had an early success but is unable to repeat it. Here again there is a cant explanation which is offered whenever this difficulty is met: this type of writer, we are assured, is a 'one-book author'; he has written a fragment of autobiography, has unburdened himself of his animus against his parents and his background, and, being relieved, cannot repeat his tour de force ... His first impatience at being unable to repeat his success can pass into discouragement and go on to actual despair; and an excellent author may be lost in consequence ...

The third difficulty is a sort of combination of the first two: there are writers who can, at wearisomely long intervals, write with great effectiveness ... Those who suffer from these silences in which not one idea seems to arise, not one sentence to come irresistibly to the mind's surface, may write like artists and craftsmen when they have once broken the spell ...

The fourth difficulty has a technical aspect: it is the inability to carry a story, vividly but imperfectly apprehended, to a successful conclusion. Writers who complain of this are often able to start a story well, but find it out of control after a few pages. Or they will write a good story so drily and sparely that all its virtues are lost. Occasionally they cannot motivate their central action adequately, and the story carries no conviction.

Dorothea Brande set herself the task of remedying these four disabilities. But she adds the rider 'If you fail repeatedly [at the exercises she commends] give up writing. Your resistance is actually greater than your desire to write, and you may as well find some other outlet for your energy early as late.' Or as Alexander Woollcott put it more brutally, 'I have a distinct feeling about people who think of writing. It is this. If anything can stop them it is no great loss.'

For other pointers to a future in writing, return to the base rules set forth by those who are undisputed masters of the craft. Evelyn Waugh identified three essential qualities:

> **Lucidity** – which can be acquired.
> **Elegance** – which you can strive all your life to achieve.
> **Distinctive voice** – for which you can only pray.

To which George Orwell adds six practicalities:

> Never use a metaphor, simile, or other figure of speech which you are used to seeing in print.
> Never use a long word when a short one will do.
> If it is possible to cut a word out, always cut it out.
> Never use the passive where you can use the active.
> Never use a foreign phrase, a scientific word, or a jargon word if you can think of an everyday English equivalent.
> Break any of these rules sooner than say anything outright barbarous.

The last word is with Dr Johnson:

> What is written without effort is in general read without pleasure.

European Publishers

Austria

Springer-Verlag GmbH
Sachsenplatz 4–6, A–1201 Vienna
☎00 43 1 3302415 Fax 00 43 1 3302426
✉ springer@springer.at
www.springer.at

Founded 1924. Austria's largest scientific publisher. Publishes academic and textbooks, journals and translations: architecture, art, cell biology, chemistry, computer science, law, medicine, neurosurgery, neurology, nursing, psychiatry, psychotherapy.

Verlag Carl Ueberreuter GmbH
Alser Strasse 24, A–1090 Vienna
☎00 43 1 404440
www.ueberreuter.de

Founded 1548. Publishes fiction and general non-fiction, children's and young adult; biography, health and nutrition, science fiction, fantasy.

Paul Zsolnay Verlag GmbH
Prinz Eugen Strasse 30, A–1040 Vienna
☎00 43 1 50576610 Fax 00 43 1 505766110
✉ info@zsolnay.at
www.zsolnay.at

Founded 1923. Publishes biography, fiction, general non-fiction, history, poetry.

Belgium

Brepols Publishers NV
Begijnhof 67, B–2300 Turnhout
☎00 32 14 448020 Fax 00 32 14 428919
✉ info@brepols.net
www.brepols.net

Founded 1796. Independent academic publisher – architecture, archaeology, art, bibliography, history, humanities, language and linguistics, literature, literary criticism, music, philosophy, reference, religion and biblical studies.

Facet NV
Willem Linnigstr 13, B–2060 Antwerp
☎00 32 3 2274028 Fax 00 32 3 2273792

Founded 1986. Publishes children's books.

Uitgeverij Lannoo NV
Kasteelstraat 97, B–8700 Tielt
☎00 32 51 424211 Fax 00 32 51 401152
✉ lannoo@lannoo.be
www.lannoo.be

Founded 1909. Publishes general non-fiction, art, architecture and interior design, cookery, biography, children's, gardening, health and nutrition, history, management, self-help, poetry, religion, travel.

Standaard Uitgeverij
Mechelsesteenweg 203, B–2018 Antwerp
☎00 32 3 2857200 Fax 00 32 3 2857299
✉ info@standaarduitgeverij.be
www.standaarduitgeverij.be

Founded 1919. Publishes education, fiction, poetry, humour, maps, children's and young adult.

Czech Republic

ABF
Václavské nám 29, 111 21 Prague 1
☎00 420 222 891 121 Fax 00 420 222 891 197
www.abf.cz

Publishes art, architecture, economics, law, management, business, entertainment, leisure interests, calendars, printing and design.

Atlantis Ltd
Ceská 15, POB 374, 602 00 Brno
☎00 420 542 213 221
✉ atlantis-brno@volny.cz
www.volny.cz/atlantis

Publishes fiction, language and linguistics, literary studies, poetry, religion, social science.

Brána Publishers Ltd
Hradešínská 30/1956, 101 00 Prague 10-Vinohrady
☎00 420 271 740 559 Fax 00 420 271 740 586
✉ info@brana-knihy.cz
www.brana-knihy.cz

Publishes fiction, non-fiction, art, architecture,

encyclopedias, language and linguistics, literary studies, medicine, health, social science, sport, tourism.

Dokorán Ltd
Zborovská 40/512, 150 00 Prague 5
☎00 420 257 320 803 Fax 00 420 257 320 805
✉ dokoran@dokoran.cz
www.dokoran.cz

Publishes fiction, non-fiction, children's, art, architecture, cartography, entertainment, geography, leisure, language and linguistics, literary studies, music, poetry, popular science, social science, sport, tourism.

Olympia Publishing Co. Inc.
Klimentská 1, 110 15 Prague 1
☎00 420 602 394 610 Fax 00 420 222 312 137
✉ olympia@mbox.vol.cz
www.iolympia.cz

Publishes fiction, non-fiction, children's, entertainment, leisure, popular science, science fiction, sport, textbooks, tourism.

Denmark

Forlaget Apostrof ApS
Postboks 2580, DK–2100 Copenhagen OE
☎00 45 39 208420 Fax 00 45 39 208453
✉ apostrof@apostrof.dk
www.apostrof.dk

Founded 1980. Publishes psychology and psychiatry.

Aschehoug Dansk Forlag A/S
Vognmagergade 11, DK–1148 Copenhagen K
☎00 45 36 156600
✉ info@aschehoug.dk
www.aschehoug.dk

Founded 1977. Merged with Egmont Lademann A/S in 2003. Publishes reference, directories, dictionaries, encyclopedias, children's and young adult, textbooks, fiction, art, biography, hobbies, how-to, health and nutrition, religion, sport.

Blackwell Munksgaard
1 Rosenørns Alle, DK–1970 Frederiksberg C
☎00 45 77 333333 Fax 00 45 77 333377
✉ info@msk.blackwellpublishing.com
www.blackwellmunksgaard.com

Founded 1917. Part of Blackwell Publishing. Publishes academic books and journals for higher education, research and professional markets.

Borgens Forlag A/S
Valbygardsvej 33, DK–2500 Valby
☎00 45 36 153615 Fax 00 45 36 153616
✉ post@borgen.dk
www.borgen.dk

Founded 1948. Publishes fiction and general non-fiction: bibliography, children's and young adult, illustrated, journals, textbooks, literature, literary criticism, essays.

Forlaget Forum
PO Box 2252, DK–1019 Copenhagen K
☎00 45 33 411800 Fax 00 45 33 411801
✉ kontakt@forlagetforum.dk
www.forlagetforum.dk

Founded 1940. Part of **Gyldendalske Boghandel-Nordisk Forlag A/S**. Publishes fiction, bibliography, history, humour, mysteries, children's and young adults.

Gyldendal
Klareboderne 3, DK–1001 Copenhagen K
☎00 45 33 755555
✉ gyldendal@gyldendal.dk
www.gyldendal.dk

Founded 1770. Publishes fiction, children's and young adult, directories, art, biography, education, history, how-to, medicine, music, poetry, philosophy, psychiatry, reference, general and social sciences, sociology, textbooks.

Høst & Søn Publishers Ltd
Købmagergade 62, DK–1150 Copenhagen K
☎00 45 33 411800 Fax 00 45 33 411801
✉ gb@gb-forlagene.dk
www.hoest.dk

Founded 1836. Imprint of **Gyldendal**. Publishes fiction, biography, children's, crafts, environmental studies, history.

Lindhardt og Ringhof Forlag A/S
Pilestræde 52, DK–1018 Copenhagen K
☎00 45 33 695000 Fax 00 45 33 695001
www.lrforlag.dk

Founded 1971. Publishes fiction and general non-fiction.

Nyt Nordisk Forlag Arnold Busck A/S
Landemærket 11, 5. sal, DK–1119 Copenhagen K
☎00 45 33 733575 Fax 00 45 33 140115
✉ nnf@nytnordiskforlag.dk
www.nytnordiskforlag.dk

Founded 1896. Publishes fiction, architecture,

art, cookery, design, education, gardening, natural history, philosophy, reference, religion, leisure, medicine, nursing, psychology, textbooks, travel.

Det Schønbergske Forlag
Landemærket 11, 5. sal, DK–1119 Copenhagen K
☎00 45 33 733585 Fax 00 45 33 733586
www.nytnordiskforlag.dk
Founded 1857. Part of **Nyt Nordisk Forlag Arnold Busck A/S**. Publishes directories, fiction, non-fiction, reference, textbooks.

Tiderne Skifter Forlag A/S
Laederstraede 5, 1, DK–1201 Copenhagen K
☎00 45 33 186390 Fax 00 45 33 186380
✉ mail@tiderneskifter.dk
www.tiderneskifter.dk
Founded 1973. Publishes fiction, literature and literary criticism, essays, poetry, drama, translations, history, art, politics, psychoanalysis, sexual politics, ethnicity, photography.

Finland

Gummerus Oy
PO Box 749, SF–00101 Helsinki
☎00 358 9 584301 Fax 00 358 9 58430200
www.gummerus.fi
Founded 1872. Publishes fiction and general non-fiction.

Karisto Oy
PO Box 102, SF–13101 Hämeenlinna
☎00 358 3 63151 Fax 00 358 3 6161565
✉ kustannusliike@karisto.fi
www.karisto.fi
Founded 1900. Publishes fiction (including crime, thrillers and fantasy), general non-fiction (including health, history, family and childcare, self improvement, pets, fishing), juvenile and young adult.

Otava Publishing Co. Ltd
Uudenmaankatu 8–12, SF–00120 Helsinki
☎00 358 9 19961
✉ otava@otava.fi
www.otava.fi
Founded 1890. Publishes fiction, translations, general non-fiction, children's and young adult, multimedia, education, textbooks.

Tammi Publishers
PL 410, SF–00101 Helsinki
☎00 358 9 6937621 Fax 00 358 9 69376266

✉ tammi@tammi.fi
www.tammi.fi
Founded 1943. Finland's third largest publisher. Publishes fiction, general non-fiction, children's and young adult, education, translations. Part of the Bonnier Group.

WSOY (Werner Söderström Osakeyhtiö)
PO Box 222, SF–00121 Helsinki
☎00 358 9 61681 Fax 00 358 9 61683560
www.wsoy.fi
Founded 1878. Publishes fiction, translation, general non-fiction, education, dictionaries, encyclopedias, textbooks, children's and young adult.

France

Éditions Arthaud
Flammarion Groupe, 87 quai Panhard-et-Levassor, F–75647 Paris Cedex 13
☎00 33 1 4051 3100
✉ contact@arthaud.fr
www.arthaud.fr
Founded 1890. Imprint of the Flammarion Groupe. Publishes illustrated books, photography; travel.

Éditions Belfond
12 avenue d'Italie, F–75013 Paris
☎00 33 1 4416 0500
www.belfond.fr
Founded 1963. Publishes fiction and general non-fiction.

Éditions Bordas
89 blvd Auguste-Blanqui, F–75013 Paris
☎00 33 1 4439 5445
www.editions-bordas.com
Founded 1946. Publishes education and general non-fiction: dictionaries, directories, encyclopedias, reference.

Éditions Calmann-Lévy
31 rue de Fleurus, F–75006 Paris
☎00 33 1 4954 3600 Fax 00 33 1 4544 8632
www.editions-calmann-levy.com
Founded 1836. Part of **Hachette-Livre**. Publishes fiction, science fiction, fantasy, biography, history, humour, economics, philosophy, psychology, psychiatry, social sciences, sociology, sport.

Éditions Denoël

9 rue du Cherche-Midi, F–75278
Paris Cedex 06
☎00 33 1 4439 7373 Fax 00 33 1 4439 7390
✉ denoel@denoel.fr
www.denoel.fr
Founded 1932. Part of **Editions Gallimard**.
Publishes fiction, science fiction, fantasy, thrillers, art, art history, biography, directories, government, history, philosophy, political science, psychology, psychiatry, reference.

Librairie Arthème Fayard

13 due du Montparnasse, F–75006
☎00 33 1 4549 8200
www.editions-fayard.fr
Founded 1857. Part of **Hachette Livre**.
Publishes fiction, biography, directories, maps, atlases, history, dance, music, philosophy, religion, reference, sociology, general science.

Éditions Flammarion

87 quai Panhard-et-Levassor, F–75647 Paris
Cedex 13
☎00 33 1 4051 3100
www.editions.flammarion.com
Imprint of the Flammarion Groupe. Publishes general fiction, science fiction, thrillers, essays, adventure, literature, literary criticism; non-fiction: art, architecture, biography, children's, cookery, crafts, design, gardening, history, lifestyle, natural history, plants, popular science, reference, medicine, nursing, wine.

Éditions Gallimard

5 rue Sébastien-Bottin, F–75328 Paris
Cedex 07
☎00 33 1 4954 4200 Fax 00 33 1 4544 9403
www.gallimard.fr
Founded 1911. Publishes fiction, poetry, art, biography, history, music, philosophy, children and young adult.

Éditions Grasset & Fasquelle

61 rue des Saints-Pères, F–75006 Paris
☎00 33 1 4439 2200 Fax 00 33 1 4222 6418
www.edition-grasset.fr
Founded 1907. Part of **Hachette-Livre**.
Publishes fiction and general non-fiction, biography, essays, literature, literary criticism, thrillers, translations, philosophy.

Hachette Livre

43 quai de Grenelle, F–75905 Paris Cedex 15
☎00 33 1 4392 3000 Fax 00 33 1 4392 3030
www.hachette.com

Founded 1826. With the acquisition of Time Warner Book Group, Hachette, already the owner of Hodder Headline and Orion, is now the biggest publisher in the British market and the third largest publisher in the world behind Pearson and Bertelsmann. Publishes fiction and general non-fiction, bibliographies, bilingual, children's, directories, education, encyclopedias, general engineering, government, language and linguistics, reference, general science, textbooks.

Éditions Robert Laffont

24 ave Marceau, F–75381 Paris Cedex 08
☎00 33 1 5367 1400
www.laffont.fr
Founded 1987. Publishes fiction and non-fiction.

Éditions Larousse

21 rue de Montparnasse, F–75283 Paris
Cedex 06
☎00 33 1 4439 4400
www.larousse.fr
Founded 1852. Publishes animals, art, bilingual, children's and young adult, childcare, cinema, cookery, dictionaries, directories, drama, encyclopedias, food, games, gardening, health, home interest, history, medicine, natural history, nursing, music, dance, self-help, psychology, reference, general science, language arts, linguistics, literature, religion, sport, technology, textbooks.

Éditions Jean–Claude Lattès

17 rue Jacob, F–75006 Paris
☎00 33 1 4441 7400 Fax 00 33 1 4325 3047
www.editions-jclattes.fr
Founded 1968. Part of **Hachette-Livre**.
Publishes fiction and general non-fiction.

Magnard SA

20 rue Berbier-du-Mets,
F–75647 Paris Cedex 13
☎00 33 1 4408 8585 Fax 00 33 1 4408 4979
www.magnard.fr
Founded 1933. Part of Groupe Albin-Michel.
Publishes education, foreign language and bilingual books, juvenile and young adults, textbooks.

Michelin Éditions des Voyages

46 ave de Breteuil, F–75007 Paris
☎00 33 1 4566 1170 Fax 00 33 1 4566 1137
Founded 1900. Publishes travel: maps and atlases.

Les Éditions de Minuit SA
7 rue Bernard-Palissy, F–75006 Paris
☎00 33 1 4439 3920 Fax 00 33 1 4544 8236
www.leseditionsdeminuit.fr
Founded 1942. Publishes fiction, essays, literature, literary criticism, philosophy, social sciences, sociology.

Les Éditions Nathan
9 rue Méchain, F–75686 Paris
☎00 33 1 4587 5000 Fax 00 33 1 4587 5343
www.nathan.fr
Founded 1881. Publishes dictionaries, directories, education, encyclopedias, history, philosophy, psychology, psychiatry, reference, general and social sciences, sociology, textbooks.

Presses de la Cité
12 ave d'Italie, F–75627 Paris Cedex 13
☎00 33 1 4416 0500 Fax 00 33 1 4416 0505
✉ pressesdelacite@placedesediteurs.com
www.pressesdelacite.com
Founded 1947. Imprint of **Editions Belfond**. Publishes fiction and general non-fiction, science fiction, fantasy, history, mysteries, romance, biography.

Presses Universitaires de France (PUF)
6 ave Reille, F–75685 Paris Cedex 14
☎00 33 1 5810 3100 Fax 00 33 1 5810 3182
www.puf.com
Founded 1921. Academic publisher of dictionaries, directories, economics, encyclopedias, essays, history, journals, law, linguistics, literature, medicine, philosophy, psychology, psychiatry, political science, reference, social science, textbooks.

Éditions du Seuil
27 rue Jacob, F–75261 Paris Cedex 06
☎00 33 1 4046 5050
www.seuil.com
Founded 1935. Publishes fiction, literature, literary criticism, essays, poetry, biography, classics, illustrated, history, how-to, juvenile and young adult, textbooks.

Les Editions de la Table Ronde
14 rue Séguier, F–75006 Paris
☎00 33 1 4046 7070
Founded 1944. Publishes fiction and general non-fiction, biography, history, psychology, psychiatry, religion, sport.

Librairie Vuibert
20 rue Berbier-du-Mets,
F–75647 Paris Cedex 13
☎00 33 1 4408 4900 Fax 00 33 1 4408 4969
www.vuibert.com
Founded 1877. Part of Groupe Albin-Michel. Publishes textbooks.

Germany

Verlag C.H. Beck (OHG)
Wilhelmstrasse 9, 80801 Munich
☎00 49 89 38 189-0 Fax 00 49 89 38 189-398
www.beck.de
Founded 1763. Publishes general non-fiction, anthropology, archaeology, art, CD-ROMs, dance, dictionaries, directories, economics, essays, encyclopedias, history, illustrated, journals, language arts, law, linguistics, literature, literary criticism, music, philosophy, professional, reference, social sciences, sociology, textbooks, theology.

C. Bertelsmann
Neumarkter Strasse 28, 81673 Munich
☎00 49 89 4136-0
Founded 1835. Imprint of the **Random House Group**. Publishes fiction and general non-fiction, art, autobiography, biography, government and politics.

Carlsen Verlag GmbH
Postfach 50 03 80, 22703 Hamburg
☎00 49 40 39804-0 Fax 00 49 40 39804-390
✉ info@carlsen.de
www.carlsen.de
Founded 1953. Publishes children's and comic books.

Deutscher Taschenbuch Verlag GmbH & Co. KG
Friedrichstrasse 1a, 80801 Munich
☎00 49 89 38167-0 Fax 00 49 89 346428
✉ verlagdtv.de
www.dtv.de
Founded 1961. Publishes fiction and general non-fiction; biography, business, child care and development, children's, dictionaries, directories, economics, education, encyclopedias, fantasy, government, health and nutrition, history, poetry, psychiatry, psychology, philosophy, politics, reference, religion, literature, literary criticism, essays, thrillers, translations, travel, young adult.

S. Fischer Verlag GmbH
Hedderichstrasse 114, 60596 Frankfurt am Main
☎00 49 69 6062-0 Fax 00 49 69 6062-214
www.fischerverlage.de
Founded 1886. Part of the Holtzbrinck Group. Publishes fiction, general non-fiction, biography, business, children's and young adult, history, literature, natural history, politics, psychology, reference.

Carl Hanser Verlag GmbH & Co. KG
Postfach 86 04 20, 81631 Munich
☎00 49 89 998300 Fax 00 49 89 984809
✉ info@hanser.de
www.hanser.de/verlag
Founded in 1928. Publishes international and German contemporary literature; children's and juveniles; specialist books on engineering and technology, natural science, computers and computer science, economics and management, CD-ROMs, journals, academic, textbooks, translations.

Heyne Verlag
Bayerstrasse 71–73, 80335 Munich
☎00 49 89 4136-0
www.heyne.de
Founded 1934. Part of Random House Group. Publishes fiction, mystery, romance, humour, science fiction, fantasy, biography, cookery, film, history, how-to, occult, psychology, psychiatry.

Hoffmann und Campe Verlag GmbH
Harvestehuder Weg 42, 20149 Hamburg
☎00 49 40 44188-0 Fax 00 49 40 44188-202
✉ email@hoca.de
www.hoca.de
Founded 1781. Publishes fiction and general non-fiction; art, audio, biography, dance, history, illustrated, journals, music, poetry, philosophy, psychology, psychiatry, general science, social sciences.

Verlagsgruppe Georg von Holtzbrinck GmbH
Gänsheidestrasse 26, 70184 Stuttgart
☎00 49 711 2150-0 Fax 00 49 711 2150-269
✉ info@holtzbrinck.com
www.holtzbrinck.com
Founded 1948. One of the world's largest publishing groups with 12 book publishing houses and 40 imprints. Also publishes the newspapers, *Handelsblatt* and *Die Zeit*.

Hüthig GmbH & Co. KG
Postfach 10 28 69, 69018 Heidelberg
☎00 49 6221 489-0 Fax 00 49 6221 489-279
www.huethig.de
Founded 1925. Germany's fourth largest professional publisher: CD-ROMs, multimedia, journals, academic, textbooks, translations.

Ernst Klett Verlag GmbH
Rotebühlstrasse 77, 70178 Stuttgart
☎00 49 711 6672 1333
Fax 00 49 711 6672 2080
www.klett.de
Founded 1897. Educational publisher: dictionaries, encyclopedias, textbooks.

Verlagsgruppe Lübbe GmbH & Co. KG
Scheidtbachstrasse 23–31, 51469 Bergisch Gladbach
☎00 49 2202 121-0 Fax 00 49 2202 121-928
www.luebbe.de
Founded 1963. Publishes fiction and general non-fiction, audio, biography, history, how-to.

Rowohlt Verlag GmbH
Hamburgerstr 17, 21465 Reinbeck
☎00 49 40 727-20 Fax 00 49 40 7272-319
✉ info@rowohlt.de
www.rowohlt.de
Founded 1908. Publishes general non-fiction.

Springer GmbH
Tiergartenstrasse 17, 69121 Heidelberg
☎00 49 6221 4870
www.springer.de
Also at: Heidelberger Platz 3, 14197 Berlin
☎ 00 49 30 827870
Founded 1842. Part of Springer Science+Business Media Deutschland GmbH. Leading specialist publisher of science, technology and medical books, journals, CD-ROMs, databases. Subjects include engineering, computer science, economics, law, architecture, construction and transport – with eighty per cent of publications in English.

Suhrkamp Verlag
Postfach 101945, 60019 Frankfurt am Main
☎00 49 69 75601-0 Fax 00 49 69 75601-314
www.suhrkamp.de
Founded 1950. Publishes fiction, poetry,

biography, cinema, film, theatre, philosophy, psychology, psychiatry, general science.

Taschen GmbH
Hohenzollernring 53, 50672 Cologne
☎00 49 221 20180-0 Fax 00 49 221 254919
✉ contact@taschen.com
www.taschen.com
Founded 1980. Publishes photography, art, erotica, architecture and interior design.

Ullstein Buchverlage GmbH
Friedrichstrasse 126, 10117 Berlin
☎00 49 30 23456-300
Fax 00 49 30 23456-303
✉ info@ullstein-buchverlage.de
www.ullsteinbuchverlage.de
Founded 1903. Publishes general fiction and non-fiction; literature, mystery, biography, business, economics, health, gift books, memoirs, politics.

WEKA Firmengruppe GmbH & Co KG
Postfach 13 31, 86438 Kissing
☎00 49 8233 23-0 Fax 00 49 8233 23-195
✉ info@weka-holding.de
www.weka-holding.de
Founded 1973. Germany's largest professional publisher.

Italy

Adelphi Edizioni SpA
Via S. Giovanni sul Muro 14, 20121 Milan
☎00 39 2 725731 Fax 00 39 2 89010337
✉ info@adelphi.it
www.adelphi.it
Founded 1962. Publishes literature, literary criticism, anthropology, art, autobiography, archaeology, architecture, biography, biology, cinema, economics, history, linguistics, mathematics, medicine, music, philosophy, photography, politics, psychiatry, religion, general science, sociology, theatre, translation.

Bompiani
Via Mecenate 91, 20138 Milan
☎00 39 2 50951 Fax 00 39 2 5065361
www.rcslibri.it
Founded 1929. Part of RCS Libri publishing group. Publishes fiction and general non-fiction, dictionaries, encyclopedias, juvenile and young adult.

Bulzoni Editore SRL
Via Dei Liburni 14, 00185 Rome
☎00 39 6 4455207 Fax 00 39 6 4450355
✉ bulzoni@bulzoni.it
www.bulzoni.it
Founded 1969. Publisher of college textbooks.

Cappelli Editore
Via Farini 14, 40124 Bologna
☎00 39 51 239060 Fax 00 39 51 239286
✉ info@cappellieditore.com
www.cappellieditore.com
Founded 1851. Publishes reference, textbooks, juvenile and young adult.

Garzanti Libri SpA
Via Gasparotto 1, 20124 Milan
☎00 39 2 674171 Fax 00 39 2 67417323
www.garzantilibri.it
Founded 1861. Publishes fiction, literature, literary criticism, encyclopedias, essays, biography, cookery, crime, dictionaries, history, memoir, philosophy, poetry, reference, textbooks.

Giunti Gruppo Editoriale
Via Bolognese 165, 50139 Florence
☎00 39 55 5062376 Fax 00 39 55 5062397
www.giunti.it
Founded 1841. Publishes fiction, literature, literary criticism, essays, art, alternative medicine, cookery, crafts, dictionaries, directories, education, encyclopedias, food, health, history, journals, language and linguistics, leisure, multimedia, music, psychology, psychiatry, reference, textbooks, tourism. Italian publishers of National Geographical Society books.

Gremese Editore
Via Virginia Agnelli 88, 00151 Rome
☎00 39 6 657 40507 Fax 00 39 6 657 40509
✉ gremese@gremese.com
www.gremese.com
Founded 1954. Publishes fiction and non-fiction; illustrated books, dictionaries, directories, encyclopedias, reference,

Casa Editrice Longanesi SpA
Via Gherardini 10, 20145 Milan
☎00 39 2 34597620 Fax 00 39 2 34597212
✉ info@longanesi.it
www.longanesi.it
Founded 1946. Mass market paperback publisher of fiction, adventure, archaeology, art, biography, fantasy, history, journalism, maritime, philosophy, popular science, thrillers.

Arnoldo Mondadori Editore SpA
Via Mondadori 1, 20090 Segrate (Milan)
☎00 39 2 75421 Fax 00 39 2 75422302
www.mondadori.it
Founded 1907. Italy's largest publisher. Publishes fiction, mystery, romance, art, biography, children's and young adult, directories, history, how-to, journals, medicine, music, poetry, philosophy, psychology, reference, religion, general science, education, textbooks.

Società Editrice Il Mulino
Strada Maggiore 37, 40125 Bologna
☎00 39 51 256011 Fax 00 39 51 256034
✉ info@mulino.it
www.mulino.it
Founded 1954. Publishes economics, government, history, law, language arts, linguistics, literature, literary criticism, philosophy, political science, psychology, psychiatry, social sciences, sociology, textbooks, journals.

Gruppo Ugo Mursia Editore SpA
Via Melchiorre Gioia 45, 20124 Milan
☎00 39 2 6737 8500 Fax 00 39 2 6737 8605
✉ info@mursia.com
www.mursia.com
Founded 1941. Publishes fiction, art, biography, directories, education, history, maritime, philosophy, reference, religion, sport, general science, social sciences, textbooks, juvenile and young adult.

Rizzoli Editore
Via Mecenate 91, 20138 Milan
☎00 39 2 50951 Fax 00 39 2 5065361
www.rcslibri.it
Founded 1945. Part of RCS Libri publishing group. Publishes fiction and non-fiction, juvenile and young adult.

Società Editrice
Internazionale – SEI
Corso Regina Margherita 176, 10152 Turin
☎00 39 11 52271 Fax 00 39 11 5211320
www.seieditrice.com
Founded 1908. Publishes children's, dictionaries, education, encyclopedias, textbooks.

Sonzogno
Via Mecenate 91, 20138 Milan
☎00 39 2 50951 Fax 00 39 2 5065361
www.rcslibri.it
Founded 1818. Part of RCS Libri publishing

group. Publishes fiction, mysteries, and general non-fiction.

Sperling e Kupfer Editori SpA
Via Marco D'Aviano 2, 20131 Milan
☎00 39 2 285231 Fax 00 39 2 28523277
www.sperling.it
Founded 1899. Publishes fiction and general non-fiction; biography, economics, history, science, sport.

Sugarco Edizioni SRL
Via don Gnocchi 4, 20148 Milan
☎00 39 2 407 8370 Fax 00 39 2 407 8493
✉ info@sugarcoedizioni.it
www.sugarcoedizioni.it
Founded 1956. Publishes fiction, biography, history, how-to, philosophy.

Todariana Editrice
Via Gardone 29, 29139 Milan
☎00 39 2 56812953 Fax 00 39 2 55213405
www.todariana-eurapress.it
Founded 1967. Publishes fiction, poetry, science fiction, fantasy, literature, literary criticism, language arts, linguistics, psychology, psychiatry, social sciences, sociology, travel.

The Netherlands

A. W. Bruna Uitgevers BV
Postbus 40203, 3504 AA Utrecht
☎00 31 30 247 0411 Fax 00 31 30 241 0018
✉ info@awwbruna.nl
www.awbruna.nl
Founded 1868. Publishes fiction and general non-fiction; mysteries, thrillers, computer science, CD-ROMs, history, philosophy, psychology, psychiatry, general science, social sciences, sociology.

Uitgeverij BZZTÔH BV
Laan van Meerdervoort 10, 2517 AJ The Hague
☎00 31 70 363 2934 Fax 00 31 70 363 1932
✉ info@bzztoh.nl
www.bzztoh.nl
Founded 1970. Publishes fiction, mysteries, romance, literature, literary criticism, foreign language, bilingual, general non-fiction, astrology, biography, cookery, finance, self-help, health and nutrition, lifestyle, occult, sport, thrillers, translations, travel.

Elsevier Science BV
Postbus 152, 1000 AD Amsterdam

☎00 31 20 515 9944 Fax 00 31 20 515 9900
www.elsevier.nl
Founded 1946. Parent company Reed Elsevier.
Publishes sciences (all fields), medicine, nursing, dentistry, economics, engineering (chemical and general), mathematics, physics, technology.

Uitgeversmaatschappij J. H. Kok BV

Postbus Box 5018, 8260 GA Kampen
☎00 31 38 339 2555
www.kok.nl
Founded 1894. Publishes fiction, history, religion, directories, encyclopedias, reference, psychology, general science, social sciences, sociology, textbooks, juvenile and young adult.

J.M. Meulenhoff BV

Postbus 100, 1000 AC Amsterdam
☎00 31 20 553 3500 Fax 00 31 20 625 1135
✉ info@meulenhoff.nl
www.meulenhoff.nl
Founded 1895. Publishes international co-productions, fiction and general non-fiction. Specialises in Dutch and translated literature.

Pearson Education Benelux

Postbus 75598, 1070 AN Amsterdam
☎00 31 20 575 5800 Fax 00 31 20 664 5334
www.pearsoneducation.nl
Founded 1942. Publishes education, business, computer science, directories, economics, management, reference, textbooks, technology.

Uitgeverij Het Spectrum BV

Postbus 2073, 3500 GB Utrecht
☎00 31 30 265 0650 Fax 00 31 30 262 0850
✉ het@spetrum.nl
www.spectrum.nl
Founded 1935. Publishes general non-fiction, children's, dictionaries, encyclopedias, health, illustrated, language, management, parenting, reference, science, sport, travel.

Springer Science+Business Media BV

Van Godewijckstraat 30, 3311 GX Dordrecht
☎00 31 78 657 6000 Fax 00 31 78 657 6555
www.springer.com
Publishes ebooks, CD-ROMs, databases and journals; computer science, economics, engineering, humanities, medicine, social sciences, mathematics, physics.

Uitgeverij Unieboek BV

Postbus 97, 3990 DB Houten
☎00 31 30 799 8300 Fax 00 31 30 799 8398
✉ info@unieboek.nl
www.unieboek.nl
Founded 1891. Publishes fiction: mysteries, romance, thrillers; general non-fiction, business, lifestyle, travel, reference, juvenile and young adults.

Norway

H. Aschehoug & Co (W. Nygaard)

Postboks 363 Sentrum, N–0102 Oslo
☎00 47 22 400400
✉ epost@aschehoug.no
www.aschehoug.no
Founded 1872. Publishes fiction and general non-fiction, children's, reference, popular science, hobbies, education and textbooks.

J.W. Cappelens Forlag AS

Postboks 350 Sentrum, N–0101 Oslo
☎00 47 22 365000 Fax 00 47 22 365040
✉ caplex@cappelen.no
www.cappelen.no
Founded 1829. Part of Bonnier AB. Publishes fiction (including foreign fiction), general non-fiction, maps and atlases, juvenile and young adult, dictionaries, directories, encyclopedias, reference, religion, textbooks.

N.W. Damm & Søn AS

Fridtjof Nansens vei 14, N–0055 Oslo
☎00 47 24 051000 Fax 00 47 24 051099
www.damm.no
Founded 1845. Owned by the Egmont Group. Publishes fiction, children's and young adult, general non-fiction, reference and translated fiction.

Gyldendal Norsk Forlag

Postboks 6860, St Olavs Plass, N–0130 Oslo
☎00 47 22 034100 Fax 00 47 22 034105
✉ gnf@gyldendal.no
www.gyldendal.no
Founded 1925. Publishes fiction, science fiction, children's, dictionaries, directories, encyclopedias, journals, reference, textbooks.

Tiden Norsk Forlag

Postboks 6704, St Olavs Plass, N–0130 Oslo
☎00 47 22 2332 7660 Fax 00 46 22 2332 7697
✉ tiden@tiden.no
www.tiden.no

Founded 1933. Part of **Gyldendal Norsk Forlag** group. Publishes Norwegian and translated fiction and general non-fiction.

Poland

Ameet Sp. zo.o.
Przybyszewskiego 176/178, 93–120 Lodz
☎00 48 42 676 2778 Fax 00 48 42 676 2819
✉ ameet@ameet.com.pl
www.ameet.pl
Children's publisher.

Publicat SA
ul. Chlebowa 24, 61-003 Poznan
☎00 48 61 652 92 52 Fax 00 48 61 652 92 00
✉ office@publicat.pl
www.publicat.pl
Publishes fiction and non-fiction; biography, children's, crime, education, geography, history, religion.

Portugal

Bertrand Editora Lda
Rua Anchieta 29–1, 1200 Lisbon
☎00 351 21 320084
Founded 1727. Publishes bilingual, dictionaries, encyclopedias, juvenile and young adult.

Editorial Caminho SARL
Avenida Almirante Gago Coutinho, n.º 121,
17100–029 Lisbon
☎00 351 21 8429830 Fax 00 351 21 8429849
✉ caminho@editorial-caminho.pt
www.editorial-caminho.pt
Founded 1977. Publishes fiction, government, political science, juvenile and young adult.

Livraria Civilização (Américo Fraga Lamares & Ca Lda)
Rua Dr Alberto Aires de Gouveia 27,
4000 Porto
☎00 351 22 20002286
Founded 1921. Publishes fiction, art, economics, history, political science, government, sociology, social sciences, juvenile and young adult.

Publicações Europa-América Lda
Rua Francisco Lyon de Castro 2, Apartado 8,
2725–354 Mem Martins
☎00 351 21 926 7700 Fax 00 351 21 926 7771
Founded 1945. Publishes fiction, children's, directories, reference, textbooks.

Gradiva–Publicações Lda
Rua Almeida e Sousa 21 R/C Esq,
1399–041 Lisbon
☎00 351 21 3974067 Fax 00 351 21 3953470
www.gradiva.pt
Founded 1981. Publishes academic, fiction, literature, literary criticism, children's, juvenile and young adult, directories, illustrated, reference, translations.

Livros Horizonte Lda
Rua das Chagas 17–1 Dto, 1200–106 Lisbon
☎00 351 1 3466917
Founded 1953. Publishes children's, education, juvenile and young adult, textbooks.

Editorial Verbo SA
Av António Augusto de Aguiar 148,
1069–019 Lisbon
☎00 351 21 380 1100 Fax 00 351 21 386 5397
www.editorialverbo.pt
Founded 1959. Publishes dictionaries, education, encyclopedias, history, general science, juvenile and young adult.

Spain

Alianza Editorial SA
Juan Ignacio Luca de Tena 15, 28027 Madrid
☎00 34 91 393 8890 Fax 00 34 91 320 4408
www.alianzaeditorial.es
Founded 1966. Part of Grupo Anaya. Publishes fiction, poetry, art, history, mathematics, philosophy, government, political science, social sciences, sociology, general science.

Ediciones Anaya SA
Juan Ignacio Luca de Tena 15, 28027 Madrid
☎00 349 1 393 8600 Fax 00 349 1 742 6631
www.anaya.es
Founded 1959. Part of Grupo Anaya. Educational publisher.

EDHASA (Editora y Distribuidora Hispano – Americana SA)
Av Diagonal 519–521, 2 piso, 08029 Barcelona
☎00 349 3 494 9720 Fax 00 349 3 419 4584
www.edhasa.es
Founded 1946. Publishes fiction, literature, literary criticism, fantasy, essays, biography, history.

Editorial Espasa-Calpe SA
Carreterade Irₓn Km 12, 200, 28049 Madrid
☎00 349 1 358 9689

www.espasa.com
Founded 1926. Publishes fiction, children's, biography, essays, education, literature, CD-ROMs, dictionaries, encyclopedias, reference, maps and atlases.

Grijalbo
Travessera de Gracia 47–49, 08021 Barcelona
☎00 349 3 366 0300
www.grijalbo.com
Founded 1962. An imprint of **Random House Mondadori**. Publishes fiction (historical and thrillers) and non-fiction (self-help and inspirational).

Ediciónes Hiperión SL
Calle de Salustiano Olózaga 14, 28001 Madrid
☎00 349 1 557 6015 Fax 00 349 1 435 8690
✉ info@hiperion.com
www.hiperion.com
Founded 1976. Publishes literature, essays, poetry, bilingual, foreign language, children's, religion, translations.

Grupo Editorial Luis Vives
Xaudaró 25, 28034 Madrid
☎00 349 1 334 4883
www.edelvives.es
Founded 1890. Educational publisher.

Editorial Molino SL
Pérez Galdós 36, 08012 Barcelona
☎00 349 3 226 0625
www.rba.es/holding
Founded 1933. Part of Grupo RBA. Publishes children's and young adults.

Pearson Educacion SA
Ribera del Loira 28, 28042 Madrid
☎00 34 91 382 8300 Fax 00 34 91 382 8325
www.pearsoneducacion.com
Founded 1942. Educational publishers.

Editorial Planeta SA
Calle Còrsega 273–279, 08008 Barcelona
☎00 349 3 228 5800
www.planeta.es
Founded 1952. Part of Groupo Planeta SA. Publishes fiction and general non-fiction.

Random House Mondadori
Travessera de Gracia 47–49, 08021 Barcelona
☎00 349 3 366 0300
www.randomhousemondadori.es
Publishes fiction and non-fiction; children's and young adult, art, bilingual dictionaries,

biography, economics, essays, guides, illustrated, literature, memoirs, poetry, reference, science, self-help, sociology, technology, thrillers,

Editorial Seix Barral SA
Avda Diagonal 662–664, 7a, 08034 Barcelona
☎00 349 3 496 7003 Fax 00 349 3 496 7004
✉ editorial@seix-barral.es
www.seix-barral.es
Founded 1911. Part of Grupo Planeta SA. Foreign language publisher of literature.

Tusquets Editores
Cesare Cantù 8, 08023 Barcelona
☎00 349 3 253 0400 Fax 00 349 3 417 6703
www.tusquets-editores.com
Founded 1969. Publishes fiction, art, autobiography, biography, cinema, cookery, food, history, essays, literature, memoirs, philosophy, poetry, social sciences, theatre.

Sweden

Bonnier Books
PO Box 3159, SE–103 63 Stockholm
☎00 46 8 696 8000 Fax 00 46 8 696 8630
✉ bonnierforlagen@bok.bonnier.se
www.bok.bonnier.se
Founded 2002. Part of the Bonnier AB group. Publishes fiction, non-fiction and children's books.

Albert Bonniers Förlag
PO Box 3159, SE–103 63 Stockholm
☎00 46 8 696 8000 Fax 00 46 8 696 8630
✉ info@abforlag.bonnier.se
www.albertbonniersforlag.com
Founded 1837. Part of Bonnier Books. Publishes fiction and general non-fiction.

Bra Böcker AB
PO Box 892, SE–20180 Malmö
☎00 46 40 665 4693
www.bbb.se
Founded 1965. Publishes fiction and non-fiction.

Brombergs Bokförlag AB
PO Box 12886, SE–112 98 Stockholm
☎00 46 8 5626 2080 Fax 00 46 8 5626 2085
✉ info@brombergs.se
www.brombergs.se
Founded 1973. Publishes literary fiction and general non-fiction.

Bokförlaget Forum AB
PO Box 70321, SE-107 23 Stockholm
☎00 46 8 696 8440 Fax 00 46 8 696 8367
www.forum.se
Founded 1944. Publishes fiction (including foreign) and general non-fiction.

Bokförlaget Natur och Kultur
PO Box 27 323, SE-102 54 Stockholm
☎00 46 8 453 8600 Fax 00 46 8 453 8790
✉ info@nok.se
www.nok.se
Founded 1922. Publishes fiction and general non-fiction; education and textbooks.

Norstedts Förlag
Box 2052, SE-103 12 Stockholm
☎00 46 8 769 8850 Fax 00 46 8 769 8864
✉ info@norstedts.se
www.norstedts.se
Founded 1823. Sweden's oldest publishing house. Publishes fiction and general non-fiction.

Rabén och Sjögren Bokförlag
PO Box 2052, SE-103 12 Stockholm
☎00 46 8 769 8800 Fax 00 46 8 769 8813
✉ raben-sjogren@raben.se
www.raben.se
Founded 1941. Part of Norstedts Förlagsgrupp. Publishes children's and young adult books.

B. Wählströms Bokförlag AB
PO Box 6630, SE-113 84 Stockholm
☎00 46 8 7283400 Fax 00 46 8 6189761
✉ info@wahlstroms.se
www.wahlstroms.se
Founded 1911. Part of Forma Publishing Group AB. Publishes fiction and general non-fiction, juvenile and young adult.

Switzerland

Arche Verlag AG
Niederdorfstr 90, CH-8001 Zurich
☎00 41 1 2522410 Fax 00 41 1 2611115
✉ info@arche-verlag.com
www.arche-verlag.com
Founded 1944. Publishes literature and literary criticism, essays, biography, fiction, poetry, music, dance, travel.

Diogenes Verlag AG
Sprecherstr 8, CH-8032 Zurich
☎00 41 1 2548511 Fax 00 41 1 2528407
✉ info@diogenes.ch
www.diogenes.ch
Founded 1952. Publishes fiction, essays, literature, literary criticism, illustrated, mysteries, art, children's, drama, theatre, philosophy.

Neptun-Verlag
Erlenstrasse 2, CH-8280 Kreuzlingen
☎00 41 71 6779655 Fax 00 41 72 6779650
✉ neptun@bluewin.ch
www.neptunart.ch
Founded 1946. Publishes non-fiction and children's books.

Orell Füssli Verlag
Dietzingerstr 3, CH-8036 Zurich
☎00 41 1 466 7711 Fax 00 41 1 466 7412
www.ofv.ch
Founded 1519. Publishes accountancy, architecture, art, art history, business, leisure, photography, politics, psychology.

Payot Libraire
Case Postale 6730, CH-1002 Lausanne
☎00 41 21 341 3252 Fax 00 41 21 341 3217
www.payot-libraire.ch
Founded 1875. Publishes fiction and general non-fiction; arts and entertainment, audio, business, children's, education, language, lifestyle, professional, reference, travel.

Sauerländer Verlage AG
Ausserfeldstr. 9, CH-5036 Oberentfelden
☎00 41 62 2836 8686 Fax 00 41 62 2836 8620
✉ verlag@sauerlaender.ch
www.sauerlaender.ch
Founded 1807. Publishes education and general non-fiction.

European Television Companies

Austria

ORF (Österreichisher Rundfunk)
Würzburggasse 30, A–1136 Vienna
☎00 43 1 87 878-0
www.orf.at

Belgium

Radio-Télévision Belge de la Communauté Française (RTBF)
Boulevard Auguste Reyers 52, B–1044 Brussels
☎00 32 2 737 2111
www.rtbf.be

Vlaamse Radio en Televisieomroep (VRT)
Auguste Reyerslaan 52, B–1043 Brussels
☎00 32 2 741 3111
www.vrt.be

Vlaamse Televisie Maatschappij (VTM) (cable)
Medialaan 1, B–1800 Vilvoorde
☎00 32 2 255 3211
✉ info@vtm.be
www.vtm.be

Denmark

DR TV & DR Radio
Emil Holms Kanal 20, DK–0999 Copenhagen C
☎00 45 35 20 3040
✉ drcommunikation@dr.dk
www.dr.dk

SBS TV A/S
Mileparken 20A, DK–2740 Skovlunde
☎00 45 70 10 1010
✉ btb@sbstv.dk
www.sbstv.dk

TV–2 Danmark
Rugaardsvej 25, DK–5100 Odense C
☎00 45 65 91 9191
✉ tv2@tv2.dk

www.tv2.dk

TV3 (Viasat)
Wildersgade 8, DK–1408 Copenhagen K
☎00 45 77 30 5500
✉ tv3@viasat.dk
www.viasat.dk

Finland

MTV3 Finland
Ilmalantori 2, FIN–00033 Helsinki
☎00 358 10 300300
www.mtv3.fi

Yleisradio Oy (YLE)
PO Box 90, FIN–00024 Yleisradio
☎00 358 9 14801
✉ fbc@yle.fi
www.yle.fi

France

Arte France (cable & satellite)
8 rue Marceau, 92785 Issy-les-Moulineaux Cedex 9
☎00 33 1 55 00 77 77
www.artefrance.fr

Canal + (pay TV)
1 place du Spectacle, 92863 Issy-les-Moulineaux Cedex 9
☎00 33 71 35 35 35
www.cplus.fr

France 5
10 rue Horace-Vernet, 92130 Issy-les-Moulineaux
☎00 33 1 56 22 91 91
www.france5.fr

France Télévision (France 2/France 3)
7 Esplanade Henri de France, 75907 Paris Cedex 15
☎00 33 1 56 22 60 00
www.france2.fr
www.france3.fr

M6 (Métropole Télévision)
89 ave Charles de Gaulle, 92575 Neuilly-sur-Seine Cedex
☎00 33 1 41 92 66 66
www.m6.fr

TF1 (Télévision Française 1)
1 quai du Pont du Jour, 92656 Boulogne
☎00 33 1 41 41 12 34
www.tf1.fr

Germany

ARD – Das Erste
Arnulfstrasse 42, 80335 Munich
☎00 49 89 5900 3344
✉ info@daserste.de
www.daserste.de

Arte Germany (cable & satellite)
Postfach 10 02 13, 76483 Baden–Baden
☎00 49 7221 93690
www.arte.de

ZDF (Zweites Deutsches Fernsehen)
Postfach 40 40, 55100 Mainz
☎00 49 61 31/701
✉ info@zdf.de
www.zdf.de

Republic of Ireland

Radio Telefís Éireann (RTÉ One – RTÉ Two)
Donnybrook, Dublin 4
☎00 353 1 208 3111
✉ info@rte.ie
www.rte.ie

TG4 (Teilefís na Gaelige)
(Irish language TV)
Baile na hAbhann, Co. na Gaillimhe
☎00 353 91 505050
✉ eolas@tg4.ie
www.tg4.ie

Italy

RAI (RadioTelevisione Italiana)
Viale Mazzini 14, 00195 Rome
☎00 39 06 3878-1
www.rai.it

The Netherlands

AVRO (Algemene Omroep Vereniging)
Postbus 2, 1200 JA Hilversum
☎00 31 35 671 79 11
www.central.avro.nl/index.asp

IKON
Postbus 10009, 1201 DA Hilversum
☎00 31 35 672 72 72
✉ ikon@ikon.nl
www.omroep.nl/ikon

NCRV (Nederlandse Christelijke Radio Vereniging)
Postbus 25000, 1202 HB Hilversum
☎00 31 35 671 99 11
info.omroep.nl/ncrv

NOS (Nederlandse Omroep Stichting)
Sumatralaan 45, 1217 GP Hilversum
☎00 31 35 677 92 22
www.nos.nl

NPS (Nederlandse Programma Stichting)
Postbus 29000, 1202 MA Hilversum
☎00 31 35 677 9333
www.omroep.nl/nps

VARA
Postbus 175, 1200 AD Hilversum
☎00 31 35 671 19 11
www.omroep.nl

VPRO
Postbus 11, 1200 JC Hilversum
☎00 31 35 671 29 11
www.vpro.nl

Norway

NRK (Norsk Rikskringkasting), N–0340 Oslo
☎00 47 23 04 7000
www.nrk.no

TVNorge
Postboks 11, Sentrum, N–0101 Oslo
☎00 47 21 02 2000
✉ tvnorge@tvnorge.no
www.tvnorge.no

TV2
Postboks 7222, N–5020 Bergen
☎00 47 55 90 8070
✉ info@tv2.no
www.tv2.no

Portugal

Radiotelevisão Portuguesa (RTP)
Avenida Marechal, Gomes da Costa 37,
1849–030 Lisbon
☎00 351 21 794 7000
www.rtp.pt

TVI (Televisão Independente)
Rua Mário Castelhano 40, Queluz de Baixo,
2734–502 Barcarena
☎00 351 21 434 7500
www.tvi.pt

Spain

RTVE (RadioTelevision Española)
Edificio Prado del Rey, E–28223 Madrid
☎00 349 1 581 7000
www.rtve.es

Sweden

Sveriges Television AB–SVT
Oxenstierngatan 26–34, S–105 10 Stockholm
☎00 46 8 784 0000
www.svt.se

TV4
Tegeluddsvägen 3, S–115 79 Stockholm
☎00 46 8 459 4000
www.tv4.se

Switzerland

RTR (Radio e Televisiun Rumantscha)
(Romansch language TV)
Via da Masans 2, Plazza dal teater,
CH–7002 Cuira
☎00 41 81 255 7575
✉ info@rtr.ch
www.rtr.ch

RTSI (Radiotelevisione svizzera di lingua Italiana) (Italian language TV)
Casella postale, CH–6903 Lugano
☎00 41 91 803 51 11
✉ info@rtsi.ch
www.rtsi.ch

Schweizer Fernsehen (SF)
(German language TV)
Postfach, CH–8052 Zurich
☎00 41 1 305 66 11
✉ sf@sf.tv
www.sf.tv

SRG SSR idée suisse (Swiss Broadcasting Corp.)
Postfach 26, CH–3000 Berne15
☎00 41 31 350 91 11
✉ info@srgssrideesuisse.ch
www.srg-ssr.ch

TSR (Télévision Suisse Romande)
Quai Ernest Ansermet 20, CH–1211 Geneva 8
☎00 41 22 708 20 20
www.tsr.ch

US Publishers

Anyone corresponding with the big American publishers should know that following the terrorist attacks of 2001 they are wary of any package or letter that looks in any way suspicious. This, of course, begs the question what is or what is not suspicious which is as difficult to answer as what makes or does not make a good novel. The best policy is to make an initial enquiry by e-mail.

International Reply Coupons (IRCs)

For return postage, send IRCs, available from post offices. Letters, 60 pence; mss according to weight. For current postal rates to the UK, go to the United States Postal Service website at www.usps.com and click on 'Calculate Postage'.

ABC–CLIO

PO Box 1911, Santa Barbara CA 93116–1911
☎001 805 968 1911 Fax 001 805 685 9685
www.abc-clio.com
President/CEO *Ronald J. Boehm*

Founded 1953. Publishes academic and reference, focusing on history and social studies; books and multimedia. UK SUBSIDIARY **ABC-Clio Ltd**, Oxford. No unsolicited mss; synopses and ideas welcome.

Abingdon Press

PO Box 801, Nashville TN 37202–0801
☎001 615 749 6290 Fax 001 615 749 6056
www.abingdonpress.com

Snr.VP/Editorial Director *Harriett Jane Olson*

Founded 1789. Publishes non-fiction: religious (Protestant), reference, professional and academic texts. Over 100 titles a year.

Harry N. Abrams, Inc.

115 West 18th Street, New York NY 10011
☎001 212 206 7715 Fax 001 212 229 0312
www.hnabooks.com

VP/Editor-in-Chief *Eric Himmel*

Founded 1950. Publishes illustrated books: art, natural history, photography. No fiction. About 200 titles a year.

Academy Chicago Publishers

363 W. Erie Street, Chicago IL 60610
☎001 312 751 7300 Fax 001 312 751 7306
www.academychicago.com
President & Senior Editor *Anita Miller*

Founded 1975. Publishes mainstream fiction; non-fiction: art, history, mysteries. No romance, children's, young adult, religious, sexist or avant-garde.

Ace Books

See **Penguin Group (USA) Inc.**

Addison Wesley

75 Arlington Street, Suite 300, Boston MA 02116
☎001 617 848 7500
www.aw-bc.com

A division of Pearson Education. Publishes academic textbooks, multimedia and learning programs in biology, astronomy, physics. See the website for submission guidelines.

University of Alabama Press

Box 870380, Tuscaloosa AL 35487–0380
☎001 205 348 5180 Fax 001 205 348 9201
www.uapress.ua.edu

Director *Daniel J.J. Ross*

Founded 1945. Publishes American history, Latin American history, American religious history; African-American and Native American studies, Judaic studies, archaeology, anthropology, enthnohistory and American letters. About 60 titles a year. Submissions are not invited in poetry, fiction or drama.

Aladdin Books

See **Simon & Schuster Children's Publishing**

University of Alaska Press

PO Box 756240, University of Alaska, Fairbanks AK 99775–6240
☎001 907 474 5831 Fax 001 907 474 5502
✉ fypress@uaf.edu

www.uaf.edu/uapress

Chair, Editorial Board *Patricia H. Partnow*

Publishes scholarly works about Alaska and the North Pacific rim, with a special emphasis on circumpolar regions, history, anthropology, natural history. No fiction or poetry. 10 titles a year. Queries and proposals welcome (see 'For Authors' page on the website for proposal guidelines).

Alpha Books
See **Penguin Group (USA) Inc.**

AMACOM Books
American Management Association, 1601 Broadway, New York NY 10019
☎001 212 586 8100
www.amacombooks.org

Editor-in-Chief *Adrienne Hickey*

Founded 1972. Owned by American Management Association. Publishes business books only, including general management, business communications, sales and marketing, finance, computers and information systems, human resource management and training, career/personal growth skills. About 80 titles a year.

Amistad
See **HarperCollins Publishers, Inc.**

Julie Andrews Collection
See **HarperCollins Publishers, Inc.**

Anvil
See **Krieger Publishing Co.**

Shaye Areheart Books
See **Crown Publishing Group**

University of Arizona Press
355 S. Euclid Avenue, Suite. 103, Tucson AZ 85719–6654
☎001 520 621 1441 Fax 001 520 621 8899
✉ uapress@uapress.arizona.edu
www.uapress.arizona.edu

Director *Christine Szuter*

Founded 1959. Publishes academic non-fiction, particularly with a regional/cultural link, plus Native-American and Hispanic literature. About 55 titles a year.

University of Arkansas Press
McIlroy House, 201 Ozark Avenue, Fayetteville AR 72701
☎001 479 575 3246 Fax 001 479 575 6044

www.uapress.com

Director *Lawrence J. Malley*

Founded 1980. Publishes scholarly monographs, poetry and general trade books. Particularly interested in scholarly works in history, politics and literary criticism. About 20 titles a year.

Atheneum Books for Young Readers
See **Simon & Schuster Children's Publishing**

Atlantic Monthly Press
See **Grove/Atlantic Inc.**

Atria Books
See **Simon & Schuster Adult Publishing Group**

Avalon Publishing Group
1400 65th Street, Suite 250, Emeryville CA 94608
☎001 510 595 3664
www.avalonpub.com

Also at: 245 West 17th Street, 11th floor, New York, NY 10011 ☎ 001 212 981 9919

Chairman *Charlie Winton*

Founded 1994. Leading independent publisher of fiction and non-fiction; current affairs, history, politics, psychology, self-help, health, science, women's studies, gay and lesbian, travel, music, mystery and popular culture.

DIVISION **Avalon Publishing Group California**: IMPRINTS **Avalon Travel Publishing** (guide books); **Seal Press** (books by and for women); **Shoemaker & Hoard Publishers** (literature, fiction, history, biography). **Avalon Publishing Group New York**: IMPRINTS **Carroll & Graf Publishers** (history, current affairs, literature, fiction, mystery); **Thunder's Mouth Press** (current affairs, popular culture, film, music, fiction, science); **Nation Books** (current world affairs, politics, science, cultural studies); **Marlowe & Company** (psychology, self-help, health). 581 titles in 2005. No unsolicited material.

Avery
375 Hudson Street, New York NY 10014
☎001 212 366 2000 Fax 001 212 366 2643
us.penguingroup.com

Publisher *Megan Newman*

Founded 1976. Imprint of **Penguin Group (USA) Inc.** Publishes alternative and complementary health care, nutrition, disease preven-

tion, diet, supplements, functional foods, mind/body therapies, holistic healing, narrative medical and science non-fiction. About 30 titles a year. No unsolicited mss; synopses and ideas welcome if accompanied by s.a.e./IRCs.
ROYALTIES twice-yearly.

Avon
See **HarperCollins Publishers, Inc.**

Back Bay Books
See **Hachette Book Group USA**

Ballantine Books
See **Random House Publishing Group**

Bantam Dell Publishing Group
1745 Broadway, New York NY 10019
☎001 212 782 9000
www.randomhouse.com/bantamdell
President & Publisher *Irwyn Applebaum*
Founded 1945. The largest mass market paperback publisher in the USA. A division of the **Random House Publishing Group**. Publishes general commercial fiction and non-fiction, young readers and children's: mysteries, science fiction and fantasy, romance, health and nutrition, self-help. DIVISIONS/IMPRINTS **Bantam Classics; Delacorte Press; Dell; Delta Books; Dial Press**.

Barron's Educational Series, Inc.
250 Wireless Boulevard, Hauppauge
NY 11788-3917
☎001 631 434 3311 Fax 001 631 434 3723
www.barronseduc.com
Chairman/CEO *Manuel H. Barron*
President *Ellen Sibley*
Acquisitions Editor *Wayne Barr*
Founded 1942. *Publishes* adult non-fiction, children's fiction and non-fiction, test preparation materials and language materials, cookbooks, pets, hobbies, sport, photography, health, business, law, computers, art and painting. No adult fiction. 400 titles a year. Unsolicited mss, synopses and ideas for books welcome.
ROYALTIES twice-yearly.

Basic Books
See **Perseus Books Group**

Basic Civitas
See **Perseus Books Group**

Beacon Press
25 Beacon Street, Boston MA 02108
☎001 617 742 2110 Fax 001 617 723 3097

www.beacon.org
Director *Helene Atwan*
Founded 1854. Publishes general non-fiction. About 60 titles a year. Does not accept unsolicited mss. For further information, refer to the website.

Berkley
See **Penguin Group (USA) Inc.**

Bison Books
See **University of Nebraska Press**

Blackbirch Press
See **Thomson Gale**

Blackwell Publishing
2121 State Avenue, Ames IA 50014
☎001 515 292 0140 Fax 001 515 292 3348
✉ acquisitions@blackwellprofessional.com
www.blackwellprofessional.com
www.blackwellpublishing.com
Vice President, Professional Publishing *Antonia Seymour*
Formerly Iowa State Press. Founded 1934 as an offshoot of the Iowa State University's journalism department. Publishes reference books and textbooks on plant science, applied chemistry, food science, human dentistry, aquaculture, agriculture, animal science and veterinary medicine. No fiction, trade books or poetry. 60 titles a year. If within subject areas listed above, submit to acquisitions@blackwellprofessional.com
ROYALTIES annually

Boyds Mills Press
815 Church Street, Honesdale PA 18431
☎001 570 253 1164 Fax 001 570 253 0179
www.boydsmillspress.com
Publisher *Stephen Roxburgh*
A subsidiary of Highlights for Children, Inc. Founded 1990 as a publisher of children's picture and activity books. Publishes children's and young adult's fiction, non-fiction and poetry under five IMPRINTS: **Boyds Mills Press; Calkins Creek Books; Front Street; Lemniscaat; Wordsong**. About 65 titles a year.

Brassey's, Inc.
See **Potomac Books, Inc.**

Bulfinch Press
See **Hachette Book Group USA**

Business Plus
See **Hachette Book Group USA**

Caedmon
See **HarperCollins Publishers, Inc.**

University of California Press
2120 Berkeley Way, Berkeley CA 94704
☎001 510 642 4247 Fax 001 510 643 7127
✉ askucp@ucpress.edu
www.ucpress.edu
Director *Lynne Withey*
Founded 1893. Publishes scholarly and scientific non-fiction; some fiction in translation. About 200 books and 50 journals annually. Preliminary letter with outline preferred.

Calkins Creek Books
See **Boyds Mills Press**

Canongate US
See **Grove/Atlantic Inc.**

Carolrhoda Books, Inc.
241 First Avenue N, Minneapolis MN 55401
☎001 612 332 3344 Fax 001 612 332 7615
www.lernerbooks.com
VP & Editor-in-Chief *Mary M. Rodgers*
Founded 1969. A division of the **Lerner Publishing Group**. Publishes: animals, biography, earth sciences, ethnology, history, geography, geology, general science, historical fiction and picture books. No longer accepting unsolicited submissions.

Carroll & Graf Publishers
See **Avalon Publishing Group**

Center Street
See **Hachette Book Group USA**

Charlesbridge Publishing
85 Main Street, Watertown MA 02472
☎001 617 926 0329 Fax 001 617 926 5775
✉ books@charlesbridge.com
www.charlesbridge.com
President/Publisher *Brent Farmer*
Vice President, School Division *Elena Dworkin Wright*
Founded 1980 as an educational publisher focused on a strategic approach to reading, writing, maths and science. Publishes children's educational programmes, non-fiction picture books and fiction for 3 to 12-year-olds. School division publishes mathematical fiction, *Maths Adventures*, in picture-book format and astronomy-related picture books.

University of Chicago Press
1427 East 60th Street, Chicago IL 60637
☎001 773 702 7700 Fax 001 773 702 9756
www.press.uchicago.edu
Founded 1891. Publishes academic non-fiction only.

Children's Press
See **Scholastic Library Publishing**

Chronicle Books LLC
680 Second Street, San Francisco CA 94107
☎001 415 537 4200 Fax 001 415 437 4460
www.chroniclebooks.com
President/Publisher *Jack Jensen*
Founded 1967. Publishes illustrated and non-illustrated adult trade and children's books as well as stationery and gift items. About 200 titles a year. Query or submit outline/synopsis and sample chapters and artwork.

Arthur H. Clarke Company
See **University of Oklahoma Press**

Clarkson Potter
See **Crown Publishing Group**

Collins
See **HarperCollins Publishers, Inc.**

Columbia University Press
61 West 62nd Street, New York NY 10023
☎001 212 459 0600 Fax 001 212 459 3678
www.columbia.edu/cu/cup
President & Director *James D. Jordan*
Associate Director *Jennifer Crewe*
Founded 1893. Publishes scholarly and general interest non-fiction, reference, translations of Asian literature. No fiction or poetry. Welcomes unsolicited material if the subject fits their programme (see website). Approach by regular mail only.

Joanna Cotler Books
See **HarperCollins Publishers, Inc.**

Counterpoint
See **Perseus Books Group**

Crocodile Books, USA
See **Interlink Publishing Group, Inc.**

Crown Publishing Group
1745 Broadway, New York NY 10019
☎001 212 782 9000
www.randomhouse.com/crown

Founded 1933. Division of the **Random House Publishing Group**. Publishes popular trade fiction and non-fiction.

IMPRINTS **Clarkson Potter** *Lauren Shakely* Illustrated books: cookery, gardening, style, decorating and design; **Crown Business** *Steve Ross* Business books; **Crown** *Steve Ross* General fiction and non-fiction; **Harmony Books** *Shaye Areheart* New Age, spirituality, religion, some fiction; **Shaye Areheart Books** *Shaye Areheart* Fiction; **Three Rivers Press** *Steve Ross* Non-fiction paperbacks. Mss submissions by agents only.

Currency
See **Doubleday Broadway Publishing Group**

Da Capo Press
See **Perseus Books Group**

DAW Books, Inc.
375 Hudson Street, 3rd Floor, New York NY 10014–3658
☎001 212 366 2096 Fax 001 212 366 2090
✉ daw@penguingroup.com
www.dawbooks.com

Publishers *Elizabeth R. Wollheim, Sheila E. Gilbert*
Associate Editor *Peter Stampfel*

Founded 1971 by Donald and Elsie Wollheim as the first mass-market publisher devoted to science fiction and fantasy. An imprint of **Penguin Group (USA) Inc.** Publishes science fiction/fantasy, and some horror. No short stories, anthology ideas or non-fiction. About 42 titles a year. Unsolicited mss, synopses and ideas for books welcome.

ROYALTIES twice-yearly.

Del Rey
See **Random House Publishing Group**

Delacorte Press
See **Bantam Dell Publishing Group**

Dell
See **Bantam Dell Publishing Group**

Delta Books
See **Bantam Dell Publishing Group**

Dial Books for Young Readers
345 Hudson Street, New York NY 10014–3657
☎001 212 366 2000
Queries *Submissions Coordinator*

Founded 1961. A division of Penguin Books for Young Readers. Publishes children's books, including picture books, beginning readers, fiction and non-fiction for middle grade and young adults. IMPRINTS Hardcover only: **Dial Books for Young Readers**; **Dial Easy-to-Read**. 50 titles a year. Accepts unsolicited picture book mss and up to ten pages for longer works with query letter. 'Do not send self-addressed envelope with submissions. Dial will respond within four months if interested in a manuscript.'

ROYALTIES twice-yearly.

Dial Press
See **Bantam Dell Publishing Group**

Doubleday Broadway Publishing Group
1745 Broadway, New York NY 10019
☎001 212 782 9000
www.randomhouse.com

President & Publisher *Stephen Rubin*

The Doubleday Broadway Publishing Group, a division of the **Random House Publishing Group**, was formed by a merger of Doubleday and Broadway Books in 1998. Publishes fiction and non-fiction. DIVISION/IMPRINTS **Currency**; **Made Simple Books**; **Nan A. Talese Books**. No unsolicited material.

Downtown Press
See **Simon & Schuster Adult Publishing Group**

Thomas Dunne Books
See **St Martin's Press LLC**

Dutton/Dutton's Children's Books
See **Penguin Group (USA) Inc.**

East Gate Books
See **M.E. Sharpe, Inc.**

Ecco
See **HarperCollins Publishers, Inc.**

Eerdmans Publishing Company
2140 Oak Industrial Drive, NE, Grand Rapids MI 49505
☎001 616 459 4591 Fax 001 616 459 6540
✉ info@eerdmans.com
www.eerdmans.com

President *William B. Eerdmans Jr*

Founded in 1911 as a theological and reference publisher. Gradually began publishing in other genres with authors like C.S. Lewis, Dorothy Sayers and Malcolm Muggeridge on its lists. Publishes religious: theology, biblical studies, ethical and social concern, social criticism and children's, religious history, religion and literature. DIVISIONS **Children's** *Judy Zylstra* Picture books, novels and biographies for the general trade market; **Other** *Jon Pott*. About 120 titles a year. Unsolicited mss, synopses and ideas welcome.

ROYALTIES twice-yearly.

Eos
See **HarperCollins Publishers, Inc.**

Faber & Faber, Inc.
19 Union Square West, New York NY 10003
☎001 212 741 6900 Fax 001 212 633 9385
www.fsgbooks.com/faberandfaber.htm
Senior Editor *Denise Oswald*
Founded 1976. An affiliate of **Farrar, Straus & Giroux, Inc.** Publishes primarily non-fiction books for adults with a focus on film, theatre, music, popular culture and literary and cultural criticism. Unsolicited mss accepted; please query first and include IRCs with letter.

Faith Words
See **Hachette Book Group USA**

Farrar, Straus & Giroux, Inc.
19 Union Square West, New York NY 10003
☎001 212 741 6900
www.fsgbooks.com
Founded 1946. Publishes general and literary fiction, non-fiction, poetry and children's books. No unsolicited material.

Firebird
See **Penguin Group (USA) Inc.**

Fireside
See **Simon & Schuster Adult Publishing Group**

First Avenue Editions
See **Lerner Publishing Group**

Five Star
See **Thomson Gale**

5–Spot
See **Hachette Book Group USA**

Forever
See **Hachette Book Group USA**

Free Press
See **Simon & Schuster Adult Publishing Group**

Samuel French, Inc.
45 West 25th Street, New York
NY 10010–2751
☎001 212 206 8990 Fax 001 212 206 1429
✉ info@samuelfrench.com
www.samuelfrench.com
Editor *Roxanne Heinz-Bradshaw*
Founded 1830. Publishes plays in paperback: London, Broadway and off-Broadway hits, light comedies, mysteries, one-act plays and plays for young audiences. Unsolicited mss welcome. No synopses. OVERSEAS ASSOCIATES in London, Toronto, Sydney and Johannesburg.

ROYALTIES annually (books); twice-yearly (amateur productions); monthly (professional productions).

Front Street
See **Boyds Mills Press**

Gale
See **Thomson Gale**

Laura Geringer Books
See **HarperCollins Publishers, Inc.**

The Globe Pequot Press
PO Box 480, Guilford CT 06437
☎001 203 458 4500 Fax 001 203 458 4601
✉ info@gobepequot.com
www.globepequot.com
Founded 1947. Publishes regional and international travel, how-to, regional and outdoor recreation. Also publishes the *Insiders'* guides. About 500 titles a year. Unsolicited mss, synopses and ideas welcome, particularly for travel and outdoor recreation books. See website for submission guidelines.

Gotham
See **Penguin Group (USA) Inc.**

Graham & Whiteside
See **Thomson Gale**

Grand Central Publishing
See **Hachette Book Group USA**

Graphic Universe
See **Lerner Publishing Group**

Great Source Education Group
See **Houghton Mifflin Co.**

Green Light Readers
See **Harcourt Trade Publishers**

Green Willow Books
See **HarperCollins Publishers, Inc.**

Greenhaven Press
See **Thomson Gale**

Griffin
See **St Martin's Press LLC**

Grolier Educational
See **Scholastic Library Publishing**

Grosset & Dunlap
See **Penguin Group (USA) Inc.**

Grove/Atlantic Inc.
841 Broadway, 4th Floor, New York NY 10003
☎001 212 614 7850 Fax 001 212 614 7886
www.groveatlantic.com
President/Publisher *Morgan Entrekin*
Managing Editor *Michael Hornburg*
Founded 1952. Publishes general fiction and non-fiction. IMPRINTS **Atlantic Monthly Press; Canongate US; Grove Press**. Mss submissions by agents only.

Gulliver Books
See **Harcourt Trade Publishers**

Hachette Book Group USA
1271 Avenue of the Americas, New York NY 10020
☎001 212 522 7200 Fax 001 212 522 7991
www.hachettebookgroupusa.com
CEO & Chairman *David Young*
Deputy Chairman & Publisher *Maureen Mahon Egen*
Founded in 2006 following the acquisition of the Time Warner Book Group by Hachette Livre. Publishes fiction and non-fiction, children's and young adult, audio books.
DIVISIONS **Grand Central Publishing; FaithWords; Center Street; Little, Brown and Company; Little, Brown Books for Young Readers; Hachette Book Group Digital Media**. IMPRINTS **Back Bay Books; Bulfinch Press; Business Plus; 5-Spot; Forever; Hachette Audio; LB Kids; Solana; Megan Tingley Books; Twelve; Vision; Wellness Central**. About 730 titles a year. No unsolicited mss.

G.K. Hall
See **Thomson Gale**

Harcourt School Publishers
6277 Sea Harbor Drive, Orlando FL 32887
☎001 407 345 2000
www.harcourtschool.com
President/CEO *Jan Spalding*
A division of Harcourt Inc., founded 1919. Publishes education materials – books, CD-ROMs, Internet and audio.

Harcourt Trade Publishers
525 B Street, Suite 1900, San Diego CA 92101
☎001 619 231 6616
www.harcourtbooks.com

Also at: 15 East 26th Street, 15th Floor, New York, NY 10010 ☎ 001 212 592 1000
President/CEO *Dan Farley*
A division of Harcourt Inc. Publishes fiction, poetry and non-fiction covering a wide range of subjects: biography, history, humour, music, dance, philosophy, psychology, religion, science, social sciences and sociology, sport, wine and spirits, women's studies.
IMPRINTS **Green Light Readers; Gulliver Books; Harcourt; Harcourt Children's Books; Harvest Books; Libros Viajeros; Magic Carpet Books; Odyssey Classics; Red Wagon Books; Silver Whistle; Voyager Books**. About 300 titles a year. No unsolicited mss.

Harmony Books
See **Crown Publishing Group**

HarperCollins Publishers, Inc.
10 East 53rd Street, New York NY 10022
☎001 212 207 7000
www.harpercollins.com
President/Chief Executive Officer *Jane Friedman*
Founded 1817. Subsidiary of News Corporation. Publishes general and literary fiction, general non-fiction, business, children's, reference and religious books.
GENERAL BOOKS GROUP IMPRINTS
Amistad; Avon; Caedmon; Collins; Collins Design; Ecco; Eos; Harper; Harper Paperbacks; Harper Perennial; Harper Perennial Modern Classics; HarperAudio; HarperEntertainment; HarperSanFrancisco; Rayo; William Morrow; William Morrow Cookbooks.
CHILDREN'S IMPRINTS
Amistad; Eos; Greenwillow Books; HarperCollins Children's Audio;

HarperCollins Children's Books; HarperFestival; HarperEntertainment; HarperTeen; HarperTrophy; Joanna Cotler Books; Julie Andrews Collection; Katherine Tegen Books; Laura Geringer Books; Rayo. About 1700 titles a year. No unsolicited material.

Harvard University Press
79 Garden Street, Cambridge MA 02138–1499
☎001 401 531 2800 Fax 001 401 531 2001
www.hup.harvard.edu

Director *William P. Sisler*

Founded 1913. Publishes scholarly non-fiction only; humanities, social sciences, sciences.

Harvest Books
See **Harcourt Trade Publishers**

University of Hawai'i Press
2840 Kolowalu Street, Honolulu
HI 96822–1888
☎001 808 956 8255 Fax 001 808 988 6052
✉ uhpbooks@hawaii.edu
www.uhpress.hawaii.edu

Director *William H. Hamilton*
Executive Editor *Patricia Crosby*

Founded 1947. Publishes scholarly books pertaining to East Asia, Southeast Asia, Hawaii and the Pacific. Unsolicited synopses and ideas welcome; approach by mail. No poetry, children's books or any topics other than Asia and the Pacific.
ROYALTIES twice-yearly.

Hill Street Press LLC
191 E. Broad Street, Suite 216, Athens
GA 30601–2848
☎001 706 613 7200 Fax 001 706 613 7204
hillstreetpress.com

VP/Editor-in-Chief *Patrick Allen*

Founded 1998. Publishes books on the American South – fiction and non-fiction. No poetry, erotica, romance, children's or young adults. About 20 titles a year. Unsolicited material welcome; approach in writing in the first instance.

Hippocrene Books, Inc.
171 Madison Avenue, New York NY 10016
☎001 212 685 4371
✉ info@hippocrenebooks.com
www.hippocrenebooks.com

President/Editorial Director *George Blagowidow*

Founded 1970. Publishes general non-fiction and reference books. Particularly strong on foreign language dictionaries, language studies and international cookbooks. No fiction. Send brief summary, table of contents and one chapter for appraisal. S.a.e. essential for response. For manuscript return include sufficient postage cover (IRCs).

Holiday House, Inc.
425 Madison Avenue, New York NY 10017
☎001 212 688 0085 Fax 001 212 421 6134
www.holidayhouse.com

Vice President/Editor-in-Chief *Regina Griffin*

Publishes children's general fiction and non-fiction (pre-school to secondary). About 50 titles a year. Send query letters only. IRCs for reply must be included. Submission guidelines available on the website.

Henry Holt & Company, Inc.
175 Fifth Avenue, New York NY 10010
☎001 646 307 5095 Fax 001 212 633 0748
www.henryholt.com

President/Publisher *John Sterling*
Editor-in-Chief, Adult Trade *Jennifer Barth*

Founded in 1866, Henry Holt is one of the oldest publishers in the United States. Part of Holtzbrinck Publishing Holdings. Publishes fiction, by both American and international authors, biographies, children's, health, science, history, politics, ecology and psychology.
DIVISIONS/IMPRINTS **Adult Trade; Books for Young Readers; Jack Macrae Books; Metropolitan Books; Owl Books; Times Books.** About 250 titles a year. No unsolicited mss.

Houghton Mifflin Co.
222 Berkeley Street, Boston MA 02116–3764
☎001 617 351 5000 Fax 001 617 351 1125
www.hmco.com

Contact *Submissions Editor*

Founded 1832. Publishes literary fiction and general non-fiction, including autobiography, biography and history. Also school and college textbooks; children's fiction and non-fiction.
DIVISIONS/SUBSIDIARY COMPANIES **Houghton Mifflin College Division; Houghton Mifflin School Division; Houghton Mifflin Trade & Reference Division; Great Source Education Group; McDougal Littell Inc.; The Riverside Publishing Co.; Promissor Inc.** About 100 titles a year. Unsolicited adult mss no longer accepted. Send synopses, outline and sample

chapters for children's non-fiction; complete mss for children's fiction. Do not include s.a.e. 'You will not hear from us regarding the status of your submission unless we are interested, in which case you can expect to hear back from us within 16 weeks. We cannot track your manuscript and regret that we cannot respond personally to each submission, but we do consider each and every submission we receive. Mss we are not interested in will be recycled.'

Howard Books
See **Simon & Schuster Adult Publishing Group**

HPBooks
See **Penguin Group (USA) Inc.**

Hudson Street Press
See **Penguin Group (USA) Inc.**

Humanity Books
See **Prometheus Books**

University of Illinois Press
1325 South Oak Street, Champaign
IL 61820–6903
☎001 217 333 0950 Fax 001 217 244 8082
✉ uipress@uillinois.edu
www.press.uillinois.edu
Director *Willis Regier*
Publishes non-fiction, scholarly and general, with special interest in Americana, women's studies, African–American studies, film, religion, American music and regional books. About 140–150 titles a year.

Indiana University Press
601 North Morton Street, Bloomington
IN 47404–3797
☎001 812 855 8817 Fax 001 812 855 8507
✉ iupress@indiana.edu
www.indiana.edu/~iupress
Director *Janet Rabinowitch*
Publishes scholarly non-fiction in the following subject areas: African studies, anthropology, Asian studies, African-American studies, bioethics, environment and ecology, film, folklore, history, Jewish studies, Middle East studies, military history, music, paleontology, philanthropy, philosophy, politics, religion, Russian and East European studies, women's studies. Query in writing in first instance.

Interlink Publishing Group, Inc.
46 Crosby Street, Northampton MA 01060
☎001 413 582 7054 Fax 001 413 582 7057
✉ info@interlinkbooks.com
www.interlinkbooks.com
Publisher *Michel Moushabeck*
Editor *Pam Thompson*
Founded 1987. Publishes international fiction, travel, politics, cookbooks. Specialises in Middle East titles and ethnicity. IMPRINTS **Crocodile Books, USA** Editorial Head *Ruth Lane Moushabeck* Children's books; **Olive Branch Press** Editorial Head *Phyllis Bennis* Political books. About 50-60 titles a year. See submission guidelines on the website before making an approach.
ROYALTIES annually.

University of Iowa Press
100 Kuhl House, 119 West Park Road, Iowa City IA 52242–1000
☎001 319 335 2000 Fax 001 319 335 2055
✉ uipress@uiowa.edu
www.uiowapress.org
Director *Holly Carver*
Founded 1969 as a small scholarly press publishing about five books a year. Now publishing about 35 annually in a variety of scholarly fields, plus local interest, short stories, creative non-fiction and poetry anthologies. No unsolicited mss; query first. Unsolicited ideas and synopses welcome.
ROYALTIES annually.

Jove
See **Penguin Group (USA) Inc.**

University Press of Kansas
2502 Westbrooke Circle, Lawrence
KS 66045-4444
☎001 785 864 4154 Fax 001 785 864 4586
✉ upress@ku.edu
www.kansaspress.ku.edu
Director *Fred M. Woodward*
Founded 1946. Became the publishing arm for all six state universities in Kansas in 1976. Publishes scholarly books in American history, legal studies, presidential studies, American studies, political philosophy, political science, military history and environmental history. About 55 titles a year. Proposals welcome.
ROYALTIES annually.

Kar-Ben Publishing
See **Lerner Publishing Group**

Kent State University Press
307 Lowry Hall, PO Box 5190, Kent
OH 44242
☎001 330 672 7913 Fax 001 330 672 3104
www.kentstateuniversitypress.com

Director *Will Underwood*
Assistant Director/Editor-in-Chief *Joanna Hildebrand Craig*

Founded 1965. Publishes scholarly works in history, literary studies and general non-fiction with an emphasis on American history and literature. 30–40 titles a year. Queries welcome; no mss.

The University Press of Kentucky
663 South Limestone Street, Lexington
KY 40508
☎001 859 257 8434 Fax 001 859 323 1873
✉ joyce.harrison@uky.edu
www.kentuckypress.com

Director *Stephen M. Wrinn*
Editor-in-Chief *Joyce Harrison*
Approx. Annual Turnover $2 million

Founded 1943. Publishes scholarly and general interest books in the humanities and social sciences. 58 titles in 2006. No unsolicited mss; send synopses and ideas for books by post or e-mail. No fiction, drama, poetry, translations, memoirs or children's books.
ROYALTIES annually.

KidHaven Press
See **Thomson Gale**

Krieger Publishing Co.
PO Box 9542, Melbourne FL 32902–9542
☎001 321 724 9542 Fax 001 321 951 3671
✉ info@krieger-publishing.com
www.krieger-publishing.com

VEO *Robert E. Krieger*
President *Donald E. Krieger*
Vice-President *Maxine D. Krieger*

Founded 1970. Publishes science, education, ecology, humanities, history, mathematics, chemistry, space science, technology and engineering.
IMPRINTS/SERIES **Anvil**; **Exploring Community History**; **Open Forum**; **Orbit**; **Professional Practices**; **Public History**. Unsolicited mss welcome. Not interested in synopses/ideas or trade type titles.

Large Print Press
See **Thomson Gale**

Lark
See **Sterling Publishing Co. Inc.**

Latino Voices
See **Northwestern University Press**

LB Kids
See **Hachette Book Group USA**

Lemniscaat
See **Boyds Mills Press**

Lerner Publishing Group
241 First Avenue N., Minneapolis MN 55401
☎001 612 332 3344 Fax 001 612 332 7615
✉ info@lernerbooks.com
www.lernerbooks.com

Chairman *Harry J. Lerner*
President & Publisher *Adam M. Lerner*

Founded 1959. Publishes children's non-fiction, fiction and curriculum material for all grade levels.
DIVISIONS/IMPRINTS **Lerner Publications**; **Carolrhoda Books** (see entry); **LernerClassroom**; **First Avenue Editions**; **Millbrook Press**; **Twenty-First Century Books**; **Kar-Ben Publishing**; **Graphic Universe**. No puzzle, song or alphabet books, text books, workbooks, or plays. No longer accepting unsolicited submissions.

Libros Viajeros
See **Harcourt Trade Publishers**

Little Simon
See **Simon & Schuster Children's Publishing**

Little, Brown and Company/Little, Brown Books for Young Readers
See **Hachette Book Group USA**

Llewellyn Publications
2143 Wooddale Drive, Woodbury MN 55125
☎001 651 291 1970 Fax 001 612 291 1908
www.llewellyn.com

President *Carl L. Weschcke*

Division of Llewellyn Worldwide Ltd. Founded 1901. Publishes self-help and how-to: astrology, alternative health, tantra, Fortean studies, tarot, yoga, Santeria, dream studies, metaphysics, magic, witchcraft, herbalism, shamanism, organic gardening, women's spirituality, graphology, palmistry, parapsychology. Also fiction with an authentic magical or metaphysical theme. About 100 titles a year. Unsolicited mss welcome;

proposals preferred. IRCs essential in all cases. Submission guidelines available on the website.

Louisiana State University Press

PO Box 25053, Baton Rouge LA 70894–5053
☎001 225 578 6295 Fax 001 225 578 6461
✉ lsupress@lsu.edu
www.lsu.edu/lsupress

Director *MaryKatherine Callaway*

Publishes fiction and non-fiction: Southern history, American history, Southern literary criticism, American literary criticism, biography, poetry, Atlantic World studies, environmental studies, political science and music (jazz). About 85 titles a year. See website for submission guidelines.

Lucent Books

See **Thomson Gale**

The Lyons Press Inc.

246 Goose Lane, Guilford CT 06347
☎001 203 458 4500
www.lyonspress.com

Associate Publisher *Gene Brissie*
Managing Editor *Alicia Solis*
Editor-in-Chief *Maureen Graney*
Executive Editor *Tom McCarthy*

Founded 1978. Imprint of The Globe Pequot Press. Publishes non-fiction; outdoor skills, hunting, fishing, sports, animals/pets, equestrian, history/current affairs, military history, nature, games, reference, health and fitness and self-reliant living. About 200 titles a year. Unsolicited mss, synopses and book proposals welcome.

ROYALTIES twice-yearly.

McDougal Littell Inc.

See **Houghton Mifflin Co.**

Margaret K. McElderry Books

See **Simon & Schuster Children's Publishing**

McFarland & Company, Inc., Publishers

PO Box 611, Jefferson NC 28640
☎001 336 246 4460 Fax 001 336 246 5018
✉ info@mcfarlandpub.com
www.mcfarlandpub.com

Executive Vice President *Rhonda Herman*
Executive Editor *Steve Wilson*
Editorial Development Chief *Virginia Tobiassen*
Acquisitions Editor *Gary Mitchem*

Founded 1979. A library reference and upper-end speciality market press publishing schol-

arly books in many fields: international studies, performing arts, popular culture, sports, automotive history, women's studies, music and fine arts, chess, history and librarianship. Specialises in general reference. Especially strong in cinema studies. No fiction, poetry, children's, New Age or inspirational/devotional works. About 300 titles a year. No unsolicited mss; send query letter first. Synopses and ideas welcome; submissions by mail preferred.

ROYALTIES annually.

The McGraw-Hill Companies, Inc.

1221 Avenue of the Americas, New York NY 10020–1095
☎001 212 512 2000
www.mcgraw-hill.com

Chairman/President/CEO *Harold W. McGraw*

Founded 1888. Parent of **McGraw-Hill Education** which has offices in the UK (see entry under *UK Publishers*). Publishes a wide range of educational, professional, business, science, engineering and computing books.

Macmillan Reference USA

See **Thomson Gale**

Jack Macrae Books

See **Henry Holt & Company, Inc.**

Made Simple Books

See **Doubleday Broadway Publishing Group**

Magic Carpet Books

See **Harcourt Trade Publishers**

Marlowe & Company

See **Avalon Publishing Group**

University of Massachusetts Press

PO Box 429, Amherst MA 01004–0429
☎001 413 545 2217 Fax 001 413 545 1226
✉ info@umpress.umass.edu
www.umass.edu/umpress

Director *Bruce Wilcox*
Senior Editor *Clark Dougan*

Founded 1964. Publishes scholarly, general interest, African-American, ethnic, women's and gender studies, cultural criticism, economics, fiction, literary criticism, poetry, philosophy, biography, history. About 40 titles a year. Unsolicited mss considered but query letter preferred in the first instance. Synopses and ideas welcome.

Metropolitan Books
See **Henry Holt & Company, Inc.**

The University of Michigan Press
839 Greene Street, Ann Arbor MI 48104–3209
☎001 734 764 4388 Fax 001 734 615 1540
www.press.umich.edu
Founded 1930. Publishes scholarly non-fiction, fiction, textbooks, translation, literary criticism, theatre, music, economics, political science, history, classics, anthropology, law studies, gender studies, English as a second language.

Milet Publishing LLC
333 North Michigan Avenue, Suite 530,
Chicago IL 60601
✉ info@milet.com
www.milet.com
Managing Directors *Sedat Turhan, Patricia Billings*
Founded 1995. Publishes children's picture books in English and dual language, and language learning books. Welcomes synopses and ideas for books. Queries may be made by e-mail but all submissions – proposal, outline or synopsis with sample text and/or artwork – by post only. 'Please review submission guidelines and existing titles on our website before submitting. We like bold, original stories and artwork, universal and/or multicultural.'

Millbrook Press
See **Lerner Publishing Group**

University of Minnesota Press
111 Third Avenue South, Suite 290,
Minneapolis MN 55401
☎001 612 627 1970 Fax 001 612 627 1980
www.upress.umn.edu
Executive Editor *Richard Morrison*
Founded 1927. Publishes academic books for scholars and selected general interest titles: American studies, anthropology, art and aesthetics, cultural theory, film and media studies, gay and lesbian studies, geography, literary theory, political and social theory, race and ethnic studies, sociology and urban studies. No original fiction or poetry. About 110 titles a year. No unsolicited mss. Welcomes synopses and proposals sent by mail (*no e-mails*). See website for submission details.

Minotaur
See **St Martin's Press LLC**

University Press of Mississippi
3825 Ridgewood Road, Jackson
MS 39211–6492
☎001 601 432 6205 Fax 001 601 432 6217
✉ press@ihl.state.ms.us
www.upress.state.ms.us
Director *Seetha Srinivasan*
Assistant Director/Editor-in-Chief *Craig Gill*
Founded 1970. Non-profit book publisher partially supported by the eight state universities. Publishes scholarly and trade titles in literature, history, American culture, Southern culture, African-American studies, women's studies, popular culture, folklife, ethnic, performance, art, architecture, photography and other liberal arts.
    REPRESENTED worldwide. UK representative: **Roundhouse Group**. About 60 titles a year. Send letter of enquiry, prospectus, table of contents and sample chapter prior to submission of full mss.
    ROYALTIES annually.

University of Missouri Press
2910 LeMone Boulevard, Columbia
MO 65201
☎001 573 882 7641 Fax 001 573 884 4498
✉ upress@umsystem.edu
www.system.missouri.edu/upress
Director *Beverly Jarrett*
Founded 1958. Publishes academic: history, intellectual history, journalism, literary criticism and related humanities disciplines, and occasional volumes of short stories. About 70 titles a year. Best approach is by letter. Send synopses for academic work together with author c.v.

Modern Library
See **Random House Publishing Group**

William Morrow
See **HarperCollins Publishers, Inc.**

NAL
See **Penguin Group (USA) Inc.**

Nation Books
See **Avalon Publishing Group**

University of Nebraska Press
1111 Lincoln Mall, Lincoln NE 68588–0630
☎001 402 472 3581 Fax 001 402 472 0308
www.nebraskapress.unl.edu
Director *Paul Royster*
Founded 1941. Publishes scholarly, Native American studies, history of the American

West, literary and cultural studies, music, Jewish studies, military history, sports history, environmental history. IMPRINT **Bison Books**. No unsolicited mss; welcomes synopses and ideas for books. Send enquiry letter in the first instance with description of project and sample material. No original fiction, children's books or poetry.

ROYALTIES annually.

University of Nevada Press
Morrill Hall Mail Stop 0166, Reno
NV 89557–0076–0166
☎001 775 784 6573
www.nvbooks.nevada.edu

Director *Joanne O'Hare*

Founded 1961. Publishes scholarly and popular books; serious fiction, Native American studies, natural history, Western Americana, Basque studies and regional studies. Unsolicited material welcome if it fits in with areas published, or offers a 'new and exciting' direction.

University Press of New England
One Court Street, Suite 250, Lebanon
NH 03766
☎001 603 448 1533 Fax 001 603 448 7006
www.upne.com

Acting Director *Michael Burton*
Editor-in-Chief *Phyllis Deutsch*

Founded 1970. A scholarly books publisher sponsored by six institutions of higher education in the region: Brandeis, Dartmouth, University of Vermont, Tufts, the University of New Hampshire and Northeastern. Publishes general and scholarly non-fiction and Hardscrabble Books fiction of New England. OVERSEAS ASSOCIATES Canada: University of British Columbia; UK, Europe, Middle East: Eurospan University Press Group; Australia, New Zealand, Asia & the Pacific: East-West Export Books. About 80 titles a year. Unsolicited material welcome.

ROYALTIES annually.

University of New Mexico Press
1312 Basehart Road SE, Albuquerque
NM 87106–4363
☎001 505 277 2346 Fax 001 505 272 7141
www.unmpress.com

Director *Luther Wilson*
Editor-in-Chief *William 'Clark' Whitehorn*

Founded 1929. Publishes scholarly, regional books and fiction. No how-to, humour, self-help or technical.

University of North Texas Press
PO Box 311336, Denton TX 76203–1336
☎001 940 565 2142 Fax 001 940 565 4590
✉ rchrisman@unt.edu
www.unt.edu/untpress

Director *Ronald Chrisman*
Managing Editor *Karen De Vinney*

Founded 1987. Publishes regional interest, contemporary, social issues, Texas history, military history, music, women's issues, multicultural. Publishes annually the winners of the Vassar Miller Poetry Prize and the Katherine Anne Porter Prize in Short Fiction. About 15 titles a year. No unsolicited mss; synopses and ideas welcome.

ROYALTIES annually.

Northwestern University Press
629 Noyes Street, Evanston IL 60208
☎001 847 491 2046 Fax 001 847 491 8150
✉ nupress@northwestern.edu
www.nupress.northwestern.edu

Chairman *Peter Hayes*
Managing Director *Donna Shear*

Publishes general and academic books: philosophy, theatre and performance studies, Slavic studies, Latino fiction and biography, contemporary fiction, poetry. No children's, art books. IMPRINTS **Latino Voices** Editorial Head *Henry Carrigan*. 60 titles in 2006. Unsolicited mss, synopses and ideas welcome; approach by mail. No unsolicited mss in fiction or poetry, please.

ROYALTIES annually.

W.W. Norton & Company, Inc.
500 Fifth Avenue, New York NY 10110
☎001 212 354 5500 Fax 001 212 869 0856
www.wwnorton.com

VP/Editor-in-Chief *Starling R. Lawrence*

Founded 1923. Publishes fiction and non-fiction, college textbooks and professional books. About 400 titles a year. Submission guidelines available on the website.

Odyssey Classics
See **Harcourt Trade Division**

Ohio University Press
19 Circle Drive, The Ridges, Athens
OH 45701–2979
☎001 740 593 1155 Fax 001 740 593 4536
www.ohiou.edu/oupress

Director *David Sanders*

Founded 1964. Publishes academic, regional and general trade books. IMPRINT **Swallow Press**.

Synopsis and ideas for books welcome. Send detailed synopsis, sample chapters and c.v. with covering letter. See website for author guidelines. No children's, how-to or genre fiction. ROYALTIES twice-yearly.

University of Oklahoma Press
2800 Venture Drive, Norman OK 73069–8216
☎001 405 325 2000 Fax 001 405 325 4000
www.oupress.com
Director *John N. Drayton*
Founded 1928. Publishes general scholarly non-fiction only: American Indian studies, American West, classical studies, anthropology, natural history and political science. IMPRINT **Arthur H. Clarke Company** Publisher *Robert Clark* About 100 titles a year. See website for submissions policy.

Olive Branch Press
See **Interlink Publishing Group, Inc.**

One World
See **Random House Publishing Group**

Open Forum
See **Krieger Publishing Co.**

Orbit
See **Krieger Publishing Co.**

Owl Books
See **Henry Holt & Company, Inc.**

Palgrave
See **St Martin's Press LLC**

Paragon House
1925 Oakcrest Avenue, Suite 7, St Paul MN 55113–2619
☎001 651 644 3087 Fax 001 651 644 0997
✉ paragon@paragonhouse.com
www.paragonhouse.com
Executive Director *Dr Gordon L. Anderson*
Founded 1982. Publishes non-fiction: reference and academic. Subjects include history, religion, philosophy, spirituality, Jewish interest, political science, international relations, psychology. ROYALTIES twice-yearly.

Pearson Scott Foresman
1900 E Lake Avenue, Glenview IL 60025
☎001 847 729 3000
✉ firstname.lastname@scottforesman.com
www.scottforesman.com
President *Paul McFall*

Founded 1896. Part of Pearson Education. Publishes elementary education materials. No unsolicited material.

Pelican Publishing Company
1000 Burmaster Street, Gretna LA 70053
☎001 504 368 1175
www.pelicanpub.com
Editor-in-Chief *Nina Kooij*
Publishes general non-fiction: popular history, cookbooks, travel, art, business, biography, children's, architecture, collectibles guides and motivational. About 75 titles a year. Initial enquiries required for all submissions.

Penguin Group (USA) Inc.
375 Hudson Street, New York NY 10014
☎001 212 366 2000 Fax 001 212 366 2666
www.penguingroup.com
CEO *David Shanks*
President *Susan Petersen Kennedy*
The second-largest trade book publisher in the world. Publishes fiction and non-fiction in hardback and paperback; adult and children's.

ADULT DIVISION IMPRINTS Hardcover: **Avery** (see entry); **Dutton; G.P. Putnam's Sons; Gotham; Hudson Street Press; Jeremy P. Tarcher/Putnam; The Penguin Press; Portfolio; Riverhead Books; Sentinel; Viking;** Trade Paperback: **Ace Books; Alpha Books; Berkley; HPBooks; NAL; Perigee; Penguin Books; Plume; Riverhead; Roc.** Mass Market Paperback: **Ace; Berkley; DAW Books** (see entry); **Jove.**

YOUNG READERS DIVISION: Hardcover: **Dial Books for Young Readers** (see entry); **Dutton Children's Books; Frederick Warne; G.P. Putnam's Sons** (see entry); **Philomel Books; Viking Children's Books**. Paperback: **Firebird; Puffin Books; Razorbill; Speak.** Mass Merchandise: **Grosset & Dunlap; Price Stern Sloan.** No unsolicited mss. ROYALTIES twice-yearly.

University of Pennsylvania Press
3905 Spruce Street, Philadelphia PA 19104–4112
☎001 215 898 6261 Fax 001 215 898 0404
✉ custserv@pobox.upenn.edu
www.pennpress.org
Director *Eric Halpern*
Editor-in-Chief *Peter Agree*
Founded 1890. Publishes serious non-fiction: scholarly, reference, professional, textbooks and semi-popular trade. No original fiction or

poetry. Over 100 titles a year. No unsolicited mss but synopses and ideas for books welcome.

ROYALTIES vary according to sales prospects and other relevant factors.

Perennial
See **HarperCollins Publisers, Inc.**

Perigee
See **Penguin Group (USA) Inc.**

Perseus Books Group
387 Park Avenue S, 12th Floor, New York NY 10016
☎001 212 340 8100 Fax 001 212 340 8115
www.perseusbooksgroup.com
President/CEO *David Steinberger*
Founded 1997. Publishes general, academic and professional. IMPRINTS **Basic Books**; **Basic Civitas**; **Counterpoint**; **Da Capo Press**; **PublicAffairs** (see entry); **Running Press**; **Vanguard**; **Westview Press**. No unsolicited mss.

Philomel Books
See **Penguin Group (USA) Inc.**

Picador USA
See **St Martin's Press LLC**

Players Press
PO Box 1132, Studio City CA 91614–0132
☎001 818 789 4980
President/CEO *Robert Gordon*
Founded 1965 as a publisher of plays; now publishes across the entire range of performing arts: plays, musicals, theatre, film, cinema, television, costume, puppetry, plus technical theatre and cinema material. No unsolicited mss; synopses/ideas welcome. Send query letter s.a.e. for response.
ROYALTIES twice-yearly.

Plume
See **Penguin Group (USA) Inc.**

Pocket Books
See **Simon & Schuster Adult Publishing Group**

Portfolio
See **Penguin Group (USA) Inc.**

Potomac Books, Inc.
22841 Quicksilver Drive, Dulles VA 20166
☎001 703 661 1548 Fax 001 703 661 1547
www.potomacbooksinc.com

Publisher *Sam Dorrance*
Formerly Brassey's, Inc., founded 1984 (acquired in 1999 by Books International of Dulles, Virginia). Publishes non-fiction titles on topics of history (especially military and diplomatic history), world and US affairs, US foreign policy, defence, intelligence, biography and sports. About 80 titles a year. No unsolicited mss; query letters/synopses welcome.
ROYALTIES annually.

Presidio Press
See **Random House Publishing Group**

Price Stern Sloan
See **Penguin Group (USA) Inc.**

Primary Source Microfilm
See **Thomson Gale**

Princeton University Press
41 William Street, Princeton NJ 08540
☎001 609 258 4900
www.pup.princeton.edu
Editor-in-Chief *Sam Elworthy*
Founded 1905. Publishes academic and trade books. About 200 titles a year. No unsolicited mss. Synopses and ideas considered. Send letter to editor-in-chief in the first instance. No fiction.
OVERSEAS ASSOCIATE Princeton University Press, 3 Market Place, Woodstock OX20 1SY, UK.
ROYALTIES annually.

Professional Practices
See **Krieger Publishing Co.**

Prometheus Books
59 John Glenn Drive, Amherst NY 14228–2197
☎001 800 421 0351 Fax 001 716 691 0137
✉ marketing@prometheusbooks.com
www.prometheusbooks.com
www.pyrsf.com
Chairman *Paul Kurtz*
Editor-in-Chief *Steven L. Mitchell*
Founded 1969. Publishes books and journals: educational, scientific professional, library, popular science, science fiction and fantasy, philosophy and young readers. IMPRINTS **Humanity Books**; **Pyr™**. About 100 titles a year. Unsolicited mss, synopses and ideas for books welcome.
ROYALTIES twice-yearly.

Promissor Inc
See **Houghton Mifflin Co.**

Public History
See **Krieger Publishing Co.**

PublicAffairs
250 West 57th Street, Suite 1321, New York
NY 10107
☎001 212 397 6666 Fax 001 212 397 4277
✉ publicaffairs@perseusbooks.com
www.publicaffairsbooks.com
Publisher *Susan Weinberg*
Founded 1997. Part of the **Perseus Books Group**. Publishes current affairs, biography, history and journalism.

Puffin Books
See **Penguin Group (USA) Inc.**

G.P. Putnam's Sons (Children's)
345 Hudson Street, New York NY 10014
☎001 212 366 2000
www.penguingroup.com
President/Publisher *Nancy Paulsen*
Associate Editorial Director *Susan Kochan*

A children's book imprint of Penguin Young Readers Group, a member of **Penguin Group (USA) Inc.** Publishes picture books, middle-grade fiction and young adult fiction.

Pyr™
See **Prometheus Books**

Rand McNally
PO Box 7600, Chicago IL 60680–7600
☎001 847 329 8100
www.randmcnally.com
President/CEO *Rob Apatoff*
Founded 1856. Publishes world atlases and maps, road atlases of North America and Europe, city and state maps of the United States and Canada, educational wall maps, atlases and globes, plus children's products. Includes electronic multimedia products. IMPRINT **Rand McNally for Kids**.

Random House Publishing Group
1745 Broadway, New York NY 10019
☎001 212 782 9000
www.randomhouse.com
President/Publisher *Gina Centrello*
Publishes fiction, non-fiction, science fiction in hardcover, trade paperback and mass market.
IMPRINTS **Ballantine Books; Del Rey; Modern Library; OneWorld; Presidio Press; Random House; Random House Trade**

Paperbacks; **Villard**. 650 titles in 2006. No unsolicited mss.

Rayo
See **HarperCollins Publishers, Inc.**

Razorbill
See **Penguin Group (USA) Inc.**

Reader's Digest Association Inc
Reader's Digest Road, Pleasantville
NY 10570–7000
☎001 914 238 1000 Fax 001 914 238 4559
www.rd.com
President/CEO *Mary Berner*
Publishes home maintenance reference, cookery, DIY, health, gardening, children's books; videos and magazines.

Red Wagon Books
See **Harcourt Trade Division**

Riverhead Books
See **Penguin Group (USA) Inc.**

The Riverside Publishing Co.
See **Houghton Mifflin Co.**

Roc
See **Penguin Group (USA) Inc.**

The Rosen Publishing Group, Inc.
29 East 21st Street, New York NY 10010
☎001 212 777 3017 Fax 001 212 777 0277
www.rosenpublishing.com
President *Roger Rosen*
Founded 1950. Publishes non-fiction books (supplementary to the curriculum, reference and self-help) for a young adult audience. Reading levels are years 7–12, 4–6 (books for teens with literacy problems), and 5–9. Subjects include conflict resolution, character building, health, safety, drug abuse prevention, self-help and multicultural titles. For all imprints, write with outline and sample chapters.

Running Press
See **Perseus Books Group**

Rutgers University Press
100 Joyce Kilmer Avenue, Piscataway
NJ 08854–8099
☎001 732 445 7762 Fax 001 732 445 7039
rutgerspress.rutgers.edu
Director *Marlie Wasserman*
Associate Director/Editor-in-Chief *Leslie Mitchner*

Founded 1936. Publishes scholarly books, regional, social sciences and humanities. About 80 titles a year. Unsolicited mss, synopses and ideas for books welcome. No original fiction or poetry.

S&S Libros eñ Espanol
See **Simon & Schuster Adult Publishing Group**

St James Press
See **Thomson Gale**

St Martin's Press LLC
175 Fifth Avenue, New York NY 10010
☎001 646 307 5151 Fax 001 212 420 9314
✉ inquiries@stmartins.com
www.stmartins.com

CEO (Holtzbrinck) *John Sargent*
President/Publisher (Trade Division) *Sally Richardson*

Founded 1952. A subsidiary of **Macmillan Publishers** (UK), St Martin's Press made its name and fortune by importing raw talent from the UK to the States and has continued to buy heavily in the UK. Publishes general fiction, especially mysteries and crime; and adult non-fiction: history, self-help, political science, travel, biography, scholarly, popular reference, college textbooks.

IMPRINTS **Picador USA**; **Griffin** (trade paperbacks); **St Martin's Paperbacks** (mass market); **Thomas Dunne Books**; **Minotaur**; **Palgrave**; **Truman Talley Books**. All submissions via legitimate literary agents only.

Scarecrow Press Inc.
4501 Forbes Boulevard, Suite 200, Lanham MD 20706
☎001 301 459 3366 Fax 001 301 429 5748
www.scarecrowpress.com

President *Jed Lyons*
Publisher/ Editorial Director *Edward Kurdyla*

Founded 1950 as a short-run publisher of library reference books. Acquired by **University Press of America, Inc.** in 1995 which is now part of Rowman and Littlefield Publishing Group. Publishes reference, scholarly and monographs (all levels) for libraries. Reference books in all areas except sciences, specialising in the performing arts, music, cinema and library science. About 160 titles a year. Unsolicited mss welcome but material will not be returned unless requested and accompanied by return postage. Unsolicited synopses and ideas for books welcome.

Schirmer Reference
See **Thomson Gale**

Scholarly Resources, Inc.
See **Thomson Gale**

Scholastic Library Publishing
90 Old Sherman Turnpike, Danbury CT 06816
☎001 203 797 3500 Fax 001 203 797 3657
www.scholastic.com/aboutscholastic/divisions/slp.htm

President *Greg Worrell*

Publishes juvenile non-fiction, encyclopedias, speciality reference sets and picture books.
DIVISIONS/IMPRINTS **Children's Press**; **Grolier Educational**; **Franklin Watts**. About 500 titles a year.

Scribner
See **Simon & Schuster Adult Publishing Group**

Charles Scribner's Sons
See **Thomson Gale**

Seal Press
See **Avalon Publishing Group**

Sentinel
See **Penguin Group (USA) Inc.**

Seven Stories Press
140 Watts Street, New York NY 10013
☎001 212 226 8760 Fax 001 212 226 1411
www.sevenstories.com

Publisher *Daniel Simon*
Subsidiary Rights *Anna Lui*

Founded 1995. Named by *Publishers Weekly* in 1999 as the fastest growing independent publisher in America. Publishes, literature, politics, media studies, popular culture, health. About 50 titles a year. No unsolicited mss; synopses and ideas from agents welcome or send query letter. No e-mail submissions. No children's or business books. OVERSEAS SUBSIDIARIES Turnaround Publishing Services, UK and EU; Palgrave Macmillan, Australia; Macmillian Publishers NZ Ltd., New Zealand; Liberty Books (Pte.) Ltd., Pakistan; Pen International Pte. Ltd., Singapore; Stephan Phillips (Pty.) Ltd., Southern Africa; Publishers Group Canada, Canada.

M.E. Sharpe, Inc.
80 Business Park Drive, Armonk NY 10504
☎001 914 273 1800 Fax 001 914 273 2106
✉ info@mesharpe.com

www.mesharpe.com

President/CEO *M.E. Sharpe*

SnrVP/COO *Vincent Fuentes*

Founded 1958. Publishes books and journals in the social sciences and humanities, both original works and translations in Asian and East European studies. IMPRINTS **East Gate Books**; **Sharpe Reference** *Patricia Kolb.* 80 titles in 2006. No unsolicited material.

ROYALTIES annually.

Shoemaker & Hoard Publishers
See **Avalon Publishing Group**

Silver Whistle
See **Harcourt Trade Publishers**

Simon & Schuster Adult Publishing Group (Division of Simon & Schuster, Inc)

1230 Avenue of the Americas, New York NY 10020

☎001 212 698 7000 Fax 001 212 698 7007

www.simonsays.com

President *Carolyn K. Reidy*

Publishes fiction and non-fiction.

DIVISIONS

Atria Books VP & Executive Editorial Director *Emily Bestler;* **Free Press** VP & Editorial Director *Dominick Anfuso;* **Fireside/Touchstone** VP & Editor-in-Chief Trish Todd; **Howard Books** EVP & Publisher *John Howard;* **Pocket Books** VP & Editorial Director *Maggie Crawford;* **Scribner** VP & Editor-in-Chief *Nan Graham;* **Simon and Schuster** VP & Editorial Director *Alice Mayhew.*

IMPRINTS

Atria Books; Downtown Press; Fireside; Free Press; Howard Books; Pocket Books; Scribner; Scribner Classics; S&S Libros eñ Espanol; Simon & Schuster; Strebor Books; Threshold Editions; Touchstone; Washington Square Press. No unsolicited mss.

ROYALTIES twice-yearly.

Simon & Schuster Children's Publishing

1230 Avenue of the Americas, New York NY 10020

☎001 212 698 7200

www.simonsayskids.com

President/Publisher *Rick Richter*

A division of the Simon & Schuster Consumer Group. Publishes pre-school to young adult, picture books, hardcover and paperback fiction, non-fiction, trade, library and mass-market titles.

IMPRINTS

Aladdin Books Picture books, paperback fiction and non-fiction reprints and originals, and limited series for ages pre-school to young adult; **Atheneum Books for Young Readers** Picture books, hardcover fiction and non-fiction books across all genres for ages three to young adult; **Little Simon** Mass-market novelty books (pop-ups, board books, colouring & activity) and merchandise (book and audio cassette) for ages birth through eight; **Margaret K. McElderry Books** Picture books, hardcover fiction and non-fiction trade books for children ages three to young adult; **Simon & Schuster Books for Young Readers** Picture books, hardcover fiction and non-fiction for children ages three to young adult. **Simon Spotlight** Devoted exclusively to children's media tie-ins and licensed properties. About 480 titles a year. No unsolicited material.

Simon Spotlight
See **Simon & Schuster Children's Publishing**

Sleeping Bear Press
See **Thomson Gale**

Solana
See **Hachette Book Group USA**

Southern Illinois University Press

PO Box 3697, Carbondale IL 62902–3697

☎001 618 453 2281 Fax 001 618 453 1221

www.siu.edu/~siupress

Director *Lain Adkins*

Founded 1956. Publishes scholarly and general interest non-fiction books and educational materials. 50 titles a year.

Speak
See **Penguin Group (USA) Inc.**

Stackpole Books

5067 Ritter Road, Mechanicsburg PA 17055

☎001 717 796 0411 Fax 001 717 796 0412

www.stackpolebooks.com

President *M. David Detweiler*

Vice President/Publisher *Judith Schnell*

Founded 1933. Publishes outdoor sports, fishing, hunting, nature, crafts, Pennsylvania and

regional, military reference, history. About 100 titles a year.
ROYALTIES twice-yearly.

Stanford University Press
1450 Page Mill Road, Palo Alto
CA 94304–1124
☎001 650 723 9434 Fax 001 650 725 3457
✉ info@www.sup.org
www.sup.org
Director *Geoffrey R.H. Burn*
Founded 1925. Publishes non-fiction: scholarly works in all areas of the humanities, social sciences, history and literature, also professional lists in business, economics and law. About 150 titles a year. No unsolicited mss; query in writing first.

State University of New York Press
194 Washington Avenue, Suite 305, Albany
NY 12210–2384
☎001 518 472 5000 Fax 001 518 472 5038
✉ info@sunypress.edu
www.sunypress.edu
Editor-in-Chief *Jane Bunker*
Founded 1966. Part of the Research Foundation of SUNY, the Press is one of the largest university presses in the USA. Publishes scholarly and trade books in the humanities, social sciences and books of regional interest on New York State. Strengths in philosophy, religious studies, education and Asian studies. 153 titles in 2006. Unsolicited submissions welcome. Send material to *Jane Bunker*, Editor-in-Chief.
ROYALTIES annually.

Sterling Publishing Co. Inc.
387 Park Avenue South, New York
NY 10016–8810
☎001 212 532 7160
www.sterlingpub.com
VP/Publisher *Andrew Martin*
President/CEO *Charles Nurnberg*
VP, Editorial *Steve Magnuson*
Executive VP/COO *Macus Leaver*
Founded 1949. A subsidiary of Barnes & Noble, Inc. Publishes illustrated non-fiction: reference and how-to books on arts and crafts, home improvement, history, photography, children's, woodworking, pets, hobbies, gardening, games and puzzles, general non-fiction. IMPRINT **Lark** Crafts, children's, photography. Submission guidelines available.

Strebor Books
See **Simon & Schuster Adult Publishing Group**

Swallow Press
See **Ohio University Press**

Syracuse University Press
621 Skytop Road, Suite 110, Syracuse
NY 13244–5290
☎001 315 443 5534 Fax 001 315 443 5545
www.SyracuseUniversityPress.syr.edu
Director *Alice R. Pfeiffer*
Founded 1943. Publishes scholarly books in the following areas: Middle East studies, Middle East literature in translation, Irish studies, Jewish studies, sports, gender and globalisation, Iroquois studies, women and religion, medieval studies, religion and politics, television, geography and regional books. Distributes for the Moshe Dayan Center, Jusoor. About 50 titles a year. No unsolicited mss. Send query letter with IRCs.
ROYALTIES annually.

The TAFT Group
See **Thomson Gale**

Nan A. Talese
See **Doubleday Broadway Publishing Group**

Jeremy P. Tarcher
See **Penguin Group (USA) Inc.**

Katherine Tegan Books
See **HarperCollins Publishers, Inc.**

Temple University Press
1601 N. Broad Street, 083–42, Philadelphia
PA 19122–6099
☎001 215 204 8787 Fax 001 215 204 4719
www.temple.edu/tempress
Editor-in-Chief *Janet M. Francendese*
Founded 1969. Publishes scholarly books. Authors generally academics. Letter of inquiry with brief outline. Include fax/e-mail address. About 60 titles a year.

University of Tennessee Press
110 Conference Center Bldg., Knoxville
TN 37996–4108
☎001 865 974 3321 Fax 001 865 974 3724
www.utpress.org
Managing Editor *Stan Ivester*
Acquisitions Editor *Scott Danforth*
Founded 1940. Publishes scholarly and regional

non-fiction. Submission guidelines are posted on the website.

University of Texas Press
PO Box 7819, Austin TX 78722
☎001 512 471 7233/471 4278 (editorial)
Fax 001 512 232 7178
✉ utpress@uts.cc.utexas.edu
www.utexas.edu/utpress/
www.utexaspress.com

Director *Joanna Hitchcock*
Assistant Director/Editor-in-Chief *Theresa J. May*

Publishes scholarly and regional non-fiction: anthropology, architecture, classics, environmental studies, humanities, social sciences, geography, language studies, literary modernism; Latin American/Latino/Mexican American/ Middle Eastern/Native American studies, natural history and ornithology, regional books (Texas and the southwest). About 90 titles a year and 11 journals. Unsolicited material welcome in above subject areas only. Author guidelines available on the website.
ROYALTIES annually.

Thomson Gale
27500 Drake Road, Farmington Hills MI 48331–3535
☎001 248 699 4253 Fax 001 248 699 8070
www.gale.com

President *Gordon Macomber*

Part of The Thomson Corporation, Thomson Gale is a world leader in information and educational publishing. Addresses all types of information needs, from homework help to health questions and business profiles, in a variety of formats: books, Web-based material and microfilm.

BRANDS/IMPRINTS **Blackbirch Press; Five Star; Graham & Whiteside; Greenhaven Press; G.K. Hall; KidHaven Press; Large Print Press; Lucent Books; Macmillan Reference USA; Primary Source Microfilm; Schirmer Reference; Scholarly Resources, Inc.; Charles Scribner's Sons; Sleeping Bear Press; St James Press; The TAFT Group; Thorndike Press; Twayne Publishers; UXL; Walker Large Print; Wheeler Publishing.**

Thorndike Press
See **Thomson Gale**

Three Rivers Press
See **Crown Publishing Group**

Threshold Editions
See **Simon & Schuster Adult Publishing Group**

Thunder's Mouth Press
See **Avalon Publishing Group**

Time Warner Book Group
See **Hachette Book Group USA**

Times Books
See **Henry Holt & Company, Inc.**

Megan Tingley Books
See **Hachette Book Group USA**

Touchstone
See **Simon & Schuster Adult Publishing Group**

Transaction Publishers Ltd
c/o Rutgers – The State University of New Jersey, 35 Berrue Circle, Piscataway NJ 08854–8042
☎001 732 445 2280 Fax 001 732 445 3138
✉ ihorowitz@transactionpub.com
www.transactionpub.com

Also at: 390 Campus Drive, Somerset, NJ 08873

Chairman *I.L. Horowitz*
President *Mary E. Curtis*
Vice President *Scott B. Bramson*

Founded 1962. Independent publisher of academic social scientific books, periodicals and serials. Publisher of record in international social research. 170 titles in 2006. All unsolicited material should be submitted in hard copy and full draft. E-mail submissions are not accepted. 'Decision-making is rapid.'
ROYALTIES Average of 10% hardcover originals; 7½% paperback.

Truman Talley Books
See **St Martin's Press LLC**

Twayne Publishers
See **Thomson Gale**

Twelve
See **Hachette Book Group USA**

Twenty-First Century Books
See **Lerner Publishing Group**

Tyndale House Publishers, Inc.
351 Executive Drive, Carol Stream IL 60188
☎001 630 668 8303

www.tyndale.com
President *Mark D. Taylor*
Founded 1962. Books cover a wide range of categories from non-fiction to gift books, theology, doctrine, Bibles, fiction, children's and youth. Also produces video material, calendars and audio books for the same market. No poetry. Non-denominational religious publisher of around 300 titles a year for the evangelical Christian market. No unsolicited mss. Synopses and ideas considered. Writer's guidelines available on the website.

University Press of America, Inc.
4501 Forbes Boulevard, Suite 200, Lanham MD 20706
☎001 301 459 3366 Fax 001 301 429 5748
www.univpress.com
VP/Director *Judith L. Rothman*
Founded 1974. Publishes scholarly monographs, college and graduate level textbooks. No children's, elementary or high school. About 300 titles a year. Submit outline or request proposal questionnaire.

UXL
See **Thomson Gale**

Vanguard Press
See **Perseus Books Group**

Viking/Viking Children's Books
See **Penguin Group (USA) Inc.**

Villard
See **Random House Publishing Group**

University of Virginia Press
PO Box 400318, Charlottesville
VA 22904–4318
☎001 434 924 3468 Fax 001 434 982 2655
✉ vapress@virginia.edu
www.upress.virginia.edu
Director *Penelope J. Kaiserlian*
Founded 1963. Publishes academic books in humanities and social science with concentrations in American history, African-American studies, architecture, Victorian literature, Caribbean literature and ecocriticism. No unsolicited mss; will consider synopses and ideas for books if in their specific areas of concentration. Approach by mail for full proposal; e-mail for short inquiry. No fiction, children's, poetry or academic books outside interests specified above.
ROYALTIES annually.

Vision
See **Hachette Book Group USA**

Voyager Books
See **Harcourt Trade Division**

J. Weston Walch, Publisher
PO Box 658, Portland ME 04104–0658
☎001 207 772 2846 Fax 001 207 772 3105
www.walch.com
President *John Thoreson*
Editor-in-Chief *Susan Blair*
Founded 1927. Publishes supplementary educational materials for middle and secondary schools across a wide range of subjects, including English/language arts, literacy, special needs, mathematics, social studies, science and school-to-career. Always interested in ideas from secondary school teachers who develop materials in the classroom. Proposal letters, synopses and ideas welcome.

Walker & Co.
104 Fifth Avenue, 7th Floor, New York NY 10011
☎001 212 727 8300 Fax 001 212 727 0984
✉ firstinitiallastname@walkerbooks.com
www.walkerbooks.com (trade non-fiction)
www.walkeryoungreaders.com (BFYR)
Contact *Submissions Editor*
Founded 1959. A division of **Bloomsbury Publishing**. Publishes children's fiction and non-fiction and adult non-fiction. Please contact the following editors in advance before sending any material to be sure of their interest, then follow up as instructed: **Trade Non-fiction** *George Gibson* Permission and documentation must be available with mss. Submit prospectus first, with sample chapters and marketing analysis. **Books for Young Readers** *Emily Easton* Fiction and non-fiction for all ages. Query before sending non-fiction proposals. Especially interested in picture books – fiction and non-fiction, historical and contemporary fiction for middle grades and young adults. BFYR will consider unsolicited submissions.

Walker Large Print
See **Thomson Gale**

Frederick Warne
See **Penguin Group (USA) Inc.**

Washington Square Press
See **Simon & Schuster Adult Publishing Group**

Washington State University Press

PO Box 645910, Washington State University,
Pullman WA 99164–5910
☎001 509 335 3518
✉ wsupress@wsu.edu
wsupress.wsu.edu
Editor-in-Chief *Glen Lindeman*
Founded 1928. Publishes hardcover originals, trade paperbacks and reprints. Publishes mainly on the history, prehistory, culture, politics and natural history of the Northwest United States (Washington, Idaho, Oregon, Montana, Alaska) and British Columbia. Subjects include history, biography, cooking/food history, nature/environment, politics. 8–10 titles a year. Queries welcome.

Franklin Watts

See **Scholastic Library Publishing**

Wellness Central

See **Hachette Book Group USA**

Westview Press

See **Perseus Books Group**

Wheeler Publishing

See **Thomson Gale**

John Wiley & Sons, Inc.

111 River Street, Hoboken NJ 07030–5774
☎001 201 748 6000 Fax 001 201 748 6088
✉ info@wiley.com
www.wiley.com
President/CEO *William J. Pesce*
Founded 1807. Wiley's core publishing programme includes scientific, technical and medical journals, encyclopedias, books and online products and services; professional and consumer books and subscription services; and educational materials for undergraduate, graduate students and life-long learners. About 1700 titles a year. Submission guidelines available on the website under 'Resources for Authors'.

The University of Wisconsin Press

1930 Monroe Street, 3rd Floor, Madison
WI 53711–2059
☎001 608 263 1110 Fax 001 608 263 1120
✉ uwiscpress@uwpress.wisc.edu
www.wisc.edu/wisconsinpress
Founded 1936. Publishes scholarly, general interest non-fiction and regional books about Wisconsin and the mid-west. About 50 titles a year. No unsolicited mss. Detailed author guidelines available on the website.

Wordsong

See **Boyds Mills Press**

Zondervan

5300 Patterson Avenue SE, Grand Rapids
MI 49530
☎001 616 698 6900 Fax 001 616 698 3439
www.zondervan.com
President/Chief Executive *Bruce E. Ryskamp*
Founded 1931. Subsidiary of **HarperCollins Publishers, Inc.** Publishes Protestant religion, Bibles, books, audio & video, computer software, calendars and speciality items.

US Literary Agents

★ = Members of the **Association of Authors' Representatives, Inc.**

Dominick Abel
Literary Agency, Inc.★
146 West 82nd Street, Suite 1B, New York
NY 10024
☎001 212 877 0710 Fax 001 212 595 3133
Contact *Dominick Abel*
Established 1975. No scripts, children's books
or poetry. COMMISSION Home 15%; Translation
20%. No unsolicited material. Send query letter
with s.a.e. in the first instance. No reading fee.

Miriam Altshuler Literary Agency★
53 Old Post Road North, Red Hook
NY 12571
☎001 845 758 9408
www.miriamaltshulerliteraryagency.com/
Founded 1994. Handles literary and commercial fiction; general non-fiction, narrative non-
fiction, memoirs, nature, psychology, biography,
travel. No romance, science fiction, mysteries,
poetry, westerns, fantasy, how-to, techno thrillers
or self-help. COMMISSION Home 15%; Foreign/
Translation 20%. Send query letter and synopsis
in the first instance with return postage or s.a.e.
(no e-mail or fax queries). No reading fee.

Malaga Baldi Literary Agency
233 West 99th Street, Suite 19C, New York
NY 10025
☎001 212 222 3213
✉ baldibooks@gmail.com
Contact *Malaga Baldi*
Founded 1986. Handles quality fiction and non-
fiction. No scripts. No westerns, men's adventure,
science fiction/fantasy, romance, how-to, young
adult or children's. COMMISSION 15%. OVERSEAS
ASSOCIATES **Abner Stein**, UK; Owl Agency;
Eliane Benisti, France; **Marsh Agency**. Writers
of fiction should send query letter describing
the novel plus IRCs. For non-fiction, approach
in writing with a proposal, table of contents and
two sample chapters. No reading fee.

The Balkin Agency, Inc.★
PO Box 222, Amherst MA 01004
☎001 413 548 9835 Fax 001 413 548 9836

✉ rick62838@crocker.com
Contact *Richard Balkin*
Founded 1973. Handles adult non-fiction only.
COMMISSION Home 15%; Foreign 20%. No
reading fee for outlines and synopses.

Loretta Barrett Books, Inc.★
101 Fifth Avenue, New York NY 10003
☎001 212 242 3420
www.lorettabarrettbooks.com
Contacts *Loretta Barrett, Nick Mullendore*
Founded 1990. Handles all non-fiction and
fiction genres except children's, poetry, science
fiction/fantasy. Specialises in women's fiction,
history, spirituality. No scripts. COMMISSION
Home 15%; Foreign 20%. No e-mail submissions. Send query letter with biography and
return postage only in the first instance.

Meredith Bernstein
Literary Agency, Inc.★
2095 Broadway, Suite 505, New York
NY 10023
☎001 212 799 1007 Fax 001 212 799 1145
Contacts *Meredith Bernstein*
Founded 1981. Handles commercial and literary
fiction, mysteries and non-fiction (women's
issues, biography, memoirs, health, current
affairs, crafts). COMMISSION Home & Dramatic
15%; Translation 20%. OVERSEAS ASSOCIATES
Abner Stein, UK; Lennart Sane, Holland,
Scandinavia and Spanish language; Thomas
Schluck, Germany; Bardon Chinese Media
Agency; William Miller, Japan; Frederique
Porretta, France; Agenzia Letteraria, Italy.

Bleecker Street Associates, Inc.★
532 LaGuardia Place, #617, New York
NY 10012
☎001 212 677 4492 Fax 001 212 388 0001
Founded 1984. Handles fiction: women's,
mystery, suspense, literary; non-fiction: history,
women's interests, parenting, health, relationships, psychology, sports, sociology, current
events, biography, spirituality, New Age, business.
No poetry, children's, westerns, science fiction,

professional, academic. COMMISSION Home 15%; Foreign 25%. Send query letter in the first instance. Will only respond if envelope and return postage enclosed. No phone calls, faxes or e-mails. No reading fee.

Georges Borchardt, Inc.★
136 East 57th Street, New York NY 10022
☎001 212 753 5785 Fax 001 212 838 6518
Founded 1967. Works mostly with established/published authors. Specialises in fiction, biography, and general non-fiction of unusual interest. COMMISSION Home, UK & Dramatic 15%; Translation 20%. UK ASSOCIATE **Sheil Land Associates Ltd** (Richard Scott Simon), London. Unsolicited mss not read.

Brandt & Hochman Literary Agents, Inc.★
1501 Broadway, Suite 2310, New York NY 10036
☎001 212 840 5760
Contacts *Carl D. Brandt, Gail Hochman, Marianne Merola, Charles Schlessiger*
Founded 1914. Handles non-fiction and fiction. No poetry. COMMISSION Home & Dramatic 15%; Foreign 20%. UK ASSOCIATE A.M. Heath & Co. Ltd. No unsolicited mss. Approach by letter describing background and ambitions; include return postage. No reading fee.

Barbara Braun Associates, Inc.★
104 Fifth Avenue, 7th Floor, New York NY 10011
☎001 212 604 9023 Fax 001 212 604 9041
✉ barbara@barbarabraunagency.com
www/barbarabraunagency.com
Contacts *Barbara Braun, John Baker*
Founded 1995. Handles literary and mainstream, women's and historical fiction, also serious non-fiction, including psychology and biography. Also young adult and mystery books. Specialises in art history, archaeology, architecture and cultural history. No scripts, poetry, science fiction. COMMISSION Home 15%; Foreign 20%. OVERSEAS ASSOCIATE Chandler Crawford Literary Agency. No unsolicited mss; send query letter in the first instance. See website for submission guidelines. No reading fee.

Browne & Miller Literary Associates★
410 S. Michigan Avenue, Suite 460, Chicago IL 60605
☎001 312 922 3063 Fax 001 312 922 1905

✉ mail@browneandmiller.com
www.browneandmiller.com
President *Danielle Egan-Miller*
Founded 1971. Formerly known as Multimedia Product Development. Handles commercial and literary fiction, and practical non-fiction with wide appeal. No scripts, juvenile, science fiction or poetry. COMMISSION Home 15%; Foreign & Translation 20%. OVERSEAS ASSOCIATES in Europe, Latin America, Japan and Asia. In the first instance, send query letter with return postage. No unsolicited material. No reading fee.

Pema Browne Ltd, Illustration and Literary Agents
11 Tena Place, Valley Cottage NY 10989
✉ ppbltd@optonline.net
www.pemabrowneltd.com
Contact *Pema Browne*
Founded 1966. ('Pema rhymes with Emma.') Handles mass-market mainstream and hardcover fiction: romance, business, children's picture books and young adult; non-fiction: how-to and reference. COMMISSION Home 20%; Translation 20%; Overseas authors 20%. No unsolicited mss; send query letter with IRCs. No fax or e-mail queries. Also handles illustrators' work. No longer accepting screenplays. 'We are accepting very few new clients at this time.'

Sheree Bykofsky Associates, Inc.★
16 West 36th Street, 13th Floor, New York NY 10018
☎001 212 244 4144
✉ submitbee@aol.com
Contact *Sheree Bykofsky*
Founded 1991. Handles adult fiction and non-fiction. No scripts. No children's, young adult, horror, science fiction, romance, westerns, occult or supernatural. COMMISSION Home 15%; UK (including sub-agent's fee) 20%. No unsolicited mss. Send query letter first with brief synopsis or outline and writing sample (1–3 pp) for fiction. IRCs essential for reply or return of material. 'Please do not send material via methods that require signature, such as FedEx, etc.' No phone calls. See website for submission guidelines. No reading fee.

Maria Carvainis Agency, Inc.★
1350 Avenue of the Americas, Suite 2905, New York NY 10019
☎001 212 245 6365 Fax 001 212 245 7196
✉ mca@mariacarvainisagency.com

President *Maria Carvainis*

Founded 1977. Handles fiction: literary and mainstream, contemporary women's, mystery, suspense, historical, young adult novels; non-fiction: business, women's issues, memoirs, health, biography, medicine. No film scripts unless from writers with established credits. No science fiction. COMMISSION Domestic & Dramatic 15%; Translation 20%. No faxed or e-mailed queries. No unsolicited mss; they will be returned unread. Queries only, with IRCs for response. No reading fee.

Castiglia Literary Agency★

1155 Camino del mar, Suite 510, Del Mar CA 92014

☎001 858 755 8761 Fax 001 858 755 7063

✉ jaclagency@aol.com

Contacts *Julie Castiglia, Winifred Golden, Sally Van Haitsma*

Founded 1993. Handles fiction: literary, mainstream, ethnic; non-fiction: narrative, biography, business, science, health, parenting, memoirs, psychology, women's and contemporary issues. Specialises in science, biography and literary fiction. No scripts, horror or fantasy. COMMISSION Home 15%; Foreign & Translation 25%. No unsolicited material; send query letter only in the first instance. No reading fee.

The Catalog Literary Agency

PO Box 2964, Vancouver WA 98668

☎001 360 694 8531

Contact *Douglas Storey*

Founded 1986. Handles popular, professional and textbook material in all subjects, especially business, health, money, science, technology, computers, electronics and women's interests; also how-to, self-help. No fiction. No scripts, articles, screenplays, plays, poetry or short stories. COMMISSION 15%. No unsolicited mss. Query with an outline and sample chapters, and include IRCs. No reading fee.

Jane Chelius Literary Agency, Inc.★

548 Second Street, Brooklyn, New York NY 11215

☎001 718 499 0236 Fax 001 718 832 7335

✉ queries@janechelius.com

www.janechelius.com

Contacts *Jane Chelius, Mark Chelius*

Founded 1995. Handles popular and literary fiction; narrative and how-to non-fiction. No children's, young adult, screenplays, scripts and

poetry. COMMISSION Home 15% Foreign 20%. Submission guidelines available on the website.

Linda Chester & Associates★

Rockefeller Center, 630 Fifth Avenue, New York NY 10111

☎001 212 218 3350 Fax 001 212 218 3343

✉ lcassoc@mindspring.com

www.lindachester.com

Contact *Linda Chester*

Founded 1978. Handles literary and commercial fiction and non-fiction in all subjects. No scripts, children's or textbooks. COMMISSION Home & Dramatic 15%; Translation 25%. No unsolicited mss or queries. No reading fee for solicited material.

William Clark Associates★

154 Christopher Street, Suite 3C, New York NY 10014

☎001 212 675 2784

✉ query@wmclark.com

www.wmclark.com

Contact *William Clark*

Founded 1997. Handles non-fiction, mainstream literary fiction and some young adult books. No scripts, horror, science fiction, fantasy, diet or mystery. COMMISSION Home 15%; Foreign & Translation 20%. OVERSEAS ASSOCIATES **Ed Victor Ltd**; **Andrew Nurnberg Associates Ltd** (translation rights). Synopses should be part of query letter; sample chapters, complete mss on request only. Contact via e-mail only with concise description of work, synopsis/outline, biographical information and publishing history, if any. No reading fee.

Frances Collin Literary Agent★

PO Box 33, Wayne PA 19087–0033

☎001 610 254 0555 Fax 001 610 254 5029

Contact *Frances Collin*

Founded 1948. Successor to Marie Rodell. Handles general fiction and non-fiction. No scripts. OVERSEAS ASSOCIATES worldwide. No unsolicited mss. Send query letter only, with IRCs for reply, for the attention of *Sarah Yake*. No fax or telephone queries, please. No reading fee. Rarely accepts non-professional writers or writers not represented in the UK.

Don Congdon Associates, Inc.★

156 Fifth Avenue, Suite 625, New York NY 10010–7002

☎001 212 645 1229 Fax 001 212 727 2688

Contacts *Don Congdon, Michael Congdon, Susan*

Ramer, Cristina Concepcion

Founded 1983. Handles fiction and non-fiction. No academic, technical, romantic fiction or scripts. COMMISSION Home 15%; UK & Translation 19%. OVERSEAS ASSOCIATES worldwide. No unsolicited mss. Query letter with return postage in the first instance. No reading fee.

Curtis Brown Ltd★

10 Astor Place, New York NY 10003

☎001 212 473 5400

Book Rights *Laura Blake Peterson, Peter L. Ginsberg, Emilie Jacobson, Ginger Knowlton, Maureen Walters, Mitchell Waters, Elizabeth Harding, Ginger Clark*

Film & TV Rights *Timothy Knowlton, Edwin Wintle*

Translation *Dave Barbor*

Founded 1914. Handles general fiction and non-fiction. Also some scripts for film, TV and theatre. OVERSEAS ASSOCIATES Representatives in all major foreign countries. No unsolicited mss; queries only, with IRCs for reply. No reading fee.

Sandra Dijkstra Literary Agency★

1155 Camino Del Mar, PMB 515, Del Mar CA 92014

☎001 858 755 3115 Fax 001 858 794 2822

Contact *Taryn Fagerness*

Founded 1981. Handles quality and commercial non-fiction and fiction, including some genre fiction. No scripts. No westerns, science fiction or poetry. Specialises in quality fiction including women's and multicultural fiction, mystery/thrillers, children's literature, narrative non-fiction, psychology, self-help, science, health, business, memoirs, biography, current affairs and history. 'Dedicated to promoting new and original voices and ideas.' COMMISSION Home 15%; Translation 20%. OVERSEAS ASSOCIATES **Abner Stein**, UK; Agence Hoffman, Germany; Licht & Burr, Scandinavia; Luigi Bernabo, Italy; Sandra Bruna, Spain/Portugal; Caroline Van Gelderen, Netherlands; La Nouvelle Agence, France; The English Agency, Japan; Bardon-Chinese Media Agency, China/Taiwan; Prava I Prevodi, Eastern Europe; Tuttle Mori, Thailand; Synopsis, Russia/Baltic States; Maxima Creative Agency, Indonesia; Graal, Poland. For fiction send brief synopsis (one page) and first 50 pages; for non-fiction send proposal with overview, chapter outline, author biog, 1–2 sample chapters and

profile of competition. All submissions should be accompanied by IRCs. No reading fee.

Dunham Literary Inc.★

156 Fifth Avenue, Suite 625, New York NY 10010

☎001 212 929 0994 Fax 001 212 929 0904

www.dunhamlit.com

Contacts *Jennie Dunham, Melanie Klessie*

Founded 2000. Handles literary fiction and non-fiction, New Age spirituality and children's (from picture books through young adult). No scripts, romance, westerns, horror, science-fiction/fantasy or poetry. COMMISSION Home 15%; Foreign & Translation 20%. OVERSEAS ASSOCIATE UK & Europe: **A.M. Heath & Co. Ltd**. The Rhoda Weyr Agency is now a division of Dunham Literary Inc. No unsolicited material. Send query letter (with return postage) giving information on the author and ms. No e-mail or faxed queries; see the website for further contact information. No reading fee.

Dystel & Goderich Literary Management★

One Union Square West, Suite 904, New York NY 10003

☎001 212 627 9100 Fax 001 212 627 9313

www.dystel.com

Contacts *Jane Dystel, Miriam Goderich, Stacey Glick, Michael Bourret, Jim McCarthy, Lauren Abramo, Adina Kahn, Chasya Milgrom*

Founded 1994. Handles non-fiction and fiction. Specialises in politics, history, biography, cookbooks, current affairs, celebrities, commercial and literary fiction. No reading fee.

Educational Design Services, LLC

PO Box 2094, Rockville MD 20852–2094

☎001 301 738 9402

✉ blinder@educationaldesignservices.com

www.educationaldesignservices.com

President *Bertram Linder*

Founded 1979. Specialises in texts and professional development materials for the education and school market. COMMISSION Home 15%; Foreign 25%. 'E-submissions' welcome. IRCs must accompany mail submissions.

Ethan Ellenberg Literary Agency★

548 Broadway, Suite 5E, New York NY 10012

☎001 212 431 4554 Fax 001 212 941 4652

✉ agent@ethanellenberg.com

www.ethanellenberg.com

Contact *Ethan Ellenberg*

Founded 1984. Handles fiction: commercial, genre, literary and children's; non-fiction: history, biography, business, science, health, cooking, current affairs. Specialises in commercial fiction, thrillers, suspense and romance. No scripts, poetry or short stories. COMMISSION Home 15%; Translation 20%. Prefers submissions by mail with return postage. For fiction send synopsis and three chapters; for non-fiction send proposal and sample chapters, if available. No reading fee. For e-mail submissions send query letter only; no attachments.

Ann Elmo Agency, Inc.★
60 East 42nd Street, New York NY 10165
☎001 212 661 2880/1 Fax 001 212 661 2883

Contacts *Lettie Lee, Mari Cronin, Andree Abecassis*

Founded in the 1940s. Handles literary and romantic fiction, mysteries and mainstream; also non-fiction in all subjects, including biography and self-help. Some children's (8–12-year-olds). COMMISSION Home 15–20%. Query letter with outline of project in the first instance. No reading fee.

The Fogelman Literary Agency★
14902 Preston Road, Suite 404, Dallas
TX 75254
☎001 214 361 9956

Also at: 445 Park Avenue, 9th Floor, New York, NY 10022

Contacts *Evan Fogelman, Linda Kruger*

Founded 1989. Handles non-fiction and fiction: romance (including historical and contemporary) and some mystery/suspense. No scripts, poetry, westerns, science fiction/fantasy or children's books. COMMISSION Home 15%; Foreign & Translation 10%. No unsolicited material. Published authors are welcome to call but unpublished authors should send query by e-mail or letter with return postage. No reading fee.

Jeanne Fredericks Literary Agency, Inc.★
221 Benedict Hill Road, New Canaan
CT 06840
☎001 203 972 3011 Fax 001 203 972 3011

Contact *Jeanne Fredericks*

Founded 1997. Handles quality adult non-fiction, usually of a practical and popular nature by authorities in their fields. Specialises in health, gardening, business, self-help, reference. No fiction, juvenile, poetry, essays, politics, academic or textbooks. COMMISSION Home 15%; Foreign

25% (with co-agent) or 20% (direct). No unsolicited material; send query by e-mail (no attachments) or letter with return postage in the first instance. No reading fee.

Robert A. Freedman Dramatic Agency, Inc.★
Suite 2310, 1501 Broadway, New York
NY 10036
☎001 212 840 5760

President *Robert A. Freedman*
Senior Vice-President *Selma Luttinger*
Vice-President *Robin Kaver*
Associate *Marta Praeger*

Founded 1928 as Brandt & Brandt Dramatic Department, Inc. Took its present name in 1984. Works mostly with established authors. Send letter of enquiry first with s.a.e. Specialises in plays, film and TV scripts. COMMISSION Dramatic 10%. Unsolicited mss not read.

Gelfman Schneider Literary Agents, Inc.★
250 West 57th Street, Suite 2515, New York
NY 10107
☎001 212 245 1993 Fax 001 212 245 8678

Contacts *Deborah Schneider, Jane Gelfman*

Founded 1919 (London), 1980 (New York). Formerly John Farquharson Ltd. Works mostly with established/published authors. Specialises in general trade fiction and non-fiction. No poetry, short stories or screenplays. COMMISSION Home 15%; Dramatic 15%; Foreign 20%. OVERSEAS ASSOCIATE **Curtis Brown Group Ltd**, UK. No reading fee for outlines. Submissions must be accompanied by IRCs. No e-mail queries please.

Frances Goldin Literary Agency, Inc.★
57 East 11th Street, Suite 5B, New York
NY 10003
☎001 212 777 0047
✉ agency@goldinlit.com
www.goldinlit.com

Contacts *Sam Stoloff, Frances Goldin, Ellen Geiger*

Founded 1977. Handles literary fiction, controversial progressive non-fiction and 'extraordinary' children's books. COMMISSION Home 15%; Foreign 10%. OVERSEAS ASSOCIATES worldwide. No unsolicited submissions; query letter in the first instance. No reading fee.

Sanford J. Greenburger Associates, Inc.★

55 Fifth Avenue, 15th Floor, New York NY 10003
☎001 212 206 5600 Fax 001 212 463 8718
www.greenburger.com

Contacts *Heide Lange, Faith Hamlin, Daniel Mandel, Matt Bialer, Peter McGuigan, Jeremy Katz, Tricia Davey*

Handles fiction and non-fiction. No unsolicited mss. First approach with query letter, sample chapter and synopsis. No reading fee.

Joy Harris Literary Agency, Inc.★

156 Fifth Avenue, Suite 617, New York NY 10010
☎001 212 924 6269 Fax 001 212 924 6609

Contact *Joy Harris*

Handles adult non-fiction and fiction. COMMISSION Home 15%; Foreign 20%. Query letter in the first instance. No reading fee.

John Hawkins & Associates, Inc.★

71 West 23rd Street, Suite 1600, New York NY 10010
☎001 212 807 7040 Fax 001 212 807 9555

Contacts *John Hawkins, William Reiss*

Founded 1893. Handles film and TV rights. COMMISSION Apply for rates. No unsolicited mss; send queries with 1–3-page outline and one-page c.v. IRCs necessary for response. No reading fee.

The Jeff Herman Agency, LLC

PO Box 1522, Stockbridge MA 01262
☎001 413 298 0077 Fax 001 413 298 8188
✉ jeff@jeffherman.com
www.jeffherman.com

Contact *Jeffrey H. Herman*

Handles all areas of non-fiction, textbooks and reference, business, spiritual and psychology. No scripts. COMMISSION Home 15%; Translation 10%. No unsolicited mss. Query letter with IRCs in the first instance. No reading fee. Jeff Herman publishes a useful reference guide to the book trade called *Jeff Herman's Guide to Book Editors, Publishers & Literary Agents* (Three Dog Press).

Frederick Hill Bonnie Nadell Inc.

1842 Union Street, San Francisco CA 94123
☎001 415 921 2910 Fax 001 415 921 2802

Contacts *Fred Hill, Bonnie Nadell, Elise Proulx*

Founded 1979. General fiction and non-fiction.

No scripts. COMMISSION Home & Dramatic 15%; Foreign 20%. OVERSEAS ASSOCIATE **Mary Clemmey Literary Agency**, UK.

Janklow & Nesbit Associates

445 Park Avenue, New York NY 10022
☎001 212 421 1700 Fax 001 212 980 3671

Partners *Morton L. Janklow, Lynn Nesbit*
Senior Vice-President *Anne Sibbald*
Agents *Tina Bennett, Luke Janklow, Richard Morris, Eric Simonoff*

Founded 1989. Handles fiction and non-fiction; commercial and literary. See also **Janklow & Nesbit (UK) Ltd** under *UK Literary Agents*. No unsolicited mss.

JCA Literary Agency, Inc.★

174 Sullivan Street, New York NY 10012
☎001 212 807 0888
www.jcalit.com/

Contacts *Tom Cushman, Melanie Meyers-Cushman*

Founded 1978. Handles general fiction and non-fiction. No scripts, poetry, science fiction/fantasy or children's books. COMMISSION Home 15%; Foreign 20%. OVERSEAS ASSOCIATE **Vanessa Holt Ltd**, UK. No unsolicited mss; send query letter with return postage. No reading fee.

The Karpfinger Agency

357 West 20th Street, New York NY 10011
☎001 212 691 2690 Fax 001 212 691 7129

Agent *Barney M. Karpfinger*

Founded 1985. Handles quality fiction and non-fiction. No scripts, poetry, romance, horror, science fiction/fantasy, children's picture books. COMMISSION Home 15%; Foreign & Translation 20%. No unsolicited mss. Send query letter with synopsis and writing samples (not exceeding 30 pages). No reading fee.

Kimberley Cameron, Reece Halsey North★

98 Main Street, #704, Tiburon CA 94920
☎001 415 789 9191 Fax 001 415 789 9177
✉ info@reecehalseynorth.com *(Phil Lang)*
www.kimberleycameron.com
www.reecehalseynorth.com

Contacts *Kimberley Cameron, Elizabeth Evans*

The Reece Halsey Agency was founded 1957. Aldous Huxley, Upton Sinclair and William Faulkner have been among their clients. Represents literary and mainstream fiction, non-fiction. No scripts, poetry or children's books. COMMISSION Home 15%; Foreign 20%. Send query letter with first 10–50 pages together with return postage. Will accept e-mail submissions from abroad. No reading fee.

Kirchoff/Wohlberg, Inc.★
866 United Nations Plaza, Suite 525, New York NY 10017
☎001 212 644 2020 Fax 001 212 223 4387
www.kirchoffwohlberg.com
Authors' Representative *Liza Pulitzer-Voges*
Founded 1930. Handles books for children and young adults. No adult material. No scripts for TV, radio, film or theatre. Send letter of enquiry with synopsis or outline and writing sample plus IRCs for reply or return. No reading fee.

Harvey Klinger, Inc.★
300 West 55th Street, Suite 11V, New York NY 10019
✉ queries@harveyklinger.com
www.harveyklinger.com
Contact *Harvey Klinger*
Founded 1977. Handles mainstream fiction and non-fiction. Specialises in commercial and literary fiction, psychology, health and science. No scripts, poetry, computer or children's books. COMMISSION Home 15%; Foreign 25%. OVERSEAS ASSOCIATES in all principal countries. Welcomes unsolicited material; send by e-mail or post (no faxes). No reading fee.

Linda Konner Literary Agency★
10 West 15 Street, Suite 1918, New York NY 10011
☎001 212 691 3419
Contact *Linda Konner*
Founded 1996. Handles non-fiction only, specialising in health, self-help, diet/fitness, pop psychology, relationships, parenting, personal finance. Also some pop culture/celebrities. COMMISSION Home 15%; Foreign 25%. Books must be written by or with established experts in their field. No scripts, fiction, poetry or children's books. No unsolicited material; send one-page query with return postage. No reading fee.

Peter Lampack Agency, Inc.
551 Fifth Avenue, Suite 1613, New York NY 10176
☎001 212 687 9106
Contact *Andrew Lampack*
Founded in 1977. Handles commercial fiction: male action and adventure, contemporary relationships, historical, mysteries and suspense, literary fiction; also non-fiction from recog-

nised experts in a given field, plus biographies, autobiographies. Handles theatrical, motion picture, and TV rights from book properties. No original scripts or screenplays, series or episodic material. COMMISSION Home & Dramatic 15%; Translation & UK 20%. Best approach by letter in first instance. No reply without s.a.e. 'We will respond within three weeks and invite the submission of manuscripts which we would like to examine.' No reading fee. No unsolicited mss.

Michael Larsen/Elizabeth Pomada Literary Agency★
1029 Jones Street, San Francisco CA 94109
☎001 415 673 0939
✉ larsenpoma@aol.com
www.larsenpomada.com
Contact (non-fiction) *Michael Larsen*
Contact (fiction) *Elizabeth Pomada*
Founded 1972. Handles adult fiction and non-fiction – literary and commercial. No scripts, poetry, children's, science fiction. COMMISSION Home 15%; Foreign 20–30%. ASSOCIATE Laurie McLean (represents science fiction and fantasy and young adult books. OVERSEAS ASSOCIATES **David Grossman Literary Agency Ltd**, British rights; Chandler Crawford (foreign rights). Fiction: send first ten pages with 2-page synopsis and s.a.e.; non-fiction: e-mail title and promotion plan. Consult website for guidelines.

Sarah Lazin Books★
126 Fifth Avenue, Suite 300, New York NY 10011
☎001 212 989 5757 Fax 001 212 989 1393
Contact *Sarah Lazin*
Handles adult narrative non-fiction in pop culture, biography, social issues, music reference, photography, fiction. Specialises in music and biography. COMMISSION Home 15%; Foreign 10%. Send query letter with references and writing sample.

The Ned Leavitt Agency★
70 Wooster Street, Suite 4F, New York NY 10012
www.nedleavittagency.com
President *Ned Leavitt*
Agent *Britta Steiner Alexander*
Ned Leavitt specialises in creativity, spirituality, health and literary fiction; Britta Alexander specialises in smart non-fiction for 20 and 30-somethings (dating, relationships, business) and commercial fiction. No screenplays or genre

fiction. COMMISSION Home 15%. See submission guidelines on the website. No reading fee.

Lescher & Lescher Ltd★

47 East 19th Street, New York NY 10003
☎001 212 529 1790 Fax 001 212 529 2716

Contacts *Robert Lescher, Susan Lescher*

Founded 1964. Handles a broad range of serious non-fiction including current affairs, history, biography, memoir, politics, law, contemporary issues, popular culture, food and wine, literary and commercial fiction including mysteries and thrillers; some children's books. Specialises in wine books and cookbooks. No poetry, science fiction, New Age, spiritual, romance. COMMISSION Home 15%; Foreign 20%. No unsolicited manuscripts – please query first. No reading fee.

Sterling Lord Literistic, Inc.

65 Bleecker Street, New York NY 10012
☎001 212 780 6050 Fax 001 212 780 6095
www.sll.com

Contacts *Philippa Brophy, Chris Calhoun, Laurie Liss*

Founded 1979. Handles all genres, fiction and non-fiction. COMMISSION Home 15%; UK & Translation 20%. No unsolicited mss. Prefers letter outlining all non-fiction. No reading fee.

Lowenstein–Yost Associates Inc.★

121 West 27th Street, Suite 601, New York NY 10001
☎001 212 206 1630 Fax 001 212 727 0280
www.lowensteinyost.com

Agents *Barbara Lowenstein, Nancy Yost, Rachel Vater, Zoe Fishman*

Founded 1976. Handles fiction: upmarket, commercial and multicultural, thrillers, mysteries, women's fiction of all kinds including historicals, paranormals and romantic suspense, fantasy and young adult. Non-fiction: narrative, business, health, spirituality, psychology, relationships, politics, history, memoirs, natural science, women's issues, social issues, pop culture, parenting, personal finance. COMMISSION Home 15%; Foreign & Translation 20%. OVERSEAS ASSOCIATES in all major countries. Fiction: send query letter with short synopsis, first chapter and s.a.e. Include any prior literary credits (previously published titles and reviews, writing courses, awards/grants); non-fiction: send query letter, project overview, list of credentials, media appearances, previous titles, reviews and s.a.e. No reading fee.

The Margret McBride Literary Agency★

7744 Fay Avenue, Suite 201, La Jolla CA 92037
☎001 858 454 1550 Fax 001 858 454 2156
✉ staff@mcbridelit.com
www.mcbrideliterary.com

Submissions Manager *Michael Daly*
Assistant to Margret McBride *Faye Atchison*
Vice President/Agent *Donna DeGutis*

Founded 1981. Handles non-fiction mostly, plus business and some fiction. No scripts, science fiction, fantasy, romance or children's books. Specialises in business and management. COMMISSION Home 15%; Overseas 15–25%; Translation 25%. No unsolicited mss. Send query letter with synopsis and s.a.e. only. Check the submission guidelines on the website before making contact.

Carol Mann Agency★

55 Fifth Avenue, New York NY 10003
☎001 212 206 5635 Fax 001 212 675 4809

Contacts *Carol Mann, Emily Nurkin, Kristy Mayer*

Founded 1977. Handles literary and commercial fiction and narrative non-fiction. No scripts or genre fiction. COMMISSION Home 15%; Foreign 20%. No unsolicited material; send query letter with return postage. No reading fee.

Manus & Associates Literary Agency, Inc.★

425 Sherman Avenue, Suite 200, Palo Alto CA 94306
✉ ManusLit@ManusLit.com
www.ManusLit.com

Also at: 444 Madison Avenue, 39th Floor, New York, NY 10022

Contacts (California) *Jillian Manus, Jandy Nelson, Stephanie Lee, Penny Nelson, Dena Fischer*
Contact (New York) *Janet Manus*

Handles commercial and literary fiction, also young adult and middle grade; non-fiction, including true crime, self-help, memoirs, history, pop culture and popular science. No scripts, science fiction/fantasy, westerns, romance, horror, poetry or children's books. COMMISSION Home 15%; Foreign 25%. No unsolicited mss. Fiction: send query letter and first 30 pages; non-fiction: query letter and proposal. Include return postage. All submissions must be made to the California office. No reading fee.

The Evan Marshall Agency*

Six Tristam Place, Pine Brook NJ 07058–9445
☎001 973 882 1122 Fax 001 973 882 3099
www.publishersmarketplace.com/members/
    evanmarshall

Contact *Evan Marshall*

Founded 1987. Handles general adult fiction.
COMMISSION Home 15%; UK & Translation
20%. No unsolicited mss; send query letter first.
No reading fee.

Mews Books Ltd

c/o Sidney B. Kramer, 20 Bluewater Hill,
Westport CT 06880
☎001 203 227 1836 Fax 001 203 227 1144
✉ mewsbooks@aol.com (initial contact only;
    submission by regular mail)

Contacts *Sidney B. Kramer, Fran Pollak*

Founded 1970. Handles adult fiction and non-
fiction, children's, pre-school and young adult.
No scripts, short stories or novellas (unless by
established authors). Specialises in cookery,
medical, health and nutrition, scientific non-
fiction, children's and young adult. COMMISSION
Home 15%; Film & Translation 20%. Unsolicited
material welcome. Presentation must be professional and should include brief summary of
plot/characters ('avoid a reviewer's point of
view when describing plot'), one or two sample
chapters, personal credentials and targeted
market, all suitable for forwarding to a publisher.
Send by regular mail, not e-mail. No reading fee.
Requests exclusivity while reading and information if material has been circulated. Charges
for photocopying, postage expenses, telephone
calls and other direct costs. Principal agent is
an attorney and former publisher (a founder of
Bantam Books, Corgi Books, London). Offers
consultation service through which writers
can get advice on a contract or on publishing
problems.

Doris S. Michaels
Literary Agency Inc.*

1841 Broadway, Suite 903, New York
NY 10023
☎001 212 265 9474 Fax 001 212 265 9480
✉ query@dsmagency.com
www.dsmagency.com

Contact *Doris Michaels*

Handles literary fiction that has a commercial
appeal and strong screen potential and women's
fiction; non-fiction: current affairs, biography
and memoirs, self-help, humour, history, health,
classical music, sports, women's issues, social

sciences and pop culture. No action/adven-
ture, suspense, science fiction, romance, New
Age, religion/spirituality, gift books, art books,
fantasy, thrillers, mysteries, westerns, occult and
supernatural, horror, historical fiction, poetry,
children's literature, humour or travel books.
COMMISSION Home 15% Send query letter via
e-mail with a one-page synopsis and include
a short paragraph detailing credentials. No
reading fee. .

Howard Morhaim
Literary Agency*

30 Pierrepont Street, Brooklyn NY 11201
☎001 718 222 8400 Fax 001 718 222 5056

Contact *Howard Morhaim*

Founded 1979. Handles general adult and young
adult fiction and non-fiction. No scripts poetry
or religious. COMMISSION Home 15%; UK &
Translation 20%. OVERSEAS ASSOCIATES worldwide. Send query letter with synopsis and sample
chapters for fiction; query letter with outline or
proposal for non-fiction. Include return postage.
No unsolicited mss. No reading fee.

Henry Morrison, Inc.

PO Box 235, Bedford Hills NY 10507–0235
☎001 914 666 3500 Fax 001 914 241 7846
✉ hmorrison1@aol.com

Contact *Henry Morrison*

Founded 1965. Handles general fiction, crime
and science fiction, and non-fiction. No scripts
unless by established writers. COMMISSION Home
15%; UK & Translation 25%. Unsolicited material welcome but send query letter with outline
(1–5 pp) in the first instance. No reading fee.

The Jean V. Naggar
Literary Agency*

216 East 75th Street, Suite 1-E, New York City
NY 10021

Contacts *Jean Naggar, Alice Tasman, Mollie Glick,*
    Jennifer Weltz, Jessica Regel

Founded 1978. Handles strong mainstream
fiction, literary fiction, memoir, biography,
sophisticated self-help, popular science and
psychology. No scripts. COMMISSION Home
15%; Foreign 20%. No unsolicited material; send
query letter *only* with return postage initially.
No reading fee.

B.K. Nelson Literary Agency

84 Woodland Road, Pleasantville NY 10570
☎001 914 741 1322 Fax 001 914 741 1324
✉ bknelson4@cs.com

www.bknelson.com

Also at: 1565 Paseo Vida, Palm Springs, CA 92264

☎ 001 760 880 8800 Fax 001 914 741 1324

President *Bonita K. Nelson*
Vice President *Leonard 'Chip' Ashbach*
Editorial Director *John W. Benson*

Founded 1979. Specialises in novels, business, self-help, how-to, political, autobiography, celebrity biography. Major motion picture and TV documentary success. COMMISSION 20%. Lecture Bureau for Authors founded 1994; Foreign Rights Catalogue established 1995; BK Nelson Infomercial Marketing Co. 1996, primarily for authors and endorsements, and BKNelson, Inc. for motion picture production in 1998. Signatory to Writers Guild of America, West (WGAW). No unsolicited mss. Letter of inquiry. Reading fee charged.

New England Publishing Associates, Inc.★

PO Box 5, Chester CT 06412
☎001 860 345 7323 Fax 001 860 345 3660
✉ nepa@nepa.com
www.nepa.com

Contacts *Elizabeth Frost-Knappman, Edward W. Knappman, Victoria S. Harlow* (photo/research editor)

Founded 1983. Handles non-fiction. Specialises in current affairs, business, history, science, women's studies, reference, psychology, politics, biography, true crime and literature. No textbooks or anthologies. No scripts, poetry or fiction. COMMISSION Home 15%. Unsolicited mss considered but query letter or phone call preferred first. No reading fee.

Richard Parks Agency★

PO Box 693, Salem NY 12865
☎001 518 854 9466 Fax 001 518 854 9466
✉ rp@richardparksagency.com

Contact *Richard Parks*

Founded 1989. Handles general trade fiction and non-fiction: literary novels, mysteries and thrillers, commercial fiction, science fiction, biography, pop culture, psychology, self-help, parenting, medical, cooking, gardening, history, etc. No scripts. No technical or academic. COMMISSION Home 15%; UK & Translation 20%. OVERSEAS ASSOCIATES **The Marsh Agency**; **Barbara Levy Literary Agency**. No unsolicited mss. Fiction read by referral only. Non-

fiction query with s.a.e. Faxed or e-mail queries will *not* be considered. No reading fee.

Alison J. Picard Literary Agent

PO Box 2000, Cotuit MA 02635
☎001 508 477 7192
Fax 001 508 477 7192 (notify before faxing)
✉ ajpicard@aol.com

Contact *Alison Picard*

Founded 1985. Handles mainstream and literary fiction, contemporary and historical romance, children's and young adult, mysteries and thrillers; plus non-fiction. No short stories or poetry. Rarely any science fiction and fantasy. Particularly interested in expanding non-fiction titles. COMMISSION 15%. OVERSEAS ASSOCIATE **John Pawsey**, UK. Approach with written query. No reading fee.

Pinder Lane & Garon-Brooke Associates Ltd★

159 West 53rd Street, Suite 14–C, New York NY 10019
☎001 212 489 0880 Fax 001 212 489 7104

Owner Agents *Dick Duane, Robert Thixton*

Founded 1951. Fiction and non-fiction. No category romance, westerns or mysteries. COMMISSION Home 15%; Dramatic 10–15%; Foreign 30%. OVERSEAS ASSOCIATES **Abner Stein**, UK; Translation: Rights Unlimited. No unsolicited mss. First approach by query letter. No reading fee.

PMA Literary & Film Management, Inc.

PO Box 1817, Old Chelsea Station, New York NY 10013
☎001 212 929 1222 Fax 001 212 206 0238
✉ queries@pmalitfilm.com
www.pmalitfilm.com

President *Peter Miller*

Founded 1976. Commercial fiction and non-fiction. Specialises in books with motion picture and television potential, and in true crime. No poetry, pornography, non-commercial or academic. COMMISSION Home 15%; Dramatic 10–15%; Foreign 20–25%. No unsolicited mss. Approach by letter with one-page synopsis.

The Aaron M. Priest Literary Agency★

708 Third Avenue, 23rd Floor, New York NY 10017
☎001 212 818 0344 Fax 001 212 373 9417

Founded 1974. Handles literary and commercial

fiction. No scripts, children's fantasy or sci-fi. Submissions by mail only. No reading fee.

Susan Ann Protter Literary Agent★

110 West 40th Street, Suite 1408, New York NY 10018
☎001 212 840 0480 Fax 001 212 840 1132
✉ sapla@aol.com
geocities.com/sapla2000

Contact *Susan Ann Protter*

Founded 1971. Handles general fiction, mysteries, thrillers, science fiction and fantasy; non-fiction: history, general reference, biography, science, health, current affairs and parenting. No romance, poetry, westerns, religious, children's or sport manuals. No scripts. COMMISSION Home & Dramatic 15%. OVERSEAS ASSOCIATES **Abner Stein**, UK; agents in all major markets. First approach with letter, including IRCs. No reading fee.

Quicksilver Books, Literary Agents

508 Central Park Avenue, Suite 5101, Scarsdale NY 10583
☎001 914 722 4664 Fax 001 914 722 4664
✉ quickbooks@optonline.net

President *Bob Silverstein*

Founded 1973. Handles literary fiction and mainstream commercial fiction: blockbuster, suspense, thriller, contemporary, mystery and historical; and general non-fiction, including self-help, psychology, holistic healing, ecology, environmental, biography, fact crime, New Age, health, nutrition, cookery, enlightened wisdom and spirituality. No scripts, science fiction and fantasy, pornography, children's or romance. COMMISSION Home & Dramatic 15%; Translation 20%. UK material being submitted must have universal appeal for the US market. Unsolicited material welcome but must be accompanied by IRCs for response, together with biographical details, covering letter, etc. No reading fee.

Raines & Raines★

103 Kenyon Road, Medusa NY 12120
☎001 518 239 8311 Fax 001 518 239 6029

Contacts *Theron Raines, Joan Raines, Keith Korman*

Founded 1961. Handles general non-fiction. No scripts. COMMISSION Home 15%; Foreign & Translation 20%. No unsolicited material; send one-page letter in the first instance. No reading fee.

Helen Rees Literary Agency★

376 North Street, Boston MA 02113–2103
☎001 617 227 9014 Fax 001 617 227 8762
✉ reesagency@reesagency.com

Contact *Helen Rees*
Associates *Ann Collette, Lorin Rees*

Founded 1982. Specialises in books on health and business; also handles biography, autobiography and history; quality fiction. No scholarly or technical books. No scripts, science fiction, children's, poetry, photography, short stories, cookery. COMMISSION Home 15%; Foreign 20%. No unsolicited mss; no e-mail queries or attachments. Send query letter with IRCs. No reading fee.

Rights Unlimited, Inc.★

6 West 37th Street, 4th Floor, New York NY 10018
☎001 212 246 0900 Fax 001 212 246 2114
✉ submissions@rightsunlimited.com

Contact *Diane Dreher*

Founded 1985. Handles adult fiction, non-fiction. No scripts, poetry, short stories, educational or literary works. COMMISSION Home & Translation 20%. Query letter with synopsis preferred in the first instance. No reading fee.

The Angela Rinaldi Literary Agency★

PO Box 7877, Beverly Hills CA 90212–7877
☎001 310 842 7665 Fax 001 310 837 8143
✉ amr@rinaldiliterary.com

Contact *Angela Rinaldi*
Associate *Lisa Cron*

Founded 1995. Handles commercial and literary fiction; narrative non-fiction, practical and pro-active self-help, memoir. No scripts, cookery, science fiction, westerns, romance, poetry, children's/young adult. COMMISSION Home 15%; Foreign 20%. Send brief e-mail or query letter with return postage in the first instance. No reading fee.

Ann Rittenberg Literary Agency, Inc.★

30 Bond Street, New York NY 10012
☎001 212 684 6936 Fax 001 212 684 6929
www.rittlit.com

Contacts *Ann Rittenberg, Penn Whaling*

Founded 1991. Handles literary fiction, serious narrative non-fiction, biography/memoir, cultural history, upmarket women's fiction and thrillers. No scripts, romance, science fiction, self-help, inspirational and nothing at genre level. COMMISSION Home 15%; Foreign 20%. Send query letter, sample chapters and synopses by post; no e-mails. Enclose s.a.e. No reading fee.

B.J. Robbins Literary Agency★
5130 Bellaire Avenue, North Hollywood CA 91607
☎001 818 760 6602
✉ robbinsliterary@aol.com

Contact *B.J. Robbins*

Founded 1992. Handles literary fiction, narrative and general non-fiction. No scripts, genre fiction, romance, horror, science fiction or children's books. COMMISSION Home 15%; Foreign & Translation 20%. OVERSEAS ASSOCIATES **Abner Stein** and **The Marsh Agency**, UK. Send covering letter with first three chapters or e-mail query in the first instance. No reading fee.

Linda Roghaar
Literary Agency, Inc.★
133 High Point Drive, Amherst MA 01002
☎001 413 256 1921
✉ info@LindaRoghaar.com
www.lindaroghaar.com

Contact *Linda L. Roghaar*

Founded 1997. Handles fiction and non-fiction, specialising in religious titles. No romance, science fiction or horror. COMMISSION Home 15%; Foreign & Translation rate varies. Send query by e-mail or letter with return postage (for fiction, include the first five pages). No reading fee.

The Rosenberg Group★
23 Lincoln Avenue, Marblehead MA 01945
☎001 781 990 1341 Fax 001 781 990 1344
www.rosenberggroup.com

Contact *Barbara Collins Rosenberg*

Founded 1998. Handles non-fiction (please see website for areas of interest), fiction, specialising in romance (single title and category) and women's; non-fiction, specialising in college textbooks. No scripts, science fiction, true crime, inspirational fiction, children's and young adult. COMMISSION Home 15%; Foreign 25%. No unsolicited material; send query letter by post only. No reading fee.

Rosenstone/Wender★
38 East 29th Street, 10th Floor, New York NY 10016
☎001 212 725 9445 Fax 001 212 725 9447

Contacts *Phyllis Wender, Susan Perlman Cohen, Sonia E. Pabley*

Founded 1981. Handles fiction, non-fiction, children's, and scripts for film, TV and theatre. No material for radio. COMMISSION Home 15%; Dramatic 10%; Foreign 20%. No unsolicited mss. Send letter outlining the project, credits, etc. No reading fee.

The Sagalyn Literary Agency★
4922 Fairmont Avenue, Suite 200, Bethesda MD 20814
☎001 301 718 6440 Fax 001 301 718 6444
✉ info@sagalyn.com
www.sagalyn.com

Founded 1980. Handles mostly upmarket nonfiction with some fiction. No screenplays, romance, science fiction/fantasy, children's literature. No unsolicited material. See website for submissions procedure. No reading fee.

Victoria Sanders
& Associates LLC★
241 Avenue of the Americas, Suite 11H, New York NY 10014
☎001 212 633 8811 Fax 001 212 633 0525
✉ queriesvsa@hotmail.com
www.victoriasanders.com

Contacts *Victoria Sanders, Diane Dickensheid*

Founded 1993. Handles general trade fiction and non-fiction, plus ancillary film and television rights. COMMISSION Home & Dramatic 15%; Translation 20%. Please send all queries via e-mail.

Jack Scagnetti Talent &
Literary Agency
5118 Vineland Avenue, Suite 102, North Hollywood CA 91601
☎001 818 762 3871
www.jackscagnetti.com

Contact *Jack Scagnetti*

Founded 1974. Works mostly with established/published authors. Handles non-fiction, fiction, film and TV scripts. No reading fee. COMMISSION Home & Dramatic 10% (scripts), 15% (books); Foreign 15%.

Schiavone Literary Agency, Inc.
Corporate Offices: 236 Trails End, West Palm Beach FL 33413–2135
☎001 561 966 9294 Fax 001 561 966 9294
✉ profschia@aol.com
www.publishersmarketplace.com/members/profschia

New York branch office: 3671 Hudson Manor Terrace, Suite 11H, Bronx, NY 10463
☎/Fax 001 718 548 5332
CEO *James Schiavone* (Florida office)
President *Jennifer Duvall* (New York; jendu77@aol.com)
Founded 1996. Handles fiction and non-fiction (all genres). Specialises in biography, autobiography, celebrity memoirs. No poetry. COMMISSION Home 15%; Foreign & Translation 20%. OVERSEAS ASSOCIATES in Europe and Asia. No unsolicited mss; send query letter only with s.a.e. and IRCs. No response without s.a.e. For fastest response, e-mail queries of one page (no attachments) are acceptable and encouraged. No reading fee.

Susan Schulman, A Literary Agency★

454 West 44th Street, New York NY 10036
☎001 212 713 1633 Fax 001 212 581 8830
Submissions Editor (books) *Emily Uhry*
Submissions Editor (plays) *Linda Migalti*
Rights & Permissions Editor *Eleanora Tevis*
Founded 1979. Specialises in non-fiction of all types but particularly in health and psychology-based self-help for men, women and families. Other interests include business, memoirs, the social sciences, biography, language and international law. Fiction interests include contemporary fiction, including women's, mysteries, historical and thrillers 'with a cutting edge'. Always looking for 'something original and fresh'. Represents properties for film and theatre, and works with agents in appropriate territories for translation rights. COMMISSION Home & Dramatic 15%; Translation 20%. OVERSEAS ASSOCIATES Plays: **Rosica Colin Ltd** and **The Agency Ltd**, UK; Commercial fiction: Laura Morris, UK. No unsolicited mss. Query first, including outline and three sample chapters with IRCs. No reading fee.

Scovil Chichak Galen Literary Agency, Inc.★

276 Fifth Avenue, Suite 708, New York NY 10001
☎001 212 679 8686 Fax 001 212 679 6710
✉ info@scglit.com
www.scglit.com
Contacts *Russell Galen, Anna M. Ghosh, Jack Scovil*
Founded 1993. Handles all categories of books. No scripts. COMMISSION Home 15%; Foreign

20%. No unsolicited material; send query by e-mail or letter. No reading fee.

Scribblers House® LLC Literary Agency

PO Box 1007 Cooper Station, New York NY 10276–1007
✉ query@scribblershouse.net
www.scribblershouse.net
Agents *Stedman Mays, Garrett Gambino*
Founded 2003 by Stedman Mays, founding member of Clausen, Mays & Tahan Literary Agency. Handles health, medical, diet, nutrition, the brain, psychology, self-help, how-to, business, personal finance, memoirs, biography, history, politics, writing books, language, relationships, sex, pop culture, spirituality, gender issues, parenting. No fiction, young adult or screenplays. COMMISSION 15%. Send e-mail query letter with brief description of the book, what's fresh and new about it, and a brief author biog including credentials for writing it. Consult the website for more submission information.

Rosalie Siegel, International Literary Agency, Inc.★

1 Abey Drive, Pennington NJ 08534
☎001 609 737 1007 Fax 001 609 737 3708
Contact *Rosalie Siegel*
Founded 1978. A one-woman, highly selective agency that takes on only a limited number of new projects. Handles fiction and non-fiction (especially narrative). Specialises in French history and literature; Europe in general; American history, social history. No science fiction, photography, illustrated art books or children's. COMMISSION Home 15%; Foreign 20%. OVERSEAS ASSOCIATE **Louise Greenberg**, UK; plus associates worldwide. No unsolicited material; send query letter citing background, previously published books and brief description of current book. Include return postage. No reading fee.

Michael Snell Literary Agency

PO Box 1206, Truro MA 02666–1206
☎001 508 349 3718
President *Michael Snell*
Vice President *Patricia Smith*
Founded 1980. Adult non-fiction, especially psychology, health, parenting, science, business and women's issues. Specialises in business and pet and animal books (professional and reference to popular trade how-to); general how-to and self-help on all topics, from diet and exercise to

parenting, relationships, health, sex, psychology, personal finance, and dogs, cats and horses, plus literary and suspense fiction. COMMISSION Home 15%. No unsolicited mss. Send outline and sample chapter with return postage for reply. No reading fee for outlines. Brochure available on how to write a book proposal. Model proposal also for sale directly to prospective clients. Author of *From Book Idea to Bestseller*, published by Prima. Rewriting, developmental editing, collaborating and ghostwriting services available on a fee basis. Send IRCs.

Spectrum Literary Agency★

320 Central Park West, Suite 1-D, New York NY 10025
☎001 212 362 4323
www.spectrumliteraryagency.com

President and Agent *Eleanor Wood*
Agent *Lucienne Diver*

Founded 1976. Handles science fiction, fantasy, mystery, suspense and romance. No scripts. Not interested in self-help, New Age, religious fiction/non-fiction, children's books, poetry, short stories, gift books or memoirs. COMMISSION Home 15%; Translation 20%. Send query letter in first instance with s.a.e. Faxed or electronic submissions are not accepted. No reading fees.

The Spieler Agency

154 West 57th Street, Room 135, New York NY 10019
☎001 212 757 4439

The Spieler Agency/West, 4096 Piedmont Avenue, Oakland, CA 94611
☎ 001 510 985 1422 Fax 001 510 985 1323

Contacts *Joseph Spieler, John Thornton, Dierdre Mullane* (NY); *Victoria Shoemaker* (Oakland)

Founded 1980. Handles literary fiction and non-fiction. No how-to, genre romance, humour or science fiction. Specialises in history, science, ecology, social and political issues and business. No scripts. COMMISSION Home 15%; Translation 20%. OVERSEAS ASSOCIATES **Abner Stein**; **The Marsh Agency**, UK. Approach in writing with IRCs. No reading fee.

Philip G. Spitzer
Literary Agency, Inc.★

50 Talmage Farm Lane, East Hampton NY 11937
☎001 631 329 3650 Fax 001 631 329 3651

Contact *Philip Spitzer*

Founded 1969. Works mostly with established/published authors. Specialises in general non-

fiction and fiction – thrillers. COMMISSION Home & Dramatic 15%; Foreign 20%. No reading fee for outlines.

Gloria Stern Agency

12535 Chandler Boulevard, Suite 3, North Hollywood CA 91607
☎001 818 508 6296 Fax 001 818 508 6296

Contact *Gloria Stern*

Founded 1984. Handles film scripts, genre (romance, detective, thriller and sci-fi) and mainstream fiction; electronic media. Accepts interactive material, games and electronic data. COMMISSION Home 15%; Offshore 20%. Currently not accepting unsolicited material. Fee required for critique.

Stimola Literary Studio, LLC★

306 Chase Court, Edgewater NJ 07020
☎001 201 945 9353 Fax 001 201 945 9353
✉ LtryStudio@aol.com

Contact *Rosemary B. Stimola*

Founded 1997. Handles children's books – preschool through young adult – fiction and non fiction. Specialises in picture books, middle/young adult novels. No adult fiction. COMMISSION Home 15%; Foreign 20%. No unsolicited material; send query e-mail (no attachments). No reading fee.

Barbara W. Stuhlmann
Author's Representative

PO Box 276, Becket MA 01223–0276
☎001 413 623 5170

Contact *Barbara Ward Stuhlmann*

Founded 1954. COMMISSION Home 10%; Foreign 15%; Translation 20%. Query first with IRCs, including sample chapters and synopsis of project. No reading fee. 'No new clients at this time.'

Mary M. Tahan
Literary Agency LLC★

PO Box 1015, New York NY 10276–1015
☎001 646 375 2483

Contact *Mary M. Tahan*

Founded 2004 by Mary M. Tahan who is also co-owner of Clausen, Mays & Tahan Literary Agency since 1997. Specialises in mainstream commercial fiction: thrillers, suspense, romance, mysteries, science fiction; narrative non-fiction: history, biography, autobiography, heroic true stories, entrepreneurial business books, health and nutrition (prospective authors must have expertise in their field). No scripts, children's, fundamental religious, humour. COMMISSION Home 15%; Foreign 25%. For non-fiction submissions send proposal and sample chapters; for fiction, synopsis and first three chapters. Include s.a.e for return of material. Initial approach should be by e-mail or post; no phone calls.

Roslyn Targ Literary Agency, Inc.★

105 West 13th Street, Suite 15-E, New York NY 10011
☎001 212 206 9390 Fax 001 212 989 6233
✉ roslyn@roslyntargagency.com

Contact *Roslyn Targ*

Founded 1970. Handles non-fiction, particularly biography, self-help, and literary fiction. No screenplays or cookbooks. COMMISSION Home 15%; Foreign 20%. No unsolicited material; send query e-mail or letter describing the work. No reading fee.

Patricia Teal Literary Agency★

2036 Vista del Rosa, Fullerton CA 92831
☎001 714 738 8333 Fax 001 714 738 8333

Contact *Patricial Teal*

Founded 1978. Handles women's fiction: series and single-title works; commercial and popular non-fiction. Specialises in romantic fiction. No scripts, science fiction, fantasy, horror, academic texts. COMMISSION Home 15%; Foreign 20%. No unsolicited material. Send query letter with s.a.e. in the first instance. No reading fee.

S©ott Treimel NY★

434 Lafayette Street, New York NY 10003
☎001 212 505 8353 Fax 001 212 505 0664

Founded 1995. Handles children's books only, from concept/board books to teen fiction. No picture book texts or filmscripts. COMMISSION Home 15%; Foreign 20%. No unsolicited material. 'Not accepting anyone unless recommended by professional authors or editors.' No reading fee.

2M Communications Ltd★

121 West 27th Street, Suite 601, New York NY 10001
☎001 212 741 1509 Fax 001 212 691 4460
✉ morel@bookhaven.com
www.2mcommunications.com

Contact *Madeleine Morel*

Founded 1982. Specialises in representing ghostwriters. No unsolicited mss; send letter with sample pages and IRCs. No reading fee.

Wales Literary Agency, Inc.★

PO Box 9428, Seattle WA 98109–0428
☎001 206 284 7114
✉ waleslit@waleslit.com
www.waleslit.com

Contacts *Elizabeth Wales, Neal Swain*

Founded 1988. Handles quality fiction and non-fiction. No genre fiction, westerns, romance, science fiction or horror. Special interest in 'Pacific Rim', West Coast and Pacific Northwest stories. COMMISSION Home 15%; Dramatic & Translation/Foreign 20%. No unsolicited mss; send query letter with publication list and writing sample. No e-mail queries longer than one page and no attachments. No reading fee.

John A. Ware Literary Agency

392 Central Park West, New York NY 10025
☎001 212 866 4733 Fax 001 212 866 4734

Contact *John Ware*

Founded 1978. Specialises in non-fiction: biography, history, current affairs, investigative journalism, science, nature, inside looks at phenomena, medicine and psychology (academic credentials required). No personal memoirs. Also handles literary fiction, mysteries/thrillers, sport, oral history, Americana and folklore. COMMISSION Home & Dramatic 15%; Foreign 20%. Unsolicited mss not read. Send query letter first with IRCs to cover return postage. No reading fee.

The Wendy Weil Agency, Inc.★

232 Madison Avenue, Suite 1300, New York NY 10016
☎001 212 685 0030 Fax 001 212 685 0765
✉ wweil@wendyweil.com
www.wendyweil.com

Agents *Wendy Weil, Emily Forland*
Associate/Assistant *Emma Patterson*

Founded 1986. Handles fiction (commercial and literary), non-fiction (journalism, memoirs, etc.). No scripts, science fiction, romance, visual books, self-help, cookery. OVERSEAS ASSOCIATES **David Higham Associates**; Paul & Peter Fritz Agency. Send query letter with synopsis. No reading fee.

Cherry Weiner Literary Agency

28 Kipling Way, Manalapan NJ 07726
☎001 732 446 2096 Fax 001 732 792 0506

Contact *Cherry Weiner*

Founded 1977. Handles all types of fiction: science fiction and fantasy, mainstream, romance, mystery, westerns. COMMISSION 15%. No submissions except through referral. No reading fee.

Rhoda Weyr Agency
See **Dunham Literary Agency**

Wieser & Elwell, Inc.★
80 Fifth Avenue, Suite 1101, New York
NY 10011
☎001 212 260 0860
President *Jake Elwell*
Founded 1976. Works mostly with established/published authors. Specialises in literary and mainstream fiction, serious and popular historical fiction, and general non-fiction. No poetry, children's, science fiction or religious. COMMISSION Home & Dramatic 15%; Foreign 20%. No unsolicited mss. First approach by letter with IRCs. No reading fee for outlines.

Ann Wright Representatives
165 West 46th Street, Suite 1105, New York
NY 10036–2501
☎001 212 764 6770 Fax 001 212 764 5125
Contact Dan Wright
Founded 1961. Specialises in material with strong film potentical. Handles screenplays and novels, drama and fiction. No academic, scientific or scholarly. COMMISSION Literary 10–20%; Screenplays 10% of gross. Approach by letter; no reply without IRCs. Include outline and credits only. 'Has reputation for encouraging new writers.' No reading fee. Signatory to the Writers Guild of America Agreement.

Writers House, LLC.★
21 West 26th Street, New York NY 10010
☎001 212 685 2400 Fax 001 212 685 1781
www.writershouse.com
Contacts *Albert Zuckerman, Amy Berkower,*

Merrilee Heifetz, Susan Cohen, Susan Ginsburg, Robin Rue, Simon Lipskar, Steven Malk, Jodi Reamer, Dan Lazar, Rebecca Sherman, Ken Wright
Founded 1974. Handles all types of fiction, including children's and young adult, plus narrative non-fiction: history, biography, popular science, pop and rock culture as well as how-to, business and finance, and New Age. Specialises in popular and literary fiction, women's novels, thrillers and children's. No scripts. No professional or scholarly. COMMISSION Home & Dramatic 15%; Foreign 20%. Albert Zuckerman is author of *Writing the Blockbuster Novel*, published by Little, Brown & Co. and Warner Paperbacks. For consideration of unsolicited mss, send one-page letter of enquiry, 'explaining why your book is wonderful, briefly what it's about and outlining your writing background'. No reading fee.

Susan Zeckendorf Associates, Inc.★
171 West 57th Street, Suite 11B, New York
NY 10019
☎001 212 245 2928
Contact Susan Zeckendorf
Founded 1979. Handles non-fiction of all kinds: self help, social history, biography; fiction. No scripts, romance, science fiction or children's books. COMMISSION Home 15%; Foreign & Translation 20%. ASSOCIATES Rosemarie Buckman (translation); **Abner Stein**, UK. No unsolicited material; send query letter with s.a.e. in the first instance. No reading fee.

AGENCY CONSULTANTS

Agent Research & Evaluation, Inc. (AR&E)
See entry under *Agency Consultants* (p. 224)

US Media Contacts in the UK

ABC News Intercontinental Inc.
3 Queen Caroline Street, London W6 9PE
☎020 8222 5000 Fax 020 8222 5020
Director of News Coverage, Europe, Middle East & Africa *Marcus Wilford*

The Associated Press
12 Norwich Street, London EC4A 1BP
☎020 7353 1515 Fax 020 7353 8118 (news)
Vice President – Global Business for Europe, Africa & Middle East *Barry Renfrew*

The Baltimore Sun
11 Kensington Court Place, London W8 5BJ
☎020 7460 2200
Bureau Chief *Todd Richissin*

Bloomberg News
City Gate House, 39–45 Finsbury Square, London EC2A 1PQ
☎020 7330 7500 Fax 020 7330 7797
Print – London Bureau Chief *Chris Collins*

Business Week
20 Canada Square, Canary Wharf, London E14 5LH
☎020 7176 6060 Fax 020 7176 6070
Bureau Chief *Stanley Reed*

Canadian Broadcasting Corporation
43/51 Great Titchfield Street, London W1P 8DD
☎020 7412 9200 Fax 020 7412 9226
London Bureau Manager *Ann Macmillan*

CBS News
68 Knightsbridge, London SW1X 7LL
☎020 7581 4801 Fax 020 7581 4431
Deputy Bureau Chief *Laura Dubowski*

Chicago Tribune Press Service
116 Brompton Road, London SW3 1JJ
☎020 7225 0345 Fax 020 7225 0345
Chief European Correspondent *Tom Hundley*

CNBC
10 Fleet Place, Limeburner Lane, London EC4M 7QS
☎020 7653 9451 Fax 020 7653 9393
Assignments Editor *Jennifer Callegher*

CNN International
See entry under **Television and Radio**

Dow Jones Newswires
10 Fleet Place, Limeburner Lane, London EC4M 7QN
☎020 7842 9300
Editor (Europe, Middle East, Africa) *Jan Boucek*

Fairchild Publications of New York
20 Shorts Gardens, London WC2H 9AU
☎020 7240 0420
Bureau Chief *Samantha Conti*

Forbes Magazine
Malta House, 36/38 Picadilly, London W1J 0DP
☎020 7534 3900
Managing Director & Publisher (Europe, Middle East & Africa) *Bob Crozier*

Fortune
Brettenham House, Lancaster Place, London WC2E 7TL
☎020 7322 1000
Europe Editor *Nelson Schwartz*

Fox News Channel
6 Centaurs Business Park, Grant Way, Isleworth TW7 5QD
☎020 7805 7143 Fax 020 7805 1111
Bureau Chief *Scott Norvell*

The Globe and Mail
6 Holly Mount, London NW3 6SG
☎020 7697 9820
Bureau Chief *Doug Saunders*

International Herald Tribune
40 Marsh Wall, London E14 9TP
☎020 7510 5718 Fax 020 7987 3470
London Correspondent *Eric Pfanner*

See entry under *National Newspapers*

Los Angeles Times
Moreau House, 116–118 Brompton Road,
London SW3 1JJ
☎020 7823 7315 Fax 020 7823 7308
Bureau Chief *Kim Murphy*

Market News International
Ocean House, 10–12 Little Trinity Lane,
London EC4A 2AR
☎020 7634 1655 Fax 020 7236 7122
✉ ukeditorial@marketnews.com
Senior UK Political Correspondent *David
Robinson*

National Public Radio
Room G-10 East Wing, Bush House, Strand,
London WC2B 4PH
☎020 7557 1087 Fax 020 7379 6486
Bureau Chief *Robert Gifford*

NBC News
4th Floor, 3 Shortlands, Hammersmith, London
W6 8HX
☎020 8600 6600 Fax 020 8600 6601
Bureau Chief *Chris Hampson*

The New York Times
66 Buckingham Gate, London SW1E 6AU
☎020 7799 5050 Fax 020 7799 2962
Acting Bureau Chief *Alan Cowell*

Newsweek
Academy House, 36 Poland Street, London
W1F 7LU
☎020 7851 9750 Fax 020 7851 9762
Bureau Chief *Stryker McGuire*

People Magazine
Brettenham House, Lancaster Place, London
WC2E 7TL
☎020 7322 1000
Bureau Chief *Simon Perry*

Reader's Digest Association Ltd
11 Westferry Circus, Canary Wharf, London
E14 4HE
☎020 7715 8000
European Bureau Chief *Robert Low*
See entries under **UK Publishers** and
Magazines

Time
Bureau Chief *Jef McAllister*
See entry under *Magazines*

Voice of America
London News Centre, 167 Fleet Street,
London EC4A 2EA
☎020 7410 0960
Bureau Chief *Michael Drudge*

Wall Street Journal
10 Fleet Place, Limeburner Lane, London
EC4M 7QN
☎020 7842 9200
London Bureau Chief *Paul Beckett*

Washington Post
Flat 3, 55–56 Hampstead High Street, London
NW3 1QH
☎020 7433 8094
Bureau Chiefs *Mary Jordan, Kevin Sullivan*

US Writers' Courses

In general, courses are open to students from overseas though the financial aid situation varies for international students.

Arizona
University of Arizona
MFA Program in Creative Writing, Department of English, Modern Languages 445, PO Box 210067, Tucson AZ 95721–0067
☎001 520 621 3880
✉ mcooksey@english.arizona.edu
cwp.web.arizona.edu

Established in 1974, the MFA in *Creative Writing* is a two-year programme with concentrations in Poetry, Fiction and Creative Non-Fiction. 'It boasts a faculty of 14 distinguished writers who share an uncommon commitment to teaching and supporting their students in the completion of publishable manuscripts.'

Arkansas
University of Arkansas
Programs in Creative Writing & Translation, Department of English, 333 Kimpel Hall, Fayetteville AR 72701
✉ mfa@uark.edu
www.uark.edu/depts/english/PCWT.html

MFA in *Creative Writing*, offering small, intensive workshops and innovative classes in fiction and poetry.

California
American Film Institute
2021 N. Western Avenue, Los Angeles CA 90027–1657
☎001 323 856 7600 Fax 001 323 467 4578
www.afi.com

Contact *Admissions Manager*

Screenwriting at AFI focuses on narrative storytelling in an environment designed to stimulate the world of the professional screenwriter. Screenwriting Fellows in the First Year are immersed in the production process in order to learn how screenplays are visualised. Initially writing short screenplays – one of which will be the basis for a first year production – writers collaborate with Producing and Directing Fellows to see their work move from page to screen. The remainder of the first year is devoted to the completion of a feature-length screenplay. Second Year Fellows may write a second feature-length screenplay, or develop materials for television, including biopics, television movies and spec scripts for sitcoms and one-hour dramas. They also have the opportunity to work closely with other disciplines by writing a Second Year thesis script.

California Institute for the Arts
MFA Writing Program, School of Critical Studies, 24700 McBean Parkway, Valencia CA 91355–2397
☎001 661 253 7716
✉ writing@calarts.edu
www.calarts.edu/~writing

Director, Writing Program *Brighde Mullins*

The two-year MFA *Writing Programme* is rooted in principles of critical thought, experimentation and innovation. It is intended as an alternative to traditional programmes, with a founding premise that distinctions between creative and critical writing should be suspended. Students are encouraged to work across genres and often work in various multi-media forms in addition to their literary production.

Chapman University
Master of Fine Arts Degree, Dept. of English and Comparative Literature, Office of Admissions, One University Drive, Orange CA 92866
☎001 714 997 6750 Fax 001 714 997 6697
www.chapman.edu

Contact *Graduate Admissions*

Three-year Master of Fine Arts (MFA) degree in *Creative Writing* is intended for graduate students who wish to pursue writing as a career and is aimed toward publishing as well as development of writing techniques.

Saint Mary's College of California
MFA Program in Creative Writing, PO Box 4686, Moraga CA 94575–4686
☎001 925 631 4762
✉ writers@stmarys–ca.edu

www.stmarys-ca.edu

Programme Coordinator *Thomas Cooney*

Two-year MFA course in *Creative Writing* with Fiction, Non-Fiction or Poetry. The core of the programme is the Writing Workshop which provides the opportunity for students to work with established writers.

San Francisco State University

Creative Writing Department, College of Humanities, 1600 Holloway Avenue, San Francisco CA 94132

☎001 415 338 1891

✉ cwriting@sfsu.edu

www.sfsu.edu/~cwriting

Offers BA and MA in *English:* with a concentration on *Creative Writing*; and MFA in *Creative Writing*. Undergraduate classes include feature writing, short story writing, the craft of poetry and the craft of playwriting while graduate classes include advanced story writing, advanced poetry writing, advanced playwriting, experimental fiction, playwright's theatre workshop and workshops in fiction, poetry and playwriting.

University of Southern California (USC)

School of Cinematic Arts, University Park, LUC 301, Los Angeles CA 90089–2211

☎001 213 740 3303 Fax 001 213 740 8035

www-cntv.usc.edu

Offers a Bachelor of Fine Arts or Master of Fine Arts degree in *Writing for Screen and Television*. There is a strong international presence, having accepted students from over 44 countries.

Colorado
Colorado State University

Creative Writing Program, 1773 Campus Delivery, 359 Eddy Hall, Fort Collins CO 80523–1773

☎001 970 491 2403

✉ english@lamar.colostate.edu

www.colostate.edu/Depts/English/programs/mfa.htm

Contact *Assistant to the Director of Creative Writing or Director of Creative Writing*

Three-year Master of Fine Arts (MFA) programme in creative writing with concentrations in fiction or poetry. The programme offers a balance of intimate and intensive writing and translation. Course work culminates in a thesis – a collection of poetry or short stories or a novel. Students have the opportunity to teach intro-

ductory creative-writing courses, intern with literary journals including the *Colorado Review* and be a part of a thriving community.

District of Columbia
American University

Department of Literature, 237 Battelle-Tompkins, 4400 Massachusetts Avenue, N.W., Washington DC 20016–8047

☎001 202 885 2971

www.american.edu/cas/lit/mfa-lit.cfm

Contact *Kristin Toburen* (Graduate Programs Assistant)

The MFA in *Creative Writing* is a 48-credit hour programme allowing students to concentrate in Poetry, Fiction or Creative Non-Fiction. Cross-genre experimentation is encouraged. All students complete a book-length thesis before graduating in two to three years. The programme is literature intensive and also exposes students to Literary Journalism and the Art of Translation. Students can elect to follow the Internship Track or the Teaching Track. The Visiting Writers Series brings writers of international renown to the campus, often to lead a workshop.

Florida
Florida International University

English Department, Biscayne Bay Campus, 3000 NE 151st Street, North Miami FL 33181

☎001 305 919 5857

✉ crwriting@fiu.edu

www.fiu.edu/crwriting

Director *Les Standiford*

The MFA Program in *Creative Writing* includes writing workshop, literature, form and theory and thesis (most students complete the course in about three years; completion of study within eight years is required). There is no language requirement. Graduate workshops include short fiction, the novel, popular fiction, screenwriting, creative non-fiction and poetry. Great emphasis is placed upon preparation and completion of a book-length thesis. Admission is based primarily on the strength of the applicant's submitted writing sample. Application deadline: January 15.

University of West Florida

Department of English and Foreign Languages, 11000 University Parkway, Building 50, Room 211, Pensacola FL 32514

☎001 850 474 2923 Fax 001 850 474 2935

uwf.edu/english

BA in *English (Writing Specialization)*: students

who choose to develop their creative writing skills or editing can take courses in poetry, fiction, creative non-fiction, magazine writing and editing, and feature writing. *MA in English (Creative Writing Specialization)*: workshop courses in the specialisation include fiction, creative non-fiction, poetry, editing, teaching creative writing and special topics in creative writing. Students also have the opportunity to work on the literary magazine *Bayou*.

Illinois
Chicago State University
MFA Program in Creative Writing, Department of English, 9501 South King Drive, SCI 320, Chicago IL 60628
☎001 773 995 2189
www.csu.edu/GraduateSchool
Program Coordinator *Dr Kelly Norman Ellis*
Offers a two-year MFA with courses in Creative Writing; writing workshops in fiction, poetry, creative non-fiction, playwriting and scriptwriting. Students undertake coursework in African American Literature, African Literature, Third World Literature and non-Black Literature. Students will show competency in the genre of their choice, choosing from fiction, creative non-fiction and poetry.

Southern Illinois University at Carbondale
Department of English, Carbondale IL 62901–4503
☎001 618 453 6849
✉ aljoseph@siu.edu
www.siu.edu
Contact *Professor Allison Joseph*
Three-year MFA in *Creative Writing*. The programme accepts a maximum of 8–12 students each year, so workshops are small and faculty members work closely with students.

Indiana
University of Notre Dame
Creative Writing Program, Department of English, Notre Dame IN 46556
☎001 574 631 7526 Fax 001 574 631 4795
✉ creativewriting@nd.edu
www.nd.edu/~alcwp
The MFA in *Creative Writing* is a two-year degree programme centred around workshops in poetry and fiction, offering literature courses, translation, a literary publishing course and twelve credits of thesis preparation with an individual faculty adviser.

Purdue University
MFA Program in Creative Writing, Department of English, West Lafayette IN 47907
☎001 765 494 3740
www.cla.purdue.edu/mfacw
Program Director *Porter Shreve*
MFA in *Creative Writing* offering 'full funding, generous stipends and editorial experience with the award-winning literary journal *Sycamore Review*'. The three-year programme in either fiction or poetry is small and intensive and includes workshops, literature and craft courses, and thesis tutorials toward a book-length manuscript.

Taylor University
Department of English, 1025 West Rudisill Blvd, Fort Wayne IN 46807–2170
☎001 260 744 8647
✉ DNHensley@TaylorU.edu
Contact *Dr Dennis E. Hensley*
Summer Honours Programme one-week seminars in *Professional Writing*; evening courses in *Freelance Writing* and *Fiction Writing*; one year college certificate in *Professional Writing*. Dr Hensley is a professor of English and director of the professional writing major.

Louisiana
Louisiana State University
English Department, 260 Allen Hall, Baton Rouge LA 70803
☎001 225 578 4086
www.english.lsu.edu
Director of Creative Writing *James Wilcox*
Master of Fine Arts in *Creative Writing* course with a focus in Poetry, Fiction, Drama, Screenwriting. Includes opportunity to edit literary journals.

Maryland
Goucher College
Welch Center for Graduate Studies, 1021 Dulaney Valley Road, Baltimore MD 21204–2794
☎001 800 697 4646 Fax 001 410 337 6085
✉ center@goucher.edu
Program Director *Patsy Sims* (☎ 001 800 697 4646)
The two-year MFA Program in *Creative Nonfiction* is a limited-residency programme that allows students to complete most of the requirements off campus while developing their skill as non-fiction writers under the close supervision

of a faculty mentor. Provides instruction in the following areas: narrative non-fiction, literary journalism, memoir, the personal essay, travel/nature/science writing and biography/profiles.

Massachusetts
Boston University
Creative Writing Program, 236 Bay State Road, Boston MA 02215
☎001 617 353 2510 Fax 001 617 353 3653
✉ crwr@bu.edu
www.bu.edu/writing
Director *Leslie Epstein*
Contact *Matthew Yost*

One-year Master of Arts in *Creative Writing*: Fiction, Poetry or Drama. The Boston University Creative Writing Program is one of the oldest in the country. Students participate in workshops or seminars concentrating on their chosen specialisation and are expected to balance that work with an equal number of graduate literature courses. Internships at the literary journal *AGNI*, assistantships at the Boston Arts Academy, as well as teaching fellowships are available on a limited basis.

Emerson College
120 Boylston Street, Boston MA 01226–4624
☎001 617 824 8610 Fax 001 617 824 8614
✉ gradapp@emerson.edu
www.emerson.edu/graduate_admission
Graduate Program Director *Douglas Whynott*

Offers MFA in *Creative Writing* with a focus on writing fiction, non-fiction and poetry. Includes writing workshops, internship opportunities, a student reading series and student teaching opportunities. Publishes literary magazines, *Ploughshares* and *Redivider*. Contact the Graduate Admission Office for more information.

Michigan
Western Michigan University
Department of English, 1903 W. Michigan Avenue, Kalamazoo MI 49008-5331
☎001 269 387 2584
✉ gwen.tarbox@wmich.edu
www.wmich.edu/english
Director of Graduate Studies *Gwen Tarbox*

BA English Major/Minor with *Creative Writing Emphasis* (poetry, fiction, playwriting). The English Major aims at giving students intensive practice in writing and criticism in various genres in a workshop format; for general writing careers or for prospective candidates for the

MFA in Creative Writing. MFA in *Creative Writing* (poetry, fiction, playwriting, non-fiction) For students who wish to become professional writers of poetry, fiction, drama or non-fiction. Qualifies them to teach the craft at college or university level. PhD in *English, with a Creative Writing Emphasis* (poetry, fiction, playwriting, non-fiction). Qualifies students to teach creative writing and literature at university level.

Minnesota
Minnesota State University Moorhead
Graduate Studies Office, MSUM, 1104 7th Avenue South, Moorhead MN 56563
☎001 218 477 2344
✉ early@mnstate.edu
www.mnstate.edu/finearts
Program Coordinator *John Early*

MFA in *Creative Writing* (Fiction, Non-fiction, Playwriting, Poetry, Screenwriting) offers the opportunity to take workshops, seminars and tutorials in chosen areas and to work with New Rivers Press (www.newriverspress.com) or with *Red Weather*, the campus literary magazine.

Minnesota State University, Mankato
Department of English, 230 Armstrong Hall, Mankato MN 56001
☎001 507 389 2117
✉ richard.robbins@mnsu.edu
www.english.mnsu.edu/cw
Programme Director *Richard Robbins*

The MFA programme in *Creative Writing* meets the needs of students who want to strike a balance between the development of individual creative talent and the close study of literature and language. The programme gives appropriate training for careers in freelancing, college-level teaching, editing and publishing and arts administration.

Missouri
University of Missouri-Columbia
Creative Writing Program, Department of English, 107 Tate Hall, Columbia MO 65211–1500
☎011 573 884 7773
✉ creativewriting@missouri.edu
creativewriting.missouri.edu
Contact *Sharon Fisher*

Creative Writing MA and PhD in English

programmes in fiction, poetry and non-fiction. Access the website for further information.

New York

Adelphi University

MFA Program in Creative Writing, Department of English, PO Box 701, Garden City NY 11530
☎001 516 877 4020
✉ mfa@adelphi.edu
academics.adelphi.edu/artsci/creativewriting

Director of Creative Writing *Judith Baumel*

The MFA in *Creative Writing* is a cross-genre programme that offers a versatile, interdisciplinary approach to prose, poetry and playwriting. Small, single-genre workshops, literature courses, thesis and one-on-one mentoring by published authors. Through the Professional Development Practicum, students are introduced to the professional and practical life of writers in multiple disciplines. Students graduate with a major piece of work along with 'a robust and realistic awareness of what a "life in letters" entails'. Scholarship, internship and teaching opportunities.

Brooklyn College of the City University of New York

MFA Program in Creative Writing, Department of English, Brooklyn NY 11210–2889
☎001 718 951 5914
✉ profmsp@msn.com
academic.brooklyn.cuny.edu/english/
index.html

Deputy Chair for Graduate Studies *Mark Patkowski*

The MFA in *Creative Writing* is a small, highly personal two-year programme which confers degrees in fiction, poetry and playwriting. Admission is highly competitive. Students must complete 12 courses (four workshops, four tutorials and four literature courses), submit a book-length work in their chosen genre near the end of the second year and pass a comprehensive examination that tests their knowledge and expertise in literature. The workshops, seminars and one-on-one tutorials with established writers particularly emphasise relationships between instructors and students.

New York University

58 West 10th Street, New York NY 10011
✉ creative.writing@nyu.edu
www.cwp.fas.nyu.edu

Contact *Allison Brotherton*

Offers MFA in *Creative Writing* and MA in *English* with focus in *Creative Writing* in poetry and fiction. Includes writing workshops and craft courses, literary outreach programmes, a public reading series, student readings, special literary seminars and student teaching opportunities. Publishes a literary journal, *Washington Square*. Contact the department via e-mail.

North Carolina

University of North Carolina at Greensboro

MFA Writing Program, 3302 Hall for Humanities and Research Administration, UNCG, Greensboro NC 27402-6170
☎001 336 334 5459
www.uncg.edu/eng/mfa

Contact *Jim Clark*, Director

MFA in *Creative Writing (Poetry, Fiction)*. One of the oldest of its kind in the country, the MFA Writing Program at Greensboro is a two-year residency with an emphasis on providing students with studio time in which to study the writing of poetry or fiction. Gives a flexibility that permits students to develop their particular talents through small classes in writing, literature and the arts.

University of North Carolina at Wilmington

Department of Creative Writing, 601 S. College Road, Wilmington NC 28403
☎001 910 962 3070
✉ mfa@uncw.edu
www.uncw.edu/writers

Contact *MFA Coordinator*

An intensive studio-academic programme in the writing of fiction, poetry and creative non-fiction leading to either the Master of Fine Arts or Bachelor of Fine Arts degree in *Creative Writing*. Courses include workshops in the three genres, special topics and forms courses as well as a range of courses in literature. Course work in publishing and editing is also offered in the Publishing Laboratory, a university press imprint which supports local, regional and national publishing projects. The MFA programme is home to the literary journal, *Ecotune: reimagining place*.

Ohio

Bowling Green State University

Creative Writing Program, English Department, Bowling Green OH 43403
☎001 419 372 8370 Fax 001 419 372 6805

www.bgsu.edu/departments/creative-writing/
Undergraduate BFA programme: a four-year programme which offers comprehensive and rigorous training in the art of writing and develops students' skills in preparation for numerous post-graduate careers. Graduate MFA programme: a two-year studio/academic composite, mostly work in writing itself in either poetry or fiction. Also offers ten new teaching assistantships each autumn. See the website for details on both programmes.

Oregon
University of Oregon
Creative Writing Program, 5243 University of Oregon, Eugene OR 97403–5243
www.uoregon.edu

Program Director *Karen J. Ford*

Offers MFA in *Creative Writing* in poetry or fiction. Includes writing workshops, craft courses, individualised tutorials with faculty, public reading series, student readings and student teaching opportunities. Admission is highly competitive.

Philadelphia
Seton Hill University
1 Seton Hill Drive, Greensburg PA 15601
☎001 724 838 4221
✉ gadmit@setonhill.edu
www.setonhill.edu

Contact *Dane Zimmer*

The MA in *Writing Popular Fiction* programme at Seton Hill University allows students to earn a graduate degree by writing fiction that people *actually* read. Students attend week-long residencies in January and June and complete writing projects off-campus, working with a faculty mentor who is a published author in the chosen genre. Students can choose to specialise in science fiction, fantasy, horror, children's literature, romance or mystery. Programmes can be completed in 24 months.

Rhode Island
Brown University
Literary Arts, Box 1923, Providence RI 02912
☎001 401 863 3260 Fax 001 401 863 1535
✉ Writing@brown.edu
www.brown.edu/cw

Contact *Director of Literary Arts*

Two-year MFA in *Fiction, Poetry, Dramatic Writing and Electronic Writing*. Students take three workshops, four electives and one independent study (through which they complete a thesis project). Application deadline: 15 December.

Tennessee
The University of Memphis
MFA Program in Creative Writing,
Department of English, 471 Patterson Hall,
Memphis TN 38152
✉ creativewriting@memphis.edu
www.mfainmemphis.com

Contact *MFA Coordinator*

'The Writing Workshop is the premier creative writing program in the South.' Concentrations on fiction, creative non-fiction and poetry. Also features an award-winning national journal, *The Pinch* and the River City Writers Series. Students work in small groups with nationally recognised authors. Students have opportunities to teach creative writing locally and abroad.

Texas
University of Houston
Creative Writing Program, Department of English, R. Cullen 229, University of Houston, Houston TX 77204-3015
☎001 713 743 3015
✉ cwp@uh.edu
www.uh.edu

Office Coordinator *Cassandra Colbert*

Offers MFA in *Creative Writing* and PhD in *Literature and Creative Writing*. Admission is highly competitive; students can apply for admission in the genres of poetry, fiction and non-fiction. Normally admits 20 students a year. The MFA is a three-year degree programme; the PhD normally takes five years. Students take courses both in creative writing and literature. Fellowships and teaching assistantships are available. In collaboration with Inprint, it hosts the Inprint/Brown Reading series and the Inprint Studio series. The programme offers opportunities to collaborate with artists in other disciplines. Publishes a literary journal, *Gulf Coast*.

Virginia
George Mason University
English Department, MSN 3E4, 4400
University Drive, Fairfax VA 22030
☎001 703 993 1180
✉ writing@gmu.edu
creativewriting.gmu.edu

Contact *Graduate Coordinator*

The MFA in *Creative Writing* is a 48-credit hour programme with flexibility for students to tailor their studies to their interests and craft development. At least 12 hours are in writing seminars in the major genre (fiction, non-fiction or poetry), including a course in the historic forms of that genre. At least 12 hours are in literature and at least three hours are in a genre other than the concentration. Six hours are in thesis. The distribution of the remaining hours is generally up to the students with consultation from the faculty.

Hollins University

MFA in Creative Writing, Hollins University Graduate Center, PO Box 9603, Roanoke VA 24020–1603
☎001 540 362 6575 Fax 001 540 362 6288
✉ hugrad@hollins.edu
www.hollins.edu/grad

Manager, Graduate Studies *Cathy Koon*

The MFA in *Creative Writing* is a small, highly selective two-year full-time programme which allows students to specialise in poetry, fiction or both, while also offering opportunities to study and write screenplays and creative non-fiction. 'The programme is characterised by an individual approach, a lively community of writers and a stimulating combination of challenge and support.' Also offers three summer-term MA/MFA programs in *Children's/Young Adult Literature*, *Playwriting* and *Screenwriting & Film Studies*. Students typically study for three to five six-week terms.

Virginia Commonwealth University

Department of English, PO Box 842005, Richmond VA 23284–2005
☎001 804 828 1329
✉ tndidato@vcu.edu
www.has.vcu.edu/eng

Graduate Programs Coordinator *Thom Didato*

Three-year MFA in *Creative Writing* with tracks in fiction and poetry, and workshops in short fiction, the novel, poetry, drama, screenwriting and creative non-fiction. Opportunities to work with *Blackbird*: an online journal of literature and the arts (www.blackbird.vcu.edu), *Stand*

Magazine, the Levis Reading Prize and the First Novelist Award.

Washington
Eastern Washington University

Inland Northwest Center for Writers, Creative Writing, 705 W. 1st Avenue, Spokane WA 99201
☎001 509 623 4221
✉ writing@mail.ewu.edu
www.creativewriting.ewu.edu

Director *Jonathan Johnson*

The MFA Program is an intensive two-year, pre-professional course of study with an emphasis on the practice of literature as a fine art. Includes course work in the study of literature from the vantage point of its composition and history, but the student's principal work is done in advanced workshops and in the writing of a book-length thesis of publishable quality in fiction, literary non-fiction or poetry. Students have the opportunity to work as interns on several projects: the literary magazine, *Willow Springs*; the community outreach programme, Writers in the Community; and Eastern Washington University Press. The MFA is a terminal degree programme.

Wyoming
University of Wyoming

MFA in Creative Writing, Department of English – 3353, 1000 E. University Avenue, Laramie WY 82071–2000
☎001 307 766 2867
✉ cw@uwyo.edu
www.uwyo.edu/creativewriting

Contact *Kris DeForest* (Program Assistant)

The two-year Master of Fine Arts in *Creative Writing* is an intensive 40-hour studio degree in Poetry, Fiction or Creative Non-Fiction. Special features include opportunities for inter-disciplinary study, supported by a wide range of university departments, and a required professional internship on campus, in the community or further afield, ensuring the acquisition or polishing of 'real-life' writing skills.

Commonwealth Publishers

Australia

ACER Press
Private Bag 55, Camberwell,Victoria 3124
☎00 61 3 9277 5555 Fax 00 61 3 9277 5500
www.acer.edu.au
Founded 1930. Publishes education, human resources, psychology, parent education, occupational therapy.

Allen & Unwin Pty Ltd
PO Box 8500, St Leonards, Sydney, NSW 1590
☎00 61 2 8425 0100 Fax 00 61 2 9906 2218
www.allenandunwin.com
Founded 1976. Independent publisher of fiction, crime, literature; general non-fiction, academic, biography, business, children's, cookery, environment, health and nutrition, history, how-to, mind, body and spirit, military history, humanities, humour, popular science, social science, women's and men's studies, professional, reference, textbooks.

Blackwell Publishing Asia
550 Swanston Street, Carlton South, Victoria 3053
☎00 61 3 8359 1011 Fax 00 61 3 8359 1120
✉ info@blackwellpublishingasia.com
Founded 1971. Part of Blackwell Science Ltd, UK. Publishes academic books, journals and CD-ROMs; business, economics, finance, general science, humanities, law, medicine, mathematics, professional, reference, textbooks.

Currency Press Pty Ltd
PO Box 2287, Strawberry Hills, NSW 2012
☎00 61 2 9319 5877 Fax 00 61 2 9319 3649
✉ enquiries@currency.com.au
www.currency.com.au
Founded 1971. Performing arts publisher – directories and reference – drama, theatre, music, dance, film and video.

Dangaroo Press
GPO Box 1209, New Lambton, NSW 2001
☎00 61 2 4965 6851 Fax 00 61 2 4951 7430
Founded 1978. Publishes general non-fiction, art, literature, literary criticism, essays, poetry, social sciences, sociology, women's studies.

Hachette Livre Australia
Level 17, 207 Kent Street, Sydney, NSW 2000
☎00 61 2 8248 0800 Fax 00 61 2 8248 0810
www.hha.com.au
Founded 1958. Part of the **Hachette Livre Publishing Group**. Publishes popular fiction, literature, general non-fiction, autobiography, biography, current affairs, health, history, self-help, sport, travel.

HarperCollins Publishers (Australia) Pty Ltd
PO Box 321, Pymble, NSW 2073
☎00 61 2 9952 5000 Fax 00 61 2 9952 5555
www.harpercollins.com.au
Founded 1872. Part of the HarperCollins Publishers Group. Publishes fiction and non-fiction, children's and illustrated books.

Macmillan Education Australia Pty Ltd
627 Chapel Street, South Yarra,Victoria 3141
☎00 61 3 9825 1025 Fax 00 61 3 9825 1010
www.macmillan.com.au
Founded 1896. Part of **Macmillan Publishers**, UK. Educational publisher for primary and secondary schools.

McGraw-Hill Australia & New Zealand Pty Ltd
Locked Bag 2233, Business Centre, North Ryde, NSW 1670
☎00 61 2 9900 1800
www.mcgraw-hill.com.au
Founded 1964 (Australia), 1974 (NZ). Owned by **The McGraw-Hill Companies, Inc**. Publishes textbooks and educational material for primary, secondary and higher education. Also professional (medical, general and reference).

Melbourne University Publishing Ltd
187 Grattan Street, Carlton South, Victoria 3053

☎00 61 3 9342 0300 Fax 00 61 3 9342 0399
✉ mup-info@unimelb.edu.au
www.mup.unimelb.edu.au

Founded 1922. Academic publishers; general non-fiction, archaeology, architecture, art, biography, business, economics, education, finance, history, law, literature, literary criticism, military history, natural history, politics, psychology, psychiatry, reference, religion, science and technology, sociology, sport, travel.

Oxford University Press (Australia, New Zealand, Singapore & the Pacific)

GPO Box 2784, Melbourne, Victoria 3001
☎00 61 3 9934 9123 Fax 00 61 3 9934 9100
www.oup.com.au

Founded 1908. Owned by **Oxford University Press**, UK. Publishes for the college, school and trade markets.

Pan Macmillan Australia Pty Ltd

Level 25, 1 Market Street, Sydney, NSW 2000
☎00 61 2 9285 9100 Fax 00 61 2 9285 9190
www.panmacmillan.com.au

Founded 1983. Part of **Macmillan Publishers**, UK. Publishes fiction, crime fiction, thrillers, essays, literature, literary criticism; general non-fiction, adventure, biography, children's, true crime, current affairs, health and nutrition, history, humour, self-help, travel.

Pearson Education Australia Pty Ltd

Locked Bag 507, Frenchs Forest, NSW 1640
☎00 61 3 9454 2200 Fax 00 61 3 9453 0089
www.pearson.com.au

Australia's largest educational publisher, formed in 1998 from a merger of Addison Wesley Longman Australia and Prentice Hall Australia.

Penguin Group (Australia)

PO Box 701, Hawthorn, Victoria 3124
☎00 61 3 9811 2400 Fax 00 61 3 9870 6086
www.penguin.com.au

Founded 1946. Publishes adult and children's general non-fiction and fiction.

University of Queensland Press

PO Box 6042, St Lucia, Queensland 4067
☎00 61 7 3365 2127
✉ uqp@uqp.uq.edu.au
www.uqp.uq.edu.au

Founded 1948. Publishes academic, textbooks, children's and young adult, general non-fiction

and fiction, literature, literary criticism, essays, poetry, biography, gardening, history, memoirs, military history, reference, sport, travel.

Random House Australia

Level 3, 100 Pacific Highway, North Sydney, NSW 2060
☎00 61 2 9954 9966 Fax 00 61 2 9954 4562
✉ random@randomhouse.com.au
www.randomhouse.com.au

Subsidiary of **Bertelsmann AG**. Publishes fiction and non-fiction.

Scholastic Australia Pty Limited

PO Box 579, Gosford, NSW 2250
☎00 61 2 4328 3555
www.scholastic.com.au

Founded 1968. Educational publisher.

Science Press

Unit 16, 102 Edinburgh Road, Marrickville, NSW 2204
☎00 61 2 9516 1122 Fax 00 61 2 9550 1915
www.sciencepress.com.au

Founded 1948. Educational publisher.

Simon & Schuster (Australia) Pty Ltd

PO Box 33, Pymble, NSW 2073
☎00 61 2 9983 6600 Fax 00 61 2 9988 4293

Founded 1987. Part of **Simon & Schuster Inc.**, USA. Publishes fiction and general non-fiction; biography, childcare, children's, gardening, health and nutrition, history, military history.

UWA Press

University of Western Australia, 35 Stirling Highway, Crawley, WA 6009
☎00 61 8 9380 3670 Fax 00 61 8 9380 1027
✉ admin@uwapress.uwa.edu.au
www.uwapress.uwa.edu.au

Founded 1935. Publishes general non-fiction, essays, literature, literary criticism, history, natural history, children's, maritime history, reference, literary studies.

John Wiley & Sons Australia Ltd

42 McDougall Street, Milton, Queensland 4064
☎00 61 7 3859 9755 Fax 00 61 7 3859 9715
✉ brisbane@johnwiley.com.au
www.johnwiley.com.au

Founded 1954. Owned by **John Wiley & Sons Inc.**, USA. Publishes general non-fiction and education books, dictionaries, encyclopedias, maps and atlases, reference, textbooks.

Canada

Canadian Scholars' Press, Inc
180 Bloor Street W, Suite 801, Toronto,
Ontario M5S 2V6
☎001 416 929 2774 Fax 001 416 929 1926
✉ info@cspi.org
www.cspi.org
Founded 1987. Publishes academic books in
English and French.

H.B. Fenn & Company Ltd
34 Nixon Road, Bolton, Ontario L7E 1W2
☎001 905 951 6600 Fax 001 905 951 6601
www.hbfenn.com
Founded 1977. Publishes fiction and non-
fiction, children's.

Firefly Books Ltd
66 Leek Crescent, Richmond Hill,
Ontario L4B 1H1
☎001 416 499 8412 Fax 001 416 499 8313
www.fireflybooks.com
Founded 1976. Publishes children's and young
adult, encyclopedias, general non-fiction,
astronomy, cookery, crafts, gardening, health,
natural history, reference, sport, transport, travel.

Fitzhenry and Whiteside Limited
195 Allstate Parkway, Markham,
Ontario L3R 4T8
☎001 905 477 9700
✉ godwit@fitzhenry.ca
www.fitzhenry.ca
Founded 1966. Publishes reference, biography,
history, poetry, photography, sport, children's and
young adult books.

Harlequin Enterprises Ltd
225 Duncan Mill Road, Don Mills,
Ontario M3B 3K9
☎001 416 445 5860 Fax 001 416 445 8655
www.eharlequin.com
Founded 1949. Canada's second largest
publishing house. Publishes romantic and
women's fiction.

HarperCollins Canada Ltd
2 Bloor Street E, 20th Floor, Toronto,
Ontario M4W 1A8
☎001 416 975 9334 Fax 001 416 975 9884
www.harpercanada.com
Founded 1989. Publishes commerical and
literary fiction, non-fiction, children's, reference,
cookery and religious books.

LexisNexis Canada Ltd
123 Commerce Valley Drive E, Suite 700,
Markham, Ontario L3T 7W8
☎001 905 479 2665 Fax 001 905 479 2826
www.lexisnexis.ca
Founded 1912. Publishes law books, CD-ROMs,
journals, newsletters, law reports.

McClelland & Stewart Ltd
75 Sherbourne Street, Fifth Floor, Toronto,
Ontario M5A 2P9
☎001 416 598 1114 Fax 001 416 598 7764
✉ mail@mcclelland.com
www.mcclelland.com
Founded 1906. Publishes fiction and general
non-fiction, poetry.

McGraw-Hill Ryerson Ltd
300 Water Street, Whitby, Ontario L1N 9B6
☎001 905 430 5000
www.mcgrawhill.ca
Founded 1944. Subsidiary of McGraw-Hill
Education. Publishes education, professional
and medical.

New Star Books Ltd
107–3477 Commercial Street, Vancouver,
British Columbia V5N 4E8
☎001 604 738 9429 Fax 001 604 738 9332
✉ info@newstarbooks.com
www.newstarbooks.com
Founded 1974. Publishes fiction and non-
fiction, literature, poetry, government and political science, history, sociology, social sciences.

Oxford University Press, Canada
70 Wynford Drive, Don Mills,
Ontario M3C 1J9
☎001 416 441 2941 Fax 001 416 444 0427
www.oup.com/ca
Founded 1904. Owned by Oxford University
Press, UK. Publishes for college, school and
trade markets.

Pearson Canada
26 Prince Andrew Place, Toronto,
Ontario M3C 2T8
☎001 416 447 5101 Fax 001 416 443 0948
www.pearsoned.canada.ca
Founded 1966. A division of Pearson Plc and
Canada's largest publisher. Publishes fiction,
non-fiction and educational material in English
and French.

Penguin Group (Canada)

90 Eglinton Avenue East, Suite 700, Toronto,
Ontario M4P 2Y3
☎001 416 925 2249 Fax 001 416 925 0068
✉ info@penguin.ca
www.penguin.ca
Founded 1974. Publishes fiction and non-fiction books and audio cassettes.

Random House of Canada Ltd

1 Toronto Street, Unit 300, Toronto,
Ontario M5C 2V6
☎001 416 364 4449 Fax 001 416 364 6863
www.randomhouse.ca
Founded 1944. Publishes fiction and non-fiction and children's.

Scholastic Canada Ltd

175 Hillmount Road, Markham,
Ontario L6C 1Z7
☎001 905 887 7323 Fax 001 905 887 3639
www.scholastic.ca
Founded 1957. Publishes (in English and French) children's books and educational material.

Thomson Nelson

1120 Birchmount Road, Scarborough,
Ontario M1K 5G4
☎001 416 752 9448 Fax 001 416 752 8101
✉ inquire@nelson.com
www.nelson.com
Part of the Thomson Corporation. Publishes directories, education, professional, reference, textbooks.

University of Toronto Press, Inc.

10 St Mary Street, Suite 700, Toronto,
Ontario M4Y 2W8
☎001 416 978 2239
✉ info@utpress.utoronto.ca
www.utpress.utoronto.ca
Founded 1901. Publishes scholarly books and journals.

Tundra Books

75 Sherbourne Street, 5th Floor, Toronto,
Ontario M5A 2P9
☎001 416 598 4786
✉ tundra@mcclelland.com
www.tundrabooks.com
Founded 1967. Division of **McClelland & Stewart Ltd**. Publishes (in English and French) children's and young adult books.

John Wiley & Sons Canada Ltd

6045 Fremont Blvd, Mississauga,
Ontario L5R 4J3
☎001 416 236 4433
www.wiley.ca
Founded 1968. Subsidiary of **John Wiley & Sons Inc.**, USA. Publishes professional, reference and textbooks.

India

Affiliated East West Press Pvt Ltd

1/16 Ansari Road, Darya Ganj,
New Delhi 110 002
☎00 91 11 2327 9113
✉ affiliate@vsnl.com
www.aewpress.com
Founded 1962. Publishes textbooks, CD-ROMs, electronic books.

Arnold Heinemann Publishers (India) Pvt Ltd

AB-9, 1st Floor, Safdaoung Enclave,
New Delhi 110 029
☎00 91 11 2638 3422
Founded 1969. Associate company of Edward Arnold (Publishers) Ltd, UK. Publishes fiction, directories, reference and textbooks.

S. Chand & Co Ltd

7361 Ram Nagar, Qutub Road, Tourist Hotel Complex, New Delhi 110 055
☎00 91 11 2367 2080 Fax 00 91 11 2367 7446
✉ info@schandgroup.com
www.schandgroup.com
Founded 1917. Publishes computer science, dictionaries, encyclopedias, engineering, reference, textbooks.

Hind Pocket Books Pvt. Ltd

18–19 Dilshad Garden, G.T. Road, Shahadara,
Delhi 110 095
☎00 91 11 229 7792
Founded 1957. Publishes fiction and general non-fiction; literature, health and self-help.

Jaico Publishing House

127 M.G. Road, Mumbai 400 023
☎00 91 22 267 6702 Fax 00 91 22 265 6412
✉ jaicobom@bom5.vsnl.net.in
www.jaicobooks.com/home.asp
Founded 1946. Publishes computer science, engineering, finance, health and nutrition, information technology, law, reference, literature, self-

help, philosophy, religion, history, government, political science, sociology.

LexisNexis India
C–33 Inner Circle, Connaught Place, New Delhi 110 001
☎00 91 11 4355 9999 Fax 00 91 11 4151 3388
✉ info@lexisnexis.co.in
www.lexisnexis.co.in

Publishes law, taxation and business books in print form, online and CD-ROM.

Macmillan India Ltd
315–316 Raheja Chambers, 12 Museum Road, Bangalore 560 011
☎00 91 80 2558 7878
www.macmillanindia.com

Founded 1893. Part of **Macmillan Publishers**, UK. Publishes education, non-fiction, reference, dictionaries, encyclopedias.

Munshiram Manoharlal Publishers Pvt Ltd
PO Box 5715, 54 Rani Jhansi Road, New Delhi 110 055
☎00 91 11 2367 1668 Fax 00 91 11 2361 2745
✉ mrml@mrmlbooks.com
www.mrmlbooks.com

Founded 1952. Publishes academic, dictionaries, art and art history, architecture, anthropology, archaeology, religion, philosophy, geography, history, humanities, language arts and linguistics, law, literature, medicine, numismatics, music, dance, drama, theatre, Asian studies, sociology, social sciences, travel.

National Publishing House
2/35 Ansari Road, Darya Ganj, New Delhi 110 002
☎00 91 11 2327 5267
✉ info@nationalpublishinghouse.com
www.nationalpublishinghouse.com

Founded 1945. Publishes non-fiction, children's, history, literature, science, textbooks.

Orient Paperbacks
5 A/8 Ansari Road, First Floor, Darya Ganj, Delhi 110 002
☎00 91 11 2327 8877 Fax 00 91 11 2327 8879
✉ mail@orientpaperbacks.com
www.orientpaperbacks.com

Founded 1975. Publishes fiction and general non-fiction; humour, health and nutrition, literature, New Age, puzzles, reference, religion, self-help.

Oxford University Press India
YMCA Library Building, 1st Floor, 1 Jai Singh Road, New Delhi 110 001
☎00 91 11 2374 2990 Fax 00 91 11 2336 4014
www.oup.co.in

Founded 1912. Owned by **Oxford University Press**, UK. Academic publishers.

Rajpal & Sons
1590 Madarasa Road, Kashmere Gate, Delhi 110 006
☎00 91 11 296 5483

Founded 1947. Publishes fiction, general science, children's, dictionaries, encyclopedias, textbooks.

Tata McGraw-Hill Publishing Co. Ltd
7 West Patel Nagar, New Delhi 110 008
☎00 91 11 2588 2743 Fax 00 91 11 2537 2841
www.tatamcgrawhill.com

Founded 1970. Educational publisher.

Vidyarthi Mithram Press
Bakar Road, Kottayarn 68 001
☎00 91 481 256 3281

Founded 1928. Publishes children's and young adult, CD-ROMs, dictionaries, directories, encyclopedias, computer science, reference.

A.H. Wheeler & Co Ltd
23 Lal Bahadur Shastri Marg, Allahabad 211 001
☎00 91 532 262 3346

Founded 1879. Publishes CD-ROMs, professional, textbooks; computer science, communications.

New Zealand

Auckland University Press
University of Auckland, Private Bag 92019, Auckland
☎00 64 9 373 7528 Fax 00 64 9 373 7465
✉ aup@auckland.ac.nz
www.auckland.ac.nz/aup

Founded 1966. Publishes academic, biography, government, political science, history, social sciences, sociology, poetry, literature, literary criticism, Maori studies.

Canterbury University Press
University of Canterbury, Private Bag 4800, Christchurch
☎00 64 3 364 2914 Fax 00 64 3 364 2044

✉ mail@cup.canterbury.ac.nz
www.cup.canterbury.ac.nz
Founded 1964. Academic publishers; general non-fiction; history, marine biology, natural history.

The Caxton Press
113 Victoria Street, Christchurch
☎00 64 3 353 0734 Fax 00 64 3 365 7840
www.caxton.co.nz
Founded 1935. Publishes general non-fiction.

Hachette Livre New Zealand Ltd
4 Whetu Place, Mairangi Bay, Auckland
☎00 64 9 478 1000 Fax 00 64 9 478 1010
Founded 1971. Part of the **Hodder Headline Group**. Publishes fiction and general non-fiction; biography, business, cookery, humour, sport.

HarperCollins Publishers (New Zealand) Ltd
31 View Road, Glenfield, Auckland
☎00 64 9 443 9400 Fax 00 64 9 443 9403
✉ editors@harpercollins.co.nz
www.harpercollins.co.nz
Founded 1888. Publishes fiction, literature, children's, business, cookery, gardening, reference, religion.

Huia (NZ) Ltd
PO Box 17-335, Wellington, Aotearoa
☎00 64 4 473 9262 Fax 00 64 4 473 9265
✉ info@huia.co.nz
www.huia.co.nz
Founded 1991. Publishes Maori cultural history and language, children's books in Maori and English, fiction.

LexisNexis New Zealand
PO Box 472, Wellington
☎00 64 4 385 1479 Fax 00 64 4 385 1598
www.lexisnexis.co.nz
Founded 1914. Publishes law, professional and textbooks in book and electronic formats.

Macmillan Publishers New Zealand
6 Ride Way, Albany, Auckland
☎00 64 9 414 0350 Fax 00 64 9 414 0351
www.macmillan.co.nz
Education publishers – general, school and academic books; fiction and non-fiction for all ages.

McGraw-Hill New Zealand Pty Ltd
See **McGraw-Hill Australia & New Zealand Pty Ltd**

Oxford University Press New Zealand
See **Oxford University Press (Australia)**

Pearson Education New Zealand Ltd
46 Hillside Road, Auckland 10
☎00 64 9 444 4968 Fax 00 64 9 444 4957
www.pearson.co.nz
Founded 1968. Educational publishers.

Penguin Books (NZ) Ltd
Private Bag 102902, North Shore Mail Centre, Auckland
☎00 64 9 442 7400 Fax 00 64 9 442 7401
www.penguin.co.nz
Founded 1976. Owned by **Penguin UK**. Adult and children's fiction and non-fiction.

Random House New Zealand
Private Bag 102950, North Shore Mail Centre, Auckland
☎00 64 9 444 7197 Fax 00 64 9 444 7524
✉ editor@randomhouse.co.nz
www.randomhouse.co.nz
Publishes fiction and non-fiction (cooking, gardening, art, natural history) and children's.

Reed Publishing (NZ) Ltd
Private Bag 34901, Birkenhead, Auckland
☎00 64 9 441 2960 Fax 00 64 9 480 4999
✉ info@reed.co.nz
www.reed.co.nz
Founded 1988. Publishes fiction and general non-fiction, biography, children's, cookery, directories, history, natural history, regional interests, reference, textbooks, travel.

Victoria University Press
PO Box 600, Wellington
☎00 64 4 463 6580 Fax 00 64 4 463 6581
✉ victoria-press@vuw.ac.nz
www.vuw.ac.nz/vup
Founded 1979. Academic publishers; new fiction and, poetry, literature, essays, New Zealand history, Maori topics.

Viking Sevenseas NZ Ltd
PO Box 152, Paraparaumu, Wellington
☎00 64 4 902 8240

Founded 1957. Publishes natural history and ethnicity.

Bridget Williams Books Ltd
PO Box 5482, Wellington
☎00 64 4 473 8128
✉ info@bwb.co.nz
www.bwb.co.nz
Founded 1990. Independent publisher of New Zealand history, Maori experience, contemporary issues and women's studies.

South Africa

Heinemann International Southern Africa
PO Box 781940, Sandton 2146
☎00 27 11 322 8600 Fax 00 27 11 322 8716
www.heinemann.co.za
Founded 1986. Educational publisher.

University of Kwa-Zulu–Natal Press
Private Bag X01, Scottsville 3209
☎00 27 33 260 5226 Fax 00 27 33 260 5801
✉ books@ukzn.ac.za
www.ukznpress.co.za
Founded 1947. Publishes academic and general books; children's, government, political science, African literature, poetry, economics, military history, natural sciences, social sciences.

LexisNexis Butterworths (Pty) Ltd South Africa
PO Box 792, Durban 4000
☎00 27 31 268 3111
www.lexisnexis.co.za

Publishes professional, accountancy, finance, business, law, taxation and economics books in print form, online and CD-ROM.

Macmillan South Africa
PO Box 32484, Braamfontein 2017
☎00 27 11 731 3300 Fax 00 27 11 731 3500
✉ info@macmillan.co.za
www.macmillan.co.za/southafrica.html

Founded 1972. Part of **Macmillan Publishers Ltd**, UK. Educational publisher.

Maskew Miller Longman
PO Box 396, Cape Town 8000
☎00 27 21 532 6000 Fax 00 27 21 531 8103
www.mml.co.za
Founded 1893. Publishes education and teacher support books.

Oxford University Press Southern Africa (Pty) Ltd
PO Box 12119, N1 City, Cape Town 7463
☎00 27 21 596 2300 Fax 00 27 21 596 1234
✉ oxford.za@oup.com
www.oup.com/za
Founded 1915. Parent company: **Oxford University Press**, UK. Publishes academic, educational and general books.

Shuter & Shooter (Pty) Ltd
21c Cascades Crescent, Pietermaritzburg 3201
☎00 27 33 347 6100 Fax 00 27 33 346 6120
www.shuter.co.za
Founded 1925. Publishes educational material.

Struik Publishers (Pty) Ltd
PO Box 1144, Cape Town 8000
☎00 27 21 462 4360 Fax 00 27 21 462 4377
✉ info@struik.co.za
www.struik.co.za
Founded 1962. Publishes general non-fiction, illustrated, art and culture, lifestyle, natural history, travel.

Wits University Press
PO Wits, Johannesburg 2050
☎00 27 11 484 5907 Fax 00 27 11 484 5971
witspress.wits.ac.za
Founded 1922. Publishes academic, art, biography and memoirs, economics, theatre studies, history, business, anthropology, archaeology, politics, law, popular science, medicine, women's writing.

Not Much Right With Copyright

I am not sure if you would call it plagiarism or daylight robbery but not long ago I had one of my books lifted in its entirety. Flicking through a magazine for writers I spotted an illustrated reference to one of my early efforts, a ghosted autobiography of the actor John Le Mesurier. One up to me, I thought, until I realised that the author of the accompanying article was claiming the book as his own. He even quoted from favourable reviews. The deception was easy since John (now dead) was given sole credit on the title page. However, it was my name on the copyright line.

A reminder that there are legal remedies available to those whose copyright is infringed brought a swift retribution. It seemed that my doppelganger, having gone over John's notes and talked about the possibility of a book, had persuaded himself that he had actually written it, adding 'It is all so long ago, it is hard to remember.' Hmmm.

There were voices urging me towards tougher action but I decided not to get too worked up. The book is long out of print and is unlikely to enjoy a second life. The record has been put straight. No great harm has been done. I then have to ask myself what I would do if, as the lawyers say, 'a substantial part' of one of my books was reproduced as someone else's work? An apology, maybe compensation, would be demanded but how much further would I be prepared to go in seeking restitution? Court appearances can be a costly and time-consuming indulgence.

This question of copyright protection is of greater moment the more we venture into the digital age. In a few short years every book, in or out of copyright, will be available to download in digital formats of one type or another. Not only will it be a simple matter to download pages at no extra cost and thus no extra payment to the originator but it will also be easy, for any particular subject, to lift paragraphs from here and there to create what looks like a new publication. If this sounds unlikely think only on what has happened in the music industry where free reproduction – legal or otherwise – is standard practice.

For writers, the warning signs are plain enough in Google's plan to scan all the books in five major research libraries including that of Stanford University which alone has eight million books. And this is only the start. Within ten years Google intends to offer up to thirty-two million titles on its database. Meanwhile, rivals Amazon and Microsoft are also digitising hundreds of thousands of books.

All this would seem to make a nonsense of copyright as currently defined – the life of the author plus seventy years. Can anything be done to protect intellectual property?

Some heavyweight protagonists believe so. In the US, Google is under legal assault from the Authors Guild and the Association of American Publishers who want to stop copyright material appearing online even when, as Google has promised, initially no more than 20 per cent of a book will be available. The fact is that to provide a chapter or two online, Google scans the entire text of the book and holds this on its servers. There is a fear that they may end up with a monopoly on access. The case may go all the way to the Supreme Court. But even if Google loses this round, which is by no means certain, it is hard to imagine that anything more will be achieved beyond a pause for regrouping before the battle resumes.

On the other hand, there are commentators who believe that an out-of-court settlement will require Google to pay the plaintiffs sufficient to guarantee a welcome additional revenue stream while, from Google's point of view, deterring competitors; indeed, that this has been the plan all along. Once the legal precedent is to offer fees based on how often books are viewed, other Internet companies will have to accede to the same principle. They might just decide that the risk and the potential rewards do not match up.

Meanwhile, the big publishers are launching their own websites which, for a fee, give access to copyright material. Revenue may or may not be divided with authors. It all depends on one's contract – something to check when you next sign up for a book. If digital electronic rights *are* covered in your contract a royalty will be payable! At Macmillan this sits at around 15 per cent of net receipts. *Some* trade publishers are applying heavy-duty DRM (Digital Rights Management) 'wrappers' around their digital files which effectively lock the file to a limited number of registered devices (PC/laptop/e-reader, etc.). The problem with this is that the experience for honest consumers is a hugely complex one since they have to fill out registration forms to download the book and then have issues if they want to move the content they've bought from one device to another, having bought a new PC or e-reader, for example. Also, publishers are doing this largely because they fear authors and agents will run scared if their content is not locked down securely. It is expensive and cumbersome and will probably restrict users rather than doing any real good. You might wonder how long it will be before such dedicated websites are swept up into Google and its like. When this happens the share of downloading revenue due to authors will again be in contention. The issue may take years to resolve.

There are those who put their faith in the safety net provided by the Authors' Licensing and Collecting Society. See *Professional Associations and Societies* (p. 484). Representing some 18,000 writers the ALCS distributes licence fees collected from institutions and businesses that use the photocopier as an in-house publisher. The system is by no means abuse proof. While, for example, universities pay up without too much protest, the fact that the copier is now such a common item of office furniture means that billions of copyright pages are reproduced without recompense to ALCS members. Even so, close on £14 million a year (including royalties from cable transmission) is gathered in. Could something on these lines be adopted for downloading of copyright material? In theory, yes, but the holes in the safety net would be much larger. With just about every home with access to a computer terminal, controls on downloading are all but impossible. Moreover, duplication is not only efficient but incredibly cheap. The capacity for immediate delivery of material across the world to thousands of people is beginning to make the photocopier look distinctly old-fashioned. There is thus a risk that the ALCS will suffer a declining income.

Much the same challenge confronts Public Lending Right (see *Professional Associations and Societies*), the government-sponsored agency which supplements the income of authors whose books are borrowed from public libraries. What happens when library services such as print-on-demand takes precedence over hard print? Does downloading count as a loan and, if so, how will the number of on-screen borrowings be calculated?

There are monitoring systems that can track the online use of copyright material but it will not be long before someone finds a way of avoiding detection. The World Intellectual Property Organization, the UN agency which administers copyright conventions, requires member states to outlaw devices aimed at frustrating effective policing. But the rule is not likely to make much impact in the Far East, China or Russia where the precedent for Internet piracy is set by the illegal reproduction of hard print, said to be costing British publishers and authors over £200 million a year. The Chinese scanning factories which make little distinction between material in or out of copyright, are churning out digital books. Bill Gates predicts that Microsoft will soon be able to offer students an affordable handheld device containing all the books they need for their course. Very soon, readers will be able to follow the lead of music fans and simply digitise their own libraries. Amazon/Mobipocket's move into the e-reader market could have a significant impact here. Will this herald in the 'iPod moment' for e-books?

On the plus side for writers, there is now in realistic prospect a world library available to anyone with an Internet connection, a research tool of unprecedented scope and power. Authors whose books have failed to take off and who count their readers in hundreds will be given a second chance to make an impact by exposure on search engines and dedicated websites. One reason why many authors will readily surrender copyright is that they will not be able to resist the opportunity to extend their reach. Their more successful competitors may well follow suit.

Such are the uncertainties of book scanning, there is little hope of a political lead. The recent Gowers Review did no more than tinker at the edges of copyright law. Yet surely now is the time for a thorough reappraisal of copyright, its value and justification.

The first thing to be said is that there is nothing in copyright that gives it the force of natural law. One writer, favourably reviewed though not strong on sales, tells me that he 'likes' the idea of his descendants profiting from his work seventy years after his death. But liking something doesn't necessarily make it right while the assumption that a century ahead anyone will be interested in the current work of a mid-list author reveals breathtaking arrogance. It can be argued that 'copyright' is already an archaic term. As soon as someone looks at a piece of content on a PC/laptop or e-reader they are making copies in computer memories. Should we be looking at granting certain limited monopoly rights to commercial exploitation? There is a balance required between providing incentives to be creative and recognising the social benefits of 'sharing'.

Anyway, where is the logic in deciding on seventy years? As in so many other media matters, America has set the pace. Congress has lengthened copyright eleven times in the last forty years. Thirty years ago the limit to US copyright was just fourteen years. It then lengthened by stages to twenty-eight, to forty-two, to fifty-six and then, in 1998, to seventy years. Why? We can be sure it was not for a Congressional love of fine literature. Those who lobbied for copyright extension were from corporations eager to protect investment in famous names, characters and titles for as long as possible. As Kevin Kelly of *Wired* magazine has argued, the new legislation, known familiarly as the 'Mickey Mouse Protection Act', was nothing less than a restrictive practice for a particular type of business model. The interests of individual authors barely rated consideration.

But surely all writers benefit if only incidentally. Only up to a point, the point being where creative work ceases to have value as a brand. For the rest of us copyright for more than, say, ten years after the death of an author can be as much a curse as a blessing, a sentiment with which any non-fiction writer who has experienced the frustration of seeking permission to quote will readily identify.

After the seventy-year rule was introduced in Britain there have been cases where work taken back into copyright has been put under embargo, to be released only on condition amounting to censorship and at a substantial price. Libertarians find it hard to appreciate why relatives of great writers should profit from an often distant family connection long after the creative minds have ceased to be. Another source of outrage is traced to those who reassert copyright by editing or amending work that otherwise would have long since entered the public domain. Some translations fall into this category.

But the most scandalous restriction imposed by copyright law on the freedom of knowledge and expression is in the orphanage of published work. It is variously calculated that between half and three quarters of out-of-print books published in the last half century have no easily identifiable copyright holder. Publishers merge or go out of business, contracts are lost, authors die without appointing literary executors to tidy their affairs. The latest generation of writers can take the risk of quoting with acknowledgement or otherwise borrowing from orphaned books after what Gowers calls a 'reasonable search' but a risk it is, particularly if a new, though indebted, work becomes a bestseller. It is then that copyright claimants are most likely to emerge, invariably with lawyers in tow.

Is this really what we want in our brave new digital world? At a recent conference on the future of publishing hosted by Google in New York, a quotation from Charles Darwin was projected on to a large screen. 'It is not the strongest of the species that survive, nor the most intelligent, but the ones most responsive to change.' Authors, as well as publishers, would be wise to take note.

Professional Associations and Societies

ABSW

Wellcome Wolfson Building, 165 Queen's Gate, London SW7 5HE
☎0870 770 3361
✉ absw@absw.org.uk
www.absw.org.uk

Chairman *Ted Nield*
Administrator & EUSJA Board Member *Barbara Drillsma*
MEMBERSHIP £40 (full) p.a.; £36 (associate); £5 (student)

ABSW has played a central role in improving the standards of science journalism in the UK over the last 40 years. The Association seeks to improve standards by means of networking, lectures and organised visits to institutional laboratories and industrial research centres. Puts members in touch with major projects in the field and with experts worldwide. A member of the European Union of Science Journalists' Associations, ABSW is able to offer heavily subsidised places on visits to research centres in most other European countries, and hosts reciprocal visits to Britain by European journalists. Membership open to those who are considered to be *bona fide* science writers/editors, or their film/TV/radio equivalents, who earn a substantial part of their income by promoting public interest in and understanding of science. Runs the administration and judging of the Syngenta ABSW Science Writers' Awards, for outstanding science journalism in newspapers, journals and broadcasting and, with The Wellcome Trust, awards bursaries for science undergraduates taking a science communication course.

Academi (Yr Academi Gymreig)

3rd Floor, Mount Stuart House, Mount Stuart Square, Cardiff CF10 5FQ
☎029 2047 2266 Fax 029 2049 2930
✉ post@academi.org
www.academi.org

Glyn Jones Centre, Wales Millenium Centre, Cardiff Bay, Cardiff

North West Wales office: Ty Newydd, Llanystumdwy, Cricieth, Gwynedd LL52 0LW
☎ 01766 522817 Fax 01766 523095

✉ olwen@academi.org
West Wales office: Dylan Thomas Centre, Somerset Place, Swansea SA1 1RR
☎ 01792 463980 Fax 01792 463993
✉ academi.dylan.thomas@business.ntl.com

Chief Executive *Peter Finch*

Academi is the trading name of Yr Academi Gymreig, the Welsh National Literature Promotion Agency and Society for Writers. Yr Academi Gymreig was founded in 1959 as an association of Welsh language writers. An English language section was established in 1968. Membership, for those who have made a significant contribution to the literature of Wales, is by invitation. Membership currently stands at 500. The Academi runs courses, competitions (including the **Cardiff International Poetry Competition**), conferences, tours by authors, festivals, and represents the interests of Welsh writers and Welsh writing both inside Wales and beyond. Its publications include *Taliesin*, a quarterly literary journal in the Welsh language, *The Oxford Companion to the Literature of Wales*, *The Welsh Academy English-Welsh Dictionary* and a variety of translated works.

The Academi won the franchise from the Arts Council of Wales to run the Welsh National Literature Promotion Agency. The new, much enlarged organisation now administers a variety of schemes including bursaries, the annual **Book of the Year Award**, critical services, writers' mentoring, Writers on Tour, Writers Residencies and a number of literature development projects. It promotes an annual literary festival alternating between North and South Wales, runs its own programme of literary activity and publishes *A470*, a bi-monthly literature information magazine. The Academi is also in receipt of a lottery grant to publish the first Welsh National Encyclopedia. This is expected to be ready in November 2007.

Those with an interest in literature in Wales can become an associate of the Academi (which carries a range of benefits). Rates are £15 p.a. (waged); £7.50 (unwaged).

ALCS
See **Authors' Licensing & Collecting Society Limited**

Alliance of Literary Societies
22 Belmont Grove, Bedhampton, Havant PO9 3PU
☎023 9247 5855
✉ honsec.als@ntlworld.com
www.allianceofliterarysocieties.org

Honorary Secretary *Rosemary Culley*

Founded 1974. Aims to help and support its 100+ member societies and, when necessary, to act as a pressure group. Produces an annual literary magazine (*ALSo*) as well as two newsletters containing useful information for its member societies.

Arts & Business (A&B)
Nutmeg House, 60 Gainsford Street, Butlers Wharf, London SE1 2NY
☎020 7378 8143 Fax 020 7407 7527
✉ head.office@AandB.org.uk
www.AandB.org.uk

Director of Press & Public Affairs *Jonathan Tuchner*
Director of Marketing & Communications *Sebastian Paul*
Media Manager *Sophie Gaskill*

A&B enables business and its people to be more successful by engaging with the arts and to increase resources for the arts from business and its people. It provides a wide range of services to over 400 business members and 1100 arts organisations through the Development Forum. Programmes include professional development for arts and business people through the skills bank, board bank and mentoring schemes, and the New Partners programme which invests funds to foster innovative long term partnerships. With the support of its President, HRH The Prince of Wales, it explores and develops new ways for business, the arts and society to interact. Arts & Business has 17 regional offices offering a range of services throughout the UK.

Arvon Foundation
See entry under *UK Writers' Courses*

ASLS
See **Association for Scottish Literary Studies**

Association for Scottish Literary Studies
c/o Department of Scottish Literature, 7 University Gardens, University of Glasgow, Glasgow G12 8QH
☎0141 330 5309 Fax 0141 330 5309
✉ office@asls.org.uk
www.asls.org.uk

Contact *Duncan Jones*
SUBSCRIPTION £38 (individual); £67 (institutional)

Founded 1970. ASLS is an educational charity promoting the languages and literature of Scotland. Publishes works of Scottish literature; essays, monographs and journals; and *Scotnotes*, a series of comprehensive study guides to major Scottish writers. Also produces *New Writing Scotland*, an annual anthology of contemporary poetry and prose in English, Gaelic and Scots (see entry under *Magazines*).

Association of American Correspondents in London
c/o People Magazine, Third Floor, Brettenham House, Lancaster Place, London WC2E 7TL
www.theaacl.co.uk

Secretary/Treasurer *Monique Jessen*
SUBSCRIPTION £100 (organisations)

Founded 1919 to serve the professional interests of its member organisations, promote social cooperation among them, and maintain the ethical standards of the profession. (An extra £40 is charged for each department of an organisation which requires separate listing in the Association's handbook and a charge of £10 for each full-time editorial staff listed, up to a maximum of £120 regardless of the number listed.)

Association of American Publishers, Inc
71 Fifth Avenue, 2nd Floor, New York, NY 10003, USA
☎001 212 255 0200 Fax 001 212 255 7007
www.publishers.org

Also at: 50 F Street, NW, Suite 400, Washington, DC 20001
☎ 001 202 347 3375 Fax 001 202 347 3690

Founded 1970. For information, visit the Association's website.

Association of Authors' Agents (AAA)

Gillon Aitken Associates Ltd, 18–21 Cavaye Place, London SW10 9PT
☎020 7373 8672
✉ aaa@gillonaitken.co.uk
www.agentsassoc.co.uk

President *Clare Alexander*
MEMBERSHIP £150 p.a. (£75 for agencies with fewer than 3 members of staff)

Founded 1974. Membership voluntary. The AAA maintains a code of practice, provides a forum for discussion and represents its members in issues affecting the profession. For a full list of members and a list of frequently asked questions visit the AAA website. The AAA is a voluntary body and unable to operate as an information service to the public.

Association of Authors' Representatives (AAR)

✉ aarinc@mindspring.com
www.aar-online.org

Contact *Administrative Secretary*

Founded in 1991 through the merger of the Society of Authors' Representatives and the Independent Literary Agents Association. Membership of this US organisation is restricted to agents of at least two years' operation. Provides information, education and support for its members and works to protect their best interests.

Association of British Editors

See **Society of Editors**

Association of British Science Writers

See **ABSW**

Association of Canadian Publishers

161 Eglinton Avenue East, Suite 702, Toronto, Ontario M4P 1J5, Canada
☎001 416 487 6116 Fax 001 416 487 8815
✉ admin@canbook.org
www.publishers.ca

Executive Director *Carolyn Wood*

Founded 1971. ACP represents over 140 Canadian-owned book publishers country-wide from the literary, general trade, scholarly and education sectors. Aims to encourage the writing, publishing, distribution and promotion of Canadian books and to support the development of a 'strong, independent and vibrant Canadian-owned publishing industry'. The organisation's website has information on getting published and links to many of their member publishers' websites. The ACP does not accept manuscripts and cannot provide assistance to authors who wish to find a Canadian publisher.

Association of Christian Writers

23 Moorend Lane, Thame OX9 3BQ
☎01844 213673
✉ admin@christianwriters.org.uk
www.christianwriters.org.uk

President *Adrian Plass*
Chairman *Brian Vincent*
Secretary *Rev. Simon Baynes*
SUBSCRIPTION Single: £22 (£18.50 Direct Debit); joint husband/wife: £25 (£21.50 DD); overseas: £30 (£25.50 DD on UK a/c)

Founded in 1971 'to inspire and equip men and women to use their talents and skills with integrity to devise, write and market excellent material which comes from a Christian worldview. In this way we seek to be an influence for good and for God in this generation.' Publishes a quarterly magazine. Runs three training events each year, biennial conference, competitions, postal workshops, area groups, prayer support and manuscript criticism. Charity No. 1069839.

Association of Freelance Editors, Proofreaders & Indexers (Ireland)

11 Clonard Road, Sandyford, Dublin 16, Republic of Ireland
☎00 353 1 295 2194/00 353 58 48458
www.afepi.ie

Contacts *Priscilla O'Connor, Winifred Power*
SUBSCRIPTION €40 p.a. (full); €20 (associate)

The organisation was established in Ireland to protect the interests of its members and to provide information to publishers on freelancers working in the relevant fields. Full membership is restricted to freelancers with experience and/or references (but the association does not test or evaluate the skills of members). A new category of membership, Associate Member, is available for trainees in proofreading/editing who are taking the Publishing Training Centre correspondence courses in Proofreading and Copy-editing.

Association of Freelance Writers

Sevendale House, 7 Dale Street, Manchester M1 1JB
☎0161 228 2362 Fax 0161 228 3533

✉ fmn@writersbureau.com
www.freelancemarketnews.com
Contact *Angela Cox*
SUBSCRIPTION £29 p.a.

Founded in 1995 to help and advise new and established freelance writers. Members receive a copy of *Freelance Market News* each month which gives news, views and the latest advice and guidelines about publications at home and abroad. Other benefits include one free appraisal of prose or poetry each year, reduced entry to **The Writers Bureau** writing competition, reduced fees for writing seminars and discounts on books for writers.

Association of Golf Writers

1 Pilgrims Bungalow, Mulberry Hill, Chilham CT4 8AH
☎01227 732496 Fax 01227 732496
✉ andyfarrell@compuserve.com
Honorary Secretary *Andy Farrell*

Founded 1938. Aims to cooperate with golfing bodies to ensure best possible working conditions.

Association of Illustrators

2nd Floor, Back Building, 150 Curtain Road, London EC2A 3AT
☎020 7613 4328 Fax 020 7613 4417
✉ info@theaoi.com
www.theaoi.com
Contact *Membership Coordinator*

The AOI is a non-profit-making trade association and members consist primarily of freelance illustrators as well as agents, clients, students and lecturers. As the only body to represent illustrators and campaign for their rights in the UK, the AOI has successfully increased the standing of illustration as a profession and improved the commercial and ethical conditions of employment. Organises annual events programme and provides an advisory service for members. Publications include: triannual magazine, *Varoom - the journal of illustration and made images*; *Rights – the illustrator's guide to professional practice*; *Survive – the illustrator's guide to a professional career*, client directories (online) and *Images*, the only jury-selected annual of British contemporary illustration.

Association of Independent Libraries

Leeds Library, 18 Commercial Street, Leeds LS1 6AL
☎0113 245 3071

www.independentlibraries.co.uk
Chairman *Geoffrey Forster*
Secretary *Carol Allison*

Established to 'further the advancement, conservation and restoration of a little-known but important living portion of our cultural heritage'. Members include the **London Library, Devon & Exeter Institution, Linen Hall Library** and **Plymouth Proprietary Library**.

Association of Learned and Professional Society Publishers

Bluebell Lodge, 8 Rickford Road, Nailsea, Bristol BS48 4PY
☎01275 856444 Fax 07968 504763
✉ ian.russell@alpsp.org
www.alpsp.org
Chief Executive *Ian Russell*
Member Services Manager *Nick Evans*
Editor-in-Chief, Learned Publishing *Sally Morris* (editor@alpsp.org)

The Association of Learned and Professional Society Publishers (ALPSP) is the international trade association for not-for-profit publishers and those who work with them. It currently has over 370 members in more than 40 countries. ALPSP provides representation of its sector, cooperative services such as the award-winning ALPSP Learned Journals Collection, professional development activities and a wealth of information and advice.

Association of Scottish Motoring Writers

c/o Scottish and Universal Newspapers, 5/15 Bank Street, Airdrie ML6 6AF
☎01236 748048 Fax 01236 748098
✉ jmurdoch@s-un.co.uk
Secretary *John Murdoch*
SUBSCRIPTION £50

Founded 1961. Aims to co-ordinate the activities of, and provide shared facilities for, motoring writers resident in Scotland. Membership is by invitation only.

Audiobook Publishing Association

c/o 18 Green Lanes, Hatfield AL10 9JT
☎07971 280788
✉ charlotte.mccandlish@ntlworld.com
www.theapa.net
Chair *Jo Forshaw*
Administrator *Charlotte McCandlish* (at address above)

Founded 1994. The Audiobook Publishing Association (formerly the Spoken Word Publishing Association) is the UK trade association for the audiobook industry with membership open to all those involved in the publishing of spoken word audio. Publishes annual *APA Resources Directory*, available from the address above, and now also available online at www.theapa.net (click on 'APA Members').

Australian Copyright Council
PO Box 1986, Strawberry Hills, NSW 2012, Australia
☎00 612 8815 9777 Fax 00 612 8815 9799
✉ info@copyright.org.au
www.copyright.org.au
Contact *Customer Service*

Founded 1968. The Council's activities and services include a range of publications, organising and speaking about copyright at seminars, research, consultancies and free legal advice. Aims include assistance for copyright owners to exercise their rights effectively, raising awareness about the importance of copyright and seeking changes to the law of copyright.

Australian Publishers Association
60/89 Jones Street, Ultimo, NSW 2007, Australia
☎00 612 9281 9788 Fax 00 612 9281 1073
www.publishers.asn.au
Chief Executive *Maree McCaskill*
SUBSCRIPTION Annual membership subscription open to Australian publishers

Founded 1948. The APA initiates programmes that contribute to the development of publishing in Australia, virgorously protects and furthers the interests of copyright owners, agents and licensees and actively represents members' interests to government and other organisations as appropriate. The Association encourages excellence in writing, editing, design, production, marketing and distribution of published works in Australia, protects freedom of expression and manages members' funds to further the interests of the industry.

Australian Society of Authors
98 Pitt Street, Redfern, NSW 2016, Australia
☎00 612 9318 0877 Fax 00 612 9318 0530
✉ asa@asauthors.org
www.asauthors.org
Executive Director *Dr Jeremy Fisher*

Founded 1963. The ASA aims to promote and protect the professional interests of Australian authors. Provides contract advice and assists authors on industry standards and practices. Publishes *Australian Author* magazine.

Authors' Club
40 Dover Street, London W1S 4NP
☎020 7499 8581 Fax 020 7409 0913
✉ stella@theauthorsclub.co.uk
www.authorsclub.co.uk
Secretary *Stella Kane*

Founded in 1891 by Sir Walter Besant, the Authors' Club welcomes as members writers, agents, publishers, critics, journalists, academics and anyone involved with literature and the written word. Administers the **Authors' Club Best First Novel Award**, the **Dolman Best First Travel Book Award** and **Sir Banister Fletcher Award**, and organises regular talks and dinners with well-known guest speakers. Membership fee: apply to secretary.

Authors' Licensing & Collecting Society Limited (ALCS)
The Writers' House, 13 Haydon Street, London EC3N 1HP
☎020 7264 5700 Fax 020 7264 5755
✉ alcs@alcs.co.uk
www.alcs.co.uk
Chief Executive *Owen Atkinson*
SUBSCRIPTION One-off membership fee: £25 incl. VAT (UK; free to members of Society of Authors, Writers' Guild)

Founded 1977. The UK collective rights management society for writers and their successors, ALCS is a non-profit organisation whose principal purpose is to ensure that hard-to-collect revenues due to writers are efficiently collected and speedily distributed. Established to give assistance to writers through the protection and exploitation of collective rights,

ALCS has distributed over £140 million in secondary royalties to writers since its creation. ALCS represents all types of writer, fiction and non-fiction, including educational, research and academic authors, scriptwriters, playwrights, poets, editors and freelance journalists across the print and broadcast media. On joining, members give ALCS a mandate to administer on their behalf those rights which the law determines must be received or which are best handled collectively. Chief among these are: photocopying, cable retransmission, rental and lending rights (but not British Public Lending Right), off-air recording, electronic rights, the performing right and public reception of broadcasts. The society is a prime resource and a leading authority on copyright matters and writers' collective interests. It maintains a watching brief on all matters affecting copyright both in Britain and abroad, making representations to UK government authorities and the EU. Visit the ALCS website or contact the office for registration forms and further information.

BAPLA (British Association of Picture Libraries and Agencies)

18 Vine Hill, London EC1R 5DZ
☎020 7713 1780 Fax 020 7713 1211
✉ enquiries@bapla.org.uk
www.bapla.org

Everything you need to know about finding, buying and selling pictures. Represents over 400 members.

The Bibliographical Society

c/o Institute of English Studies, University of London, Senate House, Malet Street, London WC1E 7HU
☎020 7862 8679 Fax 020 7862 8720
✉ secretary@bibsoc.org.uk
www.bibsoc.org.uk

President *E. Leedham-Green*
Honorary Secretary *M.L. Ford*
SUBSCRIPTION £33 p.a.

Aims to promote and encourage the study and research of historical, analytical, descriptive and textual bibliography, and the history of printing, publishing, bookselling, bookbinding and collecting; to hold meetings at which papers are read and discussed; to print and publish works concerned with bibliography; to form a bibliographical library. Awards grants and bursaries for bibliographical research. Publishes a quarterly magazine called *The Library*.

Booksellers Association of the UK & Ireland Ltd

Minster House, 272 Vauxhall Bridge Road, London SW1V 1BA
☎020 7802 0802 Fax 020 7802 0803
✉ mail@booksellers.org.uk
www.booksellers.org.uk

Chief Executive *Tim Godfray*

Founded 1895. The BA helps 4400 independent, chain and multiple retail outlets to sell more books, reduce costs and improve efficiency. It represents members' interests to the UK Government, European Commission, publishers, authors and others in the trade as well as offering marketing assistance, confer-

ences, seminars and exhibitions. Together with **The Publishers Association**, coordinates World Book Day. Publishes directories, catalogues, surveys and various other publications connected with the book trade and administers the **Costa Book Awards**.

Booktrust

Book House, 45 East Hill, London SW18 2QZ
☎020 8516 2977 Fax 020 8516 2978
✉ query@booktrust.org.uk
www.booktrust.org.uk
www.booktrusted.com

Director *Chris Meade*
Head of Promotions *Helen Hayes*

Founded 1925. Booktrust is an independent national charity that encourages readers of all ages and cultures to discover and enjoy reading. The reader is at the heart of everything they do. Their children's books website (booktrusted. com) also includes information about National Children's Book Week and the **Children's Laureate**, both of which Booktrust administers. Booktrust also administers literary prizes, including the **Orange Prize for Fiction** and the **Booktrust Teenage Prize** (see entries under *Prizes*), and promotes reading through campaigns such as Get London Reading (www. getlondonreading.com) and Story (www. theshortstory.org.uk). Booktrust runs Bookstart (www.bookstart.org.uk), the acclaimed national scheme that works through locally based organisations to give a free pack of books to babies and guidance materials for parents and carers.

British Academy of Composers and Songwriters

2nd Floor, British Music House, 25–27 Berners Street, London W1T 3LR
☎020 7636 2929 Fax 020 7636 2212
✉ info@britishacademy.com
www.britishacademy.com

Head of Membership *Fran Matthews*

The Academy represents the interests of music writers of all genres, providing advice on professional and artistic matters. Publishes bi-monthly magazines and administers the annual Ivor Novello Awards and British Composer Awards.

British Association of Communicators in Business (CiB)

Suite GA2, Oak House, Woodlands Business Park, Linford Wood, Milton Keynes MK14 6EY
☎01908 313755 Fax 01908 313661

✉ enquiries@cib.uk.com
www.cib.uk
Secretary General *Kathie Jones*
The professional body for in-house, freelance and agency staff involved in internal and corporate communications. Services to members include a business support helpline, an online forum, a monthly e-zine, the CiB Freelance Directory, an annual conference and gala dinner, automatic eligibility to FEIEA, a European network of 5000 communicators.

British Association of Journalists
89 Fleet Street, London EC4Y 1DH
☎020 7353 3003 Fax 020 7353 2310
✉ office@bajunion.org.uk
www.bajunion.org.uk
General Secretary *Steve Turner*
SUBSCRIPTION National newspaper staff, national broadcasting staff, national news agency staff: £17.50 per month. Other seniors, including magazine journalists, PRs and freelances who earn the majority of their income from journalism: £10 p.m. Journalists under 24: £7.50 p.m.
Founded 1992. Aims to protect and promote the industrial and professional interests of journalists.

British Association of Picture Libraries and Agencies
See BAPLA

British Centre for Literary Translation
University of East Anglia, Norwich NR4 7TJ
☎01603 592785 Fax 01603 592737
✉ bclt@uea.ac.uk
www.literarytranslation.com
www.uea.ac.uk
Contact *Catherine Fuller*
Founded 1989, BCLT is funded jointly by Arts Council England and the University of East Anglia. It aims to raise the profile of literary translation in the UK through events, publications, activities and research aimed at professional translators, students and the general reader. Member of the international RECIT literary translation network. Activities include the annual Sebald Lecture, Summer School, translator in residence scheme and a joint website with the British Council. BCLT has a PhD programme in literary translation as well as an MA in Literary Translation and other units at undergraduate and postgraduate level.

Joint sponsor with BCLA of the **John Dryden Translation Prize**. Publishes a journal *In Other Words* and *New Books in German*. Free mailing list.

British Copyright Council
Copyright House, 29–33 Berners Street, London W1T 3AB
☎01986 788122 Fax 01986 788847
✉ secretary@britishcopyright.org
www.britishcopyright.org
Contact *Janet Ibbotson*
Works for the national and international acceptance of copyright and acts as a lobby/watchdog organisation on behalf of creators, publishers and performers on copyright and associated matters.

The British Council
10 Spring Gardens, London SW1A 2BN
☎020 7389 3166 (Literature Dept)
Fax 020 7389 3175
✉ literatureuk@britishcouncil.org
www.britishcouncil.org/arts-literature
The British Council promotes Britain abroad. It provides access to British ideas, expertise and experience in education, the English language, literature and the arts, science and technology and governance. Works in 110 countries running a mix of offices, libraries, resource centres and English teaching operations.

British Equestrian Writers' Association
Priory House, Station Road, Swavesey, Cambridge CB24 4QJ
☎01954 232084 Fax 01954 231362
✉ gnewsumn@aol.com
Contact *Gillian Newsum*
SUBSCRIPTION £15
Founded 1973. Aims to further the interests of equestrian sport and improve, wherever possible, the working conditions of the equestrian press. Membership is by invitation of the committee. Candidates for membership must be nominated and seconded by full members and receive a majority vote of the committee.

British Film Institute
21 Stephen Street, London W1T 1LN
☎020 7255 1444 Fax 020 7436 0439
www.bfi.org.uk
Chair *Anthony Minghella CBE*
Director *Amanda Nevill*
Established in 1933 to champion moving image culture in all its richness and diversity across the

UK, for the benefit of as wide an audience as possible and to create and encourage debate. Visit the website for more information on *bfi* services or ring the enquiry line on the main switchboard between 10.00 am and 6.00 pm.

British Guild of Beer Writers

Lee Farm, Winsford TA24 7HX

✉ tierneyjones@btinternet.com

www.beerwriters.co.uk

Secretary *Adrian Tierney-Jones*

SUBSCRIPTION £40 p.a.

Founded 1988. Aims to improve standards in beer writing and at the same time extend public knowledge of beers and brewing. Publishes a directory of members with details of their publications and their particular areas of expertise; this is then circulated to newspapers, magazines, trade press and broadcasting organisations. Also publishes a monthly newsletter, the *BGBW Newsletter*. As part of the plan to improve writing standards and to achieve a higher profile for beer, the Guild offers annual awards, The Gold and Silver Tankard Awards, to writers and broadcasters judged to have made the most valuable contribution towards this end in their work.

British Guild of Travel Writers

51b Askew Crescent, London W12 9DN

☎020 8749 1128 Fax 020 8181 6663

✉ charlotte.c@virtualnecessities.com

www.bgtw.org

Chairman *Mary Anne Evans*

Secretariat *Charlotte Copeman*

The professional association of travel writers, broadcasters, photographers and editors which aims to serve its members' professional interests by acting as a forum for debate, discussion and 'networking'. The Guild publishes an annual Year Book and has a website giving full details of all its members and useful trade contacts, holds monthly meetings and has a monthly newsletter. Members are required to spend a significant proportion of their working time on travel.

British Science Fiction Association

39 Glyn Avenue, New Barnet EN4 9PJ

✉ bsfamail@gmail.com

www.bsfa.co.uk

SUBSCRIPTION £26 p.a. (reduction for unwaged)

Founded originally in 1958 by a group of authors, readers, publishers and booksellers interested in science fiction. With a worldwide membership, the Association aims to promote the reading, writing and publishing of science fiction and to encourage SF fans to maintain contact with each other. Publishes *Matrix* bi-monthly newsletter with comment and opinions, news of conventions, etc. Contributions from members welcomed; *Vector* bi-monthly critical journal – reviews of books and magazines; *Focus* biannual magazine with articles, original fiction and letters column. Also offers postal and online writer's workshop. For further information, contact the Membership Secretary *Peter Wilkinson* at the postal address above or via e-mail.

British Society of Comedy Writers

61 Parry Road, Ashmore Park, Wolverhampton WV11 2PS

☎01902 722729 Fax 01902 722729

✉ comedy@bscw.co.uk

www.bscw.co.uk

Contact *Ken Rock*

Founded 1999. The Society aims to develop good practice and professionalism among comedy writers while bringing together the best creative professionals, and working to standards of excellence agreed with the light entertainment industry. Offers a network of industry contacts and a range of products, services and training initiatives including specialised workshops, an annual international conference, script assessment service and opportunities to visit international festivals.

British Society of Magazine Editors (BSME)

137 Hale Lane, Edgware HA8 9QP

☎020 8906 4664 Fax 020 8959 2137

✉ admin@bsme.com

www.bsme.com

Contact *Gill Branston*

Holds regular industry forums and events as well as an annual awards dinner.

British Universities Film & Video Council

See **Learning on Screen**

Broadcasting Press Guild

Tiverton, The Ridge, Woking GU22 7EQ

☎01483 764895 Fax 01483 765882

✉ torin.douglas@bbc.co.uk

www.broadcastingpressguild.org

Membership Secretary *Richard Last*

Lunch Secretary *Torin Douglas*

SUBSCRIPTION £15 p.a.

Founded 1974 to promote the professional

interests of journalists specialising in writing or broadcasting about the media. Organises monthly lunches addressed by leading industry figures, and annual TV and radio awards. Membership by invitation.

BSME

See **British Society of Magazine Editors**

Bureau of Freelance Photographers

Focus House, 497 Green Lanes, London N13 4BP
☎020 8882 3315 Fax 020 8886 5174
✉ info@thebfp.com
Membership Secretary *Angela Kidd*
SUBSCRIPTION £49 p.a. (UK); £65 p.a. (overseas)

Founded 1965. Assists members in selling their pictures through monthly *Market Newsletter*, and offers advisory, legal assistance and other services.

Campaign for Press and Broadcasting Freedom

Second Floor, 23 Orford Road, London E17 9NL
☎020 8521 5932
✉ freepress@cpbf.org.uk
www.cpbf.org.uk
SUBSCRIPTION £15 p.a. (concessions available); £25 p.a. (institutions/organisations)

Broadly based pressure group working for more accountable and accessible media in Britain. Advises on right of reply and takes up the issue of the portrayal of minorities. Members receive *Free Press* (bi-monthly), discounts on publications and news of campaign progress.

Canadian Authors Association

National Office: Box 419, 320 South Shores Road, Campbellford, Ontario K0L 1L0, Canada
☎001 705 653 0323 Fax 001 705 653 0593
✉ admin@canauthors.org
www.canauthors.org
Contact *The National Director*

Founded 1921. The CAA was founded to promote recognition of Canadian writers and their works, and to foster and develop a climate favourable to the creative arts. It is Canada's national association for writers of every kind; for those actively seeking to become writers and for those who want to support writers. The Association has branches across the country providing support to local members in the form

of advice, local contests, publications and writers' circles. Publishes *National Newsline* (quarterly) and *The Canadian Writer's Guide*.

Canadian Federation of Poets

2431 Cyprus Avenue, Burlington, ON L7P 1G5, Canada
☎001 818-859-7210
✉ info@federationofpoets.com
www.federationofpoets.com
Contact *Tracy Repchuk*
SUBSCRIPTION $35 (Canada); $45 (USA); $60 (International); $45 International subscriptions available for Poetry Canada PDF option

Founded 2003. Federations and members from around the world can post messages, 'meet' via forums and live chats and learn about themselves and their international colleagues with regard to poetry. Membership includes poetry workshops, anthologies, publishing opportunities, online forums, free book promotion, calendar of events and free subscription to *Poetry Canada* magazine (www.poetrycanada.com). Also offers an online 52-week poetry certification programme to help educate on the various types of poetry and promote the diversity of poetry.

Canadian Publishers' Council

250 Merton Street, Suite 203, Toronto, Ontario M4S 1B1, Canada
☎001 416 322 7011 Fax 001 416 322 6999
✉ pubadmin@pubcouncil.ca
www.pubcouncil.ca
Executive Director, External Relations *Jacqueline Hushion*

Founded 1910. Trade association of English-language publishers which represents the domestic and international interests of member companies.

Careers Writers' Association

✉ ann@ann50.freeserve.co.uk
www.careerswriters.co.uk
Founded 1979. 'An association of professional careers writers whose work in careers writing reaches high standards of accuracy and impartiality. Membership is open only to writers with an established reputation for providing objective and up-to-date careers information.' See website for details.

Chartered Institute of Journalists

2 Dock Offices, Surrey Quays Road, London SE16 2XU
☎020 7252 1187 Fax 020 7232 2302

✉ memberservices@cioj.co.uk
www.cioj.co.uk

General Secretary *Dominic Cooper*
SUBSCRIPTION £195 p.a.; £16 (monthly)

Founded 1884. The Institute is concerned with professional journalistic standards and with safeguarding the freedom of the media. It is open to writers, broadcasters and journalists (including self-employed) in all media. Affiliate membership (£133) is available to part-time or occasional practitioners and to overseas journalists who can join the Institute's International Division. Non-employing members also belong to the IOJ (TU), an independent trade union which protects, advises and represents them in their employment or freelance work; negotiates on their behalf and provides legal assistance and support. The IOJ (TU) is a certificated independent trade union which represents members' interests in the workplace, and the CIOJ is also a constituent member of the Media Society, the **British Copyright Council** and the Journalists Copyright Fund. Editor of the Institute's quarterly magazine is *Andrew Smith*.

Chartered Institute of Linguists (IoL)

Saxon House, 48 Southwark Street, London SE1 1UN
☎020 7940 3100 Fax 020 7940 3101
✉ info@iol.org.uk
www.iol.org.uk

Chief Executive *John Hammond*
Director of Communications *Cetty Zambrano*
SUBSCRIPTION Rates on application

Founded 1910. Professional association for translators, interpreters and trainers; examining body for languages at degree level and above for vocational purposes; the National Register of Public Service Interpreters is managed by NRPSI Limited, an IoL subsidiary. The Institute's limited company, Language Services Ltd, provides customised assessments of language-oriented requirements, skills, etc.

Children's Book Circle

✉ childrensbookcircle@hotmail.co.uk
www.childrensbookcircle.org.uk

Membership Secretary *Katie Jennings*

The Children's Book Circle provides a discussion forum for anybody involved with children's books. Regular meetings are addressed by a panel of invited speakers and topics focus on current and controversial issues. Administers

the **Eleanor Farjeon Award** and the Patrick Hardy lecture.

Children's Books Ireland

17 North Great George's Street, Dublin 1, Republic of Ireland
☎00 353 1 872 7475 Fax 00 353 1 872 7476
✉ info@childrensbooksireland.com
www.childrensbooksireland.com

Contact *Mags Walsh*
SUBSCRIPTION €30 p.a. (individual);
€50 (institution); €20 (student);
€45/US$40 (overseas)

Irish national children's books organisation. Holds annual conferences as well as other occasional seminars and events. Quarterly magazine, *Inis* and bi-monthly newsletter, *Children's Book News*. Annual children's book festival in October; **CBI Bisto Book of the Year Award** (see entry under *Prizes*). Partners other organisations to promote and develop ways of bringing young people and books together.

CiB

See **British Association of Communicators in Business**

CILIP: The Chartered Institute of Library and Information Professionals

7 Ridgmount Street, London WC1E 7AE
☎020 7255 0500 Fax 020 7255 0501
✉ info@cilip.org.uk
www.cilip.org.uk

Chief Executive *Bob McKee*

The leading membership body for library and information professionals, formed in 2002 following the unification of The Library Association and the Institute of Information Scientists. **Facet Publishing** (successor to LA Publishing) produces 25–30 new titles each year and has over 150 titles in print from the LA's back catalogue. Further information from Marketing & External Relations, CILIP.

Circle of Wine Writers

5 Ingatestone Hall Cottages, Ingatestone CM4 9NR
✉ administrator@winewriters.org
www.winewriters.org

Administrator *Andrea Warren*
MEMBERSHIP £35 p.a.

Founded 1960. Membership is open to all those professionally engaged in communicating about wines and spirits, with the exception of people primarily doing so for promotional purposes. Aims to improve the standard of writing, broadcasting and lecturing about wines, spirits and beers; to contribute to the growing knowledge and interest in wine; to promote wines and spirits of quality and to comment adversely on faulty products or dubious practices; to establish and maintain good relations with the news media and the wine trade; to provide members with a strong voice with which to promote their views; to provide a programme of workshops, meetings, talks and tastings.

CLÉ – Irish Book Publishers' Association

25 Denzille Lane, Dublin 2, Republic of Ireland
☎00 353 1 639 4868
✉ info@publishingireland.com
www.publishingireland.com

President *Tony Farmar*
Administrator *Karen Kenny*
Project Manager *Jolly Ronan*

Founded 1970 to promote Irish publishing, protect members' interests and train the industry.

Comhairle nan Leabhraichean/ The Gaelic Books Council

22 Mansfield Street, Glasgow G11 5QP
☎0141 337 6211 Fax 0141 341 0515
✉ brath@gaelicbooks.net
www.gaelicbooks.net
www.ur-sgeul.com

Chairman *Professor Roibeard Ó Maolalaigh*
Director *Ian MacDonald*

Founded 1968 and now a charitable company with its own bookshop. Encourages and promotes Gaelic publishing by giving grants to publishers and writers; providing editorial and word-processing services; retailing Gaelic books; producing a catalogue of all Gaelic books in print and answering enquiries about them; mounting occasional literary evenings and training courses. Stock list on website.

Commercial Radio Companies Association

See **RadioCentre**

The Copyright Licensing Agency Ltd

Saffron House, 6–10 Kirby Street, London EC1N 8TS
☎020 7400 3100/0800 085 6644 (new licences) Fax 020 7400 3101

✉ cla@cla.co.uk
www.cla.co.uk

Chief Executive *Peter Shepherd*

CLA is the UK's reproduction rights organisation which looks after the interests of authors, publishers and artists in the photocopying and scanning of extracts from books, journals and periodicals. Founded in 1982 by the **Authors' Licensing and Collecting Society Limited (ALCS)** and the **Publishers Licensing Society Ltd (PLS)** to promote and enforce intellectual property rights of UK rightsholders both at home and abroad. CLA works closely with Reproductive Rights Organizations (RROs) from other countries and has an agency agreement with the Design and Artists Copyright Society (DACS) which represents artists and illustrators. A not-for-profit organisation, CLA licenses the use of copyright text by business, education and government and distributes fees collected via authors', publishers' and artists' collective societies. CLA has also developed licences which enable digitisation of existing print material. The licence enables users to scan and electronically send extracts from copyright works. Scanning and e-mail distribution is only available for UK works at present. Since its inception in 1982, CLA has distributed over £300 million.

Council for British Archaeology

St Mary's House, 66 Bootham, York YO30 7BZ
☎01904 671417 Fax 01904 671384
✉ info@britarch.ac.uk
www.britarch.ac.uk

Head of Information & Communications *Dan Hull*
Publications Officer *Catrina Appleby*

Founded 1944 to represent and promote archaeology at all levels. Its aims are to improve the public's awareness in and understanding of Britain's past; to carry out research; to survey, guide and promote the teaching of archaeology at all levels of education; to publish a wide range of academic, educational, general and bibliographical works (see **CBA Publishing** under *UK Publishers*).

Crime Writers' Association (CWA)

PO Box 273, Boreham Wood WD6 2XA
✉ secretary@thecwa.co.uk
www.thecwa.co.uk

Hon. Secretary *Liz Evans*
Membership Secretary *Rebecca Tope* (Crossways Cottage, Walterstone HR2 0DX)

MEMBERSHIP £50, £65 (associate); £50/$100 (overseas)

Full membership is limited to professional crime writers, but publishers, literary agents, booksellers, etc. who specialise in crime, are eligible for Associate membership. The Association has regional chapters throughout the country, including Scotland. Meetings are held regularly with informative talks frequently given by police, scenes of crime officers, lawyers, etc., and a weekend conference is held annually in different parts of the country. Produces a monthly newsletter for members called *Red Herrings* and presents various annual awards (see entries under *Prizes*).

The Critics' Circle
c/o Catherine Cooper, 69 Marylebone Lane, London W1U 2PH
☎020 7224 1410
www.criticscircle.org.uk

President *Marianne Gray*
Honorary General Secretary *Denise Silvester-Carr*
SUBSCRIPTION £25 p.a.

Membership by invitation only. Aims to uphold and promote the art of criticism (and the commercial rates of pay thereof) and preserve the interests of its members: professionals involved in criticism of film, drama, music, dance and art.

Cyngor Llyfrau Cymru
See **Welsh Books Council**

Data Publishers Association
Queen's House, 28 Kingsway, London WC2B 6JR
☎020 7405 0836
✉ christine@dpa.org.uk
www.dpa.org.uk

Contact *Christine Scott*
SUBSCRIPTION £430 to £2270 p.a.

Since 1970, the DPA has existed to serve, promote and protect the interests of all companies operating in the directory, data and search publishing sector. Today, the industry contributes well over £1 billion to the UK economy. The DPA membership not only includes mainstream data providers but also a whole host of organisations providing services and products to the data provision and publishing sector, such as printers, software solution providers and contract directory publishers. The DPA's members are predominantly UK companies but it also offers membership to overseas companies

with UK interests. It provides its members with opportunities to develop their businesses by providing a complete and diverse range of services, including communications, networking, training and seminars, statistics, representation to government, publicity and promotion, legal support and recognition.

Department for Culture, Media and Sport
2–4 Cockspur Street, London SW1Y 5DH
☎020 7211 6000 Fax 020 7211 6270
✉ matt.francis@culture.gsi.gov.uk
Director of Communications *Paddy Feeny*

The Department for Culture, Media and Sport has responsibilities for Government policies relating to the arts, museums and galleries, sport, the 2012 Olympic & Paralympic Games, gambling, broadcasting, Press freedom and regulation, the built historic environment, the film and music industries, tourism and the National Lottery. It funds the **Arts Council**, national museums and galleries, the **British Library**, the **Public Lending Right** and the Royal Commission on Historical Manuscripts. It is responsible within Government for the public library service in England, and for library and information matters generally, where they are not the responsibility of other departments.

DOI Registration Agency
3rd Floor, Midas House, 62 Goldsworth Road, Woking GU21 6LQ
☎0870 777 8712 Fax 0870 777 8714
✉ doi@nielsenbookdata.co.uk
www.doi.nielsenbookdata.co.uk

Manager, ISBN, SAN & DOI Agencies *Diana Williams*
Senior Manager, Registration Services ISBN, SAN & DOI Agencies *Julian Sowa*

DOIs (Digital Object Identifiers) are used to uniquely identify files or other resources on the Internet. The DOI Registration Agency is responsible for issuing DOI prefixes and numbers and can provide help and advice on maintaining DOIs. BookData also runs the **ISBN** and **SAN** agencies (see entries).

Drama Association of Wales
The Old Library Building, Singleton Road, Splott, Cardiff CF24 2ET
☎029 2045 2200 Fax 029 2045 2277
✉ aled.daw@virgin.net
www.amdram.co.uk/daw

Contact *Teresa Hennessy*

Runs a large playscript lending library; holds an annual playwriting competition (see entry under **Prizes**); offers a script-reading service (£25 full mss; £17.50 one-act play) which usually takes three months from receipt of play to issue of reports. From plays submitted to the reading service, selected scripts are considered for publication of a short run (70–200 copies). Writers receive a percentage of the cover price on sales and a percentage of the performance fee.

Edinburgh Bibliographical Society

National Library of Scotland, George IV Bridge, Edinburgh EH1 1EW
✉ warrenmcdougall@aol.com
www.edbibsoc.lib.ed.ac.uk

Secretary *Warren McDougall*
SUBSCRIPTION £15; £20 (institution); £10 (student)

Founded 1890. Organises lectures on bibliographical topics and visits to libraries. Publishes an annual journal, which is free to members, and other occasional publications.

Educational Publishers Council

See **The Publishers Association**

Electronic Publishers' Forum

See **The Publishers Association**

The English Association

University of Leicester, University Road, Leicester LE1 7RH
☎0116 252 3982 Fax 0116 252 2301
✉ engassoc@le.ac.uk
www.le.ac.uk/engassoc

Chief Executive *Helen Lucas*
Contact *Julia Hughes*

Founded 1906 to promote understanding and appreciation of the English language and its literatures. Activities include sponsoring a number of publications and organising lectures and conferences for teachers, plus annual sixth-form conferences. Publications include *The Year's Work in Critical and Cultural Theory*; *English, The Use of English*; *English 4–11*; *Essays and Studies* and *The Year's Work in English Studies*.

English PEN

6–8 Amwell Street, London EC1R 1UQ
☎020 7713 0023 Fax 020 7837 7838
✉ enquiries@englishpen.org
www.englishpen.org

Director *Jonathan Heawood*

MEMBERSHIP Cheque/standing order: £45/£40 (London/overseas); £40/£35 (country); £15 (students)

English PEN is part of International PEN, a worldwide association of writers and other literary professionals which promotes literature, fights for freedom of expression and speaks out for writers who are imprisoned or harassed for having criticised their governments, or for publishing other unpopular views.

Founded in London in 1921, International PEN now consists of over 130 centres in almost 100 countries. PEN originally stood for poets, essayists and novelists, but membership is now open to all literary professionals. It is also possible to become a 'Friend of English PEN'. A programme of talks and discussions, and other activities such as social gatherings, is supplemented by mailings, website and annual congress at one of the centre countries.

Federation of Entertainment Unions

1 Highfield, Twyford, Nr Winchester SO21 1QR
☎01962 713134 Fax 01962 713134
✉ harris.s@btconnect.com

Secretary *Steve Harris*

Plenary meetings six times annually. Additionally, there are Training, Equalities & European Committees. Represents the following unions: British Actors' Equity Association; Broadcasting Entertainment Cinematograph and Theatre Union; Musicians' Union; AMICUS; Professional Footballers' Association; **National Union of Journalists**; **The Writers' Guild of Great Britain**.

The Federation of Worker Writers and Community Publishers (FWWCP)

Burslem School of Art, Queen Street, Stoke on Trent ST6 3EJ
☎01782 822327
✉ thefwwcp@tiscali.co.uk
www.thefwwcp.org.uk

Administrator/Coordinator *Tim Diggles*

The FWWCP is a federation of writing groups committed to writing and publishing based on working-class experience and creativity. The FWWCP is the membership's collective national voice and has for some time been given funding by the Arts Council. Founded in 1976, it comprises around 80 member groups, each one with its own identity, reflecting its community and membership. These groups represent over 5000 people who regularly (often weekly) meet to offer constructive criticism, produce books and tapes, perform and share skills, offering creative and critical support. There are writers' workshops of long standing; adult literacy organisations; groups working mainly in oral and local history; groups and local networks of writers who come together to publish, train or perform; groups with a specific remit to further the aims of a section of the community such as the homeless or disabled.

Although diverse in nature, member organisations share the aim of making writing and publishing accessible to people and encourage them to take an active, cooperative and democratic role in writing, performing and publishing. The main activities include training days and weekends to learn and share skills, a quarterly magazine, a quarterly broadsheet of members' writing, a major annual festival of writing and networking between member organisations. The FWWCP has published a number of anthologies and is willing to work with other organisations on publishing projects. Membership is open only to groups but individuals will be put in touch with groups which can help them, and become friends of the Federation. Contact the address above for an information leaflet.

Fellowship of Authors and Artists

PO Box 158, Hertford SG13 8FA
☎0870 747 2514 Fax 0870 116 3398
www.author-fellowship.co.uk

Contact *Graham Irwin*

Founded in 2000 to promote and encourage the use of writing and all art forms as a means of therapy and self healing; to provide a valuable resource and meeting point for all interested parties including, but not limited to, writers, artists, counsellors and healers; to publish as Web pages or e-books any suitable works that may help to support or promote the aims of the fellowship.

Foreign Press Association in London

11 Carlton House Terrace, London SW1Y 5AJ
☎020 7930 0445 Fax 020 7925 0469
✉ enquiries@foreign-press.org.uk
www.foreign-press.org.uk

Director *Roy Payne*

ANNUAL SUBSCRIPTION Details available on the website

Founded 1888. Non-profit-making service association for foreign correspondents based in London, providing a variety of press-related services. Welcomes enquiries about media-related venue hire.

The Gaelic Books Council

See **Comhairle nan Leabhraichean**

The Garden Writers' Guild

c/o Institute of Horticulture, 14/15 Belgrave Square SW1X 8PS
☎020 7245 6943
✉ gwg@horticulture.org.uk
www.gardenwriters.co.uk

Contact *Erin Taylor*

SUBSCRIPTION £50; (£45 to Institute of Horticulture members); £60 (associate members)

Founded 1990. Aims to raise the quality of gardening communication, to help members operate efficiently and profitably, to improve liaison between garden communicators and the horticultural industry. Administers an annual awards scheme. Operates a mailing service and organises press briefing days.

Guild of Agricultural Journalists

Isfield Cottage, Church Road, Crowborough TN6 1BN
☎01892 610628
✉ don.gomery@btinternet.com
www.gaj.org.uk

Honorary General Secretary *Don Gomery*
SUBSCRIPTION £52 p.a.

Founded 1944 to promote a high professional standard among journalists who specialise in agriculture, horticulture and allied subjects. Represents members' interests with representative bodies in the industry; provides a forum through meetings and social activities for members to meet eminent people in the industry; maintains contact with associations of agricultural journalists overseas; promotes schemes for the education of members and for the provision of suitable entrants into agricultural journalism.

Guild of Editors

See **Society of Editors**

The Guild of Food Writers

255 Kent House Road, Beckenham BR3 1JQ
☎020 8659 0422
✉ gfw@gfw.co.uk
www.gfw.co.uk

Administrator *Jonathan Woods*

SUBSCRIPTION £70

Founded 1985. The objects of the Guild are to bring together professional food writers including journalists, broadcasters and authors, to extend the range of members' knowledge and experience by arranging discussions, tastings and visits, and to encourage new writers through competitions and awards. The Guild aims to contribute to the growth of public interest in, and knowledge of, the subject of food and to campaign for improvements in the quality of food.

Guild of Motoring Writers

39 Beswick Avenue, Ensbury Park, Bournemouth BH10 4EY

☎01202 518808 Fax 01202 518808

✉ generalsec@gomw.co.uk

www.guildofmotoringwriters.co.uk

General Secretary *Patricia Lodge*

Founded 1944. Represents members' interests and provides a forum for members to exchange information.

Horror Writers Association

244 Fifth Avenue, Suite 2767, New York, NY 10001, USA

✉ hwa@horror.org

www.horror.org

www.horror.org/UK (UK Chapter)

Founded 1987. World-wide organisation of writers and publishers dedicated to promoting the interests of writers of horror and dark fantasy. Publishes a monthly newsletter, issues e-mail bulletins, gives access to lists of horror agents, reviewers and bookstores; and keys to the 'Members Only' area of the HWA website. Presents the annual **Bram Stoker Awards** (see entry under *Prizes*).

HWA

See **Horror Writers Association**

Independent Publishers Guild

PO Box 93, Royston SG8 5GH

☎01763 247014 Fax 01763 246293

✉ info@ipg.uk.com

www.ipg.uk.com

Executive Director *Bridget Shine*

Founded 1962. Membership open to independent publishers, packagers and suppliers, i.e. professionals in allied fields. Regular meetings, annual conference, seminars, mailings and e-mail bulletin.

Independent Theatre Council

12 The Leathermarket, Weston Street, London SE1 3ER

☎020 7403 1727 Fax 020 7403 1745

✉ admin@itc-arts.org

www.itc-arts.org

Chief Executive *Charlotte Jones*

The Independent Theatre Council (ITC) is a UK management association for the performing arts. Since 1974 it has empowered and supported its diverse membership by providing management, legal and financial advice; developing tailored arts management training; creating networking opportunities and representing the sector. Publications available from ITC include *The ITC Practical Guide for Writers and Companies*. ITC negotiates contracts and has established standard agreements for theatre professionals with Equity. The rights and fee structure agreement, reached with **The Writers' Guild** in 1991, was updated in December 2002 and rates of pay are reviewed annually. Contact The Writers' Guild or visit ITC's website for further details.

Institute of Copywriting

Overbrook Business Centre, Poolbridge Road, Blackford, Wedmore BS28 4PA

☎0800 781 1715 Fax 01934 713492

✉ copy@inst.org

www.inst.org/copy

Secretary *Lynn Hall*

Founded 1991 to promote copywriters and copywriting (writing publicity material). Maintains a code of practice. Membership is open to students as well as experienced practitioners. Runs training courses (see entry under *UK Writers' Courses*). Has a list of approved copywriters. Answers queries relating to copywriting. Contact the Institute for a free booklet.

Institute of Translation and Interpreting (ITI)

Fortuna House, South Fifth Street, Milton Keynes MK9 2EU

☎01908 325250 Fax 01908 325259

✉ info@iti.org.uk

www.iti.org.uk

Founded 1986. The ITI is an association of translators and interpreters to promote the highest standards in their field. It has strong corporate membership and runs professional development courses and conferences. Membership is open to those with a genuine and proven involvement in translation and interpreting (including students). ITI's bi-monthly *Bulletin* and other publications are available from the Secretariat, which also offers a free referral service for those in need of a professional translator/interpreter. ITI's *Directory of Members* is available online. ITI is a full and active member of FIT (International Federation of Translators).

IoL
See **Chartered Institute of Linguists**

Irish Book Publishers' Association
See **CLÉ**

Irish Copyright Licensing Agency Ltd
25 Denzille Lane, Dublin 2, Republic of Ireland
☎00 353 1 662 4211 Fax 00 353 1 662 4213
✉ info@icla.ie
www.icla.ie

Executive Director *Samantha Holman*

Founded 1992 by writers and publishers in Ireland to provide a scheme through which rights holders can give permission, and users of copyright material can obtain permission, to copy.

Irish Playwrights and Screenwriters Guild
Art House, Curved Street, Temple Bar, Dublin 2, Republic of Ireland
☎00 353 1 670 9970
✉ info@script.ie
www.script.ie

Contact *David Cavanagh*
SUBSCRIPTION details available on request

Founded in 1969 to safeguard the rights of scriptwriters for radio, stage and screen.

Irish Translators' & Interpreters' Association (ITIA)
Irish Writers' Centre, 19 Parnell Square, Dublin 1, Republic of Ireland
☎00 353 1 872 1302 Fax 00 353 1 872 6282
✉ itiasecretary@eircom.net
www.translatorsassociation.ie

Chairperson *Annette Schiller*
Honorary Secretary *Mary Phelan*
Treasurer *Mirian Watchorn*
Annual Membership €120 (corporate); €75 (professional); €40 (ordinary); €20 (student)

Founded 1986. The Association is open to all translators: technical, commercial, literary and cultural, and to all classes of interpreters. It is also for those with an interest in translation such as teachers and third-level students. Information

on the profession of interpreting and translation and a Register of members are available on the website. Publishes a newsletter, *Translation Ireland* and an ezine, the *ITIA Bulletin*.

Irish Writers' Union
Irish Writers' Centre, 19 Parnell Square, Dublin 1, Republic of Ireland
☎00 353 1 872 1302
✉ iwu@ireland-writers.com
www.ireland-writers.com

Chairperson *Dr Conor Kostick*
SUBSCRIPTION €50 p.a.; €30 (associate)

Founded 1986 to promote the interests and protect the rights of writers in Ireland.

ISBN Agency
3rd Floor, Midas House, 62 Goldsworth Road, Woking GU21 6LQ
☎0870 777 8712 Fax 0870 777 8714
✉ isbn@nielsenbookdata.co.uk
www.isbn.nielsenbookdata.co.uk

Manager, ISBN, SAN & DOI Agencies *Diana Williams*
Senior Manager, Registration Services ISBN, SAN & DOI Agencies *Julian Sowa*

ISBNs are product numbers used by all sections of the book trade for ordering and listing purposes. The ISBN Agency is responsible for issuing ISBNs to publishers based in the UK and Republic of Ireland and can provide help and advice on changing from 10 to 13-digits. BookData also runs the **SAN** & **DOI** agencies (see entries).

Isle of Man Authors
11 Christian Close, Ballastowell Gardens, Ramsey IM8 2AU
☎01624 815634

Secretary *Mrs Beryl Sandwell*
SUBSCRIPTION £5 p.a.

An association of writers living on the Isle of Man, which has links with the **Society of Authors**.

ITC
See **Independent Theatre Council**

ITI
See **Institute of Translation and Interpreting**

IVCA (International Visual Communication Association)
19 Pepper Street, Glengall Bridge, London E14 9RP

☎020 7512 0571 Fax 020 7512 0591
✉ info@ivca.org
www.ivca.org
Chief Executive *Wayne Drew*
Publications and Information Officer *Philip Fey*
The IVCA is a professional association representing the interests of the users and suppliers of visual communications. In particular it pursues the interests of producers, commissioners and manufacturers involved in the non-broadcast and independent facilities industries and also business event companies. It represents all sizes of company and freelance individuals, offering information and advice services, publications, a professional network, special interest groups, a magazine and a variety of events including the UK's Film and Video Communications Festival.

Learning on Screen (British Universities Film & Video Council)

77 Wells Street, London W1T 3QJ
☎020 7393 1512 Fax 020 7393 1555
www.bufvc.ac.uk/learningonscreen.ac.uk
Learning on Screen is the title which was used by the Society for Screen-Based Learning (SSBL) for its courses and conferences. In January 2004 the SSBL merged with the British Universities Film & Video Council (BUFVC). The title Learning on Screen, now adopted by the BUFVC, will continue for a range of practical, 'hands-on' one-day courses and events around the country as well as the annual Learning on Screen conference and Awards. The BUFVC promotes the production, study and use of moving images and related media for learning, teaching and research. It offers a specialist information service, publications, online services and the unique Off-Air Recording Back-Up Service, recording 44,000 hours per year of UK television.

The Library Association

See **CILIP:The Chartered Institute of Library and Information Professionals**

literaturetraining

PO Box 23595, Leith, Edinburgh EH6 7YX
☎0131 553 2210
✉ info@literaturetraining.com
www.literaturetraining.com
Director *Philippa Johnston*
The UK's only dedicated provider of free information and advice on professional development for writers and literature professionals. Draws on the expertise of its six partner organisations: **Apples & Snakes**, Lapidus, the **National Association of Writers in Education**, the **National Association for Literature Development**, **Scottish Book Trust** and **Writernet**. Their online directory contains latest information on courses, workshops, jobs, residencies, submissions, competitions, conferences and events, organisations, books, magazines and funding for professional development. Other services include a fortnightly e-bulletin, an information and help line and a developing range of info sheets and specially commissioned features relating to creative and professional practice. literaturetraining is a partner in the CreativePeopleNetwork.

Llenyddiaeth Cymru Dramor

See **Welsh Literature Abroad**

The MCPS–PRS Alliance

29–33 Berners Street, London W1T 3AB
☎020 7306 4229 Fax 020 7306 4340
www.mcps-prs-alliance.co.uk
JOINING FEE £100 (one-off)
PRS ensures that composers, songwriters and music publishers are paid royalties when their music is used. The music does not need to be published or recorded for eligibility for PRS membership.

Medical Journalists' Association

Fairfield, Cross in Hand, Heathfield TN21 0SH
☎01435 868786 Fax 01435 865714
✉ pigache@tiscali.co.uk
www.mja-uk.org
Chairman *Oliver Gillie*
Honorary Secretary *Philippa Pigache*
SUBSCRIPTION £40 p.a. (full); £30 (associate); £10 (junior)
Founded 1967. Aims to improve the quality and practice of medical and health journalism and to improve relationships and understanding between medical and health journalists and the health and medical professions. Over 400 members. Regular meetings with senior figures in medicine and medico politics; educational workshops on important subject areas or issues of the day; debates; awards for medical journalists from commercial sponsors, plus the MJA's own annual awards for journalism and books. Publishes a newsletter five times a year.

Medical Writers' Group

The Society of Authors, 84 Drayton Gardens, London SW10 9SB
☎020 7373 6642 Fax 020 7373 5768

✉ info@societyofauthors.org
www.societyofauthors.org/medical
Contact *The Secretary*
Founded 1980. A specialist group within the **Society of Authors** offering advice and help to authors of medical books.

Mystery Writers of America, Inc.
17 East 47th Street, 6th Floor, New York, NY 10017, USA
☎001 212 888 8171 Fax 001 212 888 8107
✉ mwa@mysterywriters.org
www.mysterywriters.org
Administrative Manager *Margery Flax*
SUBSCRIPTION $95 (US)
Founded 1945. Aims to promote and protect the interests of writers of the mystery genre in all media; to educate and inform its membership on matters relating to their profession; to uphold a standard of excellence and raise the profile of this literary form to the world at large. Holds an annual banquet at which the 'Edgars' are awarded (named after Edgar Allan Poe).

National Association for Literature Development
PO Box 49657, London N8 7YZ
☎020 7272 8386
✉ dir@nald.org
www.nald.org
Contact *Melanie Abrahams*
NALD is the largest membership organisation for literary professionals. The only national body for all those involved in developing writers, readers and literary audiences. Offers individual, organisational or corporate membership.

National Association of Writers Groups
The Arts Centre, Biddick Lane, Washington NE38 2AB
☎01262 609228
✉ nawg@tesco.net
www.nawg.co.uk
Secretary *Diane Wilson*
SUBSCRIPTION £30 p.a. + £5 registration (group); £14 p.a. (individual)
Founded 1995 with the object of furthering the interests of writers' groups and individuals throughout the UK. A registered charity, No. 1059047, NAWG is strictly non-sectarian and non-political. Publishes a bi-monthly newsletter, distributed to member groups; gives free entry to competitions for group anthologies, poetry, short stories, articles, novels and sketches; holds an annual open festival of writing with 21 workshops, seminars, individual surgeries led by professional, high-profile writers. Membership is open to all writers' groups and individual writers – there are no restrictions or qualifications required for joining; 160 groups are affiliated to-date.

National Association of Writers in Education
PO Box 1, Sheriff Hutton, York YO60 7YU
☎01653 618429
✉ info@nawe.co.uk
www.nawe.co.uk
Contact *Paul Munden*
SUBSCRIPTION £20 p.a. (individual); £10 (student); £60 (institution); £30 (overseas)
Founded 1991. Aims to promote the contribution of living writers to education and to encourage both the practice and the critical appreciation of creative writing. Has over 900 members. Organises national conferences and training courses. A directory of writers who work in schools, colleges and the community is available online. Publishes a magazine, *Writing in Education*, issued free to members three times per year.

National Campaign for the Arts
1 Kingly Street, London W1B 5PA
☎020 7287 3777 Fax 020 7287 4777
✉ nca@artscampaign.org.uk
www.artscampaign.org.uk
Director *Louise de Winter*
The UK's only independent lobbying organisation representing the arts. The NCA seeks to safeguard, promote and develop the arts and win public and political recognition for their importance as a key element in the national culture. Its members shape its campaign work, provide its mandate and the core funding, through subscriptions, that enable the NCA to act independently on their behalf; the organisation receives no public subsidy. Members have access to the NCA's information, advice, seminars, conferences and publications. Membership is open to organisations and individuals working in or with an interest in the arts. Literature subscriptions available.

National Centre for Research in Children's Literature (NCRCL)

Bede House, School of Arts, Digby Stuart College, Roehampton University, Roehampton Lane, London SW15 5PH
☎020 8392 3008 Fax 020 8392 3819
✉ g.lathey@roehampton.ac.uk *or* l.sainsbury@roehampton.ac.uk
www.ncrcl.ac.uk

The National Centre for Research in Children's Literature facilitates and supports research exchange in the field of children's literature. Runs an internationally acclaimed MA Programme, an annual conference in association with the International Board on Books for Young People (IBBY) and the biennial Children's Literature International Summer School.

National Literacy Trust

Swire House, 59 Buckingham Gate, London SW1E 6AJ
☎020 7828 2435 Fax 020 7931 9986
✉ contact@literacytrust.org.uk
www.literacytrust.org.uk

Director *Jonathan Douglas*

Founded 1993. Independent registered charity 'dedicated to building a literate nation in which everyone enjoys the skills, confidence and pleasures that literacy can bring.' The only organisation concerned with raising literacy standards for all age groups throughout the UK. Maintains an extensive website with literacy news, summaries of key issues, research and examples of practice nationwide; organises conferences, courses and training events and runs a range of initiatives to turn promising ideas into effective action. These include the National Reading Campaign, funded by the government; Reading Is Fundamental, UK, which provides free books to children; Reading The Game, involving the professional football community and the Talk To Your Baby campaign.

National Union of Journalists

Headland House, 308 Gray's Inn Road, London WC1X 8DP
☎020 7278 7916 Fax 020 7837 8143
✉ info@nuj.org.uk
www.nuj.org.uk

General Secretary *Jeremy Dear*
SUBSCRIPTION £182 p.a. (freelance) or 1% of annual income if lower; or 0.5% if income less than £13,600 p.a.

Represents journalists in all sectors of publishing, print, broadcast and online media. Responsible for wages and conditions agreements which apply across the industry. Provides advice and representation for its members, as well as administering unemployment and other benefits. Publishes various guides and magazines: *On-Line Freelance Directory*; *On-Line Fees Guide*; *The Journalist* and *The Freelance*.

NCRCL

See **National Centre for Research in Children's Literature**

New Playwrights Trust

See **Writernet**

New Producers Alliance (NPA)

Room 7.03 The Tea Building, 56 Shoreditch High Street, London E1 6JJ
☎020 7613 0440 Fax 020 7729 1852
✉ queries@npa.org.uk
www.npa.org.uk

Founded 1993. National membership and training organisation for independent new filmmakers, the NPA provides a forum and focus for over 800 members, ranging from students and first timers to highly experienced feature filmmakers and industry affiliates. Services include: producer, writer and director training from 'entrance' to 'advanced' levels; seminars, masterclasses, business breakfasts, themed networking evenings and preview screenings; in addition, the NPA supports its members at film festivals including Cannes, Berlin and Edinburgh with events and industry receptions. Provides free advice services including Legal and Tax & Accounting; the NPA also publishes a monthly newsletter and online members directory included in the website.

New Writing North

Culture Lab, Grand Assembly Rooms, Newcastle University, King's Walk, Newcastle upon Tyne NE1 7RU
☎0191 222 1332 Fax 0191 222 1372
✉ mail@newwritingnorth.com
www.newwritingnorth.com

Director *Claire Malcolm*
Administrator *Catherine Lancaster*

New Writing North is the literature development agency for the Arts Council England, North East region and offers many useful services to writers, organising events, readings and workshops. NWN has a website and mailing list by which members of the public can receive news of literary events, courses and work opportunities. Administers the **Northern**

Rock Foundation Writer's Award (see entry under *Bursaries, Fellowships and Grants*) and the Northern Writers' Awards, which include tailored development packages (mentoring and financial help) for local writers at different stages of their careers. NWN works to develop theatre writing and creative radio writing projects within the region, as well as a strong education and community-based programme, working with schools, LEAs and both public and private sector organisations.

The Newspaper Society

St Andrew's House, 18–20 St Andrew Street, London EC4A 3AY
☎020 7632 7424 Fax 020 7632 7401
✉ ns@newspapersoc.org.uk
www.newspapersoc.org.uk

Director *David Newell*

The Newspaper Society is the voice of Britain's regional press – a £3 billion advertising medium read by over 40 million adults a week, It promotes the interests of the regional and local press, provides legal advice and lobbying services, holds a series of conferences and seminars, and runs the annual Local Newspaper Week.

NPA

See **New Producers Alliance**

Outdoor Writers & Photographers Guild

PO Box 520, Bamber Bridge, Preston PR5 8LF
☎01772 321243 Fax 0870 137 8888
✉ secretary@owgp.org.uk
www.owg.org.uk

Secretary *Terry Marsh*
SUBSCRIPTION £66 p.a.

Founded 1980 to promote, encourage and assist the development and maintenance of professional standards among those involved in all aspects of outdoor journalism. Members include writers, photographers, broadcasters, filmmakers, editors, publishers and illustrators. Publishes a quarterly journal, *Bootprint*, and an annual *Directory* (£30; free to members). Presents five Awards for Excellence plus other awards in recognition of achievement. Maintains a website of members' details; informal members' e-mail 'chatline' to exchange news and information; sends out regular media press releases; organises press trips.

PACT (Producers Alliance for Cinema and Television)

Procter House, 2nd Floor, 1 Procter Street, London WC1V 6DW
☎020 7067 4367 Fax 020 7067 4377
✉ enquiries@pact.co.uk
www.pact.co.uk

Chief Executive *John McVay*

Founded 1991. PACT is the trade association of the UK independent feature film, television, animation and interactive media production sector and is a key contact point for foreign producers seeking British co-production, co-finance partners and distributors. Works for producers in the industry at every level and operates a members' regional network throughout the UK. Membership services include: a dedicated industrial relations unit; discounted legal advice; a varied calendar of events; business advice; representation at international film and television markets; a comprehensive research programme; a monthly magazine, a members' online directory; affiliation with European and international producers' organisations; extensive information and production advice. Lobbies actively with broadcasters, financiers and governments to ensure that the producer's voice is heard and understood in Britain and Europe on all matters affecting the feature film, television, animation and interactive production industry.

PEN

See **English PEN**

Performing Right Society

See **The MCPS–PRS Alliance**

Periodical Publishers Association (PPA)

Queens House, 28 Kingsway, London WC2B 6JR
☎020 7404 4166 Fax 020 7404 4167
✉ info1@ppa.co.uk
www.ppa.co.uk

Founded 1913 to promote and protect the interests of its members in particular and the magazine industry as a whole.

The Personal Managers' Association Ltd

1 Summer Road, East Molesey KT8 9LX
☎020 8398 9796 Fax 020 8398 9796
✉ info@thepma.com

Co-chairs *Michelle Kass, Alan Brodie, Nicholas*

Young
Secretary *Angela Adler*
SUBSCRIPTION £275 p.a.

An association of artists' and dramatists' agents (membership not open to individuals). Monthly meetings for exchange of information and discussion. Maintains a code of conduct and acts as a lobby when necessary. Applicants screened. A high proportion of play agents are members of the PMA.

The Picture Research Association
c/o 1 Willow Court, off Willow Street, London EC2A 4QB
☎020 7739 8544 Fax 020 7782 0011
✉ chair@picture-research.org.uk
www.picture-research.org.uk
Chair *Veneta Bullen*
Membership Secretary *Frances Topp*
SUBSCRIPTION Members: £45 (introductory); £55 (full); £50 (associate). Magazine only: £16 (inland); £20 (overseas)

Founded 1977 as the Society of Picture Researchers & Editors. The Picture Research Association is a professional body for picture researchers, managers, picture editors and all those involved in the research, management and supply of visual material to all forms of the media. The Association's main aims are to promote the interests and specific skills of its members internationally; to promote and maintain professional standards; to bring together those involved in the research and publication of visual material; to provide a forum for the exchange of information and to provide guidance to its members. Free advisory service for members, regular meetings, quarterly magazine, monthly newsletter and Freelance Register.

Player–Playwrights
9 Hillfield Park, London N10 3QT
☎020 8883 0371
✉ P-P@dial.pipex.com
www.playerplaywrights.co.uk
Presidents *Laurence Marks, Maurice Gran*
Contact *Peter Thompson* (at the address above)
SUBSCRIPTION Members: £10 (joining fee); £6 p.a. thereafter, plus £2 per attendance

Founded 1948. A society giving opportunity for writers new to stage, radio, television and film, as well as others finding difficulty in achieving results, to work with writers established in those media. At weekly meetings (7.30 pm–10.00 pm, Mondays, upstairs at the Horse and Groom, 128 Great Portland Street, London W1), members'

scripts are read or performed by actor members and afterwards assessed and dissected in general discussion. New writers and new acting members are always welcome.

PLR
See **Public Lending Right**

PLS
See **Publishers Licensing Society Ltd**

PMA
See **The Personal Managers' Association Ltd**

Poetry Book Society
See under *Organisations of Interest to Poets*

Poetry Ireland
See under *Organisations of Interest to Poets*

The Poetry Society
See under *Organisations of Interest to Poets*

Press Complaints Commission
Halton House, 20/23 Holborn, London EC1N 2JD
☎020 7831 0022 Fax 020 7831 0025
✉ pcc@pcc.org.uk
www.pcc.org.uk
Director *Tim Toulmin*
Information Officer *Tonia Milton*

Founded in 1991 to deal with complaints from members of the public about the editorial content of newspapers and magazines. Administers the editors' Code of Practice covering such areas as accuracy, privacy, harrassment and intrusion into grief. Publications available: *Code of Practice, How to Complain* and *Annual Review*.

Producers Alliance for Cinema and Television
See **PACT**

Public Lending Right
Richard House, Sorbonne Close, Stockton-on-Tees TS17 6DA
☎01642 604699 Fax 01642 615641
✉ authorservices@plr.uk.com
www.plr.uk.com
Registrar *Jim Parker*

Founded 1979. Public Lending Right is funded by the Department for Culture, Media and Sport to recompense authors for books borrowed from public libraries. Authors can be registered for PLR only when application is made during the author's lifetime. To qualify, an author must be resident in a European Union member state, or in Iceland, Liechtenstein or Norway, and the book must be printed, bound and put on sale with an ISBN. In 2007, £6.81 million was distributed to over 23,800 authors (£6.54 million in the previous year) with 286 authors reaching the maximum payment threshold of £6600. The Rate Per Loan was raised in 2007 to 5.98 pence, its highest level to date. Consult the website for further information.

The Publishers Association
29B Montague Street, London WC1B 5BW
☎020 7691 9191 Fax 020 7691 9199
✉ mail@publishers.org.uk
www.publishers.org.uk
Chief Executive *Simon Juden*

The national UK trade association for books, learned journals, and electronic publications, with around 200 member companies in the industry. Very much a trade body representing the industry to Government and the European Commission, and providing services to publishers. Publishes the *Directory of Publishing* in association with **Continuum**. Also home of the Educational Publishers Council (school books), PA's International Division (BDCI), the Academic and Professional Division, the Trade Publishers Council and the Electronic Publishers' Forum.

Publishers' Association of South Africa
PO Box 106, Greenpoint 8051, Cape Town, South Africa
☎00 27 21 425 2721 Fax 00 27 21 421 3270
✉ pasa@publishsa.co.za
www.publishsa.co.za

Founded in 1992 to represent publishing in South Africa, a key industry sector. With a membership of 162 companies, the Association includes commercial organisations, university presses, one-person privately-owned publishers as well as importers and distributors.

Publishers Licensing Society Ltd
37–41 Gower Street, London WC1E 6HH
☎020 7299 7730 Fax 020 7299 7780
✉ pls@pls.org.uk
www.pls.org.uk
Chief Executive *Alicia Wise*
Operations Manager *Caroline Elmslie*

Founded in 1981, the PLS obtains mandates from publishers which grant PLS the authority to license photocopying of pages from published works. Some licences for digitisation of printed works are available. PLS aims to maximise revenue from licences for mandating publishers and to expand the range and repertoire of mandated publishers available to licence holders. It supports the **Copyright Licensing Agency Ltd (CLA)** in its efforts to increase the number of legitimate users through the issuing of licences and vigorously pursues any infringements of copyright works belonging to rights' holders.

Publishers Publicity Circle
65 Airedale Avenue, London W4 2NN
☎020 8994 1881
✉ ppc-@lineone.net
www.publisherspublicitycircle.co.uk
Contact *Heather White*

Enables book publicists from both publishing houses and freelance PR agencies to meet and share information regularly. Meetings, held monthly in central London, provide a forum for press journalists, television and radio researchers and producers to meet publicists collectively. A directory of the PPC membership is published each year and distributed to over 2500 media contacts.

Publishing Scotland
Scottish Book Centre, 137 Dundee Street, Edinburgh EH11 1BG
☎0131 228 6866 Fax 0131 228 3220
✉ katherine.naish@scottishbooks.org
www.publishingscotland.org
Director *Lorraine Fannin*
Membership Services and Marketing Manager *Liz Small*
Financial and Office Administrator *Carol Lothian*
Information and Professional Development Administrator *Katherine A. Naish*

Formerly known as the Scottish Publishers Association, Publishing Scotland is a development company and registered charity that works to promote publishing as a creative industry. It represents over 70 Scottish publishers, from multinationals to small presses, in a number of capacities, but primarily in the cooperative promotion and marketing of their books. Publishing Scotland also acts as an information centre for the trade and general public. Publishes annual *Directory of Publishing in Scotland*. Attends international book fairs; runs an extensive training programme; carries out industry research.

The Radio Academy

5 Market Place, London W1W 8AE
☎020 7255 2010 Fax 020 7255 2029
✉ info@radioacademy.org
www.radioacademy.org

Director *Trevor Dann*
SUBSCRIPTIONS £25 p.a. All patron members receive free membership.

Founded 1983. The professional body for people working in the audio industry, the Academy is dedicated to the encouragement, recognition and promotion of excellence throughout the UK audio industry. Membership ranges from students to Governors of the BBC. Hosts the annual Radio Festival which features speakers from all aspects of the industry; holds events in London and the regions; runs masterclasses for those who aspire to enter the audio industry, and seminars for the further development of professionals within the industry at various levels.

RadioCentre

77 Shaftesbury Avenue, London W1D 5DU
☎020 7306 2603 Fax 020 7306 2500

Chief Executive *Andrew Harrison*
Head of Strategy & Operations *Michael O'Brien*

RadioCentre represents commercial radio stations in the UK. Its role is to maintain and build a strong and successful commercial radio industry, both in terms of listening hours and revenues.

Romance Writers of America

16000 Stuebner Airline Road, Suite 140,
Spring, TX 77379, USA
☎001 832 717 5200 Fax 001 832 717 5201
✉ info@rwanational.org
www.rwanational.org

PR Coordinator *Nicole Kennedy*
MEMBERSHIP $75 p.a. plus $25 joining fee

Founded 1980. RWA, a non-profit association with more than 9000 members worldwide, provides a service to authors at all stages of their careers as well as to the romance publishing industry and its readers. Anyone pursuing a career in romantic fiction may join RWA. Holds an annual conference, and provides contests for both published and unpublished writers through the RITA Awards and Golden Hearts Awards.

The Romantic Novelists' Association

3 Griffin Road, Thame OX9 3LB
✉ ianandcatherinejones@btinternet.com
www.rna-uk.org

Contact *Catherine Jones* (Chairman)
SUBSCRIPTION £40 p.a. (full members); £45 (full, non-EU); £50 (associate); full and associate members who pay by standing order receive a £3 discount

Membership is open to published writers of romantic fiction (modern or historical), or those who have had one or more full-length serials published. Associate membership is open to publishers, editors, literary agents, booksellers, librarians and others having a close connection with novel writing and publishing. Membership in the New Writers' Scheme is available to a limited number of writers who have not yet had a full-length novel published. New Writers must submit a manuscript each year. The mss receive a report from experienced published members and the reading fee is paid with the annual subscription of £90 (£95 for non-EU members). Meetings are held in London and the regions with guest speakers. *Romance Matters* is published quarterly and issued free to members. The Association makes three annual awards: **The Romantic Novel of the Year**; Joan Hessayon New Writers Award for the best published novel by a new writer who has gone through the New Writers' Scheme and remains a member, and the Romance Prize for category romances.

Royal Festival Hall Literature & Talks

See entry under *Festivals*

Royal Society of Literature

Somerset House, Strand, London WC2R 1LA
☎020 7845 4676 Fax 020 7845 4679
✉ info@rslit.org
www.rslit.org

Chair *Maggie Gee, FRSL*
Secretary *Maggie Ferguson*
SUBSCRIPTION £40 p.a.

Founded 1820. Membership by application to the Secretary. Fellowships are conferred by the Society on the proposal of two Fellows. Membership benefits include lectures, discussion meetings and poetry readings. Lecturers have included Julian Barnes, Michael Holroyd, Don Paterson, Zadie Smith and Tom Stoppard. Presents the **Royal Society of Literature Ondaatje Prize**, the **Royal Society of Literature/Jerwood Awards** and the **V.S. Pritchett Memorial Prize**.

Royal Television Society

Kildare House, 3 Dorset Rise, London
EC4Y 8EN

☎020 7822 2810 Fax 020 7822 2811
✉ info@rts.org.uk
www.rts.org.uk
Membership Manager *Deborah Halls*
(membership@rts.org.uk)
MEMBERSHIP from £65 p.a.
Founded 1927. Covers all disciplines involved in the television industry. Provides a forum for debate and conferences on technical, social and cultural aspects of the medium. Presents various awards including journalism, programmes, technology and design. Publishes *Television Magazine* ten times a year for members and subscribers.

SAN Agency

3rd Floor, Midas House, 62 Goldsworth Road, Woking GU21 6LQ
☎0870 777 8712 Fax 0870 777 8714
✉ san@nielsenbookdata.co.uk
www.san.nielsenbookdata.co.uk
Manager, ISBN, SAN & DOI Agencies *Diana Williams*
Senior Manager, Registration Services ISBN, SAN & DOI Agencies *Julian Sowa*

SANs, Standard Address Numbers, are unique identifiers for geographical locations and can be assigned to the addresses of organisations involved in the book selling or publishing industries. The SAN Agency is responsible for managing the scheme on behalf of Book Industry Communication in the UK and Republic of Ireland. BookData also runs the **ISBN & DOI** agencies (see entries).

Science Fiction Foundation

37 Coventry Road, Ilford IG1 4QR
✉ sff.chair@gmail.com
www.sf-foundation.org
Founded 1970. The SFF is an international academic body for the furtherance of science fiction studies. Publishes a thrice-yearly magazine, *Foundation* (see entry under *Magazines*), which features academic articles and reviews of new fiction. Publishes a series of books on critical studies of science fiction, and arranges conferences, lectures and seminars on related topics. It also has a reference library (see entry under *Library Services*), housed at Liverpool University.

Scottish Book Trust

Sandeman House, Trunk's Close, 55 High Street, Edinburgh EH1 1SR
☎0131 524 0160 Fax 0131 524 0161
✉ info@scottishbooktrust.com
www.scottishbooktrust.com
Contact *Marc Lambert*
Scottish Book Trust exists to serve readers and writers in Scotland and works to ensure that everyone has access to good books and to related resources and opportunities. Operates 'Live Literature Scotland' which funds over 1200 visits a year by Scottish writers to a variety of institutions and groups; supports Scottish writing through a programme of professional training opportunities for writers, words@work; operates a touring programme for children's authors, Words on Wheels; works internationally promoting Scottish literature; publishes a variety of resources and leaflets to support readership; promotes other readership development opportunities. The Book Information Service provides free advice and support to readers and writers and the general public.

Scottish Daily Newspaper Society

21 Lansdowne Crescent, Edinburgh EH12 5EH
☎0131 535 1064 Fax 0131 535 1063
✉ info@sdns.org.uk
Director *Mr J.B. Raeburn*
Founded 1915. Trade association representing publishers of Scottish daily and Sunday newspapers including the major Scottish editions of UK national newspapers.

Scottish Library Association

See **CILIP in Scotland**

Scottish Newspaper Publishers Association

48 Palmerston Place, Edinburgh EH12 5DE
☎0131 220 4353 Fax 0131 220 4344
✉ info@snpa.org.uk
www.snpa.org.uk
Director *Mr S. Fairclough*
The representative body for the publishers of paid-for weekly and associated free newspapers in Scotland. Represents the interests of the industry to government, public and other bodies and provides a range of services including marketing of *The Scottish Weekly Press*, industrial relations, and education and training. It is an active supporter of the Press Complaints Commission.

Scottish Print Employers Federation

48 Palmerston Place, Edinburgh EH12 5DE
☎0131 220 4353 Fax 0131 220 4344

✉ info@spef.org.uk
www.spef.org.uk
Director *Mr S. Fairclough*

Founded 1910. Employers' organisation and trade association for the Scottish printing industry. Represents the interests of the industry to government, public and other bodies and provides a range of services including industrial relations, education, training and commercial activities. Negotiates a national wages and conditions agreement with Amicus GPM Sector. The Federation is a member of Intergraf, the international confederation for employers' associations in the printing industry, which represents its interests at European level.

Scottish Publishers Association
See **Publishing Scotland**

Scottish Screen
2nd Floor, 249 West George Street, Glasgow
G2 4QE
☎0141 302 1700 Fax 0141 302 1711
✉ info@scottishscreen.com
www.scottishscreen.com

Contact *Francis Lopez*

Scottish Screen is the national development agency for the screen industries in Scotland. 'We aim to inspire audiences, support new and existing talent and businesses, educate young people, and promote Scotland as a creative place to make great films, award-winning television and world renowned digital entertainment.'

Society for Editors and Proofreaders (SfEP)
Riverbank House, 1 Putney Bridge Approach,
London SW6 3JD
☎020 7736 3278/7736 0901 (training dept.)
Fax 020 7736 3318
✉ administration@sfep.org.uk
www.sfep.org.uk

Chair *Penny Williams*
Vice-Chair *Shena Deuchars*
Company Secretary *Val Rice*

SUBSCRIPTION £80 p.a. (individuals) plus £25 joining fee; corporate membership available. Founded 1988 in response to the growing number of freelance editors and their increasing importance to the publishing industry. Aims to promote high editorial standards by disseminating information through advice and training, and to achieve recognition of the professional status of its members. The Society also supports moves towards recognised standards of training

and accreditation for editors and proofreaders. It launched its own Accreditation in Proofreading test in 2002.

Society for Technical Communications (STC)
901 N. Stuart Street, Suite 904, Arlington,
Virginia 22203, USA
☎001 703 522 4114 Fax 001 703 522 2075
www.stc.org
www.stcuk.org

UK Chapter Membership Manager *Liz Hale*
(membership@stcuk.org)

Dedicated to advancing the arts and sciences of technical communication, the STC has more than 15,000 members worldwide, including technical writers, editors, graphic designers, videographers, multimedia artists, Web and intranet page information designers, translators and others whose work involves making technical information available to those who need it. The UK Chapter, established in 1985, hosts talks and seminars, runs an annual technical publications competition, and publishes its own newsletter six times a year.

The Society of Authors
84 Drayton Gardens, London SW10 9SB
☎020 7373 6642 Fax 020 7373 5768
✉ info@societyofauthors.org
www.societyofauthors.org

General Secretary *Mark Le Fanu*
Deputy General Secretary *Kate Pool*
SUBSCRIPTION £85/80 p.a.

The Society of Authors is an independent trade union, chaired by Tracy Chevalier, with some 8000 members. As well as campaigning for the profession, it advises members on negotiations with publishers, agents, broadcasting organisations, theatre managers and film companies and on queries or concerns members may have about the business aspects of their writing. The Society assists with complaints and takes action for breach of contract, copyright infringement, etc. Among the Society's publications are *The Author* (quarterly) and the *Quick Guides* series to various aspects of writing (all free of charge to members). Other services include vetting of contracts, emergency funds for writers, meetings and seminars, and various special discounts, including money off books, hotels and insurance. There are groups within the Society for academic writers, broadcasters, children's writers and illustrators, educational writers, medical writers and translators, as well as some regional groups. Authors under 35 or over 65, not earning a significant income from their writing, may apply for lower subscription rates (after their first year, in the case of over-65s). Contact the Society for a free booklet and a copy of *The Author* or visit the website.

The Society of Authors in Scotland

8 Briar Road, Kirkintilloch, Glasgow G66 3SA
☎0141 776 4280 Fax 0141 776 4280
✉ brian@bdosborne.fsnet.co.uk
www.writersorg.co.uk

Secretary *Brian D. Osborne*

The Scottish branch of the **Society of Authors**, which organises business meetings, social and bookshop events throughout Scotland.

Society of Children's Book Writers & Illustrators

✉ ra@britishscbwi.org
www.britishscbwi.org

British Isles Regional Adviser *Natascha Biebow*

Founded in 1968 by a group of Los Angeles-based writers, the SCBWI is the only international professional organisation for the exchange of information between writers, illustrators, editors, publishers, agents and others involved with literature for young people. With a membership of more than 12,000 worldwide, it holds two annual international conferences plus a number of regional events, publishes a bi-monthly journal and awards grants for works in progress. The British Isles region sponsors workshops and speaker events to help authors and illustrators develop their craft and market their work. It also facilitates local critique groups and publishes a quarterly regional newsletter. For membership enquiries, visit the website or contact membership@british scbwi.org

Society of Civil and Public Service Writers

17 The Green, Corby Glen, Grantham NG33 4NP
✉ joan@lewis5634.fsnet.co.uk
www.scpsw.co.uk

Membership Secretary *Mrs Joan Lewis*
SUBSCRIPTION £15 p.a.

Founded 1935. Welcomes serving and retired members of the Civil Service, armed forces, Post Office, BT, nursing profession and other public servants who are aspiring or published writers. Offers competitions for short story, article and poetry; postal folios for short story and article; AGM, occasional meetings and luncheon held in London; quarterly magazine, *Civil Service Author*, to which members may submit material; Poetry Workshop (extra £3) offers annual weekend outside London, anthology, newsletter, postal folio, competitions. S.a.e. to Secretary for details.

The Society of Creative Writers

28 Howard Mews, Denmark Road, Norwich NR3 4JU
☎01603 484424
✉ creativewriter@btconnect.com

Secretary *Inna Zabrodskaya*
SUBSCRIPTION £29 p.a.

'The Society of Creative Writers does not represent the writing profession but has been formed exclusively to promote creativity, originality and literary exploration and to help introduce and market individual writers and their work to a global audience.' Publishes a quarterly journal, *The Creative Writer* (see entry under *Magazines*). Membership is open to novelists, journalists, editors, ghost-writers, broadcasters, academics, illustrators and translators, regardless of whether or not published.

Society of Editors

University Centre, Granta Place, Mill Lane, Cambridge CB2 1RU
☎01223 304080 Fax 01223 304090
✉ info@societyofeditors.org
www.societyofeditors.org

Executive Director *Bob Satchwell*

Formed by a merger of the Association of British Editors and the Guild of Editors, the Society of Editors has nearly 500 members in national, regional and local newspapers, magazines, broadcasting, new media, journalism education and media law. Campaigns for media freedom and self-regulation. For further information call *Bob Satchwell* (☎ 07860 562815).

Society of Indexers

Woodbourn Business Centre, 10 Jessell Street, Sheffield S9 3HY
☎0114 244 9561 Fax 0114 244 9563
✉ admin@indexers.org.uk
www.indexers.org.uk

Secretary *Judith Menes*
Administrator *Wendy Burrow*
SUBSCRIPTION £88 p.a.; institutions: from £168

Founded 1957. Publishes *The Indexer* (biannual, April and October), a quarterly newsletter, an online directory, *Indexers Available (IA)*, which lists members and their subject expertise. In addition, the Society runs an open-learning course entitled *Training in Indexing* and recommends rates of pay (currently £18.50–£30 per hour or £2–£5 per page). Awards annually **The Wheatley Medal** and **The Bernard Levin Award** (see entries under *Prizes*).

Society of Picture Researchers & Editors
See **The Picture Research Association**

Society of Women Writers & Journalists
27 Braycourt Avenue, Walton-on-Thames KT12 2AZ
☎01932 702874
✉ wendy@stickler.org
www.swwj.co.uk

Membership Secretary *Wendy Hughes*
SUBSCRIPTION £35 p.a. (full); £25 (associate); £20 (probationary/student); £25 (overseas). £15 joining fee

Founded 1894. For women writers, the SWWJ upholds professional standards and literary achievements through regular workshops for all genre of writing where work-in-progress can be evaluated. Regional group meetings; residential weekends; postal critique service; competitions and outings. For Full members, membership card doubles as a press card. Publishes *The Woman Writer*. Male writers are accepted as Associate members.

Society of Young Publishers
c/o The Bookseller, Endeavour House, 189 Shaftesbury Avenue, London WC2H 8TJ
www.thesyp.org.uk

Contact *Membership Secretary*
SUBSCRIPTION £30 p.a.; £20 (student/unwaged)

Provides facilities whereby members can increase their knowledge and widen their experience of all aspects of publishing, and holds regular social events. Run entirely by volunteers, it is open to those in related occupations, students, and associate membership is available for over-35s. Publishes a bi-monthly newsletter called *InPrint* and holds meetings on the last Wednesday of each month featuring trade professionals. For other events see the website. Please enclose an s.a.e. when writing to the Society.

Spoken Word Publishing Association
See **Audiobook Publishing Association**

Sports Journalists' Association of Great Britain
c/o Start2Finish Event Management, Unit 92, Capital Business Centre, 22 Carlton Road, Croydon CR2 0BS
☎020 8916 2234 Fax 020 8916 2235
✉ stevenwdownes@btinternet.com
www.sportsjournalists.co.uk

Secretary *Steven Downes* (80 Southbridge Road, Croydon CR0 1AE ☎ 07710 428562)
SUBSCRIPTION £23.50 p.a. incl. VAT (London); £11.75 (regional)

Founded in 1948 as the Sports Writers' Association of Great Britain to promote and maintain a high professional standard among journalists who specialise in sport in all its branches and to serve members' interests. Publishes a biannual bulletin, a quarterly *Newsletter* and a Yearbook, and promotes the annual British Sports Awards each December and the British Sports Journalism Awards every March.

Tees Valley Arts
Third Floor, Melrose House, Melrose Street, Middlesbrough TS1 2HZ
☎01642 264651 Fax 01642 264955
✉ info@teesvalleyarts.org.uk
www.teesvalleyarts.org.uk

Programme Manager – Education *Janette Pratt*
Community Programme Manager *Rowena Sommerville*
Communications Officer *Simon Smith*

TVA is an arts development agency which operates throughout the Tees Valley, encompassing all art forms, working with educational and community organisations and groups, to add value to existing activities and to develop new ones. TVA works in partnership with statutory and voluntary organisations to embed cultural activity in educational and social practice, and in neighbourhood renewal and regeneration initiatives.

Theatre Writers' Union
See **The Writers' Guild of Great Britain**

Trade Publishers Council
See **The Publishers Association**

The Translators Association
84 Drayton Gardens, London SW10 9SB
☎020 7373 6642 Fax 020 7373 5768
✉ info@societyofauthors.org
www.societyofauthors.org/translators

Contact *The Secretary*

Founded 1958 as a subsidiary group within the Society of Authors to deal exclusively with the special problems of literary translators into the English language. Benefits to members include free legal and general advice and assistance on all business matters relating to translators' work, including the vetting of contracts and advice on rates of remuneration. Membership is normally confined to translators who have had their work published in volume or serial form or produced in this country for stage, television or radio. The Association administers several prizes for translators of published work (see *Prizes*) and maintains an online database of members' details for the use of publishers who are seeking a translator for a particular work.

UK Film Council

10 Little Portland Street, London W1W 7JG
☎020 7861 7861 Fax 020 7861 7863
✉ info@ukfilmcouncil.org.uk
www.ukfilmcouncil.org.uk

The UK's leading film body. Uses lottery money and Government Grant-in-Aid to encourage the development of new talent, skills and creative and technological innovation in UK film; help new and established filmmakers make distinctive British films; support the creation and growth of stable businesses in the film sector; provide access to finance and help the UK film industry to compete in the global marketplace. Also promotes enjoyment and understanding of the cinema and ensures that film's economic and creative and cultural interests are properly represented in public policy making.

Voice of the Listener & Viewer Ltd (VLV)

101 Kings Drive, Gravesend DA12 5BQ
☎01474 352835 Fax 01474 351112
✉ info@vlv.org.uk
www.vlv.org.uk

Chairman *Jocelyn Hay*
Executive Director *Peter Blackman*
Administrative Secretary *Sue Washbrook*

VLV represents the citizen and consumer interests in broadcasting. It is an independent, non-profit-making organisation working to ensure independence, quality and diversity in broadcasting. VLV is the only consumer body speaking for listeners and viewers on the full range of broadcasting issues. It is funded by its members and is free from sectarian, commercial and political affiliations. Holds public lectures, seminars

and conferences throughout the UK, and has frequent contact with MPs, civil servants, the BBC and independent broadcasters, regulators, academics and other consumer groups. Provides an independent forum where all with an interest in broadcasting can speak on equal terms. Produces a quarterly news bulletin and regular briefings on broadcasting issues. Holds its own archive and those of the former Broadcasting Research Unit (1980–90) and BACTV (British Action for Children's Television). Maintains a panel of speakers, the VLV Forum for Children's Broadcasting, the VLV Forum for Educational Broadcasting, and acts as secretariat for the European Alliance of Listeners' and Viewers' Associations (EURALVA). VLV has responded to all major public enquiries on broadcasting since 1984. The VLV does not handle complaints.

W.A.T.C.H.

See **Writers, Artists and their Copyright Holders**

Welsh Academy

See **Academi**

Welsh Books Council (Cyngor Llyfrau Cymru)

Castell Brychan, Aberystwyth SY23 2JB
☎01970 624151 Fax 01970 625385
✉ castellbrychan@cllc.org.uk
www.cllc.org.uk
www.gwales.com

Director *Gwerfyl Pierce Jones*

Founded 1961 to stimulate interest in books from Wales and to support publishing in Wales. The Council distributes publishing grants and promotes and fosters all aspects of book production in Wales in both Welsh and English. Its Editorial, Design, Marketing and Children's Books departments and wholesale distribution centre offer central services to publishers in Wales. Writers in Welsh and English are welcome to approach the Editorial Department for advice on how to get their manuscripts published.

Welsh Literature Abroad/ Llenyddiaeth Cymru Dramor

Canolfan Mercator Centre, University of Wales Aberystwyth, Llanbadarn Campus, Aberystwyth SY23 3AS
☎01970 622544 Fax 01970 621524
✉ post@welshlitabroad.org
www.welshlitabroad.org

Director *Sioned Puw Rowlands*

Founded 2000. Welsh Literature Abroad works to facilitate the translation of Wales' literature. Translation grants are available to publishers. Participates in international book fairs, and works with translators, publishers and festivals abroad to promote the literature and writers of Wales internationally.

Welsh National Literature Promotion Agency

See **Academi**

West Country Writers' Association

6 The Beals, Greenway, Woodbury, Exeter EX5 1LU
☎01395 233753
✉ secretarywcwa@aol.com
Honorary Secretary *Sue Bury*

Founded 1951 in the interest of published authors living in or writing about the West Country. Annual congress; newsletters. Regional meetings to discuss news and views.

Women in Publishing

Membership Secretary: 32 The Oaks, Swanley BR8 7YQ
✉ louisejbainbridge@googlemail.com
www.wipub.org.uk
Membership Secretary *Louise Bainbridge*

Aims to promote the status of women working in publishing and related trades by helping them to develop their careers. Through WiP there are opportunities for members to learn more about their area of work, share information and expertise, give and receive support and partake in a practical forum for the exchange of information about different industry sectors. Monthly meetings provide a forum for discussion on various topics of interest within the industry. Meetings are held on the second Wednesday of each month. See website for further information. Publishes monthly newsletter, *WiPlash*, and *Women in Publishing Directory*.

Women Writers Network (WWN)

23 Prospect Road, London NW2 2JU
☎020 7794 5861
www.womenwriters.org.uk
Membership Secretary *Cathy Smith*
SUBSCRIPTION £45 p.a. (incl. meeting admissions & 6 newsletters p.a., WWN website and online directory access); £35 p.a. (overseas); £30 p.a. ('newsletter only' UK membership')

Founded 1985. Provides a forum for the exchange

of information, support, career and networking opportunities for working women writers. Meetings, seminars, excursions, newsletter and directory. Full membership includes free admission to monthly meetings and a monthly newsletter. Details from the Membership Secretary at the address above.

Writernet (formerly **New Playwrights Trust**)

Cabin V, Clarendon Buildings, 25 Horsell Road, London N5 1XL
☎020 7609 7474 Fax 020 7609 7557
✉ info@writernet.org.uk
www.writernet.org.uk
Director *Jonathan Meth*
Chair *Bonnie Greer*
Administrator *Elizabeth Robertson*
SUBSCRIPTION Information on rates available by post or on website

Provides writers for all forms of live and recorded performance (at any stage in their career) with a range of services that enable them to pursue their careers more effectively. These include: a network connecting dramatic writers to the industry and to each other; online resources to support dramatic writers and those who work with them; a script-reading service, publications and guides. Aims to help writers from all parts of the country and a wide diversity of backgrounds to fulfil their potential both inside and outside the new-writing mainstream.

The Writers' Guild of Great Britain

15 Britannia Street, London WC1X 9JN
☎020 7833 0777 Fax 020 7833 4777
✉ admin@writersguild.org.uk
www.writersguild.org.uk
President *David Nobbs*
Chair *Katharine Way*
General Secretary *Bernie Corbett*
Deputy General Secretary *Anne Hogben*
SUBSCRIPTION Full member: 1% of earnings from professional writing (min. £150, max. £1500); Candidate member: £90; Student member: £20; Affiliate member (agent or writers' group): £275; Life member: voluntary contribution

Founded in 1959 as the Screenwriters' Guild, the Writers' Guild is a trade union, affiliated to the TUC, representing professional writers in television, radio, theatre, film, books and new media. It negotiates Minimum Terms Agreements governing writers' contracts and covering minimum fees; advances; repeat fees; royalties and residuals; rights; credits; number of drafts; script alterations and the resolution of disputes. The most important MTAs cover BBC TV Drama; BBC Radio Drama; ITV Companies; **PACT** (independent TV and film producers); **TAC** (Welsh language independent TV producers); Theatrical Management Association; **Independent Theatre Council**; and an agreement covering the **Royal National Theatre**, **Royal Shakespeare Company**, and **Royal Court Theatre**. These agreements are regularly renegotiated and in most cases the minimum fees are reviewed annually.

The Guild advises members on all aspects of their working lives, including contract vetting, legal advice, help with copyright problems and representation in disputes with producers, publishers or other writers.

Events organised by the Guild include a seminar on writing sitcoms, a networking evening for TV soap writers, a panel discussion on marketing theatre plays and lectures on forensic science aimed at TV series writers. *UK Writer*, the Guild's quarterly magazine, is free to members and contains features about professional writing, Guild news and details of work opportunities, training courses, literary competitions, etc. A detailed e-mail of news, opportunities and other information is sent to members every Friday.

Full Membership is open to anyone who has received payment for a piece of written work under a contract with terms not less than those negotiated by the Guild. Writers who do not qualify can join as Candidate Members and those on accredited writing courses or theatre attachments can become Student Members. Aged writers and those with long service in the Guild are entitled to free Life Membership.

Writers, Artists and their Copyright Holders (W.A.T.C.H.)

The Library, The University of Reading, PO Box 223, Whiteknights, Reading RG6 6AE
☎0118 378 8783 Fax 0118 378 6636
www.watch-file.com
Contact *Dr David Sutton*

Founded 1994. Provides an online database of information about the copyright holders of literary authors and artists. The database is available free of charge on the Internet and the Web. W.A.T.C.H. is the successor project to the Location Register of English Literary Manuscripts and Letters, and continues to deal with location register enquiries.

Yachting Journalists' Association

Crimsham Manor, Lagness, Chichester PO20 1LN
☎01243 264173 Fax 01243 267599
✉ jmh@dip.demon.co.uk
www.yja.co.uk
Contact *Vice Chairman/Membership Secretary*
SUBSCRIPTION £40 p.a.

To further the interest of yachting, sail and power, and to provide support and assistance to journalists in the field; current membership is just over 260 with 31 from overseas. A handbook, listing details of members and subscribing PR organisations, press facility recommendations, forthcoming events and other useful information, is published annually at a cost to non-members and non-advertisers of £10. Information for inclusion should be submitted by the end of August. The YJA organises the Yachtsman of the Year and Young Sailor of the Year Awards, presented annually at the beginning of January.

Yr Academi Gymreig

See **Academi**

Falling Foul of the Law

David Hooper gives an update on the risks of costly libel

The main area of risk in libel is in non-fiction. The best working test is whether the tendency of the words used is to diminish the reputation of the claimant. If you were in the claimant's position, could you validly object to what was written about you? It is sensible to ask yourself who might complain about what you have written and how you would respond to that complaint bearing in mind that the burden of proving the facts by legally admissible evidence will be upon you.

There is no substitute for careful research and checking. Some errors pass into mythology. A British police officer called Morton collected damages on no less than three occasions from W.H. Allen, Secker & Warburg and Weidenfeld & Nicolson for the repetition of the canard that he was responsible for the shooting in cold blood of Abram Stern, head of the Stern gang in Palestine. This tendency has been emulated by a number of Saudi businessmen falsely accused of backing terrorism.

The Court of Appeal has rejected attempts to use the freedom of expression principles under the European Convention of Human Rights Article 10, to reduce the strict application of the repetition rule in libel. If you repeat someone else's libel you are liable to have to prove that it is true even if you believed your source of information was reliable. If you repeat what someone told you or what they suspected, you are likely to have to prove the underlying truth of what was said or the facts which give rise to justifiable suspicion, not simply that this is what you were told.

The issue is what readers would reasonably conclude that the words meant. The fact that the author did not intend to libel the claimant is not a defence. The reader is, in any event, unlikely to know what the author's intention was and would form his own view on the interpretation of the words on the page. That libel is often an honest mistake is relevant to the amount of damages awarded but court proceedings can still be hideously expensive. For this reason, publishers are increasingly reluctant to risk investigative books. Cases involving the exposure of the wrongdoing of footballers, policemen or doctors normally involve newspapers or television companies but Orion Books were sued by a former policeman unhappy at his inclusion in a book entitled *Bent Coppers*. Writers need therefore to check and double check the accuracy of what they write. They would do well, for example, not to emulate the mistake of confusing the Chancellor of Glasgow University, Sir Alec Cairncross, with his brother, a suspected member of the Cambridge spy ring. Nor is it wise to suggest that a Nigerian-born singer had said that 'it was time to support apartheid' when in reality she had said nothing more sinister than 'it was time to support a party'.

The writer should focus on all people who might bring a claim. Often controversial books successfully avoid an action from the principal target only to invite a claim from some minor character over a relatively trivial indiscretion. Claims can come from unlikely sources. The *Sunday Telegraph* can scarcely have expected to be sued by the son of Colonel Gaddafi, but when he turned up at court he obtained an apology although no damages. A Russian businessman, Grigori Loutchansky, successfully sued *The Times* over a report linking him with money laundering even though he was banned from this country and had served a lengthy prison sentence in the USSR.

The Loutchansky case was a salutary reminder of the severity of English libel law. Although the limitation period for bringing libel actions is one year, the courts have upheld what is known as the single publication rule. This dates back to a case involving a nineteenth-century duke who sent his butler out to buy a book published many years previously in order to be able to establish an act of publication within the limitation period. Thus each book sale or downloading from the Internet is a fresh act of publication with its own one-year limitation period. The law is in marked contrast to the United States, where the limitation period is just one year from the first publication. The British interpretation may soon be challenged in the European Court of Human Rights.

Journalists whose material might be published electronically in an archive or otherwise accessible on a website should take care to ensure that if there is a valid libel complaint steps are taken to stop any further publication of the material electronically, otherwise they may face another claim.

Unfortunately, the libel laws in this country have attracted a number of libel tourists wishing to impress on the world their spotless reputation. Writers should bear in mind that the libel laws in the United States require proof of fault to establish a claim for libel and a knowledge of falsity in the case of a public figure or fault amounting to negligence in the case of a private figure. This explains why Dr Armand Hammer, who sued on the basis of a hostile biography, brought his action against the author not in his home country but in Britain. The fact that a book has been cleared for libel in America does not remove the risk of a claim in this country.

If a claim for libel is notified, advice should be sought from a specialist lawyer, preferably one recommended by the publisher. An outraged response can raise the level of damages. If a claim is made, immediate consideration must be given as to whether an electronic version, which can be accessed by third parties, should be amended.

Section 2 of the Defamation Act 1996 enables a swift and less expensive resolution of a claim where a mistake has been made. It involves an admission of liability and, if the parties cannot agree, an assessment of damages by the judge, but it can stop the greed of the claimant in its tracks. Recent cases have established that the court will give a 35 to 45 per cent discount on the level of damages if this procedure is promptly used.

Writers need to discover whether they are covered by the publisher's insurance and, if so, what excess attaches to any claim. If the writer believes that the claim may be covered by insurance, he must ensure that the insurers are promptly notified, that any letter of complaint is forwarded to them and that no admission of liability is made without their authority. Increasingly, libel insurance only cuts in after the claim has cost five figures – scant consolation for the author who is likely to have warranted in the publishing contract that the book is free from libel. Very often publishers will not enforce that indemnity in the absence of serious blameworthy conduct on the part of the writer but, again, this is little consolation as publishers will not commit themselves in advance to their probable reaction to a libel claim. It is important, therefore, to consider whether the book should be read for libel and, if so, whether it is necessary to have it all or simply part of it read.

Many publishing contracts are silent on the question of who pays for the libel reading. Writers who try to modify the standard form of indemnity given to publishers normally face a thankless task. But it is worth considering whether there is scope for the writer's liability to be modified in respect of potential defamations of which the publisher is aware and where the writer has complied with all the requirements of the lawyer reading the book for libel. Practical steps include sending a particular passage to the person written about. To consent to what is written is a defence to a claim for libel. The problem, of course, is that normally such persons will not give consent.

Libel actions cannot be brought on behalf of the dead. The death of a plaintiff in the course of a libel action, as happened with Robert Maxwell's claim against Faber, brings the claim to an immediate halt, but each side is left bearing their own legal costs. Writers are sometimes well advised to consult a helpful volume called *Who Was Who*. The Government are currently reviewing whether the law should be changed, something writers should oppose.

Another defence is justification, which involves the author proving that what was written was true. If it was fair comment on a matter of public interest based on facts which were substantially true, the writer will have a defence. The 2005 case of Lowe v. Associated Newspapers has shown a greater willingness of the court to accept this defence. By virtue of the Human Rights Act 1998, the courts increasingly take note of the decisions made under Article 10 of the European Convention of Human Rights which upholds the freedom of speech. There is also a tendency to rule that criticisms made of a claimant are matters of comment rather than allegations of fact which have to be justified.

If a court is told that the disputed passage in a libel claim will be defended, the court will not grant an interim injunction pending trial. The downside is that if the defence fails the damages are likely to be that much greater. It may be appropriate and less expensive to deal with the claim at an early stage, possibly by altering the disputed passage, if that can still be done, or revising it in a later edition.

One of the most promising developments has been the expansion of the defence of qualified privilege in the libel action brought by the former Irish Prime Minister Albert Reynolds against the *Sunday Times*, sometimes summarised as a defence of responsible journalism. If the writer can prove that on a matter of public interest there was a duty to inform the public who had a corresponding interest in receiving that information, there will be a defence which does not require proving that the particular allegation was true. The court will, however, look very carefully at the research carried out, the language used and the attempt to put both sides of the matter.

Qualified privilege was the issue in the Loutchansky case where the newspaper argued that it required the protection of qualified privilege to write about the alleged activities of Loutchansky which were by their nature very difficult to prove. The judge concluded, however, that the paper had made insufficient attempts to contact Loutchansky and should not have published until it had done so.

The most helpful development for writers is the recognition by the courts of the importance of freedom of speech. The press has to discharge vital functions as a bloodhound as well as a watchdog and any lingering doubts should be resolved in favour of publication. The courts have recognised that freedom of speech is essential to informed political debate and that restrictions imposed upon that freedom must be proportionate and no more than is necessary to promote the legitimate object of the restriction.

The courts also recognise that news is a perishable commodity and that the decision to publish must be assessed in the light of the facts then known. Until late 2006, despite all the ringing endorsements of the freedom of the press, the courts were often unwilling to uphold defences of qualified privilege. Too often they found some step which ought to have been taken before going into print. However, in 2006 the House of Lords ruled in a case brought by a Saudi businessman called Jameel that the defence did apply to a report in the *Wall Street Journal* about steps being taken to monitor bank accounts in the wake of 9/11. The court held that it was a balanced report and did not impute wrongdoing to Mr Jameel.

Journalists with publication deadlines are likely to have a better prospect of establishing qualified privilege than authors who may be expected to undertake more research to get to the truth of the matter. The existence of the defence and the unpredictability of the judge's view of the research are likely to deter many claimants, particularly those in public life. The Court of Appeal has held that a balanced account of the allegations, which it termed neutral reportage, made by a Saudi dissident was protected by qualified privilege.

The Reynolds qualified privilege has been instrumental in the decrease in the number of libel actions brought. However, it is uncertain in outcome and often spawns satellite litigation where the responsibility or otherwise of the journalism is pored over in minute but expensive detail. If the coverage is considered by the court to be partisan the defence will fail as in the case George Galloway brought against the *Daily Telegraph*. In 2007 the Court of Appeal will rule on the extent to which the Reynolds defence applies to books, where there is not the pressure of newsroom deadlines.

Writers of fiction face fewer libel problems. However, their use of autobiographical material can lead to characters being identifiable. The inadvertent use of the name of a real peer with fictitious sexual predilections has led to a novel being pulped. Directories should, where possible, be consulted to ensure there are no similarly named people in a comparable occupation. Care should be taken to see on whom characters are based and whether any of the surrounding events actually happened. Often there is much to be said for a carefully worded disclaimer of reference to living individuals. Compton Mackenzie used to pick names from old telephone directories. Unfortunately, when this expedient was used by the novelist Paul Watkins in his book *Stand Before Your God*, a randomly chosen name of a villainous character was by ill-fortune the name of one of his contemporaries at Eton College. Damages had to be paid as checks in the school directories could have avoided this error. Choosing the names of friends or acquaintances and involving them in defamatory escapades may be very difficult to defend and could result in the payment of damages and costs. A novelist who recently used the name and some identifying features of a film producer believing his friend would not object found himself paying libel damages and even being threatened with a baseball bat.

The growth of faction and the introduction of living people into works of fiction do increase the risk of libel claims by blurring the distinction between fact and imagination. A roman-à-clef can present significant libel problems. It was perhaps not surprising that a publisher could not be found for a novel featuring unattractive characteristics of the wife of a Labour Prime Minister described as 'a young chap with a phoney smile'.

Changes introduced by the Defamation Act 1996 and procedural changes to make libel actions less tortuous and expensive and to require each side to disclose the strengths and weaknesses of their cases at an earlier stage are to be welcomed. Libel nevertheless remains a very costly pitfall. Damages are now capped but are slowly moving upwards for the most serious libels. Two nursery workers accused of child abuse were awarded £200,000 each and a company that was falsely linked to Al-Qaeda was reputed to have recovered £500,000 from the BBC, although part of those damages may have related to loss of business contracts. On top of that there are the legal costs – the cap on general damages for libel has now moved up to £250,000 but is reserved for the worst cases.

Damages can be higher if there is a financial loss directly attributable to the libel. This enabled the stockbrokers Collins Stewart to recover £300,000 damages against the *Financial Times*. Most cases settle for a fraction of that. There are fast-track procedures where libel damages are capped at £10,000. But these can actually encourage claims as can the willingness of lawyers to work on a conditional fee basis – that is to say the lawyer does not get paid unless he wins the case, but can recover from the defendant a success fee on top of his not inconsiderable normal legal fees. This has resulted in some lawyers seeking to charge £800 or more per hour. Claims that attract astronomic fees may have to be set against the impossibility of recovering costs from an impecunious defendant. In Naomi Campbell's privacy case she recovered £3,500 damages in respect of photographs of her leaving a drugs rehabilitation clinic, but her lawyers sought £1 million in legal costs.

One saving in costs has followed the tendency of the courts to favour trial by judge alone rather than by jury. In Orion Books' case where they were sued by a police officer suspected of corruption, the judge considered the action involving a detailed reading of the book by a jury was best heard by a judge alone. If this gloomy assessment of the reading skills of jurors is followed, trial by jury in libel cases concerning books may become a thing of the past. Things are improving, but at present the only certainty about libel is its expense.

Article 8 of the European Convention of Human Rights protects the right to respect for private and family life. Initially, claims related either to intrusive tabloid exposés or to celebrities exploiting publicity rights, such as Michael Douglas in his spat with *Hello!* magazine which published unauthorised paparazzi photographs. That case was really about the right to control publicity. The court felt that there was no public interest in such intrusive behaviour on the part of *Hello!* and Douglas and his wife were entitled to £7,250 damage each for distress. Damages for privacy tend to be low, but legal costs can be enormous particularly if there is a conditional fee involved. The House of Lords did however uphold *OK!*'s claim against *Hello!* based on commercial confidence, when *Hello!* had published its own spoiler article and photos of the wedding.

A recent case brought by the Canadian folksinger Loreena McKennitt against the publication of an unauthorised biography by a former friend secured her an award of £5,000 damages as well as enormous costs, but more importantly an injunction against the intrusive parts of the book which included details of her home, business contacts, her personal relationships and her health and diet. The judgment, upheld by the Court of Appeal, shows how the law of privacy can impact on writers. The test is whether the information is private information and whether the complainant has a reasonable expectation of privacy. If so, a balancing exercise has to be carried out to weigh up the right to privacy against freedom of speech. Factors favouring publication include evidence that the information is in the public domain (particularly if put there by the claimant), the triviality of the information or of any infringement or some genuine public interest. The mere fact that the public would be interested is not sufficient.

There have been higher awards where the tabloid press have behaved particularly badly but that is unlikely to apply to authors. Amanda Holden and her husband, for example, received £40,000 from the *Daily Star* which had published intrusive pictures of them on holiday. Sara Cox was paid £50,000 in respect of particularly intrusive photos of her while on honeymoon.

The English courts are beginning to enforce the rights of privacy recognised elsewhere in Europe, most notably in Germany where the award of damages to Princess Caroline for breach of her privacy was upheld by the European Court of Human Rights. The next year is likely to see an increasing number of privacy claims.

David Hooper is media partner of Reynolds Porter Chamberlain and author of Reputations under Fire, *published by Little Brown (2001).*

Literary Societies

Margery Allingham Society

12 Barnfield Road, Orpington BR5 3LR
✉ costellorosemary@hotmail.com
www.margeryallingham.org.uk
Contact *Mrs Rosemary Costello*
Subscription £14 p.a.

Founded 1988 to promote interest in and study of the works of Margery Allingham. The Society publishes two issues of the journal, *The Bottle Street Gazette*, per year. Contributions welcome. Two social events a year. Open membership.

Jane Austen Society

9 Nicola Close, South Croydon CR2 6NA
www.janeaustensociety.org.uk
Secretary *Mrs Maureen Stiller*
Membership Secretary *Mrs Rosemary Culley*
Subscription UK: £7.50 (student for 3 years); £15 (standard annual); £12 (annual, members of JAS branches/groups); £20 (joint); £45 (corporate); £250 (life); Overseas: £18 (annual) or £50/€75 (for 3 years); £50 (corporate); £300/€450 (life) all by credit card or UK banker's order only

Founded 1940 to promote interest in and enjoyment of Jane Austen's novels and letters. The Society has the following Branches/Groups: Bath and Bristol, Cambridge, Midlands, London, Norfolk, Kent, Hampshire, Isle of Wight, Southern Circle, Wales and Scotland. There are independent Societies in North America and Australia.

The Baskerville Hounds (The Dartmoor Sherlock Holmes Study Group)

6 Bramham Moor, Hill Head, Fareham PO14 3RU
☎ 01329 667325
✉ baskervillehounds@acd-221b.info
www.acd-221b.info
Chairman *Philip Weller*

Founded 1989. An international Sherlock Holmes society specialising solely in studies of *The Hound of the Baskervilles* and its Dartmoor associations. Organises many study functions, mostly on Dartmoor. Currently involved in several large-scale research projects. Membership is open only to those who are willing to be actively involved, by correspondence and/or attendance at functions, in the group's study activities.

The BB Society

Secretary: 8 Park Road, Solihull B91 3SU
☎ 0121 704 1002
✉ enquiries@roseworldproductions.com
Chairman *Brian Mutlow*
Secretary *Bryan Holden*
Subscription £10 (individual); £17.50 (family); £50 (corporate); £5 (student); £17.50 (overseas)

Founded in 2000 to bring together devotees of the writer/illustrator BB (Denys Watkins-Pitchford). BB's oeuvre included books on wildfowling, angling, children's fantasy and the countryside. The Society holds two meetings a year and publishes newsletters and an annual journal, *Sky Gypsy*.

The Beckford Society

The Timber Cottage, Crockerton, Warminster BA12 8AX
☎ 01985 213195
✉ Sidney.Blackmore@btinternet.com
Secretary *Sidney Blackmore*
Subscription £20 (minimum) p.a.

Founded 1995 to promote an interest in the life and works of William Beckford (1760–1844) and his circle. Encourages Beckford studies and scholarship through exhibitions, lectures and publications, including an annual journal, *The Beckford Journal* and occasional newsletters.

Thomas Lovell Beddoes Society

9 Amber Court, Belper DE56 1HG
☎ 01773 828066 Fax 01773 828066
✉ john@beddoes.demon.co.uk
www.phantomwooer.org
Chairman *John Lovell Beddoes*
Secretary *Christine Hunkinson*

Formed to research the life, times and work of poet Thomas Lovell Beddoes (1803–1849), encourage relevant publications, further the reading and appreciation of his works by a wider public and liaise with other groups and organisations. Publishes an annual journal.

The Adrian Bell Society

3 The Maltings, Church Close, Coltishall
NR12 7DZ
☎01603 737168

Secretary *Moya Leighton*
Subscription £5 p.a.

Founded 1995, the Society aims to promote the study and enjoyment of the writing of Adrian Bell (1901–80); to publish journals twice a year and hold meetings to help members obtain copies of out of print titles; to assemble a collection of photocopies of his 1500 *Countryman's Notebooks* that appeared in the *Eastern Daily Press* and to index them; to commemorate his career as *The Times* first crossword compiler; to share knowledge of the places and factual background mentioned in his books. The society has 250 members worldwide who keep in touch through the journal. *A Centenary Countryman's Notebook*, published 2001 (£7 + p&p).

Hilaire Belloc Society

1 Hillview, Elsted, Midhurst GU29 0JX
☎01730 825575
✉ HilaireBelloc1@aol.com

Contact *Dr Grahame Clough*

Founded in 1996 to promote the life and work of Hilaire Belloc through the publication of newsletters containing rare and previously unpublished material. Organises walks, social events, a Belloc weekend and a three-day conference. Currently 70 members, of which 30% are from overseas.

Arnold Bennett Society

4 Field End Close, Trentham, Stoke on Trent
ST4 8DA
✉ arnoldbennettsociety@btinternet.com
www.arnoldbennettsociety.org.uk

Secretary *Mrs Carol Gorton*
Subscription £12 p.a. (single); £14 (family)
   plus £2 for membership outside the UK

Aims to promote interest in the life and works of 'Five Towns' author Arnold Bennett and other North Staffordshire writers. Annual dinner. Regular functions and talks in and around Burslem, plus annual seminar at Wedgwood College, Barlaston and annual conference at Staffordshire University.

E. F. Benson Society

The Old Coach House, High Street, Rye
TN31 7JF
☎01797 223114
www.efbensonsociety.org

Secretary *Allan Downend*
Subscription £7.50 (UK/Europe); £12.50
   (overseas)

Founded 1985 to promote the life and work of E. F. Benson and the Benson family. Organises social and literary events, exhibitions, talks and Benson interest walks in Rye. Publishes a quarterly newsletter and annual journal, *The Dodo*, postcards and reprints of E.F. Benson articles and short stories in a series called 'Bensoniana' plus other books of Benson interest. Holds an archive which includes the Seckersen Collection (transcriptions of the Benson collection at the Bodleian Library in Oxford).

The Betjeman Society

6 St Annes Road, Shrewsbury SY3 6AU
☎01743 350372
✉ honsecbetjeman@fsmail.net
www.johnbetjeman.com

Honorary Secretary *Colin Wright*
Chairman *John Heald*
Subscription £10 (individual); £12 (family);
   £3 (student); £3 additional for overseas
   members

Aims to promote the study and appreciation of the work and life of Sir John Betjeman. Annual programme includes poetry readings, lectures, discussions, visits to places associated with Betjeman, and various social events. Meetings are held in London and other centres. Regular newsletter and annual journal, *The Betjemanian*.

The Bewick Society

c/o The Hancock Museum, Newcastle upon Tyne NE2 4PT
☎01207 562196
✉ juneholmes@lineone.net
www.bewicksociety.org.uk

Membership Secretary *June Holmes*
Subscription £10 p.a. (individual); £12
   (family)

Founded 1988 to promote an interest in the life and work of Thomas Bewick, wood-engraver and naturalist (1753–1828). Organises related events and meetings, and is associated with the Bewick birthplace museum at Cherryburn, Northumberland.

Birmingham Central Literary Association

23 Arden Grove, Ladywood, Birmingham
B16 8HG
☎0121 454 9352
✉ bruce@bakerbrum.co.uk.
Contact *The Secretary*
Holds fortnightly meetings in central Birmingham to discuss the lives and work of authors and poets. Holds an annual dinner to celebrate Shakespeare's birthday.

The George Borrow Society

60 Upper Marsh Road, Warminster BA12 9PN
www.clough5.fsnet.co.uk/gb.html
Chairman/Bulletin Editor *Dr Ann M. Ridler*
Membership Secretary *Michael Skillman*
Honorary Treasurer *David Pattinson*
Bulletin Editor: St Mary's Cottage, 61 Thame Road, Warborough, Wallingford, Oxford OX10 7EA ☎ 01865 858379 Fax 01865 858575
SUBSCRIPTION £15 p.a.
Founded 1991 to promote knowledge of the life and works of George Borrow (1803–81), traveller, linguist and writer. The Society holds biennial conferences (with published proceedings) and informal intermediate gatherings, all at places associated with Borrow. Publishes the *George Borrow Bulletin* twice yearly, containing scholarly articles, reviews of publications relating to Borrow, reports of past events and news of forthcoming events. Member of the **Alliance of Literary Societies** and corporate associate member of the Centre of East Anglian Studies (CEAS) at the University of East Anglia, Norwich (Borrow's home city for many years).

Elinor Brent-Dyer

See **Friends of the Chalet School** and **The New Chalet Club**

British Fantasy Society

5 Greenbank, Barnt Green, Birmingham
B45 8DH
✉ cook.vicky@yahoo.co.uk
www.britishfantasysociety.org.uk
President *Ramsey Campbell*
Chairman *Marie O'Regan*
Secretary *Vicky Cook*
SUBSCRIPTION from £25 p.a.
Founded 1971 for devotees of fantasy, horror and related fields in literature, art and the cinema. Publishes a regular newsletter with information and reviews of new books and films, plus related fiction and non-fiction magazines. Annual conference at which the **British Fantasy Awards** are presented. These awards are voted on by the membership and are not an open competition.

The Brontë Society

Brontë Parsonage Museum, Haworth, Keighley
BD22 8DR
☎01535 640195 Fax 01535 647131
✉ bronte@bronte.org.uk
www.bronte.info
Contact *Membership Officer*
SUBSCRIPTION details from the Membership Officer or the website
Founded 1893. Aims and activities include the preservation of manuscripts and other objects related to or connected with the Brontë family, and the maintenance and development of the museum and library at Haworth. The Society holds regular meetings, lectures and exhibitions; publishes information relating to the family and a triannual *Gazette*. Freelance contributions for either publication should be sent to the Publications Secretary at the address above. Members can receive the journal, *Brontë Studies*, at a reduced subscription.

The Rupert Brooke Society

The Orchard, 45/47 Mill Way, Grantchester
CB3 9ND
☎01223 551118 Fax 01223 551119
✉ rbs@callan.co.uk
www.rupertbrooke.com
Contacts *Claire Pidoux, Karen Smith*
SUBSCRIPTION £7.50 (UK); £10.50 (overseas)
Founded in 1999 to foster an interest in the work of Rupert Brooke, help preserve places associated with him and to increase the knowledge and appreciation of the village of Grantchester. Members receive a newsletter with information about events, new books and activities.

The Browning Society

38b Victoria Rd, London NW6 6PX
☎020 7604 4257
✉ v.l.greenaway@btinternet.com
Honorary Secretary *Vicky Greenaway*
SUBSCRIPTION £15 p.a.
Founded 1969 to promote an interest in the lives and poetry of Robert and Elizabeth Barrett Browning. Meetings are arranged in the London area, one of which occurs in December at Westminster Abbey to commemorate Robert Browning's death.

The John Buchan Society

Barnack, Goring Road, Steyning BN44 3GF
☎01903 813603
www.johnbuchansociety.co.uk
Secretary *Mrs Glennis McClemont*
Membership Secretary *Diana Durdon*
SUBSCRIPTION £15 (full/overseas); £120
(10 years)

To perpetuate the memory of John Buchan and to promote a wider understanding of his life and works. Holds regular meetings and social gatherings, publishes a journal, and liaises with the John Buchan Centre at Broughton in the Scottish borders.

The Robert Burns World Federation Ltd

Dean Castle Country Park Dower House,
Kilmarnock KA3 1XB
☎01563 572469 Fax 01563 572469
✉ member@kilmarnock26.freeserve.co.uk
www.worldburnsclub.com
Chief Executive *Shirley Bell*
Office Administrator *Margaret Craig*
SUBSCRIPTION £25 p.a.(individual); £27
(family); £46 (club subscription)

Founded 1885 to encourage interest in the life and work of Robert Burns and keep alive the old Scottish Tongue. The Society's interests go beyond Burns himself in its commitment to the development of Scottish literature, music and arts in general. Publishes the triannual *Burns Chronicle*.

Randolph Caldecott Society

Clatterwick House, Clatterwick Lane, Little
Leigh, Northwich CW8 4RJ
☎01606 891303 (day)/781731 (evening)
Honorary Secretary *Kenneth N. Oultram*
SUBSCRIPTION £10–£15 p.a.

Founded 1983 to promote the life and work of artist/book illustrator Randolph Caldecott. Meetings held in the spring and autumn in Caldecott's birthplace, Chester. Guest speakers, outings, newsletter, exchanges with the Society's American counterpart. (Caldecott died and was buried in St Augustine, Florida.) A medal in his memory is awarded annually in the US for children's book illustration.

Lewis Carroll Society

69 Cromwell Road, Hertford SG13 7DP
☎01992 584530
✉ alanwhite@tesco.net
www.lewiscarrollsociety.org.uk

Secretary *Alan White*
SUBSCRIPTION Refer to website for details

Founded 1969 to bring together people with an interest in Charles Dodgson and promote research into his life and works. Publishes bi-annual journal *The Carrollian*, featuring scholarly articles and reviews; a newsletter (*Bandersnatch*) which reports on Carrollian events and the Society's activities; and *The Lewis Carroll Review*, a book-reviewing journal. Regular meetings held in London with lectures, talks, outings, etc.

Lewis Carroll Society (Daresbury)

Clatterwick House, Clatterwick Lane, Little
Leigh, Northwich CW8 4RJ
☎01606 891303 (day)/781731 (evening)
Honorary Secretary *Kenneth N. Oultram*
SUBSCRIPTION £6–10 p.a.

Founded 1970.To promote the life and work of Charles Dodgson, author of the world-famous *Alice's Adventures*. Holds meetings in the spring and autumn in Carroll's birthplace, Daresbury, Cheshire. Guest speakers, a newsletter and theatre visits.

The New Chalet Club

18 Nuns Moor Crescent, Newcastle upon
Tyne NE4 9BE
www.newchaletclub.co.uk
Membership Secretary *Mrs Rona S.S. Falconer*
SUBSCRIPTION £6 p.a. (UK under 18); £10 (UK
adult & Europe); £12 (RoW)

Founded 1995 for all those with an interest in the books of Elinor Brent-Dyer. Publishes a quarterly journal and occasional supplements, including *Children's Series Fiction*, and regularly holds local and national meetings.

Friends of the Chalet School

4 Rock Terrace, Coleford, Bath BA3 5NF
☎01373 812705
✉ focs@rockterrace.demon.co.uk
www.rockterrace.demon.co.uk/FOCS
Contacts *Ann Mackie-Hunter, Clarissa Cridland*
SUBSCRIPTION Details on website or on
application

Founded 1989 to promote the works of Elinor Brent-Dyer. The society has members world-wide; publishes four magazines a year and runs a lending library.

The Chesterton Society UK

11 Lawrence Leys, Bloxham, Near Banbury
OX15 4NU
☎01295 720869/07766 711984 (mobile)

Fax 01295 720869

Honorary Secretary *Rev. Deacon Robert Hughes, KCHS*

SUBSCRIPTION £12.50 p.a.

Founded 1964 to promote the ideas and writings of G.K. Chesterton.

The Children's Books History Society

26 St Bernards Close, Buckfast, Buckfastleigh TQ11 0EP

☎01364 643568

✉ cbhs@abcgarrett.demon.co.uk

Chair/Membership Secretary *Mrs Pat Garrett*

SUBSCRIPTION £10 p.a. (UK/Europe); write for overseas subscription details

Established 1969. Aims to promote an appreciation of children's books and to study their history, bibliography and literary content. Meetings held in London and the provinces, plus a summer meeting to a collection, or to a location with a children's book connection. Three substantial newsletters issued annually, sometimes with an occasional paper. Review copies should be sent to Newsletter co-editor *Mrs Pat Garrett* (address above). The Society constitutes the British branch of the Friends of the Osborne and Lillian H. Smith Collections in Toronto, Canada, and also liaises with **CILIP** (formerly The Library Association). In 1990, the Society established its biennial Harvey Darton Award for a book, published in English, which extends our knowledge of some aspect of British children's literature of the past. 2006 winner: Lawrence Darton for *The Dartons. An Annotated Check-List of Children's Books Issued by Two Publishing Houses 1787–1876.*

The John Clare Society

9 The Chase, Ely CB6 3DR

☎01353 668438

www.johnclare.org.uk

human.ntu.ac.uk/clare/clare.html

Honorary Secretary *Miss Sue Holgate*

SUBSCRIPTION £10 (individual); £13 (joint); £8 (fully retired); £10 (joint retired); £13 (group); £15 (library); £5 (student, full-time); £15 sterling draft/$30/€25 (eurocheque) (overseas)

Founded 1981 to promote a wider appreciation of the life and works of the poet John Clare (1793–1864). Organises an annual festival in Helpston in July; arranges exhibitions, poetry readings and conferences; and publishes an annual society journal and quarterly newsletter.

William Cobbett Society

10 Grenehurst Way, Petersfield GU31 4AZ

☎01730 262060

✉ williamcobbett@fsmail.net

Chairman *Molly Townsend*

Also: Boynell House, Outlands Lane, Curdridge, Southampton SO30 2HR

☎ 01489 782453

Contact *David Chun*

SUBSCRIPTION £8 p.a.

Founded in 1976 to bring together those with an interest in the life and works of William Cobbett (1763–1835) and to extend the interest to a wider public. Society activities include an annual Memorial Lecture; publication of an annual journal (*Cobbett's New Register*) containing articles on various aspects of his life and times; an annual expedition retracing routes taken by Cobbett on his Rural Rides in the 1820s; visits to his birthplace and his tomb in Farnham, Surrey. In association with the Society, the Museum of Farnham holds bound volumes of *Cobbett's Political Register*, a large collection of Cobbett's works, books about Cobbett, and has various Cobbett artefacts on display.

The Friends of Coleridge

87 Richmond Road, Montpelier, Bristol BS6 5EP

☎0117 942 6366

✉ gcdd@blueyonder.co.uk

www.friendsofcoleridge.com

Membership Secretary/Website Manager *Paul Cheshire* (74 Wells Road, Bath BA2 3AR

✉ friendscol@btconnect.com)

Editor (*Coleridge Bulletin*) *Graham Davidson*

SUBSCRIPTION Refer to website for details

Founded in 1987 to advance knowledge about the life, work and times of Samuel Taylor Coleridge and his circle, and to support his Nether Stowey Cottage, with the National Trust, as a centre of Coleridge interest. Holds literary evenings, study weekends and a biennial international academic conference. Publishes *The Coleridge Bulletin* biannually. Short articles on Coleridge-related topics may be sent to the editor at the (Bristol) address above.

Wilkie Collins Society

4 Ernest Gardens, London W4 3QU

☎020 8747 0115

✉ paul@wilkiecollins.org

www.wilkiecollins.org

Chairman *Andrew Gasson*

Membership Secretary *Paul Lewis* (at address

above)

Subscription £10 (UK/Europe); £18 (RoW; remittance must be made in UK sterling or by PayPal to paul@paullewis.co.uk)

Founded 1980 to provide information on and promote interest in the life and works of Wilkie Collins, one of the first English novelists to deal with the detection of crime. *The Woman in White* appeared in 1860 and *The Moonstone* in 1868. Publishes newsletters, reprints of Collins' work and an annual academic journal.

The Arthur Conan Doyle Society

PO Box 1360, Ashcroft, British Columbia, Canada V0K 1A0

☎001 250 453 2045 Fax 001 250 453 2075

✉ sirhenry@telus.net

www.ash-tree.bc.ca/acdsocy.html

Joint Organisers *Christopher Roden, Barbara Roden*

Founded 1989 to promote the study and discussion of the life and works of Sir Arthur Conan Doyle. Occasional meetings, functions and visits. Publishes an occasional journal together with reprints of Conan Doyle's writings.

Joseph Conrad Society (UK)

c/o The Polish Social and Cultural Association (POSK), 238–246 King Street, London W6 0RF

✉ theconradian@aol.com

www.josephconradsociety.org

Honorary Secretary *Hugh Epstein*

Treasurer/Editor (*The Conradian*) *Allan Simmons*

Subscription £20 p.a. (individual)

Founded in 1973 to promote the study of the works and life of Joseph Conrad (1857–1924). A scholarly society, supported by the Polish Library at the Polish Cultural Association where a substantial library of Conrad texts and criticism is held in the Study Centre. Publishes a journal of Conrad studies (*The Conradian*) biannually and holds an annual International Conference in the first week of July. Awards an essay prize and travel and study grants to scholars on application.

The Rhys Davies Trust

10 Heol Don, Whitchurch, Cardiff CF14 2AU

☎029 2062 3359

Contact *Professor Meic Stephens*

Founded 1990 to perpetuate the literary reputation of the Welsh prose writer, Rhys Davies (1901–78), and to foster Welsh writing in

English. Organises competitions in association with other bodies such as the **Welsh Academy**, puts up plaques on buildings associated with Welsh writers, offers grant-aid for book production, etc.

The Walter de la Mare Society

Flat 15, Trinity Court, Vicarage Road, Twickenham TW2 5TY

www.bluetree.co.uk/wdlmsociety

Honorary President *Professor John Bayley, CBE*

Honorary Secretary & Treasurer *Julie de la Mare*

Subscription £15 p.a.

Founded in 1997 to honour the memory of Walter de la Mare; to promote the study and deepen the appreciation of his works; to widen the readership of his works; to facilitate research by making available the widest range of contacts and information about de la Mare; and to encourage and facilitate new Walter de la Mare publications. Produces a regular newsletter and organises events. Membership information from the address above.

Warwick Deeping Appreciation Society

23 Merton Road, Enfield EN2 0LS

☎020 8367 0263

✉ geoffrey@gillam.fsworld.co.uk

Secretary *Geoffrey Gillam*

Subscription £3.50 p.a.

Open to all with an interest in the life and work of Warwick Deeping who produced 70 novels and many short stories. A quarterly newsletter includes reviews of his books and results of research into his life.

The Dickens Fellowship

The Charles Dickens Museum, 48 Doughty Street, London WC1N 2LX

☎020 7405 2127

✉ dickens.fellowship@btinternet.com

www.dickens.fellowship.org

Joint Honorary General Secretaries *Mrs Lee Ault, Mrs Joan Dicks*

Founded 1902. The Society's particular aims and objectives are: to bring together lovers of Charles Dickens; to spread the message of Dickens, his love of humanity ('the keynote of all his work'); to remedy social injustice for the poor and oppressed; to assist in the preservation of material and buildings associated with Dickens. Annual conference. Publishes journal called *The Dickensian* (founded 1905 and available at special rate to members) and organises a full programme of lectures, discussions, visits and conducted walks throughout the year. Branches worldwide.

Dymock Poets
See **The Friends of the Dymock Poets**

Early English Text Society
Lady Margaret Hall, Oxford OX2 6QA
Fax 01865 286581
www.eets.org.uk
Executive Secretary *Professor Vincent Gillespie* (at address above)
Editorial Secretary *Dr H.L. Spencer* (at Exeter College, Oxford OX1 3DP)
Membership Secretary *Mrs J.M.Watkinson* (at 12 North End, Durham DH1 4NJ)
SUBSCRIPTION £20 p.a. (UK); $30 (US); $35 (Canada)

Founded 1864. Concerned with the publication of early English texts. Members receive annual publications (one or two a year) or may select titles from the backlist in lieu.

The George Eliot Fellowship
71 Stepping Stones Road, Coventry CV5 8JT
☎024 7659 2231
www.george-eliot-fellowship.com
Contact *Mrs Kathleen Adams*
SUBSCRIPTION £10 p.a.; £100 (life); concession for pensioners

Founded 1930. Exists to honour George Eliot and promote interest in her life and works. Readings, memorial lecture, birthday luncheon and functions. Issues a quarterly newsletter and an annual journal. Awards an annual prize for a George Eliot essay.

Rev. G. Bramwell Evens
See **The Romany Society**

The John Meade Falkner Society
Greenmantle, Main Street, Kings Newton,
Melbourne DE73 8BX
☎01332 865315
www.johnmeadefalknersociety.co.uk
Secretary *Kenneth Hillier*
SUBSCRIPTION £5 (UK); $10 (overseas)

Founded in 1999 to promote the appreciation and study of John Meade Falkner's life, times and works. Produces three newsletters a year and an annual journal.

Folly (Fans of Light Literature for the Young)
21 Warwick Road, Pokesdown, Bournemouth BH7 6JW
☎01202 432562
✉ folly@sims.abel.co.uk
Contact *Mrs Sue Sims*
SUBSCRIPTION £9 p.a. (UK); £11 (Europe); £14 (worldwide)

Founded 1990 to promote interest in a wide variety of collectable children's authors – with a bias towards writers of girls' books and school stories. Publishes three magazines a year.

The Ford Madox Ford Society
c/o Dr Sara Haslam, Dept of Literature, The Open University, Milton Keynes MK7 6AA
☎01908 653453 Fax 01908 653750
✉ s.j.haslam@open.ac.uk
www.rialto.com/fordmadoxford_society
Chairman *Professor Max Saunders*
Treasurer *Dr Sara Haslam*
SUBSCRIPTION £12 or £6 concession

Founded 1996 to promote the works of Ford Madox Ford and to increase knowledge of his writing and impact on writing in the 20th century. Meets for academic conferences and more popular events annually. Distributes *International Ford Madox Ford Studies* free to members. Welcomes all with an interest in Ford and his works. Has members in the UK, USA, Italy, France and Germany and holds events in as many different places as possible.

The Franco–Midland Hardware Company
6 Bramham Moor, Hill Head, Fareham PO14 3RU
☎01329 667325
✉ fmhc@acd-221b.info
www.acd-221b.info
Chairman *Philip Weller*

Founded 1989. A federation of societies in four continents. Two core groups, '221B' (Holmesian/Sherlockian) and 'The Arthur Conan Doyle Study Group' (Doylean), form the UK base. Membership is open only to those interested in being actively involved in the programme of correspondence studies and/ or functions. Arranges certificated self-study projects and assists group and individual research programmes, plus scholarly gatherings.

The Friars' Club
33 Grenville Court, Chorleywood WD3 5PZ

☎01923 283795
✉ henry.quelch@westlodge.cdr-i.net
Secretary *Frances-Mary Blake*
SUBSCRIPTION £10 (first year); £8.50 (renewals)

Founded in 1982 to promote the writings of Frank Richards (Charles Hamilton), author of the Greyfriars School stories in *The Magnet* and creator of Billy Bunter. The Club produces a quarterly magazine for members; articles and comments are welcomed.

The Friends of Shandy Hall (The Laurence Sterne Trust)
Shandy Hall, Coxwold, York YO61 4AD
☎01347 868465 Fax 01347 868465
✉ shandyhall@dial.pipex.com
www.asterisk.org.uk
Curator *Patrick Wildgust*
SUBSCRIPTION £7 (annual); £70 (life)

Promotes interest in the works of Laurence Sterne and aims to preserve the house in which they were created (open to the public). Publishes annual journal, *The Shandean*. An Annual Memorial Lecture is delivered each summer.

The Friends of the Dymock Poets
The Rectory, St. Mary's Close, Dymock
GL18 2AX
☎01531 892967
✉ cateluck2003@yahoo.com
www.dymockpoets.co.uk
Chairman *Roy Palmer*
Hon. Secretary *Catharine Lumby*
Membership Secretary *Jeff Cooper*
SUBSCRIPTION £7 (individual); £12 (couple); £3 (student); £12 (society/family)

Founded 1993. Established to foster an interest in the work of the Dymock Poets – Edward Thomas, Robert Frost, Wilfrid Gibson, Rupert Brooke, John Drinkwater, Lascelles Abercrombie; help preserve places and things associated with them; keep members informed of literary and other matters relating to the poets; increase knowledge and appreciation of the landscape between May Hill (Gloucestershire) and the Malvern Hills. Members are offered lectures, poetry readings, social meetings, newsletters and annual journal, guided walks in the countryside around Dymock; links with other literary societies; and annual event to commemorate the first meeting between Edward Thomas and Robert Frost on 6 October 1913.

The Gaskell Society
Far Yew Tree House, Chester Road, Tabley, Knutsford WA16 0HN
☎01565 634668
✉ joanleach@aol.com
gaskellsociety.users.btopenworld.com
lang.nagoya-u.ac.jp/~matsuoka/EG-Society. html
Honorary Secretary *Joan Leach*
SUBSCRIPTION £15 p.a.; £20 (corporate & overseas)

Founded 1985 to promote and encourage the study and appreciation of the life and works of Elizabeth Cleghorn Gaskell. Meetings held in Knutsford, Manchester, Bath and London; annual journal and biannual newsletter. On alternate years holds either a residential weekend conference or overseas visit.

The Ghost Story Society
PO Box 1360, Ashcroft, British Columbia, Canada V0K 1A0
☎001 250 453 2045 Fax 001 250 453 2075
✉ nebuly@telus.net
www.ash-tree.bc.ca/GSS.html
Joint Organisers *Barbara Roden, Christopher Roden*
SUBSCRIPTION UK: £25 (airmail); $40 (US$); $45 (Canadian$)

Founded 1988. Devoted mainly to supernatural fiction in the literary tradition of M.R. James, Walter de la Mare, Algernon Blackwood, E.F. Benson, A.N.L. Munby, R.H. Malden, etc. Publishes a thrice-yearly journal, *All Hallows*, which includes new fiction in the genre and non-fiction of relevance to the genre.

Graham Greene Birthplace Trust
Rhenigidale, Ivy House Lane, Berkhamsted
HP4 2PP
☎01442 865158
✉ secretary@grahamgreenebt.org
www.grahamgreenebt.org
Secretary *Ken Sherwood*
SUBSCRIPTION £9 (UK, £23 for 3 years); £13 (Europe, £31); £17 (RoW, £43)

Founded on 2 October 1997, the 93rd anniversary of Graham Greene's birth, to promote the appreciation and study of his works. Publishes a quarterly newsletter, occasional papers, videos and compact discs. Organises the annual four-day Graham Greene Festival during the weekend nearest to the writer's birthday (2nd October) and administrates the Graham Greene Memorial Awards.

The Ivor Gurney Society
2 Turrall Street, Barbourne, Worcester
WR3 8AJ
☎01497 831038
✉ jp-hay@beeb.net
www.ivor.gurney.net
SUBSCRIPTION £12.50 (individual); £5
(student); £12.50 (group/library); rates
for joint & retired memberships set out on
membership leaflet

To promote interest in Ivor Gurney and his
context and to make his music and poetry available
to a wider audience by way of performances,
readings, conferences, recordings and publications. To enhance and promote informed scholarship on all aspects of his life and work through
the publication of a regular newsletter and an
annual journal, available to society members.
To maintain and expand the Gurney archive at
Gloucester Record Office.

Rider Haggard Society
27 Deneholm, Whitley Bay NE25 9AU
☎0191 252 4516 Fax 0191 252 4516
✉ rb27allen@blueyonder.co.uk
www.riderhaggardsociety.org.uk

Contact *Roger Allen*
SUBSCRIPTION £9 p.a. (UK); £12 (overseas)

Founded 1985 to promote appreciation of the
life and works of Sir Henry Rider Haggard,
English novelist, 1856–1925. News/books
exchange and meetings every 18 months.
Journal can now be e-mailed.

James Hanley Network
Old School House, George Green Road,
George Green, Wexham SL3 6BJ
☎01753 578632
✉ gostick@london.com
www.jameshanley.inspiron.co.uk/
INDEX.HTM

Network Coordinator *Chris Gostick*

An informal international association founded
in 1997 for all those interested in exploring and
publicising the works and contribution to literature of the novelist and dramatist James Hanley
(1901–1985). Publishes an annual newsletter.
Occasional conferences are planned for the
future. All enquiries welcome.

The Thomas Hardy Society
PO Box 1438, Dorchester DT1 1YH
☎01305 251501 Fax 01305 251501
✉ info@hardysociety.org
www.hardysociety.org

Honorary Secretary *Mike Nixon*
SUBSCRIPTION £18 (individual); £25
(corporate); £22.50 (individual, overseas);
£30 (corporate, overseas)

Founded 1967 to promote the reading and study
of the works and life of Thomas Hardy. Thrice-yearly journal, events and a biennial conference.
An international organisation.

The Hazlitt Society
c/o The Guardian, 119 Farringdon Road,
London EC1R 3ER
✉ correspondence@williamhazlitt.org
www.williamhazlitt.org

Contact *Helen Hodgson* (Secretary and
Correspondent)

Established to encourage appreciation of Hazlitt's
work and to promote his values. The first *Hazlitt
Review*, to be launched in the spring of 2008,
will aim to foster and sustain the restitution of
Hazlitt as a canonical author and to stimulate
new scholarship in his work.

The Henty Society
205 Ickneild Way, Letchworth SG6 4TT

Honorary Secretary *David Walmsley*
SUBSCRIPTION £15 p.a. (UK); £18 (overseas)

Founded 1977 to study the life and work of
George Alfred Henty, and to publish research,
bibliographical data and lesser-known works,
namely short stories. Organises conferences and
social gatherings in the UK and North America,
and publishes bulletins to members. Published in
1996: *G.A. Henty (1832–1902) a Bibliographical
Study* by Peter Newbolt (2nd edition with
addenda and corrigenda 2005).

James Hilton Society
49 Beckingthorpe Drive, Bottesford,
Nottingham NG13 0DN
www.jameshiltonsociety.co.uk

Honorary Secretary *J.R. Hammond*
SUBSCRIPTION £10 (UK/EU); £7 concession

Founded 2000 to promote interest in the life and
work of novelist and scriptwriter James Hilton
(1900–1954). Publishes *The Hiltonian* (annually)
and *The James Hilton Newsletter* (quarterly) and
organises meetings and conferences.

The Dartmoor Sherlock Holmes Study Group
See **The Baskerville Hounds**

Sherlock Holmes Society (The Musgraves)
Hallas Lodge, Greenside Lane, Cullingworth, Bradford BD13 5AP
☎01535 273468
✉ hallaslodge@btinternet.com

Contact *Anne Jordan*
SUBSCRIPTION £10 p.a.; £12 (joint)

Founded 1987 to promote enjoyment and study of Sir Arthur Conan Doyle's Sherlock Holmes through publications and meetings. One of the largest Sherlock Holmes societies in Great Britain. Honorary members include Bert Coules, Edward Hardwicke, Clive Merrison and Douglas Wilmer. Past honorary members: Dame Jean Conan Doyle, Peter Cushing, Jeremy Brett, Michael Williams and Richard Lancelyn Green. Open membership. Lectures, presentations and consultation on matters relating to Holmes and Conan Doyle available.

Sherlock Holmes
See **The Baskerville Hounds** and **The Franco-Midland Hardware Company**

Hopkins Society
41 North Drive, Rhyl LL18 4SW
☎01745 354151
✉ bill&meljones@aol.com
www.hopkinsoc.freeserve.co.uk

Contact *Imelda Jones*
SUBSCRIPTION £7 p.a. (UK); £10 (overseas)

Founded 1990 to celebrate the life and work of Gerard Manley Hopkins; to inform members of any publications, courses or events about the poet. Holds an annual lecture on Hopkins in the spring; produces two newsletters a year; sponsors and organises educational projects based on Hopkins' life and works.

Housman Society
80 New Road, Bromsgrove B60 2LA
☎01527 874136
✉ info@housman-society.co.uk
www.housman-society.co.uk

Contact *Jim Page*
SUBSCRIPTION £10 (UK); £12.50 (overseas)

Founded 1973 to promote knowledge and appreciation of the lives and work of A.E. Housman and other members of his family, and to promote the cause of literature and poetry. Sponsors a lecture at the **Hay Festival** each year under the title of 'The Name and Nature of Poetry'. Publishes an annual journal and biannual newsletter.

W.W. Jacobs Appreciation Society
3 Roman Road, Southwick BN42 4TP
☎01273 596217
Contact *A.R. James*

Founded 1988 to encourage and promote the enjoyment of the works of W.W. Jacobs, and stimulate research into his life and works. No subscription charge. Material available for purchase includes *W.W. Jacobs*, a biography published in 1999, price £12, post paid, and *WWJ Book Hunter's Field Guide*, a narrative bibliography published in 2001, price £6, post paid.

Richard Jefferies Society
Pear Tree Cottage, Longcot SN7 7SS
☎01793 783040
✉ R.Jefferies_Society@tiscali.co.uk
www.bath.ac.uk/~lissmc/rjeffs.htm

Honorary Secretary *Jean Saunders*
Membership Secretary *Mrs Margaret Evans*
SUBSCRIPTION £7 p.a. (individual); £8 (joint); life membership for those over 50

Founded 1950 to promote understanding of the work of Richard Jefferies, nature/country writer, novelist and mystic (1848–87). Produces newsletters, reports and an annual journal; organises talks, discussions and readings. Library and archives. Assists in maintaining the museum in Jefferies' birthplace at Coate near Swindon. Membership applications should be sent to *Margaret Evans*, 23 Hardwell Close, Grove, Nr Wantage OX12 0BN.

Jerome K. Jerome Society
c/o Fraser Wood, Mayo and Pinson, 15/16 Lichfield Street, Walsall WS1 1TS
☎01922 629000 Fax 01922 721065
✉ tonygray@jkj.demon.co.uk
www.jeromekjerome.com

Honorary Secretary *Tony Gray*
SUBSCRIPTION £7.50 p.a. (ordinary); £25 (corporate); £3.75 (under 21/over 65)

Founded 1984 to stimulate interest in Jerome K. Jerome's life and works (1859–1927). One of the Society's principal activities is the support of a small museum in the author's birthplace, Walsall. Meetings, lectures, events and a newsletter, *Idle Thoughts*. Annual dinner in Walsall near Jerome's birth date (2nd May).

The Captain W.E. Johns Appreciation Society
221 Church Road, Northolt UB5 5BE
✉ brian@zhong-ding.com

Contact (Derby meeting) *Brian Woodruff* (at address above ☎ 07843 680048)
Contact (Twyford) *Joy Tilley* (☎ 01785 240299) Society for the appreciation of W.E. Johns, creator of Biggles. Meets twice a year in Derby and Twyford, near Reading (see above for contacts). Biannual magazine, *Biggles Flies Again* (Editor *Roger Davies*, ☎ 01722 320761; rda@ salisbury75.freeserve.co.uk).

Johnson Society
Johnson Birthplace Museum, Breadmarket Street, Lichfield WS13 6LG
☎01543 264972
✉ sjmuseum@lichfield.gov.uk
www.lichfieldrambler.co.uk
Chairman *Mary Baker*
SUBSCRIPTION £10 p.a.; £15 (joint); £100/£150 (life: individual/joint)
Founded 1910 to encourage the study of the life, works and times of Samuel Johnson (1709–1784) and his contemporaries. The Society is committed to the preservation of the Johnson Birthplace Museum and Johnson memorials.

Johnson Society of London
255 Baring Road, Grove Park, London SE12 0BQ
☎020 8851 0173
✉ JSL@nbbl.demon.co.uk
www.nbbl.demon.co.uk/index.html
President *Lord Harmsworth*
Honorary Secretary *Mrs Z.E. O'Donnell*
SUBSCRIPTION £20 p.a.; £25 (joint); £15 (student)
Founded 1928 to promote the knowledge and appreciation of Dr Samuel Johnson and his works. Publishes an annual journal, *New Rambler* and occasional newsletter. Regular meetings from October to April in the meeting room of Wesley's Chapel, City Road, London EC1 on the second Saturday of each month, and a commemoration ceremony around the anniversary of Johnson's death (December) held in Westminster Abbey.

The David Jones Society
22 Gower Road, Sketty, Swansea SA2 9BY
☎01792 206144 Fax 01792 475037
✉ anne.price-owen@sihe.ac.uk
www.sihe.ac.uk/davidjones
Contact *Anne Price-Owen*
SUBSCRIPTION £18 (individual); £30 (corporate)
Founded 1996, the Society aims to promote and

encourage knowledge of the painter-poet David Jones. The Society hosts annual scholarly meetings. The annual subscription includes a copy of the *David Jones Journal*. Unsolicited material relating to David Jones, art, literature or any of his philosophies may be sent for consideration for publication in the journal.

The Just William Society
Easter Badbea, Dundonnell IV23 2QX
✉ philandpaula@easter-badbea.co.uk
Secretary/Treasurer *Paula Cross*
SUBSCRIPTION £7 p.a. (UK); £10 (overseas); £5 (juvenile/student); £15 (family)
Founded 1994 to further knowledge of Richmal Crompton's *William* and *Jimmy* books. The *Just William Society Magazines* are published throughout the year and an annual 'William' meeting is held in April.

The Keats–Shelley Memorial Association (Inc)
Registered office: Bedford House, 76A Bedford Street, Leamington Spa CV32 5DT
☎01926 427400 Fax 01926 335133
Contact *Honorary Secretary*
SUBSCRIPTION £12 p.a.
Founded 1903 to promote appreciation of the works of Keats and Shelley, and their circle. One of the Society's main tasks is the preservation of 26 Piazza di Spagna in Rome as a memorial to the British Romantic poets in Italy, particularly Keats and Shelley. Publishes an annual review of Romantic Studies called the *Keats-Shelley Review*, arranges events and lectures for Friends and promotes bursaries and competitive writing on Romantic Studies (see **Keats–Shelley Prize** under *Prizes*). The *Review* is edited by *Stephen Hebron*, c/o Wordsworth Trust, Dove Cottage, Grasmere LA22 9SH

Kent & Sussex Poetry Society
39 Rockington Way, Crowborough TN6 2NJ
☎01892 662781
✉ john@kentandsussexpoetrysociety.org
www.kentandsussexpoetrysociety.org
Publicity Secretary *John Arnold*
SUBSCRIPTION £10 p.a. (full); £6 (concessionary; country members living farther afield, senior citizen, under-16, unemployed)
Founded 1946 to promote the enjoyment of poetry. Monthly meetings are held in Tunbridge Wells, including readings by major poets, a monthly workshop and an annual writing retreat

week. Publishes an annual folio of members' work based on Members' Competition, adjudicated and commented upon by a major poet. Runs an annual **Open Poetry Competition** (see entry under *Prizes* and details on website) and Saturday workshops twice a year with leading poets.

The Kilvert Society
Sandalwood, North End Road, Steeple Claydon, Buckingham MK18 2PG
☎01296 730498
Secretary *Mr D. Elvins*
SUBSCRIPTION £12 p.a.; £15 (two persons at same address)
Founded 1948 to foster an interest in the Diary, the diarist and the countryside he loved. Publishes three journals each year; during the summer holds three weekends of walks, commemoration services and talks.

The Kipling Society
6 Clifton Road, London W9 1SS
☎020 7286 0194 Fax 020 7286 0194
✉ jane@keskar.fsworld.co.uk
www.kipling.org.uk
Honorary Secretary *Jane Keskar*
SUBSCRIPTION £22 p.a. (£20 p.a. by standing order)
Founded 1927. This is a literary society for all who enjoy the prose and verse of Rudyard Kipling (1865–1936) and are interested in his life and times. The Society's main activities are: maintaining a specialised library at the City University in Islington, London; answering enquiries from the public (schools, publishers, writers and the media); arranging a regular programme of lectures, especially in London and in Sussex, and an annual luncheon with guest speaker; maintaining a small museum and reference at The Grange, in Rottingdean near Brighton; issuing a quarterly journal. (For the Kipling mailbox discussion list, sends e-mail to Rudyard-Kipling@jiscmail.ac.uk) Please contact the Secretary by letter, telephone, fax or e-mail for further information.

The Kitley Trust
Woodstock, Litton Dale, Litton SK17 8QL
☎01298 871564
✉ stottie2@waitrose.com
Contact *Rosie Ford*
Founded 1990 by a teacher in Sheffield to promote the art of creative writing, in memory of her mother, Jessie Kitley. Activities include:

biannual poetry competitions; a 'Get Poetry' day (distribution of children's poems in shopping malls); annual sponsorship of a writer for a school; campaigns; organising conferences for writers and teachers of writing. Funds are provided by donations and profits (if any) from competitions.

The Charles Lamb Society
BM ELIA, London WC1N 3XX
Chairman *Nicholas Powell*
SUBSCRIPTION UK: £12 (single); £18 (double); £18 (corporate)
Founded 1935. Publishes studies of the life, works and times of Charles Lamb and his circle. Holds meetings in London five times a year. *The Charles Lamb Bulletin* is published four times a year (editor: *Professor Richard S. Tomlinson* ✉ romanticism@insightbb.com).

Lancashire Authors' Association
Heatherslade, 5 Quakerfields, Westhoughton, Bolton BL5 2BJ
☎01942 791390
✉ eholt@cwctv.net
General Secretary *Eric Holt*
SUBSCRIPTION £10 p.a.; £13 (joint); £1 (junior)
Founded 1909 for writers and lovers of Lancashire literature and history. Aims to foster and stimulate interest in Lancashire history and literature as well as in the preservation of the Lancashire dialect. Meets three times a year on Saturday at various locations. Publishes a quarterly journal called *The Record*, which is issued free to members, and holds eight annual competitions (open to members only) for both verse and prose. Comprehensive library with access for research to members.

The Landor Society of Warwick
'Little Acre', Golf Lane, Whitnash CV31 2PY
☎01926 426712
Honorary Secretary *Mrs Jean Field*
SUBSCRIPTION £7 p.a. (UK/EU); £10 (joint); £12 (overseas)
Founded 2000 to promote interest in the life and works of the Warwick-born writer Walter Savage Landor (1775–1864). Holds a Landor Birthday Lunch each year, and reading and discussion meetings most months. Publishes newsletter twice a year.

The Philip Larkin Society
16 Mere View Avenue, Hornsea HU18 1RR

☎01964 533324
www.philiplarkin.com
General Secretary *Andrew Eastwood*
SUBSCRIPTION £20 (full rate); £14 (unwaged/
senior citizen); £6 (student)
Founded in 1995 to promote awareness of the
life and work of Philip Larkin (1922–1985) and
his literary contemporaries; to bring together all
those who admire Larkin's work as a poet, writer
and librarian; to bring about publications on all
things Larkinesque. Organises a programme
of events ranging from lectures to rambles
exploring the countryside of Larkin's schooldays
and publishes a biannual journal, *About Larkin*.

The D.H. Lawrence Society
24 Briarwood Avenue, Nottingham NG3 6JQ
☎0115 950 3008
Secretary *Ron Faulks*
SUBSCRIPTION £14; £12 (concession); £16
(European); £19 (RoW)
Founded 1974 to increase knowledge and
the appreciation of the life and works of D.H.
Lawrence. Monthly meetings, addressed by guest
speakers, are held in the library at Eastwood
(birthplace of DHL). Organises visits to places
of interest in the surrounding countryside,
supports the activities of the D.H. Lawrence
Centre at Nottingham University, and has close
links with DHL Societies worldwide. Publishes
two newsletters and one journal each year, free
to members.

The T.E. Lawrence Society
PO Box 728, Oxford OX2 9ZJ
✉ info@telsociety.org.uk
www.telsociety.org
www.telawrence.net
Chairman *Peter Leney*
Honorary Secretary *Ian Heritage*
SUBSCRIPTION £13/18 (UK); £18/23
(overseas) Higher price includes newsletter.
Founded 1985, an educational charity, formed
to advance awareness of the life and work of
Thomas Edward Lawrence and to promote
research into his life and work. Publishes two
journals and issues four internal newsletters
a year. There is a biennial symposium, usually
in Oxford. Regional groups include three in
England (Northwest, London, Dorset), one in
Europe (Netherlands), two in the USA (Eastern
and Western States) and one in Japan.

The Leamington Literary Society
52 Newbold Terrace East, Leamington Spa
CV32 4EZ
☎01926 425733
Honorary Secretary *Mrs Margaret Watkins*
SUBSCRIPTION £10 p.a.
Founded 1912 to promote the study and appreciation of literature and the arts. Holds regular
meetings every second Tuesday of the month
(from September to June) at the Royal Pump
Rooms, Leamington Spa. Also smaller groups
which meet regularly to study poetry and the
modern novel. The Society has published various
books of local interest.

Lewes Monday Literary Club
c/o 1c Prince Edward's Road, Lewes BN7 1BJ
☎01273 478512
✉ chris.lutrario@btinternet.com
Contact *Christopher Lutrario*
SUBSCRIPTION £20 p.a.; £5 (guest, per meeting)
Founded in 1948 for the promotion and enjoyment of literature. Seven meetings are held
during the winter generally on the last Monday
of each month (from October to April) at the
Pelham House Hotel in Lewes. The Club
attracts speakers of the highest quality and a
balance between all forms of literature is aimed
for. Guests are welcome to attend meetings.

The Friends of Arthur Machen
Apt 5, 26 Hervey Road, Blackheath, London
SE3 8BS
www.machensoc.demon.co.uk
Contact *Jeremy Cantwell*
SUBSCRIPTION £17 p.a. (UK); £20 (Europe/
RoW); $36 (US)
Brings together those who appreciate Machen's
writings and generally promotes discussion and
research. Publishes two journals and two news-
letters annually, plus occasional publications for
the membership only.

The Marlowe Society
9 Middlefield Gardens, Hurst Green Road,
Halesowen B62 9QH
☎0121 421 1482 Fax 0121 421 1482
✉ marsocpt@aol.com
www.marlowe-society.org
Membership Secretary *Frieda Barker*
Treasurer *Bruce Young*
SUBSCRIPTION £12 p.a. (individual); £7 p.a.
(pensioner/student/unwaged); £15 p.a.
(overseas); £200 (group); £100 (individual
life membership)

Founded 1955. Holds meetings, lectures and discussions, stimulates research into Marlowe's life and works, encourages production of his plays and publishes a biannual newsletter. At a ceremony on 11th July 2002 the Society celebrated their success in establishing a memorial to the playwright and poet in Poets' Corner in Westminster Abbey.

The John Masefield Society

The Frith, Ledbury HR8 1LW
☎01531 631647 Fax 01531 631647
www2.sas.ac.uk/ies/cmps/Projects/Masefield/
Society/jms1.htm
Chairman *Peter Carter*
Subscription £5 p.a. (individual); £8 (family, institution, library); £10 (overseas); £2.50 (junior, student)

Founded in 1992 to stimulate the appreciation of and interest in the life and works of John Masefield (Poet Laureate 1930–1967). The Society is based in Ledbury, the Herefordshire market town of his birth and holds various public events in addition to publishing a journal and occasional papers.

William Morris Society

Kelmscott House, 26 Upper Mall,
Hammersmith, London W6 9TA
☎020 8741 3735 Fax 020 8748 5207
✉ william.morris@care4free.net
www.morrissociety.org
Curator *Helen Elletson*
Subscription £18 p.a.; £8 (student); £30 (corporate)

Founded 1955 to promote interest in the life, work and ideas of William Morris (1834–1896), English poet and craftsman. Organises events and educational programmes. Members receive newsletters and biannual journal. Archive and library open by appointment.

The Neil Munro Society

8 Briar Road, Kirkintilloch, Glasgow G66 3SA
☎0141 776 4280
✉ brian@bdosborne.fsnet.co.uk
www.neilmunro.co.uk
Secretary *Brian D. Osborne*
Subscription £12 (annual); £7 (unwaged); £15 (institutional)

Founded in 1996 to encourage interest in the works of Neil Munro (1863–1930), the Scottish novelist, short story writer, poet and journalist. An annual programme of meetings is held in Glasgow and Munro's home-town of Inveraray.

Publishes *ParaGraphs*, a twice-yearly magazine, sponsors reprints of Munro's work and is developing a Munro archive.

Violet Needham Society

c/o 19 Ashburnham Place, London SE10 8TZ
☎020 8692 4562
✉ richardcheffins@aol.com
Honorary Secretary *R.H.A. Cheffins*
Subscription £7.50 p.a. (UK & Europe); £11 (RoW)

Founded 1985 to celebrate the work of children's author Violet Needham and stimulate critical awareness of her work. Publishes thrice-yearly *Souvenir*, the Society journal with an accompanying newsletter; organises meetings and excursions to places associated with the author and her books. The journal includes articles about other children's writers of the 1940s and 1950s and on ruritanian fiction. Contributions welcome.

The Edith Nesbit Society

26 Strongbow Road, Eltham, London SE9 1DT
www.pete-colman.com/trc/
Contact *Mrs Marion Kennett*
Subscription £7 p.a.; £9 (joint)

Founded in 1996 to celebrate the life and work of Edith Nesbit (1858–1924), best known as the author of *The Railway Children*. The Society's activities include a regular newsletter, booklets, talks and visits to relevant places.

The Wilfred Owen Association

29 Arthur Road, London SW19 7DN
☎020 8947 0476
www.1914-18.co.uk/owen
Chairman *Mrs Meg Crane*
Subscription Adults £6 (£10 overseas); £4 (senior citizen/student/unemployed); £15 (UK group/institution); £25 (overseas group/institution)

Founded 1989 to commemorate the life and works of Wilfred Owen by promoting readings, visits, talks and performances relating to Owen and his work. The Association offers practical support for students of literature and future poets through links with education, support for literary foundations and information on historical and literary background material. Membership is international with 700 members. Publishes a regular newsletter and annual journal. Speakers are available.

The Elsie Jeanette Oxenham Appreciation Society

32 Tadfield Road, Romsey SO51 5AJ
☎01794 517149
✉ abbey@bufobooks.demon.co.uk
www.bufobooks.demon.co.uk/abbeylnk.htm
Membership Secretary/Treasurer *Ms Ruth Allen*
Editor (*The Abbey Chronicle*) *Fiona Dyer*
   (fionadyer@btopenworld.com)
SUBSCRIPTION £7.50 p.a.; enquire for overseas
   rates

Founded 1989 to promote the works of Elsie J.
Oxenham. Publishes a newsletter for members,
The Abbey Chronicle, three times a year. 500+
members.

Thomas Paine Society

43 Eugene Gardens, Nottingham NG2 3LF
☎0115 986 0010
President *The Rt. Hon. Michael Foot*
Honorary Secretary *R. W. Morrell, MBE* (at
   address above)
Treasurer *Stuart Wright*
SUBSCRIPTION (minimum) £15
   p.a. (UK); $35 (overseas); £5
   (unwaged/pensioner/student)

Founded 1963 to promote the life and work
of Thomas Paine, and continues to expound
his ideals. Meetings, newsletters, lectures and
research assistance. The Society has members
worldwide and keeps in touch with American
and French Thomas Paine associations. Publishes
magazine, *The Journal of Radical History*, twice
yearly (Editor, *R. W. Morrell*) and a newsletter.
Holds occasional exhibitions and lectures,
including the biannual Thomas Paine Memorial
Lecture and the annual Eric Paine Memorial
Lecture.

The Beatrix Potter Society

The Lodge, Salisbury Avenue, Harpenden
AL5 2PS
☎01582 769755
✉ beatrixpottersociety@tiscali.co.uk
www.beatrixpottersociety.org.uk
Membership Secretary *Jenny Akester*
SUBSCRIPTION UK: £20 p.a. (individual); £25
   (institution); Overseas: £25 (individual);
   £30 (institution)

Founded 1980 to promote the study and appreciation of the life and works of Beatrix Potter
(1866–1943). Potter was not only the author
of *The Tale of Peter Rabbit* and other classics of
children's literature; she was also a landscape and
natural history artist, diarist, farmer and conser-
vationist, and was responsible for the preservation
of large areas of the Lake District through her
gifts to the National Trust. The Society upholds
and protects the integrity of the unique work of
Potter, her aims and bequests; holds regular talks
and meetings in London and elsewhere with
visits to places connected with Beatrix Potter.
International Study Conferences are held in
the UK and the USA. The Society has an active
publishing programme. (UK Registered Charity
No. 281198.)

Anthony Powell Society

76 Ennismore Avenue, Greenford UB6 0JW
☎020 8864 4095 Fax 020 8864 6109
✉ secretary@anthonypowell.org
www.anthonypowell.org
Patron *John M.A. Powell*
President *Simon Russell Beale*
Honorary Secretary *Dr Keith C. Marshall*
SUBSCRIPTION £20 p.a. (individual); £30 (joint/
   gold); £12 (student); £100 (organisation)

Founded in June 2000 to advance educa-
tion and interest in the life and works of the
English author Anthony Powell (1905–2000).
The Society's major activity is a biennial Powell
conference, the first three of which were at Eton
College (2001), Balliol College, Oxford (2003)
and The Wallace Collection, London (2005).
The Society organises events for members,
ranging from 'pub meets' to talks and visits to
places of Powell interest as well as publishing
Secret Harmonies (annual journal) and a quarterly
Newsletter. Member of the **Alliance of Literary
Societies**.

The Powys Society

25 Mansfield Road, Taunton TA1 3NJ
☎01823 278177
✉ peter_lazare@hotmail.com
www.powys-society.org
Honorary Secretary *Peter Lazare*
SUBSCRIPTION £18.50 (UK); £22 (overseas);
   £10 (student)

The Society (with a membership of 300) aims
to promote public education and recognition of
the writings, thought and contribution to the
arts of the Powys family; particularly of John
Cowper, Theodore and Llewelyn, but also of
the other members of the family and their close
associates. The Society holds two major collections of Powys published works, letters, manuscripts and memorabilia. Publishes the *Powys
Society Newsletter* in April, June and November
and *The Powys Journal* in August. Organises an

annual conference as well as lectures and meetings in Powys places.

The J.B. Priestley Society
Eldwick Crag Farm, Otley Road, Bingley
BD16 3BB
☎01274 563078
✉ reavill@globalnet.co.uk
www.jbpriestley-society.com
President *Tom Priestley*
Chairman *Dr Ken Smith*
Honorary Secretary *R.E.Y. Slater*
Membership Secretary *Tony Reavill*
SUBSCRIPTION £12 (individual); £7
(concession); £18 (group/family)

Founded 1997 to widen the knowledge and understanding of Priestley's works; promote the study of his life and his social, cultural and political influences; provide members of the Society with lectures, seminars, films, journals and stimulate education projects; promote public performances of his works and the distribution of material associated with him. For further information, contact the Membership Secretary at the address above.

The Barbara Pym Society
St Hilda's College, Oxford OX4 1DU
☎01865 276828 Fax 01865 276820
✉ eileen.roberts@st-hildas.oxford.ac.uk
www.pym.org
Chairman *Deirdre Bryan-Brown*
SUBSCRIPTION £15 p.a. (individual); £22 p.a.
(household); £8 p.a. (concession)

Aims to promote interest in and scholarly research into the works of Barbara Pym; to bring together like-minded people to enjoy the exploration of all aspects of her novels and to continue to encourage publishers to keep her novels in print. Annual weekend conference at St. Hilda's College in September, focusing on a theme or a particular novel. Annual North American Conference at Harvard Law School. Annual one-day spring meeting in London, with speaker. Publishes a newsletter, *Green Leaves*, biannually. In addition to reports on conferences and society activities, the newsletter includes scholarly papers and various unpublished items from the Pym archives at the Bodleian Library (i.e. short stories).

The Queen's English Society
The Clergy House, Hide Place, London
SW1P 4NJ
☎020 7630 1819
✉ enquiries@queens-english-society.com

www.queens-english-society.com
Honorary Secretary *Mr G.J. Hardwick*
SUBSCRIPTION £15 p.a. (ordinary); £20 (joint)

Founded in 1972 to promote and uphold the use of good English and to encourage the enjoyment of the language. Holds regular meetings and conferences to which speakers are invited, an annual luncheon and publishes a quarterly journal, *Quest*, for which original articles are welcome. (Registered Charity no. 272901.)

Rainbow Poetry Recitals
14 Lewes Crescent, Brighton BN2 1FH
☎01424 444072/01273 687053
✉ beyondcloister@hotmail.co.uk
Administrator *Hugh Hellicar*
SUBSCRIPTION £6.50/€10 (individual); £10/
€15 (joint/family); £12 (school)

Founded 1994. Regular recitals of poetry and other literature are held in Sussex, Kent and London. Seminars in some branches. Research library in Sussex. Quarterly magazine with overseas distribution.

The Arthur Ransome Society Ltd
Abbot Hall Art Gallery & Museum, Kendal
LA9 5AL
✉ tarsinfo@arthur-ransome.org
www.arthur-ransome.org/ar
Trustee Chairman *Geraint Lewis*
Company Secretary *Kath Eastman*
SUBSCRIPTION UK: £5 (junior); £10 (student);
£15 (adult); £20 (family); £40 (corporate);
Overseas: £5 (junior); £10 (student);
£20 (adult); £25 (family) Payable in local
currency in US, Canada, Australia, Japan and
New Zealand

Founded in 1990 to celebrate the life and to promote the works and ideas of Arthur Ransome, author of *Swallows and Amazons* titles for children, biographer of Oscar Wilde, works on the Russian Revolution and extensive articles on fishing. TARS seeks to encourage children and adults to engage in adventurous pursuits, to educate the public about Ransome and his works, and to sponsor research into his literary works and life.

The Romany Society
10 Haslam Street, Bury BL9 6EQ
☎0161 764 7078
✉ phil_shelley@btopenworld.com
www.romanysociety.org.uk
Honorary Secretary *John Thorpe* (at address above)

Publications Officer *Phil Shelley*
SUBSCRIPTION £5 (individual); £9 (family); £10 (institution); £3.50 (student/unwaged) Promotes the life, work and conservation message of the Rev. G. Bramwell Evens – 'Romany' – the first broadcasting naturalist who influenced generations of listeners with his *Out With Romany* radio programmes on the BBC during the 1930s and 1940s and with his series of natural history books. The Romany Society was established originally following Evens' death at the age of 59 in 1943 and ran until 1965. Revived in 1996, the Society holds an annual members' weekend to areas of significance in the Romany story, erects memorial plaques where appropriate, encourages media coverage of Romany and supports young naturalists with the Romany Memorial Grant.

The Followers of Rupert

31 Whiteley, Windsor SL4 5PJ
☎01753 865562
✉ followersofrupert@hotmail.com
www.rupertthebear.org.uk
Membership Secretary *Mrs Shirley Reeves*
SUBSCRIPTION Europe: £30 (individual); £23 (joint); RoW: £35 (individual); £37 (joint)
Founded in 1983. The Society caters for the growing interest in the Rupert Bear stories, past, present and future. Publishes the *Nutwood Newsletter* quarterly which gives up-to-date news of Rupert and information on Society activities. A national get-together of members – the Followers Annual – is held during the summer.

The Ruskin Society of London

20 Parmoor Court, Summerfield, Oxford
OX2 7XB
☎01865 310987
Honorary Secretary *Miss O.E. Forbes-Madden*
SUBSCRIPTION £15 p.a.
Founded 1986 to promote interest in John Ruskin (1819–1900) and his contemporaries. All aspects of Ruskinia are introduced. Functions are held in London. Publishes the annual *Ruskin Gazette*, a journal concerned with Ruskin's influence. Affiliated to other literary societies.

The Ruskin Society

49 Hallam Street, London W1W 6JP
☎020 7580 1894
✉ cgamble@britishlibrary.net
www.lancs.ac.uk/depts/ruskin/links.htm
Chairman *Professor Michael Wheeler*

Honorary Secretary *Dr Cynthia J. Gamble*
SUBSCRIPTION £10 p.a. (payable on 1st Jan.)
Founded in 1997 to encourage a wider understanding of John Ruskin and his contemporaries. Organises lectures and events which seek not only to explain to the public at large the nature of Ruskin's theories but also to place these in a modern context.

The Malcolm Saville Society

78a Windmill Road, Mortimer RG7 3RL
✉ mystery@witchend.com
www.witchend.com
Chairman *Richard Griffiths*
SUBSCRIPTION £10 p.a. (UK); £12 (EU); £16 (RoW)
Founded in 1994 to remember and promote interest in the work of the popular children's author. Regular social activities, booksearch, library, contact directory and four magazines per year.

The Dorothy L. Sayers Society

Rose Cottage, Malthouse Lane, Hurstpierpoint BN6 9JY
☎01273 833444 Fax 01273 835988
www.sayers.org.uk
Contact *Christopher Dean*
SUBSCRIPTION £14 p.a. (UK); £16.50 (Europe); $34 (US)
Founded 1976 to promote the study of the life, works and thoughts of Dorothy Sayers; to encourage the performance of her plays and publication of her books and books about her; to preserve original material and provide assistance to researchers. Acts as a forum and information centre, providing material for study purposes which would otherwise be unavailable. Annual conventions, usually in August and other meetings. Co-founder of the Dorothy L. Sayers Centre in Witham. Publishes bi-monthly bulletin, annual proceedings and other papers.

The Shaw Society

Flat F, 10 Compton Road, London N1 2PA
☎020 7226 4266
✉ shawsociety@blueyonder.so.uk
Honorary Secretary *Alan Knight*
SUBSCRIPTION £15 p.a. (individual); £22 (joint)
Founded 1941 to promote interest in the life and works of G. Bernard Shaw. Meetings are held on the last Friday of every month (except July, August and December) at Conway Hall, Red Lion Square, London WC1 (6.30 pm for 7.00 pm) at which speakers are invited to talk

on some aspect of Shaw's life or works. Monthly playreadings are held on the first Friday of each month (except August). Over 40 years ago the Society began the annual open-air perform-ance held at Shaw's Corner, Ayot St Lawrence in Hertfordshire, on the weekend nearest to Shaw's birthday (26th July). Publishes a quarterly news-letter and a biannual magazine, *The Shavian*. (No payment for contributors.)

The Robert Southey Society

1 Lewis Terrace, Abergarwed, Neath SA11 4DL
☎01639 711480

Contact *Robert King*
SUBSCRIPTION £10 p.a.

Founded 1990 to promote the work of Robert Southey. Publishes an annual newsletter and arranges talks on his life and work. Open membership.

The Laurence Sterne Trust

See **The Friends of Shandy Hall**

Robert Louis Stevenson Club

12 Dean Park, Longniddry EH32 0QR
☎01875 852976 Fax 01875 853328
✉ alan@amarchbank.freeserve.co.uk
www.rlsclub.org.uk

Secretary *Alan Marchbank*
SUBSCRIPTION £20 p.a. (individual); £26 p.a.
    (overseas); £150 (10-year)

Founded in 1920 to foster interest in Robert Louis Stevenson's life and works. The Club organises an annual lunch and other events. Publishes *RLS Club News* twice a year.

The R.S. Surtees Society

Manor Farm House, Nunney, Near Frome BA11 4NJ
☎01373 836937 Fax 01373 836574
✉ rssurtees@fsmail.net
www.r.s.surteessociety.org

Contact *Orders and Membership Secretary*
    (☎ 01373 302155)

Founded 1979 to republish the works of R.S. Surtees and others.

The Tennyson Society

Central Library, Free School Lane, Lincoln LN2 1EZ
☎01522 552862 Fax 01522 552858
✉ kathleenjefferson@lincolnshire.gov.uk
www.tennysonsociety.org.uk

Honorary Secretary *Miss K. Jefferson*
SUBSCRIPTION £10 p.a. (individual); £12

(family); £15 (corporate); £160 (life)

Founded 1960. An international society with membership worldwide. Exists to promote the study and understanding of the life and work of Alfred, Lord Tennyson. The Society is concerned with the work of the Tennyson Research Centre, 'probably the most significant collection of mss, family papers and books in the world'. Publishes annually the *Tennyson Research Bulletin*, which contains articles and critical reviews; and organ-ises lectures, visits and seminars. Annual memo-rial service at Somersby in Lincolnshire.

The Angela Thirkell Society

54 Belmont Park, London SE13 5BN
☎020 8244 9339
✉ penny.aldred@ntlworld.com
www.angelathirkellsociety.com
www.angelathirkell.org (N. American branch)

Honorary Secretary *Mrs. P. Aldred*
SUBSCRIPTION £10 p.a.

Founded in 1980 to honour the memory of Angela Thirkell as a writer and to make her works available to new generations. Publishes an annual journal, holds an AGM in the autumn and a spring meeting which usually takes the form of a visit to a location associated with Thirkell. Has a flourishing North American branch which has frequent contact with the UK parent society.

The Dylan Thomas Society of Great Britain

Fern Hill, 24 Chapel Street, Mumbles, Swansea SA3 4NH
☎01792 363875

Contact *Mrs Cecily Hughes*
SUBSCRIPTION £5 (individual); £8 (two adults
    from same household)

Founded 1977 to foster an understanding of the work of Dylan Thomas and to extend members' awareness of other 20th century writers, espe-cially Welsh writers in English. Meetings take place monthly, mainly in Swansea.

The Edward Thomas Fellowship

1 Carfax, Undercliff Drive, St Lawrence, Isle of Wight PO38 1XG
☎01983 853366
✉ colingthornton@btopenworld.com
www.edward-thomas-fellowship.org.uk

Hon. Secretary *Colin G. Thornton*
SUBSCRIPTION £7 p.a. (single); £10 p.a. (joint)

Founded 1980 to perpetuate and promote the memory of Edward Thomas and to encourage an appreciation of his life and work. The

Fellowship holds a commemorative birthday walk on the Sunday nearest the poet's birthday (3rd March) and an autumn walk; issues newsletters and holds various events and seminars.

The Tolkien Society
210 Prestbury Road, Cheltenham GL52 3ER
✉ secretary@tolkiensociety.org
www.tolkiensociety.org
Secretary *Sally Kennett*
SUBSCRIPTION £21 p.a. (UK); £24 (overseas)

An international organisation which aims to encourage and further interest in the life and works of the late Professor J.R.R. Tolkien, CBE, author of *The Hobbit* and *Lord of the Rings*. Current membership stands at 1100. Publishes *Mallorn* annually and *Amon Hen* bi-monthly.

The Trollope Society
Maritime House, Old Town, Clapham, London SW4 0JW
☎020 7720 6789 Fax 020 7627 2965
✉ info@trollopesociety.org
www.trollopesociety.org
Contact *Pelham Ravenscroft*
Founded 1987 to study and promote Anthony Trollope's works. Publishes the complete works of Trollope's novels and travel books.

Wainwright Society
Kendal Museum, Station Road, Kendal LA9 6BT
☎01539 721374 Fax 01539 737976
✉ membership@wainwright.org.uk
www.wainwright.org.uk
Membership Secretary *Morag Clement*
SUBSCRIPTION £10 p.a. (per household, from 1st Jan.)

Founded in 2002 'to keep alive the things that Alfred Wainwright (1907–1991) promoted through his guidebooks (*Pictorial Guides to the Lakeland Fells*), started 50 years ago, and the many other publications which were the "labour of love" of a large portion of his life'. Produces a newsletter three times per year, organises walks, events, annual dinner and lecture.

The Walmsley Society
April Cottage, No 1 Brand Road, Hampden Park, Eastbourne BN22 9PX
☎01323 506447
✉ walmsley@haughshw.demon.co.uk
Honorary Secretary *Fred Lane*
SUBSCRIPTION £12 p.a.; £14 (family); £11 (student/senior citizen); £17 (overseas, £18,

one year; £30, two years)

Founded 1985 to promote interest in the writings of Leo Walmsley and to foster an appreciation of the work of his father, the artist Ulric Walmsley. Two annual meetings – one held in Robin Hood's Bay on the East Yorkshire coast, spiritual home of the author Leo Walmsley. Publishes a journal twice-yearly and newsletters, and is involved in other publications which benefit the aims of the Society. A biography of Leo Walmsley is now available.

Sylvia Townsend Warner Society
2 Vicarage Lane, Fordington, Dorchester DT1 1LH
☎01305 266028
✉ judith@bond.vispa.com
www.townsendwarner.com
Contact *Eileen Johnson*
SUBSCRIPTION £10 p.a.; $20 (overseas)
Founded in 2000 to promote a wider readership and better understanding of the writings of Sylvia Townsend Warner.

Mary Webb Society
8 The Knowe, Willaston, Neston CH64 1TA
☎0151 327 5843
✉ suehigginbotham@yahoo.co.uk
www.marywebb.VZE.com
Secretary *Sue Higginbotham*
SUBSCRIPTION UK: £10 p.a. (individual); £13 p.a. (joint); Overseas: £13 p.a. (individual); £15 p.a. (joint)

Founded 1972. Attracts members from the UK and overseas who are devotees of the literature of Mary Webb and of the beautiful Shropshire countryside of her novels. Publishes biannual journal, organises summer schools in various locations related to the authoress's life and works. Archives; lectures; tours arranged for individuals and groups.

H.G. Wells Society
Flat 3, 27b Church Road, London NW4 4EB
✉ secretaryhgwellsociety@hotmail.com
www.hgwellsusa.50megs.com/UK/index.html
Hon. General Secretary *Mark Egerton*
SUBSCRIPTION £16 (UK/EU); £19 (RoW); £20 (corporate); £10 (concessions);
Founded 1960 to promote an interest in and appreciation of the life, work and thought of Herbert George Wells. Publishes *The Wellsian* (annual) and *The H.G. Wells Newsletter* (three issues yearly). Organises meetings and conferences.

The Oscar Wilde Society
19 South Hill Road, Gravesend DA12 1LA
✉ vanessasalome@blueyonder.co.uk
Honorary Secretary *Vanessa Heron*
Founded 1990 to promote knowledge, appreciation and study of the life, personality and works of the writer and wit Oscar Wilde. Activities include meetings, lectures, readings and exhibitions, and visits to locations associated with Wilde. Members receive a journal of Oscar Wilde studies, *The Wildean*, twice yearly and a newsletter journal *Intentions* (six per year).

The Charles Williams Society
35 Broomfield, Stacey Bushes, Milton Keynes MK12 6HA
✉ charles_wms_soc@yahoo.co.uk
www.geocities.com/charles_wms_soc
Contact *Honorary Secretary*
SUBSCRIPTION
Founded 1975 to promote interest in, and provide a means for the exchange of views and information on the life and work of Charles Walter Stansby Williams (1886–1945).

The Henry Williamson Society
7 Monmouth Road, Dorchester DT1 2DE
☎01305 264092
✉ zseagull@aol.com
www.henrywilliamson.co.uk
General Secretary *Mrs Sue Cumming*
Membership Secretary *Mrs Margaret Murphy*
(16 Doran Drive, Redhill RH1 6AX
☎ 01737 763228
✉ mm@misterman.freeserve.co.uk)
SUBSCRIPTION £12 p.a.; £15 (family); £5 (student)
Founded 1980 to encourage, by all appropriate means, a wider readership and deeper understanding of the literary heritage left by the 20th-century English writer Henry Williamson (1895–1977). Publishes annual journal.

The P.G. Wodehouse Society (UK)
26 Radcliffe Road, Croydon CR0 5QE
✉ christinehewitt@waitrose.com
www.pgwodehousesociety.org.uk
www.eclipse.co.uk/wodehouse
Membership Secretary *Christine Hewitt*
SUBSCRIPTION £15 p.a. (£20 Dec.to March, for membership extended to May the following year)
Formed in 1997 to promote enjoyment of the works of P.G. Wodehouse, author, lyricist, playwright and journalist, creator of Lord Emsworth, Jeeves & Wooster and many more. Membership of 1000+. Publications include the quarterly journal, *Wooster Sauce* and regular *By The Way* papers. Meetings and events are held in London and around the country. The Society is allied to Wodehouse societies around the world.

The Parson Woodforde Society
22 Gaynor Close, Wymondham NR18 0EA
☎01953 604124
✉ mabrayne@supanet.com
www.parsonwoodforde.org.uk
Membership Secretary *Mrs Ann Elliott*
SUBSCRIPTION £12.50 (UK); £25 (overseas)
Founded 1968. Aims to extend and develop knowledge of James Woodforde's life and the society in which he lived and to provide the opportunity for fellow enthusiasts to meet together in places associated with the diarist. Publishes a quarterly journal and newsletter. The Society has produced a complete edition of the diary of James Woodforde in 17 volumes covering the period 1759–1802.

The Virginia Woolf Society of Great Britain
Fairhaven, Charnleys Lane, Banks, Southport PR9 8HJ
✉ stuart.n.clarke@btinternet.com
www.virginiawoolfsociety.co.uk
Contact *Stuart N. Clarke*
SUBSCRIPTION £15 p.a.; £20 (overseas)
Founded 1998 to promote interest in the life and work of Virginia Woolf, author, essayist and diarist. The Society's activities include trips away, walks, reading groups and talks. Publishes a literary journal, *Virginia Woolf Bulletin*, three times a year.

The Wordsworth Trust
Dove Cottage, Grasmere LA22 9SH
☎015394 35544 Fax 015394 63508
✉ enquiries@wordsworth.org.uk
www.wordsworth.org.uk
Contacts *Allan King, Ann Pease*
Founded in 1890, the Trust is a living memorial to the life and poetry of William Wordsworth and his contemporaries. As Centre for British Romanticism, the Wordsworth Trust, with its wealth of manuscripts, books, drawings and pictures, provides 'the full context for understanding and celebrating a major cultural moment in history in which Britain played a profound role'. (Registered Charity No. 1066184.)

WW2 HMSO PPBKS Society

3 Roman Road, Southwick BN42 4TP
☎01273 596217

Contact A.R. James

Founded 1994 to encourage collectors and to promote research into HMSO's World War II series of paperbacks. Most of them were written by well-known authors, though in many cases anonymously. No subscription charge. Available for purchase: Collectors' Guide (£5); Handbook, *Informing the People* (£10).

The Yeats Society Sligo

Yeats Memorial Building, Hyde Bridge, Sligo, Republic of Ireland
☎00 353 71 914 2693 Fax 00 353 71 914 2780
✉ info@yeats-sligo.com
www.yeats-sligo.com

President *Aleck Crichton*
SUBSCRIPTION €25 (single); €40 (couple)

Founded in 1958 to promote the heritage of W.B. Yeats and the Yeats family. Attractions include a permanent Yeats Exhibition; films for public viewing throughout the year; the annual Yeats International Summer School in July/August; the Winter School in January. The Yeats Festival is also held in the summer, and lectures, poetry readings, workshops, etc. are held in the autumn and spring, together with a variety of outings and other events for members. Visits are made to schools, and contacts are made with Yeats scholars and students worldwide.

The Charlotte M.Yonge Fellowship

8 Anchorage Terrace, Durham DH1 3DL
☎0191 384 7857
www.cmyf.org.uk

Contact *Dr C.E. Schultze*
SUBSCRIPTION £9 p.a.

Founded in 1996 to provide the opportunity for all who enjoy and admire the work of Charlotte M. Yonge (1823–1901), author of *The Heir of Radclyffe*, to learn more about her life and wrtings. Holds two meetings annually, one in November in London, and the other, the spring AGM, at venues associated with Yonge's life, works or interests, or where buildings or gallery and museum collections relate to Victorian history, art and society. Publishes *Review* twice-yearly and an occasional *Journal*. A loan collection of Yonge's works enables members to borrow publications that are hard to obtain. The Fellowship's Archive is held at St Hugh's College, Oxford and material is available to members and *bona fide* researchers.

Yorkshire Dialect Society

51 Stepney Avenue, Scarborough YO12 5BW
www.ydsociety.org.uk

Secretary *Michael Park*
SUBSCRIPTION £10 p.a.

Founded 1897 to promote interest in and preserve a record of the Yorkshire dialect. Publishes dialect verse and prose writing. Two journals to members annually. Details of publications are available from YDS at address above.

Francis Brett Young Society

92 Gower Road, Halesowen B62 9BT
☎0121 422 8969
www.fbysociety.co.uk

Honorary Secretary *Mrs Jean Hadley*
SUBSCRIPTION £7 p.a. (individual); £10 (couple sharing a journal); £5 (student); £7 (organisation/overseas); £70 (life); £100 (joint, life)

Founded 1979. Aims to provide a forum for those interested in the life and works of English novelist Francis Brett Young and to collate research on him. Promotes lectures, exhibitions and readings; publishes a regular newsletter.

Arts Councils and Regional Offices

Arts Council England
14 Great Peter Street, London SW1P 3NQ
☎0845 300 6200 Textphone 020 7973 6564
✉ enquiries@artscouncil.org.uk
www.artscouncil.org.uk
Chairman *Professor Sir Christopher Frayling*
Chief Executive *Peter Hewitt*
Director of Literature Strategy *Antonia Byatt*
Founded 1946. Arts Council England is the national development agency for the arts in England, distributing public money from government and the National Lottery to artists and arts organisations. ACE works independently and at arm's length from government. Information about Arts Council England funding is available on the website, by e-mail or by contacting the enquiry line on 0845 300 6200.

Arts Council England has 9 regional offices:

Arts Council England, East
Eden House, 48–49 Bateman Street,
Cambridge CB2 1LR
☎ 0845 300 6200 Fax 0870 242 1271
Textphone 01223 306893

Arts Council England, East Midlands
St Nicholas Court, 25–27 Castle Gate,
Nottingham NG1 7AR
☎ 0845 300 6200 Fax 0115 950 2467

Arts Council England, London
2 Pear Tree Court, London EC1R 0DS
☎ 0845 300 6200 Fax 020 7608 4100
Textphone 020 7973 6564

Arts Council England, North East
Central Square, Forth Street, Newcastle upon Tyne NE1 3PJ
☎ 0845 300 6200 Fax 0191 230 1020
Textphone 0191 255 8585

Arts Council England, North West
Manchester House, 22 Bridge Street,
Manchester M3 3AB
☎ 0845 300 6200 Fax 0161 834 6969
Textphone 0161 834 9131

Arts Council England, South East
Sovereign House, Church Street, Brighton
BN1 1RA
☎ 0845 300 6200 Fax 0870 242 1257

Textphone 01273 710659

Arts Council England, South West
Senate Court, Southernhay Gardens, Exeter
EX1 1UG
☎ 0845 300 6200 Fax 01392 229229
Textphone 01392 433503

Arts Council England, West Midlands
82 Granville Street, Birmingham B1 2LH
☎ 0845 300 6200 Fax 0121 643 7239
Textphone 0121 643 2815

Arts Council England, Yorkshire
21 Bond Street, Dewsbury WF13 1AX
☎ 0845 300 6200 Fax 01924 466522
Textphone 01924 438585

The Arts Council/ An Chomhairle Ealaíon
70 Merrion Square, Dublin 2,
Republic of Ireland
☎00 353 1 618 0200 Fax 00 353 1 676 1302
✉ artstsservices@artscouncil.ie
www.artscouncil.ie
Director *Mary Cloake*
Literature Specialist (English language) *Bronwen Williams*
Literature Specialist (Irish language) *Róisin Ní Mhianáin*

The Arts Council is the Irish government agency for developing the arts. It provides financial assistance to artists, arts organisations, local authorities and others for artistic purposes. It offers advice and information on the arts to Government and to a wide range of individuals and organisations. As an advocate for the arts and artists, the Arts Council undertakes projects and research, often in new and emerging areas of arts practice, and increasingly in cooperation with partner organisations. Its funding from government for 2007 was €80 million.

Of particular interest to individual writers is the Council's free booklet, *Support for Artists 2007*, which describes bursaries, awards and schemes on offer and how to apply for them. Applicants to these awards must have been born in, or be resident in, the Republic of Ireland.

The Arts Council of Northern Ireland

MacNeice House, 77 Malone Road, Belfast BT9 6AQ
☎028 9038 5200 Fax 028 9066 1715
✉ dsmyth@artscouncil-ni.org
www.artscouncil-ni.org

Literature and Language Arts Officer *Damian Smyth*

Funds book production by established publishers, programmes of readings, literary festivals, mentoring services, writers-in-residence schemes, network service providers, literary magazines and periodicals. Annual awards and bursaries for writers are available. Holds information also on various groups associated with regional arts, workshops and courses.

Scottish Arts Council

12 Manor Place, Edinburgh EH3 7DD
☎0131 226 6051 Fax 0131 225 9833
✉ help.desk@scottisharts.org.uk
www.scottisharts.org.uk

Chief Executive *Graham Berry*
Head of Literature *Gavin Wallace*
Literature Officers *Jenny Attala, Aly Barr, Emma Turnbull*
Literature Administrator *Catherine Allan*

Principal channel for government funding of the arts in Scotland. The Scottish Arts Council is funded by the Scottish Executive and National Lottery. It aims to develop and improve the knowledge, understanding and practise of the arts, and to increase their accessibility throughout Scotland. It offers grants to artists and arts organisations concerned with the visual arts, crafts, dance and mime, drama, literature, music, festivals and traditional, ethnic and community arts. Scottish Arts Council's support for Scottish-based writers with a track record of publication includes bursaries, writing fellowships and book awards (see entries under *Bursaries, Fellowships and Grants* and *Prizes*). Information offered includes lists of literature awards, literary magazines, agents and publishers.

The Arts Council of Wales / Cyngor Celfyddydau Cymru

9 Museum Place, Cardiff CF10 3NX
☎029 2037 6500 Fax 029 2022 1447
www.artswales.org.uk
www.celfcymru.org.uk

The Arts Council of Wales (ACW) is the development body for the arts in Wales. ACW's Creative Wales Awards offer substantial grants for established writers and playwrights. Funds the **Welsh Academy** and **Ty Newydd Writers' Centre** to provide services to individual writers, including bursaries, mentoring, the critical writers services and writers in residence/on tour. Responsibility for promoting the publishing and sales of books from Wales and funding literary magazines rests with the **Welsh Books Council**.

UK and Irish Writers' Courses

ENGLAND

Berkshire

University of Reading
The School of Continuing Education, London Road, Reading RG1 5AQ
☎0118 378 8347
✉ Cont-Ed@reading.ac.uk
www.reading.ac.uk/ContEd

An expanding programme of creative writing courses, including *Life into Fiction*; *Poetry Workshop*; *Getting Started*; *Writing Fiction*; *Publishing Poetry*; *Scriptwriting*; *Playwriting, Travel Writing*; *Comedy Writing* and *Writing for Radio*. Readings by students of their work, and various Saturday workshops. Tutors include novelist Leslie Wilson and poets Jane Draycott, Susan Utting, David Grubb and Paul Bavister. Fees vary depending on the length of course. Concessions available.

The Write Coach
2 Rowan Close, Wokingham RG41 4BH
☎0118 978 4904
✉ enquiries@thewritecoach.co.uk
www.thewritecoach.co.uk

Contact *Bekki Hill*

Workshops and one-to-one coaching (both in person and by telephone) to assist both professional and aspiring writers to become more successful, break through their blocks, build confidence, increase motivation and expand creativity, define direction and find time and space to write. Free e-zine and free initial consultation available. See website for details.

Buckinghamshire

Missenden Abbey
Evreham Adult Learning Centre, Swallow Street, Iver SL0 0HS
☎01296 383582
✉ dcevreham@buckscc.gov.uk
www.arca.uk.net/missendenabbey

Residential and non-residential weekend workshops, Easter and summer school. Programmes have included *Writing Stories for Children*; *Short*

Story Writing; *Poetry Workshop*; *Writing Comedy for Television*; *Life Writing*; *Travel Tales*.

National Film & Television School
Beaconsfield Studios, Station Road, Beaconsfield HP9 1LG
☎01494 731425 Fax 01494 674042
✉ info@nfts.co.uk
www.nfts.co.uk

Two-year programme covering all aspects of screenwriting from the development of ideas through to final production. Studying alongside other filmmaking students allows writers to have their work tested in workshops and productions. Unlike a Screenwriting MA set in an academic institution, this course is set in a working studio and emphasises practical filmmaking and contact with industry personnel through seminars and pitching sessions. The course requires and encourages a high level of dedication and a prolific output. Year One deals with the basic principles of storytelling, the craft of screenwriting for film and television and the collaborative nature of production, and includes several short writing assignments. Year Two focuses on longer writing assignments, with students writing a feature script and TV project as well as their MA dissertation. Opportunities may be available to write short fiction or animation scripts for production. In partnership with **The Script Factory**, The NFTS also offers an 18-month, part-time Diploma in *Script Development*.

Cambridgeshire

National Extension College
Michael Young Centre, Purbeck Road, Cambridge CB2 8HN
☎0800 389 2839 Fax 01223 400321
✉ info@nec.ac.uk
www.nec.ac.uk/courses

Contact *Customer Relations Adviser*

Runs a number of home-study courses on writing which include: *Essential Editing*; *Creative Writing* and *Writing Short Stories*. Contact the NEC for a free copy of the *Guide to Courses* which includes details of fees and course enrolment.'You can enrol at any time, study at home, work at your own pace and fit learning into your lives.'The NEC is accredited by the Open Distance Learning Quality Council.

University of Cambridge Institute of Continuing Education

Madingley Hall, Madingley, Cambridge
CB3 8AQ
☎01954 280399 Fax 01954 280200
✉ registration@cont-ed.cam.ac.uk
www.cont-ed.cam.ac.uk

A wide range of weekend, five-day and week-long creative writing courses for adults is offered by the University at the Institute of Continuing Education's residential headquarters at Madingley Hall. Evening courses are also available in Cambridgeshire and surrounding areas. Details of all courses can be found on the website or phone for a brochure.

Cheshire

Burton Manor

The Village, Burton, Neston CH64 5SJ
☎0151 336 5172 Fax 0151 336 6586
✉ enquiry@burtonmanor.com
www.burtonmanor.com

Wide variety of short courses, residential and non-residential, on writing and literature, including *Creative Writing Workshop* and *Writing for Pleasure*. Full details in brochure.

Cornwall

University College Falmouth

Woodlane, Falmouth TR11 4RH
☎01326 211077
www.falmouth.ac.uk
www.bloc-online.com (magazine)
Contact *Admissions*

MA professional writing programme. An intensive vocational writing programme developing skills in fiction, magazine journalism/features, screenwriting. Students work on an extended writing project and form links with other postgraduate programmes such as television production and broadcast journalism.

Cumbria

Higham Hall College

Bassenthwaite Lake, Cockermouth CA13 9SH
☎01768 776276 Fax 01768 776013
✉ admin@highamhall.com
www.highamhall.com

Winter and summer residential courses. Programme includes *Creative Writing*; *Writing for Radio and TV*. Brochure available.

Derbyshire

Real Writers

PO Box 170, Chesterfield S40 1FE
☎01246 520834 Fax 01246 520834
✉ info@real-writers.com
www.real-writers.com

Correspondence service with personal tuition from working writers. Send s.a.e. for details.

Swanwick – The Writers' Summer School

The Hayes Conference Centre, Nr Alfreton
✉ jeanfsutton@btinternet.com
www.wss.org.uk
Secretary *Jean Sutton*

Offers six-days of informal talks, discussion groups, interactive workshops and quizzes. Competitions and 'a lot of fun'. All levels welcome. Held mid-August from Saturday to Friday morning. Cost (2007) £345–440 per person, all inclusive. S.a.e. to the Secretary at 10 Stag Road, Lake, Sandown, Isle of Wight PO36 8PE (☎ 01983 406759/e-mail as above).

University of Derby

Admissions Office, Kedleston Road, Derby
DE22 1GB
☎01332 622236 Fax 01332 622754
✉ J.Bains@derby.ac.uk
www.derby.ac.uk
Contact *Carl Tighe*

With upwards of 300 students, this is one of the oldest *Creative Writing* operations at degree level in the UK. The subject offers a BA Hons *Creative Writing* with particular strengths in Short Stories, Writing and New Technologies and Storytelling. All teaching is done through practical workshops led by established and experienced writers. In the final year students produce an independent research project on a subject of their choice. The subject also contributes to the BA Hons Combined Studies.

Devon

Arvon Foundation (Devon)

See entry under **London**

Dartington College of Arts

Totnes TQ9 6EJ
☎01803 862224 Fax 01803 861666

✉ registry@dartington.ac.uk
www.dartington.ac.uk
Director of Writing *Dr Mark Leahy*
BA (Hons) *Writing* or *Writing (Contemporary Practices)* or *Writing (Scripted Media)*; *Textual Practices* minor award; *MA Performance Writing*: exploratory approaches to writing as it relates to performance, visual arts, sound arts and contemporary culture. Encourages the interdisciplinary, with minor awards and electives at BA level in arts and cultural management, choreography, music, theatre, visual performance. Contact the Director of Writing (see www.dartington. ac.uk/pw/).

Exeter Phoenix
Bradninch Place, Gandy Street, Exeter
EX4 3LS
☎01392 667080 Fax 01392 667599
www.exeterphoenix.org.uk

Regular literature events, focusing on performances by living poets and writers, often linked to wider programmes. Tutors in a wide range of writing skills run classes and workshops. 'Uncut Poets' group holds monthly meetings.

Fire in the Head Courses & Writers' Services
PO Box 17, Yelverton PL20 6YF
www.fire-in-the-head.co.uk
Contact *Roselle Anguin*

Comprehensive year-round writing programme in poetry, fiction (short and novel-writing), reflective writing and creative development. Also available, online and snailmail correspondence courses.

University of Exeter
Room 206, Department of English, Queen's Building, Queen's Drive, Exeter EX4 4QH
☎01392 264263 Fax 01392 264361
✉ soe.pgoffice@ex.ac.uk
www.ex.ac.uk/english

Offers BA (Hons) in *English* with 2nd and 3rd-year options in creative writing, poetry, short fiction, screenwriting and creative non-fiction. MA *English*; MA *Creative Writing*: poetry, novella, screenwriting, life writing and novel. PhD *Creative Writing*.

Dorset

Bournemouth University
The Media School, Weymouth House, Talbot Campus, Fern Barrow, Poole BH12 5BB

☎01202 965553 Fax 01202 965099
Programme Administrator *Katrina King*
Three-year, full-time BA(Hons) course in *Scriptwriting for Film and Television*.

Essex

National Council for the Training of Journalists
The New Granary, Station Road, Newport, Saffron Walden CB11 3PL
☎01799 544014 Fax 01799 544015
✉ info@nctj.com
www.nctj.com

For details of journalism courses, both full-time and via distance learning, please write to the NCTJ enclosing a large s.a.e. or visit the website.

Gloucestershire

Chrysalis – The Poet In You
5 Oxford Terrace, Uplands, Stroud GL5 1TW
☎01453 759436/020 7794 8880
✉ jay@ramsay3892.fsnet.co.uk
www.lotusfoundation.org.uk

Contact *Jay Ramsay, BAHons (Oxon), PGDip, UKCP member*

Two-part correspondence course combining poetry and personal development. Offers postal courses, day and weekend workshops (including 'The Sacred Space of the Word'), an on-going poetry group based in London and Gloucestershire and individual therapy related to the participant's creative process. The Chrysalis course itself consists of Part 1, 'for those who feel drawn to reading more poetry as well as wanting to start to write their own', and Part 2, 'a more in-depth course designed for those who are already writing and who want to go more deeply into its process and technique, its background and cultural history'. Both courses combine course notes with in-depth individual correspondence and feedback. Editing and information about publication also provided. Brochure and workshop dates available from the address above.

Wye Valley Arts Centre
Hephzibah Gallery, Llandogo NP25 4TW
☎01594 530214/01291 689463
Fax 01594 530321
✉ wyeart@cwcom.net
www.wyeart.cwc.net
Courses (held at Hephzibah Gallery, Llandogo

in the Wye Valley and 'at our house in Cornwall') include *Creative Writing* and *Fiction Workshop*. All styles and abilities.

Hampshire

Highbury College, Portsmouth

Dovercourt Road, Cosham, Portsmouth
PO6 2SA
☎023 9238 3131 Fax 023 9237 8382
✉ media.journalism@highbury.ack.uk
www.highbury.ac.uk

Course Administrator *Christine Stallard*
(☎ 023 9231 3287)

The 20-week fast-track postgraduate courses include: *Pre-entry Magazine Journalism*; *Pre-entry Newspaper Journalism*; and Diploma in *Broadcasting Journalism*, run under the auspices of the Periodicals Training Council, the National Council for Training of Journalists and the Broadcast Journalism Training Council respectively.

Southampton Solent University

East Park Terrace, Southampton SO14 0YN
☎023 8031 9000
✉ Richard.Hudson@Solent.ac.uk
www.solent.ac.uk

Contact *Rick Hudson* (☎ 023 8031 9097)

Courses offered: BA(Hons) *Media Writing*; BA(Hons) *Writing Fashion & Culture*; BA(Hons) *Journalism*. Writing may be taken as a specialism in MA *Media* or BA *Popular Fiction* and BA *Screenwriting*; BA *Magazine Journalism and Feature Writing*.

University of Portsmouth

School of Creative Arts, Film and Media,
Portsmouth PO1 2EG
☎023 9284 5138 Fax 023 9284 5152
✉ creative@port.ac.uk
www.port.ac.uk/departments/academic/scafm

Contact *School of Creative Arts, Film and Media*

Offers creative writing and combined creative writing degrees across a wide range of undergraduate programmes and in all genres. BA, MA and PhD study is available. The School is a key partner in a national AHRC Research training project in Creative Writing. Staff include a number of national and/or international award-winning writers, short story writers/novelists, playwrights, screenwriters, new-media writers and poets. The School runs regular national and international creative writing events.

University of Winchester

Winchester SO22 4NR
☎01962 841515 Fax 01962 842280
www.winchester.ac.uk

Contact *Enquiries* (☎ 01962 827232)

Offers a range of courses for budding writers both at undergraduate and postgraduate level. The three-year degree course in *Creative Writing* is available as a Single, Combined or Joint Honours programme. It covers a range of genres including writing for films, TV, short stories, fiction and poetry. Other three-year courses of possible interest include *English*; *English Literature and Language*; *Journalism*; *English with American Literature*. MA courses in *Writing for Children* and *Creative and Critical Writing* and *English Contemporary Literature* are available on a one or two-year basis.

Winchester Writers' Conference, Bookfair & Week-long Writing Workshops

University of Winchester, Faculty of Arts,
Winchester SO22 4NR
☎01962 827238
✉ barbara.large@winchester.ac.uk
www.Writersconference.co.uk

Conference Director *Barbara Large, MBE, FRSA, HFUW*

Honorary Patron *Dame Beryl Bainbridge* Held on 27th, 28th, 29 June in 2008, followed by week-long writing workshops, 30th June to 5th July. This Festival of Writing, now in its 28th year, attracts authors, playwrights, poets, literary agents, commissioning editors and book production specialists who give workshops, mini courses, lectures, seminars and one-to-one appointments to help writers harness their creative ideas and to develop their writing, editing and marketing skills. Fifteen writing competitions are attached to the conference. All first-place winners are published in the anthology *The Best of* series. The Bookfair offers delegates a wide choice of exhibits including authors' services, publishers, societies, booksellers, printers and trade associations. See also **Pitstop Refuelling Writers' Weekend Workshops** under *Writers' Circles and Workshops*.

Hertfordshire

Liberato Breakaway Writing Courses

16 Middle King, Braintree CM7 3XY
☎01376 551379

✉ liberato@talktalk.net
www.liberato.co.uk
Contact *Maureen Blundell*

Specialises in beginner fiction writers with weekend and week-long courses. Emphasis on individual writing with written ms critiques and one-to-one sessions. Weekends held at Polstead in Suffolk throughout the year. Greek weeks in June and/or September on the Saronic island of Agistri, near Aegina – a relaxing, informal holiday with one-to-one sessions and editing service. B&B accommodation. Also offers postal and e-mail ms critiques on all fiction/autobiography.

Isle of Wight

Annual Writers' Writing Courses & Workshops

F * F Productions, 39 Ranelagh Road, Sandown PO36 8NT
☎01983 407772 Fax 01983 407772
✉ felicity@writeplot.co.uk
www.writeplot.co.uk
www.learnwriting.co.uk

Contact *Felicity Fair Thompson*

Regular residential weeks and weekends on creative writing for beginners and experienced writers – individual advice and workshops. Also offers postal ms critiques and one-to-one advice on fiction and film scripts

Kent

North West Kent College

Oakfield Lane, Dartford DA1 2JT
☎01322 629436/0800 074 1447 (Freephone helpline) Fax 01322 629468
www.nwkcollege.ac.uk

Contact *Neil Nixon*, Head of School, Media & Communications

Two-year, full-time course that explores writing from a number of angles, teaching essential skills, market and academic aspects of the subject. Successful students progress to work or the University of Greenwich, the latter option allowing them to gain a BA(Hons) in Humanities from a further year of study. Staff include script-writers, novelists and a book publisher. Students compile a portfolio in the final year.

University of Kent

The Registry, Canterbury CT2 7NZ
☎01227 827272
✉ information@kent.ac.uk
www.kent.ac.uk/studying

www.kent.ac.uk/english
Contact *Dr Emma Bainbridge* (☎ 01227 823402)

Diploma and degree level course in English and American Literature with Creative Writing in a vibrant department. Undergraduate certificate courses in *Creative Writing, Practical* and *Imaginative Writing*. Also Combined Studies courses in *English and Creative Writing*.

Lancashire

Alston Hall College

Alston Lane, Longridge, Preston PR3 3BP
☎01772 784661 Fax 01772 785835
✉ alston.hall@ed.lancscc.gov.uk
www.alstonhall.com

Holds regular day and residential *Creative Writing* workshops. Full colour brochure available.

Edge Hill University

St Helen's Road, Ormskirk L39 4QP
☎01695 575171
✉ shepparr@edgehill.ac.uk
www.edgehill.ac.uk

Contact *Professor Robert Sheppard*

Offers a two-year, part-time MA in *Writing Studies*. Combines advanced-level writers' workshops with closely related courses in the poetics of writing and contemporary writing in English. There is also provision for MPhil and PhD-level research in writing and poetics. A full range of creative writing courses is available at undergraduate level, in poetry and fiction writing which may be taken as part of a modular BA.

Lancaster University

English & Creative Writing, Bowland College, Bailrigg, Lancaster LA1 4YN
☎01524 594169 Fax 01524 594247
✉ l.kellett@lancaster.ac.uk
www.lancs.ac.uk/depts/english/crew/index.htm

Contact *Lyn Kellett*

Offers practical graduate and undergraduate courses in writing fiction, poetry and scripts. All based on group workshops – students' work-in-progress is circulated and discussed. Distance learning MA now available. Graduates include Andrew Miller, Justin Hill, Monique Roffey, Alison MacLeod, Jacob Polley.

Leicestershire

Writing School Leicester

c/o Leicester Adult Education College, 2
Wellington Street, Leicester LE1 6HL
☎0116 233 4343 Fax 0116 233 4344
✉ vm1@laec.ac.uk
www.laec.ac.uk

Contact *Valerie Moore*

Offers a wide range of part-time creative writing
and journalism courses throughout the year in
Leicester and elsewhere. The writing school
offers a mix of critical workshops, one-day and
term-length courses and short craft modules.
Supports writers through to publication and has
strong links with local media.

London

Arvon Foundation

National Administration: 2nd Floor,
42A Buckingham Palace Road, London
SW1W 0RE
☎020 7931 7611 Fax 020 7963 0961
www.arvonfoundation.org
Devon: Totleigh Barton, Sheepwash,
Beaworthy EX21 5NS
☎ 01409 231338 Fax 01409 231144
✉ t-barton@arvonfoundation.org

Yorkshire: Lumb Bank, Heptonstall, Hebden
Bridge HX7 6DF
☎ 01422 843714 Fax 01422 843714
✉ l-bank@arvonfoundation.org

Inverness-shire: Moniack Mhor, Teavarran,
Kiltarlity, Beauly IV4 7HT
☎ 01463 741675
✉ m-mhor@arvonfoundation.org

Shropshire: The Hurst, Clunton, Craven Arms
SY7 0JA
☎ 01588 640658 Fax 01588 640509
✉ hurst@arvonfoundation.org

Joint Presidents *Terry Hands, Sir Robin
Chichester-Clark*
Chairman *Nigel Pantling*
National Director *Ariane Koek*

Founded 1968. Offers people of any age (over
16) and any background the opportunity to live
and work with professional writers. Four-and-a-
half-day residential courses are held throughout
the year at Arvon's four centres, covering poetry,
fiction, drama, writing for children, songwriting
and the performing arts. Bursaries towards the
cost of course fees are available for those on
low incomes, the unemployed, students and

pensioners. Runs a biennial international poetry
competition (see entry under *Prizes*).

Birkbeck College, University of London

School of English and Humanities, Malet
Street, London WC1E 7HX
☎020 77079 0689
✉ A.Whiting@bbk.ac.uk
www.bbk.ac.uk/eh/eng

Contact *Anne Marie Whiting*

Taught by published writers, Birkbeck offers
an MA course in *Fiction Writing*. The course
will extend and cultivate existing writing skills,
help develop writing to a professional level
and is supported by masterclasses and readings from visiting professionals. All classes are
held in the evening. Study part-time over two
years or full-time over one year. Applications
must be supported by a portfolio of creative
writing. Download an application form from
the website.

The Central School of Speech and Drama

Embassy Theatre, Eton Avenue, London
NW3 3HY
☎020 7722 8183 Fax 020 7722 4132
✉ enquiries@cssd.ac.uk

Contact *Academic Registry*

MA in *Advanced Theatre Practice*. One-year, full-
time course aimed at providing a grounding in
principal areas of professional theatre practice
– *Writing for Performance, Dramaturgy, Directing,
Performance, Puppetry* and *Design*, with an
emphasis on collaboration between the various
strands. *Writing for Performance* students have
the opportunity of working with companies to
create new and innovative work for the theatre.
Prospectus available. Also MA in *Writing for Stage
& Broadcast* Course Leader: *Dymphna Callery*
(d.callery@cssd.ac.uk).

City Lit

Keeley Street, Covent Garden, London
WC2B 4BA
☎020 7492 2652 Fax 020 7492 8256
✉ humanities@citylit.ac.uk

The Writing School offers a wide range of
courses: *Ways Into Creative Writing; Writing
for Children; Playwriting; Writing Short Stories;
Screenwriting; Comedy Writing* and *Poetry.* Various
lengths of course available. The Department
offers information and advice during term
time.

City University

Education and Lifelong Learning,
Northampton Square, London EC1V 0HB
☎020 7040 8268 Fax 020 7040 8256
✉ ell@city.ac.uk
www.city.ac.uk/ell/cfa/write

The Courses for Adults evening programme includes: *Certificate in Novel Writing* (three-term course); *Novel Writing and Longer Works*; *Towards Publication*; *Writing Television Drama*; *Writing Situation Comedy*; *Food Writing*; *Feature Writing*.

The Complete Creative Writing Course at the Groucho Club

☎020 7249 3711 Fax 020 7683 8141
✉ maggie@writingcourses.org.uk
www.writingcourses.org.uk

Contact *Maggie Hamand*

Courses of ten two-hour sessions held at the Groucho Club in London's Soho, starting in January, April and September, Monday or Saturday afternoons, 2.30 pm – 4.30 pm. Beginners and advanced courses offered. Courses include stimulating exercises, discussion and weekly homework. Fee: £225 for whole course.

The Intensive Course/ Fiction Tutorials

5 Queen Elizabeth Close, London N16 0HL
☎020 8809 4725
✉ henrietta@writtenwords.net
www.WrittenWords.net

Contact *Henrietta Soames*

One-year course for writers working on a novel or collection of short stories. Eight classes from 10.00 am to 4.00 pm spread throughout the year. Also private one-to-one fiction tutorials for students who require concentrated attention and feedback on their work. These can be held monthly or as required.

Literary Lions

PO Box 40, 61 Praed Street, London W2 1NS
✉ info@literary-lions.com *and*
jane@literary-lions.com

Tours and hotel-based courses constructed round the following authors and the places associated with them: *Cumbria:* Wordsworth, Coleridge and Southey, John Ruskin, Beatrix Potter; *Yorkshire:* the Brontë sisters, Sylvia Plath and Ted Hughes, Charles Kingsley, W.H. Auden; *Scotland:* Jane and Thomas Carlyle, Robert Louis Stevenson. Discount for seniors and chil-

dren; small groups or large classes are acceptable. Initial contact and details by e-mail or letter.

London College of Communication

Elephant & Castle, London SE1 6SB
☎020 7514 6500
✉ info@lcc.arts.ac.uk
www.lcctraining.co.uk

Intensive courses in writing, editing and journalism. Courses include: *News Writing Practice*; *Feature Writing*; *How to Write and Sell Travel Features*; *Brush Up Your Grammar*. Prospectus and information leaflets available; telephone 020 7514 6569 or access the website.

London School of Journalism

126 Shirland Road, London W9 2BT
☎020 7289 7777 Fax 020 7432 8141
✉ info@lsjournalism.com
www.home-study.com
www.lsj.org

Contact *Student Administration Office*

Distance learning courses with an individual and personal approach. Students remain with the same tutor throughout the course. Options include: *Novel Writing*; *Short Story Writing*; *Writing for Children*; *Poetry*; *Freelance Journalism*; *Media Law*; *Improve Your English*; *Cartooning*; *Thriller Writing*. Fees vary but range from £295 for *Enjoying English Literature* to £395 for *Journalism and Newswriting*. Postgraduate Diploma Courses taught in London (three month full-time, six month part-time, nine month evening classes). Online postgraduate diploma course (24 months) also available.

Middlesex University

Trent Park, Bramley Road, London N14 4YZ
☎020 8411 5000 Fax 020 8411 6652
✉ tpadmissions@mdx.ac.uk
www.mdx.ac.uk

The UK's longest established writing degree offers a Single or Joint Honours programme in *Creative and Media Writing* (full or part-time). This modular programme gives an opportunity to explore journalism, poetry, prose fiction and dramatic writing for a wide range of genres and audiences. Option for work experience in the media and publishing industries. Contact Admissions or *David Rain* (d.rain@mdx.ac.uk).

MA in *Writing* (full-time, part-time; day and evening classes) includes writing workshops; critical seminars; lectures and workshops from established writers; introduction to agents and publishers. Options available: Fiction, Poetry or Scriptwriting. Contact *Sue Gee* ☎ 020 8411 5941 (s.gee@mdx.ac.uk).

Also offer research degrees M.Phil/PhD in *Creative Writing*. Contact: Maggie Butt (m.butt@mdx.ac.uk). The University has a thriving Writing Centre running an annual literary festival, weekly talks, community projects and writers in residence. 'All of our writing courses take place in the setting of a beautiful country park, within easy reach of central London.'

PMA Training

The PMA Centre for Media Excellence, 7a Bayham Street, London NW1 0EY
☎01480 300653 Fax 01480 496022
✉ training@pma-group.com
www.pma-group.com
www.becomeajournalist.co.uk

Contacts *Vicky Chandler, Melanie Gilbert*

Fast-track nine-week Postgraduate Diploma and more than 150 one and two-day editorial, PR, design and publishing courses held in central London. Intensive workshops run by top journalists, print and online, designers and PR professionals. All short courses are designed to lead to the PMA Gold Standard qualification. Apple, Adobe, Quark and the Periodical Publishers' Association accreditation. NCJJ, NUJ and Communicators in Business recommended. Edexel Exam Centre. Special discount for freelances. See website for dates and fees.

Roehampton University

Roehampton Lane, London SW15 5PUH
☎020 8392 3000
www.roehampton.ac.uk

Three-year BA(Hons) programmes in *Drama, Theatre and Performance Studies*; *Film Studies and Screen Practice* include courses on writing for stage and screen, creative writing, cultural and news studies and journalism. Also offers postgraduage programmes in *Children's Literature*; MPhil, PhD in *English, (Literature and Language)*.

The Script Factory

66–67 Wells Street, London W1T 3PY
☎020 7323 1414
✉ general@scriptfactory.co.uk
www.scriptfactory.co.uk

Established in 1996, The Script Factory is a screenwriter and script developer organisation set up to bridge the gap between writers and the industry, and to promote excellence in screenwriting. Specialising in training, screenings, masterclasses and various services from its base

in central London, The Script Factory operates throughout the UK and internationally. For the best source of information on upcoming activities, courses and latest news, and to join the free mailing list, check out the website

Soho Theatre Company

See entry under *Theatre Producers*

Travellers' Tales

92 Hillfield Road, London NW6 1QA
✉ info@travellerstales.org
www.travellerstales.org

Travellers' Tales is Britain's foremost provider of travel writing and travel photography training for non-professionals. Offers practical courses with top professionals. Tutors include award-winning authors William Dalrymple and Colin Thubron, travel editors Simon Calder (*The Independent*), Lyn Hughes (*Wanderlust*) and Jonathan Lorie (*Traveller*). Courses include beginners' weekends, UK masterclasses and creative holidays overseas.

University of Westminster

School of Media, Arts and Design, Harrow Campus, Watford Road, Harrow HA1 3TP
☎020 7911 5903 Fax 020 7911 5955
✉ harrow-admissions@wmin.ac.uk
www.wmin.ac.uk

Courses include part-time MAs available in *Journalism Studies*; *Film and Television Studies*; *Screenwriting and Producing*; *Public Communication and Public Relations*; *Communication and Communication Policy*.

Greater Manchester

Manchester Metropolitan University – The Writing School

Department of English, Geoffrey Manton Building, Rosamond Street West, off Oxford Road, Manchester M15 6LL
☎0161 247 1732/1 Fax 0161 247 6345
✉ a.biswell@mmu.ac.uk (campus course) *or* h.beck@mmu.ac.uk (online course)

Course Convenors *Andrew Biswell* (campus address), *Heather Beck* (online)

The Writing School offers two 'routes' for students to follow: *Poetry* and *The Novel*. A key feature of the programme is regular readings, lectures, workshops and masterclasses by writers, publishers, producers, booksellers, librarians and agents. Tutors include Simon Armitage, Heather Beck, Carol Ann Duffy, Paul Magrs, Michael Symmons Roberts, Jackie Roy and Jeffrey Wainwright. A new *Children's Writing* route will soon be offered. The course is available online as well as through the campus (contact *Heather Beck*, Online Convenor: h.beck@mmu.ac.uk).

University of Manchester

English & American Studies,School of Arts, Histories and Cultures, Humanities Lime Grove, Oxford Road, Manchester M13 9PL
☎0161 306 1259 Fax 0161 275 5987
✉ englishpg@manchester.ac.uk
www.manchester.ac.uk/english

Course Directors *John McAuliffe, Patricia Duncker*

Offers a one-year MA in *Creative Writing* (the novel, short story and poetry) and a PhD.

University of Salford

Postgraduate Admissions, School of Media, Music & Performance,Adelphi Building, Peru Street, Salford M3 6EQ
☎0161 295 6026 Fax 0161 295 6023
✉ r.humphrey@salford.ac.uk
www.smmp.salford.ac.uk

MA in *Television and Radio Scriptwriting*. Two-year, part-time course taught by professional writers and producers. Also offers masterclasses with leading figures in the radio and television industry.

The Writers Bureau

Sevendale House, 7 Dale Street, Manchester M1 1JB
☎0161 228 2362 Fax 0161 236 9440
✉ studentservices@writersbureau.com
www.writersbureau.com

Contact Diana Nadin

Comprehensive home-study writing course with personal tuition service from professional writers. Fiction, non-fiction, articles, short stories, novels, TV, radio and drama all covered in detail. Trial period, guarantee and no time limits.Writing for children, using the Internet to sell your writing and biographies, memoirs and family history courses also available. ODLQC accredited. Quote Ref. EH07. Free enquiry line: 0800 389 7360.

The Writers Bureau
College of Journalism

Address etc. as The Writers Bureau above

Home-study course covering all aspects of journalism. Real-life assignments assessed by qualified tutors with the emphasis on getting into print. Comprises 28 modules and three supple-

ments. Ref: EHJ07. Free enquiry line: 0800 389 7360.

The Writers College

Address etc. as The Writers Bureau above

The Art of Writing Poetry Course from The Writers Bureau sister college.A home-study course with a more 'recreational' emphasis.The 60,000-word course has 17 modules and lets you complete six written assignments for tutorial evaluation. Quote Ref. EHP07. Free enquiry line: 0800 389 7360.

Merseyside

University of Liverpool

Continuing Education, 126 Mount Pleasant, Liverpool L69 3GR
☎0151 794 6900/6952 (24 hours)
Fax 0151 794 2544
✉ conted@liverpool.ac.uk
www.liv.ac.uk/conted

Course Organiser *Dr John Redmond*

Courses include: *Introduction to Creative Writing*; *Scriptwriting*; *Journalism*; *Writing for Children*; *Writing Your Life Story* and a series of Saturday courses on aspects of writing. Most courses take place on one evening or daytime meeting weekly, with some Saturdays and linked days. Courses may be taken to pursue a personal interest or to gain university credit towards an award. CE offers a Certificate in Higher Education (*Creative Writing*) – 120 credits. For most courses no previous knowledge is required. There are fee concessions for those who are receiving certain benefits or are retired. Free prospectus on request or see the website.

Norfolk

University of East Anglia

School of Literature and Creative Writing, Norwich NR4 7TJ
☎01603 592154 Fax 01603 250599
✉ pgt.hum@uea.ac.uk
www.uea.ac.uk/eas

Contact *Jack Camplin*, Postgraduate Admissions

UEA has a history of concern with contemporary literary culture. Among its programmes is the MA in *Creative Writing* (founded by Angus Wilson and Malcolm Bradbury in 1970/71). The course has three parallel entry points: Prose fiction, poetry and scriptwriting. A series of weekly workshops provide intensive examination of students' own work, and also draw on aspects of teaching in nineteenth and twentieth century literature, literary theory and film and cultural studies.

Northamptonshire

Knuston Hall Residential College for Adult Education

Irchester, Wellingborough NN29 7EU
☎01933 312104 Fax 01933 357596
✉ enquiries@knustonhall.org.uk
www.knustonhall.org.uk

Writing courses have included: *Articles for Magazines*; *My Life in Poems and Stories*; *Writer's Workshops* and *Creative Writing*.

Northumberland

Community Creative Writing

'Sea Winds', 2 St Helens Terrace, Berwick-upon-Tweed TD15 1RJ
☎01289 305213
✉ mavismaureen@aol.com

Contact/Tutor *Maureen Raper, MBE*

The courses, which are held at the Community Centre College, Berwick-upon-Tweed as well as by distance learning for those unable to travel into class, include: *Creative Writing for Beginners*; *Writing for Children*; *Writing Comedy*; *Writing for Radio and Television*; *Writing Crime and Mystery*. All courses are verified by North East Open College Networks.

Nottinghamshire

The Nottingham Trent University

College of Arts, Humanities and Education, Clifton Campus, Nottingham NG11 8NS
☎0115 848 3111
✉ acc.postgrad@ntu.ac.uk
www.human.ntu.ac.uk/writing

MA in *Creative Writing*. Hands-on and work-shop-based, the course concentrates primarily on the practice and production of writing. A choice of options from *Fiction*, *Poetry*, *Creative Non-Fiction*, *New Media Writing*, *Children's Writing* and *Scriptwriting*. Assignments and a dissertation, but no formal exams. There is a full programme of visiting speakers. Study either full-time or part-time; all classes held in the evenings.

Oxfordshire

University of Oxford Department for Continuing Education

Rewley House, 1 Wellington Square, Oxford OX1 2JA

☎01865 280356 Fax 01865 270309
✉ pp@conted.ox.ac.uk
www.conted.ox.ac.uk

Creative writing classes held during the autumn and spring terms. There are also one-week summer school courses, a two-year part-time Diploma and a two-year part-time MSt in *Creative Writing*. Early booking is advised.

Shropshire

Arvon Foundation (Shropshire)

See entry under **London**

Somerset

Ammerdown Conference and Retreat Centre

Ammerdown Park, Radstock, Bath BA3 5SW
☎01761 433709 Fax 01761 433094
✉ centre@ammerdown.org
www.ammerdown.org
www.ammerdown-conference.co.uk

Courses include a five-day creative writing course. En suite residential facilities. Brochure available or full details on the website.

Bath Spa University

Newton Park, Bath BA2 9BN
☎01225 875573 Fax 01225 875503
✉ r.kerridge@bathspa.ac.uk
www.bathspa.ac.uk

Contact *Admissions Officer* (☎ 01225 875821)

MA in *Creative Writing*. A course for creative writers wanting to develop their work. Teaching is by published writers in the novel, poetry, short stories and scriptwriting. In recent years, several students from this course have received contracts from publishers for novels, awards for poetry and short stories and have had work produced on BBC Radio. MA in *Writing for Young People*. A course for writers for children of all ages, from the picture-book age through to adolescent and 'crossover' writing, which aims at markets among adults as well as young people. An experienced teaching team helps and encourages students to create a significant body of writing, with practical plans for its place in the real world of publishing.

Dillington House

Ilminster TA19 9DT
☎01460 52427/Minicom: 01460 258640
Fax 01460 52433
✉ dillington@somerset.gov.uk
www.dillington.com

Dillington House is one of the finest historic houses in Somerset. Provides short residential courses across a wide range of subjects, including writing and literary appreciation. Full details of the programme are available in the free brochure and on the website.

Institute of Copywriting
Overbrook Business Centre, Poolbridge Road, Blackford, Wedmore BS28 4PA
☎0800 781 1715 Fax 01934 713492
✉ copy@inst.org
www.inst.org/copy

Comprehensive copywriting home-study course, including advice on becoming a self-employed copywriter. Each student has a personal tutor who is an experienced copywriter and who provides detailed feedback on the student's assignments. Other courses include: Diploma in *Creative Writing* and Diploma in *Screenwriting*.

University of Bristol
Department of English, 3/5 Woodland Road, Bristol BS8 1TB
☎0117 954 6969
www.bris.ac.uk/english
Contact *Lifelong Learning Organiser*

A variety of short courses and day schools designed for both experienced writers and for absolute beginners, including courses exploring writing for therapeutic purposes. Also offers *Diploma in Creative Writing*. Detailed brochure available.

Staffordshire

Keele University
The Centre for Continuing and Professional Education, Keele University, (Freepost ST1666), Newcastle under Lyme ST5 5BR
☎01782 583436

Evening and weekend courses on literature and creative writing. The 2007 programme included courses on novel writing, writers workshops and sessions on poetry writing.

Surrey

The Guildford Institute of the University of Surrey
Guildford Institute of the University of Surrey, Ward Street, Guildford GU1 4LH
☎01483 562142 Fax 01483 451034
✉ guildford-institute@surrey.ac.uk
www.guildford-institute.org.uk

The Guildford Institute is the venue for various creative writing courses. It also hosts Guildford Writers, a writers' circle meeting on alternate Tuesday evenings from 7.30 pm to 9.30 pm. Members of the group are writing short stories, poetry or novels, and bring their work to read aloud to the group for other members' advice, constructive criticism and general comments. New members are always welcome.

Royal Holloway University of London
Department of Drama and Theatre, Egham Hill, Egham TW20 0EX
☎01784 443922 Fax 01784 431018
✉ drama@rhul.ac.uk
www.rhul.ac.uk/Drama
www.rhul.ac.uk/english
Contact *Dan Rebellato*

Three-year BA courses in *Drama and Creative Writing* or *English and Creative Writing*, during which students progressively specialise in playwriting, poetry or fiction. Playwriting can be studied as part of the BA *Drama and Creative Writing* degree and poetic practice is an option in the *English* programme. Playwriting can be studied at postgraduate level in the MA in *Theatre* and there are MAs in *Poetic Practice* and *Screenwriting*.

Sussex

The Earnley Concourse
Earnley, Chichester PO20 7JL
☎01243 670392 Fax 01243 670832
✉ info@earnley.co.uk
www.earnley.co.uk

Offers a range of residential and non-residential courses throughout the year. Previous programme has included *Creative Writing: Getting Started*. Brochure available.

The University of Chichester
Bishop Otter Campus, College Lane, Chichester PO19 6PE
☎01243 816000 Fax 01243 816080
✉ S.Norgate@chi.ac.uk
www.chi.ac.uk

MA Programme Coordinator (Creative Writing) *Stephanie Norgate* (01243 816296)

Postgraduate Certificate/Diploma/MA in *Creative Writing*, both full and part-time. Also, MPhil/PhD in *Creative Writing, Creative/Critical*. Contact: *Dr Bill Gray* (b.gray@chi.ac.uk).

University of Sussex

Centre for Continuing Education, The Sussex Institute, Essex House, Brighton BN1 9QQ
☎01273 606755
✉ cce@sussex.ac.uk
www.sussex.ac.uk/cce

Contact *Sue Roe*

MA in *Creative Writing and Authorship*: a unique opportunity for graduate writers to develop writing practice in the context of the study of cultural and aesthetic issues of authorship, past and present, in workshops, masterclasses and seminars. One year, full-time, two years, part-time. Convenor: *Sue Roe*. Certificate in *Creative Writing*: short fiction, novel and poetry for imaginative writers. Two-years, part-time. Convenor: *Mark Slater*. Both courses include CCE Agents' and Publishers' Day.

Tyne & Wear

University of Sunderland

Centre for Lifelong Learning, Joseph Cowen House, Newcastle upon Tyne NE1 7RU
☎0191 515 2800 Fax 0191 515 2890
cll.sunderland.ac.uk

Courses, held in Newcastle and across the North East, include: *Creative Writing: Feature Writing*; *Screenwriting*; *Writing and Illustrating for Children* and *Writing From the Inside Out*, a workshop for women. Contact the Centre for Lifelong Learning.

West Midlands

National Academy of Writing

(based at the **University of Central England**)

University of Central England, School of English, Perry Barr Campus, Birmingham B42 2SU
☎0121 331 5540 Fax 0121 331 6692
✉ nicola.monaghan@uce.ac.uk
www.thenationalacademyofwriting.org.uk

Diploma in *Writing*. This course has a strong professional focus and aims to produce working writers. Modules are available in a number of disciplines, including fiction, life writing and screenwriting. Teaching includes taught modules and supervision by UCE staff, all of whom are established writers. There are also regular masterclasses with Academy patrons. Applications are welcome from all, regardless of previous academic experience. Admission is based on talent and commitment to a career

in writing. (See also **University of Central England**).

Starz! – Film and Theatre Performing Arts

Christmas House, Chester Road, Castle Bromwich, Solihull B36 0ET
☎0121 749 7147
www.gavinprime.mac.com

Creative Director *Gavin Prime*

Teaching disabled, disadvantaged and mainstream children. The only totally free theatre and film school of this type in England. Students range in age from eight to 23 and work in all ways connected to performing arts. This includes writing and showing them the structure of the business and how to try and get work accepted.

University of Birmingham

Department of Drama and Theatre Arts, Edgbaston, Birmingham B15 2TT
☎0121 414 5998
✉ drama@contacts.bham.ac.uk
www.drama.bham.ac.uk

The MPhil in *Playwriting Studies*, established by playwright David Edgar in 1989, was the UK's first postgraduate course in playwriting. An intensive course which encourages students to think critically about dramatic writing, assisting them to put these insights into practice in their own plays.

University of Central England

School of English, Perry Barr Campus, Birmingham B42 2SU
☎0121 331 5540 Fax 0121 331 6692
✉ ruth.page@uce.ac.uk
www.lhds.uce.ac.uk/english/
    index.php?page=ma_creative_writing

The *Creative Writing* MA is staffed entirely by established writers and can be studied full or part time. The course has core modules of *Prose Fiction* and *Scriptwriting*, but there is also the opportunity to study within the wider context of reading and literature. With opportunities to get feedback in small groups and from staff, participants receive invaluable editorial advice. (See also **National Academy of Writing**).

University of Warwick

Open Studies, Centre for Lifelong Learning, Coventry CV4 7AL
☎024 7657 3739
✉ k.rainsley@warwick.ac.uk *or*
openstudies@warwick.ac.uk
www.warwick.ac.uk/cll/OpenStudies

Creative writing courses held at the university or in regional centres. Subjects include: *Creative Writing; Publishing and Editing; Creative Writing for All* and *Writing for Pleasure*. One-year certificates in *Creative Writing* and *Journalism* are available; individual modules can be taken.

Wiltshire

Marlborough College Summer School
Marlborough SN8 1PA
☎01672 892388 Fax 01672 892476
✉ admin@mcsummerschool.org.uk
www.mcsummerschool.org.uk
Summer School with literature and creative writing included in its programme. Caters for residential and day students. Brochure available giving full details and prices.

Urchfont Manor College
Urchfont, Devizes SN10 4RG
☎01380 840495 Fax 01380 840005
✉ urchfontmanor@wiltshire.gov.uk
www.urchfontmanor.co.uk
Short courses – days, residential weeks and weekends – offered in a varied programme which includes literature and creative writing. 'Beautiful location; historic environment; delicious home cooking.' Send for a brochure.

Yorkshire

Arvon Foundation (Yorkshire)
See entry under **London**

Leeds Metropolitan University
School of Film, Television & Performing Arts, H505, Civic Quarter, Calverley Street, Leeds LS1 3HE
☎0113 283 2600 ext 3860
✉ screenwriting@leedsmet.ac.uk
www.leedsmet.ac.uk
Administrator *Chris Pugh*
Offers a Diploma/MA in *Screenwriting (Fiction)*.

Open College of the Arts
Unit 1B, Redbrook Business Park, Wilthorpe Road, Barnsley S75 1JN
☎0800 731 2116 Fax 01226 730838
✉ open.arts@ukonline.co.uk
www.oca-uk.com
The OCA correspondence course, *Starting to Write*, offers help and stimulus from experienced writers/tutors. Emphasis is on personal development rather than commercial genre. Subsequent

levels available include specialist poetry, fiction, autobiographical and children's writing courses. OCA writing courses are accredited by the University of Glamorgan. Prospectus and Guide to Courses available on request.

Sheffield Hallam University
Faculty of Development & Society, Sheffield Hallam University, Collegiate Crescent, Sheffield S10 2BP
☎0114 225 5555 Fax 0114 225 2430
✉ fdsenquiries@shu.ac.uk
www.shu.ac.uk
Offers MA in *Creative Writing* (one-year, full-time; also part-time).

University of Hull
School of Arts and New Media, Scarborough Campus, Filey Road, Scarborough YO11 3AZ
☎01723 362392
✉ a.head@hull.ac.uk
www.hull.ac.uk
Director of Studies *Dr Stuart Andrews*
BA Single Honours in *Theatre and Performance Studies* incorporates opportunities in writing and other media across each level of the programme. Works closely with the Stephen Joseph Theatre and its artistic director Alan Ayckbourn. The theatre sustains a policy for staging new writers (see entry under *Theatre Producers*). The campus hosts the annual National Student Drama Festival which includes the International Student Playscript Competition (details from The National Information Centre for Student Drama; nsdf@hull.ac.uk).

University of Leeds
Lifelong Learning Centre, Leeds LS2 9JT
☎0113 343 3212
✉ part-time@leeds.ac.uk
www.leeds.ac.uk/lifelonglearningcentre
Contacts *Rebecca O'Rourke, Pat Owens*
The Lifelong Learning Centre provides accredited part-time courses in creative writing on the Leeds campus during the day and evening. Introductory workshop courses are offered each year with follow-on and advanced courses providing the opportunity to focus on particular aspects of creative writing. These more specialised courses change from year to year and can include poetry, fiction, script and lifewriting or themed work. These courses form part of the Lifelong Learning Centre's Open Studies programme, which is designed to provide adults with opportunities for continuing education

and to create routes into higher education. The Centre also offers a dedicated Part-time Degree in Combined Arts, which currently includes a creative writing strand. Tutors include: Rosanna Blagg, Nasser Hussain, Sophie Nicholls, Rebecca O'Rourke, Rommi Smith and Adam Strickson.

University of Leeds, Bretton Hall Campus

School of Performance and Cultural Industries, Bretton Hall Campus, West Bretton, Wakefield WF4 4LG
☎0113 343 9109 Fax 0113 343 9186
✉ enquiries-pci@leeds.ac.uk
www.leeds.ac.uk/paci

Contact *Garry Lyons* or *Jane Richardson* (Admissions Secretary)

MA in *Writing for Performance and Publication*. This new postgraduate programme (launched in September 2006) is particularly relevant to aspiring writers with professional ambitions, especially in the areas of theatre, film, television and radio drama, as well as the published novel and other culturally significant genres. Studies are offered over one-year full-time and two-years part-time and the tutors are established authors in their chosen fields. The course director is award winning playwright and screenwriter Garry Lyons (*The Bill*, *The Worst Witch*, *Leah's Trials*). The MA is one of a new portfolio of post-graduate degrees to be offered by Leeds University's School of Performance and Cultural Industries, which will relocate to a new £4 million theatre complex on the main Leeds campus in the autumn of 2007. Students are not only given the opportunity to work on their own writing projects but are also encouraged to collaborate with colleagues on other MAs such as *Performance Studies*, with a view to seeing their work staged.

University of Sheffield

Institute for Lifelong Learning, 196–198 West Street, Sheffield S1 4ET
☎0114 222 7000 Fax 0114 222 7001
www.shef.ac.uk/till

Certificate in *Creative Writing* (Degree Level 1) and a wide range of courses, from foundation level to specialist writing areas, open to all. Courses in poetry, journalism, scriptwriting, comedy, short story writing, travel writing. Brochures and information available from the address above.

Yorkshire Art Circus

School Lane, Glasshoughton, Castleford WF10 4QH
☎01977 550401
✉ admin@artcircus.org.uk
www.artcircus.org.uk

Administrator *Angela Sibbit*

Yorkshire Art Circus is a community arts organisation and a registered charity. Runs courses, forums and masterclasses that aim to meet the needs of writers and artists who are looking to learn more about creative writing, ICT and visual arts. All tutors are professional writers and artists who make a living working in the field of arts that they teach. Also runs outreach projects, a Writer Development Programme (for writers who wish to pursue a career in writing), and sessions for groups on request. An annual training brochure is available.

IRELAND

Dingle Writing Courses

Ballintlea, Ventry Co. Kerry
☎00 353 66 915 9815
✉ info@dinglewritingcourses.ie
www.dinglewritingcourses.ie

Directors *Abigail Joffe*, *Nicholas McLachlan*

An autumn programme of weekend residential courses for beginners and experienced writers alike. Tutored by professional writers the courses include poetry, fiction, starting to write and writing for theatre as well as special themed courses. Past tutors have included Michael Donaghy, Paul Durcan, Anne Enright, Nuala Ni Dhomhnaill, Carlo Gébler, Jennifer Johnston, Paula Meeham. Also organises tailor-made courses for schools, writers' groups or students on a *Creative Writing* programme.

INKwell Writers' Workshops

The Old Post Office, Kilmacanogue
Co. Wicklow
☎00 353 1 276 5921
www.inkwellwriters.ie

Offers a series of one-day intensive fiction writing workshops with bestselling Irish writers, held at the Fitzpatrick's Castle Hotel, Killiney, Co. Dublin. 'Designed to inspire and guide new and accomplished writers, giving them invaluable access to authors at the top of their field.' Also, Pure Fiction Weekends: full board, single accommodation weekend workshops run at

Kippure Lodge located on a 240-acre private estate in the heart of the Wicklow Mountains. 2007 workshops include: *Start Writing* with Sarah Webb and Julie Parsons (8th September); *Memoir: Tell your own story* with playwright Miriam Gallagher (1st December); *Pure Fiction Writers' Weekend* with Alex Barclay and Tracy Culleton (21st–23rd September).

Queen's University of Belfast

School of Education, Belfast BT7 1NN
☎028 9097 3323 Fax 028 9097 1084
✉ ill@qub.ac.uk
www.qub.ac.uk/edu

Courses have included *Creative Writing*; *Writing for Profit and Pleasure* and *Scriptwriting*.

University of Dublin (Trinity College)

Graduate Studies Office, Arts Building, Trinity College, Dublin 2
☎00 353 1 896 1166 Fax 00 353 1 671 2821
✉ gradinfo@tcd.ie
www.tcd.ie/owc

Contact *Admissions*

Offers an MPhil *Creative Writing* course. A one-year, full-time course intended for students who are seriously committed to writing or prospective authors.

The Writer's Academy

Carrig-on-Bannow, Co. Wexford
☎00 353 51 561789
✉ thewritersacademy@eircom.net
www.thewritersacademy.net

Distance learning freelance article writing and short story writing courses, critique service and marketing advice. Personal tuition plus expert information and support for writers of all abilities.

SCOTLAND

Arvon Foundation (Inverness-shire)

See entry under **London**

Edinburgh University

Office of Lifelong Learning, 11 Buccleuch Place, Edinburgh EH8 9LW
☎0131 650 4400 Fax 0131 667 6097
✉ oll@ed.ac.uk
www.lifelong.ed.ac.uk

Several writing-orientated courses and summer

schools. Full course information available on the website.

7:84 Summer School

See **7:84 Theatre Company Scotland** under *Theatre Producers*

University of Dundee

Continuing Education, Nethergate, Dundee DD1 4HN
☎01382 384809
www.dundee.ac.uk/learning/conted

Various creative writing courses held at the University and elsewhere in Tayside. Detailed course brochure available from end of June.

University of Glasgow

Department of Adult and Continuing Education, 11 Eldon Street, Glasgow G3 6NH
☎0141 330 1835 Fax 0141 330 1821
✉ dace-query@educ.gla.ac.uk
www.gla.ac.uk/adulteducation

Runs writers' workshops and courses at all levels; all friendly and informal. Daytime and evening meetings. Tutors are all experienced published writers. Call 0141 330 1829 for course brochure.

University of St Andrews

School of English, The University, St Andrews KY16 9AL
☎01334 462666 Fax 01334 462655
✉ english@st-andrews.ac.uk
www.st-andrews.ac.uk

Offers postgraduate study in *Creative Writing*. Modules in Writing Fiction and Writing Poetry. Students submit a dissertation of original writing – prose fiction of 15,000 words or a collection of around 30 short poems. Taught by Professor Douglas Dunn, John Burnside, Kathleen Jamie, A.L. Kennedy, Meaghan Delahunt and Don Paterson. Also offers PhD in *Creative Writing*.

WALES

Ty Newydd Writers' Centre

Llanystumdwy, Cricieth LL52 0LW
☎01766 522811 Fax 01766 523095
✉ post@tynewydd.org
www.tynewydd.org

Residential writers' centre set up by the Taliesin Trust with the support of the **Arts Council of Wales** to encourage and promote writing in both English and Welsh. Most courses run from Monday evening to Saturday morning. Each course has two tutors and a maximum of 16 participants. A wide range of courses for all levels of experience. Early booking essential. Fees start at £205 for weekends and £410 for week-long courses, all inclusive. People on low incomes may be eligible for a grant or bursary. Course leaflet available. (See also *Organisations of Interest to Poets*.)

University of Glamorgan

Department of English, Treforest, Pontypridd CF37 1DL
☎01443 483598
www.glam.ac.uk

Director, The National Centre for Writing *Professor Tony Curtis, FRSL*

MPhil in *Writing*: a two-year part-time Masters degree for writers of fiction and poets. Established 1993. Contact *Professor Tony Curtis* at the School of Humanities, Law and Social Sciences. BA in *Creative and Professional Writing*: a three-year course for undergraduates. Contact *Sheenagh Pugh*. MA in *Scriptwriting (Theatre, Film, TV or Radio)*: a two-year part-time Masters degree for scriptwriters (held at the Cardiff School for Creative and Cultural Industries). Contact: *Wyn Mason* ☎ 01443 654292 (wmason@glam. ac.uk).

University of Wales, Aberystwyth

Department of English, Hugh Owen Building, Aberystwyth SY23 3DY
☎01970 622534/5 Fax 01970 622530
www.aber.ac.uk/english

BA in *English and Creative Writing*, a three-year course taught in part by practising writers: Director of Creative Writing, novelist and poet, Jem Poster and acclaimed poets Tiffany Atkinson, Matthew Francis and Kelly Grovier. Also offers PhD in Creative Writing, and taught MA in *Creative Writing* with modules in writing poetry, writing fiction, research for writers, and writing and publication.

University of Wales, Bangor

School of English, College Road, Bangor LL57 2DG
☎01248 382102
✉ els029@bangor.ac.uk *or*
postgrad-english@bangor.ac.uk
www.bangor.ac.uk

The School of English offers: MPhil/PhD *Creative and Critical Writing*; Diploma/MA *Creative Studies (Creative Writing)*; BA (Hons) *English with Creative Writing*; BA (Hons) *English with Journalism*. The Centre for Creative and Performing Arts offers *Creative Writing* courses from undergraduate level to MA and PhD.

John Wilson's Writing Courses

Argoed Hall, Tregaron SY25 6JR
☎01974 298070
✉ john.wilson@virgin.net

Residential writing intensives ranging from basic skills to workshops in creative and business writing and journalism. For advanced writers an opportunity to understand and develop the creative process is provided. The courses normally run from Thursday evening to Sunday afternoon, with B&B accommodation and lunch at Argoed Hall, with evening meals (or full board) at nearby hotels. Phone or e-mail for details.

Writers' Holiday at Caerleon

School Bungalow, Church Road, Pontnewydd, Cwmbran NP44 1AT
☎01633 489438
✉ writersholiday@lineone.net
www.writersholiday.net

Contact *Anne Hobbs*

Annual six-day comprehensive conference including 12 courses for writers of all standards held in the summer at the University of Wales' Caerleon Campus. Courses, lectures, concert and excursion all included in the fee. Private, single and en-suite, full board accommodation. Courses have included *Writing for Publication*; *Writing Poetry*; *Writing Romantic Fiction* and *Writing for the Radio*.

Writers' Circles and Workshops

Directory of Writers' Circles, Courses and Workshops
39 Lincoln Way, Harlington LU5 6NG
☎01525 873197
✉ diana@writers-circles.com
www.writers-circles.com

Editor *Diana Hayden*
Directory of UK writers' circles, courses and workshops.

Carmarthen Writers' Circle
Lower Carfan, Tavernspite, Whitland SA34 0NP
☎01994 240441

Contact *Jenny White*
Founded 1989. The Circle meets monthly on the second Monday of the month at the Indoor Bowls Centre, Carmarthen. All levels and genres welcome. Holds occasional workshops.

Caron Writers
Argoed Hall, Tregaron SY25 6JR
☎01974 298070
✉ john.wilson@virgin.net

Contact *John Wilson*
Founded in 2002, the group meets from 2.00 pm to 4.00 pm on the second Sunday of most months (not July or August). Each session comprises announcements and a writing/reading workshop. Emphasis is on fun, discussion and achievement. 'Outstanding results have been achieved and members are gaining considerable success in creative writing competitions and independent publishing.' All genres welcome. Fee: £15 p.a. and £3.50 per session (includes light refreshments). Phone or e-mail for details.

Chiltern Writers' Group
151 Chartridge Lane, Chesham HP5 2SE
☎01494 772308
✉ info@chilternwriters.org
www.chilternwriters.org

Guest speakers, workshops, manuscript critiques and monthly meetings, held at Wendover Library every second Thursday of the month at 8.00 pm. Regular newsletter and competitions.

SUBSCRIPTION £15 p.a.; £10 (concessions); £3 (non-members meetings).

Coleg Harlech WEA
Harlech, LL46 2PU 01766 781900
✉ info@fc.harlech.ac.uk
www.harlech.ac.uk

Coleg Harlech WEA was formed in 2001 with the merger of Coleg Harlech and the Workers' Educational Association North Wales.

The Cotswold Writers' Circle
Bliss's Cottage, Lower Chedworth, Cheltenham GL54 4AN
☎01285 720668
✉ elaine@pandelunt.co.uk

Patron *Elizabeth Webster*
Membership Secretary *Elaine Lunt*
Competition Secretary *Mrs Anne Brookes*

The Circle meets every Tuesday morning (except second Tuesday of the month) in Cirencester. Activities include workshops with well-known authors and an International Open Writing Competition; closing date: 31 January annually (send s.a.e. for details). Winners published in the Circle's anthology, *Pen Ultimate*.

Cumbrian Literary Group
'Calgarth', The Brow, Flimby, Maryport CA15 8TD
☎01900 813444

President *Glyn Matthews*
Secretary *Joyce E. Fisher*

Founded 1946 to provide a meeting place for readers and writers in Cumbria. The Group meets once a month (April to November) in Keswick. Invites speakers to meetings and holds annual competitions for poetry and prose. Publishes *Bookshelf* magazine. Further details from the Secretary at the address above.

'Sean Dorman' Manuscript Society
3 High Road, Britford, Salisbury SP5 4DS

Director *Jan Smith*
Founded 1957. Provides mutual help among writers and aspiring writers in England, Wales and Scotland. By means of circulating manu-

script parcels, members receive constructive comment on their own work and read and comment on the work of others. Full details and application forms available on receipt of s.a.e.

East Anglian Writers
77 Marlborough Road, Norwich NR3 4PL
✉ chair@eastanglianwriters.org.uk
www.eastanglianwriters.org.uk
Chair *Victoria Manthorpe*

A group for professional writers living in Norfolk, Suffolk, Essex, Cambridgeshire and Bedfordshire. Affiliated to the **Society of Authors**. Aims to help writers socialise and promote their work. Informal social events, speakers' evenings and contact point for professional writers in the area.

Eastbourne's Anderida Writers
20 Vian Avenue, Eastbourne BN23 6EY
☎01323 737677
Secretary *Stella Freshney*

Creative workshops for Sussex authors. Talks and competitions.

éQuinoxe TBC
85 Avenue Kléber, 75116 Paris, France
☎00 33 1 47 55 11 89 Fax 00 33 1 44 05 74 74
✉ equinoxetbc@equinoxetbc.fr
www.equinoxetbc.fr
President *Noëlle Deschamps*

Week-long intensive screenwriting workshops, held twice a year in English and French, open to experienced European screenwriters. Participants are selected by an international jury: candidates must have written a script for a feature film, which is sufficiently developed and ready to go into production. Entry form available on the website.

Euroscript
PO Box 3117, Gloucester GL4 0WW
☎0780 336 9414
✉ enquiries@euroscript.co.uk
www.euroscript.co.uk

Script development organisation offering creative and editorial input to writers and production companies. Develops screenplays through an intensive consultancy programme, including residential script workshops; also offers a broad programme of short courses, provides script reports, and runs an annual Screen Story Competition. Open to writers of any nationality. E-mail, telephone, or access the website for further information.

Foyle Street Writers Group
See **See Sunderland City Library and Arts Centre** under *Library Services*

Gay Authors Workshop
BM Box 5700, London WC1N 3XX
✉ eandk@lineone.net
Contact *Kathryn Byrd*

Established 1978 to encourage and support lesbian/gay writers. Regular meetings and a newsletter. GAW gave rise to **Paradise Press** (see entry under *Small Presses*).

Guildford Writers
See **The Guildford Institute of the University of Surrey** under *UK and Irish Writers' Courses*

Historical Novel Folio
17 Purbeck Heights, Mount Road, Parkstone, Poole BH14 0QP
☎01202 741897
Contact *Doris Myall-Harris*

An independent postal workshop – single folio dealing with any period before World War II. Send s.a.e. for details.

'How to Self-Publish Your Book' Workshops
Faculty of Arts, University of Winchester, Winchester SO22 4NR
☎01962 827238
✉ barbara.large@winchester.ac.uk
www.writersconference.co.uk
Contact *Barbara Large, MBE, FRSA, HFUW*

One-day workshops to inform writers who wish to self-publish their books about the digital and lithographic processes. Participants will learn the skills of researching, writing and revising their mss; the use of photographs, maps, diagrams, illustrations, design and formatting; types of paper, fonts, sizes, ISBN numbers and costs, and marketing their books. 2008 workshops: Friday, 9th May and Friday, 19th September.

Janus Writers
See **See Sunderland City Library and Arts Centre** under *Library Services*

Bernard Kops and Tom Fry Drama Writing Workshops
41B Canfield Gardens, London NW6 3JL
☎020 7624 2940/8533 2472
✉ bernardkops@tiscali.co.uk
Tutors *Bernard Kops, Tom Fry*

Three ten-week terms per year. Small group drama writing workshops for stage, screen and television with actors in attendance. Tutorials also available. Call for details.

New Writing South
9 Jew Street, Brighton BN1 1UT
☎01273 735353
✉ enquiries@newwritingsouth.com
www.newwritingsouth.com
Contact *Chris Taylor*

Works throughout the South East offering resources and development to all creative writers in the region. Also builds partnerships between writers and those able to produce their work. Membership open to professional, emerging and aspiring creative writers in the region and to companies with a professional interest in new writing.

North West Playwrights (NWP)
18 Express Networks, 1 George Leigh Street, Manchester M4 5DL
☎0161 237 1978
✉ newplaysnw@hotmail.com
www.newplaysnw.co.uk

Founded in 1982, NWP is the regional development agency for new theatre writing in the north west of England. NWP operates a script-reading service, classes and script development scheme and *The Lowdown* newsletter. Services available to writers in the region only.

The Original Writers Group
Garfield Community Centre, 64 Garfield Rd, London SW11 5PN
✉ info@theoriginalwriter.com
www.theoriginalwriter.com
Contact *Rupert Davies-Cooke*

The group meets at the Garfield Community Centre every second and fourth Wednesday of the month from 7.00 pm to 9.00 pm. £2 charge per person to cover the cost of the room. The evening is made up of reading and criticism. Everything; poetry, novels, screenplays and even 'how-to' books. 'It is also a great place to find inspiration to write.'

Pitstop Refuelling Writers' Weekend Workshops
Faculty of Arts, University of Winchester, Winchester SO22 4NR
☎01962 827238
✉ barbara.large@winchester.ac.uk
www.writersconference.co.uk

Director *Barbara Large, MBE, FRSA, HFUW*

Following on from the **Winchester Writers' Conference** in Winchester, these are small-group writing workshops under the guidance of professional writers. 2007 workshops: 26th–28th October; 2008: 14th–16th March and 24th–26th October.

Player–Playwrights
See entry under *Professional Associations*

Scribo
1/31 Hamilton Road, Bournemouth
BH1 4EQ
☎01202 302533
Contacts *K. & P. Sylvester*

Scribo (established over 20 years ago) is a postal workshop for novelists giving criticism and support via manuscript folios (e.g. fantasy/sci-fi, mainstream, women's fiction, crime, literary). Joining fee: £5. No annual subscription. Send s.a.e. for further details.

Script Yorkshire
Membership Administrator: 9 Barker's Road, Sheffield S7 1SD
✉ members@scriptyorkshire.co.uk
www.scriptyorkshire.co.uk
Membership *Caroline Small*

Formerly known as Yorkshire Playwrights. Re-launched in 2005 as Script Yorkshire. A support and advocacy organisation for scriptwriters across performance and broadcast media which aims to empower Yorkshire's scriptwriters by giving them the skills and insights they need to develop their own careers. Open to professional or aspiring scriptwriters (theatre, radio, TV and film) who live or work in Yorkshire. Company membership also available. Visit the website for further information or write to the address above.

Short Story Writers' Folio/ Children's Novel Writers' Folio
5 Park Road, Brading, Sandown, Isle of Wight
PO36 0HU
☎01983 407697
✉ nott.dawn-wortley@tiscali.co.uk
Contact *Mrs Dawn Wortley-Nott*

Postal workshops; members receive constructive criticism of their work and read and offer advice on fellow members' contributions. Send an s.a.e. for further details.

Society of Sussex Authors

Dolphin House, 51 St Nicholas Lane, Lewes
BN7 2JZ
☎01273 470100 Fax 01273 470100
✉ sussexbooks@aol.com

Contact *David Arscott*

Founded 1968. Six meetings per year, held in
Lewes, plus social events. Membership restricted
to Sussex-based writers only.

Southwest Scriptwriters

☎0117 909 5522
✉ info@southwest-scriptwriters.co.uk
www.southwest-scriptwriters.co.uk

Secretary *John Colborn*

Founded 1994 to offer support to regional
writers for all media. The group meets at the
Bristol Old Vic.

Speakeasy – Milton Keynes Writers' Group

46 Wealdstone Place, Springfield, Milton
Keynes MK6 3JG
☎01908 663860
✉ speakeasy@writerbrock.co.uk
www.mkweb.co.uk/speakeasy

Contact *Martin Brocklebank*

Monthly meetings on the first Friday of each
month at 8.00 pm. Full and varied programme
includes Local Writer Nights where work can
be read and peformed and Guest Nights where
writers, poets and journalists are invited to speak.
Mini-workshops and information nights are
also in the programme. Invites entries to Open
Creative Writing Competitions. Phone, e-mail
or send s.a.e. for details to address above.

Spread the Word

77 Lambeth Walk, London SE11 6DX
☎020 7735 3111 Fax 020 7735 2666
✉ info@spreadtheword.org.uk
www.spreadtheword.org.uk

General Manager *Nick Murza*

Develops new writing and writers in London
throughout their careers through creative
writing workshops, talks, reading groups, cross
arts projects, advice sessions and one-to-one
surgeries. Also runs annual creative writing
competitions and provides online resources for
writers.

Sussex Playwrights' Club

2 Brunswick Mews, Hove BN3 1HD
☎01273 730106
www.sussexplaywrights.com

Secretary *Dennis Evans*

Founded 1935. Monthly readings of members'
work by experienced actors. Membership open
to all. Meetings held at New Venture Theatre,
Bedford Place, Brighton.

Ver Poets

15 Brampton Road, St Albans AL1 4PP
☎01727 864898
✉ daphne.schiller@virgin.net

Secretary *Daphne Schiller*

Founded 1966. Postal and local members. Meets
in St Albans, runs evening meetings and daytime
workshops and organises competitions.

Walton Wordsmiths

27 Braycourt Avenue, Walton on Thames
KT12 2AZ
☎01932 702874
✉ wendy@stickler.org.uk

Contact *Wendy Hughes*

Founded in 1999 by Wendy Hughes. Supports
writers of all grades and capabilities by offering
constructive criticism and advice.

Workers' Educational Association

National Office: 3rd Floor, 70 Clifton Street,
London EC2A 4HB
☎020 7426 3450
✉ national@wea.org.uk
www.wea.org.uk

Founded in 1903, the WEA is a charitable
provider of adult education with students drawn
from all walks of life. It runs writing courses and
workshops in many parts of the country which
are open to everyone. Contact your local WEA
office for details of courses in your region.

Eastern Botolph House, 17 Botolph Lane,
Cambridge CB2 3RE
☎ 01223 350978 ✉ eastern@wea.org.uk

East Midlands 39 Mapperley Road,
Mapperley Park, Nottingham NG3 5AQ
☎ 0115 962 8400
✉ eastmidlands@wea.org.uk

London 4 Luke Street, London EC2A 4XW
☎ 020 7426 1950 ✉ london@wea.org.uk

North East 1st Floor, Unit 6, Metro Riverside
Park, Delta Bank Road, Gateshead NE11 9DJ
☎ 0191 461 8100 ✉ northeast@wea.org.uk

North West Suite 405–409, The Cotton
Exchange, Old Hall Street, Liverpool L3 9JR
☎ 0151 243 5340 ✉ northwest@wea.org.uk

Southern Unit 57 Riverside 2, Sir Thomas

Longley Road, Rochester ME2 4DP
☎ 01634 298600 ✉ southern@wea.org.uk
South West Bradninch Court, Castle Street,
Exeter EX4 3PL
☎ 01392 490970 ✉ southwest@wea.org.uk
West Midlands 78/80 Sherlock Street,
Birmingham B5 6LT
☎ 0121 666 6101
✉ westmidlands@wea.org.uk
Yorkshire and Humber 6 Woodhouse
Square, Leeds LS3 1AD
☎ 0113 245 3304
✉ yorkshumber@wea.org.uk

Workers' Educational Association North Wales
See **Coleg Harlech WEA**

Workers' Educational Association Northern Ireland
1 Fitzwilliam Street, Belfast BT9 6AW
☎028 9032 9718
✉ info@wea-ni.com
www.wea-ni.com
Autonomous from the WEA National
Association, WEA Northern Ireland was
founded in 1910.

Workers' Educational Association Scotland
Riddles Court, 322 Lawnmarket, Edinburgh
EH1 2PG
☎0131 226 3456
✉ hq@weascotland.org.uk
www.weascotland.org.uk
WEA Scotland was founded in 1905 and
is part of the national Workers' Educational
Association.

Workers' Educational Association South Wales
7 Coopers Yard, Curran Road, Cardiff
CF10 5NB
☎029 2023 5277 Fax 029 2023 3986
✉ weasw@swales.wea.org.uk
www.swales.wea.org.uk
Autonomous from the WEA National
Association, WEA South Wales has been active
in community education for over 100 years.

Writers in Oxford
www.writersinoxford.org
Membership Secretary *Donna Dickenson*
Chair *Julie Summers*
SUBSCRIPTION £20 p.a.
Founded 1992. Open to published authors,
playwrights, poets and journalists. Literary
seminars and social functions. Publishes *The
Oxford Writer* newsletter.

Yorkshire Playwrights
See **Script Yorkshire**

Miscellany

Apple Coaching (inc. CoachingWriters.co.uk)
8 Feering Road, Billericay CM11 2DR
☎01277 632085
✉ eve@applecoaching.com
www.CoachingWriters.co.uk
Contact *Eve Menezes Cunningham*

Helping professional and aspiring writers increase their success and happiness through life coaching, business coaching and NLP. Writing and editorial services also available. Sign up for free e-newsletter on the website. Rates negotiable.

Combrógos
10 Heol Don, Whitchurch, Cardiff CF14 2AU
☎029 2062 3359
Contact *Professor Meic Stephens*

Founded 1990. Arts and media research, editorial services, specialising in books about Wales or by Welsh authors. 'Encyclopaedic knowledge of Welsh history, language, literature and culture.'

Jacqueline Edwards
104 Earlsdon Avenue South, Coventry CV5 6DQ
✉ twigsbranches@yahoo.co.uk
Contact *Jacqueline Edwards, MA, LLB(Hons)*

Historical research: family, local and 19th and 20th century legal history. Covers Warwickshire, Gloucestershire, Northamptonshire, Worcestershire and the National Archives, Kew, London.

Caroline Landeau
6 Querrin Street, London SW6 2SJ
☎07050 600420
✉ winmacweb@hotmail.com
Contact *Caroline Landeau*

Experienced research and production – films, multimedia, books, magazines, exhibitions, animation, general interest, art, music, crime, travel, food, film, theatre.

M-Y Books Ltd
187 Ware Road, Hertford SG13 7EQ
☎01992 586279
✉ jonathan@m-ybooks.co.uk
www.m-ybooks.co.uk
Contact *Jonathan Miller*

Offers promotional and marketing services for authors or small publishers; also distribution services within the UK and English-speaking Europe. Includes agents in 20 different countries; also attends all major book fairs including Frankfurt, USA and London Book Fair, representing authors and publishers and their titles, negotiating foreign rights agreements on their behalf.

Julia McCutchen, Writers' Coach & Professional Publishing Consultant
PO Box 3703, Trowbridge
☎01380 871331 Fax 01380 871331
✉ julia@juliamccutchen.com
www.JuliaMcCutchen.com
Contact *Julia McCutchen*

Julia McCutchen is the author of *The Writer's Journey: From Inspiration to Publication* and has 20 years experience of publishing. Specialises in helping writers who want to write a book for publication by offering individual coaching, courses and classes to provide information, guidance, feedback and support for each stage of the writing journey. Primary areas of expertise include how to write a first-class book proposal and how to approach the right people in the right way for the best possible chances of success. See the website for more information and a range of free resources for writers.

Murder Files
Dommett Hill Farm, Hare Lane, Buckland St. Mary, Chard TA20 3JS
☎01460 234065
✉ enquiry@murderfiles.com
www.murderfiles.com
Contact *Paul Williams*

Founded 1994. Crime writer and researcher specialising in British murders. Holds information on thousands of well-known and less well-known murders dating from 1400 to the present day. Copies of press cuttings available from 1920 onwards. Details of executions, particularly at the Tyburn and Newgate. Information on British hangmen. Specialist in British police murders since 1700. CD-ROM *The Ultimate Price – The Unlawful Killing of British Police Officers*, Part 1 (1700–1899) & Part 2 (1900–2000) available. Service available to general enquirers, writers, researchers, TV, radio, video, etc.

Nielsen BookNet

3rd Floor, Midas House, 62 Goldsworth Road, Woking GU21 6LQ
☎0870 777 8710 Fax 0870 777 8711
✉ sales@nielsenbookdata.co.uk
www.nielsenbooknet.co.uk

Head of BookNet Sales *Stephen Long*

BookNet provides a range of e-commerce services that allows electronic trading between booksellers, publishers/distributors, libraries and other suppliers. Services include BookNet Web for booksellers and publishers/distributors, TeleOrdering and EDI messaging.

Nielsen BookScan

3rd Floor, Midas House, 62 Goldsworth Road, Woking GU21 6LQ
☎01483 712222 Fax 01483 712220
✉ info@nielsenbookscan.co.uk
www.nielsenbookscan.co.uk

Publisher Account Manager *Reeta Windsor*

BookScan collects transactional data at the point of sale from tills and despatch systems of all the major book retailers in the UK, Ireland, USA, South Africa, Spain and Italy. Each week data is coded and analysed, producing complete market information for retailers, publishers, libraries, agents and the media within 72 hours of the week ending Saturday.

Ormrod Research Services

Weeping Birch, Burwash TN19 7HG
☎01435 882541
✉ richardormrod@aol.com
www.writeonservices.co.uk

Contact *Richard Ormrod*

Established 1982. Comprehensive research service: literary, historical, academic, biographical, commercial. Verbal quotations available. Also editing, indexing, ghost-writing and critical reading.

Patent Research

Dachsteinstr. 12a, D–81825 Munich, Germany
☎00 49 89 430 7833

Contact *Gerhard Everwyn*

All world, historical patents for researchers, authors, archives, museums and publishers. Rates on application.

The United Kingdom Copyright Bureau

110 Trafalgar Road, Portslade BN41 1GS
☎01273 277333
✉ info@copyrightbureau.co.uk
www.copyrightbureau.co.uk

Contacts *Ralph de Straet von Kollman, Petra Ginman*

The UKCB provides a secure copyright service at reasonable cost, enabling multiple copyrights to be registered nominally when required. Prices are advertised on the website including the UKCB's solicitors, etc. Copyrights preferred on floppy disk or CD-ROM; mss are not accepted due to storage space.

Press Cuttings Agencies

Cision

Cision House, 16–22 Baltic Street West,
London EC1Y 0UL
☎0870 736 0010 Fax 020 7689 1164
✉ info.uk@cision.com
www.cision.com

Formerly Romeike, Cision monitors national and international dailies and Sundays, provincial papers, consumer magazines, trade and technical journals, teletext services as well as national radio and TV networks. Back research, advertising checking and Internet monitoring, plus analysis and editorial summary service available.

Durrants

Discovery House, 28–42 Banner Street,
London EC1Y 8QE
☎020 7674 0200 Fax 020 7674 0222
✉ contact@durrants.co.uk
www.durrants.co.uk

Wide coverage of all print media sectors including foreign press plus Internet, newswire and broadcast monitoring. High speed, early morning press cuttings from the national press by Web or e-mail. Overnight delivery via courier to most areas or first-class mail. Well presented, laser printed, A4 cuttings. Rates on application.

International Press–Cutting Bureau

224–236 Walworth Road, London SE17 1JE
☎020 7708 2113 Fax 020 7701 4489
✉ info@ipcb.co.uk
www.ipcb.co.uk

Contact *Robert Podro*

Covers national, provincial, trade, technical and magazine press. Cuttings are normally sent twice weekly by first-class post. Basic charges are £75 per month + £1.10 per cutting.

We Find It (Press Clippings)

40 Galwally Avenue, Belfast BT8 7AJ
☎028 9064 6008 Fax 028 9064 6008

Contact *Avril Forsythe*

Specialises in Northern Ireland press and magazines, both national and provincial. Rates on application.

Bursaries, Fellowships and Grants

The Arts Council of Wales Bursaries
See entry under **Arts Councils and Regional Offices**

The Authors' Contingency Fund
The Society of Authors, 84 Drayton Gardens, London SW10 9SB
☎020 7373 6642 Fax 020 7373 5768
✉ info@societyofauthors.org
www.societyofauthors.org

This fund makes modest grants to published authors who find themselves in sudden financial difficulties. Contact the **Society of Authors** for an information sheet and application form.

The Authors' Foundation
The Society of Authors, 84 Drayton Gardens, London SW10 9SB
☎020 7373 6642 Fax 020 7373 5768
✉ info@societyofauthors.org
www.societyofauthors.org

Grants to writers whose publisher's advance is insufficient to cover the costs of research involved. Application by letter to The Authors' Foundation giving details, in confidence, of the advance and royalties, together with the reasons for needing additional funding. Grants are sometimes given even if there is no commitment by a publisher, so long as the applicant has had a book published and the new work will almost certainly be published. About £80,000 is distributed each year. Contact the **Society of Authors** for full entry details. Final entry dates: 30 April and 30 September.

The K. Blundell Trust
The Society of Authors, 84 Drayton Gardens, London SW10 9SB
☎020 7373 6642 Fax 020 7373 5768
✉ info@societyofauthors.org
www.societyofauthors.org

Grants to writers whose publisher's advance is insufficient to cover the costs of research. Author must be under 40, has to submit a copy of his/her previous book and the work must 'contribute to the greater understanding of existing social and economic organisation'. Application by letter. Contact the **Society of Authors** for full entry details. Final entry dates: 30 April and 30 September.

Alfred Bradley Bursary Award
c/o BBC Radio Drama, Room 2130, New Broadcasting House, Oxford Road, Manchester M60 1SJ
☎0161 244 4253 Fax 0161 244 4248
Contact *Coordinator*

Established 1992. Biennial award in commemoration of the life and work of the distinguished radio producer Alfred Bradley. Aims to encourage and develop new radio writing talent in the BBC North region. There is a change of focus for each award, e.g. previous years have targeted comedy drama, verse drama, etc. Entrants must live in the north of England. The award is given to help writers to pursue a career in writing for radio. Next award will be launched summer 2008. Further information can be found on bbc.co.uk/writersroom Previous winners: Mark Shand, Anthony Cropper, Julia Copus, Michael Stewart, Ben Tagoe, Katie Douglas.
AWARD Up to £6000 over two years; potential BBC Radio Drama commissions and opportunities for mentoring with producers.

British Academy Small Research Grants
10 Carlton House Terrace, London SW1Y 5AH
☎020 7969 5217 Fax 020 7969 5414
✉ grants@britac.ac.uk
www.britac.ac.uk
Contact *Assistant Secretary, Research Grants*

Award to further original academic research at postdoctoral level in the humanities and social sciences. Entrants must be resident in the UK. See website for final entry dates. Three competitions a year.
AWARD £7500 (maximum).

Cholmondeley Awards
The Society of Authors, 84 Drayton Gardens, London SW10 9SB

☎020 7373 6642 Fax 020 7373 5768
✉ info@societyofauthors.org
www.societyofauthors.org
Founded in 1965 by the late Dowager Marchioness of Cholmondeley. Annual honorary awards to recognise the achievement and distinction of individual poets. 2006 winners: Alan Jenkins, Mimi Khalvati, Jo Shapcott.
    AWARD £8000 (total).

Olive Cook Prize
See **Tom–Gallon Trust Award**

The Economist/Richard Casement Internship
The Economist, 25 St James's Street, London SW1A 1HG
☎020 7830 7000
✉ casement@economist.com
www.economist.com
Contact *Geoffrey Carr,* Science Editor (re. Casement Internship)

For an aspiring journalist to spend three months in the summer writing for *The Economist* about science and technology. Applicants should write a letter of introduction along with an article of approximately 600 words suitable for inclusion in the Science and Technology Section. 'Our aim is more to discover writing talent in a scientist or science student than scientific aptitude in a budding journalist.' Competition details normally announced in the magazine late January or early February and 4–5 weeks allowed for application.

European Jewish Publication Society
PO Box 19948, London N3 3ZJ
Fax 020 8346 1776
✉ cs@ejps.org.uk
www.ejps.org.uk
Contact *Dr Colin Shindler*

Established in 1995 to help fund the publication of books of European Jewish interest which would otherwise remain unpublished. Helps with the marketing, distribution and promotion of such books. Publishers who may be interested in publishing works of Jewish interest should approach the Society with a proposal and manuscript in the first instance. Books which have been supported recently include: *The History of Zionism* Walter Laqueur; *Photographing the Holocaust* Janina Struk; *The Arab-Israeli Cookbook* Robin Soans; *Daughters of Sarah: An Anthology of Jewish Women Writing in French* eds. Eva

Martin Sartori and Madeleine Cottenet-Hage; *Whistleblowers and the Bomb: Vanunu, Israel and Nuclear Secrecy* Yoel Cohen. Also supports the publication of poetry, and translations from and into other European languages.
    GRANT £3000 (maximum).

Fulbright Awards
The Fulbright Commission, Fulbright House, 62 Doughty Street, London WC1N 2JZ
☎020 7404 6880 Fax 020 7404 6834
✉ programmes@fulbright.co.uk
www.fulbright.co.uk
Contact *Programme Manager*

The Fulbright Commission offers a number of scholarships given at postgraduate level and above, open to any field (science and the arts) of study/research to be undertaken in the USA. Length of award is typically an academic year. Application deadline for postgraduate awards is usually late October/early November of preceding year of study; and mid-March/early April for postdoctoral awards. Further details and application forms are available on the Commission's website. Alternatively, send A4 envelope with sufficient postage for 100g with a covering letter explaining which level of award is of interest.

Tony Godwin Memorial Trust
c/o 38 Lyttelton Court, Lyttelton Road, London N2 0EB
☎020 8209 1613
✉ info@tgmt.org.uk
www.tgmt.org.uk
Chairman *Iain Brown*

Biennial award established to commemorate the life of Tony Godwin, a prominent publisher in the 1960s/70s. Open to all young people (under 35 years old) who are UK nationals and working, or intending to work, in publishing. The award provides the recipient with the means to spend at least one month as the guest of an American publishing house in order to learn about international publishing. The recipient is expected to submit a report upon return to the UK. Next award: 2009; final entry date: 31 December 2008. Previous winners: George Lucas (Hodder), Clive Priddle (Fourth Estate), Richard Scrivener (Penguin), Lisa Shakespeare (Weidenfeld & Nicolson), Fiona Stewart (HarperCollins).
    AWARD Bursary of approx. US$5000.

Eric Gregory Trust Fund
The Society of Authors, 84 Drayton Gardens, London SW10 9SB

☎020 7373 6642 Fax 020 7373 5768
✉ info@societyofauthors.org
www.societyofauthors.org
Annual awards of varying amounts are made for the encouragement of poets under the age of 30 on the basis of a submitted collection. Open only to British-born subjects resident in the UK. Final entry date: 31 October. Contact the Society of Authors for full entry details. 2006 winners: Fiona Benson, Retta Bowen, Frances Leviston, Jonathan Morley, Eoghan Walls.
AWARD £20,000 (total).

The Guardian Research Fellowship
Nuffield College, Oxford OX1 1NF
☎01865 278542 Fax 01865 278666
Contact *The Academic Administrator*
One-year fellowship endowed by the Scott Trust, owner of *The Guardian*, to give someone working in the media the chance to put their experience into a new perspective, publish the outcome and give a *Guardian* lecture. Applications welcomed from journalists and management members, in newspapers, periodicals or broadcasting. Research or study proposals should be directly related to experience of working in the media. Accommodation and meals in college will be provided and a stipend. Advertised biennially in November.

Hawthornden Literary Institute
Hawthornden International Retreat for Writers, Lasswade EH18 1EG
☎0131 440 2180 Fax 0131 440 1989
Contact *The Administrator*
Established 1982 to provide a peaceful setting where published writers can work in silence. The Castle houses up to six writers at a time, who are known as Hawthornden Fellows. Writers from any part of the world may apply for the fellowships. No monetary assistance is given, nor any contribution to travelling expenses, but once arrived at Hawthornden, the writer is the guest of the Retreat. Applications on forms provided must be made by the end of November for the following calendar year. Previous winners include: Les Murray, Alasdair Gray, Helen Vendler, David Profumo, Hilary Spurling.

Francis Head Bequest
The Society of Authors, 84 Drayton Gardens, London SW10 9SB
☎020 7373 6642 Fax 020 7373 5768
✉ info@societyofauthors.org
www.societyofauthors.org

Provides grants to published British authors over the age of 35 who need financial help during a period of illness, disablement or temporary financial crisis. Contact the Society of Authors for an information sheet and application form.

Jerwood Awards
See **The Royal Society of Literature/ Jerwood Awards**

Journalists' Charity
Dickens House, 35 Wathen Road, Dorking RH4 1JY
☎01306 887511 Fax 01306 888212
✉ enquiries@journalistscharity.org.uk
www.journalistscharity.org.uk
Director/Secretary *David Ilott*
Aims to relieve distress among journalists and their dependants. Continuous and/or occasional financial grants; also retirement homes for eligible beneficiaries. Further information available from the Director.

Ralph Lewis Award
University of Sussex Library, Brighton BN1 9QL
☎01273 678158 Fax 01273 873413
✉ a.timoney@sussex.ac.uk
Established 1985. Occasional award set up by Ralph Lewis, a Brighton author and art collector who left money to fund awards for promising manuscripts which would not otherwise be published. The award is given in the form of a grant to a UK-based publisher in respect of a publication of literary works by new authors. No direct applications from writers. Previous winners: **Peterloo Poets**; **Serpent's Tail**; **Stride Publications**.

The Elizabeth Longford Grants
The Society of Authors, 84 Drayton Gardens, London SW10 9SB
☎020 7373 6642 Fax 020 7373 5768
✉ info@societyofauthors.org
www.societyofauthors.org
Biannual grant, sponsored by Flora Fraser and Peter Soros, to a historical biographer whose publisher's advance is insufficient to cover the costs of research involved. Contact the Society of Authors for full details. Final entry dates: 30 April and 30 September.
GRANT £2500.

The John Masefield Memorial Trust
The Society of Authors, 84 Drayton Gardens, London SW10 9SB

☎020 7373 6642 Fax 020 7373 5768
✉ info@societyofauthors.org
www.societyofauthors.org

This trust makes occasional grants to professional poets (or their immediate dependants) who are faced with sudden financial problems. Contact the **Society of Authors** for an information sheet and application form.

Somerset Maugham Trust Fund

The Society of Authors, 84 Drayton Gardens, London SW10 9SB
☎020 7373 6642 Fax 020 7373 5768
✉ info@societyofauthors.org
www.societyofauthors.org

Annual awards designed to encourage writers under the age of 35 to travel. Given on the basis of a published work of fiction, non-fiction or poetry. Open only to British-born subjects resident in the UK. Final entry date: 20 December. 2006 winners: Chris Cleave *Incendiary;* Owen Sheers *Skirrid Hill;* Zadie Smith *On Beauty.*
  AWARDS £10,000 (total).

The Airey Neave Trust

PO Box 36800, 40 Bernard Street, London WC1N 1WJ
☎020 7833 4440
✉ hanthoc@aol.com
www.theaireyneavetrust.org.uk

Contact *Hannah Scott*

Initiated 1989. Annual research fellowships for up to three years – towards a book or paper – for serious research connected with national and international law, and human freedom. Preferably attached to a particular university in Britain.

North East Literary Fellowship

Arts Council England, North East, Central Square, Forth Street, Newcastle upon Tyne NE1 3PJ
☎0191 255 8542 Fax 0191 230 1020
www.artscouncil.org.uk

Contact *Literature Officer*

A competitive fellowship in association with the Universities of Durham and Newcastle upon Tyne. Contact **Arts Council England, North East,** for details.

Northern Rock Foundation Writer's Award

New Writing North, Newcastle University, Culture Lab, Grand Assembly Rooms, King's Walk, Newcastle upon Tyne NE1 7RU

☎0191 222 1332 Fax 0191 222 1372
✉ mail@newwritingnorth.com
www.nr-foundationwriters.com

Contact *Holly Hooper*

Annual award founded in 2002 with the aim of liberating established writers who live in the region from work other than writing. Applicants must have at least two books published by a recognised publisher and *must* live and work in Northumberland, Tyne and Wear, County Durham, Cumbria or Teesside. 2007 winner: Sean O'Brien.
  AWARD £60,000 (£20,000 a year for three years).

Northern Writers' Awards

See **New Writing North** under *Professional Associations and Societies*

PAWS (Public Awareness of Science) Drama Fund

The PAWS Office, OMNI Communications, First Floor, 155 Regents Park Road, London NW1 8BB
✉ pawsomni@btconnect.com
www.pawsdrama.com

Contacts *Andrew Millington, Andree Molyneux*

Established 1994. PAWS encourages and supports television drama drawing on science, engineering and technology. It offers a range of activities to bring science and technology to TV drama writers and producers in an easily accessible way. Events: covering the latest science and technology topics and enabling writers to meet scientists and engineers; Contacts & Information Service: aims to put writers and producers in 'one-to-one' contact with specialists who can help them develop their TV drama ideas; New Funding Scheme: rolling funding support primarily intended to help writers and producers who have a recent track record of successful TV drama experience to bring their ideas closer to production. People with lesser experience may also apply. Contact the PAWS Office or check out the website for further information.

Pearson Playwrights' Scheme

c/o Pearson Plc, 80 Strand, London WC2R 0RL
✉ playwrightscheme@tiscali.co.uk
www.pearson.com

Administrator *Jack Andrews, MBE*

Awards five bursaries to playwrights annually, each worth £6500. Applicants must be sponsored by a theatre which then submits the play for consideration by a panel. Each award allows the playwright a 12-month attachment. Applications invited via theatres in October each year. E-mail for up-to-date information.

The Charles Pick Fellowship
School of Literature and Creative Writing, University of East Anglia, Norwich NR4 7TJ
☎01603 592286 Fax 01603 507728
✉ charlespickfellowship@uea.ac.uk
www.uea.ac.uk/eas/fellowships/pick.shtml
Fellowship Administrator *Shawn Alexander*

Founded in 2001 by the Charles Pick Consultancy in memory of the publisher and literary agent who died in 2000, to support a new unpublished writer of fictional or non-fictional prose. This residential Fellowship is awarded annually and lasts six months. There is no interview; candidates will be judged on the quality and promise of their writing, the project they describe and the strength of their referee's report. 2006 winner: Lois Williams. Deadline for applications: 31 January each year.
AWARD £10,000 plus accommodation on campus.

Peggy Ramsay Foundation
Hanover House, 14 Hanover Square, London W1S 1HP
☎020 7667 5000 Fax 020 7667 5100
✉ laurence.harbottle@harbottle.com
www.peggyramsayfoundation.org
Contact *G. Laurence Harbottle*

Founded 1992 in accordance with the will of the late Peggy Ramsay, the well-known agent. Grants are made to writers for the stage who have some experience and who need time and resources to make writing possible. Grants are also made for writing projects by organisations connected with the theatre. The Foundation does not support production costs or any project that does not have a direct benefit to playwriting. Writers applying must have had one full-length play professionally produced for adults.
GRANTS total £150,000 to £200,000 per year.

The Royal Literary Fund
3 Johnson's Court, off Fleet Street, London EC4A 3EA
☎020 7353 7150 Fax 020 7353 1350
✉ egunnrlf@globalnet.co.uk
www.rlf.org.uk
Secretary *Eileen Gunn*

Grants and pensions are awarded to published authors of several works in financial need, or to their dependants. Examples of author's works are needed for assessment by Committee. Contact the Secretary for further details and application form.

The Royal Society of Literature/Jerwood Awards
The Royal Society of Literature, Somerset House, Strand, London WC2R 1LA
☎020 7845 4676 Fax 020 7845 4679
✉ paulaj@rslit.org
www.rslit.org
Submissions *Paula Johnson*

The awards offer financial assistance to authors engaged in writing their first major commissioned works of non-fiction. Three awards: one of £10,000 and two of £5000 will be offered annually to writers working on substantial non-fiction projects. Open to UK and Irish writers and writers who have been resident in the UK for at least three years. Applications for the awards should be submitted by end August. Further details available on the website.

Scottish Arts Council Creative Scotland Awards
Scottish Arts Council, 12 Manor Place, Edinburgh EH3 7DD
☎0131 226 6051/ Help Desk: 0845 603 6000 Fax 0131 225 9833
✉ help.desk@scottisharts.org.uk
www.scottisharts.org.uk

The scheme offers awards of £30,000. Available to established artists based in Scotland working in any medium, including writing.

Scottish Arts Council New Writers' Bursaries
Scottish Arts Council, 12 Manor Place, Edinburgh EH3 7DD
☎0131 226 6051 Fax 0131 225 9833
✉ gavin.wallace@scottisharts.org.uk
www.scottisharts.org.uk
Head of Literature *Gavin Wallace*

Ten bursaries of £2000 awarded annually to enable previously unpublished writers of literary work more time to devote to their writing. Applicants should be based in Scotland.

Scottish Arts Council Writers' and Playwrights' Bursaries
Scottish Arts Council, 12 Manor Place, Edinburgh EH3 7DD
☎0131 226 6051 Fax 0131 225 9833

✉ gavin.wallace@scottisharts.org.uk
www.scottisharts.org.uk

Head of Literature *Gavin Wallace*

Bursaries to enable published writers of literary work and recognised playwrights to devote more time to their writing. Around 20 bursaries of up to £15,000 awarded annually; deadline for applications in July and January. Application open to writers based in Scotland.

Laurence Stern Fellowship

Department of Journalism, City University, Northampton Square, London EC1V 0HB
☎020 7040 4036
✉ a.r.mckane@city.ac.uk
www.city.ac.uk/journalism

Contact *Anna McKane*

Founded 1980. Awarded each year to a young journalist experienced enough to work on national stories. It gives a chance to work on the national desk of the *Washington Post*. A senior executive from the newspaper selects from a shortlist drawn up in February/March. 2007 winner: Paul Lewis of *The Guardian*. Full details about how to apply available on the City University website in January.

Tom-Gallon Trust Award and the Olive Cook Prize

The Society of Authors, 84 Drayton Gardens, London SW10 9SB
☎020 7373 6642 Fax 020 7373 5768
✉ info@societyofauthors.org
www.societyofauthors.org

An award of £1000 is made on the basis of a submitted story to fiction writers of limited means who have had at least one short story accepted for publication. Both awards are biennial and are awarded in alternate years. Contact the **Society of Authors** for an entry form. Final entry date 31 October.

The Betty Trask Awards

The Society of Authors, 84 Drayton Gardens, London SW10 9SB
☎020 7373 6642 Fax 020 7373 5768

✉ info@societyofauthors.org
www.societyofauthors.org

These annual awards are for authors who are under 35 and Commonwealth citizens, awarded on the strength of a first novel (published or unpublished) of a traditional or romantic nature. The awards must be used for a period or periods of foreign travel. Final entry date: 31 January. Contact the **Society of Authors** for an entry form. 2006 winners: Nick Laird *Utterly Monkey*; Nicola Monaghan *The Killing Jar*; Peter Hobbs *The Short Day Dying*.
AWARD £20,000 (total).

The Travelling Scholarships

The Society of Authors, 84 Drayton Gardens, London SW10 9SB
☎020 7373 6642 Fax 020 7373 5768
✉ info@societyofauthors.org
www.societyofauthors.org

Annual honorary grants to established British writers. No submissions. 2006 winners: Jenny Diski, Robert McFarlane, Helen Simpson.
AWARD £5000 (total).

The David T.K. Wong Fellowship

School of Literature and Creative Writing, University of East Anglia, Norwich NR4 7TJ
☎01603 592286 Fax 01603 507728
✉ davidtkwongfellowship@uea.ac.uk
www.uea.ac.uk/eas/fellowships/wong/wong.shtml

Fellowship Administrator *Shawn Alexander*

Named for its sponsor, Mr. David Wong (retired Hong Kong businessman, teacher, journalist, senior civil servant and writer of short stories); this unique and generous award was launched in 1997 to enable a fiction writer who wants to write in English about the Far East. This residential Fellowship is awarded annually and lasts one academic year. There is no interview; candidates will be judged on the quality and promise of their writing and the project they describe. 2006 winner: Mulaika Hijjas. Deadline for applications: 31 January each year.
AWARD £25,000.

Prizes

Academi Book of the Year Awards

Academi, 3rd Floor, Mount Stuart House, Mount Stuart Square, Cardiff CF10 5FQ
☎029 2047 2266 Fax 029 2047 0691
✉ post@academi.org
www.academi.org

Contacts *Peter Finch* (Chief Executive), *Lleucu Siencyn* (Deputy)

Annual prizes awarded for works of exceptional literary merit written by Welsh authors (by birth or residence), published in Welsh or English during the previous calendar year. There is one major prize in English, the Welsh Book of the Year Award, and one major prize in Welsh, Gwobr Llyfr y Flwyddyn.
PRIZES £10,000 to each winner.

Academi Cardiff International Poetry Competition

Academi, PO Box 438, Cardiff CF10 5YA
☎029 2047 2266 Fax 029 2049 2930
✉ post@academi.org
www.academi.org

Contact *Peter Finch* (Chief Executive)

Established 1986. An annual competition supported by Cardiff Council for unpublished poems in English of up to 50 lines. Closing date in January.
PRIZE £6000 (total).

J.R. Ackerley Prize

English PEN, 6–8 Amwell Street, London EC1R 1UQ
☎020 7713 0023 Fax 020 7837 7838
✉ enquiries@englishpen.org
www.englishpen.org

Commemorating the novelist/autobiographer J.R. Ackerley, this prize is awarded for a literary autobiography, written in English and published in the year preceding the award. Entry restricted to nominations from the Ackerley Trustees only ('please do not submit books'). 2006 winner: Alan Bennett *Untold Stories*.
PRIZE £1000, plus silver pen.

Aldeburgh Poetry Festival Prize

See **Jerwood Aldeburgh First Collection Prize**

Alexander Prize

Royal Historical Society, University College London, Gower Street, London WC1E 6BT
☎020 7387 7532 Fax 020 7387 7532
✉ rhs.info@sas.ac.uk
www.rhs.ac.uk/prizes

Contact *Executive Secretary*

Established 1897. Awarded for a published journal article or essay based upon original research. The article/essay must have been published during the period 1 January 2006–31 December 2007. Competitors may choose their own subject for the essay. Closing date: 31 December.
PRIZE £250.

ALPSP Awards and ALPSP/ Charlesworth Awards

ALPSP, 47 Vicarage Road, Old Moulsham, Chelmsford CM2 9BS
☎01245 260571 Fax 01245 260935
✉ events@alpsp.org
www.alpsp.org

Contact *Lesley Ogg*

Presented in recognition of significant achievement and innovation in the field of learned and professional publishing by the **Association of Learned and Professional Society Publishers** and the Charlesworth Group. The awards are international and open to publishers, organisations and individuals. Closing date: 31 May. Details available on the Association's website.

Hans Christian Andersen Awards

IBBY, Nonnenweg 12, Postfach, CH-4003 Basel, Switzerland
☎00 41 61 272 2917 Fax 00 41 61 272 2757
✉ ibby@ibby.org
www.ibby.org

Administrative Director *Estelle Roth*
Director, Member Services, Communications & New Projects *Liz Page*

The highest international prizes for children's literature: The Hans Christian Andersen Award for Writing, established 1956; The Hans Christian Andersen Award for Illustration, established 1966. Candidates are nominated by National Sections of IBBY (The International Board on Books for Young People). Biennial prizes are awarded, in even-numbered years, to an author and an illustrator whose body of work has made a lasting contribution to children's literature. 2006 winners: Award for Writing: Margaret Mahy (New Zealand); Award for Illustration: Wolf Erlbruch (Gemany).

AWARD Gold medals.

Angus Book Award

Angus Council Cultural Services, County Buildings, Forfar DD8 3WF
☎01307 461460 Fax 01307 462590
✉ cultural.services@angus.gov.uk
www.angus.gov.uk/bookaward
Contact *Moyra Hood*, Educational Resources Librarian

Established 1995. Designed to try to help teenagers develop an interest in and enthusiasm for reading. Eligible books are read and voted on by third-year schoolchildren in all eight Angus secondary schools. 2006 winner: Graham Joyce *TWOC*.

PRIZE £500 cheque, plus trophy in the form of a replica Pictish stone.

Annual Theatre Book Prize

See **The Society for Theatre Research Annual Theatre Book Prize**

Arts Council Children's Award

See **Brian Way Award**

Arvon Foundation International Poetry Competition

2nd Floor, 42a Buckingham Palace Road, London SW1W 0RE
☎020 7931 7611 Fax 020 7963 0961
✉ london@arvonfoundation.org
www.arvonfoundation.org
Contact *The London Office*

Established 1980. Biennial competition (next in 2008) for poems written in English and not previously broadcast or published. There are no restrictions on the number of lines, themes, age of entrants or nationality. No limit to the number of entries. Entry fee: £7 per poem. Previous winners: Paul Farley *Laws of Gravity*; Don Paterson *A Private Bottling*.

PRIZE (1st) £5000 and £5000 worth of other prizes.

Asham Award for Women

Asham Literary Endownment Trust, c/o Town Hall, High Street, Lewes BN7 2QS
☎01273 483159
www.ashamaward.com
Contact *Carole Buchan*

Founded in 1996, the Award (named after the house in Sussex where Virginia Woolf lived) is a biennial short story competition for women and is administered by the Asham Literary Endownment Trust which encourages new writing through competitions, mentoring, training and publication. Candidates must be female, over 18, resident in the UK and must not have had a novel or complete anthology of work previously published. Next award to be launched in January 2008. Details on the website from October. 2005 winner: Annie Kirby.

PRIZE money up to £3600; 12 winning writers are published by Bloomsbury to include specially commissioned stories by leading professional writers.

Authors' Club First Novel Award

Authors' Club, 40 Dover Street, London W1S 4NP
☎020 7499 8581 Fax 020 7409 0913
✉ stella@theauthorsclub.co.uk
Contact *Stella Kane*

Established 1954. This award is made for the most promising work published in Britain by a British author, and is presented at a dinner held at The Arts Club. Entries for the award are accepted from publishers from September of the year in question and must be full-length (short stories are not eligible). For further details/ application form, contact *Stella Kane* at the e-mail address above or access the website. 2006 winner: Nicola Monaghan *The Killing Jar*.

Award £1000.

The BA/Nielson BookData Author of the Year Award

Booksellers Association Ltd, 272 Vauxhall Bridge Road, London SW1V 1BA
☎020 7802 0801 Fax 020 7802 0803
✉ anna.okane@booksellers.org.uk
www.booksellers.org.uk
Contact *Naomi Gane*

Founded as part of the BA Annual Conference to involve authors more closely in the event. Authors must be British or Irish. Not an award open to entry but voted on by the BA's membership. 2006 winner: Alan Bennett.

AWARD £1000, plus trophy.

BAAL Book Prize

BAAL Publications Secretary, Department of Linguistics and English Language, Lancaster University, Lancaster LA1 4YT
✉ v.koller@lancaster.ac.uk
www.baal.org.uk

Contact *Veronika Koller*

Annual award made by the British Association for Applied Linguistics to an outstanding book in the field of applied linguistics. Final entry at the end of October/November. Nominations from publishers only. 2006 winner: Aneta Pavlenko *Emotions and Multilingualism*.

Banipal Prize

See **The Translators Association Awards**

Verity Bargate Award

Soho Theatre Company, 21 Dean Street, London W1D 3NE
☎020 7287 5060 Fax 020 7287 5061
www.sohotheatre.com

The award was set up to commemorate the late Verity Bargate, co-founder and director of the **Soho Theatre Company**. This national award is presented biennially for a new and unperformed play (next submission deadline: July 2009). Access details on the website. Previous winners include: Matt Charman, Shan Khan, Fraser Grace, Lyndon Morgans, Adrian Pagan, Diane Samuels, Judy Upton and Toby Whithouse.

BBC Wildlife Magazine Poet of the Year Awards

BBC Wildlife Magazine, Bristol Magazines Ltd, 14th Floor, Tower House, Fairfax Street, Bristol BS1 3BN
☎0117 927 9009 Fax 0117 933 8032
✉ wildlifemagazine@bbcmagazinesbristol.com
www.bbcwildlifemagazine.com

Contact *Sophie Stafford*

Annual award for a poem, the subject of which must be the natural world and/or our relationship with it. Entrants may submit one poem only of no more than 50 lines with the entry form which is published in the April issue. Closing date for entries varies from year to year. See website and the magazine for entry details.

PRIZES Poet of the Year: a wildlife break, publication in the magazine, plus the possibility of a reading of your poem on Radio 4's *Poetry Please*; runners-up: books and publication in the magazine; four young poets awards, categories: age 7 and under, 8–11, 12–14, 15–17.

BBC Wildlife Magazine Travel Writing Award

BBC Wildlife Magazine, Bristol Magazines Ltd, 14th Floor, Tower House, Fairfax Street, Bristol BS1 3BN
☎0117 927 9009 Fax 0117 934 9008
✉ jamesfair@bbcmagazinesbristol.com
www.bbcwildlifemagazine.com

Awarded to a travel essay that is a true account involving an intimate encounter with wildlife, either local or exotic. The essay should convey a strong impression of the environment and incorporate the idea of travel and discovery. Maximum 800 words. See website and the magazine for entry details. Call for entries appears in the January issue of the magazine.

PRIZE Publication in the magazine, plus 'holiday of a lifetime'.

BBC Wildlife Magazine Young Environmental Journalist of the Year

BBC Wildlife Magazine, Bristol Magazines Ltd, 14th Floor, Tower House, Fairfax Street, Bristol BS1 3BN
☎0117 927 9009 Fax 0117 933 8032
✉ jamesfair@bbcmagazinesbristol.com
www.bbcwildlifemagazine.com

Contact *James Fair*

Established to give young people a chance to get into environmental journalism. Entrants must be aged 16–25 and should submit an original 750-word profile, based on an interview with 'someone you regard as an environmental hero, not necessarily famous or renowned, who has contributed to conservation in some way'. See website and the March issue for entry details.

PRIZE Publication in the magazine, plus a 12–14-day Earthwatch expedition.

The BBCFour Samuel Johnson Prize for Non-Fiction

Colman Getty, Middlesex House, 28 Windmill Street, London W1T 2JJ
☎020 7631 2666 Fax 020 7631 2699
✉ lois@colmangetty.co.uk

Contact *Lois Tucker*

Established 1998. Annual prize sponsored by BBCFour. Eligible categories include the arts, autobiography, biography, business, commerce, current affairs, history, natural history, popular science, religion, sport and travel. Entries submitted by publishers only. 2006 winner:

James Shapiro *1599: A Year in the Life of William Shakespeare*.

PRIZE £30,000; £1000 to each shortlisted author.

David Berry Prize

Royal Historical Society, University College London, Gower Street, London WC1E 6BT
☎020 7387 7532 Fax 020 7387 7532
✉ rhs.info@sas.ac.uk
www.rhs.ac.uk/prizes

Contact *Executive Secretary*

Annual award for an essay of not more than 10,000 words on Scottish history. Closing date: 31 October.

PRIZE £250,

Besterman/McColvin Medal

43 Yardington, Whitchurch SY13 1BL
☎01948 663570
✉ millbrookend-awards@yahoo.co.uk
www.cilip.org.uk

Contact *Awards Administrator* (at address above)

ISG (CILIP)/BookData Reference Awards. The Besterman McColvin medals are awarded annually for an outstanding reference work first published in the UK during the preceding year. Consists of two categories: printed and electronic. Works eligible for consideration include: encyclopedias, general and special dictionaries; annuals, yearbooks and directories; handbooks and compendia of data; atlases. Nominations are invited from members of **CILIP**, publishers and others. 2005 winners: *Oxford Dictionary of National Biography* eds. H.C.G. Matthew and Brian Harrison (electronic category); *The Design Encyclopaedia* Mel Byars (printed category).

AWARD Medal and cash prize for each category.

The Biographers' Club Prize

119A Fordwych Road, London NW2 3NJ
☎020 8452 4993
✉ anna@annaswan.co.uk
www.biographersclub.co.uk

Contact *Anna Swan*

Established 1999 by literary agent, biographer and founder of the Biographers' Club, Andrew Lownie, to finance and encourage first-time writers researching a biography. Sponsored by the *Daily Mail*. Open to previously unpublished writers, applicants should submit (preferably by e-mail) a proposal of 15–20 pages, including outline, sample chapter, a note on the market for the book, sources consulted, competing books

and a c.v. Entry fee: £10 (cheques made payable to the Biographers' Club). 2006 joint-winners: Birna Helgadottir and Helen Smith.

PRIZE £1000.

Birdwatch Bird Book of the Year

c/o Birdwatch Magazine, B403A The Chocolate Factory, 5 Clarendon Road, London N22 6XJ
☎020 8881 0550
✉ enquiries@birdwatch.co.uk
www.birdwatch.co.uk

Contact *Dominic Mitchell*

Established in 1992 to acknowledge excellence in ornithological publishing – an increasingly large market with a high turnover. Annual award. Entries, from publishers, must offer an original and comprehensive treatment of their particular ornithological subject matter and must have a broad appeal to British-based readers. 2006 winner: *The Sound Approach to Birding* Mark Constantine.

Bisto Book of the Year Awards

See **CBI Bisto Book of the Year Awards**

James Tait Black Memorial Prizes

University of Edinburgh, David Hume Tower, George Square, Edinburgh EH8 9JX
☎0131 650 3619 Fax 0131 650 6898
www.englit.ed.ac.uk/jtbinf.htm

Contact *Department of English Literature*

Established 1918 in memory of a partner of the publishing firm of **A.&C. Black Ltd**. Two prizes, one for biography and one for fiction. Closing date for submissions: 31 January. Each prize is awarded for a book first published in Britain in the previous calendar year (1 January–31 December). 2005 winners: Ian McEwan *Saturday* (fiction); Sue Prideaux *Edvard Munch: Behind the Scream* (biography).

PRIZES £10,000 each.

Blue Peter Book Awards

c/o Awards Administrator, Fraser Ross Associates, 6 Wellington Place, Edinburgh EH6 7EQ
☎0131 553 2759 Fax 0131 553 2759
✉ lindsey.fraser@tiscali.co.uk
www.bbc.co.uk/bluepeter

Contacts *Lindsey Fraser, Kathryn Ross*

Established in 1999 to highlight paperback fiction, illustrated books, poetry and non-fiction for young people. The initial shortlist is selected by a panel of adults and the final decisions are

taken by a panel of Blue Peter judges. Final entry date: mid-June. Previous winners: Nicky Singer *Feather Boy*; William Nicholson *The Windsinger*; Philip Reeve *Mortal Engines*; Simon Bartram *Man on the Moon*; Michael Morpurgo *Private Peaceful*; Oliver Jeffers *Lost and Found*.
AWARD Trophy.

Boardman Tasker Award

Pound House, Llangennith, Swansea SA3 1JQ
☎01792 386215 Fax 01792 386215
✉ margaretbody@lineone.net
www.boardmantasker.com

Contact *Maggie Body*, Honorary Secretary

Established 1983, this award is given for a work of fiction, non-fiction or poetry, whose central theme is concerned with the mountain environment and which can be said to have made an outstanding contribution to mountain literature. Authors of any nationality are eligible, but the book must have been published or distributed in the UK for the first time between 1 November 2006 and 31 October 2007. Entries from publishers only. 2006 winner: Charles Lind *An Afterclap of Fate*.

PRIZE £2000 (at Trustees' discretion).

Bollinger Everyman Wodehouse Prize

Everyman's Library, Northburgh House, 10 Northburgh Street, London EC1V 0AT
☎020 7566 6350 Fax 020 7490 3708
✉ dcampbell@randomhouse.co.uk *or* sarah@everyman.uk.com

Contact *Sarah Peacock*

Established in 2000 by Everyman's Library, Bollinger and the Hay Festival to celebrate comic writing in memory of P.G. Wodehouse. Books are nominated by readers of the *Sunday Times* and visitors to www.bol.com. 2007 winner: Paul Torday, *Salmon Fishing in the Yemen*.

The Booker Prize for Fiction

See **The Man Booker Prize for Fiction**

Booktrust Early Years Awards

Booktrust, Book House, 45 East Hill, London SW18 2QZ
☎020 8516 2972 Fax 020 8516 2978
✉ tarryn@booktrust.org.uk
www.booktrust.org.uk

Contact *Tarryn McKay*

Formerly the Sainsbury's Baby Book Award, established in 1999. Annual awards with three categories: the Baby Book Award, the Best Book

for Pre-School Children (up to the age of 5), and an award for the Best New Illustrator. Books to be submitted by publishers only; authors and illustrators must be of British nationality or other nationals who have been resident in the UK for at least five years. 2006 winners: Mandy Stanley (Baby Book); Sam Lloyd (Pre-School); Catherine Rayner (Best New Illustrator).

PRIZE £2000 for each category; in addition the Best New Illustrator receives a specially commissioned piece of artwork.

Booktrust Teenage Prize

Book House, 45 East Hill, London SW18 2QZ
☎020 8516 2986 Fax 020 8516 2978
✉ hannah@booktrust.org.uk
www.bookheads.org.uk

Contact *Hannah Rutland*

Established 2003. Annual prize that recognises and celebrates the best in teenage fiction. Funded and administered by Booktrust. Open to works of fiction for young adults in the UK, the books to be published between 1 July 2005 and 30 June 2006. Final entry date in March. 2006 winner: Anthony McGowan *Henry Tumour*.

PRIZE £2500.

Harry Bowling Prize

c/o Coseley House, Munslow, Craven Arms SY7 9ET
✉ dana@mbalit.co.uk
www.harrybowlingprize.net

Contact *Dana Arnott*

Established 2000 in honour of Harry Bowling, 'the king of Cockney sagas' (died 1999). Biennial award (next in 2008), sponsored by **Headline Book Publishing**, to encourage writers of adult fiction set in London. Open to anyone who has not been published previously. Final entry date: 31 March. Entry fee charged; forms from address above (enclose s.a.e.) or via the website. 2006 winner: Jean Fullerton.

PRIZES Winner, £1000; two runners-up, £100 each.

The Branford Boase Award

8 Bolderwood Close, Bishopstoke, Eastleigh SO50 8PG
☎01962 826658 Fax 01962 856615
✉ anne.marley@tiscali.co.uk
www.branfordboaseaward.org.uk

Administrator *Anne Marley*

Established in 2000 in memory of children's novelist, Henrietta Branford and editor and publisher, Wendy Boase. To be awarded annually to encourage and celebrate the most promising novel by a new writer of children's books, while at the same time highlighting the importance of the editor in nurturing new talent. 2006 winner: Frances Hardinge *Fly By Night* (author); Ruth Alltimes, **Macmillan** (editor).

AWARD Specially commissioned box, carved and inlaid in silver with the Branford Boase Award logo; winning author receives £1000.

The Bridport Prize

Bridport Arts Centre, South Street, Bridport DT6 3NR
☎01308 485064
✉ frances@poorton.demon.co.uk
www.bridportprize.org.uk

Contact *Frances Everitt*, Administrator

Annual competition for poetry and short story writing. Unpublished work only, written in English. Winning stories are read by a literary agent, the winning poems are put forward to the **Forward Prize**, and an anthology of winning entries is published. Final entry date: 30 June. Send s.a.e. for entry forms.

PRIZES £5000, £1000 & £500 in each category, plus 10 supplementary prizes of £50 each. Winning stories are submitted to the **National Short Story Prize**.

Katharine Briggs Folklore Award

The Folklore Society, c/o The Warburg Institute, Woburn Square, London WC1H 0AB
☎020 7862 8564
✉ enquiries@folklore-society.com
www.folklore-society.com

Contact *The Convenor*

Established 1982. An annual award in November for the book, published in Britain and Ireland between 1 June in the previous calendar year and 30 May, which has made the most distinguished non-fiction contribution to folklore studies. Intended to encourage serious research in the field which Katharine Briggs did so much to establish. The term folklore studies is interpreted broadly to include all aspects of traditional and popular culture, narrative, belief, custom and folk arts. 2006 winner: Catherine Rider *Magic and Impotence in the Middle Ages*.

PRIZE £200, plus engraved goblet.

British Book Awards

See **Galaxy British Book Awards**

British Czech & Slovak Association Prize

The BCSA Prize Administrator, 24 Ferndale, Tunbridge Wells TN2 3NS
☎01892 543206
✉ prize@bcsa.co.uk
www.bcsa.co.uk

Contact *Prize Administrator*

The British Czech & Slovak Association offers an annual prize for the best piece of original writing, in English, on the links between Britain and the Czech and Slovak Republics, or describing society in transition in those Republics since the Velvet Revolution in 1989. Entries can be fiction or factual, should not have been previously published and should be up to 2000 words in length. Submissions are invited from individuals of any age, nationality or educational background. Closing date: 30 June. Entry details for 2008 should be checked with the Prize Administrator. 2006 winners: Adam Daniel Mezei *Mayor Sulc's Astounding 2010 Directive*; Jarmila Hlavkova *Home Cooking in Britain & Slovakia – Traditional or International?*

PRIZE £300, presented at the BCSA's annual dinner in London; 2nd prize, £100. The winning entry is published in the *British Czech & Slovak Review*.

British Fantasy Awards

5 Greenbank, Barnt Green, Birmingham B45 8DH
✉ cook.vicky@yahoo.co.uk
www.britishfantasysociety.org.uk

Secretary *Vicky Cook*

Awarded by the **British Fantasy Society** by members at its annual conference for Best Novel and Best Short Story categories, among others. Not an open competition. Previous winners include: Ramsey Campbell, Dan Simmons, Michael Marshall Smith, Thomas Ligotti.

British Press Awards

Press Gazette, 6–14 Underwood Street, London N1 7JQ
☎020 7549 8719 Fax 020 7566 5780
✉ franb@pressgazette.co.uk
www.pressgazette.co.uk

'The Oscars of British journalism.' Open to all British national newspapers and news agencies. April event. Run by *Press Gazette*.

British Science Fiction Association Awards

16 Napier Road, Oxford OX4 3JA

☎01865 749378
✉ bsfa.awards@gmail.com
www.bsfa.co.uk
Awards Administrator *Ian Snell*
Established 1970. Categories for novel, short fiction, non-fiction and artwork. The awards are announced and presented at the British National Science Fiction Convention every Easter. 2006 winners: Jon Courtenay *End of the World Blues* (novel); Ian McDonald *The Djinn's Wife* (short fiction); Fangorn *Angelbot* (artwork - for cover of *Time Pieces*, ed. Ian Whates).

British Sports Book Awards
National Sporting Club, Café Royal, 68 Regent Street, London W1B 5EL
☎020 7437 0144 Fax 020 7437 5441
✉ david@nationalsportingclub.co.uk
www.nationalsportingclub.co.uk
Chairman *David Willis*
Established 2003. Annual awards presented at a Café Royal lunch in London in March. Four categories: Best Autobiography, Best Biography, Best Illustrator , Best New Writer. Nominations received in November each year by e-mail (address above). Sponsors include Skysports, *The Times*, Llanllyr Spring Water, Littlehampton Book Services and Ladbrokes.

British Sports Journalism Awards
See **Sports Writers' Association of Great Britain** under *Professional Associations and Societies*

The Browning Society Poetry Prize
84 Addison Gardens, London W14 0DR
☎020 7602 3094 Fax 020 7602 3771
✉ pamela@tvdox.com
www.browningsociety.org
Contact *Pamela Neville-Sington*
Established in 2004 to encourage interest in the Brownings' poetry among young people. Held annually, the competition focuses on two different Browning poems – one by Elizabeth and one by Robert; visit the website for details. Open to students between the ages of 9 and 19 who are citizens of or resident in the UK. Final entry date: 15 March.
PRIZE £100 for students aged 9–13; £200 for students 14–19.

The Caine Prize for African Writing
51a Southwark Street, London SE1 1RU
☎020 7378 6234 Fax 020 7378 6235
✉ info@caineprize.com
www.caineprize.com
Administrator *Nick Elam*
Secretary *Jan Hart*
Annual award founded in 1999 in memory of Sir Michael Caine, former chairman of Booker plc, to recognise the worth of African writing in English. Awarded for a short story by an African writer, published in English anywhere in the world. An 'African writer' is someone who was born in Africa, or who is a national of an African country, or whose parents are African, and whose work has reflected African sensibilities. Final entry date: 31 January; submissions by publishers only. 2006 winner: Mary Watson *Jungfrau*.
PRIZE $15,000.

The Calouste Gulbenkian Prize
See **The Translators Association Awards**

James Cameron Award
City University, Department of Journalism, Northampton Square, London EC1V 0HB
☎020 7040 8221 Fax 020 7040 8594
✉ H.Stephenson@city.ac.uk
Contact *Hugh Stephenson*
Annual award for journalism to a reporter of any nationality, working for the British media, whose work is judged to have contributed most during the year to the continuance of the Cameron tradition. 2006 winner: Patrick Cockburn.

Canadian Poetry Association (Annual Poetry Contest)
Canadian Poetry Association, 331 Elmwood Dr., Suite 4-212, Moncton, New Brunswick E1A 1X6, Canada
✉ info@canadianpoetryassoc.com
www.canadianpoetryassoc.com
Annual contest open only to members of the CPA worldwide. Submission fee: $5 per poem. See the website for entry details. All winning poems are published on the CPA website and in *Poemata*. Three cash PRIZES.

Cardiff Book of the Year Awards
See **Academi Book of the Year Awards**

Cardiff International Poetry Competition
See **Academi Cardiff International Poetry Competition**

Carey Award

Society of Indexers, Woodbourn Business Centre, 10 Jessell Street, Sheffield S9 3HY
☎0114 244 9561 Fax 0114 244 9563
✉ admin@indexers.org.uk
www.indexers.org.uk
Secretary *Judith Menes*

A private award made by the Society to a member who has given outstanding services to indexing. The recipient is selected by the Executive Board with no recommendations considered from elsewhere.

Carnegie Medal

See **CILIP: The Chartered Institute of Library and Information Professionals Carnegie Medal**

CBI Bisto Book of the Year Awards

17 North Great Georges Street, Dublin 1, Republic of Ireland
☎00 353 1 872 7475 Fax 00 353 1 872 8486
✉ info@childrensbooksireland.com
www.childrensbooksireland.com

Contact *Jenny Murray*

Founded 1990 as Bisto Book of the Decade Awards. This led to the establishment of an annual award made by the Irish Children's Book Trust, later to become Children's Books Ireland. Open to any author or illustrator of children's books born or resident in Ireland; open to English or Irish languages. 2006/7 winners: John Boyne *The Boy In the Striped Pyjamas* (Bisto Book of the Year); Siobhan Dowd *A Swift Pure Cry* (Eilís Dillon Award).

PRIZES €10,000 (Bisto Book of the Year); €3000 (Eilís Dillon Award); three honour awards of €1000 each.

Sid Chaplin Short Story Competition

Shildon Town Council, Civic Hall Square, Shildon DL4 1AH
☎01388 772563 Fax 01388 775227

Contact *Mrs J.M. Stafford*

Established 1986. Annual short story competition. Maximum 3000 words; £2.50 entrance fee (juniors free). All stories must be unpublished and not broadcast and/or performed. Application forms available from March; closing date: May.

PRIZES £300 (1st); £150 (2nd); £75 (3rd); £30 (Junior).

Chapter One Promotions International Open Short Story Competition

PO Box 43667, London SE22 9XU
☎0845 456 5364 Fax 0845 456 5347
✉ info@chapteronepromotions.com
www.chapteronepromotions.com

Contact *Johanna Bertie*

Established in 2005, the competition is open to new and established writers to submit unpublished short stories of fewer than 2500 words. Author details on separate sheet. Submissions and payment accepted online. Closing date: 14 January. 2005 winner: Pablo Stewart.

PRIZES £2500, £1000, £500, plus top 13 entries published in anthology.

Chapter One Promotions Open Poetry Competition

PO Box 43667, London SE22 9XU
☎0845 456 5364 Fax 0845 456 5347
✉ poetry@chapteronepromotions.com
www.chapteronepromotions.com

Contact *Johanna Bertie*

Established 2005. Unpublished poems of no more than 30 lines. Judge decides on the best 20 poems which are displayed on the website and the public votes for their favourite poem. The three poems with the most votes wins. Closing date: 1 June. Online voting period: 1–15 July. Winning poems appear on the website in August. Submissions and payment accepted online. 2005 winner: Graham Burchell.

PRIZES £1000, £500, £250.

Children's Book Circle Eleanor Farjeon Award

See **Eleanor Farjeon Award**

The Children's Laureate

Booktrust, Book House, 45 East Hill, London SW18 2QZ
☎020 8516 2976 Fax 020 8516 2978
✉ childrenslaureate@booktrust.org.uk
www.childrenslaureate.org

Contact *Nikki Marsh*

Established 1998. The Laureate is awarded biennially to an eminent British writer or illustrator of children's books both in celebration of a lifetime's achievement and to highlight the role of children's book creators in inspiring, informing and entertaining young readers. 2007–09 winner: Michael Rosen.

AWARD Medal and £10,000.

CILIP: The Chartered Institute of Library and Information Professionals Carnegie Medal

7 Ridgmount Street, London WC1E 7AE
☎020 7255 0650 Fax 020 7255 0651
✉ ckg@cilip.org.uk
www.ckg.org.uk

Established 1936. Presented for an outstanding book for children written in English and first published in the UK during the preceding year. Fiction, non-fiction and poetry are all eligible. 2005 winner (presented in 2006): Mal Peet *Tamar*.

AWARD Medal.

CILIP: The Chartered Institute of Library and Information Professionals Kate Greenaway Medal

7 Ridgmount Street, London WC1E 7AE
☎020 7255 0650 Fax 020 7255 0651
✉ ckg@cilip.org.uk
www.ckg.org.uk

Established 1955. Presented annually for the most distinguished work in the illustration of children's books first published in the UK during the preceding year. 2005 winner (presented in 2006): Emily Graves *Wolves*.

AWARD Medal. The Colin Mears Award (£5000 cash) is given annually to the winner of the Kate Greenaway Medal.

Arthur C. Clarke Award for Science Fiction

60 Bournemouth Road, Folkestone
CT19 5AZ
☎01303 252939
✉ clarkeaward@googlemail.com
www.clarkeaward.com

Administrator *Paul Kincaid*

Established 1986. The Arthur C. Clarke Award is given annually to the best science fiction novel with first UK publication in the previous calendar year. Both hardcover and paperback books qualify. Made possible by a generous donation from Arthur C. Clarke, this award is selected by a rotating panel of judges nominated by the **British Science Fiction Association**, the **Science Fiction Foundation** and the Science Museum. 2005 winner: China Miéville *Iron Curtain*.

AWARD £2006 (award increases by £1 per year), plus trophy.

David Cohen Prize for Literature

Arts Council England, 14 Great Peter Street, London SW1P 3NQ
☎020 7973 5325 Fax 020 7973 6983
✉ info.literature@artscouncil.org.uk
www.artscouncil.org.uk

Literature Administrator *Jessica Ryan*

Established 1993 by the Arts Council and awarded biennially, the David Cohen Prize for Literature is one of the most distinguished literary prizes in Britain. It recognises writers who use the English language and who are citizens of the UK and the Republic of Ireland, encompassing dramatists as well as novelists, poets and essayists. The prize is for a lifetime's achievement and is donated by the David Cohen Family Charitable Trust. Set up in 1980 by David Cohen, general practitioner and son of a property developer, the Trust has helped composers, choreographers, dancers, poets, playwrights and actors. The Council is providing a futher £12,500 (The Clarissa Luard Award) to enable the winner to commission new work, with the dual aim of encouraging young writers and readers. Previous winners: William Trevor, Dame Muriel Spark, Harold Pinter, V.S. Naipaul, Doris Lessing, Beryl Bainbridge and Thom Gunn. 2005 winner: Michael Holroyd.

AWARD £40,000, plus £12,500 towards new work.

The Commonwealth Writers Prize

Commonwealth Foundation, Marlborough House, Pall Mall, London SW1Y 5HY
☎020 7747 6262
✉ j.sobol@commonwealth.int
www.commonwealthfoundation.com/
 culturediversity/writersprize/

Established 1987. An annual award to reward and encourage the upsurge of new Commonwealth fiction. Any work of prose or fiction is eligible, i.e. a novel or collection of short stories. No drama or poetry. The work must be first written in English by a citizen of the Commonwealth and be first published in the year before its entry for the prize. Entries must be submitted by the publisher to the region of the writer's Commonwealth citizenship. The four regions are: Africa, Europe and South Asia, South East Asia and South Pacific, Caribbean and Canada. 2007 winners: Lloyd Jones (New Zealand) *Mister Pip* (Best Book Award); D.Y. Béchard (Canada) *Vandal Love* (Best First Book Award).

PRIZES £10,000 for Best Book; £5000 for

Best First Book; 8 prizes of £1000 for each best and best first book in four regions.

The Duff Cooper Prize

54 St Maur Road, London SW6 4DP
☎020 7736 3729
✉ artemiscooper@btopenworld.com

Contact *Artemis Cooper*

An annual award for a literary work of biography, history, politics or poetry, published by a recognised publisher (member of the **Publishers Association**) during the previous 12 months. The book must be submitted by the publisher, not the author. Financed by the interest from a trust fund commemorating Duff Cooper, first Viscount Norwich (1890–1954). 2006 winner: William Dalrymple *The Last Mughal*.
PRIZE £5000.

Costa Book Awards

The Booksellers Association, Minster House, 272 Vauxhall Bridge Road, London SW1V 1BA
☎020 7802 0802 Fax 020 7802 0803
✉ naomi.gane@booksellers.org.uk
www.costa.co.uk/bookawards

Contact *Anna O'Kane*

Established 1971. Formerly the Whitbread Book Awards. The awards celebrate and promote the best contemporary British writing. They are judged in two stages and offer a total of £50,000 prize money. The awards are open to novel, first novel, biography, poetry and children's book, each judged by a panel of three judges, with two young judges joining the panel for the Costa Children's Book Award. The winner of each award receives £5000. The Costa Book of the Year (£25,000) is chosen from the category winners. Writers must have lived in Britain and Ireland for three or more years. Submissions received from publishers only. Closing date: early July. Sponsored by Costa. 2006 winners: William Boyd *Restless* (novel); Stef Penney *The Tenderness of Wolves* (first novel & overall winner); Brian Thompson *Keeping Mum* (biography); John Haynes *Letter to Patience* (poetry); Linda Newbery *Set in Stone* (children's).

Rose Mary Crawshay Prize

The British Academy, 10 Carlton House Terrace, London SW1Y 5AH
☎020 7969 5200 Fax 020 7969 5300
www.britac.ac.uk

Contact *British Academy Chief Executive and Secretary*

Established 1888 by Rose Mary Crawshay, this prize is given for an historical or critical work to a woman of any nationality on English literature, with particular preference for a work on Keats, Byron or Shelley. The work must have been published in the preceding three years.

John Creasey Dagger

See **Crime Writers' Association (The New Blood Dagger for Best First Crime Novel)**

Crime Writers' Association (Cartier Diamond Dagger)

PO Box 273, Boreham Wood WD6 2XA
✉ secretary@thecwa.co.uk
www.thecwa.co.uk

Contact *The Secretary*

Established 1986. An annual award for a lifetime's outstanding contribution to the genre. 2007 winner: John Harvey.

Crime Writers' Association (The CWA Gold Dagger for Non-Fiction)

PO Box 273, Boreham Wood WD6 2XA
✉ secretary@thecwa.co.uk
www.thecwa.co.uk

Contact *The Secretary*

Biennial award for the best non-fiction crime book published during the year. Nominations from publishers only. 2006 winner: Linda Rhodes, Lee Shelden and Kathryn Abnett *The Dagenham Murder*.
AWARD Dagger, plus cheque (sum varies).

Crime Writers' Association (The Dagger in the Library)

PO Box 273, Boreham Wood WD6 2XA
✉ secretary@thecwa.co.uk
www.thecwa.co.uk

Contact *The Secretary*

Reinstated 2002. Annual award (sponsored by **Random House**) to the author whose work has given most pleasure to readers. Nominated and judged by librarians. 2006 winner: Jim Kelly.
AWARD Dagger, plus cheque.

Crime Writers' Association (The Debut Dagger)

The Debut Dagger Competition, PO Box 165, Wirral CH31 9BD
✉ debut.dagger@thecwa.co.uk
www.thecwa.co.uk

Contact *The Secretary*

Annual competition (sponsored by **Orion**) for unpublished writers to submit the first 3000 words and 500 word outline of a crime novel (entry fee and form required). For full details see website or send s.a.e. to address above. 2006 winner: D.V.Wesselmann (aka Otis Twelve) *Imp*.
AWARD Dagger, plus cheque.

Crime Writers' Association (The Ian Fleming Steel Dagger)

PO Box 273, Boreham Wood WD6 2XA
✉ secretary@thecwa.co.uk
www.thecwa.co.uk

Contact *The Secretary*

Founded 2002. Annual award for the best thriller, adventure or spy novel. Sponsored by Ian Fleming (Glidrose) Publications Ltd to celebrate the best of contemporary thriller writing. 2006 winner: Nick Stone *Mr Clarinet*.
AWARD Dagger, plus cheque.

Crime Writers' Association (The Gold and Silver Daggers for Fiction)

These awards have now been superseded by the **Duncan Lawrie Dagger** (see entry).

Crime Writers' Association (The New Blood Dagger for Best First Crime Novel)

PO Box 273, Boreham Wood WD6 2XA
✉ secretary@thecwa.co.uk
www.thecwa.co.uk

Contact *The Secretary*

Established in 1973 following the death of crime writer John Creasey, founder of the **Crime Writers' Association**. This award, sponsored by **BBC Audio Books**, is given annually for the best crime novel by an author who has not previously published a full-length work of fiction. Fomerly known as the John Creasey Dagger. Nominations from publishers only. 2006 winner: Louise Penny *Still Life*.
AWARD Dagger, plus cheque.

Crime Writers' Association (The CWA Ellis Peters Award)

PO Box 273, Boreham Wood WD6 2XA
✉ secretary@thecwa.co.uk
www.thecwa.co.uk

Contact *The Secretary*

Sponsored by the Estate of Ellis Peters, Time Warner and **Headline**. Established 1999. Annual award for the best historical crime novel.

Nominations from publishers only. 2006 winner: Edward Wright *Red Sky Lament*.
AWARD plus cheque.

Daily Mail First Novel Award

Transworld Publishers, 61–63 Uxbridge Road, London W5 5SA
www.dailymail.co.uk/books

Founded 2007. Open competition for writers aged 16 or over, resident in the UK or Republic of Ireland. The winning novel will be published by Transworld in 2008 with an advance of £30,000.

Hunter Davies Prize

See **Lakeland Book of the Year Awards**

Felix Dennis Prize for Best First Collection

See **The Forward Prizes for Poetry**

George Devine Award

9 Lower Mall, Hammersmith, London W6 9DJ

Contact *Christine Smith*

Annual award for a promising new playwright writing for the stage in memory of George Devine, artistic director of the **Royal Court Theatre**, who died in 1965. The play, which can be of any length, does not need to have been produced. Send two copies of the script, plus outline of work, to *Christine Smith*. Closing date: 1 March 2008. Send s.a.e. for the script to be returned if required. Information leaflet available from January on receipt of s.a.e.
PRIZE £10,000.

Dingle Prize

British Society for the History of Science, 5 Woodcote Green, Fleet GU51 4EY
☎ 01252 641135
✉ execsec@bshs.org.uk
www.bshs.org.uk

Biennial award made by the BSHS to the best book in the history of science (broadly construed) which is accessible to a wide audience of non-specialists. Next award: 2007. Previous winners: Ken Alder, *The Measure of All Things*; Deborah Cadbury *The Dinosaur Hunters*; Steven Shapin *The Scientific Revolution*.
PRIZE £300.

Dolman Best First Travel Book Award

Authors' Club, 40 Dover Street, London W1S 4NP
☎ 020 7408 5092 Fax 020 7409 0913

✉ stella@theauthorsclub.co.uk

Contact *Stella Kane*

William Dolman, a former chairman of the **Authors' Club**, instituted this new prize for the most promising first book of travel literature. Books published in Great Britain by British writers are eligible and submissions are accepted in January of each year. Inaugural winner: Nicholas Jubber *The Prester Quest*.

AWARD £1000.

Drama Association of Wales Playwriting Competition

The Old Library, Singleton Road, Splott, Cardiff CF24 2ET

☎029 2045 2200 Fax 029 2045 2277

✉ aled.daw@virgin.net

Contact *Teresa Hennessy*

Annual competition held to promote the writing of one-act plays in English and Welsh of between 20 and 50 minutes' playing time. Application forms from the address above. Closing date: 31 January.

The John Dryden Competition

School of Literature and Creative Writing, University of East Anglia, Norwich NR4 7TJ

Fax 01603 250599

✉ transcomp@uea.ac.uk

www.bcla.org

Competition Organiser *Dr Jean Boase-Beier*

Established 1983. Annual competition open to unpublished literary translations from all languages. Maximum submission: 25 pages.

PRIZES £350 (1st); £200 (2nd); £100 (3rd); plus publication for all winning entries in the Association's journal. Other entries may receive commendations.

The Duke of Westminster's Medal for Military Literature

Royal United Services Institute for Defence and Security Studies, Whitehall, London SW1A 2ET

☎020 7747 2602 Fax 020 7321 0943

www.rusi.org

Established in 1997, this annual award is sponsored by the Duke of Westminster and aims to mark a notable and original contribution to the study of international or national security, or the military profession. Work must be in English, by a living author, and have been published as a book, rather than an article, in the preceding or next six months of the closing date for entries.

2006 winner: *The Pursuit of Victory* Professor Roger Knight.

PRIZE Silver medal, £1000. Winning author is invited to give lecture at RUSI where the Duke of Westminster will present the Medal.

Edge Hill Prize for the Short Story

Dept. of English, Edge Hill University, St Helen's Road, Ormskirk L39 4QP

☎01695 584121 Fax 01695 579997

✉ coxa@edgehill.ac.uk

www.edgehill.ac.uk

Contact *A. Cox*

Annual award founded in 2007 following a one-day conference on the short story. Its aim is to reward high achievement in writing the short story and to promote the genre. Awarded to the author of a published short story collection from the UK or Ireland. Entries are submitted through publishers and must be published in the previous year. Final entry date: February 2008.

PRIZE £5000.

T.S. Eliot Prize

Truman State University Press, 100 East Normal Street, Kirksville, MO 63501, USA

☎001 660 785 7336 Fax 001 660 785 4480

✉ tsup@truman.edu

tsup.truman.edu

Contact *Nancy Rediger*

An annual award, established in 1997 in honour of native Missourian, T.S. Eliot, to publish and promote contemporary English-language poetry regardless of a poet's nationality, reputation, stage in career or publication history. Entry requirements: 60–100 pages of original poetry with $25 fee. Final entry date: 31 October. 2007 winner: Carol V. Davis *Into the Arms of Pushkin: Poems of St Petersburg*.

PRIZE $2000, plus publication.

The Encore Award

The Society of Authors, 84 Drayton Gardens, London SW10 9SB

☎020 7373 6642 Fax 020 7373 5768

✉ info@societyofauthors.org

www.societyofauthors.org

Established 1990. Awarded biennially for the best second published novel or novels of the year. Final entry date: 30 November 2008. Details from the **Society of Authors**. 2005 winner: Nadeem Aslam *Maps for Lost Lovers*.

PRIZE £10,000.

Envoi Poetry Competition

Ty Meirion, Glan yr afon,Tanygrisiau, Blaenau Ffestiniog LL41 3SU

☎01766 832112

Contact *Roger Elkin*

Run by *Envoi* poetry magazine. Competitions are featured regularly, with prizes of £300, plus three annual subscriptions to *Envoi*. Winning poems along with full adjudication report are published. Send s.a.e. to Competition Secretary at the address above.

Geoffrey Faber Memorial Prize

Faber & Faber Ltd, 3 Queen Square, London WC1N 3AU

☎020 7465 0045 Fax 020 7465 0034

Established 1963 as a memorial to the founder and first chairman of **Faber & Faber**, this prize is awarded in alternate years for the volume of verse and the volume of prose fiction published in the UK in the preceding two years, which is judged to be of greatest literary merit. Authors must be under 40 at the time of publication and citizens of the UK, Commonwealth, Republic of Ireland or South Africa. 2005 winner: David Mitchell *Cloud Atlas*.

PRIZE £1000.

The Alfred Fagon Award

The Royal Court Theatre, Sloane Square, London SW1W 8AS

www.talawatheatrecompany.co.uk/afa

First presented in 1997. An annual award, in memory of playwright Alfred Fagon, which is open to any playwright of Caribbean descent, resident in the UK, for the best new stage play in English, which need not have been produced (television and radio plays and film scripts not eligible).Two copies of the script (plus s.a.e. for return), together with a brief history of the play and c.v. (including author's Caribbean connection), should be sent to the address above by 31 August. 2006 winner: Lorna French.

AWARD £5000.

Eleanor Farjeon Award

✉ childrensbookcircle@hotmail.co.uk
www.childrensbookcircle.org.uk

This award, named in memory of the much-loved children's writer, is for distinguished services to children's books either in this country or overseas, and may be given to a librarian, teacher, publisher, bookseller, author, artist, reviewer, television producer, etc. or occasionally to an organisation. Nominations from members of the **Children's Book Circle**. 2006 winner: Wendy Cooling.

AWARD £750.

Fish Fiction Prizes

Fish Publishing, Durrus, Bantry, Co. Cork, Republic of Ireland

✉ info@fishpublishing.com
www.fishpublishing.com

Contact *Clem Cairns*

Offers several writing contests including the International Short Story Prize, an annual award, founded in 1994, which aims to discover, encourage and publish new literary talent. The best 15 stories are published in an anthology. Also the Historical Short Fiction Prize, run in conjunction with the Historical Novel Society, and the Fish-Knife Award run in conjunction with the **Crime Writers' Association**. Details of these and other contests can be found on the website.

Sir Banister Fletcher Award

Authors' Club, 40 Dover Street, London W1S 4NP

☎020 7408 5092 Fax 020 7409 0913

✉ stella@theauthorsclub.co.uk

Contact *Sarah Kane*

Founded in 1954, this award was created by the late Sir Banister Fletcher, former President of the **Authors' Club** and the Royal Institute of British Architects, and is presented for 'the most deserving book on architecture or the arts'.The Award is open to titles written by British authors or those resident in the UK and published under a British imprint. 2006 winner: Julian Spalding *The Art of Wonder*.

PRIZE £1000.

The John Florio Prize

See **The Translators Association Awards**

The Paul Foot Award

Private Eye, 6 Carlisle Street, London W1D 3BN

www.private-eye.co.uk

Contact *Ben Tisdall* (Midas PR ☎ 020 7584 7474)

Annual award, established in 2005 by *The Guardian* and *Private Eye* for campaigning journalism in memory of former contributor Paul Foot. Submissions can be made by individual journalists, teams of journalists or publications for work appearing between October 2006 and August 2007. Single pieces or entire campaigns are eligible. Final entry date: 12 September 2007. No broadcast material. 'Please do not send original material as no correspondence can be entered into.' 2006 winner: David Harrison.

AWARD £5000 with 5 runners-up receiving £1000.

The Forward Prizes for Poetry

Administrator: Colman Getty, 28 Windmill Street, London W1T 2JJ
☎020 7631 2666 Fax 020 7631 2699
✉ kate@colmangetty.co.uk
www.forwardartsfoundation.co.uk

Contact *Kate Wright-Morris*

Established 1992. Three awards: the Forward Prize for Best Collection, the Felix Dennis Prize for Best First Collection and the Forward Prize for Best Single Poem in memory of Michael Donaghy, which is not already part of an anthology or collection. All entries must be published in the UK or Republic of Ireland and submitted by poetry publishers (collections) or newspaper and magazine editors (single poems). Individual entries of poets' own work are not accepted. 2006 winners: Robin Robertson (best collection), Tishani Doshi (best first collection), Sean O'Brien (best single poem).

PRIZES £10,000 (best collection); £5000 (best first collection); £1000 (best single poem).

The Frogmore Poetry Prize

42 Morehall Avenue, Folkestone CT19 4EF
☎07751 251689
www.frogmorepress.co.uk

Contact *Jeremy Page*

Established 1987. Awarded annually and sponsored by the Frogmore Foundation. The winning poem, runners-up and short-listed entries are all published in the magazine. Previous winners: Bill Headdon, John Latham, Diane Brown, Tobias Hill, Mario Petrucci, Gina Wilson, Ross Cogan, Joan Benner, Ann Alexander, Gerald Watts, Katy Darby, David Angel, Howard Wright, Caroline Price, Julie-ann Rowell, Arlene Ang.

PRIZE The winner receives 200 guineas and a two-year subscription to the biannual literary magazine, *The Frogmore Papers*.

FT & Goldman Sachs Business Book of the Year Award

Financial Times, One Southwark Bridge, London SE1 9HL
☎020 7873 3000 Fax 020 7873 3072
✉ bookaward@ft.com
www.ft.com/bookaward

Contacts *Lizzie Allen*

Established in 2005 to identify the book that provides the most compelling and enjoyable insight into modern business issues, including management, finance and economics. Titles must be published for the first time in the English language, or in English translation, between 31 October 2006 and 1 November 2007. Submissions by a publisher or *bona fide* imprint which holds English language rights in the book. 2006 winner: James Kynge *China Shakes the World*.

AWARD £30,000 (winner); shortlisted authors receive £5000 each.

Galaxy British Book Awards

Publishing News, 7 John Street, London WC1N 2ES
☎0870 870 2345 Fax 0870 870 0385
✉ mailbox@publishingnews.co.uk
www.britishbookawards.com

Established 1988. Viewed by the book trade as the one to win, 'The Nibbies' are presented annually. The awards are made in various categories. Each winner receives the prestigious Nibbie and the awards are presented to those who have made the most impact in the book trade during the previous year. 2007 winners included: Richard Dawkins, John Grisham, Victoria Hislop, Ricky Gervais, Marian Keys, Ian Rankin. For further information contact: Merric Davidson, PO Box 60, Cranbrook TN17 2ZR (☎/Fax 01580 212041; nibbies@mdla.co.uk).

Martha Gellhorn Trust Prize

Crosscombe, Town's Lane, Loddiswell TQ7 4QY
☎01548 550344 Fax 01548 550344
✉ sandyandshirlee@tiscali.co.uk

Annual prize for journalism in honour of one of the twentieth century's greatest reporters. Open for journalism published in English, giving 'the view from the ground – a human story that penetrates the established version of events and illuminates an urgent issue buried by prevailing fashions of what makes news'. The subject matter can involve the UK or abroad. Six copies of each entry should be sent to the address above by 15 March 2008. Previous winners include: Hala Jaber, Michael Tierney, Ghaith Abdul-Ahad, Patrick Cockburn, Robert Fisk, Jeremy Harding, Geoffrey Lean.

PRIZE £5000.

The Gladstone History Book Prize

Royal Historical Society, University College London, Gower Street, London WC1E 6BT
☎020 7387 7532 Fax 020 7387 7532
✉ rhs.info@sas.ac.uk
www.rhs.ac.uk/prizes

Contact *Executive Secretary*

Established 1998. Annual award for the best new work on any historical subject which is not primarily related to British history, published in the UK in the preceding calendar year. The book must be the author's first (solely written) history book and be an original and scholarly work of historical research. Closing date: 31 December.
PRIZE £1000.

Glenfiddich Food & Drink Awards

c/o Wild Card PR, Brettenham House, 5 Savoy Street, London WC2E 7AE
www.glenfiddich.com/foodanddrink

Known as the 'Cooker Bookers' or the 'Oscars' of the gastronomic world, the awards aim to recognise excellence in writing, publishing and broadcasting on the subjects of food and drink. There were 13 category winners in 2007 from work published or broadcast in the UK and the Republic of Ireland. 2007 winners: Food Book: *Made in Italy Food & Stories* Giorgio Locatelli; Drink Book: *Wine Behind the Label* Philip Williamson and David Moore; Food Writer: Clarissa Hyman for work in the *Financial Times*; Cookery Writer: Elisabeth Luard for work in *The Oldie*; Drink/Bar Writer: Simon Difford *difford's-guide to Cocktails #5.4 Liquor & City Drinking*; Wine Writer: Jamie Goode *World of Fine Wine/Harpers*; Restaurant Critic: Terry Durack *The Independent on Sunday*: *Review*; Regional Writer: Alastair Gilmour for work in the *The Journal*, Newcastle; TV: *Heston Blumenthal: In Search of Perfection: Fish & Chips*, BBC2; Radio: *The Jungle*, BBC Radio 4; Photography: Jonathan Lovekin *Feasts*; Independent Spirit Award: Myrtle Allen; GQ/Glenfiddich Food & Drink Personality of the Year: Heston Blumenthal; Glenfiddich Trophy: Elisabeth Luard.

AWARD Overall winner (chosen from the category winners) £3000, plus the Glenfiddich Trophy (which is held for one year); category winners £1000 each, plus a special bottling of Glenfiddich Gran Reserva 21 Year Old Single Malt Scotch Whisky.

Golden Hearts Awards

See **Romance Writers of America** under *Professional Associations and Societies*

Golden PEN Award for Lifetime Distinguished Service to Literature

English PEN, 6–8 Amwell Street, London EC1R 1UQ
☎020 7713 0023 Fax 020 7837 7838
✉ enquiries@englishpen.org
www.englishpen.org

Awarded to a senior writer, with a distinguished body of work written over many years, who has made a significant and constructive impact on fellow writers, the reading public and the literary world. Nominations by members of English PEN only. Previous winners include: Harold Pinter, Doris Lessing, Michael Frayn, Nina Bawden. 2006 winner: Michael Holroyd.

The Phillip Good Memorial Prize

1 Blake Close, Bilton, Rugby CV22 7LJ
✉ jo.derrick@ntlworld.com
www.qwfmagazine.co.uk

Contact *Competition Secretary*

Established in 1997, the competition is run by Jo Derrick, former editor of *QWF Magazine*. The prize commemorates the memory of Phillip Good (her late husband) and is for short stories of less than 5000 words in any style or genre (except children's). Open entry. Entrants may request in-depth critique of their stories for an extra fee. For entry forms, send s.a.e. to the address above. Closing date: 31 December.
PRIZES (total) at least £525 and publication in a special anthology.

Gourmand World Cookbook Awards

Pintor Rosales 36, 8°A, 28008 Madrid, Spain
☎00 34 91 541 6768 Fax 00 34 91 541 6821
✉ icr@virtualsw.es
www.cookbookfair.com

Contact *Edouard Cointreau*

Founded in 1995 by Edouard Cointreau to reward those who 'cook with words'. The only world competition for food and wine books in all languages. Annual event. In 2004 there were 53 local or regional competitions worldwide, with the winners competing for the 'Best Book in the World' award.

Kate Greenaway Medal

See **CILIP: The Chartered Institute of Library and Information Professionals Kate Greenaway Medal**

The Griffin Poetry Prize

6610 Edwards Boulevard, Mississauga, Ontario,
Canada L5T 2V6
☎001 905 565 5993 Fax 001 905 564 3645
✉ info@griffinpoetryprize.com
www.griffinpoetryprize.com
Contact *Ruth Smith*, Manager

Annual award established in 2000 by Toronto-based entrepreneur, Scott Griffin, for books of poetry written in or translated into English. Trustees include Margaret Atwood and Michael Ondaatje. Submissions from publishers only.

PRIZES A total of C$100,000, divided into two categories: International and Canadian.

The Guardian Children's Fiction Award

The Guardian, 119 Farringdon Road, London
EC1R 3ER
☎020 7239 9694 Fax 020 7239 9933
Children's Book Editor *Julia Eccleshare*

Established 1967. Annual award for an outstanding work of fiction for children aged seven and over by a British or Commonwealth author, first published in the UK in the year of the award, excluding picture books. No application form necessary. 2006 winner: Philip Reeve *A Darkling Plain*.

AWARD £1500.

The Guardian First Book Award

The Guardian, 119 Farringdon Road, London
EC1R 3ER
☎020 7886 9317
Contact *Thea Skelton*

Established 1999. Annual award for first time authors published in English in the UK. All genres of writing eligible, apart from academic, guidebooks, children's, educational, manuals, reprints and TV, radio and film tie-ins. 2006 winner: Yiyun Li *A Thousand Years of Good Prayers*. All books must be published between January and December 2007 and have an ISDN number or equivalent. Submissions are only received direct from publishers, not from individual authors. Self-published work is not eligible.

AWARD £10,000, plus *Guardian/Observer* advertising package.

Guild of Food Writers Awards

255 Kent House Road, Beckenham BR3 1JQ
☎020 8659 0422
✉ awards@gfw.co.uk
www.gfw.co.uk
Contact *Jonathan Woods*

Established 1985. Annual awards in recognition of outstanding achievement in all areas in which food writers work and have influence. Entry is not restricted to members of the Guild. Entry form available from the address above. 2006 winners: Michael Smith Award for Work on British Food: *Best of British Fish* by Hattie Ellis; Jeremy Round Award for Best First Book: *Dough* by Richard Bertinet; Evelyn Rose Award for Cookery Journalist of the Year: Alex Mackay, for work in *Sainsbury's Magazine*; Food Book of the Year: *Culinary Pleasures* by Nicola Humble; Cookery Book of the Year: *The River Cottage Family Cookbook* by Hugh Fearnley-Whittingstall and Fizz Carr; Food Journalist of the Year: Fuchsia Dunlop, for work in the *Financial Times* and *Observer Food Monthly*; and Miriam Polunin Award for Work on Healthy Eating: *The Dinner Lady* by Jeanette Orrey.

Gwobr Llyfr y Flwyddyn

See **Academi Book of the Year Awards**

The Anthony Hecht Poetry Prize

The Waywiser Press, 9 Woodstock Road,
London N4 3ET
☎020 8374 5526 Fax 020 8374 5536
✉ waywiserpress@aol.com
www.waywiser-press.com/hechtprize.html
Contact *Philip Hoy*, Managing Editor

Established 2005. Annual prize awarded for an outstanding, unpublished, full collection of poems. Entrants must be at least 18 years of age and may not have published more than one previous collection. Postmark deadline for submissions is 1 December with the winner announced the following May. Detailed guidelines and entry forms available from July on the website or by sending an A4-sized s.a.e.

PRIZE £1750 and publication by Waywiser in the UK and USA.

Hellenic Foundation Prize

See **The Translators Association Awards**

Felicia Hemans Prize for Lyrical Poetry

University of Liverpool, PO Box 147,
Liverpool L69 7WZ
☎0151 794 2458 Fax 0151 794 2454
✉ wilderc@liv.ac.uk
Contact *The Sub-Dean, Faculty of Arts*

Established 1899. Annual award for published or unpublished verse. Open to past or present members and students of the University of

Liverpool. One poem per entrant only. Closing date 1 May.

PRIZE £30.

The Hessell-Tiltman Prize for History

English PEN, 6–8 Amwell Street, London EC1R 1UQ

☎020 7713 0023 Fax 020 7837 7838

✉ enquiries@englishpen.org

www.englishpen.org

Founded 2002. Awarded for a history book covering any period up to the end of the Second World War, written in English (including translations) and aimed at a wide audience. Submissions cannot be made as books are nominated by PEN Literary Foundation Patrons and members of PEN's Executive Committee. 2006 winner: Bryan Ward Perkins *The Fall of Rome and the End of Civilisation.*

PRIZE £3000.

Hidden Brook Press International Poetry Anthology Contests

109 Bayshore Road, RR#4, Brighton, Ontario, Canada K0K 1H0

☎001 613 475 2368

✉ writers@hiddenbrookpress.com

www.HiddenBrookPress.com

International poetry competitions: the Open Window Poetry Anthology Contest and Seeds International Poetry Anthology Contest. E-mail for details. (HBP is also a contract publisher and print broker.)

William Hill Sports Book of the Year

Greenside House, Station Road, Wood Green, London N22 7TP

☎020 8918 3731 Fax 020 8918 3728

✉ pressoffice@williamhill.co.uk

Contact *Graham Sharpe*

Established 1989. Annual award introduced by Graham Sharpe of bookmakers William Hill. Sponsored by William Hill and thus dubbed the 'Bookie' prize, it is the first, and only, Sports Book of the Year award. Final entry date: September. 2006 winner: Geoffrey C. Ward *Unforgivable Blackness.*

PRIZE (reviewed annually) £20,000 package including £16,000 cash, hand-bound copy, £2000 free bet. Runners-up prizes.

Calvin & Rose G. Hoffman Prize

King's School, Canterbury CT1 2ES

☎01227 595544

Contact *The Bursar*

Annual award for distinguished publication on Christopher Marlowe, established by the late Calvin Hoffman, author of *The Man Who was Shakespeare* (1955) as a memorial to himself and his wife. For unpublished works of at least 5000 words written in English for their scholarly contribution to the study of Christopher Marlowe and his relationship to William Shakespeare. Final entry date: 1 September each year.

David C. Horn Prize

See **The Yale Drama Series**

L. Ron Hubbard's Writers of the Future Contest

PO Box 218, East Grinstead RH19 4GH

Contest Administrator *Andrea Grant-Webb*

Established 1984 by L. Ron Hubbard to encourage new and amateur writers of science fiction and fantasy. Quarterly awards with an annual grand prize. Entrants must submit a short story of up to 10,000 words, or a novelette of fewer than 17,000 words, which must not have been published previously. The contest is open only to those who have not been published professionally. Previous winners: Roge Gregory, Malcolm Twigg, Tom Brennan, Alan Smale, Janet Barron. Send s.a.e. for entry form.

PRIZES £500 (1st); £375 (2nd); £250 (3rd) each quarter; Annual Grand Prize: £2500. All winners are awarded a trip to the annual L. Ron Hubbard Achievement Awards which include a series of professional writers' workshops, and are published in the *L. Ron Hubbard Presents Writers of the Future* anthology.

The Imison Award

The Society of Authors, 84 Drayton Gardens SW10 9SB

☎020 7373 6642 Fax 020 7373 5768

✉ jhodder@societyofauthors.org

www.societyofauthors.org

Contact *Jo Hodder*

Annual award established 'to perpetuate the memory of Richard Imison, to acknowledge the encouragement he gave to writers working in the medium of radio, and in memory of the support and friendship he invariably offered writers in general, and radio writers in particular'. Administered by the **Society of Authors** and generally sponsored by the **Peggy Ramsay Foundation**, the purpose is 'to encourage new talent and high standards in writing for radio by selecting the radio drama by a writer new to radio which, in the opinion of the judges, is the best of those submitted.' An adaptation for radio of a piece originally written for the stage, television or film is not eligible. Any radio drama first transmitted in the UK between 1 January and 31 December, by a writer or writers new to radio, is eligible, provided the work is an original piece for radio and it is the first dramatic work by the writer(s) that has been broadcast. Submission may be made by any party to the production in the form of three copies of both script and recording (non-returnable), accompanied by a nomination form and 250 word synopsis and CV. 2006 winner: Nazrin Choudhury's *Mixed Blood*.

PRIZE £1500.

The Independent Foreign Fiction Prize

c/o Literature Department, Arts Council England, 14 Great Peter Street, London SW1P 3NQ
☎020 7973 5204 Fax 020 7973 6983
✉ info.literature@artscouncil.org.uk
www.artscouncil.org.uk

Contact *Bethany King*

Awarded for translated fiction by living authors first published in Britain in the year preceding the award. 2006 winner: *Out Stealing Horses* by Per Petterson, translated by Anne Born.

Prize £10,000 shared equally between author and translator.

The International Dundee Book Prize

City of Discovery Campaign, 3 City Square, Dundee DD1 3BA
☎01382 434214 Fax 01382 434650
✉ book.prize@dundeecity.gov.uk
www.dundeebookprize.com

Contact *Karin Johnston*

Launched in 1996, this is a biennial award. Previous winners include Andrew Murray Scott for *Tumulus*, Claire-Marie Watson for *The Curewife* and Malcolm Archibald for *Whales for the Wizard*. Entry qualifications are detailed in the entry form. Launch date: April 2007. Final entry date: March 2008.

PRIZE £10,000, plus publication of novel.

The International IMPAC Dublin Literary Award

Dublin City Library & Archive, 138–144 Pearse Street, Dublin 2, Republic of Ireland
☎00 353 1 674 4802 Fax 00 353 1 674 4879
✉ literaryaward@dublincity.ie
www.impacdublinaward.ie

Established 1995. Sponsored by Dublin City Council and US-based productivity improvement firm, IMPAC, this prize is awarded for a work of fiction written and published in the English language or written in a language other than English and published in English translation. Initial nominations are made by municipal public libraries in major and capital cities worldwide, each library putting forward up to three books to the international panel of judges in Dublin. 2006 winner: Colm Toibin *The Master*.

PRIZE €100,000 (if the winning book is in English translation, the prize is shared €75,000 to the author and €25,000 to the translator).

International Student Playscript Competition

See **University of Hull** under *UK and Irish Writers' Courses*

Jelf Group First Novel Award

Guildford Book Festival, c/o Tourist Information Centre, 14 Tunsgate, Guildford GU1 3QT
☎01483 444334
✉ deputy@guildfordbookfestival.co.uk
www.guildfordbookfestival.co.uk

Contacts *Glenis Pycraft, Pamela Thomas*

Established in 1998 and sponsored by the Jelf Group, this annual award was originally to encourage local talent but now all writers in the UK are eligible. Submissions must be from agents or publishers with accompanying letter (proofs accepted). Books to be published between 1 November–31 October and shortlisted authors must be prepared to attend the presentation dinner. 2006 winner: Mike Stocks *White Man Falling*.

PRIZE £2500 (presented during the Festival).

Jerwood Aldeburgh First Collection Prize

The Poetry Trust, The Cut, 9 New Cut, Halesworth IP19 8BY
☎01986 835950
✉ info@thepoetrytrust.org
www.thepoetrytrust.org

Contact *Naomi Jaffa*
Funded by Jerwood Charitable Foundation, the prize is awarded to the author of what in the opinion of the judges is the best first full collection of poetry published in Great Britain and the Republic of Ireland in the preceding twelve months. The winner receives £3000 plus an invitation to read (fee paid) at the **Aldeburgh Poetry Festival** the following year. 2006/7 winner: Roger Moulson *Waiting for the Night Rowers.*

Jewish Quarterly Literary Prize
PO Box 37645, London NW7 1WB
☎020 8343 4675
www.jewishquarterly.org
Administrator *Pam Lewis*
Formerly the H.H. Wingate Prize. Annual award (for fiction or non-fiction) for a work that best stimulates an interest in and awareness of themes of Jewish interest. Books must have been published in the UK in the year of the award (written in English originally or in translation) by an author resident in Britain, the Commonwealth, Israel, Republic of Ireland or South Africa. 2006 winner: Imre Kertesz *Fatelessness* (fiction).
PRIZES £5000.

Samuel Johnson Prize for Non-Fiction
See **The BBCFour Samuel Johnson Prize for Non-Fiction**

Mary Vaughan Jones Award
Cyngor Llyfrau Cymru (Welsh Books Council), Castell Brychan, Aberystwyth SY23 2JB
☎01970 624151 Fax 01970 625385
✉ wbc.children@wbc.org.uk
www.wbc.org.uk
Contact *The Administrator*
Triennial award for distinguished services in the field of children's literature in Wales over a considerable period of time. 2006 winner: Mair Wynn Hughes.
AWARD Silver trophy.

Keats–Shelley Prize
Keats–Shelley Memorial Association, 117 Cheyne Walk, London SW10 0ES
☎020 7352 2180 Fax 020 7352 6705
✉ harrietcullenuk@yahoo.com
www.keats-shelley.com
Contact *Harriet Cullen*

Established 1998. Annual award to promote the study and appreciation of Keats and Shelley, especially in the universities, and of creative writing inspired by the younger Romantic poets. Two categories: essay and poem; open to all ages and nationalities. Recent winners: Martin McRitchie, Edmund Cusick (poems), Alison Pearce, David Taylor (essays).
PRIZE £3000 distributed between the winners of the two categories.

Kelpies Prize
Floris Books, 15 Harrison Gardens, Edinburgh EH11 1SH
☎0131 337 2372 Fax 0131 347 9919
✉ floris@florisbooks.co.uk
www.florisbooks.co.uk/kelpiesprize
Contact *Prize Administrator*
Established 2004. Annual prize to encourage and reward new Scottish writing for children. The prize is for an unpublished novel (40–60,000 words) for children aged 9–12, set wholly or mainly in Scotland. The author does not need to be Scottish. Application form, guidelines, terms and conditions are available on the website.
PRIZE £2000 and publication in Floris Books' Kelpies series.

The Petra Kenney Poetry Competition
PO Box 32, Filey YO14 9YG
✉ morgan@kenney.uk.net
www.petrapoetrycompetition.co.uk
Contact *Secretary*
Established 1995. Annual poetry award. Original, unpublished poems up to 80 lines on any theme. Closing date: 1 December. Entry fee: £3 per poem. Send s.a.e. for rules and entry form.
PRIZES £1000 (1st); £500 (2nd); £250 (3rd) plus inscribed Royal Brierley Crystal Vase; and three highly commended prizes of £125 each. New prizes for comic verse: £250 (1st) and Young Poets (14–18): £250 (1st); £125 (2nd).

Kent & Sussex Poetry Society Open Competition
13 Ruscombe Close, Southborough, Tunbridge Wells TN4 0SG
☎01892 543862
Chairman *Clive R. Eastwood*
Annual competition. Entry fee: £4 per poem, maximum 40 lines.
PRIZES £1350 (total).

Kiriyama Pacific Rim Book Prize

Pacific Rim Voices, 300 Third Street, Suite 822, San Francisco, CA 94107, USA

☎001 415 777 1628

✉ jeannine@kiriyamaprize.org

www.kiriyamaprize.org

Contact *Jeannine Stronach*, Prize Manager

Founded 1996 with the aim of promoting books that contribute to greater understanding and cooperation among the peoples and nations of the Pacific Rim and South Asia, this annual award takes its name from the Reverend Seiyu Kiriyama. Entry details may be obtained from the address above or from the website. 2007 winners: Greg Mortenson and David Oliver Relin *Three Cups of Tea: One Man's Mission to Promote Peace … One School at a Time*; Haruki Murakami *Blind Willow, Sleeping Woman* (fiction).

PRIZES $30,000, divided between both winners.

Kraszna-Krausz Book Awards

The Rectory, Ripley, Harrogate HG3 3AY

☎01423 772217

✉ awards@k-k.org.uk

www.k-k.org.uk

Coordinator *Margaret Brown*

Established 1985. Annual award to encourage and recognise oustanding achievements in the publishing and writing of books on the art, practice, history and technology of still photography and the moving image (film, television, video and related screen media). Books in English, distributed in the UK, are eligible. Entries must be submitted by publishers only.

Lakeland Book of the Year Awards

Cumbria Tourism, Windermere Road, Staveley LA8 9PL

☎01539 825052 Fax 01539 825076

✉ slindsay@cumbria tourism.org

www.golakes.co.uk

Contact *Sheila Lindsay*

Established in 1984 by local author and broad-caster Hunter Davies in conjunction with the Cumbria Tourist Board, the books entered can be about any aspect of life in the county of Cumbria, from local history books and walking guides to novels and poetry. The contest attracts entries from both new and established authors. Since the establishment of the awards they have grown in importance and are now attracting in the region of 60 entries annually, all competing for the Hunter Davies Prize for the Lakeland Book of the Year.

In addition to the Hunter Davies Prize there are currently five categories including Award for Guides, Walks and Places; Award for People and Social History; Award for Arts and Culture; Award for Heritage and Tradition; and the Best Illustrated Book. Closing date for entries is mid-March. The awards are presented at a charity luncheon in early June.

AWARDS £100 for each category together with a framed certificate. Overall winner of the Hunter Davies Prize for the Lakeland Book of the Year also receives a cheque for £100 and a framed certificate.

Lancashire County Library and Information Service Children's Book of the Year Award

Lancashire County Library Headquarters, County Hall, PO Box 61, Preston PR1 8RJ

☎01772 534751 Fax 01772 534880

✉ jacob.hope@lcl.lancscc.gov.uk

Award Coordinator *Jake Hope*

Established 1986. Annual award, presented in June for a work of original fiction suitable for 12–14-year-olds. The winner is chosen by 13–14-year-old secondary school pupils in Lancashire. Books must have been published between 1 September and 31 August in the previous year of the award and authors must be UK and Republic of Ireland residents. Final entry date: 1 September each year. 2006 winner: Anthony Horowtiz *Raven's Gate*.

PRIZE £1000, plus engraved glass decanter.

Lannan Literary Award

Lannan Foundation, 313 Read Street, Santa Fe, New Mexico 87501, USA

☎001 505 986 8160

www.lannan.org

Established 1989. Annual awards given to writers of exceptional poetry, fiction and non-fiction who have made a significant contribution to English-language literature, as well as emerging writers of distinctive literary merit who have demonstrated potential for outstanding future work. On occasion, the Foundation recognises a writer for lifetime achievement. Candidates for the awards and fellowships are recommended to the Foundation by a network of writers, literary scholars, publishers and editors. Applications or unsolicited nominations for the awards and fellowships are not accepted.

The Duncan Lawrie Dagger (in association with Crime Writers' Association)

PO Box 273, Boreham Wood WD6 2XA
✉ secretary@thecwa.co.uk
www.thecwa.co.uk

Contact *The Secretary*

Established 2006. Sponsored by Duncan Lawrie Bank. An annual award for the best crime fiction published during the year. Nominations from publishers only. Inaugural winner: Ann Cleeves *Raven Black.*

AWARD Dagger, plus cheque for £20,000.

The Duncan Lawrie International Dagger (in association with Crime Writers' Association)

PO Box 273, Boreham Wood WD6 2XA
✉ secretary@thecwa.co.uk
www.thecwa.co.uk

Contact *The Secretary*

Established 2006. Sponsored by Duncan Lawrie Bank. An annual award for the best foreign crime fiction translated into English during the year. Nominations from publishers only. Inaugural winner: Fred Vargas *The Three Evangelists.*

AWARD Dagger, plus cheque for £5000 to the author; £1000 to the translator.

Le Prince Maurice Prize

Mason Rose, 8a Bradbrook House, Studio Place, Knightsbridge, London SW1X 8EL
☎020 7235 3245 Fax 020 7235 3246
✉ comm@constancehotels.com
www.constancehotels.com

Contact *Claire Barrett*

Founded in 2003 and sponsored by one of Mauritius's five-star resorts, Le Prince Maurice. Annual award designed to celebrate the literary love story. Administered in both the UK and France, it is awarded alternately to an English-speaking and French-speaking writer. The aim is to strengthen the cultural links between Mauritius and Europe. Submissions are made by publishers only; closing date for next English award is September 2007. 2004 winner: Anne Donovan *Buddha Da.*

PRIZE Trophy, plus all-expenses-paid two-week 'writer's retreat' at Le Prince Maurice.

Legend Writing Award

39 Emmanuel Road, Hastings TN34 3LB
www.legendwritingaward.com

Contact *Legend Coordinator*

Established 2001. Annual award to encourage new fiction writers resident in the UK. The competition is for short stories of 2000 words maximum and there is no set theme. Closing date: 31 August. Entry fee: £5. Rules/entry form available from website or by sending s.a.e. to address above. The competition is organised and judged by Hastings Writers' Group.

PRIZES £500 (1st); £250 (2nd); £100 (3rd); plus three runners-up prizes of £50.

The Bernard Levin Award

Society of Indexers, Woodbourn Business Centre, 10 Jessell Street, Sheffield S9 3HY
☎0114 244 9561 Fax 0114 244 9563
✉ admin@indexers.org.uk
www.indexers.org.uk

Secretary *Judith Menes*

Established in 2000 to celebrate the late Bernard Levin, a journalist and author whose writings showed untiring and eloquent support for indexers and indexing. An occasional award for outstanding services to the Society of Indexers. Last awarded in 2005 to John Halliday.

The Library Association Awards

See **CILIP: The Chartered Institute of Library and Information Professionals** individual awards

The Astrid Lindgren Memorial Award for Literature (ALMA)

Swedish Arts Council, PO Box 27215, SE-102 53 Stockholm, Sweden
☎00 46 8 519 264 00 Fax 00 46 8 519 264 99
✉ literatureaward@alma.se
www.alma.se

Director *Anna Cokorilo*

Established 2002 by the Swedish government in memory of the children's author Astrid Lindgren. Administered by the Swedish Arts Council, it is an international award for children's and young people's literature given annually to one or more recipients, irrespective of language or nationality. Writing, illustrating and storytelling, as well as reading promotion activities may be awarded. Selected organisations worldwide are invited to submit nominations once a year; jury members may also contribute nominations. 2007 winner: Banco del Libro.

AWARD SEK 5 million (approx. €550,000)

John Llewellyn Rhys Prize

Booktrust, Book House, 45 East Hill, London SW18 2QZ
☎020 8516 2972 Fax 020 8516 2978

✉ tarryn@booktrust.org.uk
www.booktrust.org.uk
Contact *Tarryn McKay*
Established 1942. An annual young writer's award for a memorable work of any kind. Entrants must be 35 or under at the time of publication; books must have been published in the UK in the year of the award (the award runs a year behind; the next prize will be 2006). The author must be a citizen of the UK or the Commonwealth, writing in English. 2005 winner: Uzodinma Iweala *Beasts of No Nation*.
    PRIZE £5000 (1st); £500 for shortlisted entries.

The Elizabeth Longford Prize for Historical Biography

The Society of Authors, 84 Drayton Gardens, London SW10 9SB
☎020 7373 6642 Fax 020 7373 5768
✉ info@societyofauthors.org
www.societyofauthors.org

Established in 2003 in memory of Elizabeth Longford and sponsored by Flora Fraser and Peter Soros. Awarded annually for a historical biography published in the year preceding the prize. No unsolicited submissions. 2007 winner: Jessie Childs *Henry VIII's Last Victim – The Life and Times of Henry Howard, Earl of Surrey*.
    PRIZE £3000.

Longman–History Today Book of the Year Award

c/o History Today, 20 Old Compton Street, London W1D 4TW
☎020 7534 8000
www.historytoday.com
Contact *Peter Furtado*

Established 1993. Annual award set up as a joint initiative between the magazine *History Today* and the publisher Longman (**Pearson Education**) to mark the past links between the two organisations, to encourage new writers, and to promote a wider public understanding of, and enthusiasm for, the study and publication of history. Award for author's first or second book.
    PRIZE £2000 (see *History Today* from July 2006).

The Clarissa Luard Award

See **David Cohen Prize for Literature**

The Lulu Blooker Prize

✉ blookerprize@lulu.com
www.lulublookerprize.com

Established in 2006 by **Lulu.com**, the publish-on-demand website, the prize is the first to be devoted to 'blooks', bound and printed books based on either blogs or websites. Awarded in three categories: fiction, non-fiction and comic books. Entries are accepted from publishers or individual authors from any country but must be printed in English. E-books are not accepted. Full entry details on the website. 2007 winners: *My War: Killing Time in Iraq* Colby Buzzell (non-fiction/overall winner); *Monster Island: A Zombie Novel* David Wellington (non-fiction); *Mom's Cancer* Brian Fies (comic book).
    PRIZES $2,500 (category); $10,000 (overall winner).

Sir William Lyons Award

The Guild of Motoring Writers, 39 Beswick Avenue, Ensbury Park, Bournemouth BH10 4EY
☎01202 518808 Fax 01202 518808
✉ chris@whizzco.freeserve.co.uk
www.guildofmotoringwriters.co.uk
Contact *Patricia Lodge*

An annual competitive award, sponsored by Jaguar, to encourage young people in automotive journalism and to foster interests into motoring and the motor industry. Entrance by two essays and interview with Awards Committee. Applicants must be British, aged 17–23 and resident in UK. Final entry date: 1 October.

McColvin Medal

See **Besterman/McColvin Medal**

W.J.M. Mackenzie Book Prize

Political Studies Association, Dept. of Politics, University of Newcastle, Newcastle upon Tyne NE1 7RU
☎0191 222 8021 Fax 0191 222 3499
✉ psa@ncl.ac.uk
www.psa.ac.uk
PSA Executive Director *Jack Arthurs*

Established 1987. Annual award to best work of political science published in the UK during the previous year. Submissions from publishers only. Final entry date: 31 October. Prizes are judged in the year following publication and awarded the year after that. 2004 winner: Andrew Vincent *The Nature of Political Theory*.

McKitterick Prize

Society of Authors, 84 Drayton Gardens, London SW10 9SB
☎020 7373 6642 Fax 020 7373 5768
✉ info@societyofauthors.org

www.societyofauthors.org

Contact *Awards Secretary*

Annual award for a full-length novel in the English language, first published in the UK or unpublished. Open to writers over 40 who have not had any novel published other than the one submitted (excluding works for children). Closing date: 20 December. 2006 winner: Peter Pouncey *Rules for Old Men Waiting*.

PRIZE £4000.

Enid McLeod Prize

Franco-British Society, 2 Dovedale Studios, 465 Battersea Park Road, London SW11 4LR

☎020 7924 3511

www.francobritishsociety.org.uk

Executive Secretary *Kate Brayn*

Established 1982. Annual award to the author of the work of literature published in the UK which, in the opinion of the judges, has contributed most to Franco-British understanding. Any full-length work written in English by a citizen of the UK, Commonwealth, Republic of Ireland, Pakistan, Bangladesh and South Africa. No English translation of a book written originally in any other language will be considered. Nominations from publishers for books published between 1 January and 31 December of the year of the prize. Closing date: 31 December. 2005 winner: Maria Fairweather *Madame de Staël*

PRIZE Cheque.

Macmillan Prize for a Children's Picture Book Illustration

Macmillan Children's Books, 20 New Wharf Road, London N1 9RR

☎020 7014 6124 Fax 020 7014 6142

✉ d.pinner@macmillan.co.uk

www.panmacmillan.com

Contact *Dianne Pinner*, Macmillan Children's Books

Set up in order to stimulate new work from young illustrators in art schools, and to help them start their professional lives. Fiction or non-fiction. Macmillan have the option to publish any of the prize winners.

PRIZES £1000 (1st); £500 (2nd); £250 (3rd).

Macmillan Writer's Prize for Africa

Macmillan Education, 4 Between Towns Road, Oxford OX4 3PP

☎01865 405700 Fax 01865 405788

www.write4africa.com

Contacts *Victoria Tait, Tom Hardy*

Founded in 2001 to encourage and to recognise original writing for children and young people by African writers. Sponsored by Macmillan Publishers Ltd, which has publishing companies throughout sub-Saharan Africa. The prize is for previously unpublished works of fiction by African writers, and aims to promote and to celebrate story writing from all over the continent. Two main awards – for children's literature and teenage fiction – and an additional award dedicated to new, previously unpublished writers. See website for entry qualifications. 2006 winners: Glaydah Namukasa *Voice of a Dream* (Senior Award); Elizabeth-Irene Baitie *A Saint in Brown Sandals* (Junior); Ngozi Ifeyinwa Razak-Soyebi *The House that Kojo Built* (New Children's Writer).

PRIZES US$ 5000 each (Senior and Junior awards); US$3000 (New Children's Writer).

The Mail on Sunday Novel Competition

Postal box address may changes annually (see below)

Annual award established 1983. Judges look for a story/character that springs to life in the 'tantalising opening 50–150 words of a novel'. Details of the competition, including the postal box address, are published in *The Mail on Sunday* in July/August. 2006 winner: Jac Jones.

AWARDS £400 book tokens and a writing course at the **Arvon Foundation** (1st); £300 tokens (2nd); £200 tokens (3rd); three further prizes of £150 tokens each.

The Man Asian Literary Prize

23A Success Commercial Building, 245–251 Hennessy Road, Hong Kong

☎00 852 2877 8444 Fax 00 852 2598 6604

✉ info@manasianliteraryprize.org

www.manasianliteraryprize.org

Chairman *Peter Gordon*

Initiated by the Man Group and the Hong Kong Literary Festival in 2007. An annual award which aims to recognise the best of new Asian literature and to bring it to the attention of the world literary community. Open to a single work of Asian fiction in English (but unpublished in English) of no less than 30,000 words by an Asian author residing in an Asian country or territory. Final entry date: end March.

The Man Booker International Prize

Colman Getty, 28 Windmill Street, London
W1T 2JJ
☎020 7631 2666 Fax 020 7631 2699
✉ info@colmangetty.co.uk
www.manbookerinternational.com

Established in 2004 to complement **The Man Booker Prize for Fiction** by recognising one writer's achievement in literature and their significant influence on writers and readers worldwide. Sponsored by the Man Group, this biennial award is given to a living author who has published fiction either originally in English or whose work is generally available in translation into the English language. Submissions for the prize are not invited. Where the winning author's work has been translated into English an additional prize of £15,000 is awarded to the translator. The winning author chooses who the translator's prize should go to and whether it is to be awarded to one translator or divided between several. 2007 winner: Chinua Achebe
PRIZE £60,000.

The Man Booker Prize for Fiction

Colman Getty, 28 Windmill Street, London
W1T 4JE
☎020 7631 2666 Fax 020 7631 2699
✉ info@colmangetty.co.uk
www.themanbookerprize.com

Contact *Lois Tucker* (Submissions)

The Booker Prize for Fiction was originally set up by Booker plc in 1968 to reward merit, raise the stature of the author in the eyes of the public and encourage an interest in contemporary fiction. In April 2002 it was announced that the Man Group had been chosen by the Booker Prize Foundation as the new sponsor of the Booker Prize. The sponsorship is due to run until 2011. United Kingdom publishers may enter up to two full-length novels, with scheduled publication dates between 1 October 2006 and 30 September 2007. In addition, any title by an author who has previously won the Booker or Man Booker Prize and any title by an author who has been shortlisted in the last ten years may be submitted. 2006 winner: Kiran Desai *The Inheritance of Loss*.

PRIZE The winner receives £50,000. The six shortlisted authors each receive £2500.

Marsh Award for Children's Literature in Translation

National Centre for Research in Children's Literature, Roehampton University, Froebel College, Roehampton Lane, London SW15 5PJ
☎020 8392 3008 Fax 020 8392 3819
✉ g.lathey@roehampton.ac.uk

Contact *Dr Gillian Lathey*

Established 1995 and sponsored by the Marsh Christian Trust, the award aims to encourage translation of foreign children's books into English. It is a biennial award (next award: 2009), open to British translators of books for 4–16-year-olds, published in the UK by a British publisher. Any category will be considered with the exception of encyclopedias and reference books. No electronic books. 2007 winner: Anthea Bell for her translation of *The Flowing Queen* by Kai Meyer.
PRIZE £1000.

Marsh Biography Award

The English-Speaking Union, Dartmouth House, 37 Charles Street, London W1J 5ED
☎020 7529 1563 Fax 020 7495 6108
✉ katie_brock@esu.org
www.esu.org

Contact *Katie Brock*

A biennial award for the most significant biography published over a two-year period by a British publisher. Next award October 2007. 2005 winner: John Guy *My Heart is My Own: The Life of Mary Queen of Scots*.
AWARD Membership of the ESU and £4000, plus a silver trophy presented at a gala dinner.

MCA Management Writing Awards

49 Whitehall, London SW1A 1BX
☎020 7321 3990 Fax 020 7321 3991
✉ natalia.kay@mca.org.uk
www.mca.org.uk

Contact *Natalia Kay*

Annual awards, established in 2004 by the Management Consultancies Association in association with *Management Today* magazine in order to recognise and reward excellence in management writing. Books and articles submitted must have been first published in the UK in the previous 12 months. Entries can be accepted from journalists, authors or their publishers. Full entry details on the website. 2005 winners: 'The organic milk of human kindness overflows at Pret' Sathnam Sanghera, *Financial Times* (Best Management Article); *Growth Gamble* Andrew

Campbell and Robert Park (Best Management Book); Stefan Stern (Best Management Interview); Lisa Miles (Best Young Writer).

Colin Mears Award

See **CILIP: The Chartered Institute of Library and Information Professionals Kate Greenaway Medal**

Medical Book Awards

The Society of Authors, 84 Drayton Gardens, London SW10 9SB
☎020 7373 6642 Fax 020 7373 5768
✉ info@society of authors.org
www.societyofauthors.org

Contact *Secretary, Medical Writers Group*

Annual awards sponsored by the Royal Society of Medicine. Nine categories for medical textbooks published in the twelve months preceding the deadline. Contact the **Society of Authors** for entry details. Closing date: 20 April.
PRIZES £6500 (total).

The Mercedes-Benz Award for the Montagu of Beaulieu Trophy

Guild of Motoring Writers, 39 Beswick Avenue, Ensbury Park, Bournemouth BH10 4EY
☎01202 518808 Fax 01202 518808
✉ chris@whizzco.freeserve.co.uk
www.guildofmotoringwriters.co.uk

Contact *Patricia Lodge*

First presented by Lord Montagu on the occasion of the opening of the National Motor Museum at Beaulieu in 1972. Awarded annually to a member of the **Guild of Motoring Writers** who, in the opinion of the nominated jury, has made the greatest contribution to recording in the English language the history of motoring or motor cycling in a published book or article, film, television or radio script, or research manuscript available to the public. Cash PRIZE sponsored by Mercedes-Benz UK.

Mere Literary Festival Open Competition

'Lawrences', Old Hollow, Mere BA12 6EG
☎01747 860475
www.merewilts.org.uk

Contact *Mrs Adrienne Howell* (Events Organiser)

Annual open competition which alternates between short stories and poetry. The winners are announced at the **Mere Literary Festival** during the second week of October. The 2008 competition is for short fiction. Closing date for

entries: July. For further details, including entry fees and form, access the website or contact the address above from 1 March with s.a.e. Cash PRIZES.

Meyer-Whitworth Award

Playwrights' Studio Scotland, CCA, 350 Sauchiehall Street, Glasgow G2 3JD
☎0141 332 4403
✉ info@playwrightsstudio.co.uk
www.playwrightsstudio.co.uk

Contact *Claire Burkitt*

This annual award is intended to help further the careers of UK playwrights who are not yet established, and to draw contemporary theatre writers to the public's attention. Nominations are made by directors of professional theatre companies. Plays must have been written in the English language and produced professionally in the UK during the past 12 months. Candidates will have had no more than two of their plays professionally produced. No writer who has won the award previously may re-apply and no play that has been submitted previously for the award is eligible. Apply for further details and application form.
AWARD £10,000.

MIND Book of the Year

Granta House, 15–19 Broadway, London E15 4BQ
☎020 8215 2301 Fax 020 8215 2269
✉ j.bird@mind.org.uk
www.mind.org.uk

Established 1981. Annual award, in memory of Sir Allen Lane, for the author of a book published in the current year (fiction or non-fiction), which furthers public understanding of mental health problems. 2007 winner: Michele Hanson *Living With Mother: Right to the Very End*.

The Mitchell Prize for Art History/ The Eric Mitchell Prize

c/o The Burlington Magazine, 14–16 Duke's Road, London WC1H 9SZ
☎020 7388 8157 Fax 020 7388 1230
✉ annette.bradshaw@burlington.org.uk

Chairman *Caroline Elam*
Contact *Sara Heaton*

The Mitchell Prize is awarded for a book which has made an outstanding and original contribution to the understanding of the visual arts, and The Eric Mitchell Prize is awarded for the best exhibition catalogue. Both must be on western art, written in English and published in the previous two years. Nominations should be submitted by publishers before the end of April. 2004/5 winners: Mark P. McDonald *The Print Collection of Ferdinand Columbus* (The Mitchell Prize); Elena Phipps, Johanna Hecht, Christina Esteras Martin *The Colonial Andes: Tapestry & Silverware 1530–1830*, The Metropolitan Museum of Art, New York in association with Yale University Press 2004 (The Eric Mitchell Prize).

PRIZES $10,000 each.

Momaya Press Short Story Writing Competition

Momaya Press, Flat 1, 189a Balham High Road, Rear Building, London SW12 9BE
☎020 8673 9616
✉ infouk@momayapress.com
www.momayapress.com

Contact *Monisha Saldanha*

Established 2004. Annual short story competition sponsored by Momaya Press. Open to writers in the English language worldwide. Entries, which should not have been published previously, can be in any style and format and on any subject; 2500 words maximum. Entry fee: £7; final entry date: 30 April 2008. Submissions by post or via entry form on the website.

PRIZES £110 (1st); £60 (2nd); £30 (3rd); all winners are published in the *Momaya Annual Review*.

Scott Moncrieff Prize

See **The Translators Association Awards**

The Oscar Moore Screenwriting Prize

The prize is currently under review.

Nasen & TES Special Educational Needs Book Awards

Nasen House, 4–5 Amber Business Village, Amber Close, Amington, Tamworth B77 4RP
☎01827 311 500 Fax 01827 313 005
✉ welcome@nasen.org.uk
www.nasen.org.uk

Organised by the Nasen and the *Times Educational Supplement*. Five awards: The Children's Book Award, for the book that most successfully provides a positive image of children with special educational needs; The Academic Book Award celebrates the work of authors and editors who have made an outstanding contribution to the theory and practice of special education; The Books for Teaching and Learning

Award is presented for curriculum materials for pupils or teachers in early years, primary or secondary phases; the Inclusive Resource for Primary Classrooms Award is given to the educational resource considered to be the best tool to support and promote inclusive practice in primary classrooms; and the Inclusive Resource for Secondary Classrooms Award. Deadline: 21 June each year. Eligibility: books must have been published in the UK within the year preceding the awards.

PRIZE £500 each category.

National Poetry Anthology

United Press, Admail 3735, London EC1B 1JB
☎0870 240 6190 Fax 0870 240 6191
www.unitedpress.co.uk

Contact *Julie Embury*

Free-to-enter annual poetry competition. Organisers United Press allow up to three poems (20 lines and 160 words maximum each) by annual closing date of 30 June. They select around 250 regional winners in the UK. These receive a free copy of the annual book, *The National Poetry Anthology* and vote for the overall winner who receives £1000 and a trophy to keep for life.

National Poetry Competition

The Poetry Society, 22 Betterton Street, London WC2H 9BX
☎020 7420 9895 Fax 020 7240 4818
✉ marketing@poetrysociety.org.uk
www.poetrysociety.org.uk

Contact *Competition Organiser (WH)*

One of Britain's major open poetry competitions. Closing date: 31 October. Poems on any theme, up to 40 lines. For rules and entry form send s.a.e. to the competition organiser at the address above or enter the competition via the website.

PRIZES £5000 (1st); £1000 (2nd); £500 (3rd); plus 10 commendations of £50.

The National Short Story Prize

Room 316, BBC Henry Wood House, 3–6 Langham Place, London W1B 3DF
www.bbc.co.uk/radio4

Launched at the 2005 Edinburgh International Book Festival, this annual short story award – the largest for a single story – is funded by NESTA (the National Endowment for Science, Technology and the Arts) and supported by BBC Radio 4 and *Prospect* magazine. The award, which is open to UK nationals or residents, aged

18 or over, is for stories of no more than 8000 words. Entrants must have a prior record of publication in creative writing; only two stories (written in English) will be accepted per author. Full entry details from the address above or via the website. 2007 winner: Julian Gough *The Orphan & The Mob.*

PRIZES £15,000 (overall); £3000 (runner up).

Nestlé Children's Book Prize

Booktrust, Book House, 45 East Hill, London SW18 2QZ
☎020 8516 2986 Fax 020 8516 2978
✉ hannah@booktrust.org.uk
www.booktrusted.com

Contact *Hannah Rutland*

Established in 1985 to encourage high standards and stimulate interest in books for children, this prize is given for a children's book (fiction or poetry), written in English by a citizen of the UK or an author resident in the UK, and published in the UK in the year ending 30 September. There are three age-group categories: 5 and under, 6–8 and 9–11. Uniquely, the shortlist for each age category is judged by classes of schoolchildren, who enter a competition to win a chance to be Young Judges. 50 classes from each age category judge the books, deciding who gets Gold, Silver and Bronze. The class projects entered for the judging process are then judged to see which classes will come to London for the prize presentation. 2006 Gold Award winners: Cressida Cowell and Neal Layton *That Rabbit Belongs to Emily Brown* (5 and under); Daren King and illustrator David Roberts *Mouse Noses on Toast* (6–8); Julia Golding *The Diamond of Drury Lane* (9–11).

PRIZES in each category: £2500 (gold); £1500 (silver); £500 (bronze).

The New Writer Prose & Poetry Prizes

The New Writer, PO Box 60, Cranbrook TN17 2ZR
☎01580 212626 Fax 01580 212041
✉ admin@thenewwriter.com
www.thenewwriter.com

Contact *Merric Davidson*

Established 1997. Annual award. Open to all poets writing in the English language for an original, previously unpublished poem or collection of six to ten poems. Also open to writers of short stories and novellas/serials, features, articles, essays and interviews. Final entry date:

30 November. Full guidelines on the website. Previous winners: Mario Petrucci, Ros Barber, Celia de Fréine, Andrew McGuinness, Katy Darby, David Grubb.

PRIZES (total) £2000, plus publication in annual collection published by *The New Writer.*

New Writing Ventures

c/o Booktrust, Book House, 45 East Hill, London SW18 2QZ
☎020 8516 2972 Fax 020 8516 2978
✉ tarryn@booktrust.org.uk
www.booktrust.org.uk
www.newwritingpartnership.org.uk

Contact *Tarryn McKay*

Established in 2005 by The New Writing Partnership in association with Arts Council England, and administered by Booktrust, this annual award is aimed at emerging writers of adult fiction, non-fiction and poetry, written in English. Open only to unpublished writers who are resident in the UK. Final entry date to be confirmed.

PRIZES £5000 for each category

'The Nibbies'

See **Galaxy British Book Awards**

Nielsen Gold & Platinum Book Awards

Nielsen BookScan, 3rd Floor, Midas House, 62 Goldsworth Road, Woking GU21 6LQ
☎01483 712222 Fax 01483 712220
✉ gold&platinumawards@nielsenbookscan.co.uk
www.nielsenbookscan.co.uk

Contact *Mo Siewcharran*

Established in 2000 to award actual consumer purchases of a title through UK bookshops. Awarded to any title, in all its editions, that sells more than 500,000 copies (Gold) or one million copies (Platinum) over a period of five consecutive years.

AWARDS Commemorative plaque issued by the publisher to the author.

Nobel Prize

The Nobel Foundation, PO Box 5232, 102 45 Stockholm, Sweden
☎00 46 8 663 0920 Fax 00 46 8 660 3847
www.nobel.se

Contact *Information Section*

Awarded yearly for outstanding achievement in physics, chemistry, physiology or medicine, literature and peace. Founded by Alfred Nobel, a chemist who proved his creative ability by inventing dynamite. In general, individuals cannot nominate someone for a Nobel Prize.The rules vary from prize to prize but the following are eligible to do so for Literature: members of the Swedish Academy and of other academies, institutions and societies similar to it in constitution and purpose; professors of literature and of linguistics at universities or colleges; Nobel Laureates in Literature; presidents of authors' organisations which are representative of the literary production in their respective countries. British winners of the literature prize, first granted in 1901, include Rudyard Kipling, John Galsworthy and Winston Churchill. Winners since 1996:Wislawa Szymborska (Poland); Dario Fo (Italy);José Saramago (Portugal);Günter Grass (Germany); Gao Xingjian (France);V.S. Naipaul (UK); Imre Kertész (Hungary); J.M. Coetzee (South Africa); Elfriede Jelinek (Austria); Harold Pinter (UK). Nobel Laureate in Literature 2006: Orhan Pamuk (Turkey).

The Noma Award for Publishing Africa

PO Box 128,Witney OX8 5XU
☎01993 775235 Fax 01993 709265
✉ maryljay@aol.com
www.nomaaward.org

Contact *Mary Jay*, Secretary to the Managing Committee

Established 1979.Annual award, founded by the late Shoichi Noma, President of Kodansha Ltd, Tokyo. The award is for an outstanding book, published in Africa by an African writer, in three categories: scholarly and academic; literature and creative writing; children's books. Entries, by publishers only, by 31 March for a title published in the previous year. Maximum number of three entries. Previous winners: Hamdi Sakkut *The Arabic Novel: Bibliography and Critical Introduction 1865–1995*; Elinor Sisulu *Walter and Albertina Sisulu – In Our Lifetime*;Were Liking *La memoire amputee*; Lebogang Mashile *In a Ribbon of Rhythm*.
PRIZE US$10,000 and presentation plaque.

C.B. Oldman Prize

Special Libraries & Archives, University of Aberdeen, King's College, Aberdeen AB24 3SW
☎01224 274266 Fax 01224 273891
✉ r.turbet@abdn.ac.uk

Contact *Richard Turbet*

Established 1989 by the International Association of Music Libraries, UK & Ireland Branch. Annual award for best book of music bibliography, librarianship or reference published the year before last (i.e. books published in 2004 considered for the 2006 prize). Previous winners: Pamela Thompson, Malcolm Lewis, Andrew Ashbee, Michael Talbot, Donald Clarke, John Parkinson, John Wagstaff, Stanley Sadie, William Waterhouse, Richard Turbet, John Gillaspie, David Fallows, Arthur Searle, Graham Johnson, Michael Twyman, David Wyn Jones.
PRIZE £200.

Ondaatje Prize

See **The Royal Society of Literature Ondaatje Prize**

Open Window Poetry Anthology Contest

See **Hidden Brook Press International Poetry Anthology Contests**

Orange Broadband Prize for Fiction/Orange Broadband Award for New Writers

Booktrust, 45 East Hill, London SW18 2QZ
☎020 8516 2972 Fax 020 8516 2978
✉ tarryn@booktrust.org.uk
www.orangeprize.co.uk

Contact *Tarryn McKay*

Established 1996. Annual award founded by a group of senior women in publishing to 'create the opportunity for more women to be rewarded for their work and to be better known by the reading public'. Awarded for a full-length novel written in English by a woman of any nationality, and published in the UK between 1 April and 31 March of the following year. 2007 winner: Chimamanda Ngozi Adichie *Half of a Yellow Sun*.

PRIZE £30,000 and a work of art (a limited edition bronze figurine known as 'The Bessie' in acknowledgement of anonymous prize endowment). Established 2005, the **Orange Broadband Award for New Writers** is open to all first works of fiction, written by women of any age or nationality, published in the UK between 1 April and 31 March (short story collections and novellas also eligible). 2007 winner: Karen Connelly *The Lizard Cage*.

The Orwell Prize

Blackwell Publishing, 9600 Garsington Road, Oxford OX4 2DQ
☎01865 476255 Fax 01865 471255
✉ lucie.crowther@oxon.blackwellpublishing. com

www.blackwellpublishing.com/poqu

Contact *Lucie Crowther*

Jointly established in 1993 by the George Orwell Memorial Fund and *Political Quarterly* to encourage and reward writing in the spirit of Orwell's 'What I have most wanted to do ... is to make political writing into an art'. Two categories: book or pamphlet; sustained journalism, reporting, comment or blogs (on a theme) in broadcast, online, newspaper, periodicals, features or columns. Submissions by editors, publishers or authors. 2005 winners (for work published in 2004): Delia Jarrett-Macauley *Moses, Citizen and Me* (book); Timothy Garton Ash (journalism).

PRIZES £1000 for each category.

The Wilfred Owen Award for Poetry

21 Culverden Avenue, Tunbridge Wells TN4 9RE
☎01892 532712 Fax 01892 532712
✉ mmccrane@ukonline.co.uk
www.1914-18.co.uk/owen

Contact *Mrs Meg Crane*

Established in 1988 by the **Wilfred Owen Association**. Given to a poet whose poetry reflects the spirit of Owen's work in its thinking, expression and inspiration. Applications are not sought; the decision is made by the Association's committee. Previous winners: Seamus Heaney, Christopher Logue, Michael Longley, Harold Pinter, Tony Harrison.

AWARD A silver and gunmetal work of art, suitably decorated and engraved.

OWPG Awards for Excellence

Outdoor Writers & Photographers Guild, PO Box 520, Bamber Bridge, Preston PR5 8LF
☎01772 321243 Fax 0870 137 8888
✉ sec@owpg.org.uk
www.owpg.org.uk

Secretary *Terry Marsh*

Established 1980. Annual awards by the **Outdoor Writers & Photographers Guild** to raise the standard of outdoor writing, journalism, broadcasting and photography. Categories include guidebook, outdoor book, outdoor feature, travel feature, words and pictures, photography. Open to OWPG members only. Final entry date: June.

The Oxford Weidenfeld Translation Prize

St Anne's College, Oxford OX2 6HS

☎01865 274820 Fax 01865 274899
✉ sandra.madley@st-annes.ox.ac.uk
www.stannes.ox.ac.uk/about/translationprize.html

Contact *The Fellows' Secretary*

Established in 1996 by publisher Lord Weidenfeld to encourage good translation into English. Annual award to the translator(s) of a work of fiction, poetry or drama written in any living European language. Translations must have been published in the previous calendar year. Submissions from publishers only.

PRIZE £2000.

PEN Awards

See **J.R. Ackerley Prize**; **Golden PEN Award for Lifetime Distinguished Service to Literature**; **The Hessell-Tiltman Prize for History**

Samuel Pepys Award

Samuel Pepys Award Trust, Montreal House, Winson, Cirencester GL7 5EL
☎01285 740331

Contact *Jolyon Dromgoole, MA (Oxon), FRSA*

Established 2003. Biennial award (closing date: May 2009) given by the Samuel Pepys Award Trust for a book that makes the greatest contribution to the understanding of Samuel Pepys, his times or his contemporaries. 2005 winner: Frances Harris *The Transformations of Love*.

AWARD £2000, plus commemorative medal.

Peterloo Poets Open Poetry Competition

The Old Chapel, Sand Lane, Calstock PL18 9QX
☎01822 833473
✉ publisher@peterloopoets.com
www.peterloopoets.com

Contact *Harry Chambers*

Established 1986. Annual competition for unpublished English language poems of not more than 40 lines. Final entry date: 1 March. Send s.a.e. for rules and entry form. Previous winners: Susan Utting, David Craig, Rodney Pybus, Debjani Chatterjee, Donald Atkinson, Romesh Gunesekera, Anna Crowe, Carol Ann Duffy, Mimi Khalvati, John Lyons, M.R. Peacocke, Alison Pryde, John Weston, Maureen Wilkinson, Chris Woods, Judy Gahagan, Carol Rumens, John Godfrey.

PRIZES £4100 (total): £1500 (1st); £1000 (2nd); £500 (3rd); £100 (4th); plus 10 prizes of £50; 15–19 age group: 5 prizes of £100.

Ben Pimlott Prize for Political Writing

Fabian Society, 11 Dartmouth Street, London
SW1H 9BN
☎020 7227 4900 Fax 020 7976 7153
www.fabians.org.uk
www.guardian.co.uk
Contact *Claire Willgress* (Office Manager)

Founded 2005. Annual award in memory of Ben Pimlott, political writer, regular contributor to *Guardian Review*, and a major intellectual force in the Fabian Society. The aim of the prize is to encourage young/new writers and the political essay as a literary form. The topic for the award is announced each January. The 2006 theme was 'Who do you think you are? Can history help us to define British identity today, or is it part of the problem?' Open to all. Final entry date: mid-March. Inaugural winner: Mark Hayhurst on Aneurin Bevan.

AWARD £3000, plus publication in *Guardian Review* and on the Fabian Society website.

Poetry Business Competition

The Studio, Byram Arcade, Westgate,
Huddersfield HD1 1ND
☎01484 434840 Fax 01484 426566
✉ edit@poetrybusiness.co.uk
www.poetrybusiness.co.uk
Contact *The Competition Administrator*

Established 1986. Annual award which aims to discover and publish new writers. Entrants should submit a short manuscript of poems. Winners will have their work published by the **Poetry Business** under the Smith/Doorstop imprint. Final entry date: end of October. Contact for conditions of entry. Previous winners include: Pauline Stainer, Michael Laskey, Mimi Khalvati, David Morley, Moniza Alvi, Selima Hill, Catherine Smith, Daljit Nagra.

PRIZES Publication of full collection; runners-up have pamphlets; 20 complimentary copies. Also cash prize (£1000) to be shared equally between all winners.

The Poetry Society's National Poetry Competition
See **National Poetry Competition**

The Portico Prize

The Portico Library, 57 Mosley Street,
Manchester M2 3HY
☎0161 236 6785 Fax 0161 236 6803
✉ librarian@theportico.org.uk
www.theportico.org.uk

Contact *Miss Emma Marigliano*

Established 1985. Administered by the Portico Library in Manchester. Biennial award for a work of fiction or non-fiction published between the two closing dates. Set wholly or mainly in the North West of England, including Cumbria and the High Peak District of Derbyshire. Previous winners include: Anthony Burgess *Any Old Iron*; Jenny Uglow *Elizabeth Gaskell: A Habit of Stories*. 2006 winner: Andrew Biswell *The Real Life of Anthony Burgess*.

PRIZE £3000.

The Dennis Potter Screenwriting Award

BBC Broadcasting House, Whiteladies Road,
Bristol BS8 2LR
☎0117 974 7586

Contact *Jeremy Howe*, Executive Producer,
Drama

Annual award established in 1995 in memory of the late television playwright to 'nurture and encourage the work of new writers of talent and personal vision'. Submissions should be made through a BBC TV drama producer or an independent production company. 2006 winner: Russell T. Davies.

Practical Art Book of the Year

PO Box 3, Huntingdon PE28 0QX
☎01832 710201 Fax 01832 710488
✉ award@acaward.com
www.acaward.com
Contact *Henry Malt*

Jointly sponsored by Artists' Choice book club and *Leisure Painter* and *The Artist* magazines. A short list is drawn up by the editors and the winner voted by readers. Shortlist will be announced in June and the winner in November.

The Premio Valle Inclán
See **The Translators Association Awards**

V.S. Pritchett Memorial Prize

The Royal Society of Literature, Somerset House, Strand, London WC2R 1LA
☎020 7845 4676 Fax 020 7845 4679
✉ info@rslit.org
www.rslit.org

Established 1999. Awarded for a previously unpublished short story of between 2000 and 5000 words. For entry forms, please contact the Secretary from 15 November onwards.

Closing date: 31 February. Open to UK and Irish writers.
PRIZE £1000.

The Projection Box Essay Awards for Research into the Projected and Moving Image

12 High Street, Hastings TN34 3EY
☎01424 204144 Fax 01424 204144
✉ admin@pbawards.co.uk
www.pbawards.co.uk

Contact *Mo Heard*

Founded 2007 by small independent publishers, The Projection Box. Annual open competition to encourage new research and thinking into any historical, artistic or technical aspect of projected and moving images up to 1915. The prize is for an essay in English, not previously published, of between 5000 and 8000 words (including notes). Further information available on the website.

PRIZE £250 plus publication in *Early Popular Visual Culture*.

Pulitzer Prizes

The Pulitzer Prize Board, 709 Journalism Building, Columbia University, 2950 Broadway, New York, NY 10027, USA
☎001 212 854 3841 Fax 001 212 854 3342
✉ pulitzer@www.pulitzer.org
www.pulitzer.org

Awards for journalism in US newspapers, and for published literature, drama and music by American nationals. 2007 winners include: Cormac McCarthy *The Road* (fiction); Debby Applegate *The Most Famous Man in America: The Biography of Henry Ward Beecher* (biography); *The Wall Street Journal* (public service).

The Red House Children's Book Award

The Federation of Children's Book Groups, The Old Malt House, Aldbourne SN8 2DW
☎01672 540629 Fax 01672 541280
✉ marianneadey@aol.com
www.redhousechildrensbookaward.co.uk

Coordinator *Marianne Adey*

Established 1980. Awarded annually for best book of fiction suitable for children. Unique in that it is judged by the children themselves. 2006 winner: Rick Riordan *Percy Jackson and the Olympians: Lightning Thief*.

AWARD Portfolio of letters, drawings and comments from the children who took part in the judging. Silver bowls and trophy.

Trevor Reese Memorial Prize

Institute of Commonwealth Studies, School of Advanced Studies, University of London, 28 Russell Square, London WC1B 5DS
☎020 7862 8844 Fax 020 7862 8820
commonwealth.sas.ac.uk/reese.htm

Established in 1979 with the proceeds of contributions to a memorial fund to Dr Trevor Reese, Reader in Commonwealth Studies at the Institute and a distinguished scholar of Imperial History (d.1976). Biennial award (next award 2008 for works published 2005–06) for a scholarly work, usually by a single author, which has made a wide-ranging, innovative and scholarly contribution in the broadly-defined field of Imperial and Commonwealth History. All correspondence relating to the prize should be marked 'Trevor Reese Memorial Prize'.

PRIZE £1000.

Regional Press Awards

Press Gazette, 6–14 Underwood Street, London N1 7JQ
☎020 7549 8719 Fax 020 7566 5780
✉ franb@pressgazette.co.uk
www.pressgazette.co.uk

Open to all regional newspapers and regional journalists, whether freelance or staff. June event. Run by the *Press Gazette*.

Renault UK Journalist of the Year Award

Guild of Motoring Writers, 39 Beswick Avenue, Ensbury Park, Bournemouth BH10 4EY
☎01202 518808 Fax 01202 518808
✉ chris@whizzco.freeserve.co.uk
www.guildofmotoringwriters.co.uk

Contact *Patricia Lodge*

Originally the Pierre Dreyfus Award, established in 1977. Awarded annually by Renault UK Ltd in honour of Pierre Dreyfus, president director general of Renault 1955–75, to the member of the **Guild of Motoring Writers** who is judged to have made the most outstanding journalistic effort in any medium during the year. Particular emphasis is placed on initiative and endeavour.

RITA Awards

See **Romance Writers of America** under *Professional Associations and Societies*

Romantic Novel of the Year

RNA Award Organiser: PO Box 50421, London
W8 5XW
www.rna-uk.org
Honorary Administrator *Mrs P. Fenton*
Established 1960. Annual award for the best
romantic novel of the year, open to non-
members as well as members of the **Romantic
Novelists' Association**. Novels must be first
published in the UK between specified dates.
Full details on the RNA website. 2007 winner:
Rosie Thomas *Iris & Ruby*. Send s.a.e. to the
organiser for entry form.

Rossica Translation Prize

Academia Rossica, 151 Kensington High
Street, London W8 6SU
☎020 7937 5001 Fax 020 7937 5001
✉ rossica-prize@academia-rossica.org
www.academia-rossica.org

Contacts *Svetlana Adjoubei, Bettina Wrichert*

Founded in 2005 by Academia Rossica (AR),
a UK registered charity that supports cultural
collaboration between Russia and the West. A
biennial prize, which is awarded for the best
new literary translation from Russian into
English, published anywhere in the world. The
aim is to promote the best of Russian literature
and a better understanding of Russian culture in
English-speaking countries. Four copies of the
(published) English translation and three copies
of the Russian original should be submitted to
Academia Rossica. Final entry date for the 2009
award: 31 December 2008. 2005 winner: Oliver
Ready for his translation of *The Prussian Bride*
by Yuri Buida.

PRIZES £3000 (translator); £1000 (publisher).

Royal Economic Society Prize

The Economic Journal, Department of
Economics, London Business School, Regent's
Park, London NW1 4SA
☎020 7000 8413 Fax 020 7000 8401
✉ econjournal@london.edu
www.res.org.uk/society.resprize.asp

Contact *Heather Daly*

Annual award for the best article published in
The Economic Journal. Open to members of
the Royal Economic Society only. Previous
winners: Professors Marcos Rangal, Tilman
Börgers, Christian Dustmann, Paul Cheshire,
Stephen Sheppard.

PRIZE £3000.

Royal Mail Awards for Scottish Children's Books (Administrated by BRAW, Scottish Book Trust in partnership with the Scottish Arts Council)

Scottish Book Trust, Sandeman's House, Trunk's
Close, 55 High Street, Edinburgh EH1 1SR
☎0131 524 0160 Fax 0131 524 0161
✉ anna.gibbons@scottishbooktrust.com
www.braw.org.uk

Manager, BRAW *Anna Gibbons*

Awards are given to new and established authors
of published books in recognition of high
standards of writing for children in three age
group categories: younger children (0–7 years);
younger readers (8–11), older readers (12–16).
A shortlist is drawn up by a panel of children's
book experts and the winner in each category
is selected by children and young people voting
for their favourites in schools and libraries across
Scotland. Authors should be Scottish or resident
in Scotland, but books of particular Scottish
interest by other authors are eligible. Final entry
date: 31 January; guidelines available on request.

Royal Society of Literature Awards

**The Royal Society of Literature Ondaatje
Prize, V.S. Pritchett Memorial Prize** and
(under *Bursaries, Fellowships and Grants*)
**The Royal Society of Literature/Jerwood
Awards**

The Royal Society of Literature Ondaatje Prize

The Royal Society of Literature, Somerset
House, Strand, London WC2R 1LA
☎020 7845 4676 Fax 020 7845 4679
✉ paulaj@rslit.org
www.rslit.org

Submissions *Paula Johnson*

Administered by the **Royal Society of
Literature** and endowed by Sir Christopher
Ondaatje, the prize is awarded annually to a book
of literary merit, fiction, non-fiction or poetry,
best evoking the spirit of a place. All entries must
be published within the calendar year 2007 and
should be submitted between 1 September and
1 December 2007. The writer must be a citizen
of the UK, Commonwealth or Ireland. Further
details available on the website. 2007 winner:
Hisham Matar *In the Country of Men*.

PRIZE £10,000.

The Royal Society Prizes for Science Books

c/o The Royal Society, 6–9 Carlton House Terrace, London SW1Y 5AG
☎020 7451 2513 Fax 020 7930 2170
✉ sciencebooks@royalsoc.ac.uk
www.royalsociety.ac.uk

Contact *Aosaf Afzal*

Annual prizes established in 1988 to celebrate the best in popular science writing. Awarded to books that make science more accessible to readers of all ages and backgrounds. Owned and managed by the Royal Society and sponsored by the Aventis Foundation. All entries must be written in English and their first publication must have been between 1 January and 31 December; submission by publishers only. Educational textbooks published for professional or specialist audiences are not eligible. 2007 winners: Richard Hammond *Can You Feel the Force?* (Junior Prize); Daniel Gilbert *Stumbling on Happiness* (General Prize).

PRIZES (total) £30,000: £10,000 to each winner; £1000 to each of the five shortlisted authors in each prize.

Runciman Award

The Anglo-Hellenic League, c/o The Hellenic Centre, 16–18 Paddington Street, London W1U 5AS
☎020 7486 9410
Fax 020 7486 4254 (c/o Hellenic Centre)
✉ info@anglohellenicleague.org

Contact *The Administrator*

Established 1985. Annual award, sponsored by the National Bank of Greece. Founded by the Anglo-Hellenic League to promote Anglo-Greek understanding and friendship, for a work wholly or mainly about some aspect of Greece or the world of Hellenism, published in English in any country of the world in its first edition during 2006. Books published anywhere in the world are eligible. It is a condition of the award that shortlisted books should be available for purchase to readers in the UK at the time of the award ceremony. Named after the late Sir Steven Runciman, former chairman of the Anglo-Hellenic League. No category of writing will be excluded from consideration. Works in translation, with the exception of translations from Greek literature, will not be considered. Final entry date in late January; award presented in May/June.

AWARD £9000.

Sainsbury's Baby Book Award

See **Booktrust Early Years Awards**

The David St John Thomas Charitable Trust & Awards

The David St John Thomas Charitable Trust.
PO Box 6055, Nairn IV12 4YB
☎01667 453351 Fax 01667 452365
✉ dsjtcharitynairn@fsmail.net
www.dsjtcharitynairn.net

Competition & Awards Manager *Lorna Edwardson*

A programme of writing competitions, some of them run in association with others such as *Writing Magazine*. Includes £1000 first prize for a ghost story (1600–1800 words) and for poetry (up to 32 lines). All winning entries are published. The annual Self-Publishing Awards are open to anyone who has self-published a book during the preceding calendar year. There are several categories each with a £250 prize; the overall winner is declared Self-Publisher of the Year with a total award of £1000. For details of all competitions and awards send a large s.a.e. to address above.

The Saltire Literary Awards

Saltire Society, 9 Fountain Close, 22 High Street, Edinburgh EH1 1TF
☎0131 556 1836 Fax 0131 557 1675
✉ saltire@saltiresociety.org.uk
www.saltiresociety.org.uk

Administrator *Kathleen Munro*

Established 1982 and 1988. Annual awards, one for Book of the Year and one for a First Book by an author publishing for the first time. Open to any author of Scottish descent or living in Scotland, or to anyone who has written a book which deals with either the work and life of a Scot or with a Scottish problem, event or situation. Nominations are invited from editors of leading newspapers, magazines and periodicals. 2006 winners: The Faculty of Advocates/Saltire Society Scottish Book of the Year: John Burnside *A Lie About My Father*; Royal Mail/Saltire Society Scottish First Book of the Year: Maggie Fergusson *George Mackay Brown: The Life*.

PRIZES £5000 (Scottish Book); £1500 (First Book).

Schlegel–Tieck Prize

See **The Translators Association Awards**

Science Writer Awards

The Daily Telegraph, 111 Buckingham Palace Road, London SW1W 0DT
☎020 7931 2000/0845 094 6367 (Hotline: 10.00 am to 4.00 pm Mon–Fri)
✉ enquiries@science-writer.co.uk
www.science-writer.co.uk

Contact *Roger Highfield*

Established 1987, this award is designed to bridge the gap between science and writing, challenging the writer to come up with a piece of no more than 700 words that is friendly, informative and, above all, understandable. Sponsored by Bayer, the award is open to two age groups: 16–19 and 20–28.

AWARD Winners and runners-up receive cash prizes and have the opportunity to have their pieces published on the science pages of *The Daily Telegraph*. The winner in each category also gets a cash prize and a chance to meet the judges, which include Fay Weldon, Sir David Attenborough and Adam Hart-Davis. There is also a prize for schools and a prize for teachers. To check launch date, visit the website, telephone the hotline number or e-mail for further information.

The Scotsman Short Story Award

Currently seeking new sponsorship.

Scottish Arts Council Book of the Year Awards

Scottish Arts Council, 12 Manor Place, Edinburgh EH3 7DD
☎0131 226 6051 Fax 0131 225 9833
✉ gavin.wallace@scottisharts.org.uk
www.scottisharts.org.uk

Contact *Gavin Wallace*, Head of Literature

Awards are made annually and are given in recognition of high standards in fiction, poetry and literary non-fiction. Authors should be Scottish or resident in Scotland, but books of Scottish interest by other authors are eligible for consideration. Applications are made by publishers only and the closing date is 31 January for books published in the previous calendar year. 2006 winner: James Meek *The People's Act of Love* (Book of the Year).

AWARDS Three shortlisted adult writers each receive an award of £2000. The Scottish Arts Council Book of Year Award is worth a total of £10,000. (The Awards were due to be relaunched in a different format in 2007.)

Scottish Book of the Year

See **The Saltire Literary Awards**

Scottish History Book of the Year

The Saltire Society, 9 Fountain Close, 22 High Street, Edinburgh EH1 1TF
☎0131 556 1836 Fax 0131 557 1675
✉ saltire@saltiresociety.org.uk
www.saltiresociety.org.uk

Administrator *Kathleen Munro*

Established 1965. Annual award in memory of the late Dr Agnes Mure Mackenzie for a published work of distinguished Scottish historical research of scholarly importance (including intellectual history and the history of science). Editions of texts are not eligible. Nominations are invited and should be sent to the Administrator. 2005 winner: Cynthia J. Neville *Native Lordship in Medieval Scotland: The Earldoms of Strathearn and Lennox c. 1140–1365*.

PRIZE Bound and inscribed copy of the winning publication and £1500.

Seeds International Poetry Anthology Contest

See **Hidden Brook Press International Poetry Anthology Contests**

SES Book Prizes

24 Ireton Grove, Attenborough, Nottingham NG9 6BJ
☎0115 925 5959 Fax 0115 925 5959
✉ grahamlittler@msn.com

Honorary Secretary *Professor Graham Littler*

Annual awards given by the Society for Educational Studies for the best books on education published in the UK during the preceding year. Nominations by publishers or by individual authors based in the UK.

PRIZES £2000 (1st); £1000 (2nd); £400 (highly commended).

Bernard Shaw Translation Prize

See **The Translators Association Awards**

André Simon Memorial Fund Book Awards

1 Westbourne Gardens, Glasgow G12 9XT
☎0141 342 4929
✉ katie@andresimon.co.uk

Contact *Katie Lander*

Established 1978. Awards given annually for the best book on drink, best on food and special commendation in either. 2006 winners: Andrew

Whitley *Bread Matters*; Stephen Brook *Bordeaux - Medoc and Graves*.
AWARDS £2000 (best book); £1000 (special commendation); £200 to shortlisted books.

The Society for Theatre Research Annual Theatre Book Prize

The Society for Theatre Research, PO Box 53971, London SW15 6UL
✉ theatrebookprize@btinternet.com
www.str.org.uk

Established 1997. Annual award for books, in English, of original research into any aspect of the history and technique of British or British-related theatre. Not restricted to authors of British nationality nor books solely from British publishers. Books must be first published in English (no translations) during the calendar year. Play texts and those treating drama as literature are not eligible. Publishers submit books directly to the independent judges and should contact the Book Prize Administrator for further details. 2006 winner: *John Osborne: A Patriot for Us* John Heilpern.
AWARD £400.

Sony Radio Academy Awards

Alan Zafer & Associates, 47–48 Chagford Street, London NW1 6EB
☎020 7723 0106 Fax 020 7724 6163
✉ secretariat@radioawards.org
www.radioawards.org

Contact *The Secretariat*

Established 1982 in association with the **Society of Authors** and Sony UK. Presented in association with the **Radio Academy**. Annual awards to recognise excellence in radio broadcasting. Entries must have been broadcast in the UK between 1 January and 31 December in the year preceding the award. The categories for the awards are reviewed each year and announced in November.

Southport Writers' Circle Open Short Story Competition

16 Ormond Avenue, Westhead LA40 6HT
☎01695 577938
✉ southportwriterscircle@yahoo.co.uk

Contact *Daphne Chappell*

Founded 2005. Annual award that replaces the Southport Writers' Annual Seminar which incorporated a short story competition. Open to previously unpublished work, the story must be entered anonymously. No entry form required; include a cover sheet supplying title of story, name and contact details (send s.a.e. for results if no e-mail). Fee: £3 per story (payable to Southport Writers' Circle). Final entry date: 31 October. 2006 winner: R.V. Jones.
PRIZES £150 (1st); £75 (2nd); £25 (3rd); additional £25 Local Prize.

Southport Writers' Circle Poetry Competition

32 Dover Road, Southport PR8 4TB
Contact *Mrs Hilary Tinsley*

For previously unpublished work. Entry fee: £2 per poem. Any subject, any form; maximum 40 lines. Closing date: end April. Poems must be entered anonymously, accompanied by a sealed envelope marked with the title of poem, containing s.a.e. Entries must be typed on A4 paper and be accompanied by the appropriate fee payable to Southport Writers' Circle. No application form is required. Envelopes should be marked 'Poetry Competition'. Postal enquiries only. No calls.
PRIZES £200 (1st); £100 (2nd); £50 (3rd); additional £25 Humour Prize.

Bram Stoker Awards for Superior Achievement

Horror Writers Association, 244 Fifth Ave., Suite 2767, New York, NY 10001, USA
✉ hwa@horror.org
www.horror.org

Founded 1988 and named in honour of Bram Stoker, author of *Dracula*. Presented annually by the **Horror Writers Association** (HWA) for works of horror first published in the English language. Works are eligible during their first year of publication. HWA members recommend works for consideration in eight categories: Novel, First Novel, Short Fiction, Long Fiction, Fiction Collection, Poetry Collection, Anthology and Non-fiction. In addition, Lifetime Achievement Stokers are occasionally presented to individuals whose entire body of work has substantially influenced horror.

Strokestown International Poetry Competition

Strokestown International Poetry Festival Office, Strokestown, Co. Roscommon, Republic of Ireland
☎00 353 71 963 3759/963 8540
✉ petersirr@eircom.net
www.strokestownpoetry.org

Administrator *Sheila Lawe*

Annual poetry festival and competition. The

festival takes place over the first weekend in May with readings and competitions. A centrepiece of the festival is the Strokestown International Poetry Competition for unpublished poems not exceeding 70 lines. Entry forms available on the website or call the Festival Office. Entry fee: €5.

PRIZES €4000, €2000 and €1000 for a poem in English; €4000, €2000 and €1000 for a poem in Irish or Scottish Gaelic.

Sunday Times Writer of the Year Award

The Sunday Times, 1 Pennington Street, London E1 9XW
☎020 7782 5770 Fax 020 7782 5798
www.societyofauthors.org

Established 1987. Annual award to fiction and non-fiction writers. The panel consists of *Sunday Times* journalists and critics. Previous winners: Anthony Burgess, Seamus Heaney, Stephen Hawking, Ruth Rendell, Muriel Spark, William Trevor, Martin Amis, Margaret Atwood, Ted Hughes, Harold Pinter, Tom Wolfe, Robert Hughes. No applications; prize at the discretion of the Literary Editor.

Sunday Times Young Writer of the Year Award

The Society of Authors, 84 Drayton Gardens, London SW10 9SB
☎020 7373 6642 Fax 020 7373 5768
✉ info@societyofauthors.org

Contact *Awards Secretary*

Established 1991. Annual award given on the strength of the promise shown by a full-length published work of fiction, non-fiction, poetry or drama. Entrants must be British citizens, resident in Britain and under the age of 35. The panel consists of *Sunday Times* journalists and critics. Closing date: 31 October. The work must be by one author, in the English language, and published in Britain. Applications by publishers via the **Society of Authors**.

Syngenta ABSW Science Writers' Awards,

See **ABSW** under *Professional Associations and Societies*

Reginald Taylor and Lord Fletcher Essay Prize

Journal of the British Archaeological Association, Institute of Archaeology, c/o School of Art History, St Andrew's University, 9 The Scorel St Andrew's KY16 9AR

Contact *Dr Julian Luxford*

A biennial prize, in memory of the late E. Reginald Taylor and of Lord Fletcher, for the best unpublished scholarly essay, not exceeding 7500 words, on a subject of archaeological, art history or antiquarian interest within the period from the Roman era to AD 1830. The essay should show *original* research on its chosen subject, and the author will be invited to read the essay before the Association. The essay may be published in the journal of the Association if approved by the Editorial Committee. Closing date for entries is 30 April 2008. All enquiries by post, please. No phone calls. Send s.a.e. for details.

PRIZE £300 and a medal.

Theakstons Old Peculier Prize for the Crime Novel of the Year

Raglan House, Raglan Street, Harrogate HG1 1LE
☎01423 562303 Fax 01423 521264
✉ crime@harrogatefestival.org.uk
www.harrogate-festival.org.uk/crime

Festival Manager *Sharon Canavar*
Event Manager *Adina Watt*

Established 2005. Sponsored by Theakstons Old Peculier in association with Waterstone's, the award is open to full-length crime or mystery novels by British authors, published in the UK. It is the only crime fiction prize to be voted for by the general public following announcement of a long list in April. 2006 winner: (announced on the opening night of the **Theakstons Old Peculier Harrogate Crime Festival**) Val McDermid *The Torment of Others*.

PRIZE £3000 cash.

The Dylan Thomas Prize

The Dylan Thomas Centre, Somerset Place, Swansea SA1 1RR
☎01792 474051 Fax 01792 463993
✉ tim@dylanthomasprize.com
www.dylanthomasprize.com

Contact *Tim J. Prosser*

Founded 2004. An award of £60,000 will be given to the winner of this prize, which was established to encourage, promote and reward exciting new writing in the English-speaking world and to celebrate the poetry and prose of Dylan Thomas. Entrants should be the author of a published book (in English), under the age of 30 (when the work was published), writing within one of the following categories: poetry, novel, collection of short stories by one author, play that has been professionally performed, a broadcast radio play, a professionally produced screenplay that has resulted in a feature-length film. Authors need to be nominated by their publishers, or producers in the case of performance art. Final entry date: 30 April. The award will be presented at the Dylan Thomas Literary Festival in Swansea on 5th November 2008. Further entry details can be found on the website.

The Tinniswood Award

The Society of Authors, 84 Drayton Gardens, London SW10 9SB
☎020 7373 6642 Fax 020 7373 5768
✉ jhodder@societyofauthors.org.uk
www.societyofauthors.net

Contact *Jo Hodder*

Annual award established in 2004 by the Society of Authors and the Writers' Guild of Great Britain to perpetuate the memory of playwright Peter Tinniswood as well as to celebrate and encourage high standards in radio drama. Producers are invited to send in any radio drama first transmitted within the UK and Northern Ireland during the period 1 January–31 December 2006. Submissions must come from the producers and are restricted to a maximum of *two entries only* per producer. The work must be an original piece for radio, and may also include the first episode from an original series or serial. If submitting 15-minute episodes from a series or serial, consecutive episodes are required (including the first episode) to make up at least 45 minutes. An adaptation for radio of a piece originally written for any other medium e.g. stage, television, film, novel, poem or a short story will not be eligible. Final entry date: 28 January. Previous winner: *Beast* Nick Warburton.

PRIZE £1500, donated by the **ALCS**.

The Tir Na N-Og Award

Cyngor Llyfrau Cymru (Welsh Books Council), Castell Brychan, Aberystwyth SY23 2JB
☎01970 624151 Fax 01970 625385
✉ wbc.children@wbc.org.uk
www.wbc.org.uk

An annual award given to the best original book published for children in the year prior to the announcement. There are three categories: Welsh Language Book – Primary Sector; Welsh Language Book – Secondary Sector; Best English Book with an authentic Welsh background.

AWARDS £1000 (each category).

The Translators Association Awards

The Translators Association, 84 Drayton Gardens, London SW10 9SB
☎020 7373 6642 Fax 020 7373 5768
✉ info@societyofauthors.org
www.societyofauthors.org

Contact *Awards Secretary*

Various awards for published translations into English from Arabic (Banipal Prize), Dutch and Flemish (The Vondel Translation Prize), French (Scott Moncrieff Prize), German (Schlegel-Tieck Prize), Modern Greek (Hellenic Foundation Prize), Italian (The John Florio Prize), Portuguese (The Calouste Gulbenkian Prize), Spanish (The Premio Valle Inclán) and Swedish (Bernard Shaw Translation Prize). Contact the **Translators Association** for full details.

The Betty Trask Awards

See entry under *Bursaries, Fellowships and Grants*

The Trollope Society Short Story Prize

Maritime House, Old Town, Clapham, London SW4 0JW
☎020 7720 6789
✉ pamela@tvdox.com
www.trollopestoryprize.org

Contacts *Pamela Neville-Sington, John Williams*

Established in 2001 to encourage interest in Trollope's novels among young people with the emphasis on reading – and writing – for fun. The competition, which is held annually, focuses on a different Trollope book each year; visit the website for details. Open to students (aged 21 and younger) of all countries. Final entry date: 15 January. The winning story will be published in the Society's quarterly journal, *Trollopiana*.

PRIZE £1000.

Undiscovered Authors Literary Competition

See **Discovered Authors** under *UK Publishers*

Sir Peter Ustinov Television Scriptwriting Award

Foundation of the International Academy of Television Arts & Sciences, 888 Seventh Avenue, 5th Floor, New York, NY 10019, USA
☎001 212 489 6969 Fax 001 212 489 6557

✉ info@iemmys.tv

www.iemmys.tv

Contact *Award Administrator*

Established 1998. The late Sir Peter Ustinov gave his name to the Foundation's Television Scriptwriting Award. This annual competition is designed to motivate novice writers worldwide. The scriptwriter cannot be a United States citizen nor resident and must be below 30 years of age. Further details and entry form available on the website.

PRIZE The award winner will receive US$2500, a trip to New York and the opportunity to work with an established writer as mentor.

Ver Poets Open Competition

181 Sandridge Road, St Albans AL1 4AH

☎01727 762601

✉ gillknibbs@yahoo.co.uk

www.verpoets.org.uk

Contact *Gillian Knibbs*

Various competitions are organised by **Ver Poets**, the main one being the annual Open for unpublished poems of no more than 30 lines written in English. Entry fee: £3 per poem. Entry form available from address above. Two copies of poems typed on A4 white paper. The anthology of winning and selected poems, and the adjudicators' report are normally available from mid-June. Final entry date: 30 April. Back numbers of the anthology are available for £4, post-free; one copy each free to those included.

PRIZES £500 (1st); £300 (2nd); £100 (3rd). Also runs High Lights, an open competition for younger poets with an October 31 closing date. Details available from address above.

Vogue Talent Contest

Vogue, Vogue House, Hanover Square, London W1S 1JU

☎020 7152 3003 Fax 020 7408 0559

Contact *Frances Bentley*

Established 1951. Annual award for young writers and journalists (under 25 on 1 January in the year of the contest). Final entry date is in April. Entrants must write three pieces of journalism on given subjects.

PRIZES £1000, plus a month's paid work experience with *Vogue*; £500 (2nd).

The Vondel Translation Prize

See **The Translators Association Awards**

Wadsworth Prize for Business History

Dept. of Management, HumSS, University of Reading, PO Box 218, Whiteknights, Reading RG6 6AA

✉ p.m.scott@reading.ac.uk

Contact *Dr Peter Scott*

Now in its 31st year, the Wadsworth Prize is awarded annually by the Business Archives Council to an individual judged to have made an outstanding contribution to the study of British business history. Books are nominated by publishers. 2005 winner: Geoffrey Jones *Renewing Unilever. Transformation and Tradition*.

Wales Book of the Year Award

See **Academi Wales Book of the Year Awards**

Walford Award

43 Yardington, Whitchurch SY13 1BL

☎01948 663570

✉ millbrookend-awards@yahoo.co.uk

www.cilip.org.uk

Contact *Awards Administrator* (at address above)

Part of the ISG (CILIP)/BookData Reference Awards. Awarded to an individual who has made a sustained and continual contribution to British bibliography over a period of years. The nominee need not be resident in the UK. The award is named after Dr A.J. Walford, a bibliographer of international repute. 2006 winner: Dr Diana Dixon.

AWARD Cash prize and certificate.

The David Watt Prize

Rio Tinto plc, 6 St James's Square, London SW1Y 4LD

☎01985 844613 Fax 01985 844002

✉ davidwattprize@riotinto.com *or* celiabeale@globalnet.co.uk

www.riotinto.com

Contact *The Administrator*

Initiated in 1988 to commemorate the life and work of David Watt. Annual award, open to writers currently engaged in writing for English language newspapers and journals, on international and national affairs. The winner is judged as having made 'an outstanding contribution towards the greater understanding of national, international or global issues'. Entries must have been published during the year preceding the award. Final entry date 31 March. 2006 winner:

Sophie Pedder of *The Economist* for her article 'Spot the difference'.
PRIZE £10,000.

Brian Way Award

c/o Theatre Centre, Shoreditch Town Hall, 380 Old Street, London EC1V 9LT
☎020 7729 3066
✉ admin@theatre-centre.co.uk
www.theatre-centre.co.uk

Contact *Theatre Writing Section*

Formerly the Arts Council Children's Award, founded 2000. An annual award for playwrights who write for children and young people. The plays, which must have been produced professionally, must be at least 45 minutes long. The playwright must be resident in the UK. Contact email address/website for full details and application form. 2007 winner: Tim Crouch *Shopping for Shoes*.
AWARD £6000.

The Harri Webb Prize

10 Heol Don, Whitchurch, Cardiff CF14 2AU
☎029 2062 3359

Contact *Professor Meic Stephens*

Established 1995. Annual award to commemorate the Welsh poet, Harri Webb (1920–94), for a single poem in any of the categories in which he wrote: ballad, satire, song, polemic or a first collection of poems. The poems are chosen by three adjudicators; no submissions. Previous winner: Grahame Davies.
PRIZES £100/£200.

The Wheatley Medal

Society of Indexers, Woodbourn Business Centre, 10 Jessell Street, Sheffield S9 3HY
☎0114 244 9561 Fax 0114 244 9563
✉ admin@indexer.org.uk
www.indexers.org.uk

Marketing Director *Ann Kingdom*

The Wheatley Medal is awarded for an outstanding index and was established by the **Society of Indexers** and the Library Association (now **CILIP**) to highlight the importance of good indexing and confer recognition on the most highly regarded practitioners and their publishers. First awarded in 1963, it has since been presented for indexes to a wide range of publications, from encyclopedias to journals.
PRIZE Cash, plus medal and certificate.

Whitbread Book Awards

See **Costa Book Awards**

Whitfield Prize

Royal Historical Society, University College London, Gower Street, London WC1E 6BT
☎020 7387 7532 Fax 020 7387 7532
✉ rhs.info@sas.ac.uk
www.rhs.ac.uk/prizes

Contact *Executive Secretary*

Established 1977. An annual award for the best new work within a field of British or Irish history, published in the UK in the preceding calendar year. The book must be the author's first (solely written) history book and be an original and scholarly work of historical research. Final entry date: 31 December.
PRIZE £1000.

John Whiting Award

Hampstead Theatre, Eton Avenue, London NW3 3EU
☎020 7749 4200
✉ info@hampsteadtheatre.com
www.hampsteadtheatre.com

Contact *Brian Savery* (Executive Director)

Founded 1965. Annual award to commemorate the life and work of the playwright John Whiting (*The Devils, A Penny for a Song*). Open to any writer who has received an award during the previous two years from **Arts Council England** or a commission or production by a theatre in receipt of Arts Council subsidy. Awarded to the writer whose play most nearly satisfies the following criteria: a play in which the writing is of special quality; a play of relevance and importance to contemporary life; a play of potential value to the British theatre. No writer who has won the award previously may reapply and no play that has been submitted for the award previously is eligible. Contact the theatre writing section for full details and application form.
PRIZE £6000.

Wilkins Memorial Poetry Prize

Birmingham & Midland Institute, 9 Margaret Street, Birmingham B3 3BS
☎0121 236 3591 Fax 0121 212 4577
www.bmi.org.uk

Administrator *Mr P.A. Fisher*

The structure of the Wilkins Memorial Poetry Prize is currently under discussion. For further information, contact the Administrator.

Winchester Writers' Conference Prizes

Faculty of Arts, University of Winchester, Winchester SO22 4NR
☎01962 827238
www.writersconference.co.uk

Fifteen writing competitions sponsored by major publishers who offer 56 prizes and trophies for entries under categories of: The First Three Pages of the Novel; Poetry; Writing can be Murder; Feature Articles and Scriptwriting. Competitions open for all writers in January; closing date: 29 May. Phone or write for booklet giving details of each competition and the entry blanks or access them on the website.

H.H. Wingate Prize

See **Jewish Quarterly Literary Prize**

Wisden (Cricket) Book of the Year

John Wisden & Co., 13 Old Aylesfield, Froyle Road, Alton GU34 4BY
☎01420 83415
✉ almanack@wisdengroup.com
www.wisden.com

Contact *Hugh Chevallier*

Founded 2002. Annual award. The Wisden Book of the Year is chosen exclusively by the Wisden Cricketers' Almanack book reviewer. In each annual *Wisden Almanack*, a different person is commissioned to review all cricket books published in the previous calendar year, and that reviewer selects the Wisden Book of the Year. Any cricket book sent to John Wisden & Co. for review in Wisden Cricketers' Almanack will be considered. Final entry date: 1st December. 2005 winner: *Ashes 2005* by Gideon Haigh, selected by book reviewer Ed Smith.

Wolfson History Prize

Wolfson Foundation, 8 Queen Anne Street, London W1G 9LD
☎020 7323 5730 Fax 020 7323 3241
www.wolfson.org.uk

Contact *Prize Administrator*

The Wolfson History Prize, established in 1972, is awarded annually to promote and encourage standards of excellence in the writing of history for the general reading public. Submissions are made through publishers. 2005 winners (awarded in 2006): Evelyn Welch *Shopping in the Renaissance*; Christopher Wickham, FBA *Framing the Early Middle Ages*.

The Writers Bureau Poetry and Short Story Competition

The Writers Bureau, Sevendale House, 7 Dale Street, Manchester M1 1JB
☎0161 228 2362 Fax 0161 228 3533
✉ studentservices@writersbureau.com
www.writersbureau.com/competition

Competition Secretary *Angela Cox*

Established 1994. Annual award. Poems should be no longer than 40 lines and short stories no more than 2000 words. £5 entry fee. Closing date: 30 June 2008.

PRIZES in each category: £1000 (1st); £400 (2nd); £200 (3rd); £100 (4th); £50 (x 6).

Writers' Forum Short Story & Poetry Competitions

See *Writers' Forum* under *Magazines*.

The Yale Drama Series/ David C. Horn Prize

PO Box 209040, New Haven, CT 06520–9040, USA
www.yalebooks.com/drama

Major new annual playwriting competition intended to support emerging playwrights in the United States, Canada, the UK and the Republic of Ireland. Submissions must be original, unpublished full-length plays written in English (translations, musicals and children's plays are not accepted). Only one manuscript may be submitted per year; plays that have had professional productions are not eligible. Entry fee: $25, cheques should be made out to Yale University Press. 2008 competition deadline: 15 August 2007. Further information available on the website.

PRIZE The David C. Horn Prize of $10,000, publication by Yale University Press and a staged reading at Yale Rep.

Yorkshire Post Book Awards

Yorkshire Post Newspapers Ltd, PO Box 168, Wellington Street, Leeds LS1 1RF

Contact *Duncan Hamilton*, Deputy Editor

Annual awards: **Yorkshire Post Novel of the Year Award**; **Yorkshire Post Non-Fiction Book of the Year Award**; **Best Title With a Yorkshire Theme**. Awarded to the book which, in the opinion of the judges, is the best work published in the preceding year.

PRIZE £1200 (Novel of the Year); £1200 (Non-Fiction Book of the Year); £500 (Best Title with a Yorkshire Theme) .

YoungMinds Book Award

Youngminds, 48–50 St John Street, London EC1M 4DG

☎020 7336 8445 Fax 020 7336 8446

✉ bookaward@youngminds.org.uk

www.youngminds.org.uk/bookaward

Contact *Jessica Peters*

Established 2003. This award is given to a published work of literature that throws fresh light on the ways a child takes in and makes sense of the world he or she is growing into – novels, memoirs, diaries, poetry collections which portray something of the unique subtlety of a child's experience. 2006 winner: Uzo Dinma Iweale *Beasts of No Nation*.

PRIZE £3000.

Library Services

Aberdeen Central Library

Rosemount Viaduct, Aberdeen AB25 1GW
☎01224 652500 Fax 01224 641985
✉ centrallibrary@aberdeencity.gov.uk
www.aberdeencity.gov.uk

OPEN Central Library Lending Services: 9.00 am to 7.00 pm Monday to Thursday; 9.00 am to 5.00 pm Friday & Saturday. Business Information, Community Reference & Local Studies: 9.00 am to 8.00 pm Monday to Thursday; 9.00 am to 5.00 pm Friday & Saturday. Branch library opening hours vary

OPEN ACCESS
General reference and loans. Books, pamphlets, periodicals and newspapers; videos, CDs, DVDs; arts equipment lending service; Internet and Learning Centre for public access; photographs of the Aberdeen area; census records, maps, newspapers; online databases, patents and standards. The library offers special services to housebound readers. Non-resident administrative fee.

Armitt Collection, Museum & Library

Rydal Road, Ambleside LA22 9BL
☎015394 31212 Fax 015394 31313
✉ info@armitt.com
www.armitt.com

OPEN 10.00 am to 5.00 pm Tuesday and Friday (last admission 4.30 pm)

FREE ACCESS (Prior appointment for research)
A small but unique reference library of rare books, manuscripts, pictures, antiquarian prints, maps and museum items, mainly about the Lake District. It includes early guidebooks and topographical works, books and papers relating to Ruskin, H. Martineau, Charlotte Mason and others; fine art including work by W. Green, J.B. Pyne, John Harden, K. Schwitters, and Victorian photographs by Herbert Bell; also a major collection of Beatrix Potter's scientific watercolour drawings and microscope studies. Museum and Exhibition open seven days per week from 10.00 am to 5.00 pm. Entry charge for museum.

The Athenaeum, Liverpool

Church Alley, Liverpool L1 3DD
☎0151 709 7770 Fax 0151 709 0418
✉ info@theathenaeum.org.uk
www.theathenaeum.org.uk

OPEN 9.00 am to 4.00 pm Monday and Tuesday; 9.00 am to 9.00 pm Wednesday to Friday

ACCESS To club members; researchers by application only
General collection, with books dating from the 15th century, now concentrated mainly on local history with a long run of Liverpool directories and guides. SPECIAL COLLECTIONS Liverpool playbills; William Roscoe; Blanco White; Robert Gladstone; 18th-century plays; 19th-century economic pamphlets; the Norris books; Bibles; Yorkshire and other genealogy. Some original drawings, portraits, topographical material and local maps.

Bank of England Information Centre

Threadneedle Street, London EC2R 8AH
☎020 7601 4715 Fax 020 7601 4356
✉ informationcentre@bankofengland.co.uk
www.bankofengland.co.uk

OPEN 9.00 am to 5.30 pm Monday to Friday

ACCESS For research workers by prior arrangement only, when material is not readily available elsewhere
50,000 volumes of books and periodicals. 2000 periodicals taken. UK and overseas coverage of banking, finance and economics. SPECIAL COLLECTIONS Central bank reports; UK 17th–19th-century economic tracts; government reports in the field of banking.

Barbican Library

Barbican Centre, London EC2Y 8DS
☎020 7638 0569/7638 0568 (24-hr renewals)
Fax 020 7638 2249
✉ barbicanlib@cityoflondon.gov.uk
www.cityoflondon.gov.uk/libraries
Librarian *John Lake*

OPEN 9.30 am to 5.30 pm Monday and Wednesday; 9.30 am to 7.30 pm Tuesday and Thursday; 9.30 am to 2.00 pm Friday; 9.30 am to 4.00 pm Saturday

OPEN ACCESS

Situated on Level 2 of the Barbican Centre, this is the Corporation of London's largest lending library. Study facilities are available plus free Internet access. In addition to a large general lending department, the library seeks to reflect the Centre's emphasis on the arts and includes strong collections (including DVDs, videos and CD-ROMs) on painting, sculpture, theatre, cinema and ballet, as well as a large music library with books, scores and CDs (sound recording loans available at a small charge). Also houses the City's main children's library and has special collections on basic skills, materials for young adults, finance, natural resources, conservation, socialism and the history of London. Service available for housebound readers. A literature events programme is organised by the Library which supplements and provides cross-arts planning opportunities with the Barbican Centre artistic programme. Reading groups meet in the library on the first Thursday of every month and a weekly Basic Skills advice service is offered during term time.

Barnsley Public Library

Central Library, Shambles Street, Barnsley
S70 2JF
☎01226 773930 Fax 01226 773955
✉ barnsleylibraryenquiries@barnsley.gov.uk
www.barnsley.gov.uk/bguk/Leisure_Culture/Libraries

OPEN Lending & Reference: 9.30 am to 7.00 pm Monday and Wednesday; 9.30 am to 5.30 pm Tuesday, Thursday, Friday; 9.30 am to 4.00 pm Saturday. Telephone to check hours of other departments and other branch libraries.

OPEN ACCESS

General library, lending and reference. Archive collection of family history and local firms; local studies: coal mining, local authors, Yorkshire and Barnsley; large junior library. (Specialist departments are closed on certain weekday evenings and Saturday afternoons.)

BBC Written Archives Centre

Caversham Park, Reading RG4 8TZ
☎0118 948 6281 Fax 0118 946 1145
✉ heritage@bbc.co.uk
www.bbc.co.uk/heritage

Contact *Jacqueline Kavanagh*

OPEN 9.30 am to 5.30 pm Monday to Friday

ACCESS For reference, by appointment only, Wednesday to Friday

Holds the written records of the BBC, including internal papers from 1922 to the 1990s and published material to date. 20th century biography, social history, popular culture and broadcasting. Charges for certain services.

Bedford Central Library

Harpur Street, Bedford MK40 1PG
☎01234 350931/270102 (Reference Library)
Fax 01234 342163
www.bedfordshire.gov.uk

OPEN 9.00 am to 6.00 pm Monday, Tuesday, Wednesday, Friday; 9.00 am to 1.00 pm Thursday; 9.00 am to 5.00 pm Saturday

OPEN ACCESS

Lending library with a wide range of stock, including books, music, audiobooks, DVDs and videos; reference and information library, children's library, local history library and Internet facilities.

Belfast Public Libraries: Central Library

Royal Avenue, Belfast BT1 1EA
☎028 9050 9150 Fax 028 9033 2819
✉ info.belb@ni-libraries.net
www.belb.org.uk
www.ni-libraries.net

OPEN 9.00 am to 8.00 pm Monday and Thursday; 9.00 am to 5.30 pm Tuesday, Wednesday, Friday; 9.00 am to 1.00 pm Saturday

OPEN ACCESS To lending libraries; reference libraries by application only

Over two million volumes for lending and reference. SPECIAL COLLECTIONS United Nations depository; complete British Patent Collection; Northern Ireland Newspaper Library; British and Irish government publications. The Central Library provides the following Reference Departments: General Reference; Belfast, Ulster and Irish Studies; Music. A Learning Gateway includes public Internet facilities and a Learndirect Centre. The Lending Library is one of over 20 branches along with a range of outreach services to hospitals, care homes and housebound readers.

BFI National Library

21 Stephen Street, London W1T 1LN
☎020 7255 1444 Fax 020 7436 2338
✉ library@bfi.org.uk
www.bfi.org.uk

OPEN 10.30 am to 5.30 pm Monday and Friday; 10.30 am to 8.00 pm Tuesday and Thursday; 1.00 pm to 8.00 pm Wednesday; Telephone Enquiry Service operates from 10.00 am to 5.00 pm (closed 1.00 pm to 2.00 pm)

ACCESS For reference only; annual, 5-day and limited day membership available

The world's largest collection of information on film and television including periodicals, cuttings, scripts, related documentation, personal papers. Main library catalogue available via website.

Birmingham and Midland Institute
9 Margaret Street, Birmingham B3 3BS
☎0121 236 3591 Fax 0121 212 4577
✉ admin@bmi.org.uk
www.bmi.org.uk

Administrator & General Secretary *Philip Fisher*
ACCESS Members only

Established 1854. Later merged with the Birmingham Library which was founded in 1779. The Library specialises in the humanities, with approximately 100,000 volumes in stock. Founder member of the **Association of Independent Libraries**. Meeting-place of many affiliated societies devoted to poetry and literature.

Birmingham Library Services
Central Library, Chamberlain Square, Birmingham B3 3HQ
☎0121 303 4511
✉ central.library@birmingham.gov.uk
www.birmingham.gov.uk/libraries

OPEN 9.00 am to 8.00 pm Monday to Friday; 9.00 am to 5.00 pm Saturday

Over a million volumes. RESEARCH COLLECTIONS include the Shakespeare Library; War Poetry Collection; Parker Collection of Children's Books and Games; Johnson Collection; Milton Collection; Cervantes Collections; Early and Fine Printing Collection (including the William Ridler Collection of Fine Printing); Joseph Priestley Collection; Loudon Collection; Railway Collection; Wingate Bett Transport Ticket Collection; Labour, Trade Union and Co-operative Collections. PHOTOGRAPHIC ARCHIVES Sir John Benjamin Stone; Francis Bedford; Francis Frith; Warwickshire Photographic Survey; Boulton and Watt Archive. Also, Charles Parker Archive; Birmingham Repertory Theatre Archive and Sir Barry Jackson Library; Local Studies (Birmingham); Patents Collection; Song

Sheets Collection; Oberammergau Festival Collection.

Bournemouth Library
22 The Triangle, Bournemouth BH2 5RQ
☎01202 454848 Fax 01202 454840
✉ bournemouth@bournemouthlibraries.org.uk
www.bournemouth.gov.uk/libraries

OPEN 10.00 am to 7.00 pm Monday; 9.30 am to 7.00 pm Tuesday, Thursday, Friday; 9.30 am to 5.00 pm Wednesday; 10.00 am to 4.00 pm Saturday

OPEN ACCESS

Main library for Bournemouth with lending, reference and music departments, plus the Heritage Zone – local and family history.

Bradford Central Library
Princes Way, Bradford BD1 1NN
☎01274 433600 Fax 01274 395108
✉ public.libraries@bradford.gov.uk

Wide range of books and media loan services. Comprehensive reference and information services, including major local history collections and specialised business information service.

Brighton Jubilee Library
Jubilee Street, Brighton BN1 1GE
☎01273 290800
www.citylibraries.info/libraries/jubilee.asp

OPEN 10.00 am to 7.00 pm Monday and Tuesday; 10.00 am to 5.00 pm Wednesday and Friday; 10.00 am to 8.00 pm Thursday; 10.00 am to 4.00 pm Saturday

ACCESS Stock on open access and in onsite store; material for reference use and lending

Specialisations include art and antiques, history of Brighton, local illustrations, Hebrew and Oriental literature, natural history, children's books, World War Two and large bequests of rare and historical books.

Bristol Central Library
College Green, Bristol BS1 5TL
☎0117 903 7200 Fax 0117 922 1081
www.bristol.gov.uk

OPEN 9.30 am to 7.30 pm Monday, Tuesday and Thursday; 10.00 am to 5.00 pm Wednesday; 9.30 am to 5.00 pm Friday and Saturday; 1.00 pm to 5.00 pm Sunday

OPEN ACCESS

Lending, reference, art, music, business and local studies are particularly strong. DVD, video and CD collections on site. Facilities available:

PCs (large screen with Jaws and Zoomtext), Internet, printing; videophone on site; black & white and colour photocopiers.

British Architectural Library

Royal Institute of British Architects, 66 Portland Place, London W1B 1AD
☎020 7580 5533 Fax 020 7631 1802
✉ info@inst.riba.org
www.architecture.com

OPEN 10.00 am to 8.00 pm Tuesday; 10.00 am to 5.00 pm Wednesday to Friday; 10.00 am to 1.30 pm Saturday; Closed Sunday, Monday and any Saturday preceding a Bank Holiday; full details on the website

ACCESS Free to RIBA members; non-members must buy a day ticket (£10/£7 concessions, but on Tuesdays between 5.00 pm–8.00 pm and Saturdays £7/£3.50); subscriber membership available (write for details); loans available to RIBA and library members only

Collection of books, photographs and periodicals. All aspects of architecture, current and historical. Material both technical and aesthetic, covering related fields including: interior design, landscape architecture, topography, the construction industry and applied arts. Brochure available; queries by telephone, letter, e-mail or in person. Charge for research (min. charge £40 + VAT).

RIBA British Architectural Library Drawings & Archives Collections Drawings and manuscripts can be consulted at the RIBA Study Rooms, Henry Cole Wing, Victoria and Albert Museum: ☎ 020 7307 3708 ✉ drawings&archives@inst.riba.org

ACCESS Free to all.

The British Cartoon Archive

See entry under *Picture Libraries*

The British Library

Admission to St Pancras Reading Rooms – British Library Readers' Passes

Everyone is welcome to visit the British Library exhibition galleries or to tour the building. However, to use the reading rooms you will need to apply for a reader's pass, for which identification is required. The British Library issues passes to those who want to use its collections – researchers, innovators and entrepreneurs across all fields of study, and in academic, commerce or personal research – whether or not they are affiliated to a research institution. Two pieces of identification are required (original documents

only). One proof of home address: e.g. a utility bill, bank statement or driving licence; and proof of signature, i.e. a bank or credit card, passport, driving licence or national identity card.

It would also be helpful to take with you anything to support your application (such as a student card, business card, professional membership card or details of the items you wish to see).

For further information, visit the website at www.bl.uk or contact the Reader Admissions Office, The British Library, 96 Euston Road, London NW1 2DB ☎ 020 7412 7676 Fax 020 7412 7794; reader-admissions@bl.uk

British Library Asia, Pacific and Africa Collections

96 Euston Road, London NW1 2DB
☎020 7412 7873 Fax 020 7412 7641
✉ apac-enquiries@bl.uk
www.bl.uk

OPEN 10.00 am to 5.00 pm Monday; 9.30 am to 5.00 pm Tuesday to Saturday; closed for public holidays

ACCESS By British Library reader's pass

An extensive collection of printed volumes and manuscripts in the languages of Africa, the Near and Middle East and all of Asia, plus records of the East India Company and British government in India until 1947. Also prints, drawings and paintings by British artists of India. For information on British Library collections and services, visit the website.

British Library Business & IP Centre

96 Euston Road, London NW1 2DB
☎020 7412 7454 (free enquiry service)
Fax 020 7412 7453 (free enquiry service)
✉ bipc@bl.uk
www.bl.uk/bipc

OPEN 10.00 am to 8.00 pm Monday; 9.30 am to 8.00 pm Tuesday to Thursday; 9.30 am to 5.00 pm Friday and Saturday; closed for public holidays

ACCESS By British Library reader's pass

The Business & IP Centre holds the most comprehensive collection of business information literature and patent specifications in the UK. Includes market research reports and journals, directories, company annual reports, trade and business journals, up-to-date literature on patents, trade marks, designs and copyright.

British Library Early Printed Collections/Rare Books and Music Reading Room

96 Euston Road, London NW1 2DB
☎020 7412 7564 Fax 020 7412 7691
✉ rare-books@bl.uk
www.bl.uk/collections/early.html

General enquiries about reader services & advance reservations:
☎ 020 7412 7676 Fax 020 7412 7609
✉ reader-services-enquiries@bl.uk

OPEN 10.00 am to 8.00 pm Monday; 9.30 am to 8.00 pm Tuesday to Thursday; 9.30 am to 5.00 pm Friday and Saturday; closed for public holidays

ACCESS By British Library reader's pass

Early Printed Collections selects, acquires, researches and provides access to material printed in Britain and Western Europe from the 15th to early 20th centuries. The collections are available in the Rare Books and Music Reading Room at St Pancras which also functions as the focus for the British Library's extensive collection of humanities microforms. Further information about Early Printed Collections can be found at the British Library website.

British Library Humanities Reading Room

96 Euston Road, London NW1 2DB
☎020 7412 7676 Fax 020 7412 7789
✉ humanities-enquiries@bl.uk
www.bl.uk/resources/humanities

OPEN 10.00 am to 8.00 pm Monday; 9.30 am to 8.00 pm Tuesday, Wednesday, Thursday; 9.30 am to 5.00 pm Friday and Saturday; closed for public holidays

ACCESS By British Library reader's pass

This reading room is the focus for the Library's modern collections service in the humanities. It is on two levels, Humanities 1 and Humanities 2 and provides access to the Library's comprehensive collections of books and periodicals in all subjects in the humanities and social sciences and in all languages apart from Oriental. These collections are not available for browsing at the shelf. Material is held in closed access storage and needs to be identified and ordered from store using an online catalogue. A selective open access collection on most humanities subjects can be found in Humanities 1 whilst in Humanities 2 there are open access reference works relating to periodicals and theses, to recorded sound and to

librarianship and information science. To access British Library catalogues, go to the website.

British Library Manuscript Collections

96 Euston Road, London NW1 2DB
☎020 7412 7513 Fax 020 7412 7745
✉ mss@bl.uk
www.bl.uk

OPEN 10.00 am to 5.00 pm Monday; 9.30 am to 5.00 pm Tuesday to Saturday; closed for public holidays

ACCESS Reading facilities only, by British Library reader's pass; a written letter of recommendation and advance notice is required for certain categories of material

Two useful publications, *Index of Manuscripts in the British Library,* Cambridge 1984–6, 10 vols, and *The British Library: Guide to the Catalogues and Indexes of the Department of Manuscripts* by M.A.E. Nickson, help to guide the researcher through this vast collection of manuscripts dating from Ancient Greece to the present day. Approximately 300,000 mss, charters, papyri and seals are housed here. For information on British Library collections and services and to access British Library catalogues, including the Manuscripts online catalogue, visit the website.

British Library Map Collections

96 Euston Road, London NW1 2DB
☎020 7412 7702 Fax 020 7412 7780
✉ maps@bl.uk
www.bl.uk/collections/maps

OPEN 10.00 am to 5.00 pm Monday; 9.30 am to 5.00 pm Tuesday to Saturday; closed for public holidays

ACCESS By British Library reader's pass

A collection of about 4.5 million maps, charts and globes, manuscript, printed and, increasingly, digital, with particular reference to the history of British cartography. Maps for all parts of the world in a wide range of scales, formats and dates, including the most comprehensive collection of Ordnance Survey maps and plans. SPECIAL COLLECTIONS King George III Topographical Collection and Maritime Collection, the Crace Collection of maps and plans of London and the cartographic archive of the Ministry of Defence (i.e. GSGS). For information on British Library collections and services, visit the website. To access main British Library catalogues, go to the website at catalogue.bl.uk

British Library Music Collections

96 Euston Road, London NW1 2DB
☎020 7412 7772 Fax 020 7412 7751
✉ music-collections@bl.uk
www.bl.uk
OPEN 10.00 am to 8.00 pm Monday; 9.30 am
   to 8.00 pm Tuesday to Thursday; 9.30 am
   to 5.00 pm Friday and Saturday; closed for
   public holidays
ACCESS By British Library reader's pass
   SPECIAL COLLECTIONS The Royal Music
Library (containing almost all Handel's surviving
autograph scores), The Zweig Collection of
Music & Literary Mss, The Royal Philharmonic
Society Archive and the Paul Hirsch Music
Library. Also a large collection (about one and
a half million items) of printed music (UK
via legal deposit) and about 100,000 items of
manuscript music, both British and foreign.
The British Library website contains details of
collections and services, and provides access to
the catalogues.

British Library Newspapers

Colindale Avenue, London NW9 5HE
☎020 7412 7353 Fax 020 7412 7379
✉ newspaper@bl.uk
www.bl.uk/collections/newspapers.html
OPEN 10.00 am to 5.00 pm Monday to
   Saturday (last newspaper issue 4.15 pm);
   closed for public holidays
ACCESS By British Library reader's pass or
Newspaper Library pass (available from and
valid only for Colindale)
   Major collections of English provincial,
Scottish, Welsh, Irish, Commonwealth and
selected overseas foreign newspapers from
c.1700 are housed here. Some earlier holdings
are also available. London newspapers from 1801
and many weekly and fortnightly periodicals are
also in stock. (London newspapers pre-dating
1801 are housed at the new library building in
St Pancras – 96 Euston Road, NW1 – though
many are available at Colindale Avenue on
microfilm.) Readers are advised to check availability of material in advance. For information
on British Library Newspapers collections and
services, visit the website.

British Library Science, Technology and Business Collections

96 Euston Road, London NW1 2DB
☎020 7412 7676 (General Enquiries)
Fax 020 7412 7495
✉ scitech@bl.uk
www.bl.uk
Business enquiries: ☎ 020 7412 7454
   (Free enquiry service)
OPEN 10.00 am to 8.00 pm Monday; 9.30 am
   to 8.00 pm Tuesday to Thursday; 9.30 am
   to 5.00 pm Friday and Saturday; closed for
   public holidays
Engineering, business information on companies, markets and products, physical science
and technologies. See also **British Library
Business & IP Centre**. To access British Library
catalogues go to the website at catalogue.bl.uk

British Library Social Sciences & Official Publications

96 Euston Road, London NW1 2DB
☎020 7412 7676 Fax 020 7412 7761
✉ social-sciences@bl.uk
www.bl.uk/collections/social/social.html
OPEN Reading Room: 10.00 am to 8.00 pm
   Monday; 9.30 am to 8.00 pm Tuesday to
   Thursday; 9.30 am to 5.00 pm Friday and
   Saturday; closed for public holidays
ACCESS By British Library reader's pass
   Provides an information service on the
social sciences, law, public administration, and
current and international affairs, and access to
current and historical official publications from
all countries and intergovernmental bodies.
Maerial available in the reading room includes
House of Commons sessional papers, UK legislation, UK electoral registers, up-to-date reference books on official publications and on the
social sciences, a major collection of statistics and
a browsing collection of recent social science
books and periodicals; other collections are kept
in closed stores and items have to be ordered for
delivery to the reading room. To access British
Library catalogues, go to the website at cata-
logue.bl.uk

British Library Sound Archive

96 Euston Road, London NW1 2DB
☎020 7412 7676 Fax 020 7412 7441
✉ sound-archive@bl.uk
www.bl.uk/soundarchive
OPEN 10.00 am to 8.00 pm Monday; 9.30 am
   to 8.00 pm Tuesday to Thursday; 9.30 am
   to 5.00 pm Friday and Saturday; closed for
   public holidays
Listening service (by appointment)
Northern Listening Service British Library
Document Supply Centre, Boston Spa: 9.15 am
to 4.30 pm Monday to Friday

OPEN ACCESS

An archive of over 1,000,000 discs and more than 200,000 hours of tape recordings, including all types of music, oral history, drama, literature, poetry, wildlife, selected BBC broadcasts and BBC Sound Archive material. Produces a twice-yearly newsletter, *Playback*. For information on British Library Sound Archive collections and services, visit the website.

British Psychological Society Library

c/o Psychology Library, Senate House Library, University of London, Senate House, Malet Street, London WC1E 7HU

☎020 7862 8451/8461 Fax 020 7862 8480

✉ enquiries@shl.lon.ac.uk

www.shl.lon.ac.uk

OPEN Term-time: 9.00 am to 9.00 pm Monday to Thursday; 9.00 am to 6.30 pm Friday; 9.30 am to 5.30 pm Saturday (Holidays: 9.00 am to 6.00 pm Monday to Friday; 9.30 am to 5.30 pm Saturday)

ACCESS Members only; Non-members £5 day ticket

Reference library, containing the British Psychological Society collection of periodicals – over 140 current titles housed alongside the University of London's collection of books and journals. Largely for academic research. General queries referred to **Swiss Cottage Library** in London which has a good psychology collection.

Benjamin Britten Collection

See **Suffolk County Council – Suffolk Libraries**

Bromley Central Library

High Street, Bromley BR1 1EX

☎020 8460 9955 Fax 020 8466 7860

✉ central.library@bromley.gov.uk

www.bromley.gov.uk

OPEN 9.30 am to 6.00 pm Monday, Wednesday, Friday; 9.30 am to 8.00 pm Tuesday and Thursday; 9.30 am to 5.00 pm Saturday

OPEN ACCESS

A large selection of fiction and non-fiction books for loan, both adult and children's. Also DVDs, videos, CDs, cassettes, language courses, open learning packs, CD-ROM and Playstation games for hire. Other facilities include CD-ROMs, computer hire, People's Network Internet, local studies library, 'Upfront' teenage section, large reference library with photocop-

ying, fax, microfiche and film facilities, 'Bromley Knowledge' – online community information, reading groups and Local Links (access to council services). Library and Archives catalogues online, 'Bromley Training Truck' – free computer and basic skills training. SPECIALIST COLLECTIONS include: H.G. Wells, Walter de la Mare, Crystal Palace, The Harlow Bequest, and the history and geography of Asia, America, Australasia and the Polar regions.

Bromley House Library

Angel Row, Nottingham NG1 6HL

☎0115 947 3134

✉ nfl@bromho.freeserve.co.uk

Librarian *Carol Allison*

OPEN 9.30 am to 5.00 pm Monday to Friday; also first Saturday of each month from 10.00 am to 12.30 pm

ACCESS For members only

Founded 1816 as the Nottingham Subscription Library. Collection of 35,000 books including local history, topography, biography, travel and fiction.

Robert Burns Collection

See **The Mitchell Library**

CAA Library and Information Centre

Aviation House, Gatwick Airport South, Gatwick RH6 0YR

☎01293 573725 Fax 01293 573181

✉ infoservices@caa.co.uk

www.caa.co.uk

OPEN 9.00 am to 5.00 pm Monday to Friday

OPEN ACCESS

A collection of books, reports, directories, statistics and periodicals on most aspects of civil aviation and related subjects.

Cambridge Central Library (Reference Library & Information Service)

7 Lion Yard, Cambridge CB2 3QD

☎0845 045 5225 Fax 01223 712011

✉ cambridge.central.library@cambridgeshire.gov.uk

www.cambridgeshire.gov.uk/leisure/libraries

The Central Library is closed until spring 2008 for major redevelopment. During this period a full range of services is available through the network of 31 libraries in the county (details on the website) and by telephone, post, e-mail and online referral.

Large stock of books, periodicals, newspapers, maps, plus comprehensive collection of directories and annuals covering UK, Europe and the world. Microfilm and fiche reading and printing services. Online access to news and business databases. News databases on CD-ROM; Internet access. Monochrome and colour photocopiers.

Camomile Street Library

12–20 Camomile Street, London EC3A 7EX
☎020 7247 8895
✉ camomile@cityoflondon.gov.uk
www.cityoflondon.gov.uk/camomilestlibrary

OPEN 9.30 am to 5.30 pm Monday, Tuesday, Thursday, Friday; 9.30 am to 6.30 pm Wednesday

OPEN ACCESS
City of London Corporation lending library. Wide range of fiction and non-fiction books and language courses on cassette and CD, foreign fiction, paperbacks, maps and guides for travel at home and abroad, children's books, a selection of large print, and collections of DVDs, videos and music CDs, books in Bengali. Spoken word recordings on cassette and CD. Free Internet access.

Cardiff Central Library

John Street, Cardiff CF10 5BA
☎029 2038 2116 Fax 029 2087 1599
✉ rboddy@cardiff.gov.uk
www.cardiff.gov.uk/libraries

OPEN 9.00 am to 6.00 pm Monday, Tuesday, Wednesday, Friday; 9.00 am to 7.00 pm Thursday; 9.00 am to 5.30 pm Saturday

General lending library with the following departments: leisure, music, children's, local studies, information, science and humanities.

Carmarthen Public Library

St Peter's Street, Carmarthen SA31 1LN
☎01267 224824 Fax 01267 221839
✉ wtphillips@carmarthenshire.gov.uk
www.carmarthenshire.gov.uk

OPEN 9.30 am to 7.00 pm Monday, Tuesday, Wednesday, Friday; 9.30 am to 5.00 pm Thursday and Saturday

OPEN ACCESS
Comprehensive range of fiction, non-fiction, children's books and reference works in English and in Welsh. Large local history library. Free Internet access and computer facilities. Large Print books, audiobooks, CDs, CD-ROMs, DVDs and videos available for loan.

Catholic Central Library

St Michaels Abbey, Farnborough Road, Farnborough GU14 7NQ
✉ library@catholic-library.org.uk
www.catholic-library.org.uk

OPEN ACCESS For reference (non-members must sign in; loans restricted to members)
Contains books, many not readily available elsewhere, on theology, religions worldwide, scripture and the history of churches of all denominations.

City Business Library

1 Brewers' Hall Garden, off Aldermanbury Square, London EC2V 5BX
☎020 7332 1812/(3803 textphone)
Fax 020 7332 1847
✉ cbl@cityoflondon.gov.uk
www.cityoflondon.gov.uk/citylibrary

OPEN 9.30 am to 5.00 pm Monday to Friday (except public holidays)

OPEN ACCESS
Local authority free public reference library run by the Corporation of London. Books, directories, periodicals, newspapers and electronic databases of current business interest. Provided for anyone with a business informatin enquiry and is one of the leading public resource centres in Britain in its field. Large directory collection for both the UK and overseas, plus companies information, market research reports, management, banking, insurance, investment and statistics. Free public Internet access. No academic journals or textbooks.

Commonwealth Secretariat Library

Marlborough House, Pall Mall, London SW1Y 5HX
☎020 7747 6164 Fax 020 7747 6168
✉ library@commonwealth.int
www.thecommonwealth.org
Library Services Manager *David Blake*

OPEN 10.00 am to 4.45 pm Monday to Friday

ACCESS For reference only, by appointment
Extensive reference source concerned with economy, development, trade, production and industry of Commonwealth countries; also human resources including women, youth, health, management and education. Includes the archives of the Secretariat.

Corporation of London Libraries
See **Barbican Library**; **Camomile Street Library**; **City Business Library**; **Guildhall Library**

Coventry Central Library
Smithford Way, Coventry CV1 1FY
☎024 7683 2314/2395 (Minicom)
Fax 024 7683 2440
✉ central.library@coventry.gov.uk
www.coventry.gov.uk
OPEN 9.00 am to 8.00 pm Monday to Friday;
9.00 am to 4.30 pm Saturday; 12.00 am to
4.00 pm Sunday
OPEN ACCESS
Located in the middle of the city's main
shopping centre. Approximately 120,000 items
(books, cassettes, CDs and DVDs) for loan; plus
reference collection of business information
and local history. SPECIAL COLLECTIONS Cycling
and motor industries; George Eliot; Angela
Brazil; Tom Mann Collection (trade union and
labour studies); local newspapers on microfilm
from 1740 onwards. Over 300 periodicals taken.
'Peoplelink' community information database
available.

Crace Collection
See **British Library Map Collections**

Department for Environment, Food and Rural Affairs
Nobel House, 17 Smith Square, London
SW1P 3JR
☎020 7238 3000 Fax 020 7238 6591
DEFRA Helpline 08459 335577 (local call rate):
general contact point which can provide information on the work of DEFRA, either directly
or by referring callers to appropriate contacts.
Available 9.00 am to 5.00 pm Monday to Friday
(excluding Bank Holidays)
OPEN 9.30 am to 5.00 pm Monday to Friday
ACCESS For reference (but at least 24 hours
notice must be given for intended visits)
Large stock of volumes on temperate
agriculture.

Derby Central Library
Wardwick, Derby DE1 1HS
☎01332 255398 Fax 01332 369570
www.derby.gov.uk/libraries
OPEN 9.30 am to 7.00 pm Monday, Tuesday,
Thursday, Friday; 9.30 am to 1.00 pm
Wednesday; 9.30 am to 4.00 pm Saturday

Local Studies Library
25B Irongate, Derby DE1 3GL
☎ 01332 255393 Fax 01332 255381
OPEN 9.30 am to 7.00 pm Monday and Tuesday;
9.30 am to 5.00 pm Wednesday, Thursday, Friday;
9.30 am to 4.00 pm Saturday
OPEN ACCESS
General library for lending, information and
Children's Services. The Central Library also
houses specialist private libraries: Derbyshire
Archaeological Society; Derby Philatelic Society.
The Local Studies Library houses the largest
multimedia collection of resources in existence
relating to Derby and Derbyshire. The collection includes mss deeds, family papers, business
records including the Derby Canal Company,
Derby Board of Guardians and the Derby China
Factory. Both libraries offer free Internet access.

Devon & Exeter Institution Library
7 Cathedral Close, Exeter EX1 1EZ
☎01392 251017
✉ J.P.Gardner@exeter.ac.uk
www.devonandexeterinstitution.org.uk
OPEN 9.30 am to 5.00 pm Monday to Friday
ACCESS Members only (temporary membership
available)
Founded 1813. Under the administration of
Exeter University Library. Contains over 36,000
volumes, including long runs of 19th-century
journals, theology, history, topography, early
science, biography and literature. A large and
growing collection of books, journals, newspapers, prints and maps relating to the South West.

Doncaster Library and Information Services
Central Library, Waterdale, Doncaster DN1 3JE
☎01302 734305 Fax 01302 369749
✉ Reference.Library@doncaster.gov.uk
library.doncaster.gov.uk
OPEN 9.00 am to 6.00 pm Monday; 8.30 am
to 6.00 pm Tuesday and Friday; 8.30 am to
8.00 pm Wednesday and Thursday; 9.00 am
to 5.00 pm Saturday
OPEN ACCESS
Books, spoken word cassettes/CDs, DVDs,
videos. Reading aids unit for people with visual
impairment; activities for children during school
holidays, including visits by authors, readers'
groups, etc. Also reference library and Local
Studies library.

Dorchester Library (part of Dorset County Library)

Colliton Park, Dorchester DT1 1XJ
☎01305 224440 (lending)/224448 (reference)
Fax 01305 266120
✉ dorchesterreferencelibrary@dorsetcc.gov.uk
www.dorsetforyou.com/libraries
OPEN 10.00 am to 7.00 pm Monday; 9.30 am to 7.00 pm Tuesday, Wednesday, Friday; 9.30 am to 5.00 pm Thursday; 9.00 am to 4.00 pm Saturday

OPEN ACCESS
General lending and reference library, including special collections on Thomas Hardy, the Powys Family and William Barnes. Periodicals, children's library, CD-ROMs, free Internet access. Video lending service.

Dundee Central Library

The Wellgate, Dundee DD1 1DB
☎01382 431500 Fax 01382 431558
✉ central.library@dundeecity.gov.uk
www.dundeecity.gov.uk
OPEN Lending & Local Studies Departments and General Reference: 9.30 am to 6.00 pm Monday, Tuesday, Friday; 10.00 am to 6.00 pm Wednesday; 9.30 am to 8.00 pm Thursday; 9.30 am to 5.00 pm Saturday. Commerce & Technology: 9.30 am to 9.00 pm Monday, Tuesday, Thursday, Friday; 10.00 am to 9.00 pm Wednesday; 9.30 am to 5.00 pm Saturday.

ACCESS Reference services available to all; lending services to those who live, work, study or were educated within Dundee City
Adult lending, reference and children's services. Art, music, audio, video and DVD lending services. Internet access. Schools service (Agency). Housebound and mobile services. SPECIAL COLLECTIONS The Wighton Collection of National Music; The Wighton Heritage Centre; The Wilson Photographic Collection; The Lamb Collection.

Durning-Lawrence Library

See Senate House Library

English Nature

See Natural England

Equal Opportunities Commission

Arndale House, Arndale Centre, Manchester M4 3EQ
☎0845 601 5901 Fax 0161 838 8312
✉ info@eoc.org.uk

www.eoc.org.uk
The EOC is open to the public via the Helpline (0845 601 5901) 9.00 am to 5.00 pm Mondays to Fridays.

Essex County Council Libraries

Goldlay Gardens, Chelmsford CM2 0EW
☎01245 284981 Fax 01245 492780
✉ essexlib@essexcc.gov.uk
www.essexcc.gov.uk
Essex County Council Libraries has 73 static libraries throughout Essex as well as 13 mobile libraries and three special-needs mobiles. Services to the public include books, newspapers, periodicals, CDs, cassettes, videos, CD-ROMs and Internet access. Specialist subjects and collections are listed below at the relevant library.

Chelmsford Library

PO Box 882, Market Road, Chelmsford CM1 1LH
☎ 01245 492758 Fax 01245 492536
✉ chelmford.library@essexcc.gov.uk
OPEN 8.30 am to 7.00 pm Monday to Friday; 8.30 am to 5.30 pm Saturday; 12.30 pm to 4.30 pm Sunday

Colchester Library

Trinity Square, Colchester CO1 1JB
☎ 01206 245900 Fax 01206 245901
✉ colchester.library@essexcc.gov.uk
OPEN 8.30 am to 7.30 pm Monday to Friday; 8.30 am to 5.00 pm Saturday; 12.30 pm to 4.30 pm Sunday

Local studies; Castle collection (18th-century subscription library); Cunnington collection; Margaret Lazell collection; Taylor collection.

Harlow Library

The High, Harlow CM20 1HA
☎ 01279 413772 Fax 01279 424612
✉ harlow.library@essexcc.gov.uk
OPEN 9.00 am to 7.00 pm Monday to Friday; 9.00 am to 5.00 pm Saturday; 1.00 pm to 4.00 pm Sunday
Sir John Newson Memorial collection; Maurice Hughes Memorial collection.

Loughton Library

Traps Hill, Loughton IG10 1HD
☎ 020 8502 0181 Fax 020 8508 5041
✉ loughton.library@essexcc.gov.uk
OPEN 9.00 am to 7.00 pm Monday to Friday; 9.30 am to 5.30 pm Saturday; 11.00 am to 3.00 pm Sunday
National Jazz Foundation Archive.

Saffron Walden Library
2 King Street, Saffron Walden CB10 1ES
☎ 01799 523178 Fax 01799 513642
OPEN 9.00 am to 7.00 pm Monday, Tuesday, Friday; 9.00 am to 8.00 pm Thursday; 9.00 am to 5.00 pm Saturday; 1.00 pm to 4.00 pm Sunday (closed Wednesday)
Victorian studies collection.

Witham Library
18 Newland Street, Witham CM8 2AQ
☎ 01376 519625 Fax 01376 501913
OPEN 9.00 am to 7.00 pm Monday to Friday; 9.00 am to 5.00 pm Saturday; 1.00 pm to 4.00 pm Sunday
Dorothy L. Sayers and Maskell collections.

Family Records Centre
1 Myddleton Street, London EC1R 1UW
☎020 8392 5200 Fax 020 8487 9214
✉ frc@nationalarchives.gov.uk
www.familyrecords.gov.uk/frc
OPEN 9.00 am to 5.00 pm Monday, Wednesday, Friday; 10.00 am to 7.00 pm Tuesday; 9.00 am to 7.00 pm Thursday; 9.30 am to 5.00 pm Saturday (closed Sunday)
ACCESS for reference; no i.d. required
The Centre provides a family history service to visitors, advising on how to use the wealth of genealogical records available, including births, marriages and deaths and census returns. Part of the **National Archives** and the **Office for National Statistics** (see entries).

The Fawcett Library
See **The Women's Library**

Edward Fitzgerald Collection
See **Suffolk County Council – Suffolk Libraries**

Forestry Commission Library
Forest Research Station, Alice Holt Lodge, Wrecclesham, Farnham GU10 4LH
☎01420 22255 Fax 01420 23653
✉ library@forestry.gsi.gov.uk
www.forestry.gov.uk
www.forestresearch.gov.uk
OPEN 9.00 am to 5.00 pm Monday to Thursday; 9.00 am to 4.30 pm Friday
ACCESS By appointment for personal visits
Approximately 20,000 books on forestry and arboriculture, plus 500 current journals. CD-ROMS include TREECD (1939 onwards). Offers a Research Advisory Service for advice and enquiries on forestry (☎ 01420 23000) with

a charge for consultations and diagnosis of tree problems exceeding ten minutes.

French Institute Library
Institut français du Royaume Uni, 17 Queensberry Place, London SW7 2DT
☎020 7073 1350 Fax 020 7073 1363
✉ library@ambafrance.org.uk
www.institut-francais.org.uk
OPEN 12 noon to 7.00 pm Tuesday to Friday; 12 noon to 6.00 pm Saturday; Children's Library: 12 noon to 6.00 pm Tuesday to Saturday; closed in August; closed for one week at Christmas
OPEN ACCESS For reference and consultation (loans restricted to members; leaflet available on demand)
A collection of over 55,000 volumes mainly centred on French cultural interests with special emphasis on language, literature and history. Books, mainly in French, a few in English and some bilingual. Collection of DVDs, videos, periodicals, CDs (French music), CD-ROMs, audiobooks; special collections: 'France Libre'. Denis Saurat MSS, recordings of lectures, press-cuttings on French current affairs. Inter-library loans; quick information service; Edufrance; Internet access to members. Group visits on request. Children's library (8000 documents).

The Froebel Archive for Childhood Studies
See entry under *Useful Websites*

John Frost Newspapers
22b Rosemary Avenue, Enfield EN2 0SS
☎020 8366 1392/0946 Fax 020 8366 1379
✉ andrew@johnfrostnewspapers.com
www.johnfrostnewspapers.co.uk
Contacts *Andrew Frost, John Frost*
A collection of 80,000 original newspapers (1630 to the present day) and 200,000 press cuttings available, on loan, for research and rostrum/stills work (TV documentaries, book and magazine publishers and audiovisual presentations). Historic events, politics, sports, royalty, crime, wars, personalities, etc., plus many in-depth files.

German Historical Institute Library
17 Bloomsbury Square, London WC1A 2NJ
☎020 7309 2050 Fax 020 7404 5573
✉ library@ghil.ac.uk
www.ghil.ac.uk

OPEN 10.00 am to 5.00 pm Monday, Tuesday, Wednesday, Friday; 10.00 am to 8.00 pm Thursday

OPEN ACCESS Visitors must bring proof of address and recent photograph to be issued with a reader's ticket

70,000 volumes; around 200 journals; databases. Devoted primarily to German history from the Middle Ages to the present day, with special emphasis on the 19th and 20th centuries, in particular Germany between 1933 and 1945, the development of the two German states after 1945/49 and German unification after 1989.

Gloucestershire County Council Libraries & Information

Quayside House, Shire Hall, Gloucester GL1 2HY

☎08452 305420 Fax 01452 425042

✉ libraryhelp@gloucestershire.gov.uk

www.libraries.gloucestershire.gov.uk/

Head of Libraries & Information *David Paynter*

OPEN ACCESS

The service includes 39 local libraries and five mobile libraries. The website includes library opening hours, mobile library route schedules; the library catalogue; book renewal/reservations facility; and information about news and events.

Goethe-Institut Library

50 Princes Gate, Exhibition Road, London SW7 2PH

☎020 7596 4040 Fax 020 7594 0230

✉ library@london.goethe.org

www.goethe.de/london

Librarian *Elisabeth Pyroth*

OPEN 1.00 pm to 8.00 pm Monday to Thursday; 1.00 pm to 5.00 pm Saturday

Library specialising in German literature and books/audiovisual material on German culture and history: 20,000 books (4000 of them in English), 120 periodicals, 13 newspapers, 3700 audiovisual media (including 1200 videos/DVDs), selected press clippings on German affairs from the German and UK press, information service, photocopier, video facility. Also German language teaching material for teachers and students of German. See website for membership details.

Goldsmiths' Library

See **Senate House Library**

Greater London Record Office

See **London Metropolitan Archives Library Services**

Guildford Institute of the University of Surrey Library

Ward Street, Guildford GU1 4LH

☎01483 562142 Fax 01483 451034

✉ guildford-institute@surrey.ac.uk

OPEN 10.00 am to 3.00 pm Tuesday to Friday

OPEN ACCESS To members only but open to enquirers for research purposes

Founded 1834. Some 14,000 volumes of which 7500 were printed before the First World War. The remaining stock consists of recently published works of fiction and non-fiction. Newspapers and periodicals also available. SPECIAL COLLECTIONS include an almost complete run of the *Illustrated London News* from 1843–1906, a collection of Victorian and early 20th century local history ephemera albums, and about 400 photos and other pictures relating to the Institute's history and the town of Guildford.

Guildhall Library

Aldermanbury, London EC2V 7HH

☎See below Fax 020 7600 3384

www.cityoflondon.gov.uk/guildhalllibrary

ACCESS For reference (but much of the material is kept in storage areas and is supplied to readers on request; proof of identity is required for consultation of certain categories of stock). Free, *limited* enquiry service available.

Also a fee-based service for in-depth research:

☎ 020 7332 1854 Fax 020 7600 3384

✉ search.guildhall@cityoflondon.gov.uk

www.cityoflondon.gov.uk/search_guildhall

Part of the City of London libraries. Seeks to provide a basic general reference service but its major strength, acknowledged worldwide, is in its historical collections. The library is divided into three sections, each with its own catalogues and enquiry desks. These are: Printed Books; Manuscripts; the Print & Maps Room.

PRINTED BOOKS

☎ 020 7332 1868/1870

✉ printed books.guildhall@cityoflondon. gov.uk

OPEN 9.30 am to 5 pm Monday to Saturday; NB closes on Saturdays preceding Bank Holidays; check for details

Strong on all aspects of London history, with wide holdings of English history, topography and genealogy, including local directories, poll books and parish register transcripts. Also good collections of English statutes, law reports, parliamentary debates and journals, and House of Commons papers. Home of several important collections deposited by London institutions: the Marine collection of the Corporation of Lloyd's, the Stock Exchange's historical files of reports and prospectuses, the Clockmakers' Company library and museum, the Gardeners' Company, Fletchers' Company, the Institute of Masters of Wine, International Wine and Food Society and Gresham College.

MANUSCRIPTS
☎ 020 7332 1862/3
✉ manuscripts.guildhall@cityoflondon.gov.uk
www.history.ac.uk/gh/

OPEN 9.30 am to 5.00 pm Monday to Saturday (no requests for records after 4.30 pm; no manuscripts can be produced between 12 noon and 2 pm on Saturdays); NB closes on Saturdays preceding Bank Holidays; check for details

The official repository for historical records relating to the City of London (except those of the City of London Corporation itself, which are housed at the London Metropolitan Archives). Records date from the 11th century to the present day. They include archives of most of the City's parishes, wards and livery companies, and of many individuals, families, estates, schools, societies and other institutions, notably the Diocese of London and St Paul's Cathedral, as well as the largest collection of business archives in any public repository in the UK. Although mainly of City interest, holdings include material for the London area as a whole and beyond. Many of the records are of national and international significance.

PRINTS & MAPS ROOM
☎ 020 7332 1839
✉ prints&maps@cityoflondon.gov.uk
OPEN 9.30 am to 5.00 pm Monday to Friday

An unrivalled collection of prints and drawings relating to London and the adjacent counties. The emphasis is on topography, but there are strong collections of portraits and satirical prints. The map collection includes maps of the capital from the mid-16th century to the present day and various classes of Ordnance Survey maps. Other material includes photographs, theatre bills and programmes, trade cards, book plates and playing cards as well as a sizeable collection of Old Master prints. Over 30,000 items have been digitally imaged on the 'Collage' website, including topographical prints, some maps, a small number of photographs and all the Guildhall Art Gallery collection. 'Collage' website: collage.cityoflondon.gov.uk

Guille–Alles Library
Market Street, St Peter Port, Guernsey
GY1 1HB
☎01481 720392 Fax 01481 712425
✉ ga@library.gg
www.library.gg
OPEN 9.00 am to 5.00 pm Monday, Thursday, Friday, Saturday; 10.00 am to 5.00 pm Tuesday; 9.00 am to 8.00 pm Wednesday

OPEN ACCESS For residents; payment of returnable deposit by visitors. Music CD collection: £10 for two-year subscription

Lending, reference and information services. Public Internet service.

Herefordshire Libraries
Shirehall, Hereford HR1 2HX
☎01432 261644 Fax 01432 260744
✉ libraries@herefordshire.gov.uk
www.libraries.herefordshire.gov.uk

OPEN Opening hours vary in the libraries across the county

ACCESS Information and reference services open to anyone; loans to members only (membership criteria: resident, being educated, working, or an elector in the county or neighbouring authorities. Proof of identity and address required.) Temporary membership to visitors is also available.

Information service, reference and lending libraries. Non-fiction and fiction for all age groups, including normal and large print, spoken word cassettes, and CDs, music CDs, DVDs, playstation2. Hereford Library houses the largest reference section and the county local history collection, although some reference material and local history is available at all libraries. Internet access at all libraries. *Special collections* Cidermaking; Beekeeping; Alfred Watkins; John Masefield; Pilley.

University of Hertfordshire Library
College Lane, Hatfield AL10 9AB
☎01707 284678 Fax 01707 284666
www.herts.ac.uk/lis
OPEN See website for term-time and vacation opening hours

ACCESS For reference use of printed collections. Appropriate ID required for Visitor's pass.

For further information please refer to the website.

Highgate Literary and Scientific Institution Library
11 South Grove, London N6 6BS

☎020 8340 3343 Fax 020 8340 5632
✉ librarian@hlsi.net
OPEN 10.00 am to 5.00 pm Tuesday to Friday;
10.00 am to 4.00 pm Saturday (closed
Sunday and Monday)
ANNUAL MEMBERSHIP £55 (individual); £90
(household)
25,000 volumes of general fiction and non-
fiction, with a children's section and extensive
local archives. SPECIAL COLLECTIONS on local
history, London, and local poets Samuel Taylor
Coleridge and John Betjeman.

Highland Libraries, The Highland Council, Education, Culture and Sport Service

Library Support Unit, 31a Harbour Road,
Inverness IV1 1UA
☎01463 235713 Fax 01463 236986
✉ libraries@highland.gov.uk
www.highland.gov.uk
OPEN Library opening hours vary to suit local
needs. Contact administration and support
services for details (8.00 am to 6.00 pm
Monday to Friday)
OPEN ACCESS
Comprehensive range of lending and reference stock: books, pamphlets, periodicals, newspapers, compact discs, audio and video cassettes,
maps, census records, genealogical records,
photographs, educational materials, etc. Free
access to the Internet in all libraries. Highland
Libraries provides the public library service
throughout the Highlands with a network of 43
static and 12 mobile libraries.

Paul Hirsch Music Collection

See **British Library Music Collections**

Holborn Library

32–38 Theobalds Road, London WC1X 8PA
☎020 7974 6345
OPEN 10.00 am to 7.00 pm Monday and
Thursday; 10.00 am to 6.00 pm Tuesday,
Wednesday and Friday; 10.00 am to 5.00
pm Saturday
OPEN ACCESS
London Borough of Camden public library.
Includes the London Borough of Camden Local
Studies and Archive Centre.

Sherlock Holmes Collection (Westminster)

Marylebone Library, Marylebone Road,
London NW1 5PS

☎020 7641 1206 Fax 020 7641 1019
✉ ccooke@westminster.gov.uk
www.westminster.gov.uk/libraries/special/
sherlock.cfm
OPEN 9.30 am to 8.00 pm Monday, Tuesday,
Thursday, Friday; 10.00 am to 8.00 pm
Wednesday; closed Saturday and Sunday
(unless by prior arrangement)
ACCESS By appointment only
Located in Westminster's Marylebone
Library. An extensive collection of material from
all over the world, covering Sherlock Holmes
and Sir Arthur Conan Doyle. Books, pamphlets,
journals, newspaper cuttings and photos, much
of which is otherwise unavailable in this country.
Some background material.

IHR Library

See **The Institute of Historical Research**

Imperial College Central Library

See **Science Museum Library**

Imperial War Museum

Department of Printed Books, Lambeth Road,
London SE1 6HZ
☎020 7416 5342 Fax 020 7416 5246
✉ books@iwm.org.uk
www.iwm.org.uk
OPEN 10.00 am to 5.00 pm Monday to
Saturday (restricted service Saturday; closed
on Bank Holiday Saturdays and two weeks
during the year for annual stock check)
ACCESS For reference (but at least 24 hours'
notice must be given for intended visits)
A large collection of material on British
and Commonwealth 20th-century life with
detailed coverage of the two World Wars and
other conflicts. This collection includes substantial holdings of European language material.
Books, pamphlets and periodicals, including
many produced for short periods in unlikely
wartime settings; also maps, biographies and
privately printed memoirs, and foreign language
material. Additional research material available
in the departments of Art, Documents, Exhibits
and Firearms and in the Film, Photographs and
Sound Archives. See www.iwmcollections.
org.uk for their online catalogues. Publishing
programme is part based on reprints of rare
books held in library.

The Institute of Historical Research

Senate House, Malet Street, London
WC1E 7HU

☎020 7862 8760 Fax 020 7862 8762
✉ IHR.Library@sas.ac.uk
www.history.ac.uk/library
OPEN 9.00 am to 8.45 pm Monday to Friday;
9.30 am to 5.15 pm Saturday
ACCESS For reference only. Non-members are
advised to telephone to check availability of
items before visiting.

Reference collection of printed primary
sources, bibliographies, guides to archives,
periodicals and works covering the history of
Western Europe from the fall of the Roman
Empire. Holds a substantial microform collection of mainly British material from repositories
outside London.

Instituto Cervantes
102 Eaton Square, London SW1W 9AN
☎020 7201 0757 Fax 020 7235 0329
✉ biblon@cervantes.es
londres.cervantes.es
OPEN 12 noon to 7.30 pm Monday to
Thursday; 12 noon to 6.30 pm Friday; 9.30
am to 2.00 pm Saturday
OPEN ACCESS For reference and lending
Spanish language and literature, history, art,
philosophy. The library houses a collection of
books, periodicals, videos, DVDs, slides, tapes,
CDs, cassettes, CD-ROMs specialising entirely
in Spain and Latin America.

Italian Institute Library
39 Belgrave Square, London SW1X 8NX
☎020 7396 4425 Fax 020 7235 4618
www.icilondon.esteri.it
OPEN 10.00 am to 1.30 pm and 2.30 pm to
5.00 pm Monday to Friday. Term-time:
10.00 am to 1.30 pm and 2.30 pm to 5.00
pm Monday, Tuesday, Thursday, Friday; 2.30
pm to 8.00 pm Wednesday; 10.30 am to
4.30 pm Saturday (first and third of each
month). The Library is now open to the
general public every Wednesday evening
and on the first and third Saturday of each
month during term time. Call 020 7396
4425 to confirm exact opening times.
OPEN ACCESS For reference
A collection of over 30,000 volumes relating
to all aspects of Italian culture, including DVDs
and CDs relating to Italian cinema. Texts are
mostly in Italian, with some in English.

Jersey Library
Halkett Place, St Helier, Jersey JE2 4WH
☎01534 448700 (Jersey Library)/448701

(Reference)/448702 (Open Learning)/448733
(Branch Library)
Fax 01534 448730
✉ je.library@.gov.je
www.gov.je/library
OPEN 9.30 am to 5.30 pm Monday, Wednesday,
Thursday, Friday; 9.30 am to 7.30 pm
Tuesday; 9.30 am to 4.00 pm Saturday
OPEN ACCESS
Books, periodicals, newspapers, CDs,
DVDs and language packs, cassettes, videos,
microfilm, specialised local studies collection,
public Internet access. Branch Library at Les
Quennevais School, St Brelade. Mobile library
and homes services. Open Learning Centre.

Kent County Central Library
Kent Libraries and Archives, Springfield,
Maidstone ME14 2LH
☎01622 696511 Fax 01622 696494
✉ countycentrallibrary@kent.gov.uk
www.kent.gov.uk/libs
OPEN 9.00 am to 6.00 pm Monday to Friday;
9.00 am to 5.00 pm Saturday
OPEN ACCESS
50,000 volumes available on the floor of the
library plus 250,000 volumes of non-fiction,
mostly academic, available on request to staff.
English literature, poetry, classical literature,
drama (including play sets), music (including
music sets). Strong, too, in sociology, art history,
business information and government publications. Loans to all who live or work in Kent;
those who do not may consult stock for reference or arrange loans via their own local library
service.

King George III Topographic Collection and Maritime Collection
See **British Library Map Collections**

Leeds Central Library
Calverley Street, Leeds LS1 3AB
☎0113 247 8911 Fax 0113 247 8426
www.leeds.gov.uk/libraries
OPEN 9.00 am to 8.00 pm Monday, Tuesday,
Wednesday; 9.30 am to 5.30 pm Thursday;
9.00 pm to 5.00 pm Friday; 10.00 am to
5.00 pm Saturday; 12.00 noon to 4.00 pm
Sunday
OPEN ACCESS to lending libraries; reference
material on request. Free public Internet access.
Lending Library.
☎ 0113 247 8270

✉ centrallending@leedslearning.net

Music Library
☎ 0113 247 8273
✉ musiclibrary@leedslearning.net
Scores, books, video and audio.

Business & Research Library
☎ 0113 247 8282
✉ businessandresearch@leedslearning.net

Company information, market research, statistics, directories, journals and computer-based information. Extensive files of newspapers and periodicals plus all government publications since 1960. SPECIAL COLLECTIONS include military history, Judaic, early gardening books.

Art Library
☎ 0113 247 8247
✉ artlibrary@leedslearning.net
Major collection of material on fine and applied arts.

Local Studies Library
☎ 0113 247 8290
✉ localstudies@leedslearning.net

Extensive collection on Leeds and Yorkshire, including maps, books, pamphlets, local newspapers, illustrations and playbills. Census returns for the whole of Yorkshire also available. International Genealogical Index and parish registers. Leeds City Libraries has an extensive network of 65 branch and mobile libraries.

Leeds Library

18 Commercial Street, Leeds LS1 6AL
☎0113 245 3071 Fax 0113 245 1191
OPEN 9.00 am to 5.00 pm Monday to Friday
ACCESS To members; research use upon application to the librarian
Founded 1768. Contains over 125,000 books and periodicals from the 15th century to the present day. SPECIAL COLLECTIONS include Reformation pamphlets, Civil War tracts, Victorian and Edwardian children's books and fiction, European language material, spiritualism and psychical research, plus local material.

Library of the Religious Society of Friends

Friends House, 173 Euston Road, London NW1 2BJ
☎020 7663 1135 Fax 020 7663 1001
✉ library@quaker.org.uk
www.quaker.org.uk
OPEN 1.00 pm to 5.00 pm Monday, Tuesday, Thursday, Friday; 10.00 am to 5.00 pm Wednesday

OPEN ACCESS Reader registration required with proof of permanent address
Quaker history, thought and activities from the 17th century onwards. Supporting collections on peace, anti-slavery and other subjects in which Quakers have maintained long-standing interest. Also archives and manuscripts relating to the Society of Friends.

Lincoln Central Library

Free School Lane, Lincoln LN2 1EZ
☎01522 510800/782010 Fax 01522 535882
✉ lincoln.library@lincolnshire.gov.uk
www.lincolnshire.gov.uk
OPEN 9.30 am to 7.00 pm Monday to Friday; 9.30 am to 4.00 pm Saturday
OPEN ACCESS to the library; appointment required for the Tennyson Research Centre
Lending and reference library. Special collections include Lincolnshire local history (printed and published material, photographs, maps, directories and census data) and the Tennyson Research Centre (contact *Grace Timmins*, grace.timmins@lincolnshire.gov.uk).

Linen Hall Library

17 Donegall Square North, Belfast BT1 5GB
☎028 9032 1707 Fax 028 9043 8586
✉ info@linenhall.com
www.linenhall.com
Librarian *John Gray*
OPEN 9.30 am to 5.30 pm Monday to Friday; 9.30 am to 1.00 pm Saturday
OPEN ACCESS For reference (loans restricted to members)
Founded 1788. Contains about 200,000 books. Major Irish and local studies collections, including the Northern Ireland Political Collection relating to the current troubles (c. 250,000 items).

Literary & Philosophical Society of Newcastle upon Tyne

23 Westgate Road, Newcastle upon Tyne NE1 1SE
☎0191 232 0192 Fax 0191 261 4494
✉ library@litandphil.org.uk
www.litandphil.org.uk
Librarian *Kay Easson*
OPEN 9.30 am to 7.00 pm Monday, Wednesday, Thursday; 9.30 am to 8.00 pm Tuesday; 9.30 am to 5.00 pm Friday; 9.30 am to 1.00 pm Saturday
ACCESS Members; research facilities for *bona fide* scholars on application to the Librarian

200-year-old library of 140,000 volumes, periodicals (including 130 current titles), classical music on vinyl recordings and CD, plus a collection of scores. Free public lectures, events and recitals. Recent publications include: *The Reverend William Turner: Dissent and Reform in Georgian Newcastle upon Tyne* Stephen Harbottle; *History of the Literary and Philosophical Society of Newcastle upon Tyne, Vol. 2 (1896–1989)* Charles Parish; *Bicentenary Lectures 1993* ed. John Philipson.

Liverpool Libraries and Information Services

William Brown Street, Liverpool L3 8EW
☎0151 233 5829 Fax 0151 233 5886
✉ refbt.central.library@liverpool.gov.uk
www.liverpool.gov.uk/libraries
OPEN 9.00 am to 6.00 pm Monday to Friday;
     9.00 am to 5.00 pm Saturday; 12 noon to
     4.00 pm Sunday
OPEN ACCESS

Learn Direct Centre – UK Online Centre
Free broadband internet access.

Humanities Reference Library
A total stock in excess of 120,000 volumes and 24,000 maps, plus book plates, prints and autographed letters. SPECIAL COLLECTIONS Walter Crane and Edward Lear illustrations, Kelmscott Press, Audubon's *Birds of America*.

Business and Technology Reference Library
Extensive stock dealing with all aspects of science, commerce and technology, including British and European standards and patents and trade directories.

Audio Visual Library
Extensive stock relating to all aspects of music. Includes 128,000 volumes and music scores, over 3000 CDs, 2000 videos and 800 DVDs.

Record Office and Local History Department
Material relating to Liverpool, Merseyside, Lancashire and Cheshire, together with archive material mainly on Liverpool. Proof of name and address required to obtain reader's ticket.

Lending Library
Graphic novels, large print collection, children's collections, audio books, study support collections, Reader friendly displays of bestsellers and out of print titles.

University of the Arts London – London College of Communication

Library and Learning Resources, Elephant and Castle, London SE1 6SB
☎020 7514 6527 Fax 020 7514 6527
www.lcc.arts.ac.uk
ACCESS Appointment required

Library and Learning Resources provides books, periodicals, slides, CD-ROMs, videos and computer software on all aspects of the art of the book, printing, management, film/photography, graphic arts, plus retailing. SPECIAL COLLECTIONS History and development of published and unpublished scripts and the art of the western book.

The London Library

14 St James's Square, London SW1Y 4LG
☎020 7930 7705 Fax 020 7766 4766
✉ membership@londonlibrary.co.uk
www.londonlibrary.co.uk
Librarian *Miss Inez Lynn*
OPEN 9.30 am to 7.30 pm Monday, Tuesday,
     Wednesday; 9.30 am to 5.30 pm Thursday,
     Friday, Saturday
ACCESS For members only (2007: £210 pa; £105 pa for under-25s). Day and weekly reference tickets available for non-members (£10 and £30)

With over a million books and 8000 members, The London Library 'is the most distinguished private library in the world; probably the largest, certainly the best loved'. Founded in 1841, it is a registered charity and wholly independent of public funding. Its permanent collection embraces most European languages as well as English. Its subject range is predominantly within the humanities, with emphasis on literature, history, fine and applied art, architecture, bibliography, philosophy, religion, and topography and travel. Some 8000–9000 titles are added yearly. Most of the stock is on open shelves to which members have free access. Members may take out up to 10 volumes; 15 if they live more than 20 miles from the Library. The comfortable Reading Room has an annexe for users of personal computers. There are photocopiers, CD-ROM workstations, free access to the Internet, and the Library also offers a postal loans service. The London Library has recently embarked on its most ambitious redevelopment project in over a century; it includes the integration of a new contiguous building which will increase the total area of the site by approximately 30%. Membership is open to all: prospective members are required to submit a refereed application form in advance of admission, but there is at present no waiting list for membership. The London Library Trust may make grants to those who are unable to afford the full annual fee; details on application.

London Metropolitan Archives Library Services

History Library: 40 Northampton Road, London EC1R 0HB
☎020 7332 3820 Fax 020 7833 9136
✉ ask.lma@cityoflondon.gov.uk
www.cityoflondon.gov.uk/lma

Contact *The Enquiry Team*
ACCESS For reference only
This 100,000 volume library covers all aspects of the life and development of London, with strong holdings on the history and organisation of London local government. As the former Greater London Council History Library, the collection covers all subjects of London life, from architecture and biography to theatres and transport. The collection includes London directories from 1677 to the present, Acts of Parliament, statistical returns, several hundred periodical titles and public reports.

Lord Louis Library

Orchard Street, Newport, Isle of Wight PO30 1LL
☎01983 527655/823800 (Reference Library)
Fax 01983 825972
✉ reflib@postmaster.co.uk
OPEN 9.00 am to 5.30 pm Monday, Tuesday, Wednesday and Friday; 10.00 am to 8.00 pm Thursday; 9.00 am to 5.00 pm Saturday; 10.00 am to 1.00 pm Sunday

OPEN ACCESS
General adult and junior fiction and non-fiction collections; local history collection at Library HQ (☎ 01983 203880 for details). Internet access in all branches of the library on the Isle of Wight. Also the county's main reference library.

Manchester Central Library

St Peters Square, Manchester M2 5PD
☎0161 234 1900 Fax 0161 234 1963
✉ mclib@libraries.manchester.gov.uk
www.manchester.gov.uk/libraries
OPEN 9.00 am to 8.00 pm Monday to Thursday; 9.00 am to 5.00 pm Friday and Saturday. Commercial and European Units:

9.00 am to 6.00 pm Monday to Thursday; 9.00 am to 5.00 pm Friday and Saturday
OPEN ACCESS
One of the country's leading reference libraries with extensive collections covering all subjects. Departments include: Commercial, European, Technical, Social Sciences, Arts, Music, Local Studies, Chinese, General Readers, Language & Literature. Large lending stock and VIP (visually impaired) service available. Free Internet access.

Tom Mann Collection

See **Coventry Central Library**

Marylebone Library (Westminster)

See **Sherlock Holmes Collection**

Ministry of Defence Cartographic Archive

See **British Library Map Collections**

The Mitchell Library

North Street, Glasgow G3 7DN
☎0141 287 2999 Fax 0141 287 2815
www.glasgowlibraries.org
OPEN 9.00 am to 8.00 pm Monday to Thursday; 9.00 am to 5.00 pm Friday and Saturday

OPEN ACCESS
One of Europe's largest public reference libraries with stock of over 1,200,000 volumes. It subscribes to 48 newspapers and more than 1200 periodicals. There are collections in microform, records, tapes and videos, as well as CD-ROMs, electronic databases, illustrations, photographs, postcards, etc. The library contains a number of special collections, e.g. the Robert Burns Collection (5000 vols), the Scottish Poetry Collection (12,000 items) and the Scottish Drama Collection (1650 items).

Morrab Library

Morrab House, Morrab Gardens, Penzance TR18 4DA
☎01736 364474
Librarian *Annabelle Read*
OPEN 10.00 am to 4.00 pm Tuesday to Friday; 10.00 am to 1.00 pm Saturday

ACCESS Non-members may use the library for a small daily fee but may not borrow books
Formerly known as the Penzance Library. An independent subscription lending library of over 40,000 volumes covering virtually all subjects except modern science and technology, with large collections on history, literature and

religion. There is a comprehensive Cornish collection of books, newspapers and manuscripts including the Borlase letters; a West Cornwall photographic archive; many runs of 18th and 19th-century periodicals; a collection of over 2000 books published before 1800.

The National Archives

Kew, Richmond TW9 4DU
☎020 8876 3444
www.nationalarchives.gov.uk
www.nationalarchives.gov.uk/contact/form

OPEN 9.00 am to 5.00 pm Monday, Wednesday, Friday; 10.00 am to 7.00 pm Tuesday; 9.00 am to 7.00 pm Thursday; 9.30 am to 5.00 pm Saturday (closed public holidays and 7 to 10 December for annual stocktaking). In 2007 ad-hoc closures of the reading rooms may be required for building works in connection with the relocation of the Family Records Centre services in 2008.

ACCESS for reference, by reader's ticket, available free of charge on production of proof of identity (UK citizens: banker's card or driving licence; non-UK: passport or national identity card. Telephone for further information)

Over 168 kilometres of shelving house the national repository of records of central government in the UK and law courts of England and Wales, which extend in time from the 11th to the 20th century. Medieval records and the records of the State Paper Office from the early 16th to late 18th century, plus the records of the Privy Council Office and the Lord Chamberlain's and Lord Steward's departments. Modern government department records, together with those of the Copyright Office dating mostly from the late 18th century. Under the Public Records Act, records are normally only open to inspection when they are 30 years old.

National Library of Ireland

Kildare Street, Dublin 2, Republic of Ireland
☎00 353 1 603 0200 Fax 00 353 1 676 6690
✉ info@nli.ie
www.nli.ie

OPEN 9.30 am to 9.00 pm Monday, Tuesday, Wednesday; 9.30 am to 5.00 pm Thursday and Friday; 9.30 am to 1.00 pm Saturday

ACCESS Passes are issued for genealogical research or to consult newspapers; Reader's Ticket required for access to other material.

Collections include books, manuscripts, prints and drawings, maps, photographs, news-papers, music, ephemera and genealogical materials.

National Library of Scotland

George IV Bridge, Edinburgh EH1 1EW
☎0131 623 3700 Fax 0131 623 3701
✉ enquiries@nls.uk
www.nls.uk

OPEN Main Reading Room: 9.30 am to 8.30 pm Monday, Tuesday, Thursday, Friday; 10.00 am to 8.30 pm Wednesday; 9.30 am to 1.00 pm Saturday. Map Library: 9.30 am to 5.00 pm Monday, Tuesday, Thursday, Friday; 10.00 am to 5.00 pm Wednesday; 9.30 am to 1.00 pm Saturday

ACCESS to all reading rooms, for research not easily done elsewhere, by reader's ticket

Collection of over seven million volumes. The library receives all British and Irish publications. Large stock of newspapers and periodicals. Many special collections, including early Scottish books, theology, polar studies, baking, phrenology and liturgies. Also large collections of maps, music and manuscripts including personal archives of notable Scottish persons.

National Library of Wales

Aberystwyth SY23 3BU
☎01970 632800 Fax 01970 615709
✉ holi@llgc.org.uk
www.llgc.org.uk

OPEN 9.30 am to 6.00 pm Monday to Friday; 9.30 am to 5.00 pm Saturday (closed Bank Holidays and the week after Christmas)

ACCESS to reading rooms by reader's ticket, available on application. Open access to a wide-ranging exhibition programme

Collection of over four million books and including large collections of periodicals, maps, manuscripts and audiovisual material. Particular emphasis on humanities in printed foreign material, and on Wales and other Celtic areas in all collections.

National Meteorological Library and Archive

FitzRoy Road, Exeter EX1 3PB
☎01392 884841 Fax 0870 900 5050
✉ metlib@metoffice.gov.uk
www.metoffice.gov.uk

OPEN Library: 8.30 am to 4.30 pm Monday to Friday. Archive: 10.00 am to 6.00 pm

ACCESS By Visitor's Pass available from the reception desk; advance notice of a planned visit is appreciated

The major repository of most of the important literature on the subjects of meteorology, climatology and related sciences from the 16th century to the present day. The Library houses a collection of books, journals, articles and scientific papers, plus published climatological data from many parts of the world.

The Technical Archive (National Meteorological Archive, Great Moor House, Sowton Industrial Estate, Bittern Road, Exeter EX2 7NL ☎ 01392 360987, Fax 0870 900 5050; metarc@metoffice.gov.uk) holds the document collection of meteorological data and charts from England, Wales and British overseas bases, including ships' weather logs. Records from Scotland are stored in Edinburgh and those from Northern Ireland in Belfast.

Natural England
1 East Parade, Sheffield S1 2ET
☎0114 241 8920 Fax 0114 241 8921
✉ enquiries@naturalengland.org.uk
www.naturalengland.org.uk
Contact *Enquiry Service* (☎ 0845 600 3078 Fax: 01733 455103)
OPEN 8.30 am to 5.00 pm Monday to Thursday; 8.30 am to 4.30 pm Friday
ACCESS *Bona fide* students only. Telephone library for appointment on 01733 455094

Information on nature conservation, nature reserves, SSSIs, planning, legislation, countryside, recreation, stewardship schemes and advice to farmers.

The Natural History Museum Library
Cromwell Road, London SW7 5BD
☎020 7942 5460 Fax 020 7942 5559
✉ library@nhm.ac.uk
www.nhm.ac.uk/library/index.html
OPEN 10.00 am to 4.30 pm Monday to Friday
ACCESS To *bona fide* researchers, by reader's ticket on presentation of identification (telephone first to make an appointment)

The library is in five sections: general; botany; zoology; entomology; earth sciences. The sub-department of ornithology is housed at the Zoological Museum, Akeman Street, Tring HP23 6AP (☎ 020 7942 6156). Resources available include books, journals, maps, manuscripts, drawings and photographs covering all aspects of natural history, including palaeontology and mineralogy, from the 14th century to the present day. Also archives and historical collection on the museum itself.

Norfolk Library & Information Service
Norfolk and Norwich Millennium Library, The Forum, Millennium Plain, Norwich NR2 1AW
www.norfolk.gov.uk/council/departments/lis/libhome.htm
OPEN Lending Library, Reference and Information Service and Norfolk Studies: 9.00 am to 8.00 pm Monday to Friday; 9.00 am to 5.00 pm Saturday. EXPRESS: 9.00 am to 9.30 pm Monday to Friday; 9.00 am to 8.30 pm Saturday; 10.30 am to 4.30 pm Sunday
OPEN ACCESS

Reference lending library (stock merged together) with wide range, including books, recorded music, music scores, plays and videos. Houses the 2nd Air Division Memorial Library and has a strong Norfolk Heritage Library. Extensive range of reference stock including business information. Online databases. Public fax and colour photocopying, free access to the Internet. EXPRESS (fiction, sound & vision library within a library): selection of popular fiction, videos, CDs and DVDs available, with extended opening hours.

Northamptonshire Libraries & Information Service
Library HQ, PO Box 216, John Dryden House, 8–10 The Lakes, Northampton NN4 7DD
☎01604 237959 Fax 01604 237937
✉ nlis@northamptonshire.gov.uk *and* kwilkinson@northamptonshire.gov.uk
www.northamptonshire.gov.uk/Leisure/Libraries/home.htm
Literature Development Officer *Kate Wilkinson*

Since 1991, the Libraries and Information Service has offered its 'Wordworks' diary of literature events. The rolling programme now attracts exciting literary names as well as new and locally-based writers. Writers have an opportunity to read at a variety of venues around the country. Literature workshops, activities and other events are supported. Regular book displays and dedicated notice boards in libraries support the programme across the county.

Northumberland County Library
Beechfield, Gas House Lane, Morpeth NE61 1TA
☎01670 534518/534514 Fax 01670 534513
✉ libraries@northumberland.gov.uk
www.northumberlandlibraries.com

OPEN 9.30 am to 7.30 pm Monday, Tuesday, Wednesday, Friday; 9.30 am to 12.30 pm Saturday (closed Thursday)

OPEN ACCESS
Books, periodicals, newspapers, story cassettes, CD-ROMs, DVDs, CDs, videos, Free Internet access, word processing facilities, prints, microforms, vocal scores, playsets. SPECIAL COLLECTIONS Northern Poetry Library: 15,000 volumes of modern poetry (see entry under *Organisations of Interest to Poets*); Cinema: comprehensive collection of about 5000 volumes covering all aspects of the cinema; Family History.

Nottingham Central Library
Angel Row, Nottingham NG1 6HP
☎0115 915 2828 Fax 0115 915 2840
✉ enquiryline@nottinghamcity.gov.uk
www.nottinghamcity.gov.uk/libraries
OPEN 9.00 am to 7.00 pm Monday to Friday; 9.00 am to 1.00 pm Saturday

OPEN ACCESS
City Centre Library; includes wide range of stock. Strengths: Business collection; Sound and Vision collection; comprehensive Nottinghamshire Local Studies. Drama and music sets for loan to groups. Free Internet access for visitors. Contemporary Art Gallery (not administered by the library service).

Nottingham Subscription Library Ltd
See **Bromley House Library**

Office for National Statistics, National Statistics Information and Library Service
Customer Contact Centre, Room 1.015 Office for National Statistics, Cardiff Road, Newport NP10 8XG
☎0845 601 3034/01633 812399
Fax 01633 652747
✉ info@statistics.gov.uk
www.statistics.gov.uk
OPEN 9.00 am to 5.00 pm; appointment required; visitors must supply some form of identification
Also: National Statistics Information and Library Service, Government Buildings, Cardiff Road, Newport NP9 1XG
OPEN as above
Wide range of government statistical publications and access to government Internet-based data. Census statistical data from 1801; population and health data from 1837; govern-

ment social survey reports from 1941; recent international statistical data (UN, Eurostat, etc.); monograph and periodical collections of statistical methodology. The library in south Wales holds a wide range of government economic and statistical publications.

Orkney Library and Archive
44 Junction Road, Kirkwall KW15 1AG
☎01856 873166 Fax 01856 875260
✉ general.enquiries@orkneylibrary.org.uk *and* archives@orkneylibrary.org.uk
www.orkneylibrary.org.uk
Principal Archivist *Alison Fraser*
Principal Librarian *Karen Walker*
OPEN 9.00 am to 7.00 pm Monday to Thursday; 9.00 am to 5.00 pm Friday and Saturday. Archives: 9.00 am to 5.00 pm Monday, Tuesday, Wednesday, Friday; 9.00 am to 7.00 pm Thursday; 9.00 am to 5.00 pm Saturday

OPEN ACCESS
Local studies collection. Archive includes sound and photographic departments.

Oxford Central Library
Westgate, Oxford OX1 1DJ
☎01865 815549 Fax 01865 721694
✉ oxfordcentral.library@oxfordshire.gov.uk
www.oxfordshire.gov.uk
OPEN 9.00 am to 7.00 pm Monday to Thursday; 9.00 am to 5.30 pm Friday and Saturday

General lending and reference library including Oxfordshire Studies. Also periodicals, audio visual materials, music library, children's library and Business Information Point.

PA News Centre
Central Park, New Lane, Leeds LS11 5DZ
☎0870 830 6824 Fax 0870 830 6825
✉ palibrary@pressassociation.co.uk
www.pa.press.net
OPEN 8.00 am to 6.00 pm Monday to Friday; 8.00 am to 4.00 pm Saturday (closed Sunday)

OPEN ACCESS
PA News, the 24-hour national news and information group, offers the PA Digital Library which holds Press Association stories. Research undertaken by in-house staff.

Penzance Library
See **Morrab Library**

City of Plymouth Library and Information Services

Central Library, Drake Circus, Plymouth
PL4 8AL
☎01752 305923
✉ library@plymouth.gov.uk
www.plymouthlibraries.info

OPEN ACCESS

CENTRAL LIBRARY LENDING DEPARTMENTS:

Lending
☎ 01752 305912
✉ lendlib@plymouth.gov.uk

Children's Department
☎ 01752 305916
✉ childrens.library@plymouth.gov.uk

Music & Drama Department
☎ 01752 305914
✉ music@plymouth.gov.uk

OPEN 9.00 am to 7.00 pm Monday and Friday;
9.00 am to 5.30 pm Tuesday, Wednesday,
Thursday; 9.00 am to 5.00 pm Saturday

The Lending departments offer books on all subjects; language courses on cassette and foreign language books; the Holcenberg Jewish Collection; books on music and musicians, drama and theatre; music parts and sets of music parts; play sets; DVDs, videos; song index; cassettes and CDs; public Internet access.

CENTRAL LIBRARY REFERENCE DEPARTMENTS:

Reference
☎ 01752 305907/305908
✉ ref@plymouth.gov.uk

Local Studies & Naval History Department
☎ 01752 305909
✉ localstudies@plymouth.gov.uk
OPEN 9.00 am to 7.00 pm Monday to Friday;
9.00 am to 5.00 pm Saturday

The Reference departments include an extensive collection of Ordnance Survey maps and town guides; community and census information; marketing and statistical information; Patents; books on every aspect of Plymouth; naval history; Mormon Index on microfilm; Baring Gould manuscript of 'Folk Songs of the West'; public Internet access, including some electronic subscriptions.

Plymouth Proprietary Library

Alton Terrace, 111 North Hill, Plymouth
PL4 8JY
☎01752 660515
Librarian *John R. Smith*

OPEN Monday to Saturday from 9.30 am (closing time varies)
ACCESS To members; visitors by appointment only
Founded 1810. The library contains approximately 17,000 volumes of mainly 19th and 20th century work. Member of the **Association of Independent Libraries**.

The Poetry Library

See entry under *Organisations of Interest to Poets*

Polish Library POSK

238–246 King Street, London W6 0RF
☎020 8741 0474 Fax 020 8741 7724
✉ polish.library@posk.org
Librarian *Mrs Jadwiga Szmidt*
OPEN 10.00 am to 8.00 pm Monday and Wednesday; 10.00 am to 5.00 pm Friday;
10.00 am to 1.00 pm Saturday (library closed Tuesday and Thursday)

ACCESS For reference to all interested in Polish affairs; limited loans to members and *bona fide* scholars only through inter-library loans

Books, pamphlets, periodicals, maps, music, photographs on all aspects of Polish history and culture. SPECIAL COLLECTIONS Emigré publications; Joseph Conrad and related works; Polish underground publications; bookplates.

Poole Central Library

Dolphin Centre, Poole BH15 1QE
☎01202 262424 Fax 01202 262442
✉ poolelibrary@poole.gov.uk
www.boroughofpoole.com/libraries
OPEN 9.00 am to 6.00 pm Monday to Thursday; 9.00 am to 7.00 pm Friday; 9.00 am to 5.00 pm Saturday

OPEN ACCESS

General lending and reference library, including Healthpoint health information centre, business information, children's library, periodicals and newspapers, cafe, IT suite and meeting room.

Press Association Library

See **PA News Centre**

Public Record Office

See **The National Archives**

Reading Central Library

Abbey Square, Reading RG1 3BQ
☎0118 901 5950 Fax 0118 901 5954
✉ info@readinglibraries.org.uk

www.readinglibraries.org.uk

OPEN 9.30 am to 5.30 pm Monday and Friday;
9.30 am to 7.00 pm Tuesday and Thursday;
9.30 am to 5.00 pm Wednesday and
Saturday

OPEN ACCESS
Ground Floor: Fiction, audio-visual material,
children's library; First Floor: Newspapers, non-
fiction – biography, business, careers, cookery,
DIY, engineering, gardening, health, languages,
law, mind, body and spirit, pets, science, social
studies, sport, transport, travel; Second Floor:
LearnDirect, non-fiction – art, music, literature, plays, computing; Third floor: Non-fiction
– world history, national history, local history.
Magazines and periodicals and Internet access
on all floors.

RIBA British Architectural Library Drawings & Archives Collection
See **British Architectural Library**

Richmond Central Reference Library
Old Town Hall, Whittaker Avenue, Richmond
TW9 1TP
☎020 8940 5529 Fax 020 8940 6899
✉ reference.services@richmond.gov.uk
www.richmond.gov.uk

OPEN 9.30 am to 6.00 pm Monday, Thursday,
Friday; 9.30 am to 5.00 pm Tuesday; 9.30
am to 8.00 pm Wednesday; 9.30 am to 5.00
pm Saturday

OPEN ACCESS
General reference library serving the needs of
local residents and organisations. Internet access
and online databases for public use. Enquiries
received by visit, telephone and e-mail.

Royal Geographical Society (with the Institute of British Geographers)
1 Kensington Gore, London SW7 2AR
☎020 7591 3044 Fax 020 7591 3001
www.rgs.org

A collection of over 150,000 volumes, dating
primarily from the foundation of the Society
in 1830 onwards, focusing on the history and
geography of places worldwide. For information
on the Picture Library see entry under *Picture
Libraries*.

Royal Institute of Philosophy
See **Senate House Library, University of London**

The Royal Philharmonic Society Archive
See **British Library Music Collections**

Royal Society Library
6–9 Carlton House Terrace, London
SW1Y 5AG
☎020 7451 2606 Fax 020 7930 2170
✉ library@royalsoc.ac.uk
www.royalsoc.ac.uk

OPEN 10.00 am to 5.00 pm Monday to Friday

ACCESS Open to all researchers with an interest
in the history of science, the Fellowship of the
Royal Society and science policy. Researchers
are advised to contact the Library in advance of
their first visit.

History of science, scientists' biographies,
science policy reports, and publications of international scientific unions and national academies
from all over the world.

RSA (Royal Society for the Encouragement of Arts, Manufactures & Commerce)
8 John Adam Street, London WC2N 6EZ
☎020 7930 5115 Fax 020 7839 5805
www.theRSA.org

OPEN Library: 8.30 am to 8.00 pm every weekday. Archive material by appointment

ACCESS to Fellows of RSA; Archive: by appointment to all researchers (contact the Archivist, ☎
020 7451 6847; archive@rsa.org.uk)

Archives of the Society since 1754. A collection of approximately 15,000 items including
minutes of the Society, correspondence, prints,
original drawings and international exhibition material and an early library of over 700
volumes.

Royal Society of Medicine Library
1 Wimpole Street, London W1G 0AE
☎020 7290 2940 Fax 020 7290 2939
✉ library@rsm.ac.uk
www.rsm.ac.uk

Contact *Director of Information Services*

OPEN 9.00 am to 5.00 pm Monday to
Thursday; 9.00 am to 5.30 pm Friday; 10.00
am to 4.30 pm Saturday

ACCESS For reference only, on introduction by
Fellow of the Society or temporary membership is available to non-members; £12 per day;
£35 per week; £90 per month. Identification
required.

Books, periodicals, databases on postgraduate

biomedical information. Extensive historical collection dating from the fifteenth century and medical portrait collection.

Eric Frank Russell Archive

See **Science Fiction Foundation Research Library**

St Bride Library

Bride Lane, Fleet Street, London EC4Y 8EE
☎020 7353 4660 Fax 020 7583 7073
✉ library@stbridefoundation.org
www.stbridefoundation.org
OPEN 12 noon to 5.30 pm Tuesday and Thursday; 12 noon to 9.00 pm Wednesday
OPEN ACCESS
A public reference library maintained by the St Bride Foundation. Appointments advisable for consultation of special collections. Every aspect of printing and related matters: publishing and bookselling, newspapers and magazines, graphic design, calligraphy and typography, papermaking and bookbinding. One of the world's largest specialist collections in its field, with over 50,000 volumes, over 3000 periodicals (200 current titles), and extensive collection of drawings, manuscripts, prospectuses, patents and materials for printing and typefounding. Noted for its comprehensive holdings of historical and early technical literature.

Science Fiction Foundation Research Library

Liverpool University Library, PO Box 123, Liverpool L69 3DA
☎0151 794 3142 Fax 0151 794 2681
✉ asawyer@liverpool.ac.uk
www.sfhub.ac.uk
www.sf-foundation.com

Contact *Andy Sawyer*
ACCESS For research, by appointment only (telephone first)
This is the largest collection outside the US of English-language science fiction and related material – including autobiographies and critical works. SPECIAL COLLECTIONS Runs of 'pulp' magazines dating back to the 1920s. Foreign-language material (including a large Russian collection), and the papers of the Flat Earth Society. The collection also features a growing range of archive and manuscript material, including material from Stephen Baxter, Ramsey Campbell and John Brunner. The University of Liverpool also holds the Olaf Stapledon, Eric Frank Russell and John Wyndham archives.

Science Museum Library

Imperial College Road, London SW7 5NH
☎020 7942 4242 Fax 020 7942 4243
✉ smlinfo@nmsi.ac.uk
www.sciencemuseum.org.uk/library
OPEN 8.30 am to 11.00 pm Monday to Friday (closes 5.30 pm outside academic terms); 9.30 am to 5.30 pm Saturday (NB Opening times due to change in October 2007)
OPEN ACCESS Reference only; no loans
National reference library for the history and public understanding of science and technology, with a large collection of source material. Operates jointly with Imperial College Central Library.

Scottish Poetry Library

See entry under *Organisations of Interest to Poets*

Seckford Collection

See **Suffolk County Council – Suffolk Libraries**

2nd Air Division Memorial Library

See **Norfolk Library & Information Service**

Senate House Library, University of London

Senate House, Malet Street, London WC1E 7HU
☎020 7862 8461/62 (Information Centre)
Fax 020 7862 8480
✉ enquiries@shl.lon.ac.uk (Information Centre)
www.shl.lon.ac.uk
MEMBERSHIP DESK: ☎ 020 7862 8439/40
✉ userservices@shl.lon.ac.uk
OPEN Term-time: 9.00 am to 9.00 pm Monday to Thursday; 9.00 am to 6.30 pm Friday; 9.30 am to 5.30 pm Saturday. Vacation: 9.00 am to 6.00 pm Monday to Friday; 9.30 am to 5.30 pm Saturday (closed on Sundays and at certain periods during Bank Holidays)
The Senate House Library is a major academic research library predominantly based across the Humanities and Social Sciences. Housed within its 16 floors are some two million titles including 5500 current periodicals and a wide range of electronic resources. It contains a number of outstanding research collections which, as well as supporting the scholarly activities of the University, attract researchers from throughout the UK and internationally. These include:

English (e.g. the Durning-Lawrence Library and Sterling Collection of first editions); Economic and Social History (the Goldsmiths' Library, containing 70,000 items ranging from 15th to early 19th century); Modern Languages (primarily Romance and Germanic); Palaeography (acclaimed as being the best open access collection in its field in Europe); History (complementary to the Institute of Historical Research); Music, Philosophy (acts as the Library of the Royal Institute of Philosophy); Psychology (includes the BPS library); Major area studies collections (Latin-American, including Caribbean; United States and Commonwealth Studies, British Government Publications and maps). The Library has a wide range of Special Collections holdings. Check the website for full details of collections and current access arrangements.

Sheffield Libraries, Archives and Information

Central Library, Surrey Street, Sheffield S1 1XZ
☎0114 273 4712 Fax 0114 273 5009
✉ libraries@sheffield.gov.uk
www.sheffield.gov.uk (click on 'In your area')

Central Lending Library
☎ 0114 273 4727 (enquiries)/4729 (book renewals)
OPEN 10.00 am to 8.00 pm Monday; 9.30 am to 5.30 pm Tuesday, Thursday and Friday; 9.30 am to 8.00 pm Wednesday; 9.30 am to 5.30 pm Saturday

Books, talking books, large print, language courses, European fiction, books in cultural languages, play sets. Free Internet access. Writers' Resource Centre, Wednesday evenings, 5.00 pm to 7.00 pm. Proof of signature and a separate proof of address required to join.

Sheffield Archives
52 Shoreham Street, Sheffield S1 4SP
☎ 0114 203 9395 Fax 0114 203 9398
✉ archives@sheffield.gov.uk

OPEN 10.00 am to 5.30 pm Monday; 9.30 am to 5.30 pm Tuesday to Thursday; 9.00 am to 1.00 pm and 2.00 pm to 5.00 pm Saturday (documents should be ordered by 5.00 pm Thursday for Saturday); closed Friday

ACCESS By reader's card

Holds documents relating to Sheffield and South Yorkshire, dating from the 12th century to the present day, including records of the City Council, churches, businesses, landed estates, families and individuals, institutions and societies. Free Internet access.

Arts and Social Sciences and Sports Reference Service
☎ 0114 273 4747/8
OPEN 10.00 am to 8.00 pm Monday; 9.30 am to 5.30 pm Tuesday, Thursday, Friday, Saturday; 9.30 am to 8.00 pm Wednesday
ACCESS Mainly reference but some lending material

A comprehensive collection of books, periodicals and newspapers covering all aspects of the arts (excluding music), sports, social sciences and free Internet access.

Music and Video Service
☎ 0114 273 4733
✉ musicandav.library@sheffield.gov.uk
OPEN As for Central Lending Library above
ACCESS For reference and lending

An extensive range of books, CDs, cassettes, scores, etc. related to music. Also a video cassette and DVD loan service. Free Internet access.

Local Studies Service
☎ 0114 273 4753
✉ localstudies.library@sheffield.gov.uk
OPEN As for Arts & Social Sciences above (except Wednesday 9.30 am to 5.30 pm)
ACCESS For reference

Extensive material covering all aspects of Sheffield and its population, including maps, photos and videos. Free Internet access. Photograph collection available on www.picturesheffield.co.uk

Business, Science and Technology Reference Services
☎ 0114 273 4736/7 or 273 4743
✉ businessandtech.library@sheffield.gov.uk
OPEN As for Arts & Social Sciences above
ACCESS For reference only

Extensive coverage of science and technology as well as commerce and commercial law. British patents and British and worldwide standards with emphasis on metals. Hosts the World Metal Index. The business section holds a large stock of business and trade directories, and reference works with business emphasis. Free Internet access.

Sheffield Information Service
☎ 0114 273 4712
Fax 0114 275 7111
✉ sis@sheffield.gov.uk
OPEN 10.00 am to 5.30 pm Monday; 9.30 am to 5.30 pm Tuesday to Saturday

Full local information service covering all aspects of the Sheffield community. Free Internet access.

Central Children's Library

☎ 0114 273 4734

✉ kidsandteens.library@sheffield.gov.uk

OPEN 10.30 am to 5.00 pm Monday and
Friday; 1.00 pm to 5.00 pm Tuesday,
Wednesday,Thursday; 9.30 am to 5.30 pm
Saturday

Books, spoken word cassettes, DVDs, videos;
under-five play area; teenage reference section;
readings and promotions; storytime and
Babytime sessions. Free Internet access.

Shetland Library

Lower Hillhead, Lerwick ZE1 0EL

☎01595 743868 Fax 01595 694430

✉ shetlandlibrary@sic.shetland.gov.uk

www.shetland-library.gov.uk

OPEN 9.30 am to 8.00 pm Monday and
Thursday; 9.30 am to 5.00 pm Tuesday,
Wednesday, Friday, Saturday

General lending and reference library; extensive
local interest collection including complete set
of *The Shetland Times*, *The Shetland News* and
other local newspapers on microfilm and many
old and rare books; audio collection including
talking books/newspapers. Junior room for children. Disabled access and Housebound Readers
Service (delivery to reader's home). Mobile
library services to rural areas. Open Learning
Service. Same day photocopying service.
Publishing programme of books in dialect,
history, literature. Learning centre providing
access to learning opportunities including
Internet.

Shoe Lane Library

Hill House, Little New Street, London
EC4A 3JR

☎020 7583 7178 Fax 020 7353 0884

✉ shoelane@cityoflondon.gov.uk

www.cityoflondon.gov.uk/shoelanelibrary

OPEN 9.00 am to 5.30 pm Monday,Wednesday,
Thursday, Friday; 9.00 am to 6.30 pm
Tuesday

OPEN ACCESS
Corporation of London general lending
library, with a comprehensive stock of 50,000
volumes, most of which are on display. Free
Internet access.

Shrewsbury Library and Reference & Information Service

Castlegates, Shrewsbury SY1 2AS

☎01743 255300 Fax 01743 255309

✉ shrewsbury.library@shropshire-cc.gov.uk

www.shropshire.gov.uk/library.nsf

OPEN 9.30 am to 5.00 pm Monday,Wednesday,
Friday; 9.30 am to 8.00 pm Tuesday and
Thursday; 9.00 am to 5.00 pm Saturday;
1.00 pm to 4.00 pm Sunday

OPEN ACCESS
The largest public library in Shropshire.
Books, cassettes, CDs, talking books, DVDs,
videos, language courses. Open Learning and
study centre with public use computers for word
processing and Internet access. Music, literature
and art book collection for lending and reference. The West Midlands Literary Heritage
Collection is housed at Shrewsbury Library.

Spanish Institute Library
See **Instituto Cervantes**

Olaf Stapledon
See **Science Fiction Foundation Research
Library**

Sterling Collection
See **Senate House Library**

Suffolk County Council – Suffolk Libraries

Endeavour House, Russell Road, Ipswich
IP1 2BX

☎01473 584563 Fax 01473 583700

✉ help@suffolklibraries.co.uk

www.suffolk.gov.uk/LeisureAndCulture/
Libraries/SuffolkLibrariesDirect

OPEN See website for details of individual
libraries or contact Endeavour House.
Major libraries open seven days a week; all
libraries open Sunday

ACCESS A single library card gives access to the
lending service of 43 libraries and resource
centres across the county. Loans can be collected
and/or returned at any service point. Details on
website
Full range of lending and reference services,
free public access to the Internet. Wide range
of online services for registered library users
through the Suffolk Libraries Direct pages, e.g.
self-service reservations, renewals, free access
to subscription services. Suffolk InfoLink Plus
database gives details of local organisations
throughout the county. SPECIAL COLLECTIONS
include Suffolk Archives and Local History
Collection;Benjamin Britten Collection;Edward
Fitzgerald Collection; Seckford Collection and
Racing Collection (Newmarket). The Suffolk
Infolink service gives details of local groups and

societies and is available in libraries throughout the county and on the website.

Sunderland City Library and Arts Centre

28–30 Fawcett Street, Sunderland SR1 1RE
☎0191 514 1235 Fax 0191 514 8444
✉ enquiry.desk@sunderland.gov.uk
www.sunderland.gov.uk/libraries

OPEN 9.30 am to 7.30 pm Monday and Wednesday; 9.30 am to 5.00 pm Tuesday, Thursday, Friday; 9.30 am to 4.00 pm Saturday

The city's main library for lending and reference services. Local studies and children's sections, plus Sound and Vision department (CDs, DVDs, CD-ROMs, talking books). Sunderland Public Libraries also maintains community libraries of varying size, offering a range of services, plus mobile libraries. Free Internet access is available in all libraries across the city. A Books on Wheels service is available to housebound readers; the Schools Library Service serves teachers and schools. Two writers' groups meet at the City Library and Arts Centre: Janus Writers, every Wednesday, 1.30 pm to 3.30 pm; Foyle Street Writers Group, every Wednesday, 10.00 am to 12 noon.

Swansea Central Reference Library

Alexandra Road, Swansea SA1 5DX
☎01792 516753/516757 Fax 01792 516759
✉ central.library@swansea.gov.uk
www.swansea.gov.uk/libraries

OPEN 9.00 am to 6.00 pm Monday, Tuesday, Thursday; 9.00 am to 8.00 pm Wednesday and Friday; 9.00 am to 5.00 pm Saturday. The Library has a lending service open the same hours, including books, DVDs, videos, music CDs and talking books (☎ 01792 516750/1)

ACCESS For reference only (many local studies items now available on open access; other items must be requested on forms provided)

General reference material; also Welsh Assembly information, statutes, company information, maps, European Community information. Local studies: comprehensive collections on Wales; Swansea & Gower; Dylan Thomas. Local maps, periodicals, illustrations, local newspapers from 1804. B&w and colour photocopying and fax facilities, free computer and Internet access available (library membership required and pre-booking recommended) and microfilm/micro-fiche copying facility.

Swiss Cottage Central Library

88 Avenue Road, London NW3 3HA
☎020 7974 6522 Fax 020 7974 6532

OPEN 10.00 am to 7.00 pm Monday and Thursday; 10.00 am to 6.00 pm Tuesday, Wednesday, Friday; 10.00 am to 5.00 pm Saturday

OPEN ACCESS Over 300,000 volumes in the lending and reference libraries. Home of the London Borough of Camden's Information and Reference Services.

Tennyson Research Centre
See **Lincoln Central Library**

Thurrock Communities, Libraries & Cultural Services

Grays Library, Orsett Road, Grays RM17 5DX
☎01375 383611 Fax 01375 370806
✉ grays.library@thurrock.gov.uk
www.thurrock.gov.uk/libraries

OPEN 10.00 am to 7.00 pm Monday; 9.00 am to 7.00 pm Tuesday and Thursday; 9.00 am to 5.00 pm Wednesday, Friday, Saturday; branch library opening times vary

OPEN ACCESS General library lending and reference through ten libraries and a mobile library. Services include books, magazines, newspapers, audiocassettes, CDs, videos and language courses. Large collection of Thurrock materials. Internet and Microsoft Office.

Truro Library

Union Place, Truro TR1 1EP
☎01872 279205 (lending)/272702 (reference)/0845 607 2119 (24hr-renewals)
✉ truro.library@cornwall.gov.uk
www.cornwall.gov.uk/library

OPEN 8.30 am to 6.00 pm Monday, Tuesday, Thursday, Friday; 9.30 am to 6.00 pm Wednesday; 9.00 am to 4.00 pm Saturday

Books, cassettes, CDs, videos, DVDs and pc games for loan through branch or mobile networks. Internet access and IT support and training. Reference collection. SPECIAL COLLECTIONS on local studies.

West Midlands Literary Heritage Collection
See **Shrewsbury Library and Reference & Information Service**

Western Isles Libraries

Public Library, 19 Cromwell Street, Stornoway HS1 2DA

☎01851 708631 Fax 01851 708676

www.cne-siar.gov.uk

OPEN 10.00 am to 5.00 pm Monday to Wednesday; 10.00 am to 6.00 pm Thursday and Friday; 10.00 am to 5.00 pm Saturday

OPEN ACCESS

General public library stock, plus local history and Gaelic collections including maps, videos, printed music, cassettes and CDs; census records and Council minutes; music collection (CDs and cassettes). Branch libraries on the isles of Barra, Benbecula, Harris and Lewis.

City of Westminster Archives Centre

10 St Ann's Street, London SW1P 2DE

☎020 7641 5180/4879 (Minicom)

Fax 020 7641 5179

✉ archives@westminster.gov.uk

www.westminster.gov.uk/archives

OPEN 10.00 am to 7.00 pm Tuesday Wednesday, Thursday, 10.00 am to 5.00 pm Friday and Saturday (closed Monday)

ACCESS For reference

Comprehensive coverage of the history of Westminster and selective coverage of general London history. 22,000 books, together with a large stock of maps, prints, photographs, local newspapers, theatre programmes and archives.

Westminster Music Library

Victoria Library, 160 Buckingham Palace Road, London SW1W 9UD

☎020 7641 1300 Fax 020 7641 4281

✉ musiclibrary@westminster.gov.uk

www.westminster.gov.uk/libraries/special/music

OPEN 11.00 am to 7.00 pm Monday to Friday; 10 am to 5.00 pm Saturday

OPEN ACCESS

Located at Victoria Library, this is the largest public music library in the South of England, with extensive coverage of all aspects of music, including books, periodicals and printed scores. No recorded material, notated only. Lending library includes a small collection of CDs and DVDs.

Westminster Reference Library

35 St Martin's Street, London WC2H 7HP

☎020 7641 1300 Fax 020 7641 4606

✉ referencelibrarywc2@westminster.gov.uk

www.westminster.gov.uk/libraries

OPEN Main Library: 10.00 am to 8.00 pm Monday to Friday. Art & Design: 1.00 pm to 8.00 pm Monday to Friday; 10.00 am to 5.00 pm Saturday

ACCESS For reference only

A general reference library with emphasis on the following: Art & Design – fine and decorative arts, architecture, graphics and design; Performing Arts – theatre, cinema, radio, television and dance; Official Publications – major collection of HMSO publications from 1947, plus parliamentary papers dating back to 1906 (TSO subscription ceased April 2006); Business – UK directories, trade directories, company and market data; Periodicals – long files of many titles. One working day's notice is required for some government documents and most older periodicals. Extensive picture resource library.

The Wiener Library

4 Devonshire Street, London W1W 5BH

☎020 7636 7247 Fax 020 7436 6428

✉ info@wienerlibrary.co.uk

www.wienerlibrary.co.uk

Director *Ben Barkow*

Education and Outreach Coordinator *Katherine Klinger*

OPEN 10.00 am to 5.30 pm Monday to Friday

ACCESS By letter of introduction (readers needing to use the Library for any length of time should become members)

Private library – one of the leading research centres on European history since the First World War, with special reference to the era of totalitarianism and to Jewish affairs. Founded by Dr Alfred Wiener in Amsterdam in 1933, it holds material that is not available elsewhere. Books, periodicals, press archives, documents, pamphlets, leaflets, photo archive, audiovisual material, brochures.

Vaughan Williams Memorial Library

English Folk Dance and Song Society, Cecil Sharp House, 2 Regent's Park Road, London NW1 7AY

☎020 7485 2206 ext. 33 Fax 020 7284 0523

✉ library@efdss.org

www.efdss.org

Contact *Malcolm Taylor*

OPEN 9.30 am to 5.30 pm Tuesday to Friday; 10.00 am to 4.00 pm 1st & 3rd Saturday (sometimes closed between 1.00 pm and 2.00 pm)

ACCESS For reference to the general public, on payment of a daily fee; EFDSS members may borrow books and use the library free of charge

A multimedia collection: books, periodicals, manuscripts, tapes, records, CDs, films, videos. Mostly British traditional culture and how this has developed around the world. Some foreign language material, and some books in English about foreign cultures. Also, the history of the English Folk Dance and Song Society.

Dr Williams's Library

14 Gordon Square, London WC1H 0AR
☎020 7387 3727
✉ enquiries@dwlib.co.uk

OPEN 10.00 am to 5.00 pm Monday, Wednesday, Friday; 10.00 am to 6.30 pm Tuesday and Thursday

OPEN ACCESS to reading room (loans restricted to subscribers). Visitors required to supply identification. Requests to see manuscripts and rare books must be made in advance; separate registration required. Annual subscription £10; ministers of religion and undergraduate students £5

Primarily a library of theology, religion and ecclesiastical history. Also philosophy, history (English and Byzantine). Particularly important for the study of English Nonconformity. Also major manuscript collections. Trustees of Dr Williams's Library manage the Congregational Library on behalf of the Memorial Hall Trustees. The Dr Williams's Centre for Dissenting Studies is a collaboration with Queen Mary, University of London.

Wolverhampton Central Library

Snow Hill, Wolverhampton WV1 3AX
☎01902 552025 (lending)/552026 (reference)
Fax 01902 552024
✉ wolverhampton.libraries@dial.pipex.com
www.wolverhampton.gov.uk/libraries

OPEN 9.00 am to 7.00 pm Monday to Thursday; 9.00 am to 5.00 pm Friday and Saturday

Archives & Local Studies Collection

42–50 Snow Hill, Wolverhampton WV2 4AG
☎ 01902 552480
OPEN 10.00 am to 5.00 pm Monday, Tuesday, Friday, 1st and 3rd Saturday of each month; 10.00 am to 7.00 pm Wednesday; closed Thursday

General lending and reference libraries, plus children's library and audiovisual library holding cassettes, CDs, videos and music scores. Internet access.

The Women's Library

London Metropolitan University, Old Castle Street, London E1 7NT
☎020 7320 2222 Fax 020 7320 2333
✉ moreinfo@thewomenslibrary.ac.uk
www.thewomenslibrary.ac.uk

Director *Antonia Byatt*
OPEN Reading Room: 9.30 am to 5.00 pm Tuesday to Friday (8.00 pm Thursday); 10.00 am to 4.00 pm Saturday

OPEN ACCESS Exhibition: 9.30 am to 5.30 pm Monday to Friday (8.00 pm Thursday); 10.00 am to 4.00 pm Saturday

The Women's Library, national research library for women's history, is the UK's oldest and most comprehensive research library on all aspects of women in society, with both historical and contemporary coverage. The Library includes materials on feminism, work, education, health, the family, law, arts, sciences, technology, language, sexuality, fashion and the home. The main emphasis is on Britain but many other countries are represented, especially the Commonwealth and the developing countries. Established in 1926 as the library of the London Society of Women's Service (formerly Suffrage), a non-militant organisation led by Millicent Fawcett. In 1953 the Society was renamed after her and the library became the Fawcett Library. Collections include: women's suffrage, work, education, women and the church, the law, sport, art, music, abortion, prostitution. Mostly British materials but some American, Commonwealth and European works. Books, journals, pamphlets, archives, photographs, posters, postcards, audiovisual materials, artefacts, scrapbooks, albums and press cuttings dating mainly from the 19th century although some materials date from the 17th century. The Library's new building, which opened in 2002, includes a reading room, exhibition space, café, education areas and a conference room, and is the cultural and research centre for anyone interested in women's lives and achievements.

Worcestershire Libraries and Information Service

Cultural Services, Worcestershire County Council, County Hall, Spetchley Road, Worcester WR5 2NP
☎01905 766231 Fax 01905 766244
✉ libraries@worcestershire.gov.uk
www.worcestershire.gov.uk/libraries

OPEN Opening hours vary in the 22 libraries, the History Centre and mobile libraries covering the county; all full-time libraries open at least one evening a week until 8.00 pm, and on Saturday until 5.30 pm; part-time libraries vary

ACCESS Information and reference services open to anyone; loans to members only (membership criteria: resident, being educated, working, or an elector in the county or neighbouring authorities; temporary membership to visitors. Proof of identity and address required. No charge for membership or for borrowing books.)

Information service, and reference and lending libraries. Non-fiction and fiction for all age groups, including normal and large print, spoken word cassettes, sound recordings (CD, cassette), videos, maps, local history, CD-ROMs for reference at main libraries, free public Internet access in all libraries. Joint Libraries Service/County Record Office History Centre with resources for local and family history. SPECIAL COLLECTIONS Carpets and Textiles; Needles & Needlemaking; Stuart Period; A.E. Housman.

John Wyndham Archive
See **Science Fiction Foundation Research Library**

York Central Library
Museum Street, York YO1 7DS
☎01904 655631 Fax 01904 552835
✉ reference.library@york.gov.uk

Lending Library
OPEN 9.30 am to 8.00 pm Monday, Tuesday, Friday; 9.30 am to 5.30 pm Wednesday and Thursday; 9.30 am to 4.00 pm Saturday

General lending library including CDs, DVDs, audio books, children's storytapes language courses and printed music. Large print books. Photocopying, Internet and fax facilities.

Reference Library

OPEN 9.00 am to 8.00 pm Monday, Tuesday, Wednesday, Friday; 9.00 am to 5.30 pm Thursday; 9.00 am to 4.00 pm Saturday

General reference library; periodicals, newspapers, local newspaper index, EU information, organisations database; local studies library for York and surrounding area; microfilm/fiche readers for national and local newspapers; census returns and family history resource; general reference collection. Maintains strong links with other local history resource centres, namely the Borthwick Institute, York City Archive and York Minster Library. CD-ROM and Internet facilities. Room 18: IT resource centre available to the public. In addition, 14 branch libraries and one mobile, serving the City of York Council area.

Zoological Society Library
Regent's Park, London NW1 4RY
☎020 7449 6293 Fax 020 7586 5743
✉ library@zsl.org
www.zsl.org

OPEN 9.30 am to 5.30 pm Monday to Friday

ACCESS To members and staff; non-members by application

160,000 volumes on zoology including 5000 journals (1300 current) and a wide range of books on animals and particular habitats. Slide collection available and many historic zoological prints. Library catalogue available online (library.zsl.org).

The Zweig Collection of Music & Literary Mss
See **British Library Music Collections**

Picture Libraries

Acme

See **Popperfoto.com**

actionplus sports images

54–58 Tanner Street, London SE1 3PH
☎020 7403 1558 Fax 020 7403 1526
✉ pictures@actionplus.co.uk
www.actionplus.co.uk

Founded 1986. Specialist sports and action library providing complete and creative international coverage of over 300 varieties of professional and amateur sport. Elite, junior, professional, amateur, extreme, disabled, minority, offbeat, major and minor events, adults, children, high and low, fast and slow. Millions of images covering over 30 years of sport.

Lesley & Roy Adkins Picture Library

Ten Acre Wood, Whitestone, Exeter EX4 2HW
☎01392 811357
✉ mail@adkinsarchaeology.com
www.adkinsarchaeology.com

Colour and some b&w coverage of archaeology, antiquity, heritage and related subjects in the UK, Europe, Egypt and Turkey. Subjects include towns, villages, housing, landscape and countryside, churches, temples, castles, monasteries, art and architecture, gravestones and tombs, inscriptions, naval, nautical and antiquarian views. Images now supplied in digital form. No service charge if pictures are used.

The Advertising Archive Limited

45 Lyndale Avenue, London NW2 2QB
☎020 7435 6540 Fax 020 7794 6584
✉ suzanne@advertisingarchives.co.uk
www.advertisingarchives.co.uk

Contacts *Suzanne Viner, Larry Viner*

With over one million images, the largest collection of British and American press ads, TV commercial stills and magazine cover illustrations in Europe. Material spans the period from 1850 to the present day. In-house research; rapid service, competitive rates. On-line database and digital delivery available.

akg-images Ltd, The Arts and History Picture Library

5 Melbray Mews, 158 Hurlingham Road, London SW6 3NS
☎020 7610 6103 Fax 020 7610 6125
✉ enquiries@akg-images.co.uk
www.akg-images.co.uk

Contact *Ute Krebs*

250,000 images online with direct access to ten million kept in the Berlin AKG Library. Specialises in art, archaeology, history, topography, music, personalities and film.

Bryan & Cherry Alexander Photography

Higher Cottage, Manston, Sturminster Newton DT10 1EZ
☎01258 473006 Fax 01258 473333
✉ alexander@arcticphoto.co.uk
www.arcticphoto.co.uk

Contact *Cherry Alexander*

Arctic and Antarctic specialists; indigenous peoples, wildlife and science in polar regions; Norway, Iceland, Siberia and Alaska.

Alpine Garden Society

AGS Centre, Avon Bank, Pershore WR10 3JP
☎01386 554790 Fax 01386 554801
✉ ags@alpinegardensociety.net
www.alpinegardensociety.net

Contact *Peter Sheasby*

Over 28,000 colour transparencies (35mm) covering plants in the wild from many parts of the world; particularly strong in plants from mountain and sub-alpine regions, and from Mediterranean climates; South Africa, Australia, Patagonia, California and the Mediterranean. Extensive coverage of show alpines in pots and in gardens and of European orchids. Full slide list available.

Alvey & Towers

The Springboard Centre, Mantle Lane, Coalville LE67 3DW
☎01530 450011 Fax 01530 450011
✉ office@alveyandtowers.com
www.alveyandtowers.com

Contact *Emma Rowen*

Houses one of the country's most comprehensive collections of transport images depicting not only actual transport systems but their surrounding industries as well. Also specialist modern railway image collection.

Andes Press Agency
26 Padbury Court, London E2 7EH
☎020 7613 5417 Fax 020 7739 3159
✉ apa@andespressagency.com
www.andespressagency.com

Contacts *Val Baker, Carlos Reyes*

80,000 colour transparencies and 300,000 b&w, specialising in social documentary, world religions, Latin America and Britain.

Heather Angel/Natural Visions
Highways, 6 Vicarage Hill, Farnham GU9 8HJ
☎01252 716700 Fax 01252 727464
✉ hangel@naturalvisions.co.uk
www.naturalvisions.co.uk

Contact *Heather Angel*

Constantly expanding worldwide natural history, wildlife and landscapes: polar regions, tropical rainforest flora and fauna, all species of plants and animals in natural habitats from Africa, Asia (notably China and Malaysia), Australasia, South America and USA, urban wildlife, pollution, biodiversity, global warming. Also worldwide gardens and cultivated flowers. Can send a digital lightbox to authors with an e-mail. The library then supplies high resolution digital files direct to the publisher.

Aquarius Library
PO Box 5, Hastings TN34 1HR
☎01424 721196 Fax 01424 717704
✉ aquarius.lib@clara.net
www.aquariuscollection.com

Contact *David Corkill*

A unique collection of film stills, star portraits and candids covering the entire history of the cinema to the present day. Available as high resolution downloads from the Aquarius Library website containing thousands of film and TV titles and over 100,000 high quality stills. Postal deliveries and free searches also available.

Architectural Association Photo Library
36 Bedford Square, London WC1B 3ES
☎020 7887 4066 Fax 020 7414 0782
✉ valerie@aaschool.ac.uk
www.aaschool.ac.uk/photlib

Contacts *Valerie Bennett, Sarah Franklin, Henderson Downing*

100,000 35mm transparencies on architecture, historical and contemporary. Archive of large-format b&w negatives from the 1920s and 1930s.

ArenaPAL
Lambert House, 55 Southwark Street, London SE1 1RU
☎020 7403 8542 Fax 020 7403 8561
✉ enquiries@arenapal.com
www.arenapal.com

'Probably the best entertainment images in the world.' Continually updated performing arts image collection covering classical music, opera, theatre, musicals, film, pop, rock, jazz, instruments, festivals, venues, circus, ballet and contemporary dance, props and personalities. Over two million images from late 19th century onwards. Phone, fax or e-mail to make a selection.

ArkReligion.com
57 Burdon Lane, Cheam SM2 7BY
☎020 8642 3593 Fax 020 8395 7230
✉ images@artdirectors.co.uk
www.arkreligion.com

Contacts *Helene Rogers, Bob Turner*

Extensive coverage of all religions.

The Art Archive
2 The Quadrant, 135 Salusbury Road, London NW6 6RJ
☎020 7624 3500 Fax 020 7624 3355
✉ info@picture-desk.com
www.picture-desk.com

Picture library holding over 80,000 high-resolution images covering fine art, history and ancient civilisations.

Art Directors & Trip Photo Library
57 Burdon Lane, Cheam SM2 7BY
☎020 8642 3593 Fax 020 8395 7230
✉ images@artdirectors.co.uk
www.artdirectors.co.uk

Contacts *Helene Rogers, Bob Turner*

Extensive coverage, with over 750,000 images, of all countries, lifestyles, peoples, etc. with detailed coverage of all religions. Backgrounds a speciality.

Aspect Picture Library Ltd
40 Rostrevor Road, London SW6 5AD
☎020 7736 1998/7731 7362
Fax 020 7731 7362

✉ Aspect.Ldn@btinternet.com
www.aspect-picture-library.co.uk

Colour and b&w worldwide coverage of countries, events, industry and travel, with large files on art, namely paintings, space, China, the Middle East, French villages, English villages and Ireland.

Australia Pictures

28 Sheen Common Drive, Richmond
TW10 5BN
☎020 7602 1989 Fax 020 7602 1989
✉ equilibrium.films@virgin.net

Contact *John Miles*

Collection of 4000 transparencies covering all aspects of Australia: Aboriginal people, paintings, Ayers Rock, Kakadu, Tasmania, underwater, reefs, Arnhem Land, Sydney. Also Africa, Middle East and Asia.

aviation–images.com

42B Queens Road, London SW19 8LR
☎020 8944 5225 Fax 020 8944 5335
✉ pictures@aviation-images.com
www.aviation-images.com

Contacts *Mark Wagner, Steve Lake*

500,000+ aviation images, civil and military, archive and modern, from the world's best aviation photographers. Member of **BAPLA** and RAeS.

Barnaby's Photographic Library
See **Mary Evans Picture Library**

Barnardo's Photographic and Film Archive

Barnardo's House, Tanners Lane, Barkingside, Ilford IG6 1QG
☎020 8498 7345 Fax 020 8550 0429
✉ stephen.pover@barnardos.org.uk
www.barnardos.org.uk

Image Librarian *Stephen Pover*

The Barnardo's image archive is a unique resource of images of social history dating from 1874. Images can be sent either by post, ISDN or e-mail.

Colin Baxter Photography Limited

Woodlands Industrial Estate, Grantown-on-Spey PH26 3NA
☎01479 873999 Fax 01479 873888
✉ sales@colinbaxter.co.uk
www.colinbaxter.co.uk

Contact *Mike Rensner* (Editorial)

Over 50,000 images specialising in Scotland.

Also the Lake District, Yorkshire, France, Iceland and a special collection on Charles Rennie Mackintosh's work. Publishes guidebooks plus books, calendars, postcards and greetings cards on landscape, cityscape and natural history containing images which are primarily, but not exclusively, Colin Baxter's. Also publishers of the *Worldlife Library* of natural history books, and a range of books and stationery based on reproductons of the designs of Charles Rennie Mackintosh.

BBC Natural History Unit Picture Library
See **Nature Picture Library**

The Photographic Library Beamish, The North of England Open Air Museum

The North of England Open Air Museum, Beamish DH9 0RG
☎0191 370 4000 Fax 0191 370 4001
✉ museum@beamish.org.uk
www.beamish.org.uk

Comprehensive collection; images relate to the North East of England and cover agricultural, industrial, topography, advertising and shop scenes, people at work and play. On laser disk for rapid searching. Visitors by appointment weekdays.

Francis Bedford
See **Birmingham Library Services** under *Library Services*

Ivan J. Belcher Colour Picture Library

57 Gibson Close, Abingdon OX14 1XS
☎01235 521524 Fax 01235 521524

Extensive colour picture library specialising in top-quality medium-format transparencies depicting the British scene. Particular emphasis on tourist, holiday and heritage locations, including famous cities, towns, picturesque harbours, rivers, canals, castles, cottages, rural scenes and traditions photographed throughout the seasons. Mainly of recent origin and constantly updated.

bfi Stills, Posters and Designs

British Film Institute, 21 Stephen Street, London W1T 1LN
☎020 7957 4797 Fax 020 7323 9260
✉ stills.films@bfi.org.uk
www.bfi.org.uk/collections/stills/index.html

'*bfi* Stills, Posters and Designs is the world's most

comprehensive collection of film and television images.' The collection captures on and off screen moments, portraits of the world's most famous stars – and those behind the camera who made them famous – as well as publicity posters, set designs, images of studios, cinemas, special events and early film and TV technologies. Rapid access to these images can be provided by photographic or digital reproduction. Visits by appointment only.

Anthony Blake Photo Library

20 Blades Court, Deodar Road, Putney,
London SW15 2NU
☎020 8877 1123 Fax 020 8877 9787
✉ info@abpl.co.uk
www.abpl.co.uk

'Europe's premier source' of food and wine related images. From the farm and the vineyard to the plate and the bottle. Cooking and kitchens, top chefs and restaurants, country trades and markets, worldwide travel with an extensive Italian section.

Peter Boardman Collection

See **Chris Bonington Picture Library**

Chris Bonington Picture Library

Badger Hill, Hesket Newmarket, Wigton
CA7 8LA
☎016974 78286 Fax 016974 78238
✉ frances@bonington.com
www.bonington.com

Contact *Frances Daltrey*

Based on the personal collection of climber and author Chris Bonington and his extensive travels and mountaineering achievements; also work by Doug Scott and other climbers, including the Peter Boardman and Joe Tasker Collections. Full coverage of the world's mountains, from British hills to Everest, depicting expedition planning and management stages, the approach march showing inhabitants of the area, flora and fauna, local architecture and climbing action shots on some of the world's highest mountains.

Boulton and Watt Archive

See **Birmingham Library Services** under *Library Services*

The Bridgeman Art Library

17–19 Garway Road, London W2 4PH
☎020 7727 4065 Fax 020 7792 8509
✉ research@bridgeman.co.uk
www.bridgemanart.co.uk

Head of Picture Research *Jenny Page*

Fine art photo archive representing more than 1000 museums, galleries and picture owners around the world. High res digital files and large-format colour transparencies of paintings, sculptures, prints, manuscripts, antiquities photographs and the decorative arts. From prehistoric sculpture to contemporary paintings. Offices in London, Paris, New York and Berlin. Collections represented include the British Library, National Galleries of Scotland, Boston Museum of Fine Arts, the Wallace Collection, The Courtauld, Detroit Institute of Arts, The Barnes Foundation, the National Army Museum, the National Trust as well as the Giraudon archive.

The British Cartoon Archive

The Templeman Library, University of Kent,
Canterbury CT2 7NU
☎01227 823127 Fax 01227 823127
✉ N.P.Hiley@kent.ac.uk *or*
J.M.Newton@kent.ac.uk
www.kent.ac.uk/cartoons

Contacts *Dr Nicholas Hiley, Jane Newton*

A national research archive of over 120,000 original cartoons and caricatures by 350 British cartoonists, supported by a library of books, papers, journals, catalogues, cuttings and assorted ephemera. A computer database of 120,000 cartoons provides quick and easy catalogued access via the Web. A source for exhibitions and displays as well as a picture library service. Specialises in historical, political and social cartoons from British newspapers and magazines.

British Library Picture Library and Images Online/Reproductions

British Library, 96 Euston Road, London
NW1 2DB

Images Online ☎ 020 7412 7614
(Research)/7755 (Reproduction rights)
Fax 020 7412 7771
✉ imagesonline@bl.uk
www.bl.uk/imagesonline

The British Library Images Online offers instant access to thousands of images from the British Library's historic worldwide collections which include manuscripts, rare books, music scores and maps spanning almost 3000 years. A collection of 20,000 images including digital images of drawings, illustrations and photographs. Specialities: historical images.

Brooklands Museum Picture Library

Brooklands Museum, Brooklands Road,
Weybridge KT13 0QN
☎01932 857381 Fax 01932 855465
✉ info@brooklandsmuseum.com
www.brooklandsmuseum.com

Contacts *John Pulford* (Curator of Collections),
Julian Temple (Curator of Aviation)

About 40,000 b&w and colour prints and
slides. Subjects include: Brooklands Motor
Racing 1907–1939; British aviation and aero-
space, 1908 to the present day, particularly BAC,
Hawker, Sopwith and Vickers aircraft built at
Brooklands.

Hamish Brown MBE, D.Litt, FRSGS Scottish Photographic

26 Kirkcaldy Road, Burntisland KY3 9HQ
☎01592 873546 Fax 01592 873546

Contact *Hamish Brown*

Coverage of most topics and areas of Scotland
(sites, historic, buildings, landscape, mountains),
also travel, mountains, general (50,000 items)
and Morocco. Commissions undertaken.

Capital Pictures

85 Randolph Avenue, London W9 1DL
☎020 7286 2212
✉ sales@capitalpictures.com
www.capitalpictures.com

Contact *Phil Loftus*

Specialises in photographs of famous people
from the worlds of showbusiness, rock and pop,
television, politics, royalty and film stills.

Cephas Picture Library

A1 Kingsway Business Park, Oldfield Road,
Hampton TW12 2HD
☎020 8979 8647 Fax 020 8941 4001
✉ pictures@cephas.com
www.cephas.com

The wine industry and vineyards of the world
is the subject on which Cephas has made its
reputation. 100,000 images make this one of the
most comprehensive and up-to-date archives
in Britain. Almost all wine-producing countries and all aspects of the industry are covered
in depth. Spirits, beer and cider also included. A
major food and drink collection now also exists,
through preparation and cooking, to eating and
drinking.

Giles Chapman Library

25 Homefield Road, Sevenoaks TN13 2DU
☎01732 452547
✉ chapman.media@virgin.net
www.gileschapman.com

Contact *Giles Chapman*

Some 150,000 colour and b&w images of cars
and motoring, from 1945 to the present day. No
research fees.

Christian Aid Photo Section

PO Box 100, London SE1 7RT
☎020 7523 2232/5 Fax 020 7620 0719
✉ photos@christian-aid.org
www.christian-aid.org

Contacts *J. Cabon, B. Nicholson,*
M. Gonzalez-Noda

Pictures are mainly from Africa, Asia and Latin
America, relating to small-scale, community-
based programmes. Mostly development themes:
health, agriculture, education, urban and rural
life.

Christie's Images Ltd

1 Langley Lane, London SW8 1TJ
☎020 7582 1282 Fax 020 7582 5632
✉ imageslondon@christies.com
www.christiesimages.com

Contact *Mark Lynch*

The collection spans 80 categories representing
every culture, from the distant past to the present
day. An unrivalled collection from Old Masters
to Impressionists and Twentieth Century masterpieces. Antiquities, Art Nouveau and Decorative
Art, Books and Manuscripts, Contemporary Art
and Furniture, Music and Movie Memorabilia,
Textiles, Toys. Experienced researchers will
search for specific requests.

The Cinema Museum

The Master's House, Old Lambeth Workhouse,
2 Dugard Way, off Renfrew Road, London
SE11 4TH
☎020 7840 2200 Fax 020 7840 2299
✉ martin@cinemamuseum.org.uk *and*
pixdesk@rgapix.com
www.ronaldgrantarchive.com

Colour and b&w coverage (including stills)
of the motion picture industry throughout its
history, including the Ronald Grant Archive.
Smaller collections on theatre, variety, television
and popular music.

Classical Collection Ltd

22 Avon, Hockley, Tamworth B77 5QA
☎01827 286086/07963 194921
Fax 01827 286086

✉ neil@classicalcollection.co.uk

Managing Director *Neil Arthur Williams, MA (Hum), MA (Mus)*

Archive specialising in classical music ephemera, particularly portraits of composers, musicians, conductors and opera singers, comprising old and very rare photographs, postcards, antique prints, cigarette cards, stamps, First Day Covers, concert programmes, Victorian newspapers, etc. Also modern photos of composer references such as museums, statues, busts, paintings, monuments, memorials and graves. Other subjects covered include ballet, musical instruments, concert halls, opera houses, 'music in art', manuscripts, opera scenes, music-caricatures, bands, orchestras and other music groups. Neil Arthur Williams is a qualified music historian, musicologist and freelance writer of music articles, concert programme notes and CD as well as being a commissionable composer.

John Cleare/Mountain Camera

Hill Cottage, Fonthill Gifford, Salisbury SP3 6QW

☎01747 820320 Fax 01747 820320

✉ cleare@btinternet.com

www.mountaincamera.com

Colour and b&w coverage of mountains and wild places, climbing, ski-touring, trekking, expeditions, wilderness travel, landscapes, people and geographical features from all continents with Himalaya, Andes, Antarctic, Alps and the British countryside in depth. Topics range from reindeer in Lapland and camels in Australia to whitewater rafting in Utah, ski-mountaineering in China and abstract illustration for poetry and Japanese haiku. Commissions, presentations and consultancy work undertaken. Researchers welcome by appointment. Member of **BAPLA** and the **OWPG**.

Michael Cole Camerawork

The Coach House, 27 The Avenue, Beckenham BR3 5DP

☎020 8658 6120 Fax 020 8658 6120

✉ mikecole@dircon.co.uk

Contacts *Michael Cole, Derrick Bentley*

Probably the largest and most comprehensive collection of tennis pictures in the world. Over 50 years' coverage of the Wimbledon Championships. M.C.C. incorporates the tennis archives of Le Roye Productions, established in 1945. Picture requests and enquiries by e-mail.

Collections

13 Woodberry Crescent, London N10 1PJ

☎020 8883 0083 Fax 020 8883 9215

✉ collections@btinternet.com

www.collectionspicturelibrary.co.uk

www.collectionspicturelibrary.com

Contact *Simon Shuel*

Extensive coverage of the British Isles and Ireland, from the Shetlands to the Channel Islands and Connemara to East Anglia, including people, traditional customs, landscapes, buildings old and new – both well known and a bit obscure, 'plus a considerable collection of miscellaneous bits and pieces which defy logical filing'. Images supplied digitally or as original transparencies. Visitors welcome but please call first.

Corbis Images

111 Salusbury Road, London NW6 6RG

☎020 7644 7644 Fax 020 7644 7645

✉ sales.uk@corbis.com

www.corbis.com

A unique and comprehensive resource containing more than 65 million images, with over 2.1 million of them available online. The images come from professional photographers, museums, cultural institutions and public and private collections worldwide. Subjects include history, travel, celebrities, events, science, world art and cultures.

Sylvia Cordaiy Photo Library

45 Rotherstone, Devizes SN10 2DD

☎01380 728327 Fax 01380 728328

✉ info@sylvia-cordaiy.com

www.sylvia-cordaiy.com

www.alamy.com/sylviacordaiyphotolibrary

Over 170 countries on file from the obscure to main stock images – Africa, North, Central and South America, Asia, Atlantic, Indian and Pacific Ocean islands, Australasia, Europe, polar regions. Covers travel, architecture, ancient civilisations, world heritage sites, people worldwide, environment, wildlife, natural history, Antarctica, domestic pets, livestock, marine biology, veterinary treatment, equestrian, ornithology, flowers. UK files cover cities, towns villages, coastal and rural scenes, London collection. Transport, railways, shipping and aircraft (military and civilian). Aerial photography. Backgrounds and abstracts. Also the Paul Kaye B/W archive.

Country Images Picture Library

27 Camwood, Bamber Bridge, Preston PR5 8LA

☎01772 321243 Fax 0870 137 8888
✉ terrymarsh@wpu.org.uk
www.countryimages.info
Contact *Terry Marsh*

35mm film and digital colour coverage of landscapes and countryside features generally throughout the UK (Cumbria, North Yorkshire, Lancashire, southern Scotland, Isle of Skye, St Kilda and Scottish islands, Wales, Cornwall), France (Alps, Pyrenees, Provence, Charente-Maritime, Hérault, Aube-en-Champagne, Loire valley, Somme), Madeira and Australia. Commissions undertaken.

Country Life Picture Library
The Blue Fin Building, 110 Southwark Street, London SE1 0SU
☎020 3148 5000
✉ camilla_costello@ipcmedia.com
www.clpicturelibrary.co.uk
Contact *Camilla Costello*

Over 150,000 b&w negatives dating back to 1897, and 80,000 colour transparencies. Country houses, stately homes, churches and town houses in Britain and abroad, interiors of architectural interest (ceilings, fireplaces, furniture, paintings, sculpture), and exteriors showing many landscaped gardens, sporting and social events, crafts, people and animals. Visitors by appointment. Open Tuesday to Friday.

Philip Craven Worldwide Photo-Library
Surrey Studios, 21 Nork Way, Nork, Banstead SM7 1PB
☎0870 220 2121
www.philipcraven.com
Contact *Philip Craven*

Extensive coverage of British scenes, cities, villages, English countryside, gardens, historic buildings and wildlife. Worldwide travel and wildlife subjects on medium and large-format transparencies.

Sue Cunningham Photographic
56 Chatham Road, Kingston upon Thames KT1 3AA
☎020 8541 3024 Fax 020 8541 5388
✉ info@scphotographic.com
www.scphotographic.com
Contacts *Patrick Cunningham, Sue Cunningham*

Extensive coverage of many geographical areas: South America (especially Brazil), Eastern Europe from the Baltic to the Balkans, various

African countries, Western Europe including the UK. Colour and b&w. Member of **BAPLA**.

Dale Concannon Collection
See **Phil Sheldon Golf Picture Library**

Dalton–Watson Collection
See **Ludvigsen Library**

The Defence Picture Library
14 Mary Seacole Road, The Millfields, Plymouth PL1 3JY
☎01752 312061 Fax 01752 312063
✉ picdesk@defencepictures.com
www.defencepictures.com
Contacts *David Reynolds, Jessica Kelly, James Rowlands, Andrew Chittock*

Leading source of military photography covering all areas of the UK Armed Forces, supported by a research agency of facts and figures. More than one million images. Visitors welcome by appointment.

Douglas Dickins Photo Library
2 Wessex Gardens, Golders Green, London NW11 9RT
☎020 8455 6221
Sole Proprietor *Douglas Dickins, FRPS*

Worldwide colour and b&w coverage, specialising in Asia, particularly India, Indonesia and Japan. *In Grandpa's Footsteps*, highly illustrated book of world travel published by The Book Guild in 2000.

Dominic Photography
4B Moore Park Road, London SW6 2JT
☎020 7381 0007 Fax 020 7381 0008
Contacts *Zoë Dominic, Catherine Ashmore*

Colour and b&w coverage of the entertainment world from 1957 onwards: dance, opera, theatre, ballet, musicals and personalities.

E&E Picture Library – Ecclesiastical and Eccentricities
Beggars Roost, Woolpack Hill, Brabourne Lees, Ashford TN25 6RR
☎01303 812608 Fax 01303 812608
✉ info@picture-library.freeserve.co.uk
www.heritage-images.com (click on E&E)
picture-library.mysite.wanadoo-members.co.uk
www.eeimages.com
Contact *Isobel Sinden*

Religions (buildings, artifacts, clothes, festivals, clergy, arts, culture, history, pilgrimages); Manuscripts & Illustrations; Bible lands; Saints,

Stained Glass (religious and secular); Ancient (buildings, stones); Architecture (worldwide with historical, literary, artistic, commemorative, design, important connections); Death & Commemorative; Eccentricities (symbols, carvings, follies, knights, signs, illustrations, the unusual)l; Festivals (religious and secular); Heritage (castles, bridges, houses, temples, industrial and farming archaeology), from Guatemala to Japan. Also nature, including wind, water, sunsets and transport.

Patrick Eagar Photography

1 Queensberry Place, Richmond TW9 1NW
☎020 8940 9269 Fax 020 8332 1229
✉ mail@patrickeagar.com
www.patrickeagar.com

The cricket library consists of Patrick Eagar's work over the last 30 years with coverage of over 290 Test matches worldwide, unique coverage of all eight World Cups, countless one-day internationals and player action portraits of over 2000 cricketers. The wine library consists of vineyards, grapes and festivals from Argentina to New Zealand. France and Australia are specialist areas. Photographs can be supplied by e-mail, on CD or DVD.

Ecoscene

Empire Farm, Throop Road, Templecombe BA8 0HR
☎01963 371700
✉ pix@ecoscene.com
www.ecoscene.com

Contact *Sally Morgan*

Expanding colour library of over 80,000 transparencies specialising in all aspects of the environment: pollution, conservation, recycling, restoration, wildlife (especially underwater), habitats, education, landscapes, industry and agriculture. All parts of the globe are covered with specialist collections covering Antarctica, Australia, North America. Sally Morgan, who runs the library, is a professional ecologist and expert source of information on all environmental topics. Photographic and writing commissions undertaken. Images delivered by e-mail or available for download.

Edifice

Cutterne Mill, Evercreech BA4 6LY
☎01749 831400
✉ info@edificephoto.com
www.edificephoto.com

Contacts *Philippa Lewis, Gillian Darley*

Colour material on exteriors of all possible types of building worldwide from grand landmarks to the small and simple. Specialists in domestic architecture, garden features, architectural detail, ornament, historical and period style, building materials and techniques. Website searchable online, but expert help and advice happily given over the phone or by e-mail.

Education Photos

8 Whitemore Road, Guildford GU1 1QT
☎01483 511666
✉ johnwalmsley@educationphotos.co.uk
www.educationphotos.co.uk

Formerly the John Walmsley Photo Library. Specialist library of learning/training/working subjects. Comprehensive coverage of learning environments such as playgroups, schools, colleges and universities. Images reflect a multi-racial Britain. Commissions undertaken.

English Heritage Photo Library

Kemble Drive, Swindon SN2 2GZ
☎01793 414903 Fax 01793 414606
✉ photo.library@english-heritage.org.uk
www.english-heritage.org.uk/photolibrary

Contact *Duncan Brown*

Images of English castles, abbeys, houses, gardens, Roman remains, ancient monuments, battlefields, industrial and post-war buildings, interiors, paintings, artifacts, architectural details, conservation, archaeology, scenic views, landscapes.

Mary Evans Picture Library

59 Tranquil Vale, Blackheath, London SE3 0BS
☎020 8318 0034 Fax 020 8852 7211
✉ pictures@maryevans.com
www.maryevans.com

Specialist historical archive of illustrations, photographs, prints and ephemera documenting all aspects of the past, from ancient times to the later decades of the 20th century. Subject areas: social and political history, portraits, events, transport, costume, trade and industry, places worldwide and natural history plus specialist material on folklore and paranormal phenomena. Notable collections include the Weimar Archive documenting the Third Reich and Barnaby's Photographic Library covering social scenes and events from the 1930s to the 1970s. MEPL's own material is complemented by many contributors such as Sigmund Freud Copyrights, the **Women's Library** (women's rights) and the Meledin Collection of 20th century Russian history. Over 150,000 images searchable online with 60,000 scanned in high-resolution for immediate download. Brochure on request. Founder member of **BAPLA**. Compilers of the *Picture Researcher's Handbook* by Pira International.

Eye Ubiquitous
65 Brighton Road, Shoreham BN43 6RE
☎01273 440113 Fax 01273 440116
✉ library@eyeubiquitous.com
www.eyeubiquitous.com

General stock specialising in social documentary worldwide, and an extensive travel related collection.

Faces and Places
28 Sheen Common Drive, Richmond TW10 5BN
☎020 7602 1989/07930 622964 (mobile)
✉ equilibrium.films@virgin.net *or* john@facesandplacespix.com
www.facesandplacespix.com

Extensive worldwide library built up over 20 years which covers 40,000 photographs focusing mainly on travel, tourism, unusual locations, indigenous peoples, scenery and underwater photography; Australia, Tibet, Mali, Yemen and Iran.

Famous Pictures
& Features Agency
13 Harwood Road, London SW6 4QP
☎020 7731 9333 Fax 020 7731 9330
✉ info@famous.uk.com
www.famous.uk.com

'Famous is a long-established celebrity features and pictures agency that has worked successfully for many years with writers who value our integrity and efficiency.' Represents top celebrity writers from the UK, LA, New York, Europe and Australia, syndicating their copy worldwide. 'We are always interested in new showbiz material, so please contact us if you are a journalist or freelancer looking to sell your celebrity interviews, features or gossip stories.'

ffotograff
10 Kyveilog Street, Pontcanna, Cardiff CF11 9JA
☎029 2023 6879
✉ ffotograff@easynet.co.uk
www.ffotograff.com

Contact *Patricia Aithie*

Library and agency specialising in travel, exploration, the arts, architecture, traditional culture,

archaeology and landscape. Based in Wales but specialising in the Middle and Far East; Africa, Central and South America; Yemen and Wales are strong aspects of the library. Churches and cathedrals of Britain and Crusader castles.

Financial Times Pictures
One Southwark Bridge, London SE1 9HL
☎020 7873 3671 Fax 020 7873 4606
✉ photosynd@ft.com

Contacts *Nicky Burr, Richard Pigden*

Photographs from around the world ranging from personalities in business, politics and the arts, people at work and other human interests and activities. Delivery via ISDN or e-mail.

Fine Art Photographic Library Ltd
2A Milner Street, London SW3 2PU
☎020 7589 3127 Fax 020 7584 1944
✉ info@fineartphotolibrary.com
www.fineartphotolibrary.com

Over 30,000 large-format transparencies, with a specialist collection of 19th and 20th century paintings. CD-ROM available.

Firepix International
68 Arkles Lane, Anfield, Liverpool L4 2SP
☎0151 260 0111/0777 5930419 (mobile)
Fax 0151 260 0111
✉ info@firepix.com
www.firepix.com

Contact *Tony Myers*

The UK's only fire photo library. 23,000 images of fire-related subjects, firefighters, fire equipment manufacturers. Website contains 15 categories from industrial fire, domestic, digital images and abstract flame.

Fogden Wildlife Photographs
16 Locheport, North Uist, Western Isles HS6 5EU
☎01876 580245 Fax 01876 580777
✉ susan.fogden@fogdenphotos.co.uk
www.fogdenphotos.com

Contact *Susan Fogden*

Natural history collection, with special reference to rain forests and deserts. 'Emphasis on quality rather than quantity'; growing collection of around 25,000 images.

Food Features
Stream House, West Flexford Lane, Wanborough, Guildford GU3 2JW
☎01483 810840 Fax 01483 811587
✉ frontdesk@foodpix.co.uk

www.foodfeatures.net

Contacts *Steve Moss, Alex Barker*

Specialised high-quality food and drink photography, features and tested recipes. Clients' specific requirements can be incorporated into regular shooting schedules.

Forestry Commission Picture Library

231 Corstorphine Road, Edinburgh EH12 7AT

☎0131 314 6411

✉ neill.campbell@forestry.gsi.gov.uk

www.forestry.gov.uk/pictures

Contact *Neill Campbell*

The official image bank of the Forestry Commission, the library provides a single source for all aspects of forest and woodland management. The comprehensive subject list includes tree species, scenic landscapes, employment, wildlife, flora and fauna, conservation, sport and leisure.

Werner Forman Archive Ltd

36 Camden Square, London NW1 9XA

☎020 7267 1034 Fax 020 7267 6026

✉ wfa@btinternet.com

www.werner-forman-archive.com

Colour and b&w coverage of ancient civilisations, oriental and primitive societies around the world. A number of rare collections. Searchable website.

Formula One Pictures

2013 Pomaz, Buzavirag U.6. Hungary

☎00 36 26 322 826/07747 862606 (UK mobile)

✉ jt@f1pictures.com

www.f1pictures.com

Contact *John Townsend*

500,000 35mm colour slides, b&w and colour negatives and digital images of all aspects of Formula One Grand Prix racing from 1980 including driver profiles and portraits.

Robert Forsythe Picture Library

16 Lime Grove, Prudhoe NE42 6PR

☎01661 834511 Fax 01661 834511

✉ robert@forsythe.demon.co.uk

www.forsythe.demon.co.uk

Contacts *Robert Forsythe, Fiona Forsythe*

30,000 transparencies of industrial and transport heritage; plus a unique collection of 100,000 items of related publicity ephemera from 1945. Image finding service available. Robert Forsythe

is a transport/industrial heritage historian and consultant. Nationwide coverage, particularly strong on northern Britain. A bibliography of published material is available.

The Francis Frith Collection

Frith's Barn, Teffont, Salisbury SP3 5QP

☎01722 716376 Fax 01722 716881

✉ julia_skinner@francisfrith.co.uk

www.francisfrith.co.uk

Contact *Julia Skinner*, Managing Editor

Publishers of *Frith's Photographic Memories* series of illustrated local books, all featuring nostalgic photographs from the archive, founded by Frith in 1860. The archive contains over 360,000 images of 7000 British towns.

John Frost Newspapers

See entry under Library Services

Andrew N. Gagg's PHOTO FLORA

Town House Two, Fordbank Court, Henwick Road, Worcester WR2 5PF

☎01905 748515

✉ info@photoflora.co.uk

www.photoflora.co.uk

Contact *Andrew Gagg*

Specialist in British and European wild plants, flowers, ferns, grasses, trees, shrubs, etc. with colour coverage of most British and many European species (rare and common) and habitats; also travel in India, Sri Lanka, Nepal, Egypt and North Africa, China, Mexico, Thailand, Tibet, Vietnam and Cambodia.

Galaxy Picture Library

34 Fennels Way, Flackwell Heath, High Wycombe HP10 9BY

☎01628 521338 Fax 01628 520132

✉ robin@galaxypix.com

www.galaxypix.com

Contact *Robin Scagell*

Specialises in astronomy, space, telescopes, observatories, the sky, clouds and sunsets. Composites of foregrounds, stars, moon and planets prepared to commission. Editorial service available.

Garden and Wildlife Matters Photo Library

'Marlham', Henley's Down, Battle TN33 9BN

☎01424 830566 Fax 01424 830224

✉ gardens@gmpix.com

www.gmpix.com

Contact *Dr John Feltwell*

Collection of 110,000 6x4" and 35mm images. General gardening techniques and design; cottage gardens and USA designer gardens. 10,000 species of garden plants and over 1000 species of trees. Flowers, wild and house plants, trees and crops. Environmental, ecological and conservation pictures, including sea, air, noise and freshwater pollution, SE Asian and Central and South American rainforests; Eastern Europe, Mediterranean. Recycling, agriculture, forestry, horticulture and oblique aerial habitat shots from Europe and USA. Digital images supplied worldwide.

Garden Picture Library

Unit 12, Ransome's Dock, 35 Parkgate Road, London SW11 4NP
☎020 7228 4332 Fax 020 7924 3267
✉ info@gardenpicture.com
www.gardenpicture.com

Contact *Ruth Brown* (Editor)

'Our inspirational images of gardens, plants and gardening lifestyle offer plenty of scope for writers looking for original ideas to write about.' The collection covers all garden related subjects; everything from plant portraits to floral graphics and garden design details to whole landscapes. Brings together the work of over 100 professional photographers from across the gardening globe. Holds approximately 400,000 fully captioned images of which around 60,000 are available digitally. Free in-house picture research can be undertaken on request or searches can be made online via keyword or subject category to create lightboxes which can be e-mailed or downloaded. Visitors to the library are welcome by appointment and copies of promotional literature are available on request.

Ed Geldard Photo Collection

9 Sunderland Bridge Village, Durham DH6 5HB
☎0191 378 2592
✉ ed@camera-one.freeserve.co.uk

Contact *Ed Geldard*

Approximately 30,000 colour transparencies and b&w negs, all by Ed Geldard, specialising in mountain landscapes: particularly the mountain regions of the Lake District, and the Yorkshire limestone areas, from valley to summit. Commissions undertaken. Books published: *Wainwright's Tour of the Lake District; Wainwright in the Limestone Dales; The Lake District.*

Genesis Space Photo Library

20 Goodwood Park Road, Bideford EX39 2RR
☎01237 477883
✉ tim@spaceport.co.uk
www.spaceport.co.uk

Contact *Tim Furniss*

Contemporary and historical colour and b&w spaceflight collection including rockets, spacecraft, spacemen, Earth, moon and planets. Catalogue of 775 images on website.

Geo Aerial Photography

4 Christian Fields, London SW16 3JZ
☎020 8764 6292/0115 981 9418
Fax 020 8764 6292/0115 981 9418
✉ geo.aerial@geo-group.co.uk
www.geo-group.co.uk

Contact *Kelly White*

Established 1990 and now a growing collection of aerial oblique photographs from the UK, Scandinavia, Asia and Africa – landscapes, buildings, industrial sites, etc. Commissions undertaken.

GeoScience Features

6 Orchard Drive, Wye TN25 5AU
☎01233 812707 Fax 01233 812707
✉ gsf@geoscience.demon.co.uk
www.geoscience.demon.co.uk

Fully computerised and comprehensive library containing the world's principal source of volcanic phenomena. Extensive collections, providing scientific detail with technical quality, of rocks, minerals, fossils, microsections of botanical and animal tissues, animals, biology, birds, botany, chemistry, earth science, ecology, environment, geology, geography, habitats, landscapes, macro/microbiology, peoples, sky, weather, wildlife and zoology. Over 450,000 original colour transparencies in medium and 35mm-format. Subject lists and CD-ROM catalogue available. Incorporates the RIDA photolibrary and Landform Slides.

Geoslides Photography

4 Christian Fields, London SW16 3JZ
☎020 8764 6292/0115 981 9418
Fax 020 8764 6292/0115 981 9418
✉ geoslides@geo-group.co.uk
www.geo-group.co.uk

Contact *John Douglas*

Established in 1968. Landscape and human interest subjects from the Arctic, Antarctica, Scandinavia, UK, Africa (south of Sahara),

Middle East, Asia (south and southeast). Also specialist collections of images from British India (the Raj) and Boer War.

Getty Images

101 Bayham Street, London NW1 0AG
☎0800 376 7981 Fax 020 7428 6175
✉ bbi@gettyimages.com
www.gettyimages.com

Contact *Sales Department*

'Getty Images is the world's leading imagery company, creating and providing the largest collection of still and moving images to communication professionals around the globe.' From sports and news photography to archival and contemporary imagery. For those who wish to commission photographers to fulfil specific needs, the company maintains a full-service department for custom-shot images.

Martin and Dorothy Grace

Boxwood Cottage, The Row, Lyth, Kendal
LA8 8DD
☎01539 568569
✉ graces@lineone.net

Colour coverage of natural history in Britain, the Galapagos Islands, France and southern Spain, specialising in trees, shrubs and wild flowers. Also ferns, birds and butterflies, habitats, landscapes, ecology.

Ronald Grant Archive

See **The Cinema Museum**

Sally and Richard Greenhill

357 Liverpool Road, London N1 1NL
☎020 7607 8549
✉ sr.greenhill@virgin.net
www.srgreenhill.co.uk

Photo Librarian *Denise Lalonde*

Social documentary photography in colour and b&w of working lives: pregnancy and birth, child development, education, work, old people, medical, urban. Also Modern China, 1971 to the present; most London statues. Some material from Borneo, USA, India, Israel, Philippines and Sri Lanka.

V.K. Guy Ltd

Browhead Cottage, Troutbeck LA23 1PG
☎015394 33519 Fax 015394 32971
✉ admin@vkguy.co.uk
www.vkguy.co.uk

Contacts *Vic Guy, Mike Guy*

25,000 5x4″ UK and Ireland scenic transparen-cies from Shetland in the north to the Channel Isles in the south, suitable for tourism brochures, calendars, etc. Can be supplied digitally and browsed through via the online database.

Robert Harding Picture Library

58–59 Great Marlborough Street, London
W1F 7JY
☎020 7478 4000 Fax 020 7478 4161
✉ info@robertharding.com
www.robertharding.com

A leading source of stock photography with over two million colour images covering a wide range of subjects – worldwide travel and culture, geography and landscapes, people and lifestyle, architecture. Rights protected and royalty-free images. Visitors welcome; telephone or visit the website.

Dennis Hardley Photography, Scottish Photo Library

Rosslynn, Benderloch, Oban PA37 1ST
☎01631 720434 Fax 01631 720434
✉ dennis.hardley@btinternet.com
www.ineedanimage.com

Contacts *Dennis Hardley, Tony Hardley*

Established 1974. About 30,000 images (6x7″, 6x9″ format colour transparencies) of Scotland: castles, historic, scenic landscapes, islands, transport, etc. Also English views – Liverpool, Chester, Bath, Weston Super Mare, Sussex, Somerset and Cambridge. All images available to buy and instantly download from the website. Includes Scotland, England and North Wales, covering lifestyle, landscapes, transport, cities, etc.

Jim Henderson Photography

Crooktree, Kincardine O'Neil, Aboyne
AB34 4JD
☎01339 882149 Fax 01339 882149
✉ JHende7868@aol.com
www.jimhendersonphotography.com

Contact *Jim Henderson*

Scenic and general activity coverage of north east Scotland (Aberdeenshire) and Highlands for tourist, holiday and activity illustration. Specialist collection of over 300 Aurora Borealis displays from 1989–to date on Royal Deeside and co-author of *The Aurora* (pub. 1997). Author and photographer for *Aberdeen* and *Aberdeen & Royal Deeside* titles for Aberdeen Journals. Recent images of ancient Egyptian sites: Cairo through to Abu-Simbel. **BAPLA** and Alamy member. Commissions undertaken.

John Heseltine Archive

Mill Studio, Frogmarsh Mill, South
Woodchester GL5 5ET
☎01453 873792
✉ john@heseltine.co.uk
www.heseltine.co.uk

Contact *John Heseltine*

Over 200,000 colour transparencies and digital files of landscapes, architecture, food and travel with particular emphasis on Italy and the UK.

Christopher Hill Photographic

17 Clarence Street, Belfast BT2 8DY
☎028 9024 5038 Fax 028 9023 1942
✉ sales@scenicireland.com
www.scenicireland.com

Contact *Christopher Hill*

A comprehensive collection of scenic landscapes of Ireland. Every aspect of Irish life is shown, concentrating on the positive. Also large miscellaneous section. The website contains over 7000 images available to buy online.

Hobbs Golf Collection

5 Winston Way, New Ridley, Stocksfield NE43 7RF
☎01661 842933/07941 445993
Fax 01661 842933
✉ info@hobbsgolfcollection.com
www.hobbsgolfcollection.com

Contact *Margaret Hobbs*

Specialist golf collection: players, courses, art, memorabilia and historical topics (1300–present). 40,000+ images, mainly 35mm colour transparencies and b&w prints. All images can be supplied in digital format. Commissions undertaken. Author of 30 golf books.

David Hoffman Photo Library

c/o BAPLA, 18 Vine Hill, London EC1R 5DZ
☎020 8981 5041
✉ info@hoffmanphotos.com
www.hoffmanphotos.com

Contact *David Hoffman*

Commissioned photography and stock library with a strong emphasis on social issues built up from 35mm journalistic and documentary work dating from the late 1970s. Files on drugs and drug use, policing, disorder, riots, youth, prostitution, protest, homelessness, housing, environmental demonstrations and events, waste disposal, alternative energy, industry and pollution. Wide range of images especially from UK and Europe but also USA, Canada, Venezuela, Mexico and Thailand. General files on topical issues and current affairs plus specialist files from leisure cycling to local authority services. Many photographs available for online delivery from www.alamy.com/davidhoffman

Holt Studios International Ltd

See **Frank Lane Picture Agency Ltd**

Houghton's Horses/ Kit Houghton Photography

Radlet Cottage, Spaxton, Bridgwater TA5 1DE
☎01278 671362 Fax 01278 671739
✉ kit@enterprise.net
www.houghtonshorses.com

Contacts *Kit Houghton, Kate Houghton*

Specialist equestrian library of over 300,000 transparencies and digital images on all aspects of the horse world, with images ranging from the romantic to the practical and competition pictures in all equestrian disciplines worldwide. Online picture delivery is now the norm. All transparencies in the process of being scanned. Commissions undertaken.

Chris Howes/Wild Places Photography

PO Box 100, Abergavenny NP7 9WY
☎01873 737707
✉ photos@wildplaces.co.uk

Contacts *Chris Howes, Judith Calford*

Expanding collection of over 50,000 colour transparencies, b&w prints and digital photos covering travel, topography and natural history worldwide, plus action sports such as climbing. Supply now fully digital. Specialist areas include caves, caving and mines (with historical coverage using engravings and early photographs), wildlife, landscapes and the environment, including pollution and conservation. Europe (including Britain), Canada, USA, Africa and Australia are all well represented within the collection. Commissions undertaken.

Huntley Film Archive

22 Islington Green, London N1 8DU
☎020 7226 9260 Fax 020 7359 9337
✉ films@huntleyarchives.com
www.huntleyarchives.com

Contact *Amanda Huntley*

Originally a private collection, the library is now a comprehensive archive of rare and vintage documentary film dating from 1895. 50,000 films on all subjects of a documentary nature. Online catalogue available.

Jacqui Hurst

66 Richford Street, Hammersmith, London
W6 7HP
☎020 8743 2315/07970 781336 (mobile)
✉ jacquihurst@yahoo.co.uk
www.jacquihurstphotography.co.uk

Contact *Jacqui Hurst*

A specialist library of traditional and contemporary applied arts, regional food producers and markets. The photos form illustrated essays of how something is made and finish with a still life of the completed object. The collection is always being extended and a list is available on request. Commissions undertaken.

Hutchison Picture Library

65 Brighton Road, Shoreham-by-Sea
BN43 6RE
☎01273 440113
✉ library@hutchisonpictures.co.uk
www.hutchisonpictures.co.uk

Worldwide contemporary images from the straight-forward to the esoteric and quirky. Over half a million documentary colour photographs on file, covering people, places, customs and faiths, agriculture, industry and transport. Special collections include the environment and climate, family life (including pregnancy and birth), ethnic minorities worldwide (including Disappearing World archive), conventional and alternative medicine, and music around the world. Search service available.

Illustrated London News Picture Library

20 Upper Ground, London SE1 9PF
☎020 7805 5585 Fax 020 7805 5905
✉ research@ilnpictures.co.uk
www.ilnpictures.co.uk

Engravings, photographs and illustrations from 1842 to the present day, taken from magazines published by Illustrated Newspapers: *Illustrated London News*; *Graphic*; *Sphere*; *Tatler*; *Sketch*; *Illustrated Sporting and Dramatic News*; *Illustrated War News 1914–18*; *Bystander*; *Britannia & Eve*. Social history, London, Industrial Revolution, wars, travel. Visitors occasionally admitted by appointment. Research and scanning services available.

Images of Africa Photobank

11 The Windings, Lichfield WS13 7EX
☎01543 262898 Fax 01543 417154
✉ info@imagesofafrica.co.uk
www.imagesofafrica.co.uk

Contact *David Keith Jones, FRPS*

Over 135,000 images covering Botswana, Chad, Egypt, Ethiopia, Kenya, Lesotho, Madagasca, Malawi, Morocco, Namibia, Rwanda, South Africa, Swaziland, Tanzania, Uganda, Zaire, Zambia, Zanzibar and Zimbabwe. 'Probably the best collection of photographs of Kenya in Europe.' A wide range of topics are covered. Strong on African wildlife with over 80 species of mammals including many sequences showing action and behaviour. Popular animals like lions and elephants are covered in encyclopædic detail. More than 100 species of birds and many reptiles are included. Other strengths include National Parks and reserves, natural beauty, tourism facilities, traditional and modern people. Most work is by David Keith Jones, FRPS; several other photographers are represented. Colour brochure available. The Library offers next day delivery by post or same day by e-mail when requested.

Imperial War Museum Photograph Archive

All Saints Annexe, Austral Street, London
SE11 4SJ
☎020 7416 5333 Fax 020 7416 5355
✉ photos@iwm.org.uk
www.iwm.org.uk

A national archive of ten million photographs illustrating all aspects of 20th and 21st century conflict. Emphasis on the two World Wars but includes material from other conflicts involving Britain and the Commonwealth. Majority of material is b&w, although holdings of colour material increase with more recent conflicts. Visitors welcome by appointment, Monday to Friday, 10.00 am to 5.00 pm.

International Photobank

PO Box 6554, Dorchester DT1 9BS
☎01305 854145 Fax 01305 853065
✉ peter@internationalphotobank.co.uk
www.internationalphotobank.co.uk

Contacts *Peter Baker, Gary Goodwin*

Over 450,000 images, in digital and transparency format. Colour coverage of travel subjects: places, people, folklore, events. Digital broadband service available for newspapers, magazines and other users. Pictures can also be selected from the comprehensive website.

Robbie Jack Photography

45 Church Road, Hanwell, London W7 3BD
☎020 8567 9616
✉ robbie@robbiejack.com

www.robbiejack.com

Contact *Robbie Jack*

Built up over the last 25 years, the library contains over 500,000 colour images of the performing arts – theatre, dance, opera and music. Includes West End shows, the RSC and Royal National Theatre productions, English National Opera and Royal Opera. The dance section contains images of the Royal Ballet, English National Ballet, the Rambert Dance Company, plus many foreign companies. Also holds the largest selection of colour material from the Edinburgh International Festival. Researchers are welcome to visit by appointment. From 2001 began offering colour transparencies as digital images which are being added to on a daily basis.

Jayawardene Travel Photo Library

7A Napier Road, Wembley HA0 4UA

☎020 8795 3581 Fax 020 8795 4083

✉ jaytravelphotos@aol.com

www.jaytravelphotos.com

Contact *Rohith Jayawardene*

160,000 travel and travel-related images – digital and original transparencies. Many places photographed in depth, with more than 800 pictures per country. Over 7000 images available online.

Paul Kaye B/W Archive

See **Sylvia Cordaiy Photo Library**

David King Collection

90 St Pauls Road, London N1 2QP

☎020 7226 0149 Fax 020 7354 8264

✉ davidkingcollection@btopenworld.com

www.davidkingcollection.com

Contact *David King*

250,000 b&w original and copy photographs and colour transparencies of historical and present-day images. Russian history and the Soviet Union from 1900 to the fall of Khrushchev; the lives of Lenin, Trotsky and Stalin; the Tzars, Russo-Japanese War, 1917 Revolution, World War I, Red Army, the Great Purges, Great Patriotic War, etc. Special collections on China, Eastern Europe, the Weimar Republic, John Heartfield, American labour struggles, Spanish Civil War. Open to qualified researchers by appointment, Monday to Friday, 10.00 am to 6.00 pm. Staff will undertake research; negotiable fee for long projects. David King's latest photographic books: *The Commissar Vanishes*, documenting the falsification of photographs and art in Stalin's Russia, and *Ordinary Citizens*, mugshots of victims shot without trial from the archives of Stalin's secret

police. The 1930s Soviet photographic magazine, *USSR in Construction*, from the David King Collection is on display throughout 2007 at Tate Modern, London.

The Kobal Collection

2 The Quadrant, 135 Salusbury Road, London NW6 6RJ

☎020 7624 3500 Fax 020 7624 3355

✉ info@picture-desk.com

www.picture-desk.com

Picture library holding colour and b&w coverage of Hollywood films, portraits, stills, publicity shots, posters and ephemera.

Kos Picture Source Ltd

Po Box 52854, 7 Spice Court, London SW11 3UU

☎020 7801 0044 Fax 020 7801 0055

✉ images@kospictures.com

www.kospictures.com

Contact *Chris Savage*

Specialists in water-related images including international yacht racing and cruising, classic boats and superyachts, and extensive range of watersports. Also worldwide travel including seascapes, beach scenes, underwater photography and the weather.

Ed Lacey Collection

See **Phil Sheldon Golf Picture Library**

Landform Slides

See **GeoScience Features**

Frank Lane Picture Agency Ltd

Pages Green House, Wetheringsett, Stowmarket IP14 5QA

☎01728 860789 Fax 01728 860222

✉ pictures@flpa-images.co.uk

www.flpa-images.co.uk

Colour coverage of natural history, environment, pets and weather. Represents Sunset from France, Foto Natura from Holland, Minden Pictures from the US, Holt Studios and works closely with Eric and David Hosking, plus 270 freelance photographers. Website with 110,000 images.

Last Resort Picture Library

Manvers Studios, 12 Ollerton Road, Tuxford, Newark NG22 0LF

☎01777 870166 Fax 01777 871739

✉ dick@dmimaging.co.uk

www.dmimaging.co.uk

Contacts *Jo Makin, Dick Makin*

Subject areas include agriculture, architecture, IT, education, food, industry, landscapes, people at work, skiing, trees, flowers, mountains and winter landscapes. Images cover a wide variety of topics, ranging from the everyday to the obscure. 'Bespoke service available through our linked photographic studio. Contact us for details.'

LAT Photographic

Teddington Studios, Broom Road, Teddington TW11 9BE
☎020 8251 3000 Fax 020 8251 3001
✉ lat.photo@haynet.com
www.latphoto.co.uk
Contact *Zoë Mayho*

Motor sport collection of over nine million images dating from 1895 to the present day.

Lebrecht Music and Arts

3 Bolton Road, London NW8 0RJ
☎020 7625 5341
✉ pictures@lebrecht.co.uk
www.lebrecht.co.uk
Contact *Elbie Lebrecht*

Classical music, opera, jazz, rock, musicians, instruments, performers, writers, artists, architects, sculptors, historical personalities, politicians, society and glamorous showbusiness personalities.

The Erich Lessing Archive of Fine Art & Culture

c/o akg-images Ltd, The Arts and History Picture Library, 5 Melbray Mews, 158 Hurlingham Road, London SW6 3NS
☎020 7610 6103 Fax 020 7610 6125
✉ enquiries@akg-images.co.uk
www.akg-images.co.uk

Top quality high resolution scans depicting the contents of many of the world's finest art galleries as well as ancient archaeological and biblical sites available in the UK via the akg-images website.

Lindley Library, Royal Horticultural Society

80 Vincent Square, London SW1P 2PE
☎020 7821 3051 Fax 020 7821 3022
Contact *Picture Librarian*

22,000 original drawings and approx. 8000 books with hand-coloured plates of botanical illustrations. Appointments are necessary to visit the collection of unpublished material; all photography is carried out by their own photographer.

Link Picture Library

41A The Downs, London SW20 8HG
☎020 8944 6933
✉ library@linkpicturelibrary.com
www.linkpicturelibrary.com
Contact *Orde Eliason*

100,000 images of South Africa, India, China, Vietnam and Israel. A more general collection of colour transparencies from 100 countries worldwide. Link Picture Library has an international network and can source material not in its file from Japan, Scandinavia, India and South Africa. Original photographic commissions undertaken.

London Aerial Photo Library

Studio D1, Fairoaks Airport, Chobham, Woking GU24 8HU
☎01276 855997/855344 Fax 01276 855455
✉ info@londonaerial.co.uk
www.londonaerial.co.uk
www.flightimages.com
Contact *Amanda Campbell*
Librarian *Glyn Tassell*

Extensive collections of aerial imagery. 450,000 images including continually updated photography of London plus excellent coverage of the UK in general. Covers landmarks, industrial/retail properties, sporting venues/football stadiums, conceptual shots. Library searches by expert staff, free of charge. Selection of digital images also available via website. Commissioned photography undertaken.

London Metropolitan Archives

40 Northampton Road, London EC1R 0HB
☎020 7332 3820 Fax 020 7833 9136
✉ ask.lma@cityoflondon.gov.uk
www.cityoflondon.gov.uk/lma
Contact *The Enquiry Team*

London Metropolitan Archives (LMA) is the largest local authority record office in the UK. Holds over 32 miles of archives – an enormous amount of information about the capital and its people. These include records of London government, hospitals, charities, businesses and parish churches. Types of record range from books and manuscript documents to photographs, maps and drawings. 'Nearly 900 years of London history can be brought to life at LMA.' There is also a 100,000 volume reference library specialising in London history. See entry under *Library Services*.

London's Transport Museum Photographic Library

39 Wellington Street, London WC2E 7BB
☎020 7379 6344 Fax 020 7565 7252
✉ photo@ltmuseum.co.uk
www.ltmuseum.co.uk

Contacts *Hugh Robertson, Simon Murphy*

Around 100,000 b&w images from the 1860s and 20,000 colour images from c.1975. Specialist collections: Poster archive, Underground construction, corporate design and architecture, street scenes, London Transport during the war. Collection available for viewing by appointment on Monday and Tuesday. No loans system but prints and transparences can be purchased. Digital images available on CD-ROM.

Ludvigsen Library

Scoles Gate, Hawkedon, Bury St Edmunds IP29 4AU
☎01284 789246 Fax 01284 789246
✉ library@ludvigsen.com
www.ludvigsen.com

Contact *Karl Ludvigsen*

Extensive information research facilities for writers and publishers. Approximately 400,000 images (both b&w and many colour transparencies) of automobiles and motorsport, from 1890s through 1980s. Glass plate negatives from the early 1900s; Formula One, Le Mans, motor car shows, vintage, antique and classic cars from all countries. Includes the Dalton-Watson Collection and the work of noted photographers such as John Dugdale, Edward Eves, Peter Keen, Max le Grand, Karl Ludvigsen, Rodolfo Mailander, Ove Nielsen, Stanley Rosenthall and others.

MacQuitty International Photographic Collection

7 Elm Lodge, River Gardens, Stevenage Road, London SW6 6NZ
☎020 7385 5606 Fax 020 7385 5606
✉ miranda.macquitty@btinternet.com

Contact *Dr Miranda MacQuitty*

Colour and b&w collection on aspects of life in over 70 countries: dancing, music, religion, death, archaeology, buildings, transport, food, drink, nature. Visitors by appointment.

Magnum Photos Ltd

Ground Floor, 63 Gee Street, London EC1V 3RS
☎020 7490 1771 Fax 020 7608 0020
✉ magnum@magnumphotos.co.uk

www.magnumphotos.com

Head of Library *Nick Galvin*

Founded 1947 by Cartier Bresson, George Rodger, Robert Capa and David 'Chim' Seymour. Represents over 70 of the world's leading photo-journalists. Coverage of all major world events from the Spanish Civil War to present day. Also a large collection of travel images and personalities.

The Raymond Mander & Joe Mitchenson Theatre Collection

Jerwood Library of the Performing Arts, Trinity College of Music, King Charles Court, Old Royal Naval College, London SE10 9JF
☎020 8305 4426 Fax 020 8305 9426
✉ rmangan@tcm.ac.uk
www.mander-and-mitchenson.co.uk

Contact *Richard Mangan*

Archive Officer/Cataloguer *Kristy Davis*

Enormous collection covering all aspects of the theatre: plays, actors, dramatists, music hall, theatres, singers, composers, etc. Visitors welcome by appointment.

The Roger Mann Collection

Wensley Court, 48 Barton Road, Torquay TQ1 4DW
☎01803 323868 Fax 01803 616448
✉ rogermann48bart@aol.com
www.therogermanncollection.co.uk

Contact *R.F. Mann*

Comprehensive collection of cricket photographs covering the period 1750 to 1945. The photographs feature most of the first-class players, teams, Test match action and overseas tours of the period. This collection includes almost 2000 original match scorecards, cartoons, images, prints, postcards, cigarette cards, letters and the personal memorabilia of many of the best-known players of the time. Also some coverage of the period 1946 to 1970.

S&O Mathews Photography

Little Pitt Place, Brighstone, Isle of Wight PO30 4DZ
☎01983 741098
✉ oliver@mathews-photography.com
www.mathews-photography.com

Specialist stock library of fine photographs of botanical and horticultural subjects, plants, plant portraits and plant associations, as well as gardens, including views, details and features.

Institution of Mechanical Engineers

1 Birdcage Walk, London SW1H 9JJ
☎020 7973 1274 Fax 020 7222 8762
✉ library@imeche.org
www.imeche.org

Historical images and archives on mechanical engineering. Open 9.15 am to 5.30 pm, Monday to Friday.

Meledin Collection
See **Mary Evans Picture Library**

The MerseySlides Collection
See **Tropix Photo Library**

Lee Miller Archives

Farley Farm House, Chiddingly, Near Lewes BN8 6HW
☎01825 872691 Fax 01825 872733
✉ archives@leemiller.co.uk
www.leemiller.co.uk

The work of Lee Miller (1907–77). As a photojournalist she covered the war in Europe from early in 1941 to VE Day with further reporting from the Balkans. Collection includes photographic portraits of prominent Surrealist artists: Ernst, Eluard, Miró, Picasso, Penrose, Carrington, Tanning, and others. Surrealist and contemporary art, poets and writers, fashion, the Middle East, Egypt, the Balkans in the 1930s, London during the Blitz, war in Europe and the liberation of Dachau and Buchenwald.

Mirrorpix

21 Bruton Street, London W1J 6QD
☎020 7293 3700 Fax 020 7293 0357
✉ desk@mirrorpix.com
www.mirrorpix.com

Account Manager *Mel Knight*

Archive of photographic glass plates and negatives spanning over 100 years of UK and world history. Key themes include social and political history (domestic and foreign), the arts, culture, industry, fashion, sport and royalty. Also includes a collection of cityscapes, landscapes, pastoral scenes and still life.

Monitor Picture Library

The Forge, Roydon, Harlow CM19 5HH
☎01279 792700 Fax 01279 792600
✉ info@monitorpicturelibrary.com
www.monitorpicturelibrary.com

Colour and b&w coverage of 1960s, '70s and '80s personalities and celebrities from: music, entertainment, sport, politics, royals, judicial, commerce etc. Specialist files on Lotus cars. Syndication to international, national and local media.

Motoring Picture Library

National Motor Museum, Beaulieu SO42 7ZN
☎01590 614656 Fax 01590 612655
✉ motoring.pictures@beaulieu.co.uk
www.motoringpicturelibrary.com
www.alamy.com/mpl

Contacts *Jonathan Day, Tim Woodcock, Tom Wood*

Three-quarters of a million b&w images, plus over 100,000 colour images covering all forms of motoring history from the 1880s to the present day. Commissions undertaken. Own studio.

Mountain Camera
See **John Cleare**

Moving Image Communications

9 Faversham Reach, Faversham ME14 7LA
☎0845 257 2968 Fax 01795 534306
✉ mail@milibrary.com *and*
nathalie@milibrary.com *and*
mike@milibrary.com
www.milibrary.com

Contact *Nathalie Banaigs*

Over 16,000 hours of quality archive and contemporary footage, including: Channel X; TVAM Archive 1983–92; Drummer Films (travel classics, 1950–70); The Freud Archive (1930–39); Film Finders (early cinema); Adrian Brunel Films; Cuban Archives; Stockshots (timelapse, cityscapes, land and seascapes, chroma-key); Space Exploration (NASA); Wild Islands; Flying Pictures; National Trust.

Museum of Antiquities Picture Library

University and Society of Antiquaries of Newcastle upon Tyne, Newcastle upon Tyne NE1 7RU
☎0191 222 7846 Fax 0191 222 8561
✉ m.o.antiquities@ncl.ac.uk
www.ncl.ac.uk/antiquities

Contact *Lindsay Allason-Jones*

25,000 images, mostly b&w, of special collections including: Hadrian's Wall Archive (b&ws taken over the last 100 years); Gertrude Bell Archive (during her travels in the Near East, 1900–26); and aerial photographs of archaeological sites in the North of England. Visitors welcome by appointment.

Museum of London
Picture Library

150 London Wall, London EC2Y 5HN
☎020 7814 5604/5612 Fax 020 7600 1058
✉ picturelib@museumoflondon.org.uk
www.museumoflondon.org.uk

Contacts *Sarah Williams*

The Museum of London picture library holds over 35,000 images illustrating the history of London and the life of its people from prehistoric times to the present day. The images are drawn from the Museum's extensive and unique collections of oil paintings, historic photographs, drawings, prints maps and artefacts including costume, jewellery and ceramics.

The National Archives
Image Library

Ruskin Avenue, Kew, Richmond TW9 4DU
☎020 8392 5225 Fax 020 8487 1974
✉ image-library@nationalarchives.gov.uk
www.nationalarchives.gov.uk/imagelibrary

Contacts *Paul Johnson, Hugh Alexander*

British and colonial history from the Domesday Book to the 1970s, shown in photography, maps, illuminations, posters, advertisements, textiles and original manuscripts. Approximately 30,000 5x4˝ and 35mm colour transparencies and b&w negatives. Open: 9.00 am to 5.00 pm, Monday to Friday.

National Galleries of Scotland
Picture Library

The Scottish National Gallery of Modern Art, 75 Belford Road, Edinburgh EH4 3DR
☎0131 624 6258/6260 Fax 0131 623 7135
✉ picture.library@nationalgalleries.org
www.nationalgalleries.org

Contact *Shona Corner*

Over 80,000 b&w and several thousand images in colour of works of art from the Renaissance to present day. Specialist subjects cover fine art (painting, sculpture, drawing), portraits, Scottish, historical, still life, photography and landscape.

National Maritime Museum
Picture Library

Greenwich, London SE10 9NF
☎020 8312 6631/6704 Fax 020 8312 6533
✉ picturelibrary@nmm.ac.uk
www.nmm.ac.uk/picturelibrary

Contacts *David Taylor, Doug McCarthy*

Over 400,000 images from the leading collection of maritime art and artefacts, including oil paintings from the 16th century to present day, prints and drawings, historic photographs, ships plans, models, rare maps and charts, globes, manuscripts and navigation and scientific instruments. Images are available as resolution digital files. Contact for further information or for picture research assistance.

National Media Museum
See **Science & Society Picture Library**

National Monuments Record

National Monuments Record Centre, Kemble Drive, Great Western Village, Swindon SN2 2GZ
☎01793 414600 Fax 01793 414606
www.english-heritage.org.uk/nmr

'The National Monuments Record is the first stop for photographs and information on England's heritage.' Over 10 million photographs, documents and drawings are held. English architecture from the first days of photography to the present, air photographs covering every inch of England from the first days of flying to the present, and archaeological sites. The Record is the public archive of English Heritage (see **English Heritage Photo Library**).

National Portrait Gallery
Picture Library

St Martin's Place, London WC2H 0HE
☎020 7312 2474/5/6 Fax 020 7312 2464
✉ picturelibrary@npg.org.uk
www.npg.org.uk

Contact *Tom Morgan*

Pictures of brilliant, daring and influential characters who have made British history are available for publication. Images can be searched, viewed and ordered on the website. Copyright clearance is arranged for all images supplied.

National Railway Museum
Research Centre

Leeman Road, York YO26 4XJ
☎01904 686235 Fax 01904 686233
✉ nrm.researchcentre@nrm.org.uk
www.nrm.org.uk

The National Railway Museum and the **Science and Society Picture Library** are both part of the National Museum of Science and Industry (NMSI) whose other constituents are the Science Museum in London and the National Media Museum in Bradford (formerly the National Museum of Photography, Film & Television). 1.5 million images, mainly b&w,

covering every aspect of railways from 1850s to the present day. The Research Centre is closed for refurbishment until October 2007 but is taking e-mail and postal enquiries.

The National Trust Photo Library
Heelis, Kemble Drive, Swindon SN2 2NA
☎01793 817700 Fax 01793 817401
✉ photo.library@nationaltrust.org.uk
www.ntpl.org.uk
Contact *Chris Lacey*

The National Trust Photo Library houses a unique collection of contemporary photography which vividly illustrates the rich diversity and historical range of properties in the National Trust's care, throughout England, Wales and Northern Ireland. The Library has an exceptional choice of images, created by commissioned specialist photographers, suitable for a broad range of creative applications. 40,000 images can be searched and ordered online.

Natural History Museum Picture Library
Cromwell Road, London SW7 5BD
☎020 7942 5401/5324 Fax 020 7942 5212
✉ nhmpl@nhm.ac.uk
www.nhm.ac.uk/piclib
Contacts *Elanor Carrington, Jamie Owen*

Pictures from the Museum's collections, including dinosaurs, man's evolution, extinct species and fossil remains. Also pictures of gems, minerals, birds and animals, plants and insect specimens, plus historical artworks depicting the natural world.

Nature Photographers Ltd
West Wit, New Road, Little London, Tadley RG26 5EU
☎01256 850661
✉ info@naturephotographers.co.uk
www.naturephotographers.co.uk
Contact *Dr Paul Sterry*

Over 150,000 images, digitised to order, on worldwide natural history and environmental subjects. The library is run by a trained biologist and experienced author on his subject.

Nature Picture Library
BBC Broadcasting House, Whiteladies Road, Bristol BS8 2LR
☎0117 974 6720 Fax 0117 923 8166
✉ info@naturepl.com
www.naturepl.com
Contact *Helen Gilks*

A collection of 300,000 nature photos from around the world, including strong coverage of animal portraits and behaviour. Other subjects covered include plants, pets, landscapes and travel, environmental issues and wildlife film-makers at work. Thousands of images can be viewed online and downloaded direct for reproduction.

Peter Newark's Picture Library
3 Barton Buildings, Queen Square, Bath BA1 2JR
☎01225 334213 Fax 01225 480554

Over one million images covering world history from ancient times to the present day. Includes an extensive military collection of photographs, paintings and illustrations. Also a special collection on American history covering Colonial times, exploration, social, political and the Wild West and Native-Americans in particular. Subject list available. Telephone, fax or write for further information.

NHPA
See **Photoshot**

Odhams Periodicals Library
See **Popperfoto.com**

Offshoot
See **Skishoot**

Only Horses Picture Agency
27 Greenway Gardens, Greenford UB6 9TU
☎020 8578 9047 Fax 020 8575 7244
✉ onlyhorsespics@aol.com
www.onlyhorsespictures.com

Colour and b&w coverage of all aspects of the horse. Foaling, retirement, racing, show jumping, eventing, veterinary, polo, breeds, personalities.

Oxford Picture Library
15 Curtis Yard, North Hinksey Lane, Oxford OX2 0LX
☎01865 723404 Fax 01865 725294
✉ opl@cap-ox.com
www.cap-ox.co.uk
Contacts *Chris Andrews, Annabel Matthews*

Specialist collection on Oxford: the city, university and colleges, events, people, spires and shires. Also, the Cotswolds, architecture and landscape from Stratford-upon-Avon to Bath; the Thames and Chilterns, including Henley on Thames and Windsor; Channel Islands, especially Guernsey and Sark. Aerial views of all areas specified above. General collection includes wildlife, trees, plants, clouds, sun, sky, water and teddy bears. Commissions undertaken.

Oxford Scientific (OSF)

Ground Floor, Network House, Station Yard, Thame OX9 3UH
☎01844 262370 Fax 01844 262380
✉ enquiries@osf.co.uk
www.osf.co.uk

Account Executive (stills) *Lorel Ward* (l.ward@osf.co.uk)
Account Executive (footage) *Vicky Turner* (v.turner@osf.co.uk)

Collection of 350,000 colour transparencies and digital files of wildlife and natural science images supplied by over 300 photographers worldwide, covering all aspects of wildlife plus landscapes, weather, seasons, plants, pets, environment, anthropology, habitats, science and industry, space, creative textures and backgrounds, and geology. Macro and micro photography. UK agents for Animals Animals, USA, Okapia, Germany and Dinodia, India. Research by experienced researchers for specialist and creative briefs. Visits welcome, by appointment.

Panos Pictures

1 Honduras Street, London EC1Y 0TH
☎020 7253 1424 Fax 020 7253 2752
✉ pics@panos.co.uk
www.panos.co.uk

Documentary colour and b&w library specialising in Third World and Eastern Europe, with emphasis on environment and development issues. Leaflet available. Fifty per cent of all profits from this library go to the Panos Institute to further its work in international sustainable development.

Charles Parker Archive

See **Birmingham Library Services** under *Library Services*

Ann & Bury Peerless Picture Library

St David's, 22 King's Avenue, Minnis Bay, Birchington-on-Sea CT7 9QL
☎01843 841428 Fax 01843 848321
www.peerlessimages.com

Contacts *Ann Peerless, Bury Peerless*

Specialist collection on world religions: Hinduism, Buddhism, Confucianism, Taoism, Jainism, Christianity, Islam, Sikhism, Zoroastrianism (Parsees of India). Geographical areas covered: India, Afghanistan (Bamiyan Valley

of the Buddhas), Pakistan, Bangladesh, Sri Lanka, Cambodia (Angkor), Java (Borobudur), Bali, Thailand, Taiwan, Russia, China, Spain, Poland, Uzbekistan (Samarkand and Bukhara), Vietnam. Basis of collection (35mm colour transparencies), historical, cultural, extensive coverage of art (sculpture and miniature paintings), architecture including Pharaonic Egypt.

Photofusion

17A Electric Lane, London SW9 8LA
☎020 7733 3500 Fax 020 7738 5509
✉ library@photofusion.org
www.photofusionpictures.org

Contact *Liz Somerville*

Colour and b&w coverage of contemporary social and environmental UK issues including babies and children, disability, education, the elderly, environment, family, health, housing, homelessness, people and work. Brochure available.

The Photolibrary Wales

2 Bro-nant, Church Road, Pentyrch, Cardiff CF15 9QG
☎029 2089 0311 Fax 029 2089 0311
✉ info@photolibrarywales.com
www.photolibrarywales.com

Contacts *Steve Benbow, Kate Benbow*

Over 100,000 digital images covering all areas and subjects of Wales. Represents the work of 260 photographers, living and working in Wales.

Photos Horticultural

PO Box 105, Ipswich IP1 4PR
☎01473 257329 Fax 01473 233974
✉ library@photos-horticultural.com
www.photos-horticultural.com

Pictures *Ashley Warren*
Editorial *Michael Warren*

Wide selection of horticultural subjects, gardens, practical, plants cultivated and wild from around the world. Now available online via their website. Commissions for photography and illustrated features undertaken.

Photoshot

29–31 Saffron Hill, London EC1N 8SW
☎020 7421 6000 Fax 020 7421 6006
www.photoshot.com
www.nhpa.co.uk
www.staystill.com
www.worldpictures.co.uk

Contacts *Charles Taylor* (U.P.P.A.); *Emma Hier*

(Stay Still); *Tracey Howells* (Starstock); *Colin Finlay* (World Illustrated); *Tim Harris* (NHPA); *David Brenes* (World Pictures)

Photoshot collections include U.P.P.A. (daily national and international business, political and establishment news); Stay Still (exclusive celebrity portraiture and TV publicity images); Starstock (live images of celebrity and entertainment personalities and events from around the world); World Illustrated (the world in pictures, art, culture, environment and heritage); NHPA (wildlife and nature); World Pictures (comprehensive archive of practical and stylish travel images).

PictureBank Photo Library Ltd

Parman House, 30–36 Fife Road, Kingston upon Thames KT1 1SY

☎020 8547 2344 Fax 020 8974 5652

✉ info@picturebank.co.uk

www.picturebank.co.uk

Over 400,000 images covering people (girls, couples, families, children), travel and scenic (UK and world), moods (sunsets, seascapes, deserts, etc.), industry and technology, environments and general. Commissions undertaken. Visitors welcome. Member of **BAPLA**. New material in digital format welcome.

Pictures Colour Library

10 James Whatman Court, Turkey Mill, Ashford Road, Maidstone ME14 5SS

☎01622 609809 Fax 01622 609806

✉ enquiries@picturescolourlibrary.co.uk

www.picturescolourlibrary.co.uk

Travel and travel-related images depicting lifestyles and cultures, people and places, attitudes and environments from around the world, including a comprehensive section on Great Britain.

Axel Poignant Archive

115 Bedford Court Mansions, Bedford Avenue, London WC1B 3AG

☎020 7636 2555 Fax 020 7636 2555

✉ Rpoignant@aol.com

Contact *Roslyn Poignant*

Anthropological and ethnographic subjects, especially Australia and the South Pacific. Also Scandinavia (early history and mythology), Sicily and England.

H.G. Ponting

See **Popperfoto.com**

Popperfoto.com

The Old Mill, Overstone Farm, Overstone, Northampton NN6 0AB

☎01604 670670 Fax 01604 670635

✉ inquiries@popperfoto.com

www.popperfoto.com

Home to over 14 million images, covering 150 years of photographic history. Renowned for its archival material, a world-famous sports library and stock photography. POPPERFOTO's credit line includes Bob Thomas Sports Photography, UPI, Acme, INP, Planet, Paul Popper, Exclusive News Agency, Victory Archive, Odhams Periodicals Library, Illustrated, Harris Picture Agency, and H.G. Ponting. Colour from 1940, b&w from 1870 to the present. Major subjects covered worldwide include events, personalities, wars, royalty, sport, politics, transport, crime, history and social conditions. Material available on the same day to clients throughout the world. Nearly 200,000 high-resolution images online available by direct download, e-mail, FTP and CD. Researchers welcome by appointment.

PPL (Photo Agency) Ltd

Bookers Yard, The Street, Walberton, Arundel BN18 0PF

☎01243 555561 Fax 01243 555562

✉ ppl@mistral.co.uk

www.pplmedia.com

Contacts *Barry Pickthall, Emma Brenton*

Two million pictures covering watersports, sub-aqua, business and commerce, travel and tourism; pictures of yesteryear and a fast growing archive on Sussex and the home counties. Pictures available in high resolution directly from the website.

Premaphotos Wildlife

Amberstone, 1 Kirland Road, Bodmin PL30 5JQ

☎01208 78258 Fax 01208 72302

✉ enquiries@premaphotos.com

www.premaphotos.com

Contact *Jean Preston-Mafham*, Library Manager

Natural history worldwide. Subjects include flowering and non-flowering plants, fungi, slime moulds, fruits and seeds, galls, leaf mines, seashore life, mammals, birds, reptiles, amphibians, insects, spiders, habitats, scenery and cultivated cacti. Commissions undertaken. Searchable website. Visitors welcome.

Professional Sport UK Ltd

18–19 Shaftesbury Quay, Hertford SG14 1SF

☎01992 505000 Fax 01992 505020
✉ pictures@prosport.co.uk
www.professionalsport.com

Photographic coverage of tennis, soccer, athletics, golf, cricket, rugby, winter sports and many minor sports. Major international events including the Olympic Games, World Cup soccer and all Grand Slam tennis events. Also news and feature material supplied worldwide. Online photo archive; photo transmission services available for editorial and advertising.

Public Record Office Image Library

See **The National Archives**

Punch Cartoon Library

87–135 Brompton Road, London SW1X 8XL
☎020 7225 6710 Fax 020 7225 6712
✉ punch.library@harrods.com
www.punch.co.uk

Owner *Punch Limited*

Gives access to the 500,000 cartoons published in *Punch* magazine between 1841–1992. The library has a 500+ subject listing and can search on any topic. Social history, politics, fashion, fads, famous people and more by the world's most famous cartoonists, including Tenniel, du Maurier, Pont, Fougasse, E.H. Shepard and Emmett.

Redferns Music Picture Library

7 Bramley Road, London W10 6SZ
☎020 7792 9914 Fax 020 7792 0921
✉ info@redferns.com
www.redferns.com

Picture library covering every aspect of music, from 18th century classical to present day pop. Over one million archived artists and other subjects including musical instruments, recording studios, crowd scenes, festivals, etc. Brochure available. Over 200,000 images available on the website.

Retna Pictures Ltd

Units 1a & 1b, Farm Lane Trading Estate, 101 Farm Lane, London SW6 1QJ
☎0845 034 0645 Fax 0845 034 0646
✉ info@retna.co.uk
www.retna.co.uk

Established 1978, Retna Pictures Ltd is a leading picture agency with two libraries: celebrity/music and lifestyle. The former specialises in images of international and national celebrities, music from the '60s to the current day, films

and personalities. The lifestyle library specialises in people, family life, work, leisure and food. Both libraries are constantly receiving new material from established and up and coming photographers.

Rex Features Ltd

18 Vine Hill, London EC1R 5DZ
☎020 7278 7294 Fax 020 7696 0974
✉ library@rexfeatures.com
www.rexfeatures.com

Contact *Glen Marks*, Sales Manager

Extensive picture library established in the 1950s. Daily coverage of news, politics, personalities, showbusiness, glamour, humour, art, medicine, science, landscapes, royalty, etc.

RIDA Photolibrary

See **GeoScience Features**

Royal Air Force Museum

Grahame Park Way, Hendon, London NW9 5LL
☎020 8205 2266 Fax 020 8200 1751
✉ photographic@rafmuseum.org
www.rafmuseum.org

About a quarter of a million images, mostly b&w, with around 1500 colour in all formats, on the history of aviation. Particularly strong on the activities of the Royal Air Force from the 1870s to 1970s. Researchers are requested to enquire in writing only.

The Royal Collection, Photographic Services

St. James's Palace, London SW1A 1JR
☎020 7839 1377 Fax 020 7024 5643
✉ picturelibrary@royalcollection.org.uk
www.royalcollection.org.uk
www.royal.gov.uk

Contacts *Shruti Patel, Karen Lawson*

Photographic material of items in the Royal Collection, particularly oil paintings, drawings and watercolours, works of art, and interiors and exteriors of royal residences. Over 35,000 colour transparencies, plus 25,000 b&w negatives.

Royal Geographical Society Picture Library

1 Kensington Gore, London SW7 2AR
☎020 7591 3060 Fax 020 7591 3001
✉ images@rgs.org
www.rgs.org/images

Contact *Justin Hobson*

A strong source of geographical and historical

images, both archival and modern, showing the world through the eyes of photographers and explorers dating from the 1830s to the present day. The RGS Contempory Collection provides up-to-date transparencies from around the world, highlighting aspects of cultural activity, environmental phenomena, anthropology, architectural design, travel, mountaineering and exploration. Offers a professional and comprehensive service for both commercial and academic use.

Royal Photographic Society Collection
See **Science & Society Picture Library**

RSPB Images
The Old Dairy, Broadfield Road, Sheffield S8 0XQ
☎0114 258 0001 Fax 0114 258 0101
✉ rinfo@rspb-images.com
www.rspb-images.com

Contact *Naddy Tweed*

RSPB Images represents some of the UK's leading wildlife photographers, and holds stunning images ranging from birds, butterflies, moths, mammals, reptiles and their habitats to most RSPB reserves, plants and abstract subjects. High resolution downloads are now available for many of the images and a free picture research service is also provided.

RSPCA Photolibrary
RSPCA Trading Limited, Wilberforce Way, Southwater, Horsham RH13 9RS
☎0870 754 0150 Fax 0870 753 0150
✉ pictures@rspcaphotolibrary.com
www.rspcaphotolibrary.com

Photolibrary Manager *Andrew Forsyth*

With over 150,000 colour images, the RSPCA Photolibrary has a comprehensive collection of natural history images whose subjects include mammals, birds, domestic and farm animals, amphibians, insects and the environment, as well as a unique photographic record of the RSPCA's work. Also includes the Wild Images collection. Downloadable website and e-mail lightboxes. No search fees.

Russia and Eastern Images
'Sonning', Cheapside Lane, Denham, Uxbridge UB9 5AE
☎01895 833508
✉ easteuropix@btinternet.com
www.easteuropix.com

Architecture, cities, landscapes, people and travel

images of Russia and the former Soviet Union. Considerable background knowledge available and Russian language spoken.

Peter Sanders Photography Ltd
24 Meades Lane, Chesham HP5 1ND
☎01494 773674/771372 Fax 01494 773674
✉ photos@petersanders.com
www.petersanders.com

Contacts *Peter Sanders, Hafsa Garwatuk*

Specialises in the world of Islam in all its aspects from culture, arts, industry, lifestyles, celebrations, etc. Areas included are north, east and west Africa, the Middle East (including Saudi Arabia), China, Asia, Europe and USA. A continually expanding library.

Science & Society Picture Library
Science Museum, Exhibition Road, London SW7 2DD
☎020 7942 4400 Fax 020 7942 4401
✉ piclib@nmsi.ac.uk
www.scienceandsociety.co.uk

Contact *David Thompson*

'The Science & Society Picture Library has one of the widest ranges of photographs, paintings, prints, posters and objects in the world.' The images come from the Science Museum, the **National Railway Museum** and the National Media Museum (formerly the National Museum of Photography, Film & Television) which now includes the Royal Photographic Society collection. Images are available as high or low resolution files via e-mail, FTP or direct from the website.

Science Museum
See **Science & Society Picture Library**

Science Photo Library
327–329 Harrow Road, London W9 3RB
☎020 7432 1100 Fax 020 7286 8668
✉ info@sciencephoto.com
www.sciencephoto.com

Subjects covered include the human body, health and medicine, research, genetics, technology and industry, space exploration and astronomy, earth science, satellite imagery, environment, flowers, plants and gardens, nature and wildlife and the history of science. The whole collection, more than 250,000 images, is available online.

Seaco Picture Library
Sea Containers House, 20 Upper Ground, London SE1 9PF
☎020 7805 5831 Fax 020 7805 5905

✉ seaco.pictures@seacontainers.com
Contact *Picture Library Manager*

Approx. 250,000 images of containerisation, shipping, fast ferries, manufacturing, fruit farming, ports, hotels and leisure.

Mick Sharp Photography
Eithinog, Waun, Penisarwaun, Caernarfon
LL55 3PW
☎01286 872425 Fax 01286 872425
✉ mick.jean@virgin.net

Contacts *Mick Sharp, Jean Williamson*

Archaeology, ancient monuments, buildings, churches, countryside, environment, history, landscape, past cultures and topography. Emphasis on British Isles but material also from other countries. Features the photos of both Mick Sharp and Jean Williamson. Access to other specialist collections on related subjects. Commissions undertaken. Medium format and 35mm colour transparencies plus b&w prints from 5x4 negatives.

Phil Sheldon Golf Picture Library
40 Manor Road, Barnet EN5 2JQ
☎020 8440 1986 Fax 020 8440 9348
✉ gill@philsheldongolfpics.co.uk *or*
info@philsheldongolfpics.co.uk
www.philsheldongolfpics.co.uk

An expanding collection of over 600,000 quality images of the 'world of golf'. In-depth worldwide tournament coverage including every Major championship and Ryder Cup since 1976. Instruction, portraits, trophies and over 400 golf courses from around the world. Also the Dale Concannon collection covering the period 1870 to 1940, the classic 1960s collection by photographer Sidney Harris and the Ed Lacey Collection.

Skishoot–Offshoot
Hall Place, Upper Woodcott, Whitchurch
RG28 7PY
☎01635 255527 Fax 01635 255528
✉ pictures@skishoot.co.uk
www.skishoot.co.uk

Contact *Claire Randall*

Skishoot ski and snowboarding picture library has 500,000 images. Offshoot travel library specialises in France.

The Skyscan Photolibrary
Oak House, Toddington, Cheltenham
GL54 5BY
☎01242 621357 Fax 01242 621343

✉ info@skyscan.co.uk
www.skyscan.co.uk

As well as the Skyscan Photolibrary collection of unique balloon's-eye views of Britain, the library now includes the work of photographers from across the aviation spectrum; air to ground, aviation, aerial sports – 'in fact, anything aerial!' Links have been built with photographers across the world; photographs can be handled on an agency basis and held in house, or as a brokerage where the collection stays with the photographer; terms 50/50 for both. Commissioned photography arranged. Enquiries welcome.

Snookerimages (Eric Whitehead Photography)
10 Brow Close, Bowness on Windermere
LA23 2HA
☎01539 448894
✉ snooker@snookerimages.co.uk
www.snookerimages.co.uk

Over 30,000 images of snooker from 1982 to the present day.

Solo Syndication Ltd
17–18 Haywards Place, Clerkenwell, London
EC1R 0EQ
☎020 7566 0360 Fax 020 7566 0388

Syndication Director *Trevor York*
Sales *Danny Howell, Nick York*
Online transmissions *Geoff Malyon*
   (☎ 020 7566 0370)

Three million images from the archives of the *Daily Mail, Mail on Sunday, Evening Standard* and *Evening News*. Hard prints or Mac-to-Mac delivery. 24-hour service.

Sotheby's Picture Library
Level 2, Olympia 2, Hammersmith Road,
London W14 8UX
☎020 7293 5383 Fax 020 7293 5062
✉ piclib@sothebys.com
www.sothebys.com

Contacts *Joanna Ling, Sue Daly*

The library consists of over one million subjects sold at Sotheby's. Images from the 15th to the 20th century. Oils, drawings, watercolours, prints and decorative items. 'Happy to do searches or, alternatively, visitors are welcome by appointment.'

South American Pictures
48 Station Road, Woodbridge IP12 4AT
☎01394 383963
✉ morrison@southamericanpictures.com

www.southamericanpictures.com www.nonesuchinfo.info (specialist site)

Contact *Marion Morrison*

Colour and b&w images of South/Central America, Cuba, Mexico, New Mexico (USA), Dominican Republic and Haiti, including archaeology and the Amazon. There is an archival section, with pictures and documents from most countries. Now with 40 contributing photographers. All images are supplied digitally.

Starstock
See **Photoshot**

Stay Still
See **Photoshot**

Still Digital
1c Castlehill, Doune FK16 6BU
☎01786 842790
✉ john@stillmovingpictures.com
www.stilldigital.co.uk

Contact *John Hutchinson*

Fully searchable and downloadable service for thousands of Scottish images.

Still Pictures' Whole Earth Photolibrary
199 Shooters Hill Road, London SE3 8UL
☎020 8858 8307 Fax 020 8858 2049
✉ info@stillpictures.com
www.stillpictures.com

Contacts *Minh Ai Ton, Sarah Hodgkins*

Founded 1970. High profile photo library specialising in environment, the Third World, social issues and nature. Represents 15 leading European and US agencies and over 400 photographers as well as the United Nations Environment Programme (UNEP) archive, the **Christian Aid** collection (see entry) and a growing selection of images from **Woodfall Wild Images** (see entry). The website has nearly 250,000 images online, ready for instant download.

Stockfile
'Bearsden', Bourneside, Virginia Water GU25 4LZ
☎01344 844428 Fax 01344 843513
✉ info@stockfile.co.uk
www.stockfile.co.uk

Contacts *Jill Behr, Steven Behr*

Specialist cycling collection with emphasis on mountain biking. Expanding adventure sports section covering snow, land, air and water activities.

Stockscotland.com
Croft Studio, Croft Roy, Crammond Brae, Tain IV19 1JG
☎01862 892298 Fax 01862 892298
✉ info@stockscotland.com
www.stockscotland.com

Contact *Hugh Webster*

150,000 Scottish images with 10,000 currently available online.

Sir John Benjamin Stone
See **Birmingham Library Services** under *Library Services*

Jessica Strang Photo Library
504 Brody House, Strype Street, London E1 7LQ
☎020 7247 8982 Fax 020 7247 8982
✉ jessica@jessicastrang.com

Contact *Jessica Strang*

Approximately 60,000 transparencies covering architecture, interiors (contemporary), gardens, 'obsessive and not just small but tiny, or from almost no space at all', men, women, couples and animals in architecture, and vanishing London details. Recycled ideas for the home.

Joe Tasker Collection
See **Chris Bonington Picture Library**

Tate Images
Top Floor, The Lodge, Tate Britain, Millbank, London SW1P 4RG
☎020 7887 8871/8890/4933
Fax 020 7887 8805
✉ tate.images@tate.org.uk
www.tate-images.com

Contact *Alison Fern*

Tate is one of the world's leading visual arts organisations and its collection encompasses the national collection of historic British art from 1500, including iconic masterpieces by Gainsborough, Constable, Turner, David Hockney and Henry Moore, and the national collection of international modern art which includes works by Dali, Picasso, Matisse, Rothko, Emin, Hirst, Warhol and Andreas Gursky. This vast collection of art imagery is available from the Tate Images website. Clients can browse the entire Tate collection using a new, keyword-based search engine; select images and save their selections to a personal light box; download low-resolution imagery for layout purposes. E-commerce coming soon.

Bob Thomas Sports Photography

See **Popperfoto.com**

Thoroughbred Photography Ltd

The Hornbeams, 2 The Street, Worlington
IP28 8RU
☎01638 713944
✉ mail@thoroughbredphoto.com
www.thoroughbredphoto.com

Contacts *Trevor Jones, Gill Jones, Laura Green*

Extensive library of high-quality colour images depicting all aspects of thoroughbred horseracing dating from 1987. Major group races, English Classics, studs, stallions, mares and foals, early morning scenes, personalities, jockeys, trainers and prominent owners. Also international work: USA Breeders' Cup, Arc de Triomphe, French Classics, Irish Derby, Dubai racing scenes, Japan Cup and Hokkaido stud farms; and more unusual scenes such as racing on the sands at low tide, Ireland, and on the frozen lake at St Moritz. Visitors by appointment.

TopFoto

PO Box 33, Edenbridge TN8 5PF
☎01732 863939 Fax 01732 860215
✉ admin@topfoto.co.uk
www.topfoto.co.uk

Contact *Alan Smith*

International editorial distributor with over one million pictures available online to download and 12 million in hard copy, representing 40 leading suppliers.

B.M. Totterdell photography

Constable Cottage, Burlings Lane, Knockholt
TN14 7PE
☎01959 532001 Fax 01959 532001
✉ btrial@btinternet.com
whatvolleyball.co.uk

Contact *Barbara Totterdell*

Specialist volleyball library covering all aspects of the sport.

Tessa Traeger Picture Library

7 Rossetti Studios, 72 Flood Street, London
SW3 5TF
☎020 7352 3641 Fax 020 7352 4846
✉ info@tessatraeger.com
www.tessatraeger.com

Food, gardens, travel and artists.

Travel Ink Photo & Feature Library

The Old Coach House, 14 High Street, Goring on Thames, Nr Reading RG8 9AR
☎01491 873011 Fax 01491 875558
✉ info@travel-ink.co.uk
www.travel-ink.co.uk

Contacts *Frances Honnor, Felicity Bazell*

A collection of over 120,000 travel, tourism and lifestyle images, carefully edited and constantly updated, from countries worldwide. Specialist collections from the UK, Greece, France, Far East and Caribbean. The website offers a fully captioned and searchable selection of over 31,000 images and is ideal for picture researchers.

Peter Trenchard's Image Store Ltd

The Studio, West Hill, St Helier, Jersey
JE2 3HB
☎01534 769933 Fax 01534 789191
✉ peter-trenchard@jerseymail.co.uk
www.peter-trenchard.com

Contact *Peter Trenchard, FBIPP, AMPA, PPA*

Slide library of the Channel Islands – mainly tourist and financial-related. Commissions undertaken.

Tropix Photo Library

44 Woodbines Avenue, Kingston upon Thames
KT1 2AY
☎020 8546 0823/07740 426 620
✉ veronica@tropix.co.uk
www.tropix.co.uk

Managing Director *Veronica Birley*

Specialises in images of developing nations: travel and editorial pictures emphasising the attractive and progressive. Fully searchable, keyworded website. Evocative photos concerning the economies, environment, culture and society of 100+ countries across Africa, Central and South America, Caribbean, Eastern Europe, Middle East, Indian sub-continent, South East Asia, CIS and Far East. Worldwide travel collections also include UK, Europe, North America and Antarctica. Assignment photography available. All photos supplied with detailed captions. Established 1982. **BAPLA** member.

True North

Louper Weir, Ghyll Head, Windermere
LA23 3LN
☎01539 443017/07941 630420
✉ hurlmere@btinternet.com
www.northpix.co.uk

Contact *John Morrison*

The collection features the life and landscape

of the north of England, photographed by John Morrison. No other photographer's work required.

U.P.P.A.
See **Photoshot**

Ulster Museum Picture Library
Botanic Gardens, Belfast BT9 5AB
☎028 9038 3000 ext 3114 Fax 028 9038 3103
✉ michelle.ashmore@magni.org.uk
www.ulstermuseum.org.uk

Contact *Mrs Michelle Ashmore*

Specialist subjects: art (fine and decorative, late 17th–20th century), particularly Irish art, archaeology, ethnography, treasures from the Armada shipwrecks, geology, botany, zoology, local history and industrial archaeology.

United Nations Environment Programme (UNEP)
See **Still Pictures' Whole Earth Photolibrary**

Universal Pictorial Press & Agency Ltd
29–31 Saffron Hill, London EC1N 8SW
☎020 7421 6000
✉ contact@uppa.co.uk
www.photoshot.com

News Editor *Peter Dare*

Photo archive dates back to 1944 and contains approximately four million pictures. Colour and b&w coverage of news, royalty, politics, sport, arts, and many other subjects. Commissions undertaken for press and public relations. Fully interactive digital photo archive accessible via ISDN or modem. Full digital scanning, retouching and transmission facilities.

UPI
See **Popperfoto.com**

V&A Images
Victoria and Albert Museum, Cromwell Road, South Kensington, London SW7 2RL
☎020 7942 2489 (commercial)/2479 (academic)
Fax 020 7942 2482
✉ vaimages@vam.co.uk
www.vandaimages.com

A vast collection of photographs from the world's largest museum of decorative and applied arts, reflecting culture and lifestyle spanning over 1000 years of history to the present time. Digital delivery of contemporary and histor-ical textiles, costumes and fashions, ceramics, furniture, metalwork, glass, sculpture, toys, and games, design and photographs from around the world. Unique photographs include 1960s fashion by John French, Harry Hammond's behind the scenes pop idols, Houston Rogers theatrical world of the 1930s to 1970s, images of royalty by Lafayette, Cecil Beaton, and the 19th century pioneer photographers. Images from the National Art Library and Library of Art & Design, and from the Theatre Museum and Museum of Childhood are readily available.

Victory Archive
See **Popperfoto.com**

Vin Mag Archive Ltd
84–90 Digby Road, London E9 6HX
☎020 8533 7588 Fax 020 8533 7283
✉ piclib@vinmag.com
www.vinmagarchive.com

Formerly the Vintage Magazine Company. A collection of half a million movie, TV, celebrity and sports images available online. Contact *Angela Maguire* for code and password.

John Walmsley Photo Library
See **Education Photos**

Warwickshire Photographic Survey
See **Birmingham Library Services** under *Library Services*

Waterways Photo Library
39 Manor Court Road, Hanwell, London W7 3EJ
☎020 8840 1659 Fax 020 8567 0605
✉ watphot39@aol.com
www.waterwaysphotolibrary.com

Contact *Derek Pratt*

A specialist photo library on all aspects of Britain's inland waterways. Top-quality 35mm and medium-format colour transparencies, plus a large collection of b&w and an increasing collection of digital photography. Rivers and canals, bridges, locks, aqueducts, tunnels and waterside buildings. Town and countryside scenes, canal art, waterway holidays, boating, fishing, windmills, watermills, watersports and wildlife.

Weimar Archive
See **Mary Evans Picture Library**

Wellcome Images
183 Euston Road, London NW1 2BE
☎020 7611 8348 Fax 020 7611 8577

✉ medphoto@wellcome.ac.uk
medphoto.wellcome.ac.uk

Contact *Venita Paul*

Approximately 180,000 images on the history of medicine and human culture worldwide, including religion, astronomy, botany, genetics, landscape and cell biology.

Westminster Reference Library
See entry under *Library Services*

Eric Whitehead Photography
20 Brow Close, Bowness on Windermere
LA23 2HA
☎01539 448894
✉ snooker@snookerimages.co.uk
www.snookerimages.co.uk

The agency covers local news events, PR and commercial material, also leading library of snooker images (see **Snookerimages**).

Wild Images
See **RSPCA Photolibrary**

Wild Places Photography
See **Chris Howes**

David Williams Picture Library
50 Burlington Avenue, Glasgow G12 0LH
☎0141 339 7823 Fax 0141 337 3031
✉ david@scotland-guide.co.uk

Specialises in travel photography with wide coverage of Scotland, Iceland and Spain. Many other European countries also included plus smaller collections of Western USA and Canada. The main subjects in each country are: cities, towns, villages, 'tourist haunts', buildings of architectural or historical interest, landscapes and natural features. The Scotland and Iceland collections include many pictures depicting physical geography and geology. Photographic commissions and illustrated travel articles undertaken. Catalogue available.

Vaughan Williams Memorial Library
English Folk Dance and Song Society, Cecil Sharp House, 2 Regent's Park Road, London NW1 7AY
☎020 7485 2206 ext. 18/19
Fax 020 7284 0523
✉ library@efdss.org
www.efdss.org

Mainly b&w coverage of traditional/folk music, dance and customs worldwide, focusing on Britain and other English-speaking nations.

Photographs date from the late 19th century to the present day.

The Wilson Photographic Collection
See **Dundee Central Library** under *Library Services*

Woodfall Wild Images
17 Bull Lane, Denbigh LL16 3SN
☎01745 815903 Fax 01745 814581
www.woodfall.com

Contact *David Woodfall*

A comprehensive and specialist collection of wildlife, landscape and environmental photographs from both the UK and the rest of the world. Award-winning photography by the world's more imaginative photographers. All formats, 35mm to panoramic. 'Personal and friendly service.' Subjects include: birds, animals, insects and marine life, trees and forests, wildflowers, all habitats worldwide and canals. Environmental issues such as pollution, conservation and habitat destruction, the weather and climate, landscapes and scenics. Suitable for advertising, editorial, calendars and design purposes.

World Illustrated
See **Photoshot**

World Pictures
See **Photoshot**

Yemen Pictures
28 Sheen Common Drive, Richmond TW10 5BN
☎020 7602 1989 Fax 020 7602 1989
www.facesandplacespix.com

Large collection (4000 transparencies) covering all aspects of Yemen – culture, people, architecture, dance, qat, music. Also Africa, Australia, Middle East, and Asia.

York Archaeological Trust Picture Library
47 Aldwark, York YO1 7BXFG
☎01904 663006 Fax 01904 663024
✉ ckyriacou@yorkarchaeology.co.uk
www.yorkarchaeology.co.uk

Specialist library of rediscovered artifacts, historic buildings and excavations, presented by the creators of the highly acclaimed Jorvik Viking Centre. The main emphasis is on the Roman, Anglo-Saxon, Medieval and Viking periods.

John Robert Young Collection

Paxvobiscum, 16 Greenacres Drive, Ringmer,
Lewes BN8 5LX

☎01273 814172

✉ johnrobert@paxvobiscum.fsnet.co.uk

Contacts *Jennifer Barrett, John Robert Young*

50,000 colour and B&W images. Military
(French Foreign Legion, Spanish Foreign
Legion, Royal Marines), religion (Christian),
travel, China, personalities of the 1960s and
'70s.

Settling Accounts

Ian Spring takes an expert look at the latest budget and explains how writers can be tax-wise

When he was Chancellor of the Exchequer, Norman Lamont said:

'Tax should be
- Simple and certain
- Fair and reasonable
- Easy to collect'

Unfortunately over the years, tax law has become ever more complicated and it has become more and more difficult for the 'ordinary' person to understand it. Until recently it was inconceivable that tax changes would be passed which had retrospective effect but this is no longer the case and is happening. With the recent merger of the Inland Revenue and Customs and Excise, the former have taken on some of the powers and practices of the latter and have become more aggressive in enforcing the law, as they see it, in their never ending endeavour to increase the tax take.

Tax is not simple and a taxpayer cannot be certain that a tax planning action legally taken now will be legal in years to come. Tax and its ramifications such as tax credits are ever increasingly viewed by the general public as being unfair and unreasonable and whilst tax collection is regarded by the Revenue as being easier this is only because taxpayers are now responsible for paying rather than the Revenue being responsible for collecting.

It is against this background that authors have to comply with the law and complete and submit a tax return each year.

Income Tax

What is a professional writer for tax purposes?

Writers are professionals while they are writing regularly with the intention of making a profit; or while they are gathering material, researching or otherwise preparing a publication.

A professional freelance writer is taxed under section 5 Income Tax (Trading and Other Income) Act 2005. The taxable income is the amount receivable, either directly or by an agent, on his behalf, less expenses wholly and exclusively laid out for the purpose of the profession. If expenses exceed income, the loss can either be set against other income of the same or preceding years or carried forward and set against future income from writing. If tax has been paid on that other income, a repayment can be obtained, or the sum can be offset against other tax liabilities. Special loss relief can apply in the opening years of the profession. Losses made in the first four years can be set against income of up to three earlier years.

Where a writer receives very occasional payments for isolated articles, it may not be possible to establish that these are profits arising from carrying on a continuing profession.

In such circumstances these 'isolated transactions' may be assessed under section 687 Income Tax (Trading and Other Income) Act 2005. Again, expenses may be deducted in arriving at the taxable income but, if expenses exceed income, the loss can only be set against the profits from future isolated transactions or other income assessable under section 687.

In the tax year 1996/97 a new tax system came into effect called Self Assessment. Under Self Assessment the onus is on the individual to declare income and expenses correctly. Each writer therefore has to decide whether profits arise from a professional or occasional activity. The consequences of getting it wrong can be expensive by way of interest, penalties and surcharges on additional tax subsequently found to be due. If in any doubt the writer should seek professional advice.

Income

A writer's income includes fees, advances, royalties, commissions, sale of copyrights, reimbursed expenses, etc., from any source anywhere in the world whether or not brought to the UK (non UK resident or domiciled writers should seek professional advice).

Agents

It should be borne in mind that the agent stands in the shoes of the principal. It is not always realised that when the agent receives royalties, fees, advances, etc. on behalf of the author those receipts became the property of the author on the date of their receipt by the agent. This applies for Income Tax and Value Added Tax purposes.

Expenses

A writer can normally claim the following expenses:

(a) Secretarial, typing, proof-reading, research. Where payment for these is made to the author's wife or husband they should be recorded and entered in the spouse's tax return as earned income which is subject to the usual personal allowances. If payments reach relevant levels, PAYE should be operated.

(b) Telephone, faxes, Internet costs, computer software, postage, stationery, printing, equipment maintenance, insurance, dictation tapes, batteries, any equipment or office requisites used for the profession.

(c) Periodicals, books (including presentation copies and reference books) and other publications necessary for the profession, but amounts received from the sale of books should be deducted.

(d) Hotels, fares, car running expenses (including repairs, petrol, oil, garaging, parking, cleaning, insurance, road fund tax, depreciation), hire of cars or taxis in connection with:
   (i)   business discussions with agents, publishers, co-authors, collaborators, researchers, illustrators, etc.
   (ii) travel at home and abroad to collect background material.
   As an alternative to keeping details of full car running costs, a mileage rate can be claimed for business use. This rate depends on the engine size and varies from year to year. This is known as the Fixed Profit Car Scheme and is available to writers whose turnover does not exceed the VAT registration limit, currently £64,000

(e) Publishing and advertising expenses, including costs of proof corrections, indexing, photographs, etc.

(f) Subscriptions to societies and associations, press cutting agencies, libraries, etc., incurred wholly for the purpose of the profession.

(g) Rent, council tax and water rates, etc., the proportion being determined by the ratio of the number of rooms used exclusively for the profession, to the total number of rooms in the residence. But see note on Capital Gains Tax below.

(h) Lighting, heating and cleaning. A carefully calculated figure of the business use of these costs can be claimed as a proportion of the total.

(i) Agent's commission, accountancy charges and legal charges incurred wholly in the course of the profession including cost of defending libel actions, damages in so far as they are not covered by insurance, and libel insurance premiums. However, where in a libel case, damages are awarded to punish the author for having acted maliciously, the action becomes quasi-criminal and costs and damages may not be allowed.

(j) TV and video rental (which may be apportioned for private use), and cinema or theatre tickets, if wholly for the purpose of the profession.

(k) Capital allowances
   (i) On motor cars the allowance is 25% in the first year and 25% of the reducing balance in each successive year, limited to £3000 each year.
   (ii) For all other business equipment, e.g. TV, radio, hi-fi sets, tape and video recorders, Dictaphones, office furniture, photographic equipment, etc. for small businesses (which most authors will be), there is a First Year Allowance of 50%. After the first year there is an annual Writing Down Allowance of 25% of the reducing balance. The allowances for both categories mentioned above will be reduced to exclude personal (non-professional) use where necessary. These allowances are going to change with effect from 6th April 2008.

(l) Lease rent. The cost of lease rent of equipment is allowable; also on cars, subject to restrictions for private use, and for expensive cars.

(m) Other expenses incurred wholly and exclusively for professional purposes. (Entertaining expenses are not allowable in any circumstances.)

NB It essential to keep detailed records. Diary entries of appointments, notes of fares and receipted bills are much more convincing to the Inland Revenue who are very reluctant to accept estimates.

The Self Assessment regime makes it a legal requirement for proper accounting records to be kept. These records must be sufficient to support the figures declared in the tax return.

In addition to the above, tax relief is available on:

(a) Premiums to a pension scheme. At 6th April 2006 a new pension scheme tax regime came into effect which replaced all previous rules for occupational , personal pension and retirement annuity schemes. An individual can make (and tax relief is available on) contributions up to the higher of the full amount of relevant income or £3,600, subject to a maximum annual limit. That limit for 2006/07 was £215,000 and for 2007/08 is £225,000.

(b) Gift Aid payments to charities. Any amount.

Capital Gains Tax

The exemption from Capital Gains Tax which applies to an individual's main residence does not apply to any part of that residence which is used exclusively for business purposes. The appropriate proportion of any increase in value of the residence, since purchase or 31 March 1982 if later, can be taxed when the residence is sold, subject to adjustment for inflation to March 1998 and subsequent period of ownership, at the individual's highest rate of tax.

Writers who own their houses should bear this in mind before claiming expenses for the use of a room for writing purposes. Arguments in favour of making such claims are that they afford some relief now, while Capital Gains Tax in its present form may not stay for ever. Also, where a new house is bought in place of an old one, the gain made on the sale of the first study may be set off against the cost of the study in the new house, thus postponing the tax payment until the final sale. For this relief to apply, each house must have a study and the author must continue his profession throughout. On death there is an exemption of the total Capital Gains of the estate.

Alternatively, writers can claim that their use is non-exclusive and restrict their claim to the cost of extra lighting, heating and cleaning to avoid any Capital Gains Tax liability.

Can a writer average out his income over a number of years for tax purposes?
The Budget in March 2001 introduced measures which enable writers to average their profits (made wholly or mainly from creative works) over two or more consecutive years. If the profits of the lower year are less than 70% of the profits of the higher year or the profits of one year (but not both) are nil, the author will be able to claim to have the profits averaged. Where the profits of the lower year are more than 70% but less than 75% of the profits of the higher year a pro-rata adjustment is made to both years to reduce the difference between them.

It is also possible to average out income within the terms of publishers' contracts, but professional advice should be taken before signature. Where a husband and wife collaborate as writers, advice should be taken as to whether a formal partnership agreement should be made or whether the publishing agreement should be in joint names.

Is a lump sum paid for an outright sale of the copyright or part of the copyright exempt from tax?
No. All the money received from the marketing of literary work, by whatever means, is taxable. Some writers, in spite of clear judicial decisions to the contrary, still seem to think that an outright sale of, for instance, the film rights in a book is not subject to tax. The averaging relief described above should be considered.

Remaindering
To avoid remaindering authors can usually purchase copies of their own books from the publishers. Monies received from sales are subject to income tax but the cost of books sold should be deducted because tax is only payable on the profit made.

Is there any relief where old copyrights are sold?
No. There was relief available until April 2001 but was then withdrawn. The averaging relief described above should be considered.

Are royalties payable on publication of a book abroad subject to both foreign tax as well as UK tax?
Where there is a Double Taxation Agreement between the country concerned and the UK, then on the completion of certain formalities no tax is deductible at source by the foreign payer, but such income is taxable in the UK in the ordinary way. When there is no Double Taxation Agreement, credit will be given against UK tax for overseas tax paid. A

complete list of countries with which the UK has conventions for the avoidance of double taxation may be obtained from the Centre for Non-Residents, Inland Revenue, St John's House, Merton Road, Bootle, Merseyside L69 9BB, or a local tax office.

Residence abroad

Writers residing abroad will, of course, be subject to the tax laws ruling in their country of residence, and as a general rule royalty income paid from the United Kingdom can be exempted from deduction of UK tax at source, providing the author is carrying on his profession abroad. A writer who is intending to go and live abroad should make early application for future royalties to be paid without deduction of tax to the Centre for Non-Residents, address as above. In certain circumstances writers resident in the Irish Republic are exempt from Irish Income Tax on their authorship earnings.

Are grants or prizes taxable?

The law is uncertain. Some Arts Council grants are now deemed to be taxable, whereas most prizes and awards are not, though it depends on the conditions in each case. When submitting the Self Assessment annual returns, such items should be excluded, but reference made to them in the 'Additional Information' box on the self-employment (or partnership) pages.

What is the item 'Class 4 N.I.C.' which appears on my Self Assessment return?

All taxpayers who are self-employed pay an additional national insurance contribution if their earned income exceeds a figure which varies each year. This contribution is described as Class 4 and is calculated when preparing the return. It is additional to the self-employed Class 2 contribution but confers no additional benefits and is a form of levy. It applies to men aged under 65 and women under 60.

Should an author use a limited company?

The tax regime has made the incorporation of businesses attractive and there can be advantages in so doing even for businesses with relatively low levels of profit although these advantages have been reduced in recent Budgets. However, there are disadvantages in all cases and there are particular considerations for authors. The advice of an accountant, knowledgeable about the affairs of authors, should be sought if incorporation is contemplated.

Value Added Tax

Value Added Tax (VAT) is a tax currently levied at 17.5% on:

(a)   the total value of taxable goods and services supplied to consumers,
(b)   the importation of goods into the UK,
(c)   certain services or goods from abroad if a taxable person receives them in the UK for the purpose of their business.

Who is taxable?

A writer resident in the UK whose turnover from writing and any other business, craft or art on a self-employed basis is greater than £64,000 annually, before deducting agent's commission, must register with HM Revenue & Customs as a taxable person. Turnover includes fees, royalties, advances, commissions, sale of copyright, reimbursed expenses, etc.

A business is required to register:
- at the end of any month if the value of taxable supplies in the past twelve months has exceeded the annual threshold; or
- if there are reasonable grounds for believing that the value of taxable supplies in the next twelve months will exceed the annual threshold.

Inputs (Expenses)

Taxable at the standard rate if supplier is registered	*Taxable at the zero or special rate*	*Not liable to VAT*
Rent of certain commercial premises	Books (zero)	Rent of non-commercial premises
Advertisements in newspapers, magazines, journals and periodicals	Coach, rail and air travel (zero)	Postage
Agent's commission (unless it relates to monies from overseas)	Agent's commission (on monies from overseas)	Services supplied by unregistered persons
Accountant's and solicitor's fees for business matters	Domestic gas and electricity (5%)	Subscriptions to the Societyof Authors, PEN, NUJ, etc.
Agency services (typing, copying, etc.)		Insurance
Word processors, typewriters and stationery		
Artists' materials		
Photographic equipment		
Tape recorders and tapes		
Hotel accommodation		
Taxi fares		
Motorcar expenses		*Outside the scope of VAT*
Telephone		PLR (Public Lending
Theatres and concerts		Profit shares
		Investment income
NB This list is not exhaustive		

Penalties will be claimed in the case of late registration. A writer whose turnover is below these limits is exempt from the requirements to register for VAT but may apply for voluntary registration and this will be allowed at the discretion of HM Revenue & Customs.

A taxable person collects VAT on outputs (turnover) and deducts VAT paid on inputs (taxable expenses) and where VAT collected exceeds VAT paid, must remit the difference to HM Revenue & Customs. In the event that input exceeds output, the difference will be refunded by HM Revenue & Customs

Outputs (Turnover)

A writer's outputs are taxable services supplied to publishers, broadcasting organisations, theatre managements, film companies, educational institutions, etc. A taxable writer must invoice all the persons (either individuals or organisations) in the UK to whom supplies have been made, for fees, royalties or other considerations, plus VAT.

An unregistered writer cannot and must not invoice for VAT. A taxable writer is not obliged to collect VAT on royalties or other fees paid by publishers or others overseas. In practice, agents usually collect VAT for the registered author.

Remit to Customs

The taxable writer adds up the VAT which has been paid on taxable inputs, deducts it from the VAT received and remits the balance to Customs. Business with HM Customs is conducted through the local VAT offices of HM Revenue & Customs which are listed in local telephone directories, except for VAT returns which are sent direct to the HM Revenue & Customs VAT Central Unit, Alexander House, 21 Victoria Avenue, Southend on Sea, Essex SS99 1AA.

Accounting

A taxable writer is obliged to account to HM Revenue & Customs at quarterly intervals. Returns must be completed and sent to VAT Central Unit by the dates shown on the return. Penalties can be charged if the returns are late.

It is possible to account for the VAT liability under the Cash Accounting Scheme (leaflet 731), whereby the author accounts for the output tax when the invoice is paid or royalties, etc., are received. The same applies to the input tax, but as most purchases are probably on a 'cash basis', this will not make a considerable difference to the author's input tax. This scheme is only applicable to those with a taxable turnover of less than £1,350,000 and, therefore, is available to the majority of authors. The advantage of this scheme is that the author does not have to account for VAT before receiving payments, thereby relieving the author of a cash flow problem.

Also, if turnover is less than or expected to be less than £1,350,000 it is possible to pay VAT by monthly instalments, with a final balance at the end of the year (see leaflet 732). This annual accounting method also means that only one VAT return is submitted..

Flat Rate Scheme

Small businesses can elect to pay VAT under a flat rate scheme (FRS). This is open to businesses with business income up to £150,000 a year. Under the normal VAT accounting rules, each item of turnover and every claimed expense must be recorded and supported by evidence, e.g. invoices, receipts, etc. Under the FRS, detailed records of sales and purchases do not have to be kept. A record of gross income (including zero rated and excepted income) is maintained and a flat rate percentage is applied to the total. This percentage is then paid over to HM Revenue & Customs. The percentage varies from one profession or business to another but for authors is 11%. In the first year of registration this percent is reduced by 1%.

The aim of the scheme is to reduce the amount of time and money spent in complying with VAT regulations and this is to be welcomed. However, there are disadvantages:

- The detailed records of income and expenses are still going to be required for taxation purposes.
- Invoices on sales are issued in the normal way.
- The percentage is applied to all business income. So 11% VAT will effectively be paid on income from abroad, zero rated under the normal basis, and PLR, otherwise exempt.

For many authors, normal VAT accounting has imposed a good, timely discipline for dealing with accounting and taxation matters.

Registration

A writer will be given a VAT registration number which must be quoted on all VAT correspondence. It is the responsibility of those registered to inform those to whom they make supplies of their registration number. The taxable turnover limit which determines whether a person who is registered for VAT may apply for cancellation of registration is £62,000.

Voluntary registration

A writer whose turnover is below the limits may apply to register. If the writer is paying a relatively large amount of VAT on taxable inputs – agent's commission, accountant's fees, equipment, materials, or agency services, etc. – it may make a significant improvement in the net income to be able to offset the VAT on these inputs. A writer who pays relatively little VAT may find it easier, and no more expensive, to remain unregistered.

Fees and royalties

A taxable writer must notify those to whom he makes supplies of the VAT Registration Number at the first opportunity. One method of accounting for and paying VAT on fees and royalties is the use of multiple stationery for 'self-billing', one copy of the royalty statement being used by the author as the VAT invoice. A second method is for the recipient of taxable outputs to pay fees, including authors' royalties, without VAT. The taxable writer then renders a tax invoice for the VAT element and a second payment, of the VAT element, will be made. This scheme is cumbersome but will involve only taxable authors. Fees and royalties from abroad will count as payments for exported services and will accordingly be zero-rated.

Agents and accountants

A writer is responsible to HM Revenue & Customs for making VAT returns and payments. Neither an agent nor an accountant nor a solicitor can remove the responsibility, although they can be helpful in preparing and keeping VAT returns and accounts. Their professional fees or commission will, except in rare cases where the adviser or agent is himself unregistered, be taxable at the standard rate and will represent some of a writer's taxable inputs.

Income Tax

An unregistered writer can claim some of the VAT paid on taxable inputs as a business expense allowable against income tax. However, certain taxable inputs fall into categories which cannot be claimed under the income tax regulations. A taxable writer, who has already claimed VAT on inputs, cannot charge it as a business expense for the purposes of income tax.

Certain services from abroad

A taxable author who resides in the United Kingdom and who receives certain services from abroad must account for VAT on those services at the appropriate tax rate on the sum paid for them. Examples of the type of services concerned include: services of lawyers, accountants, consultants, provision of information and copyright permissions.

Inheritance Tax

Inheritance Tax was introduced in 1984 to replace Capital Transfer Tax, which had in turn replaced Estate Duty, the first of the death taxes of recent times. Paradoxically, Inheritance Tax has reintroduced a number of principles present under the old Estate Duty. The general principle now is that all assets owned at death are chargeable to tax (currently 40%) except for the first £300,000 of the estate and any assets passed to a surviving spouse or a charity. Gifts made more than seven years before death are exempt, but those made within this period may be taxed on a sliding scale. No tax is payable at the time of making the gift.

In addition, each individual may currently make gifts of up to £3000 in any year and these will be considered to be exempt. A further exemption covers any number of annual gifts not exceeding £250 to any one person.

If the £3000 is not fully utilised in one year, any unused balance can be carried forward to the following year (but no later). Gifts out of income, which do not reduce one's living standards, are also exempt if they are part of normal expenditure.

At death all assets are valued; they will include any property, investments, life policies, furniture and personal possessions, bank balances and, in the case of authors, the value of copyrights. All, with the sole exception of copyrights, are capable (as assets) of accurate valuation and, if necessary, can be turned into cash. The valuation of copyright is, of course, complicated and frequently gives rise to difficulty. Except where they are bequeathed to the owner's husband or wife, very real problems can be left behind by the author.

Experience has shown that a figure based on two to three years' past royalties may be proposed by the Inland Revenue in their valuation of copyright. However, this may not be reasonable and may require negotiation. If a book is running out of print or if, as in the case of educational books, it may need revision at the next reprint, these factors must be taken into account. In many cases the fact that the author is no longer alive and able to make personal appearances, or provide publicity, or write further works, will result in lower or slower sales. Obviously, this is an area in which help can be given by the publishers, and in particular one needs to know what their future intentions are, what stocks of the books remain, and what likelihood there will be of reprinting.

There is a further relief available to authors who have established that they have been carrying on a business for at least two years prior to death. It has been possible to establish that copyrights are treated as business property and in these circumstances Inheritance Tax 'business property relief' is available. This relief at present is 100% so that the tax saving can be quite substantial. The Inland Revenue may wish to be assured that the business is continuing and consideration should therefore be given to the appointment, in the author's will, of a literary executor who should be a qualified business person or, in certain circumstances, the formation of partnership between the author and spouse, or other relative, to ensure that it is established the business is continuing after the author's death.

If the author has sufficient income, consideration should be given to building up a fund to cover future Inheritance Tax liabilities. One of a number of ways would be to take out a whole life assurance policy which is assigned to the children, or other beneficiaries, the premiums on which are within the annual exemption of £3000. The capital sum payable on the death of the assured is exempt from inheritance tax.

Tax credits

Working authors may also be eligible to claim Child Tax Credit and Working Tax Credit.

Child tax credit is the main way that families receive money for their younger children and for 16 - 18 year olds in education. A claim is based on your income and you can claim whether or not you are working. All families (with children) with an income up to £58,175 a year (or up to £66,350 a year if your child is under one year old) can claim. To qualify, you must be aged 16 or over, usually live in the UK and if single, (or separated) claim based on your individual circumstances. If you are married or a man and woman living together (or a same sex couple from December 2005) you must claim together based on joint circumstances and income.

Working tax credit is a payment to top up earnings of the lower paid (whether employed or self employed including those who do not have children). To qualify, you must be aged 16 or over and you or your partner responsible for a child and you must work at least 16 hours a week. If you are part of a couple with children, greater amounts may be claimed if you jointly work at least 30 hours a week provided one of you works for at least 16 hours. Childless couples cannot add their hours together to qualify for the 30 hour element. If you do not have children and you do not have a disability, you must be aged 25 or over and work at least 30 hours a week. It is also possible that your working tax credit will be increased to assist with the cost of registered or approved childcare

Anyone wondering how best to order his affairs for tax purposes should consult an accountant with specialised knowledge in this field. Experience shows that a good accountant is well worth his fee which, incidentally, so far as it relates to professional matters, is an allowable expense.

The information contained in this section has been prepared by Ian Spring of Moore Stephens, Chartered Accountants, who will be pleased to answer questions on tax problems. Please write to Ian Spring, c/o The Writer's Handbook, 34 Ufton Road, London N1 5BX.

Index of Entries

Subject Index